GUN TRADER'S GUIDE

20th Edition — Completely Revised and Updated

STOEGER PUBLISHING COMPANY
Wayne, New Jersey

EDITORIAL STAFF:

Editor
John Traister

Production & Design
John E. Traister Associates

Editorial Assistant
Ruby Updike

Art
Keeler Chapman
John Karns

Cover Photographer
Ray Wells

Publisher
David C. Perkins

President
Brian T. Herrick

FRONT COVER: The two beauties pictured on the front cover were both produced by the world famous English firm of Westley Richards. Both are ejector shotguns in 28 and .410 gauge. Receivers are scroll engraved with gold inlays of game scenes by Geoffrey Casbard.

Published by:
Stoeger Publishing Company
5 Mansard Court
Wayne, New Jersey 07470

International Standard Book Number: 0-88317-193-7
Library of Congress Catalog Card No. 85-641040

In the United States, distributed to the book trade and to the sporting goods trade by:
Stoeger Industries
5 Mansard Court
Wayne, New Jersey 07470
201-872-9500 Fax: 201-872-2230

In Canada, distributed to the book trade and to the sporting goods trade by:
Stoeger Canada Ltd.
1801 Wentworth Street, Unit 16
Whitby, Ontario, L1N 8R6, Canada

NOTE

All prices shown in this book are for guns in excellent condition (almost new) and the prices are retail (what a dealer would normally charge for them). A dealer will seldom pay the full value shown in this book. If a gun is in any condition other than excellent, the price in this book must be multiplied by the appropriate factor to obtain a true value of the gun in question.

INTRODUCTION

Nearly fifty years have passed since the first edition of *Gun Trader's Guide* appeared in print. That's half a century — enough time to elect nine Presidents, fight three major conflicts, enter into the space and computer ages, and find a cure for polio — just to name a few! This same amount of time allowed many firearm restrictions to become law in the United States, and what had once been low-cost used guns to bang around now have become collector items that bring many times the gun's originial value.

The first edtion of *Gun Trader's Guide* contained 225 pages and some 1,360 listings — accompanied by about 100 illustrations. Now, after twenty revisions, the book has evolved into a complete catalog of rifles, shotguns and handguns of the twentieth century. The current edition of *Gun Trader's Guide* has been expanded to include more listings than ever before with nearly 600 pages, over 5,000 listings, and nearly 2700 illustrations, representing an enlargement greater than 100 percent over the first edtion. No wonder hundreds of thousands of gun buffs have made *Gun Trader's Guide* their chief source for firearm identification and comparison for sporting, military, law enforcement, commemoratives and other types of firearms. Furthermore, many of the following items are also found throughout this comprehensive guide:

- Production data
- Specifications
- Variations of different models
- Dates of manufacture
- Current values
- Tabbed sections for user-friendly reference
- Complete INDEX of all firearms

The format of *Gun Grader's Guide* is simple and straightforward. It lists thousands of firearms that have been manufactured in the United States and abroad since about 1900. Most entries include complete specifications: model number and name, caliber/gauge, barrel length, overall length, weight, distinguishing features, variations, plus the dates of manufacture (when they can

be accurately determined). Many illustrative photos and drawings accompany the text to help the reader with identifications and comparisons.

Gun Trader's Guide is revised annually to ensure that its wealth of information is the most up to date available. The highlight for many users is the current price of used guns. This feature is essential in determining the value of old firearms that may be family heirlooms or firearms that the reader wishes to sell or buy. Values shown are based on national averages, obtained by conferring with hundreds of different gun dealers and auctioneers; not by some formula which could be way off the mark. The values listed accurately reflect the prices being charged nationwide at the time of publication. In other words, the prices are what the various models are sold for — not what someone *thinks* they should be.

In some rare cases, however — like the Winchester Model 1873 "One of One Thousand" rifle or the Parker AA1 Special shotgun in 28 gauge — where very little (if any) trading took place, gun collectors were consulted to obtain fair market values.

ORGANIZATION OF LISTINGS

In the early editions of *Gun Trader's Guide*, firearms were frequently organized chronologically by date of production within manufacturers' listings. Firearms aficionados know that many gunmaking companies used the date that a particular model was introduced as the model number. For example, the Colt U.S. Model 1911 semiautomatic pistol was introduced in 1911; the French Model 1936 military rifle was introduced in 1936; and the Remington Model 32 shotgun debuted in 1932. However, during the first quarter of this century, gunmakers began assigning names and numbers that did not relate to the year a gun was introduced. And as the models and their variations multiplied through the years, it became increasingly difficult to track them by date — especially for the less experienced shooting enthusiasts.

To overcome any confusion and to provide information most accurately, *Gun Trader's Guide* was dramatically reorganized to simplify use for the reader. In today's edition, guns are:

- Grouped by category first: Handguns, Rifles and Shotguns.
- They are then arranged alphabetically by name of manufacturer. Or, in the case of some military weapons, by country.
- Within each manufacturer's entries, *Model Numbers* appear first in consecutive numerical order (Model 58, Model 66, Model 629), followed by *Model Names* in alphabetical order (Single-Action Army, Target, Woodsmaster).
- Large handgun manufacturers, such as Colt, Smith & Wesson, etc., are broken down further into separate groupings of PISTOLS and RE-VOLVERS. The index in the back of the book parallels these refinements, so you can find with ease the page on which any gun appears.

Some Winchester and Remington firearms are grouped differently in this edition. For example, The Winchester Model 1894, in its many variations, has been produced since 1894 and is still being manufactured under "Model 94" by U.S. Repeating Arms Co. In general, Winchester used the year of introduction to name its firearms; that is, Model 1890, 1892, 1894, 1895, etc. Then shortly after World War I, Winchester dropped the first two digits and listed the models as 90, 92, 94, 95 etc. Furthermore, new models were given model numbers that had no relation to the date of manufacture. Marlin and some other manufacturers used a similar approach in handling model designations.

Consequently, Winchester rifles are grouped alphanumerically in two different groups: Early Winchesters that were manufactured from 1873 until about 1920 and those manufactured after 1920. If any difficulty is encountered in locating a particular model, look in the INDEX; the different models and their variations are cross-referenced.

Readers in the past have had difficulty in locating certain Remington rifles. In this edition, Remington rifles have been grouped according to action type; that is, single-shot rifles, slide-actions, autoloaders, etc. A survey revealed this to be the easiest way to locate a particular firearm. Again, use the INDEX if any difficulty is encountered.

In researching data for firearms, we have found through the years that not all the information is obtainable. Some manufacturers' records may have been lost, or just not kept up accurately. The result is that some listings may not be complete, and production dates, for example, may only be approximate. We apologize for any inconvenience this may cause you as users of *Gun Trader's Guide*, but we encourage you to communicate with us at the Stoeger offices and send in any clues you may come across, especially in relation to older, out-of-production models.

CAUTION TO READERS: To comply with new Federal regulations, all manufacturers who produce firearms that are intended for disposition to the general public and that are designed to accept large-capacity ammunition feeding devices are required to redesign those models to limit their capacities to 10 rounds or less, or discontinue production or importation. This amendment to the Gun Control Act prohibits the manufacture, transfer or possession of all such devices manufactured after October 13, 1994. The "grandfather" clause of this amendment exempts all such devices lawfully possessed at the time the legislation became law. These "pre-ban" arms (those manufactured before October 13, 1994) may therefore be bought, sold or traded without any additional restrictions imposed by this law.

All "post-ban" feeding devices must meet the new requirements. *For purposes of this book:* Models previously designed to accept high-capacity feeding devices will be listed at their original specifications and capacities if only the feeding device was modified to reduce that capacity.

Regarding shotguns, the general public should be aware that shotgun barrels must be 18 inches or longer; anything shorter is illegal, except for use by military and law-enforcement personnel. A special permit from the BATF is required for all others.

ACKNOWLEDGMENTS

The Publisher wishes to express special thanks to the numerous collectors, dealers, manufacturers, shooting editors and others whose suggestions and advice always contribute to making this a better book.

A big thank you is extended, in particular, to the firearms firms and distributors — their public relations and product personnel, and all the research people that we work with throughout the year — we are especially grateful to all of you for your assistance and cooperation in compiling information for *Gun Trader's Guide* and for allowing us to reproduce photographs and illustrations of your firearms. Finally, thank you to all the dedicated readers who take the time to write in with comments, suggestions and queries about various firearms. We appreciate them all.

HOW TO USE THIS GUIDE

When a gun enthusiast is ready to buy or sell a used gun, he inevitably turns to *GUN TRADER'S GUIDE*. He opens the book, then silently asks two questions: "How much will I be able to get (or expect to pay) for a particular gun?" and, "How was that price obtained?"

First, be aware that the prices contained in this book are "retail"; that is, the price the consumer may expect to pay for a similar item. However, many variables must be considered when buying or selling any gun. In general, scarcity, demand, geographical location, the buyer's position and the gun's condition will govern the selling price of a particular gun. Sentiment also enters into the value of an individual's gun, but cannot be logically cataloged.

To illustrate how the price of a particular gun may fluctuate, let's take the popular Winchester Model 94 and see what its value might be.

In general, the Model 1894 (94) is a lever-action, solid-frame repeater. Round or octagon barrels of 26 inches were standard when the rifle was first introduced in 1894. However, half-octagon barrels were available for a slight increase in price. Various magazine lengths were also available.

Fancy grade versions in all Model 94 calibers were available with 26-inch round, octagon or half-octagon nickel-steel barrels. This grade used a checkered fancy walnut pistol-grip stock and forearm, and was available with either shotgun or rifle-type buttplates.

In addition, Winchester turned out this model in carbine-style with a saddle ring on the left side of the receiver. The carbine had a 20-inch round barrel and full- or half-magazine. Some carbines were supplied with standard grade barrels, while others were made of nickel steel. Trapper models were also available with shortened 14-, 16-, and 18-inch barrels.

In later years, the rifle and trapper versions were dropped and only the carbine remained. Eventually, the saddle ring was eliminated from this model and the carbine buttstock was replaced with a shotgun-type buttstock and shortened forend. After World War II, the finish on Winchester Model 94 carbines changed to strictly hot-caustic bluing; thus, prewar models usually demand a premium over postwar models.

Then in 1964, beginning with serial number 2,700,000, the action on Winchester Model 94s was redesigned for easier manufacturing. Many collectors and firearms enthusiasts considered the change inferior to former models. Whether this is true or not is not the issue; the main reason for a price increase of pre-1964 models was that they were no longer available. This put them immediately in the "scarce" class and made them desirable to collectors.

Shortly after the 1964 transition, Winchester started producing Model 94 commemoratives in an almost endless number — further adding to the confusion on prices. If this were not enough, the Winchester Company was sold in the 1980s and the name changed to U.S. Repeating Arms Co. This firm still manufactured the Model 94 in both standard carbine and Big Bore, and later introduced its "Angle-Eject" model to allow for the mounting of telescopic sights directly over the action.

With the above facts in mind, let's see how to use *GUN TRADER'S GUIDE* to find out the approximate value of a particular Winchester Model 94. Let's say that you recently inherited a rifle that has the inscription "Winchester Model 94" on the barrel. You turn to the rifle section of this book and look under the W's until you find "Winchester." The Contents pages will also tell you where Winchester Rifles begin. The Index in the back of the book is another possible means of locating your rifle. Since the listings in *GUN TRADER'S GUIDE* are arranged within each manufacturer's entry first by Model Numbers in consecutive numerical order (followed by Model Names in alphabetical order), you brief through the pages until you come to "Model 94." At first glance, you realize there are two pages of Model 94 listings, not including the commemoratives. Which of these is yours?

The first step is to try to match the appearance of your model with an illustration in the book. They may all look similar at first, but paying careful attention to detail will soon weed out the models that don't apply. You look at your gun and see that the buttplate is kind of curved, or crescent-shaped. Matching up the appearance leads you to the "Winchester Model 94 Lever Action Rifle."

You think you have your model, but, to be sure, you read through the specifications and see that the barrel on the rifle was 26 inches long — either round, octagonal or half-octagonal. Upon measuring, you find that yours is approximately 26 inches long, maybe a trifle under, and it is obviously round. (Please note that the guns are not always shown in proportion to one another; that is, a carbine might not appear shorter than a rifle.)

Your rifle is marked ".38-55"— the caliber designation. Since the caliber offerings include 38-55, you are further convinced. You read on to find that this rifle was manufactured from 1894 to 1937. After this date, only the shorter-barreled carbine was offered by Winchester and only in calibers 30-30, 32 Special and 25-35.

At this point you know you have a Winchester Model 94 rifle manufactured before World War II. You read the value as $1295 and decide to take the rifle to your local dealer and collect your money. Here are some of the scenarios you may encounter:

1. If the rifle is in excellent condition — that is, if it contains at least 95 percent of its original finish on both the metal and wood and has a perfect bore — then the gun does have a retail value of $1295. However, the dealer is in business to make some profit. If he pays you $1295 for the gun, he will have to charge more than this when he sells it. If more is charged than the fair market value, then either the gun will not sell, or someone will pay more than the gun is worth. Therefore, an honest dealer will have to offer you less than the retail price for the gun to make a fair profit. However, the exact amount will vary. For example, if this dealer already has a dozen or so of the same model on his shelf and they have been slow moving, his offer will probably be low. On the other hand, if the dealer does not have any of this model in stock, but knows several collectors who want it, chances are the dealer may raise his offer.

2. Perhaps you overlooked the rifle's condition. Although the gun apparently functions flawlessly, not much of the original bluing is left. Rather, there are several shiny bright spots mixed with a brown patina finish over the remaining metal. You also notice that much of the original varnish on the wood has disappeared. Consequently, your rifle is not in "excellent" condition, and you will have to settle for less than the value shown in this book.

3. So your Winchester Model 94 rifle looks nearly new, just out of the box, and the rifle works perfectly. Therefore, you are convinced that the dealer is going to pay you full value, less a reasonable profit of between 25% and 35%. When the dealer offers you about half of what you expected, you are shocked! Perhaps you were not aware that the gun had recently been refinished, and although the finish looks new to you, you did not notice the rounding of the formerly sharp edges on the receiver, or the slight funneling of some screw holes — all of which are a dead giveaway that the rifle had at one time been refinished. Therefore, your rifle has less than "book" value.

A knowledgeable gun dealer will check the rifle for proper functioning; the condition of interior parts will also be a factor in determining the value of any firearm.

While any gun's exterior condition is a big factor in determining its value, internal parts also play an important role in pricing.

Now if you are somewhat of an expert and know for certain that your rifle has never been refinished or otherwise tampered with, and there is still at least 95% of its original finish left, and you believe you have a firearm that is worth full book value, a dealer will still offer you from 25% to 35% less; perhaps even less if he is overstocked with this model.

Another alternative is to advertise in a local newspaper, selling the firearm directly to a private individual. However, this approach may prove both frustrating and expensive. In addition, there are federal and local restrictions on the sale of firearms. Chances are, the next time you have a firearm to sell, you will be more than happy to sell to a dealer, letting him make his fair share of profit.

CONDITION

The condition of a firearm is a big factor in determining its value. In some rare collector models, a jump from one condition to another can mean a value difference of several thousand dollars. Therefore, you must be able to determine condition before you can accurately evaluate firearms. Several sets of standards are available, with the National Rifle Association Standards of Condition of Modern Firearms probably being the most popular. However, in recent years, condition has been specified by percentage of original finish remaining on the firearm — both on the wood and metal. Let's see how these standards stack up against each other.

NRA STANDARDS OF CONDITION OF MODERN FIREARMS

- **New:** Not previously sold at retail, in same condition as current factory production.
- **New, Discontinued:** Same as New, but discontinued model.
- **Perfect:** In new condition in every respect; sometimes referred to as mint.
- **Excellent:** New condition, used very little, no noticeable marring of wood or metal, bluing perfect (except at muzzle or sharp edges).
- **Very Good:** In perfect working condition, no appreciable wear on working surfaces, no corrosion or pitting, only minor surface dents or scratches.
- **Good:** In safe working condition, minor wear on working surfaces, no broken parts, no corrosion or pitting that will interfere with proper functioning.
- **Fair:** In safe working condition, but well worn, perhaps requiring replacement of minor parts or adjustments that should be indicated in advertisement; no rust, but may have corrosion pits that do not render the gun unsafe or inoperable.
- **Poor:** Badly worn, rusty and battered, perhaps requiring major adjustment or repairs to place in operating condition.

When a collector firearm has been expertly refinished to "excellent" condition, a rule of thumb is to deduct 50% from the value indicated in this book; if poorly done, deduct 90%.

For the purpose of assigning comparative values as a basis for trading, firearms listed in this book are assumed to be in "excellent" condition, with 95% or better remaining overall finish, no noticeable marring of wood or metal, and bores excellent with no pits. To the novice, this means a practically new gun, almost as though you had removed it from the factory carton. The trained eye, however, will know the difference between "new or mint" condition, and "excellent."

From the previous paragraph, any other defects, regardless of how minor, lower the value from those listed in this book. For example, if more than 5% of the original finish is gone and there are minor surface dents or scratches — regardless of how small — the gun is no longer in "excellent" condition, rather it takes on the condition of "very good," provided the gun is in perfect working order. Even in this state, other than for the minor defects, the gun will still look relatively new to the uninitiated gun buyer.

If the gun is in perfect working condition — functions properly, does not jam and is accurate — but has minor wear on working surfaces, perhaps some bad scratches on the wood or metal, etc., then the gun takes on the condition of "good," one grade below "very good," according to the NRA Standards. Again, the price in this book for that particular firearm must be lowered more to obtain its true value.

The two remaining NRA conditions fall under the headings of "fair" and "poor," respectively.

Previous editions of *GUN TRADER'S GUIDE* gave multiplication factors to use for firearms in other than "excellent" condition. While these factors are still listed below, please be aware that they are not infallible. They are only one "rough" means of establishing a value.

For guns in other than "excellent" condition, multiply the price in this book for the model in question by the following appropriate factors:

Multiplication Factors For Guns In Other Than Excellent Condition	
Condition	**Multiplication Factor**
Mint or New	1.25
Excellent	1.00
Very Good	0.85
Good	0.68
Fair	0.35
Poor	0.15

The above examples present some of the factors that influence firearms' values. There are countless others, and the brief examples given here are meant to provide you with only a basic understanding of the process. Remember, the word "Guide" in *GUN TRADER'S GUIDE* should be taken literally. It is a guide only, not gospel. We sincerely hope, however, that it is helpful when you do decide to buy or sell a used firearm.

CONTENTS

Section II
RIFLES

Section III
SHOTGUNS

Section I
HANDGUNS

ACCU-TEK
Chino, California

Accu-Tek Model AT-9 Auto Pistol
Caliber: 8mm Parabellum, 8-shot magazine. Double action only. 3.2-inch bbl. 6.25 inches overall. Weight: 28 oz. Sights: fixed blade front; adj. rear w/3-dot system. Firing-pin block with no external safety. Stainless or black over stainless finish. Checkered black nylon grips. Announced 1992, but introduced 1995.
Satin Stainless Model **$195**
Matte Black Stainless **200**

Accu-Tek Model AT-25 Auto Pistol
Similar to Model AT-380, except for caliber 25 ACP with 7-shot magazine. Made from 1991 to date.
Lightweight w/aluminum frame **$115**
Bright Stainless (Disc. 1991) **120**
Satin Stainless Model **115**
Matte Black Stainless **120**

Accu-Tek Model AT-32 Auto Pistol
Similar to Model AT-380, except in 32 ACP. Made from 1990 to date.
Lightweight w/aluminum Frame (Disc. 1991). . . . . **$ 95**
Satin Stainless Model **130**
Matte Black Stainless **135**

Accu-Tek Model AT-40 DA Auto Pistol
Caliber: 40 S&W. 7-shot magazine. 3.2-inch bbl., 6.25 inches overall. Weight: 28 oz. Sights: fixed blade front adj. rear w/3-dot system. Firing-pin block with no external safety. Stainless or black over stainless finish. Checkered black nylon grips. Made from 1992 to date.
Satin Stainless Model **$200**
Matte Black Stainless **205**

Accu-Tek Model AT-380 Auto Pistol
Caliber: 380 ACP. 5-shot magazine. 2.75-inch bbl., 5.6 inches overall. Weight: 20 oz. External hammer with slide safety. Grooved black composition grips. Stainless finish. Made from 1992 to date.
Standard Alloy Frame (Disc. 1992) **$130**
Satin Stainless Model **135**
Matte Black Stainless **140**

Accu-Tek Model HC-380SS Auto Pistol **$170**
Caliber: 380 ACP. 13-shot magazine. 2.75-inch bbl., 6 inches overall. Weight: 28 oz. External hammer with slide safety. Checkered black composition grips. Stainless finish. Made from 1993 to date.

NOTE

The following abbreviations are used throughout the Handgun Section: *DA* = Double Action; *SA* = Single Action; *LR* = Long Rifle; *WMR* = Winchester Magnum Rimfire; *adj.* = adjustable; *avail.* = available; *bbl.* = barrel.

ACTION ARMS
Philadelphia, Pennsylvania

See also listings under CZ pistols. Action Arms stopped importing firearms in 1994.

Action Arms AT-84 with Prototype of Model AT-84P in background

Action Arms AT-84 DA Automatic Pistol $400
Caliber: 9mm Parabellum. 15-shot magazine. 4.75-inch bbl., 8 inches overall. Weight: 35 oz. Fixed front sight; drift adj. rear. Checkered walnut stocks. Blued finish. Made in Switzerland 1987-89.

Action Arms AT-84P DA Automatic Pistol $2400
Compact version of the Model AT-84. Only a few prototypes of this model were manufactured in 1985.

Action Arms AT-88S DA Automatic Pistol $450
Calibers: 9mm Parabellum or .41 Action Express, 10-shot magazine. 4.6-inch bbl., 8.1 inches overall. Weight: 35.3 oz. (empty). Fixed blade front sight; adj. rear. Checkered walnut stocks. Imported 1989-91.

Action Arms AT-88P DA Automatic Pistol $465
Compact version of the AT-88S with 3.7-inch bbl. Imported 1989-1991.

ADVANTAGE ARMS
St. Paul, Minnesota

Advantage Arms Model 6 Double Derringer $245
Calibers: .410 and 45 Colt. 6-inch bbl., 8.2 inches overall. Weight: 21 oz. Satin or high-polished stainless steel.

Advantage Arms Model 7 Ultra Lightweight
Calibers: 38 S&W, 380 Auto, 32 S&W Long, 32 Mag., 38 Special, 22 LR and 44 Mag. Same general specifications as Model 6, except weighs 7.5 oz. and chambered for different calibers.
38 S&W, 380 Auto and 32 S&W **$125**
32 Magnum **135**
38 Special **140**
22 Long Rifle **135**
44 Special **345**

Advantage Arms Model 11 Lightweight $140
Same general specifications as Model 7, except weighs 11 oz. and chambered for 38 Special only.

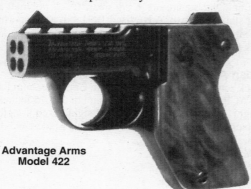

Advantage Arms
Model 422

Advantage Arms Model 422 . . . . $220
Hammerless, top-break, 4-bbl. derringer w/rotating firing pin. Calibers: 22 LR and 22 Mag. 4-cartridge capacity. Bbl: 2.5 inches, 4.5 inches overall. Weight: 15 oz. Fixed sights. Walnut grips. Blued, nickel or PDQ matte black finish. Made 1985-87.

S. A. ALKARTASUNA FABRICA DE ARMAS
Guernica, Spain

Alkartasuna Ruby

Alkartasuna "Ruby" Automatic Pistol $250
Caliber: 32 Automatic (7.65mm). 9-shot magazine. 3.63-inch bbl., 6.38 inches overall. Weight: about 34 oz. Fixed sights. Blued finish. Checkered wood or hard rubber stocks. Made 1917-1922. *Note:* Mfd. by a number of Spanish firms, the Ruby was a secondary standard service pistol of the French Army in World Wars I and II. Specimens made by Alkartasuna bear the "Alkar" trademark.

AMERICAN ARMS
Kansas City, Missouri

American Arms Buckhorn SA Revolver $255
Caliber: 44 Mag., 6-shot cylinder. 7.5-inch bbl., blade front sight; fixed rear sight. Made from 1993 to date.

American Arms CX22

American Arms CX-22 DA Automatic Pistol
Similar to Model PX-22, except with 8-shot magazine. 3.33-inch bbl., 6.5 inches overall. Weight: 22 oz. Made from 1990 to 1995.
Standard w/Chrome Slide (Disc. 1990) $130
Classic Model 125

American Arms EP-380

American Arms EP-380 DA Automatic Pistol . . . $320
Caliber: 380 Automatic. 7-shot magazine. 3.5-inch bbl., 6.5 inches overall. Weight: 25 oz. Fixed front sight; square-notch adj. rear. Stainless finish. Checkered wood stocks. Made 1989-91.

American Arms Escort DA Auto Pistol $250
Caliber: 380 ACP, 7-shot magazine. 3.38-inch bbl., 6.13 inches overall. Weight: 19 ounces. Fixed, low-profile sights. Stainless steel frame, slide, and trigger; nickel-steel bbl. Soft polymer grips. Loaded chamber indicator. Made from 1995 to date.

American Arms P-98

American Arms P-98 DA Automatic Pistol $155
Caliber: 22 LR. 8-shot magazine. 5-inch bbl., 8.25 inches overall. Weight: 25 oz. Fixed front sight; square-notch adj. rear. Blued finish. Serrated black polymer stocks. *See* illustration preceding page.

American Arms PK 22

American Arms PK-22 DA Automatic Pistol $145
Caliber: 22 LR. 8-shot magazine. 3.33-inch bbl. 6.33 inches overall. Weight: 22 oz. Fixed front sight; V-notch rear. Blued finish. Checkered black polymer stocks. Made from 1989 to date.

American Arms PX-22 DA Automatic Pistol $135
Caliber: 22 LR. 7-shot magazine. 2.75-inch bbl. 5.33 inches overall. Weight: 15 oz. Fixed front sight; V-notch rear. Blued finish. Checkered black polymer stocks. Made from 1989 to date.

American Arms PX-25 DA Automatic Pistol $145
Same general specifications as the Model PX-22, except chambered for 25 ACP. Made from 1991 to date.

American Arms Regulator SA Revolver
Similar in appearance to the Colt Single-Action Army. Calibers: 357 Mag., 44-40, 45 Long Colt. 6-shot cylinder. 4.75- and 7.5-inch bbl. Blade front sight, fixed rear sight. Brass trigger guard/backstrap on Standard model. Casehardened steel on Deluxe model. Made from 1992 to date.

Standard Model $215
Standard Combo Set
   (45 LC/45 ACP & 44-40/44 Spec.) 245
Deluxe Model 240
Deluxe Combo Set
   (45 LC/45 ACP & 44-40/44 Spec.) 275
Stainless Steel 265

American Arms Sabre

American Arms Sabre DA Automatic Pistol
Calibers: 9mm Luger, 40 S&W. 8-shot magazine in 9mm, 9-shot in 40 S&W. 3.75-inch bbl. 6.9 inches overall. Weight: 26 oz. Fixed blade front sight; square-notch adj. rear. Black polymer stocks. Blued or stainless finish. Advertised 1991, but not imported.
Blued Finish $235
Stainless Steel 265

American Arms Spectre DA Auto Pistol
Blowback action, fires from closed bolt. Calibers: 9mm Parabellum, 45 ACP, 30-shot magazine. 6-inch bbl., 13.75 inches overall. Weight: 4 lbs. 8 oz. Adj. post front sight, fixed U-notch rear sight. Black nylon stocks. Matte black finish. Made 1993-1994.
9mm Parabellum $295
40 S&W (Disc. 1991) 320
45 ACP 350

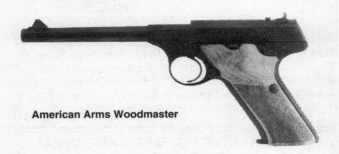

American Arms Woodmaster

American Arms Woodmaster SA Auto Pistol . . . $140
Caliber: 22 LR. 10-shot magazine. 5.88-inch bbl. 10.5 inches overall. Weight: 31 oz. Fixed front sight, square-notch adj. rear. Blued finish. Checkered wood stocks. Discontinued 1989.

AMERICAN DERRINGER CORPORATION
Waco, Texas

American Derringer
Model 1

American Derringer Model 1, Stainless
Single-action pocket pistol. 2-shot capacity. Bbl.: 3 inches, 4.82 inches overall. Weight: 15 oz. Automatic bbl. selection. Satin or high-polished stainless steel. Rosewood grips. Made from 1985 to date.
45 Colt, 44-40 Win., 44 Special, .410 × 2.5" $265
45-70, 44 Mag., 41 Mag., 30-30 Win., 223 Rem. 225
357 Max., 357 Mag., 45 Win Mag., 9mm Luger 195
38 Special, 38 Super, 32 Mag., 22 LR, 22 Rim. Mag. 175

American Derringer Model 2 Steel "Pen" Pistol

Calibers: 22 LR, 25 Auto, 32 Auto (7.65mm). Single shot. 2-inch bbl. 5.6 inches overall (4.2 inches in pistol format). Weight: 5 oz. Stainless finish. Made 1993 to 1994.

22 Long Rifle	$195
25 Auto	205
32 Auto	225

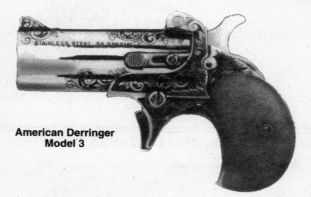

**American Derringer
Model 3**

American Derringer Model 3 Stainless Steel $75

Single Shot. Caliber: 38 Special. Bbl.: 2.5 inches. 4.9 inches overall. Weight: 8.5 oz. Rosewood grips. Made from 1984 to date.

American Derringer Model 4 Double Derringer

Calibers: 357 Mag., 357 Max., 44 Mag., 45 LC, 45 ACP (upper bbl. and 3-inch .410 shotshell (lower bbl.). 4.1-inch bbl. 6 inches overall. Weight: 16.5 oz. Stainless steel. Stag horn grips. Made from 1984 to date.

357 Mag., 357 Max.	$260
44 Mag., 45 LC, 45 ACP	325

**American Derringer
Model 6**

American Derringer Model 6 . . . . $250

Caliber: .410 or 45 Colt. Bbl.: 6 inches. 8.2 inches overall. Weight: 22 oz. Satin or high-polished stainless steel with rosewood grips. Made from 1986 to date.

American Derringer Model 7

Same general specifications as the Model 1, except high-strength aircraft aluminum is used to replace some of the stainless steel parts, which reduces its weight to 7.5 oz. Made from 1986 to date.

22 Long Rifle, 22 WMR.	$150
38 Calibers, 32 Mag., 32 S&W Long.	140

American Derringer Model 10

Same general specifications as the Model 7, except chambered for 45 ACP or 45 Long Colt.

45 ACP	$165
45 Long Colt	180

American Derringer Model 11 . . . . $130

Same general specifications as Model 7, except chambered for .38 Special only, and weighs 11 oz. Made 1980 to date.

American Derringer 25 Automatic Pistol $310

Calibers: 25 ACP or 250 Mag. Bbl.: 2.1 inches. 4.4 inches overall. Weight: 15.5 oz. Smooth rosewood grips. Made from 1984 to date.

**American Derringer
Model 38 DA**

American Derringer Model 38 DA Derringer

Hammerless, double action, double bbl (over/under). Calibers: 38 Special, 9mm Luger, 357 Mag., 40 S&W. 3-inch bbl. Weight: 14.5 oz. Made from 1990 to date.

38 Special	$155
9mm Luger	175
357 Mag.	210
40 S&W	220

American Derringer Alaskan Survival Model $225

Same general specifications as the Model 4, except upper bbl. comes in 45-70 or 3-inch .410 and 45 Colt lower bbl. Also available in 45 Auto, 45 Colt, 44 Special, 357 Mag. and .357 Max. Made from 1985 to date.

American Derringer Cop DA Derringer $235

Hammerless, double-action, four-bbl. derringer. Caliber: 357 Mag. 3.15-inch bbl., 5.5 inches overall. Weight: 16 oz. Blade front sight; open, notched rear sight. Rosewood grips. Made from 1990 to date.

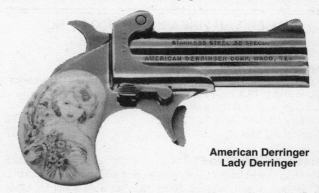

**American Derringer
Lady Derringer**

American Derringer Lady Derringer

Same general specifications as Model 1, except with custom-tuned action fitted with scrimshawed synthetic ivory grips. Calibers: 32 H&R Mag., 32 Special, 38 Special (additional calibers on request). Deluxe Grade engraved and highly polished with French fitted jewelry box. Made from 1991 to date. *See* illustration previous page.

Lady Derringer **$175**
Deluxe Engraved **560**

American Derringer Mini-Cop DA Derringer $195

Same general specifications as the American Derringer Cop, except chambered for 22 Magnum. Made 1990-1995.

**American Derringer
Semmerling LM-4**

American Derringer Semmerling LM-4

Manually operated repeater. Calibers: 45 ACP or 9mm. 5-shot (45 ACP) or 7-shot magazine (9mm). 3.6-inch bbl. 5.2 inches overall. Weight: 24 oz. Made from 1986 to date. Limited availability.

Blued Finish **$2395**
Stainless Steel **2650**

American Derringer Texas Commemorative

Same general specifications as Model 1, except with solid brass frame, stainless bbls. and rosewood grips. Calibers: 38 Special, 44-40 Win. or 45 Colt. Made 1991 to date.

38 Special **$175**
44-40 or 45 Colt **250**

AMERICAN FIREARMS MFG. CO., INC.
San Antonio, Texas

American 25 Auto Pistol

Caliber: 25 Auto. 8-shot magazine. 2.1-inch bbl. 4.4 inches overall. Weight: 14.5 oz. Fixed sights. Stainless or blued ordnance steel. Smooth walnut stocks. Made 1966-1974.

Stainless Steel Model **$170**
Blued Steel Model **135**

American 380 Auto Pistol $325

Stainless steel. Caliber: 380 Auto. 8-shot magazine. 3.5-inch bbl. 5.5 inches overall. Weight: 20 oz. Smooth walnut stocks. Made 1972-74.

American 380 Auto Pistol

AMT (ARCADIA MACHINE & TOOL)

AMT Hardballer

AMT 45 ACP Hardballer $375

Caliber: 45 ACP. 7-shot magazine. 5-inch bbl. 8.5 inches overall. Weight: 39 oz. Adj. or fixed sights. Serrated matte slide rib. Wraparound rubber grips.

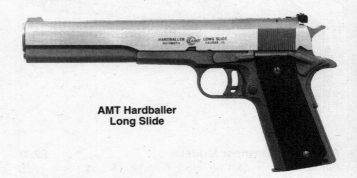

**AMT Hardballer
Long Slide**

AMT 45 ACP Hardballer Long Slide $460

Similar to the standard AMT Hardballer except with 2-inch longer bbl. and slide. Discontinued 1991.

AMT 1911 Government Model Auto Pistol

Caliber: 45 ACP. 7-shot magazine. 5-inch bbl. 8.5 inches overall. Weight: 38 ounces. Fixed sights. Made from 1979 to date.

Standard Model **$325**
Stainless (Disc. 1991) **375**

AMT Automag II Automatic Pistol $225
Caliber: 22 WRF. 9-shot magazine. Bbl. lengths: 3.38-,4.5-, 6-inch. Weight: 32 oz. Fully adj. Millett sights. Stainless finish. Smooth black composition stocks. Made from 1986 to date.

AMT Automag III Automatic Pistol $275
Calibers: 30 M1 and 9mm Win., 8-shot magazine. 6.38-inch bbl. 10.5 inches overall. Weight: 43 ounces. Millet adj. sights. Stainless finish. Carbon fiber grips. Made from 1989 to date.

AMT Automag IV Automatic Pistol $450
Calibers: 10mm Mag., 45 Win. Mag. 7-shot magazine. 6.5- or 8.63-inch bbl. 10.5 inches overall. Weight 46 oz. Millet adj. sights. Stainless finish. Carbon fiber grips. Made from 1990 to date.

AMT Automag V Automatic Pistol $675
Caliber: 50 A.E. 5-shot magazine. 7-inch bbl. 10.5 inches overall. Weight: 46 oz. Custom adj. sights. Stainless finish. Carbon fiber grips. Made from 1994 to 1995.

AMT Backup

AMT Backup Automatic Pistol $160
Caliber: 380, 5-shot magazine. 2.5-inch bbl. 5 inches overall. Weight: 18 oz. Open sights. Carbon fiber Grips. Made from 1990 to date.

AMT Backup II Automatic Pistol
Caliber: 380 ACP, 5-shot magazine, 2.5-inch bbl., 5 inches overall. Weight: 18 oz. Fixed open sights. Carbon-fiber grips. Stainless steel finish. Made from 1993 to 1995.
Single Action. $250
DA 265

AMT Backup DAO

AMT Backup DAO Auto Pistol $170
Similar to the AMT Backup, except double action only with re-contoured slide and enlarged trigger guard. Made from 1992 to date.

**AMT Bull's Eye
Target Model**

AMT Bull's Eye Target Model $290
Caliber: 40 S&W. 8-shot magazine. 5-inch bbl. 8.5 inches overall. Weight: 38 oz. Millet adjustable sights. Wide adj. trigger. Wraparound Neoprene grips. Made 1990-92.

AMT Javelina $425
Caliber: 10mm, 8-shot magazine. 7-inch bbl. 10.5 inches overall. Weight: 48 oz. Long grip safety, beveled magazine well, wide adj. trigger. Millet adj. sights. Wraparound Neoprene grips. Stainless finish. Made 1991-93.

AMT Lightning Auto Pistol
Caliber: 22 LR. 10-shot magazine. 5-, 6.5-, 8.5-, 10-inch bbls. 10.75 inches overall w/6.5-inch bbl. Weight: 45 oz. w/6.5-inch bbl. Millett adj. sights. Checkered rubber grips. Stainless finish. Made 1984-87.
Standard Model $185
Bull's-Eye Model 275

AMT On Duty DA Pistol
Calibers: 40 S&W, 9mm Luger, 45 ACP. 15-shot (9mm), 13-shot (40 S&W) or 9-shot (45 ACP) magazine. 4.5-inch bbl. 7.75 inches overall. Weight: 32 oz. Hard anodized aluminum frame. Stainless steel slide and bbl. Carbon fiber grips. Made 1991-94.
9mm or 40 S&W $325
45 ACP 380

AMT Skipper Auto Pistol

AMT Skipper Auto Pistol **$300**
Calibers: 40 S&W and 45 ACP. 7-shot magazine. 4.25-inch bbl.
7.5 inches overall. Weight: 33 oz. Millet adj. sights. Walnut
grips. Matte finish stainless steel. Made 1990-92.

ANSCHUTZ PISTOLS
Ulm, Germany
Mfd. by J.G. Anschutz GmbH Jagd und Sportwaffenfabrik

Anschutz Exemplar

Anschutz Exemplar Bolt-Action Pistol
Calibers: 22 LR, 5-shot clip. 10- or 14-inch bbl. 19 inches overall
(w/10-inch bbl.). Weight: 3.33 lbs. Match 64 action. Slide safety.
Hooded ramp post front sight, adjustable open notched rear.
European walnut contoured grip. Made from 1990 to 1995. *Note:*
The 22 WMR chambering was also advertised, but never manufactured.

22 LR with 10-inch bbl.	**$315**
22 LR with 14-inch bbl.	350
Left-Hand Model.	330

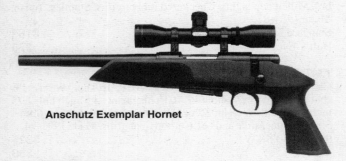

Anschutz Exemplar Hornet

Anschutz Exemplar Hornet **$595**
Based on the Anschutz Match 54 action, tapped and grooved for
scope mounting; no open sights. Caliber: 22 Hornet, 5-shot
magazine. 10-inch bbl. 20 inches overall. Weight: 4.35 lbs.
Checkered European walnut stock. Winged safety. Made from
1990 to 1995.

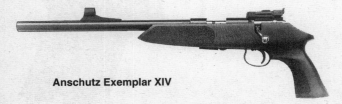

Anschutz Exemplar XIV

Anschutz Exemplar XIV **$325**
Same general specifications as the standard Exemplar Bolt Action Pistol, except with 14-inch bbl., weight 4.15 lbs. Made from
1989 to 1995.

ASTRA PISTOLS
Guernica, Spain
Manufactured by Unceta y Compania

Astra Model 41 DA Revolver **$200**
Same general specifications as Model 44 (below), except in 41
Mag. Made 1980-1985.

Astra Model 44 DA Revolver

Astra Model 44 DA Revolver
Similar to Astra 357, except chambered for 44 Magnum. Bbls.:
6-, 8.5-inch. 11.5 inches overall with 6-inch bbl. Weight: 44 oz.
with 6-inch bbl. Made 1980-93.

Blued Finish (Disc. 1987)	**$225**
Stainless Finish (Disc. 1993).	275

Astra Model 45 DA Revolver, ... **$220**
Similar to Astra 357, except chambered for 45 Colt or 45 ACP.
Bbls.: 6- or 8.5-inch. 11.5 inches overall w/6-inch bbl. Weight:
44 oz. w/6-inch bbl. Made 1980-87.

Astra Model 200 Firecat

Astra Model 200 Firecat Vest Pocket
Auto Pistol **$175**
Caliber: 25 Automatic (6.35mm). 6-shot magazine. 2.25-inch
bbl. 4.38 inches overall. Weight: 11.75 oz. Fixed sights. Blued
finish. Plastic stocks. Made from 1920 to date; U.S. importation
discontinued in 1968.

Astra Model 202

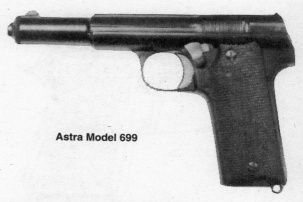

Astra Model 699

Astra Model 202 Firecat Vest Pocket Auto Pistol . . $495

Same general specifications as the Model 200 except chromed and engraved with pearl grips.

Astra Model 357
3-inch barrel

Astra Model 357 DA Revolver $190

Caliber: 357 Magnum. 6-shot cylinder. Bbls.: 3-, 4-, 6-, 8.5-inch. 11.25 inches overall w/6-inch bbl. Weight: 42 oz. w/6-inch bbl. Ramp front sight, adj. rear sight. Blued finish. Checkered wood stocks. Made 1972-1988.

Astra Model 600 Mil./Police Type Auto Pistol . . . $300

Calibers: 32 Automatic (7.65mm),9mm Luger. Magazine: 10-(32 cal.) or 8-shot (9mm). 5.25-inch bbl. 8 inches overall. Weight: about 33 oz. Fixed sights. Blued finish. Checkered wood or plastic stocks. Made 1944-45.

Astra Model 800 Condor

Astra Model 800 Condor Military Auto Pistol . . . $895

Similar to Models 400 and 600, except has an external hammer. Caliber: 9mm Luger. 8-shot magazine. 5.25-inch bbl. 8.25 inches overall. Weight: 32.5 oz. Fixed sights. Blued finish. Plastic stocks. Made 1958-1965.

Astra Model 400

Astra Model 400 Auto Pistol $260

Caliber: 9mm Bayard Long (38 ACP, 9mm Browning Long, 9mm Glisenti, 9mm Luger and 9mm Steyr cartridges may be used interchangeably in this pistol because of its chamber design).9-shot magazine. 6-inch bbl.10 inches overall. Weight: 35 oz. Fixed sights. Blued finish. Plastic stocks. Made 1922-1945. *Note:* This pistol, as well as Astra Models 600 and 3000, is a modification of the Browning Model 1912.

Astra Model 2000 Camper

Camper Automatic Pistol. $255

Same as Model 2000 Cub, except chambered for 22 Short only, has 4-inch bbl, overall length, 6.25 inches, weight, 11.5 oz. Made 1955-1960.

Astra Model 2000 Cub

Astra Model 2000 Cub Pocket Auto Pistol $200
Calibers: 22 Short, 25 Auto. 6-shot magazine. 2.25-inch bbl. 4.5 inches overall. Weight: about 11 oz. Fixed sights. Blued or chromed finish. Plastic stocks. Made from 1954 to date; U.S. importation discontinued in 1968.

Astra Model 3000 Pocket Auto Pistol $265
Calibers: 22 LR, 32 Automatic (7.65mm), 380 Auto (9mm Short). 10-shot magazine (22 cal.), 7-shot (32 cal.), 6-shot (380 cal.). 4-inch bbl. 6.38 inches overall. Weight: about 22 oz. Fixed sights. Blued finish. Plastic stocks. Made 1947-1956.

Astra Model 3003

Astra Model 3003 Pocket Auto Pistol $425
Same general specifications as the Model 3000 except chromed and engraved with pearl grips. Discontinued 1956.

Astra Model 4000 Falcon

Astra Model 4000 Falcon Auto Pistol $350
Similar to Model 3000, except has an external hammer. Calibers: 22 LR, 32 Automatic (7.65mm), 380 Auto (9mm Short). 10-shot magazine (22 LR), 8-shot (32 Auto), 7-shot (380 Auto). 3.66-inch bbl. 6.5 inches overall. Weight: 20 oz. (22 cal.) or 24.75 oz. (32 and 380). Fixed sights. Blued finish. Plastic stocks. Made 1956-1971.

Astra Model A-60 DA Automatic Pistol $265
Similar to the Constable, except in 380 only, with 13-shot magazine and slide-mounted ambidextrous safety. Blued finish only. Made 1980-1991.

Astra Model A-70 Compact Auto Pistol
Calibers: 9mm Parabellum, 40 S&W. 8-shot (9mm) or 7-shot (40 S&W) magazine. 3.5-inch bbl. 6.5 inches overall. Blued, nickel or stainless finish. Weight: 29.3 oz. Made from 1992 to date.
Blued Finish	**$255**
Nickel Finish	275
Stainless Finish	295

Astra Model A-75 Decocker Auto Pistol
Similar to the Model 70, except in 9mm, 40 S&W and 45 ACP with decocking system and contoured pebble-textured grips. Made from 1993 to date.
Blued Finish, 9mm or 40 S&W	**$295**
Nickel Finish, 9mm or 40 S&W.	325
Stainless, 9mm or 40 S&W	375
Blued Finish, 45 ACP	325
Nickel Finish, 45 ACP	360
Stainless, 45 ACP	395

Astra Model A-75 Ultralight $385
Similar to the standard Model 75, except 9mm only with 24-oz. alloy frame. Made from 1994 to date.

Astra Model A-80

Astra Model A-80 Auto Pistol $280
Calibers: 9mm Parabellum, 38 Super, 45 ACP. 15-shot magazine or 9-shot (45 ACP). Bbl.: 3.75 inches. 7 inches overall. Weight: 36 oz. Made 1982-89.

Astra Model A-90 DA Automatic Pistol $295
Calibers: 9mm Parabellum, 45 ACP. 15-shot (9mm) or 9-shot (45 ACP) magazine. 3.75-inch bbl. 7 inches overall. Weight: about 40 oz. Fixed sights. Blued finish. Checkered plastic stocks. Made 1985-1990.

Astra Model A-100 DA Auto Pistol

Same general specifications as the Model A-90, except selective double action chambered for 9mm Luger, 40 S&W or 45 ACP. Made in 1991.

Blued Finish	**$295**
Nickel Finish	330
For Night Sights, **add**	100

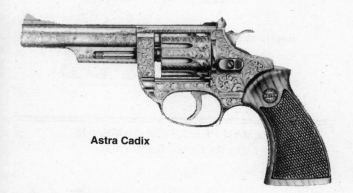

Astra Cadix

Astra Cadix DA Revolver **$150**

Calibers: 22 LR, 38 Special. 9-shot (22 LR) or 5-shot (38 cal.) cylinder. Bbls.: 4- or 6-inch. Weight: about 27 oz. w/6-inch bbl. Ramp front sight, adj. rear sight. Blued finish. Plastic stocks. Made 1960-68.

Standard Model	**$ 150**
Lightly Engraved Model	245
Heavily Engraved Model (shown)	+400

Astra Constable

Astra Constable DA Auto Pistol

Calibers: 22 LR, 32 Automatic (7.65mm), 380 Auto (9mm Short). Magazine capacity: 10-shot (22 LR), 8-shot (32), 7-shot (380). 3.5-inch bbl. 6.5 inches overall. Weight: about 24 oz. Blade front sight, windage adj. rear. Blued or chromed finish. Made 1965-1992.

Stainless Finish	**$290**
Blued or Chrome	235
Chrome (Disc. 1990)	250

AUTO-ORDNANCE CORPORATION
West Hurley, New York

**Auto-Ordnance 1911A1
Government Auto Pistol**

Auto-Ordnance 1911A1 Government Auto Pistol

Copy of Colt 1911A1 semiautomatic pistol. Calibers: 9mm Para., 38 Super, 10mm, 45 ACP. 9-shot (9mm, 38 Super) or 7-shot (10mm, 45 ACP) magazine. 5-inch bbl. 8.5 inches overall. Weight: 39 oz. Fixed blade front sight; rear adj. Blued finish. Checkered plastic stocks.

45 ACP Caliber	**$270**
9mm, 10mm, 38 Super	305

Auto-Ordnance 1911A1 40 S&W Pistol **$325**

Similar to the Model 1911A1, except has 4.5-inch bbl. with 7.75-inch overall length. 8-shot magazine. Weight: 37 oz. Blade front and adj. rear sights with 3-dot system. Checkered black rubber wraparound grips. Made from 1991 to date.

Auto-Ordnance 1911 "The General" **$295**

Caliber: 45 ACP. 7-shot magazine. 4.5-inch bbl. 7.75 inches overall. Weight: 37 oz. Blued nonglare finish. Made from 1992 to date.

**Auto-Ordnance Model 1927
A-5 w/drum magazine**

Auto-Ordnance 1927 A-5 Semiautomatic Pistol

Similar to Thompson Model 1928A submachine gun, except has no provision for automatic firing and does not have detachable buttstock. Caliber: 45 ACP, 5-, 15-, 20- and 30-shot detachable box magazines; 30-shot drum also available. 13-inch finned bbl., 26 inches overall. Weight: about 6.75 lbs. Adj. rear sight, blade front. Blued finish. Walnut grips. Made 1977-1991.

With box magazine	**$1000**
With drum magazine (illustrated)	1295

Auto-Ordnance Pit Bull Automatic Pistol $285
Caliber: 45 ACP. 7-shot magazine. 3.5-inch bbl. 7 inches overall.
Weight: 32 oz. Fixed front sight; square-notch rear. Blued finish.
Checkered plastic stocks. Made from 1991 to date.

Auto-Ordnance ZG-51 Government Auto Pistol . . $290
Caliber: 45 ACP. 7-shot magazine. 3.5-inch bbl. 7.25 inches
overall. Weight: 36 oz. Fixed blade front sight; drift adj. rear.
Blued finish. Checkered plastic stocks. Made 1989-1990.

BAUER FIREARMS CORPORATION
Fraser, Michigan

Bauer 25 Automatic

Bauer 25 Automatic Pistol $145
Stainless steel. Caliber: 25 Automatic. 6-shot magazine. 2.13-
inch bbl. 4 inches overall. Weight: 10 oz. Fixed sights. Checkered walnut or simulated pearl stocks. Made 1972-1984.

BAYARD PISTOLS
Herstal, Belgium
Mfd. by Anciens Etablissements Pieper

Bayard Model 1908 Pocket Automatic Pistol $225
Calibers: 25 Automatic (6.35mm), 32 Automatic (7.65mm), 380
Automatic (9mm Short). 6-shot magazine. 2.25-inch bbl. 4.88
inches overall. Weight: about 16 oz. Fixed sights. Blued finish.
Hard rubber stocks.

Bayard Model 1923 Pocket 25 Automatic Pistol . . $195
Caliber: 25 Automatic (6.35mm). 2.13-inch bbl. 4.31 inches
overall. Weight: 12 oz. Fixed sights. Blued finish. Checkered
hard-rubber stocks.

Bayard Model 1923 Pocket Automatic Pistol $235
Calibers: 32 Automatic (7.65mm), 380 Automatic (9mm Short).
6-shot magazine. 3.31-inch bbl. 5.5 inches overall. Weight:
about 19 oz. Fixed sights. Blued finish. Checkered hard-rubber
stocks.

Bayard Model 1930 Pocket 25 Automatic Pistol . . $210
This is a modification of the Model 1923, which it closely resembles.

Bayard Model 1930

BEEMAN PRECISION ARMS, INC.
Santa Rosa, California

**Beeman P08 Automatic
Pistol**

Beeman P08 Automatic Pistol $270
Caliber: 22 LR. 10-shot magazine. 3.8-inch bbl. 7.8 inches overall. Weight: 25 oz. Fixed sights. Blued finish. Checkered hardwood grips. Imported 1986-1991.

Beeman Mini P08 Automatic Pistol $265
Caliber: Same general specifications as P08, except shorter 3.5-
inch bbl., 7.4 inches overall and weight of 20 oz. Imported 1986-
1991.

Beeman SP Deluxe Metallic Silhouette
Caliber: 22 LR. Single shot. Bbl.: 6, 8, 10 or 15 inches. Adj. rear
sight; receiver ground for scope mount. Walnut target grips
w/adj. palm rest. Made 1985-86.
With 8-or 10-inch bbl. $195
With 12-inch bbl. 215
With 15-inch bbl. 235

Beeman/FAS 601 Semiautomatic
Caliber: 22 Short. 9.25-inch sight radius. Weight: about 41 oz.
Top loading magazine. Ventilated with gas vents. Adj. trigger.
Right $650
Left 675

Beeman/FAS 602 Semiautomatic
Caliber: 22 LR. 8.5-inch sight radius. Weight: 40 oz.
Right **$620**
Left **650**

**Beeman/Hämmerli Model 150
Free Pistol**

Beeman/Hämmerli Model 150 Free Pistol $1300
Caliber: 22 LR. Free-floating precision bbl. w/low axis relative to hand. Martini-type locking action w/sidemounted locking lever. Sight radius 14.8 inches. Micrometer rear sight adj. for windage and elevation. Select walnut grip with handrest. Made from 1990 to date.

Beeman/Hämmerli Model 152 Electronic Pistol
Same general specifications as Model 150, except with electronic trigger.
Right Hand **$1400**
Left Hand **1450**

Beeman/Hämmerli Model 208S

Beeman/Hämmerli Model 208S Target Pistol . . $1095
Caliber: 22 LR. 8-shot magazine. 6-inch bbl. 10.2 inches overall. Weight: 37.3 oz. Micrometer rear sight, ramp front sight. Blued finish. Stippled walnut stocks with adj. heel plate. Imported from 1990 to date.

Beeman/Hämmerli Model 212 Hunter Pistol $925
Caliber: 22 LR. 8-shot magazine. 5-inch bbl. 8.6 inches overall. Weight: 31 oz. Blade front sight, square-notched rear. Blued finish. Checkered walnut stocks. Imported from 1990 to date.

Beeman/Hämmerli Model 215 Target Pistol $910
Same general specifications as Model 208S, except with fewer deluxe features. Imported from 1990 to date.

Beeman/Hämmerli Model 232 Rapid Fire Pistol . $995
Caliber: 22 Short. 6-shot magazine. 5.2-inch bbl. 10.5 inches overall. Weight: 44 oz. Fully adj. target sights. Blued finish. Stippled walnut wraparound target stocks. Imported from 1990 to date.

**Beeman/Hämmerli Model 280
Sport Pistol**

Beeman/Hämmerli Model 280 Sport Pistol $1095
Calibers: 22 LR, 32 S&W. 5-shot (32 S&W) or 6-shot (22 LR) clip. 4.5-inch bbl. Weight: 35 to 39 oz. Handrest grip. Made from 1990 to date.

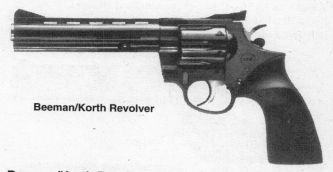

Beeman/Korth Revolver

Beeman/Korth Revolver $2195
Calibers: 357 Mag. or 22 LR with interchangeable combo cylinders of 357 Mag./9mm Para. or 22 LR/22 WMR. Bbl.: 6-inch target; 3-, 4-inch combat. Walnut grips. Discontinued 1993.

Beeman/Korth Semiauto Pistol

Beeman/Korth Semiauto Pistol $1895
Calibers: 30 Luger, 9mm Para. 14-shot magazine. 4- or 5-inch bbl. All-steel construction, recoil-operated; adj. rear sight. Imported from 1990 to date.

Beeman/Unique 32U Rapid Fire Pistol
Caliber: 32 S&W Long (wadcutter). 5.9-inch bbl. Weight: 40 oz. Blade front, adj. rear target sights. Trigger adj. for weight and position. Blued finish. Stippled handrest grips. Imported from 1990 to date.
Right-Hand Model . . . . $ 995
Left-Hand Model. 1025

Beeman/Unique DES/69-U Target Pistol

Beeman/Unique DES/69-U Target Pistol
Caliber: 22 LR. 5-shot magazine. 5.9-inch bbl. Trigger adjusts for position and pull weight. Comes with 250 gm counterweight. Weight: about 36 oz. Adj. grips. Imported 1990-93.
Right-Hand Model $950
Left-Hand Model. 975

Beeman/Unique 2000-U Match Pistol

Beeman/Unique 2000-U Match Pistol
Caliber: 22 Short. Designed for rapid fire. Weight: 2.7 lbs. Special light alloy frame, solid steel slide and shock absorber. Five vents for recoil reduction. Handrest grip. Imported 1990-93.
Right-Hand Model $695
Left-Hand Model. 750

BEHOLLA PISTOL
Suhl, Germany
Mfd. by both Becker and Holländer and Stenda-Werke GmbH

Beholla Pocket Automatic Pistol $175
Caliber: 32 Automatic (7.65mm). 7-shot magazine. 2.9-inch bbl. 5.5 inches overall. Weight: 22 oz. Fixed sights. Blued finish. Serrated wood or hard rubber stocks. Made by Becker and Hollander 1915-1920, by Stenda-Werke circa 1920-25. *Note:* Essentially the same pistol was manufactured concurrently with the Stenda version as the "Leonhardt" by H. M. Gering and as the "Menta" by August Menz.

Beholla Pocket Pistol*

BERETTA USA CORP.
Accokeek, Maryland

Beretta pistols are manufactured by Fabbrica D'Armi Pietro Beretta S. p. A. in the Gardone Valtrompia (Brescia), Italy. This prestigious firm has been in business for over 300 years. Since the late 1970s, many of the models sold in the U.S have been made at the Accokeek (MD) plant.

Beretta Model 20 Double-Action Auto Pistol $135
Caliber: 25 ACP. 8-shot magazine. 2.5-inch bbl. 4.9 inches overall. Weight: 10.9 oz. Plastic or walnut grips. Fixed sights. Made 1984-85.

Beretta Model 21

Beretta Model 21 Double-Action Auto Pistol
Calibers: 22 LR and 25 ACP. 7-shot (22 LR) or 8-shot (25 ACP) magazine. 2.5-inch bbl. 4.9 inches overall. Weight: about 12 oz. Blade front sight, V-notch rear. Walnut grips. Made from 1985 to date.
Blued Finish $160
Nickel Finish (22 LR only) 200
Model 21EL Engraved Model. 205

Beretta Model 70 Automatic Pistol $195
Improved version of Model 1935. Steel or lightweight alloy. Calibers: 32 Auto (7.65mm), 380 Auto (9mm Short). 8-shot (32) or 7-shot (380) magazine. 3.5-inch bbl. 6.5 inches overall. Weight: steel, 22.25 oz., alloy, 16 oz. Fixed sights. Blued finish. Checkered plastic stocks. Made 1959-1985. *Note:* Formerly marketed in U.S. as "Puma" (alloy model in 32) and "Cougar" (steel model in 380).

Beretta Model 70

Beretta Model 72

Beretta Model 70S **$215**
Similar to Model 70T, except chambered for 22 Auto and 380 Auto. Longer bbl. guide, safety lever blocking hammer; front and rear sight blade fixed on breechblock. Weight: 1 lb. 7 oz. Made 1977-1985.

Beretta Model 72 . . . . **$220**
Same as Model 71, except has 6-inch bbl., weighs 18 oz. Made from 1959 to date. *Note:* Formerly marketed in U.S as "Jaguar Plinker." Discontinued.

Beretta Model 70T

Beretta Model 76

Beretta Model 70T Automatic Pistol **$250**
Similar to Model 70. Caliber: 32 Automatic (7.65mm). 9-shot magazine. 6-inch bbl. 9.5 inches overall. Weight: 19 oz. adj. rear sight, blade front sight. Blued finish. Checkered plastic stocks. Introduced in 1959. Discont.

Beretta Model 76 Auto Target Pistol
Caliber: 22 LR. 10-shot magazine. 6-inch bbl. 8.8 inches overall. Weight: 33 oz. Adj. rear sight, front sight with interchangeable blades. Blued finish. Checkered plastic or wood grips (Model 76W). Made 1966-1985. *Note:* Formerly marketed in the U.S. as the "Sable."
Model 76 w/Plastic Grips **$330**
Model 76W w/Wood Grips. **345**

Beretta Model 71

Beretta Model 81

Beretta Model 71 Automatic Pistol **$220**
Same general specifications as alloy Model 70. Caliber: 22 LR. 6-inch bbl. 8-round magazine. Adj. rear sight frame. Single action. Made 1959-1989. *Note:* Formerly marketed in U.S. as the "Jaguar Plinker."

Beretta Model 81 Double-Action Auto Pistol **$250**
Caliber: 32 Automatic (7.65mm). 12-shot magazine. 3.8-inch bbl. 6.8 inches overall. Weight: 23.5 oz. Fixed sights. Blued finish. Plastic stocks. Made principally for the European market 1975-1984, with similar variations to the Model 84.

Beretta Model 84 Double-Action Auto Pistol . . . $365

Same as Model 81, except made in caliber 380 Automatic with 13-shot magazine. 3.82-inch bbl. 6.8 inches overall. Weight: 23 oz. Fixed front and rear sights. Made from 1975 to about 1982.

Beretta Model 84B

Beretta Model 84B DA Auto Pistol $385

Improved version of Model 84 with strengthened frame and slide, and firing-pin block safety added. Ambidextrous reversible magazine release. Blued or nickel finish. Checkered black plastic or wood grips. Other specifications same. Made about 1982-84.

Beretta Model 84BB Double-Action Auto Pistol

Improved version of Model 84B, with further strengthened slide, frame and recoil spring. Caliber: 380 ACP. 13-shot magazine. Bbl.: 3.82 inches. 6.8 inches overall. Weight: 23 oz. Checkered black plastic or wood grips. Blued or nickel finish. Fixed sights. Made c. 1984 to date.

Blued Finish **$350**
Blued w/Wood Grips **370**
Nickel Finish **390**

Beretta Model 85

Beretta Model 85 Double-Action Auto Pistol $295

This is basically the same gun as the Model 84 and has seen a similar evolution. However, this 8-shot version has no ambidextrous magazine release, has a slightly narrower grip and weighs 21.8 oz. It was introduced a little later than the Model 84.

Beretta Model 85BB

Beretta Model 85B DA Auto Pistol $310

Improved version of the Model 85. Made about 1982-85.

Beretta Model 85BB Double-Action Pistol

Improved version of the Model 85B, with strengthened frame and slide. Caliber: 380 ACP. 8-shot magazine. 3.82 inch bbl. 6.8 inches overall. Weight: 21.8 oz. Blued or nickel finish. Checkered black plastic or wood grips. Made from 1985 to date.

Blued Finish w/Plastic Grips. **$325**
Blued Finish w/Wood Grips **345**
Nickel Finish **360**

Beretta Model 85F Double-Action Pistol

Similar to the Model 85BB, except has re-contoured trigger guard and manual ambidextrous safety with decocking device. Made in 1990.

Blued Finish w/Plastic Grips. **$360**
Blued Finish w/Wood Grips **380**
Nickel Finish w/Wood Grips **410**

Beretta Model 86

Beretta Model 86 Double-Action Auto Pistol $355

Caliber: 380 auto. 8-shot magazine. Bbl.: 4.33 inches, tip-up. 7.33 inches overall. Weight: 23 oz. Made 1986-89. (Reintroduced 1990 in the Cheetah Series.)

Beretta Model 87BB

Beretta Model 92

Beretta Model 87BB Auto Pistol

Similar to the Model 85, except in 22 LR with 8-shot magazine and optional extended 6-inch bbl. (in single action). Overall length: 6.8 inches; 8.9 w/6-inch bbl. Weight: 20.8 oz., 23 oz. w/6-inch bbl. Checkered wood grips. Made from 1977 to date.

Blued Finish (Double-Action) **$340**
Long bbl. (Single Action) **350**

Beretta Model 89 Target Automatic Pistol **$485**

Caliber: 22 LR. 8-shot magazine. 6-inch bbl. 9.5 inches overall. Weight: 41 oz. Adj. target sights. Blued finish. Target-style walnut stocks. Made 1990 to date.

Beretta Model 90

Beretta Model 90 DA Auto Pistol **$220**

Caliber: 32 Auto (7.65mm). 8-shot magazine. 3.63-inch bbl. 6.63 inches overall. Weight: 19.5 oz. Fixed sights. Blued finish. Checkered plastic grips. Made 1969-1975.

Beretta Model 92 DA Auto Pistol **$395**

Caliber: 9mm Luger. 15-shot magazine. 4.9-inch bbl. 8.5 inches overall. Weight: 33.5 oz. Fixed sights. Blued finish. Plastic stocks. Made from 1976 to date.

Beretta Model 92D DA Auto Pistol

Same general specifications as Model 92F, except DA only with bobbed hammer and 3-Dot Sight.

Model 92D **$420**
Model 92D w/Triticon Sight **470**

Beretta Model 92F Compact DA Auto **$375**

Caliber: 9mm Parabellum. 12-shot magazine. 4.3-inch bbl. 7.8 inches overall. Weight: 31.5 oz. Wood grips. Square-notched bar rear sight; blade front sight, integral with slide. Made from 1986 to date.

Beretta Model 92F DA Auto Pistol

Same general specifications as Model 92, except with slide-mounted safety and repositioned magazine release. Replaced Model 92SB. Blued or stainless finish. Made from 1985 to date.

Blued Finish **$410**
Stainless Finish **495**

Beretta Model 92F-EL DA Auto Pistol

Deluxe version of Model 92F with gold trim and logo inlay. Deluxe walnut stocks.

Model 92F-EL Gold **$595**
Model 92F-EL Stainless **930**

Beretta Model 92SB DA Auto Pistol **$395**

Same general specifications as standard Model 92, except has slide-mounted safety and repositioned magazine release. Discontinued 1985.

Beretta Model 92 SB-F

Beretta Model 92 SB-F DA Auto Pistol **$415**

Caliber: 9mm Parabellum. 15-shot magazine. Bbl.: 4.9 inches. 8.5 inches overall. Weight: 34 oz. Plastic or Beretta Model 92 SB-F DA Auto Pistol wood grips. Square-notched bar rear sight; blade front sight, integral with slide. This model, also called **Model 92S-1**, is the standard-issue sidearm for the U.S. Armed Forces. Made from 1985 to date.

Beretta Model 96 Double-Action Auto Pistol

Same general specifications as Model 92F, except in 40 S&W. 10-shot magazine (9-shot in Compact Model).

Model 96 Standard	**$425**
Model 96 Centurion (Compact)	435
Model 96 D (DA only)	420
Model 96 w/Triticon Sights	485

Beretta Model 101 . . . . $215

Same as Model 70T, except caliber 22 LR, has 10-shot magazine. Introduced in 1959. Discontinued.

Beretta Model 950B

Beretta Model 318 (1934)

Beretta Model 318 (1934) Auto Pistol $255

Caliber: 25 Automatic (6.35mm). 8-shot magazine. 2.5-inch bbl. 4.5 inches overall. Weight: 14 oz. Fixed sights. Blued finish. Plastic stocks. Made from 1934 to c. 1939.

Beretta Model 950-BS-EL

Beretta Model 950 BS Single Action Semiautomatic

Calibers: 25 ACP or 22 Short. Magazine capacity: 7 rounds (22 short); 8 rounds (25 ACP). 2.5- or 4-inch bbl. 4.5 inches overall (2.5-inch bbl.) Weight: about 10 oz. Blade front sight, V-notch in rear. Checkered black plastic grips. Made from 1987 to date.

Blued Finish	**$125**
Nickel Finish	160
With 4-inch bbl. (22 short)	140
Model 950 EL gold-etched version	210

Beretta Model 949 Olimpionico

Beretta Model 949 Olimpionico Auto Pistol $525

Calibers: 22 Short, 22 LR. 5-shot magazine. 8.75-inch bbl. 12.5 inches overall. Weight: 38 oz. Target sights. Adj. bbl. weight. Muzzle brake. Checkered walnut stocks with thumbrest. Made 1959-1964.

Beretta Model 950B Auto Pistol $125

Same general specifications as Model 950CC, except caliber 25 Auto, has 7-shot magazine. Made from 1959 to date. *Note:* Formerly marketed in the U.S. as "Jetfire."

Beretta Model 950CC

Beretta Model 950CC Auto Pistol **$125**
Caliber: 22 Short. 6-shot magazine. Hinged, 2.38-inch bbl. 4.75
inches overall. Weight: 11 oz. Fixed sights. Blued finish. Plastic
stocks. Made from 1959 to date. *Note:* Formerly marketed in the
U.S. as "Minx M2."

Beretta Model 950CC Special

Beretta Model 950CC Special Auto Pistol **$130**
Same general specifications as Model 950CC Auto, except has
4-inch bbl. Made from 1959 to date. *Note:* Formerly marketed in
the U.S. as "Minx M4."

Beretta Model 951 (1951)

Beretta Model 951 (1951) Military Auto Pistol . . . **$245**
Caliber: 9mm Luger. 8-shot magazine. 4.5-inch bbl. 8 inches
overall. Weight: 31 oz. Fixed sights. Blued finish. Plastic stocks.
Made from 1952 to date. *Note:* This is the standard pistol of the
Italian Armed Forces; also used by Egyptian and Israeli armies
and by the police in Nigeria. Egyptian and Israeli models usually
command a premium. Formerly marketed in the U.S. as the
"Brigadier."

Beretta Model 1915 Auto Pistol **$285**
Calibers: 9mm Glisenti and 32 ACP (7.65mm). 8-shot magazine.
4-inch bbl. 6.7 inches overall (9mm), 5.7 inches (32 ACP).
Weight: 30 oz. (9mm), 20 oz. (32 ACP). Fixed sights. Blued finish. Wood grips. Made 1915-1922. An improved postwar
1915/1919 version in caliber 32 ACP was later offered for sale in
1922 as the Model 1922.

Beretta Model 1915

Beretta Model 1923

Beretta Model 1923 Auto Pistol **$565**
Caliber: 9mm Glisenti (Luger). 8-shot magazine. 4-inch bbl. 6.5
inches overall. Weight: 30 oz. Fixed sights. Blued finish. Plastic
stocks. Made from 1923-c to 1936.

Beretta Model 1934

Beretta Model 1934 Auto Pistol

Caliber: 380 Automatic (9mm Short). 7-shot magazine. 3.38-inch bbl. 5.88 inches overall. Weight: 24 oz. Fixed sights. Blued finish. Plastic stocks. Official pistol of the Italian Armed Forces. Wartime pieces not as well made and finished as commercial models. Made 1934-1959. *See* illustration preceding page.

Commercial Model **$265**
War Model **325**

Beretta Model 1935

Beretta Model 1935 Auto Pistol

Caliber: 32 ACP (7.65mm). 8-shot magazine. 3.5-inch bbl. 5.75 inches overall. Weight: 24 oz. Fixed sights. Blued finish. Plastic stocks. A roughly finished version of this pistol was produced during WW II. Made 1935-1959.

Commercial Model **$245**
War Model **225**

VINCENZO BERNARDELLI, S.P.A.
Gardone V. T. (Brescia), Italy

Bernardelli Model 60

Bernardelli Model 60 Pocket Automatic Pistol . . $185

Calibers: 22 LR, 32 Auto (7.65mm), 380 Auto (9mm Short). 8-shot magazine (22 and 32), 7-shot (380). 3.5-inch bbl. 6.5 inches overall. Weight: about 25 oz. Fixed sights. Blued finish. Bakelite stocks. Made 1959-1990.

Bernardelli Model 68 Automatic Pistol $120

Caliber: 6.35. 5- and 8-shot magazine. 2.13-inch bbl. 4.13 inches overall. Weight: 10 oz. Fixed sights. Blued or chrome finish. Bakelite or pearl stocks. This model, like its smaller bore 22-counterpart, was known as the "Baby" Bernardelli.

Bernardelli Model 69 Automatic Target Pistol . . . $385

Caliber: 22 LR. 10-shot magazine. 5.9-inch bbl. 9 inches overall. Weight: 2.2 lbs. Fully adj. target sights. Blued finish. Stippled right- or left-hand wraparound walnut grips. Made from 1987 to date. *Note:* This was previously Model 100.

Bernardelli Model 80

Bernardelli Model 80 Automatic Pistol $165

Calibers: 22 LR, 32 ACP (7.65mm), 380 Auto (9mm Short). Magazine capacity: 10-shot (22), 8-shot (32), 7-shot (380). 3.5-inch bbl. 6.5 inches overall. Weight: 25.6 oz. adj. rear sight, white dot front sight. Blued finish. Plastic thumbrest stocks. *Note:* Model 80 is a modification of Model 60 designed to conform with U.S. import regulations. Made 1968-1988.

Bernardelli Model 90

Bernardelli Model 90 Sport Target $175

Same as Model 80, except has 6-inch bbl., is 9 inches overall, weighs 26.8 oz. Made 1968-1990.

Bernardelli Model 100

Bernardelli P018

Bernardelli Model 100 Target Automatic Pistol . . . $315
Caliber: 22 LR. 10-shot magazine. 5.9-inch bbl. 9 inches overall. Weight: 37.75 oz. Adj. rear sight, interchangeable front sights. Blued finish. Checkered walnut thumbrest stocks. Made 1969-1986. *Note:* Formerly Model 69.

Bernardelli P018 Compact Model $395
Slightly smaller version of the Model P018 standard DA automatic, except has 14-shot magazine and 4-inch bbl. 7.68 inches overall. Weight: 33 oz. Walnut grips only. Imported 1987-1991.

Bernardelli P018 Double-Action Automatic Pistol
Caliber: 9mm Parabellum. 16-shot magazine. 4.75-inch bbl. 8.5 inches overall. Weight: 36 oz. Fixed combat sights. Blued finish. Checkered plastic or walnut stocks. Imported 1987-1991.
With Plastic Grips $370
With Walnut Grips 380

Bernardelli Model P010

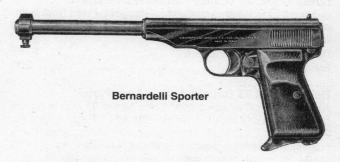

Bernardelli Sporter

Bernardelli Sporter Automatic Pistol $245
Caliber 22 LR. 8-shot magazine. Bbl. lengths: 6-, 8- and 10-inch. 13 inches overall with 10-inch bbl. Weight about 30 oz. with 10-inch bbl. Target sights. Blued finish. Walnut stocks. Made from 1949 to 1968.

Bernardelli "Baby" Automatic Pistol $175
Calibers: 22 Short, 22 Long. 5-shot magazine. 2.13-inch bbl. 4.13 inches overall. Weight: 9 oz. Fixed sights. Blued finish. Bakelite stocks. Made 1949-1968.

Bernardelli Model P010 Automatic Pistol $405
Caliber: 22 LR. 5- and 10-shot magazine. 5.9-inch bbl. with 7.5-inch sight radius. Weight: 40.0 oz. Interchangeable front sight, adj. rear. Blued finish. Textured walnut stocks. Discontinued 1990.

Bernardelli Vest Pocket

Bernardelli Vest Pocket Automatic Pistol $190
Caliber: 25 Auto (6.35mm). 5- or 8-shot magazine. 2.13-inch bbl. 4.13 inches overall. Weight: 9 oz. Fixed sights. Blued finish. Bakelite stocks. Made 1945-1968.

BERSA PISTOLS
Imported from Argentina by Eagle Imports

Bersa firearms have been imported by other distributors, including Interarms and Outdoor Sports Headquarters.

Bersa Model 23

Bersa Model 23 Double-Action Auto Pistol
Caliber: 22 LR. 10-shot magazine. 4-inch bbl. Fixed front sight; square-notch adj. rear. Blued or satin nickel finish. Textured wood stocks. Imported 1989 to date.
Blued Finish **$185**
Satin Nickel **200**

Bersa Model 83 Double-Action Auto Pistol
Almost identical in appearance to the Model 23 except for the following specifications: Caliber: 380 ACP. 7-shot magazine. 3.5-inch bbl. Front blade sight integral on slide; square-notch rear adj. for windage. Blued or satin nickel finish. Custom wood stocks. Imported 1990 to date.
Blued Finish **$185**
Satin Nickel **205**

Bersa Model 85

Bersa Model 85 Double-Action Auto Pistol
Same general specifications as Model 83, except 13-shot magazine. Imported 1990 to date.
Blued Finish **$230**
Satin Nickel **275**

Bersa Model 86 Double-Action Auto Pistol
Same general specifications as Model 85, except available in matte blue finish and with neoprene grips.
Matte Blue Finish **$235**
Nickel Finish **265**

Bersa Model 97 Auto Pistol $275
Caliber: 380 ACP. 7-shot magazine. 3.3-inch bbl. 6.5 inches overall. Weight: 28 oz. Introduced 1982; disc.

Bersa Model 223
Same general specifications as Model 383, except in 22 LR w/10-round magazine capacity. Discontinued 1987.
Double-Action **$170**
Single Action **160**

Bersa Model 224
Caliber: 22 LR. 10-shot magazine. 4-inch bbl. Weight: 26 oz. Front blade sight; square-notched rear adj. for windage. Blued finish. Checkered nylon or custom wood grips. Made from 1984; SA discontinued 1986.
Double-Action **$170**
Single Action **165**

Bersa Model 383

Bersa Model 226
Same general specifications as Model 224, but with 6-inch bbl. Discontinued.
Double-Action **$170**
Single Action **160**

Bersa Model 383 Auto Pistol
Caliber: 380 Auto. 7-shot magazine. 3.5-inch bbl. Front blade sight integral on slide; square-notched rear sight adj. for windage. Custom wood grips on double-action, nylon grips on single action. Blued or satin nickel finish. Made from 1984; SA discontinued 1989.
Double-Action **$145**
Single Action **125**
Satin Nickel **155**

Bersa Model 622 Auto Pistol $125
Caliber: 22 LR. 7-shot magazine. 4- or 6-inch bbl. 7 or 9 inches overall. Weighs 2.25 pounds. Blade front sight; square-notch rear adj. for windage. Blued finish. Nylon grips. Made 1982-87.

Bersa Model 644 Auto Pistol $135
Caliber: 22 LR. 10-shot magazine. 3.5-inch bbl. Weight: 26.5 oz. 6.5 inches overall. Adj. rear sight, blade front. Contoured black nylon grips. Made 1980-88.

Bersa Thunder 9 Auto Pistol $295
Caliber: 9mm Parabellum. 15-shot magazine. 4-inch bbl. 7.38 inches overall. Weight: 30 oz. Blade front sight, adj. rear w/3-dot system. Ambidextrous safety and decocking devise. Matte blued finish. Checkered black polymer grips. Made from 1993 to date.

Bersa Thunder 22 Auto Pistol $255
Caliber: 22 LR, 10-shot magazine. 3.5-inch bbl., 6.63 inches overall. Weight: 24.5 oz. Notched-bar dovetailed rear; blade integral with slide front. Black polymer grips. Made 1995 to date.

Bersa Thunder 380 Auto Pistol
Caliber: 380 ACP, 7-shot magazine. 3.5-inch bbl., 6.63 inches overall. Weight: 25.75 oz. Notched-bar dovetailed rear; blade integral with slide front. Blue, satin nickel, or duo-tone finish. Made from 1995 to date.
Blue Finish $230
Satin Nickel Finish 255
Duo-Tone Finish 240

Bersa Thunder 380 Plus Auto Pistol
Same general specifications as standard Thunder 380 except has 10-shot magazine and weighs 26 oz. Made from 1995 to date.
Matte Finish $275
Satin Nickel Finish 285
Duo-Tone Finish 290

BRNO PISTOLS
Manufactured in Czechoslovakia

Also see listings under CZ Pistols.

Brno CZ 75

Brno CZ 75 Double-Action Automatic Pistol
Caliber: 9mm Parabellum. 15-shot magazine. 4.75-inch bbl. 8 inches overall. Weight: 35 oz. Fixed sights. Blued or black polymer finish. Checkered wood or high-impact plastic stocks.
Black Polymer Finish $365
High-Polish Blued Finish 395
Matte Blue Finish 375

Brno CZ 83 Engraved

Brno CZ 83 Double-Action Automatic Pistol
Calibers: 32 ACP, 380 ACP. 15-shot (32 ACP) or 13-shot (380 ACP) magazine. 3.75-inch bbl. 6.75 inches overall. Weight: 26.5 oz. Fixed sights. Blued finish. Checkered black plastic stocks. Imported 1985-92.
Standard finish $395
Engraved (shown) 795

Brno CZ 85 Combat DA Automatic Pistol
Similar to the standard CZ 85 Model, except with 13-shot magazine, combat-style hammer, fully adj. rear sight and walnut grips.
Black Polymer Finish $415
High-Polish Blued Finish 465
Matte Blued Finish 440

Brno CZ 85 Double-Action Automatic Pistol
Same as CZ 75, except with ambidextrous slide release and safety. Calibers: 9mm Parabellum, 7.65mm. Made from 1986 to date.
Black Polymer Finish $400
High-Polish Blued Finish 450
Matte Blued Finish 425

Bronco 25 Auto Pistol

BRONCO PISTOL
Eibar, Spain
Manufactured by Echave y Arizmendi

Bronco Model 1918 Pocket Automatic Pistol . . . $115
Caliber: 32 ACP (7.65mm). 6-shot magazine. 2.5-inch bbl. 5 inches overall. Weight: 20 oz. Fixed sights. Blued finish. Hard rubber stocks. Made circa 1918-1925.

Bronco Semiautomatic Pistol $130
Caliber: 25ACP, 6-shot magazine. 2.13-inch bbl., 4.13 inches overall. Weight: 11 oz. Fixed sights. Blued finish. Hard rubber grips. Made 1919-1935. *See* photo preceding page.

BROWNING PISTOLS
Morgan, Utah

The following Browning pistols have been manufactured by Fabrique Nationale d'Armes de Guerre (now Fabrique Nationale Herstal) of Herstal, Belgium, by Arms Technology Inc. of Salt Lake City and by J. P. Sauer & Sohn of Eckernforde, W. Germany. (See also FN Browning and J.P. Sauer & Sohn listings.)

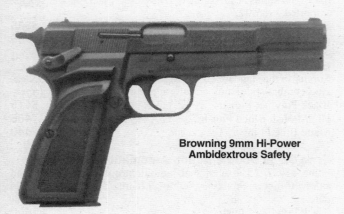

**Browning 9mm Hi-Power
Ambidextrous Safety**

Browning 9mm Hi-Power

Browning 9mm Classic

**Browning 25 Automatic
Standard Model**

Browning 9mm Hi-Power Ambidextrous Safety . . $345
Same general specifications as standard 9mm Hi-Power, except with matte blued finish and ambidextrous safety. Made from 1987 to date.

Browning 9mm Hi-Power Automatic Pistol
Same general specifications as FN Browning Model 1935 (see separate listing). DA or SA. 13-shot. Bbl.: about 5 inches. 7.75 inches overall. Weight: 32 oz. Fixed sights; also available with rear sight adj. for windage and elevation and ramp front sight. Standard Model, blued finish, checkered walnut or contour-molded stocks. Renaissance Engraved Model, chrome-plated, Nacrolac pearl stocks. Made by FN from 1955 to date.
Standard Model, fixed sights $335
Standard Model, adj. sights. 375
Renaissance Model, fixed sights. 725
Renaissance Model, adj. sights. 765

Browning 9mm Classic
Same general specifications as 9mm Auto (Hi-Power), except for high-grade engraving, finely checkered walnut grips with double border, and limited to 5000 production. Gold Classic limited to 500 production. Made 1985-86.
Gold Classic $1695
Standard Classic 895

Browning 25 Automatic Pistol
Same general specifications as FN Browning Baby (*see* separate listing). Standard Model, blued finish, hard rubber grips. Lightweight Model, nickel-plated, Nacrolac pearl grips. Renaissance Engraved Model, nickel-plated, Nacrolac pearl grips. Made by FN 1955-1969.
Standard Model $260
Lightweight Model 355
Renaissance Model 695

**Browning 380 Automatic
Standard Model (1955-Type)**

Browning 380 Automatic Pistol, 1955 Type

Same general specifications as FN Browning 380 Pocket Auto.
Standard Model, Renaissance Engraved Model, as furnished in
25 Automatic. Made by FN 1955-1969.
Standard Model $325
Renaissance Model 895

Browning BDA Automatic

Browning 380 Automatic Pistol, 1971 Type

Same as 380 Automatic, 1955 Type, except has longer slide,
4.44-inch bbl., is 7.06 inches overall, weighs 23 oz. Rear sight
adj. for windage and elevation, plastic thumbrest stocks. Made
1971-75.
Standard Model $295
Renaissance Model 795

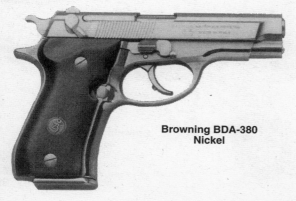

**Browning BDA-380
Nickel**

Browning BDA DA Automatic Pistol $375

Similar to SIG-Sauer P220. Calibers: 9mm Luger, 38 Super
Auto, 45 Auto. 9-shot magazine (9mm and 38),7-shot (45 cal).
4.4-inch bbl. 7.8 inches overall. Weight: 29.3 oz. Fixed sights.
Blued finish. Plastic stocks. Made from 1977-79 by J. P. Sauer.

**Browning BDM 9mm DA
Automatic**

Browning BDA-380 DA Automatic Pistol

Caliber: 380 Auto. 13-shot magazine. Bbl. length: 3.81 inches.
6.75 inches overall. Weight: 23 oz. Fixed blade front sight,
square-notch drift adj. rear sight. Made from 1982 to date.
Blued finish $335
Nickel finish 350

Browning BDM 9mm DA Automatic Pistol $395

Caliber: 9mm Luger. 15-shot magazine. 4.73-inch bbl. 7.85 inches
overall. Weight: 31 oz. Low-profile removable blade front sight and
windage-adj. rear sight w/3-dot system. Matte blue finish. Features
selectable shooting mode. Made from 1991 to date.

Browning Buck Mark 22 Micro

Browning Buck Mark 22 Automatic Pistol $155

Caliber: 22 LR. 10-shot magazine. Bbl.: 5.5 inches. 9.5 inches
overall. Weight: 32 oz. Black molded grips. Adj. rear sight.
Made from 1985 to date.

Browning Buck Mark 22 Field Auto $165

Same general specifications as the standard Buck Mark 22, except with hoodless ramp-style front and low-profile rear sights.
Contoured walnut grips. Made 1991 to date.

Browning Buck Mark 22 Micro

Same general specifications as standard Buck Mark 22 except with 4-inch bbl. 8 inches overall. Weight: 32 oz. Molded composite grips. Ramp front sight; Pro Target rear sight. Made from 1992 to date.

Blued Finish **$145**
Nickel finish **180**

Browning Buck Mark 22 Plus $175

Same general specifications as standard Buck Mark 22 except for black molded, impregnated hardwood grips. Made from 1987 to date.

**Browning Buck Mark 22
Silhouette**

Browning Buck Mark 22 Silhouette $250

Same general specifications as standard Buck Mark 22, except for 9.88-inch bbl., 53-oz. weight, target sights mounted on full-length scope base, and laminated hardwood grips and forend. Made from 1987 to date.

Browning Buck Mark 22 Target 5.5 . . . . $235

Same general specifications as Buck Mark 22, except 5.5-inch bbl., 35.5 oz. weight and target sights mounted on full-length scope base. Made from 1989 to date.

Standard **$235**
Gold Model **255**

Browning Buck Mark 22 Unlimited Silhouette $295

Same general specifications as standard Buck Mark 22 Silhouette, except with 14-inch bbl. 18.69 inches overall. Weight: 64 oz. Interchangeable post front sight and Pro Target rear. Nickel finish. Made 1992 to date.

Browning Buck Mark 22 Varmint Auto Pistol . . . $225

Same general specifications as standard Buck Mark 22, except for 9.88-inch bbl., 48-oz. weight, no sights, full-length scope base, and laminated hardwood grips. Made from 1987 to date.

Browning Challenger Automatic Pistol

Caliber: 22 LR. 10-shot magazine. Bbl. lengths: 4.5 and 6.75-inch. 11.44 inches overall w/6.75-inch bbl. Weight: 38 oz. w/6.75-inch bbl. Removable blade front sight, screw adj. rear. Standard finish, blue, also furnished gold inlaid (Gold Model) and engraved and chrome-plated (Renaissance Model). Checkered walnut stocks; finely figured and carved stocks on Gold and Renaissance Models. Standard made by FN 1962-1975, higher grades intro. in 1971, discontinued.

Standard Model . . . . **$ 275**
Gold Model **995**
Renaissance Model **1095**

**Browning Challenger
Standard Model**

**Browning Challenger
Gold Medal**

**Browning Challenger
Renaissance Model**

Browning Challenger II

**Browning Challenger III
Sporter 22**

Browning Challenger II Automatic Pistol $185

Same general specifications as Challenger Standard Model with 6.75-inch bbl., changed grip angle and impregnated hardwood stocks. Original Challenger design modified for lower production costs. Made by ATI 1976-1983.

Browning Challenger III Automatic Pistol $175

Same general description as Challenger II, except has 5.5 inch bull bbl., alloy frame and new sight system. Weight: 35 oz. Made 1982-84. **Sporter Model** w/6.75-inch bbl. made 1984-86.

Browning Hi-Power 40 S&W Auto Pistol $395

Similar to the standard 9mm Hi-Power, except in caliber 40 S&W with 10-shot magazine. 4.63-inch bbl. 7.75 inches overall. Weight: 35 oz. Matte blued finish. Molded Polyamide grips. Made from 1993 to date.

Browning Hi-Power Capitan Automatic $395

Similar to the standard Hi-Power, except fitted with adj. 500-meter tangent rear sight and rounded serrated hammer. Made from 1993 to date.

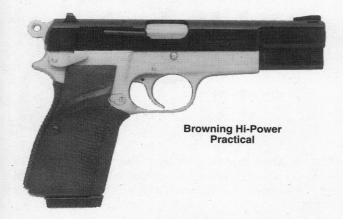

Browning Hi-Power Practical

Browning Hi-Power Practical Automatic Pistol

Similar to the standard Hi-Power, except has silver-chromed frame and blued slide with Commander-style hammer. Made from 1991 to date.

With Fixed Sights $395
With adj. Sights. 445

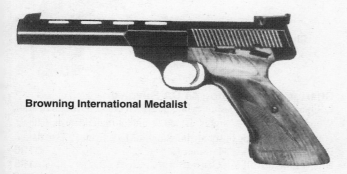

Browning International Medalist

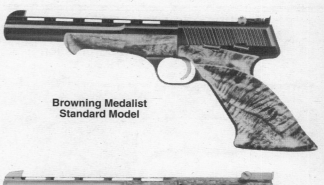

**Browning Medalist
Standard Model**

**Browning Medalist
Renaissance Model**

Browning International Medalist Automatic Target Pistol. $575

Modification of Medalist to conform with International Shooting Union rules; has 5.9-inch bbl., smaller grip, no forearm. Weight: 42 oz. Made 1970-73.

Browning Medalist Automatic Target Pistol

Caliber: 22 LR. 10-shot magazine. 6.75-inch bbl. w/vent rib. 11.94 inches overall. Weight: 46 oz. Removable blade front sight, click-adj. micrometer rear. Standard finish, blue; also furnished gold-inlaid (Gold Model) and engraved and chrome-plated (Renaissance Model). Checkered walnut stocks with thumbrest (for right- or left-handed shooter); finely figured and carved stocks on Gold and Renaissance Models. Made by FN 1962-1975; higher grades introduced in 1971.

Standard Model . . . . $ 585
Gold Model 1200
Renaissance Model 1650

Browning Nomad

Browning Nomad Automatic Pistol $265

Caliber: 22 LR. 10-shot magazine. Bbl. lengths: 4.5 and 6.75-inch. 8.94 inches overall w/4.5-inch bbl. Weight: 34 oz. (4.5-inch bbl.). Removable blade front sight, screw adj. rear. Blued finish. Plastic stocks. Made by FN 1962-1974.

BUDISCHOWSKY PISTOL
Mt. Clemens, Michigan
Mfd. by Norton Armament Corporation

Budischowsky TP-70

Charter Arms Bonnie

Budischowsky TP-70 DA Automatic Pistol
Calibers: 22 LR, 25 Auto. 6-shot magazine. 2.6-inch bbl. 4.65 inches overall. Weight: 12.3 oz. Fixed sights. Stainless steel. Plastic stocks. Made 1973-77.
22 Long Rifle **$365**
25 Automatic. 250

CALICO LIGHT WEAPONS SYSTEMS
Bakersfield, California

Calico Model 110 Auto Pistol **$300**
Caliber: 22 LR. 100-shot magazine. 6-inch bbl. 17.9 inches overall. Weight: 3.75 lbs. Sights: adj. post front; fixed U-notch rear. Black finish aluminum frame. Molded composition grip. Made 1986-1994.

Calico Model M-950 Auto Pistol **$395**
Caliber 9mm Parabellum. 50- or 100-shot magazine. 7.5-inch bbl. 14 inches overall. Weight: 2.25 lbs. sights: adj. post front; fixed U-notch rear. Glass-filled polymer grip. Made 1989-1994.

Charter Arms Clyde

Charter Arms Bonnie and Clyde Set **$395**
Matching pair of shrouded 2.5-inch bbl. revolvers, chambered for 32 Magnum and 38 Special. Blued finish with scrolled name on bbls.

Charter Arms Bulldog 44

CHARTER ARMS CORPORATION
Stratford, Connecticut

Charter Arms Model 40 Automatic Pistol **$235**
Caliber: 22 RF. 8-shot magazine. 3.3-inch bbl. 6.3 inches overall. Weight: 21.5 oz. Fixed sights. Checkered walnut grips. Stainless steel finish. Made 1985-86.

Charter Arms Model 79K Automatic Pistol **$295**
Calibers: 380 or 32 Auto. 7-shot magazine. 3.6-inch bbl. 6.5 inches overall. Weight: 24.5 oz. Fixed sights. Checkered walnut grips. Stainless steel finish. Made 1985-86.

Charter Arms Bulldog 44 DA Revolver
Caliber: 44 Special. 5-shot cylinder. 3-inch bbl. 7.5 inches overall. Weight: 19 oz. Fixed sights. Blued or nickel-plated finish. Checkered walnut Bulldog or square buttstocks. Made from 1973 to date.
Blued Finish/Pocket Hammer (2.5") **$190**
Blued Finish/Bulldog Grips (3") 195
Stainless Steel/Bulldog Grips 210
Neoprene Grips/Pocket Hammer 205

Charter Arms Bulldog 357

Charter Arms Bulldog 357 DA Revolver $165

Caliber: 357 Magnum. 5-shot cylinder. 6-inch bbl. 11 inches overall. Weight: 25 oz. Fixed sights. Blued finish. Square, checkered walnut grips. Intro. 1977; discontinued.

Charter Arms Bulldog New Police DA Revolver

Same general specifications as Bulldog Police, except chambered for 44 Special. 5-shot cylinder. 2.5- or 3.5-inch bbl. Made 1990-92.

Blued Finish $180
Stainless Finish (2.5-inch bbl. only) 220

**Charter Arms Police Bulldog
32 H&R Magnum**

Charter Arms Bulldog Police DA Revolver

Caliber: 38 Special or 32 H&R Magnum. 6-shot cylinder. 4-inch bbl. 8.5 inches overall. Weight: 20.5 oz. Adj. rear sight, ramp front. Blued or stainless finish. Square checkered walnut grips. Made from 1976 to date. Shroud dropped on new model.

Blued Finish $160
Stainless Finish 195
32 H&R Magnum (Discontinued 1992) 210

Charter Arms Bulldog Pug

Charter Arms Bulldog Pug DA Revolver

Caliber: 44 Special. 5-shot cylinder. 2.5 inch bbl. 7.25 inches overall. Weight: 20 oz. Blued or stainless finish. Fixed ramp front sight, fixed square-notch rear. Checkered neoprene or walnut grips. Made from 1988 to date.

Blued Finish $195
Stainless Finish 220

Charter Arms Bulldog Target

Charter Arms Bulldog Target DA Revolver

Calibers: 357 Magnum, 44 Special (latter introduced in 1977). 4-inch bbl. 8.5 inches overall. Weight: in 357, 20.5 oz. Adj. rear sight, ramp front. Blued finish. Square checkered walnut grips. Made 1976-1992.

Blued Finish $180
Stainless Steel 225

Charter Arms Bulldog Tracker

Charter Arms Bulldog Tracker DA Revolver $160

Caliber: 357 Mag. 5-shot cylinder. 2.5-, 4- or 6-inch bbl. 11 inches overall w/6-inch bbl. Weight: 21 oz., 2.5-inch bbl. Adj. rear sight, ramp front. Checkered walnut grips. Blued finish. 4- and 6-inch bbls. Discontinued 1986.

**Charter Arms Explorer II
Standard Model**

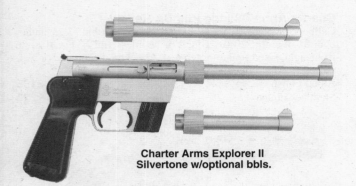

**Charter Arms Explorer II
Silvertone w/optional bbls.**

Charter Arms Explorer II Semiauto Survival Pistol
Caliber: 22 RF. 8-shot magazine. 6-, 8- or 10-inch bbl. 13.5 inches overall w/6-inch bbl. Weight: 28 oz. Finishes: black, heat cured, semigloss textured enamel or silvertone anticorrosion. Discontinued 1987.
Standard Model **$75**
Silvertone (w/optional 6- and 10-inch bbls.). **95**

Charter Arms Off-Duty DA Revolver
Calibers: 22 LR or 38 Special. 6-shot (22 LR) or 5-shot (38 Spec.) cylinder. 2-inch bbl. 6.25 inches overall. Weight: 16 oz. Fixed rear sight, Patridge-type front sight. Plain walnut grips. Matte black, electroless nickel or stainless steel finish.
Matte Black Finish **$130**
Electroless Nickel **185**
Stainless Steel **175**

**Charter Arms Pathfinder
New Model**

Charter Arms Pathfinder DA Revolver
Calibers: 22 LR, 22 WMR. 6-shot cylinder. Bbl. lengths: 2-, 3-, 6-inch. 7.13 inches overall w/3-inch bbl. and regular stocks. Weight: 18.5 oz. w/3-inch bbl. Adj. rear sight, ramp front. Blued or stainless finish. Plain walnut regular, checkered Bulldog or square buttstocks. Made from 1970 to date. *Note:* Originally designated "Pocket Target," name was changed in 1971 to "Pathfinder." Grips changed in 1984. Disc. 1993.
Blued Finish **$145**
Stainless Finish **175**

Charter Arms Pitbull DA Revolver
Calibers: 9mm, 357 Magnum, 38 Special. 5-shot cylinder. 2.5-, 3.5- or 4-inch bbl. 7 inches overall w/2.5-inch bbl. Weight: 21.5 to 25 oz. All stainless steel frame. Fixed ramp front sight; fixed square-notch rear. Checkered neoprene grips. Blued or stainless finish. Made 1989-1993.
Blued Finish **$175**
Stainless Finish **195**

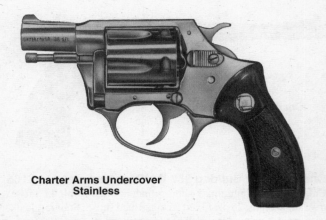

**Charter Arms Undercover
Stainless**

Charter Arms Undercover DA Revolver
Caliber: 38 Special. 5-shot cylinder. bbl. lengths: 2-, 3-, 4-inch. 6.25 inches overall w/2-inch bbl and regular grips. Weight: 16 oz. w/2-inch bbl. Fixed sights. Plain walnut, checkered Bulldog or square buttstocks. Made 1965-1994.
Blued or Nickel-plated Finish **$155**
Stainless Finish **185**

**Charter Arms Undercover
32 S&W Long**

Charter Arms Undercover 32 H&R Magnum or S&W Long
Same general specifications as standard Undercover, except chambered for 32 H&R Magnum or 32 S&W Long, has 6-shot cylinder and 2.5-inch bbl.
32 H&R Magnum (Blued) **$140**
32 H&R Magnum (Stainless) **180**
32 S&W Long (Blued) Disc. 1989 . . . . **125**

Charter Arms Undercover Pocket Police DA Revolver
Same general specifications as standard Undercover, except has 6-shot cylinder and pocket-type hammer. Blued or stainless steel finish.
Blued Finish **$150**
Stainless Steel **180**

Charter Arms Undercover Police DA Revolver
Same general specifications as standard Undercover, except has 6-shot cylinder. (*See* photo, opposite page.)
Blued, 38 Special **$165**
Stainless, 38 Special **195**
32 H&R Magnum **160**

**Charter Arms Police Undercover
32 H&R Magnum**

Charter Arms Undercoverette DA Revolver. **$135**
Same as Undercover model with 2-inch bbl., except caliber 32
S&W Long, 6-shot cylinder, blued finish only; weighs 16.5 oz.
Made 1972-1983.

COLT MANUFACTURING CO., INC.
Hartford, Connecticut

*Previously Colt Industries, Firearms Division. Production of
some Colt handguns spans the period from before World War
II to the postwar years. Values shown for these models are for
earlier production. Those manufactured c. 1946 and later generally are less desirable to collectors, and values are approximately 30 percent lower.*

NOTE

For ease in finding a particular firearm, Colt handguns
are grouped into three sections: Automatic Pistols (below) Single Shot Pistols and Deringers (page 50), and
Revolvers (page 51). For a complete listing, please refer to the Index.

AUTOMATIC PISTOLS

Colt Model 1900

Colt Model 1900 38 Automatic Pistol **$4600**
Caliber: 38 ACP (modern high-velocity cartridges should not be
used in this pistol). 7-shot magazine. 6-inch bbl. 9 inches overall.
Weight: 35 oz. Fixed sights. Blued finish. Plain walnut stocks.
Sharp-spur hammer. Combination rear sight and safety. Made
1900-1903.

Colt Model 1902 Sporting

Colt Model 1902 Military 38 Automatic Pistol. . . **$1350**
Caliber: 38 ACP (modern high-velocity cartridges should not be
used in this pistol). 8-shot magazine. 6-inch bbl. 9 inches overall.
Weight: 37 oz. Fixed sights, knife-blade and V-notch. Blued finish. Checkered hard rubber stocks. Round back hammer,
changed to spur type in 1908. No safety. Made 1902-1929.

Colt Model 1902 Sporting 38 Automatic Pistol . . **$1495**
Caliber: 38 ACP (modern high-velocity cartridges should not be
used in this pistol). 7-shot magazine. 6-inch bbl. 9 inches overall.
Weight: 35 oz. Fixed sights, knife-blade and V-notch. Blued finish. Checkered hard rubber stocks. Round back hammer. No
safety. Made 1902-1908.

**Colt Model 1903 Pocket
Hammer Model**

**Colt Model 1903 Pocket 38 Hammer
Automatic Pistol** **$495**
Caliber: 38 ACP (modern high-velocity cartridges should not be
used in this pistol). Similar to Model 1902 Sporting 38, but with
4.5-inch bbl. 7.5 inches overall. Weight: 31 oz. Fixed sights,
knife-blade and V-notch. Blued finish. Checkered hard rubber
stocks. Round back hammer, changed to spur type in 1908. No
safety. Made 1903-1929.

**Colt Model 1903 Pocket
Hammerless Model**

Colt Model 1903 Pocket Hammerless
Automatic Pistol $475

Calibers: 32 and 38 ACP, 8- and 7-shot magazines, respectively. Similar to Model 1903 except hammerless and equipped with slide-lock and grip safety. 3.75-inch bbl. Weight: 24 oz. Fixed sights, knife-blade and V-notch. Blued finish. Checkered hard rubber stocks. Made 1903-1945.

Colt Model 1905 Military

Colt Model 1905 Military 45 Automatic Pistol . . $2250

Caliber: 45 Automatic. 7-shot magazine. 5-inch bbl. 8 inches overall. Weight: 32.5 oz. Fixed sights, knife-blade and V-notch. Blued finish. Checkered walnut stocks. Similar to Model 1902 38 Auto Pistol. Made 1905-1911.

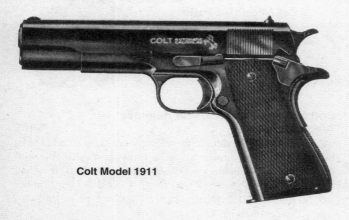

Colt Model 1911

Colt Model 1911 Automatic Pistol

Caliber: 45 Auto. 7-shot magazine. 5-inch bbl. 8.5 inches overall. Weight: 39 oz. Fixed sights. Blued finish on Commercial Model Parkerized or similar finish on most military pistols. Checkered walnut stocks (early production), plastic grips (later production). Checkered, arched mainspring housing and longer grip safety spur adopted in 1923 (on M1911A1).
Model 1911 Commercial $1050
Model 1911A1   750
   Note: During both World Wars, Colt licensed other firms to make these pistols under government contract: Ithaca Gun Co., North American Arms Co. Ltd. (Canada) Remington-Rand Co., Remington-UMC, Singer Sewing Machine Co., and Union Switch & Signal Co.; M1911 also produced at Springfield Armory.

U.S. Government Model 1911

Colt manufacture	$ 845
North American manufacture	8500
Remington-UMC manufacture	995
Springfield manufacture	875
Commercial Model M1911 Type	995

U.S. Government Model 1911A1

Singer manufacture	$9275
Colt, Ithaca, Remington-Rand, Union Switch	
manufacture	610
Commercial Model, M1911A1 Type	595

Colt Model M1991 A1

Colt Model M1991 A1 Semiauto Pistol

Reissue of Model l911A1 (*see* above) with a continuation of the original serial number range from 1945. Caliber: 45 ACP. 7-shot magazine. 5-inch bbl. 8.5 inches overall. Weight: 39 oz. Fixed blade front sight; square notch rear. Parkerized finish. Black composition stocks. Made from 1991 to date. (Commander and Compact variations introduced 1993).
Standard Model $350
Commander w/4.5-inch bbl.   355
Compact w/3.5-inch bbl. (6-shot)   360

Colt Ace Automatic Pistol

Caliber: 22 LR (regular or high speed). 10-shot magazine. Built on the same frame as the Government Model 45 Auto, with same safety features, etc. Hand-honed action, target bbl., adj. rear sight. 4.75-inch bbl. 8.25. inches overall. Weight: 38 oz. Made 1930-1940.
Commercial Model . . . . $ 795
Service Model (1938-1942)   1500

Colt All American Model 2000 DA Pistol

Colt Commander Lightweight

Colt All American Model 2000 DA Pistol **$375**
Caliber: 9mm Luger. 15-shot magazine. Semiautomatic. 4.5-inch bbl. 7.5 inches overall. Weight: 29 oz. Fixed blade front sight; square-notch rear w/3-dot system. Blued slide with polymer receiver. Made 1992-94.

Colt Commander Lightweight Automatic Pistol . . **$435**
Same basic design as Government Model, but shorter and lighter in weight, receiver and mainspring housing are forged from a special lightweight metal, "Coltalloy." Calibers: 45 Auto, 38 Super Auto, 9mm Luger. 7-shot magazine in 45 cal., 9-shot in 38 Auto and 9mm Luger. 4.25-inch bbl. 8 inches overall. Weight: 26.5 oz. Fixed sights. Round spur hammer. Improved safety lock. Blued finish. Checkered plastic or walnut stocks. Made 1951 to date.

Colt Conversion Unit—22-45 . . . . **$2100**
Converts Service Ace 22 to National Match 45 Auto. Unit consists of match-grade slide assembly and bbl., bushing, recoil spring, recoil spring guide and plug, magazine and slide stop. Made 1938-1942.

Colt Cadet 22

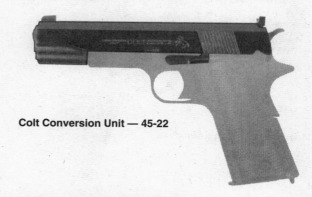

Colt Conversion Unit — 45-22

Colt Cadet 22 Automatic Pistol **$165**
Caliber: 22 LR. 11-shot magazine. 4.5-inch vent-rib bbl. 8.63 inches overall. Weight: 48 oz. Sights: blade front; dovetailed rear. Stainless steel. Textured black polymer grips with Colt medallion. Made from 1993 to date.

Colt Challenger Automatic Pistol **$295**
Same basic design as Woodsman Target, Third Issue, but lacks some of the refinements. Fixed sights. Magazine catch on butt as in old Woodsman. Does not stay open on last shot. Lacks magazine safety. 4.5- or 6-inch bbl. 9 to 10.5 inches overall. Weight: 30 oz., 4.5-inch bbl.; 31.5 oz., 6-inch bbl. Blued finish. Checkered plastic stocks. Made 1950-55.

Colt Combat Commander Automatic Pistol **$425**
Same as Lightweight Commander, except has steel frame available in blued, nickel-plated or stainless steel finish. Weighs 36 oz. Made from 1970 to date.

Colt Conversion Unit — 45-22 . . . . **$395**
Converts Government Model 45 Auto to a 22 LR target pistol. Unit consists of slide assembly, bbl., floating chamber (as in Service Ace), bushing, ejector, recoil spring recoil spring guide and plug, magazine and slide stop. Made from 1938 to date. *Note:* Now designated "22 Conversion Unit," postwar model of this unit is also adaptable to the Super 38 pistols.

Colt Delta Elite Semiauto Pistol
Caliber: 10 mm. 5-inch bbl. 8.5 inches overall. 8-round cylinder. Weight: 38 oz., empty. Checkered rubber combat grips with Delta medallion. 3-dot, high-profile front and rear combat sights. Blued or stainless finish.
Blued Finish **$495**
Stainless Finish **615**

Colt Delta Gold Cup Semiauto Pistol

Same general specifications as Delta Elite, except weighs 39 oz. with 6.75-inch sight radius. Adjustable rear sight. Made 1989 to date.

Blued Finish	**$550**
Stainless Steel Finish	**625**

Colt Huntsman

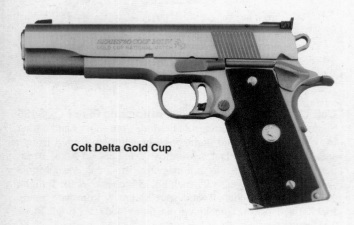

Colt Delta Gold Cup

Colt Gold Cup Mark III National Match $685

Similar to Gold Cup National Match 45 Auto, except chambered for 38 Special mid-range. 5-shot magazine. Made 1961-1974.

Colt MK II/Series '90 Double Eagle Combat Commander $475

Calibers: 40 S&W, 45 ACP. 7-shot magazine. 4.25-inch bbl. 7.75 inches overall. Weight: 36 oz. Fixed blade front sight; square-notch rear. Checkered Xenoy grips. Stainless finish. Made from 1992 to date.

Colt MK II/Series '90 Double Eagle DA Semiauto Pistol

Calibers: 38 Super, 9mm, 40 S&W, 10mm, 45 ACP. 7-shot magazine. 5-inch bbl. 8.5 inches overall. Weight: 39 oz. Fixed or Accro adj. sights. Matte stainless finish. Checkered Xenoy grips. Made from 1991 to date.

38 Super, 9mm, 40 S&W (Fixed Sights)	**$450**
45 ACP (Adjustable Sights)	**475**
45 ACP (Fixed Sights)	**455**
10mm (Adjustable Sights)	**470**
10mm (Fixed Sights)	**450**

Colt Gold Cup National Match 45

Colt MK II/Series '90 Double Eagle

Colt Gold Cup National Match 45 Auto $595

Match version of Government Model 45 Auto with same general specifications, except: match grade bbl. with new design bushing, flat mainspring housing, long wide trigger with adj. stop, hand-fitted slide with improved ejection port, adj. rear sight, target front sight checkered walnut grips with gold medallions. Weight: 37 oz. Made 1957-1970.

Colt Government Model 1911/1911A1

See Colt Model 1911.

Colt Huntsman $285

Same specifications as the Challenger. Made 1955-1976.

Colt MK II/Series '90 Double Eagle Officer's ACP $460

Same general specifications as Double Eagle Combat Commander, except chambered for 45 ACP only. 3.5-inch bbl. 7.25 inches overall. Weight: 35 oz. Also available in lightweight (25 oz.) with blued finish (same price).

Colt MK IV/Series '70 Combat Commander

Same general specifications as the Lightweight Commander, except made from 1970-1983.

Blued Finish	**$355**
Nickel Finish	**365**
Stainless	**395**

Colt MK IV/Series '70 Gold Cup National Match 45

Colt MK IV/Series '70 Gov't.

Colt MK IV/Series '80 380

Colt MK IV/Series '80 Combat Commander

Colt MK IV/Series '70 Gold Cup National Match 45 Auto $595
Match version of MK IV/Series '70 Government Model. Caliber: 45 Auto only. Flat mainspring housing. Accurizor bbl. and bushing. Solid rib, Colt-Elliason adj. rear sight undercut front sight. Adj. trigger, target hammer. 8.75 inches overall. Weight: 38.5 oz. Blued finish. Checkered walnut stocks. Made 1970-1984.

Colt MK IV/Series '70 Gov't. Auto Pistol $435
Calibers: 45 Auto, 38 Super Auto, 9mm Luger. 7-shot magazine in 45, 9-shot in 38 and 9mm. 5-inch bbl. 8.38 inches overall. Weight: 38 oz., 45, 39 oz., 38 and 9mm. Fixed rear sight and ramp front sight. Blued or nickel-plated finish. Checkered walnut stocks. Made 1970-1984.

Colt MK IV/Series '80 380 Automatic Pistol
Caliber: 380 ACP. 3.29-inch bbl. 6.15 inches overall. Weight: 21.8 oz. Composition grips. Fixed sights. Made from 1984 to date.
Blued Finish $250
Bright Nickel. 295
Satin Nickel. 275
Stainless Finish 325
Pocketlite (Blued, 14.75 oz.). 305

Colt MK IV/Series '80 Combat Commander
Updated version of the MK IV/Series '70 with same general specifications. Blued or stainless steel with "pebbled" black neoprene wraparound grips.
Blued Finish $405
Stainless Finish 460

Colt MK IV/Series '80 Combat Elite
Same general specifications as MK IV/Series '80 Combat Commander, except with Elite enhancements. Calibers: 38 Super, 40 S&W, 45 ACP. Stainless frame with blued steel slide. Accro adj. sights and beavertail grip safety. Made from 1992 to date.
38 Super, 45 ACP $495
40 S&W. 485

Colt MK IV/Series '80 Gold Cup National Match
Same general specifications as Match '70 version, except with additional finishes and "pebbled" wraparound neoprene grips.
Blued Finish $525
Bright Blue Finish. 575
Stainless Finish 585

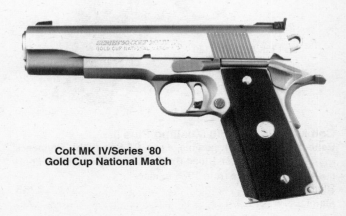

Colt MK IV/Series '80 Gold Cup National Match

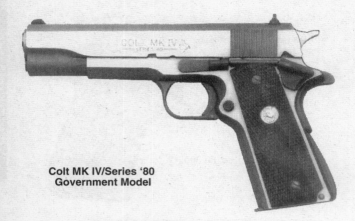

**Colt MK IV/Series '80
Government Model**

**Colt MK IV/Series '80
Mustang Pocketlite**

Colt MK IV/Series '80 Government Model
Same general specifications as Government Model Series '70, except also chambered in 40 S&W, with "pebbled" wraparound neoprene grips, blue or stainless finish.
Blued Finish **$425**
Bright Blue Finish 450
Bright Stainless Finish 510
Matte Stainless Finish 495

Colt MK IV/Series '80 Lightweight Commander . . . $475
Updated version of the MK IV/ cries '70 with same general specifications.

Colt MK IV/Series '80 Mustang 380 Automatic
Caliber: 380 ACP. 5-round magazine. 2.75-inch bbl. 5.5 inches overall. Weight: 18.5 oz. Black composition grips.
Blued Finish **$275**
Nickel Finish 305
Stainless Finish 295

Colt MK IV/Series '80 Mustang Pocketlite
Same general specifications as the Mustang 30, except weighs only 12.5 oz. with aluminum alloy receiver. Blued or stainless finish. Optional wood grain grips. Made from 1988 to date.
Blued Finish **$265**
Stainless Finish 295

Colt MK IV/Series '80 Officer's ACP

Colt MK IV/Series '80 Officer's ACP Automatic Pistol
Calibers: 40 S&W and 45 ACP. 3.63-inch bbl. 7.25 inches overall. Weight: 34 oz. Made from 1984 to date. 40 S&W discontinued 1992.
Matte Finish **$415**
Satin Nickel Finish 425
Stainless Steel 455

Colt National Match Automatic Pistol
Identical with the Government Model 45 Auto, but with hand-honed action, match-grade bbl., adj. rear and ramp front sights or fixed sights. Made 1932-1940.
With Adjustable Sights **$1795**
With Fixed Sights 1295

Colt NRA Centennial 45 Gold Cup
National Match **$875**
2500 produced in 1971.

**Colt MK IV/Series '80
Mustang Plus II**

Colt MK IV/Series '80 Mustang Plus II
Caliber: 380 ACP, 7-round magazine. 2.75-inch bbl. 5.5 inches overall. Weight: 20 oz. Blued finish with checkered black composition grips. Made from 1988 to date.
Blued Finish **$265**
Stainless Finish 295

Colt Pocket Model 25

Colt Pocket Junior

Colt Pocket Model 25 (1908) Auto Pistol $395
Caliber: 25 Auto. 6-shot magazine. 2-inch bbl. 4.5 inches overall. Weight: 13 oz. Flat-top front, square-notch rear sight in groove. Blued or nickel finish. Checkered hard rubber stocks on early models, checkered walnut on later type, special pearl stocks illustrated. Disconnector added in 1916 at pistol No. 141000. Made 1908-1941.

Colt Pocket Model 32 (1903) Automatic Pistol, First Issue $425
Caliber: 32 Auto. 8-shot magazine. 4-inch bbl. 7 inches overall. Weight: 23 oz. Fixed sights. Blued finish. Checkered hard rubber stocks. Hammerless. Slide lock and grip safeties. Barrel-lock bushing similar to that on Government Model 45 Auto. Made 1903-1911. *See* Colt Model 1903.

Colt Pocket Model 32 Automatic Pistol, Second Issue $440
Same as First Issue but without bbl.-lock bushing. Made 1911-1926.

Colt Pocket Model 32 Automatic Pistol, Third Issue $375
Caliber: 32 Auto. Similar to First and Second Issues, but has safety disconnector on all pistols above No. 468097 which prevents firing of cartridge in chamber if magazine is removed. 3.75-inch bbl. 6.75 inches overall. Weight: 24 oz. Fixed sights. Blued or nickel finish. Checkered walnut stocks. Made 1926-1945.

Colt Pocket Model 380 (1908) Automatic Pistol
Same as Pocket 32 Auto, First, Second and Third Issues, respectively, except chambered for caliber 380 Auto with 7-shot magazine.
First Issue (made 1908-1911) $600
Second Issue (made 1911-1926) 345
Third Issue (Safety disconnector on all pistols
   above No. 92,894; made 1926-1945) 375

Colt Pocket Junior Model Automatic Pistol $245
Made in Spain by Unceta y Cia (Astra). Calibers: 22 Short, 25 Auto. 6-shot magazine. 2.25 inch bbl. 4.75 inches overall. Weight: 12 oz. Fixed sights. Checkered walnut grips. Made 1958-1968.

Colt Super 38 Automatic Pistol
Identical with Government Model 45 Auto, except for caliber and magazine capacity. Caliber: 38 Automatic. 9-shot magazine. Made 1928-1970.
Pre-war $1225
Post-war 550

Colt Super Match 38

Colt Super Match 38 Automatic Pistol
Identical to Super 38 Auto, but with hand-honed action, match grade bbl., adjustable rear sight and ramp front sight or fixed sights. Made 1933-1940.
With Adjustable Sights $1395
With Fixed Sights 795

Colt Targetsman

Colt Targetsman $325
Similar to Woodsman Target but has "economy" adj. rear sight, lacks automatic slide stop. Made 1959-1976.

**Colt Woodsman Match Target
First Issue**

**Colt Woodsman Sport Model
First Issue**

Colt Woodsman Match Target Automatic Pistol, First Issue. $950

Same basic design as other Woodsman models. Caliber: 22 LR. 10-shot magazine. 6.5-inch bbl., slightly tapered with flat sides. 11 inches overall. Weight: 36 oz. Adjustable rear sight. Blued finish. Checkered walnut one-piece stock w/extended sides. Made 1938-1942.

**Colt Woodsman Sport Model
Second Issue**

**Colt Woodsman Match Target
Second Issue**

**Colt Woodsman Target
First Issue**

Colt Woodsman Match Target Auto Pistol, Second Issue $595

Same basic design as Woodsman Target, Third Issue. Caliber: 22 LR (reg. or high speed). 10-shot magazine. 6-inch flat-sided heavy bbl. 10.5 inches overall. Weight: 40 oz. Click adj. rear sight, ramp front. Blued finish. Checkered plastic or walnut grips. Made 1948-1976.

Colt Woodsman Match Target "4½" Automatic Pistol $550

Same as Match Target, 2nd Issue, except w/4.5-inch bbl. 9 inches overall. Weight: 36 oz. Made 1950-1976.

Colt Woodsman Sport Model Automatic Pistol, First Issue $495

Caliber: 22 LR (reg. or high speed). Same as Woodsman Target, Second Issue, except has 4.5-inch bbl. Adjustable rear sight; fixed or adjustable front sight. Weight: 27 oz. 8.5 inches overall. Made 1933-1948.

Colt Woodsman Sport Model Automatic Pistol, Second Issue $500

Same as Woodsman Target, 3rd Issue, but with 4.5-inch bbl. 9 inches overall. Weight: 30 oz. Made 1948-1976.

Colt Woodsman Target Model Automatic, First Issue $495

Caliber: 22 LR (reg. velocity). 10-shot magazine. 6.5-inch bbl. 10.5 inches overall. Weight: 28 oz. Adjustable sights. Blued finish. Checkered walnut stocks. Made 1915-1932. *Note:* The mainspring housing of this model is not strong enough to permit safe use of high-speed cartridges.

Change to a new heat-treated mainspring housing was made at pistol No. 83,790. Many of the old models were converted by installation of new housings. The new housing may be distinguished from the earlier type by the checkering in the curve under the breech; new housing is grooved straight across, while the old type bears a diagonally checkered oval.

**Colt Woodsman Target
Second Issue**

Colt Woodsman Target Model Automatic, Second Issue $425

Caliber: 22 LR (reg. or high speed). Same as original model except has heavier bbl. and high-speed mainspring housing. *See* note under Woodsman, First Issue. Weight: 29 oz. Made 1932-1948.

Colt Woodsman Target Third Issue

Colt World War II 50th Anniversary Commemorative

Colt Woodsman Target Model Automatic, Third Issue $375

Same basic design as previous Woodsman pistols, but with longer grip, magazine catch on left side, larger thumb safety, slide stop, slide stays open on last shot, magazine disconnector thumbrest stocks. Caliber: 22 LR (reg. or high speed). 10-shot magazine. 6-inch bbl. 10.5 inches overall. Weight: 32 oz. Click adjustable rear sight, ramp front sight. Blued finish. Checkered plastic or walnut stocks. Made 1948-1976.

Colt World War I 50th Anniversary Commemorative Series 45 Auto

Limited production replica of Model 1911 45 Auto engraved with battle scenes, commemorating Battles at Chateau Thierry, Belleau Wood Second Battle of the Marne, Mouse Argonne. In special presentation display cases. Production: 7,400 standard model, 75 deluxe, 25 special deluxe grade. Match numbered sets offered. Made in 1967, 1968, 1969. Values indicated are for commemoratives in new condition.

Standard Grade	$ 595
Deluxe Grade	1350
Special Deluxe Grade	2600

Colt World War II Commemorative 45 Auto $695

Limited production replica of Model l911A1 45 Auto engraved with respective names of locations where historic engagements occurred during WW II, as well as specific issue and theater identification. European model has oak leaf motif on slide, palm leaf design frames the Pacific issue. Cased. 11,500 of each model were produced. Made in 1970. Value listed is for gun in new condition.

Colt World War II 50th Anniversary Commemorative 45 Auto $1500

Same general specifications as the Colt World War II Commemorative 45 Auto, except slightly difference scroll engraving, 24-karat gold-plate trigger, hammer, slide stop, magazine catch, magazine catch lock, safety lock, and four grip screws. Made in 1995 only.

Colt WW II D-Day Commemorative

Colt World War II D-Day Invasion Commemorative $800

High-luster and highly decorated version of the Colt Model 1911A1. Caliber: 45 ACP. Same general specifications as the Colt Model 1911 except for 24-karat gold-plated hammer, trigger, slide stop, magazine catch, magazine catch screw, safety lock and four grip screws. Also has scrolls and inscription on slide. Made in 1991 only.

Colt WW II V-J Day Commemorative

Colt World War II Golden Anniversary V-J Day Tribute 45 Auto $1600

Basic Colt Model 1911A1 design with highly-polished bluing and decorated with specialized tributes to honor V-J Day. Two 24-karat gold scenes highlight the slide; 24-karat gold-plated hammer. Checkered wood grips with gold medallion on each side. Made 1995.

COLT SINGLE-SHOT PISTOLS AND DERINGERS

NOTE

For ease in finding a particular firearm, Colt handguns are grouped into three sections: Automatic Pistols (which precedes this one), this section, and Revolvers, which follows. For a complete listing, please refer to the Index.

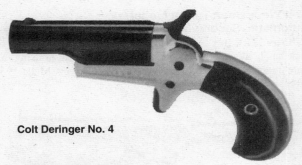

Colt Deringer No. 4

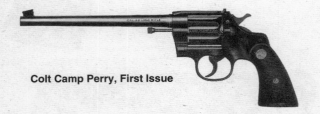

Colt Camp Perry, First Issue

Colt Camp Perry Model Single-Shot Pistol, First Issue **$995**

Built on Officers' Model frame. Caliber: 22 LR (embedded head chamber for high-speed cartridges after 1930). 10 inch bbl. 13.75 inches overall. Weight: 34.5 oz. Adj. target sights. Hand-finished action. Blued finish. Checkered walnut stocks. Made 1926-1934.

Colt Camp Perry, Second Issue

Colt Camp Perry Model, Second Issue **$915**

Same general specifications as First Issue, except has shorter hammer fall and 8-inch bbl. 12 inches overall. Weight: 34 oz. Made 1934-1941 (about 440 produced).

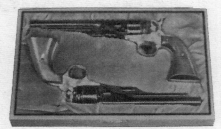

Colt Civil War Centennial (Cased Pair)

Colt Civil War Centennial Model Pistol

Single-shot replica, 7/8 scale, of Colt Model 1860 Army Revolver. Caliber: 22 Short. 6-inch bbl. Weight: 22 oz. Blued finish with gold-plated frame, grip frame, and trigger guard, walnut grips. Cased. 24,114 were produced. Made in 1961.
Single Pistol **$150**
Pair with consecutive serial numbers 350

Colt Deringer No. 4

Replica of Deringer No. 3 (1872). Single-shot with sideswing bbl. Caliber: 22 Short. 2.5-inch bbl. 4.9 inches overall. Weight: 7.75 oz. Fixed sights. Gold-finished frame, blued barrel, walnut grips, also nickel-plated with simulated ivory grips. Cased. Made 1959-1963.
Single Pistol **$125**
Pair with consecutive serial numbers 250

Colt Deringer No. 4 (Cased Pair)

Colt Deringer No. 4 Commemorative Models

Limited production version of 22 Deringer issued, with appropriate inscription, to commemorate historical events.

1961 Issue

Geneseo, Illinois, 125th Anniversary (104 produced) . . . **$625**

1962 Issue

Fort McPherson, Nebraska, Centennial (300 produced) . . **$375**

Colt Lord and Lady Deringers

Same as Deringer No. 4. Lord model is blued with gold-plated frame and walnut stocks. Lady model is gold-plated with simulated pearl stocks. Furnished in cased pairs. Made 1970-72.
Lord Deringer, pair in case **$200**
Lady Deringer, pair in case 200
Lord and Lady Deringers, one each, in case 200

Colt Rock Island Arsenal Centennial Pistol **$250**

Limited production (550 pieces) version of Civil War Centennial Model single shot 22 pistol, made exclusively for Cherry's Sporting Goods, Geneseo, Illinois, to commemorate the centennial of the Rock Island Arsenal in Illinois. Cased. Made in 1962.

REVOLVERS

NOTE

This section of Colt handguns contains only revolvers. For automatic pistols or single-shot pistols and derringers, please see the two sections that precede this. For a complete listing, please refer to the Index.

Colt Anaconda

Colt Agent First Issue

Colt Agent DA Revolver, First Issue **$335**
Same as Cobra, First Issue, except has short-grip frame 38 Special only, weighs 14 oz. Made 1962-1973.

Colt Agent, Second Issue

Colt Agent DA Revolver, Second Issue **$250**
Same as Cobra, Second Issue, except has short service stocks, 6.63 inches overall, weighs 16 oz. Made 1973-1981.

Colt Anaconda DA Revolver
Calibers: 44 Mag., 45 Colt. Bbl. lengths: 4, 6 or 8 inches. 11.63 inches overall w/6-inch bbl. Weight: 53 oz. w/6-inch bbl. Adj. white outline rear sight, red insert rampstyle front. Matte stainless finish. Black neoprene combat grips with finger grooves. Made from 1992 to date.
44 Magnum **$425**
45 Colt (6-inch bbl. only **445**

Colt Anaconda Titanium DA Revolver **$1800**
Caliber: 44 Mag. Same general specifications as the standard Anaconda except that it was the first titanium-plated Colt handgun and manufactured on a limited basis. Gold-plated trigger, hammer, cylinder release, and inscription on bbl. Made in 1996 only.

Colt Army Special DA Revolver **$395**
41-caliber frame. Calibers: 32-20, 38 Special (41 Colt). 6-shot cylinder, right revolution. Bbl. lengths: 4-, 4.5, 5-, and 6-inch. 9.25 inches overall w/4-inch bbl. Weight: 32 oz. w/4-inch bbl. Fixed sights. Blued or nickel-plated finish. Hard rubber stocks. Made 1908-1927. *Note:* This model has a somewhat heavier frame than the New Navy, which it replaced. Serial numbers begin with 300,000. The heavy 38 Special High Velocity loads should not be used in 38 Special arms of this model.

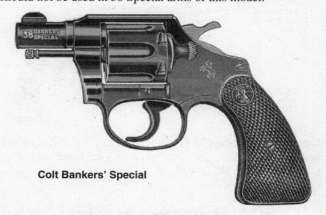

Colt Bankers' Special

Colt Bankers' Special DA Revolver
This is the Police Positive with a 2-inch bbl., otherwise specifications same as that model, rounded butt introduced in 1933. Calibers: 22 LR (embedded head-cylinder for high speed cartridges introduced 1933), 38 New Police. 6.5 inches overall. Weight: 23 oz. (22 LR), 19 oz. (38). Made 1926-1940.
38 Caliber . . . . **$ 585**
22 Caliber **1195**

Colt Bisley Model SA Revolver
Variation of the Single-Action Army, developed for target shooting; grips, trigger and hammer changed. Calibers: general specifications same as SA Army. Target Model made w/flat-topped frame and target sights. Made 1894-1915. *See* illustration next page.
Standard Model **$3795**
Target Model **6450**

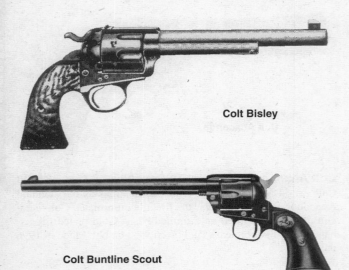

Colt Bisley

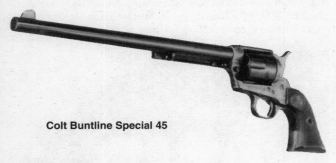

Colt Buntline Scout

Colt Buntline Scout $350
Same as Frontier Scout, except has 9.5-inch bbl. Made from 1959-1971.

Colt Buntline Special 45

Colt Buntline Special 45 . . . . $695
Same as standard SA Army, except has 12-inch barrel, caliber 45 Long Colt. Made 1957-1975.

Colt Cobra, Round Butt First Issue

Colt Cobra DA Revolver, Round Butt, First Issue $325
Lightweight Detective Special with same general specifications as that model, except with Colt-alloy frame. 2-inch bbl. Calibers: 38 Special, 38 New Police, 32 New Police. Weight: 15 oz., 38 cal. Blued finish. Checkered plastic or walnut stocks. Made 1951-1973.

Colt Cobra, Second Issue

Colt Cobra DA Revolver, Second Issue $295
Lightweight version of Detective Special, Second Issue has aluminum alloy frame. 16.5 oz. Made 1973-1981.

Colt Cobra DA Revolver Square Butt $315
Lightweight Police Positive Special with same general specifications, except has Colt-alloy frame. 4-inch bbl. Calibers: 38 Special, 38 New Police, 32 New Police. Weight: 17 oz. in 38 caliber. Blued finish. Checkered plastic or walnut stocks. Made 1951-1973.

Colt Commando Special

Colt Commando Special DA Revolver $295
Caliber: 38 Special. 6-shot cylinder. 2-inch barrel; 6.88 inches overall. Weight: 21.5 oz. Fixed sights. Low-luster blue finish. Made 1982-86.

**Colt Detective Special
First Issue**

Colt Detective Special DA Revolver, First Issue .. $450

This is the Police Positive Special with 2-inch bbl., otherwise specifications same as that model, rounded butt intro. 1933. Originally supplied in 38 Special only; also made in calibers 32 New Police, 38 New Police. Weight: 17 oz. (38 cal.). 6.75 inches overall. Made 1926-1972.

**Colt Detective Special
2nd Issue**

Colt Detective Special DA Revolver, 2nd Issue

"D" frame, shrouded ejector rod. Caliber: 38 Special. 6-shot cylinder. 2-inch bbl. 6.88 inches overall. Weight: 21.5 oz. Fixed rear sight, ramp front. Blued or nickel-plated finish. Checkered walnut wraparound stocks. Made 1972-1984. Reintroduced in 1993 with checkered black composition grips.

Second Issue $295
Reissue 325

Colt Diamondback

Colt Diamondback DA Revolver $325

"D" frame, shrouded ejector rod. Calibers: 22 LR, 38 Special. 6-shot cylinder. Bbls.: 2.5-, 4-inch; vent rib. 9 inches overall w/4-inch bbl. Weight: w/4-inch bbl., 22 cal., 31.75 oz., 38 cal., 28.5 oz. Adj. rear sight, ramp front. Blued or nickel finish. Checkered walnut stocks. Made 1966-1984.

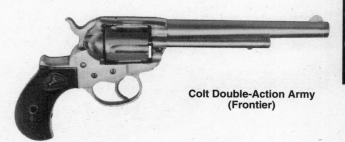

**Colt Double-Action Army
(Frontier)**

Colt DA Army Revolver $2250

Also called DA Frontier. Similar in appearance to the smaller Lightning Model, but has heavier frame of different shape, round disc on left side of frame, lanyard loop in butt. Calibers: 38-40, 44-40, 45 Colt. 6-shot cylinder. Bbl. lengths: 3.5- and 4-inch without ejector; 4.75-, 5.5- and 7.5-inch with ejector. 12 .5 inches overall with 7.5-inch bbl. Weight: 45 cal. with 7.5-inch bbl., 39 oz. Fixed sights. Hard rubber bird's-head grips. Blued or nickel finish. Made 1878-1905.

Colt Frontier Scout

Colt Frontier Scout Revolver

SA Army replica, 7/8 scale. Calibers: 22 Short, Long, LR; 22 WMR (interchangeable cylinder available). 6-shot cylinder. 4.75-inch bbl. 9.9 inches overall. Weight: 24 oz. Fixed sights. Plastic stocks. Originally made with bright alloy frame; since 1959 with steel frame, blued finish, also in all-nickel finish with wood stocks. Made 1958-1971.

Blued Finish, plastic stocks. $295
Nickel Finish, wood stocks 315
Extra interchangeable cylinder 55

Colt Frontier Scout Revolver Commemorative Models

Limited production versions of Frontier Scout issued, with appropriate inscription, to commemorate historical events. Cased. *Note:* Values indicated are for commemoratives in new condition.

1961 Issues

Kansas Statehood Centennial (6201 produced) $350
Pony Express Centennial (1007 produced). 460

Colt Frontier Scout Commemoratives *(cont.)*

1962 Issues

Columbus, Ohio, Sesquicentennial (200 produced) . . . $ 595
Fort Findlay, Ohio, Sesquicentennial (130 produced) . . . 730
Fort Findlay Cased Pair, 22 Long Rifle and 22
  Magnum (20 produced) 2950
New Mexico Golden Anniversary 395
West Virginia Statehood Centennial (3452 produced) . . 375

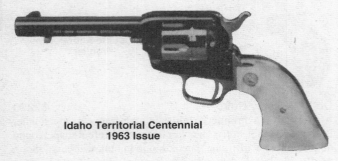

**Idaho Territorial Centennial
1963 Issue**

1963 Issues

Arizona Territorial Centennial (5355 produced) $365
Battle of Gettysburg Centennial (1019 produced) 375
Carolina Charter Tercentenary (300 produced) 395
Fort Stephenson, Ohio, Sesquicentennial (200 produced) . . 575
General John Hunt Morgan Indiana Raid 675
Idaho Territorial Centennial (902 produced) 395

**General Hood Centennial
1964 Issue**

New Jersey Tercentenary — 1964 Issue

Colt Frontier Scout Commemoratives *(cont.)*

1964 Issues

California Gold Rush (500 produced) $375
Chamizal Treaty (450 produced) 410
General Hood Centennial (1503 produced) 385
Montana Territorial Centennial (2300 produced) 375
Nevada "Battle Born" (981 produced) 375
Nevada Statehood Centennial (3984 produced) 375
New Jersey Tercentenary (1001 produced) 365
St. Louis Bicentennial (802 produced) 375
Wyoming Diamond Jubilee (2357 produced) 375

1965 Issues

Appomattox Centennial (1001 produced) $375
Forty-Niner Miner (500 produced) 375
General Meade Campaign (1197 produced) 365
Kansas Cowtown Series—Wichita (500 produced) 365
Old Fort Des Moines Reconstruction (700 produced) . . . 375
Oregon Trail (1995 produced) 365
St. Augustine Quadricentennial (500 produced) 375

1966 Issues

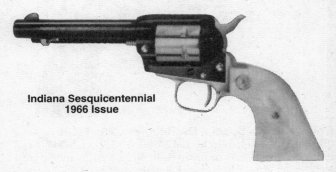

**Indiana Sesquicentennial
1966 Issue**

Colorado Gold Rush (1350 produced) $375
Dakota Territory (1000 produced) 375
Indiana Sesquicentennial (1500 produced) 375
Kansas Cowtown Series—Abilene (500 produced) 375
Kansas Cowtown Series—Dodge City (500 produced) . . 365
Oklahoma Territory (1343 produced) 365

1967 Issues

Alamo (4500 produced) $365
Kansas Cowtown Series—Coffeyville (500 produced) . . 365
Kansas Trail Series—Chisholm Trail (500 produced) . . . 365
Lawman Series—Bat Masterson (3000 produced) 385

1968 Issues

Kansas Trail Series—Santa Fe Trail (501 produced) $365
Kansas Trail Series—Pawnee Trail (501 produced) 365
Lawman Series—Pat Garrett (3000 produced) 385
Nebraska Centennial (7001 produced) 350

Colt Frontier Scout Commemoratives (cont.)

**Golden Spike Centennial
1969 Issue**

1969 Issues

Alabama Sesquicentennial (3001 produced). **$365**
Arkansas Territory Sesquicentennial (3500 produced). . . **365**
California Bicentennial (5000 produced) **350**
General Nathan Bedford Forrest (3000 produced) **365**
Golden Spike (11,000 produced) **370**
Kansas Trail Series—Shawnee Trail (501 produced) . . . **365**
Lawman Series—Wild Bill Hickock (3000 produced) . . **375**

1970 Issues

Kansas Fort Series—Fort Lamed (500 produced) **$365**
Kansas Fort Series—Fort Hays (500 produced) **365**
Kansas Fort Series—Fort Riley (500 produced). **365**
Lawman Series—Wyatt Earp (3000 produced) **475**
Maine Sesquicentennial (3000 produced). **350**
Missouri Sesquicentennial (3000 produced) **365**

1971 Issues

Kansas Fort Series—Fort Scott (500 produced) **$365**

1972 Issues

Florida Territory Sesquicentennial (2001 produced) . . . **$365**

1973 Issues

Arizona Ranger (3001 produced) **$350**

Colt King Cobra Revolver

Caliber: 357 Mag. Bbl. lengths: 2.5-, 4-, 6- or 8-inch. 9 inches overall w/4-inch bbl. Weight: 42 oz., average. Matte stainless steel finish. Black neoprene combat grips. Made from 1986 to date. 2.5-inch barrel, and "Ultimate" bright or blued finish made 1988-1992.
Matte Stainless **$325**
Ultimate Bright Stainless **350**
Blued. **295**

Colt King Cobra

Colt Lawman MK III

Colt Lawman MK III DA Revolver **$220**

"J" frame, shrouded ejector rod on 2-inch barrel only. Caliber: 357 Magnum. 6-shot cylinder. Bbl. lengths: 2-, 4-inch. 9.38 inches overall with 4-inch bbl. Weight: with 4-inch bbl., 35 oz. Fixed rear sight, ramp front. Service trigger and hammer or target trigger and wide-spur hammer. Blued or nickel-plated finish. Checkered walnut service or target stocks. Made 1969-1982.

Colt Lawman MK V

Colt Lawman MK V DA Revolver **$245**

Similar to Trooper MK V. Caliber: 357 Mag. 6-shot cylinder. 2- or 4-inch barrel, 9.38 inches overall w/4-inch bbl. Weight: 35 oz. w/4-inch bbl. Fixed sights. Checkered walnut grips. Made 1983-85.

Colt Marine Corps Model (1905) DA Revolver .. $1995

General specifications same as New Navy, Second Issue, except this has round butt, was supplied only in 38 caliber (38 Short & Long Colt, 38 Special) with 6-inch bbl. Made 1905-1909.

Colt Metropolitan MK III

Colt Metropolitan MK III DA Revolver $245

Same as Official Police MK III, except has 4-inch barrel, service or target stocks; weighs 36 oz. Made 1969-1972.

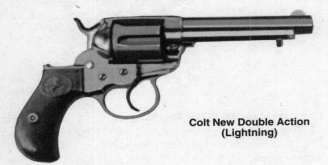

**Colt New Double Action
(Lightning)**

Colt New DA Central Fire Revolver.......... $1280

Also called Lightning Model. Calibers: 38 and 41 Centerfire. 6-shot cylinder. Bbl. lengths: 2.5-, 3.5-, 4.5- and 6-inch without ejector, 4.5- and 6-inch w/ejector. 8 .5 inches overall w/3.5-inch bbl. Weight: 38 cal. w/3.5-inch bbl., 23 oz. Fixed sights. Blued or nickel finish. Hard rubber bird's-head grips. Made 1877-1909.

Colt New Frontier Buntline Special

Same as New Frontier SA Army, except has 12-inch bbl.
Second Generation (1962-1975)..................... $995
Third Generation (1976-1992) 695

**Colt New Frontier SA Army
Second Generation**

Colt New Frontier SA Army Revolver

Same as SA Army, except has flat-top frame, adj. target rear sight, ramp front sight, smooth walnut grips. 5.5- or 7.5-inch bbl. Calibers: 357 Magnum, 44 Special, 45 Colt. Made 1961-1992.
Second Generation (1961-75)..................... $1295
Third Generation (1976-92) 650

Colt New Frontier SA 22

Colt New Frontier SA 22 Revolver $260

Same as Peacemaker 22, except has flat-top frame, adj. rear sight, ramp front sight. Made 1971-76.

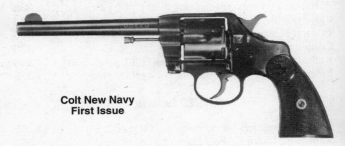

**Colt New Navy
First Issue**

Colt New Navy DA, First Issue $945

Also called New Army. Calibers: 38 Short & Long Colt, 41 Short & Long Colt. 6-shot cylinder, left revolution. Bbl. lengths: 3-, 4.5- and 6-inch. 11.25 inches overall w/6-inch bbl. Weight: 32 oz., 6-inch bbl. Fixed sights, knife-blade and V-notch. Blued or nickel-plated finish. Walnut or hard rubber grips. Made 1889-1894. *Note:* This model, which was adopted by both the Army and Navy, was Colt's first revolver of the solid frame, swing-out cylinder type. It lacks the cylinder-locking notches found on later models made on this 41 frame, ratchet on the back of the cylinder is held in place by a double projection on the hand.

Colt New Navy DA, Second Issue $735

Also called New Army. General specifications same as First Issue except has double cylinder notches and double locking bolt. Calibers: 38 Special added in 1904 and 32-20 in 1905. Made 1892-1907. *Note:* The heavy 38 Special High Velocity loads should not be used in 38 Special arms of this model.

Colt New Pocket DA Revolver $395

Caliber: 32 Short & Long Colt. 6-shot cylinder. Bbl. lengths: 2.5, 3.5- and 6-inch. 7 .5 inches overall with 3.5-inch bbl. Weight: 16 oz., 3.5-inch bbl. Fixed sights knife-blade and V-notch. Blued or nickel finish. Rubber stocks. Made 1893-1905.

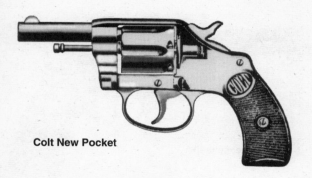

Colt New Pocket

Colt New Service Target

Colt New Police DA Revolver $325

Built on New Pocket frame, but with larger grip. Calibers: 32 Colt New Police, 32 Short & Long Colt. Bbl. lengths: 2.5-, 4- and 6-inch. 8.5 inches overall w/4-inch bbl. Weight: 17 oz., 4-inch bbl. Fixed sights: knife-blade, V-notch. Blued or nickel finish. Rubber stocks. Made 1896-1905.

Colt New Police Target DA Revolver $595

Target version of the New Police with same general specifications. Target sights. 6-inch bbl. Blued finish only. Made 1896-1905.

Colt New Service

Colt New Service DA Revolver

Calibers: 38 Special, 357 Magnum (intro. 1936), 38-40, 44-40, 44 Russian, 44 Special, 45 Auto, 45 Colt, 450 Eley, 455 Eley, 476 Eley. 6-shot cylinder. Bbl. lengths: 4-, 5- and 6-inch in 38 Special and 357 Magnum, 4.5-, 5.5- and 7.5 inch in other calibers. 9.75 inches overall w/4.5-inch bbl. Weight: 39 oz., 45 cal. w/4.5-inch bbl. Fixed sights. Blued or nickel finish. Checkered walnut stocks. Made 1898-1942. *Note:* More than 500,000 of this model in caliber 45 Auto (designated "Model 1917 Revolver") were purchased by the U.S. Govt. during WW I. These arms were later sold as surplus to National Rifle Association members through the Director of Civilian Marksmanship. Price was $16.15 plus packing charge. Supply exhausted during the early 1930s.

Commercial Model $950
Magnum 695
1917 Army 795

Colt New Service Target $1195

Target version of the New Service; general specifications same as that model. Calibers: originally chambered for 44 Russian, 450 Eley 455 Eley and 476 Eley, later models in 44 Special, 45 Colt and 45 Auto. Bbl. lengths: 6- and 7.5-inch. 12.75 inches overall with 7.5-inch bbl. Adj. target sights. Hand-finished action. Blued finish. Checkered walnut stocks. Made 1900-1940.

Colt Officers' Model Match

Colt Officers' Model Match $395

Same general design as Officers' Model revolvers. Has tapered heavy barrel, wide hammer spur, Accrued rear sight ramp front sight, large target stocks of checkered walnut. Calibers: 22 LR, 38 Special. 6-inch bbl. 11.25 inches overall. Weight: 43 oz., 22 cal.; 39 oz., 38 cal. Blued finish. Made 1953-1970.

Colt Officers' Model Special $495

Target arm replacing Officers' Model, Second Issue; basically the same as that model, but with heavier, nontapered barrel, redesigned hammer, ramp front sight and Colt Officers' Model Special "Coltmaster" rear sight adj. for windage and elevation. Calibers: 22 LR, 38 Special. 6-inch bbl. 11.25 inches overall. Weight: 39 oz., 38 cal., 43 oz., 22 cal. Blued finish. Checkered plastic stocks. Made 1949-1953.

Colt Officers' Model Target DA Revolver, First Issue $995

Caliber: 38 Special. 6-inch bbl. Hand-finished action. Adj. target sights. Checkered walnut stocks. General specifications same as New Navy, Second Issue. Made 1904-1908.

**Colt Officers' Model Target
Second Issue**

Colt Officers' Model Target, Second Issue $750

Calibers: 22 LR (intro. 1930, embedded head-cylinder for high-speed cartridges after 1932), 32 Police Positive (made 1932-1942), 38 Special. 6-shot cylinder. Bbl. lengths: 4-, 4.5-, 5-, 6- and 7.5-inch in 38 Special; 6-inch only in 22 LR and 32 PP. 11.25 inches overall w/6-inch bbl. (38 Special). Adj. target sights. Blued finish. Checkered walnut stocks. Hand-finished action. General features same as Army Special and Official Police of same date. Made 1908-1949 (with exceptions noted).

Colt Official Police

Colt Official Police DA Revolver

Calibers: 22 LR (intro. 1930, embedded head-cylinder for high-speed cartridges after 1932), 32-20 (discontinued 1942), 38 Special, 41 Long Colt (discontinued 1930). 6-shot cylinder. Bbl. lengths: 4-, 5-, and 6-inch; 2-inch and 6-inch heavy barrel in 38 Special only, 22 LR w/4 and 6-inch barrels only. 11.25 inches overall. Weight: 36 oz. w/standard 6-inch bbl. in 38 Special. Fixed sights. Blued or nickel-plated finish. Checkered walnut stocks on all revolvers of this model, except some of postwar production had checkered plastic stocks. Made 1927-1969. Note: This model is a refined version of the Army Special, which it replaced in 1928 at about serial number 520,000. The Commando 38 Special was a wartime adaptation of the Official Police made to Government specifications. Commando can be identified by its sandblasted blued finish; serial numbers start with number 1 (1942).
Commercial Model **$395**
Commando Model **350**

Colt Official Police MK III

Colt Official Police MK III DA Revolver $175

"J" frame, without shrouded ejector rod. Caliber: 38 Special. 6-shot cylinder. Bbl. lengths: 4-, 5-, 6-inch. 9.25 inches overall with 4-inch bbl. Weight: 34 oz. w/4-inch bbl. Fixed rear sight, ramp front. Service trigger and hammer or target trigger and wide-spur hammer. Blued or nickel-plated finish. Checkered walnut service stocks. Made 1969-1975.

Colt Peacekeeper

Colt Peacekeeper DA Revolver $265

Caliber: 357 Mag. 6-shot cylinder. 4- and 6-inch barrels; 11.25 inches overall with 6-inch bbl. Weight: 46 oz. with 6-inch bbl. Adj. white outline rear sight, red insert ramp-style front. Non-reflective matte blued finish. Made 1985-89.

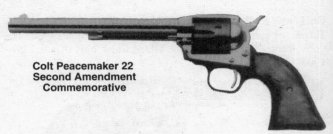

**Colt Peacemaker 22
Second Amendment
Commemorative**

Colt Peacemaker 22 Second Amendment Commemorative $350

Peacemaker 22 SA Revolver with 7.5-inch bbl. Nickel-plated frame, barrel, ejector rod assembly, hammer and trigger, blued cylinder, backstrap and trigger guard. Black pearlite stocks. Bbl. inscribed "The Right to Keep and Bear Arms." Presentation case. Limited edition of 3000 issued in 1977. Value is for revolver in new condition.

Colt Peacemaker 22

Colt Peacemaker 22 SA Revolver $260

Calibers: 22 LR and 22 WMR. Furnished with cylinder for each caliber. 6-shot. Bbl.: 4.38-, 6- or 7.5-inch. 11.25 inches overall w/6-inch bbl. Weight: 30.5 oz. w/6-inch bbl. Fixed sights. Black composite stocks. Made 1971-76.

Colt Pocket Positive

Colt Pocket Positive DA Revolver $375

General specifications same as New Pocket, except this model has positive lock feature (see Police Positive). Calibers: 32 Short & Long Colt (discontinued 1914), 32 Colt New Police (32 S&W Short & Long). Fixed sights, flat top and square notch. Made 1905-1940.

**Colt Police Positive
First Issue**

Colt Police Positive DA, First Issue $345

Improved version of the New Police with the "Positive Lock," which prevents the firing pin from coming in contact with the cartridge except when the trigger is pulled. Calibers: 32 Short & Long Colt (discontinued 1915), 32 Colt New Police (32 S&W Short & Long), 38 New Police (38 S&W). 6-shot cylinder. Bbl. lengths: 2.5- (32 cal. only), 4-, 5- and 6-inch. 8 .5 inches overall w/4-inch bbl. Weight 20 oz. w/4-inch bbl. Fixed sights. Blued or nickel finish. Rubber or checkered walnut stocks. Made 1905-1947.

Colt Police Positive DA, Second Issue $285

Same as Detective Special, Second Issue, except has 4-inch barrel, is 9 inches overall, weighs 26 .5 oz. Introduced in 1977. Note: Original Police Positive (First Issue) has a shorter frame, is not chambered for 38 Special.

Colt Police Positive Special DA Revolver $315

Based on the Police Positive with frame lengthened to permit longer cylinder. Calibers: 32-20 (discontinued 1942), 38 Special, 32 New Police and 38 New Police (introduced 1946). 6-shot cylinder. Bbl. lengths: 4- (only length in current production), 5- and 6-inch. 8.75 inches overall w/4-inch bbl. Weight: 23 oz. (38 Special) w/4-inch bbl. Fixed sights. Checkered stocks of hard rubber, plastic or walnut. Made 1907-1973.

Colt Police Positive Special

Colt Police Positive Target

Colt Police Positive Target DA Revolver $595

Target version of the Police Positive. Calibers: 22 LR (introduced 1910, embedded head-cylinder for high-speed cartridges after 1932), 22 WRF (intro. 1910, disc. 1935), 32 Short & Long Colt. 1915), 32 New Police (32 S&W Short & Long). 6-inch bbl. Blued finish only. 10.5 inches overall. Weight: 26 oz. in 22 cal. Adj. target sights. Checkered walnut stocks. Made 1905-1940.

Colt Python

Colt Python DA Revolver

"I" frame, shrouded ejector rod. Calibers: 357 Magnum, 38 Special. 6-shot cylinder. Bbls.: 2.5-, 4-, 6-, 8-inch; vent rib. 11.25 inches overall w/6-inch bbl. Weight: 44 oz. w/6-inch bbl. Adj. rear sight, ramp front. Blued, nickel-plated or stainless finish. Checkered walnut target stocks. Made from 1955 to date. Ultimate stainless finish made from 1985 to date.

Blued Finish	**$395**
Royal Blue Finish	445
Nickel Finish	385
Stainless Finish	525

Colt Shooting Master DA Revolver. $950

Deluxe target arm based on the New Service model. Calibers: originally made only in 38 Special, 44 Special, 45 Auto and 45 Colt added in 1933, 357 Magnum in 1936. 6-inch bbl. 11.25 inches overall. Weight: 44 oz., 38 cal. Adj. target sights. Hand-finished action. Blued finish. Checkered walnut stocks. Rounded butt. Made 1932-1941.

Colt SA Army

Colt SA Army Revolver

Also called Frontier Six-Shooter and Peacemaker. Calibers: 22 Rimfire (Short, Long, LR), 22 WRF, 32 Rimfire, 32 Colt, 32 S&W, 32-20, 38 Colt, 38 S&W, 38 Special, 357 Magnum, 38-40, 41 Colt, 44 Rimfire, 44 Russian, 44 Special, 44-40, 45 Colt, 45 Auto, 450 Boxer, 450 Eley, 455 Eley, 476 Eley. 6-shot cylinder. Bbl. lengths: 4.75, 5 .5 and 7.5 inches with ejector; 3 and 4 inches w/o ejector. 10.25 inches overall w/4.75-inch bbl. Weight: 36 oz., 45 cal. w/4.75-inch bbl. Fixed sights. Also made in Target Model with flat top-strap and target sights. Blued finish with casehardened frame or nickel-plated. One-piece smooth walnut or checkered black rubber stocks.

   S.A. Army Revolvers with serial numbers above 165,000 (circa 1896) are adapted to smokeless powder; cylinder pin screw was changed to spring catch at about the same time. Made 1873-1942; production resumed in 1955 with serial number 1001SA. Current calibers: 357 Magnum, 44 Special, 45 Long Colt.

Frontier Six-Shooter, 44-40	**$4550**
Storekeeper's Model, 3-inch/4-inch barrel, no ejector . .	**4595**
Target Model, flat top strap, target sights	**9850**
U.S. Artillery Model, 45 Colt, 5.5-inch bbl.	**6595**
U.S. Cavalry Model, 45, 7.5-inch bbl.	**8995**

(Above values apply only to original models, not to similar S.A.A. revolvers of recent manufacture.)

Standard Model, pre-1942	**$2950**
Standard Model (1955-1982)	**1595**
Standard Model (Reissued 1992)	**795**

Colt SA Army Flat Top

Colt SA Army — 125th Anniversary $1050

Limited production deluxe version of SA Army issued in commemoration of Colt's 125th Anniversary. Caliber: 45 Long Colt. 7.5-inch bbl. Gold-plated frame trigger, hammer, cylinder pin, ejector rod tip, and stock medallion. Presentation case with anniversary medallion. Serial numbers from "50AM." 7368 were made in 1961. *See* illustration opposite page.

Colt SA Army Commemorative Models

Limited production versions of SA Army 45 issued, with appropriate inscription to commemorate historical events. Cased. *Note:* Values indicated are for commemorative revolvers in new condition.

1963 Issues

Arizona Territorial Centennial (1280 produced)	**$1125**
West Virginia Statehood Centennial (600 produced) . . .	**1100**

1964 Issues

Chamizal Treaty (50 produced)	**$1325**
Colonel Sam Colt Sesquicentennial Presentation (4750 produced)	**1100**
Deluxe Presentation (200 produced)	**2150**
Special Deluxe Presentation (50 produced)	**3200**
Montana Territorial Centennial (851 produced)	**1125**
Nevada "Battle Born" (100 produced)	**1425**
Nevada Statehood Centennial (1877 produced)	**1100**
New Jersey Tercentenary (250 produced)	**1125**
Pony Express Presentation (1004 produced)	**1200**
St. Louis Bicentennial (450 produced)	**1100**
Wyatt Earp Buntline (150 produced)	**1995**

1965 Issues

Appomattox Centennial (500 produced).	**$1100**
Old Fort Des Moines Reconstruction (200 produced) . .	**1125**

1966 Issues

Abercrombie & Fitch Trailblazer—Chicago (100 produced)	**$1125**
Abercrombie & Fitch Trailblazer—New York (200 produced)	**1125**
Abercrombie & Fitch Trailblazer—San Francisco (100 produced)	**1125**
California Gold Rush (130 produced)	**1325**
General Meade (200 produced)	**1100**
Pony Express Four Square (4 guns)	**4950**

1967 Issues

Alamo (1000 produced)	**$1100**
Lawman Series—Bat Masterson (500 produced)	**1325**

1968 Issues

Lawman Series—Pat Garrett (500 produced)	**$1150**

Colt 150th Anniversary Commemorative

1969 Issues

Lawman Series—Wild Bill Hickok (500 produced) . . . **$1125**

1970 Issues

Lawman Series—Wyatt Earp (501 produced) **$1950**
Missouri Sesquicentennial (501 produced). **1050**
Texas Ranger (1000 produced). **2000**

1971 Issues

NRA Centennial, 357 or 45 (5001 produced) **$1125**

1975 Issues

Peacemaker Centennial 45 (1501 produced) **$1150**
Peacemaker Centennial 44-40 (1501 produced) **1225**
Peacemaker Centennial Cased Pair (501 produced) . . . **2500**

1979 Issues

Ned Buntline 45 (3000 produced) **$895**

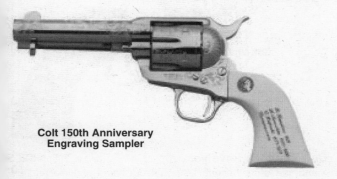

**Colt 150th Anniversary
Engraving Sampler**

1986 Issues

Colt 150th Anniversary (standard) **$2700**
Colt 150th Anniversay (Engraved). **3500**

**Colt 150th Anniversay
Deluxe Model**

Colt SA Sheriff's Model 45

Limited edition of replica of Storekeeper's Model in caliber 45 Colt, made exclusively for Centennial Arms Corp. Chicago, Illinois. Numbered from "1SM." Blued finish with casehardened frame or nickel-plated. Walnut stocks. 478 were produced in blue, 25 in nickel. Made in 1961.
Blued Finish **$1595**
Nickel Finish **4250**

Colt Three-Fifty-Seven DA Revolver

Heavy frame. Caliber: 357 Magnum. 6-shot cylinder. 4 or 6-inch bbl. Quick-draw ramp front sight, Accro™ rear sight. Blued finish. Checkered walnut stocks. 9.25 or 11.25 inches overall. Weight: 36 oz., 4-inch bbl.; 39 oz., 6 inch bbl. Made 1953-1961.
With standard hammer and service stocks **$325**
With wide-spur hammer and target stocks **375**

Colt Trooper DA Revolver **$320**

Same specifications as Officers' Model Match, except has 4-inch barrel with quick-draw ramp front sight, weighs 34 oz. in 38 caliber. Made 1953-1969. *(See* photo, next page.)

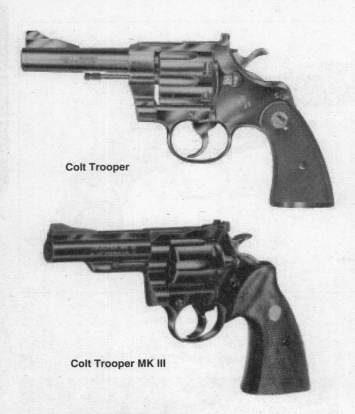

Colt Trooper

Colt Trooper MK III

Colt U.S. Bicentennial Commemorative Set

Colt Trooper MK III DA Revolver **$225**
"J"frame, shrouded ejector rod. Calibers: 22 LR, 22 Magnum, 38 Special, 357 Magnum. 6-shot cylinder. Bbl. lengths: 4-, 6-inch. 9.5 inches overall w/4-inch bbl. Weight: 39 oz. w/4-inch bbl. Adj. rear sight, ramp front. Target trigger and hammer. Blued or nickel-plated finish. Checkered walnut target stocks. Made 1969-1978.

Colt Trooper MK IV DA Revolver **$265**
Same general specifications as Trooper MK III with action modifications. Introduced in 1978; discontinued.

Colt U.S. Bicentennial Commemorative Set . . . **$2100**
Replica Colt 3rd Model Dragoon Revolver with accessories, Colt SA Army Revolver, and Colt Python Revolver. Matching roll-engraved unfluted cylinders, blued finish, and rosewood stocks with Great Seal of the United States silver medallion. Dragoon revolver has silver grip frame. Serial numbers 0001 to 1776, all revolvers in set have same number. Deluxe drawer-style presentation case of walnut, with book compartment containing a reproduction of "Armsmear." Issued in 1976. Value is for revolvers in new condition.

Colt Trooper MK V

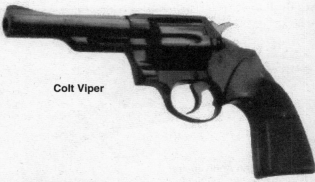

Colt Viper

Colt Trooper MK V Revolver **$260**
Re-engineered Mark III for smoother, faster action. Caliber: 357 Magnum. 6-shot cylinder. Bbl. lengths: 4-, 6-, 8-inch w/vent rib. Adj. rear sight, ramp front, red insert. Checkered walnut stocks. Made 1982-86.

Colt Viper DA Revolver **$295**
Same as Cobra, Second Issue, except has 4-inch barrel, is 9 inches overall, weighs 20 oz. Made 1977-1984.

COONAN ARMS, INC.
St. Paul, Minnesota

**Coonan Arms Model 357
Magnum Auto**

Coonan Arms Model 357 Magnum Auto Pistol

Caliber: 357 Mag. 7-round magazine. 5- or 6-inch bbl. 8.3 inches overall (w/5-inch bbl.). Weight: 42 oz. Front ramp interchangeable sight; fixed rear sight, adj. for windage. Black walnut grips.

Model A Std. Grade w/o Grip Safety (Disc. 1991) **$775**
Model B Competition Grade **820**
Model B Std. Grade w/5-inch Bbl. **550**
Model B Std. Grade w/6-inch Bbl. **575**

Coonan Arms 357 Magnum Cadet Compact **$560**

Similar to the standard 357 Magnum Model, except with 3.9-inch bbl. 6-shot magazine and compact frame. Weight: 39 oz., 7.8 inches overall. Made from 1993 to date.

CZ PISTOLS
Uhersky Brod (formerly Strakonice), Czechoslovakia
Mfd. by Ceska Zbrojovka-Nardoni Podnik (formerly Bohmische Waffenfabrik A. G.)

Currently manufactured models are imported by Magnum Research, Inc.; prior to 1994 were imported by Action Arms. Vintage importation is by Century International Arms.

CZ Model 27 Auto Pistol

CZ Model 27 Auto Pistol **$395**

Caliber: 32 Automatic (7.65mm). 8-shot magazine. 4-inch bbl. 6 inches overall. Weight: 23.5 oz. Fixed sights. Blued finish. Plastic stocks. Made 1927-1951. *Note:* After the German occupation, March 1939, Models 27 and 38 were marked with manufacturer code "fnh." Designation of Model 38 was changed to "Pistole 39(t)."

CZ Model 38 DA Auto Pistol

CZ Model 38 DA Auto Pistol **$335**

Caliber: 380 Automatic (9mm). 9-shot magazine. 3.75-inch bbl. 7 inches overall. Weight: 26 oz. Fixed sights. Blued finish. Plastic stocks. Made 1939-1945.

CZ Model 50 DA Auto Pistol

CZ Model 50 DA Auto Pistol **$320**

Caliber: 32 ACP, 8-round magazine. 3.13-inch barrel, 6.5 inches overall. Weight: 24.5 oz. Fixed sights. Blued finished. Introduced in 1948.

CZ Model 52 SA Auto Pistol **$135**

Roller-locking breech system. Caliber: 7.62mm. 8-shot magazine. 4.7-inch bbl. 8.1 inches overall. Weight: 31 oz. Fixed sights. Blued finish. Grooved composition grips.

CZ 75 DA Automatic Pistol

Caliber: 9mm Parabellum. 15-shot magazine. 4.75-inch bbl. 8 inches overall. Weight: 35 oz. Fixed sights. Blued or black polymer finish. Checkered wood or high-impact plastic stocks.

Black Polymer Finish **$365**
High-Polish Blued Finish **395**
Matte Blue Finish **375**

CZ 75 DA Auto Pistol

CZ Model 1945 DA Pocket Auto

CZ 82 DA Auto Pistol $250
Similar to the standard CZ 83 Model, except chambered in 9 ×18 Makarov. This model currently is the Czech military sidearm.

CZ 83 DA Automatic Pistol $295
Calibers: 32 ACP, 380 ACP. 15-shot (32 ACP) or 13-shot (380 ACP) magazine. 3.75-inch bbl. 6.75 inches overall. Weight: 26.5 oz. Fixed sights. Blued finish. Checkered black plastic stocks.

CZ 85 Automatic DA Pistol
Same as CZ 75, except with ambidextrous slide release and safety. Calibers: 9mm Parabellum, 7.65mm. Made from 1986 to date.

Black Polymer Finish	$395
High-Polish Blued Finish	450
Matte Blued Finish	425

CZ Duo Pocket Auto Pistol

CZ 85 Combat DA
Automatic Pistol

CZ Duo Pocket Auto Pistol $195
Caliber: 25 Automatic (6.35mm). 6-shot magazine. 2.13 inch bbl. 4.5 inches overall. Weight: 14 .5 oz. Fixed sights. Blued or nickel finish. Plastic stocks. Made 1926 to c. 1960.

CZ New Model .006 DA Auto

CZ 85 Combat DA Automatic Pistol
Similar to the standard CZ 85 Model, except with 13-shot magazine, combat-style hammer, fully adj. rear sight and walnut grips.

Black Polymer Finish	$400
High-Polish Blued Finish	465
Matte Blued Finish	440

CZ Model 1945 DA Pocket Auto Pistol $195
Caliber: 25 Auto (6.35mm). 8-shot magazine. 2.5-inch bbl. 5 inches overall. Weight: 15 oz. Fixed sights. Blued finish. Plastic stocks. Introduced 1945; discontinued.

CZ New Model .006 DA Auto Pistol $395
Caliber: 32 Automatic (7.65mm). 8-shot magazine. 3.13-inch bbl. 6 .5 inches overall. Weight: 24 oz. Fixed sights. Blued finish. Plastic stocks. Introduced 1951. Discont. *Note:* Official designation of this pistol, used by the Czech National Police, is "VZ50." "New Model .006" is export designation.

DAEWOO PISTOLS
Seoul, Korea
Mfd. by Daewoo Precision Industries Ltd.

Daewoo DH40 Auto Pistol

Daewoo DH40 Auto Pistol **$275**
Caliber: 40 S&W. 12-shot magazine. 4.25-inch bbl. 7 inches overall. Weight: 28 oz. Sights: blade front; dovetailed rear w/3-dot system. Blued finish. Checkered composition grips. DH/DP series feature a patented "fastfire" action with 5-6 lb. trigger pull. Made from 1994 to date.

Daewoo DH45 Auto Pistol **$265**
Caliber: 45 ACP. 13-shot magazine. 5-inch bbl. 8.1 inches overall. Weight: 35 oz. Sights: blade front; dovetailed rear w/3-dot system. Blued finish. Checkered composition grips. Announced 1994.

Daewoo DP51 Auto Pistol **$255**
Caliber: 9mm Parabellum. 13-shot magazine. 4.1-inch bbl. 7.5 inches overall. Weight: 28 oz. Blade front and square-notch rear sights. Matte black finish. Checkered composition grips. Made from 1991 to date.

Daewoo DP52 Auto Pistol **$235**
Caliber: 22 LR. 10-shot magazine. 3.8-inch bbl. 6.7 inches overall. Weight: 23 oz. Sights: blade front; dovetailed rear w/3-dot system. Blued finish. Checkered wood grips. Made from 1994 to date.

DAKOTA/E.M.F. CO.
Santa Ana, California

Dakota Model 1873 SA Revolver
Calibers: 22 LR, 22 Mag., 357 Mag., 45 Long Colt, 30 M1 carbine, 38-40, 32-20, 44-40. Bbl. lengths: 3.5, 4.75, 5.5, 7.5 inches. Blue or nickel finish. Engraved models avail.
Standard Model **$295**
With Extra Cylinder **445**

Dakota Model 1875 Outlaw SA Revolver **$335**
Calibers: 45 Long Colt, 357 Mag., 44-40. 7.5-inch bbl. Casehardened frame, blued finish. Walnut grips. This is an exact replica of the Remington #3 revolver produced 1875-1889.

Dakota Model 1890 Remington Police
Calibers: 357 Mag., 44-40, 45 Long Colt. 5.75-inch bbl. Blue or nickel finish. Exact replica of Colt original with lanyard ring.
Standard Model **$355**
Nickel Model **425**
Engraved Model **465**

Dakota Bisley SA Revolver
Calibers: 44-40, 45 Long Colt, 357 Mag. 5.5- or 7.5-inch bbl. Discontinued 1992; reintroduced 1994.
Standard Model **$255**
Target Model **295**

**Dakota Hartford
SA Revolver**

Dakota Hartford SA Revolver
Calibers: 22 LR, 32-20, 357 Mag., 38-40, 44-40, 44 Special, 45 Long Colt. These are exact replicas of the original Colts, with steel backstraps, trigger guards and forged frames. Blued or nickel finish.
Standard Model **$350**
Engraved Model **495**
Hartford Artillery, U.S. Cavalry Models **320**

Dakota Sheriff's Model SA Revolver **$290**
Calibers: 32-20, 357 Mag., 38-40, 44 Special, 44-40, 45 LC. 3.5-inch bbl. Reintroduced 1994.

Dakota Target SA Revolver **$295**
Calibers: 45 Long Colt, 357 Mag., 22 LR. 5.5- or 7.5-inch bbl. Polished, blued finish, casehardened frame. Walnut grips. Ramp front, blade target sight, adj. rear sight.

DAVIS INDUSTRIES, INC.
Chino, California

Davis Model D Derringer
Single-action double derringer. Calibers: 22 LR, 22 Mag., 25 ACP, 32 Auto, 32 H&R Mag., 9mm, 38 Special. 2-shot capacity. 2.4-inch or 2.75-inch bbl. 4 inches overall (2.4-inch bbl.). Weight: 9 to 11.5 oz. Laminated wood grips. Black Teflon or chrome finish. Made from 1987 to date.
22 LR or 25 ACP **$50**
22 Mag., 32 H&R Mag., 38 Spec. **65**
32 Auto **70**
9mm Parabellum **75**

Davis Model P-32

Davis Long Bore Derringer $85
Similar to Model D, except in calibers 22 Mag., 32 H&R Mag., 38 Special, 9mm Parabellum. 3.75-inch bbl. Weight: 16 oz. Made from 1995 to date.

Davis Model P-38

Davis Model P-32 . . . . $70
Caliber: 32 Auto. 6-round magazine. 2.8-inch bbl. 5.4 inches overall. Weight: 22 oz. Black teflon or chrome finish. Laminated wood grips. Made from 1987 to date.

Davis Model P-380 . . . . $85
Caliber: 380 Auto. 5-shot magazine. 2.8-inch bbl. 5.4 inches overall. Weight: 22 oz. Black teflon or chrome finish. Made from 1990 to date.

DESERT INDUSTRIES, INC.
Las Vegas, Nevada

Desert Industries Double Deuce DA Pistol $275
Caliber: 22 LR. 6-shot magazine. 2.5-inch bbl. 5.5 inches overall. Weight: 15 oz. Matte-finish stainless steel. Rosewood grips.

Desert Industries Two-Bit Special Pistol $295
Similar to the Double Deuce Model, except chambered in 25 ACP with 5-shot magazine.

Desert Industries War Eagle DA Pistol $495
Calibers: 9mm Parabellum, 10mm, 40 S&W, 45 ACP. Magazine: 14-shot, 9mm/40 S&W; 13-shot, 10mm; and 12-shot, 45 ACP. 4-inch bbl. 7.5 inches overall. Weight: 35.5 oz. Fixed sights. Matte-finish stainless steel. Rosewood grips. Made from 1986 to date.

(NEW) DETONICS MFG. CORP
Phoenix, Arizona
(Formerly Detonics Firearms Industries, Bellevue, WA)

Detonics Combat Master

Detonics Combat Master
Calibers: 45 ACP, 451 Detonics Mag. 6-round magazine. 3.5-inch bbl. 6.75 inches overall. Combat-type with fixed or adjustable sights. Checkered walnut stock. Stainless steel construction. Discontinued 1992.

MK I Matte Stainless, Fixed Sights	**$425**
MK I Stainless Steel Finish.	**400**
MK IV Polished Blue, Adj. Sights, Disc.	**415**
MK V Matte Stainless, Fixed Sights, Disc.	**530**
MK VI Polished Stainless, Adj. Sights	**560**
MK VI in 451 Magnum	**825**
MK VII Matte Stainless Steel, No Sights	**750**
MK VII in 451 Magnum	**995**

Detonics Pocket 9 . . . . $350
Calibers: 9mm Parabellum, 380. 6-round magazine. 3-inch bbl. 5.88 inches overall. Fixed sights. Double- and single-action trigger mechanism. Discontinued 1986.

Detonics Scoremaster

Detonics Scoremaster $845
Calibers: 45 ACP, 451 Detonics Mag. 7-round magazine. 5- or 6-inch heavyweight match bbl. 8.75 inches overall. Weight: 47 oz. Stainless steel construction, self-centering bbl. system. Discontinued 1992.

Detonics Service Master $525
Caliber: 45 ACP. 7-round magazine. 4.25-inch bbl. Weight: 39 oz. Interchangeable front sight, millett rear sight. Discontinued 1986.

Detonics Service Master II $625
Same general specifications as standard Service Master, except comes in polished stainless steel with self-centering bbl. system. Discontinued 1992.

DREYSE PISTOLS
Sommerda, Germany
Mfd. by Rheinische Metallwaren und Maschinen-fabrik ("Rheinmetall")

Dreyse Model 1907

Dreyse Model 1907 Automatic Pistol $200
Caliber: 32 Auto (7.65mm). 8-shot magazine. 3.5-inch bbl. 6.25 inches overall. Weight: about 24 oz. Fixed sights. Blued finish. Hard rubber stocks. Made 1907-c. 1914.

Dreyse Vest Pocket Automatic Pistol $195
Conventional Browning type. Caliber: 25 Auto (6.35mm). 6-shot magazine. 2-inch bbl. 4.5 inches overall. Weight: about 14 oz. Fixed sights. Blued finish. Hard rubber stocks. Made from c. 1909-1914.

DWM PISTOL
Berlin, Germany
Mfd. by Deutsche Waffen-und-Munitionsfabriken

DWM Pocket Automatic

DWM Pocket Automatic Pistol $595
Similar to the FN Browning Model 1910. Caliber: 32 Automatic (7.65mm). 3.5-inch bbl. 6 inches overall. Weight: about 21 oz. Blued finish. Hard rubber stocks. Made from c. 1921-1931.

ENFIELD REVOLVER
Enfield Lock, Middlesex, England
Manufactured by Royal Small Arms Factory

Enfield (British Service) No. 2 MK 1 Revolver

Enfield (British Service) No. 2 MK 1 Revolver . . . $205
Webley pattern. Hinged frame. Double action. Caliber: 380 British Service (38 S&W w/200-grain bullet). 6-shot cylinder. 5-inch bbl. 10.5 inches overall. Weight: about 27.5 oz. Fixed sights. Blued finish. Vulcanite stocks. First issued in 1932, this was the standard revolver of the British Army in WW II. Now obsolete. *Note:* This model also produced w/spurless hammer as No. 2 Mk 1* and Mk 1**.

ERMA-WERKE
Dachau, Germany

Erma Model ER-772 Match Revolver

Erma Model ER-772 Match Revolver $795
Caliber: 22 LR. 6-shot cylinder. 6-inch bbl. 12 inches overall. Weight: 47.25 oz. Adjustable micrometer rear sight and front sight blade. Adjustable trigger. Interchangeable walnut sporter or match grips. Polished blue finish. Made from 1991 to date.

Erma Model ER-773 Match Revolver $765
Same general specifications as Model 772, except chambered for 32 S&W. Made from 1991 to date.

Erma Model ER-777 Match Revolver $700
Caliber: 357 Magnum. 6-shot cylinder. 4- or 5.5-inch bbl. 9.7 to 11.3 inches overall. Weight: 43.7 oz. w/5.5-inch bbl. Micrometer adj. rear sight. Checkered walnut sporter or match-style grip (interchangeable). Made from 1991 to date.

Erma Model ESP-85A

Erma Model ESP-85A Competition Pistol
Calibers: 22 LR and 32 S&W Wadcutter. 8- or 5-shot magazine. 6-inch bbl. 10 inches overall. Weight: 40 oz. Adj. rear sight, blade front sight. Checkered walnut grip with thumbrest. Made from 1991 to date.

Match Model	$825
Chrome Match.................................	875
Sporting Model	810
Conversion Unit 22 LR.........................	765
Conversion Unit 32 S&W.......................	800

Erma-Werke Model KGP68

Erma-Werke Model KGP68 Automatic Pistol.... $275
Luger type. Calibers: 32 Auto (7.65mm), 380 Auto (9mm Short).6-shot magazine in 32; 5-shot in 380. 4-inch bbl. 7.38 inches overall. Weight: 22.5 oz. Fixed sights. Blued finish. Checkered walnut stocks. Made from 1968 to date.

Erma-Werke Model KGP69 Automatic Pistol.... $285
Luger type. Caliber: 22 LR. 8-shot magazine. 4-inch bbl. 7.75 inches overall. Weight: 29 oz. fixed sights. Blued finish. Checkered walnut stocks. Made from 1969 to date.

EUROPEAN AMERICAN ARMORY
Hialeah, Florida

See also listings under Astra Pistols.

European American Armory Model 380 DA Auto Pistol
Similar to the standard European Model, except double action and chambered in 380 only. Made 1992 to date.

Blued Finish	$125
Chrome	135
Ladies Model	150

European American Armory Big Bore Bounty Hunter

European American Armory Big Bore Bounty Hunter SA Revolver
Calibers: 357 Mag., 41 Mag., 44-40, 44 Mag.,45 Colt. Bbl. lengths: 4.63, 5.5, 7.5 inches. Blade front and grooved topstrap rear sights. Blued or chrome finish with color casehardened or gold-plated frame. Smooth walnut grips. Made from 1992 to date.

Blued Finish	$195
Blued w/Color-Casehardened Frame	215
Blued w/Gold-Plated Frame	235
Chrome Finish.................................	240

European American Armory Bounty Hunter SA Revolver
Calibers: 22 LR, 22 WRF. Bbl. lengths: 4.75, 6 or 9 inches. Blade front and dovetailed rear sights. Blued finish or blue with gold-plated frame. European hardwood grips. Made from 1991 to date.

Blued Finish (4.75-inch bbl.)	$ 90
Blued 22 LR/22 WRF Combo (4.75-inch bbl.)	115
Blued 22 LR/22 WRF Combo (6-inch bbl.)	120
Blued 22 LR/22 WRF Combo (9-inch bbl.)	125
For Gold-Plated Frame, **add**	10%

European American Armory EA22 Target $295
Caliber: 22 LR. 12-shot magazine. 6-inch bbl. 9.10 inches overall. Weight: 40 oz. Ramp front sight, fully adj. rear. Blued finish. Checkered walnut grips with thumbrest.

European American Armory European Model Auto Pistol
Calibers: 32 ACP, 380 ACP. 7-shot magazine. 3.85-inch bbl. 7.75 inches overall. Weight: 26 oz. Blade front sight rear sight drift-adj. for windage. Blued or chrome finish. European hardwood grips.

Blued Finish SA	$125
Chrome SA	135
Ladies Model SA	165
Blued Finish DA only; Disc. 1995	160

European American Armory FAB 92 Auto Pistol

Similar to the Witness Model, except chambered in 9mm only with slide-mounted safety and no cock-and-lock provision.

FAB 92 Standard **$265**
FAB 92 Compact **245**

European American Armory Standard Grade Revolver

Calibers: 22 LR, 22 WRF, 32 H&R Mag., 38 Special. 2-, 4- or 6-inch bbl. Blade front sight, fixed or adj. rear. Blued finish. European hardwood grips with finger grooves. Made from 1991 to date.

22 LR (4-inch bbl.) **$135**
22 LR (6-inch bbl.) **145**
22 LR Combo (4-inch bbl.) **195**
22 LR Combo (6-inch bbl.) **205**
32 H&R, 38 Special (2-inch bbl.) **140**
38 Special (4-inch) **150**

European American Armory Tactical Grade Revolver

Similar to the Standard Model, except chambered in 38 Special only. 2- or 4-inch bbl. Fixed sights. Available with compensator. Made from 1991 to date.

Tactical Revolver **$185**
Tactical Revolver w/Compensator **275**

European American Armory Windicator

European American Armory Windicator Target Revolver **$295**

Calibers: 22 LR, 38 Special, 357 Magnum. 8-shot cylinder in 22 LR, 6-shot in 38 Special/357 Magnum. 6-inch bbl. w/bbl. weights. 11.8 inches overall. Weight: 50.2 oz. Interchangeable blade front sight, fully adj. rear. Walnut competition-style grips. Made from 1991 to date.

European American Armory Witness

European American Armory Witness DA Auto Pistol

Similar to the Brno CZ-75 with a cocked-and-locked system. Double or single action. Calibers: 9mm Parabellum 38 Super, 40 S&W, 10mm, 41 AE and 45 ACP. 16-shot magazine in 9mm; 12 shot in 38 Super/40 S&W; 10-shot in 10mm/45 ACP. 4.75-inch bbl. 8.10 inches overall. Weight: 35.33 oz. Blade front sight, rear sight adj. for windage with 3-dot sighting system. Blued, satin chrome, blue/chrome or stainless finish. Checkered rubber grips. Made from 1991 to date.

9mm Blue **$280**
9mm Chrome or Blue/Chrome **290**
9mm Stainless **335**
38 Super and 40 S&W Blued **295**
38 Super and 40 S&W Chrome or Blue/Chrome **325**
38 Super and 40 S&W Stainless **345**
10mm, 41 AE and 45 ACP Blued **365**
10mm, 41 AE and 45 ACP Chrome or Blue/Chrome . . . **380**
10mm, 41 AE and 45 ACP Stainless **425**

European American Armory Witness Subcompact DA Auto Pistol

Calibers: 9mm Para., 40 S&W, 41 AK, 45 ACP. 13-shot magazine in 9mm, 9-shot in 40 S&W. 3.66-inch bbl. 7.25 inches overall. Weight: 30 oz. Blade front sight, rear sight adj. for windage. Blued, satin chrome or blue/chrome finish.

9mm Blue **$270**
9mm Chrome or Blue/Chrome **295**
40 S&W Blue **295**
40 S&W Chrome or Blue/Chrome **325**
41 AE Blue **350**
41 AE Chrome or Blue/Chrome **375**
45 ACP Blue **360**
45 ACP Chrome or Blue/Chrome **385**

European American Armory Witness Target Pistol

Similar to standard Witness Model, except fitted with 2- or 3-port compensator, competition frame and S/A target trigger. Calibers: 9mm Parabellum, 9×21, 40 S&W, 10mm and 45 ACP. 5.25-inch match bbl. 10.5 inches overall. Weight: 38 oz. Square post front sight, fully adj. rear or drilled and tapped for scope. Blued or hard chrome finish. Low-profile competition grips.

Silver Team (Blued w/2-Port Compensator) . . . . **$ 660**
Gold Team (Chrome w/3-Port Compensator) **1255**

FEATHER INDUSTRIES, INC.
Boulder. Colorado

Feather Guardian Angel Derringer

Feather Guardian Angel Derringer

Double-action over/under derringer with interchangeable drop-in loading blocks. Calibers: 22 LR, 22 WMR, 9mm, 38 Spec., 2-shot capacity. 2-inch bbl. 5 inches overall. Weight: 12 oz. Stainless steel. Checkered black grip. Made from 1988 to date.
22 LR, 22 WMR **$85**
9mm, 38 Special (Disc. 1989) **95**

FEG (FEGYVERGYAN) PISTOLS
Budapest, Soroksariut, Hungary

Currently imported by KBI, Inc. and Century International Arms (previously by Interarms).

FEG Model GKK-9 Auto Pistol **$245**

Improved version of the double-action FEG Model MBK. Caliber: 9mm Parabellum. 14-shot magazine. 4-inch bbl. 7.4 inches overall. Weight: 34 oz. Blade front sight; rear sight adj. for windage. Checkered wood grips. Blued finish. Imported 1992-93.

FEG Model GKK-45 Auto Pistol

Improved version of the double-action FEG Model MBK. Caliber: 45 ACP. 8-shot magazine. 4.1-inch bbl. 7.75 inches overall. Weight: 36 oz. Blade front sight; rear sight adj. for windage w/3-Dot system. Checkered walnut grips. Blued or chrome finish.
Blued Model (Discontinued 1994). **$255**
Chrome Model **265**

FEG Model MBK-9HP Auto Pistol **$265**

Similar to the double-action Browning Hi-Power. Caliber: 9mm Parabellum. 14-shot magazine. 4.6-inch bbl. 8 inches overall. Weight: 36 oz. Blade front sight; rear sight adj. for windage. Checkered wood grips. Blued finish. Imported 1992-93.

FEG Model PJK-9HP Auto Pistol

FEG Model PJK-9HP Auto Pistol

Similar to the single-action Browning Hi-Power. Caliber: 9mm Parabellum. 13-shot magazine. 4.75-inch bbl. 8 inches overall. Weight: 21 oz. Blade front sight, rear sight adj. for windage w/3-Dot system. Checkered walnut or rubber grips. Blued or chrome finish.
Blued Model **$245**
Chrome Model. **285**

FEG Model PSP-25 Auto Pistol

Similar to the Browning 25. Caliber: 25 ACP. 6-shot magazine. 2.1-inch bbl. 4.1 inches overall. Weight: 9.5 oz. Fixed sights. Checkered composition grips. Blued or chrome finish.
Blued Model **$185**
Chrome Model. **215**

FEG Model SMC-22 Auto Pistol **$195**

Same general specifications as FEG Model SMC-380, except in 22 LR. 8-shot magazine. 3.5-inch bbl. 6.1 inches overall. Weight: 18.5 oz. Blade front sight, rear sight adj. for windage. Checkered composition grips w/thumbrest. Blued finish.

FEG Model SMC-380 Auto Pistol **$195**

Similar to the Walther DA PPK with alloy frame. Caliber: 380 ACP. 6-shot magazine. 3.5-inch bbl. 6.1 inches overall. Weight: 18.5 oz. Blade front sight, rear sight adj. for windage. Checkered composition grips w/ thumbrest. Blued finish. Imported 1993 to date.

FEG Model SMC-918 Auto Pistol **$195**

Same general specifications as FEG Model SMC-380, except chambered in 9×18mm Makarov. Imported 1994 to date.

FIALA OUTFITTERS, INC.
New York, New York

Fiala Repeating Pistol **$395**

Despite its appearance, which closely resembles that of the early Colt Woodsman and High-Standard, this arm is not an automatic pistol. It is hand-operated by moving the slide to eject, cock and load. Caliber: 22 LR. 10-shot magazine. bbl. lengths: 3-, 7.5- and 20-inch. 11.25 inches overall w/7.5-inch bbl. Weight: 31 oz. w/7.5-inch bbl. Target sights. Blued finish. Plain wood stocks. Shoulder stock was originally supplied for use with 20-inch bbl. Made 1920-23. Value shown is for pistol with one bbl. and no shoulder stock.

F.I.E. CORPORATION
Hialeah, Florida

The F.I.E Corporation became QFI (Quality Firearms Corp.) of Opa Locka, Fl., about 1990, when most of F.I.E's models were discontinued.

F.I.E. Model A27BW

F.I.E. Model A27BW "The Best" Semiauto $90
Caliber: 25 ACP. 6-round magazine. 2.5-inch bbl. 6.75 inches overall. Weight: 13 oz. Fixed sights. Checkered walnut stock. Discontinued 1990.

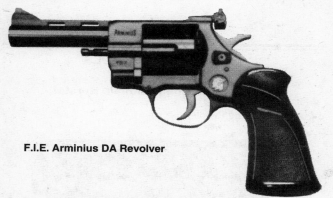

F.I.E. Arminius DA Revolver

F.I.E. Arminius DA Revolver
Calibers: 22 LR; 22 combo w/interchangeable cylinder; 32 S&W, 38 Special, 357 Magnum.6, 7 or 8 rounds depending on caliber. Swingout cylinder.Bbl. lengths: 2-, 3-, 4, 6-inch. Vent rib on calibers other than 22.11 inches overall w/6-inch bbl. Weight: 26 to 30 oz. Fixed or micro-adjustable sights. Checkered plastic or walnut stocks. Blued finish. Made in Germany; discontinued.

22 LR.	$ 90
22 Combo	100
32 S&W.	105
38 Special	110
357 Magnum.	135

F.I.E. Buffalo Scout SA Revolver
Calibers: 22 LR, 22 WRF, 22 combo w/interchangeable cylinder. 4.75-inch bbl. 10 inches overall. Weight: 32 oz. Adjustable sights. Blued or chrome finish. Smooth walnut or black checkered nylon grips. Made in Italy.

Blued Standard	$ 50
Blued Convertible.	100
Chrome Standard.	65
Chrome Convertible	110

F.I.E. Hombre SA Revolver $160
Calibers: 357 Magnum, 44 Magnum, 45 Colt. 6-shot cylinder. Bbl. lengths: 6 or 7.5 inches. 11 inches overall w/6-inch bbl. Weight: 45 oz. w/6-inch bbl. Fixed sights. Blued bbl. with color-casehardened receiver. Smooth walnut stocks. Made 1979-1990.

F.I.E. Little Ranger SA Revolver
Same as the Texas Ranger, except with 3.25-inch bbl. and bird's-head grips. Made 1986-1990.

Standard.	$80
Convertible	95

F.I.E. Super Titan II
Caliber: 32 ACP or 380 ACP. 3.25-inch bbl. Weight: 28 oz. Blued or chrome finish. Discontinued 1990.

32 ACP in Blue.	$130
32 ACP in Chrome	145
380 ACP in Blue.	160
380 ACP in Chrome	175

F.I.E. Texas Ranger Single Action Revolver
Calibers: 22 LR, 22 WRF, 22 combo w/interchangeable cylinder. Bbl. lengths: 4.75-, 6.5-, 9-inch. 10 inches overall w/4.75-inch bbl. Weight: 32 oz. w/4.75-inch bbl. Fixed sights. Blued finish. Smooth walnut stocks. Made 1983-1990.

Standard	$60
Convertible	90

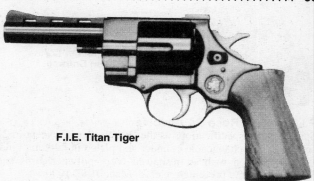

F.I.E. Titan Tiger

F.I.E. Titan Tiger Double Action Revolver $100
Caliber: 38 Special. 6-shot cylinder. 2- or 4-inch bbl. 8.25 inches overall w/4-inch bbl. Weight: 30 oz. w/4inch bbl. Fixed sights. Blued finish. Checkered plastic or walnut stocks. Made in the U.S. Discontinued 1990.

F.I.E. Titan II

F.I.E. Titan II Semiautomatic
Caiibers: 22 LR, 32 ACP, 380 ACP. 10-round magazine. Integral tapered post front sight, windage-adjustable rear sight. European walnut grips. Blued or chrome finish. Discontinued 1990.

22 LR in Blue	$ 95
32 ACP in Blue	135
32 ACP in Chrome	155
380 ACP in Blue	155
380 ACP in Chrome	175

F.I.E. Model TZ75 DA Semiautomatic
Double action. Caliber: 9mm. 15-round magazine. 4.5-inch bbl. 8.25 inches overall. Weight: 35 oz. Ramp front sight, windage-adjustable rear sight. European walnut or black rubber grips. Discontinued 1989. *See* illustration next page.

Blued Finish	$275
Satin Chrome.	325

**F.I.E. Model TZ75
Satin Chrome**

F.I.E. Yellow Rose SA Revolver

Same general specifications as the Buffalo Scout, except in 22 combo w/interchangeable cylinder and plated in 24-karat gold. Limited Edition with scrimshawed ivory polymer grips and American walnut presentation case. Made 1987-1990.

Yellow Rose 22 Combo **$100**
Yellow Rose Ltd. Edition **250**

FIREARMS INTERNATIONAL CORP.
Washington, D.C.

Firearms Int'l. Model D

Firearms Int'l. Model D Automatic Pistol **$175**

Caliber: 380 Automatic.6-shot magazine. 3.3-inch bbl. 6.13 inches overall. Weight: 19.5 oz. Blade front sight, windage-adjustable rear sight. Blued, chromed, or military finish. Checkered walnut stocks. Made 1974-77.

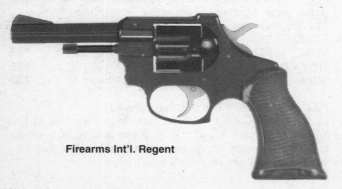

Firearms Int'l. Regent

Firearms Int'l. Regent DA Revolver **$90**

Calibers: 22 LR, 32 S&W Long. 8-shot cylinder (22 LR). 7-shot (32). Bbls.: 3-, 4-, 6-inch (22 LR); 2.5-, 4-inch (32). Weight: with 4-inch bbl., 28 oz. Fixed sights. Blue finish. Plastic stocks. Made 1966-1972.

FN BROWNING PISTOLS
Liege, Belgium
Mfd. by Fabrique Nationale Herstal

See also Browning Pistols.

FN Browning 6.35mm

FN Browning 6.35mm Pocket Auto Pistol **$325**

Same specifications as Colt Pocket Model 25 Automatic.

FN Browning Model 1900

FN Browning Model 1900 Pocket Auto Pistol . . . **$345**

Caliber: 32 Automatic (7.65mm). 7-shot magazine. 4-inch bbl. 6.75 inches overall. Weight: 22 oz. Fixed sights. Blued finish. Hard rubber stocks. Made 1899-1910.

FN Browning Model 1903 Military Auto Pistol . . . **$400**

Caliber: 9mm Browning Long. 7-shot magazine. 5-inch bbl. 8 inches overall. Weight: 32 oz. Fixed sights. Blued finish. Hard rubber stocks. *Note:* Aside from size, this pistol is of the same basic design as the Colt Pocket 32 and 380 Automatic pistols. Made 1903-1939.

FN Browning Model 1910

FN Browning Model 1910 Pocket Auto Pistol . . . $540
Calibers: 32 Auto (7.65mm), 380 Auto (9mm). 7-shot magazine (32 cal.), 6-shot (380 cal.). 3.5-inch bbl. 6 inches overall. Weight: 20.5 oz. Fixed sights. Blued finish. Hard rubber stocks. Made 1910-1922.

FN Browning Model 1922

FN Browning Model 1922 Police/Military Auto . . $255
Calibers: 32 Auto (7.65mm), 380 Auto (9mm). 9-shot magazine (32 cal.), 8-shot (380 cal.). 4.5-inch bbl. 7 inches overall. Weight: 25 oz. Fixed sights. Blued finish. Hard rubber stocks. Made 1922-1959.

**FN Browning Model 1935
Hi-Power**

FN Browning Model 1935 Military Hi-Power Pistol
Variation of the Browning-Colt 45 Auto design. Caliber: 9mm Luger.13-shot magazine. 4.63-inch bbl. 7.75 inches overall. Weight: about 35 oz. Adjustable rear sight and fixed front, or both fixed. Blued finish (Canadian manufacture Parkerized). Checkered walnut or plastic stocks. *Note:* Above specifications in general apply to both the original FN production and the pistols made by John Inglis Company of Canada for the Chinese Government. A smaller version, with shorter bbl. and slide and 10-shot magazine, was made by FN for the Belgian and Rumanian Governments about 1937-1940. Both types were made at the FN plant during the German Occupation of Belgium.

With adjustable rear sight **$645**
FN manufacture, with fixed rear sight 555
Inglis manufacture, with fixed rear sight 640

FN Browning Baby

FN Browning Baby Auto Pistol $335
Caliber: 25 Automatic (6.35mm). 6-shot magazine. 2.13-inch bbl. 4 inches overall. Weight: 10 oz. Fixed sights. Blued finish. Hard rubber stocks. Made 1931-1983.

FOREHAND & WADSWORTH
Worcester, Massachusetts

Forehand & Wadsworth Revolvers
See listings of comparable Harrington & Richardson and Iver Johnson revolvers for values.

LE FRANCAIS PISTOLS
St. Etienne, France
Produced by Manufacture Francaise
d'Armes et Cycles

Le Francais Army Model Automatic Pistol $995
Similar in operation to the Le Francais 25 Automatics. Caliber: 9mm Browning Long. 8-shot magazine. 5-inch bbl. 7.75 inches overall. Weight: about 34 oz. Fixed sights. Blued finish. Checkered walnut stocks. Made from 1928-1938.

Le Francais Policeman Model Automatic Pistol . . . $695
DA. Hinged bbl. Caliber: 25 Automatic (6.35mm). 7shot magazine. 3.5-inch bbl. 6 inches overall. Weight: about 12 oz. Fixed sights. Blued finish. Hard rubber stocks. Intro. 1914; discontinued.

Le Francais Staff Officer Model

Le Francais Staff Officer Model
Automatic Pistol $235
Caliber: 25 Automatic. Similar to the "Policeman" Model except does not have cocking-piece head, bbl. is about an inch shorter and weight is an oz. less. Intro. 1914; disc.

FREEDOM ARMS
Freedom, Wyoming

Freedom Arms Model FA-44 SA Revolver
Similar to Model 454 Casull, except chambered in 44 Mag. Made from 1988 to date.

Field Grade	**$725**
Premier Grade	765
Silhouette Class (w/10-inch bbl.)	695
Silhouette Pac (10-inch bbl., access.)	750
For Fixed Sights, deduct	95

Freedom Arms Model FA-45 SA Revolver
Similar to Model 454 Casull, except chambered in 45 Long Colt. Made 1988-1990.

Field Grade	**$695**
Premier Grade	760
For Fixed Sights, deduct	95

**Freedom Arms Model FA-252
Silhouette Class**

Freedom Arms Model FA-252 SA Revolver
Calibers: 22 LR w/optional 22 Mag. cylinder. Bbl. lengths: 5.13 and 7.5 (Varmint Class), 10 inches (Silhouette Class). Adjustable express or competition silhouette sights. Brushed or matte stainless finish. Black micarta (Silhouette) or black and green laminated hardwood grips (Varmint). Made from 1991 to date.

Silhouette Class	**$ 895**
Silhouette Class w/extra 22 Mag. cyl	1125
Varmint Class	870
Varmint Class w/extra 22 Mag. cyl	1095

**Freedom Arms Model FA-353
Field Grade**

Freedom Arms Model FA-353 SA Revolver
Caliber: 357 Mag. Bbl. lengths: 4.75, 6, 7.5 or 9 inches. Removable blade front sight; adjustable rear sight. Brushed or matte stainless finish. Pachmayr Presentation or impregnated hardwood grips.

Field Grade	**$725**
Premier Grade	765
Silhouette Class (w/9-inch bbl.)	695

**Freedom Arms
Model FA-454 Casull**

Freedom Arms Model FA-454AS Revolver
Caliber: 454 Casull (w/optional 45 ACP, 45 LC, 45 Win. Mag. cylinders). 5-shot cylinder. Bbl. lengths: 4.75, 6, 7.5 or 10 inches. Adjustable express or competition silhouette sights. Pachmayr presentation or impregnated hardwood grips. Brushed or matte stainless steel finish.

Field Grade	**$730**
Premier Grade	775
Silhouette Class (w/10-inch bbl.)	735
For Fixed Sights, deduct	95
For Extra Cylinder, add..................	250

Freedom Arms Model FA-454FS Revolver...... $950
Same general specifications as Model FA-454AS, except with fixed sight.

**Freedom Arms FA-454AS
Field Grade**

Freedom Arms Model FA-454GAS Revolver $895
Field Grade version of Model FA-454AS, except not made w/12-inch bbl. Matte stainless finish, Pachmayr presentation grips. Adj. sights; fixed sight on 4.75-inch bbl.

Freedom Arms Model FA-555 Revolver
Similar to Model 454 Casull, except chambered in 50 AK. Made 1994 to date.
Field Grade $725
Premier Grade 765

Freedom Arms Model FA-BG-22LR Mini-Revolver $120
Caliber: 22 LR. 3-inch tapered bbl. Partial high-gloss stainless steel finish. Discontinued 1987.

Freedom Arms Model FA-BG-22M Mini-Revolver . . $135
Same general specifications as model FA-BG-22LR, except in caliber 22 WMR.

Freedom Arms Model FA-BG-22P Mini-Revolver . . $120
Same general specifications as Model FA-BG-22LR, except in 22 percussion. Discontinued 1987.

**Freedom Arms
Model FA-L-22LR**

Freedom Arms Model FA-L-22LR Mini-Revolver . . $85
Caliber: 22 LR. 13/4-inch contoured bbl. Partial high-gloss stainless steel finish. Bird's-head-type grips. Discontinued 1987.

Freedom Arms Model FA-L-22M Mini-Revolver . . $120
Same general specifications as Model FA-L-22LR, except in caliber 22 WMR. Discontinued 1987.

Freedom Arms Model FA-L-22P Mini-Revolver . . . $95
Same general specifications as Model FA-L-22LR, except in 22 percussion. Discontinued 1987.

Freedom Arms Model FA-S-22LR Mini-Revolver . . $110
Caliber: 22 LR. 1-inch contoured bbl. Partial high-gloss stainless steel finish. Discontinued.

Freedom Arms Model FA-S-22M Mini-Revolver . $120
Same general specifications as Model FA-S-22LR, except in caliber 22 WMR. Discontinued.

Freedom Arms Model FA-S-22P Mini-Revolver . . . $95
Same general specifications as Model FA-S-22LR, except in percussion. Discontinued.

FRENCH MILITARY PISTOLS
Cholet, France
Mfd. originally by Société Alsacienne de Constructions Mécaniques (S.A.C.M.); currently made by Manufacture d'Armes Automatiques, Lotissement Industriel des Pontots, Bayonne

French Model 1935A

French Model 1935A Automatic Pistol $235
Caliber: 7.65mm Long. 8-shot magazine. 4.3-inch bbl. 7.6 inches overall. Weight: 26 oz. Two-lug locking system similar to the Colt U.S. M1911A1. Fixed sights. Blued finish. Checkered stocks. Made 1935-1945. *Note:* This pistol was used by French troops during WW II and in Indo-China 1945-1954.

French Model 1935S Automatic Pistol $250
Similar to Model 1935A, except shorter (4.1-inch bbl. and 7.4 inches overall) and heavier (28 oz.). Single-step lug locking system.

French Model 1950 Automatic Pistol $250
Caliber: 9mm Parabellum. 9-shot magazine. 4.4-inch bbl. 7.6 inches overall. Weight: 30 oz. Fixed sights; tapered post front and U-notched rear. Similar in design and function to the U.S. 45 service automatic, except no bbl. bushing.

French Model MAB F1 Automatic Pistol $550
Similar to Model MAB P-15, except with 6-inch bbl. and 9.6 inches overall. Adjustable target-style sights. Parkerized finish.

French Model MAB P-8 Automatic Pistol $375
Similar to Model MAB P-15, except with 8-shot magazine.

French Model MAB P-15 Automatic Pistol $465
Caliber: 9mm Parabellum. 9-shot magazine. 4.5-inch bbl. 7.9 inches overall. Weight: 38 oz. Fixed sights; tapered post front and U-notched rear.

FROMMER PISTOLS
Budapest, Hungary
Mfd. by Fémáru-Fegyver-és Gépgyár R.T.

Frommer Baby Pocket Automatic Pistol $185
Similar to Stop model, except has 2-inch bbl., is about 4.75 inches overall, weighs about 17.5 oz. Magazine capacity is one round less. Introduced shortly after WW I.

Frommer Liliput Pocket Automatic Pistol $195
Caliber: 25 Automatic (6.35mm). 6-shot magazine. 2.14-inch
bbl. 4.33 inches overall. Weight: 10.13 oz. Fixed sights. Blued
finish. Hard rubber stocks. Made during early 1920s. *Note:* Although similar in appearance to the Stop and Baby, this pistol is
blowback operated.

Frommer Stop Pocket Auto

Frommer Stop Pocket Automatic Pistol. $165
Locked-breech action, outside hammer. Calibers: 32 Automatic
(7.65mm), 380 Auto (9mm short). 7-shot (32 cal.) or 6-shot (380
cal.) magazine.3.88-inch bbl. 6.5 inches overall. Weight: about
21 oz. Fixed sights. Blued finish. Hard rubber stocks. Made
1912-1920.

GALESI PISTOLS
Collebeato (Brescia), Italy
Mfd. by Industria Armi Galesi

Galesi Model 6

Galesi Model 6 Pocket Automatic Pistol $125
Calibers: 22 Long, 25 Automatic (6.35mm). 6-shot magazine.
2.25-inch bbl. 4.38 inches overall. Weight: about 11 oz. Fixed
sights. Blued finish. Plastic stocks. Made from 1930 to date.

Galesi Model 9 Pocket Automatic Pistol
Calibers: 22 LR,32 Auto (7.65mm), 380 Auto (9mm Short). 8-
shot magazine. 3.25-inch bbl. 5.88 inches overall. Weight: about
21 oz. Fixed sights. Blued finish. Plastic stocks. Made from 1930
to date. *Note:* Specifications vary; those shown are for 32 Automatic of common type.
22 Long Rifle or 380 Automatic. $160
32 Automatic. **150**

GLISENTI PISTOL
Carcina (Brescia), Italy
Mfd. by Societa Siderurgica Glisenti

Glisenti Model 1910

Glisenti Model 1910 Italian Service Automatic . . $495
Caliber: 9mm, Glisenti. 7-shot magazine. 4-inch bbl. 8.5 inches
overall. Weight: about 32 oz. Fixed sights. Blued finish. Hard
rubber or plastic stocks. Adopted 1910 and used through WWII.

GLOCK, INC.
Smyrna, Georgia

Glock Model 17

Glock Model 17 DA Automatic Pistol $385
Caliber: 9mm Parabellum. 17-shot magazine. 4.5-inch bbl. 7.2
inches overall. Weight: about 22 oz., empty. Hi-tech polymer
frame and receiver; steel bbl., slide and springs. Fixed or adj. rear
sights. Matte, nonglare finish. Made of only 33 components, including 3 internal safety devices. This gun received the "Best
Pistol Award of Merit" in 1987 by the American Firearms Indus-
try. Made in Austria from 1983 to date.

Glock Model 17L Competition

Glock Model 17L Competition $535
Same general specifications as Model 17, except weighs 23.35 oz. with 6-inch bbl.; 8.85 inches overall. Currentlymanufactured.

Glock Model 19

Glock Model 19 Compact $395
Same general specifications as Model 17, except smaller version with 4-inch bbl., 6.85 inches overall and 21-oz. weight. Made from 1988 to date.

Glock Model 20

Glock Model 20 DA Auto Pistol $475
Caliber: 10mm.15-shot. Hammerless. 4.6-inch bbl. 7.59 inches overall. Weight: 26.3 oz. Fixed or adj. sights. Matte, nonglare finish. Made from 1991 to date.

Glock Model 21 Automatic Pistol $470
Same general specifications as Model 17, except chambered in 45 ACP. 13-shot magazine. 7.59 inches overall. Weight: 25.2 oz. Made from 1991 to date.

Glock Model 22 Automatic Pistol $360
Same general specifications as Model 17, except chambered for 40 S&W. 15-shot magazine. 7.4 inches overall. Made from 1992 to date.

Glock Model 23 Automatic Pistol $395
Same general specifications as Model 19 except chambered for 40 S&W. 13-shot magazine. 6.97 inches overall. Made from 1992 to date.

Glock Model 24 Automatic Pistol $465
Caliber: 40 S&W, 10- and 15-shot magazines; the latter for law enforcement and military use only. 8.85 inches overall. Weight: 26.5 oz. Manual trigger safety; passive firing block and drop safety. Made 1995 to date.

Glock Model 24 Competitions Automatic Pistol $605
Caliber: 40 S&W, 10- and 15-shot magazines; the latter for law enforcement and military use only. 8.85 inches overall. Weight: 26.5 oz. Manual trigger safety; passive firing block and drop safety. Made from 1995 to date.

Glock Model 26 DA Automatic Pistol $425
Caliber: 9mm, 10-round magazine. 3.47-inch bbl. 6.3 inches overall. Weight: 19.77 oz. Made 1995 to date.

Glock Desert Storm Commemorative $750
Same specifications as Model 17, except "Operation Desert Storm, January 16-February 27, 1991" engraved on side of slide with list of coalition forces. Limited issue of 1,000 guns. Made in 1991.

GREAT WESTERN ARMS CO.
North Hollywood, California

Great Western Double Barrel Derringer $195
Replica of Remington Double Derringer. Caliber: 38 S&W. Double bbls. (superposed), 3-inch. Overall length: 5 inches. Fixed sights. Blued finish. Checkered black plastic grips. Made 1953-1962.

Great Western SA Frontier Revolver $575
Replica of the Colt Single Action Army Revolver. Calibers: 22 LR, 357 Magnum, 38 Special 44 Special, 44 Magnum 45 Colt. 6-shot cylinder. Bbl. lengths: 4.75-, 5.5 and 7.5-inch. Weight: 40 oz., 22 cal. w/5.5-inch bbl. Overall length: 11.13 inches w/5.5-inch bbl. Fixed sights. Blued finish. Imitation stag grips. Made 1951-1962. *Note:* Value shown is for improved late model revolvers; early Great Westerns are variable in quality and should be evaluated accordingly. It should also be noted that, beginning about July 1956, these revolvers were offered in kit form, values of guns assembled from these kits will, in general, be of less value than for factory-completed weapons.

GRENDEL, INC.
Rockledge, Florida

Grendel Model P-12

Grendel Model P-12 DA Automatic Pistol
Caliber: 380 ACP. 11-shot Zytel magazine. 3-inch bbl. 5.3 inches overall. Weight: 13 oz. Fixed sights. Polymer DuPont ST-800 grip. Made from 1991 to date.
Standard Model **$135**
Electroless Nickel **145**

Grendel Model P-30 Automatic Pistol
Caliber: 22 WMR. 30-shot magazine. 5-or 8-inch bbl. 8.5 inches overall with 5-inch bbl. Weight: 21 oz. Blade front sight, fixed rear sight. Made from 1991 to date.
With 5-inch Bbl. **$165**
With 8-inch Bbl. **195**

Grendel Model P-31 Automatic Pistol **$245**
Caliber: 22 WMR. 30-shot Zytel magazine. 11-inch bbl. 17.3 inches overall. Weight: 48 oz. Adj. blade front sight; fixed rear sight. Checkered black polymer DuPont ST-800 grip and forend. Made from 1991 to 1995.

H&R 1871, INC.
Gardner, Massachusetts

See listings under Harrington & Richardson, Inc.

HÄMMERLI AG JAGD-UND SPORTWAFFENFABRIK
Lenzburg, Switzerland

Hämmerli Model 33MP

Hämmerli Model 33MP Free Pistol **$820**
System Martini single-shot action, set trigger. Caliber: 22 LR. 11.5-inch octagon bbl. 16.5 inches overall. Weight: 46 oz. Micrometer rear sight, interchangeable front sights. Blued finish. Walnut grips, forearm. Made 1933-1949.

Hämmerli Model 100 Free Pistol
Same general specifications as Model 33MP. Improved action and sights, redesigned stock. Standard model has plain stocks and forearm, deluxe model has carved stocks and forearm. Made 1950-56.
Standard Model **$645**
Deluxe Model **755**

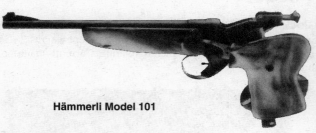

Hämmerli Model 101

Hämmerli Model 101. . . . . **$625**
Similar to Model 100, except has heavy round bbl. with matte finish, improved action and sights, adj. stocks. Weight: about 49 oz. Made 1956-1960.

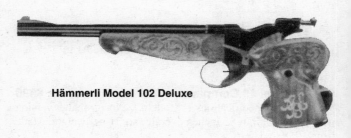

Hämmerli Model 102 Deluxe

Hämmerli Model 102
Same as Model 101, except bbl. has highly polished blued finish. Deluxe model (illustrated) has carved stocks and forearm. Made 1956-1960.
Standard Model **$635**
Deluxe Model **735**

Hämmerli Model 103. . . . . **$645**
Same as Model 101, except has lighter octagon bbl. (as in Model 100) with highly polished blued finish, stocks and forearm of select French walnut. Weight: about 46 oz. Made 1956-1960.

Hämmerli Model 104. . . . . **$585**
Similar to Model 102, except has lighter round bbl., improved action redesigned stocks and forearm. Weight: 46 oz. Made 1961-1965.

Hämmerli Model 105. . . . . **$710**
Similar to Model 103, except has improved action, redesigned stocks and forearm. Made 1961-65.

Hämmerli Model 105

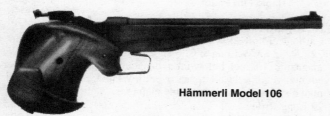

Hämmerli Model 106

Hämmerli Model 106 . . . . $595
Similar to Model 104, except has improved trigger and stocks.
Made 1966-1971.

Hämmerli Model 107 Deluxe

Hämmerli Model 107
Similar to Model 105, except has improved trigger and stock.
Deluxe model (illustrated) has engraved receiver and bbl.,
carved stocks and forearm. Made 1966-1971.
Standard Model $675
Deluxe Model 910

Hämmerli Model 120 Heavy Bbl.
Adj. Stocks

Hämmerli Model 120 Heavy Barrel
Same as Models 120-1 and 120-2, except has 5.7-inch heavy bbl.
Weight: 41 oz. Available with standard or adj. stocks. Made from
1972 to date.
With standard stocks $425
With adj. stocks 440

Hämmerli Model 120-1

Hämmerli Model 120-1 Single-Shot Free Pislol . . $385
Side lever-operated bolt action. Adj. single-stage or two-stage
trigger. Caliber: 22 LR. 9.9-inch bbl. 14.75 inches overall.
Weight: 44 oz. Micrometer rear sight, front sight on high ramp.
Blued finish bbl. and receiver, lever and grip frame anodized aluminum. Checkered walnut thumbrest stocks. Made from 1972 to
date.

Hämmerli Model 120-2 . . . . $395
Same as Model 120-1, except has hand-contoured stocks with
adj. palm rest (available for right or left hand). Made from 1972
to date.

Hämmerli Model 150

Hämmerli Models 150/151 Free Pistols
Improved Martini-type action with lateral-action cocking lever.
Set trigger adj. for weight, length and angle of pull. Caliber: 22
LR. 11.3-inch round bbl., free-floating. 15.4 inches overall.
Weight: 43 oz. (w/extra weights, 49.5 oz.). Micrometer rear
sight, front sight on high ramp. Blued finish. Select walnut fore-
arm and stocks w/adj. palm shelf. Made 1972-1993.
Model 150 (Disc. 1989) $1395
Model 151 (Disc. 1993) 1425

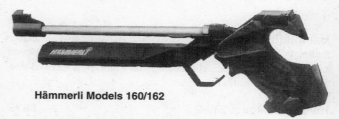

Hämmerli Models 160/162

Hämmerli Models 160/162 Free Pistols
Caliber: 22 LR. Single shot. 11.31-inch bbl. 17.5 inches overall.
Weight: 46.9 oz. Sights: interchangeable front blade; fully adj.
match rear. Match-style stippled walnut stocks w/adj. palm shelf.
Made from 1993 to date.
Model 160 w/Mechanical Set Trigger $1125
Model 162 w/Electronic Trigger 1295

Hämmerli Model 208

Hämmerli Model 232 Rapid Fire Pistol

Hämmerli Model 208 Standard Auto Pistol **$1195**
Caliber: 22 LR. 8-shot magazine. 5.9-inch bbl. 10 inches overall. Weight: 35 oz. (bbl. weight adds 3 oz.). Micrometer rear sight, ramp front. Blued finish. Checkered walnut stocks w/adj. heel plate. Made 1966-1988.

Hämmerli Model 211 . . . . **$1095**
Same as Model 208, except has standard thumbrest stocks. Made from 1966 to date.

Hämmerli Model 212 Hunter's Pistol **$945**
Caliber: 22 LR. 4.88-inch bbl. 8.5 inches overall. Weight: 31 oz. Fully adj. sights. Blued finish. Checkered walnut stocks. Made 1984-1990.

Hämmerli Model 215

Hämmerli Model 215 . . . . **$1095**
Similar to the Model 208 except w/heavier bbl. and fewer deluxe features.

Hämmerli Model 230-1 Rapid Fire Auto Pistol . . . **$595**
Caliber: 22 Short. 5-shot magazine. 6.3-inch bbl. 11.6 inches overall. Weight: 44 oz. Micrometer rear sight, post front. Blued finish. Smooth walnut thumbrest stocks. Made 1970-1983.

Hämmerli Model 230-2 . . . . **$635**
Same as Model 230-1, except has checkered walnut stocks with adj. heel plate. Made 1970-1983.

Hämmerli Model 232 Rapid Fire Auto Pistol **$995**
Caliber: 22 LR. 5-shot magazine. 5.2-inch bbl. 10.38 inches overall. Weight: 44 oz. Fully adj. target sights. Blued finish. Stippled walnut wraparound target stocks. Made from 1984 to date.

Hämmerli Model 280 Target Pistol
Carbon-reinforced synthetic frame and bbl. housing. Calibers: 22 LR, 32 S&W Long WC. 6-shot (22 LR) or 5-shot (32 S&W) magazine. 4.5-inch bbl. w/interchangeable metal or carbon fiber counterweights. 11.88 inches overall. Weight: 39 oz. Micro-adj. match sights w/interchangeable elements.
22 Long Rifle . . . . **$ 895**
32 S&W Long WC **1095**

Hämmerli International Model 206

Hämmerli International Model 206 Auto Pistol . . **$535**
Calibers: 22 Short, 22 LR. 6-shot (22 Short) or 8-shot (22 LR) magazine. 7.1-inch bbl. w/muzzle brake. 12.5 inches overall. Weight: 33 oz. (22 Short), 39 oz. (22 LR) (supplementary weights add 5 and 8 oz.). Micrometer rear sight, ramp front. Blued finish. Standard thumbrest stocks. Made 1962-69.

Hämmerli International Model 207

Hämmerli International Model 207 . . . . **$570**
Same as Model 206, except has stocks with adj. heel plate, weighs 2 oz. more. Made 1962-69.

Hämmerli International Model 209 Auto Pistol . . **$660**
Caliber: 22 Short. 5-shot mag. 4.75-inch bbl. w/muzzle brake and gas-escape holes. 11 inches overall. Weight: 39 oz. (interchangeable front weight adds 4 oz.). Micrometer rear sight, post front. Blued finish. Standard thumbrest stocks of checkered walnut. Made 1966-1970.

Hämmerli International Model 210

**Hämmerli-Walther Olympia Model 203
1958 Type**

Hämmerli International Model 210 . . . . $675
Same as Model 209, except has stocks with adj. heel plate, is 0.8-inch longer and weighs 1 ounce more. Made 1966-1970.

Hämmerli Virginian SA Revolver $495
Similar to Colt Single-Action Army, except has base pin safety system (SWISSAFE). Calibers: 357 Magnum, 45 Colt. 6-shot cylinder. Bbls.: 4.63-, 5.5-, 7.5-inch. 11 inches overall w/5.5-inch bbl. Weight: 40 oz. w/5.5-inch bbl. Fixed sights. Blued bbl. and cylinder, casehardened frame, chrome-plated grip frame and trigger guard. One-piece smooth walnut stock. Made 1973-76 for Interarms, Alexandria, Va.

Hämmerli-Walther Olympia Model 203
Same as corresponding Model 200 (1955-Type lacks muzzle brake), except has stocks with adj. heel plate. Made 1955-1963.
1955-Type $595
1958-Type 615

Hämmerli-Walther Olympia Model 204
American Model. Same as corresponding Model 200 (1956-Type lacks muzzle brake), except in 22 LR only, has slide stop and micrometer rear sight. Made 1956-1963.
1956-Type $695
1958-Type 645

**Hämmerli-Walther Olympia
Model 200, 1952 Type**

**Hämmerli-Walther Olympia Model
205**

Hämmerli-Walther Olympia Model 200
Automatic Pistol, 1952-Type $575
Similar to 1936 Walther Olympia Funfkampf Model. Calibers: 22 Short, 22 LR. 6-shot (22 Short) or 10-shot (22 LR) magazine. 7.5-inch bbl. 10.7 inches overall. Weight: 27.7 oz. (22 Short, light alloy breechblock); 30.3 oz. (22 LR), supplementary weights provided. Adj. target sights. Blued finish. Checkered walnut thumbrest stocks. Made 1952-58.

Hämmerli-Walther Olympia Model 200,
1958-Type $600
Same as Model 200, 1952 Type, except has muzzle brake, 8-shot magazine (22 LR). 11.6 inches overall. Weight: 30 oz. (22 Short); 33 oz. (22 LR). Made 1958-1963.

Hämmerli-Walther Olympia Model 201 . . . . $590
Same as Model 200, 1952 Type, except has 9.5-inch bbl. Made 1955-57.

Hämmerli-Walther Olympia Model 202 . . . . $600
Same as Model 201, except has stocks with adj. heel plate. Made from 1955-57.

Hämmerli-Walther Olympia Model 205
American Model. Same as Model 204, except has stocks with adj. heel plate. Made 1956-1963.
1956-Type $750
1958-Type 675

SIG-Hämmerli Model P240

SIG-Hämmerli Model P240 Automatic Pistol
Caliber: 38 Special (wadcutter). 5-shot magazine. 6-inch bbl. 10 inches overall. Weight: 41 oz. Micrometer rear sight, post front. Blued finish. Smooth walnut thumbrest stocks. Accessory 22 LR conversion unit available. Made from 1975 to date.
Model P240 . . . . $1095
22 Conversion Unit 500

SIG-Hämmerli Model P240 Target Auto Pistol . . $2595
Same general specifications as Model P240 Automatic except
with fully adj. target sights and stippled walnut wraparound target stocks. Weight: 49 oz.

HARRINGTON & RICHARDSON, INC.
Gardner, Massachusetts
Now H&R 1871, Inc., Gardner, Mass.

*Formerly Harrington & Richardson Arms Co. of Worcester,
Mass. One of the oldest and most distinguished manufacturers
of handguns, rifles and shotguns, H&R had suspended operations in 1986; it was purchased by New England Firearms in
the early 1990s.*

AUTOMATIC/SINGLE-SHOT PISTOLS

NOTE

For ease in finding a particular firearm, H&R handguns
are grouped into Automatic/Single-Shot Pistols, followed by Revolvers. For a complete listing, please refer
to the Index.

Harrington & Richardson SL 25 Pistol $325
Modified Webley & Scott design. Caliber: 25 Auto. 6-shot
magazine. 2-inch bbl. 4.5 inches overall. Weight: 12 oz. Fixed
sights. Blued finish. Black hard rubber stocks. Discontinued
prior to 1942.

**Harrington & Richardson
Self-Loading 32 Pistol**

Harrington & Richardson SL 32 Pistol $315
Modified Webley & Scott design. Caliber: 32 Auto. 8-shot
magazine. 3.5-inch bbl. 6.5 inches overall. Weight: about 20 oz.
Fixed sights. Blued finish. Black hard rubber stocks. Disconti-
ued prior to 1942.

**Harrington & Richardson USRA Model
Single-Shot Target Pistol $395**
Hinged frame. Caliber: 22 LR. Bbl. lengths: 7-, 8- and 10-inch.
Weight: 31 oz. with 10-inch bbl. Adj. target sights. Blued finish.
Checkered walnut stocks. Made 1928-1941.

**H&R USRA Model
Single-Shot Target Pistol**

REVOLVERS

NOTE

This section contains only H&R Revolvers. Pistols may
be found in the preceding section. For a complete listing of H&R handguns, please refer to the Index.

**H&R Model 4 (1904)
Double-Action Revolver**

Harrinoton & Richardson Model 4 (1904) DA $75
Solid frame. Calibers: 32 S&W Long, 38 S&W. 6-shot cylinder
(32 cal.), 5-shot (38 cal.). Bbl. lengths: 2.5-, 4.5- and 6-inch.
Weight: about 16 oz., 32 cal. Fixed sights. Blued or nickel finish.
Hard rubber stocks. Discontinued prior to 1942.

H&R Model 5

Harrington & Richardson Model 5 (1905) DA $80
Solid frame. Caliber: 32 S&W. 5-shot cylinder. Bbl. lengths:
2.5-,4.5- and 6-inch. Weight: about 11 oz. Fixed sights. Blued
or nickel finish. Hard rubber stocks. Discontinued prior to
1942.

H&R Model 6

Harrington & Richardson Model 6 (1906) DA $85
Solid frame. Caliber: 22 LR. 7-shot cylinder. Bbl. lengths: 2.5-4.5- and 6-inch. Weight: about 10 oz. Fixed sights. Blued or nickel finish. Hard rubber stocks. Discontinued prior to 1942.

H&R 22 Special

Harrington & Richardson 22 Special DA $140
Heavy hinged frame. Calibers: 22 LR, 22 WRF. 9-shot cylinder. 6-inch bbl. Weight: 23 oz. Fixed sights, front gold-plated. Blued finish. Checkered walnut stocks. Recessed safety cylinder on later models for high-speed ammunition. Discontinued prior to 1942.

H&R Model 199

Harrington & Richardson Model 199 Sportsman SA Revolver $155
Hinged frame. Caliber: 22 LR. 9-shot cylinder. 6-inch bbl. 11 inches overall. Weight: 30 oz. Adj. target sights. Blued finish. Checkered walnut stocks. Discontinued 1951.

Harrington & Richardson Model 504 DA $145
Caliber: 32 H&R Magnum. 5-shot cylinder. 4- or 6-inch bbl., square butt; 3- or 4-inch bbl., round butt. Made 1984-1986.

Harrington & Richardson Model 532 DA $85
Caliber: 32 H&R Magnum. 5-shot cylinder. 2.5- or 4-inch bbl. Weight: approx. 20 and 25 oz. respectively. Fixed sights. American walnut grips. Lustre blue finish. Made 1984-86.

Harrington & Richardson Model 586 DA $140
Caliber: 32 H&R Magnum. 5-shot cylinder. Bbl. lengths: 4.5, 5.5, 7.5, 10 inches. Weight: 30 oz. average. Adj. rear sight, blade front. Walnut finished hardwood grips. Made 1984-86.

Harrington & Richardson Model 603 Target $115
Similar to Model 903, except in 22 WMR. 6-shot capacity with unfluted cylinder. Made 1980-83.

Harrington & Richardson Model 604 Target $135
Similar to Model 603, except with 6-inch bull bbl. Weight: 38 oz. Made 1980-83.

H&R Model 622

Harrington & Richardson Model 622/623 DA $85
Solid frame. Caliber: 22 Short, Long, LR, 6-shot cylinder. Bbl. lengths: 2.5-, 4-, 6-inch. Weight: 26 oz. w/4-inch bbl. Fixed sights. Blued finish. Plastic stocks. Made 1957-1986. *Note:* Model 623 is same, except chrome or nickel finish.

H&R Model 632

Harrington & Richardson Model 632/633 Guardsman DA Revolver $90
Solid Frame. Caliber: 32 S&W Long. 6-shot cylinder. Bbl. lengths: 2.5- or 4-inch. Weight: 19 oz. w/2.5-inch bbl. Fixed sights. Blued or chrome finish. Checkered Tenite stocks (round butt on 2.5-inch, square butt on 4-inch). Made 1953-1986. *Note:* Model 633 is the same, except for chrome or nickel finish.

H&R Model 649

H&R Model 650

Harrington & Richardson Model 649/650 DA.... $115
Solid frame. Side loading and ejection. Convertible model with two 6-shot cylinders. Calibers: 22 LR, 22 WMR. 5.5-inch bbl. Weight: 32 oz. Adj. rear sight, blade front. Blued finish. One-piece, Western-style walnut stock. Made 1976-1986. *Note:* **Model 650** is same, except nickel finish.

H&R Model 666, Nickel Finish

Harrington & Richardson Model 666 DA $90
Solid frame. Convertible model with two 6-shot cylinders. Calibers: 22 LR, 22 WMR. 6-inch bbl. Weight: 28 oz. Fixed sights. Blued finish. Plastic stocks. Made 1976-78.

H&R Model 676

Harrington & Richardson Model 676 DA $120
Solid frame. Side loading and ejection. Convertible model with two 6-shot cylinders. Calibers: 22 LR, 22 WMR. Bbl. lengths: 4.5-, 5.5-, 7.5-, 12-inch. Weight: 32 oz. w/5.5-inch bbl. Adj. rear sight, blade front. Blued finish, color-casehardened frame. One-piece, Western-style walnut stock. Made 1976-1980.

H&R Model 686

Harrington & Richardson Model 686 DA $145
Caliber: 22 LR and 22 WMR. Bbls.: 4.5-, 5.5-, 7.5-, 10- and 12-inches. 6-shot magazine. Adj. rear sight, ramp and blade front. Blued, color-casehardened frame. Weight: 31 oz. w/4.5-inch bbl. Made 1980-86.

H&R Model 733, Nickel Finish

Harrington & Richardson Model 732/733 DA $90
Solid frame, swing-out 6-shot cylinder. Calibers: 32 S&W, 32 S&W Long. Bbl. lengths: 2.5-, 4-inch. Weight: 26 oz. w/4-inch bbl. Fixed sights (windage adj. rear on 4-inch bbl. model). Blue finish. Plastic stocks. Made 1958-1986. *Note:* Model 733 is same, except nickel finish.

Harrington & Richardson Model 826 DA $110
Caliber: 22 WMR. 6-shot magazine. 3-inch bull bbl. Ramp and blade front sight, adj. rear. American walnut grips. Weight: 28 oz. Made 1981-83.

H&R Model 830, Nickel Finish

Harrington & Richardson Model 829/830 DA
Same as Model 826, except in 22 LR caliber. 9-shot capacity. Made 1981-83.
Model 829, Blued $115
Model 830, Nickel. **120**

Harrington & Richardson Model 832,1833 DA
Same as Model 826, except in 32 S W Long. Blued or nickel finish. Made 1981-83.
Model 832, Blued $125
Model 833, Nickel. **130**

H&R Model 900

Harrington & Richardson Model 900/901 DA. $75
Solid frame, snap-out cylinder. Calibers: 22 Short, Long, LR. 9-shot cylinder. Bbl. lengths: 2.5-, 4-, 6-inch. Weight: 26 oz. w/6-inch bbl. Fixed sights. Blued finish. Blade Cycolac stocks. Made 1962-1973. *Note:* **Model 901** (discontinued in 1963) is the same, except has chrome finish and white Tenite stocks.

H&R Model 903

Harrington & Richardson Model 903 Target $125
Caliber: 22 LR. 9-shot capacity. SA/DA. 6-inch targetweight flat-side bbl. Swing-out cylinder. Weight: 35 oz. Blade front sight, adj. rear. American walnut grips. Made 1980-83.

H&R Model 904

Harrington & Richardson Model 904 Target $130
Similar to Model 903, except 4- and 6-inch bull bbls. 4-inch bbl. weighs 32 oz. Made 1980-86.

H&R Model 905

Harrington & Richardson Model 905 Target $135
Same as Model 904, except with 4-inch bbl. only. Nickel finish. Made 1981-83.

H&R Model 922, First Issue

Harrington & Richardson Model 922 DA Revolver, First Issue $150
Solid frame. Caliber: 22 LR. 9-shot cylinder. Bbl.: early model, 10-inch, octagon; later production, 6-inch, round. Weight: 26 oz. w/6-inch bbl. Fixed sights. Blued finish. Checkered walnut stocks. Safety cylinder on later models. Discontinued prior to 1942.

H&R Model 922, Second Issue

Harrington & Richardson Model 922/923 DA Revolver, Second Issue $75

Solid frame. Caliber: 22 LR. 9-shot cylinder. Bbl. lengths: 2.5-, 4-, 6-inch. Weight: 24 oz. w/4-inch bbl. Fixed sights. Blued finish. Plastic stocks. Made 1950-1986. *Note:* Second Issue Model 922 has a different frame from that of the First Issue. **Model 923** is same as Model 922, Second Issue, except for nickel finish.

H&K Model 925

Harrington & Richardson Model 925 Defender . . $115

DA. Hinged frame. Caliber: 38 S&W. 5-shot cylinder. 2.5-inch bbl. Weight: 22 oz. Adj. rear sight, fixed front. Blued finish. One-piece wraparound grip. Made 1964-1978.

H&K Model 926

Harrington & Richardson Model 926 DA $115

Hinged frame. Calibers: 22 LR, 38 S&W. 9-shot (22 LR) or 5-shot (38) cylinder. 4-inch bbl. Weight: 31 oz. Adj. rear sight, fixed front. Blued finish. Checkered walnut stocks. Made 1968-1978.

H&K Model 929

Harrington & Richardson Model 929/930 Sidekick DA Revolver $85

Caliber: 22 LR. Solid frame, swing-out 9-shot cylinder. Bbl. lengths: 2.5-, 4-, 6-inch. Weight: 24 oz. w/4-inch bbl. Fixed sights. Blued finish. Checkered plastic stocks. Made 1956-1986. *Note:* **Model 930** is same, except nickel finish.

H&K Model 939

Harrington & Richardson Model 939/940 Ultra Sidekick DA Revolver $110

Solid frame, swing-out 9-shot cylinder. Safety lock. Calibers: 22 Short, Long, LR. Flat-side 6-inch bbl. w/vent rib. Weight: 33 oz. Adj. rear sight, ramp front. Blued finish. Checkered walnut stocks. Made 1958-1986, reintroduced by H&R 1871 in 1992. *Note:* **Model 940** is same, except has round bbl.

H&K Model 949

H&K Model 950

Harrington & Richardson Model 949/950 Forty-Niner DA Revolver $110

Solid frame. Side loading and ejection. Calibers: 22 Short, Long, LR. 9-shot cylinder. 5.5-inch bbl. Weight: 31 oz. Adj. rear sight, blade front. Blue or nickel finish. One-piece, Western-style walnut grip. Made 1960-1986, reintroduced by H&R 1871 in 1992. *Note:* **Model 950** is same, except nickel finish.

Harrington & Richardson Model 976 DA $90
Same as Model 949, except has color-casehardened frame, 7.5-inch bbl., weighs 36 oz. Intro. 1977; discontinued.

**H&K Model 999
First Issue**

Harrington & Richardson Model 999 Sportsman DA Revolver, First Issue $165
Hinged frame. Calibers: 22 LR, 22 WRF. Same specifications as Model 199 Sportsman Single Action. Discontinued before 1942.

Harrington & Richardson Model 999 Sportsman DA Revolver, Second Issue $175
Hinged frame. Caliber: 22 LR. 9-shot cylinder. 6-inch bbl. w/vent rib. Weight: 30 oz. Adj. sights. Blued finish. Checkered walnut stocks. Made 1950-1986.

**H&K Model 999
Second Issue**

Harrington & Richardson (New) Model 999 Sportsman DA Revolver $170
Hinged frame. Caliber: 22 Short, Long, LR. 9-shot cylinder. 6-inch bbl. w/vent rib. Weight: 30 oz. Sights: Blade front adj. for elevation square-notched rear adj. for windage. Blued finish. Checkered hardwood stocks. Reintroduced by H&R 1871 in 1992.

Harrington & Richardson American DA $75
Solid frame. Calibers: 32 S&W Long, 38 S&W. 6-shot (32 cal.) or 5-shot (38 car.) cylinder. Bbl. lengths: 2.5-,4.5- and 6-inch. Weight: about 16 oz. Fixed sights. Blued or nickel finish. Hard rubber stocks. Discontinued prior to 1942.

Harrington & Richardson Automatic Ejecting DA Revolver $145
Hinged frame. Calibers: 32 S&W Long, 38 S&W. 6-shot cylinder (32 cal.), 5-shot (38 cal.). Bbl. lengths: 3.25-, 4-, 5- and 6-inch. Weight: about 16 oz., 32 car.; 15 oz., 38 cal. Fixed sights. Blued or nickel finish. Black hard rubber stocks. Discontinued prior to 1942.

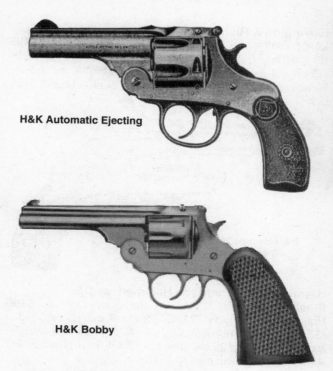

H&K Automatic Ejecting

H&K Bobby

Harrington & Richardson Bobby DA $250
Hinged frame. Calibers: 32 S&W, 38 S&W. 6-shot cylinder (32 cal.), 5-shot (38 cal.). 4-inch bbl. 9 inches overall. Weight: 23 oz. Fixed sights. Blued finish. Checkered walnut stocks. Discontinued 1946. *Note:* Originally designed and produced for use by London's bobbies.

H&K Defender 38

Harrington & Richardson Defender 38 DA $105
Hinged frame. Based on the Sportsman design. Caliber: 38 S&W. Bbl. lengths: 4- and 6-inch. 9 inches overall w/4-inch bbl. Weight: 25 oz., 4-inch bbl. Fixed sights. Blued finish. Black plastic stocks. Discontinued 1946. *Note:* This model was manufactured during WW II as an arm for plant guards, auxiliary police, etc.

Harrington & Richardson Expert Model DA $150
Same specifications as 22 Special, except has 10-inch bbl. Weight: 28 oz. Discontinued prior to 1942.

Harrington & Richardson Hammerless DA, Large Frame **$105**
Hinged frame. Calibers: 32 S&W Long 38 S&W. 6-shot cylinder (32 cal.), 5-shot (38 cal.). Bbl. lengths: 3.25-, 4-, and 6-inch. Weight: about 17 oz. Fixed sights. Blued or nickel finish. Hard rubber stocks. Discontinued prior to 1942.

**H&R Hammerless
Small Frame**

Harrington & Richardson Hammerless DA, Small Frame **$105**
Hinged frame. Calibers: 22 LR, 32 S&W. 7-shot (22 cal.) 5-shot (32 cal.) cylinder. Bbl. lengths: 2-, 3-, 4-, 5- and 6-inch. Weight: about 13 oz. Fixed sights. Blued or nickel finish. Hard rubber stocks. Discontinued. prior to 1942.

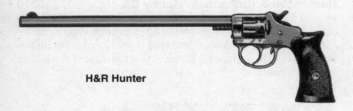

H&R Hunter

Harrington & Richardson Hunter Model DA **$105**
Solid frame. Caliber: 22 LR. 9-shot cylinder. 10-inch octagon bbl. Weight: 26 oz. Fixed sights. Blued finish. Checkered walnut stocks. Safety cylinder on later models. *Note:* An earlier Hunter Model was built on the smaller 7-shot frame. Discontinued prior to 1942.

H&R New Defender

Harrington & Richardson New Defender DA **$195**
Hinged frame. Caliber: 22 LR. 9-shot cylinder. 2-inch bbl. 6.25 inches overall. Weight: 23 oz. Adj. sights. Blued finish. Checkered walnut stocks, round butt. *Note:* Basically, this is the Sportsman DA with a short bbl. Discontinued prior to 1942.

H&R Premier

Harrington & Richardson Premier DA **$90**
Small hinged frame. Calibers: 22 LR, 32 S&W. 7-shot (22 LR) or 5-shot (32) cylinder. Bbl. lengths: 2-, 3-, 4-, 5 and 6-inch. Weight: 13 oz. (22 LR); 12 oz. (32). Fixed sights. Blued or nickel finish. Black hard rubber stocks. Discontinued prior to 1942.

Harrington & Richardson Model STR 022 Blank Revolver **$65**
Caliber: 22 RF blanks. 9-shot cylinder. 2.5-inch bbl. Weight: 19 oz. Satin blue finish.

Harrington & Richardson Model STR 032 Blank Revolver **$75**
Same general specifications as STR 022 except chambered for 32 S&W blank cartridges.

H&R Target Model

Harrington & Richardson Target Model DA **$130**
Small hinged frame. Calibers: 22 LR, 22 W.R.F. 7-shot cylinder. 6-inch bbl. Weight: 16 oz. Fixed sights. Blued finish. Checkered walnut stocks. Discontinued prior to 1942.

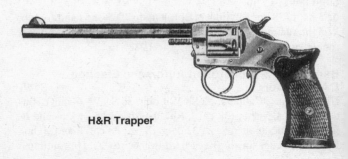

H&R Trapper

Harrington & Richardson Trapper Model DA **$115**
Solid frame. Caliber: 22 LR. 7-shot cylinder. 6-inch octagon bbl. Weight: 12.5 oz. Fixed sights. Blued finish. Checkered walnut stocks. Safety cylinder on later models. Discontinued prior to 1942.

H&R Ultra Sportsman

Harrington & Richardson Ultra Sportsman **$185**
SA. Hinged frame. Caliber: 22 LR. 9-shot cylinder. 6-inch bbl. Weight: 30 oz. Adj. target sights. Blued finish. Checkered walnut stocks. This model has short action, wide hammer spur, cylinder is length of a 22 LR cartridge. Discontinued prior to 1942.

H&R Vest Pocket

Harrington & Richardson Vest Pocket DA **$75**
Solid frame. Spurless hammer. Calibers: 22 Rimfire, 32 S&W. 7-shot (22 cal.) or 5-shot (32 cal.) cylinder. 1.13-inch bbl. Weight: about 9 oz. Blued or nickel finish. Hard rubber stocks. Discontinued prior to 1942.

H&R Young American

Harrington & Richardson Young America DA **$75**
Solid frame. Calibers: 22 Long, 32 S&W. 7-shot (22 car.) or 5-shot (32 car.) cylinder. Bbl. lengths: 2-, 4.5- and 6-inch. Weight: about 9 oz. Fixed sights. Blued or nickel finish. Hard rubber stocks. Discont. prior to 1942.

HARTFORD ARMS & EQUIPMENT CO.
Hartford, Connecticut

Hartford pistols were the forebears of the original High Standard line, since High Standard Mfg. Corp. acquired Hartford Arms & Equipment Co. in 1932. The High Standard Model B is essentially the same as the Hartford Automatic.

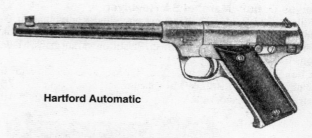

Hartford Automatic

Hartford Automatic Target Pistol **$545**
Caliber. 22 LR. 10-shot magazine. 6.75-inch bbl. 10.75 inches overall. Weight: 31 oz. Target sights. Blued finish. Black rubber stocks. This arm closely resembles the early Colt Woodsman and High Standard pistols. Made 1929-1930.

Hartford Repeating Pistol **$430**
Same general design as the automatic pistol of this manufacture, but this model is a hand-operated repeating pistol on the order of the Fiala. Made 1929-1930.

Hartford Single Shot Target Pistol **$455**
Similar in appearance to the Hartford Automatic. Caliber: 22 LR. 6.75-inch bbl. 10.75 inches overall. Weight: 38 oz. Target sights. Mottled frame and slide, blued bbl. Black rubber or walnut stocks. Made 1929-1930.

HAWES FIREARMS
Van Nuys, California

Hawes Deputy Denver Marshal

Hawes Deputy Denver Marshal

Same as Deputy Marshal SA, except has brass frame.

22 LR (plastic grips) **$75**
Combination, 22 LR/22 WMR (plastic) **75**
Extra for walnut stocks **10**

Hawes Deputy Marshal

Hawes Deputy Marshal SA Revolver

Calibers: 22 LR, also 22 WMR in two-cylinder combination. 6-shot cylinder. 5.5-inch bbl. 11 inches overall. Weight: 34 oz. Adj. rear sight, blade front. Blued finish. Plastic or walnut grips. Made from 1973 to date.

22 Long Rifle (plastic grips) **$70**
Combination, 22 LR/22 WMR (plastic) **75**
Extra for walnut stocks **10**

Hawes Deputy Montana Marshal

Hawes Deputy Montana Marshal

Same as Deputy Marshal, except has brass grip frame. Walnut grips only.

22 Long Rifle **$75**
Combination, 22 LR/22 WMR **95**

Hawes Deputy Silver City Marshal

Hawes Deputy Silver City Marshal

Same as Deputy Marshal, except has chrome-plated frame, brass grip frame, blued cylinder and bbl.

22 Long Rifle (plastic grips) **$70**
Combination, 22 LR/22 WMR (plastic) **90**
Extra for walnut grips **10**

Hawes Deputy Texas Marshal

Hawes Deputy Texas Marshal

Same as Deputy Marshal, except has chrome finish.

22 Long Rifle (plastic grips) **$70**
Combination, 22 LR/22 WMR (plastic) **85**
Extra for walnut grips **10**

Hawes Favorite

Hawes Favorite Single-Shot Target Pistol **$130**

Replica of Stevens No. 35. Tip-up action. Caliber: 22 LR. 8-inch bbl. 12 inches overall. Weight: 24 oz. Target sights. Chrome-plated frame. Blued bbl. Plastic or rosewood grips (**add** $5). Made 1968-1976.

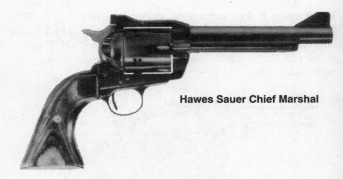

Hawes Sauer Chief Marshal

Hawes Sauer Chief Marshal SA Target Revolver

Same as Western Marshal, except has adj. rear sight and front sight, oversized rosewood grips. Not made in 22 caliber.

357 Magnum or 45 Colt **$200**
44 Magnum **225**
Combination, 357 Magnum and 9mm Luger
   45 Colt and 45 Auto **250**
Combination, 44 Magnum and 44-40 . . . . **245**

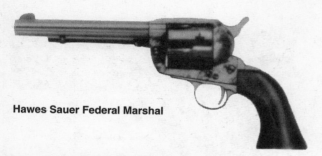

Hawes Sauer Federal Marshal

Hawes Sauer Texas Marshal

Hawes Sauer Federal Marshal

Same as Western Marshal, except has color-casehardened frame, brass grip frame, one-piece walnut grip. Not made in 22 caliber.

357 Magnum or 45 Colt	**$200**
44 Magnum	**230**
Combination, 357 Magnum and 9mm Luger, 45 Colt and 45 Auto	**250**
Combination, 44 Magnum and 44-40	**245**

Hawes Sauer Texas Marshal

Same as Western Marshal, except nickel-plated, has pearlite grips. 22 caliber discontinued.

357 Magnum or 45 Colt	**$225**
44 Magnum	**240**
Combination, 357 Magnum and 9mm Luger, 45 Colt and 45 Auto	**260**
Combination, 44 Magnum and 44-40	**275**
22 Long Rifle	**195**
Combination, 22 LR and 22 WMR	**230**

Hawes Sauer Montana Marshal

Hawes Sauer Montana Marshal

Same as Western Marshal, except has brass grip frame. 22 caliber discontinued.

357 Magnum or 45 Colt	**$200**
44 Magnum	**225**
Combination, 357 Magnum and 9mm Luger, 45 Colt and 45 Auto	**240**
Combination, 44 Magnum and 44-40	**250**
22 LR	**195**
Combination, 22 LR and 22 WMR	**210**

Hawes Sauer Montana Marshal

Hawes Sauer Montana Marshal 22

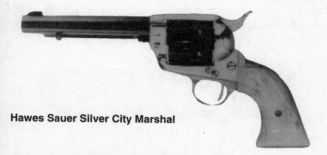

Hawes Sauer Silver City Marshal

Hawes Sauer Silver City Marshal

Same as Western Marshal except has nickel-plated frame, brass grip frame, blued cylinder and bbl., pearlite grips.

44 Magnum	**$240**
Combination, 357 Magnum and 9mm Luger 45 Colt and 45 Auto	**225**
Combination, 44 Magnum and 44-40	**260**

Hawes Sauer Western Marshal SA Revolver

Calibers: 22 LR (discont.), 357 Magnum, 44 Magnum, 45 Auto. Also in two-cylinder combinations: 22 WMR (discont.),9mm Luger, 44-40, 45 Auto.6-shot cylinder. Bbl. lengths: 5.5-inch (discont.), 6-inch. 11.75 inches overall w/6-inch bbl. Weight: 46 oz. Fixed sights. Blued finish. Originally furnished with simulated stag plastic stocks; recent production has smooth rosewood stocks. Made 1968 to date by J. P. Sauer & Sohn, Eckernforde, Germany.

357 Magnum or 45 Colt	**$200**
44 Magnum	**230**
Combination, 357 Magnum and 9mm Luger, 45 Colt and 45 Auto	**225**
Combination, 44 Magnum and 44-40	**240**
22 Long Rifle	**195**
Combination, 22 LR and 22 WMR	**210**

HECKLER & KOCH
Oberndorf/Neckar, West Germany, and Chantilly, Virginia

Heckler & Koch HK4

Heckler & Koch Model HK4 DA Auto Pistol
Calibers: 380 Automatic (9mm Short); also 22 LR, 25 Automatic (6.35mm), 32 Automatic (7.65mm) with conversion kits. 7-shot magazine in 380; 8-shot in other calibers. 3.4-inch bbl. 6.19 inches overall. Weight: 18 oz. Fixed sights. Blued finish. Plastic stock. Discontinued 1984.

380 Automatic	$295
380 Automatic with 22 conversion unit	425
380 Automatic with 22, 25, 32 conversion units	695

Heckler & Koch Model P7K3

Heckler & Koch Model P7K3 DA Auto Pistol
Caliber: 380 ACP. 8-round magazine. 3.8 inch-bbl. 6.3 inches overall. Weight: about 26 oz. Adj. rear sight. Made from 1988 to date.

P7K3 in 380 Cal.	$750
22 LR Conversion Kit	495

Heckler & Koch Model P7M8 . . . . $750
Caliber: 9mm. 8-shot magazine. 4.13-inch bbl. 6.73 inches overall. Weight: 29.9 oz. Matte black finish. Adj. rear sight. Made 1985 to date.

Heckler & Koch P7M8

Heckler & Koch Model P7M10
Caliber: 40 S&W. 9-shot magazine. 4.2-inch bbl. 6.9 inches overall. Weight: 43 oz. Sights: fixed front blade; adj. rear w/3-dot system. Made from 1992 to date.

Blued Finish	$895
Nickel Finish	950

Heckler & Koch Model P7M13

Heckler & Koch Model P7M13 . . . . $850
Caliber: 9mm. 13-shot magazine. 4.13-inch bbl. 6.65 inches overall. Weight: 34.42 oz. Matte black finish. Adj. rear sight. Made 1985-89.

Heckler & Koch Model P7 (PSP)

Heckler & Koch Model P7(PSP) Auto Pistol $895

Caliber: 9mm Parabellum/Luger. 8-shot magazine. DA. 4.13-inch bbl. 6.54 inches overall. Weight: about 33.5 oz. Blue finish. Made 1983-85.

**Heckler & Koch Model P9S
DA**

Heckler & Koch Model P9S DA Automatic Pistol

Calibers: 9mm Luger, 45 Automatic. 9-shot (9mm) or 7-shot (45 Auto) magazine. 4-inch bbl. 7.63 inches overall. Weight: 32 ounces. Fixed sights. Blued finish. Plastic grips. Discontinued 1986.

9mm $650
45 Automatic. 695

**Heckler & Koch Model P9S
9mm Target**

Heckler & Koch Model P9S 9mm Target $995

Same as standard Model P9S 9mm, except has adj. trigger, trigger stop, adj. rear sight.

Heckler & Koch Model P9S 9mm Target Competition Kit

Same as Model P9S 9mm Target, except comes with extra 5.5-inch bbl. and bbl. weight. Also available with walnut competition stock.

With Standard stock $850
With Competition stock 950

Heckler & Koch Model SP89 . . . . $2100

Semiautomatic, recoil-operated, delayed roller-locked bolt system. Caliber: 9mm Luger. 15-shot magazine. 4.5-inch bbl. 13 inches overall. Weight: 68 oz. Hooded front sight; adj. rotary-aperture rear. Made from 1989 to date.

Heckler & Koch Model USP Auto Pistol

Polymer integral grip/frame design with recoil reduction system. Calibers: 9mm Parabellum, 40 S&W. 15-shot (9mm) or 13-shot (40 S&W) magazine. 4.75-inch bbl. 6.88 inches overall. Weight: 28 oz. Sights: blade front, adj. rear w/3-dot system. Matte black finish. Stippled black polymer grip. Available in SA/DA or DAO. Made from 1993 to date.

Right-Hand Model $550
Left-Hand Model 575

Heckler & Koch Model VP'70Z

Heckler & Koch Model VP'70Z Auto Pistol $325

Caliber: 9mm Luger. 18-shot magazine. DA. 4.5-inch bbl. 8 inches overall. Weight: 32.5 oz. Fixed sights. Blued slide, plastic receiver and stock. Discontinued 1986.

HELWAN PISTOL
See Interarms

HERITAGE MANUFACTURING
Opa Locka, Florida

Heritage Model HA25 Auto Pistol

Caliber: 25 ACP. 6-shot magazine. 2.5-inch bbl. 4.63 inches overall. Weight: 12 oz. Fixed sights. Blued or chrome finish. Made from 1993 to date.

Blued $60
Chrome 70

Heritage Rough Rider

Heritage Rough Rider SA Revolver

Calibers: 22 LR, 22 WRF. 6-shot cylinder. Bbl. lengths: 3, 4.75, 6.5, 9 inches. Weight: 31-38 oz. Sights: blade front; fixed rear. High-polished blued finish with gold accents. Smooth walnut grips. Made from 1993 to date.

22 Long Rifle . . . . **$ 75**
22 WRF. **100**

Heritage Sentry DA

Heritage Sentry DA Revolver

Caliber: 38 Special. 6-shot cylinder. 2- or 4-inch bbl. 6.25 inches overall w/2-inch bbl. Sights: ramp front; fixed rear. Blued or chrome finish. Checkered plastic grips. Made from 1993 to date.

Blued . . . . **$ 95**
Chrome **100**

HI-POINT FIREARMS
Mansfield, Ohio

Hi-Point Model JS-9mm

Hi-Point Model JS-9mm Auto Pistol **$100**
Caliber: 9mm Parabellum. 8-shot magazine. 4.75-inch bbl. 7.75 inches overall. Weight: 42 oz. Fixed low-profile sights. Matte black finish. Checkered plastic grips. Made from 1994 to date.

Hi-Point Model JS-9mm Compact Pistol **$90**
Similar to standard JS-9, except with 3.5-inch bbl. 6.72 inches overall. Weight: 32 oz. 3-dot type sights. Made from 1994 to date.

Hi-Point Model 380 Polymer **$110**
Caliber: 380 ACP, 8-shot magazine. 3.5-inch bbl. 6.72 inches overall. Weight: 32 oz. 3-dot sights. Made from 1994 to date.

Hi-Point Model JS-40 Auto Pistol **$115**
Similar to Model JS-9mm, except in caliber 40 S&W.

Hi-Point Model JS-45 Auto Pistol **$115**
Similar to Model JS-9mm, except in caliber 45 ACP with 7-shot magazine and two-tone Polymer finish.

J. C. HIGGINS HANDGUNS
See Sears, Roebuck & Company

HIGH STANDARD SPORTING FIREARMS
East Hartford, Connecticut
Formerly High Standard Mfg. Co., Hamden, Connecticut

A long-standing producer of sporting arms, High Standard discontinued its operations in 1984. See new High Standard models under separate entry that follows.

AUTOMATIC PISTOLS

> ─── **NOTE** ───
>
> For ease in finding a particular firearm, High Standard handguns are grouped into three sections: Automatic Pistols (below), Derringers, and Revolvers which follow. For a complete listing, please refer to the index.

High Standard Model A

High Standard Model A Automatic Pistol **$495**
Hammerless. Caliber: 22 LR. 10-shot magazine. Bbl. lengths: 4.5-, 6.75-inch. 11.5 inches overall w/6.75-inch bbl. Weight: 36 oz. w/6.75-inch bbl. Adj. target sights. Blued finish. Checkered walnut stocks. Made 1938-1942.

High Standard Model B Automatic Pistol **$445**
Original Standard pistol. Hammerless. Caliber: 22 LR. 10-shot magazine. Bbl. lengths: 4.5-, 6.75-inch. 10.75 inches overall w/6.75-inch bbl. Weight: 33 oz. w/6.75-inch bbl. Fixed sights. Blued finish. Hard rubber stocks. Made 1932-1942.

High Standard Model C Automatic Pistol **$535**
Same as Model B, except in 22 Short. Made 1935-1942.

High Standard Model B

High Standard Model D

High Standard Dura-Matic

High Standard Model E

High Standard Model G-380

High Standard Model D Automatic Pistol $495
Same general specifications as Model A, but heavier bbl. Weight: 40 oz. w/6.75-inch bbl. Made 1937-1942.

High Standard Dura-Matic Automatic Pistol $285
Takedown. Caliber: 22 LR. 10-shot magazine. Bbls.: 4.5 or 6.5 inches, interchangeable. 10.88 inches overall w/6.5-inch bbl. Weight: 35 oz. w/6.5-inch bbl. Fixed sights. Blued finish. Checkered grips. Made 1952-1970.

High Standard Model E Automatic Pistol $695
Same general specifications as Model A, but with extra heavy bbl. and thumbrest stocks. Weight: 42 oz. w/6.75inch bbl. Made 1937-1942.

High Standard Field-King Automatic Pistol
Same general specifications as Sport-King but with heavier bbl. and target sights. Late model 6.75-inch bbls. have recoil stabilizer feature. Weight: 43 oz. w/6.75 inch bbl. Made 1951-58.
With One Bbl. $395
With Both Bbls. 445

High Standard Flite-King Automatic Pistol — First Model
Same general specifications as Sport-King, except in caliber 22 Short with aluminum alloy frame and slide; weighs 26 oz. w/6.5-inch bbl. Made 1953-58.
With One Bbl. $335
With Both Bbls. 375

High Standard Flite-King Automatic Pistol — Second Model $295
Same as Sport-King—Second Model, except caliber 22 Short and weighs 2 oz. lighter. Made 1958-1966.

High Standard Model G-380 Automatic Pistol $495
Lever takedown. Visible hammer. Thumb safety. Caliber: 380 Automatic. 6-shot magazine. 5-inch bbl. Weight: 40 oz. Fixed sights. Blued finish. Checkered plastic stocks. Made 1943-1950.

High Standard Model G-B

High Standard Model G-B Automatic Pistol
Lever takedown. Hammerless. Interchangeable bbls. Caliber: 22 LR. 10-shot magazine. Bbl. lengths: 4.5, 6.75 inches. 10.75 inches overall w/6.75-inch bbl. Weight: 36 oz. w/6.75-inch bbl. Fixed sights. Blued finish. Checkered plastic stocks. Made 1948-1951.
With One Bbl. $435
With Both Bbls. 480

High Standard Model G-D Automatic Pistol
Lever takedown. Hammerless. Interchangeable bbls. Caliber: 22 LR. 10-shot magazine. Bbl. lengths: 4.5, 6.75 inches. 11.5 inches overall w/6.75-inch bbl. Weight: 41 oz. w/6.75-inch bbl. Target sights. Blued finish. Checkered walnut stocks. Made 1948-1951.
With One Bbl. **$525**
With Both Bbls.. . . . . **585**

High Standard Model G-E

High Standard Model G-E Automatic Pistol
Same general specifications as Model G-D, but with extra heavy bbl. and thumbrest stocks. Weight: 44 oz. w/6.75inch bbl. Made 1949-1951.
With One Bbl. **$750**
With Both Bbls.. . . . . **835**

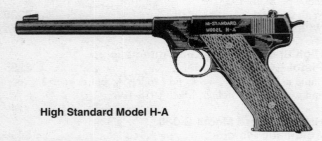

High Standard Model H-A

High Standard Model H-A Automatic Pistol. **$550**
Same as Model A, but with visible hammer, no thumb safety. Made 1939-1942.

High Standard Model H-B

High Standard Model H-B Automatic Pistol. **$415**
Same as Model B, but with visible hammer, no thumb safety. Made 1940-42.

High Standard Model H-D Automatic Pistol. **$795**
Same as Model D, but with visible hammer, no thumb safety. Made 1939-1942.

High Standard Model H-DM Automatic Pistol . . . $395
Also called H-D Military. Same as Model H-D, but with thumb safety. Made 1941-1951.

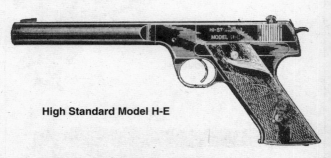

High Standard Model H-E

High Standard Model H-E Automatic Pistol. . . . $1150
Same as Model E, but with visible hammer, no thumb safety. Made 1939-1942.

High Standard Olympic, First Model

High Standard Olympic Automatic — First Model
Same general specifications as Model G-E, but in 22 Short with light alloy slide. Made 1950-51.
With one bbl.. . . . . **$395**
With both bbls. **465**

High Standard Olympic, Second Model

High Standard Olympic Automatic — Second Model
Same general specifications as Supermatic, but in 22 Short with light alloy slide. Weight: 39 oz. w/6.75-inch bbl. Made 1951-58.
With one bbl.. . . . . **$525**
With both bbls. **600**

High Standard Olympic Automatic
Pistol — Third Model **$615**
Same as Supermatic Trophy with bull bbl., except in caliber 22 Short. Made 1963-66.

High Standard Olympic Commemorative

Limited edition of Supermatic Trophy Military issued to commemorate the only American-made rimfire target pistol ever to win an Olympic Gold Medal. Highly engraved with Olympic rings inlaid in gold. Deluxe presentation case. Two versions issued: in 1972 (22 LR) and 1980 (22 Short). *Note:* Value shown is for pistol in new, unfired condition.

1972 Issue **$3495**
1980 Issue **1250**

High Standard Olympic I.S.U.

High Standard Olympic I.S.U. **$695**

Same as Supermatic Citation, except caliber 22 Short. 6.75- and 8-inch tapered bbls. with stabilizer, detachable weights. Made from 1958 to date; 8-inch bbl. discontinued in 1964.

High Standard Olympic I.S.U. Military

High Standard Olympic I.S.U. Military **$725**

Same as Olympic I.S.U., except has military grip and bracket rear sight. Introduced in 1965. Discontinued.

High Standard Olympic Military

High Standard Olympic Military **$625**

Same as Olympic — Third Model, except has military grip and bracket rear sight. Made in 1965.

High Standard Plinker

High Standard Plinker **$295**

Similar to Dura-Matic with same general specifications. Made 1971-73.

High Standard Sharpshooter

High Standard Sharpshooter Automatic Pistol . . **$350**

Takedown. Hammerless. Caliber: 22 LR. 10-shot magazine. 5.5-inch bull bbl. 9 inches overall. Weight: 42 oz. Micrometer rear sight, blade front sight. Blued finish. Plastic stocks. Made 1971-1983.

High Standard Sport-King First Model

High Standard Sport-King Automatic — First Model

Takedown. Hammerless. Interchangeable bbls. Caliber: 22 LR. 10-shot magazine. Bbl. lengths: 4.5-, 6.75-inch. 11.5 inches overall w/6.75-inch bbl. Weight: 39 oz. w/6.75-inch bbl. Fixed sights. Blued finish. Checkered plastic thumbrest stocks. Made 1951-58. *Note:* 1951-54 production has lever takedown as in "G" series; later version (illustrated) has push-button takedown.

With One Bbl. **$295**
With Both Bbls. **375**

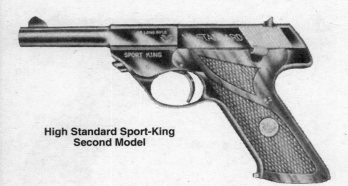

**High Standard Sport-King
Second Model**

High Standard Sport-King Automatic Pistol
Second Model **$250**
Caliber: 22 LR. 10-shot magazine. Bbls.: 4.5- or 6.75 inch, inter-
changeable. 11.25 inches overall w/6.75-inch bbl. Weight: 42 oz.
w/6.75-inch bbl. Fixed sights. Blued finish. Checkered grips.
Made 1958-1970.

**High Standard Sport-King
Third Model**

High Standard Sport-King Automatic Pistol
Third Model **$265**
Similar to Sport-King — Second Model, with same general
specifications. Blued or nickel finish. Introduced in 1974. Discontinued.

High Standard Sport-King Lightweight
Same as standard Sport-King, except has forged aluminum alloy
frame, weighs 30 oz. with 6.75-inch bbl. Made 1954-1965.
With One Bbl. **$350**
With Both Bbls. **425**

High Standard Supermatic

High Standard Supermatic Automatic Pistol
Takedown. Hammerless. Interchangeable bbls. Caliber: 22 LR.
10-shot magazine. Bbl. lengths: 4.5-, 6.75-inch. Late model
6.75-inch bbls. have recoil stabilizer feature. Weight: 43 oz.
w/6.75-inch bbl. 11.5 inches overall w/6.75-inch bbl. Target
sights. Elevated serrated rib between sights. Adj. bbl. weights
add 2 or 3 oz. Blued finish. Checkered plastic thumbrest stocks.
Made 1951-58.
With One Bbl. **$395**
With Both Bbls. **445**

**High Standard Supermatic Citation
Bull Barrel**

High Standard Supermatic Citation
Same as Supermatic Tournament, except 6.75-, 8-, 10-inch tapered bbls. with stabilizer and two removable weights. Also furnished with Tournament's 5.5-inch bull bbl., adj. trigger pull,
recoil-proof click-adj. rear sight (bbl.-mounted on 8- and 10-inch
bbls.), checkered walnut thumbrest grips on bull bbl. model. Currently mfd. with only bull bbl. Made 1958 to date.
With Bull Bbl. **$510**
With Tapered Bbl. **550**

**High Standard Supermatic Citation
Military Fluted Barrel**

High Standard Supermatic Citation Military
Same as Supermatic Citation, except has military grip and
bracket rear sight, bbls. as in Supermatic Trophy. Made from
1965 to date.
With Bull Bbl. **$450**
With Fluted Bbl. **500**

**High Standard Supermatic Tournament
Bull Barrel**

High Standard Supermatic Tournament $425

Takedown. Caliber: 22 LR. 10-shot magazine. Bbls. (interchangeable): 5.5-inch bull, 6.75-inch heavy tapered, notched and drilled for stabilizer and weights. 10 inches overall w/5.5-inch bbl. Weight: 44 oz. w/5.5-inch bbl. Click adj. rear sight, undercut ramp front. Blued finish. Checkered grips. Made 1958-1966.

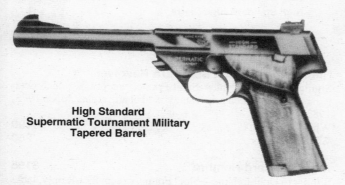

**High Standard
Supermatic Tournament Military
Tapered Barrel**

High Standard Supermatic Tournament Military $425

Same as Supermatic Tournament, except has military grip. Made 1965-1971.

**High Standard
Supermatic Trophy Bull Barrel**

High Standard Supermatic Trophy

Same as Supermatic Citation except 5.5-inch bull bbl. or 7.25-inch fluted bbl. with detachable stabilizer and weights, extra magazine. High-luster blued finish, checkered walnut thumbrest grips. Made 1963-66.

With Bull Bbl. **$575**
With Fluted Bbl. **615**

**High Standard Supermatic
Military Fluted Barrel**

High Standard Supermatic Trophy Military

Same as Supermatic Trophy, except has military grip and bracket rear sight. Made 1965-1984.

With Bull Bbl. **$550**
With Fluted Bbl. **600**

**High Standard Victor
Solid Rib Barrel**

High Standard Victor Automatic Pistol $525

Takedown. Caliber: 22 LR. 10-shot magazine. Bbls.: 4.5-inch solid or vent rib, 5.5-inch vent rib; interchangeable. 9.75 inches overall w/5.5-inch bbl. Weight: 52 oz. w/5.5-inch bbl. Rib-mounted target sights. Blued finish. Checkered walnut thumbrest stocks. Standard or military grip configuration. Made from 1972 to date (standard-grip model, 1974-75).

DERRINGER

NOTE

High Standard Automatic Pistols can be found in the preceding section, while Revolvers immediately follow this Derringer listing.

**High Standard
Derringer**

High Standard Derringer

Hammerless, double action, double bbl. (over/under). Calibers: 22 Short, Long, LR; 22 Magnum Rimfire. 2-shot. 3.5-inch bbls. 5 inches overall. Weight: 11 oz. Standard model has blued or nickel finish, plastic grips; presentation model is gold-plated in walnut case. Standard model made from 1963 (22 S-L-LR) and 1964 (22 MRF) to date; gold model, 1965-1983.

Gold Presentation, one derringer **$350**
Gold Presentation, matched pair,
    consecutive numbers **595**
Standard Model **185**

REVOLVERS

NOTE

Only High Standard Revolvers can be found in this section. For Automatic Pistols and Derringers see the preceding sections. For a complete listing of High Standard handguns, please refer to the Index.

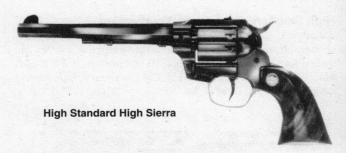

High Standard High Sierra

High Standard Camp Gun **$200**
Same as Sentinel Mark I/Mark IV, except has 6-inch bbl., adj. rear sight, target-style checkered walnut stocks. Caliber: 22 LR or 22 WMR. Made 1976-1983.

**High Standard Double-Nine DA Revolve
—Aluminum Frame** **$215**
Western-style version of Sentinel. Blued or nickel finish with simulated ivory, ebony or stag grips. 5.5-inch bbl. 11 inches overall. Weight: 27.25 oz. Made 1959-1971.

High Standard Double-Nine Deluxe **$225**
Same as Double-Nine — Steel Frame, except has adj. target rear sight. Introduced in 1971. Discontinued.

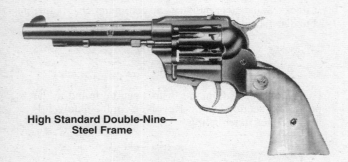

**High Standard Double-Nine—
Steel Frame**

High Standard Double-Nine—Steel Frame **$250**
Similar to Double-Nine—Aluminum Frame, with same general specifications, except has extra cylinder for 22 WMR, walnut stocks. Introduced in 1971. Discontinued.

High Standard Durango **$190**
Similar to Double-Nine—Steel Frame, except 22 LR only, available with 4.5- and 5.5-inch bbls. Made 1971-73.

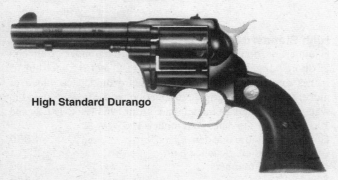

High Standard Durango

High Standard High Sierra DA Revolver
Similar to Double-Nine—Steel Frame, except has 7-inch octagon bbl., gold-plated grip frame; fixed or adj. sights. Made 1973-1983.
With fixed sights **$190**
With adj. sights **250**

High Standard Hombre **$195**
Similar to Double-Nine—Steel Frame, except 22 LR only, lacks single-action type ejector rod and tube, has 4.5-inch bbl. Made 1971-73.

High Standard Kit Gun

High Standard Kit Gun DA Revolver **$175**
Solid frame, swing-out cylinder. Caliber: 22 LR. 9-shot cylinder. 4-inch bbl. 9 inches overall. Weight: 19 oz. Adj. rear sight, ramp front. Blued finish. Checkered walnut stocks. Made 1970-73.

**High Standard Longhorn
Aluminum Frame**

High Standard Longhorn — Aluminum Frame
Similar to Double-Nine—Aluminum Frame. Longhorn hammer spur. Blued finish 4.5-inch bbl. with simulated pearl grips; 5.5-inch, simulated stag grips; 9.5-inch, walnut grips. Latter model made 1960-1971, others made 1961-66.
With 4.5- or 5.5-inch bbl. **$160**
With 9.5-inch bbl. **225**

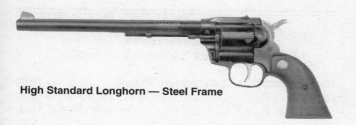

High Standard Longhorn — Steel Frame

High Standard Longhorn — Steel Frame
Similar to Double-Nine — Steel Frame, except has 9.5-inch bbl.; available with fixed or adj. sights. Made 1971-1983
With Fixed Sights **$180**
With Adj. Sights **295**

High Standard Natchez

High Standard Natchez **$130**
Similar to Double-Nine — Aluminum Frame, except 4.5-inch bbl. (10 inches overall, weighs 25.25 oz.), blued finish, simulated ivory bird'shead grips. Made 1961-66.

High Standard Posse

High Standard Posse **$135**
Similar to Double-Nine — Aluminum Frame, except 3.5-inch bbl. (9 inches overall, weighs 23.25 oz.), blued finish, brass-grip frame and trigger guard, walnut grips. Made 1961-66.

High Standard Sentinel

High Standard Sentinel DA Revolver **$315**
Solid frame, swing-out cylinder. Caliber: 22 LR. 9-shot cylinder. Bbls.: 3-, 4- or 6-inch. 9 inches overall w/4inch-bbl. Weight: 19 oz. w/4-inch bbl. Fixed sights. Aluminum frame. Blued or nickel finish. Checkered grips. Made 1955-56.

High Standard Sentinel Deluxe

High Standard Sentinel Deluxe **$260**
Same as Sentinel, except 4- or 6-inch bbls. only, has wide trigger, movable rear sight, two-piece square-butt grips. Made 1957-1974. *Note:* Designated Sentinel after 1971.

High Standard Sentinel Imperial **$245**
Same as Sentinel, except has onyx-black or nickel finish two-piece checkered walnut grips, ramp front sight. Made 1962-65.

High Standard Sentinel I

High Standard Sentinel I DA Revolver
Steel frame. Caliber: 22 LR. 9-shot cylinder. Bbl. lengths: 2-, 3-, 4-inch. 6.88 inches overall w/2-inch bbl. Weight: 21.5 oz. w/2-inch bbl. Ramp front sight, fixed or adj. rear. Blued or nickel finish. Smooth walnut stocks. Made 1974-1983.
With Fixed Sights **$255**
With Adj. Sights **275**

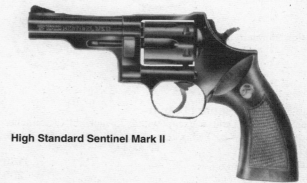

High Standard Sentinel Mark II

High Standard Sentinel Mark II DA Revolver **$295**
Caliber: 357 Magnum. 6-shot cylinder. Bbl. lengths: 2.5-, 4-, 6-inch. 9 inches overall with 4-inch bbl. Weight: 38 oz. w/4-inch bbl. Fixed sights. Blued finish. Walnut service or combat-style stocks. Made 1974-76.

High Standard Sentinel Mark III

High Standard Sentinel Mark III **$300**
Same as Sentinel Mark II, except has ramp front and adj. rear sights. Weight: 40 oz. w/4-inch bbl. Blued finish. Made 1974-1976.

High Standard Sentinel Mark IV
Same as Sentinel Mark I, except in caliber 22 WMR. Made 1974-1983.
With Fixed Sights **$250**
With Adj. Sights 275

High Standard Sentinel Snub

High Standard Sentinel Snub
Same as Sentinel Deluxe, except with 2.75-inch bbl. (7.25 inches overall, weighs 15 oz.), checkered bird's head-type grips. Made 1957-1974.
Blued Finish **$180**
Nickel Finish 200

HIGH STANDARD MFG. CO., INC.
Houston, Texas
Distributed from Hartford, Connecticut

High Standard 10X Automatic Pistol **$560**
Caliber: 22 LR. 10-shot magazine. 5.5-inch bbl. 9.5 inches overall. Weight: 45 oz. Checkered walnut grips. Blued finish. Made from 1994 to date.

High Standard Citation MS Auto Pistol **$325**
Similar to the Supermatic Citation, except has 10-inch bbl. 14 inches overall. Weight: 49 oz. Made from 1994 to date.

High Standard Olympic I.S.U. Automatic Pistol
Same specifications as the 1958 I.S.U. issue. *See* listing under previous High Standard Section.
Olympic I.S.U. Model **$425**
Olympic I.S.U. Military Model 335

High Standard Sport King Auto Pistol **$260**
Caliber: 22 LR. 10-shot magazine. 4.5- or 6.75-inch bbl. 8.5 or 10.75 inches overall. Weight: 44 oz. (4.5-inch bbl.); 46 oz. (6.75-inch bbl.). Fixed sights, slide mounted. Checkered walnut grips. Parkerized finish. Made from 1994 to date.

High Standard Supermatic Citation Auto Pistol
Caliber: 22 LR. 10-shot magazine. 5.5- or 7.75-inch bbl. 9.5 or 11.75 inches overall. Weight: 44 oz. (5.5-inch bbl.); 46 oz. (7.75-inch bbl.). Frame-mounted, micro-adj. rear sight; undercut ramp front sight. Blued or Parkerized finish. Made from 1994 to date.
Supermatic Citation Model **$295**
22 Short Conversion 260

High Standard Supermatic Tournament **$295**
Caliber: 22 LR. 10-shot magazine. Bbl. length: 4.5, 5.5, or 6.75 inches. Overall length: 8.5, 9.5 or 10.75 inches. Weight: 43, 44 or 45 oz. depending on bbl. length. Micro-adj. rear sight; undercut ramp front sight. Checkered walnut grips. Parkerized finish. Made from 1994 to date.

High Standard Supermatic Trophy
Caliber: 22 LR. 10-shot magazine. 5.5 or 7.25-inch bbl. 9.5 or 11.25 inches overall. Weight: 44 oz. w/5.5-inch bbl. Micro-adj. rear sight, undercut ramp front sight. Checkered walnut grips w/thumbrest. Blued or Parkerized finish. Made from 1994 to date.
Supermatic Trophy **$345**
22 Short Conversion 250

High Standard Victor Automatic
Caliber: 22 LR. 10-shot magazine. 4.5- or 5.5-inch bbl. 8.5 or 9.5 inches overall. Weight: 45 oz. (4.5-inch bbl.); 46 oz. (5.5-inch bbl.). Bbl.-mounted rib w/micro-adj. rear sight; post front sight. Checkered walnut grips. Blued or Parkerized finish. Made from 1994 to date.
Victor Model **$355**
22 Short Conversion 265

NOTE

After June 1, 1995 all High Standard pistols were drilled and tapped to accept scope mounts.

HOPKINS & ALLEN ARMS CO.
Norwich, Connecticut

Hopkins & Allen Revolvers
See listings of comparable Harrington & Richardson and Iver Johnson models for values.

INTERARMS
Alexandria, Virginia

See also Bersa Pistol.

Interarms/Helwan Brigadier Auto Pistol

Interarms/Helwan Brigadier Auto Pistol **$175**
Caliber: 9mm Parabellum. 8-shot magazine. 4.25-inch bbl. 8 inches overall. Weight: 32 oz. Sights: blade front; dovetailed rear. Blued finish. Grooved plastic grips.

Interarms Virginian Dragoon SA Revolver
Calibers: 357 Magnum, 44 Magnum, 45 Colt. 6-shot cylinder. Bbs.: 5- (not available in 44 Magnum), 6-, 7.5-, 8.38-inch (latter only in 44 Magnum w/adj. sights). 11.88 inches overall w/6-inch bbl. Weight: 48 oz. w/6-inch bbl. Fixed sights or micrometer rear and ramp front sights. Blued finish with color-casetreated frame. Smooth walnut stocks. SWISSAFE base pin safety system. Manufactured by Interarms Industries Inc., Midland, VA. 1977-1984.
Standard Dragoon **$250**
Engraved Dragoon. 495
Deputy Model 260

**Interarms Virginian
SA Revolver**

Interarms Virginian Revolver Silhouette Model . . **$395**
Same general specifications as regular model except designed in stainless steel with untapered bull bbl., lengths of 7.5, 8.38 and 10.5 inches. Made 1985-86.

Interarms Virginian SA Revolver **$295**
See listing under Hammerli (manufacturer). Similar to Colt Single-Action Army, except has base pin safety system.

INTRATEC U.S.A. INC.
Miami, Florida

Intratec Category 9 DAO Semiautomatic **$195**
Blowback action w/polymer frame. Caliber: 9mm Parabellum. 8-shot magazine. 3-inch bbl. 7.7 inches overall. Weight: 18 oz. Textured black polymer grips. Matte black finish. Made from 1993 to date.

Intratec Category 40 DAO Semiautomatic **$215**
Locking-breech action w/polymer frame. Caliber: 40 S&W. 7-shot magazine. 3.25-inch bbl. 8 inches overall. Weight: 21 oz. Textured black polymer grips. Matte black finish. Made from 1994 to date.

Intratec Category 45 DAO Semiautomatic **$215**
Locking-breech action w/polymer frame. Caliber: 45 ACP. 6-shot magazine. 3.25-inch bbl. 8 inches overall. Weight: 21 oz. Textured black polymer grips. Matte black finish. Made from 1994 to date.

Intratec Model ProTec 22 DA Semiautomatic
Caliber: 25 ACP. 10-shot magazine. 2.5-inch bbl. 5 inches overall. Weight: 14 oz. Wraparound composition grips. Black Teflon, satin grey or Tec-Kote finish. Made from 1992 to date.
ProTec 22 Standard **$65**
ProTec 22 w/Satin or Tec-Kote. 70

Intratec Model ProTec 25 DA Semiautomatic
Caliber: 25 ACP. 8-shot magazine. 2.5-inch bbl. 5 inches overall. Weight: 14 oz. Fixed sights. Wraparound composition grips. Black Teflon, satin grey or Tec-Kote finish. Made from 1991 to date. *Note:* Formerly Model Tec-25; name changed about 1995.
ProTec 25 Standard **$70**
ProTec 25 w/Satin or Tec-Kote. 75

Intratec Model Tec-9 Semiautomatic
Caliber: 9mm Luger/Parabellum. 20- or 36-round magazine. 5-inch bbl. Weight: 50-51 oz. Open fixed front sight, adj. rear. Military nonglare blued or stainless finish.
Tec-9 w/Blued Finish **$245**
Tec-9 w/Electroless Nickel Finish 295
Tec 9S w/Stainless Finish 305

Intratec Model Tec-9M Semiautomatic
Same specifications as Model Tec-9, except has 3-inch bbl. without shroud and 20-round magazine. Blued or stainless finish.
Tec-9M w/Blued Finish **$235**
Tec-9MS w/Stainless Finish 280

Intratec Model Tec-22T Semiautomatic

Caliber: 22 LR. 10/22-type 30-shot magazine. 4-inch bbl. 11.19 inches overall. Weight: 30 oz. Protected post front sight, adj. rear sight. Matte black or Tec-Kote finish. Made from 1989 to date.
Tec-22T Standard **$155**
Tec-22TK Tec-Kote **175**

Intratec Model Tec Double Derringer **$90**

Calibers: 22 WRF, 32 H&R Mag., 38 Special. 2-shot capacity. 3-inch bbl. 4.63 inches overall. Weight: 13 oz. Fixed sights. Matte black finish.

JAPANESE MILITARY PISTOLS
Tokyo, Japan
Manufactured by Government Plant

Japanese Model 14 (1925)

Japanese Model 14 (1925) Automatic Pistol **$495**

Modification of the Nambu Model 1914, changes chiefly intended to simplify mass production. Standard round trigger guard or oversized guard for use with gloves. Caliber: 8mm Nambu. 8-shot magazine. 4.75-inch bbl. 9 inches overall. Weight: about 29 oz. Fixed sights. Blued finish. Grooved wood stocks. Introduced 1925; mfd. through WW II.

Japanese Model 26

Japanese Model 26 DAO Revolver **$355**

Top-break frame. Caliber: 9mm, 6-shot cylinder w/automatic extractor/ejector. 4.7-inch bbl. Adopted by the Japanese Army from 1893 to 1914, when replaced by the Model 14 Automatic Pistol, but remained in service through World War II.

Japanese Model 94

Japanese Model 94 (1934) Automatic Pistol **$225**

Poorly design and constructed, this pistol can be fired merely by applying pressure on the sear, which is exposed on the left side. Caliber: 8mm Nambu. 6-shot magazine. 3.13-inch bbl. 7.13 inches overall. Weight: about 27 oz. Fixed sights. Blued finish. Hard rubber or wood stocks. Introduced in 1934, principally for export to Latin American countries, production continued thru WW II.

Japanese Nambu Model 1914 Automatic Pistol . . **$465**

Original Japanese service pistol, resembles Luger in appearance and Glisenti in operation. Caliber: 8mm Nambu. 7-shot magazine. 4.5-inch bbl. 9 inches overall. Weight: about 30 oz. Fixed front sight, adj. rear sight. Blued finish. Checkered wood stocks. Made 1914-1925.

JENNINGS FIREARMS INC.
Irvine, California

Jennings Model J
Auto Pistol

Jennings Model J Auto Pistol

Calibers: 22 LR, 25 ACP. 6-shot magazine. 2.5-inch bbl. About 5 inches overall. Weight: 13 oz. Fixed sights. Chrome, satin nickel or black Teflon finish. Walnut, grooved black Cycolac or resin-impregnated wood grips. Made from 1981 to date.
Model J-22. . . . . **$75**
Model J-25. . . . . **60**

Jennings Model M38 Bryco Auto Pistol **$100**
Calibers: 32 ACP, 380 ACP. 6-shot magazine. 2.81-inch bbl. 5.31 inches overall. Weight: 15 oz. Fixed sights. Chrome, satin nickel or black Teflon finish. Walnut, grooved black Cycolac or resin-impregnated wood grips. Made from 1988 to date.

Jennings Model M48 Bryco Auto Pistol **$110**
Calibers: 380 ACP, 9mm. 7-shot magazine. 4-inch bbl. 6.69 inches overall. Weight: 20 oz. Fixed sights. Chrome, satin nickel or black Teflon finish. Smooth wood or black Teflon grips. Made from 1989 to date.

Jennings Model M58 Bryco Auto Pistol **$120**
Caliber: 380 ACP. 13-shot magazine. 3.75-inch bbl. 5.5 inches overall. Weight: 30 oz. Fixed sights. Chrome, satin nickel, blued or black Teflon finish. Smooth wood or black Teflon grips. Made from 1993 to date.

Jennings Model M59 Bryco Auto Pistol **$125**
Caliber: 9mm Parabellum. 13-shot magazine. 4-inch bbl. 6.5 inches overall. Weight: 33 oz. Fixed sights. Chrome, satin nickel, blued or black Teflon finish. Smooth wood or black Teflon grips. Made from 1994 to date.

IVER JOHNSON'S ARMS, INC.
Jacksonville, Arkansas

Operation of this company dates back to 1871, when Iver Johnson and Martin Bye partnered to manufacture metallic cartridge revolvers. Johnson became the sole owner and changed the name to Iver Johnson's Arms & Cycle Works which it was known as for almost 100 years. Modern management shortened the name, and after several owner changes, the firm was moved from Massachusetts, its original base, to Jacksonville, Arkansas. In 1987, the American Military Arms Corporation (AMAC) acquired the operation, which subsequently ceased in 1993.

AUTOMATIC PISTOLS

> **NOTE**
>
> For ease in finding a particular firearm, Iver Johnson handguns are divided into two sections: Automatic Pistols (below) and Revolvers, which follows. For the complete handgun listing, please refer to the Index.

Iver Johnson 9mm DA Automatic

Iver Johnson 9mm DA Automatic **$295**
Caliber: 9mm. 6-round magazine. 3-inch bbl. 6.5 inches overall. Weight: 26 oz. Sights: blade front, adj. rear. Smooth hardwood grip. Blued or matte blued finish. Introduced in 1986.

Iver Johnson Compact 25 ACP **$150**
Bernardelli V/P design. Caliber: 25 ACP. 5-shot magazine. 2.13-inch bbl. 4.13 inches overall. Weight: 9.3 oz. Fixed sights. Checkered composition grips. Blued slide, matte blue frame and color-casehardened trigger. Made from 1991 to 1993.

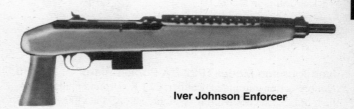

Iver Johnson Enforcer

Iver Johnson Enforcer **$345**
Caliber: 30 US Carbine. 5-, 15-, or 30-round magazine. Semiautomatic. 9.5-inch bbl. Weight: 5.5 lbs. Adj. sights. Walnut stock. Made mid-1980s to 1993.

Iver Johnson PP30 Super Enforcer Automatic . . **$395**
Caliber: 30 US Carbine. 15- or 30-shot magazine. 9.5-inch bbl. 17 inches overall. Weight: 4 pounds. Adj. peep rear sight; blade front. American walnut stock. Made 1984-86.

Iver Johnson Pony

Iver Johnson Pony Automatic Pistol **$260**
Caliber: 380 Auto. 6-shot magazine. 3.1-inch bbl. 6.1 inches overall. Blue, matte or nickel finish. Weight: 20 oz. Wooden grips. Smallest of the locked breech automatics. Made 1982-88; reintroduced 1990-1993.

Iver Johnson Model TP DA Automatic **$165**
Calibers: 22 LR, 25 ACP. 7-shot magazine. 2.85-inch bbl. 5.39 inches overall. Blue finish. Weight: 14.46 oz. Introduced in 1982. Discontinued.

Iver Johnson Model TP

Iver Johnson Model 55-S

Iver Johnson Model TP22 DA Pocket Pistol **$150**
Double-action automatic. Caliber: 22 LR. 7-round magazine. 3-inch bbl. 5.5 inches overall. Weight: 12 oz. Black plastic grips and blued finish. Discontinued 1990.

Iver Johnson Model TP25 Pocket Pistol **$115**
Same general specifications as the Model TP22, except made in 25 ACP caliber. Discontinued.

Iver Johnson Trailsman Automatic Pistol
Caliber: 22 LR. 10-shot magazine. 4.5 or 6-inch bbl. 8.75 inches overall w/4.5-inch bbl. Weight: 46 oz. Fixed target-type sights. Checkered composition grips. Made 1984-1990.
Standard Model $175
Deluxe Model **195**

REVOLVERS

> **NOTE**
>
> Only Iver Johnson Revolvers can be found in the section below. For Pistols, please see the preceding pages. For a complete listing, please refere to the Index.

Iver Johnson Model 55-S Revolver **$125**
Same general specifications as the Model 55 except for 2.5-inch bbl. and small molded pocket-size grip.

**Iver Johnson Model 56
Blank Revolver**

Iver Johnson Model 56 Blank Revolver **$65**
Solid frame. Caliber: 22 blanks only. 8-shot cylinder. 2.5-inch solid bbl., 6.75 inches overall. Weight: 10 oz.

Iver Johnson Model 57A

Iver Johnson Model 55A

Iver Johnson Model 55 Target DA Revolver **$115**
Solid frame. Caliber: 22 LR. 8-shot cylinder. Bbl. lengths: 4.5-, 6-inch. 10.75 inches overall (6-inch bbl.). Weight: 30.5 oz. (6-inch bbl.). Fixed sights. Blued finish. Walnut stocks. *Note:* Original model designation was 55 changed to 55A when loading gate was added in 1961. Made 1955-1977.

Iver Johnson Model 57A Target DA Revolver . . . **$135**
Solid frame. Caliber: 22 LR. 8-shot cylinder. Bbl. lengths: 4.5-, 6-inch. 10.75 inches overall (6-inch bbl.). Weight: 30.5 oz., 6-inch bbl. Adj. sights. Blued finish. Walnut stocks. *Note:* Original model designation was 57, changed to 57A when loading gate was added in 1961. Made 1956-1975.

Iver Johnson Model 66 Trailsman

**Iver Johnson Model 1900
Double Action**

Iver Johnson Model 66 Trailsman DA Revolver . . $95
Hinged frame. Rebounding hammer. Caliber: 22 LR. 8-shot cylinder. 6-inch bbl. 11 inches overall. Weight: 34 oz. Adj. sights. Blued finish. Walnut stocks. Made 1958-1975.

Iver Johnson Model 1900 Target DA Revolver . . $150
Solid frame. Caliber: 22 LR. 7-shot cylinder. Bbl. lengths: 6- and 9.5-inch. Fixed sights. Blued finish. Checkered walnut stocks. This earlier model does not have counterbored chambers as in the Target Sealed 8. Made 1925-1942.

Iver Johnson Model 67 Viking

Iver Johnson American Bulldog

Iver Johnson Model 67 Viking DA Revolver $110
Hinged frame. Caliber: 22 LR. 8-shot cylinder. Bbl. lengths: 4.5- and 6-inch. 11 inches overall w/6-inch bbl. Weight: 34 oz. w/6-inch bbl. Adj. sights. Walnut stocks w/thumbrest. Made 1964-1975.

Iver Johnson American Bulldog DA Revolver
Solid frame. Calibers: 22 LR, 22 WMR, 38 Special. 6-shot cylinder in 22, 5-shot in 38. Bbl. lengths: 2.5-, 4-inch. 9 inches overall w/4-inch bbl. Weight: 30 oz. w/4-inch bbl. Adj. sights. Blued or nickel finish. Plastic stocks. Made 1974-76.
38 Special $145
Other calibers 125

Iver Johnson Armsworth Model 855 SA $135
Hinged frame. Caliber: 22 LR. 8-shot cylinder. 6-inch bbl. 10.75 inches overall. Weight: 30 oz. Adj. sights. Blued finish. Checkered walnut one-piece grip. Adj. finger rest. Made 1955-57.

**Iver Johnson Model 67S
Viking Snub**

Iver Johnson Model 67S Viking Snub Revolver . . $125
DA. Hinged frame. Calibers: 22 LR, 32 S&W Short and Long, 38 S&W. 8-shot cylinder in 22, 5-shot in 32 and 38 calibers. 2.75-inch bbl. Weight: 25 oz. Adj. sights. Tenite grips. Made 1964-1975.

Iver Johnson Model 1900 DA Revolver $110
Solid frame. Calibers: 22 LR, 32 S&W, 32 S&W Long, 38 S&W. 7-shot cylinder (22 cal.), 6-shot (32 S&W), 5-shot (32 S&W Long, 38 S&W). Bbl. lengths: 2.5-, 4.5- and 6-inch. Weight: 12 oz., 32 S&W w/2.5-inch bbl. Fixed sights. Blued or nickel finish. Hard rubber stocks. Made 1900-1947.

Iver Johnson Cadet

Iver Johnson Cattleman Buntline

Iver Johnson Cadet DA Revolver **$135**
Solid frame. Calibers: 22 LR, 22 WMR, 32 S&W Long, 38 S&W, 38 Special. 6- or 8-shot cylinder in 22, 5-shot in other calibers. 2.5-inch bbl. 7 inches overall. Weight: 22 oz. Fixed sights. Blued finish; nickel finish also available in 32 and 38 Special models. Plastic stocks. *Note:* Loading gate added in 1961, 22 cylinder capacity changed from 8 to 6 rounds in 1975. Made 1955-1977. *See* illustration preceding page.

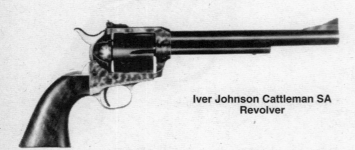

Iver Johnson Cattleman SA Revolver

Iver Johnson Cattleman SA Revolver
Patterned after the Colt Army SA Revolver. Calibers: 357 Magnum, 44 Magnum, 45 Colt. 6-shot cylinder. Bbl. lengths: 4.75-, 5.5- (not available in 44), 6- (44 only), 7.25-inch. Weight: about 41 oz. Fixed sights. Blued bbl. and cylinder color-casehardened frame, brass grip frame. One-piece walnut stock. Made by Aldo Uberti, Brescia, Italy, 1973-78.
44 Magnum **$260**
Other calibers 195

Iver Johnson Cattleman Buckhorn SA Revolver
Same as standard Cattleman except has adj. rear and ramp front sights. Bbls.: 4.75- (44 only), 5.75- (not available in 44), 6- (44 only), 7.5-, 12-inch. Weight: almost 44 oz. Made 1973-78.
357 Magnum or 45 Colt, 12-inch bbl. **$300**
357 Magnum or 45 Colt, other bbls. 330
44 Magnum, 12-inch bbl. 300
44 Magnum, other bbls. 330

Iver Johnson Cattleman Buntline SA Revolver
Same as Cattleman Buckhorn, except has 18-inch bbl., walnut shoulder stock with brass fittings. Weight: about 56 oz. Made 1973-78.
44 Magnum **$385**
Other calibers 345

Iver Johnson Cattleman Trailblazer **$170**
Similar to Cattleman Buckhorn, except 22 caliber has interchangeable 22 LR and 22 WMR cylinders, 5.5- or 6.5-inch bbl. Weight: about 40 oz. Made 1973-78.

Iver Johnson Champion

Iver Johnson Champion 22 Target SA **$185**
Hinged frame. Caliber: 22 LR. 8-shot cylinder. Single action. Counterbored chambers as in Sealed 8 models. 6-inch bbl. 10.75 inches overall. Weight: 28 oz. Adj. target sights. Blued finish. Checkered walnut stocks, adj. finger rest. Made 1938-1948.

Iver Johnson Deluxe Target

Iver Johnson Deluxe Target **$170**
Same as Sportsman, except has adj. sights. Made 1975-76.

Iver Johnson Sealed 8

Iver Johnson Protector Sealed 8 DA Revolver . . $150
Hinged frame. Caliber: 22 LR. 8-shot cylinder. 2.5-inch bbl. 7.25 inches overall. Weight: 20 oz. Fixed sights. Blued finish. Checkered walnut stocks. Made 1933-1949.

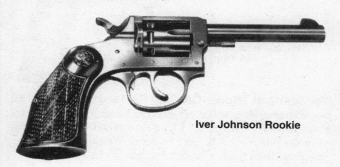

Iver Johnson Rookie

Iver Johnson Rookie DA Revolver $95
Solid frame. Caliber: 38 Special. 5-shot cylinder. 4-inch bbl. 9-inches overall. Weight: 30 oz. Fixed sights. Blued or nickel finish. Plastic stocks. Made 1975-77.

Iver Johnson Safety Hammer

Iver Johnson Safety Hammer DA Revolver $125
Hinged frame. Calibers: 22 LR, 32 S&W, 32 S&W Long, 38 S&W. 7-shot cylinder (22 cal.), 6-shot (32 S&W Long), 5-shot (32 S&W, 38 S&W). Bbl. lengths: 2, 3, 3.25, 4, 5 or 6 inches. Weight with 4-inch bbl.: 15 oz., 22, 32 S&W; 19.5 oz., 32 S&W Long, 19 oz., 38 S&W. Fixed sights. Blued or nickel finish. Hard rubber stocks, round butt; square butt, rubber and walnut stocks available. *Note:* 32 S&W Long and 38 S&W models built on heavy frame. Made 1892-1950.

Iver Johnson Safety Hammer

Iver Johnson Safety Hammerless DA Revolver . . $135
Hinged frame. Calibers: 22 LR, 32 S&W, 32 S&W Long, 38 S&W. 7-shot cylinder (22 cal), 6-shot (32 S&W Long), 5-shot (32 S&W, 38 S&W). Bbl. lengths: 2, 3, 3.25, 4, 5 or 6 inches. Weight with 4-inch bbl.: 15 oz., 22, 32 S&W; 20.5 oz., 32 S&W Long, 20 oz., 38 S&W. Fixed sights. Blued or nickel finish. Hard rubber stocks, round butt. Square butt, rubber and walnut stocks available. *Note:* 32 S&W Long & 38 S&W models built on heavy frame. Made 1895-1950.

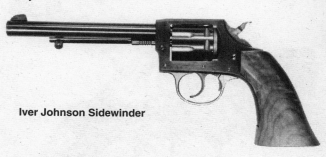

Iver Johnson Sidewinder

Iver Johnson Sidewinder DA Revolver $135
Solid frame. Caliber: 22 LR. 6- or 8-shot cylinder. Bbl. lengths: 4.75-, 6-inch. 11.25 inches overall w/6-inch bbl. Weight: 31 oz. w/6-inch bbl. Fixed sights. Blued or nickel finish w/plastic "staghorn" stocks; also color-casehardened frame with walnut stocks. *Note:* Cylinder capacity changed from 8 to 6 rounds in 1975. Intro. 1961; disc.

Iver Johnson Sidewinder "S" $145
Same as Sidewinder, except has interchangeable cylinders in 22 LR and 22 WMR, adj. sights. Introduced 1974; discontinued.

Iver Johnson Sportsman DA Revolver $95
Solid frame. Caliber: 22 LR. 6-shot cylinder. Bbl. lengths: 4.75-, 6-inch. 10.75 inches overall w/6-inch bbl. Weight: 30.5 oz. w/6-inch bbl. Fixed sights. Blued finish. Plastic stocks. Made 1974-76.

Iver Johnson Supershot 9-Shot DA Revolver . . . $135
Same as Supershot Sealed 8, except has nine non-counterbored chambers. Made 1929-1949.

Iver Johnson Supershot 22 DA Revolver $105
Hinged frame. Caliber: 22 LR. 7-shot cylinder. 6-inch bbl. Fixed sights. Blued finish. Checkered walnut stocks. This earlier model does not have counterbored chambers as in the Supershot Sealed 8. Made 1929-1949.

Iver Johnson Supershot Model 844 DA $230
Hinged frame. Caliber: 22 LR. 8-shot cylinder. Bbl. lengths: 4.5- or 6-inch. 9.25 inches overall w/4.5-inch bbl. Weight: 27 oz. w/4.5-inch bbl. Adj. sights. Blued finish. Checkered walnut one-piece grip. Made 1955-56.

Iver Johnson Supershot Sealed 8 DA Revolver . . $175
Hinged frame. Caliber: 22 LR. 8-shot cylinder. 6-inch bbl. 10.75 inches overall. Weight: 24 oz. Adj. target sights. Blued finish. Checkered walnut stocks. Postwar model does not have adj. finger rest as earlier version. Made 1931-1957.

Iver Johnson Supershot Sealed 8

Iver Johnson Swing Out DA Revolver

Iver Johnson Swing Out DA Revolver
Calibers: 22 LR, 22 WMR, 32 S&W Long, 38 Special. 6-shot cylinder in 22, 5-shot in 32 and 38. Bbls.: plain, 2-, 3-, 4-inch, vent rib, 4- 6-inch. 8.75 inches overall w/4-inch bbl. Fixed or adj. sights. Blued or nickel finish. Walnut stocks. Made in 1977.
w/plain Barrel, Fixed Sights **$135**
w/ventilated Rib, Adj. Sights **195**

Iver Johnson Target 9-Shot DA Revolver $145
Same as Target Sealed 8, except has nine non-counterbored chambers. Made 1929-1946.

Iver Johnson Target Sealed 8

Iver Johnson Target Sealed 8 DA Revolver $155
Solid frame. Caliber: 22 LR. 8-shot cylinder. Bbl. lengths: 6- and 10-inch. 10.75 inches overall w/6-inch bbl. Weight: 24 oz. w/6-inch bbl. Fixed sights. Blued finish. Checkered walnut stocks. Made 1931-1957.

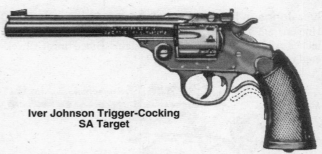

**Iver Johnson Trigger-Cocking
SA Target**

Iver Johnson Trigger-Cocking SA Target $165
Hinged frame. First pull on trigger cocks hammer, second pull releases hammer. Caliber: 22 LR. 8-shot cylinder, counterbored chambers. 6-inch bbl. 10.75 inches overall. Weight: 24 oz. Adj. target sights. Blued finish. Checkered walnut stocks. Made 1940-47.

KAHR ARMS
Blauvelt, New York

Kahr Model K9

Kahr Model K9 DA Auto Pistol $450
Caliber: 9mm Parabellum. 8-shot magazine. 3.5-inch bbl. 6 inches overall. Weight: 24 oz. Fixed sights. Blued finish. Wraparound smooth hardwood grips. Made from 1994 to date.

KBI, INC
Harrisburg, Pennsylvania

KBI Model PSP-25 Auto Pistol $195
Caliber: 25 ACP, 6-shot magazine. 2.13-inch bbl., 4.13 inches overall. Weight: 9.5 oz. All-steel construction with dual safety system. Made from 1994 to date.

KIMBER OF AMERICA, INC
Clackamas, Oregon

Kimber Model Classic .45
Caliber: 45 ACP, 8- and 10-shot magazines. 5-inch bbl., 8.5 inches overall. McCormick low-profile type sights. Made from 1994 to date.
Custom **$430**
Custom Stainless **490**
Royal **535**
Gold Match **690**

LAHTI PISTOLS
Mfd. by Husqvarna Vapenfabriks A. B. Huskvarna, Sweden, and Valtion Kivaar Tedhas ("VKT") Jyväskyla, Finland

Lahti Automatic Pistol

Lahti Automatic Pistol
Caliber: 9mm Luger. 8-shot magazine. 4.75-inch bbl. Weight: about 46 oz. Fixed sights. Blued finish. Plastic stocks. Specifications given are those of the Swedish Model 40 but also apply in general to the Finnish Model L-35, which differs only slightly. A considerable number of Swedish Lahti pistols were imported and sold in the U.S., the Finnish Model, somewhat better made, is a rather rare pistol. Finnish Model L-35 adopted 1935; Swedish Model 40 adopted 1940; mfd. through 1944.
Finnish Model **$1180**
Swedish Model **475**

L.A.R. MANUFACTURING, INC.
West Jordan, Utah

L.A.R. Mark I Grizzly Win. Mag. Automatic Pistol
Calibers: 357 Mag., 45 ACP, 45 Win. Mag. 7-shot magazine. 6.5-inch bbl. 10.5 inches overall. Weight: 48 oz. Fully adj. sights. Checkered rubber combat-style grips. Blued finish. Made from 1983 to date. 8-inch and 10-inch barrels made from 1987 to date.
357 Mag. (6.5" barrel) **$660**
45 Win. Mag.(6.5" barrel) **635**
8-inch barrel **920**
10-inch barrel **995**

**L.A.R. Mark I
Grizzly Win. Mag.**

L.A.R. Mark IV Grizzly Automatic Pistol **$745**
Same general specifications as the L.A.R. Mark I, except chambered for 44 Magnum- has 5.5- or 6.5-inch bbl. beavertail grip safety, matte blue finish. Made from 1991 to date.

L.A.R. Mark V Auto Pistol **$795**
Similar to the Mark I, except chambered in 50 Action Express. 6-shot magazine, 5.4- or 6.5-inch bbl. 10.6 inches overall w/5.4-inch bbl. Weight: 56 oz. Checkered walnut grips. Made 1993 to date.

LIGNOSE PISTOLS
Suhl, Germany
Aktien-Gesellschaft "Lignose" Abteilung

The following Lignose pistols were manufactured from 1920 to the mid-1930s. They were also marketed under the Bergmann name.

Lignose Model 2 Pocket Auto Pistol **$160**
Conventional Browning type. Same general specifications as Einhand Model 2A, but lacks the one-hand operation.

Lignose Einhand Model 2A

Lignose Einhand Model 2A Pocket Auto Pistol . . **$225**
As the name implies, this pistol is designed for one-hand operation, pressure on a "trigger" at the front of the guard retracts the slide. Caliber: 25 Automatic (6.35 mm). 6-shot magazine. 2-inch bbl. 4.75 inches overall. Weight: about 14 oz. Blued finish. Hard rubber stocks.

Lignose Model 3A

Lignose Einhand Model 3A Pocket Auto Pistol. . . **$245**
Same as the Model 2A except has longer grip, 9-shot magazine,
weighs about 16 oz.

LLAMA HANDGUNS
Mfd. by Gabilondo y Cia, Vitoria, Spain
Imported by S.G.S., Wanamassa, New Jersey

AUTOMATIC PISTOLS

NOTE

For ease in finding a particular Llama handgun, the listings are divided into two groupings: Automatic Pistols
(below) and Revolvers, which follows. For a complete
listing of Llama handguns, please refer to the Index.

Llama Model IIIA Automatic Pistol **$250**
Caliber: 380 Auto. 7-shot magazine. 3.69-inch bbl. 6.5 inches
overall. Weight: 23 oz. Adj. target sights. Blued finish. Plastic
stocks. Intro. 1951; discontinued.

Llama Model IIIA
Second Issue

Llama Models IIIA, XA, XV Deluxe
Same as standard Model IIIA, XA and XV, except finish—
chrome engraved or blue engraved—and simulated pearl stocks.
Disc. 1984. (*See* photos, preceding page.)
Chrome-engraved Finish. **$260**
Blue-engraved Finish **220**

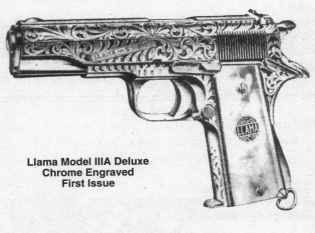

Llama Model IIIA Deluxe
Chrome Engraved
First Issue

Llama Model IIIA Deluxe
Blue Engraved
Second Issue

Llama Model VIII Automatic Pistol **$295**
Caliber: 38 Super. 9-shot magazine. 5-inch bbl. 8 1/2 inches
overall. Weight: 40 oz. Fixed sights. Blued finish. Wood stocks.
Introduced in 1952; discontinued.

Llama Models VIII, IXA, XI Deluxe
Same as standard Models VIII, IXA and XI, except fin-
ish—chrome engraved or blue engraved—and simulated pearl
stocks. Discontinued 1984.
Chrome-engraved Finish. **$335**
Blue-engraved Finish **370**

Llama Model IXA Automatic Pistol **$275**
Same as Model VIII, except caliber 45 Automatic, 7-shot magazine.

Llama Model XA Automatic Pistol **$220**
Same as Model IIIA, except caliber 32 Automatic, 8-shot magazine.

**Llama Model XA
First Issue**

Llama Model XI Automatic Pistol **$245**
Same as Model VIII, except caliber 9mm Luger.

Llama Model XV Automatic Pistol **$220**
Same as Model XA, except caliber 22 LR.

Llama Models BE-IIIA, BE-XA, BE-XV **$250**
Same as Models IIIA, XA and XV, except with blue-engraved
finish. Made 1977-1984.

Llama Models BE-VIII, BE-IXA, BE-XI Deluxe . . . **$320**
Same as Models VIII, IXA and XI, except with blue-engraved
finish. Made 1977-1984.

Llama Models C-IIIA, C-XA, C-XV **$320**
Same as Models IIIA, XA and XV, except in satin-chrome.

Llama Models C-VIII, C-IXA, C-XI **$320**
Same as Models VIII, IXA and XI, except in satin-chrome.

Llama Models CE-IIIA, CE-XA, CE-XV **$315**
Same as Models IIIA, XA and XV, except w/chrome-engraved
finish. Made 1977-1984.

Llama Models CE-VIII, CE-IXA, CE-XI **$395**
Same as Models VIII, IXA and XI, w/except chrome-engraved
finish. Made 1977-1984.

Llama Model C-XI

Llama Compact Frame Auto Pistol **$365**
Calibers: 9mm Para., 38 Super, 45 Auto. 7-, 8- or 9-shot. 5-inch
bbl. 7.88 inches overall. Weight: 34 oz. Blued, satin-chrome or
Duo-Tone finishes. Made 1990 to date; Duo-Tone discontinued
1993.

Llama Model CE-IIIA

Llama Duo-Tone Large Frame Auto Pistol **$295**
Caliber: 45 ACP. 7-shot magazine. 5-inch bbl. 8.5 inches overall.
Weight: 36 oz. Adj. rear sight. Blued finished with satin chrome.
Polymer black grips. Made 1990-93.

Llama Compact

Llama Duo-Tone Small Frame Auto Pistol **$295**
Calibers: 22 LR, 32 and 380 Auto. 7- or 8-shot magazine 3.69
inch bbl. 6.5 inches overall. Weight: 23 oz. Square-notch rear
sight, Patridge-type front. Blued finish with chrome. Made 1990-
1993.

Llama Model G-IIIA Deluxe **$850**
Same as Model IIIA, except is gold-damascened w/simulated
pearl stocks. Discontinued 1982.

Llama Large-Frame Automatic Pistol (IXA)
Caliber: 45 Auto. 7-shot magazine. 5-inch bbl. Weight: 2 lbs. 8
oz. Adj. rear sight, Patridge-type front. Walnut grips; teakwood
on satin chrome model; Later models with polymer grips. Made
from 1984 to date.
Blued Finish **$320**
Satin Chrome Finish **310**

Llama Large-Frame

Llama M-82 DA Auto

Llama M-82 DA Automatic Pistol $425
Caliber: 9mm Parabellum. 15-shot magazine. 4.25-inch bbl. 8 inches overall. Weight: 39 oz. Drift adj. rear sight. Matte blue finish. Matte black polymer grips. Made from 1988 to date.

Llama M-87 Comp Pistol $745
Caliber: 9mm Parabellum. 15-shot magazine. 5.5-inch bbl. 9.5 inches overall. Weight: 40 oz. Low-profile combat sights. Satin nickel finish. Matte black grip panels. Built-in ported compensator to minimize recoil and muzzle rise. Made 1989-1993.

Llama Omni 9mm Double-Action Automatic . . . $350
Same general specifications as 45 Omni, except chambered for 9mm with 13-shot magazine. Discontinued 1986.

Llama Omni

Llama Omni 45 Double-Action Automatic Pistol $375
Caliber: 45 Auto. 7-shot magazine. 4.25-inch bbl. 7.75 inches overall. Weight: 40 oz. Adj. rear sight, ramp front. Highly polished deep blue finish. Made 1984-86.

Llama Single-Action Automatic Pistol $345
Calibers: 38 Super, 9mm, 45 Auto. 9-shot magazine (7-shot for 45 Auto). 5-inch bbl. 8.5 inches overall. Weight: 2 lhs. 8 oz. Introduced in 1981.

Llama Small-Frame Automatic Pistol
Calibers: 380 Auto (9mm)- 7-shot magazine; 22 RF (8 shot magazine). 3.69-inch bbl. Weight: 23 oz. Adjust able rear sight, Patridge-type front. Blued or satin-chrome finish.
Blued Finish **$265**
Satin-Chrome Finish **325**

REVOLVERS

> **NOTE**
>
> This section contains only Llama Revolvers. Pistols may be found in the preceding section. For a complete listing of Llama handguns, please refer to the Index.

Llama Comanche I

Llama Comanche I Double-Action Revolver $180
Same general specifications as Martial 22. Made 1977-1983.

Llama Comanche II $195
Same general specifications as Martial 38. Made 1977-1983.

Llama Comanche III Double-Action Revolver . . . $250
Caliber: 357 Magnum. 6-shot cylinder. 4-inch bbl. 9.25 inches overall. Weight: 36 oz. Adj. rear sight, ramp front. Blued finish. Checkered walnut stocks. Made from 1975 to date. *Note:* Prior to 1977, this model was designated "Comanche."

Llama Comanche III Chrome $295
Same gen. specifications as Comanche III, except has satin chrome finish, 4- or 6-inch barrels. Made 1979 to date.

Llama Comanche III Chrome

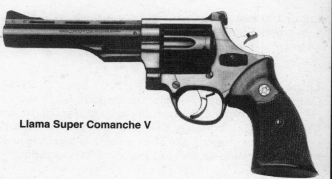

Llama Super Comanche V

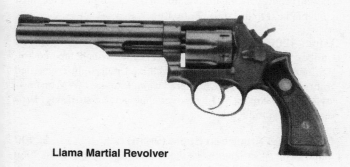

Llama Martial Revolver

Llama Martial Double-Action Revolver **$215**
Calibers: 22 LR, 38 Special. 6-shot cylinder. Bbl. lengths: 4-inch (38 Special only), 6-inch. 11.25 inches overall with 6-inch bbl. Weight: about 36 oz. with 6-inch bbl. Target sights. Blued finish. Checkered walnut stocks. Made 1969-1976.

**Llama Martial Deluxe
Gold Damascened**

Llama Martial Double-Action Deluxe
Same as standard Martial, except finish—satin chrome chrome engraved, blue engraved, gold damascened; has simulated pearl stocks. Discontinued 1978.

Satin-chrome Finish	$ 275
Chrome-engraved Finish	325
Blue-engraved Finish	300
Gold-damascened Finish	1500

Llama Super Comanche IV DA Revolver **$295**
Caliber: 44 Magnum. 6-shot cylinder. 6-inch bbl. 11.75 inches overall. Weight: 3 lbs. 2 oz. Sights: adj. rear ramp front. Polished deep blue finish. Checkered walnut grips. Made from 1980 to date.

Llama Super Comanche V DA Revolver **$275**
Caliber: 357 Mag. 6-shot cylinder. 4-, 6- or 8.5-inch bbl. Weight: 3 pounds. Sights: click-adj. rear, ramped blade front.

LUGER PISTOLS

Mfd. by Deutsche Waffen und Munitionsfabriken (DWM), Berlin, Germany; also by Koniglich Gewehrfabrik Erfurt, Heinrich Krieghoff Waffenfabrik, Mauser-Werke, Simson & Co., Vickers Ltd., Waffenfabrik, Bern.

Luger 1900 American Eagle

Luger 1900 American Eagle **$2400**
Caliber: 7.65 mm. 8-shot magazine. Thin, 4.75-inch long, tapered bbl. 9.5 inches overall. Weight: 32 oz. Fixed rear sight, dovetailed front sight. Grip safety. Checkered walnut grips. Early-style toggle, narrow trigger, wide guard, no stock lug. American Eagle over chamber. Estimated 8000 production.

Luger 1900 Commercial **$1495**
Same specifications as Luger 1900 American Eagle, except DWM on early-style toggle, no chamber markings. Estimated 8000 production.

Luger 1900 Swiss $2100
Same specifications as Luger 1900 American Eagle, except Swiss cross in sunburst over chamber. Estimated 9000 production.

Luger 1902 American Eagle $3750
Caliber: 9mm Luger. 8-shot magazine. 4-inch, heavy tapered bbl. 8.75 inches overall. Weight: 30 oz. Fixed rear sight, dovetailed front sight. Grip safety. Checkered walnut stocks. American Eagle over chamber, DWM on early-style toggle, narrow trigger, wide guard, no stock lug. Estimated 700 production.

Luger 1902 Carbine $6300
Caliber: 7.65mm. 8-shot magazine. 11.75-inch tapered bbl. 16.5 inches overall. Weight: 46 oz. Adj. 4-position rear sight, long ramp front sight. Grip safety. Checkered walnut stocks and forearm. DWM on early-style toggle, narrow trigger, wide guard, no chamber markings, stock lug. Estimated 3200 production.

Luger 1902 Cartridge Counter $8000
Caliber: 9mm Luger. 8-shot magazine. Heavy, tapered 4-inch bbl. 8.75 inches overall. Weight: 30 oz. Fixed rear sight, dovetailed front sight. Grip safety. Checkered walnut stocks. DWM on dished toggle with lock, American Eagle over chamber when marked; no stock lug. Estimated production unknown.

Luger 1902 Commercial $4480
Same basic specifications as Luger 1902 Cartridge Counter, except DWM on early-style toggle, narrow trigger, wide guard, no chamber markings, no stock lug. Estimated 400 production.

Luger 1903 American Eagle $5500
Same basic specifications as Luger 1902 Cartridge Counter, except American Eagle over chamber, DWM on early-style toggle, narrow trigger, wide guard, no stock lug. Estimated 700 production.

Luger 1904 GL "Baby"

Luger 1904 GL "Baby" $150,000
Caliber: 9mm Luger. 7-shot magazine. 3.25-inch bbl. 7.75 inches overall. Weight: approx. 20 oz. Serial number 10077B. "GL" marked on rear of toggle. Georg Luger's personal sidearm. Only one made in 1904.

Luger 1904 Naval (Reworked) $6500
Caliber: 9mm Luger. 8-shot magazine. Bbl. length altered to 4 inches. 8.75 inches overall. Weight: 30 oz. Adj. two-position rear sight, dovetailed front sight. Thumb lever safety. Checkered walnut stocks. Heavy tapered bbl. DWM on new-style toggle with lock, 1902 over chamber. With or without grip safety and stock lug. Estimated 800 production.

Luger 1906 (11.35) $90,000
Caliber: 45 ACP. 6-shot magazine. 5-inch bbl. 9.75 inches overall. Weight: 36 oz. Fixed rear sight, dovetailed front sight. Grip safety. Checkered walnut stocks. GL monogram on rear toggle link, larger frame with altered trigger guard and trigger, no proofs, no markings over chamber. No stock lug. Estimated production is only 2. *Note:* this version of the Luger pistol is the most valuable next to the "GL" Baby Luger.

Luger 1906 American Eagle (7.65) $1400
Caliber: 7.65mm. 8-shot magazine. Thin, 4.75-inch, tapered bbl. 9.5 inches overall. Weight: 32 oz. Fixed rear sight dovetailed front sight. Grip safety. Checkered walnut stocks. DWM on new-style toggle, American Eagle over chamber; no stock lug. Estimated 8000 production.

Luger 1906 American Eagle (9mm) $2400
Same basic specifications as the 7.65mm 1906, except in 9mm Luger with 4-inch barrel, 8.75 inches overall and weight of 30 ounces. Estimated 3500 production.

Luger 1906 Bern (7.65mm) $750
Same basic specifications as the 7.65mm 1906 American Eagle, except checkered walnut stocks with .38-inch borders, Swiss Cross on new-style toggle, Swiss proofs, no markings over chamber, no stock lug. Estimated 17,874 production.

Luger 1906 Brazilian (7.65mm) $1300
Same general specifications as the 7.65mm 1906 American Eagle, except with Brazilian proofs, no markings over chamber, no stock lug. Estimated 4500 production.

Luger 1906 Brazilian (9mm) $1625
Same basic specifications as the 9mm 1906 American Eagle, except with Brazilian proofs, no markings over chamber, no stock lug. Estimated production unknown, but less than 4000 is estimated by collectors.

Luger 1906 Commercial
Calibers: 7.65mm, 9mm. Same specifications as the 1906 American Eagle versions, above, except no chamber markings, no stock lug. Estimated production: 6000 (7.65mm); 3500 (9mm).
7.65mm $1200
9mm 1350

Luger 1906 Dutch $1425
Caliber: 9mm Luger. Same specifications as the 9mm 1906 American Eagle, except tapered bbl. with proofs, no markings over chamber, no stock lug. Estimated 3000 production.

Luger 1906 Loewe and Company **$3100**
Caliber: 7.65mm. 8-shot magazine. 6-inch tapered bbl. 10.75 inches overall. Weight: 35 oz. Adj. two-position rear sight, dovetailed front sight. Grip safety. Checkered walnut stocks. Loewe & Company over chamber, Naval proofs, DWM on new-style toggle, no stock lug. Estimated production unknown.

Luger 1906 Naval **$2600**
Caliber: 9mm Luger. 8-shot magazine. 6-inch tapered bbl. 10.75 inches overall. Weight: 35 oz. Adj. two-position rear sight, dovetailed front sight. Grip safety and thumb safety with lower marking (1st issue), higher marking (2nd issue). Checkered walnut stocks. No chamber markings, DWM on new-style toggle without lock; with stock lug. Est. production: 8000 (lst issue); 12,000 (2nd issue).

Luger 1906 Naval Commercial **$2850**
Same as the 1906 Naval, except lower marking on thumb safety, no chamber markings DWM on new-style toggle, with stock lug and commercial proofs. Estimated 3000 production.

Luger 1906 Portuguese Army **$995**
Same specifications as the 7.65mm 1906 American Eagle except with Portuguese proofs, crown and crest over chamber; no stock lug. Estimated 3500 production.

Luger 1906 Portuguese Naval **$7500**
Same as the 9mm 1906 American Eagle except with Portuguese proofs, crown and anchor over chamber; no stock lug.

Luger 1906 Russian **$9500**
Same general specifications as the 9mm 1906 American Eagle, except thumb safety has markings concealed in up position, DWM on new-style toggle, DWM bbl. proofs, crossed rifles over chamber. Estimated production unknown.

Luger 1906 Swiss **$2200**
Same general specifications as the 7.65mm 1906 American Eagle Luger, except Swiss Cross in sunburst over chamber, no stock lug. Estimated 10,300 production.

Luger 1906 Swiss (Rework) **$3000**
Same basic specifications as the 7.65mm 1906 Swiss, except in bbl. lengths of 3.63, 4 and 4.75 inches, overall length 8.38 inches and up, weight 32 oz. and up. DWM on new-style toggle, bbl. with serial number and proof marks, Swiss Cross in sunburst or shield over chamber, no stock lug. Estimated production unknown.

Luger 1906 Swiss Police **$2400**
Same general specifications as the 7.65mm 1906 Swiss except DWM on new-style toggle, Swiss Cross in matted field over chamber, no stock lug. Estimated 10,300 production.

Luger 1908 Bulgarian **$2145**
Caliber: 9mm Luger. 8-shot magazine. 4-inch tapered barrel. 8.75 inches overall. Weight: 30 oz. Fixed rear sight dovetailed front sight. Thumb safety with lower marking concealed. Checkered walnut stocks. DWM chamber marking, no proofs, crown over shield on new-style toggle lanyard loop, no stock lug. Estimated production unknown.

Luger 1908 Commercial **$995**
Same basic specifications as the 1908 Bulgarian, except higher marking on thumb safety. No chamber markings, commercial proofs, DWM on new-style toggle; no stock lug. Estimated 4000 production.

Luger 1908 Erfurt Military **$995**
Caliber: 9mm Luger. 8-shot magazine. 4-inch tapered bbl. 8.75 inches overall. Weight: 30 oz. Fixed rear sight dovetailed front sight. Thumb safety with higher marking concealed. Checkered walnut stocks. Serial number and proof marks on barrel, crown and Erfurt on new-style toggle, dated chamber; no stock lug. Estimated production unknown.

Luger 1908 Military
Same general specifications as the 9mm 1908 Erfurt Military Luger, except *1st and 2nd Issue* have thumb safety with higher marking concealed, serial number on bbl. no chamber markings, proofs on frame, DWM on new style toggle; no stock lug. Estimated production: 10,000 (lst issue); 5000 (2nd issue). *3rd Issue* has serial number and proof marks on barrel, dates over chamber, DWM on new-style toggle; no stock lug. Estimated 3000 production.
1st Issue. **$1200**
2nd Issue   1400
3rd Issue   995

Luger 1908 Naval **$3100**
Same basic specifications as the 9mm 1908 Military Lugers, except with 6-inch barrel, adj. two-position rear sight, no chamber markings, DWM on new-style toggle; with stock lug. Estimated 26,000 production.

Luger 1908 Naval (Commercial) **$3750**
Same specifications as the 1908 Naval Luger, except no chamber markings or date. Commercial proofs, DWM on new-style toggle; with stock lug. Estimated 1900 produced.

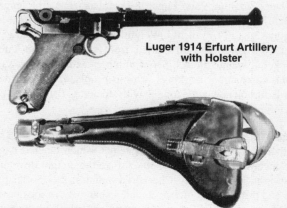

Luger 1914 Erfurt Artillery
with Holster

Luger 1914 Erfurt Artillery **$1500**
Caliber: 9mm Luger. 8-shot magazine. 8-inch tapered bbl. 12.75 inches overall. Weight: 40 oz. Artillery rear sight, Dovetailed front sight. Thumb safety with higher marking concealed. Checkered walnut stocks. Serial number and proof marks on barrel, crown and Erfurt on new-style toggle, dated chamber, with stock lug. Estimated production unknown.

Luger 1914 Erturt Military $795
Same specifications as the 1914 Erfurt Artillery, except with 4-inch bbl. and corresponding length, weight, etc., and fixed rear sight. Estimated 3000 production.

Luger 1914 Naval $2195
Same specifications as 9mm 1914 Lugers, except has 6-inch bbl. with corresponding length and weight, and adj. two-position rear sight. Dated chamber, DWM on new-style toggle; with stock lug. Estimated 40,000 produced.

Luger 1914-1918 DWM Artillery $1175
Caliber: 9mm Luger.8-shot magazine.8-inch tapered bbl. 12.75 inches overall. Weight: 40 oz. Artillery rear sight, dovetailed front sight. Thumb safety with higher marking concealed. Checkered walnut stocks. Serial number and proof marks on barrel, DWM on new-style toggle, dated chamber; with stock lug. Estimated 3000 production.

Luger 1914-1918 DWM Military $995
Same specifications as the 9mm 1914-1918 DWM Artillery, except with 4-inch tapered bbl. and corresponding length, weight, etc., and fixed rear sight. Estimated production unknown.

Luger 1920 Carbine
Caliber: 7.65mm. 8-shot magazine. 11.75-inch tapered bbl. 15.75 inches overall. Weight: 44 oz. Four-position rear sight, long ramp front sight. Grip (or thumb) safety. Checkered walnut stocks and forearm. Serial numbers and proof marks on barrel, no chamber markings, various proofs, DWM on new-style toggle; with stock lug. Estimated production unknown.
Carbine With Forearm $7500
Carbine Less Forearm 3500

Luger 1920 Commercial $610
Calibers: 7.65mm, 9mm Luger. 8-shot magazine. Bbl. lengths: 3.63, 3.75, 4, 4.75, 6, 8, 10, 12 16, 18, 20 inches; tapered. Overall length: 8 3/8 to 24.75 inches. Weight: 30 oz. and up. Varying rear sight configurations, dovetailed front sight. Thumb safety. Checkered walnut stocks. Serial numbers and proof marks on barrel, no chamber markings, various proofs, DWM or crown over Erfurt on new-style toggle; with stock lug. Estinmated production not documented.

Luger 1920 DWM and Erfurt Military $795
Cariber: 9mm Luger. 8-shot magazine. 4-inch tapered barrel. 8.75 inches overall. Weight: 30 oz. Fixed rear sight dovetailed front sight. Thumb safety. Checkered walnut stocks. Serial numbers and proof marks on barrel, dated chamber, various proofs, DWM or crown over Erfurt on new-style toggle; with stock lug. Esimated 3000 production.

Luger 1920 Police $900
Same specifications as 9mm 1920 DWM with some dated chambers, various proofs, DWM or crown over Erfurt on new-style toggle, identifying marks on grip frame; with stock lug. Estimated 3000 production.

Luger 1923 Commerical $695
Calibers: 7.65mm and 9mm Luger.8-shot magazine. Bbl. lengths: 3.63, 3.75, 4, 6, 8, 12 and 16 inches; tapered. Overall length: 8.38 inches and up. Weight: 30 oz. and up. Various rear sight configurations, dovetailed front sight. Thumb lever safety. Checkered walnut stocks. DWM on new-style toggle, serial number and proofs on barrel, no chamber markings, with stock lug. Estimated 15,000 production.

Luger 1923 Dutch Commerical $2000
Same basic specifications as 1923 Commercial Luger, with same caliber offerings, but only 3.63- or 4-inch bbl. Fixed rear sight, thumb lever safety with arrow markings. Estimated production unknown.

Luger 1923 Krieghoff Commercial $1600
Same specifications as 1923 Commercial Luger, with same caliber offerings but bbl. lengths of 3.63, 4, 6, and 8 inches. "K" marked on new-style toggle; serial number, proofs and Germany on barrel; no chamber markings; with stock lug. Estimated production unknown.

Luger 1923 Safe and Loaded $1100
Same caliber offerings, bbl. lengths and specifications as the 1923 Commercial, except thumb lever safety with safe markings. Other markings the same, with stock lug. Estimated 10,000 production.

1923 Stoeger Luger

Luger 1923 Stoeger $2900
Same general specifications as the 1923 Commercial Luger, with the same caliber offerings and bbl. lengths of 3.75, 4, 6, and 8 inches. Thumb lever safety. DWM on new-style toggle, serial number and/or proof marks on barrel, American Eagle over chamber usually; no stock lug. Estimated production unknown.

Luger 1926 "Baby" Prototype $85,000
Calibers: 7.65mm Browning and 9mm Browning (short). 5-shot magazine. 2.31-inch bbl. About 6.25 inches overall. Small-sized frame and toggle assembly. Prototype for a Luger "pocket pistol," but never manufactured commercially. Checkered walnut grips, slotted for safety. Only four known to exist, but possibly as many as a dozen could have been made.

Luger 1929 Swiss **$1350**
Caliber: 7.65mm. 8-shot magazine. 4.75-inch tapered bbl. 9.5 inches overall. Weight: 32 oz. Fixed rear sight, dovetailed front sight. Long grip safety and thumb lever with S markings. Stepped receiver and straight grip frame. Checkered plastic stocks. Swiss Cross in shield on new-style toggle, serial numbers and proofs on barrel, no markings over chamber; no stock lug. Estimated 1900 produuction.

Luger 1934 Krieghoff Commercial (Side Frame) . . **$6995**
Caliber: 7.65mm and 9mm Luger. 8-shot magazine. Bbl. lengths: 4, 6, and 8 inches. Overall length: 8.75 inch and up. Weight: 30 oz. and up. Various rear sight configurations, dovetailed front sight. Thumb lever safety. Checkered brown plastic stocks. Anchor with H K Krieghoff Suhl on new-style toggle, no chamber markings, tapered bbl. with serial number and proofs; with stock lug. Estimated 1700 production.

Luqer 1934 Krieghoff S
Caliber: 9mm Luger. 8-shot magazine. 4-inch tapered barrel. 8.75 inches overall. Weight: 30 oz. Fixed rear sight, dovetailed front sight. Thumb lever safety. Anchor with H K Krieghoff Suhl on new-style toggle, S dated chamber, bbl. proofs; stock lug. *Early Model:* Checkered walnut or plastic stocks. Estimated 2500 production. *Late Model:* Checkered brown plastic stocks. Est. 1200 production.
Early Model **$1695**
Late Model **1495**

Luger 1934 byf **$895**
Caliber: 9mm Luger. 8-shot magazine. 4-inch tapered bbl. 8.75 inches overall. Weight: 30 oz. Fixed rear sight, dovetailed front sight. Thumb lever safety. Checkered walnut or plastic stocks. byf on new-style toggle, serial number and proofs on bbl. 41-42 dated chamber; stock lug. Estimated 3000 productlon.

Luger 1934 Mauser 42 . . . . **$1500**
Caliber: 9mm Luger. 8-shot magazine. 4-inch tapered bbl. 8.75 inches overall. Weight: 30 oz. Fixed rear sight dovetailed front sight. Thumb lever safety. Checkered walnut or plastic stocks. 42 on new-style toggle, serial number and proofs on barrel, 1939-40 dated chamber markings; stock lug. Estimated 3000 production.

Luger 1934 Mauser 42 (Dated) **$2300**
Same specifications as Luger 1934 Mauser 42, above, except 41 dated chamber markings; stock lug. Estimated production unknown.

Luger 1934 Mauser Banner (Military) **$1495**
Same specifications as Luger 1934 Mauser 42, except Mauser in banner on new-style toggle, tapered bbl. with serial number and proofs usually, dated chamber markings; stock lug. Estimated production unknown.

Luger 1934 Mauser Commercial **$2800**
Same specifications as Luger 1934 Mauser 42, except checkered walnut stocks. Mauser in banner on new-style toggle, tapered bbl. with serial number and proofs usually, no chamber markings; stock lug. Estimated production unknown.

Luger 1934 Mauser Dutch **$1395**
Same specifications as Luger 1934 Mauser 42, except checkered walnut stocks. Mauser in banner on new-style toggle, tapered bbl. with caliber, 1940 dated chamber markings; stock lug. Estimated production unknown.

Luger 1934 Mauser Latvian **$3000**
Caliber: 7.65mm. 8-shot magazine. 4-inch tapered bbl. 8.75 inches overall. Weight: 30 oz. Fixed square-notched rear sight, dovetailed Patridge front sight. Thumb lever safety. Checkered walnut stosks. Mauser in banner on new-style toggle,1937 dated chamber markings; stock lug. Estimated production unknown.

Luger 1934 Mauser (Oberndorf) **$2100**
Same as 1934 Mauser 42, except checkered walnut stocks. Oberndorf 1934 on new-style toggle, tapered bbl. with proofs and caliber, Mauser in banner over chamber; stock lug.

Luger 1934 Simson-S Toggle **$1800**
Same as 1934 Mauser 42, except checkered walnut stocks. S on new-style toggle, tapered bbl. with serial number and proofs, no chamber markings; stock lug. Estimated 10,000 production.

Luger 42 Mauser Banner **$1350**
Same specifications as Luger 1934 Mauser 42, except weight 32 oz.; Mauser in banner on new-style toggle, tapered bbl. with serial number and proofs usually, dated chamber markings; stock lug. Estimated production unknown.

Luger Abercrombie and Fitch **$4795**
Calibers: 7.65mm and 9mm Luger. 8-shot magazine. 4.75-inch tapered bbl. 9.5 inches overall. Weight: 32 oz. Fixed rear sight, dovetailed front sight. Grip safety. Checkered walnut stocks. DWM on new-style toggle Abercrombie & Fitch markings on barrel, Swiss Cross in sunburst over chamber; no stock lug. Est.100 production.

Luger Dutch Royal Air Force **$1150**
Caliber: 9mm Luger. 8-shot magazine. 4-inch tapered bbl. 8.75 inches overall. Weight: 30 oz. Fixed rear sight dovetailed front sight. Grip safety and thumb safety with markings and arrow. Checkered walnut stocks. DWM on new-style toggle, bbl. dated with serial number and proofs, no markings over chamber, no stock lug. Estimated 4000 production.

Luger DWM (G Date) **$825**
Caliber: 9mm Luger. 8-shot magazine. 4-inch tapered bbl. 8.75 inches overall. Weight: 30 oz. Fixed rear sight; dovetailed front sight. Thumb lever safety. Checkered walnut stocks. DWM on new-style toggle, serial number and proofs on barrel, G (1935 date) over chamber; with stock lug. Estimated production unknown.

Luger DWM and Erfurt **$895**
Caliber: 9mm Luger. 8-shot magazine. Bbl. length: 4 or 6 inches, tapered. Overall length: 8.75, 10.75 inches. Weight: 30 or 38 oz. Fixed rear sight, dovetailed front sight. Thumb safety. Checkered walnut stocks. Serial numbers and proof marks on barrel, double dated chamber, various proofs, DWM or crown over Erfurt on new-style toggle; with stock lug. Estimated production unknown.

Luger Krieghoff 36 . . . . $2170
Caliber: 9mm Luger. 8-shot magazine. 4-inch tapered bbl. 8.75
inches overall. Weight: 30 oz. Fixed rear sight dovetailed front
sight. Thumb lever safety. Checkered brown plastic stocks. Anchor with H K Krieghoff Suhl on new-style toggle, 36 dated
chamber, serial number and proofs on barrel; stock lug. Estimated 700 production.

Luger Krieghoff-Dated 1936-1945 . . . . $1920
Same specifications as Luger Krieghoff 36, except 1936-1945
dated chamber, bbl. proofs. Est. 8600 production.

Luger Krieghoff (Grip Safety) $3645
Same specifications as Luger Krieghoff 36, except grip safety
and thumb lever safety. No chamber markings, tapered bbl. with
serial number, proofs and caliber, no stock lug. Estimated production unknown.

Luger Mauser Banner (Grip Safety) $2850
Caliber: 7.65mm. 8-shot magazine. 4.75-inch tapered bbl. 9.5
inches overall. Weight: 30 oz. Fixed rear sight, dovetailed front
sight. Grip safety and thumb lever safety. Checkered walnut
stocks. Mauser in banner on new-style toggle, serial number and
proofs on barrel, 1939 dated chamber markings; no stock lug. Estimated production unknown.

Luger Mauser Banner 42 (Dated) $1295
Caliber: 9mm Luger. 8-shot magazine. 4-inch tapered bbl. 8.75
inches overall. Weight: 30 oz. Fixed rear sight dovetailed front
sight. Thumb lever safety. Checkered walnut or plastic stocks.
Mauser in banner on new-style toggle serial number and proofs
on bbl. usually, 42 dated chamber markings; stock lug. Estimated
production unknown.

Luger Mauser Banner (Swiss Proof) $1830
Same specifications as Luger Mauser Banner 42, above except
checkered walnut stocks and 1939 dated chamber.

Luger Mauser Freise $3550
Same specifications as Mauser Banner 42, except checkered
walnut stocks tapered bbl. with proofs on sight block and Freise
above chamber. Estimated production unknown.

**German Luger S/42
Dated 1936**

Luger S/42
Caliber: 9mm Luger. 8-shot magazine. 4-inch tapered barrel.
8.75 inches overall. Weight: 30 oz. Fixed rear sight, dovetailed
front sight. Thumb lever safety. Checkered walnut stocks. S/42
on new-style toggle, serial number and proofs on barrel; stock
lug. *Dated Model:* has dated chamber; estimated 3000 production. *G Date:* has G (1935 date) over chamber; estimated 3000
production. *K Date:* has K (1934 date) over chamber; prod. figures unknown.

Dated Model . . . . $ 895
G Date Model   845
K Date Model   1895

Luger Russian Commercial $2100
Caliber: 7.65mm. 8-shot magazine. 3.63-inch tapered bbl. 8.38
inches overall. Weight: 30 oz. Fixed rear sight, dovetailed front
sight. Thumb lever safety. Checkered walnut stocks. DWM on
new-style toggle, Russian proofs on barrel, no chamber markings; with stock lug. Estimated production unknown.

Luger Simson and Company $1295
Calibers: 7.65mm and 9mm Luger. 8-shot magazine. Weight: 32
oz. Fixed rear sight, dovetailed front sight. Thumb lever safety.
Checkered walnut stocks. Simson & Company Suhl on new-
style toggle, serial number and proofs on barrel, date over chamber usually; with stock lug. Estimated 10,000 production.

Luger Vickers-Dutch $2460
Caliber: 9mm Luger. 8-shot magazine. 4-inch tapered bbl. 8.75
inches overall. Weight: 30 oz. Fixed rear sight, dovetailed front
sight. Grip safety and thumb lever with arrow markings. Checkered walnut stocks (coarse). Vickers LTD on new-style toggle,
no chamber markings, dated barrel; no stock lug. Estimated
10,000 production.

**LUNA FREE PISTOL
Zella-Mehlis, Germany
Originally mfd. by Ernst Friedr. Buchel and later
by Udo Anschutz**

Luna Model 300 Free Pistol

Luna Model 300 Free Pistol $1200
Single shot. System Aydt action. Set trigger. Caliber: 22 LR. 11-
inch bbl. Weight: 40 oz. Target sights. Blued finish. Checkered
and carved walnut stock and forearm improved design with adj.
hand base on later models of Udo Anschutz manufacture. Made
prior to WW II.

M.A.C./DEFENSE SYSTEMS INTL.
Marietta, Georgia

M.A.C. Ingram Model 10A1S

M.A.C. Ingram Model 10A1S Semiautomatic $795

Caliber: 9mm or 45 ACP. 30- or 32-round magazine. 5.75 inch bbl. 10.5 inches overall. Weight: 6.25 pounds. Front protected post sight, fixed aperture rear sight. Manually operated Garand-type safety in trigger guard. Based on Military Armament Corporation's Ingram 10 design.

MAGNUM RESEARCH INC.
Minneapolis, Minnesota

Magnum Research Baby Eagle

Magnum Research Baby Eagle Semiautomatic . . . $460

DA. Calibers: 9mm, 40 S&W, 41 AE. 15-shot magazine (9mm), 9-shot magazine (40 S&W), 10-shot magazine (41 AE). 4.75-inch bbl. 8.15 inches overall. Weight: 35.4 oz. Combat sights. Matte blued finish.

Magnum Research Desert Eagle Semiautomatic

Calibers: 357 Mag., 41 Mag., 44 Mag., 50 Action Express (AE). 8- or 9-shot magazine. Gas-operated. Bbl. lengths: 6 (standard), 10 and 14 inches; polygonal. 10.6 inches overall w/6-inch bbl. Weight (w/6-inch bbl.): 357 Mag. — 52 oz. w/alum. alloy frame, 62 oz. w/steel frame 41/44 Mag. — 56 oz. w/alloy; 67 oz. w/steel. Fixed or adj. combat sights. Combat-type trigger guard.

Magnum Research Desert Eagle

Magnum Research Desert Eagle *(Cont.)*

Finish: Military black oxide, nickel, chrome, stainless or blued. Wraparound rubber stocks. Made by Israel Military Industries from 1984 to date.

357 Standard (steel) or Alloy (6-inch bbl.)	$ 595
357 Stainless Steel (6-inch bbl.)	725
41 Mag. Standard (steel) or Alloy (6-inch bbl.)	695
41 Mag. Stainless Steel (6-inch bbl.)	675
44 Mag. Standard (steel) or Alloy (6-inch bbl.)	650
44 Mag. Stainless Steel (6-inch bbl.)	710
50 AE Magnum Standard	1000
Add for 10-inch Bbl.	100
Add for 14-inch Bbl.	125

Magnum Research Mountain Eagle

Magnum Research Mountain Eagle
Semiautomatic $195

Caliber: 22 LR.15-shot polycarbonate resin magazine. 6.5-inch injection-molded polymer and steel bbl. 10.6 inches overall. Weight: 21 oz. Sights: ramp blade front, adj. rear. Injection-molded, checkered and textured grip. Matte black finish. Made from 1992 to date.

Magnum Research SSP-91 Lone Eagle Pistol

Single-shot action with interchangeable rotating breech bbl. assembly. Calibers: 22 LR, 22 Mag., 22 Hornet, 22-250, 223 Rem., 243 Rem., 6mm BR, 7mm-08, 7mm BR, 30-06, 30-30, 308 Win., 35 Rem., 357 Mag., 44 Mag., 444 Marlin. 14-inch interchangeable bbl. assembly. 15 inches overall. Weight: 4.5 lbs. *See* illustration next page.

SSP-91 S/S Pistol (Complete)	$255
14-inch Bbl. Assembly	190
Stock Assembly	65

Magnum Research Lone Eagle

MAUSER PISTOLS
Oberndorf, Germany
Waffenfabrik Mauser of Mauser-Werke A.G.

Mauser Model 80-SA

Mauser Model 80-SA Automatic **$330**
Caliber: 9mm Para. 13-shot magazine. 4.66-inch bbl. 8 inches overall. Weight: about 31.5 oz. Blued finish. Hardwood grips. Made 1991-94.

Mauser Model 90-DA

Mauser Model 90-DA Automatic **$375**
Caliber: 9mm Para. 14-shot magazine. 4.66-inch bbl. 8 inches overall. Weight: 35 oz. Blued finish. Hardwood grips. Made 1991-94.

Mauser Model 90 DAC Compact **$395**
Caliber: 9mm Para. 14-shot magazine. 4.13-inch bbl. 7.4 inches overall. Weight: 33.25 oz. Blued finish. Hardwood grips. Made 1991-94.

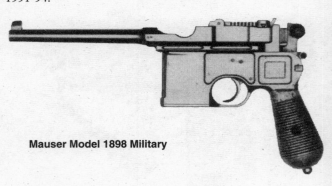

Mauser Model 1898 Military

Mauser Model 1898 Military Auto Pistol **$2475**
Caliber: 7.63mm Mauser; also chambered for 9mm Mauser and 9mm Luger; the latter is identified by a large red "9" in the stocks. Box magazine, 10-shot. 5.25-inch bbl. 12 inches overall. Weight: 45 oz. Adj. rear sight. Blued finish. Walnut stocks. Made 1898-1945. *Note:* Specialist collectors recognize a number of variations at higher values. Price here is for more common type.

Mauser Model HSc

Mauser Model HSc DA Auto Pistol **$450**
Calibers: 32 Auto (7.65mm), 380 Auto (9mm Short). 8-shot (32) or 7-shot (380) magazine. 3.4-inch bbl. 6.4 inches overall. Weight: 23.6 oz. Fixed sights. Blued or nickel finish. Checkered walnut stocks. Made 1938-1945; from 1968 to date.

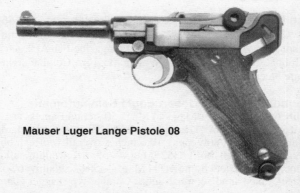

Mauser Luger Lange Pistole 08

Mauser Luger Lange Pistole 08 . . . . $1995
Caliber: 9mm Para. 8-inch bbl. Checkered grips. Blued finish. Accessorized w/walnut shoulder stock, front sight tool, spare magazine, leather case. Currently in production. Commemorative version made in limited quantities with ivory grips and 14-carat gold monogram plate.

**Mauser Luger Lange Pistole 08
Commemorative**

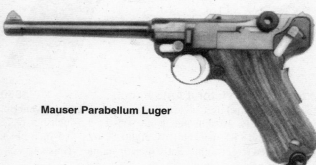

Mauser Parabellum Luger

Mauser Parabellum Luger Auto Pistol $1000
Current commercial model. Swiss pattern with grip safety. Calibers: 7.65mm Luger, 9mm Luger. 8-shot magazine. Bbl. lengths: 4-,6-inch. 8.75 inches overall w/4-inch bbl. Weight: 30 oz. w/4-inch bbl. Fixed sights. Blued finish. Checkered walnut stocks. Made from 1970 to date. *Note:* Pistols of this model sold in the U.S. have the American Eagle stamped on the receiver.

Mauser Pocket Model 1910 Auto Pistol $345
Caliber: 25 Auto (6.35mm). 9-shot magazine. 3.1-inch bbl. 5.4 inches overall. Weight: 15 oz. Fixed sights. Blued finish. Checkered walnut or hard rubber stocks. Made 1910-34.

Mauser Pocket Model 1914 Automatic $325
Similar to Pocket Model 1910. Caliber: 32 Auto (7.65mm). 8-shot magazine. 3.4-inch bbl. 6 inches overall. Weight: 21 oz. Fixed sights. Blued finish. Checkered walnut or hard rubber stocks. Made 1914-34.

Mauser Pocket Model 1934 . . . . $345
Similar to Pocket Models 1910 and 1914 in the respective calibers. Chief difference is in the more streamlined one-piece stocks. Made 1934-c. 1939.

Mauser WTP Model I

Mauser WTP Model I Auto Pistol $395
"Westentaschen-Pistole" (Vest Pocket Pistol). Caliber: 25 Automatic (6.35mm). 6-shot magazine. 2.5-inch bbl. inches overall. Weight: 11.5 oz. Blued finish. Hard rubber stocks. Made 1922-37.

Mauser WTP Model II Auto Pistol $550
Similar to Model I, but smaller and lighter. Caliber: 25 Automatic (6.35mm). 6-shot magazine. 2-inch bbl. 4 inches overall. Weight: 9.5 oz. Blued finish. Hard rubber stocks. Made 1938-40.

MITCHELL ARMS, INC.
Santa Ana, California

Mitchell Arms Model 1911 Gold Signature
Caliber: 45 ACP. 8-shot magazine. 5-inch bbl. 8.75 inches overall. Weight: 39 oz. Interchangeable blade front sight; drift adj. combat or fully adj. rear sight. Smooth or checkered walnut grips. Blued or stainless finish. Made from 1994 to 1996.
Blued Model w/Fixed Sights. $365
Blued Model w/Adj. Sights. 400
Stainless Model w/Fixed Sights 390
Stainless Model w/Adj. Sights 425

Mitchell Arms Alpha Model
Dual action w/interchangeable trigger modules. Caliber: 45 ACP. 8-shot magazine. 5-inch bbl. 8.75 inches overall. Weight: 39 oz. Interchangeable blade front sight; drift adj. rear. Smooth or checkered walnut grips. Blued or stainless finish. Made from 1994 to 1996.
Blued Model w/Fixed Sights. $495
Blued Model w/Adj. Sights. 550
Stainless Model w/Fixed Sights 540
Stainless Model w/Adj. Sights 575

Mitchell Arms American Eagle Pistol $525
Stainless-steel re-creation of the American Eagle Parabellum auto pistol. Caliber: 9mm Parabellum. 7-shot magazine. 4-inch bbl. 9.6 inches overall. Weight: 26.6 oz. Blade front sight, fixed rear. Stainless finish. Checkered walnut grips. Discontinued 1994.

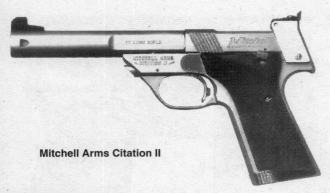

Mitchell Arms Citation II

Mitchell Arms Citation II Auto Pistol **$340**
Re-creation of the High Standard Supermatic Citation Military.
Caliber: 22 LR. 10-shot magazine. 5.5-inch bull bbl. or 7.25
fluted bbl. 9.75 inches overall (5.5-inch bbl.). Weight: 44.5 oz.
Ramp front sight, slide-mounted micro-adj. rear. Satin blue or
stainless finish. Checkered walnut grips w/thumbrest. Made
from 1992 to 1996.

Mitchell Arms Olympic I.S.U. Auto Pistol **$435**
Similar to the Citation II Model, except chambered in 22 Short.
6.75-inch round tapered bbl. with stabilizer and removable counterweights. Made from 1992 to 1996.

Mitchell Arms Sharpshooter II

Mitchell Arms Sharpshooter II Auto Pistol **$275**
Re-creation of the High Standard Sharpshooter. Caliber: 22 LR.
10-shot magazine. 5-inch bull bbl. 10.25 inches overall. Weight:
42 oz. Ramp front sight, slide-mounted micro-adj. rear. Satin
blue or stainless finish. Checkered walnut grips w/thumbrest.
Made from 1992 to 1996.

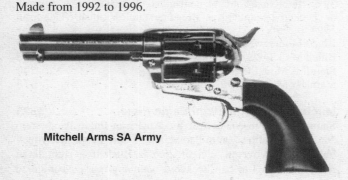

Mitchell Arms SA Army

Mitchell Arms SA Army Revolver
Calibers: 357 Mag., 44 Mag., 45 Colt/45 ACP. 6-shot cylinder.
Bbl. lengths: 4.75, 5.5, 7.5 inches. Weight: 40-43 oz. Sights:
blade front; grooved topstrap or adj. rear. Blued or nickel finish
w/color-casehardened frame. Brass or steel backstrap/trigger
guard. Smooth one-piece walnut grips.
Standard Model w/Blued Finish **$320**
Standard Model w/Nickel Finish 395
Standard Model w/Stainless Backstrap 420
45 Combo w/Blued Finish 445
45 Combo w/Nickel Finish 495

Mitchell Arms Trophy II Auto Pistol **$395**
Similar to the Citation II Model, except with gold-plated trigger
and gold-filled markings. Made from 1992 to 1996.

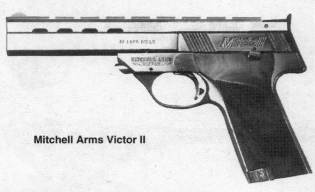

Mitchell Arms Victor II

Mitchell Arms Victor II Auto Pistol **$350**
Re-creation of the High Standard Victor with full-length vent rib.
Caliber: 22 LR. 10-shot magazine. 4.5- or 5.5-inch bbl. 9.75
inches overall (5.5-inch bbl.). Weight: 52 oz., (5.5-inch bbl.).
Rib-mounted target sights. Satin blue or stainless finish. Check-
ered walnut grips w/thumbrest.

MKE PISTOL
Ankara, Turkey
Mfd. by Makina ve Kimya Endüstrisi Kurumu

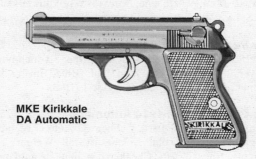

MKE Kirikkale
DA Automatic

MKE Kirikkale DA Automatic Pistol **$295**
Similar to Walther PP. Calibers: 32 Auto (7.65mm), 380 Auto
(9mm Short). 7-shot magazine. 3.9-inch bbl. 6.7 inches overall.
Weight: 24 oz. Fixed sights. Blued finish. Checkered plastic
stocks. Made 1948 to date. *Note:* This is a Turkish Army standard service pistol.

MOA CORPORATION
Dayton, Ohio

MOA Maximum Single-Shot Pistol **$470**
Calibers: 22 Hornet to 358 Win. 10- or 14-inch Douglas bbl. Weight: 3 lbs. 13 oz.-4 lbs. 3 oz. Smooth walnut grips. Currently in production.

MOA Maximum Carbine Pistol

MOA Maximum Carbine Pistol **$445**
Similar to Maximum Pistol, but with 18-inch bbl. Currently in production.

O.F. MOSSBERG & SONS, INC.
North Haven, Connecticut

Mossberg Brownie

Mossberg Brownie "Pepperbox" Pistol **$445**
Hammerless, top-break, double-action, four bbls. with revolving firing pin. Caliber: 22 LR, 4-shot. 2.5-inch bbls.. Weight: 14 oz. Blued finish. Serated grips. Approximately 37,000 made from 1919 to 1932.

NAVY ARMS COMPANY
Martinsburg, West Virginia

Navy Arms Model 1873 SA Revolver
Calibers: 44-40, 45 Colt. 6-sfiot cylinder. Bbl. lengths: 3, 4.75, 5.5, 7.5 inches. 10.75 inches overall (5.5-inch bbl.). Weight: 36 oz. Sights: blade front-grooved topstrap rear. Blued w/color-casehardened frame or nickel finish. Smooth walnut grips. Made from 1991 to date.
Blued Finish w/Brass Backstrap **$295**
U.S. Artillery Model w/5-inch bbl. **395**
U.S. Cavalry Model w/7-inch bbl **400**

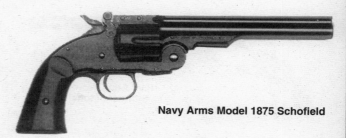

Navy Arms Model 1875 Schofield

Navy Arms Model 1875 Schofield Revolver
Replica of S&W Model 3, Top-break single-action w/auto ejector. Calibers: 44-40 or 45 LC. 6-shot cylinder, 5- or 7-inch bbl. 10.75 or 12.75 inches overall. Weight: 39 oz. Blade front sight; square-notched rear. Polished blued finish. Smooth walnut stocks. Made 1994 to date.
Cavalry Model (7-inch bbl.). **$525**
Wells Fargo Model (5-inch bbl.) **495**

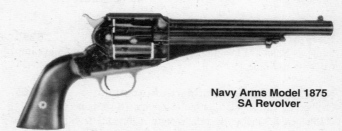

Navy Arms Model 1875 SA Revolver

Navy Arms Model 1875 SA Revolver **$325**
Replica of Remington Model 1875. Calibers: 357 Magnum, 4440, 45 Colt. 6-shot cylinder. 7.5-inch bbl. 13.5 inches overall. Weight: about 48 oz. Fixed sights. Blued or nickel finish. Smooth walnut stocks. Made in Italy c.1955-1980. *Note:* Originally marketed in the U.S. as Replica Arms Model 1875; that firm was acquired by Navy Arms Co.

Navy Arms Buntline Frontier

Navy Arms Buntline Frontier. **$375**
Same as Target Frontier, except has detachable shoulder stock and 16.5-inch bbl. Calibers: 357 Magnum and 45 Colt only. Made 1975-79.

Navy Arms Frontier SA Revolver **$230**
Calibers: 22 LR, 22 WMR, 357 Mag., 45 Colt. 6-shot cylinder. Bbl. lengths: 4 .5-, 5.5-, 7.5-inch. 10.25 inches overall w/4.5-inch bbl. Weight: about 36 oz. w/4.5-inch bbl. Fixed sights. Blued bbl. and cylinder, color-casehardened frame, brass grip frame. One-piece smooth walnut stock. Made 1975-79.

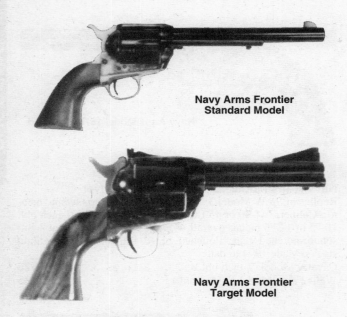

**Navy Arms Frontier
Standard Model**

**Navy Arms Frontier
Target Model**

Navy Arms Frontier Target Model. $250
Same as Standard Frontier, except has adj. rear sight and ramp front sight. Made 1975-79.

Navy Arms Luger (Standard) Automatic $165
Caliber: 22 LR, standard or high velocity. 10-shot magazine. Bbl.: 4.5 inches. 8.9 inches overall. Weight: 1 lb. 13.5 oz. Square blade front sight w/square notch, stationary rear sight. Walnut checkered grips. Non-reflecting black finish. Discontinued 1983.

Navy Arms Rolling Block

Navy Arms Rolling Block Single-Shot Pistol. . . . $180
Calibers: 22 LR, 22 Hornet, 357 Magnum. 8-inch bbl. 12 inches overall. Weight: about 40 oz. Adjustable sights. Blued bbl., color-casehardened frame, brass trigger guard. Smooth walnut stock/forearm. Made 1965-1980.

Navy Arms TT-Olympia

Navy Arms TT-Olympia Pistol. $250
Reproduction of the Walther Olympia Target Pistol. Caliber: 22 LR. 4.6-inch bbl. 8 inches overall. Weight: 28 oz. Blade front sight, adj. rear. Blued finish. Checkered hardwood grips. Made from 1992 to 1994.

NEW ENGLAND FIREARMS
Gardner, Massachusetts

**New England Firearms
Model R73**

New England Firearms Model R73 Revolver $125
Caliber: 32 H&R Mag. 5-shot cylinder. 2.5- or 4-inch bbl. 8.5 inches overall w/4-inch bbl. Weight: 26 oz. w/4 inch bbl. Fixed or adjustable sights. Blued or nickel finish. Walnut-finish hardwood stocks. Made from 1988 to date.

New England Firearms Model R92 Revolver $110
Same general specifications as Model R73, except chambered for 22 LR. 9-shot cylinder. Weight: 28 oz. with 4 inch bbl.

**New England Firearms Model 832
Starter Pistol**

New England Firearms Model 832
Starter Pistol $75
Calibers: 22 Blank, 32 Blank. 9- and 5-shot cylinders, respectively. Push-pin swing-out cylinder. Solid wood grips with NEF medallion insert.

New England Firearms Ultra Revolver $130
Calibers: 22 LR, 22 WRF. 9-shot cylinder in 22 LR, 6-shot cylinder in 22 WRF. 4- or 6-inch ribbed bull bbl. 10.75 inches overall w/6-inch bbl. Weight: 36 oz. w/6-inch bbl. Blade front sight; adj. square-notched rear. Blued or nickel finish. Walnut-finish hardwood grips. Made from 1989 to date.

New England Firearms Lady Ultra

New England Firearms Lady Ultra Revolver **$155**
Same basic specifications as the Ultra, except in 32 H&R Mag. w/5-shot cylinder and 3-inch ribbed bull bbl. 7.5 inches overall. Weight: 31 oz. Made from 1992 to date.

NORTH AMERICAN ARMS
Spanish Fork, Utah

**North American Arms
Model 22LR**

North American Arms Model 22LR **$125**
Same as Model 22S, except chambered for 22 LR, is 3.88 inches overall, weighs 4.5 oz. Made 1976 to date.

**North American Arms
Model 22S**

North American Arms Model 22S Mini Revolver . . **$155**
SA. Caliber: 22 Short. 5-shot cylinder. 1.13-inch bbl. 3.5 inches overall. Weight: 4 oz. Fixed sights. Stainless steel. Plastic stocks. Made from 1975 to date.

North American Arms 450 Magnum Express . . . **$850**
SA. Calibers: 450 Magnum Express, 45 Win. Mag. 7.5 inch bbl. Matte stainless steel finish. Cased. Discontinued 1986.

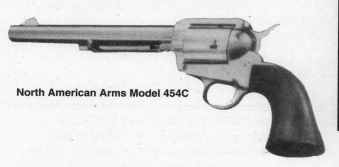

North American Arms Model 454C

North American Arms Model 454C SA Revolver . . **$755**
Caliber: 454 Casull. 5-shot cylinder. 7.5-inch bbl. 14 inches overall. Weight: 50 oz. Fixed sights. Stainless steel. Smooth hardwood stocks. Introduced 1977.

**North American Arms
Black Widow**

North American Arms Black Widow Revolver
SA. Calibers: 22 LR, 22 WMR. 5-shot cylinder. 2-inch heavy vent bbl. 5.88 inches overall. Weight: 8.8 oz. Fixed or adj. sights. Full-size black rubber grips. Stainless steel brush finish. Made from 1990 to date.
Adj. Sight Model **$210**
Adj. Sight Combo Model **220**
Fixed Sight Model **195**
Fixed Sight Combo Model **210**

**North American Arms
Mini-Master**

North American Arms Mini-Master Revolver

SA. Calibers: 22 LR, 22 WMR. 5-shot cylinder. 4-inch heavy vent-rib bbl. 7.75 inches overall. Weight: 10.75 inches. Fixed or adj. sights. Black rubber grips. Stainless steel brush finish. Made from 1990 to date.

Adj. Sight Model	$215
Adj. Sight Combo Model	250
Fixed Sight Model	220
Fixed Sight Combo Model	255

NORWEGIAN MILITARY PISTOLS
Mfd. by Kongsberg Vaapenfabrikk, the government arsenal at Kongsberg, Norway

Norwegian Model 1914

Norwegian Model 1914 Automatic Pistol $340

Similar to Colt Model 1911 45 Automatic with same general specifications, except has lengthened slide stop. Made 1919-46.

Norwegian Model 1912 . . . . $2100

Same as the Model 1914 except has conventional slide stop. Only 500 were made.

ORTGIES PISTOLS
Erfurt, Germany
Manufactured by Deutsche Werke A.G.

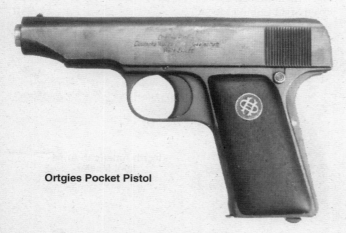

Ortgies Pocket Pistol

Ortgies Pocket Automatic Pistol $225

Calibers: 32 Automatic (7.65mm), 380 Automatic (9mm) 7-shot magazine (380 cal.), 8-shot (32 cal.). 3.25-inch bbl. 6.5 inches overall. Weight: 22 oz. Fixed sights. Blued finish. Plain walnut stocks. Made in 1920s.

Ortgies Vest Pocket Automatic Pistol $225

Caliber: 25 Automatic (6.35mm). 6-shot magazine. 2.75-inch bbl. 5.19 inches overall. Weight: 13.5 oz. Fixed sights. Blued finish. Plain walnut stocks. Made in 1920s.

PARA-ORDNANCE MFG., INC.
Scarborough, Ontario, Canada

Para-Ordnance P-12

Para-Ordnance P-12 Compact Auto Pistol

Caliber: 45 ACP. 11-shot magazine. 3.5-inch bbl. 7 inches overall. Weight: 24 oz. (alloy frame). Blade front sight, adj. rear w/3-Dot system. Textured composition grips. Matte black alloy or steel finish. Made from 1990 to date.

Model P1245 (Alloy)	$565
Model P1245C (Steel)	595

Para-Ordnance P-13 Auto Pistol

Same general specifications as Model P-12, except with 12-shot magazine. 4.5-inch bbl. 8 inches overall. Weight: 25 oz. (alloy frame). Blade front sight, adj. rear w/3-dot system. Textured composition grips. Matte black alloy or steel finish. Made from 1990 to date.

Model P1345 (Alloy)	$520
Model P1345C (Steel)	555

Para-Ordnance P-14 Auto Pistol

Caliber: 45 ACP. 13-shot magazine. 5-inch bbl. 8.5 inches overall. Weight: 28 oz. Alloy frame. Blade front sight, adj. rear w/3-dot system. Textured composition grips. Matte black alloy or steel finish. Made from 1990 to date.

Model P1445 (Alloy)	$495
Model P1445C (Steel)	570

PLAINFIELD MACHINE COMPANY
Dunellen, New Jersey

This firm discontinued operation about 1982.

Plainfield Model 71

Plainfield Model 71 Automatic Pistol
Calibers: 22 LR, 25 Automatic; conversion kit available. 10-shot magazine in 22, 8-shot in 25. 2.5-inch bbl. 5.13 inches overall. Weight: 25 oz. Fixed sights. Stainless steel frame/slide. Checkered walnut stocks. Made 1970-1982.

22 LR or 25 Auto only **$135**
With Conversion Kit **160**

Plainfield Model 72

Plainfield Model 72 Automatic Pistol
Same as Model 71, except has aluminum slide, 3.5-inch bbl., is 6 inches overall. Made 1970-1982.

22 LR or 25 Auto only **$145**
With Conversion Kit **170**

RADOM PISTOL
Radom, Poland
Manufactured by the Polish Arsenal

Radom P-35 Automatic Pistol **$610**
Variation of the Colt Government Model 45 Auto. Caliber: 9mm Luger. 8-shot magazine. 4.75-inch bbl. 7.75 inches overall. Weight: 29 oz. Fixed sights. Blued finish. Plastic stocks. Made 1935 thru WW II.

Radom P-35 Automatic

RECORD-MATCH PISTOLS
Zella-Mehlis, Germany
Manufactured by Udo Anschütz

Record-Match Model 200

Record-Match Model 200 Free Pistol **$940**
Basically the same as Model 210 except plainer, with different stock design and conventional set trigger, spur trigger guard. Made prior to WW II.

Record-Match Model 210 Free Pistol **$1295**
System Martini action, set trigger with button release. Caliber: 22 LR. Single shot. 11-inch bbl. Weight: 46 oz. Target sights micrometer rear. Blued finish. Carved and checkered walnut stock and forearm, adj. hand base. Also made with dural action (Model 210A); weight of this model, 35 oz. Made prior to WWII.

REISING ARMS CO.
Hartford, Connecticut

Reising Target Automatic Pistol **$430**
Hinged frame. Outside hammer. Caliber: 22 LR. 12-shot magazine. 6.5-inch bbl. Fixed sights. Blued finish. Hard rubber stocks. Made 1921-24.

Remington Arms Company
Ilion, New York

Remington Model 51

Remington Model 51 Automatic Pistol $525
Calibers: 32 Auto, 380 Auto. 7-shot magazine. 3.5-inch bbl. 6.63 inches overall. Weight: 21 oz. Fixed sights. Blued finish. Hard rubber stocks. Made 1918-1934.

Remington Model 95 Double Derringer

Remington Model 95 Double Derringer
SA. Caliber: 41 Short Rimfire. 3-inch double bbls. (superposed). 4.88 inches overall. Early models have long hammer spur and two-armed extractor; later production have short hammer spur and sliding extractor (a few have no extractor). Fixed sights: front blade integral with bbls., rear groove. Finish: all blued, blued w/nickel-plated frame, fully nickel-plated; also with factory engraving. Grips: walnut, checkered hard rubber, pearl, ivory. Weight: 11 oz. Made 1866-1935. Approximately 150,000 were manufactured. *Note:* During the 70 years of its production, serial numbering of this model was repeated two or three times. Therefore, aside from hammer and extractor differences between the earlier and later models, the best clue to the age of a Double Derringer is the stamping of the company's name on the top of the bbl. or side rib. Prior to 1888, derringers were stamped "E. Remington & Sons"; 1888-1910, "Remington Arms Co."; 1910-1935, "Remington Arms-U.M.C. Co."
Plain Model. $1150
Factory-engraved Model with ivory or pearl grips. **1895**

Remington New Model Single-Shot
Target Plstol $1670
Also called Model 1901 Target. Rolling-block action. Calibers: 22 Short, 22 LR, 44 S&W Russian. 10-inch bbl., half-octagon. 14 inches overall. Weight: 45 oz. (22 cal.). Target sights. Blued finish. Checkered walnut grips and forearm. Made 1901-1909.

**Remington Model 1901
Rolling Block Pistol**

**Remington Model XP-100
Custom Pistol**

**Remington Model XP-100
Custom Heavy Barrel**

Remington Model XP-100 Custom Pistol $695
Bolt-action, single-shot, long-range pistol. Calibers: 223 Rem., 7mm-08 or 35 Rem. 14.5-inch bbl., standard contour or heavy. Weight: about 4.25 pounds. Currently in production.

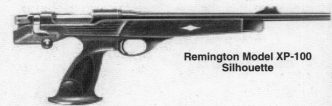

**Remington Model XP-100
Silhouette**

Remington Model XP-100 Silhouette $345
Same general specifications as Model XP-100, except chambered for 7mm BR Rem., 14.75-inch bbl. and weighs 4.13 lbs.

**Remington Model XP-100
Single-Shot Pistol**

Remington Model XP-100 Single-Shot Pistol . . . $280
Bolt action. Caliber: 221 Rem. "Fire Ball." 10.5-inch vent rib bbl. 16.75 inches overall. Weight: 3.75 pounds. Adj. rear sight, blade front, receiver drilled and tapped for scope mounts. Blued finish. One-piece brown nylon stock. Made 1963-88.

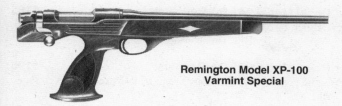

Remington Model XP-100 Varmint Special

RG Model 38S

Remington Model XP-100 Varmint Special $295
Bolt-action, single-shot, long-range pistol. Calibers: 223 Rem., 7mm BR. 14.5-inch bbl. 21.25 inches overall. Weight: about 4.25 pounds. One-piece Du Pont nylon stock with universal grips. Discontinued 1991.

Remington Model XP-100R KS Custom Repeater $555
Same general specifications as Model XP-100 Custom, except chambered for 22-250, 223 Rem., 250 Savage, 7mm-08 Rem., 308 Win., 35 Rem. and 350 Rem. Mag. Kevlar-reinforced synthetic stock with blind magazine and sling swivel studs. Made from 1990 to date.

Remington XP-22R Rimfire Repeater $310
Bolt-action clip repeater built on Model 541-style action. Calibers: 22 Short, Long, LR. 5-shot magazine. 14.5-inch bbl. Weight: 4.25 pounds. Rem. synthetic stock. Made 1991-92.

RG REVOLVERS
Miami, Florida

RG Model 23

RG Model 23
SA/DA. 6-shot magazine, swing-out cylinder. Caliber: 22 LR. 1.75-and 3.38-inch bbls. Overall length: 5.13 and 7.5 inches. Weight: 16-17 oz. Fixed sights. Blued or nickel finish. Discontinued.
Blued Finish $80
Nickel Finish 85

RG Model 38S
SA/DA. 6-shot magazine, swing-out cylinder. Caliber: 38 Special. 3-and 4-inch bbls. Overall length: 8.25 and 9.25 inches. Weight: 32-34 oz. Windage-adj. rear sight. Blued finish. Discontinued.
With Plastic Grips $105
With Wood Grips 120

ROSSI REVOLVERS
Sáo Leopoldo, Brazil
Manufactured by Amadeo Rossi S.A.

Rossi Model 31 DA Revolver $125
Caliber: 38 Special. 5-shot cylinder. 4-inch bbl. Weight: 20 oz. Blue or nickel finish. Discontinued 1985.

Rossi Model 51 DA Revolver $140
Caliber: 22 LR. 6-shot cylinder. 6-inch bbl. Weight: 28 oz. Blued finish.

Rossi Model 68 . . . . $145
Caliber: 38 Special. 5-round magazine. 2- or 3-inch bbl. Overall length: 6.5 and 7.5 inches. Weight: 21-23 oz. Blued finish. Nickel finish available with 3-inch bbl.

Rossi Model 84 DA Revolver $185
Caliber: 38 Special. 6-shot. 3-inch bbl. 8 inches overall. Weight: 27.5 oz. Stainless steel finish. Made 1984-86.

Rossi Model 85 DA Revolver $195
Same as Model 84 except has ventilated rib.

Rossi Model 88 DA Revolver $185
Caliber: 38 Special. 5-shot cylinder. 2- or 3-inch bbl. Weight: 21 oz. Stainless steel finish.

Rossi Model 88 DA Revolver

Rossi Model 88/2 DA Revolver $225
Caliber: 38 Special. 5-shot cylinder. 2- or 3-inch bbl. 6.5 inches overall. Weight: 21 oz. Stainless steel finish. Made 1985-87.

Rossi Model 89 DA Revolver $155
Caliber: 32 S&W. 6-shot cylinder. 3-inch bbl. 7.5 inches overall. Weight: 17 oz. Stainless steel finish. Disc. 1986.

Rossi Model 94 DA Revolver $175
Caliber: 38 Special. 6-shot cylinder. 3-inch bbl. 8 inches overall. Weight: 29 oz. Discontinued 1986.

Rossi Model 95 Revolver $170
Caliber: 38 Special. 6-round magazine. 3-inch bbl. 8 inches overall. Weight: 27.5 oz. Ventilated rib. Blued finish. Discontinued 1986.

Rossi Model 511 DA Revolver $155
Similar to the Model 51, except in stainless steel. Made 1986-1990.

Rossi Model 515 DA Revolver $185
Calibers: 22 LR, 22 WRF. 6-shot cylinder. 4-inch bbl. 9 inches overall. Weight: 30 oz. Red ramp front sight; adj. square-notched rear. Stainless finish. Checkered hardwood stocks. Made from 1992 to date.

Rossi Model 518 DA Revolver $175
Similar to the Model 515, except in caliber 22 LR. Made 1993 to date.

Rossi Model 720 DA Revolver $205
Caliber: 44 Special. 5-shot cylinder. 3-inch bbl. 8 inches overall. Weight: 27.5 oz. Red ramp front sight; adj. square-notched rear. Stainless finish. Checkered neoprene combat-style stocks. Made from 1992 to date.

Rossi Model 841 DA Revolver $195
Same general specifications as Model 84, except has 4-inch bbl. (9 inches overall), weighs 30 oz. Made 1985-86.

Rossi Model 851

Rossi Model 851 DA Revolver $185
Same general specifications as Model 85, except with 3-or 4-inch bbl. 8 inches overall w/3-inch bbl. Weight: 27.5 oz. w/3-inch bbl. Red ramp front sight; adj. square-notched rear. Stainless finish. Checkered hardwood stocks. Made from 1991 to date.

Rossi Model 941 DA Revolver $155
Caliber: 38 Special. 6-shot cylinder. 4-inch bbl. 9 inches overall. Weight: 30 oz. Blue finish. Made 1985-86.

Rossi Model 951 DA Revolver $195
Same general specifications as Model 941 except has ventilated rib.

Rossi Model 971 DA Revolver

Rossi Model 971 DA Revolver
Caliber: 357 Magnum. 6-shot cylinder. 2.5-, 4- or 6-inch bbl. 9 inches overall w/4-inch bbl. Weight: 36 oz. w/4-inch bbl. Blade front sight, adj. square-notched rear. Blued or stainless finish. Checkered hardwood stocks. Made from 1990 to date.
Blued Finish **$210**
Stainless Finish **245**

Rossi DA Revolver

Rossi DA Revolver $130
Calibers: 22 LR, 32 S&W Long, 38 Special. 5-shot (38) or 6-shot cylinder (other calibers). Bbl. lengths: 3-, 6-inch. Weight: 22 oz. w/3-inch bbl. Sights: adj. rear, ramp front. Blued or nickel finish. Wood or plastic stocks. Made 1965-1991.

Rossi Sportsman's 22

Rossi Sportsman's 22 . . . . **$185**
Caliber: 22 LR. 6-round magazine. 4-inch bbl. 9 inches overall. Weight: 30 oz. Stainless steel finish. Disc. 1991. *See* illustration preceding page.

RUBY PISTOL
Manufactured by Gabilondo y Urresti, Eibar, Spain, and others

Ruby 7.65mm Automatic Pistol **$180**
Secondary standard service pistol of the French Army in World Wars I and II. Essentially the same as the Alkartasuna (*see* separate listing). Other manufacturers: Armenia Elgoibarresa y Cia., Eceolaza y Vicinai y Cia., Hijos de Angel Echeverria y Cia., Bruno Salaverria y Cia., Zulaika y Cia., all of Eibar, Spain-Gabilondo y Cia., Elgoibar Spain; Ruby Arms Company, Guernica, Spain. Made 1914-1922.

RUGER HANDGUNS
Southport, Connecticut
Manufactured by Sturm, Ruger & Co.

Rugers made in 1976 are designated "Liberty" in honor of the U.S. Bicentennial and bring a premium of approximately 25 percent in value over regular models.

AUTOMATIC/SINGLE-SHOT PISTOLS

NOTE

For ease in finding a particular Ruger handgun, the listings are divided into two groupings: Automatic/Single-Shot Pistols (below) and Revolvers, which follow. For a complete listing, please refer to the Index.

Ruger Hawkeye
Single-Shot Pistol

Ruger Hawkeye Single-Shot Pistol **$1100**
SA. Cylinder replaced by rotating breechblock; chamber is in bbl. Caliber: 256 Magnum. 8.5-inch bbl. 14.5 inches overall. Weight: 45 oz. Blued finish. Click adj. rear sight, ramp front sight. Smooth walnut stocks. Made 1963-65.

Ruger Mark I Target
w/6.88-inch heavy tapered barrel

Ruger Mark I Target
w/5.5-inch untapered bull barrel

Ruger Mark I Target Model Automatic Pistol
Caliber: 22 LR. 9-shot magazine. Bbls.: 5.25 or 6.88 inch heavy tapered, 5.5-inch untapered bull bbl. 10.88 inches overall w/6.88-inch bbl. Weight: 42 oz. w/5.5- or 6.88-inch bbl. Sights: adj. rear, under-cut target front. Blued finish. Hard rubber stocks or checkered walnut thumbrest stocks (add $10 to value for latter). Made 1951-1981.
Standard **$185**
With Red Medallion 495

Ruger Mark II Automatic Pistol

Ruger Mark II Automatic Pistol
Caliber: 22 LR, standard or high velocity. 4.75- or 6-inch tapered bbl. 10-shot magazine. 8.31 inches overall w/4.75-inch bbl. Weight: 36 oz. Fixed front sight, square notch rear. Blued or stainless finish. Made 1982 to date.
Blued **$175**
Stainless 225
Bright Stainless (Ltd. prod. 5,000 in 1982) 360

Ruger Mark II 22/45 Automatic Pistol

Same general specifications as Ruger Mark II 22 LR, except with stainless receiver and bbl. in three lengths: 4.75-inch tapered w/fixed sights, 5.25-inch tapered w/adj. sights and 5.5-inch bull. Fitted with Zytel grip frame of the same design as the Model 191145 ACP.

Model KP4 . . . . **$165**
Model KP512, KP514 . . . . **220**

Ruger Mark II Bull Barrel Model
Stainless w/10-inch barrel

Ruger Mark II Bull Barrel Model

Same as standard Mark II, except for bull bbl. (5.5- or 10-inch). Weight: about 2.75 pounds.

Blued Finish **$195**
Stainless Model, introduced 1985 . . . . **260**

Ruger Mark II Government Model Auto Pistol

Civilian version of the Mark II used by U.S. Armed Forces. Caliber: 22 LR rimfire. 10-shot magazine. 6.88-inch bull bbl. 11.13 inches overall. Weight: 44 oz., empty. Made from 1986 to date.

Blued **$240**
Stainless Steel **275**

Ruger Mark II Target Model

Ruger Mark II Target Model

Caliber: 22 LR. 10-shot magazine. 5.25- or 6.88-inch bbl. Weight: 38 oz. with 5.25-inch bbl.; 42 oz. with 6.88-inch bbl. 11.13 inches overall with 6.88-inch bbl. Made from 1982 to date. Same as standard Mark II, except has 6.88-inch tapered bbl. Made from 1982 to date.

Blued Finish **$200**
Stainless Steel Finish **255**

Ruger Model P-85 Automatic Pistol

Caliber: 9mm. DA, recoil-operated. 15-shot capacity. 4.5 inch bbl. 7.84 inches overall. Weight: 32 oz. Fixed rear sight, square-post front. Available with decocking levers, ambidextrous safety or in DA only. Blued or stainless finish. Made 1987 to date.

Blued Finish **$265**
Stainless Steel Finish **290**

Ruger Model P-85 Automatic
Pistol

Ruger Model P-89 Automatic Pistol

Caliber: 9mm. DA with slide-mounted safety levers. 15-shot magazine. 4.5-inch bbl. 7.84 inches overall. Weight: 32 oz. Square-post front sight, adj. rear w/3-dot system. Blued or stainless steel finish. Grooved black Xenoy grips. Made from 1986 to date; stainless introduced in 1990.

P-89 Blued **$315**
P-89 Stainless **365**

Ruger Model P-89 DAC

Ruger Model P-89 DAC/DAO Auto Pistols

Similar to the standard Model P-89, except the P-89 DAC has ambidextrous decocking levers. The P-89 DAO operates in double-action-only mode, has stainless finish only and was introduced in 1991.

P-89 DAC Blued **$315**
P-89 DAC Stainless **375**
P-89 DAO Stainless **360**

Ruger Model P-90 DA Automatic Pistol

Caliber: 45 ACP. 7-shot magazine. 4.5-inch bbl. 7.88 inches overall. Weight: 33.5 oz. Square-post front sight adj. square-notched rear w/3-dot system. Grooved black Xenoy composition stocks. Stainless finish. DAC model has ambidextrous decocking levers. Made 1991 to date.

Model P-90 Standard **$315**
Model P-90 DAC (Decockers) **320**

Ruger Model P-91 DA Automatic Pistol

Same general specifications as the Model P-90, except chambered for 40 S&W with 12-shot double-column magazine. Made from 1992 to date.

Model P-91 Standard	$315
Model P-91 DAC (Decockers)	320
Model P-91 DAO (DA Only)	325

Ruger Model P-93 Compact Auto Pistol

Similar to the standard Model P-89, except with 3.9-inch bbl. (7.3 inches overall) and weighs 31 oz. Stainless steel finish. Made from 1993 to date.

Model P-93 DAC (Decocker) (Disc. 1994)	$395
Model P-93 DAO (DA Only)	375

Ruger Model P-94 Automatic Pistol

Similar to the Model P-91, except with 4.25-inch bbl. Calibers: 9mm or 40 S&W. Stainless steel finish. Made from 1994 to date.

Model P-94 DAC (Decocker)	$340
Model P-94 DAO (Double Action Only)	335

Ruger Standard Model Automatic Pistol

Caliber: 22 LR. 9-shot magazine. 4.75- or 6-inch bbl. 8.75 inches overall w/4.75-inch bbl. Weight: 36 oz. w/4.75 inch bbl. Fixed sights. Blued finish. Hard rubber or checkered walnut stocks. Made from 1949 to date. *Note:* In 1951, after the death of Alexander Sturm, the color of the eagle on the stock medallion was changed from red to black as a memorial. Known as the "Red Eagle Automatic," this early type is now a collector's item. Discontinued 1981.

With Red Eagle Medallion	$495
With Black Eagle Medallion	145
Extra for Walnut Stocks	15

REVOLVERS

> **NOTE**
>
> This section contains only Ruger Revolvers. Automatic and Single-Shot Pistols may be found on the preceding pages. For a complete listing of Ruger handguns, please refer to the Index.

Ruger Bearcat SA (Old Model)

Ruger Bearcat SA (Old Model) $295

Aluminum frame. Caliber: 22 LR. 6-shot cylinder. 4-inch bbl. 8.88 inches overall. Weight: 17 oz. Fixed sights. Blued finish. Smooth walnut stocks. Made 1958-1973.

Ruger Bearcat, Super. $330

Same general specifications as Bearcat, except has steel frame. Weight: 25 oz. Made 1971-73.

Ruger Bisley, Large Frame

Ruger Bisley SA Revolver, Large Frame $265

Calibers: 357 Mag., 41 Mag. 44 Mag., 45 Long Colt. 7.5-inch bbl. 13 inches overall. Weight: 48 oz. Non-fluted or fluted cylinder, no engraving. Sights: adj. rear, ramp front. Blued satin finish. Made from 1986 to date.

Ruger Bisley, Small Frame

Ruger Bisley Single-Six Revolver, Small Frame $225

Calibers: 22 LR and 32 Mag. 6-shot cylinder. 6.5-inch bbl. 11.5 inches overall. Weight: 41 oz. Sights: fixed rear, blade front. Made from 1986 to date.

Ruger Blackhawk SA Convertible. $295

Same as Blackhawk, except has extra cylinder. Caliber combinations: 357 Magnum and 9mm Luger, 45 Colt and 45 Automatic. Made 1967-1972.

Ruger Blackhawk

Ruger Blackhawk SA Revolver $230

Calibers: 30 Carbine, 357 Magnum, 41 Magnum, 45 Colt. 6-shot cylinder. Bbl. lengths: 4.63-inch (357, 41, 45 caliber), 6.5-inch (357, 41 caliber), 7.5-inch (30, 45 caliber). 10.13 inches overall (357 Mag. w/4.63-inch bbl.). Weight: 38 oz. (357 w/4.63-inch bbl.). Sights: adj. rear, ramp front. Blued finish. Checkered hard rubber or smooth walnut stocks. Made 1956-1973.

Ruger Blackhawk SA 44

Ruger New Model Blackhawk

Ruger Blackhawk SA 44 Magnum Revolver

SA with heavy frame and cylinder. Caliber: 44 Magnum. 6-shot cylinder. 6.5-inch bbl. 12.13 inches overall. Weight: 40 oz. Adj. rear sight, ramp front. Blued finish. Smooth walnut stocks. Made 1956-73.

Standard **$400**
Flat Top. **625**

Ruger GP-100 DA Revolver

Ruger New Model Blackhawk SA Revolver

Interlocked mechanism. Calibers: 30 Carbine, 357 Magnum, 41 Magnum, 44 Magnum, 44 Special, 45 Colt. 6-shot cylinder. Bbl. lengths: 4.63-inch (357, 41, 45 Colt); 5.5 inch (44 Mag., 44 Spec.); 6.5-inch (357, 41, 45 Long Colt); 7.5-inch (30, 45, 44 Special, 44 Mag.); 10.5-inch in 44 Mag. 10.38 inches overall in 357 Mag. w/4.63-inch bbl. Weight: 40 oz. (357 w/4.63-inch bbl.). Adj. rear sight, ramp front. Blued finish or stainless steel; latter only in 357. Smooth walnut stocks. Made from 1973 to date.

Blued finish. **$220**
Stainless steel **295**
357 Maximum. **280**
44 Magnum, introduced 1987 . . . . **295**

Ruger GP-100 DA Revolver

Caliber: 357 Magnum. 4-inch heavy bbl., or 6-inch standard or heavy bbl. Overall length: 9.38 or 11.38 inches. Cushioned grip panels. Made from 1986 to date.

Blued Finish **$240**
Stainless Steel Finish. **280**

Ruger New Model Single-Six SSM
32 H&R Magnum

Ruger New Model Single-Six SSM Revolver **$195**

Same general specifications as standard Single-Six, except chambered for 32 H&R Magnum cartridge. Bbl. lengths: 4.63, 5.5, 6.5 or 9.5 inches.

Ruger New Model Blackhawk
Convertible

Ruger New Model Super
Blackhawk

Ruger New Model Blackhawk Convertible. **$240**

Same as New Model Blackhawk, except has extra cylinder; blued finish only. Caliber combinations: 357 Magnum and 9mm Luger, 45 Colt and 45 Automatic. 45 Colt and 45 Automatic discontinued 1983.

Ruger New Model Super Blackhawk SA Revolver

Interlocked mechanism. Caliber: 44 Magnum. 6-shot cylinder. 5.5-inch, 7.5-inch and 10.5-inch bull bbl. 13.38 inches overall. Weight: 48 oz. Adj. rear sight, ramp front. Blued and stainless steel finish. Smooth walnut stocks. Made from 1973 to date. 5.5-inch bbl. made from 1987 to date.

Blued Finish **$245**
Stainless Steel **285**

**Ruger New Model Super Single-Six
Convertible**

Ruger New Model Super Single-Six Convertible Revolver

SA with interlocked mechanism. Calibers: 22 LR and 22 WMR. Interchangeable 6-shot cylinders. Bbl. lengths: 4.63, 5.5, 6.5, 9.5 inches. 10.81 inches overall w/4.63 inch bbl. Weight: 33 oz. w/4.63-inch bbl. Adj. rear sight, ramp front. Blued finish or stainless steel; latter only with 5.5- or 6.5-inch bbl. Smooth walnut stocks. Made from 1972 to date.

Blued Finish **$195**
Stainless Steel **235**

**Ruger Police Service-Six
Stainless Steel**

Ruger Police Service-Six

Same general specifications as Speed-Six, except has square butt. Stainless steel models and 9mm Luger caliber available with only 4-inch bbl. Made 1971-1988.

38 Special, Blued Finish **$185**
38 Special, Stainless Steel **195**
357 Magnum or 9mm Luger, Blued Finish **200**
357 Magnum, Stainless Steel **225**

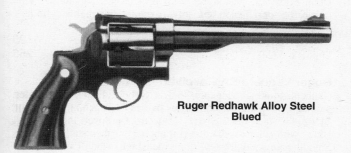

**Ruger Redhawk Alloy Steel
Blued**

Ruger Redhawk DA Revolver

Calibers: 357 Mag., 41 Mag., 44 Mag. 6-shot cylinder. 5.5-and 7.5-inch bbl. 11 and 13 inches overall, respectively. Weight: about 52 oz. Adj. rear sight, interchangeable front sights. Stainless finish. Made 1979 to date; 357 Mag. discontinued 1986. Alloy steel model with blued finish introduced in 1986 in 41 Mag. and 44 Mag. calibers.

Blued Finish **$285**
Stainless Steel **335**

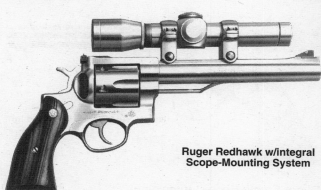

**Ruger Redhawk w/integral
Scope-Mounting System**

Ruger Redhawk Stainless DA Scope-Ring Revolver **$355**

Same general specifications as standard Redhawk, except chambered for 44 Mag. only, and has integral mounting system.

Ruger Security-Six

Ruger Security-Six DA Revolver

Caliber: 357 Magnum, handles 38 Special. 6-shot cylinder. Bbl. lengths: 2.25-, 4-, 6-inch. 9.25 inches overall w/4-inch bbl. Weight: 33.5 oz. w/4-inch bbl. Adj. rear sight, ramp front. Blued finish or stainless steel. Square butt. Checkered walnut stocks. Made 1971-85.

Blued Finish **$200**
Stainless Steel **225**

Ruger Single-Six

Ruger Single-Six SA Revolver

Calibers: 22 LR, 22 WMR. 6-shot cylinder. Bbl. lengths: 4.63, 5.5, 6.5, 9.5 inches. 10.88 inches overall w/5.5-inch bbl. Weight: about 35 oz. Fixed sights. Blued finish. Checkered hard rubber or smooth walnut grips. Made 1953-73. *Note:* Pre-1956 model with flat loading gate is worth about twice as much as later version. *See* illustration preceding page.

Standard **$195**
Convertible (w/2 cylinders, 22 LR/22 WMR) **225**

Ruger Single-Six — Lightweight

Ruger Single-Six — Lightweight **$260**

Same general specifications as Single-Six, except has 4.75-inch bbl., lightweight alloy cylinder and frame, 10 inches overall length, weighs 23 oz. Made in 1956.

Ruger SP101

Ruger SP101 DA Revolver

Calibers: 22 LR, 32 Mag., 9mm, 38 Special+P, 357 Mag. 5- or 6-shot cylinder. 2.25-, 3.06- or 4-inch bbl. Weight: 25-34 oz. Stainless steel finish. Cushioned grips. Made from 1988 to date.

Standard Model **$270**
DAO Model (DA only, spurless hammer) **275**

Ruger Speed-Six

Ruger Speed-Six DA Revolver

Calibers: 38 Special, 357 Magnum, 9mm Luger. 6-shot cylinder. Bbl. lengths: 2.75-, 4-inch; 9mm available only with 2.75-inch bbl. 7.75 inches overall w/2.75-inch bbl. Weight: 31 oz. w/2.75-inch bbl. Fixed sights. Blued or stainless steel finish; latter available in 38 Special w/2.75 inch bbl., 357 Magnum and 9mm with either bbl. Round butt. Checkered walnut stocks. Made 1973-87.

38 Special, Blued Finish **$150**
38 Special, Stainless Steel **180**
357 Magnum or 9mm Luger, Blued Finish **215**
357 Magnum or 9mm Luger, Stainless Steel **245**

Ruger Super Bearcat

See Ruger Bearcat, Super.

Ruger Super Blackhawk SA Revolver **$250**

Caliber: 44 Magnum. 6-shot cylinder. 7.5-inch bbl. 13.38 inches overall. Weight: 48 oz. Click adj. rear sight, ramp front. Blued finish. Steel or brass grip frame. Plain walnut stocks. Made 1959-73.

Ruger Super Redhawk

Ruger Super Redhawk Revolver **$395**

Caliber: 44 Magnum. 7.5- or 9.5-inch bbl. 13 or 15 inches overall. Weight: 53-58 oz. Cushioned grips. Satin polished stainless steel finish. Made from 1987 to date.

Ruger Super Single-Six

Ruger Super Single-Six Convertible Revolver

Same general specifications as Single-Six, except has ramp front, click-adj. rear sights with protective ribs integral with frame, 5.5- or 6.5-inch bbl. only; two interchangeable cylinders, 22 LR and 22 WMR. Made from 1973 to date.

Blued **$195**
Stainless Steel **255**

Ruger Vaquero SA Revolver

Calibers: 44-40, 44 Magnum, 45 Colt. 6-shot cylinder. Bbl. lengths: 4.63, 5.5, 7.5 inches. 13.63 inches overall (7.5-inch bbl.). Weight: 41 oz. (7.5-inch bbl.). Sights: blade front-grooved topstrap rear. Blued with color casehardened frame or polished stainless finish. Smooth rosewood grips w/Ruger medallion. Made 1993 to date.

Blued w/Color-casehardened Frame **$268**
Stainless Finish **268**

RUSSIAN SERVICE PISTOLS
Mfd. by Government plants at Tula and elsewhere

Tokarev-type pistols have also been made in Hungary, Poland, Yugoslavia, People's Republic of China, N. Korea.

Russian Model 30 Tokarev

Russian Model 30 Tokarev Service Automatic . . $375
Modified Colt-Browning type. Caliber: 7.62mm Russian Automatic (also uses 7.63mm Mauser Automatic cartridge). 8-shot magazine. 4.5-inch bbl. 7.75 inches overall. Weight: about 29 oz. Fixed sights. Made 1930 mid-1950s. *Note:* A slightly modified version with improved locking system and different disconnector was adopted in 1933.

**Russian Model PM
Makarov Auto**

Russian Model PM Makarov Auto Pistol $135
Double-action, blowback design. Caliber: 9mm Makarov. 8-shot magazine. 3.8-inch bbl. 6.4 inches overall. Weight: 26 oz. Blade front sight; square-notched rear. Checkered composition grips.

SAKO HANDGUNS
Riihimaki, Finland
Manufactured by Oy Sako Ab

Sako 22-32 Olympic Pistol
Calibers: 22 LR, 22 Short, 32 S&W Long. 5-round magazine. Bbls.: 6 or 8.85 (22 Short) inches. Weight: about 46 oz. (22 LR); 44 oz. (22 Short); 48 oz. (32). Steel frame. ABS plastic, anatomically designed grip. Non-reflecting matte black upper surface and chromium-plated slide. Equipped w/carrying case and tool set. Made 1983-89.
Sako 22-32 Single Pistol. $1045
Sako Triace, triple-barrel set w/wooden grip **1840**

Sako 22-32 Olympic Pistol

SAUER HANDGUNS
Mfd. through WW II by J. P. Sauer & Sohn, Suhl, Germany. Now mfd. by J. P. Sauer & Sohn, GmbH, Eckernförde, West Germany

See **also listings under Sig-Sauer.**

Sauer Model 1913

Sauer Model 1913 Pocket Automatic Pistol $260
Caliber: 32 Automatic (7.65mm). 7-shot magazine. 3-inch bbl. 5.88 inches overall. Weight: 22 oz. Fixed sights. Blue finish. Black hard rubber stocks. Made 1913-1930.

Sauer Model 1930

Sauer Model 1930 Pocket Automatic Pistol $295
Authority Model (Behorden Modell). Successor to Model 1913, has improved grip and safety. Caliber: 32 Auto (7.65mm). 7-shot magazine. 3-inch bbl. 5.75 inches overall. Weight: 22 oz. Fixed sights. Blued finish. Black hard rubber stocks. Made 1930-38. *Note:* Some pistols made with indicator pin showing when cocked. Also mfd. with dural slide and receiver; this type weighs about 7 oz. less than the standard model.

**Sauer Model 38H
Wartime Model**

Sauer Model 38H DA Automatic Pistol **$395**
Calibers: 25 Auto (6.35mm), 32 Auto (7.65mm), 380 Auto
(9mm). Specifications shown are for 32 Auto model. 7-shot
magazine. 3.25-inch bbl. 6.25 inches overall. Weight: 20 oz.
Fixed sights. Blued finish. Black plastic stocks. Also made in
dural model weighing about 6 oz. less. Made 1938-1945. *Note:*
This pistol, designated Model 38, was mfd. during WW II for
military use. Wartime models are inferior to earlier production,
as some lack safety lever.

Sauer Pocket 25 Automatic Pistol **$295**
Smaller version of Model 1913, issued about same time as 32
caliber model. Caliber: 25 Auto (6.35mm). 7-shot magazine.
2.5-inch bbl. 4.25 inches overall. Weight: 14.5 oz. Fixed sights.
Blued finish. Black hard rubber stocks. Made 1913-1930.

Sauer Single-Action Revolvers *See* listings under Hawes.

SAVAGE ARMS CO.
Utica, New York

Savage Model 101

Savage Model 101 SA Single-Shot Pistol **$150**
Barrel integral with swing-out cylinder. Calibers: 22 Short,
Long, LR. 5.5-inch bbl. Weight: 20 oz. Blade front sight, slotted
rear, adj. for windage. Blued finish. Grips of compressed, impregnated wood. Made 1960-68.

Savage Model 1907 Automatic Pistol **$295**
Caliber: 32 ACP, 10-shot magazine. 3.25-inch bbl., 6.5 inches
overall. Weight: 19 oz. Checkered steel grips marked "Savage
Quality," circling an Indian-head logo. Made from 1908 to 1920.

Savage Model 1910

Savage Model 1910 Automatic Pistol **$195**
Calibers: 32 Auto, 380 Auto. 10-shot magazine (32 cal.), 9-shot
(380 cal.). 3.75-inch bbl. (32 cal.), 4.25-inch (380 cal.). 6.5
inches overall (32 cal.), 7 inches (380 cal.). Weight: about 23 oz.
Fixed sights. Blued finish. Hard rubber stocks. Made in hammerless type with grip safety or with exposed hammer spur.
Made 1910-17.

Savage Model 1915 Automatic Pistol **$320**
Same general specifications as the Savage Model 1907 except
the Model 1915 is hammerless and has a grip safety. It is also
chambered for both the 32 and 380 ACP.

Savage U.S. Army Test Model **$5000**
Caliber: 45 ACP, 7-shot magazine with exposed hammer. An enlarged version of the Model 1910 manufactured for military tri-
als between 1907 and 1911.

Savage Model 1917

Savage Model 1917 Automatic Pistol **$305**
Same specifications as 1910 Model, except has spur-type hammer and redesigned heavier grip. Made 1917-1928.

SEARS, ROEBUCK & COMPANY
Chicago, Illinois

Sears/J.C. Higgins Model 80 Auto Pistol **$150**
Caliber: 22 LR. 10-shot magazine. 4.5- or 6.5-inch interchange-able bbl. 10.88 inches overall w/6.5-inch bbl. Weight: 41 oz. w/6.5-inch bbl. Fixed Patridge sights. Blued finish. Checkered stocks with thumbrest.

J.C. Higgins Model 88 Revolver

Sears/J.C. Higgins Model 88 DA Revolver **$95**
Caliber: 22 LR. 9-shot cylinder. 4- or 6-inch bbl. 9.5 inches w/4-inch bbl. Weight: 23 oz. w/4-inch bbl. Fixed sights. Blued or nickel finish. Checkered plastic stocks.

Sears/J.C. Higgins Ranger DA Revolver **$115**
Caliber: 22 LR. 9-shot cylinder. 5.5-inch bbl. 10.75 inches over-all. Weight: 28 oz. Fixed sights. Blued or chrome finish. Check-ered plastic stocks.

SECURITY INDUSTRIES OF AMERICA
Little Ferry, New Jersey

Security Model PM357

Security Model PM357 DA Revolver **$195**
Caliber: 357 Magnum. 5-shot cylinder. 2.5-inch bbl. 7.5 inches overall. Weight: 21 oz. Fixed sights. Stainless steel. Walnut stocks. Introduced 1975; discontinued.

Security Model PPM357 DA Revolver **$180**
Caliber: 357 Magnum. 5-shot cylinder. 2-inch bbl. 6.13 inches overall. Weight: 18 oz. Fixed sights. Stainless steel. Walnut stocks. Made from 1976 to date. *Note:* Spurless hammer (illus-trated) was discontinued in 1977; this model now has the same conventional hammer as other Security revolvers.

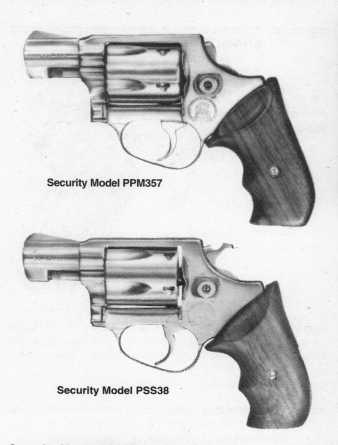

Security Model PPM357

Security Model PSS38

Security Model PSS38 DA Revolver **$180**
Caliber: 38 Special. 5-shot cylinder. 2-inch bbl. 6.5 inches over-all. Weight: 18 oz. Fixed sights. Stainless steel. Walnut stocks. Introduced 1973. Discontinued.

R. F. SEDGLEY. INC.
Philadelphia, Pennsylvania

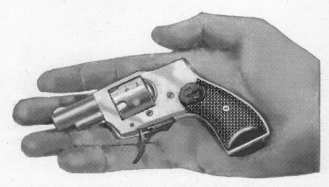

Sedgley Baby Hammerless Ejector Revolver . . . **$395**
DA. Solid frame. Folding trigger. Caliber: 22 Long. 6-shot cylin-der. 4 inches overall. Weight: 6 oz. Fixed sights. Blued or nickel finish. Rubber stocks. Made c. 1930-39.

SHERIDAN PRODUCTS, INC.
Racine, Wisconsin

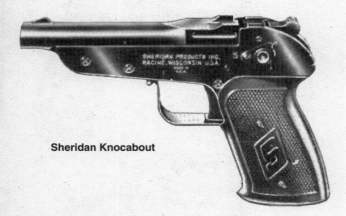

Sheridan Knocabout

Sheridan Knocabout Single-Shot Pistol $140
Tip-up type. Caliber: 22 LR, Long, Short. 5-inch bbl. 6.75 inches overall. Weight: 24 oz. Fixed sights. Checkered plastic stocks. Blue finish. Made 1953-60.

SIG PISTOLS
Neuhausen am Rheinfall, Switzerland
Mfd. by SIG Schweizerische Industrie-Gesellschaft

See also listings under SIG-Sauer.

SIG Model P210-1

SIG Model P210-1 Automatic Pistol $1495
Calibers: 22 LR, 7.65mm Luger, 9mm Luger. 8-shot magazine.4.75-inch bbl. 8.5 inches overall. Weight: 33 oz. (22 cal.); 35 oz. (7.65mm, 9mm). Fixed sights. Polished blued finish. Checkered wood stocks. Made 1949-86.

SIG Model P210-2 . . . . $1250
Same as Model P210-1, except has sandblasted finish, plastic stocks; not avail. in 22 LR. Discont. 1987.

SIG Model P210-5 Target Pistol $1495
Same as Model P210-2, except has 6-inch bbl., micrometer adj. rear sight, target front sight, adj. trigger stop. 9.7 inches overall. Weight: about 38.3 oz. Discontinued.

SIG Model P210-6

SIG Model P210-6 Target Pistol $1495
Same as Model P210-2, except has micrometer adj. rear sight, target front sight, adj. trigger stop. Weight: about 37 oz. Discontinued 1987.

SIG P210 22 Conversion Unit $595
Converts P210 pistol to 22 LR. Consists of bbl. with recoil spring, slide and magazine.

SIG-Hämmerli Model P240 Automatic Pistol . . . $1095
For data *see* listing under Hämmerli. Discont. 1986.

SIG-SAUER HANDGUNS
Mfd. by J. P. Sauer & Sohn of West Germany, SIG of Switzerland, and other manufacturers

SIG-Sauer Model P220

SIG-Sauer Model P220 DA Automatic Pistol $545
Calibers: 9mm Luger, 38 Super, 45 Automatic. 7-shot in 45, 9-shot in other calibers. 4.4-inch bbl. 8 inches overall. Weight: 9mm, 26.5 oz. Fixed sights. Blued finish Checkered plastic stocks. Made from 1976 to date. *Note:* Also sold in U.S. as Browning BDA.

SIG-Sauer Model P225

SIG-Sauer Model P225 DA Automatic **$560**
Caliber: 9mm Parabellum. 8-shot magazine. 3.85-inch bbl. 7 inches overall. Weight: 26.1 oz. Blue finish.

SIG-Sauer Model P226 DA Automatic **$550**
Caliber: 9mm Parabellum. 15-shot magazine. 4.4-inch bbl. 7.75 inches overall. Weight: 26.5 oz. Blue finish. Made from1985 to date.

SIG-Sauer Model P228 DA Automatic
Same general specifications as Model P226, except with 3.86-inch bbl. 7.13 inches overall. Blued or K-Kote finish. Made from 1990 to date.
Blued Finish **$525**
K-Kote Finish 570
For Siglite Nite Sights, **add** 80

Sig-Sauer Model P229 DA Automatic
Same general specifications as Model P226, except chambered in 40 S&W with 12-shot magazine. 3.86-inch bbl. 7.13 inches overall. Weight: 30.5 oz. Blued finish. Made from 1991 to date.
Blued Finish **$650**
Blued Finish DAO (double action only) 650
For Siglite Nite Sights, **add** 80

SIG-Sauer Model P230

SIG-Sauer Model P230 DA Automatic Pistol
Calibers: 22 LR, 32 Automatic (7.65mm), 380 Automatic (9mm Short), 9mm Police.10-shot magazine in 22, 8-shot in 32, 7-shot in 9mm. 3.6-inch bbl. 6.6 inches overall. Weight: 32 Auto, 18.2 oz. Fixed sights. Blued or stainless finish. Plastic stocks. Made from 1976 to date.
Blued Finish **$350**
Stainless Finish 395

SMITH & WESSON, INC.
Springfield, Massachusetts

NOTE

For ease in locating a particular S&W handgun, the listings are divided into two groupings: Automatic/Single-Shot Pistols (below) and Revolvers (page 151). For a complete handgun listing, please refer to the Index.

AUTOMATIC/SINGLE-SHOT PISTOLS

Smith & Wesson 32 Automatic

Smith & Wesson 32 Automatic Pistol **$1850**
Caliber: 32 Automatic. Same general specifications as 35 caliber model, but barrel is fastened to the receiver instead of hinged. Made 1924-1937.

Smith & Wesson 35 Automatic

Smith & Wesson 35 Automatic Pistol **$675**
Caliber: 35 S&W Automatic. 7-shot magazine. 3.5-inch bbl. (hinged to frame). 6.5 inches overall. Weight: 25 oz. Fixed sights. Blued or nickel finish. Plain walnut stocks. Made 1913-1921.

Smith & Wesson Model 39

Smith & Wesson Model 39 9mm DA Auto Pistol

Caliber: 9mm Luger. 8-shot magazine. 4-inch bbl. Overall length: 7.44 inches. Weight: 26.5 oz. Click adjustable rear sight, ramp front. Blued or nickel finish. Checkered walnut stocks. Made 1954-1982. *Note:* Between 1954 and 1966, 927 pistols of this model were made w/steel instead of alloy frames.

With Steel Frame **$835**
With Alloy Frame **335**

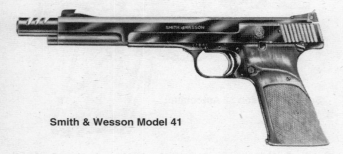

Smith & Wesson Model 41

Smith & Wesson Model 41 22 Auto Pistol $565

Caliber: 22 LR, 22 Short (not interchangeable). 10-shot magazine. Bbl. lengths: 5-, 5.5-, 7.38-inch; latter has detachable muzzle brake. 12 inches overall (7.38-inch bbl.). Weight: 43.5 oz. (7.38-inch bbl.). Click adj. rear sight, undercut Patridge front. Blued finish. Checkered walnut stocks w/thumbrest. Made from 1957 to date.

Smith & Wesson Model 46

Smith & Wesson Model 46 22 Auto Pistol $435

Caliber: 22 LR. 10-shot magazine. Barrel lengths: 5, 5.5, 7 inches. 10.56 inches overall (7-inch bbl.). Weight: 42 oz. (7-inch bbl.). Click adj. rear sight, undercut Patridge front. Blue finish. Molded nylon stocks w/thumbrest. Only 4,000 produced. Made 1957-1966.

Smith & Wesson Model 52

Smith & Wesson Model 52 38 Master Auto $760

Caliber: 38 Special (midrange wadcutter only). 5-shot magazine. 5-inch bbl. Overall length: 8.63 inches. Weight: 41 oz. Micrometer click rear sight, Patridge front on ramp base. Blued finish. Checkered walnut stocks. Made 1961-1994.

Smith & Wesson Model 59

Smith & Wesson Model 59 9mm DA Auto $335

Similar specifications as Model 39, except has 14-shot magazine, checkered nylon stocks. Made 1971-1981.

Smith & Wesson Model 61

Smith & Wesson Model 61 Escort Pocket Automatic Pistol $230

Caliber: 22 LR. 5-shot magazine. 2.13-inch bbl. 4.69 inches overall. Weight: 14 oz. Fixed sights. Blued or nickel finish. Checkered plastic stocks. Made 1970-74.

Smith & Wesson Model 411 Auto Pistol $360

Similar to S&W Model 915, except in caliber 40 S&W. 11-shot magazine. Made from 1994 to date.

Smith & Wesson Model 422

Smith & Wesson Model 422 SA Auto Pistol

Caliber: 22 LR. 10-shot magazine. 4.5- or 6-inch bbl. 7.5 inches overall w/4.5-inch bbl. Weight: 22-23.5 oz. Fixed or adjustable sights. Checkered plastic or walnut grips. Blued finish. Made from 1987 to date.

Standard Model $175
Target Model 195

Smith & Wesson Model 439

Smith & Wesson Model 439 9mm Automatic. . . . $295

DA. Caliber: 9mm Luger. Two 8-round magazines. 4-inch bbl. 7.44 inches overall. Weight: 30 oz. Serrated ramp square front sight, square notch rear. Checkered walnut grips. Blue or nickel finish. Discontinued 1988.

Smith & Wesson Model 459 DA Automatic

Caliber: 9mm Luger. Two 14-round magazines. 4-inch bbl. 7.44 inches overall. Weight: 28 oz. Blued or nickel finish. Discontinued 1988.

Standard Model $325
FBI Model 550

Smith & Wesson Model 459

Smith & Wesson Model 469

Smith & Wesson Model 469 9mm Automatic. . . . $345

DA. Caliber: 9mm Luger. Two 12-round magazines. 3.5-inch bbl. 6.88 inches overall. Weight: 26 oz. Yellow ramp front sight, dovetail mounted square-notch rear. Sandblasted blue finish. Optional ambidextrous safety. Discontinued 1988.

Smith & Wesson Model 622 SA Auto Pistol

Same general specifications as Model 422, except with stainless finish. Made from 1990 to date.

Standard Model $175
Target Model 225

Smith & Wesson Model 639

Smith & Wesson Model 639 Automatic $340

Caliber: 9mm Luger Parabellum. Two 12-round magazines. 3.5-inch bbl. 6.9 inches overall. Weight: 26 oz. Nonglare blued finish. Discontinued 1988.

SMITH & WESSON — 3RD Generation, Semiautomatic Pistol

Models... 10XX 39XX 40XX 45XX 59XX
Calibers: 9mm, 10mm, 40 S&W, or 45 ACP
Barrel Lengths: 3 .5", 4", or 5"
Finish: Blue or Stainless
Capacity: 7-, 8-, 9-, 11-, 12-, or 15-Shot Magazine

See Note A

MODEL NOMENCLATURE

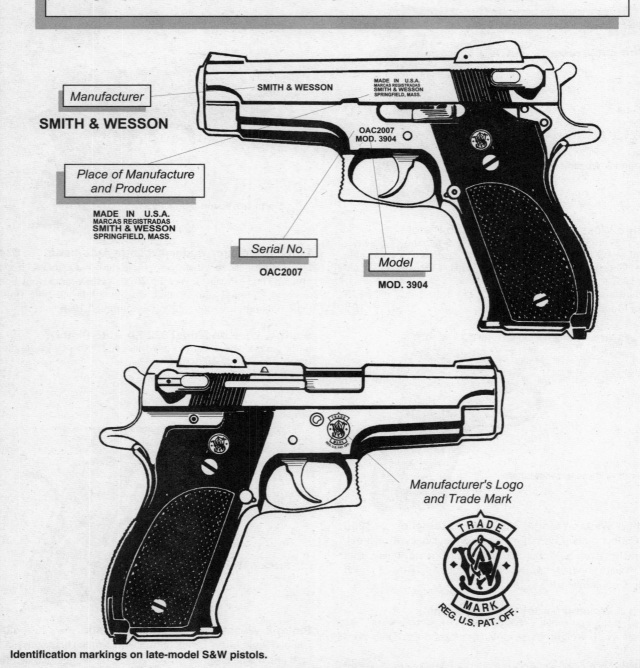

Manufacturer

SMITH & WESSON

SMITH & WESSON

MADE IN U.S.A.
MARCAS REGISTRADAS
SMITH & WESSON
SPRINGFIELD, MASS.

*Place of Manufacture
and Producer*

**MADE IN U.S.A.
MARCAS REGISTRADAS
SMITH & WESSON
SPRINGFIELD, MASS.**

OAC2007
MOD. 3904

Serial No.

OAC2007

Model

MOD. 3904

*Manufacturer's Logo
and Trade Mark*

TRADE MARK
REG. U.S. PAT. OFF.

Identification markings on late-model S&W pistols.

SMITH & WESSON 3RD Generation, Semiautomatic Pistols

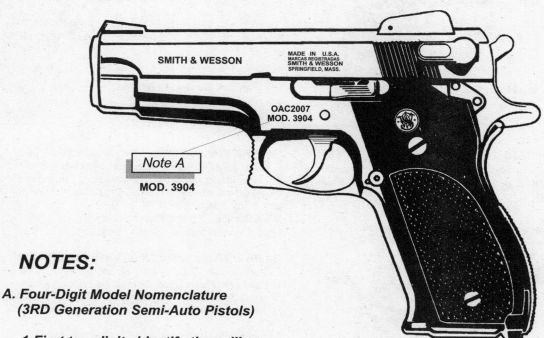

SMITH & WESSON

MADE IN U.S.A.
MARCAS REGISTRADAS
SMITH & WESSON
SPRINGFIELD, MASS.

OAC2007
MOD. 3904

Note A

MOD. 3904

NOTES:

A. Four-Digit Model Nomenclature
(3RD Generation Semi-Auto Pistols)

1-First two digits identify the caliber.
39 - 9mm
40 - 40 S&W
45 - 45 ACP
59 - 9mm
69 - 9mm

2-Third digit identifies the model type.
0 - Standard
1 - Compact
2 - Standard with Decocking Lever
3 - Compact with Decocking Lever
4 - Standard Double Action Only
5 - Compact Double Action Only
6 - Non-Standard Barrel Length
7 - Non-Standard Barrel Length w/Decocking Lever
8 - Non-Standard Barrel Length Double Action Only

3-Fourth digit identifies frame and slide composition.
3 - Aluminum Frame w/Stainless Slide
4 - Aluminum Frame w/Carbon Steel Slide
5 - Carbon Steel Frame & Slide
6 - Stainless Frame & Slide
7 - Stainless Frame w/Carbon Steel Slide

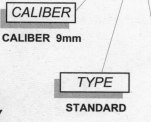

EXAMPLE

MODEL 3904

CALIBER

CALIBER 9mm

TYPE

STANDARD

COMPOSITION

ALUMINUM FRAME
w/CARBON STEEL SLIDE

Identification markings on late-model S&W pistols. *(Cont.)*

Smith & Wesson Model 645

Smith & Wesson Model 745

Smith & Wesson Model 645 DA Automatic $375
Caliber: 45 ACP. 8-shot. 5-inch bbl. Overall length: 8.5 inches. Weight: Approx. 38 oz. Red ramp front, fixed rear sights. Stainless. Made 1986-88.

Smith & Wesson Model 745 Automatic Pistol
Caliber: 45 ACP. 8-shot magazine. 5-inch bbl. 8.63 inches overall. Weight: 38.75 oz. Fixed sights. Blued slide, stainless frame. Checkered walnut grips. Similar to the model 645, but w/o DA capability. Made 1987-1990.
With Standard Competition Features **$450**
IPSC Commemorative (first 5,000) **545**

Smith & Wesson Model 909/910 Auto Pistols
Caliber: 9mm Parabellum. 9-shot (Model 909) or 10-shot (Model 910) magazine. 4-inch barrel. 7.38 inches overall. Weight: 28 oz. Post front sight; fixed rear. Delrin straight backstrap grips. Blued steel slide with alloy frame. Made 1994 to date.
Model 909 . . . . **$270**
Model 910 . . . . **285**

Smith & Wesson Model 659

Smith & Wesson Model 915 Auto Pistol $295
DA. Caliber: 9mm Luger. 15-shot magazine. 4-inch bbl. 7.5 inches overall. Weight: 28.5 oz. Post front sight, fixed square-notched rear w/3-dot system. Xenoy® wraparound grip. Blued steel slide and alloy frame. Made 1992-94.

Smith & Wesson Model 659 9mm Automatic $345
DA. Similar to S&W Model 459, except weight is 39.5 oz. and finish is satin stainless steel. Discontinued 1988.

Smith & Wesson Model 1026

Smith & Wesson Model 669

Smith & Wesson Model 669 Automatic $310
Caliber: 9mm. 12-shot magazine. Bbl.: 3.5 inches. 6.9 inches overall. Weight: 26 oz. Serrated ramp front sight with red bar, fixed rear. Nonglare stainless-steel finish. Made 1986-88.

Smith & Wesson Model 1000 Series DA Auto
Caliber: 10mm. 9-shot magazine. 4.25- or 5-inch bbl. 7.88 or 8.63 inches overall. Weight: about 38 oz. Post front sight, adj. or fixed square-notched rear w/3-dot system. One-piece Xenoy® wraparound grips. Stainless slide and frame. Made 1990-94.
Model 1006 (Fixed Sights, 5" bbl.) **$445**
Model 1006 (Adj. Sights, 5" bbl.) **475**

Smith & Wesson Model 1000 Series *(Cont.)*

Model 1026 (Fixed Sights, 5" bbl.,
  Decocking Lever) **475**
Model 1066 (Fixed Sights, 4.25" bbl.) **450**
Model 1076 (Fixed Sights, 4.25" bbl., Frame-mounted
  Decocking Lever, Straight Backstrap) **465**
Model 1076 (same as above w/Tritium Night Sight) **495**
Model 1086 (same as Model 1076 in DA only) **450**

Smith & Wesson Model 2206 SA Automatic Pistol

Similar to Model 422, except w/stainless-steel slide and frame, weighs 35-39 oz., has Patridge front sight on adj. sight model; post w/white dot on fixed sight model, plastic grips.
Standard Model **$200**
Target Model **245**

Smith & Wesson Model 2213 Sportsman Auto . . **$190**

Caliber: 22 LR. 8-shot magazine. 3-inch bbl. 6.13 inches overall. Weight: 18 oz. Patridge front sight, fixed square-notched rear w/3-Dot system. Black synthetic molded grips. Stainless steel slide w/alloy frame. Made 1992 to date.

Smith & Wesson Model 2214 Sportsman Auto . . **$185**

Same general specifications as Model 2214, except with blued slide and matte black alloy frame. Made from 1990 to date.

S&W Model 3906

Smith & Wesson Model 3904/3906 DA Auto Pistol

Caliber: 9mm. 8-shot magazine. 4-inch bbl. 7.5 inches overall. Weight: 25.5 oz. (Model 3904); 34 oz. (Model 3906). Fixed or adj. sights. Delrin one-piece wraparound, checkered grips. Alloy frame w/blued carbon steel slide (Model 3904) or satin stainless (Model 3906). Made 1989-1991.
Model 3904 w/Adjustable Sights **$365**
Model 3904 w/Fixed Sights **325**
Model 3904 w/Novak LC Sight **360**
Model 3906 w/Adjustable Sights **410**
Model 3906 w/Novak LC Sight **400**

Smith & Wesson Model 3913/3914 DA Automatic

Caliber: 9mm Parabellum (Luger). 8-shot magazine. 3.5-inch barrel. 6.88 inches overall. Weight: 25 oz. Post front sight, fixed or adj. square-notched rear. One-piece Xenoy® wraparound grips w/straight backstrap. Alloy frame with stainless or blued slide. Made 1990 to date.

S&W Model 3914

Smith & Wesson Model 3913/3914 *(Cont.)*

Model 3913 Stainless **$395**
Model 3913LS Lady Smith Stainless w/contoured
  Trigger Guard **410**
Model 3914 Blued. **370**

Smith & Wesson Model 3953/3954 DA Auto Pistol

Same general specifications as Model 3913/3914, except double action only. Made from 1991 to date.
Model 3953 Stainless, Double Action Only **$395**
Model 3954 Blued, Double Action Only **350**

S&W Model 4046

Smith & Wesson Model 4000 Series DA Auto

Caliber: 40 S&W. 11-shot magazine. 4-inch bbl. 7.88 inches overall. Weight: 28-30 oz. (alloy frame); 36 oz. (stainless frame). Post front sight; adj. or fixed square-notched rear w/2 white dots. Straight backstrap. One-piece Xenoy wraparound grips. Blued or stainless finish. Made between 1990/1992 to date.
Model 4003 Stainless w/Alloy Frame **$475**
Model 4004 Blued w/Alloy Frame **450**
Model 4006 Stainless Frame, Fixed Sights **395**
Model 4006 Stainless Frame, Adj. Sights **495**
Model 4026 w/Decocking Lever (disc. 1994) **535**
Model 4043 DA only, Stainless w/Alloy Frame. **465**
Model 4044 DA only, Blued w/Alloy Frame **440**
Model 4046 DA only, Stainless Frame, Fixed Sights. . . . **400**
Model 4046 DA only, Stainless Frame, Tritium
  Night Sight **565**

Smith & Wesson Model 4013/4014 DA Automatic

Caliber: 40 S&W.8-shot capacity. 3.5-inch bbl. 7 inches overall. Weight: 26 oz. Post front sight; fixed Novak LC rear w/3-dot system. One-piece Xenoy wraparound grips. Stainless or blued slide w/alloy frame. Made 1991 to date.

Model 4013 w/Stainless Slide **$455**
Model 4014 w/Blued Slide **445**

Smith & Wesson Model 4053/4054 DA Auto Pistol

Same general specifications as Model 4013/4014, except double action only. Alloy frame fitted with blued steel slide. Made from 1991 to date.

Model 4053 DA only w/Stainless Slide **$465**
Model 4054 DA only w/Blued Slide **395**

S&W Model 4506

Smith & Wesson Model 4500 Series DA Automatic

Caliber: 45 ACP. 7-shot magazine (Model 4516); 8-shot magazine (Model 4506). Bbl. lengths: 3.75, 4.25 or 5 inches. 7.13 to 8.63 inches overall. Weight: 34.5 to 38.5 oz. Post front sight; fixed Novak LC rear w/2-Dot system or adj. One-piece Xenoy wraparound grips. Satin stainless finish. Made from 1990 to date.

Model 4506 w/Fixed Sights, 5-inch bbl **$435**
Model 4506 w/Novak LC Sight, 5-inch bbl **445**
Model 4516 w/3.75-inch bbl. **475**
Model 4526 w/5-inch bbl., Alloy Frame, Decocking
  Lever, Fixed Sights **425**
Model 4536 w/Anodized frame, Decocking Lever **415**

S&W Model 5904

Smith & Wesson Model 4500 Series *(Cont.)*

Model 4556 w/3.75-inch bbl., DA only, Alloy Frame . . . **395**
Model 4566, 4.25-inch bbl., Ambidextrous Safety,
  Fixed Sights **435**
Model 4576 w/4.25-inch bbl., Decocking Lever **485**
Model 4586 w/4.25-inch bbl., DA only **495**

Smith & Wesson Model 5900 Series DA Automatic

Caliber: 9mm. 15-shot magazine. 4-inch bbl. 7.5 inches overall. Weight: 26-38 oz. Fixed or adj. sights. One-piece Xenoy wraparound grips. Alloy frame w/stainless-steel slide (Model 5903) or blued slide (Model 5904) stainless-steel frame and slide (Model 5906). Made from 1989/1990 to date.

Model 5903 w/Adjustable Sights **$435**
Model 5903 w/Novak LC Rear Sight. **425**
Model 5904 w/Adjustable Sights **430**
Model 5904 w/Novak LC Rear Sight. **405**
Model 5905 w/Adjustable Sights **430**
Model 5905 w/Novak LC Rear Sight. **415**
Model 5906 w/Adjustable Sights **440**
Model 5906 w/Novak LC Rear Sight. **405**
Model 5906 w/Tritium Night Sight **550**
Model 5924 Anodized frame, Blued Slide **385**
Model 5926 Stainless frame, Decocking Lever **460**
Model 5943 Alloy Frame/Stainless Slide, DA only **450**
Model 5944 Alloy Frame/Blued Slide, DA only **395**
Model 5946 Stainless Frame/Slide, DA only **445**

S&W Model 6906

Smith & Wesson Model 6900 Compact Series

Double action. Caliber: 9mm. 12-shot magazine. 3.5-inch bbl. 6.88 inches overall. Weight: 26.5 oz. Ambidextrous safety. Post front sight, fixed Novak LC rear w/3-Dot system. Alloy frame w/blued carbon steel slide (Model 6904) or stainless steel slide (Model 6906). Made from 1989 to date.

Model 6904 . . . . **$385**
Model 6906 w/Fixed Sights **425**
Model 6906 w/Tritium Night Sight **495**
Model 6926 Same as Model 6906 w/Decocking
  Lever. **853**
Model 6944 Same as Model 6904 in DA only **395**
Model 6946 Same as Model 6906 in DA only,
  Fixed Sights. **425**
Model 6946 w/Tritium Night Sight **495**

**S&W Model 1891
Single-Shot Pistol**

Smith & Wesson Model 1891 Single-Shot Target Pistol, First Model

Hinged frame. Calibers: 22 LR, 32 S&W, 38 S&W. Bbl. lengths: 6-, 8- and 10-inch. Approx. 13.5 inches overall w/10-inch bbl. Weight: about 25 oz. Target sights, barrel catch rear adj. for windage and elevation. Blued finish. Square butt, hard rubber stocks. Made 1893-1905. *Note:* This model was available also as a combination arm w/accessory 38 revolver bbl. and cylinder enabling conversion to a pocket revolver. It has the frame of the 38 SA Revolver Model 1891 w/side flanges, hand and cylinder stop slots.

Single-shot Pistol, 22 LR . . . . **$ 550**
Single-shot Pistol, 32 S&W or 38 S&W **1170**
Combination Set, Revolver and Single-shot Barrel **1395**

Smith & Wesson Model 1891 Single-Shot Target Pistol, Second Model **$475**

Similar to the First Model, except side flanges, hand and stop slots eliminated, cannot be converted to revolver, redesigned rear sight. Caliber: 22 LR only. 10-inch bbl. only. Made 1905-1909.

Smith & Wesson Perfected Single-Shot Target Pistol

Similar to the Second Model, except has double-action lockwork. Caliber: 22 LR only. 10-inch bbl. Checkered walnut stocks, extended square-butt target type. Made 1909-1923. *Note:* In 1920 and thereafter, this model was made w/barrels having bore diameter of .223 instead of .226 and tight, short chambering. The first group of these pistols was produced for the U.S. Olympic Team of 1920, thus the designation Olympic Model.

Pre-1920 Type **$495**
Olympic Model **695**

**S&W Straight Line
Target Pistol**

Smith & Wesson Straight Line Single-Shot Target Pistol **$1250**

Frame shaped like that of an automatic pistol, barrel swings to the left on pivot for extracting and loading, straight line trigger and hammer movement. Caliber: 22 LR. 10-inch bbl. 11.25 inches overall. Weight: 34 oz. Target sights. Blued finish. Smooth walnut stocks. Supplied in metal case with screwdriver and cleaning rod. Made 1925-1936.

REVOLVERS

NOTE

The following section contains only S&W Revolvers. Both Automatic and Single-Shot Pistols may be found in the preceding section. For a complete listing of S&W handguns, please refer to the index.

S&W Model 1

Smith & Wesson Model 1 Hand Ejector DA Revolver **$375**

First Model. Forerunner of the 32 Hand Ejector and Regulation Police models, this was the first S&W revolver of the solid-frame, swing-out cylinder type. Top strap of this model is longer than those of later models, and it lacks the usual S&W cylinder latch. Caliber: 32 S&W Long. Bbl. lengths: 3.25-, 4.25-, and 6-inch. Fixed sights. Blued or nickel finish. Round butt, hard rubber stocks. Made 1896-1903.

S&W No. 3 Frontier

Smith & Wesson No. 3 SA Frontier **$1470**

Caliber: 44-40 WCF. Bbl. lengths: 4-, 5- and 6.5-inch. Fixed or target sights. Blued or nickel finish. Round, hard rubber or checkered walnut grips. Made 1885-1908.

**S&W No. 3 SA
New Model**

Smith & Wesson No. 3 SA (New Model) $1345
Hinged frame. 6-shot cylinder. Caliber: 44 S&W Russian. Bbl. lengths: 4-, 5-, 6-, 6.5-, 7.5- and 8-inch. Fixed or target sights. Blued or nickel finish. Round, hard rubber or checkered walnut grips. Made 1878-1908. *Note:* Value shown is for standard model. Specialist collectors recognize numerous variations with a range of higher values.

Smith & Wesson No. 3 SA Target $1695
Hinged frame. 6-shot cylinder. Calibers: 32/44 S&W, 38/44 S&W Gallery & Target. 6.5-inch bbl. only. Fixed or target sights. Blued or nickel finish. Round, hard rubber or checkered walnut grips. Made 1887-1910.

**S&W Model 10
2-inch Barrel**

Smith & Wesson Model 10 38 Military & Police DA
Also called Hand Ejector Model of 1902, Hand Ejector Model of 1905, Model K. Manufactured substantially in its present form since 1902, this model has undergone numerous changes, most of them minor. Round- or square-butt models, the latter introduced in 1904. Caliber: 38 Special. 6-shot cylinder. Bbl. lengths: 2-(introduced 1933), 4-, 5-, 6- and 6.5-inch (latter discontinued 1915) also 4-inch heavy bbl. (introduced 1957). 11.13 inches overall in square-butt model w/6-inch bbl. Round-butt model is ¼-inch shorter, weighs about ½ oz. less. Fixed sights. Blued or nickel finish. Checkered walnut stocks, hard rubber available in round-butt style. Current Model 10 has short action. Made 1902 to date. *Note:* S&W Victory Model, wartime version of the M & P 38, was produced for the U.S. Government from 1940 to the end of the war. A similar revolver, designated 38/200 British Service Revolver, was produced for the British Government during the same period. These arms have either brush-polish or sandblast blue finish, and most of them have plain, smooth walnut stocks, lanyard swivels.

Model of 1902 (1902-05)	**$460**
Model of 1905 (1905-1940)	**395**
38/200 British Service (1940-1945)	**295**
Victory Model (1942-45)	**235**
Model of 1944 (1945-1948)	**175**
Model 10 (1948 - date)	**180**

Smith & Wesson Model 10 38 Military & Police Heavy Barrel $195
Same as standard Model 10, except has heavy 4-inch bbl., weighs 34 oz. Made from 1957 to date.

Smith & Wesson Model 12 38 M & P Airweight . . $215
Same as standard Military & Police, except has light alloy frame, furnished with 2- or 4-inch bbl. only, weighs 18 oz. (with 2-inch bbl.). Made 1952-1986.

**S&W Model 12
2-inch Barrel**

Smith & Wesson Model 13 357 Military/Police . . . $200
Same as Model 10 38 Military & Police Heavy Barrel except chambered for 357 Magnum and 38 Special with 3- or 4-inch bbl. Made 1974 to date.

**S&W Model 13
Heavy Barrel**

Smith & Wesson Model 13 (Heavy Barrel) DA Revolver $225
Calibers: 357 Mag. and 38 S&W Special. DA. 6-shot cylinder. Bbl. lengths: 3 and 4 inches, 9.25 inches overall. Weight: 34 oz. Square-notch rear sight, ramp front.

S&W Model 14

Smith & Wesson Models 14 (K38) and 16 (K32) Masterpiece Revolvers
Calibers: 22 LR, 22 Magnum Rimfire, 32 S&W Long, 38 Special. 6-shot cylinder. DA/SA. Bbl. lengths: 4- (22 WMR only), 6-, 8.38-inch (latter not available in K32). 11.13 inches overall (6-inch bbl.). Weight: 38.5 oz. w/6-inch bbl. Click adj. rear sight, Patridge front. Blued finish. Checkered walnut stocks. Made 1947 to date. (Model 16 discontinued 1974, with only 3,630 produced; reissued 1990-93.)

Model 14 (K-38 Double-Action)	**$225**
Model 14 (K-38 Single Action, 6-inch bbl.)	**245**
Model 14 (K-38 Single Action, 8.38-inch bbl.)	**260**
Model 16 (K-32 Double-Action)	**245**

S&W Model 15

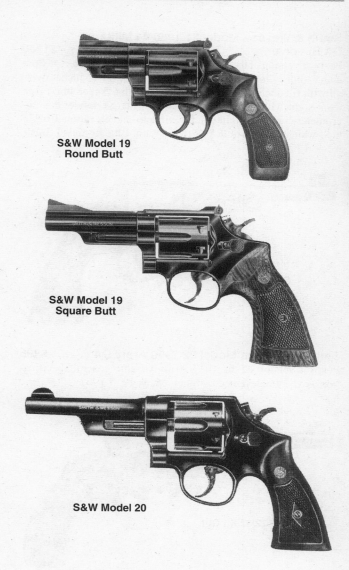

**S&W Model 19
Round Butt**

**S&W Model 19
Square Butt**

S&W Model 20

Smith & Wesson Models 15 (38) and 18 (22) Combat Masterpiece DA Revolvers

Same as K-22 and K-38 Masterpiece but with 2- (38) or 4-inch bbl. and Baughman quick-draw front sight. 9.13 inches overall with 4-inch bbl. Weight: 34 oz. (38 cal.). Introduced 1950, Model 18 (22 LR) discontinued 1985.

Model 15 . . . . **$255**
Model 18 . . . . **275**

S&W Model 17 K-22 Masterpiece

Smith & Wesson Model 17 K-22 Masterpiece
DA Revolver **$250**
Caliber: 22 LR. 6-shot cylinder. Bbl. lengths: 4, 6 or 8.38 inches. 11.13 inches overall w/6-inch bbl. Weight: 38.5 oz. w/6-inch bbl. Patridge-type front sight; S&W micrometer click rear. Checkered walnut Service grips w/S&W monogram. S&W blued finish. Made 1947 to date.

S&W Model 18
(*See* **S&W Model 15 for description**)

Smith & Wesson Model 19 357 Combat Magnum
DA Revolver **$265**
Caliber: 357 Magnum. 6-shot cylinder. Bbl lengths: 2.5 (round butt), 4, 6 inches, 9.5 inches overall (4-inch bbl.). Weight: 35 oz. (4-inch bbl.). Click adj. rear sight; ramp front. Blued or nickel finish. Target stocks of checkered Goncalo Alves. Made from 1956 to date. The 2.5- and 6-inch bbls. were discontinued in 1991.

Smith & Wesson Model 20 38/44 Heavy Duty DA
Caliber: 38 Special. 6-shot cylinder. Bbl. lengths: 4, 5 and 6.5 inches. 10.38 inches overall w/5-inch bbl. Weight: 40 oz. w/5-inch bbl. Fixed sights. Blued or nickel finish. Checkered walnut stocks. Short action after 1948. Made 1930-1967.

Pre-World War II **$570**
Postwar **255**

S&W Model 21

Smith & Wesson Model 21 1950 44 Military DA Revolver **$1280**
Postwar version of the 1926 Model 44 Military. Caliber: .44 Special, 6-shot cylinder. Bbl.: 4-, 5- and 6.5-inch, 11.75 inches overall with 6.5-inch bbl. Weight: 39.5 oz. with 6.5-inch bbl. Fixed front sight with square-notch rear sight; target model has micrometer click rear sight adj. for windage and elevation. Checkered walnut grips with S&W monogram. Blue or nickel finish. Made 1950-1967.

S&W Model 22

Smith & Wesson Model 22 1950 Army DA **$895**
Postwar version of the 1917 Army w/same general specifications, except redesigned hammer. Made 1950-1967.

S&W 22/32 Kit Gun

Smith & Wesson 22/32 Kit Gun **$495**
Same as 22/32 Target, except has 4-inch bbl., round grips, 8 inches overall, weighs 21 oz. Made 1935-1953.

S&W 22/32
Target Revolver

Smith & Wesson 22/32 Target DA Revolver **$695**
Also known as the Bekeart Model. Design based upon "32 Hand Ejector." Caliber: 22 LR (recessed head cylinder for high-speed cartridges introduced 1935). 6-shot cylinder. 6-inch bbl. 10.5 inches overall. Weight: 23 oz. Adj. target sights. Blued finish. Checkered walnut stocks. Made 1911-1953. *Note:* In 1911, San Francisco gun dealer Phil Bekeart, who suggested this model, received 292 pieces. These are the true "Bekeart Model" revolvers worth about double the value shown for the standard 22/32 Target.

S&W Model 23

Smith & Wesson Model 23 38/44 Outdoorsman DA Revolver
Target version of the 38/44 Heavy Duty. 6-inch bbl. only. Weight: 41.75 oz. Target sights, micrometer-click rear on postwar models. Blued finish only. 1950 model has ribbed barrel, redesigned hammer. Made 1930-1967.
Prewar **$595**
Postwar **475**

S&W Model 24 Target

Smith & Wesson Model 24 1950 44 Target DA Revolver **$575**
Postwar version of the 1926 Model 44 Target w/same specifications, except has redesigned hammer, ribbed bbl., micrometer click rear sight. Made 1950-1967.

S&W Model 25 Target

Smith & Wesson Model 25 1950 45 Target
DA Revolver **$365**
Same as 1950 Model 44 Target but chambered for 45 ACP cartridge, and later, the 45 LC cartridge. Made 1950, in several variations, to 1991.

S&W Model 29

S&W Model 27

Smith & Wesson Model 27 357 Magnum DA
Caliber: 357 Magnum. 6-shot cylinder. Bbl. lengths: 3.5-, 5-, 6-, 6.5-and 8.38-inch. 11.38 inches overall w/6-inch bbl. Weight: 44 oz. w/6-inch bbl. Adj. target sights, Baughman quick-draw ramp front sight on 3.5-inch bbl. Blued or nickel finish. Checkered walnut stocks. Made 1935 to date. *Note:* Until 1938, the 357 Magnum was custom made in any barrel length from 3.5-inch to 8.75-inch, each of these revolvers was accompanied by a registration certificate and has its registration number stamped on the inside of the yoke. Postwar Magnums have a redesigned hammer with shortened fall and the new S&W micrometer click rear sight.

Prewar Registered Model	**$825**
Prewar Model without Registration Number	**495**
Current Model with 8.38-inch bbl	**325**
Current Model, other bbl. lengths	**295**

S&W Model 30

Smith & Wesson Model 30 32 Hand Ejector DA
Revolver **$235**
Caliber: 32 S&W Long. 6-shot cylinder. Bbl. lengths: 2- (introduced 1949), 3-, 4- and 6-inch. 8 inches overall w/4-inch bbl. Weight: 18 oz. w/4-inch bbl. Fixed sights. Blued or nickel finish. Round, checkered walnut or hard rubber stocks. Made 1903-1976. Numerous changes, mostly minor, as in M & P model.

**S&W Model 28
Highway Patrolman**

S&W Model 31

Smith & Wesson Model 28 DA Revolver **$235**
Caliber: 357 Magnum. 6-shot cylinder. Bbl. lengths: 4- or 6-inch. 11.25 inches overall w/6-inch bbl. Weight: 44 oz. w/6-inch bbl. Adj.rear sight, ramp front. Blued finish. Checkered walnut stocks, Magna or target type. Made 1954-1986.

Smith & Wesson Model 29 44 Magnum DA Revolver
Caliber: 44 Magnum. 6-shot cylinder. Bbl. lengths: 4-, 6.5-, 8.38-inch. 11.88 inches overall (6.5-inch bbl.). Weight: 47 oz., 6.5-inch bbl. Click adj. rear sight, ramp front. Blued or nickel finish. Checkered Goncalo Alves target stocks. Made 1956-1991.

With 8.38-inch bbl.	**$345**
Other bbl. lengths	**320**

Smith & Wesson Models 31 & 33 Regulation
Police DA Revolver **$190**
Same basic type as 32 Hand Ejector, except has square buttstocks. Calibers: 32 S&W Long (Model 31) 38 S&W (Model 33). 6-shot cylinder in 32 cal., 5-shot in 38 caliber. Bbl. lengths: 2- (introduced 1949), 3-, 4- and 6-inch in 32 cal., 4-inch only in 38 cal. 8.5 inches overall w/4-inch bbl. Weight: 18 oz., 38 cal. w/4-inch bbl., 32 cal., ¾-oz. heavier. Fixed sights. Blued or nickel finish. Checkered walnut stocks. Made from 1917. Model 33 discontinued in 1974; Model 31 discontinued in 1992.

Smith & Wesson 32 Double-Action Revolver . . . **$195**
Hinged frame. Caliber: 32 S&W. 5-shot cylinder. Bbl. lengths: 3-, 3.5- and 6-inch. Fixed sights. Blued or nickel finish. Hard rubber stocks. Made from 1880-1919. *Note:* Value shown applies generally to the several varieties. Exception is the rare first issue of 1880 (identified by squared sideplate and serial no. 1 to 30) valued at **$2,500**.

SMITH & WESSON   N Series...................Large Frame Revolver

Models 25 27 29 57 625-2 629 657
Calibers: 357 Mag., 41 Mag., 44 Mag., 44 Spl., 45 Long Colt, 45 ACP
Barrel Lengths: 3", 4", 5", 6", 8 3/8" or 10 5/8"
Finish: Blue, Nickel or Stainless
Capacity: 6-Shot

SMITH & WESSON

Manufacturer

SMITH & WESSON

44 MAGNUM

Caliber

44 MAGNUM

**Place of Manufacture
and Producer**

MADE IN U.S.A.
MARCAS REGISTRADAS
SMITH & WESSON
SPRINGFIELD, MASS.

**Manufacturer's Logo
and Trade Mark**

Identification markings on late-model S&W revolvers.

SMITH & WESSON   N Series...........Large Frame Revolver

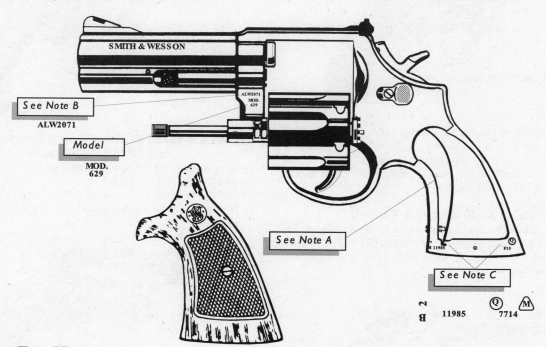

See Note B

ALW2071

Model

MOD.
629

See Note A

See Note C

Top View

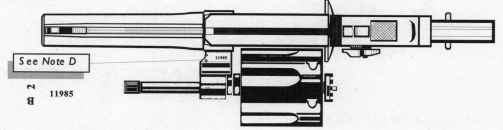

See Note D

Bottom View

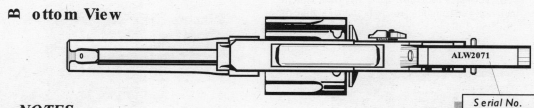

Serial No.

ALW2071

NOTES:

A. *Target or Custom grips must be removed to reveal the serial number on the butt of the frame. (Record this number.)*

B. *Numbers stamped inside the frame area above the model number may be production, series or serial numbers.*

C. *Numbers stamped on either side of the grip frame may be production numbers or inspector stamps but not serial numbers.*

D. *Numbers stamped on the yoke may refer to production or series but are not serial numbers.*

Identification markings on late-model S&W revolvers. *(Cont.)*

S&W Model 32 Terrier

S&W Model 36 Chiefs
Special

Smith & Wesson Model 32 Terrier DA $260
Caliber: 38 S&W. 5-shot cylinder. 2-inch bbl., 6.25 inches over-all. Weight: 17 oz. Fixed sights. Blued or nickel finish. Checkered walnut or hard rubber stocks. Built on 32 Hand Ejector frame. Made 1936-1974.

Smith & Wesson 32-20 Military & Police DA
Same as M & P 38, except chambered for 32-20 Winchester cartridge. First introduced in the 1899 model, M & P Revolvers were produced in this caliber until about 1940. Values same as for corresponding M & P 38 models.

Smith & Wesson Model 36 Chiefs Special DA . . . $235
Based on 32 Hand Ejector with frame lengthened to permit longer cylinder for 38 Special cartridge. Caliber: 38 Special. 5-shot cylinder. Bbl. lengths: 2- or 3-inch. 6.5 inches overall w/2-inch bbl. Weight: 19 oz. Fixed sights. Blued or nickel finish. Checkered walnut stocks, round or square butt. Made 1952-1991.

S&W Model 34

S&W Model 37

Smith & Wesson Model 34 1953 22/32 Kit Gun . . $255
Same general specifications as previous 22/32 Kit Gun, except with 2-inch or 4-inch bbl. and round or square buttstocks, blue or nickel finish. Made 1953-1991.

Smith & Wesson Model 37 Airweight Chiefs
Special $225
Same general specifications as standard Chiefs Special except has light alloy frame, weighs 12.5 oz. with 2-inch bbl., blued finish only. Made 1954 to date.

S&W Model 35

S&W Model 38 Airweight

Smith & Wesson Model 35 1953 22/32 Target . . . $295
Same general specifications as previous model 22/32 Target, except has micrometer-click rear sight Magna-type target stocks, weighs 25 oz. Made 1953-1974.

Smith & Wesson Model 38 Airweight DA $235
Caliber: 38 Special. 5-shot cylinder. Bbl. length: 2 or 4 inches. 6.88 inches (2-inch bbl.) overall. Weight: 18 oz. Square-notch rear sight, ramp front sight.

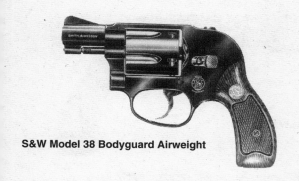

S&W Model 38 Bodyguard Airweight

Smith & Wesson Model 38 Bodyguard Airweight DA Revolver $225
"Shrouded" hammer. Light alloy frame. Caliber: 38 Special. 5-shot cylinder. 2-inch bbl. 6.38 inches overall. Weight: 14.5 oz. Fixed sights. Blued or nickel finish. Checkered walnut stocks. Made 1955 to date.

Smith & Wesson 38 DA Revolver $860
Hinged frame. Caliber: 38 S&W. 5-shot cylinder. Bbl. lengths: 4-, 4.25-, 5-, 6-, 8- and 10- inch. Fixed sights. Blued or nickel finish. Hard rubber stocks. Made 1880-1911. *Note:* Value shown applies generally to the several varieties. Exceptions are the first issue of 1880 (identified by squared sideplate and serial no. 1 to 4,000) and the 8- and 10-inch bbl. models of the third issue (1884-1895).

Smith & Wesson Model 38 Hand Ejector DA $675
Military & Police — First Model. Resembles Colt New Navy in general appearance, lacks bbl. lug and locking bolt common to all later S&W hand ejector models. Caliber: 38 Long Colt. 6-shot cylinder. Bbl. lengths: 4-, 5-, 6- and 6.5-inch. 11.5 inches overall w/6.5-inch bbl. Fixed sights. Blued or nickel finish. Round, checkered walnut or hard rubber stocks. Made 1899-1902.

Smith & Wesson 38 Military & Police Target DA $960
Target version of the Military & Police with standard features of that model. Caliber: 38 Special. 6-inch bbl. Weight: 32.25 oz. Adj. target sights. Blued finish. Checkered walnut stocks. Made 1899-1940. For values, **add $175** to those shown for corresponding M&P 38 models.

Smith & Wesson Model 38 Perfected DA $555
Hinged frame. Similar to earlier 38 DA Model, but heavier frame, side latch as in solid-frame models improved lockwork. Caliber: 38 S&W. 5-shot cylinder. Bbl. lengths: 3.25 , 4, 5 and 6 inches. Fixed sights. Blued or nickel finish. Hard rubber stocks. Made 1909-1920.

Smith & Wesson Model 40 Centennial DA Hammerless Revolver $360
Similar to Chiefs Special, but has Safety Hammerless-type mechanism with grip safety. 2-inch bbl.. Weight: 19 oz. Made 1953-1974.

Smith & Wesson Model 42 Centennial Airweight $395
Same as standard Centennial model, except has light alloy frame, weighs 13 oz. Made 1954-1974.

Smith & Wesson Model 43 1955 22/32 Kit Gun Airweight $395
Same as Model 34 Kit Gun, except has light alloy frame, furnished with 3.5-inch bbl. only, weighs 14.25 oz., square butt-stock. Made 1954-1974.

Smith & Wesson Model 44 1926 Military DA Revolver
Basically the same as the early New Century model, having the extractor rod casing but lacking the "Triple Lock" feature. Caliber: 44 S&W Special. 6-shot cylinder. Bbl. lengths: 4, 5 and 6.5 inches. 11.75 inches overall w/6.5-inch bbl. Weight: 39.5 oz., 6.5-inch bbl. Fixed sights. Blued or nickel finish. Checkered walnut stocks. Made 1926-1941.
Standard Model . . . . $ 695
Target Model w/6.5-inch bbl., Target Sights, Blued . . . 1195

Smith & Wesson 44 DA Revolver
Also called Wesson Favorite (lightweight model), Frontier (caliber 44-40). Hinged frame. 6-shot cylinder. Calibers: 44 S&W Russian, 38-40, 44-40. Bbl. lengths: 4-, 5-, 6- and 6.5-inch. Weight: 37.5 oz. w/6.5-inch bbl. Fixed sights. Blued or nickel finish. Hard rubber stocks. Made 1881-1913, Frontier discontinued 1910.
Standard Model, 44 Russian . . . . $ 870
Standard Model, 38-40 1995
Frontier Model 1350
Favorite Model 3595

Smith & Wesson 44 Hand Ejector, Second Model DA Revolver $595
Basically the same as New Century, except crane lock ("Triple Lock" feature) and extractor rod casing eliminated. Calibers: 44 S&W Special 44-40 Win. 45 Colt. Bbl. lengths: 4-, 5-, 6.5- and 7.5-inch. 11.75 inches overall w/6.5-inch bbl. Weight: 38 oz. w/6.5-inch bbl. Fixed sights. Blued or nickel finish. Checkered walnut stocks. Made 1915-1937.

S&W Model 48

Smith & Wesson Model 48 (K-22) Masterpiece M.R.F. DA Revolver $270
Caliber: 22 Mag. and 22 RF. 6-shot cylinder. Bbl. lengths: 4 and 6 inches. 11.13 inches overall. Weight: 39 oz. Adj. rear sight, ramp front.

S&W Model 49 Bodyguard

S&W Model 60

S&W Model 63

Smith & Wesson Model 49 Bodyguard **$245**
Same as Model 38 Bodyguard Airweight, except has steel frame,
weighs 20.5 oz. Made 1959 to date.

Smith & Wesson Model 51 1960 22/32 Kit Gun . . **$395**
Same as Model 34 Kit Gun, except chambered for 22 WMR; has
3.5-inch bbl., weighs 24 oz. Made 1960-74.

Smith & Wesson Model 53 22 Magnum DA **$595**
Caliber: 22 Rem. Jet C.F. Magnum. 6-shot cylinder (inserts permit use of 22 Short, Long, or LR cartridges). Bbl. lengths: 4-, 6-,
8.38-inches. 11.25 inches w/6-inch bbl. Weight: 40 oz. w/6-inch
bbl. Micrometer-click rear sight ramp front. Checkered walnut
stocks. Made 1960-1974.

**Smith & Wesson Model 63 (1977) Kit
Gun DA** **$245**
Caliber: 22 LR. 6-shot cylinder. 4-inch bbl. 6.5 inches overall.
Weight: 24.5 oz. Adj. rear sight, ramp front.

S&W Model 57

S&W Model 64

Smith & Wesson Model 57 41 Magnum DA Revolver
Caliber: 41 Magnum. 6-shot cylinder. Bbl. lengths: 4-, 6-, 8.38-
inches. Weight: with 6-inch bbl., 40 oz. Micrometer click rear
sight, ramp front. Target stocks of checkered Goncalo Alves.
Made 1964 to date.
With 8.38-inch bbl. **$375**
Other bbl. lengths **295**

**Smith & Wesson Model 58 41 Military & Police
DA Revolver** **$335**
Caliber: 41 Magnum. 6-shot cylinder. 4-inch bbl.. 9.25 inches
overall. Weight: 41 oz. Fixed sights. Checkered walnut stocks.
Intro. 1964; discontinued.

Smith & Wesson Model 60 Stainless DA **$260**
Caliber: 38 Special. 5-shot cylinder. Bbl. lengths: 2 or 3 inches
(Lady Smith Model). 6.5 or 7.5 inches overall. Weight: 19 oz.
Square-notch rear sight, ramp front. Satin finish stainless steel.
Made 1965 to date.

Smith & Wesson Model 64 38 M&P Stainless . . . **$195**
Same as standard Model 10, except satin-finished stainless steel,
square butt w/4-inch heavy bbl. or round butt w/2-inch bbl.
Made 1970 to date.

S&W Model 65

Smith & Wesson Model 65 357 Military/Police Stainless $210

Same as Model 13, except satin-finished stainless steel. Made 1974 to date.

S&W Model 66 Combat Magnum

Smith & Wesson Model 66 357 Combat Magnum Stainless $260

Same as Model 19, except satin-finished stainless steel. Made 1971 to date.

S&W Model 67 Combat Masterpiece

Smith & Wesson Model 67 38 Combat Masterpiece Stainless $225

Same as Model 15, except satin-finished stainless steel available only with 4-inch bbl. Made 1972-1988.

Smith & Wesson 125th Anniversary Commemorative

Issued to celebrate the 125th anniversary of the 1852 partnership of Horace Smith and Daniel Baird Wesson. Standard Edition is Model 25 revolver, caliber 45 Colt with 6.5-inch bbl., bright blued finish, gold-filled bbl. roll mark "Smith & Wesson 125th Anniversary," sideplate marked with gold-filled Anniversary seal, smooth Goncalo Alves stocks, in presentation case with nickel silver Anniversary medallion and book, *125 Years with Smith & Wesson,* by Roy Jinks. Deluxe Edition is same, except revolver is Class A engraved with gold-filled seal on si deplate, ivory stocks, Anniversary medallion is sterling silver and book is leather bound; limited to 50 units. Total issue is 10,000 units, of which 50 are Deluxe Edition and two are a Custom Deluxe Edition not for sale. Made in 1977. Values are for revolvers in new condition.

Standard Edition . . . . $ 595
Deluxe Edition 1640

S&W 125th Anniversary Commemorative, Deluxe Edition

Smith & Wesson Model 547 DA Revolver $270

Caliber: 9mm. 6-shot cylinder. Bbl. lengths: 3 or 4 inches. 7.31 inches overall. Weight: 32 oz. Square-notch rear sight, ramp front. Discontinued 1986.

Smith & Wesson Models 581 Revolver

Caliber: 357 Magnum. Bbl.: 4 inches. Weight: 34 oz. Serrated ramp front sight, square notch rear. Checkered walnut grips.
Blued Finish **$195**
Nickel Finish **230**

**S&W Model 586
Distinguished Combat Magnum**

Smith & Wesson Model 586 Distinguished Combat Magnum $275

Caliber: 357 Magnum. 6-shot. Bbl. lengths: 4, 6 and 8.38 inches. Overall length: 9.75 inches w/4-inch bbl.; 13.81 inches w/8.38-inch bbl. Weight: 42, 46, 53 oz., respectively. Red ramp front sight, micrometer-click adj. rear. Checkered grip. S&W blue or nickel finish.

Smith & Wesson Model 610 DA Revolver $385

Similar to Model 625, except in caliber 10mm. Magna classic grips.

Smith & Wesson Model 617 DA Revolver

Similar to Model 17, except in stainless. Made 1992-93.
Semi-Target Model with 4- or 6-inch bbl. $275
Target Model with 6-inch bbl. 295
Target Model with 8.38-inch bbl. 315

Smith & Wesson Model 624 Double-Action Revolver

Same general specifications as Model 24, except satin-finished stainless steel. Limited production of 10,000 made in 1985 only.
Standard Model $375
Semi-target Model 325
Target Model 395

S&W Model 625

**S&W Model 642
Centennial Airweight**

Smith & Wesson Model 625 DA Revolver $375
Same general specifications as Model 25, except 3-, 4- or 5-inch bbl., round-butt Pachmayr grips and satin stainless steel finish. Made from 1989 to date.

Smith & Wesson Model 627 DA Revolver $355
Same general specifications as Model 27, except satin stainless steel finish. Made 1989-1991.

S&W Model 629

Smith & Wesson Model 629 DA Revolver
Same as Model 29 in 44 Magnum, except in stainless steel. Classic made from 1990 to date.
Model 629 (4- and 6-inch bbl.) $375
Model 629 (8.38-inch bbl.) 385
Model 629 Classic (5- and 6.5-inch bbl.) 395
Model 629 Classic (8.38-inch bbl.) 425

Smith & Wesson Model 631 DA Revolver
Similar to Model 31, except chambered for 32 H&R Mag. Goncalo Alves combat grips. Made 1991-92.
Fixed Sights, 2-inch bbl. $270
Adjustable Sights, 4-inch bbl. 295

Smith & Wesson Model 632 Centennial DA $295
Same general specifications as Model 640, except chambered for 32 H&R Mag. 2-inch bbl. Weight: 15.5 oz. Stainless slide with alloy frame. Santoprene combat grips. Made in 1991.

Smith & Wesson Model 640 Centennial DA $335
Caliber: 38 Special. 5-shot cylinder. 2- or 3-inch bbl. 6.31 inches overall. Weight: 20-22 oz. Fixed sights. Stainless finish. Smooth hardwood service stocks. Made 1990 to date.

Smith & Wesson Model 642 Centennial Airweight DA Revolver $315
Same general specifications as Model 640, except with 2-inch bbl. only, weight of 15.8 oz. with stainless steel/aluminum alloy frame and finish. Santoprene combat grips. Made 1990-93.

Smith & Wesson Model 648 DA Revolver $295
Same general specifications as Models 17/617, except in stainless and chambered for 22 Magnum. Made 1992-93.

Smith & Wesson Model 649 Bodyguard DA $250
Caliber: 38 Special. 5-shot cylinder. Bbl. length: 2 inches. 6.25 inches overall. Weight: 20 oz. Square-notch rear sight ramp front. Stainless frame and finish.

Smith & Wesson Model 650 Revolver $275
Caliber: 22 Mag. 6-shot cylinder. 3-inch bbl. 7 inches overall. Weight: 23.5 oz. Serrated ramp front sight, fixed square-notch rear. Round butt, checkered walnut monogrammed stocks. Stainless steel finish. Made 1983-85.

Smith & Wesson Model 651 Stainless DA $265
Caliber: 22 Mag. Rimfire. 6-shot cylinder. Bbl. length: 3 and 4 inches. 7 and 8.63 inches, respectively, overall. Weight: 24.5 oz. Adj. rear sight, ramp front.

Smith & Wesson Model 657 Revolver
Caliber: 41 Mag. 6-shot cylinder. Bbl.: 4, 6 or 8.4 inches. 9.6, 11.4, and 13.9 inches overall. Weight: 44.2, 48 and 52.5 oz. Serrated black ramp front sight on ramp base click rear, adj. for windage and elevation. Satin finished stainless steel.
With 4- or 6-inch bbl. $295
With 8.4-inch bbl. 350

S&W Model 681

Smith & Wesson Model 681 .... $215
Same as S&W Model 581, except in stainless finish only.

Smith & Wesson Model 686 .... $275
Same as S&W Model 586 Distinguished Combat Magnum except in stainless finish w/additional 2.5-inch bbl.

Smith & Wesson Model 940 Centennial DA $285
Same general specifications as Model 640, except chambered for 9mm. 2- or 3-inch bbl. Weight: 23 oz. w/2-inch bbl. Santoprene combat grips. Made 1991 to date.

Smith & Wesson Model 1891 SA Revolver
Hinged frame. Caliber: 38 S&W. 5-shot cylinder. Bbl. lengths: 3.25, 4-, 5- and 6-inch. Fixed sights. Blued or nickel finish. Hard rubber stocks. Made 1891-1911. *Note:* Until 1906, an accessory single-shot target bbl. *(see* Model 1891 Single-Shot Target Pistol) was available for this revolver.

Revolver only .... $ 895
Set with 22 single-shot bbl. 1295

Smith & Wesson 1917 Army DA Revolver
Caliber: 45 Automatic, using 3-cartridge half-moon clip; 45 Auto Rim, without clip. 6-shot cylinder. 5.5-inch bbl. 10.75 inches overall. Weight: 36.25 oz. Fixed sights. Blued finish (blue-black finish on commercial model, brush polish on military). Checkered walnut stocks (commercial model, smooth on military). Made under U.S. Government contract 1917-19; produced commercially 1919-1941. *Note:* About 175,000 of these revolvers were produced during WW I. The DCM sold these to NRA members during the 1930s at $16.15 each.

Commercial Model $395
Military Model 385

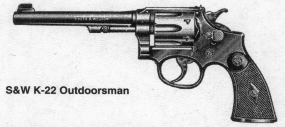

S&W K-22 Outdoorsman

Smith & Wesson K-22 Masterpiece DA $895
Improved version of K-22 Outdoorsman with same specifications but with micrometer-click rear sight, short action and anti-backlash trigger. Manufactured in 1940.

Smith & Wesson K-22 Outdoorsman DA $495
Design based on the 38 Military & Police Target. Caliber: 22 LR. 6-shot cylinder Bbl..11.13 inches overall. Weight: 35 oz. Adj. target sights. Blued finish. Checkered walnut stock. Made 1931-1940.

Smith & Wesson K32 and K38 Heavy Masterpieces
Same as K32 and K38 Masterpiece, but with heavy bbl. Weight: 38.5 oz. Made 1950-53. *Note:* All K32 and K38 revolvers made after September 1953 have heavy bbls. and the "Heavy Masterpiece" designation was discontinued. Values for Heavy Masterpiece models are the same as shown for Models 14 and 16. *(See* separate listing).

Smith & Wesson K-32 Target DA Revolver $995
Same as 38 Military & Police Target, except chambered for 32 S&W Long cartridge, slightly heavier bbl. Weight: 34 oz. Only 98 produced. Made 1938-1940.

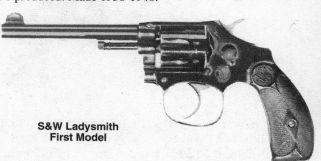

**S&W Ladysmith
First Model**

Smith & Wesson Ladysmith (Model M Hand Ejector) DA Revolver
Caliber: 22 LR. 7-shot cylinder. Bbl. lengths: 2.25-, 3-, 3.5- and 6-inch (Third Model only). Approximately 7 inches overall w/3.5-inch bbl. Weight: about 9.5 oz. Fixed sights, adj. target sights available on Third Model. Blued or nickel finish. Round butt, hard rubber stocks on First and Second Model; checkered walnut or hard rubber square buttstocks on Third Model. First Model — 1902 to 1906: cylinder locking bolt operated by button on left side of frame, no bbl. lug and front locking bolt. Second Model — 1906 to 1911: rear cylinder latch eliminated, has bbl. ug, forward cylinder lock with draw-bolt fastening. Third Model — 1911 to 1921: same as Second Model except has square buttstocks, target sights and 6-inch bbl. available. *Note:* Legend has it that a straight-laced D.B. Wesson ordered discontinuance of the Ladysmith when he learned of the little revolver's reputed popularity with ladies of the evening. The story, which undoubtedly has enhanced the appeal of this model to collectors, is not true: Wesson Ladysmith was discontinued because of difficulty of manufacture and high frequency of repairs.

First Model $1195
Second Model 1035
Third Model, fixed sights, 3- or 3.5-inch bbl........ 995
Third Model, fixed sights, 2.25- or 6-inch bbl. 1160
Third Model, adj. sights, 6-inch bbl. 1195

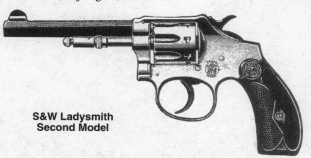

**S&W Ladysmith
Second Model**

Smith & Wesson New Century Model Hand Ejector DA Revolver $895
Also called "Triple Lock" because of its third cylinder lock at the crane. 6-shot cylinder. Calibers: 44 S&W Special, 450 Eley, 455 Mark II. Bbl. lengths: 4-, 5-, 6.5- and 7.5-inch. Weight: 39 oz. w/6.5-inch bbl. Fixed sights. Blued or nickel finish. Checkered walnut stocks. Made 1907-1915.

S&W Regulation Police Target

S&W Safety Hammerless

Smith & Wesson Regulation Police Target DA . . $325
Target version of the Regulation Police with standard features of
that model. Caliber: 32 S&W Long. 6-inch bbl. 10.25 inches
overall. Weight: 20 oz. Adj. tar get sights. Blued finish. Checkered walnut stocks. Made about 1917-1940.

Smith & Wesson Safety Hammerless Revolver . . $595
Also called New Departure Double Action. Hinged frame. Calibers: 32 S&W, 38 S&W. 5-shot cylinder. Bbl. lengths: 32 cal.—2,
3- and 3.5-inch; 38 cal. — 2-, 3.25-, 4-, 5- and 6-inch. Length
overall: 6.75 inches, 32 cal. w/3-inch bbl., 7.5 inches, 38 cal.
w/3.25-inch bbl. Weight: 14.25 oz., 32 cal. w/3-inch bbl.; 18.25

Smith & Wesson Safety Hammerless *(Cont.)*
oz., 38 cal. .25-inch bbl. Fixed sights. Blued or nickel finish.
Hard rubber stocks. 32 cal. made 1888-1937; 38 cal. 1887-1941.
Various minor changes.

**Smith & Wesson Texas Ranger
Commemorative $895**
Issued to honor the 150th anniversary of the Texas Rangers.
Model 19 357 Combat Magnum with 4-inch bbl., sideplate
stamped with Texas Ranger Commemorative Seal, smooth Goncalo Alves stocks. Special Bowie knife. In presentation case.
8,000 sets made in 1973. Value is for set in new condition.

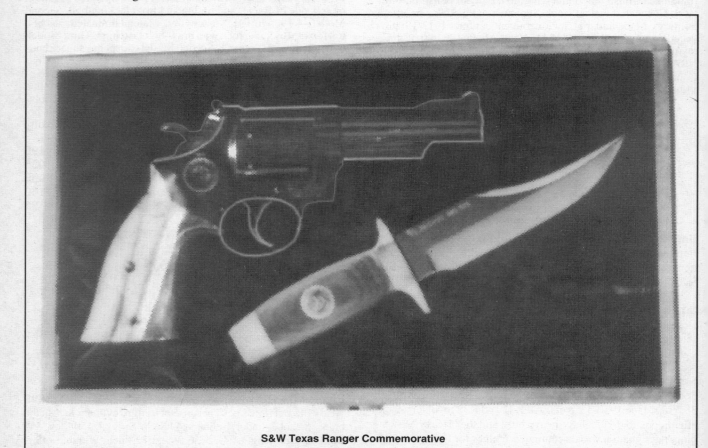

S&W Texas Ranger Commemorative

SPRINGFIELD, INC.
Colona, Illinois
(Formerly Springfield Armory of Geneseo, IL.)

**Springfield Armory 1911-A1
Auto Pistol**

Springfield Armory 1911-A1 Automatic Pistol
Calibers: 9mm Parabellum, 38 Super, 40 S&W, 45 ACP., 7-, 8- or 10-shot magazine. 5-inch bbl. 8.5 inches overall. Weight: 36 oz. Fixed combat sights. Blued or parkerized finish. Checkered walnut stocks. *Note:* This is an exact duplicate of the Colt M1911-A1 that was used by the U.S. Armed Forces for many years.
Blued Finish **$395**
Parkerized Finish. **360**

**Springfield Armory
Bobcat**

Springfield Armory Bobcat Automatic Pistol . . . **$340**
Caliber: 380 ACP. 13-shot magazine. 3.5-inch bbl. 6.6 inches overall. Weight: 21.95 oz. Blade front sight; rear adj. for windage. Textured composition grip. Matte blue finish. Made 1991-93.

Springfield Armory Firecat Automatic Pistol
Calibers: 9mm, 40 S&W. 8-shot magazine (9mm); 7-shot magazine (40 S&W). 3.5-inch bbl. 6.5 inches overall. Weight: 25.75 oz. Fixed sights w/3-Dot system. Checkered walnut grip. Matte blue finish. Made 1991-93.
9mm **$375**
40 S&W. **395**

Springfield Armory Lynx Automatic Pistol **$195**
Caliber: 25 ACP. 7-shot magazine. 2.25-inch bbl. 4.45 inches overall. Weight: 10.55 oz. Blade front sight, rear adj. for windage w/3-Dot system. Checkered composition grip. Matte blue finish. Made 1991-93.

Springfield Armory Panther

Springfield Armory Panther Automatic Pistol . . . **$465**
Calibers: 9mm, 40 S&W. 15-shot magazine (9mm); 11-shot magazine (40 S&W). 3.8-inch bbl. 7.5 inches overall. Weight: 28.95 oz. Blade front sight; rear adj. for windage w/3-Dot system. Checkered walnut grip. Matte blue finish. Made 1991-93.

Springfield Armory P9

Springfield Armory Model P9 DA Automatic Pistol
Calibers: 9mm, 40 S&W, 45 ACP. Magazine capacity: 15-shot (9mm); 11-shot (40 S&W); 10-shot (45 ACP). 4.75-inch bbl. 8 inches overall. Weight: 32 oz. Fixed sights w/3-Dot system. Checkered walnut grip. Finishes: Matte blue, Parkerized or stainless. Made 1990-94.
9mm Blued **$395**
9mm Parkerized **425**
9mm Stainless **425**
40 S&W or 45 ACP Blued. **415**
40 S&W or 45 ACP Parkerized **420**
40 S&W or 45 ACP Stainless **450**

Springfield Armory Model P9 Ultra LPS Pistol

Same general specifications as Model P9, except with dual port compensator system, extended safety and magazine release.

9mm Bi-Tone	**$525**
9mm Stainless	**525**
40 S&W Bi-Tone	**535**
40 S&W Stainless	**540**
45 ACP Bi-Tone	**555**
45 ACP Stainless	**550**

STAR PISTOLS
Eibar, Spain
Star, Bonifacio Echeverria, S.A.

Star Model 30M

Star Model 30M DA Auto Pistol $325

Caliber: 9mm Parabellum. 15-shot magazine. 4.38-inch bbl. 8 inches overall. Weight: 40 oz. Steel frame with combat features. Adj. sights. Checkered composition stocks. Blued finish. Made 1984-91.

Star Model 30PK

Star Model 30PK DA Auto Pistol $325

Same gen. specifications as Star Model 30M, except 3.8-inch bbl. 30-oz. weight and alloy frame. Made 1984-89.

Star Model 31P DA Auto Pistol

Same general specifications as Model 30M, except removable backstrap houses complete firing mechanism. Weight: 39.4 oz. Made 1990 to date.

Blued Fininh	**$275**
Starvel Finish	**375**

Star Model 31 PK DA Auto Pistol $295

Same general specifications as Model 31P, except with alloy frame. Weight: 30 oz. Made 1990 to date.

Star Model A Automatic Pistol $205

Modification of the Colt Government Model 45 Auto, which it closely resembles; lacks grip safety. Caliber: 38 Super. 8-shot magazine. 5-inch bbl. 8-inches overall. Weight: 35 oz. Fixed sights. Blued finish. Checkered stocks. Made 1934 to date. No longer imported.

Star Model AS

Star Models AS, BS, PS $295

Same as Models A, B and P, except have magazine safety. Made in 1975.

Star Model B $235

Same as Model A, except in 9mm Luger. Made 1934-75.

Star Model BKM $240

Similar to Model BM, except has aluminum frame and weighs 25.6 oz. Made 1976-92.

Star Model BKS

Star Model BKS Starlight Automatic Pistol $235
Light alloy frame. Caliber: 9mm Luger. 8-shot magazine. 4.25-inch bbl. 7 inches overall. Weight: 25 oz. Fixed sights. Blued or chrome finish. Plastic grips. Made 1970-81.

Star Model BM Automatic Pistol
Caliber: 9mm. 8-shot magazine. 3.9-inch bbl. 6.95 inches overall. Weight: 34.5 oz. Fixed sights. Checkered walnut stocks. Blued or Starvel finish. Made 1976-92.
Blued Finish **$245**
Starvel Finish. **260**

Star Model CO Pocket Automatic Pistol $180
Caliber: 25 Automatic (6.35mm). 2.75-inch bbl. 4.5 inches overall. Weight: 13 oz. Fixed sights. Blued finish. Plastic stocks. Made 1941-57.

Star Model CU Starlet Pocket Pistol $195
Light alloy frame. Caliber: 25 Automatic (6.35mm). 8-shot magazine. 2.38-inch bbl. 4.75 inches overall. Weight: 10.5 oz. Fixed sights. Blued or chrome-plated slide; frame anodized in black, blue, green, gray or gold. Plastic stocks. Made 1957 to date. U.S. importation discont. 1968.

Star Model F Automatic

Star Model F Automatic Pistol $165
Caliber: 22 LR. 10-shot magazine. 4.5-inch bbl. 7.5 inches overall. Weight: 25 oz. Fixed sights. Blued finish. Plastic stocks. Made 1942-67.

Star Model F Olympic

Star Model F Olympic Rapid-Fire $315
Caliber: 22 Short. 9-shot magazine. 7-inch bbl. 11.06 inches overall. Weight: 52 oz. with weights. Adj. target sight. Adj. 3-piece bbl. weight. Aluminum alloy slide. Muzzle brake. Plastic stocks. Made 1942-67.

Star Model FM

Star Model FM $175
Similar to Model FR, except has heavier frame with web in front of trigger guard, 4.25-inch heavy bbl.; weighs 32 oz. Made 1972-91.

Star Model FR $185
Similar to Model F with same general specifications, but restyled, has slide stop and adj. rear sight. Made 1967-72.

Star Model FRS

Star Model FRS $170
Same as Model FR, except has 6-inch bbl., weighs 28 oz.; also avail. in chrome finish. Made 1967-91.

Star Model FS

Star Model FS $165
Same as regular Model F, but with 6-inch bbl. and adj. sights. Weight: 27 oz. Made 1942-67.

Star Model H **$175**
Same as Model HN except caliber 32 Automatic (7.65mm). 7-shot magazine. Weight: 20 oz. Made 1934-41.

Star Model HK Lancer Automatic Pistol **$220**
Similar to Starfire with same general specifications, except caliber 22 LR. Made 1955-68.

Star Model HN Automatic Pistol **$165**
Caliber: 380 Automatic (9mm Short). 6-shot magazine. 2.75-inch bbl. 5.56 inches overall. Weight: 20 oz. Fixed sights. Blued finish. Plastic stocks. Made 1934-41.

Star Model I Automatic Pistol **$175**
Caliber: 32 Automatic (7.65mm). 9-shot magazine. 4.81-inch bbl. 7.5 inches overall. Weight: 24 oz. Fixed sights. Blued finish. Plastic stocks. Made 1934-36.

Star Model IN **$185**
Same as Model I, except caliber 380 Automatic (9mm Short), 8-shot magazine, weighs 24.5 oz. Made 1934-36.

Star Model M Military

Star Model M Military Automatic Pistol **$295**
Modification of the Colt Government Model 45 Auto, which it closely resembles; lacks grip safety. Calibers: 9mm Bergmann, 38 Super, 9mm Luger. 8-shot magazine, except 7-shot in 45 caliber. 5-inch bbl. 8.5 inches overall. Weight: 36 oz. Fixed sights. Blued finish. Checkered stocks. Made 1934-39.

Star Models M40, M43, M45 Firestar Auto Pistols
Calibers: 9mm, 40 S&W, 45 ACP. 7-shot magazine (9mm); 6-shot (other calibers). 3.4-inch bbl., 6.5 inches overall. Weight: 30.35 oz. Blade front sight, adj. rear w/3-Dot system. Checkered rubber grips. Blued or Starvel finish. Made 1990 to date.
M40 Blued (40 S&W). $265
M40 Starvel (40 S&W) 285
M43 Blued (9mm). 260
M43 Starvel (9mm) 275
M45 Blued (45 ACP) 295
M45 Starvel (45 ACP). 325

Star Megastar Automatic Pistol
Calibers: 10mm, 45 ACP. 12-shot magazine. 4.6-inch bbl. 8.44 inches overall. Weight: 47.6 oz. Sights: blade front; adj. rear. Checkered composition grip. Finishes: Blued or Starvel. Made from 1992 to date.
Blued Finish, 10mm or 45 ACP. $375
Starvel Finish,. 10mm or 45 ACP 395

Star Model P **$290**
Same as Model A, except caliber 45 Automatic, has 7-shot magazine. Made 1934-75.

Star Model PD

Star Model PD Automatic Pistol
Caliber: 45 Automatic. 6-shot magazine. 3.75-inch bbl. 7 inches overall. Weight: 25 oz. Adj. rear sight, ramp front. Blued or Starvel finish. Checkered walnut stocks. Made 1975-92.
Blued Finish $235
Starvel Finish. 265

Star Model S

Star Model S **$175**
Same as Model SI except caliber 380 Automatic (9mm), 7-shot magazine, weighs 19 oz. Made 1941-65.

Star Model SI Automatic Pistol **$225**
Reduced-size modification of the Colt Government Model 45 Auto, lacks grip safety. Caliber: 32 Automatic (7.65mm). 8-shot magazine. 4-inch bbl. 6.5 inches overall. Weight: 20 oz. Fixed sights. Blued finish. Plastic stocks. Made 1941-65. *See* illustration next page.

Star Model SI

Super Star Auto Pistol

Star Starfire Automatic Pistol **$365**
Light alloy frame. Caliber: 380 Automatic (9mm Short). 7-shot magazine. 3.13-inch bbl.. 5.5 inches overall. Weight: 14.5 oz. Fixed sights. Blued or chrome-plated slide; frame anodized in black, blue, green, gray or gold. Plastic stocks. Made 1957 to date. U.S. importation discontinued 1968.

Star Models Super A, Super B, Super **$240**
Same as Models A, B and P, except with improvements described under Super Star. Made c. 1946-89/90.

Star Models Super SI, Super S **$245**
Same general specifications as the regular Model SI and S, except with improvements described under Super Star. Made c. 1946-72.

Star Model Super SM

Star Model Super SM **$235**
Similar to Model Super S, except has adj. rear sight, wood stocks. Made 1973-81.

Super Star Automatic Pistol **$295**
Improved version of the Model M with same general specifications; has disarming bolt permitting easier takedown, indicator of cartridge in chamber, magazine safety, take-down magazine, improved sights with luminous spots for aiming in darkness. Calibers: 38 Super, 9mm Luger. This is the standard service pistol of the Spanish Armed Forces adopted 1946.

Super Star Target Model **$395**
Same as regular Super Star, except with adj. target rear sight. Discontinued.

STENDA-WERKE PISTOL
Suhl, Germany

Stenda Pocket Automatic Pistol **$230**
Essentially the same as the Beholla, *see* listing of that pistol for specifications. Made c. 1920-25. *Note:* This pistol may be marked "Beholla" along w/the Stenda name and address.

STERLING ARMS CORPORATION
Gasport, New York

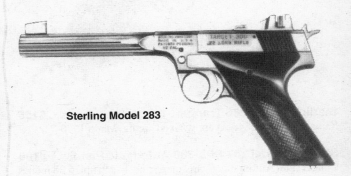

Sterling Model 283

Sterling Model 283 Target 300 Auto Pistol **$145**
Caliber: 22 LR. 10-shot magazine. Bbl. lengths: 4.5-, 6- 8-inch. 9 inches overall with 4.5-inch bbl. Weight: 36 oz. with 4.52-inch bbl. Adj. sights. Blued finish. Plastic stocks. Made 1970-71.

Sterling Model 284 Target 300L **$160**
Same as Model 283, except has 4.5- or 6-inch "Luger"-type bbl. Made 1970-71.

Sterling Model 284

Sterling Model 285

Sterling Model 285 Husky $155
Same as Model 283, except has fixed sights, 4.5-inch bbl only. Made 1970-71.

Sterling Model 286

Sterling Model 286 Trapper $155
Same as Model 284, except w/fixed sights. Made 1970-71.

Sterling Model 287 PPL-380 Automatic Pistol . . . $100
Caliber: 380 Automatic. 6-shot magazine. l-inch bbl. 5.38 inches overall. Weight: 22.5 oz. Fixed sights. Blued finish. Plastic stocks. Made 1971-72.

Sterling Model 300 Automatic Pistol $125
Caliber: 25 Automatic. 6-shot magazine. 2.33-inch bbl. 4.5 inches overall. Weight: 13 oz. Fixed sights. Blued or nickel finish. Plastic stocks. Made 1972-83.

Sterling Model 300S $115
Same as Model 300, except in stainless steel. Made 1976-83.

Sterling Model 300

Sterling Model 302 . . . . $125
Same as Model 300, except in 22 LR. Made 1973-83.

Sterling Model 302S $125
Same as Model 302 except in stainless steel. Made 1976-1983.

Sterling Model 400

Sterling Model 400 DA Automatic Pistol $195
Caliber: 380 Automatic. 7-shot magazine. 3.5-inch bbl. 6.5 inches overall. Weight: 24 oz. Adj. rear sight. Blued or nickel finish. Checkered walnut stocks. Made 1975-83.

Sterling Model 400S $245
Same as Model 400, except stainless steel. Made 1977-83.

Sterling Model 450 DA Auto Pistol $295
Caliber: 45 Automatic. 8-shot magazine. 4-inch bbl. 7.5 inches overall. Weight: 36 oz. Adj. rear sight. Blued finish. Smooth walnut stocks. Made 1977-83.

Sterling Model PPL-22 Automatic Pistol $160
Caliber: 22 LR. 10-shot magazine. 1-inch bbl. 5.5 inches overall. Weight: about 24 oz. Fixed sights. Blued finish. Wood stocks. *Note:* Only 382 made 1970-71. *See* illustration next page.

Sterling Model PPL-22

J. STEVENS ARMS & TOOL CO.
Chicopee Falls, Mass.

This firm was established in Civil War days by Joshua Stevens, for whom the company was named. In 1936 it became a subsidiary of Savage Arms.

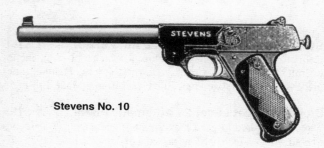

Stevens No. 10

Stevens No. 10 Single-Shot Target Pistol $270
Caliber: 22 LR. 8-inch bbl. 11.5 inches overall. Weight: 37 oz. Target sights. Blued finish. Hard rubber stocks. In external appearance this arm resembles an automatic pistol; it has a tip-up action. Made 1919-39.

Stevens No. 35

Stevens No. 35 Offhand Model Single-Shot Target Pistol. $350
Tip-up action. Caliber: 22 LR. Bbl. lengths: 6, 8, 10, 12.25 inches. Weight: 24 oz. with 6-inch bbl. Target sights. Blued finish. Walnut stocks. *Note:* This pistol is similar to the earlier "Gould" model. Made 1907-39.

Stevens Offhand No. 35 Single-Shot Pistol/Shotgun $260
Same general specifications as the standard No. 35 pistol except chambered for the 410 shotshell. 6-, 8-, 10-, or 12-inch half-ocatagonal barrel. Iron frame either blued, nickel plated, or case-hardened. BATF Class 3 license required to purchase or dispose of. Made 1923 to 1942.

Stevens-Lord No. 36

Stevens-Lord No. 36 Single-Shot Pistol $575
Tip-up action. Calibers: 22 Short and LR, 22 WRF, 25 Stevens, 32 Short Colt, 38 Long Colt, 44 Russian. 10- or 12-inch half-octagonal bbl. Iron or brass frame with nickel plated finish. Blued bbl. Checkered walnut grips. Made from 1880 to 1911.

Stevens-Gould No. 37 Single-Shot Pistol $750
Similar specifications to the No. 38 except the finger spur on the trigger guard has been omitted. Made from 1889 to 1903.

Stevens-Conlin No. 38

Stevens-Conlin No. 38 Single-Shot Pistol. $450
Tip-up action. Calibers: 22 Short and LR, 22 WRF, 25 Stevens, 32 Stevens, 32 Short Colt. Iron or brass frame. Checkered grips. Made from 1884 to 1903.

Stevens No. 41 Tip-Up Single-Shot Pistol. $235
Tip-up action. Caliber: 22 Short. 3.5-inch half-octagonal bbl. Blued metal parts with optional nickel frame. Made 1896 to 1915.

STEYR PISTOLS
Steyr, Austria

Steyr GB Semiautomatic Pistol. $495
Caliber: 9mm Parabellum. 18-round magazine. 5.4-inch bbl. 8.9 inches overall. Weight: 2.9 pounds. Post front sight; fixed, notched rear. Double, gas-delayed, blow-back action. Made 1981-88.

Steyr GB Semiautomatic

Steyr-Hahn M12

Steyr-Hahn M12 Automatic Pistol. **$455**
Caliber: 9mm Steyr. 8-shot fixed magazine, charger loaded. 5.1-inch bbl. 8.5 inches overall. Weight: 35 oz. Fixed sights. Blued finish. Checkered wood stocks. Made 1911-19. Adopted by the Austro-Hungarian Army in 1912. *Note:* Confiscated by the Germans in 1938, an estimated 250,000 of these pistols were converted to 9mm Luger and stamped with an identifying "08" on the left side of the slide. Mfd. by Osterreichische Waffenfabrik-Gesellschaft.

STOEGER LUGERS
Formerly mfd. by Stoeger Industries, So. Hackensack, N.J.; then Classic Arms, Union City, N.J.

Stoeger American Eagle Luger

Stoeger American Eagle Luger
Caliber: 9mm Parabellum. 7-shot magazine. 4- or 6-inch bbl. 8.25 inches (w/4-inch bbl.) or 10.25 inches (w/6-inch bbl.) overall. Weight: 30 or 32 oz. Checkered walnut grips. Stainless steel frame. Made from 1994 to date.
P-08 Model (4-inch bbl.). **$525**
Navy Model (6-inch bbl.) **535**

Stoeger Standard Luger 22 Automatic Pistol . . . **$150**
Caliber: 22 LR. 10-shot magazine. Bbls.: 4.5, 5.5 inches. 8.88 inches overall w/4.5-inch bbl. Weight: 29.5 oz. w/4.5-inch bbl. Fixed sights. Black finish. Smooth wood stocks. Made 1969-86.

Stoeger Standard Luger

Stoeger Steel Frame Luger 22 Auto Pistol. **$165**
Caliber: 22 LR. 10-shot magazine. 4.5-inch bbl. 8.88 inches overall. Blued finish. Checkered wood stocks. Features one-piece solidly forged and machined steel frame. Made 1980-86.

Stoeger Target Luger 22 Automatic Pistol. **$195**
Same as Standard Luger 22, except has target sights. 9.38 inches overall with 4.5-inch bbl. Checkered wood stocks. Made 1975-86.

TARGA PISTOLS
Italy
Manufactured by Armi Tanfoglio Guiseppe

Targa Model GT26S Auto Pistol **$75**
Caliber: 25 ACP. 6-shot magazine. 2.5-inch bbl. 4.63 inches overall. Weight: 15 oz. fixed sights. Checkered composition stocks. Blued or chrome finish. Discontinued 1990.

Targa Model GT 380XE

Targa Model GT32 Auto Pistol
Caliber: 32 ACP. 6-shot magazine. 4.88-inch bbl. 7.38 inches overall. Weight: 26 oz. fixed sights. Checkered composition or walnut stocks. Blued or chrome finish.
Blued finished . . . . $ 95
Chrome finish **110**

Targa Model GT380 Automatic Pistol
Same as the Targa GT32, except chambered for 380 ACP.
Blued finish $115
Chrome finish **125**

Targa Model GT380XE Automatic Pistol $135
Caliber: 380 ACP. 11-shot magazine. 3.75-inch bbl. 7.38 inches overall. Weight: 28 oz. Fixed sights. Blued or satin nickel finish. Smooth wooden stocks. Made 1980-1990.

FORJAS TAURUS S.A.
Porto Alegre, Brazil

Taurus Model 44 DA Revolver
Caliber: 44 Mag. 6-shot cylinder. 4-, 6.5-, or 8.38-inch bbl. Weight: 44.75 oz. (4-inch bbl.), 52.5 or 57.25 oz. Brazilian hardwood grips. Blued or stainless steel finish. Made 1994 to date.
Blued Finish $295
Stainless **355**

Taurus Model 65
Satin Model

Taurus Model 65 DA Revolver
Caliber: 357 Magnum. 6-shot cylinder. 3- or 4-inch bbl. Weight: 32 oz. Front ramp sight, square notch rear. Checkered walnut target stock. Royal blue or satin nickel finish. Currently in production.
Blue $175
Stainless **235**

Taurus Model 66 DA Revolver
Calibers: 357 Magnum, 38 Special. 6-shot cylinder. Bbls.: 3, 4 and 6 inches. Weight: 35 oz. Serrated ramp front sight, rear click adj. Checkered walnut grips. Royal blue or nickel finish. Currently in production.
Blue $195
Stainless **255**

Taurus Model 66

Taurus Model 73 DA Revolver $175
Caliber: 32 Long. 6-shot cylinder. 3-inch heavy bbl. Weight: 20 oz. Checkered grips. Blued or satin finish. Discontinued 1993.

Taurus Model 74

Taurus Model 74 Target Grade DA Revolver $155
Caliber: 32 S&W Long. 6-shot cylinder. 3-inch bbl. 8.25 inches overall. Weight: 20 oz. Adj. rear sight, ramp front. Blued or nickel finish. Checkered walnut stocks. Made 1971-90.

Taurus Model 80

Taurus Model 80 DA Revolver
Caliber: 38 Special. 6-shot cylinder. Bbl. lengths: 3, 4, inches. 9.25 inches overall with 4-inch bbl. Weight: w/4-inch bbl., 30 oz. Fixed sights. Blued or nickel finish. Checkered walnut stocks. Made 1971 to date.
Blued $150
Stainless **175**

Taurus Model 82

Taurus Model 85
Concealed Hammer

Taurus Model 82 Heavy Barrel **$165**
Same as Model 80, except has heavy bbl. Weight: with 4-inch
bbl., 33 oz. Made 1971 to date.

Taurus Model 83

Taurus Model 85
w/Spur Hammer

Taurus Model 86

Taurus Model 83 Heavy Barrel Target Grade. . . . **$245**
Same as Model 84, except has heavy bbl., weighs 34.5 oz. Made
1977 to date.

Taurus Model 84

Taurus Model 86 Target Master DA Revolver . . . **$195**
Caliber: 38 Special. 6-shot cylinder. 6-inch bbl. 11.25 inches
overall. Weight: 34 oz. Adj. rear sight, Patridge-type front. Blued
finish. Checkered walnut stocks. Made 1971 to date.

Taurus Model 94 Target Grade
Same as Model 74, except caliber 22 LR, with 9-shot cylinder. 3-
or 4-inch bbl. Weight: 25 oz. Blued or stainless finish. Made
1971 to date.
Blued Finish **$185**
Stainless Finish   235

Taurus Model 96 Target Master **$215**
Same as Model 86, except in 22 LR. Made 1971 to date.

Taurus Model 84 Target Grade Revolver **$225**
Caliber: 38 Special. 6-shot cylinder. 4-inch bbl. 9.25 inches overall. Weight: 31 oz. Adj. rear sight, ramp front. Blued or nickel
finish. Checkered walnut stocks. Made 1971-89.

Taurus Model 85 DA Revolver
Caliber: 38 Special. 5-shot cylinder. Bbl.. 2- or 3-inch. Weight:
21 oz. Fixed sights. Checkered walnut grips. Blued, satin nickel
or stainless-steel finish. Currently in production. **Model 85CH** is
the same as the standard version except for concealed hammer.
Blued or Satin Nickel **$195**
Stainless Steel   230

Taurus Model 431 DA Revolver
Caliber: 44 Spec. 5-shot cylinder. 3- or 4-inch solid-rib bbl. with
ejector shroud. Weight: 35 oz.with 4-inch bbl. Serrated ramp
front sight, notched topstrap rear. Blued or stainless finish. Made
1992 to date.
Blued Finish **$195**
Stainless Finish   245

Taurus Model 441 DA Revolver

Similar to the Model 431, except w/6-inch bbl. and fully adj. target sights. Weight: 40 oz. Made 1991 to date.

Blued Finish **$225**
Stainless Finish **275**

Taurus Model 669

Taurus Model 669/669VR DA Revolver

Caliber: 357 Mag. 6-shot cylinder. 4- or 6-inch solid-rib bbl. with ejector shroud; Model 669VR has vent-rib bbl. Weight: 37 oz. with 4-inch bbl. Serrated ramp front sight, micro-adj. rear. Royal blue or stainless finish. Checkered Brazilian hardwood grips. Model 669 made 1989 to date; Model 669VR from 1990.

Model 669 Blued. **$195**
Model 669 Stainless **260**
Model 669VR Blued **240**
Model 669VR Stainless. **265**

Taurus Model 741/761 DA Revolver

Caliber: 32 H&R Mag. 6-shot cylinder. 3- or 4-inch solid-rib bbl. with ejector shroud. Weight: 20 oz. with 3-inch bbl. Serrated ramp front sight, micro-adj. rear. Blued or stainless finish. Checkered Brazilian hardwood grips. Made 1991 to date.

Model 741 Blued. **$200**
Model 741 Stainless **295**
Model 761 (6-inch bbl., blued, 34 oz.) **255**

Taurus Model 941 Target Revolver

Caliber: 22 Magnum. 8-shot cylinder. Solid-rib bbl. with ejector shroud. Micro-adj. rear sight. Brazilian hardwood grips. Blued or stainless finish.

Blued Finish **$210**
Stainless Finish **260**

Taurus Model PT 22

Taurus Model PT 22 DA Automatic Pistol $135

Caliber: 22 LR. 9-shot magazine. 2.75-inch bbl. Weight: 12.3 oz. Fixed open sights. Brazilian hardwood stocks. Blued finish. Made 1991 to date.

Taurus Model PT 25 DA Automatic Pistol $145

Same general specifications as Model PT 22, except in 25 ACP with 8-shot magazine. Made from 1992 to date.

Taurus Model PT-58

Taurus Model PT-58 Semiautomatic Pistol

Caliber: 380 ACP. 12-shot magazine. 4-inch bbl. 7.2 inches overall. Weight: 30 oz. Blade front sight; rear adj. for windage w/3-Dot sighting system. Blued, satin nickel or stainless finish. Made 1988 to date.

Blued Finish **$185**
Satin Nickel Finish **135**
Stainless Finish **335**

Taurus Model PT 92AF

Taurus Model PT 92AF Semiautomatic Pistol

Caliber: 9mm Parabellum. 15-round magazine. Double action. Bbl.: about 5 inches. 8.5 inches overall. Weight: 34 oz. Blade front sight, notched bar rear. Smooth Brazilian walnut grips. Blued, satin nickel or stainless finish. Made 1991 to date.

Blued Finish **$325**
Satin Nickel Finish **355**
Stainless Finish **375**

Taurus Model PT-92AFC Compact Pistol

Same general specifications as Model PT-92AF, except with 13-shot magazine. 4.25-inch bbl. 7.5 inches overall. Weight: 31 oz. Made 1991 to date.

Blued Finish **$340**
Satin Nickel Finish **355**
Stainless Finish **375**

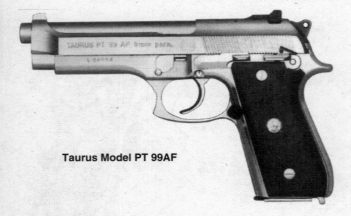

Taurus Model PT 99AF

Taurus Model PT 99AF Semiautomatic Pistol   . . $295

Same general specifications as Model PT 92AF, except rear sight is adj. for elevation and windage, and finish is blued or satin nickel. Discontinued 1993.

Taurus Model PT 100 DA Automatic Pistol

Caliber: 40 S&W. 11-shot magazine. 5-inch bbl. Weight: 34 oz. Fixed front sight; adj. rear w/3-Dot system. Smooth hardwood grip. Blued, satin nickel or stainless finish. Made 1991 to date.

Blued Finish **$330**
Satin Nickel Finish **365**
Stainless Finish **385**

Taurus Model PT 908

Taurus Model PT 101 DA Automatic Pistol

Same general specifications as Model 100, except w/micrometer click adj. sights.

Blued **$360**
Satin Nickel **385**
Stainless **425**

Taurus Model PT 908 Semiautomatic Pistol

Caliber: 9mm Parabellum. 8-shot magazine. 3.8-inch bbl. 7 inches overall. Weight: 30 oz. Sights: drift-adj. front; combat rear w/3-Dot system. Blued, satin nickel or stainless finish. Made from 1993 to date.

Blued Finish **$325**
Satin Nickel Finish **345**
Stainless Finish **375**

Texas Arms Defender Derringer

TEXAS ARMS
Waco, Texas

Texas Arms Defender Derringer **$215**
Calibers: 9mm, 357 Mag., 44 Mag., 45 ACP, 45 Colt/.410. 3-inch bbl. 5 inches overall. Weight: 21 oz. Sights: blade front; fixed rear. Matte gun-metal grey finish. Smooth grips. Made from 1993 to date.

TEXAS LONGHORN ARMS
Richmond, Texas

**Texas Longhorn Arms Keith No. 5
SA Revolver** **$750**
Caliber: 44 Magnum. 6-shot. 5.5-inch bbl. 11 inches overall. Weight: 44 oz. Adj. rear sight, blade front. One-piece deluxe walnut stock. Blued finish. Introduced 1987.

**Texas Longhorn Arms Sesquicentennial
SA Revolver** **$1895**
Same as South Texas Army Limited Edition, except engraved and nickel-plated with one-piece ivory stock. Introduced in 1986.

**Texas Longhorn Arms SA
Revolver Cased Set**
Set contains one each of the Texas Longhorn Single Actions. Each chambered in the same caliber and with the same serial number. Introduced in 1984.

Standard Set **$4400**
Engraved Set **5750**

Texas Longhorn Arms South Texas Army Limited Edition SA Revolver $1295

Calibers: all popular centerfire pistol calibers. 6-shot cylinder. 4.75-inch bbl. 10.25 inches overall. Weight: 40 oz. Fixed sights. Color casehardened frame. One-piece deluxe walnut stocks. Blued bbl. Introduced in 1984.

Texas Longhorn Arms Texas Border Special SA Revolver $1195

Same as South Texas Army Limited Edition, except with 3.5-inch bbl. and bird's-head grips. Introduced in 1984.

Texas Longhorn Arms West Texas Flat Top Target SA Revolver $1525

Same as South Texas Army Limited Edition, except with choice of bbl. lengths from 7 .5 to 15 inches. Same special features with flat-top style frame and adj. rear sight. Introduced in 1984.

THOMPSON PISTOL
West Hurley, New York
Mfd. by Auto-Ordnance Corporation

Thompson Model 27A-5 Semiautomatic Pistol

Similar to Thompson Model 1928A submachine gun, except has no provision for automatic firing, does not have detachable buttstock. Caliber: 45 Automatic. 20-shot detachable box magazine (5-, 15- and 30-shot box magazine, 39-shot drum also available). 13-inch finned bbl. Overall length: 26 inches. Weight: about 6.75 pounds. Adj. rear sight, blade front. Blued finish. Walnut grips. Introduced 1977. *See* Auto-Ordnance in Handgun Section.

With box magazine $1000
With drum magazine 1295

THOMPSON/CENTER ARMS
Rochester, New Hampshire

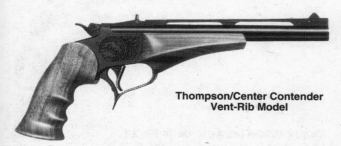

**Thompson/Center Contender
Vent-Rib Model**

Thompson/Center Contender Single-Shot Pistol

Break frame, underlever action. Calibers: (rimfire) 22 LR 22 WMR, 5mm RRM; (standard centerfire), 218 Bee, 22 Hornet, 22 Rem. Jet, 221 Fireball, 222 Rem., 25-35, 256 Win. Mag., 30 M1 Carbine, 30-30, 38 Auto, 38 Special 357 Mag./Hot Shot, 9mm Luger, 45 Auto, 45 Colt, 44 Magnum/Hot Shot; (wildcat centerfire) 17 Ackley Bee, 17 Bumblebee, 17 Hornet, 17 K Hornet, 17 Mach IV, 17-222, 17-223, 22 K Hornet, 30 Herrett, 357 Herrett,

**Thompson/Center Contender
Bull Barrel**

Thompson/Center Contender Single-Shot Pistol *(Cont.)*

357-4 B&D. Interchangeable bbls.: 8.75- or 10-inch standard octagon (357 Mag., 44 Mag. and 45 Colt available with detachable choke for use with Hot Shot cartridges); 10-inch with ventilated rib and detachable internal choke tube for Hot Shots, 357 and 44 Magnum only; 10-inch bull bbl., 30 or 357 Herrett only. 13.5 inches overall with 10-inch bbl. Weight: with standard 10-inch bbl., about 43 oz. Adj. rear sight, ramp front; vent-rib model has folding rear sight, adj. front; bull bbl. available with or w/o sights; Lobo 1½ X scope and mount (**add** $40 to value). Blued finish. Receiver photoengraved. Checkered walnut thumbrest stock and forearm (pre-1972 model has different stock with silver grip cap). Made 1967 to date, with the following revisions and variations.

Standard Model $220
Ventilated-Rib Model 250
Bull Bbl. Model, with sights 255
Bull Bbl. Model, without sights 225
Extra standard bbl. 85
Extra ventilated rib or bull bbl. 90

Thompson/Center Contender — Bull Barrel $260

Caliber offerings of the bull bbl. version expanded in 1973, with another bump in 1978, making it the Contender model with the widest range of caliber options: 22 LR, 22 Win. Mag., 22 Hornet, 223 Rem., 7mm T.C.U., 7×30 Waters, 30 M1 Carbine, 30-30 Win., 32 H&R Mag., 32-20 Win., 357 Rem. Max., 357 Mag., 10mm Auto, 44 Magnum, 445 Super Magnum. 10-inch heavy bbl. Patridge-style iron sights. Contoured Competitor grip. Blued finish.

Thompson/Center Contender — Internal Choke Model

Originally made in 1968-69 with octagonal bbl., this Internal Choke version in 45 Colt/.410 caliber only was reintroduced in 1986 with 10-inch bull bbl. Vent rib also available. Iron sights: fixed rear, bead front. Detachable choke screws into muzzle. Blued finish. Contoured American black walnut Competitor Grip, also introduced in 1986, has nonslip rubber insert permanently bonded to back of grip.

With Bull Bbl. $285
With Vent Rib 340

**Thompson/Center Contender
Octagon Barrel**

Thompson/Center Contender — Octagon Barrel $245

The original Contender design, this octagonal bbl. version began to see the discontinuance of caliber offerings in 1980, so that now it is available in 22 LR only. 10-inch octagonal bbl. Patridge-style iron sights. Contoured Competitor Grip. Blued finish.

Thompson/Center Contender — Stainless

Similar to the standard Contender Models, except stainless steel with blued sights. Black Rynite forearm and ambidextrous finger-groove grip. Made from 1993 to date.

Standard SS Model (10-inch bbl.). $315
SS Super 14..   325
SS Super 16   335

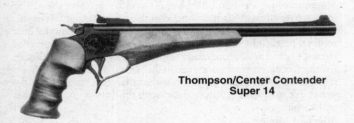

Thompson/Center Contender Super 14

Thompson/Center Contender Super 14 . . . . $275

Calibers: 22 LR, 222 Rem., 223 Rem., 6mm T.C.U., 6.5mm T.C.U., 7mm T.C.U., 7× 30 Waters, 30 Herrett, 30-30 Win., 357 Herrett, 357 Rem. Max., 35 Rem., 10mm Auto, 44 Mag., 445 Super Mag. 14-inch bull bbl. 18 inches overall. Weight: 56 oz. Patridge-style ramp front sight, adj. target rear. Blued finish. Made 1978 to date.

Thompson/Center Contender TC Alloy II with Vent Rib

Thompson/Center Contender TC Alloy II

Calibers: 22 LR, 223 Rem., 357 Magnum, 357 Rem. Max., 44 Magnum, 7mm T.C.U., 30-30 Win.; 45 Colt/.410 with internal choke, 35 Rem. and 7×30 Waters (14-inch bbl.). 10- or 14-inch bull bbl. or 10-inch vent-rib bbl. (w/internal choke). All metal parts permanently electroplated with T/C Alloy II, which is harder than stainless steel, ensuring smoother action, 30 percent longer bbl. life. Other design specifications the same as late model Contenders. Made 1986-89.

T/C Alloy II 10-inch Bull Bbl. $315
T/C Alloy II Vent-rib Bbl. w/Choke   350
T/C Alloy II Super 14   370

UNIQUE PISTOLS
Hendaye, France
Mfd. by Manufacture d'Armes des Pyrénées

Unique Model B/cf

Unique Model B/cf Automatic Pistol. $185

Calibers: 32 ACP, 380 ACP, 9-shot (32) or 8-shot (38) magazine. 4-inch bbl. 6.6 inches overall. Weight: 24.3 oz. Blued finish. Plain or thumbrest plastic stocks. Introduced 1954; discontinued.

Unique Model D2 . . . . $235

Same as Model D6, except has 4.5-inch bbl., 7.5 inches overall, weighs 24.5 oz. Made 1954 to date.

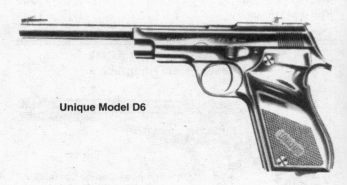

Unique Model D6

Unique Model D6 Automatic Pistol. $225

Caliber: 22 LR. 10-shot magazine. 6-inch bbl. 9.25 inches overall. Weight: about 26 oz. Adj. sights. Blued finish. Plain or thumbrest plastic stocks. Introduced in 1954; discontinued.

Unique Model DES/69 Standard Match Automatic Pistol $875

Caliber: 22 LR. 5-shot magazine. 5.9-inch bbl. 10.6 inches overall. Weight: 35 oz. (bbl. weight adds about 9 oz.). Click adj. rear sight, ramp front. Blued finish. Checkered walnut thumbrest stocks w/adj. handrest. Made 1969 to date.

Unique Model DES/69 Standard Match

Unique Model DES/VO

Unique Model DES/VO Rapid Fire Match Automatic Pistol $750
Caliber: 22 Short. 5-shot magazine. 5.9-inch bbl. 10.4 inches overall. Weight: 43 oz. Click adj. rear sight blade front. Checkered walnut thumbrest stocks w/adj. handrest. Trigger adj. for length of pull. Made from 1974 to date.

Unique Kriegsmodell

Unique Kriegsmodell Automatic Pistol. $245
Caliber: 32 Automatic (7.65mm). 9-shot magazine. 3.2-inch bbl. 5.8 inches overall. Weight: 26.5 oz. Fixed sights. Blued finish. Plastic stocks. Mfd. during German occupation of France 1940-45. *Note:* Bears the German military acceptance marks and may have stocks marked "7.65m/m 9 SCHUSS."

Unique Model L

Unique Model L Automatic Pistol $235
Calibers: 22 LR, 32 Auto (7.65mm), 380 Auto (9mm Short). 10-shot magazine in 22, 7 in 32, 6 in 380. 3.3-inch bbl. 5.8 inches overall. Weight: about 16.5 oz. (380) w/light alloy frame; 23 oz. with steel frame. Fixed sights. Blued finish. Plastic stocks. Introduced 1955; discontinued.

Unique Model Mikros

Unique Model Mikros Pocket Automatic Pistol . . $160
Calibers: 22 Short, 25 Auto (6.35mm). 6-shot magazine. 2.25-inch bbl. 4.44 inches overall. Weight: 9.5 oz. w/light alloy frame; 12.5 oz. w/steel frame. Fixed sights. Blued finish. Plastic stocks. Introduced 1957; discontinued.

Unique Model Rr

Unique Model Rr Automatic Pistol $185
Postwar commercial version of WWII Kriegsmodell with same general specifications. Introduced 1951; discontinued.

UNITED STATES ARMS CORPORATION
Riverhead, New York

U.S. Arms Abilene SA Revolver

U.S. Arms Abilene SA Revolver

Safety Bar action. Calibers: 357 Mag., 41 Mag., 44 Mag., 45 Colt; also 9mm Luger and 357 convertible model with two cylinders. 6-shot cylinder. Bbl. lengths: 4.63-, 5.5-, 6.5-inch, 7.5- and 8.5-inch in 44 Mag. only. Weight: about 48 oz. Adj. rear sight, ramp front. Blued finish or stainless steel. Smooth walnut stocks. Made 1976 to date.

44 Magnum, blued finish	**$250**
44 Magnum, stainless steel	**275**
Other calibers, blued finish	**225**
357 Magnum, stainless steel	**250**
Convertible, 357 Mag./9mm Luger, blued finish	**215**

UNIVERSAL FIREARMS CORPORATION
Hialeah, Florida

This company was purchased by Iver Johnson's Arms in the mid-1980s, when the Enforcer listed below was discontinued. An improved version was issued under the Iver Johnson name (see separate listing).

Universal Enforcer

Universal Enforcer Semiautomatic Pistol $275

M-1 Carbine-type action. Caliber: 30 Carbine. 5-, 15- or 30-shot clip magazine. 10.25-inch bbl. 17.75 inches overall. Weight: 4.5 pounds w/30-shot magazine. Adj. rear sight, blade front. Blued finish. Walnut stock with pistol grip and handguard. Made 1964-83.

UZI PISTOLS
Mfd. by Israel Military Industries, Israel

Uzi Semiautomatic Pistol. $995

Caliber: 9mm Parabellum. 20-round magazine. 4.5-inch bbl. About 9.5 inches overall. Weight: 3.8 pounds. Front post-type sight; rear open-type, both adj. Discontinued.

Uzi 9mm Semiautomatic

WALTHER PISTOLS
Manufactured by German, French and Swiss firms

The following Walther pistols were made before and during World War II by Waffenfabrik Walther, Zella-Mehlis (Thür.), Germany.

Walther Model 1

Walther Model 1 Automatic Pistol $385

Caliber: 25 Auto (6.35mm). 6-shot. 2.1-inch bbl. 4.4 inches overall. Weight: 12.8 oz. Fixed sights. Blued finish. Checkered hard rubber stocks. Introduced 1908.

Walther Model 2

Walther Model 2 Automatic Pistol $405

Caliber: 25 Auto (6.35mm). 6-shot magazine. 2.1-inch bbl. 4.2 inches overall. Weight: 9.8 oz. Fixed sights. Blued finish. Checkered hard rubber stocks. Intro. 1909.

Walther Model 3 Automatic Pistol $995

Caliber: 32 Auto (7.65mm). 6-shot magazine. 2.6-inch bbl. 5 inches overall. Weight: 16.6 oz. Fixed sights. Blued finish. Checkered hard rubber stocks. Intro. 1910.

Walther Model 6 Automatic Pistol $1995

Caliber: 9mm Luger. 8-shot magazine. 4.75-inch bbl. 8.25 inches overall. Weight: 34 oz. Fixed sights. Blued finish. Checkered hard rubber stocks. Made 1915-1917. *Note:* Since the powerful 9mm Luger cartridge is too much for the simple blow-back system of this pistol, firing is not recommended.

Walther Model 4

Walther Model 7

Walther Model 4 Automatic Pistol $250

Caliber: 32 Automatic (7.65mm). 8-shot magazine. 3.5-inch bbl. 5.9 inches overall. Weight: 18.6 oz. Fixed sights. Blued finish. Checkered hard rubber stocks. Made 1910-18.

Walther Model 7 Automatic Pistol $425

Caliber: 25 Auto. (6.35mm). 8-shot magazine. 3-inch bbl. 5.3 inches overall. Weight: 11.8 oz. Fixed sights. Blued finish. Checkered hard rubber stocks. Made 1917-18.

Walther Model 5

Walther Model 8

Walther Model 5 Automatic Pistol $290

Improved version of Model 2 with same general specifications, distinguished chiefly by better workmanship and appearance. Introduced in 1913.

Walther Model 8 Automatic Pistol $335

Caliber: 25 Auto. (6.35mm). 8-shot magazine. 2.88-inch bbl. 5.13 inches overall. Weight: 12.38 oz. Fixed sights. Blued finish. Checkered plastic stocks. Made 1920-45.

Walther Model 8 Lightweight Automatic Pistol . . $390

Same as standard Model 8 except about 25 percent lighter due to use of aluminum alloys.

Walther Model 6

Walther Model 9 Vest Pocket Automatic Pistol . . $350

Caliber: 25 Automatic (6.35mm). 6-shot magazine. 2-inch bbl. 3.94 inches overall. Weight: 9 oz. Fixed sights. Blue finish. Checkered plastic stocks. Made 1921-1945. *See* illustration next page.

Walther Model 9

Walther Model HP

Walther Model HP Double-Action Automatic. . . $1050
Prewar commercial version of the P38. "HP" is abbreviation of "Heeres Pistole" (Army Pistol). Caliber: 9mm Luger. 8-shot magazine. 5-inch bbl. 8.38 inches overall. Weight: about 34.5 oz. Fixed sights. Blued finish. Checkered wood or plastic stocks. The Model HP is distinguished by its notably fine material and workmanship. Made 1937-44.

Walther Olympia Funfkampf Model Automatic . . $895
Caliber: 22 LR. 10-shot magazine. 9.6-inch bbl. 13 inches overall. Weight: 33 oz., less weight. Set of 4 detachable weights. Adj. target sights. Blued finish. Checkered stocks. Introduced 1936.

Walther Olympia Hunting Model Automatic $695
Same general specifications as Olympia Sport Model, but with 4-inch bbl. Weight: 28.5 oz.

Walther Olympia Rapid Fire Model Automatic . . $795
Caliber: 22 Short. 6-shot magazine. 7.4-inch bbl. 10.7 inches overall. Weight: without 12.38 oz. detachable muzzle weight, 27.5 oz. Adj. target sights. Blued finish. Checkered stocks. Made about 1936-40.

Walther Olympia Sport Model Automatic. $995
Caliber: 22 LR. 10-shot magazine. 7.4-inch bbl. 10.7 inches overall. Weight: 30.5 oz., less weight. Adj. target sights. Blued finish. Checkered stocks. Set of four detachable weights was supplied at extra cost. Made about 1936-40.

Walther P38 Military DA Automatic $625
Modification of the Model HP adopted as an official German Service arm in 1938 and produced throughout WW II by Walther (code "ac"), Mauser (code "byf") and a few other manufacturers. General specifications and appearance same as Model HP, but with a vast difference in quality, the P38 being a mass-produced military pistol; some of the late wartime models were very roughly finished and tolerances were quite loose.

Walther Model PP (Prewar)

Walther Model PP DA Automatic Pistol
Polizeipistole (Police Pistol). Calibers: 22 LR (5.6mm), 25 Auto (6.35mm), 32 Auto (7.65mm), 380 Auto (9mm). 8-shot magazine, 7-shot in 380. 3.88-inch bbl. 6.94 inches overall. Weight: 23 oz. Fixed sights. Blued finish. Checkered plastic stocks. *Note:* Wartime models are inferior in quality to prewar commercial pistols. Made 1929-45.

22 caliber, commercial model	$475
25 caliber, commercial model	495
32 and 380 caliber, commercial model	810
Wartime model	400

Walther Model PP Lightweight
Same as standard Model PP, except about 25 percent lighter due to use of aluminum alloys. Values 50 percent higher.

Walther Model PP 7.65mm Presentation $1400
Made of soft aluminum alloy in green-gold color, these pistols were not intended to be fired.

Walther Model PPK (WW II)

Walther Model PPK Double-Action Automatic Pistol

Polizeipistole Kriminal (Detective Pistol). Calibers: 22 LR (5.6mm), 25 Auto (6.35mm), 32 Auto (7.65mm), 380 Auto (9mm). 7-shot magazine, 6-shot in 380. 3.25-inch bbl. 5.88 inches overall. Weight: 19 oz. Fixed sights. Blued finish. Checkered plastic stocks. *Note:* Wartime models are inferior in workmanship to prewar commercial pistols. Made 1931-45.

25, commercial model. . . . . $ 795
32, commercial model. 475
22 LR & 380 1500

Walther Model PPK Lightweight

Same as standard Model PPK, except about 25 percent lighter due to aluminum alloys. Values 50 percent higher.

Walther Model PPK 7.65mm Presentation $1095

Made of soft aluminum alloy in green-gold color, these pistols were not intended to be fired.

Walther Self-Loading Sport Pistol $610

Caliber: 22 LR. 10-shot magazine. Bbl. lengths: 6- and 9-inch. 9.88 inches overall with 6-inch bbl. Target sights. Blued finish. One-piece, wood or plastic stocks, checkered. Introduced in 1932.

NOTE

The following Walther pistols are now manufactured by Carl Walther Waffenfabrik, Ulm/Donau, Germany.

Walther Free Pistol

Walther Model Free Pistol $1250

Single-Shot. Caliber: 22 LR. 11.7-inch heavy barrel. Weight: 48 oz. Adj. grips and sights; electronic trigger. Importation discontinued 1991.

Walther Model GSP

Walther Model GSP Target Automatic Pistol

Calibers: 22 LR, 32 S&W Long Wadcutter. 5-shot magazine. 4.5-inch bbl. 11.8 inches overall. Weights: 44.8 oz., 22 cal.; 49.4 oz., 32 cal. Adj. target sights. Black finish. Walnut thumbrest stocks w/adj. handrest. Made 1969-94.

22 Long Rifle . . . . $ 995
32 S&W Long Wadcutter 1250
Conversion unit. 22 Short or 22 LR extra. 1000

Walther Model OSP Rapid Fire Target Pistol . . . $1095

Caliber: 22 Short. 5-shot magazine. 4.5-inch bbl. 11.8 inches overall. Weight: 42.3 oz. Adj. target sights. Black finish. Walnut thumbrest stocks w/adj. handrest. 22 LR conversion unit available (**add** $275). Made 1968-94.

Walther Model P4 (P38-IV) DA Pistol $425

Similar to P38, except has an uncocking device instead of a manual safety. Caliber: 9mm Luger only. 4.3-inch bbl. 7.9 inches overall. Other general specifications same as for current model P38. Made 1974-82.

Walther Model P5

Walther Model P5 DA Pistol $600

Alloy frame with frame-mounted decocking levers. Caliber: 9mm Parabellum. 8-shot magazine. 3.5-inch bbl. 7 inches overall. Weight: 28 oz. blued finish. Checkered walnut or synthetic grips. Made from 1988 to date.

Walther P5 Compact Pistol $600

Similar to model P5, except with 3.1-inch bbl. and weighs 26 oz. Made from 1988 to date.

Walther Model P38 (P1) DA Automatic

Postwar commercial version of the P38, has light alloy frame. Calibers: 22 LR, 7.65mm Luger, 9mm Luger. 8-shot magazine. Bbl. lengths: 5.1-inch in 22 caliber, 4.9- inch in 7.65mm and 9mm. 8.5 inches overall. Weight: 28.2 oz. Fixed sights. Nonreflective black finish. Checkered plastic stocks. Made 1957-89. *Note:* The "P1" is W. German Armed Forces official pistol.

22 Long Rifle $575
Other calibers 445

**Walther Model P38 Standard
Current Production**

Walther Model P38 Deluxe Engraved Pistol

Elaborately engraved. Available in blued, chrome-, silver- or gold-plated finish.

Blued finish.	**$1095**
Chrome-plated.	**1110**
Silver-plated	**1195**
Gold-plated	**1600**

Walther Model P38K

Walther Model P38K. $595

Short-barreled version of current P38, the "K" standing for kurz (short). Same general specifications as standard model, except 2.8-inch bbl., 6.3 inches overall, weighs 27.2 oz., front sight is slide mounted. Caliber: 9mm Luger only. Made 1974-80.

Walther Model P88

Walther Model P 88 DA Automatic $795

Caliber: 9mm Luger. 15-shot magazine. 4-inch bbl. 7.38 inches overall. Weight: 31.5 oz. Blade front sight; adj. rear. Checkered black composition grip. Ambidextrous decocking levers. Blued finish. Made 1987 to date.

Walther Model P 88 DA Compact $895

Similar to the standard P 88 Model, except with 13-shot magazine. 3.8-inch bbl. 7.1 inches overall. Weight: 29 oz. Blued finish.

Walther Model PP (Current)

Walther Model PP DA Automatic Pistol

Calibers: 22 LR, 32 Auto (7.65mm), 380 Auto (9mm Short). 8-shot magazine in 22 and 32, 7-shot in 380. 3.9-inch bbl. 6.7 inches overall. Weight: 32 cal., 23.3 oz. Fixed sights. Blued finish. Checkered plastic stocks. Made 1963 to date.

22 Long Rifle	**$355**
Other calibers	**325**

Walther Model PP Super DA Pistol $425

Caliber: 9×18mm. 7-shot magazine. 3.6-inch bbl. 6.9 inches overall. Weight: 30 oz. Fixed sights. Blued finish. Checkered plastic stocks. Made 1974-81.

Walther Model PPK (Current)

Walther Model PPK DA Automatic Pistol

Steel or dural frame. Calibers: 22 LR, 32 Auto (7.65mm) 380 Auto (9mm Short); latter caliber not available in model with dural frame. 3.3-inch bbl.6.1 inches overall. Weight (32 caliber): with steel frame, 20.8 oz., with dural frame,16.6 oz. Fixed sights.

Walther Model PPK DA Automatic Pistol *(Cont.)*

Blued finish. Checkered plastic stocks. German-made 1963 to date, U.S. importation discontinued in 1968. U.S. version made by Interarms since 1986 incl. a stainless-steel model.

22 Long Rifle **$650**
Other calibers **595**

Walther Model PPK/S DA Automatic Pistol

Designed to meet the requirements of the U.S. Gun Control Act of 1968, this model has the frame of the PP and the shorter slide and bbl. of the PPK. Overall length: 6.1 inches. Weight: 23 oz. Other specifications are the same as those of standard PPK, except steel frame only. German-made 1971 to date. U.S. version made by Interarms 1979 to date.

22 Long Rifle **$315**
Other calibers **295**

Walther Models PP, PPK, PPK/S Deluxe Engraved

These elaborately engraved models are available in blued finish, chrome-, silver- or gold-plated.

Blued finish.. **$ 875**
Chrome-plated **995**
Silver-plated **1000**
Gold-plated..................................... **1145**
Add for 22 Long Rifle **50**

Walther Model TPH

Walther Model TPH DA Pocket Pistol......... **$325**

Light alloy frame. Calibers: 22 LR, 25 ACP (6.35mm). 6-shot magazine. 2.25-inch bbl. 5.38 inches overall. Weight: 14 oz. Fixed sights. Blued finish. Checkered plastic stocks. Made 1968 to date. *Note:* Few Walther-made models reached the U.S. because of import restrictions; a U.S.-made version has been mfd. by Interarms since 1986.

NOTE

The following Mark IIs have been made in France since 1950 by Manufacture de Machines du Haut-Rhin (MANURHIN) at Mulhouse-Bourtzwiller. The designation "Mark II" is used here to distinguish between these and the prewar models. Early (1950-54) production bears MANURHIN trademark on slide and grips. Later models are marked "Walther Mark II." U.S. importation discontinued.

Walther Mark II Model PP Auto Pistol......... **$410**
Same general specifications as prewar Model PP.

Walther Mark II Model PPK Auto Pistol **$475**
Same general specifications as prewar Model PPK.

Walther Mark II Model PPK Lightweight........ **$510**
Same as standard PPK except has dural receiver. Calibers: 22 LR and 32 Auto.

NOTE

The Walther Olympia Model pistols were manufactured 1952-1963 by Hämmerli AG Jagd-und Sportwaffenfabrik, Lenzburg, Switzerland, and marketed as "Hämmerli-Walther." See Hämmerli listings for specific data.

**Hämmerli-Walther Olympia
Model 200, 1952 Type**

**Hämmerli-Walther Olympia Model 200
Auto Pistol, 1952 Type.....................** **$575**
Similar to 1936 Walther Olympia Funfkampf Model.

**Hämmerli-Walther Olympia
Model 200, 1958 Type.....................** **$595**
Hämmerli-Walther Olympia Model 201........ **$575**
Hämmerli-Walther Olympia Model 202........ **$550**
Hämmerli-Walther Olympia Model 203
1955 Type **$625**
1958 Type **625**

Hämmerli-Walther Olympia American Model 204
1956 Type **$695**
1958 Type **650**

Hämmerli-Walther Olympia American Model 205
1956 Type **$750**
1958 Type **675**

WARNER PISTOL
Norwich, Connecticut
Warner Arms Corp. (or Davis-Warner Arms Co.)

Warner Infallible Pocket Automatic Pistol **$275**
Caliber: 32 Automatic. 7-shot magazine. 3-inch bbl. 6.5 inches overall. Weight: about 24 oz. Fixed sights. Blued finish. Hard rubber stocks. Made 1917-19.

WEBLEY & SCOTT LTD.
London and Birmingham, England

Webley 9mm Military & Police

Webley 9mm Military & Police Auto Pistol $795
Caliber: 9mm Browning Long. 8-shot magazine. 8 inches overall. Weight: 32 oz. Fixed sights. Blued finish. Checkered vulcanite stocks. Made 1909-30.

Webley 25 Hammer

Webley 25 Hammer Model Automatic Pistol $225
Caliber: 25 Automatic. 6-shot magazine. Overall length: 4.75 inches. Weight: 11.75 oz. No sights. Blued finish. Checkered vulcanite stocks. Made 1906-40.

Webley 25 Hammerless

Webley 25 Hammerless Model Auto Pistol $220
Caliber: 25 Automatic. 6-shot magazine. Overall length: 4.25 inches. Weight: 9.75 oz. Fixed sights. Blued finish. Checkered vulcanite stocks. Made 1909-40.

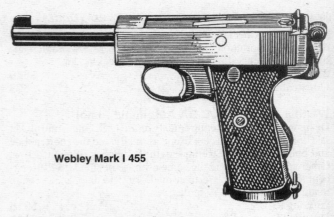

Webley Mark I 455

Webley Mark I 455 Automatic Pistol $995
Caliber: 455 Webley Automatic. 7-shot magazine. 5-inch bbl. 8.5 inches overall. Weight: about 39 oz. Fixed sights. Blued finish. Checkered vulcanite stocks. Made 1913-31. Reissued during WWII. Total production about 9,300. *Note:* **Mark I No. 2** is same pistol with adj. rear sight and modified manual safety.

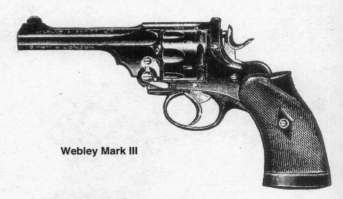

Webley Mark III

Webley Mark III 38 Military & Police Revolver . . . $275
Hinged frame. DA. Caliber: 38 S&W. 6-shot cylinder. Bbl. lengths: 3- and 4-inch. 9.5 inches overall w/4-inch bbl. Weight: 21 oz. w/4-inch bbl. Fixed sights. Blued finish. Checkered walnut or vulcanite stocks. Made 1897-45.

Webley Mark IV 22

Webley Mark IV 22 Caliber Target Revolver $345
Same frame and general appearance as Mark IV 38. Caliber: 22 LR. 6-shot cylinder. 6-inch bbl. 10.13 inches overall. Weight: 34 oz. Target sights. Blued finish. Checkered stocks. Discontinued 1945.

Webley Mark IV 38 Military & Police Revolver... $250

Identical in appearance to the Mark IV 22 on the preceding page. Hinged frame. DA. Caliber: 38 S&W. 6-shot cylinder. Bbl. lengths: 3-, 4- and 5-inch. 9.13 inches overall w/5-inch bbl. Weight: 27 oz. w/5-inch bbl. Fixed sights. Blued finish. Checkered stocks. Made 1929-c. 1957.

Webley Mark VI No. 1

Webley Mark VI No. 1 British Service Revolver.. $275

DA. Hinged frame. Caliber: 455 Webley. 6-shot cylinder. Bbl. lengths: 4-, 6- and 7.5-inch. 11.25 inches overall w/6-inch bbl. Weight: 38 oz. w/6-inch bbl. Fixed sights. Blued finish. Checkered walnut or vulcanite stocks. Made 1915-1947.

Webley Mark VI 22 Target Revolver $250

Same frame and general appearance as the Mark VI 455. Caliber: 22 LR. 6-shot cylinder. 6-inch bbl. 11.25 inches overall. Weight: 40 oz. Target sights. Blued finish. Checkered walnut or vulcanite stocks. Discontinued 1945.

Webley Metropolitan Police

Webley Metropolitan Police Automatic Pistol ... $675

Calibers: 32 Auto, 380 Auto. 8-shot (32) or 7-shot (380) magazine. 3.5-inch bbl. 6.25 inches overall. Weight: 20 oz. Fixed sights. Blued finish. Checkered vulcanite stocks. Made 1906-40 (32); 1908-20 (380).

Webley RIC Model DA Revolver $295

Royal Irish Constabulary or Bulldog Model. Solid frame. Caliber: 455 Webley. 5-shot cylinder. 2.25-inch bbl. Weight: 21 oz. Fixed sights. Blued finish. Checkered walnut or vulcanite stocks. Discont.

Webley RIC Model

Webley "Semiautomatic" Single-Shot Pistol.... $225

Similar in appearance to the Webley Metropolitan Police Automatic, this pistol is "semiautomatic" in the sense that the fired case is extracted and ejected and the hammer cocked as in a blow-back automatic pistol; it is loaded singly and the slide manually operated in loading. Caliber: 22 Long. Bbl. lengths: 4.5- and 9-inch. 10.75 inches overall w/9-inch bbl. Weight: 24 oz. w/9-inch bbl. Adj. sights. Blued finish. Checkered vulcanite stocks. Made 1911-27.

Webley Single-Shot Target

Webley Single-Shot Target Pistol $250

Hinge frame. Caliber: 22 LR. 10-inch bbl. 15 inches overall. Weight: 37 oz. Fixed sights on earlier models, current production has adj. rear sight. Blued finish. Checkered walnut or vulcanite stocks. Made 1909 to date.

Webley-Fosbery Automatic Revolver

Webley-Fosbery Automatic Revolver......... $2500

Hinged frame. Recoil action revolves cylinder and cocks hammer. Caliber: 455 Webley. 6-shot cylinder. 6-inch bbl. 12 inches overall. Weight: 42 oz. Fixed sights. Blued finish. Checkered walnut stocks. Made 1901-1939. *Note:* A few were produced in caliber 38 Colt Auto with an 8-shot cylinder; this is a very rare collector's item.

WESSON FIREARMS CO., INC.
Palmer, Massachusetts
Formerly Dan Wesson Arms, Inc.

Dan Wesson Model 8 Service

Same general specifications as Model 14, except caliber 38 Special. Made 1971-75. Values same as for Model 14.

Dan Wesson Model 8-2 Service

Same general specifications as Model 14-2, except caliber 38 Special. Made 1975 to date. Values same as for Model 14-2.

Dan Wesson Model 9 Target

Same as Model 15, except caliber 38 Special. Made 1971-75. Values same as for Model 15.

Dan Wesson Model 9-2 Target

Same as Model 15-2, except caliber 38 Special. Made 1975 to date. Values same as for Model 15-2.

Dan Wesson Model 9-2H Heavy Barrel

Same general specifications as Model 15-2H, except caliber 38 Special. Made 1975 to date. Values same as for Model 15-2H. Discontinued 1983.

Dan Wesson Model 9-2HV Vent-Rib Heavy Barrel

Same as Model 15-2HV, except caliber 38 Special. Made 1975 to date. Values same as for Model 15-2HV.

Dan Wesson Model 9-2V Ventilated Rib

Same as Model 15-2V, except caliber 38 Special. Made 1975 to date. Values same as for Model 15-2H.

Dan Wesson Model 11

Dan Wesson Model 11 Service DA Revolver

Caliber: 357 Magnum. 6-shot cylinder. Bbl. lengths: 2.5-, 4-, 6-inch- interchangeable bbl. assemblies. 9 inches overall w/4-inch bbl.; Weight: 38 oz. w/4-inch bbl. Fixed sights. Blued finish. Interchangeable stocks. Made 1970-71. *Note:* The Model 11 has an external bbl. nut.

With one bbl. assembly and stock **$185**
Extra bbl. assembly 60
Extra stock 45

Dan Wesson Model 12 Target

Same general specifications as Model 11, except has adj. sights. Made 1970-71.

With one-bbl. assembly and stock **$215**
Extra bbl. assembly 50
Extra stock 25

Dan Wesson Model 14

Dan Wesson Model 14 Service DA Revolver

Caliber: 357 Magnum. 6-shot cylinder. Bbl. lengths: 2.25-, 3.75, 5.75-inch; interchangeable bbl. assemblies. 9 inches overall w/3.75-inch bbl. Weight: 36 oz. w/3.75-inch bbl. Fixed sights. Blued or nickel finish. Interchangeable stocks. Made 1971-75. *Note:* Model 14 has recessed bbl. nut.

With one-bbl. assembly and stock **$220**
Extra bbl. assembly 50
Extra stock 25

Dan Wesson Model 14-2

Dan Wesson Model 14-2 Service DA Revolver

Caliber: 357 Magnum. 6-shot cylinder. Bbl. lengths: 2.5-, 4-, 6-, 8-inch; interchangeable bbl. assemblies. 9.25 inches overall w/4-inch bbl. Weight: 34 oz. w/4-inch. Fixed sights. Blued finish. Interchangeable stocks. Made 1975 to date. *Note:* Model 14-2 has recessed bbl. nut.

W/one-bbl. assembly (8") and stock **$195**
W/one-bbl. assembly (other lengths) and stock 185
Extra bbl. assembly, 8" 65
Extra bbl. assembly, other lengths 50
Extra stock 25

Dan Wesson Model 15 Target

Same general specifications as Model 14, except has adj. sights. Made 1971-75.

With one-bbl. assembly and stock **$230**
Extra bbl. assembly 50
Extra stock 25

Dan Wesson Model 15

Dan Wesson Model 15-2

Dan Wesson Model 15-2 Target

Same general specifications as Model 14-2 except has adj. rear sight and interchangeable blade front; also avail. with 10-, 12- and 15-inch bbls. Made 1975 to date.

With one-bbl. assembly (8") and stock	$250
With one-bbl. assembly (10") and stock	265
With one-bbl. assembly (12")/stock. Disc.	250
With one-bbl. assembly (15")/stock. Disc.	275
With one-bbl. assembly (other lengths)/stock	190
Extra bbl. assembly (8")	75
Extra bbl. assembly (10")	95
Extra bbl. assembly (12"). Discontinued	100
Extra bbl. assembly (15"). Discontinued	115
Extra bbl. assembly (other lengths)	50
Extra stock	20

**Dan Wesson Model 15-2H
Interchangeable Heavy Barrel
Assemblies**

Wesson Model 15-2H Heavy Barrel

Same as Model 15-2, except has heavy bbl. assembly weight, with 4-inch bbl., 38 oz. Made 1975-83.

With one-bbl. assembly (8") and stock	$240
With one-bbl. assembly (10") and stock	245
With one-bbl. assembly (12") and stock	265

Dan Wesson Model 15-2H Heavy Barrel *(Cont.)*

With one-bbl. assembly (15") and stock	$295
With one-bbl. assembly (other lengths)/stock	260
Extra bbl. assembly (8")	80
Extra bbl. assembly (10")	100
Extra bbl. assembly (12")	110
Extra bbl. assembly (15")	135
Extra bbl. assembly (other lengths)	60
Extra stock	20

Dan Wesson Model 15-2HV Vent-Rib Heavy Barrel

Same as Model 15-2, except has ventilated-rib heavy bbl. assembly; weight, with 4-inch bbl., 37 oz. Made 1975 to date.

With one-bbl. assembly (8") and stock	$275
With one-bbl. assembly (10") and stock	290
With one-bbl. assembly (12") and stock	295
With one-bbl. assembly (15") and stock	335
With one-bbl. assembly (other lengths) and stock	270
Extra bbl. assembly (8")	90
Extra bbl. assembly (10")	110
Extra bbl. assembly (12")	125
Extra bbl. assembly (15")	140
Extra bbl. assembly (other lengths)	70
Extra stock	20

Dan Wesson Model 15-2V Ventilated Rib

Same as Model 15-2, except has vent-rib bbl. assembly weighs 35 oz. w/4-inch bbl. Made 1975 to date. Values same as for 15-2H.

Dan Wesson Hunter Pacs

Dan Wesson Hunter Pacs are offered in all Magnum calibers and include heavy vent 8-inch shroud bbl. revolver Burris scope mounts, bbl. changing tool in a case.

HP22M-V	$525
HP22M-2	485
HP722M-V	565
HP722M-2	545
HP32-V	525
HP32-2	455
HP732-V	550
HP732-2	515
HP15-V	515
HP15-2	475
HP715-V	555
HP715-2	515
HP41-V	450
HP741-V	595
HP741-2	515
HP44-V	585
HP44-2	515
HP744-V	645
HP744-2	625
HP40-V	395
HP40-2	565
HP740-V	675
HP740-2	625
HP375-V	385
HP375-2	565
HP45-V	495

WHITNEY FIREARMS COMPANY
Hartford, Connecticut

Whitney Wolverine

Whitney Wolverine Automatic Pistol **$335**
Dural frame/shell contains all operating components. Caliber: 22 LR. 10-shot magazine. 4.63-inch bbl. 9 inches overall. Weight: 23 oz. Patridge-type sights. Blue or nickel finish. Plastic stocks. Made 1955-62.

WICHITA ARMS
Wichita, Kansas

Wichita Classic Pistol
Caliber: Chambered to order. Bolt-action, single-shot. 11.25-inch octagonal bbl. 18 inches overall. Weight: 78 oz. Open micro sights. Custom-grade checkered walnut stock. Blued finish. Made 1980 to date.
Standard **$2295**
Presentation Grade (engraved) **3695**

Wichita Hunter Pistol **$470**
Bolt-action, single-shot. Calibers: 22 LR, 22 WRF, 7mm Super Mag., 7-30 Waters, 30-30 Win., 32 H&R Mag., 357 Mag., 357 Super Mag. 10.5-inch bbl. 16.5 inches overall. Weight: 60 oz. No sights (scope mount only). Stainless steel finish. Walnut stock. Made 1983 to date.

Wichita International Pistol

Wichita International Pistol **$495**
Top-break, single-shot. SA. Calibers: 7-30 Waters, 7mm Super Mag., 7R (30-30 Win. necked to 7mm), 30-30 Win. 357 Mag., 357 Super Mag., 32 H&R Mag., 22 Mag. RF, 22 LR. 10- and 14-inch bbl. (10.5" for centerfire calibers). Weight: 50-71 oz. Patridge front sight; adj. rear. Walnut forend and grips.

Wichita MK-40 Silhouette Pistol **$820**
Calibers: 22-250, 7mm IHMSA, 308 Win. Bolt-action, single-shot. 13-inch bbl. 19.5 inches overall. Weight: 72 oz. Wichita Multi-Range sight system. Aluminum receiver with blued bbl. Gray fiberthane glass stock. Made 1981 to date.

Wichita Silhouette Pistol **$840**
Calibers: 22-250, 7mm IHMSA 308 Win. Bolt-action, single-shot. 14.94-inch bbl. 21.38 inches overall. Weight: 72 oz. Wichita Multi-Range sight system. Blued finish. Walnut or gray fiberthane glass stock. Walnut center or rear grip. Made 1979 to date.

WILKINSON ARMS
Parma, Idaho

Wilkinson Linda

Wilkinson "Linda" Semiautomatic Pistol **$295**
Caliber: 9mm Luger Parabellum. 31-shot magazine. 8.25-inch bbl. 12.25 inches overall. Weight: 77 oz., empty. Rear peep sight with blade front. Blued finish. Checkered composition stocks.

Wilkinson Sherry

Wilkinson "Sherry" Semiautomatic Pistol **$145**
Caliber: 22 LR. 8-shot magazine. 2.13-inch bbl. 4.38 inches overall. Weight: 9.25 oz., empty. Crossbolt safety. Fixed sights. Blued or blue-gold finish. Checkered composition stocks. Made 1985 to date.

Section II
RIFLES

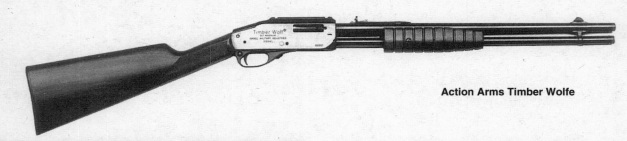

Action Arms Timber Wolfe

ACTION ARMS
Philadelphia, Pennsylvania

Action Arms Model B Sporter Semiautomatic Carbine **$525**
Similar to the Uzi Carbine (*see* separate listing), except with thumbhole stock. Caliber: 9mm Parabellum, 10-shot magazine. 16-inch bbl. Weight: 8.75 lbs. Post front sight; adj. rear. Imported 1993-94.

Action Arms Timber Wolfe Repeating Rifle
Calibers: 357 Mag./38 Special and 44 mag. Slide action. Tubular magazine holds 10 and 8 rounds, respectively. 18.5-inch bbl. 36.5 inches overall. Weight: 5.5 lbs. Fixed blade front sight; adj. rear. Receiver w/integral scope mounts. Checkered walnut stock. Imported 1989-94.
Blued Model **$225**
Chrome Model 295
44 Mag., **Add** 150

Alpha Arms Alaskan

Alpha Arms Custom

Alpha Arms Jaguar

ALPHA ARMS, INC.
Dallas, Texas

Alpha Alaskan Bolt-Action Rifle **$1095**
Same as Custom model, except w/stainless-steel bbl. and receiver and all other parts coated with Nitex; sling swivel stud attached to bbl. Left-hand model available. Made 1984-89.

Alpha Custom Bolt-Action Rifle **$1050**
Calibers: 17 Rem. thru 338 Win. Mag. Three action lengths w/three-lug locking system and 60-degree bolt rotation. 20- to 24-inch bbl.; round or octagonal. Weight: 6 to 7.25 lbs. No sights. Pistol-grip stock of presentation-grade California claro walnut; hand-rubbed oil finish. Custom inletted sling swivel stud attached to forend. Ebony forend tip. Left-hand models avail. Made 1984-89.

Alpha Grand Slam Bolt-Action Rifle **$945**
Same as Custom model, except w/Alphawood (fiberglass and wood) classic-style stock featuring Niedner-style grip cap. Weight: 6.5 lbs. Left-hand models. Made 1984-89.

Alpha Jaguar Bolt-Action Rifle
Same as Custom Rifle, except designed on Mauser-style action w/claw extractor, drilled and tapped and for scope. Originally designated Alpha Model 1. Calibers: 243, 7mm-08, 308 original chambering (1984-85) up to 338 Win. Mag. in the standard model; 338 thru 458 Win. Mag. in the Big Five model (1984-85). 20- to 24-inch bbl. Weights: 6 lbs. (min.) in standard model. 39.5 inches overall with 20-inch bbl. Teflon coated trigger guard/floorplate assembly. Made 1984-88.
Model 1 . . . . **$ 525**
Jaguar Standard Model 795
Big Five Model 1125

AMT Magnum Hunter Auto Rifle

AMT (ARCADIA MACHINE & TOOL)
Irwindale, California

AMT Challenger Edition Autoloading Target Rifle $625
Similar to the Small Game Hunter, except with McMillan target fiberglass stock. Caliber: 22 LR. 10-shot magazine. 16.5-, 18-, 20- or 22-inch bull bbl. Drilled and tapped for scope mount; no sights. Stainless steel finish. Made 1994 to date.

AMT Lightning 25/22 Autoloading Rifle $175
Caliber: 22 LR. 25-shot magazine. 18-inch tapered or bull bbl. Weight: 6 lbs. 37 inches overall. Sights: adj. rear; ramp front. Folding stainless-steel stock with matte finish. Made 1984-1994.

AMT Lightning

AMT Lightning Small Game Hunter $185
Similar to the AMT 25/22, except with conventional matte black fiberglass/nylon stock. 10-shot rotary magazine. 22-inch bbl. 40.5 inches overall. Weight: 6 lbs. Grooved for scope; no sights. Made 1987-1994.

AMT Lightning Small Game Hunter II $190
Similar to the original Small Game Hunter, except with free-floated 22-inch heavy target bbl. Weight: 6.75 lbs. Made 1992-93.

AMT Magnum Hunter Auto Rifle $290
Similar to the Lightning Small Game Hunter II Model, except chambered in 22 WRF with 22-inch match-grade bbl. Made from 1993 to date.

ANSCHUTZ RIFLES
Ulm, Germany
Mfd. by J.G. Anschutz GmbH Jagd und Sportwaffenfabrik

Anschutz Models 1407 ISU, 1408-ED, 1411, 1413, 1418, 1432, 1433, 1518 and 1533 were marketed in the U.S by Savage Arms. Further, Anschutz Models 1403, 1416, 1422D, 1441, 1516 and 1522D were sold as Savage/Anschutz with Savage model designations (see also listings under Savage Arms.) Precision Sales Int'l., Inc. of Westfield, Mass., is now the U S. distributor for all Anschutz rifles.

Anschutz Model 54.18MS $925
Bolt action, single shot. Caliber: 22 LR. 22-inch bbl. European hardwood stock w/cheekpiece. Forend and Wundhammer swell pistol grip stipple checkered. Receiver grooved, drilled and tapped for scope blocks. Weight: 8.38 lbs. Made 1982 to date.

Anschutz Model 54.18MS-REP Repeating Rifle
Same as the Model 54.18MS, except with repeating action and 5-shot magazine. 22- to 30-inch bbl. 41-49 inches overall. Avg. weight: 7 lbs. 12 oz. Hardwood or synthetic gray thumbhole stock. Made 1989 to date.
Standard MS-REP Model $1095
MS-REP Deluxe w/Fibergrain Stock 1295

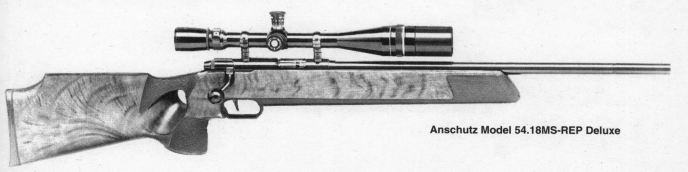

Anschutz Model 54.18MS-REP Deluxe

Anschutz Model 64MS Bolt-Action Single-Shot Rifle

Bolt action, single shot. Caliber: 22 LR. 21.25-inch bbl. European hardwood silhouette-style stock w/cheekpiece. Forend base and Wundhammer swell pistol grip, stipple checkered. Adj. two-stage trigger. Receiver grooved, drilled and tapped for scope blocks. Weight: 8 lbs. Made 1982-1990.

Standard or Featherweight **$550**
Left-hand Model **595**

Anschutz Model 520/61 Semiautomatic $215

Caliber: 22 LR. 10-shot magazine. 24-inch bbl. Sights: folding leaf rear, hooded ramp front. Receiver grooved for scope mounting. Rotary-style safety. Monte Carlo stock and beavertail forend, checkered. Weight: 6.5 lbs. Imported 1982-83.

Anschutz Model 525 Autoloading Rifle $365

Caliber: 22 LR. 10-shot magazine. 24-inch bbl. 43 inches overall. Weight: 6.5 lbs. Adj. folding rear sight; hooded ramp front. Checkered European hardwood Monte Carlo style buttstock and beavertail forend. Sling swivel studs. Imported since 1982.

Anschutz Model 1403B $695

A lighter weight model designed for Biathlon competition. Caliber: 22 LR. 21.5-inch bbl. Adj. two-stage trigger. Adj. grooved wood buttplate, stipple-checkered deep thumbrest flute and straight pistol grip. Weight: about 9 lbs. with sights. Made 1982-1992.

Anschutz Model 1403D Match Single-Shot Target Rifle

Caliber: 22 LR. 25-inch bbl. 43 inches overall. Weight: 8.6 lbs. No sights, receiver grooved for Anschutz target sights. Walnut finished hardwood target stock w/adj. buttplate. Discontinued 1992.

Standard Model **$505**
W/Match Sights **695**

Anschutz Model 1407 ISU Match 54 Rifle $395

Bolt action, single shot. Caliber: 22 LR. 26.88-inch bbl. Scope bases. Receiver grooved for Anschutz sights. Single-stage adj. trigger. Select walnut target stock w/deep forearm for position shooting, adj. buttplate, hand stop and swivel. Model 1407-L has left hand stock. Weight: about 10 lbs. Made 1970, discontinued. Value is for rifle less sights; **add** $65 for Anschutz International sight set.

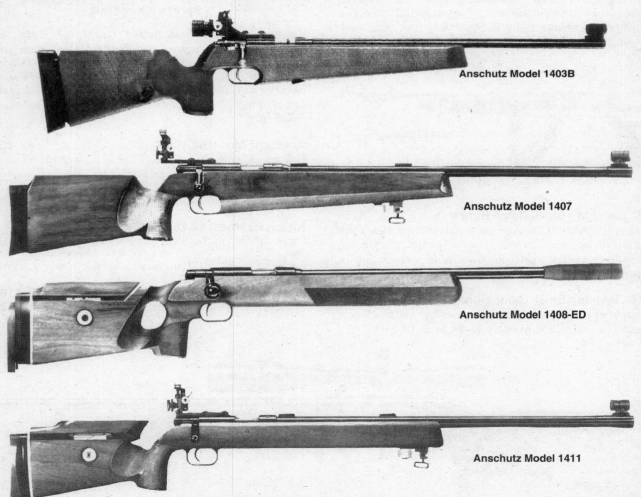

Anschutz Model 1403B

Anschutz Model 1407

Anschutz Model 1408-ED

Anschutz Model 1411

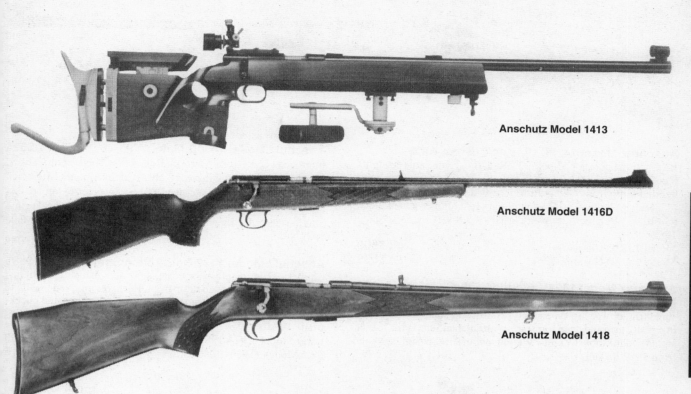

Anschutz Model 1413

Anschutz Model 1416D

Anschutz Model 1418

RIFLES

Anschutz Model 1408-ED Super Running Boar . . $425
Bolt action, single shot. Caliber: 22 LR. 23.5-inch bbl. w/sliding weights. No metallic sights. Receiver drilled and tapped for scope-sight bases. Single-stage adj. trigger. Oversize bolt knob. Select walnut stock w/thumbhole, adj. comb and buttplate. Weight: about 9.5 lbs. Introduced 1976; discontinued.

Anschutz Model 1411 Match 54 Rifle
Bolt action, single shot. Caliber: 22 LR. 27.5-inch extra heavy bbl. w/mounted scope bases. Receiver grooved for Anschutz sights. Single-stage adj. trigger. Select walnut target stock w/cheekpiece (adj. in 1973 and later production), full pistol grip, beavertail forearm, adj. buttplate, hand stop and swivel. Model 1411-L has left-hand stock. Weight: about 11 lbs. Discontinued.

W/non-adjustable cheekpiece **$425**
W/adjustable cheekpiece 455
Extra for Anschutz International sight set 125

Anschutz Model 1413 Super Match 54 Rifle
Freestyle international target rifle w/specifications similar to those of Model 1411, except has special stock with thumbhole, adj. pistol grip, adj. cheekpiece in 1973 and later production, adj. hook buttplate, adj. palmrest. Model 1413-L has left-hand stock. Weight: about 15.5 lbs. Discontinued.

W/non-adjustable cheekpiece **$725**
W/adjustable cheekpiece 755
Extra for Anschutz International sight set 125

Anschutz Model 1416D **$395**
Bolt-action sporter. Caliber: 22 LR. 22.5-inch bbl. Sights: folding leaf rear; hooded ramp front. Receiver grooved for scope mounting. Select European stock w/cheekpiece, skip-checkered pistol grip and forearm. Weight: 6 lbs. Made 1982 to date.

Anschutz Model 1416D Classic/Custom Sporters
Same as Model 1416D, except w/American classic-style stock (Classic) or modified European-style stock w/Monte Carlo rollover cheekpiece and schnabel forend (Custom). Weight: 5.5 lbs. (Classic); 6 lbs. (Custom). Made 1986 to date.
Model 1416D Classic **$450**
Model 1416D Classic, "True" Left-Hand 465
Model 1416D Custom 425
Model 1416D Fiberglass (1991-92) 425

Anschutz Model 1418 Bolt-Action Sporter **$355**
Caliber: 22 LR. 5- or 10-shot magazine. 19.75-inch bbl. Sights: folding leaf rear; hooded ramp front. Receiver grooved for scope mounting. Select walnut stock, Mannlicher type, w/cheekpiece, pistol grip and forearm skip checkered. Weight: 5.5 lbs. Intro. 1976; discontinued.

Anschutz Model 1418D Bolt-Action Sporter **$625**
Caliber: 22 LR. 5- or 10-shot magazine. 19.75-inch bbl. European walnut Monte Carlo stock, Mannlicher type w/cheekpiece, pistol grip and forend skip-line checkered buffalo horn schnabel tip. Weight: 5.5 lbs. Made from 1982 to date.

Anschutz Model 1422D

Anschutz Model 1422D Classic/Custom Rifle

Bolt-action sporter. Caliber: 22 LR. 5-shot removable straight-feed clip magazine. 24-inch bbl. Sights: folding leaf rear; hooded ramp front. Select European walnut stock, classic type (Classic); Monte Carlo w/hand-carved rollover cheekpiece (Custom). Weight: 7.25 lbs. (Classic) 6.5 lbs. (Custom). Made 1982-89.

Model 1422D Classic **$550**
Model 1422D Custom 595

Anschutz Model 1427B Biathlon Rifle $1095

Bolt-action clip repeater. Caliber: 22 LR. 21.5-inch bbl. Two-stage trigger w/wing-type safety. Hardwood stock w/deep fluting, pistol grip and deep forestock with adj. hand stop rail. Target sights w/adjustable weights. Weight: about 9 lbs. w/sights. Made from 1982 to date.

Anschutz Model 1430D Match $525

Improved version of Model 64S. Bolt-action, single shot. Caliber: 22 LR. 26-inch medium-heavy bbl. Walnut Monte Carlo stock w/cheekpiece, adj. buttplate, deep midstock tapered to forend. Pistol-grip and contoured thumb groove w/stipple checkering. Single-stage adj. trigger. Target sights. Weight: 8.38 lbs. Made 1982-83.

Anschutz Model 1432 Bolt-Action Sporter $895

Caliber: 22 Hornet. 5-shot box magazine. 24-inch bbl. Sights: folding leaf rear, hooded ramp front. Receiver grooved for scope mounting. Select walnut stock w/Monte Carlo comb and cheekpiece, pistol grip and forearm skip checkered. Weight: 6.75 lbs. Made 1974-1989.

Early Model (1974-1985) **$895**
Late Model (1986-1989) 815

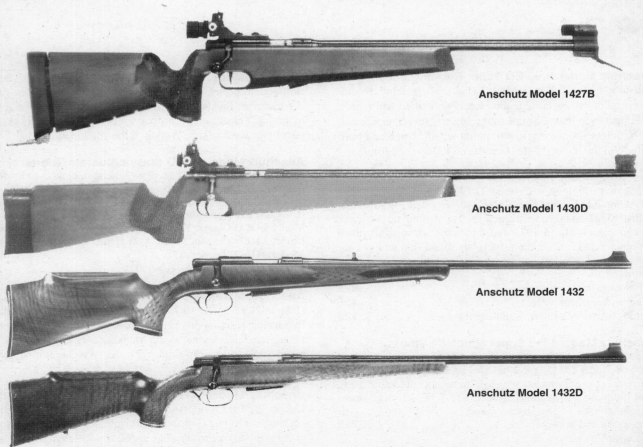

Anschutz Model 1427B

Anschutz Model 1430D

Anschutz Model 1432

Anschutz Model 1432D

Anschutz Model 1433

Anschutz Model 1432D Classic/Custom Rifle
Bolt-action sporter similar to Model 1422D except chambered for 22 Hornet. 4-shot magazine. 23.5-inch bbl. Weight: 7.75 lbs. (Classic); 6.5 lbs. (Custom). Classic stock on Classic model; fancy-grade Monte Carlo w/hand-carved rollover cheekpiece (Custom). Made 1982-89.
Model 1432D Classic **$895**
Model 1432D Custom **930**

Anschutz Model 1433 Bolt-Action Sporter...... **$760**
Caliber: 22 Hornet. 5-shot box magazine. 19.75-inch bbl. Sights: folding leaf rear, hooded ramp front. Receiver grooved for scope mounting. Single-stage or double-set trigger. Select walnut Mannlicher stock; cheekpiece, pistol grip and forearm skip checkered. Weight: 6.5 lbs. Made 1976-1986.

Anschutz Model 1449 Sporter **$195**
Bolt-action sporter version of Model 2000. Caliber: 22 LR. 5-shot box magazine. 16.25-inch bbl. Weight: 3.5 lbs. Hooded ramp front sight, adj. Walnut-finished hardwood stock. Made 1989-1992.

Anschutz Model 1450B Target Rifle **$395**
Biathlon rifle developed on the 2000 Series action. 19.5-inch bbl. Weight: 5.5 lbs. Adj. buttplate. Target sights. Imported 1993-94.

Anschutz Model 1516D Bolt-Action Sporter **$480**
Same as Model 1416D, except chambered for 22 Magnum RF. Made from 1982 to date.

Anschutz Model 1516D Classic/Custom Rifle
Same as Model 1516D, except w/American classic-style stock (Classic) or modified European-style stock w/Monte Carlo rollover cheekpiece and schnabel forend (Custom). Weight: 5.5 lbs. (Classic), 6 lbs. (Custom). Made from 1986 to date.
Model 1516D Classic **$540**
Model 1516D Custom **535**

Anschutz Models 1518/1518D Sporting Rifle
Same as Model 1418, except chambered for 22 Magnum RF, 4-shot box magazine. Model 1518 introduced 1976 discontinued. Model 1518D has full Mannlicher-type stock; made from 1982 to date.
Model 1518 .... **$515**
Model 1518D **650**

Anschutz Model 1522D Classic/Custom Rifle
Same as Model 1422D, except chambered for 22 Magnum RF, 4-shot magazine. Weight: 6.5 lbs. (Custom). Classic stock on Classic Model; fancy-grade Monte Carlo stock w/hand-carved rollover cheekpiece (Custom). Made 1982-89.
Model 1522D Classic **$795**
Model 1522D Custom **725**

Anschutz Model 1532D Classic/Custom Rifle
Same as Model 1432D except chambered for 222 Rem. 3-shot mag. Weight: 6.5 lbs. (Custom). Classic stock on Classic Model; fancy-grade Monte Carlo stock w/handcarved rollover cheekpiece (Custom). Made 1982-89.
Model 1532D Classic **$625**
Model 1532D Custom **795**

Anschutz Model 1533 .... **$770**
Same as Model 1433 except chambered for 222 Rem. 3-shot box magazine. Introduced 1976; discontinued.

Anschutz Model 1700 Series Bolt-Action Repeater
Match 54 Sporter. Calibers: 22 LR, 22 Magnum, 22 Hornet, 222 Rem. Removable straight-feed clip magazine.24-inch bbl. 43 inches overall. Weight: 7.5 lbs. Folding leaf rear sight, hooded ramp front. Select European walnut stock w/cheekpiece and schnabel forend tip. Made from 1989 to date.
Standard Model 1700 Bavarian — RF calibers **$820**
Standard Model 1700 Bavarian — CF calibers **985**
Model 1700D Classic (Classic stock, 6.75 lbs.)
    Rimfire calibers **865**
Model 1700D Classic — Centerfire calibers **975**

Anschutz Model 1700

Anschutz Model 1733D

Anschutz Model 1700 Series *(Cont.)*

Model 1700D Custom — Rimfire calibers **825**
Model 1700D Custom — Centerfire calibers **995**
Model 1700D Graphite Custom (McMillian graphite
reinforced stock, 22" bbl., intro. 1991) **825**
Model 1700 FWT Featherweight (6.5 lbs.)
    Rimfire calibers **825**
Model 1700 FWT — Centerfire calibers **1025**

Anschutz Model 1733D Mannlicher **$995**

Same as the Model 1700D, except with 19-inch bbl. and Mannlicher-style stock. 39 inches overall. Weight: 6.25 lbs. Made 1993 to date.

Anschutz Model 1803D Match Single-Shot Target Rifle

Caliber: 22 LR. 25.5-inch bbl. 43.75 inches overall. Weight: 8.5 lbs. No sights, receiver grooved, drilled and tapped for scope mounts. Blonde or walnut-finished hardwood stock with adj. cheekpiece, stippled grip and forend. Left-hand version. Imported 1987-1992.
Right-hand Model **$675**
Left-hand Model **750**

Anschutz Model 1807 ISU Standard Match **$795**

Bolt action, single shot. Caliber: 22 LR. 26-inch bbl. Improved Super Match 54 action. Two-stage match trigger. Removable cheekpiece, adj. buttplate, thumbpiece and forestock w/stipple checkered. Weight: 10 lbs. Imported 1982-1988.

Anschutz Model 1808ED Super-Running Target

Bolt action, single shot. Caliber: 22 LR. 23.5-inch bbl. w/sliding weights. Improved Super Match 54 action. Heavy beavertail forend, adj. cheekpiece and buttplate. Adj. single-stage trigger. Weight: 9.5 lbs. Made from 1982 to date.
Right-Hand Model . . . .   **$ 995**
Left-Hand Model **1035**

Anschutz Model 1810 Super Match II **$1295**

A less detailed version of the Super Match 1813 Model. Tapered forend w/deep receiver area. Select European hardwood stock. Weight: about 13.5 lbs. Imported 1982-88.

Anschutz Model 1811 Prone Match **$1095**

Bolt action, single shot. Caliber: 22 LR. 27.5-inch bbl. Improved Super Match 54 action. Select European hardwood stock w/beavertail forend, adj. cheekpiece, and deep thumb flute. Thumb groove and pistol grip w/stipple checkering. Adj. buttplate. Weight: about 11.5 lbs. Imported 1982-1988.

Anschutz Model 1813 Super Match **$1250**

Bolt-action, single-shot. Caliber: 22 LR. 27.5-inch bbl. Improved Super Match 54 action w/light firing pin, one-point adj. trigger. European walnut thumbhole stock, adj. palmrest, forend and pistol grip stipple checkered. Adj. cheekpiece and hook buttplate. Weight: 15.5 lbs. Imported 1982-1988.

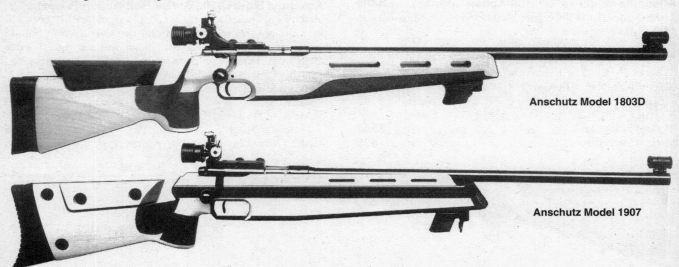

Anschutz Model 1803D

Anschutz Model 1907

Anschutz Model 2013

Anschutz Model 1827 Biathlon Rifle

Bolt action. Caliber: 22 LR. 21.5-inch bbl. 42.5 inches overall. Weight: 8.5 lbs w/sights. 6827 Sight Set w/snow caps; 10-click adj. Slide safety. European walnut stock w/cheekpiece, stippled pistol grip and forearm. Discontinued 1989.

Model 1827B w/Super Match 54 action	**$1295**
Model 1827BT w/Fortner straight-pull bolt,	
Right-hand.	**2595**
Left-hand.	**2895**

Anschutz Model 1907 International Match Rifle

Same general specifications Model 1913, except w/26-inch bbl. 44.5 inches overall. Weight: 11 lbs. Designed for ISU 3-position competition. Fitted w/vented blonde finished stock.

Right-hand Model	**$1095**
Left-hand Model	**1225**

Anschutz Model 1910 International Super Match Rifle

Same general specifications Model 1913, except w/less-detailed hardwood stock w/tapered forend. Weight: 13.5 lbs.

Right-hand Model	**$1695**
Left-hand Model	**1845**

Anschutz Model 1911 Prone Match Rifle

Same general specifications Model 1913, except w/specialized prone match hardwood stock w/beavertail forend. Weight: 11.5 lbs.

Right-hand Model	**$1295**
Left-hand Model	**1395**

Anschutz Model 1913 Super Match Rifle

Bolt action, single-shot Super Match. Caliber: 22 LR. 27.5-inch bbl. Weight: 15.2 lbs. Adj. two-stage trigger. Vented International thumbhole stock w/adj. cheekpiece, hand and palmrest, fitted w/10-way butthook. Made 1982 to date.

Right-hand Model	**$1825**
Left-hand Model	**1895**

Anschutz Model 2007 ISU Standard Rifle **$1595**

Bolt action, single shot. Caliber: 22 LR. 19.75-inch bbl. 43.5 to 44.5 inches overall. Weight: 10.8 lbs. Two-stage trigger. Standard ISU stock w/adj. cheekpiece. Made from 1992 to date.

Anschutz Model 2013 Super Match Rifle **$2595**

Bolt action, single shot. Caliber: 22 LR. 19.75-inch bbl. 43 to 45.5 inches overall. Weight: 12.5 lbs. Two-stage trigger. International thumbhole stock w/adj. cheekpiece hand and palmrest; fitted w/10-way butthook. Made from 1992 to date.

Anschutz Achiever Bolt-Action Rifle **$245**

Caliber: 22 LR. 5-shot magazine. Mark 2000-type repeating action. 19.5-inch bbl. 36.5 inches overall. Weight: 5 lbs. Adj. open rear sight; hooded ramp front. Plain European hardwood target-style stock w/vented forend and adj. buttplate. Imported since 1987.

Anschutz Achiever ST-Super Target **$350**

Same as the Achiever, except single shot with 22-inch bbl. and adj. stock. 38.75 inches overall. Weight: 6.5 lbs. Target sights. Imported since 1994.

Anschutz Model BR-50 Bench Rest Rifle. **$1495**

Single shot. Caliber: 22 LR. 19.75-inch bbl. (23 inches w/muzzle weight). 37.75-42.5 inches overall. Weight: 11 lbs. Grooved receiver, no sights. Walnut-finished hardwood or synthetic benchrest stock w/adj. cheekpiece. Made 1994 to date.

Anschutz Kadett Bolt-Action Repeating Rifle . . . **$190**

Caliber: 22 LR. 5-shot detachable box magazine. 22-inch bbl. 40 inches overall. Weight: 5.5 lbs. Adj. folding leaf rear sight; hooded ramp front. Checkered European hardwood stock w/walnut finish. Imported 1987-88.

Anschutz Achiever

Armalite AR-7 Explorer

Armalite AR-7 Explorer Custom

Armalite AR-180

Anschutz Mark 2000 Match **$275**
Takedown. Bolt action, single shot. Caliber: 22 LR. 26-inch heavy bbl. Walnut stock w/deep-fluted thumb-groove, Wundhammer swell pistol grip, beavertail-style forend. Adj. buttplate, single-stage adj. trigger. Weight: 8.5 lbs. Imported 1982-89.

ARMALITE INC.
Costa Mesa, California

Armalite AR-7 Explorer Survival Rifle **$100**
Takedown. Semiautomatic. Caliber: 22 LR. 8-shot box magazine. 16-inch cast aluminum bbl. with steel liner. Sights: peep rear; blade front. Brown plastic stock, recessed to stow barrel, action, and magazine. Weight: 2.75 lbs. Will float stowed or assembled. Made 1959-1973 by Armalite; 1974-1990 by Charter Arms; now manufactured by Survival Arms, Cocoa, FL.

Armalite AR-7 Explorer Custom Rifle **$130**
Same as AR-7 Survival Rifle except has deluxe walnut stock w/cheekpiece and pistol grip. Weight: 3.5 lbs. Made 1964-1970.

Armalite AR-10(T) Semiautomatic Rifle **$1500**
Gas-powered semiautomatic action. Caliber: 7.62 × 51mm, 10-shot magazine. 24-inch bbl., 43.5 inches overall. Weight: 12 pounds, 2 ounces. Post front sight; adj. aperature rear sight. Black plastic stock. Made from 1996 to date.

Armalite AR-180 Semiautomatic Rifle **$995**
Commercial version of full automatic AR-18 Combat Rifle. Gas-operated semiautomatic. Caliber: 223 Rem. (5.56mm). 5-, 20-, 30-round magazines. 18.25-inch bbl. w/flash hider/muzzle brake. Sights: flip-up "L" type rear, adj. for windage; post front, adj. for elevation. Accessory 3X scope and mount (add $60 to value). Folding buttstock of black nylon, rubber buttplate, pistol grip, heat-dissipating fiberglass forend (hand guard), swivels, sling. 38 inches overall, 28.75 inches folded. Weight: 6.5 lbs. *Note:* Made by Armalite Inc. 1969-1972, manufactured for Armalite by Howa Machinery Ltd., Nagoya, Japan, 1972-73; by Sterling Armament Co. Ltd., Dagenham, Essex, England, 1976 to 1994. Importation discontinued due to federal restrictions.

ARMI JAGER
Turin, Italy

Armi Jager AP-74 Commando **$185**
Similar to standard AP-74, but styled to resemble original version of Uzi 9mm submachine gun w/wood buttstock; lacks carrying handle and flash suppressor, has different type front sight mount and guards, wood stock, pistol grip and forearm. Introduced 1976; discontinued.

Armi Jager AP-74 Semiautomatic Rifle
Styled after U.S. M16 military rifle. Calibers: 22 LR, 32 Auto (pistol cartridge). Detachable clip magazine; capacity: 14 rounds 22 LR, 9 rounds 32 ACP. 20-inch bbl. with flash suppressor. Weight: about 6.5 lbs. M16 type sights. Stock, pistol grip and forearm of black plastic, swivels and sling. Introduced 1974; discontinued.
22 LR **$225**
32 Automatic **250**

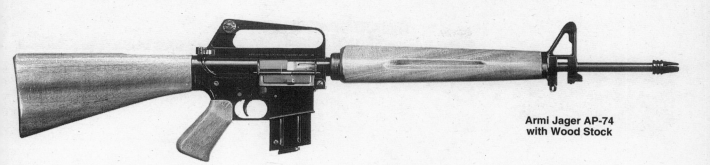

**Armi Jager AP-74
with Wood Stock**

Ami Jager Ap-74 with Wood Stock
Same as standard AP-74, except has wood stock, pistol grip and forearm, weighs about 7 lbs. Discontinued.

22 LR. **$275**
32 Automatic **290**

ARMSCOR (Arms Corp.)
Manila, Philippines

Imported until 1991 by Armscor Precision, San Mateo, CA; currently imported by Ruko Products, Inc., Buffalo, NY.

Armscor Model 20 Auto Rifle
Caliber: 22 LR. 15-shot magazine. 21-inch bbl. 39.75 inches overall. Weight: 6.5 lbs. Sights: hooded front; adj. rear. Checkered or plain walnut-finished mahogany stock. Blued finish. Imported 1990-91. Reinstated by Ruko in the M series.

Model 20 (Checkered Stock) **$110**
Model 20C (Carbine-style Stock) **105**
Model 20P (Plain Stock) **90**

Armscor Model 1600 Auto Rifle
Caliber: 22 LR. 15-shot magazine. 19.5 inch bbl. 38 inches overall. Weight: 6 lbs. Sights: post front; aperture rear. Plain mahogany stock. Matte black finish. Imported 1987-91. Reinstated by Ruko in the M series.

Standard Model **$150**
Retractable Stock Model **160**

Armscor Model AK22 Auto Rifle
Caliber: 22LR. 15- or 30-shot magazine. 18.5-inch bbl. 36 inches overall. Weight: 7 lbs. Sights: post front; adj. rear. Plain mahogany stock. Matte black finish. Imported 1987-1991.

Standard Model **$225**
Folding Stock Model **275**

Armscor/Ruko Model M14 Bolt-Action Rifle
Caliber: 22 LR. 10-shot magazine. 23-inch bbl. Weight: 6.25 lbs. Open sights. Walnut-finished mahogany stock. Imported 1991 to date.

M14P Standard Model **$80**
M14D Deluxe Model (Checkered Stock) **90**

Armscor/Ruko Model M1400 Bolt-Action Rifle
Similar to the Model 14P, except has checkered stock w/ schnabel forend. Weight: 6 lbs. Imported 1991-92.

M1400LW (Lightweight) **$165**
M1400SC (Super Classic) **195**

Armscor/Ruko Model M1500 Bolt-Action Rifle
Caliber: 22 Mag. 5-shot magazine. 21.5-inch bbl. Weight: 6.5 lbs. Open sights. Checkered mahogany stock. Imported 1991 to date.

M1500 (Standard) **$145**
M1500LW (Euro-style Walnut Stock, Disc. 1992) **155**
M1500SC (Monte Carlo Stock) **175**

Armscor/Ruko Model M1600 Auto Rifle **$145**
Similar to the Model 1600 Standard, except chambered for 22 Mag. 5-shot magazine. 21.5-inch bbl. Weight: 6.5 lbs. Open sights. Checkered mahogany stock. Imported 1991 to date.

Armscor/Ruko Model M2000 Auto Rifle
Similar to the Model 20P, except with checkered mahogany stock and adj. sights. Imported 1991 to date.

M2000 (Standard) . . . . **$ 95**
M2000SC (Checkered Walnut Stock) **175**

A-SQUARE COMPANY INC.
Bedford, Kentucky

A-Square Caesar Bolt-Action Rifle
Custom rifle built on the Remington 700 receiver. Calibers: Same as Hannibal, Groups I, II and III. 20- to 26-inch bbl. Weight: 8.5 to 11 lbs. Express 3-leaf rear sight, ramp front. Synthetic or classic Claro oil-finished walnut stock w/flush detachable swivels and Coil-Check recoil system. Three-way adj. target trigger; 3-position safety. Right- or left-hand. Made 1984 to date.

Synthetic Stock Model **$2395**
Walnut Stock Model **2195**

A-Square Genghis Khan Bolt-Action Rifle
Custom varmint rifle developed on the Winchester 70 receiver; fitted w/heavy tapered bbl. and Coil-Chek stock. Calibers: 22-250 Rem., 243 Win., 25-06 Rem., 6mm Rem. Weight: 8-8.5 lbs. Made 1994 to date.

Synthetic Stock Model **$1995**
Walnut Stock Model **1855**

A-Square Hamilcar Bolt-Action Rifle
Similar to the Hannibal Model except lighter. Calibers: 25-06, 257 Wby., 6.5×55 Swedish, 270 Wby., 7×57, 7mm Rem., 7mm STW, 7mm Wby., 280 Rem., 30-06, 300 Win., 300 Wby., 338-06, 9.3×62. Weight: 8-8.5 lbs. Made 1994 to date.

Synthetic Stock Model **$2250**
Walnut Stock Model **2095**

A-Square Hannibal

A-Square Hannibal Bolt-Action Rifle
Custom rifle built on reinforced P-17 Enfield receiver. Calibers: *Group I:* 30-06, *Group II:* 7mm Rem. Mag., 300 Win. Mag., 416 Taylor, 425 Express, 458 Win. Mag.; *Group III:* 300 H&H, 300 Wby. Mag.,8mm Rem. Mag., 340 Wby. Mag., 375 H&H, 375 Wby. Mag., 404 Jeffery, 416 Hoffman, 416 Rem Mag., 450 Ackley, 458 Lott; *Group IV:* 338 A-Square Mag., 375 A-Square Mag., 378 Wby. Mag., 416 Rigby, 416 Wby. Mag., 460 Short Square Mag., 500 A-Square Mag. 20- to 26-inch bbl. Weight: 9 to 11.75 lbs. Express 3-leaf rear sight, ramp front. Classic Claro oil-finished walnut stock, or synthetic stock w/flush detachable swivels and Coil-Check recoil system. Adj. trigger with 2-position safety. Made 1983 to date.
Synthetic Stock Model $2150
Walnut Stock Model **1995**

AUSTRIAN MILITARY RIFLES
Steyr, Austria
Manufactured at Steyr Armory

Austrian Model 90 Steyr-Mannlicher Rifle $170
Straight-pull bolt action. Caliber: 8mm. 5-shot magazine. Open sights. 10-inch bayonet. Cartridge clip forms part of the magazine mechanism. Some of these rifles were provided with a laced, canvas hand guard, others were of wood.

Austrian Model 90 Steyr-Mannlicher Carbine . . . $190
Same general specifications as Model 90 Rifle, except has 19.5-inch bbl., weighs about 7 lbs. No bayonet stud or supplemental forend grip.

Austrian Model 95 Steyr-Mannlicher
Service Rifle $130
Straight-pull bolt action. Caliber: 8×50R Mannlicher (many of these rifles were altered during World War II to use the 7.9mm German service ammunition). 5-shot Mannlicher-type box magazine. 30-inch bbl. Weight: about 8.5 lbs. Sights: blade front; rear adj. for elevation. Military-type full stock.

Austrian Model 95 Steyr-Mannlicher Carbine . . . $140
Same general specifications as Model 95 Rifle, except has 19.5-inch bbl., weighs about 7 lbs. Post front sight; adj. rear carbine sight.

AUTO-ORDNANCE CORPORATION
West Hurley, New York

Auto-Ordnance Thompson Model 22-27A-3 . . . . $395
Small-bore version of Deluxe Model 27A-1. Same general specifications, except caliber 22 LR, has lightweight alloy receiver, weighs about 6.5 lbs.; magazines include 5-, 20-, 30- and 50-shot box types, 80-shot drum. Introduced 1977.

Austrian Model 90 Rifle

Austrian Model 95 Rifle

Austrian Model 95 Carbine

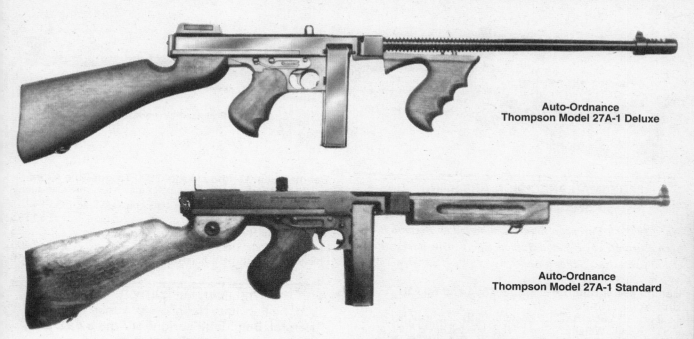

Auto-Ordnance
Thompson Model 27A-1 Deluxe

Auto-Ordnance
Thompson Model 27A-1 Standard

Auto-Ordnance Thompson Model 27A-1 Deluxe

Same as Standard Model 27A-1, except has finned bbl. w/compensator, adj. rear sight, pistol-grip forestock. Caliber: 10mm or 45 ACP. Weight: about 11.5 lbs. Made 1976 to date.

45 ACP	**$995**
10mm (Made 1991-93)	**950**
50-Round Drum Magazine, **add**	**250**
100-Round Drum Magazine, **add**	**450**
Violin Carrying Case, **add**	**100**

Auto-Ordnance Thompson Model 27A-1 Standard Semiauto Carbine **$875**

Similar to Thompson submachine gun ("Tommy Gun"), except has no provision for automatic firing. Caliber: 45 Automatic. 20-shot detachable box magazine (5-,15- and 30-shot box magazines, 39-shot drum also available). 16-inch plain bbl. Weight: about 14 lbs. Sights: aperture rear; blade front. Walnut buttstock, pistol grip and grooved forearm, sling swivels. Made 1976-1986.

Auto-Ordnance Thompson 27A-1C Lightweight Carbine **$895**

Similar to the Model 27A-1, except with lightweight alloy receiver. Weight: 9.25 lbs. Made 1984 to date.

Auto-Ordnance Thompson M1 Semiautomatic Carbine **$950**

Similar to the Model 27A-1, except in M-1 configuration w/side cocking lever and horizontal forearm. Weight: 11.5 lbs. Made 1986 to date.

BARRETT FIREARMS MFG., INC.
Murfreesboro, Tennessee

Barrett Model 82 A-1 Semiautomatic Rifle **$5155**

Caliber: 50 BMG. 10-shot detachable box magazine. 29-inch recoiling bbl. with muzzlebrake. 57 inches overall. Weight: 28.5 lbs. Open iron sights and 10X scope. Composition stock with Sorbothance recoil pad and self-leveling bipod. Blued finish. Made 1985 to date.

Barrett Model 82 A-1

Barrett Model 90 Bolt-Action Rifle **$3150**

Caliber: 50 BMG. 5-shot magazine. 29-inch match bbl. 45 inches overall. Weight: 22 lbs. Composition stock with retractable bipod. Made 1990 to date.

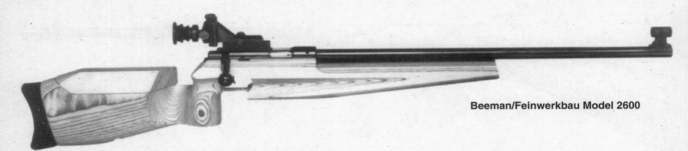

Beeman/Feinwerkbau Model 2600

BEEMAN PRECISION ARMS, INC.
Santa Rosa, California

Since 1993 all European firearms imported by Beeman have been distributed by Beeman Outdoor Sports, Div. Roberts Precision Arms, Inc., Santa Rosa, CA

Beeman/Weihrauch HW Models 60J and 60J-ST Bolt-Action Rifles
Calibers: 22 LR (60J-ST), 222 Rem. (60J).22.8-inch bbl. 41.7 inches overall. Weight: 6.5 lbs. Sights: hooded blade front; open adj. rear. Blued finish. Checkered walnut stock with cheekpiece. Made 1988-94.
Model 60J $495
Model 60J-ST 440

Beeman/Weihrauch HW Model 60M Small
Bore Rifle $475
Caliber: 22 LR. Single shot. 26.8-inch bbl. 45.7 inches overall. Weight: 10.8 lbs. Adj. trigger with push-button safety. Sights: hooded blade front on ramp, precision aperture rear. Target-style stock with stippled forearm and pistol grip. Blued finish. Made 1988-94.

Beeman/Weihrauch HW Model 660 Match Rifle . . . $595
Caliber: 22 LR.26-inch bbl.45.3 inches overall. Weight: 10.7 lbs. Adj. match trigger. Sights: globe front; precision aperture rear. Match-style walnut stock with adj. cheekpiece and buttplate. Made 1988-94.

Beeman/Feinwerkbau Model 2600 Target Rifle
Caliber: 22 LR. Single shot. 26.3-inch bbl. 43.7 inches overall. Weight: 10.6 lbs. Match trigger with fingertip weight adjustment

Beeman/Feinwerkbau Model 2600 Target Rifle *(Cont.)*
dial. Sights: globe front; micrometer match aperture rear. Laminated hardwood stock with adj. cheekpiece. Made 1988-94.
Standard Model (left-hand) **$1195**
Standard Model (right-hand) **995**
Free Rifle Model (left-hand) **1595**
Free Rifle Model (right-hand) **1450**

BELGIAN MILITARY RIFLES
Mfd. by Fabrique Nationale D'Armes de Guerre, Herstal, Belgium; Fabrique D'Armes de L'Etat, Lunich, Belgium

Hopkins & Allen Arms Co. of Norwich, Conn., as well as contractors in Birminham, England, also produced these arms during World War 1.

Belgian Model 1889 Mauser Military Rifle $125
Caliber: 7.65mm Belgian Service (7.65mm Mauser). 5-shot projecting box magazine. 30.75-inch bbl. w/jacket. Weight: about 8.5 lbs. Adj. rear sight, blade front. Straight-grip military stock. This and the carbine version were the principal weapons of the Belgian Army at the start of WWII. Made 1889 to c.1935.

Belgian Model 1916 Mauser Carbine $175
Same as Model 1889 Rifle, except has 20.75-inch bbl. weighs about 8 lbs. and has minor differences in the rear sight graduations, lower band closer to the muzzle and swivel plate found on side of buttstock.

Belgian Model 1935 Mauser Military Rifle $225
Same general specifications as F.N. Model 1924; minor differences. Caliber: 7.65mm Belgian Service. Mfd. by Fabrique Nationale D'Armes de Guerre.

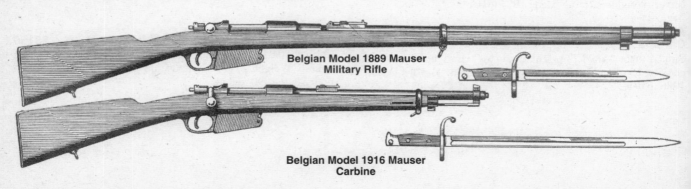

Belgian Model 1889 Mauser Military Rifle

Belgian Model 1916 Mauser Carbine

Belgian Model 1936 Mauser Military Rifle **$185**
An adaptation of the Model 1889 w/German M/98-type bolt,
Belgian M/89 protruding box magazine. Caliber: 7.65mm Bel-
gian Service. Mfd. by Fabrique Nationale D'Armes de Guerre.

BENTON & BROWN FIREARMS, INC.
Fort Worth, Texas

Benton & Brown Model 93 Bolt-Action Rifle
Similar to the Blaser Model R84 (the B&B rifle is built on the Blaser
action, *see* separate listing) with an inter-changeable bbl. system.
Calibers: 243 Win., 6mm Rem., 25-06, 257 Wby., 264 Win., 270
Win., 280 Rem., 7mm Rem Mag., 30-06, 308, 300 Wby., 300 Win.
Mag., 338 Win., 375 H&H. 22- or 24-inch bbl. 41 or 43 inches over-
all. Bbl.-mounted scope rings and one-piece base; no sights. Two-
piece walnut or fiberglass stock. Made 1993 to date.

Walnut Stock Model	$1295
Fiberglass Stock Model	1195
Extra Bbl. Assembly, **add**	475
Extra Bolt Assembly, **add**	425

BERETTA U.S.A. CORP.
Accokeek, Maryland
Manufactured by Fabbrica D'Armi Pietro Beretta
S.p.A. in the Gardone Valtrompia (Brescia), Italy

Beretta 455 SxS Express Double Rifle
Sidelock action with removable sideplates. Calibers: 375 H&H,
458 Win. Mag., 470 NE, 500 NE (3 inches), 416 Rigby. Bbls.:
23.5 or 25.5-inch. Weight: 11 lbs. Double triggers. Sights: blade
front; V-notch folding leaf rear. Checkered European walnut
forearm and buttstock with recoil pad. Color casehardened receiver with blued bbls. Made 1990 to date.

Model 455	$29,000
Model 455EELL	37,500

Beretta 500 Bolt-Action Sporter
Centerfire bolt-action rifle with a Sako AI short action. Calibers:
222 Rem., 223 Rem. 5-shot magazine. 23.63-inch bbl. Weight:
6.5 lbs. No sights. Tapered dovetailed receiver. European walnut
stock. Discontinued.

Standard	$ 465
DL Model	1095
Engraved	1195

Beretta 501 Bolt-Action Sporter
Same as Model 500, except with Sako AII medium action. Calibers: 243 Win., 308 Win. Weight: 7.5 lbs. Discontinued.

Standard	$ 495
Standard w/Iron Sights	525
DL Model	1150
Engraved	1295

Beretta 502 Bolt-Action Sporter
Same as Model 500, except w/Sako AIII long action. Calibers:
270 Win., 7mm Rem. Mag., 30.06, 375 H&H. Weight: 8.5 lbs.
Discontinued.

Standard	$ 530
DL Model	1225
Engraved	1350

Beretta AR-70 Semiautomatic Rifle $1295
Caliber: 223 Rem. (5.56mm). 30-shot magazine. 17.75-inch bbl.
Weight: 8.25 lbs. Sights: rear peep adj. for windage and elevation; blade front. High-impact synthetic buttstock. Made 1984 to
date. No longer imported.

Beretta Small Bore Sporting Carbine $250
Semiautomatic w/bolt handle raised, conventional bolt-action
repeater w/handle in lowered position. Caliber: 22 LR .4-, 8-, or
20-shot magazines. 20.5-inch bbl. Sights: 3-leaf folding rear- patridge front. Stock w/checkered pistol grip and forend, sling
swivels. Weight: 5.5 lbs.

RIFLES

Beretta 501 Bolt-Action Sporter

Beretta AR-70 Semiautomatic Rifle

Blaser Model R84 Bolt-Action Rifle

Beretta Express SSO O/U Double Rifle

Sidelock. Calibers: 375 H&H, 458 Win. Mag., 9.3 X 74R. Bbls.: 25.5-inch. Weight: 11 lbs. Double triggers. Sights: blade front, V-notch folding leaf rear. Checkered European walnut forearm with recoil pad. Color receiver with blued bbls. Made 1990 to date.

Model SS06 .... $15,995
Model SS06 Gold 18,500

BLASER USA, INC.
Fort Worth, Texas
Mfd. by Blaser Jagdwaffen GmbH, Germany

Blaser Model R84 Bolt-Action Rifle

Calibers: 22-250, 243, 6mm Rem., 25-06, 270, 280 Rem., 30-06, 257 Wby. Mag., 264 Win. Mag., 7mm Rem Mag., 300 Win. Mag., 300 Wby. Mag., 338 Win. Mag., 375 H&H. Interchangeable bbls. with standard or Magnum bolt assemblies. Bbl. length: 23 inches (standard); 24 inches (Magnum). 41 to 42 inches overall. Weight: 7 to 7.25 lbs. No sights. Bbl.-mounted scope system. Two-piece Turkish walnut stock with solid black recoil pad. Imported 1989-94.

Right-hand Model $1690
Left-hand Model 1725
Extra Bbl. Assembly 430

Blaser Model R93 Bolt-Action Rifle

Similar to the Model R84, except restyled action with straight-pull bolt. Additional chamberings: 6.5×55, 7×57, 308, 416 Rem. Optional open sights. Imported 1994 to date.

Standard Model $1725
Safari Model (375 H&H, 416 Rem.) 1795
Extra Bbl. Assembly, **add** 430

BRITISH MILITARY RIFLES
Mfd. at Royal Small Arms Factory, Enfield Lock, Middlesex, England, as well as private contractors

British Army Rifle No. 1 Mark III* $165
Short Magazine Lee-Enfield (S.M.L.E.). Bolt action. Caliber: 303 British Service. 10-shot box magazine. 25.25-inch bbl. Weight: about 8.75 lbs. Sights: adj. rear; blade front with guards. Two-piece, full-length military stock. *Note:* The earlier Mark III (approved 1907) is virtually the same as the Mark III* (adopted 1918) except for sights and different magazine cut-off that was eliminated on the latter.

British Army Rifle No. 3 Mark I* (Pattern '14) . . . $175
Modified Mauser-type bolt action. Except for caliber, 303 British Service, and long-range sights, this rifle is the same as U.S. Model 1917 Enfield. *See* listing of the latter for general specifications.

British Army Rifle No. 4 Mark I* $150
Post-World War I modification of the S.M.L.E. intended to simplify mass production. General specifications same as Rifle No. 1 Mark III* except weighs 9.25 lbs., has aperture rear sight, minor differences in construction.

British Army Light Rifle No. 4 Mark I* $135
Modification of the S.M.L.E. Caliber: 303 British Service. 10-shot box magazine. 23-inch bbl. Weight: about 6.75 lbs. Sights: micrometer click rear peep; blade front. One-piece military-type stock w/recoil pad. Made during WWII.

British S.M.L.E. No. 1 Mark III

British No. 3 Mark I

Brno Model II

Brno Model 21H

Brno Model 22F

Brno Hornet

British Army Rifle No. 5 Mark I* **$175**
Jungle Carbine. Modification of the S.M.L.E. similar to Light Rifle No. 4 Mark I* except has 20.5-inch bbl. with flash hider, carbine-type stock. Made during WWII, originally designed for use in the Pacific Theater.

BRNO SPORTING RIFLES
Brno, Czechoslovakia
Manufactured by Ceska Zbrojovka

See also CZ Rifles.

Brno Model I Bolt-Action Sporting Rifle **$495**
Caliber: 22 LR. 5-shot detachable magazine. 22.75-inch bbl. Weight: about 6 lbs. Sights: three-leaf open rear; hooded ramp front. Sporting stock w/checkered pistol grip, swivels. Discontinued.

Brno Model II **$525**
Same as Model I except with deluxe grade stock. Discontinued.

Brno Model 21H Bolt-Action Sporting Rifle **$595**
Mauser-type action. Calibers: 6.5×57mm, 7×57mm 8×57mm. 5-shot box magazine. 20.5-inch bbl. Double set trigger. Weight: about 6.75 lbs. Sights: two-leaf open rear-hooded ramp front. Half-length sporting stock with cheekpiece, checkered pistol grip and forearm, swivels. Discontinued.

Brno Model 22F **$795**
Same as Model 21H except has full-length Mannlicher-type stock, weighs about 6 lbs 14 oz. Discontinued.

Brno Hornet Bolt-Action Sporting Rifle **$725**
Miniature Mauser action. Caliber: 22 Hornet. 5-shot detachable box magazine. 23-inch bbl. Double set trigger. Weight: about 6.25 lbs. Sights: three-leaf open rear hooded ramp front. Sporting stock with checkered pistol grip and forearm, swivels. Discontinued. *Note:* This was also marketed in the U.S. as "Z-B Mauser Varmint Rifle."

Brno ZKB 680 Bolt-Action Rifle **$350**
Calibers: 22 Hornet, 222 Rem. 5-shot detachable box magazine. 23.5-inch bbl. Weight: 5.75 lbs. Double-set triggers. Adj. open rear sight, hooded ramp front. Walnut stock. No longer imported.

RIFLES

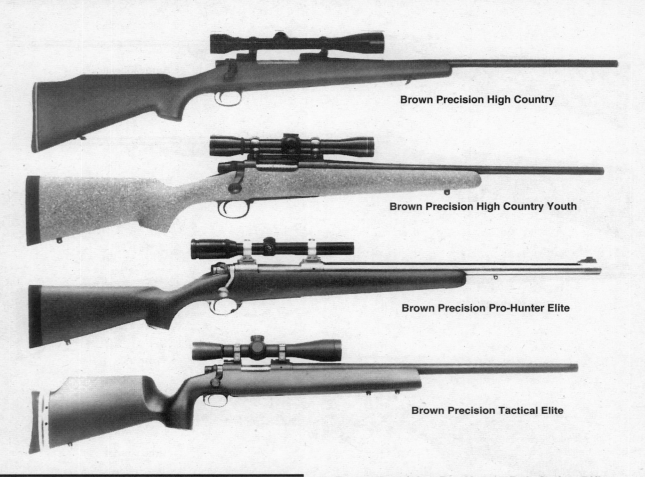

Brown Precision High Country

Brown Precision High Country Youth

Brown Precision Pro-Hunter Elite

Brown Precision Tactical Elite

BROWN PRECISION COMPANY
Los Molinos, California

Brown Precision Model 7 Super Light Sporter . . **$795**
Lightweight sporter built on a Remington Model 7 barreled action with 18-inch factory bbl. Weight: 5.25 lbs. Kevlar stock. Made 1984-92.

Brown Precision High Country Bolt-Action Sporter
Custom sporting rilfes built on Blaser, Remington 700, Ruger 77 and Winchester 70 actions. Calibers: 243 Win., 25-06, 270 Win., 7mm Rem. Mag., 308 Win., 30-06. 5-shot magazine (4-shot in 7mm Mag.). 22- or 24-inch bbl. Weight: about 6.5 lbs. Fiberglass stock with recoil pad, sling swivels. No sights. Made 1975 to date.
Standard High Country . . . . **$ 850**
Custom High Country **1450**
Left-Hand Action, **add** **100**
Stainless Bbl., **add** **100**
70, 77 or Blaser Actions, **add** **125**
70 SG Action, **add** **350**

Brown Precision High Country Youth Rifle **$850**
Similar to the standard Model 7 Super Light, except with Kevlar or graphite stock scaled-down to youth dimensions. Calibers: 223, 243, 6mm, 7mm-08, 308. Made 1992 to date.

Brown Precision Pro-Hunter Bolt-Action Rifle
Custom sporting rifle built on Remingtom 700 or Winchester 70 SG action, fitted with match-grade Shilen bbl. chambered in customer's choice of caliber. Matte blued electroless nickel or Teflon finish. Express-style rear sight hooded ramp front. Synthetic stock. Made 1989 to date
Standard Pro-Hunter **$1695**
Pro-Hunter Elite (1993 to date) **2395**

Brown Precision Pro-Varminter Bolt-Action Rifle
Custom varminter built on a Remington 700 or 40X action fitted w/Shilen stainless steel benchrest bbl. Varmint or benchrest-style stock. Made 1993 to date.
Standard Pro-Varminter . . . . **$ 1225**
Pro-Hunter w/Rem 40X Action **1650**

Brown Precision Selective Target Model **$895**
Tactical law-enforcement rifle built on a Remington 700V action. Caliber: 308 Win. 20-, 22- or 24-inch bbl. Synthetic stock. Made 1989-92.

Brown Precision Tactical Elite Rifle **$1650**
Similar to the Selective Target Model, except fitted w/select match-grade Shilen benchrest heavy stainless bbl. Calibers: 223, 308, 300 Win. Mag. Black or camo Kevlar/graphite composite fiberglass stock w/adj. buttplate. Non-reflective black Teflon metal finish. Made 1993 to date.

Browning 22 Automatic, Grade I

Browning 22 Automatic, Grade III

Browning 22 Automatic
Grade VI

BROWNING RIFLES
Morgan, Utah

Mfd. for Browning by Fabrique Nationale d'Armes de Guerre (now Fabrique Nationale Herstal), Herstal, Belgium Miroku Firearms Mfg. Co., Tokyo, Japan; Oy Sako Ab, Riihimaki, Finland.

Browning 22 Automatic Rifle, Grade I
Similar to discontinued Remington Model 241A. Autoloading. Takedown. Calibers: 22 LR, 22 Short (not interchangeably). Tubular magazine in buttstock holds 11 LR 16 Short. Bbl. lengths: 19.25 inches (22 LR), 22.25 inches (22 Short). Weight: about 4.75 lbs. (22LR); 5 lbs. (22 Short). Receiver scroll engraved. Open rear sight, bead front. Checkered pistol-grip buttstock, semibeavertail forearm. Made 1965-72 by FN; 1972 to date by Miroku. *Note:* Illustrations are of rifles manufactured by FN.
FN manufacture $350
Miroku manufacture   225

Browning 22 Automatic Rifle, Grade II
Same as Grade I, except satin chrome-plated receiver engraved w/small game animal scenes, gold-plated trigger select walnut stock and forearm. 22 LR only. Made 1972-84.
FN manufacture $595
Miroku manufacture   295

Browning 22 Automatic Rifle, Grade III
Same as Grade I, except satin chrome-plated receiver elaborately hand-carved and engraved w/dog and game-bird scenes, scrolls and leaf clusters: gold-plated trigger, extra-fancy walnut stock and forearm, skip-checkered. 22 LR only. Made 1972-84.
FN manufacture $1350
Miroku manufacture   575

Browning 22 Automatic, Grade VI $495
Same general specifications as standard 22 Automatic, except for engraving, high-grade stock with checkering and glossy finish. Made 1986 to date.

Browning Model 52 Bolt-Action Rifle $425
Limited Edition of the Winchester Model 52C Sporter. Caliber: 22 LR. 5-shot magazine. 24-inch bbl. Weight: 7 lbs. Micro-Motion trigger. No sights. Checkered select walnut stock w/rosewood forend and metal grip cap. Blued finish. Only 5000 made in 1991.

Browning Model 53 Lever-Action Rifle $450
Limited Edition of the Winchester Model 53. Caliber: 32-20. 7-shot tubular half-magazine. 22-inch bbl. Weight: 6.5 pounds. Adj. rear sight, bead front. Select walnut checkered pistol-grip stock w/high-gloss finish. Classic-style forearm. Blued finish. Only 5000 made in 1990. *See illustration next page.*

Browning Model 65 Grade I Lever-Action Rifle . . $475
Caliber: 218 Bee. 7-shot tubular half-magazine. 24-inch bbl. Weight: 6.75 lbs. Sights: adj. buckhorn-style rear, hooded bead front. Select walnut pistol-grip stock w/high-gloss finish. Semibeavertail forearm. Limited edition made in 1989 only.

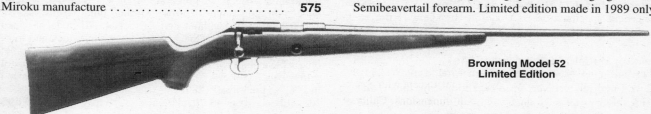

Browning Model 52
Limited Edition

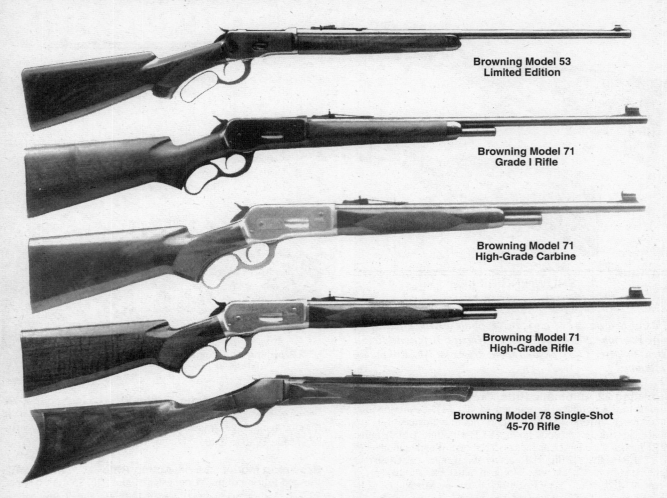

Browning Model 53
Limited Edition

Browning Model 71
Grade I Rifle

Browning Model 71
High-Grade Carbine

Browning Model 71
High-Grade Rifle

Browning Model 78 Single-Shot
45-70 Rifle

Browning Model 65 High Grade Rifle **$795**
Same general specifications as Model 65 Grade I, except w/engraving and gold-plated animals on grayed receiver. Cut-checkering on pistol grip and forearm. Limited edition made in 1989 only.

Browning Model 71 Grade I Carbine **$425**
Same general specifications as Model 71 Grade I Rifle, except carbine has 20-inch round bbl. and weighs 8 lbs. Disc. 1989.

Browning Model 71 Grade I Lever-Action Rifle . . **$450**
Caliber: 348 Win. 4-shot magazine. 24-inch round bbl. Weight: 8 lbs. 2 oz. Open buckhorn sights. Select walnut straight grip stock with satin finish. Classic-style forearm, flat metal buttplate. Made 1986-89.

Browning Model 71 High-Grade Carbine **$650**
Same general specifications as Model 71 High Grade Rifle, except carbine has 20-inch round bbl. Discontinued 1989.

Browning Model 71 High-Grade Rifle **$685**
Caliber: 348 Win. 4-shot magazine. 24-inch round bbl. Weight: 8 lbs. 2 oz. Engraved receiver. Open buckhorn sights. Select walnut checkered pistol-grip stock w/high-gloss finish. Classic-style forearm, flat metal buttplate. Made 1987 only.

Browning 78 Bicentennial Set **$2200**
Special Model 78 45-70 w/same specifications as standard type, except sides of receiver engraved w/bison and eagle, scroll engraving on top of receiver, lever, both ends of bbl. and buttplate; high-grade walnut stock and forearm. Accompanied by an engraved hunting knife and stainless steel commemorative medallion all in an alder wood presentation case. Each item in set has matching serial number beginning with "1776" and ending with numbers 1 to 1,000. Edition limited to 1,000 sets. Made in 1976. Value is for set in new condition.

Browning 78 Single-Shot Rifle
Falling-block lever action similar to Winchester 1885 High Wall single-shot rifle. Calibers: 22-250, 6mm Rem., 243 Win., 25-06, 7mm Rem. Mag., 30-06, 45-70 Govt. 26-inch octagon or heavy round bbl.; 24-inch octagon bull bbl. on 45-70 model. Weight: w/octagon bbl., about 7.75 lbs.; w/round bbl., 8.5 lbs.; 45-70, 8.75 lbs. Furnished without sights, except 45-70 model has open rear sight, blade front. Checkered fancy walnut stock and forearm. 45-70 model has straight-grip stock w/curved buttplate; others have stock w/Monte Carlo comb and cheekpiece, pistol grip w/cap, recoil pad. Made 1973-83 by Miroku. Reintroduced in 1985 as the Model 1885.
All calibers except 45-70 . . . . **$495**
45-70 . . . . **525**

Browning Model 1885 High-Wall
Single-Shot Rifle

Browning Model 1885 Single-Shot Rifle
Calibers: 22 Hornet, 223, 243, (Low Wall); 22-250, 270, 7mm Rem. Mag., 30-06, 45 Govt. (High Wall). 24- or 28-inch octagonal bbl. 39.5 or 43.5 inches overall. Weight: 6.25 to 8.75 lbs. Blued receiver. Gold-colored adj. trigger. Drilled and tapped for scope mounts, open sights on 45-70 Govt. caliber only. Walnut straight-grip stock and schnabel forearm w/cut checkering and high-gloss finish. Made 1985 to date.
Low Wall Model (Introduced 1995) **$515**
High Wall Model **525**

Browning Model 1886 Grade I Lever-Action Rifle **$625**
Caliber: 45-70 Govt. 8-round magazine. 26-inch octagonal bbl. 45 inches overall. Weight: 9 lbs. 5 oz. Deep blued finish on receiver. Open buckhorn sights. Straight-grip walnut stock. Classic-style forearm. Metal buttplate. Satin finish. Made in 1986 in limited issue 1 of 7,000 by Miroku.

Browning Model 1886 High-Grade Lever-Action Rifle **$1095**
Same general specifications as the Model 1886 Grade I, except receiver is grayed steel embellished with scroll; game scenes of elk and American bison engraving. High-gloss stock. Made in 1986 in limited issue 1 of 3,000 by Miroku.

Browning Model 1886 Montana Centennial Rifle **$1125**
Same general specifications as the Model 1886 High Grade Lever Action, except has specially engraved receiver designating Montana Centennial; also different stock design. Made in 1986 in limited issue 1 of 2,000 by Miroku.

Browning Model 1895 Grade I Lever-Action Rifle **$495**
Caliber: 30-06, 30-40 Krag. 4-shot magazine. 24-inch round bbl. 42 inches overall. Weight: 8 lbs. French walnut stock and schnabel forend. Sights: rear buckhorn; gold bead on elevated ramp front. Made in 1984 in limited issue 1 of 6,000. The 30-40 Krag caliber made in 1985 in limited issue 1 of 2,000. Mfd. by Miroku.

Browning Model 1895
High-Grade Rifle

RIFLES

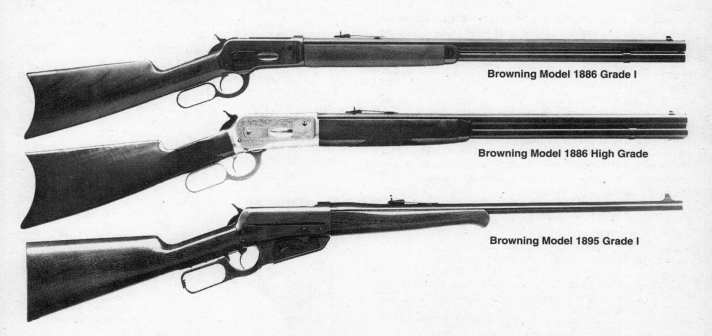

Browning Model 1886 Grade I

Browning Model 1886 High Grade

Browning Model 1895 Grade I

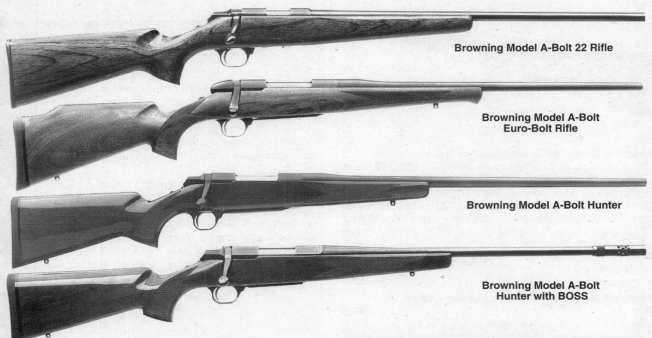

Browning Model A-Bolt 22 Rifle

Browning Model A-Bolt
Euro-Bolt Rifle

Browning Model A-Bolt Hunter

Browning Model A-Bolt
Hunter with BOSS

Model 1895 High-Grade Lever-Action
Rifle. $895
Same general specifications as Model 1895 Grade I except engraved receiver and Grade III French walnut stock and forend with fine checkering. Made in 1885 in limited issue 1 of 1000 by Miroku. *See* illustration preceding page.

Browning Model A-Bolt 22 Rifle
Calibers: 22 LR, 22 Magnum. 5- and 15-shot magazines. 22-inch round bbl. 40.25 inches overall. Weight: 5 lbs. 9 oz. Gold-colored adj. trigger. Laminated walnut stock with checkering. Rosewood forend grip cap; pistol grip. With or without sights. Ramp front and adj. folding leaf rear on open sight model. 22 LR made 1985 to date; 22 Magnum, 1990 to date.

Grade I 22 LR	$235
Grade I 22 Magnum	285
Deluxe Grade Gold Medallion	350

Browning Model A-Bolt Euro-Bolt Rifle
Same general specifications as Model A-Bolt Hunter Rifle, except has checkered satin-finished walnut stock w/continental-style cheekpiece, palm-swell grip, schnabel forend. Mannlicher-style spoon bolt handle and recontoured bolt shroud. Calibers: 270, 30-06 and 7mm Mag. only. Weight: 6.75 lbs. Made 1993 to date.

Euro-Bolt Model	$475
Euro-Bolt Model II	495
BOSS Option, **add**.	90

Browning Model A-Bolt Hunter Grade Rifle
Calibers: 22 Hornet, 22-250, 223, 243, 257 Roberts, 7mm-08, 308, (short action) 25-06, 270, 280, 30-06, 7mm Rem. 300 Win. Mag., 338 Win. 4-shot magazine (Std.), 3-shot (Mag.). 22-inch bbl. (Std.); 24-inch (Mag.). Weight: 7.5 lbs. (Std.); 8.5 lbs. (Mag.). Open sights optional. Classic-style walnut stock. Produced in two action lengths w/nine locking lugs, fluted bolt w/60

Browning Model A-Bolt Hunter Grade Rifle *(Cont.)*
degree rotation. Mfd. by Miroku since 1985. An improved variation w/anti-binding bolt and redesigned trigger system (A-Bolt II) was introduced in 1993.

Hunter	$340
Hunter II	350
BOSS Option, **add**	90
Open Sights, **add**	50

Browning Model A-Bolt Medallion Grade Rifle
Same as Hunter Grade except w/high-gloss deluxe stock rosewood grip cap and forend; high-luster blued finish. Also in 375 H&H w/open sights. Left Hand Models in 270, 30-06, 7mm Rem. Mag. Big Horn Sheep Ltd. Ed.

(600 made 1986, 270 Win.)	$895
Gold Medallion Deluxe Grade	525
Gold Medallion II Deluxe Grade	540
Medallion, Standard Grade	415
Medallion II, Standard Grade	425
Medallion, 375 H&H	575
Medallion II, 375 H&H	595
Micro Medallion	425
Micro Medallion II	430
Pronghorn Antelope Ltd. Ed.	
(500 made 1987, 243 Win.).	850
BOSS Option, **add**.	90
Open Sights, **add**	50

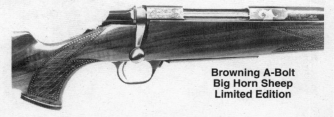

**Browning A-Bolt
Big Horn Sheep
Limited Edition**

Browning A-Bolt
Camo Stalker

Browning Model B-92
Lever-Action Rifle

Browning Model A-Bolt Stalker Rifle

Same general specifications as Model A-Bolt Hunter Rifle except w/checkered graphite-fiberglass composite stock and matte blued or stainless metal. Nonglare matte finish off all exposed metal surfaces. 3 models: Camo Stalker orig. w/multi-colored laminated wood stock, matte blued metal; Composite Stalker w/graphite-fiberglass stock, matte blued metal; Stainless Stalker w/composite stock, stainless metal. Made 1987 to date.

Camo Stalker (orig. Laminated Stock)	**$395**
Composite Stalker	415
Composite Stalker II	450
Stainless Stalker	515
Stainless Stalker II	530
Stainless Stalker, 375 H&H	600
BOSS Option, **add**	90
Left-Hand Model, **add**	90

Browning Model A-Bolt Varmint II Rifle $525

Same general specifications as the Stalker Model, except w/22-inch heavy bbl. w/BOSS system and varmint-style black laminated wood stock. Calibers: 22-250, 223 or 308. No sights. Bright blued or satin finish. Made 1994 to date.

Browning Model B-92 Lever-Action Rifle $315

Calibers: 357 Mag. and 44 Rem. Mag. 11-shot magazine. 20-inch round bbl.. 37.5 inches overall. Weight: 5.5 lbs. to 6 lbs. 6 oz. Seasoned French walnut stock w/high gloss finish. Cloverleaf rear sight; steel post front. Made 1979-1989 by Miroku.

Browning BAR Automatic Rifle, Grade I, Standard Calibers $450

Gas-operated semiautomatic. Calibers: 243 Win., 270 Win., 308 Win., 30-06. 4-round box magazine. 22-inch bbl. Weight: about 7.5 lbs. Folding leaf rear sight, hooded ramp front. French walnut stock and forearm checkered, QD swivels. Made 1967 to date by FN.

Browning BAR, Grade I, Magnum Calibers $525

Same as BAR in standard calibers, except chambered for 7mm Rem. Mag., 300 Win. Mag., has 3-round box magazine, 24-inch bbl., recoil pad. Weight: about 8.5 lbs. Made 1969 to date by FN.

Browning BAR, Grade II

Same as Grade I, except receiver engraved w/big-game heads (deer and antelope on standard-caliber rifles, ram and grizzly on Magnum-caliber) and scrollwork, higher grade wood. Made 1967-1974 by FN.

Standard calibers	**$595**
Magnum calibers	640

Browning BAR, Grade III $850

Same as Grade I, except receiver of grayed steel engraved w/big-game heads (deer and antelope on standard-caliber rifles, moose and elk on Magnum-caliber) framed in fine-line scrollwork, gold-plated trigger, stock and forearm of highly figured French walnut, hand-checkered and carved. Made 1971-74 by FN.

Browning BAR, Grade I
Standard Calibers

Browning BAR, Grade I
Magnum Calibers

RIFLES

Browning BAR, Grade IV

Browning BAR, Grade V

Browning BAR, Grade IV $1350
Same as Grade I, except receiver of grayed steel engraved w/full detailed rendition of running deer and antelope on standard-caliber rifles, moose and elk on Magnum-caliber gold-plated trigger, stock and forearm of highly figured French walnut, hand checkered and carved. Made 1971-1986 by FN.

Browning BAR, Grade V $2550
Same as Grade I, except receiver w/complete big-game scenes executed by a master engraver and inlaid with 18K gold (deer and antelope on standard-caliber rifles, moose and elk on Magnum caliber), gold-plated trigger, stock and forearm of finest French walnut, intricately hand-checkered and carved. Made 1971-74 by FN.

Browning Model BAR Mark II Semiautomatic Rifle
Same general specifications as standard BAR semiauotmatic rifle, except has redesigned gas and buffer systems, new bolt release lever, and engraved receiver. Made 1993 to date.
Standard Calibers	$475
Magnum Calibers	550
BOSS Option, **add**	90
Open Sights, **add**	15

Browning BAR-22 Automatic Rifle
Semiautomatic. Caliber: 22 LR. Tubular magazine holds 15 rounds. 20.25-inch bbl. Weight: 6.25 pounds. Sights: folding-leaf rear, gold bead front on ramp. Receiver grooved for scope mounting. French walnut pistol-grip stock and forearm checkered. Made 1977-1981.
BAR-22, Standard Version	$225
BAR-22, 1982 Version 6 lbs. (Made 1982-84)	215

Browning BBR Lightning Bolt-Action Rifle $425
Bolt-action rifle with short throw bolt of 60 degrees. Calibers: 25-06 Rem., 270 Win., 30-06, 7mm Rem. Mag., 300 Win. Mag.24-inch bbl. Weight: 8 lbs. Made 1979-1984.

Browning BL-22 Lever-Action Repeating Rifle
Short-throw lever action. Caliber: 22 LR, Long, Short. Tubular magazine holds 15 LR, 17 Long 22 Short. 20-inch bbl.. Weight: 5 pounds. Sights: folding leaf; bead front. Receiver grooved for scope mounting. Walnut straight-grip stock and forearm, bbl. band. Made 1970 to date by Miroku.
Grade I	$195
Grade II w/Scroll Engraving	225

Browning BLR Lever-Action Repeating Rifle ... $325
Calibers: 243 Win., 308 Win., 358 Win. 4-round detachable box magazine. 20-inch bbl. Weight: about 7 lbs. Sights: windage and elevation adj. open rear; hooded ramp front. Walnut straight-grip stock and forearm, checkered, bbl. band, recoil pad. Made 1971 by FN, 1972 to date by Miroku.

Browning BLR Model '81
Redesigned version of the Browning BLR. Calibers: 222-50 Rem., 243 Win., 308 Win., 358 Win; Long Action— 270 Win., 7mm Rem. Mag., 30-06. 4-round detachable box magazine. 20-inch bbl. Weight: about 7 pounds. Walnut straight-grip stock and forearm, cut checkering, recoil pad. Made 1982 to date; Long Action introduced 1991.
BLR Model '81 Standard	$350
BLR Model '81 Long Action	395

Browning BPR-22 Pump Rifle $185
Hammerless slide-action repeater. Specifications same as for BAR-22, except also available chambered for 22 Magnum RF; magazine capacity, 11 rounds. Made 1977-1982 by Miroku.

Browning High-Power Bolt-Action Rifle, Medallion Grade $1150
Same as Safari Grade, except receiver and bbl. scroll engraved, ram's head engraved on floorplate; select walnut stock w/rosewood forearm tip, grip cap. Made 1961-1974.

Browning High-Power Bolt-Action Rifle, Olympian Grade $2395
Same as Safari Grade, except bbl. engraved; receiver, trigger guard and floorplate satin chrome-plated and engraved with game scenes appropriate to caliber; finest figured walnut stock with rosewood forearm tip and grip cap, latter with 18K-gold medallion. Made 1961-1974.

Browning BAR Mark II with BOSS

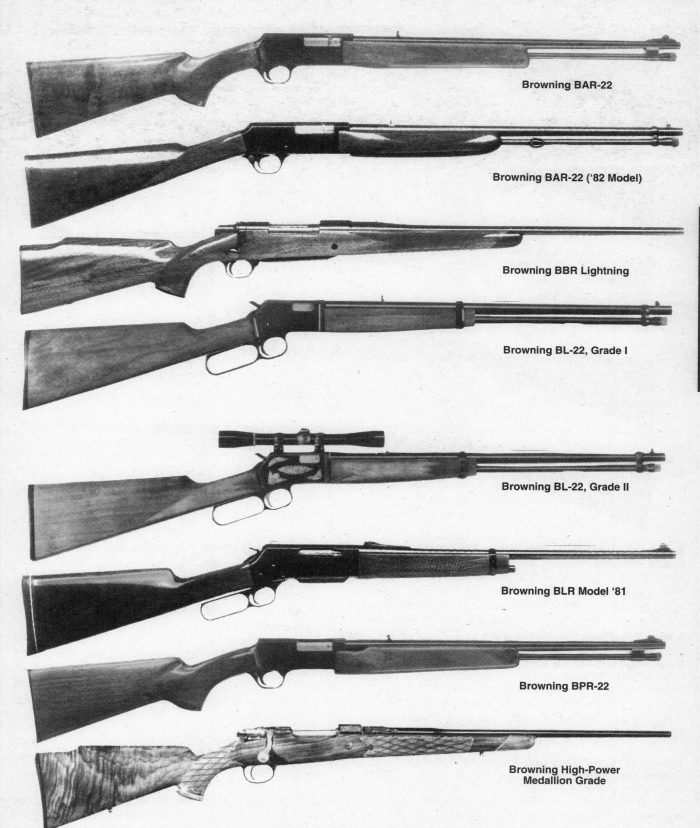

Browning BAR-22

Browning BAR-22 ('82 Model)

Browning BBR Lightning

Browning BL-22, Grade I

Browning BL-22, Grade II

Browning BLR Model '81

Browning BPR-22

Browning High-Power
Medallion Grade

RIFLES

Browning High-Power, Safari Grade
Medium Action, Heavy Barrel

Browning High-Power, Safari Grade
Short Action, Heavy Barrel

Browning High-Power, Safari Grade
Standard Action

Browning "T-Bolt" T-1

Browning "T-Bolt" T-2

Browning High-Power Bolt-Action Rifle, Safari Grade, Medium Action **$695**
Same as Standard, except medium action. Calibers: 22/250, 243 Win., 264 Win. Mag., 284 Win. Mag., 308 Win. Bbl.: 22-inch lightweight bbl.; 22/250 and 243 also available w/24-inch heavy bbl. Weight: 6 lbs. 12 oz. w/lightweight bbl.; 7 lbs.13 oz. w/heavy bbl. Made 1963-1974 by Sako.

Browning High-Power Bolt-Action Rifle, Safari Grade, Short Action **$725**
Same as Standard, except short action. Calibers: 222 Rem., 222 Rem. Mag. 22-inch lightweight or 24-inch heavy bbl. No sights. Weight: 6 lbs. 2 oz. w/lightweight bbl.; 7.5 lbs. w/heavy bbl. Made 1963-1974 by Sako.

Browning High-Power Bolt-Action Rifle, Safari Grade, Standard Action **$895**
Mauser-type action. Calibers: 270 Win., 30-06, 7mm Rem. Mag., 300 H&H Mag., 300 Win. Mag., 308 Norma Mag. 338 Win. Mag., 375 H&H Mag., 458 Win. Mag. Cartridge capacity: 6 rounds in 270, 30-06; 4 in Magnum calibers. Bbl. length: 22 in.,

Browning High-Power rifle, Safari Std. *(Cont.)*
270, 30-06, 24 in., Magnum calibers. Weight: 7 lbs. 2 oz., 270, 30-06; 8.25 lbs., Mag. calibers. Folding leaf rear sight, hooded ramp front. Checkered stock w/pistol grip, Monte Carlo cheekpiece, QD swivels; recoil pad on Magnum models. Made 1959-1974 by FN.

Browning "T-Bolt" T-122 Repeating Rifle **$325**
Straight-pull bolt action. Caliber: 22 LR. 5-shot clip magazine. 24-inch bbl. Sights: peep rear; blade/ramp front. Plain walnut stock w/pistol grip. Weight: 6 lbs. Also left hand model. Made 1965-1974 by FN.

Browning "T-Bolt" T-2 . . . . **$365**
Same as T-1, except fancy-figured walnut stock, checkered. Discontinued 1974.

F.N. Browning Semiautomatic Rifle **$2500**
Same as F.N. FAL Semiautomatic Rifle. *See* listing of that rifle for specifications. Sold by Browning for a brief period c. 1960.

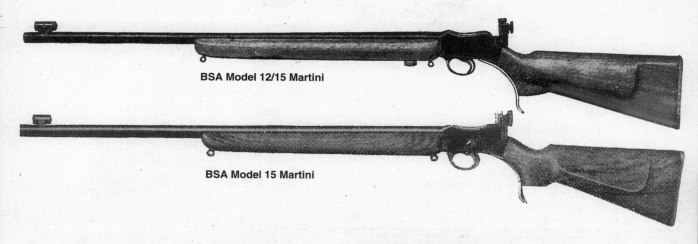

BSA Model 12/15 Martini

BSA Model 15 Martini

BSA GUNS LTD.
Birmingham, England

Importation of BSA rifles was discontinued in 1989.

BSA No. 12 Martini Single-Shot Target Rifle $295
Caliber: 22 LR. 29-inch bbl. Weight: about 8.75 lbs. Parker-Hale Model 7 rear sight and Model 2 front sight. Straight-grip stock, checkered forearm. *Note:* This model was also available with open sights or with BSA No. 30 and 20 sights. Made before WWII.

BSA Model 12/15 Martini Heavy $325
Same as Standard Model 12/15 except has extra heavy bbl., weighs about 11 lbs.

BSA Model 12/15 Martini Single-Shot Target Rifle. $330
Caliber: 22 LR. 29-inch bbl. Weight: about 9 lbs. Parker-Hale No. PH-7A rear sight and No. FS-22 front sight. Target stock w/high comb and cheekpiece, beavertail forearm. *Note:* This is a post-WWII model; however, a similar rifle, the BSA-Parker Model 12/15, was produced c. 1938.

BSA No. 13 Martini Single-Shot Target Rifle $275
Caliber: 22 LR. Lighter version of the No.12 w/same general specifications, except has 25-inch bbl., weighs 6.5lbs. Made before WWII.

BSA No. 13 Sporting Rifle
Same as No. 13 Target except fitted w/Parker-Hale "Sportarget" rear sight and bead front sight. Also available in 22 Hornet. Made before WWII.
22 Long Rifle $275
22 Hornet **340**

BSA Model 15 Martini Single-Shot Target Rifle $325
Caliber: 22 LR. 29-inch bbl. Weight: about 9.5 lbs. BSA No.30 rear sight and No. 20 front sight. Target stock w/cheekpiece and pistol grip, long semibeavertail forearm. Made before WWII.

BSA Centurion Model Match Rifle $435
Same general specifications as Model 15 except has "Centurion" match bbl. Made before WWII.

BSA CF-2 Bolt-Action Hunting Rifle $295
Mauser-type action. Calibers: 7mm Rem. Mag., 300 Win. Mag. 3-shot magazine. 23.6-inch bbl. Weight: 8 lbs. Sights: adj. rear; hooded ramp front. Checkered walnut stock w/Monte Carlo comb, rollover cheekpiece, rosewood forend tip, recoil pad, sling swivels. Made 1975 1987. *See* Ithaca-BSA CF-2.

BSA CF-2 Stutzen Rifle $375
Calibers: 222 Rem., 22/250, 243 Win., 270 Win., 308 Win. 30-06. 4-round capacity (5 in 222 Rem.). 20.6-inch bbl. 41.5 inches (approx.) overall length. Weight: 7.5 to 8 lbs. Williams front and rear sights. Hand-finished European walnut stock. Monte Carlo cheekpiece and Wundhammer palmswell. Double-set triggers. Discontinued 1987.

BSA CF-2 Stutzen Rifle

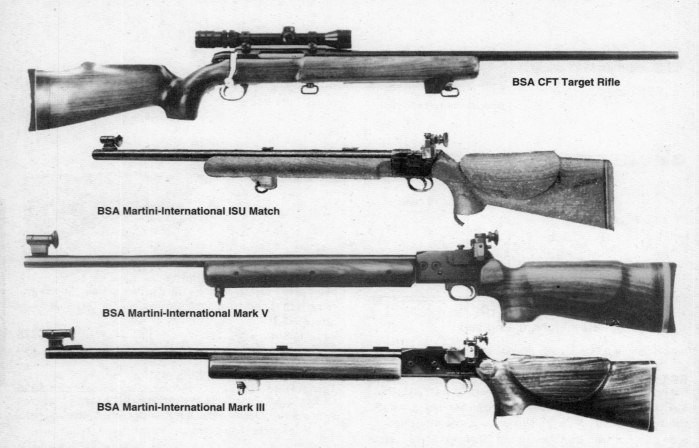

BSA CFT Target Rifle

BSA Martini-International ISU Match

BSA Martini-International Mark V

BSA Martini-International Mark III

BSA CFT Target Rifle $595
Single-shot bolt action. Caliber: 7.62mm. 26.5-inch bbl. About
47.5 inches overall. Weight: 11 lbs., incl. accessories. Bbl. and
action weight: 6 lbs. 12 oz. Discontinued 1987.

**BSA Majestic Deluxe Featherweight Bolt-Action
Hunting Rifle**
Mauser-type action. Calibers: 243 Win., 270 Win., 308 Win., 30-
06, 458 Win. Mag. 4-shot magazine. 22-inch bbl. with BESA recoil reducer. Weight: 6.25 lbs.; 8.75 lbs. in 458. Folding leaf rear
sight, hooded ramp front. Checkered European-style walnut
stock w/cheekpiece, pistol grip, schnabel forend, swivels, recoil
pad. Made 1959-1965.
458 Win. Mag. caliber $425
Other calibers 265

BSA Majestic Deluxe Standard Weight $265
Same as Featherweight Model, except heavier bbl. without recoil
reducer. Calibers: 22 Hornet, 222 Rem., 243 Win., 7×57mm, 308
Win., 30-06. Weight: 7.25 to 7.75 lbs. Discontinued.

BSA Martini-International ISU Match Rifle $695
Similar to MK III, but modified to meet International Shooting
Union "Standard Rifle" specifications. 28-inch standard weight
bbl. Weight: 10.75 lbs. Redesigned stock and forearm, latter attached to bbl. with "V" section alloy strut. Introduced 1968, discontinued.

BSA Martini-International Mark V Match Rifle . . . $495
Same as ISU model, except has heavier bbl. Weight: 12.25 lbs.
Introduced 1976, discontinued.

**BSA Martini-International Match Rifle
Single-Shot Heavy Pattern** $395
Caliber: 22 LR. 29-inch heavy bbl. Weight: about 14 pounds.
Parker-Hale "International" front and rear sights. Target
stock w/full cheekpiece and pistol grip, broad beavertail
forearm, handstop, swivels. Right- or left-hand models.
Mfd. 1950-53.

**BSA Martini-International Match Rifle —
Light Pattern** $390
Same general specifications as Heavy Pattern, except has 26-
inch lighter weight bbl. Weight: about 11 lbs. Discontinued.

BSA Martini-International MK II Match Rifle $395
Same general specifications as original model. Heavy and Light
Pattern. Improved trigger mechanism and ejection system. Re-
designed stock and forearm. Made 1953-59.

BSA Martini-International MK III Match Rifle $445
Same general specifications as MK II Heavy Pattern. Longer action frame with I-section alloy strut to which forearm is attached;
bbl. is fully floating. Redesigned stock and forearm. Made 1959-
1967.

BSA Monarch Deluxe Varmint

BSA Monarch Deluxe Bolt-Action Hunting Rifle. . **$325**
Same as Majestic Deluxe Standard Weight Model, except has redesigned stock of U.S. style with contrasting hardwood forend tip and grip cap. Calibers: 222 Rem., 243 Win., 270 Win., 7mm Rem. Mag., 308 Win., 30-06. 22-inch bbl. Weight: 7 to 7.25 pounds. Made 1965-1974.

BSA Monarch Deluxe Varmint Rifle **$335**
Same as Monarch Deluxe except has 24-inch heavy bbl. and weighs 9 pounds. Calibers: 222 Rem., 243 Win.

CALICO LIGHT WEAPONS SYSTEMS
Bakersville, California

Calico Model M-900 Semiautomatic Carbine **$495**
Caliber: 9mm Parabellum. 50- or 100-shot magazine. 16.1-inch bbl. 28.5 inches overall. Weight: 3.7 pounds. Post front sight adj. for windage and elevation, fixed notch rear. Collapsible steel buttstock and glass-filled polymer grip. Matte black finish. Made 1989-94.

Calico Model M-951 Tactical Carbine
Similar to the Model 900, except with long compensator and adjustable forward grip. Made 1990-94.
Model 951 . . . . **$495**
Model 951-S **505**

CANADIAN MILITARY RIFLES
Quebec, Canada
Manufactured by Ross Rifle Co.

Canadian Model 1907 Mark II Ross
Military Rifle **$185**
Straight-pull bolt action. Caliber: 303 British. 5-shot box magazine. 28-inch bbl. Weight: about 8.5 lbs. Sights: adj. rear; blade front. Military-type full stock. *Note:* The Ross was originally issued as a Canadian service rifle in 1907. There were several variations; it was the official weapon at the start of WWI, but has been obsolete for many years. For Ross sporting rifle, *see* listing under Ross Rifle Co.

Charter Arms Explorer
(Disassembled and Stowed in Stock)

CHARTER ARMS CORPORATION
Stratford, Connecticut

Charter AR-7 Explorer Survival Rifle **$125**
Same as Armalite AR-7, except has black, instead of brown, "wood grain" plastic stock. *See* listing of that rifle for specifications. Made 1973-90.

CHIPMUNK MANUFACTURING INC.
Medford, Oregon
Succeeded by Oregon Arms Co.

Chipmunk Bolt-Action Single-Shot Rifle
Calibers: 22 LR or 22 WMR. Bbl.: 16.13 inches. Weight: about 2.5 pounds. Sights: peep rear; ramp front. Plain American walnut stock. Made 1982 to date.
Standard Model (Discontinued 1987) **$105**
Camouflage Model **125**
Deluxe Grade **150**

Chipmunk Single-Shot Rifle

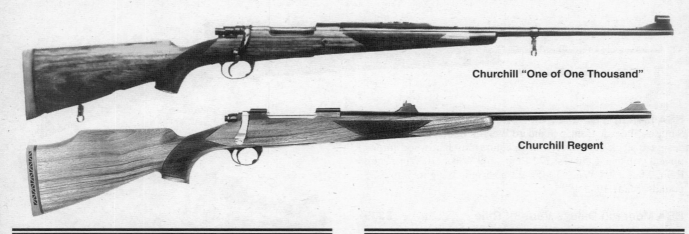

Churchill "One of One Thousand"

Churchill Regent

CHURCHILL RIFLES
Mfd. in England. Imported by Ellett Brothers, Inc., Chapin, SC (Previously by Kassnar Imports, Inc., Harrisburg, PA)

Churchill Highlander Bolt-Action Rifle **$350**
Calibers: 243 Win., 25-06 Rem., 270 Win., 308 Win., 30-06, 7mm Rem. Mag., 300 Win. Mag. 4-shot magazine (standard); 3-shot (magnum). Bbl. length: 22-inch (standard); 24-inch (magnum). 42.5 to 44.5 inches overall. Weight: 7.5 pounds. Adj. rear sight, blade front. Checkered European walnut pistol-grip stock. Imported 1986-91.

Churchill "One of One Thousand" Rifle **$1195**
Made for Interarms to commemorate that firm's 20th anniversary. Mauser-type action. Calibers: 270, 7mm Rem. Mag., 308, 30-06, 300 Win. Mag., 375 H&H Mag., 458 Win. Mag. 5-shot magagine (3-shot in Magnum calibers). 24-inch bbl. Weight: about 8 pounds. Classic-style French walnut stock with cheekpiece, black forend tip, checkered pistol grip and forearm, swivel-mounted recoil pad w/cartridge trap, pistol-grip cap w/trap for extra front sight, barrel-mounted sling swivel. Limited issue of 1,000 rifles made in 1973.

Churchill Regent Bolt-Action Rifle **$425**
Calibers: 243 Win., 25-06 Rem., 270 Win., 308 Win., 30-06, 7mm Rem. Mag.,300 Win. Mag. 4-shot magazine. 22-inch round bbl. 42.5 inches overall. Weight: 7.5 pounds. Ramp front sight w/gold bead; adj. rear. Hand-checkered Monte Carlo-style stock of select European walnut; recoil pad. Made 1986-90.

CLERKE RECREATION PRODUCTS
Santa Monica, California

Clerke Hi-Wall Single-Shot Rifle **$220**
Falling-block lever action similar to Winchester 1885 High Wall S.S. Color casehardened investment-cast receiver. Calibers: 222 Rem., 22-250, 243 Rem., 6mm Rem., 25-06, 270 Win., 7mm Rem. Mag., 30-06, 45-70 Govt. 26-inch medium-weight bbl. Weight: about 8 pounds. Furnished without sights. Checkered walnut pistol-grip stock and schnabel forearm. Made 1972-74.

Clerke Deluxe Hi-Wall **$275**
Same as standard model, except has adj. trigger, half-octagon bbl., select wood, stock w/cheekpiece and recoil pad. Made 1972-74.

CLIFTON ARMS
Medina, Texas

Clifton Arms Scout Bolt-Action Rifle **$2200**
Custom built on the Ruger Model 77 MKII stainless steel action. Calibers: 243, 7mm-08, 30-06, 308, and 350 Rem. Mag. Standard bbl. length: 19 inches, but many other lengths were made on special order. Weight: 7.5 lbs., average. Composite stock with retractable tripod and an integral butt magazine well for storage of cartridges. Forward-mounted Burris 2¾× Scout scope attached to integral scope base pedestals machined in the bbl. Reserve open sights are also installed.

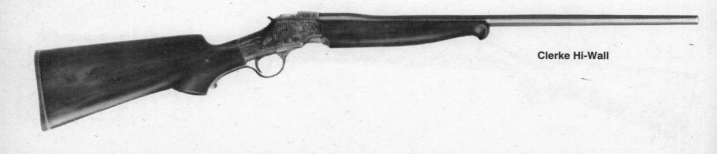

Clerke Hi-Wall

Colt AR-15 9mm Carbine

COLT INDUSTRIES, FIREARMS DIVISION
Hartford, Connecticut

Colt 22 Lightning Magazine Rifle **$1275**
Slide action. Caliber: 22 Rimfire (Short or Long). Tubular magazine holding 15 long or 16 short. 24-inch bbl., round or octagon. Weight: 5.75 lbs. (round barrel). Sights: open rear, bead front. Walnut stock and forearm. Available in small, medium and large frames. Made 1887-04.

Colt AR-15 Compact 9mm Carbine **$1025**
Semiautomatic. Caliber: 9mm NATO. 20-round detachable magazine. Bbl.: 16-inch round. Weight: 6.3 lbs. Adj. rear and front sights. Adj. buttstock. Ribbed round handguard. Made 1985-86.

Colt AR-15 Semiautomatic Sporter
Commercial version of U.S. M16 rifle. Gas-operated. Takedown. Caliber: 223 Rem. (5.56mm). 20-round magazine w/spacer to reduce capacity to 5 rounds. 20-inch bbl. w/flash suppressor. Sights: rear peep w/windage adjustment in carrying handle; front adj. for windage. 3X scope and mount optional (add $70 to value). Black molded buttstock of high-impact synthetic material, rubber buttplate. Barrel surrounded by handguards of black fiberglass w/heat-reflecting inner shield. Swivels, black web sling strap. Weight: w/o accessories, 6.3 pounds. Made 1964-94.
Standard Sporter . . . . **$ 975**
w/Adj. Stock, Redesigned Forearm (Disc. 1988) **1150**

Colt AR-15 A2 Delta Match H-BAR Rifle **$1345**
Similar to the AR-15A2 Government Model except has standard stock and heavy refined bbl. Furnished with 3-9× rubber armored scope and removeable cheekpiece.

Colt AR-15 A2 Government Model Carbine **$825**
Caliber: 223 Rem., 5- shot magazine. 16-inch bbl. with flash suppressor. 35 inches overall. Weight: 5.8 lbs. Telescoping aluminum buttstock; sling swivels. Made from 1985 to 1991.

RIFLES

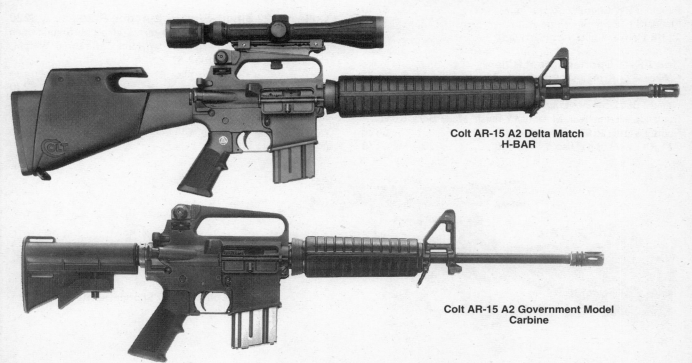

Colt AR-15 A2 Delta Match H-BAR

Colt AR-15 A2 Government Model Carbine

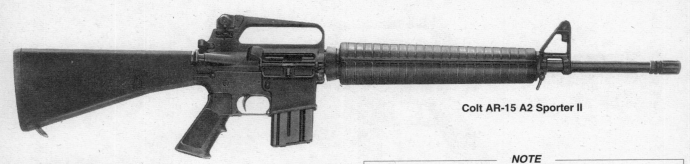

Colt AR-15 A2 Sporter II

Colt AR-15 A2 Sporter II $1095
Same general specifications as standard AR-15 Sporter except heavier bbl., improved pistol grip, weight of 7.5 pounds and optional 3X or 4X scope. Made 1985-89.

Colt AR-15 Sporter Competition H-BAR Rifle . . . $850
Similar to the AR-15 Sporter Target Model, except with integral Weaver-type mounting system on a flat-top receiver. 20-inch bbl. with counter-bored muzzle and 1:9" rifling twist. Made 1991 to date.

Coit AR-15 Sporter Competition H-BAR (RS) . . $1275
Similar to the AR-15 Sporter Competition H-BAR Model, except "Range Selected" for accuracy with 3×9 rubber-clad scope with mount. Carrying handle with iron sights. Made 1992-94.

Colt AR-15 Sporter Match Target Lightweight
Calibers: 223 Rem., 7.62×39mm, 9mm. 5-shot magazine. 16-inch bbl. (non-threaded after 1994). 34.5-35.5 inches overall. Weight: 7.1 pounds. Redesigned stock and shorter handguard. Made 1991 to date.
Standard LW Sporter (except 9mm) $750
Standard LW Sporter, 9mm 585
22 LR Conversion (Disc. 1994), **add** 175

Colt AR-15 Sporter Target Rifle
Caliber: 223 Rem. 5-shot magazine. 20-inch bbl. with flash suppressor (non-threaded after 1994). 39 inches overall. Weight: 7.5 pounds. Black composition stock, grip and handguard. Sights: post front; adj. aperture rear. Matte black finish. Made 1993 to date.
Sporter Target Rifle $825
22 LR Conversion (Disc. 1994), **add** 175

NOTE

On Colt AR-15 Sporter models currently produced (i.e., Competition H-BAR, Sporter Match Target Lightweight, and Sporter Target Rifle, **add $200** to pre-ban models made prior to 10-13-94.

Colt Lightning Carbine
Same as Lightning Magazine Rifle, except has 12-shot magazine, 20-inch bbl., weighs 6.25 pounds.
Carbine $2595
Baby Carbine (5.5 pounds) 3795

Colt Lightning Magazine Rifle $1395
Slide action. Calibers: 32-20, 38-40, 44-40. 15-shot tubular magazine. 26-inch bbl., round or octagon. Weight: 6.75 pounds (round barrel). Sights: open rear; bead or blade front. Walnut stock and forearm. Made 1884-1902.

Colt Stagecoach 22 Autoloader $265
Same as Colteer 22 Autoloader, except has engraved receiver, saddle ring, 16.5-inch bbl. Weight: 4 lbs. 10 oz. Made 1965-75.

Colteer 1-22 Single-Shot Bolt-Action Rifle $220
Caliber: 22 LR, Long, Short. 20- or 22-inch bbl. Sights: open rear; ramp front. Pistol-grip stock w/Monte Carlo comb. Weight: about 5 pounds. Made 1957-67.

Colteer 22 Autoloader $230
Caliber: 22 LR. 15-round tubular magazine. 19.38-inch bbl. Sights: open rear; hooded ramp front. Straight-grip stock, Western carbine-style forearm with barrel band. Weight: about 4.75 pounds. Made 1964-75.

Colt AR-15 A2 Sporter H-BAR

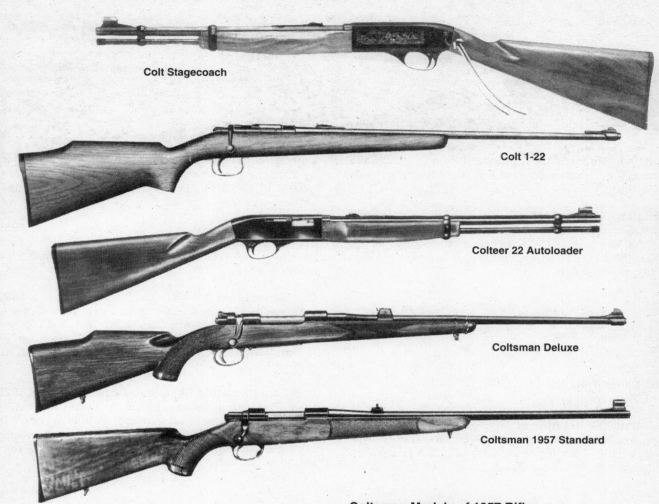

Colt Stagecoach

Colt 1-22

Colteer 22 Autoloader

Coltsman Deluxe

Coltsman 1957 Standard

Coltsman Custom Bolt-Action Sporting Rifle . . . $425
FN Mauser action, side safety, engraved floorplate. Calibers: 30-06, 300 H&H Mag. 5-shot box magazine. 24-inch bbl., ramp front sight. Fancy walnut stock, Monte Carlo comb, cheekpiece, pistol grip, checkered, QD swivels. Weight: about 7.25 pounds. Made 1957-61. Value shown is for rifle, as furnished by manufacturer, w/o rear sight.

Coltsman Deluxe Rifle $650
FN Mauser action. Same as Custom model except plain floorplate, plainer wood and checkering. Made 1957-61. Value shown is for rifle, as furnished by manufacturer, without rear sight.

Coltsman Models of 1957 Rifles
Sako Medium action. Calibers: 243, 308. Weight: about 6.75 pounds. Other specifications similar to those of models w/FN actions. Made 1957-61.

Custom	**$575**
Deluxe	450
Standard	395

Coltsman Model of 1961, Custom Rifle $460
Sako action. Calibers: 222, 222 Mag., 223, 243, 264, 270, 308, 30-06, 300 H&H. 23-, 24-inch bbl. Sights: folding leaf rear; hooded ramp front. Fancy French walnut stock w/Monte Carlo comb, rosewood forend tip and grip cap skip checkering, recoil pad, sling swivels. Weight: 6.5 - 7.5 lbs. Made 1963-65.

Coltsman 1961 Custom

Colteer 1961 Standard

Coltsman Model of 1961, Standard Rifle $395
Same as Custom model, except plainer, American walnut stock. Made 1963-65.

Coltsman Standard Rifle $395
FN Mauser action. Same as Deluxe model, except in 243, 30-06, 308, 300 Mag. and stock w/o cheekpiece, bbl. length 22 inches. Made 1957-61. Value shown is for rifle, as furnished by manufacturer, w/o rear sight.

NOTE

Colt-Sauer rifles were manufactured for Colt by J. P. Sauer & Sohn, Eckernförde, Germany.

Colt-Sauer Drillings
See Colt shotgun listings.

Colt-Sauer Grand African $1200
Same specifications as standard model, except caliber 458 Win. Mag., weighs 9.5 lbs. Sights: adj. leaf rear; hooded ramp front. Magnum-style stock of Bubinga. Made 1973-85.

Colt-Sauer Grand Alaskan $1195
Same specifications as standard model, except caliber 375 H&H, weighs 8.5 lbs. Sights: adj. leaf rear; hooded ramp front. Magnum-style stock of walnut.

Colt-Sauer Magnum $965
Same specifications as standard model, except calibers 7mm Rem. Mag., 300 Win. Mag., 300 Weatherby. Weight: 8.5 lbs. Made 1973-85.

Colt-Sauer Short Action $895
Same specifications as standard model, except shorter action to accept the following calibers: 22-250, 243 Win., 308 Win. and similar length cartridges. Weight: 7.5 lbs.; 8.25 lbs. (22-250). Drilled and tapped for scope mount. No front or rear open sights. Made 1973-88.

Colt-Sauer Sporting Rifle, Standard Model $925
Sauer 80 nonrotating bolt-action. Calibers: 25-06, 270 Win., 30-06. 3-round detachable box magazine. 24-inch bbl. Weight: 7.75 lbs., 8.5 lbs. (25-06). Furnished w/o sights. American walnut stock w/Monte Carlo cheekpiece, checkered pistol grip and forearm, rosewood forend tip and pistol-grip cap, recoil pad. Made 1973-1988.

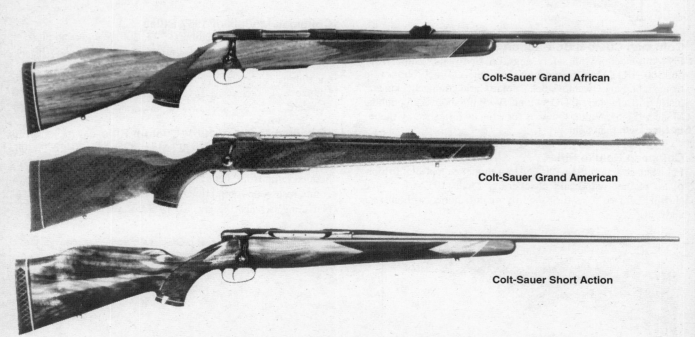

Colt-Sauer Grand African

Colt-Sauer Grand American

Colt-Sauer Short Action

COMMANDO CARBINES
Knoxville, Tennessee
Manufactured by Volunteer Enterprises, Inc.

Commando Mark III Semiautomatic Carbine
Blow-back action, fires from closed bolt. Caliber: 45 ACP. l5- or 30-shot magazine. 16.5-inch bbl. w/cooling sleeve and muzzle brake. Weight: 8 pounds. Sights: peep rear; blade front. "Tommy Gun" style stock and forearm or grip. Made I969-76.
With Horizontal Forearm **$325**
With Vertical Foregrip **415**

Commando Mark 9
Same specifications as Mark III and Mark 45, except caliber 9mm Luger. Made 1976-81.
With Horizontal Forearm **$360**
With Vertical Foregrip **375**

Commando Mark 45
Same specifications as Mark III. Has redesigned trigger housing and magazines. Made 1976-1988.
With Horizontal Forearm **$375**
With Vertical Foregrip **415**

CONTINENTAL RIFLES
Manufactured in Belgium for Continental Arms Corp., New York, N.Y.

Continental Double Rifle **$4750**
Calibers: 270, 303 Sav., 30-40, 348 Win., 30-06, 375 H&H, 400 Jeffrey, 465, 470, 475 No. 2, 500, 600. Side-by-side. Anson-Deeley reinforced boxlock action w/triple bolting lever-work. Two triggers. Nonautomatic safety. 24- or 26-inch bbls. Sights: express rear; bead front. Checkered cheekpiece stock and forend. Weight: from 7 lbs., depending on caliber.

COOPER ARMS
Stevensville, Montana

Cooper Arms Model 21
Similar to the Model 36CF, except in calibers 17 Rem., 17 Mach IV, 221 Fireball, 222, 223, 6×45, 6×47. 24-inch stainless or chrome-moly bbl. 43.5 inches overall. Weight: 8.75 lbs. Made 1994 to date.
Benchrest **$950**
Varmint Extreme **795**

Cooper Arms Model 22 Pro Varmint
Bolt-action, single-shot. Calibers: 22 BR, 22-250 Rem., 220 Swift, 243 Win., 6mm PPC, 6.5×55mm, 25-06 Rem., 7.62×39mm 26-inch bbl, 45.63 inches overall. Weight: 8 lbs., 12 oz. Single-stage trigger. AAA claro walnut stock. Made 1996 to date.
Pro Varmint. **$1595**
BR-50 Bench Rest. **1875**
Black Jack **1550**

Cooper Arms Model 22 Repeater
Calibers: 22-250, 243, 7mm-08 and 308. 23.75-inch bbl. Made from 1996 to date.
Classic. **$2100**
Custom Classic **2300**

Cooper Arms Model 36CF Bolt-Action Rifle
Calibers: 17 CCM, 22 CCM, 22 Hornet. 4-shot magazine. 23.75-inch bbl. 42.5 inches overall. Weight: 7 lbs. Walnut or synthetic stock. Made 1992-94.
Marksman **$595**
Sportsman **475**
Classic Grade **795**
Custom Grade **725**
Custom Classic Grade **825**

Cooper Arms Model 36RF Bolt-Action Rifle
Similar to the Model 36CF, except in caliber 22 LR. 5-shot magazine. Weight: 6.5-7 lbs. Made 1992 to date.
BR-50 (22-inch stainless bbl.) **$795**
Custom Grade **725**
Custom Classic Grade **825**
Featherweight **775**

Cooper Arms Model 38 Sporter
Similar to the Model 36CF, except in calibers 17 or 22 CCM w/3-shot magazine. Weight: 8 lbs. Walnut or synthetic stock. Made 1992-93.
Sporter Standard **$595**
Classic Grade **675**
Custom Grade **775**
Custom Classic Grade **850**

Cooper Arms Model 40 Classic Bolt-Action Rifle
Calibers: 17 CCM, 17 Ackley Hornet, 22 Hornet, 22K Hornet, 22 CCM, 4- or 5-shot magazine. 23.75-inch bbl. Checkered oil-finished AAA Claro walnut stock with steel grip cap and Pachmayr recoil pad. Made from 1995 to date.
Classic. **$1120**
Custom Classic **1270**
Classic Varminter **1275**

**Cooper Arms Model 22
Pro Varmint**

RIFLES

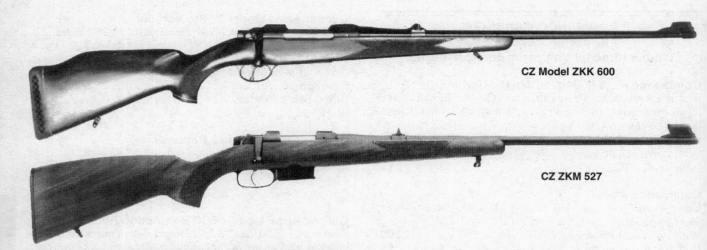

CZ Model ZKK 600

CZ ZKM 527

CZ RIFLES
Strankonice, Czechoslovakia
(Currently Uhersky Brod and Brno, Czecho.)
Mfd. by Ceska Zbrojovka-Nardoni Podnik
(formerly Bohmische Waffenfabrik A.G.)

See also listings under Brno Sporting Rifles and Springfield, Inc.

CZ ZKK 600 Bolt-Action Rifle
Calibers: 270 Win., 7×57, 7×64, 30-06. 5-shot magazine. 23.5-inch bbl. Weight: 7.5 lbs. Adj. folding-leaf rear sight, hooded ramp front. Pistol-grip walnut stock. Imported 1990 to date.
Standard Model $475
Deluxe Model 525

CZ ZKK 601 Bolt-Action Rifle
Similar to Model ZKK 600, except w/short action in calibers 223 Rem., 243 Win., 308 Win. 43 inches overall. Weight: 6 lbs. 13 oz. Checkered walnut pistol-grip stock w/Monte Carlo cheekpiece. Imported 1990 to date.
Standard Model $395
Deluxe Model 425

CZ ZKK 602 Bolt-Action Rifle
Similar to Model ZKK 600, except w/Magnum action in calibers 300 Win. Mag., 8×68S, 375 H&H, 458 Win. Mag. 25-inch bbl. 45.5 inches overall. Weight: 9.25 lbs. Imported 1990 to date.
Standard Model $550
Deluxe Model 625

CZ ZKM 452 Bolt-Action Repeating Rifle $190
Caliber: 22 LR. 5- or 10-shot magazine. 25-inch bbl. 43.5 inches overall. Weight: 6 lbs. Adj. rear sight, hooded bead front. Checkered oil-finished beechwood stock. Currently imported.

CZ ZKM 527 Bolt-Action Rifle
Calibers: 22 Hornet, 222 Rem., 223 Rem. 5-shot magazine. 23.5-inch bbl. 42.5 inches overall. Weight: 6.75 lbs. Adj. rear sight, hooded ramp front. Grooved receiver. Adj. double-set triggers. Synthetic or walnut stock w/Monte Carlo.
Synthetic Stock Model $450
Walnut Stock Model 490

CZ ZKM 537 Sporter Bolt-Action Rifle
Calibers: 270 Win., 308 Win., 30-06. 23.5-inch bbl. 44.75 inches overall. Weight: 7.5 lbs. Adj. folding leaf rear sight, hooded ramp front. Shrouded bolt and grooved. Synthetic or checkered walnut stock. Imported 1992 to date.
Synthetic Stock Model $450
Walnut Stock Model 500

CZ 550 Bolt-Action Rifle $395
Calibers: 243 Win., 270 Win., 7mm Mag., 7x57, 30-06, 300 Win Mag. 4-shot magazine. 23.6-inch bbl. Weight: 7.25 lbs. No sights. Receiver drilled and tapped for scope mount. Single-set trigger. Checkered stock with buttpad. Imported 1995 to date.

CZECHOSLOVAKIAN MILITARY RIFLES
Brno, Czechoslovakia
Manufactured by Ceska Zbrojovka

Czech Model 1924 (VZ24) Mauser Military Rifle . . $185
Basically the same as the German Kar.,98k and F.N. (Belgian Model 1924.) Caliber: 7.9mm Mauser. 5-shot box magazine. 23.25-inch bbl. Weight: about 8.5 lbs. Sights: adj. rear; blade front w/guards. Military stock of Belgian-type, full handguard. Mfd. 1924 thru WWII. Many of these rifles were made for export. As produced during the German occupation, this model was known as Gewehr 24t.

Czech Model 1933 (VZ33) Mauser Military Carbine $220
Modification of the German M/98 action with smaller receiver ring. Caliber: 7.9mm Mauser. 19.25-inch bbl. Weight: about 7.5 lbs. Sights: adj. rear; blade front w/guards. Military-type full stock. Mfd. 1933 thru WWII a similar model, produced during the German occupation, was designated Gew. 33/40.

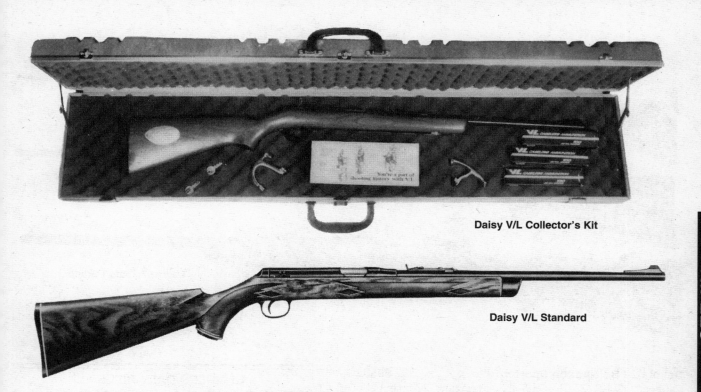

Daisy V/L Collector's Kit

Daisy V/L Standard

DAISY RIFLES
Rogers, Arkansas

Daisy V/L rifles carry the first and only commercial caseless cartridge system. These rifles are expected to appreciate considerably in future years. The cartridge, no longer made is also a collector's item.

Daisy V/L Collector's Kit **$295**
Presentation-grade rifle w/gold plate inscribed w/owner's name and gun serial number mounted on the stock. Also includes a special gun case, pair of brass gun cradles for wall-hanging, 300 rounds of 22 V/L ammunition and a certificate signed by Daisy president, Cass S. Hough. Approx. 1,000 manufactured 1968-69.

Daisy V/L Presentation Grade **$265**
Same specifications as standard model, except w/walnut stock. Approx. 4,000 manufactured 1968-69.

Daisy V/L Standard Rifle **$175**
Single shot, under-lever action. Caliber: 22 V/L (caseless cartridge, propellant ignited by jet of hot air). 18-inch bbl. Weight: 5 lbs. Sights: adj. open rear, ramp w/blade front. Wood-grained Lustran stock (foam-filled). Approx. 19,000 manufactured 1968-69.

DAKOTA ARMS, INC.
Sturgis, South Dakota

Dakota Model 10 Single-Shot Rifle **$1675**
Chambered for most commercially loaded calibers. 23-inch bbl. 39.5 inches overall. Weight: 5.5 lbs. Top tang safety. No sights. Checkered pistol-grip buttstock and semi-beavertail forearm, QD swivels, rubber recoil pad. Made 1992 to date.

Dakota Model 10 Single-Shot Rifle

Dakota 22 LR Sporter

Dakota 76 Classic Grade

Dakota 76 Safari Grade

Dakota 22 Bolt-Action Sporter Rifle **$955**
Calibers: 22 LR 22 Hornet.5-shot magazine. 22-inch bbl.
Weight: 6.5 lbs. Adj. trigger. Checkered classic-style Clara or
English walnut stock w/black recoil pad. Made 1992 to date.

Dakota Model 76 African Bolt-Action Rifle . . . **$2995**
Same general specifications as Model 76 Safari. Calibers: 404
Jeffery, 416 Rigby, 416 Dakota, 450 Dakota. 24-inch bbl.
Weight: 8 lbs. Checkered select walnut stock w/two crossbolts.
Made 1989 to date.

Dakota Model 76 Alpine Bolt-Action Rifle **$1495**
Same general specifications as Model 76 Classic, except short
action w/blind magazine. Calibers: 22-250, 243, 6mm Rem.,
250-3000, 7mm-08, 308. 21-inch bbl. Weight: 7.5 lbs. Made
1989 to date.

Dakota Model 76 Classic Bolt-Action Rifle **$1590**
Calibers: 257 Roberts, 270 Win., 280 Rem., 30-06, 7mm Rem.
Mag. 300 Win. Mag., 338 Win. Mag., 375 H&H Mag., 458 Win.
Mag. 21- or 23-inch bbl. Weight: 7.5 lbs. Receiver drilled and
tapped for sights. Adj. trigger. Classic-style checkered walnut
stock w/steel grip cap and solid recoil pad. Right- and left-hand
models. Made 1988 to date

Dakota Model 76 Safari Bolt-Action Rifle **$2495**
Calibers: 300 Win. Mag., 338 Win. Mag.,375 H&H Mag. 458
Win. Mag. 23-inch bbl. w/bbl. band swivel. Weight: 8.5 lbs.
Ramp front sight, standing leaf rear. Checkered fancy walnut
stock w/ebony forend tip and solid recoil pad. Made 1988 to
date.

CHARLES DALY RIFLE
Made by Franz Jaeger & Co., Suhl, Germany
Distributed in the U.S. by Outdoor Sports Head-
quarters, Inc., Dayton, Ohio

Charles Daly Hammerless Drilling
See listing under Charles Daly shotguns.

Charles Daly Hornet Rifle **$850**
Same as Herold Rifle. *See* listing of that rifle for specifications.
Imported during the 1930s.

DESERT INDUSTRIES, INC.
Las Vegas, Nevada
Formerly Steel City Arms, Pittsburg, PA

Desert Industries G-90 Single-Shot Rifle **$390**
Falling-block action. Calibers: 22-250, 220 Swift 223, 243 6mm,
257 Roberts, 25-06, 270 Win., 270 Wby., 280, 7×57, 7mm Rem.
Mag. 30-06, 300 Win., 300 Wby., 338 Win. Mag., 375 H&H,
45-70, 458 Win. Mag. 20-, 22-, 24-, or 26-inch bbl. in light, medium or heavy configuration. Weight: 7.5 lbs. Checkered walnut
stock. Blued finish. Made 1990 to date.

EAGLE ARMS INC.
Coal Valley, Illinois

Eagle Arms Model EA-15 Semiautomatic Rifle . . **$925**
Same general as the EA-15 Carbine except 20-inch bbl., 39
inches overall, and weighs 7 lbs. Made 1989 to date.

Eagle Arms Model EA-15 Carbine

Caliber: 223 Rem. (5.56mm). 30-shot magazine. 16-inch bbl. and collapsible buttstock. Weight: 5.75 lbs. (E1); 6.25 lbs. (E2 w/heavy bbl. & NM sights). Made 1989 to 1994.

E1 Carbine **$925**
E2 Carbine **975**

Eagle Arms Model EA-15 Golden Eagle Match Rifle **$1025**

Same general specifications as EA-15 Standard, except w/E2-style National Match sights. 20-inch Douglas Heavy Match bbl. NM trigger and bolt-carrier group. Weight: 12.75 lbs. Made 1991 to 1994.

EMF AP-74 Semiautomatic

EMF COMPANY, INC.
Santa Ana, California

EMF Model AP-74 Semiautomatic Carbine **$295**

Calibers: 22 LR or 32 ACP, 15-shot magazine. 20-inch bbl. w/flash reducer. 38 inches overall. Weight: 6.75 lbs. Protected pin front sight; protected rear peep sight. Lightweight plastic buttstock; ventilated snap-out forend.

EMF Model AP74-W Sporter Carbine **$195**

Sporterized version of the AP-75 with wood buttstock and forend.

EMF AP74 Paratrooper Model **$200**

Same general specifications as the Model AP74-W except with folding tubular buttstock. Made in 22 LR only.

ERMA-WERKE
Dachau, Germany

Erma EG72 Pump Action Repeater **$115**

Visible hammer. Caliber: 22 LR. 15-shot magazine. 18.5-inch bbl. Weight: about 5.25 lbs. Sights: open rear; hooded ramp front. Receiver grooved for scope mounting. Straight-grip stock, grooved slide handle. Made 1970-76.

Erma Model EG73 . . . . **$215**

Same as Model EG712, except chambered for 22 WMR, has 12-shot tubular magazine, 19.3-inch bbl. Made 1973 to date.

Erma Model EG712 Lever-Action Repeating Carbine **$200**

Styled after Winchester Model 94. Caliber: 22 LR, Long, Short. Tubular magazine holds 15 LR, 17 Long, 21 Short. 18.5-inch bbl. Weight: about 5.5 lbs. Sights: open rear; hooded ramp front. Receiver grooved for scope mounting. Western carbine-style stock and forearm w/ bbl. band. Made 1976 to date. *Note: A similar carbine of Erma manufacture is marketed in the U.S. as Ithaca Model 72 Saddlegun.*

EMF AP74-W Sporter Model

EMF AP74 Paratrooper Model

RIFLES

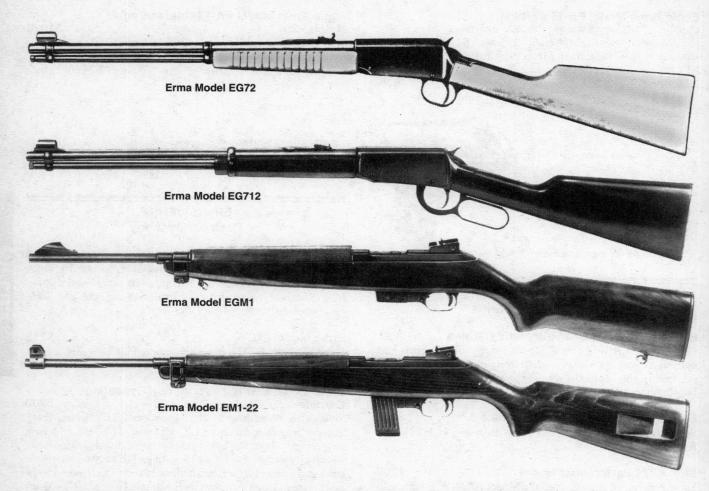

Erma Model EG72

Erma Model EG712

Erma Model EGM1

Erma Model EM1-22

Erma Model EGM1 . . . . $205
Same as Model EM1, except has unslotted buttstock, ramp front
sight, 5-shot magazine standard. Introduced 1970; discontinued.

Erma Model EM1 22 Semiautomatic Carbine . . . $265
Styled after U.S. Carbine Cal. 30 M1. Caliber: 22 LR. 10- or 15-
round magazine. 18-inch bbl. Weight: about 5.5 lbs. Carbine-
type sights. Receiver grooved for scope mounting. Military
stock/handguard. Intro. 1966; discontinued.

EUROPEAN AMERICAN ARMORY
Sharps, Florida

EAA Model HW 660 Bolt-Action
Single-Shot Rifle $595
Caliber: 22 LR. 26.8-inch bbl., 45.7 inches overall. Weight: 10.8
lbs. Match-type aperture rear sight; hooded ramp front. Stippled
walnut stock. Made from 1995 to date.

EAA HW Bolt-Action Single-Shot
Target Rifle $520
Same general specification as the Model HW 660 except
equipped with a target stock. Made from 1995 to date.

EAA HW 660 Bolt-Action
Single-Shot Rifle

FABRIQUE NATIONALE HERSTAL
Herstal, Belgium
Formerly Fabrique Nationale d'Armes de Guerre

F.N. Models 1924, 1934/30 and 1930 Mauser Military Rifles $275

Basically the same as the German Kar.98k. Straight bolt handle. Calibers: 7mm, 7.65mm and 7.9mm Mauser. 5-shot box magazine. 23.5-inch bbl. Weight: about 8.5 lbs. Sights: adj. rear; blade front. Military stock of M/98 pattern w/slight modification. Model differences are minor. Also produced in a short carbine model with 17.25-inch bbl. *Note:* These rifles were manufactured under contract for Abyssinia, Argentina, Belgium, Bolivia, Brazil, Chile, China, Colombia, Ecuador, Iran, Luxembourg, Mexico, Peru, Turkey, Uruguay and Yugoslavia. Such arms usually bear the coat of arms of the country for which they were made, together with the contractor's name and the date of manufacture. Also sold commercially and exported to all parts of the world.

F.N. Model 1949 Semiautomatic Military Rifle . . $450

Gas-operated. Calibers: 7mm, 7.65mm, 7.92mm, 30-06. 10-round box magazine, clip fed or loaded singly. 23.2-inch bbl. Weight: 9.5 lbs. Sights: tangent rear-shielded post front. Pistol-grip stock, handguard. *Note:* Adopted by Belgium in 1949; also by Belgian Congo, Brazil, Colombia, Luxembourg, Netherlands, East Indies; and Venezuela. Approx. 160,000 were made.

F.N. Model 1950 Mauser Military Rifle $295

Same as previous F.N. models of Kar. 98k type, except chambered for 30-06.

F.N. Deluxe Mauser Bolt-Action Sporting Rifle . . $550

American calibers: 220 Swift, 243 Win., 244 Rem., 250/3000, 257 Roberts, 270 Win., 7mm, 300 Sav., 308 Win. 30-06. *European calibers:* 7×57, 8×57JS, 8×60S, 9.3×62, 9.5×57, 10.75×68mm. 5-shot box magazine. 24-inch bbl. Weight: about 7.5-8.25 lbs. American model is standard w/hooded ramp front sight and Tri-Range rear; Continental model has two-leaf rear. Checkered stock w/cheekpiece, pistol grip, swivels. Made 1947-63.

F.N. Deluxe Mauser — Presentation Grade . . . $995

Same as regular model, except has select grade stock; engraving on receiver, trigger guard, floorplate and barrel breech. Discontinued 1963.

F.N. Supreme Mauser Bolt-Action Sporting Rifle . . $575

Calibers: 243, 270, 7mm, 308, 30-06. 4-shot magazine in 243 and 308; 5-shot in other calibers. 22-inch bbl. in 308; 24-inch in other calibers. Sights: hooded ramp front, Tri-Range peep rear. Checkered stock w/Monte Carlo cheekpiece, pistol grip, swivels. Weight: about 7.75 lbs. Made 1957-75.

RIFLES

F.N. Model 1949 Semiautomatic Rifle

F.N. Model 1950 Mauser

F.N. Deluxe Mauser

F.N. Supreme Mauser

F.N.-FAL Semiautomatic Rifle

F.N. Supreme Magnum Mauser **$595**
Calibers: 264 Mag., 7mm Mag., 300 Win. Mag. Specifications same as for standard-caliber model except 3-shot magazine capacity.

F.N.-FAL Semiautomatic Rifle **$1795**
Same as the standard FAL military rifle except w/o provision for automatic firing. Gas-operated. Caliber: 7.62mm NATO (.308 Win.). 10- or 20-round box magazine. 25.5-inch bbl. (including flash hider). Weight: about 9 lbs. Sights: post front; aperture rear. Wood buttstock, pistol grip, forearm/handguard; carrying handle, sling swivels. Made 1950 to date.

FEATHER INDUSTRIES, INC.
Boulder, Colorado

Feather Model AT-9 Semiautomatic Rifle
Caliber: 9mm Parabellum. 25-shot magazine. 17-inch bbl. 35 inches overall (extended). Hooded post front sight, adj. aperture rear. Weight: 5 lbs. Telescoping wire stock w/composition pistol-grip and barrel-shroud handguard. Matte black finish. Made 1988 to date.
Mode lAT-9 . . . . **$395**
Model F-9 (AT-9 w/Fixed Polymer Stock) **425**

Feather Model AT-22
Caliber: 22 LR. 20-shot magazine. 17-inch bbl. 35 inches overall (extended). Hooded post front sight; adj. aperture rear. Weight: 3.25 lbs. Telescoping wire stock w/composition pistol-grip and barrel-shroud handguard. Matte black finish.
Model AT-22 . . . . **$185**
Model F-22 (AT-22 w/Fixed Polymer Stock) **195**

FINNISH LION RIFLES
Jyväskylä, Finland
Manufactured by Valmet Oy, Tourula Works

Finnish Lion Champion Free Rifle **$475**
Bolt-action, single-shot. Double-set trigger. Caliber: 22 LR. 28.75-inch heavy bbl. Weight: about 16 lbs. Sights: extension rear peep; aperture front. Walnut free-rifle stock w/full pistol grip, thumbhole, beavertail forend, hook buttplate, palmrest, hand stop, swivel. Made 1965-72.

Finnish Lion Standard ISU Target Rifle **$295**
Bolt-action, single-shot. Caliber: 22 LR. 27.5-inch bbl. Weight: about 10.5 lbs. Sights: extension rear peep; aperture front. Walnut target stock w/full pistol grip, checkered beavertail forearm, adj. buttplate, sling swivel. Made 1966-77.

Finnish Lion Champion

Finnish Lion Match

Finnish Lion Match Rifle $410
Bolt-action, single-shot. Caliber: 22 LR. 28.75-inch heavy bbl. Weight: about 14.5 lbs. Sights: extension rear peep; aperture front. Walnut free-rifle stock w/full pistol grip, thumbhole, beavertail forearm, hook buttplate, palmrest, hand stop, swivel. Made 1937-72

Finnish Lion Standard Target Rifle
Bolt-action, single-shot. Caliber: 22 LR. 27.5-inch bbl. 44.5 inches overall. Weight: 10.5 pounds. No sights; micrometer rear and globe front International-style sights available. Select walnut stock in target configuration. Currently in production.
Standard Model $550
Thumbhole Stock Model 625

LUIGI FRANCHI, S.P.A.
Brescia, Italy

Franchi Centennial Automatic Rifle
Commemorates Franchi's 100th anniversary (1868-1968). Centennial seal engraved on receiver. Semiautomatic. Takedown. Caliber: 22 LR. 11-shot magazine in buttstock. 21-inch bbl. Weight: 5.13 lbs. Sights: open rear; goldbead front, on ramp. Checkered walnut stock and forend. Deluxe model has fully engraved receiver, premium grade wood. Made 1968.
Standard Model $250
Deluxe Model 295

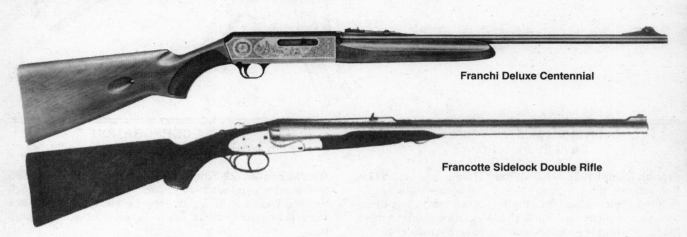

Franchi Deluxe Centennial

Francotte Sidelock Double Rifle

FRANCOTTE RIFLES
Distributed by Armes de Chasse
Herford, North Carolina

Francotte Standard Bolt-Action Rifle $4725
Calibers: 7×64mm, 270, 30-06 and similar length cartridges. Bbl. made to customer's specifications. Weight: 8 to 12 lbs. Metal engraving and finish to customer's specifications. Stock wood and checkering to customer's specifications.

Francotte Short Bolt-Action Rifle $5950
Same general specifications as the standard model except built on a shorter action and chambered for shorter cartridges such as the .17 Bee, 222 Rem., 243 Win., etc.

Francotte African Action $8500
Same general specifications as the standard model except built on a lengthened action to accept the larger African cartridges such as the 416 Rigby, 460 WM, etc.

Francotte Boxlock Double Rifle $11,550
Made in practically any caliber (for which chambering reamers and barrels are available) to customer's specifications and with any barrel lengths, weights, stock wood, etc.

Francotte Double Rifle
Made in practically any caliber to customer's specifications and with any barrel lengths, weights, stock wood, etc.
Standard Boxlock $13,000
Sidelock 22,500

**Francotte Mountain Rifle
w/claw mounts and scope**

Francotte Boxlock Mountain Rifle $16,000
Same general specifications as the standard boxlock except equipped with claw scope mounts and other minor features.

RIFLES

French Model 1935 MAS

Galil Model 223 AR
Semiautomatic Rifle

FRENCH MILITARY RIFLE
Saint Etienne, France

French Model 1936 MAS Military Rifle **$110**
Bolt-action. Caliber: 7.5mm MAS. 5-shot box magazine. 22.5-inch bbl. Weight: about 8.25 lbs. Sights: adj. rear; blade front. Two-piece military-type stock. Bayonet carried in forend tube. Made 1936-1940 by Manufacture Francaise d'Armes et de Cycles de St. Etienne (MAS).

GALIL RIFLES
Manufactured by Israel Military Industries, Israel

Galil AR Semiautomatic Rifle
Calibers: 308 Win. (7.62 NATO), 223 Rem. (5.56mm). 25-shot (308) or 35-shot (223) magazine. 16-inch (223) or 18.5-inch (308) bbl. w/flash suppressor. Weight: 9.5 lbs. Folding aperture rear sight, post front. Folding metal stock w/carrying handle. Imported early 1980s.
Model 223 AR **$1355**
Model 308 AR **1390**

Galil Sporter Semiautomatic Rifle **$995**
Same general specifications as AR Model, except w/hardwood thumbhole stock and 5-shot magazine. Weight: 8.5 lbs. Made 1991-94.

GARCIA CORPORATION
Teaneck, New Jersey

Garcia Bronco 22 Single-Shot Rifle **$85**
Swing-out action. Takedown. Caliber: 22 LR, Long, Short. 16.5-inch bbl. Weight: 3 lbs. Sights: open rear-blade front. One-piece stock and receiver, crackle finish. Introduced 1967: discontinued.

GERMAN MILITARY RIFLES
Mfd. by Ludwig Loewe & Co., Berlin, other contractors and by German arsenals and various plants under German Government control

German Model 24T (Gew. 24T) Mauser Rifle **$295**
Same general specifications as the Czech Model 24 (VZ24) Mauser Rifle w/minor modifications, has laminated woodstock. Weight: about 9.25 lbs. Made in Czechoslovakia during German occupation; adopted 1940.

German Model 29/40 (Gew. 29/40) Mauser Rifle . . **$195**
Same general specifications as Kar. 98K, with minor differences. Made in Poland during German occupation; adopted 1940.

Garcia Bronco 22

German Gew. 33/40

German Gew. 43

German Model 33/40 (Gew. 33/40) Mauser Rifle .. $550

Same general specifications as the Czech Model 33 (VZ33) Mauser Carbine with minor modifications, has laminated wood stock as found in war-time Model 98K carbines. Made in Czechoslovakia during German occupation; adopted 1940.

German Models 41 and 41-W (Gew. 41, Gew. 41-W) Semiautomatic Military Rifles

Gas-operated, muzzle cone system. Caliber: 7.9mm Mauser. 10-shot box magazine. 22.5-inch bbl. Weight: about 10.25 lbs. Sights: adj. leaf rear; blade front. Military-type stock w/semipistol grip, plastic handguard. *Note:* Model 41 lacks bolt release found on Model 41-W; otherwise, the models are the same. These early models were mfd. in Walther's Zella-Mehlis plant. Made c.1941-43.

Model 41 . . . . $2895
Model 41-W 2195

German Model 43 (Gew. 43, Kar. 43) Semiauto Military Rifles $990

Gas-operated, barrel vented as in Russian Tokarev. Caliber: 7.9mm Mauser. 10-shot detachable box magazine. 22- or 24-inch bbl. Weight: about 9 lbs. Sights: adj. rear; hooded front. Military-type stock w/semipistol grip, wooden handguard. *Note:* These rifles are alike except for minor details, have characteristic late WWII mfg. short cuts: cast receiver and bolt cover, stamped steel parts, etc. Gew. 43 may have either 22- or 24-inch bbl; the former length was standardized in late 1944, when weapon designation was changed to "Kar. 43." Made 1943-45.

German Model 1888 (Gew. 88) Mauser- Mannlicher Service Rifle $185

Bolt action, straight handle. Caliber: 7.9mm Mauser (8×57mm). 5-shot Mannlicher box magazine. 29-inch bbl. with jacket. Weight: about 8.5 lbs. Fixed front sight, adj. rear. Military-type full stock. Mfd. by Ludwig Loewe & Co., Haenel, Schilling and other contractors.

German Kar. 88

German Model 1888 (Kar. 88) Mauser-Mannlicher Carbine $195

Same general specifications as Gew. 88, except w/18-inch bbl., w/o jacket, flat turned-down bolt handle, weighs about 6.75 lbs. Mfd. by Ludwig Loewe & Co., Haenel, Schilling and other contractors.

German Model 1898 (Gew. 98) Mauser Military Rifle $255

Bolt action, straight handle. Caliber: 7.9mm Mauser (8×57mm). 5-shot box magazine. 29-inch steeped bbl. Weight: 9 lbs. Sights: blade front; adj. rear. Military-type full stock w/rounded bottom pistol grip. Adopted 1898. *See* illustration next page.

NOTE

German Mauser Military Rifles (Gew. 98, Kar. 98) were made before and during WWI at the government arsenals at Amberg, Brunn, Danzig, Erfurt and Spandau; they were also manufactured by contractors such as Haenel, Loewe, Mauser, Schilling and Steyr. These rifles bear the Imperial Crown, maker's name and date of manufacture on the receiver ring. Post-WWI Kar. 98B bears maker's name and date. During WWII as well as the years immediately before (probably from c. 1935), a letter or number code was used to indicate maker. This code and date of manufacture will be found stamped on the receiver ring of rifles of this period. German Service Mausers also bear the model number (Gew. 98 Kar. 98K, G. 33/40, etc.) on the left side of the receiver. An exception is Model VK98, which usually bears no identifying marks. Gew. is abbreviation for gewehr (rifle), Kar. for *karabiner (carbine)*.

German Model 1898A (Kar. 98A) Mauser Carbine $265

Same general specifications as Model 1898 (Gew.98) Rifle, except has turned-down bolt handle, smaller receiver ring, light 23.5-inch straight taper bbl., front sight guards, sling is attached to left side of stock, weighs 8 lbs. *Note:* Some of these carbines are marked "Kar. 98"; the true Kar. 98 is the earlier original M/98 carbine with 17-inch bbl. and is rarely encountered.

German Model 1898B (Kar. 98B) Mauser Carbine $295

Same general specifications as Model 1898 (Gew.98) Rifle, except has turned-down bolt handle and sling attached to left side of stock. This is post-WWI model.

German Gew. 98

German Kar. 98K

German Model 1898K (Kar. 98K) Mauser Carbine $245

Same general specifications as Model 1898 (Gew.98) Rifle, except has turned-down bolt handle, 23.5-inch bbl., may have hooded front sight, sling is attached to left side of stock, weighs about 8.5 lbs. Adopted in 1935, this was the standard German Service rifle of WWII. *Note:* Late-war models had stamped sheet steel trigger guards and many of the Model 98K carbines made during WWII had laminated wood stocks, these weigh about ½ to ¾ pound more than the previous Model 98K. Value shown is for earlier type.

German Model VK 98 People's Rifle ("Volksaewehr") $160

Kar. 98K-type action. Caliber: 7.9mm. Single shot or repeater (latter w/rough hole-in-the-stock 5-shot "magazine" or fitted w/10-shot clip of German Model 43 semiauto rifle). 20.9-inch bbl. Weight: 7 lbs. Fixed V-notch rear sight dovetailed into front receiver ring; front blade welded to barrel. Crude, unfinished, half-length stock w/o buttplate. Last ditch weapon made in 1945 for issue to German civilians. *Note:* Of value only as a military arms collector's item, this hastily made rifle should be regarded as *unsafe* to shoot.

Gévarm E-1

GÉVARM RIFLE
Saint Etienne, France
Manufactured by Gevelot

Gévarm E-1 Autoloading Rifle $160

Caliber: 22 LR. 8-shot clip magazine. 19.5-inch bbl. Sights: open rear; post front. Pistol-grip stock and forearm of French walnut.

GOLDEN EAGLE RIFLES
Houston, Texas
Mfd. by Nikko Firearms Ltd., Tochigi, Japan

Golden Eagle Model 7000 Grade I African $595

Same as Grade I Big Game, except calibers 375 H&H Mag. and 458 Win. Mag., 2-shot magazine in 458, weighs 8.75 lbs. in 375 and 10.5 lbs. in 458, furnished with sights. Introduced 1976; discontinued.

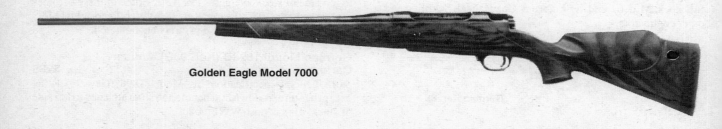

Golden Eagle Model 7000

Golden Eagle Model 7000 Grade I Big Game . . . $525

Bolt action. Calibers: 22-250, 243 Win., 25-06, 270 Win., Weatherby Mag., 7mm Rem. Mag., 30-06, 300 Weatherby Mag., 300 Win. Mag., 338 Win. Mag. Magazine capacity: 4 rounds in 22-250, 3 rounds in other calibers. 24- or 26-inch bbl. (26-inch only in 338). Weight: 7 lbs., 22-250; 8.75, lbs., other calibers. Furnished w/o sights. Fancy American walnut stock, skip checkered, contrasting wood forend tip and grip cap w/gold eagle head, recoil pad. Introduced 1976; discontinued.

GREIFELT & CO.
Suhl, Germany

Greifelt Sport Model 22 Hornet Bolt-Action Rifle $1655

Caliber: 22 Hornet. 5-shot box magazine. 22-inch Krupp steel bbl. Weight: 6 lbs. Sights: two-leaf rear; ramp front. Walnut stock, checkered pistol grip and forearm. Made before WWII.

CARL GUSTAF RIFLES
Eskilstuna, Sweden
Mfd. by Carl Gustafs Stads Gevärsfaktori

Carl Gustaf Model 2000 Bolt-Action Rifle

Calibers: 243, 6.5×55, 7×64, 270, 308 Win., 30-06, 7mm Rem. Mag., 300 Win. Mag. 3-shot magazine. 24-inch bbl. 44 inches overall. Weight: 7.5 lbs. Receiver drilled and tapped. Hooded ramp front sight, open rear. Adj. trigger. Checkered European walnut stock w/Monte Carlo cheekpiece and Wundhammer palmswell grip. Made 1991 to date.

Model 2000 w/o Sights $1195
Model 2000 with Sights 1250

Carl Gustaf Deluxe $550

Same specifications as Monte Carlo Standard. Calibers: 6.5×55, 308 Win., 30-06, 9.3×62. 4-shot magazine in 9.3×62. Jeweled bolt. Engraved floorplate and trigger guard. Deluxe French walnut stock w/rosewood forend tip. Made 1970-77.

Carl Gustaf Grand Prix Single-Shot Target Rifle . . . $475

Special bolt action with "world's shortest lock time." Single-stage trigger adjusts down to 18 oz. Caliber: 22 LR. 26.75-inch heavy bbl. w/adj. trim weight. Weight: 9.75 lbs. Furnished w/o sights. Target-type Monte Carlo stock of French walnut, adj. cork buttplate. Made 1970 to date.

Carl Gustaf Monte Carlo Standard Bolt-Action Sporting Rifle $350

Carl Gustaf 1900 action. Calibers: 6.5×55, 7×64, 270 Win., 7mm Rem. Mag., 308 Win., 30-06, 9.3×62. 5-shot magazine, except 4-shot in 9.3×62 and 3-shot in 7mm Rem. Mag. 23.5-inch bbl. Weight: about 7 lbs. Sights: folding leaf rear; hooded ramp front. French walnut Monte Carlo stock w/cheekpiece, checkered forearm and pistol grip, sling swivels. Also available in left-hand model. Made 1970-77.

Carl Gustaf Special $395

Also designated "Grade II" in U.S. and "Model 9000" in Canada. Same specifications as Monte Carlo Standard. Calibers: 22-250, 243 Win., 25-06, 270 Win., 7mm Rem. Mag., 308 Win., 30-06, 300 Win. Mag. 3-shot magazine in Magnum calibers. Select wood stock w/rosewood forend tip. Left-hand model avail. Made 1970-77.

Carl Gustaf Sporter $475

Also designated "Varmint-Target" in U.S. Fast bolt action with large bakelite bolt knob. Trigger pull adjusts down to 18 oz. Calibers: 222 Rem., 22-250, 243 Win., 6.5×55. 5-shot magazine,

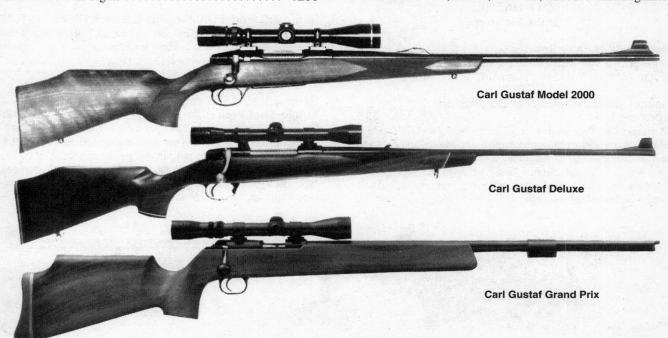

Carl Gustaf Model 2000

Carl Gustaf Deluxe

Carl Gustaf Grand Prix

Carl Gustaf Sporter

Carl Gustaf Sporter *(Cont.)*

except 6-shot in 222 Rem. 26.75-inch heavy bbl. Weight: about 9.5 lbs. Furnished w/o sights. Target-type Monte Carlo stock of French walnut. Made 1970 to date.

Carl Gustaf Standard **$425**
Same specifications as Monte Carlo Standard. Calibers: 6.5×55, 7×64, 270 Win., 308 Win., 30-06, 9.3×62. Classic-style stock w/o Monte Carlo. Made 1970-77.

Carl Gustaf Trofé **$595**
Also designated "Grade III" in U.S. and "Model 8000" in Canada. Same specifications as Monte Carlo Standard. Calibers: 22-250, 25-06, 6.5×55, 270 Win., 7mm Rem. Mag., 308 Win., 30-06, 300 Win. Mag. 3-shot magazine in Magnum calibers. Furnished w/o sights. Fancy wood stock w/rosewood forend tip, high-gloss lacquer finish. Made 1970-77.

C.G. HAENEL
Suhl, Germany

Haenel '88 Mauser Sporter **$395**
Same general specifications as Haenel Mauser-Mannlicher, except has Mauser 5-shot box magazine.

**Haenel Mauser-Mannlicher Bolt-Action
Sporting Rifle** **$350**
Mauser M/88-type action. Calibers: 7×57, 8×57, 9×57mm. Mannlicher clip-loading box magazine, 5-shot. 22- or 24-inch half or full octagon bbl. with raised matted rib. Double-set trigger. Weight: 7.5 lbs. Sights: leaf-type open rear; ramp front. Sporting stock w/cheekpiece, checkered pistol grip, raised sidepanels, schnabel tip, swivels.

HÄMMERLI AG JAGD-UND
SPORTWAFFENFABRIK
Lenzburg, Switzerland

**Hämmerli Model 45 Smallbore Bolt-Action
Single-Shot Match Rifle** **$525**
Calibers: 22 LR, 22 Extra Long. 27.5-inch heavy bbl. Weight: about 15.5 lbs. Sights: micrometer peep rear; globe front. Free-rifle stock w/cheekpiece, full pistol grip, thumbhole, beavertail forearm, palmrest, Swiss-type buttplate, swivels. Made 1945-57.

Hämmerli Model 54 Smallbore Match Rifle **$495**
Bolt-action, single-shot. Caliber: 22 LR. 27.5-inch heavy bbl. Weight: about 15 lbs. Sights: micrometer peep rear; globe front. Free-rifle stock w/cheekpiece, thumbhole, adj. hook buttplate, palmrest, swivel. Made 1954-57.

Hämmerli Model 503 Free Rifle **$475**
Bolt-action, single-shot. Caliber: 22 LR. 27.5-inch heavy bbl. Weight: about 15.5 lbs. Sight: micrometer peep rear; globe front. Free-rifle stock w/cheekpiece, thumbhole adj. hook buttplate, palmrest, swivel. Made 1957-1962.

Hämmerli Model 506 Smallbore Match Rifle **$515**
Bolt action, single shot. Caliber: 22 LR. 26.75-inch heavy bbl. Weight: about 16.5 lbs. Sights: micrometer peep rear; globe front. Free-rifle stock w/cheekpiece, thumbhole adj. hook buttplate, palmrest, swivel. Made 1963-66.

**Hämmerli Model Olympia 300 Meter Bolt-Action
Single-Shot Free Rifle** **$625**
Calibers: 30-06, 300 H&H Magnum for U.S.A.; ordinarily produced in 7.5mm, other calibers available on special order. 29.5-inch heavy bbl. Double-pull or double-set trigger. Sights: micrometer peep rear, globe front. Free-rifle stock w/cheekpiece, full pistol grip, thumbhole, beavertail forend, palmrest, Swiss-type buttplate, swivels. Made 1945-59.

Hämmerli Model 45

Hämmerli-Tanner 300M

Hämmerli-Tanner 300 Meter Free Rifle $795
Bolt-action, single-shot. Caliber: 7.5mm standard, available in most popular centerfire calibers. 29.5-inch heavy bbl. Weight: about 16.75 lbs. Sights: micrometer peep rear; globe front. Free-rifle stock w/cheekpiece, thumbhole, adj. hook buttplate, palm-rest, swivel. Introduced 1962; discontinued.

HARRINGTON & RICHARDSON, INC.
Gardner, Massachusetts
(Now H&R 1871, INC., Gardner, Mass.)

Formerly Harrington & Richardson Arms Co. of Worcester Mass. After a long and distinguished career in gunmaking, this firm suspended operation in 1986. However, in 1992, the firm was bought by New England Firearms of Gardner, Mass. Some models are mfd. under that banner as well as H&R 1871, Inc.

Harrington & Richardson Model 60 Reising Semiautomatic Rifle $350
Caliber: 45 Automatic. 12- and 20-shot detachable box magazines. 18.25-inch bbl. Weight: about 7.5 lbs. Sights: open rear; blade front. Plain pistol-grip stock. Made 1944-46.

Harrington & Richardson Model 65 Military Autoloading Rifle $255
Also called "General." Caliber: 22 LR. 10-shot detachable box magazine. 23-inch heavy bbl. Weight: about 9 lbs. Sights: Redfield 70 rear peep, blade front w/protecting "ears." Plain pistol-grip stock, "Garand" dimensions. Made 1944-46. *Note:* This model was used as a training rifle by the U.S. Marine Corps.

Harrington & Richardson Model 150 Leatherneck Autoloader $110
Caliber: 22 LR only. 5-shot detachable box magazine. 22-inch bbl. Weight: 7.25 lbs. Sights: open rear; blade front, on ramp. Plain pistol-grip stock. Made 1949-53.

Harrington & Richardson Model 151 .... $125
Same as Model 150 except with Redfield 70 rear peep sight.

Harrington & Richardson Model 155 Single-Shot Rifle $110
Model 158 action. Calibers: 44 Rem. Mag., 45-70 Govt. 24- or 28-inch bbl. (latter in 44 only). Weight: 7 or 7.5 lbs. Sights: folding leaf rear; blade front. Straight-grip stock, forearm with bbl. band, brass cleaning rod. Made 1972-82.

RIFLES

H&R Model 60 Reising

H&R Model 65

H&R Model 150

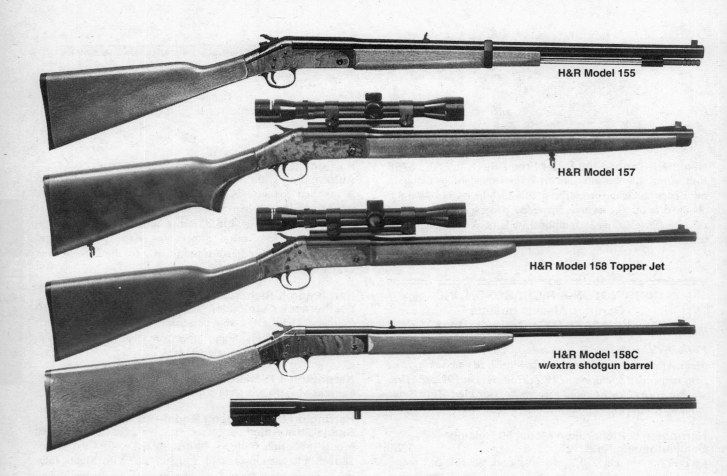

H&R Model 155

H&R Model 157

H&R Model 158 Topper Jet

H&R Model 158C
w/extra shotgun barrel

Harrington & Richardson Model 157
Single-Shot Rifle **$100**
Model 158 action. Calibers: 22 WMR, 22 Hornet, 30-30. 22-inch
bbl. Weight: 6.25 lbs. Sights: folding leaf rear; blade front.
Pistol-grip stock, full-length forearm, swivels. Made 1976-86.

Harrington & Richardson Model 158 Topper Jet
Single-Shot Combination Rifle
Shotgun-type action w/visible hammer, side lever, auto ejector.
Caliber: 22 Rem. Jet. 22-inch bbl. (interchanges with 30-30, .410
ga., 20 ga. bbls.). Weight: 5 lbs. Sights: Lyman folding adj. open
rear; ramp front. Plain pistol-grip stock and forearm, recoil pad.
Made 1963-67.
Rifle only **$130**
Interchangeable bbl.—30-30, shotgun **45**

Harrington & Richardson Model 158C **$145**
Same as Model 158 Topper Jet, except calibers 22 Hornet, 30-
30, 357 Mag., 357 Max., 44 Mag. Straight-grip stock. Made
1963-86.

Harrington & Richardson Model 163 Mustang
Single-Shot Rifle **$110**
Same as Model 158 Topper except has gold-plated hammer and
trigger, straight-grip stock and contoured forearm. Made 1964-67.

Harrington & Richardson Model 165
Leatherneck Autoloader **$125**
Caliber: 22 LR.10-shot detachable box magazine. 23-inch
bbl. Weight: about 7.5 lbs. Sights: Redfield 70 rear peep;
blade front, on ramp. Plain pistol-grip stock, swivels, web
sling. Made 1945-61.

Harrington & Richardson Model 171 . . . . **$285**
Model 1873 Springfield Cavalry Carbine replica. Caliber: 45-70.
22-inch bbl. Weight: 7 lbs. Sights: leaf rear; blade front. Plain
walnut stock. Made 1972-81.

Harrington & Richardson Model 171 Deluxe . . . **$325**
Same as Model 171, except engraved action and different sights.
Made 1972-86.

Harrington & Richardson Model 172 . . . . **$995**
Same as Model 171 Deluxe, except silver-plated, has fancy walnut stock, checkered, with grip adapter; tang-mounted aperture
sight. Made 1972-86.

Harrington & Richardson Model 173 . . . . **$325**
Model 1873 Springfield Officer's Model replica, same as 100th
Anniversary Commemorative, except w/o plaque on stock.
Made 1972-86.

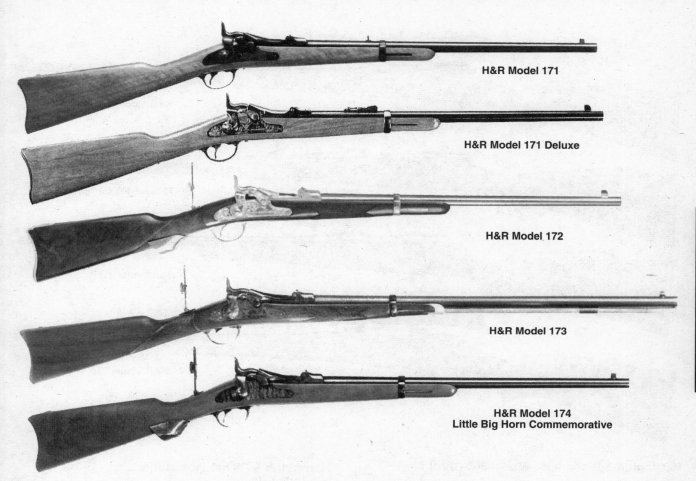

H&R Model 171

H&R Model 171 Deluxe

H&R Model 172

H&R Model 173

H&R Model 174
Little Big Horn Commemorative

Harrington & Richardson Model 174 . . . . $350
Little Big Horn Commemorative Carbine. Same as Model 171
Deluxe, except has tang-mounted aperture sight, grip adapter.
Made 1972-84. Value is for carbine in new, unfired condition.

Harrington & Richardson Model 178 . . . . $325
Model 1873 Springfield Infantry Rifle replica. Caliber: 45-70. 32-
inch bbl. Weight: 8 lbs. 10 oz. Sights: leaf rear; blade front. Full-
length stock with bbl. bands, swivels, ramrod. Made 1973-86.

**Harrington & Richardson Model 250 Sportster
Bolt-Action Repeating Rifle** $80
Caliber: 22 LR. 5-shot detachable box magazine. 23-inch bbl.
Weight: about 6.5 lbs. Sights: open rear; blade front, on ramp.
Plain pistol-grip stock. Made 1948-61.

Harrington & Richardson Model 251 . . . . $85
Same as Model 250 except has Lyman 55H rear sight.

**Harrington & Richardson Model 265 "Reg'lar" Bolt-
Action Repeating Rifle** $80
Caliber: 22 LR. 10-shot detachable box magazine. 22-inch bbl.
Weight: about 6.5 lbs. Sights: Lyman 55 rear peep; blade front,
on ramp. Plain pistol-grip stock. Made 1946-49.

**Harrington & Richardson Model 300 Ultra
Bolt-Action Rifle** $395
Mauser-type action. Calibers: 22-250, 243 Win., 270 Win., 30-06,
308 Win., 7mm Rem. Mag., 300 Win. Mag. 3-round magazine in
7mm and 300 Mag. calibers, 5-round in others. 22- or 24-inch bbl.
Sights: open rear; ramp front. Checkered stock w/rollover cheek-

H&R Model 178

H&R Model 300

H&R Model 301 Carbine

H&R Model 317P

H&R Model 330

Harrington & Richardson Model 300 (*Cont.*)

piece and full pistol grip, contrasting wood forearm tip and pistol grip, rubber buttplate, sling swivels. Weight: 7.25 lbs. Made 1965-82.

Harrington & Richardson Model 301 Carbine . . . $380

Same as Model 300, except has 18-inch bbl., Mannlicher-style stock, weighs 7.25 pounds; not available in caliber 22-250. Made 1967-82.

Harrington & Richardson Model 308
Automatic Rifle $325

Original designation of the Model 360 Ultra. Made 1965-67.

Harrington & Richardson Model 317 Ultra
Wildcat Bolt-Action Rifle $495

Sako short action. Calibers: 17 Rem., 17/223 (handload), 222 Rem., 223 Rem. 6-round magazine. 20-inch bbl. No sights, receiver dovetailed for scope mounts. Checkered stock w/cheekpiece and full pistol grip, contrasting wood forearm tip and pistol-grip cap, rubber buttplate. Weight: 5.25 lbs. Made 1968-76.

Harrington & Richardson Model 317P
Presentation Grade $595

Same as Model 317, except has select grade fancy walnut stock with basketweave carving on forearm and pistol grip. Made 1968-76.

Harrington & Richardson Model 330
Hunter's Rifle $295

Similar to Model 300, but w/plainer stock. Calibers: 243 Win., 270 Win., 30-06, 308 Win., 7mm Rem. Mag., 300 Win. Mag. Weight: about 7.13 lbs. Made 1967-72.

Harrington & Richardson Model 333 . . . . $230

Plainer version of Model 300 with uncheckered walnut-finished hardwood stock. Calibers: 7mm Rem. Mag. and 30-06. 22-inch bbl. Weight: 7.25 lbs. No sights. Made in 1974.

Harrington & Richardson Model 340 . . . . $295

Mauser-type action. Calibers: 243 Win., 308 Win., 270 Win., 30-06, 7×57mm. 22-inch bbl. Weight: 7.25 lbs. Hand-checkered, American walnut stock. Made 1982-84.

Harrington & Richardson Model 360 Ultra
Automatic Rifle $325

Gas-operated semiautomatic. Calibers: 243 Win., 308 Win. 3-round detachable box magazine. 22-inch bbl. Sights: open rear; ramp front. Checkered stock with rollover cheekpiece, full pistol grip, contrasting wood forearm tip and pistol-grip cap, rubber buttplate, sling swivels. Weight: 7.25 lbs. Made 1967-1978.

Harrington & Richardson Model 361 . . . . $355

Same as Model 360, except has full rollover cheekpiece for right- or left-hand shooters. Made 1970-73.

H&R 360 Ultra Automatic

H&R 370 Ultra Medalist

Harrington & Richardson Model 365 Ace Bolt-Action Single-Shot Rifle $100
Caliber: 22LR.22-inch bbl. Weight: about 6.5 lbs. Sights: Lyman 55 rear peep, blade front, on ramp. Plain pistol-grip stock. Made 1946-47.

Harrington & Richardson Model 370 Ultra Medalist $395
Varmint and target rifle based on Model 300. Calibers: 22-250, 243 Win., 6mm Rem. 5-round magazine. 24-inch varmint weight bbl. No sights. Target-style stock with semibeavertail forearm. Weight: 9.5 lbs. Made 1968-73.

Harrington & Richardson Model 422 Slide-Action Repeater $125
Caliber: 22 LR, Long, Short. Tubular magazine holds 21 Short, 17 Long, 15 LR. 24-inch bbl. Weight: about 6 lbs. Sights: open rear; ramp front. Plain pistol-grip stock grooved slide handle. Made 1956-58.

Harrington & Richardson Model 450 . . . . $130
Same as Model 451, except w/o front and rear sights.

Harrington & Richardson Model 451 Medalist Bolt- Action Target Rifle $155
Caliber: 22 LR. 5-shot detachable box magazine. 26-inch bbl. Weight: about 10.5 lbs. Sights: Lyman 524F extension rear; Lyman 77 front, scope bases. Target stock w/full pistol grip and forearm, swivels and sling. Made 1948-61.

Harrington & Richardson Model 465 Targeteer Special Bolt-Action Repeater $145
Caliber: 22 LR.10-shot detachable box magazine.25-inch bbl. Weight: about 9 lbs. Sights: Lyman 57 rear peep; blade front, on ramp. Plain pistol-grip stock, swivels, web sling strap. Made 1946-47.

Harrington & Richardson Model 700 Autoloader . . $175
Caliber: 22 WMR. 5-shot magazine. 22-inch bbl. Weight: about 6.5 lbs. Sights: folding leaf rear; blade front, on ramp. Monte Carlo-style stock of American walnut. Introduced 1977; discontinued.

Harrington & Richardson Model 700 Deluxe . . . $275
Same as Model 700 Standard except has select custom polished and blued finish, select walnut stock, hand ceckering, and no iron sights. Fitted with H&R Model 432 4× scope. Made 1980-86.

Harrington & Richardson Model 750 Pioneer Bolt- Action Single-Shot Rifle $90
Caliber: 22 LR, Long, Short. 22- or 24-inch bbl. Weight: about 5 lbs. Sights: open rear; bead front. Plain pistol-grip stock. Made 1954-81; redesigned 1982; discont. 1985. *See* photo next page.

Harrington & Richardson Model 751 Single-Shot Rifle $75
Same as Model 750, except has Mannlicher-style stock. Made 1971.

H&R Model 700 Deluxe

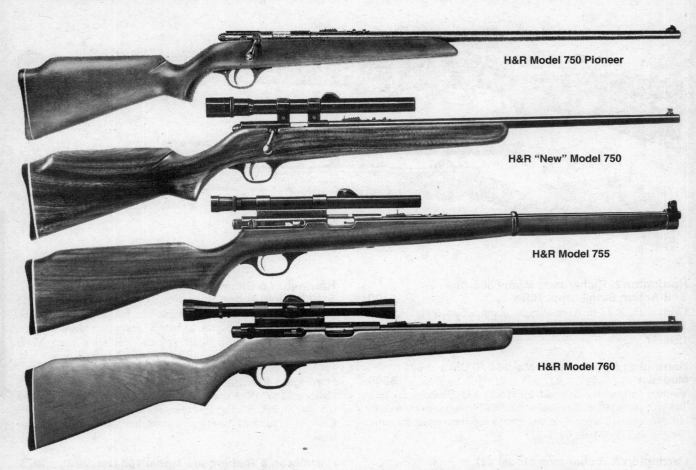

H&R Model 750 Pioneer

H&R "New" Model 750

H&R Model 755

H&R Model 760

Harrington & Richardson Model 755 Sahara Single-Shot Rifle **$75**
Blow-back action, automatic ejection. Caliber: 22 LR, Long, Short. 18-inch bbl. Weight: 4 lbs. Sights: open rear; military-type front. Mannlicher-style stock. Made 1963-71.

Harrington & Richardson Model 760 Single-Shot . . **$80**
Same as Model 755, except has conventional sporter stock. Made 1965-70.

Harrington & Richardson Model 765 Pioneer Bolt-Action Single-Shot Rifle **$60**
Caliber: 22 LR, Long, Short. 24-inch bbl. Weight: about 5 lbs. Sights: open rear; hooded bead front. Plain pistol-grip stock. Made 1948-54.

Harrington & Richardson Model 800 Lynx Autoloading Rifle **$110**
Caliber: 22 LR. 5- or 10-shot clip magazine. 22-inch bbl. Open sights. Weight: 6 lbs. Plain pistol-grip stock. Made 1958-60.

Harrington & Richardson Model 852 Fieldsman Bolt-Action Repeater **$90**
Caliber: 22 LR, Long, Short. Tubular magazine holds 21 Short, 17 Long, 15 LR. 24-inch bbl. Weight: about 5.5 lbs. Sights: open rear; bead front. Plain pistol-grip stock. Made 1952-53.

Harrington & Richardson Model 865 Plainsman Bolt-Action Repeater **$85**
Caliber 22 LR, Long, Short. 5-shot detachable box magazine. 22- or 24-inch bbl. Weight: about 5.25 lbs. Sights: open rear, bead front. Plain pistol-grip stock. Made 1949-86.

H&R Model 865

H&R Model 866

H&R Model 1873

H&R Model 5200

H&R Ultra Varmint

Harrington & Richardson Model 866 Bolt-Action Repeater **$85**
Same as Model 865, except has Mannlicher-style stock. Made 1971.

Harrington & Richardson Model 1873 100th Anniversary (1871-1971) Commemorative Officer's Springfield Replica **$595**
Model 1873 "trap door" single-shot action. Engraved breech block, receiver, hammer, lock, band and buttplate. Caliber: 45-70. 26-inch bbl. Sights: peep rear; blade front. Checkered walnut stock w/anniversary plaque. Ramrod. Weight: about 8 lbs.10,000 made 1971. Value is for rifle in new, unfired condition.

Harrington & Richardson Model 5200 Sporter . . **$495**
Turn-bolt repeater. Caliber: 22 LR. 24-inch bbl. Classic-style American walnut stock. Adj. trigger. Sights: peep receiver; hooded ramp front. Weight: 6.5 lbs. Discontinued 1983.

Harrington & Richardson Model 5200 Match Rifle **$425**
Same action as 5200 Sporter. Caliber: 22 LR. 28-inch target weight bbl. Target stock of American walnut. Weight: 11 lbs. Made 1982-86.

Harrington & Richardson Custer Memorial Issue
Limited Edition Model 1873 Springfield Carbine replica, richly engraved and inlaid with gold, fancy walnut stock, in mahogany display case. Made 1973. Value is for carbine in new, unfired condition.
Officers' Model, limited to 25 pieces **$4500**
Enlisted Men's Model, limited to 243 pieces **2250**

Harrington & Richardson Targeteer Jr. Bolt-Action Rifle **$110**
Caliber: 22 LR 5-shot detachable box magazine. 20-inch bbl. Weight: about 7 lbs. Sights: Redfield 70 rear peep; Lyman 17A front. Target stock, junior size with pistol grip, swivels and sling. Made 1948-1951.

Harrington & Richardson Ultra Single-Shot Rifle
Side-lever single shot. Calibers: 22-250 Rem., 223 Rem., 25-06 Rem., 308 Win. 22- to 26-inch bbl. Weight: 7-8 lbs. Curly maple or laminated stock. Barrel-mounted scope mount, no sights. Made 1993 to date.
Ultra Hunter (25-06, 308) **$150**
Ultra Varmint **190**

NOTE
See also New England Firearms.

HARRIS GUNWORKS
Phoenix, Arizona
(Formerly McMillan Gun Works)

Harris Signature Alaskan Bolt-Action Rifle $2490
Same general specifications as Classic Sporter, except with match-grade bbl. Rings and mounts. Sights: single-leaf rear, barrel band front. Checkered Monte Carlo stock w/palmswell and solid recoil pad. Electroless nickel finish. Calibers: LA (long): 270 Win., 280 Rem., 30-06, MA (Magnum): 7mm Rem. Mag., 300 Win. Mag., 300 Wby. Mag., 340 Wby. Mag., 358 Win., 375 H&H Mag. Made 1995 to date.

Harris Signature Classic Sporter
The "prototype" for Harris's Signature Series, this bolt-action is available in three lengths: SA (standard/ short) — from 22-250 to 350 Rem Mag.; LA (long) — 25-06 to 30-06; MA (Magnum) — 7mm STW to 416 Rem. Mag. Four-shot or 3-shot (Magnum) magazine. Bbl. lengths: 22, 24 or 26 inches. Weight: 7 lbs. (short action). No sights; rings and bases provided. Harris fiberglass stock, Fibergrain or wood stock optional. Stainless, matte black or black chrome sulfide finish. Available in right- and left-hand models. Made 1987 to date. Has pre-64 Model 70-style action for dangerous game.
Classic Sporter Standard $1695
Classic Sporter Stainless 1750
Talon Sporter 1795

Harris Signature Mountain Rifle $1675
Same general specifications as Harris (McMillan) Classic Sporter, except w/titanium action and graphite-reinforced fiberglass stock. Weight: 5.5 lbs. Calibers: 270 Win., 280 Rem., 30-06, 7mm Mag., 300 Win. Mag. Other calibers on special order. Made 1995 to date.

Harris Signature Super Varminter $1495
Same general specifications as Harris (McMillan) Classic Sporter, except w/heavy, contoured bbl., adj. trigger, fiberglass stock and field bipod. Calibers: 223, 22-250, 220 Swift, 244 Win., 6mm Rem., 25-06, 7mm-08, 308 Win., 350 Win. Mag. Made 1995 to date.

Harris Talon Safari Rifle
Same general specifications as Harris (McMillan) Classic Sporter, except w/Harris Safari-grade action, match-grade bbl. and "Safari" fiberglass stock. Calibers: Magnum — 300 H&H Mag., 300 Win Mag., 300 Wby. Mag., 338 Win. Mag., 340 Wby. Mag., 375 H&H Mag., 404 Jeffrey, 416 Rem. Mag., 458 Win., Super Mag. — 300 Phoenix, 338 Lapua, 378 Wby. Mag., 416 Rigby, 416 Wby. Mag., 460 Wby. Mag. Matte black finish. Other calibers available on special order, and at a premium, but the "used gun" value remains the same. Made 1959 to date.
Safari Magnum $2590
Safari Super Magnum 2995

HECKLER & KOCH, GMBH
Oberndorf/Neckar, Germany

Heckler & Koch Model 911 Semiauto Rifle $1095
Caliber: 308 (7.62mm). 5-shot magazine. 19.7-inch bull bbl. 42.4 inches overall. Sights: hooded post front; adj. aperture rear. Weight: 11 lbs. Kevlar reinforced fiberglass thumbhole-stock.

Heckler & Koch Model HK91 A-2 Semiauto . . . $1995
Delayed roller-locked blow-back action. Caliber: 7.62mm×51 NATO (308 Win.). 5- or 20-round box magazine. 19-inch bbl. Weight: w/o magazine, 9.37 lbs. Sights: "V" and aperture rear, post front. Plastic buttstock and forearm. No longer imported.

Heckler & Koch Model HK91 A-3 . . . . $2350
Same as Model HK91 A-2, except has retractable metal buttstock, weighs 10.56 lbs. Currently manufactured.

Heckler & Koch Model HK91 A-2

Heckler & Koch Model HK93 Semiautomatic
Delayed roller-locked blow-back action. Caliber: 5.56mm × 45 (223 Rem.). 5- or 20-round magazine. 16.13-inch bbl. Weight: w/o magazine, 7.6 lbs. Sights: "V" and aperture rear; post front. Plastic buttstock and forearm. Currently manufactured.
HK93 A-2 . . . . **$1895**
HK93 A-3 with retractable stock 2450

Heckler & Koch Model HK94 Semiautomatic Carbine
Caliber: 9mm Para. 15-shot magazine. 16-inch bbl. Weight: 6.75 lbs. Aperture rear sight, front post. Plastic buttstock and forend or retractable metal stock. Made 1983 to date.
HK94-A2 w/Standard Stock **$2395**
HK94-A3 w/Retractable Stock 2695

Heckler & Koch Model HK300 Semiautomatic . . . $525
Caliber: 22 WMR. 5- or 15-round box magazine.19.7-inch bbl. w/polygonal rifling. Weight: about 5.75 lbs. Sights: V-notch rear; ramp front. High-luster polishing and bluing. European walnut stock w/cheekpiece, checkered forearm and pistol grip. No longer imported.

Heckler & Koch Model HK630 Semiautomatic . . $680
Caliber: 223 Rem. 4- or 10-round magazine. 24-inch bbl. Overall length: 42 inches. Weight: 7 lbs. Sights: open rear; ramp front. European walnut stock w/Monte Carlo cheek-piece. Made 1983-90.

Heckler & Koch Model HK770 Semiautomatic . . . $795
Caliber: 308 Win. 3- or 10-round magazine. Overall length: 44.5 inches. Weight: 8 lbs. Sights: open rear; ramp front. European walnut stock w/Monte Carlo cheekpiece. Made 1983-90.

Heckler & Koch Model HK940 Semiautomatic . . . $875
Caliber: 30-06 Springfield. 3- or 10-round magazine. Overall length: 47 inches. Weight: 8.8 lbs. Sights: open rear; ramp front. European walnut stock w/Monte Carlo cheekpiece. Made 1983-90.

Heckler & Koch Model HK PSG-1
Marksman's Rifle $8500
Caliber: 308 (7.62mm). 5- and 20-shot magazine. 25.6-inch bbl. 47.5 inches overall. Hensoldt 6×42 telescopic sight. Weight: 17.8 lbs. Matte black composition stock w/pistol grip. Made 1988 to date.

Heckler & Koch Model SR-9 Semiauto Rifle . . . $1750
Caliber: 308 (7.62mm). 5-shot magazine. 19.7-inch bull bbl. 42.4 inches overall. Hooded post front sight; adj. aperture rear. Weight: 11 lbs. Kevlar reinforced fiberglass thumbhole-stock w/wood grain finish. Made 1989-1993.

Heckler & Koch Model SR-9 Target Rifle $1895
Same general specifications as standard SR-9, except w/ PSG-1 trigger group and adj. buttstock. Made 1992-94.

RIFLES

Heckler & Koch Model HK91 A-3

Heckler & Koch Model HK93 A-2

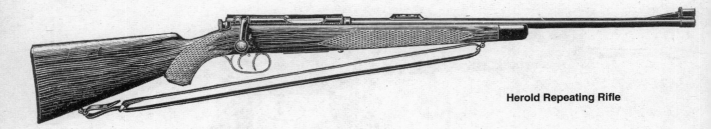

Herold Repeating Rifle

HERCULES RIFLES

See listings under "W" for Montgomery Ward.

HEROLD RIFLE
Suhl, Germany
Made by Franz Jaeger & Company

Herold Bolt-Action Repeating Sporting Rifle ... $890
"Herold-Repetierbüchse." Miniature Mauser-type action with unique 5-shot box magazine on hinged floorplate. Double-set triggers. Caliber: 22 Hornet. 24-inch bbl. Sights: leaf rear; ramp front. Weight: about 7.75 lbs. Fancy checkered stock. Made before WWII. *Note:* These rifles were imported by Charles Daly and A.F. Stoeger Inc. of New York City and sold under their own names.

HEYM AMERICA, INC.
Fort Wayne, Indiana

Currently imported by Heckler & Koch, Sterling, VA.

Heym Model 55B O/U Double Rifle
Kersten boxlock action with double cross bolt and cocking indicators. Calibers: 308 Win., 30-06, 375 H&H, 458 Win. Mag., 470 N.E. 25-inch bbl. 42 inches overall. Weight: 8.25 lbs. Sights: fixed V-type rear; front ramp with silver bead. Engraved receiver with optional sidelocks, interchangeable bbls. and claw mounts. Checkered European walnut stock. Imported from Germany.
Model 55 (boxlock) $8250
Model 55 (sidelock) 9550
Add for extra rifle bbls. 4500
Add for extra shotgun bbls. 2500

Heym Model 88B Double Rifle
Modified Anson & Deeley boxlock action with standing sears, double underlocking lugs and Greener extension w/crossbolt. Calibers: 8×57 JRS, 9.3×74R, 30-06, 375 H&H, 458 Win. Mag., 470 Nitro Express, 500 Nitro Express. Other calibers available on special order. Weight: 8 to 10 lbs. Top tang safety and cocking indicators. Double triggers with front set. Fixed or 3-leaf express rear sight, front ramp w/silver bead. Engraved receiver w/optional sidelocks. Checkered French walnut stock. Imported from Germany.
Model 88B Boxlock .... **from $ 8,775**
Model 88B/SS Sidelock .... **from 11,500**
Model 88B Safari (Magnum) 11,950

Heym Express Bolt-Action Rifle
Same general specifications as Model SR-20 Safari, except w/modified Magnum Mauser action. Checkered AAA-grade European walnut stock w/cheekpiece, solid rubber recoil pad, rosewood forend tip and grip cap. Calibers: 338 Lapua Magnum, 375 H&H, 378 Wby. Mag., 416 Rigby 450 Ackley, 460 Wby. Mag., 500 A-Square, 500 Nitro Express, 600 Nitro Express. Other calibers available on special order, but no change in "used gun value." Made 1989 to date.
Standard Express Magnum $4150
600 Nitro Express 7950
Add for Left-hand Models 600

Heym SR-20 Bolt-Action Rifle
Calibers: 243 Win., 270 Win., 308 Win., 30-06, 7mm Rem. Mag., 300 Win. Mag., 375 H&H. 5-shot (standard) or 3-shot (Magnum) magazine. Bbl. length: 20.5-inch (SR-20L); 24-inch (SR-20N); 26-inch (SR-20G). Weight: 7.75 lbs. Adj. rear sight, blade front. Checkered French walnut stock in Monte Carlo style (N&G Series) or full Mannlicher (L Series). Imported from Germany. Discontinued 1992.
SR-20L $1050
SR-20N 1195
SR-20G 1395

Heym Model SR-20 Standard

Heym SR-20L Mannlicher

RIFLES

Heym SR-20 Classic Bolt-Action Rifles

Same as SR-20, except w/22-250 and 338 Win. Mag., plus metric calibers on request. 24-inch (standard) or 25-inch (Magnum) bbl. Checkered French walnut stock. Left-hand models. Imported from Germany since 1985; Sporter version from 1989-93.

Classic (Standard) **$1395**
Classic (Magnum) 1525
Left-hand Models, **add** 300
Classic Sporter (Std. w/22-inch bbl.) 1595
Classic Sporter (Mag. w/24-inch bbl.) 1650

Heym SR-20 Alpine, Safari and Trophy Series

Same general specifications as Model SR-20 Classic Sporter, except **Alpine Series** has 20-inch bbl., Mannlicher stock, chambered in standard calibers only; **Safari Series** has 24-inch bbl., 3-leaf express sights and magnum action in calibers 375 H & H, 404 Jeffrey, 425 Express, 458 Win. Mag.; **Trophy Series** has Krupp-Special tapered octagon bbl. with quarter rib and open sights, standard and Magnum calibers. All imported from Germany 1989-93.

Alpine Series **$1450**
Safari Series 1525
Trophy Series (Standard Calibers) 1595
Trophy Series (Magnum Calibers) 1625

J.C. HIGGINS RIFLES

See Sears, Roebuck & Company.

HIGH STANDARD SPORTING FIREARMS
East Hartford, Connecticut
Formerly High Standard Mfg. Co., Hamden, CT

A long-standing producer of sporting arms, High Standard discontinued its operations in 1984.

High Standard Flite-King Pump Rifle **$115**
Hammerless slide action. Caliber: 22 LR, 22 Long, 22 Short. Tubular mag. holds 17 LR, 19 Long, or 24 Short. 24-inch bbl. Weight: 5.5 lbs. Sights: Patridge rear; bead front. Monte Carlo stock w/pistol grip, serrated semibeavertail forearm. Made 1962-75.

High Standard Hi-Power Deluxe Rifle **$295**
Mauser-type bolt action, sliding safety. Calibers: 270, 30-06. 4-shot magazine. 22-inch bbl. Weight: 7 lbs. Sights: folding open rear; ramp front. Walnut stock w/checkered pistol grip and forearm, Monte Carlo comb, QD swivels. Made 1962-66.

High Standard Hi-Power Field Bolt Action Rifle . . **$225**
Same as Hi-Power Deluxe, except has plain field style stock. Made 1962-66.

High Standard Sport-King Autoloading Carbine . . **$135**
Same as Sport-King Field Autoloader, except has 18.25-inch bbl., Western-style straight-grip stock w/bbl. band, sling and swivels. Made 1964-73.

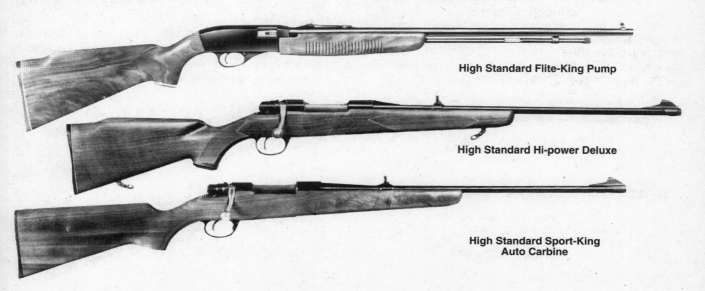

High Standard Flite-King Pump

High Standard Hi-power Deluxe

High Standard Sport-King Auto Carbine

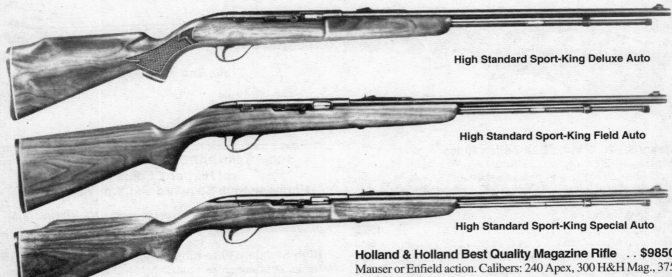

High Standard Sport-King Deluxe Auto

High Standard Sport-King Field Auto

High Standard Sport-King Special Auto

High Standard Sport-King Deluxe Autoloader . . $155
Same as Sport-King Special Autoloader, except has checkered stock. Made 1966-75.

High Standard Sport-King Field Autoloader $110
Calibers: 22 LR, 22 Long, 22 Short (high speed). Tubular magazine holds 15 LR, 17 Long, or 21 Short. 22.25-inch bbl. Weight: 5.5 lbs. Sights: open rear; beaded post front. Plain pistol-grip stock. Made 1960-66.

High Standard Sport-King Special Autoloader . . $125
Same as Sport-King Field, except stock has Monte Carlo comb and semibeavertail forearm. Made 1960-66.

HOLLAND & HOLLAND, LTD.
London, England

**Holland & Holland No. 2 Model Hammerless
Ejector Double Rifle** $12,500
Same general specifications as Royal Model, except plainer finish. Discontinued 1960.

Holland & Holland Best Quality Magazine Rifle . . $9850
Mauser or Enfield action. Calibers: 240 Apex, 300 H&H Mag., 375 H&H Magnum. 4-shot box magazine. 24-inch bbl. Weight: about 7.25 lbs., 240 Apex; 8.25 lbs., 300 Mag. and 375 Mag. Sights: folding leaf rear; hooded ramp front. Detachable French walnut stock w/cheekpiece, checkered pistol grip and forearm, swivels. Currently mfd. Specifications given apply to most models.

Holland & Holland Deluxe Magazine Rifle . . . $10,950
Same specifications as Best Quality, except has exhibition grade stock and special engraving. Currently mfd.

Holland & Holland Royal Deluxe Double Rifle . . . $45,500
Formerly designated "Modele Deluxe." Same specifications as Royal Model, except has exhibition grade stock and special engraving. Currently mfd.

**Holland & Holland Royal Hammerless
Ejector Rifle** $30,000
Sidelock. Calibers: 240 Apex, 7mm H&H Mag., 300 H&H Mag., 300 Win. Mag., 30-06, 375 H&H Mag., 458 Win. Mag., 465 H&H Mag. 24- to 28-inch bbls. Weight: from 7.5 lbs. Sights: folding leaf rear, ramp front. Cheekpiece stock of select French walnut, checkered pistol grip and forearm. Currently mfd. Same general specifications apply to prewar model.

H&H Best Quality Magazine Rifle

H&H Royal Double Rifle

Howa Model 1500 Hunter

Howa Lightning Rifle

HOWA MACHINERY LTD.
Shinkawa-Chonear, Nagoya 452, Japan

Currently imported by Interarms, Alexandria, VA

See also Mossberg (1500) Smith & Wesson (1500 & 1700) and Weatherby (Vanguard).

Howa Model 1500 Hunter
Similar to the Trophy Model, except w/standard walnut stock. No Monte Carlo cheekpiece or grip cap. Imported 1988-89.
Standard Calibers **$300**
Magnum Calibers 325

Howa Model 1500 Lightning Bolt-Action Rifle
Similar to the Hunter Model; except fitted with black Bell & Carlson Carbelite stock with checkered grip and forend. Weight: 7.5 lbs. Imported 1988-89.
Standard Calibers **$330**
Magnum Calibers 355

Howa Model 1500 Realtree Camo Rifle **$375**
Similar to the Trophy Model, except fitted with Camo Bell & Carlson Carbelite stock with checkered grip and forend. Weight: 8 lbs. Stock, action and barrel finished in Realtree camo. Available in standard calibers only. Imported 1993 to date.

Howa Model 1500 Trophy/Varmint Bolt-Action Rifle
Calibers: 22-250, 223, 243 Win., 270 Win., 308 Win., 30-06, 7mm Mag., 300 Win. Mag., 338 Win. Mag. 22-inch bbl. (standard); 24-inch bbl. (Magnum). 42.5 inches overall (standard). Weight: 7.5 lbs. Adj. rear sight hooded ramp front. Checkered walnut stock w/Monte Carlo cheekpiece. Varmint Model has 24-inch heavy bbl., weight of 9.5 lbs. in calibers 22-250, 223 and 308 only. Imported 1979-93.
Trophy Standard **$340**
Trophy Magnum 365
Varmint (Parkerized Finish) 425

Howa Model Lightning Bolt-Action Rifle
Calibers: 22-250, 223, 243, 270, 7mm Rem. Mag., 30-06, 308, 300 Win. Mag., 338 Win. Mag. 3-shot magazine (Mag.). Bbl. length: 22-inch (Std.); 24-inch (Mag.). 42- to 44-inches overall.

Howa Lightning Rifle *(Cont.)*
Weight: 7.5-7.75 lbs. Receiver drilled and tapped for scope mount, no sights. Checkered synthetic polymer stock. Imported 1993 to date.
Standard Calibers **$300**
Magnum Calibers 325
Woodgrain Stock, **add** 35

HUNGARIAN MILITARY RIFLES
Budapest, Hungary
Manufactured at Government Arsenal

Hungarian Model 1935M Mannlicher
Military Rifle **$200**
Caliber: 8×52mm Hungarian. Bolt action, straight handle. 5-shot projecting box magazine. 24-inch bbl. Weight: about 9 lbs. Adj. leaf rear sight, hooded front blade. Two-piece military-type stock. Made 1935-40.

Hungarian Model 1943M (German Gew. 98/40)
Mannlicher Military Rifle **$250**
Modification, during German occupation, of the Model 1935M. Caliber: 7.9mm Mauser. Turned-down bolt handle and Mauser M/98-type box magazine; other differences are minor. Made 1940 to end of war in Europe.

HUSQVARNA VAPENFABRIK A.B.
Huskvarna, Sweden

Husqvarna Model 456 Lightweight
Full-Stock Sporter **$415**
Same as Series 4000/4100 except has sporting-style full stock with slope-away cheekrest. Weight: 6.5 lbs. Made 1959-70.

Husqvarna Series 1000 Super Grade **$425**
Same as 1951 Hi-Power, except has European walnut sporter stock w/Monte Carlo comb and cheekpiece. Made 1952-56.

Husqvarna Series 1100 Deluxe Model Hi-Power
Bolt-Action Sporting Rifle **$435**
Same as 1951 Hi-Power, except has "jeweled" bolt, European walnut stock. Made 1952-56. *See* photo next page.

RIFLES

Husqvarna 1100 Lightweight

Husqvarna 1951 Hi-Power

Husqvarna 3000 Crown Grade

Husqvarna 4100 Lightweight

Husqvarna 6000 Imperial Custom

Husqvarna 1950 Hi-Power Sporting Rifle. **$275**
Mauser-type bolt action. Calibers: 220 Swift, 270 Win. 30-06
(*see* note below), 5-shot box magazine. 23.75-inch bbl. Weight:
about 7.75 lbs. Sights: open rear; hooded ramp front. Sporting
stock of Arctic beech, checkered pistol grip and forearm, swivels. *Note:* Husqvarna sporters were first introduced in the U.S.
about 1948; earlier models were also available in calibers
6.5×55, 8×57 and 9.3×57. Made 1946-1951.

Husqvarna 1951 Hi-Power Rifle **$365**
Same as 1950 Hi-Power, except has high-comb stock, low
safety.

Husqvarna Series 3000 Crown Grade **$430**
Same as Series 3100, except has Monte Carlo comb stock.

Husqvarna Series 3100 Crown Grade **$450**
HVA improved Mauser action. Calibers: 243, 270, 7mm, 30-06,
308 Win. 5-shot box magazine. 23.75-inch bbl. Weight: 7.75 lbs.
Sights: open rear; hooded ramp front. European walnut stock,

Husqvarna Series 3100 Crown Grade *(Cont.)*

checkered, cheekpiece, pistol-grip cap, black foretip, swivels.
Made 1954-72.

Husqvarna Series 4000 Lightweight Rifle **$450**
Same as Series 4100, except has no rear sight and has Monte
Carlo comb stock.

Husqvarna Series 4100 Lightweight Rifle **$425**
HVA improved Mauser action. Calibers: 243, 270, 7mm, 30-06,
308 Win. 5-shot box magazine. 20.5-inch bbl. Weight: about
6.25 lbs. Sights: open rear; hooded ramp front. Lightweight walnut stock w/cheekpiece, pistol grip, schnabel foretip, checkered,
swivels. Made 1954-72.

Husqvarna Series 6000 Imperial Custom Grade . . **$595**
Same as Series 3100, except fancy-grade stock, 3-leaf folding
rear sight, adj. trigger. Calibers: 243, 270, 7mm Rem. Mag. 308,
30-06. Made 1968-70.

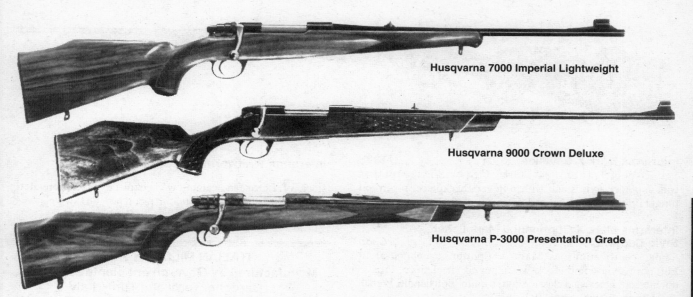

Husqvarna 7000 Imperial Lightweight

Husqvarna 9000 Crown Deluxe

Husqvarna P-3000 Presentation Grade

Husqvarna Series 7000 Imperial Monte Carlo Lightweight **$550**
Same as Series 4000 Lightweight, except fancy-grade stock, 3-leaf folding rear sight, adj. trigger. Calibers: 243, 270, 308, 30-06. Made 1968-70.

Husqvarna Model 8000 Imperial Grade Rifle . . . **$550**
Same as Model 9000, except has jeweled bolt, engraved floor-plate, deluxe French walnut checkered stock, no sights. Made 1971-72.

Husqvarna Model 9000 Crown Grade Rifle **$425**
New design Husqvarna bolt action. Adj. trigger. Calibers: 270, 7mm Rem. Mag., 30-06, 300 Win. Mag. 5-shot box magazine, hinged floorplate. 23.75-inch bbl. Sights: folding leaf rear; hooded ramp front. Checkered walnut stock w/Monte Carlo cheekpiece, rosewood forearm tip and pistol-grip cap. Weight: 7 lbs. 3 oz. Made 1971-72.

Husqvarna Series P-3000 Presentation Rifle . . . **$695**
Same as Crown Grade Series 3000, except w/selected stock, engraved action, adj. trigger. Calibers: 243, 270, 7mm Rem. Mag., 30-06. Made 1968-70.

INTERARMS RIFLES
Alexandria, Virginia

The following Mark X rifles are manufactured by Zavodi Crvena Zastava, Belgrade, Yugoslavia.

Interarms Mark X Alaskan **$430**
Same specifications as Mark X Sporter, except calibers 375 H&H Mag. and 458 Win. Mag., 3-round magazine, weighs 8.25 lbs., has stock with recoil-absorbing cross bolt and heavy duty recoil pad. Made 1976-84.

Interarms Mark X Bolt-Action Sporter Series
Mauser-type action. Calibers: 22-250, 243, 25-06, 270, 7×57, 7mm Rem. Mag., 308, 30-06, 300 Win. Mag. 5-shot magazine (3-shot in Magnum calibers). 24-inch bbl. Weight: 7.5 lbs. Sights: adj. leaf rear; ramp front, with hood. Classic-style stock of European walnut w/Monte Carlo comb and cheekpiece, checkered pistol grip and forearm, black forend tip, QD swivels. Made 1972 to date.
American Field Model, Std. (Rubber Recoil Pad) **$465**
American Field, Magnum (Rubber Recoil Pad) **495**
Mark X Standard Model **295**

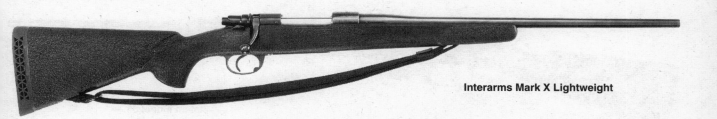

Interarms Mark X Lightweight

Interarms Mini-Mark X

Interarms Mark X Cavalier $325
Same specifications as Mark X Sporter, except has
contemporary-style stock with rollover cheekpiece, rosewood
forend tip/grip cap, recoil pad. Introduced 1974; disc.

**Interarms Mark X Continental Mannlicher
Style Carbine** $385
Same specifications as Mark X Sporter, except straight
European-style comb stock w/sculptured cheekpiece. Precise
double-set triggers and classic "butter-knife" bolt handle. French
checkering. Weight: about 7.25 lbs.

Interarms Mark X Lightweight Sporter $350
Calibers: 270, 7mm Rem. Mag., 30-06, 5-round magazine. 20-
inch bbl. Weight: 7 lbs. Importation began in 1988.

**Interarms Mark X Marquis Mannlicher
Style Carbine** $395
Same specifications as Mark X Sporter, except has 20-inch bbl.,
full-length Mannlicher-type stock with metal forend/muzzle
cap. Calibers: 270, 7X57, 308, 30-06. Made 1976 to date.

Interarms Mini-Mark X Bolt-Action Rifle $325
Miniature M98 Mauser action. Caliber: 223 Rem. 5-shot magazine. 20-inch bbl. 39.75 inches overall. Weight: 6.25 lbs. Adj.
rear sight, hooded ramp front. Checkered hardwood stock. Imported 1987 to date.

Interarms Mark X Viscount $335
Same specifications as Mark X Sporter, except has plainer field
grade stock. Made 1974-87.

**Interarms Whitworth Express Rifle,
African Series** $495
Mauser-type bolt action. Calibers: 375 H&H Mag., 458 Win.
Mag. 3-shot magazine. 24-inch bbl. Weight: about 8 lbs. Sights:
3-leaf express open rear, ramp front with hood. English-style

Interarms Whitworth Express Rifle *(Cont.)*

stock of European walnut, w/cheekpiece, black forend tip,
checkered pistol grip and forearm, recoil pad, QD swivels. Made
1974 to date by Whitworth Rifle Co., England.

ITALIAN MILITARY RIFLES
Manufactured by Government plants at Brescia,
Gardone, Terni and Turin, Italy

Italian Model 38 Military Rifle $95
Modification of Italian Model 1891 Mannlicher-Carcano Military Rifle w/turned-down bolt handle, detachable folding bayonet. Caliber: 7.35mm Italian Service (many arms of this model
were later converted to the old 6.5mm caliber). 6-shot box magazine. 21.25-inch bbl. Weight: about 7.5 pounds. Sights: adj. rear-
blade front. Military straight-grip stock. Adopted 1938.

ITHACA GUN COMPANY, INC.
King Ferry (formerly Ithaca), New York

**Ithaca Model 49 Saddlegun Lever-Action
Single-Shot Rifle** $80
Martini-type action. Hand-operated rebounding hammer. Caliber: 22 LR, Long, Short. 18-inch barrel. Open sights. Western
carbine-style stock. Weight: 5.5 pounds. Made 1961-78.

Ithaca Model 49 Saddlegun — Deluxe $95
Same as standard Model 49, except has gold-plated hammer and
trigger, figured walnut stock, sling swivels. Made 1962-75.

Ithaca Model 49 Saddlegun — Magnum $100
Same as standard Model 49, except chambered for 22 WMR cartridge. Made 1962-78.

Italian Model 38

RIFLES

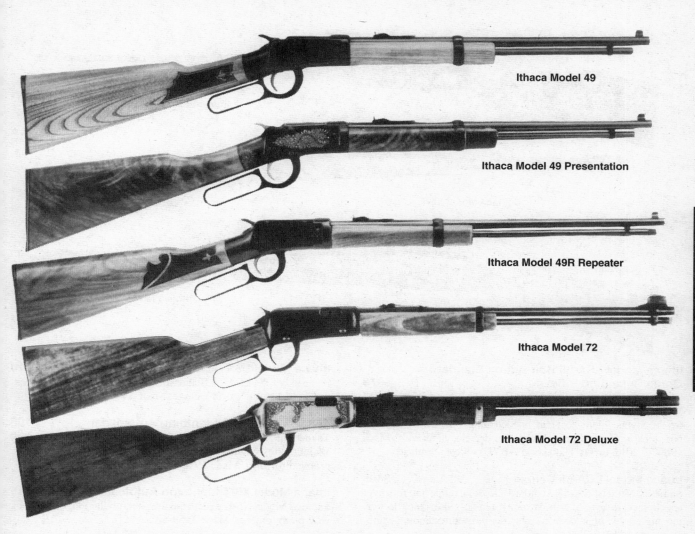

Ithaca Model 49

Ithaca Model 49 Presentation

Ithaca Model 49R Repeater

Ithaca Model 72

Ithaca Model 72 Deluxe

Ithaca Model 49 Saddlegun — Presentation **$160**
Same as standard Model 49 Saddlegun, except has gold-plated hammer and trigger, engraved receiver, full fancy-figured walnut stock w/gold nameplate. Available in 22 LR or 22 WMR. Made 1962-74.

Ithaca Model 49 Saddlegun — St. Louis Bicentennial **$180**
Same as Model 49 Deluxe, except has commemorative inscription. 200 made in 1964. Value is for rifle in new, unfired condition.

Ithaca Model 49 Youth Saddlegun **$85**
Same as standard Model 49, except shorter stock for young shooters. Made 1961-78.

Ithaca Model 49R Saddlegun Repeating Rifle . . **$140**
Similar in appearance to Model 49 Single Shot. Caliber: 22 LR, Long, Short. Tubular magazine holds 15 LR, 17 Long, 21 Short. 20-inch bbl. Weight: 5.5 lbs. Sights: open rear-bead front. Western-style stock, checkered grip. Made 1968-71.

Ithaca Model 72 Saddlegun Lever-Action Repeating Carbine **$195**
Caliber: 22 LR, Long, Short. Tubular magazine holds 15 LR, 17 Long, 21 Short. 18.5-inch bbl. Weight: about 5.5 lbs. Sights: open rear; hooded ramp front. Receiver grooved for scope mounting. Western carbine stock and forearm of American walnut. Made 1973-78.

Ithaca Model 72 Saddlegun — Deluxe **$215**
Same as standard Model 72, except has silver-finished and engraved receiver, octagon bbl., higher grade walnut stock and forearm. Made 1974-76.

Ithaca Model 72 Saddlegun — Magnum **$175**
Same as standard Model 72, except chambered for 22 WMR, has 11-shot tubular magazine, 18.5-inch bbl. Made 1975-78.

NOTE

Barrel and action for the Model 72s are manufactured by Erma-Werke, Dachau, W. Germany; wood installed by Ithaca.

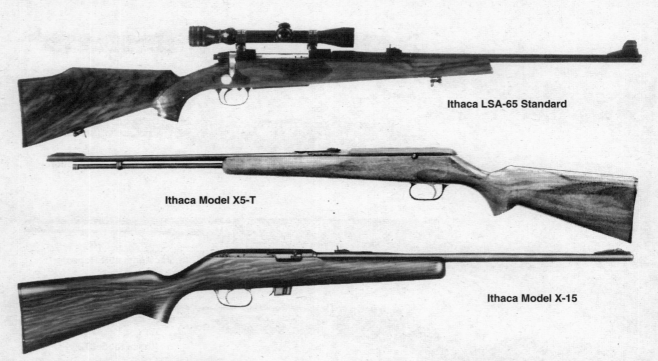

Ithaca LSA-65 Standard

Ithaca Model X5-T

Ithaca Model X-15

Ithaca Model LSA-55 Bolt-Action Standard Grade Repeating Rifle $375

Mauser-type action. Calibers: 222 Rem., 22-250, 6mm Rem. 243 Win., 308 Win. 3-shot detachable magazine. 22-inch bbl. Weight: 6.5 lbs. Sights: folding leaf rear; hooded ramp front. Checkered walnut stock w/Monte Carlo cheekpiece, detachable swivels. Made 1969-77. Mfd. by Oy Tikkakoski AB, Tikkakoski, Finland.

Ithaca Model LSA-55 Deluxe $405

Same as Model LSA-55 Standard Grade, except has roll-over cheekpiece, rosewood grip-cap and forend tip, skip-line checkering, high-luster blue, no iron sights, scope mount standard equipment. Made 1969-77.

Ithaca Model LSA-55 Heavy Barrel $400

Same as Model LSA-55, except calibers 222 Rem. and 22-250 only; has 23-inch heavy bbl., no sights, special stock with beavertail forearm, weighs about 8.5 lbs. Made 1974-77

Ithaca Model LSA-65 Bolt-Action Standard Grade $370

Same as Model LSA-55 Standard Grade, except calibers 25-06, 270, 30-06; 4-shot magazine, 23-inch bbl., weighs 7 lbs. Made 1969-77.

Ithaca Model LSA-65 Deluxe $410

Same as Model LSA-65 Standard Grade, except has special features of Model LSA-55 Deluxe. Made 1969-77.

Ithaca Model X5-C Lightning Autoloader $105

Takedown. Caliber: 22 LR. 7-shot clip magazine. 22-inch bbl. Weight: 6 lbs. Sights: open rear; Raybar front. Pistol-grip stock, grooved forearm. Made 1958-64.

Ithaca Model X5-T Lightning Autoloader $115

Same as Model X5-C except has 16-shot tubular magazine stock with plain forearm. Made 1959-63.

Ithaca Model X-15 Lightning Autoloader $110

Same general specifications as Model X5-C, except forend is not grooved. Made 1964-67.

Ithaca-BSA CF-2 Bolt-Action Repeating Rifle . . $325

Mauser-type action. Calibers: 7mm Rem. Mag., 300 Win. Mag. 3-shot magazine. 23.6-inch bbl. Weight: 8 lbs. Sights: adj. rear; hooded ramp front. Checkered walnut stock w/Monte Carlo comb, rollover cheekpiece, rosewood forend tip, recoil pad, sling swivels. Made 1976-77. Mfd. by BSA Guns Ltd., Birmingham, England.

Ithaca-BSA CF-2

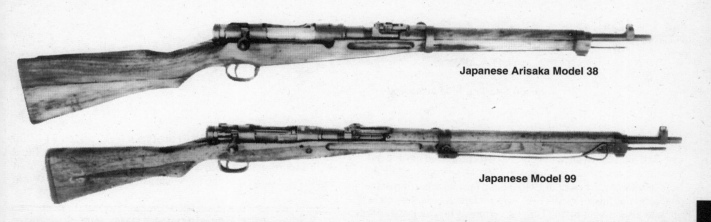

Japanese Arisaka Model 38

Japanese Model 99

JAPANESE MILITARY RIFLES
Tokyo, Japan
Manufactured by Government Plant

Japanese Model 38 Arisaka Carbine $130
Same general specifications as Model 38 Rifle, except has 19-inch bbl., heavy folding bayonet, weighs about 7.25 lbs.

Japanese Model 38 Arisaka Service Rifle $135
Mauser-type bolt action. Caliber: 6.5mm Japanese. 5-shot box magazine. Bbl. lengths: 25.38 and 31.25 inches. Weight: about 9.25 lbs w/long bbl. Sights: fixed front, adj. rear. Military-type full stock. Adopted in 1905, the 38th year of the Meiji reign; hence, the designation "Model 38."

Japanese Model 44 Cavalry Carbine $195
Same general specifications as Model 38 Rifle except has 19-inch bbl., heavy folding bayonet, weighs about 8.5 lbs. Adopted in 1911, the 44th year of the Meiji reign; hence, the designation "Model 44."

Japanese Model 99 Service Rifle $165
Modified Model 38. Caliber: 7.7mm Japanese. 5-shot box magazine. 25.75-inch bbl. Weight: about 8.75 lbs. Sights: fixed front; adj. aperture rear; anti-aircraft sighting bars on some early models; fixed rear sight on some late WWII rifles. Military-type full stock, may have bipod. Takedown paratroop model was also made during WWII. Adopted in 1939 Japanese year 2599 from which the designation "Model 99" is taken. *Note:* The last Model 99 rifles made were of poor quality; some have cast steel receivers. Value shown is for earlier type.

JARRETT CUSTOM RIFLES
Jackson, South Carolina

Jarrett Model No. 2 Bolt-Action Rifle $2140
Calibers: available in any short-action calibers. Bbl. lengths to customer's specifications. Remington Model 7 action and Jarret barrel are pillar-bedded into a McMillan Model 7-style stock.

Jarrett Model No. 3 Bolt-Action Rifle $2150
Same general specifications as the Model No. 2 except furnished with a fiberglass stock.

Jarrett Model No. 4 Bolt-Action Rifle $4500
Calibers: Any magnum caliber. Bbl. length to customer's specifications. Based on a Winchester Model 70 round-feed receiver. Sights include a quarter rib and iron sights along with two Leupold scops with quick-detachable scope rings. The action and receiver are pillar-bedded into a McMillan fiberglass stock.

Jarrett Cowden Bolt-Action Rifle $1200
Calibers: Any standard caliber. Similar to the Model No. 2 except each action is embedded into a camo McMillan stock using poured pillars.

JOHNSON AUTOMATICS, INC.
Providence, Rhode Island

Johnson Model 1941 Semiauto Military Rifle . . $1295
Short-recoil-operated. Removable, air-cooled, 22-inch bbl. Caliber: 30-06, 7mm Mauser. 10-shot rotary magazine. Two-piece, wood stock, pistol grip, perforated metal radiator sleeve over

Johnson Model 1941

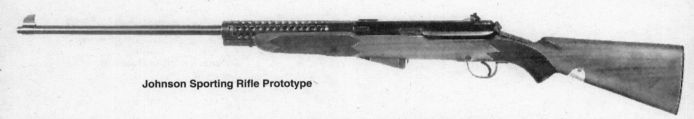

Johnson Sporting Rifle Prototype

Johnson Model 1941 Semiauto Military Rifle *(Cont.)*

rear half of bbl. Sights: receiver peep; protected post front. Weight: 9.5 lbs. *Note:* The Johnson M/1941 was adopted by the Netherlands Government in 1940-41 and the major portion of the production of this rifle, 1941-43, was on Dutch orders. A quantity was also bought by the U.S. Government for use by Marine Corps parachute troops (1943) and for Lend Lease. All these rifles were caliber 30-06; the 7mm Johnson rifles were made for the South American government.

Johnson Sporting Rifle Prototype $11,000

Same general specifications as the military rifle except fitted with a sporting stock with checkered grip and forend. Blade front sight; receiver peep sight. Less than a dozen made prior to World War II.

IVER JOHNSON'S ARMS, INC.
Jacksonville, Arkansas
Formerly of Fitchburg, Massachusetts, and Middlesex, New Jersey

Iver Johnson Li'l Champ

Iver Johnson Model 5100A1 Bolt-Action Rifle . . $3850

Single-shot long-range rifle with removable bolt for breech loading. Caliber: 50BMG. Flutted 29-inch bbl. with muzzle break. 51.5 inches overall. Adj. composition stock w/folding bipod. Scope rings; no sights.

Iver Johnson Li'l Champ Bolt-Action Rifle $75

Caliber: 22 S, L, LR. Single shot. 16.25-inch bbl. 32.5 inches overall. Weight: 3.25 lbs. Adj. rear sight, blade front. Synthetic composition stock. Made 1986-88.

Iver Johnson Model SC30FS Semiautomatic
Carbine $295

Similar to Survival Carbine except has folding stock. Made 1983 to date.

Iver Johnson Model M-1 Semiautomatic Carbine

Similar to U.S. M-1 Carbine. Calibers: 9mm Parabellum 30 U.S. Carbine. 15- or 30-shot magazine. 18-inch bbl. 35.5 inches overall. Weight: 6.5 lbs. Sights: blade front, with guards; adj. peep rear. Walnut, hardwood or collapsible wire stock. Parkerized finish.

Model M-1 (30 cal. w/hardwood)	**$265**
Model M-1 (30 cal. w/walnut)	290
Model M-1 (30 cal. w/wire)	350
Model M-1 (9mm w/hardwood)	345
Model M-1 (9mm w/walnut)	365
Model M-1 (9mm w/wire)	395
Model M-1 Spitfire - 5.7mm Johnson)	325

Iver Johnson Model PM.30 Semiautomatic
Carbine $275

Similar to U.S. Carbine, Cal. .30 M1. 18-inch bbl. Weight: about 5.5 lbs. 15- or 30-round detachable magazine. Both hardwood and walnut stock.

Iver Johnson M1 Carbine

Iver Johnson Model SC30FS

Iver Johnson Survival Carbine

Iver Johnson Trailblazer

Iver Johnson Model 2X

RIFLES

Iver Johnson Survival Semiautomatic Carbine . . **$325**
Similar to Model PM.30 except in stainless steel w/high-impact plastic, one-piece stock. Made 1983 to date. W/folding high-impact plastic stock **add $35**.

Iver Johnson Trailblazer Semiauto Rifle **$135**
Caliber: 22 LR.18-inch bbl. Weight: 5.5 lbs. Sights: open rear: blade front. Hardwood stock. Made 1983-85.

Iver Johnson Model X Bolt-Action Rifle **$110**
Takedown. Single shot. Caliber: 22 Short, Long and LR. 22-inch bbl. Weight: about 4 lbs. Sights: open rear; blade front. Pistol-grip stock w/knob forend tip. Made 1928-32.

Iver Johnson Model XX (2X) Bolt-Action Rifle . . **$115**
Improved version of the Model X, has heavier 24-inch bbl. larger stock (w/o knob tip), weighs about 4.5 lbs. Made 1932-55.

KDF Model K15

K.D.F. INC.
Sequin, Texas

KDF Model K15 Bolt-Action Rifle
Calibers: (Standard) 22-250, 243 Win., 6mm Rem., 25-06, 270 Win., 280 Rem., 7mm Mag., 30-06; (Magnum) 300 Wby., 300 Win., 338 Win., 340 Wby., 375 H&H, 411 KDF, 416 Rem., 458

KDF Model K15 Bolt Action Rifle *(Cont.)*
Win. 4-shot magazine (standard), 3-shot (magnum). 22-inch (standard) or 24-inch (magnum) bbl. 44.5 to 46.5 inches overall. Weight: 8 lbs. Sights optional. Kevlar composite or checkered walnut stock in classic, European or thumbhole-style.
Standard Model **$1150**
Magnum Model **1350**

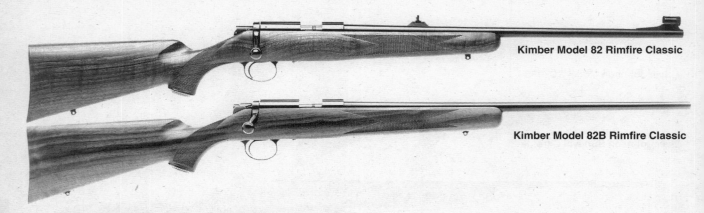

Kimber Model 82 Rimfire Classic

Kimber Model 82B Rimfire Classic

KIMBER OF AMERICA, INC.
Clackamas, Oregon
(Formerly Kimber of Oregon, Inc., Colton, OR)

Kimber Model 82 Bolt-Action Rifle

Small action based on the Kimber "A" Model 82 rimfire receiver with twin rear locking lugs. Calibers: 22 LR, 22 WRF, 22 Hornet, 218 Bee, 25-20. 5- or 10-shot magazine (22 LR); 5-shot magazine (22WRF); 3-shot magazine (22 Hornet). 218 Bee and 25-20 are single shot. 18- to 25-inch bbl. 37.63 to 42.5 inches overall. Weight: 6 lbs. (Light Sporter), 6.5 lbs. (Sporter), 7.5 lbs. (Varmint); 10.75 lbs. (Target). Right- and left-hand actions are available in distinctive stock styles.

Cascade (discontinued 1987) . . . . $ 650
Classic (discontinued 1988)   625
Continental   995
Custom Classic (discontinued 1988)   695
Mini Classic   475
Super America   875
Super Continental   1100
1990 Classifications
All-American Match   595
Deluxe Grade (discontinued 1990)   895
Hunter (Laminated Stock)   575
Super America   795
Target (Government Match)   495

Kimber Model 82C Classic Bolt-Action Rifle

Caliber: 22 LR. 4-shot or 10-shot magazine. 21-inch air-gauged bbl. 40.5 inches overall. Weight: 6.5 lbs. Receiver drilled and tapped for Warne scope mounts; no sights. Single-set trigger. Checkered Claro walnut stock w/red buttpad and polished steel grip cap. Reintroduced 1993.

Classic Model $575
Left-Hand Model, **add**   75

Kimber Model 84 Bolt-Action Rifle

Compact medium action based on a "scaled down" Mauser-type receiver, designed to accept small base centerfire cartridges. Calibers: 17 Rem., 221 Fireball, 222 Rem., 223 Rem. 5-shot magazine. Same general barrel and stock specifications as Model 82.

Classic (discontinued 1988) . . . . $ 650
Continental   895
Custom Classic (discontinued 1988)   50
Super America (discontinued 1988)   975
Super Continental (discontinued 1988)   1125
1990 Classifications
Deluxe Grade (discontinued 1990)   895
Hunter/Sporter (Laminated Stock)   725
Super America (discontinued 1991)   995
Super Varmint (discontinued 1991)   1025
Ultra Varmint (discontinued 1991)   950

Kimber Model 89 Big-Game Rifle

A large action combining the best features of the pre-64 Model 70 Winchester and the Mauser 98. Three action lengths are offered in three stock styles. Calibers: 257 Roberts, 25-06, 7×57, 270 Win., 280 Win., 30-06, 7mm Rem. Mag., 300 Win. Mag., 300 H&H, 338 Win., 35 Whelen, 375 H&H, 404 Jeffrey, 416 Rigby, 460 Wby., 505 Gibbs (308 cartridge family to follow). 5-shot magazine (standard calibers); 3-shot magazine (Magnum calibers). 22- to 24-inch bbl. 42 to 44 inches overall. Weight: 7.5 to 10.5 lbs. Model 89 African features express sights on contoured quarter rib, banded front sight. Barrel-mounted recoil lug w/integral receiver lug and twin recoil crosspins in stock.

BGR Long Action Classic (disc. 1988) . . . . $ 695
Custom Classic (discontinued 1988)   895
Super America   1095
1990 Classifications
Deluxe Grade
  Featherweight   1295
  Medium   1325

Kimber Model 84 Classic

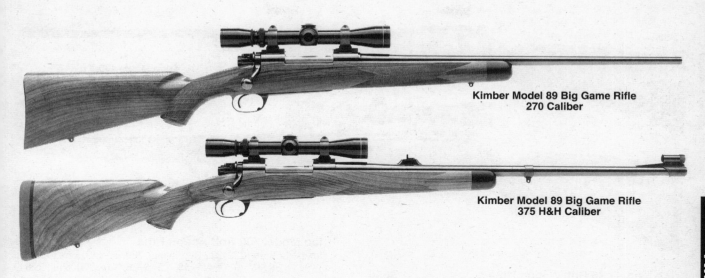

**Kimber Model 89 Big Game Rifle
270 Caliber**

**Kimber Model 89 Big Game Rifle
375 H&H Caliber**

Kimber Model 89 Big Game Rifle *(Cont.)*

375 H&H	**$1395**
Hunter Grade (Laminated Stock)	
270 and 30-06	925
375 H&H	1150
Super America	
Featherweight	1495
Medium	1570
375 H&H	2000
African — All calibers	3595

KRICO RIFLES
Stuttgart-Hedelfingen, Germany
Mfd. by Sportwaffenfabrik Kriegeskorte GmbH

Krico rifles currently imported are available thru Beeman Precision Arms, Inc., Santa Rosa, CA.

Krico Model 260 Semiautomatic Rifle **$475**
Caliber: 22 LR. 10-shot magazine. 20-inch bbl. 38.9 inches overall. Weight: 6.6 lbs. Hooded blade front sight; adj. rear. Grooved receiver. Beech stock. Blued finish. Imported 1991 to date.

Krico Model 300 Bolt-Action Rifle
Calibers: 22 LR, 22 WMR, 22 Hornet. 19.6-inch bbl. (22 LR), 23.6-inch (22 Hornet). 38.5 inches overall. Weight: 6.3 lbs. Double-set triggers. Sights: ramped blade front, adj. open rear. Checkered walnut-finished hardwood stock. Blued finish. Made 1993 to date.

Model 300 Standard	**$525**
Model 300 Deluxe	560
Model 300 SA (Monte-Carlo walnut stock)	565
Model 300 Stutzen (full-length walnut stock)	620

Krico Model 311 Small-Bore Rifle
Bolt action. Caliber: 22 LR. 5- or 10-shot clip magazine. 22-inch bbl. Weight: about 6 lbs. Single- or double-set trigger. Sights: open rear; hooded ramp front; available with factory-fitted Kaps 2.5× scope. Checkered stock w/cheekpiece, pistol grip and swivels.

W/Scope Sight	**$325**
W/Iron Sights Only	295

Krico Model 320 Bolt-Action Sporter **$550**
Caliber: 22 LR. 5-shot detachable box magazine. 19.5-inch bbl. 38.5 inches overall. Weight: 6 lbs. Adj. rear sight, blade ramp front. Checkered European walnut Mannlicher-style stock w/low comb and cheekpiece. Single or double-set triggers. Discontinued 1989.

Krico Model 340 Metallic Silhouette
Bolt-Action Rifle **$595**
Caliber: 22 LR. 5-shot magazine. 21-inch heavy, bull bbl. 39.5 inches overall. Weight: 7.5 lbs. No sights. Grooved receiver for scope mounts. European walnut stock in off-hand match-style configuration. Match or double-set triggers. Imported 1983-86.

Krico Model 360S Biathlon Rifle **$1025**
Caliber: 22 LR. Five 5-shot magazines. 21.25-inch bbl. with snow cap. 40.5 inches overall. Weight: 9.25 lbs. Straight-pull action. Match trigger with 17½-oz. pull. Sights: globe front, adj. match peep rear. Biathlon-style walnut stock with high comb and adj. butt-plate. Made 1991 to date.

Krico Model 360 S2 Biathlon Rifle **$950**
Similar to the Model 360S, except with pistol-grip activated action. Biathlon-style walnut stock with black epoxy finish. Made 1991 to date.

Krico Model 400 Bolt-Action Rifle **$695**
Caliber: 22 Hornet. 5-shot detachable box magazine. 23.5-inch bbl. Weight: 6.75 lbs. Adj. open rear sight, ramp front. European walnut stock. Discontinued 1990. *See photo next page.*

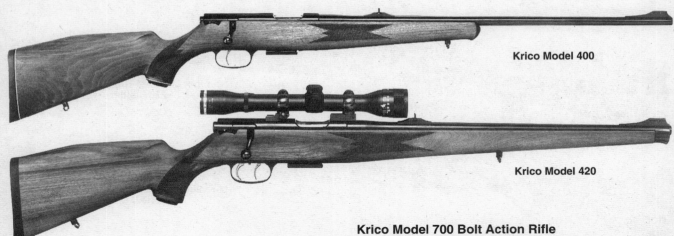

Krico Model 400

Krico Model 420

Krico Model 420 Bolt-Action Rifle $650
Same as Model 400, except has full-length Mannlicher-style stock and double-set triggers. Scope optional, extra. Discontinued 1989. *See* photo above.

Krico Model 440 S Bolt-Action Rifle $650
Caliber: 22 Hornet. Detachable box magazine. 20-inch bbl. 36.5 inches overall. Weight: 7.5 lbs. No sights. French walnut stock w/ventilated forend. Discont. 1988.

Krico Model 500 Match Rifle $3000
Caliber: 22 LR. Single shot. 23.6-inch bbl. 42 inches overall. Weight: 9.4 lbs. Kricotronic electronic ignition system. Sights: globe front; match micrometer aperture rear. Match-style European walnut stock w/adj. butt.

Krico Model 600 Bolt-Action Rifle $895
Same general specifications as Model 700, except with short action. Calibers: 17 Rem., 222, 223, 22-250, 243, 5.6×50 Mag. and 308.

Krico Model 620 Bolt-Action Rifle $925
Same as Model 600, except has short action chambered 308 Win. only and full-length Mannlicher-style stock with schnabel forend tip. 20.75-inch bbl. Weight: 6.5 pounds. No longer imported.

Krico Model 700 Bolt Action Rifle
Calibers: 17 Rem., 222, 222 Rem. Mag., 223, 22-250, 5.6×50 Mag., 243, 5.6×57 RSW, 6×62, 6.5×55, 6.5×57, 6.5×68 270 Win., 7×64, 7.5 Swiss, 7mm Mag., 30-06, 300 Win., 8×68S, 9.3×64. 24-inch (standard) or 26-inch (magnum) bbl. 44 inches overall (standard). Weight: 7.5 lbs. Adj. rear sight; hooded ramp front. Checkered European-style walnut stock w/Bavarian cheekpiece and rosewood schnabel forend tip. Imported 1983 to date.

Model 700	$ 795
Model 700 Deluxe	895
Model 700 Deluxe S	1095
Model 700 Stutzen	950

Krico Model 720 Bolt-Action Rifle
Same general specifications as Model 700, except in calibers 270 Win. and 30-06 with full-length Mannlicher-style stock and schnabel forend tip. 20.75-inch bbl. Weight: 6.75 lbs. Discontinued importing 1990.

Sporter Model	$ 895
Ltd. Edition	1750

Krico Bolt-Action Sporting Rifle $535
Miniature Mauser action. Single- or double-set trigger. Calibers: 22 Hornet, 222 Rem. 4-shot clip magazine. 22-24- or 26-inch bbl. Weight: about 6.25 lbs. Sights: open rear; hooded ramp front. Checkered stock w/cheekpiece, pistol grip, black forend tip, sling swivels. Made 1956-62.

Krico Carbine $450
Same as Krico Sporting Rifle, except has 20- or 22-inch bbl., full-length Mannlicher-type stock.

Krico Model 640 Varmint Rifle

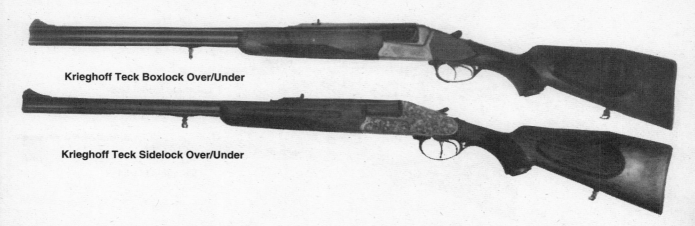

Krieghoff Teck Boxlock Over/Under

Krieghoff Teck Sidelock Over/Under

Krico Model 640 Super Sniper Bolt-Action Repeating Rifle $1095
Calibers: 223 Rem., 308 Win. 3-shot magazine. 26-inch bbl. 44.25 inches overall. Weight: 9.5 lbs. No sights drilled and tapped for scope mounts. Single or double-set triggers. Select walnut stock with adj. cheekpiece and recoil pad. Discontinued 1989.

Krico Model 640 Varmint Rifle $695
Caliber: 222 Rem. 4-shot magazine. 23.75-inch bbl. Weight: 9.5 lbs. No sights. European walnut stock. No longer imported.

Krico Special Varmint Rifle $525
Same as Krico Rifle, except has heavy bbl., no sights weighs about 7.25 lbs. Caliber: 222 Rem. only.

KRIEGHOFF RIFLES
Ulm (Donau), Germany
Mfd. by H. Krieghoff Jagd und Sportwaffenfabrik

See also combination guns under Krieghoff shotgun listings.

Krieghoff Teck Over/Under Rifle
Kersten action, double crossbolt, double underlugs. Boxlock. Calibers: 7×57r5, 7×64, 7×65r5, 30-30, 308 Win. 30-06, 300 Win. Mag., 9.3×74r5, 375 H&H Mag. 458 Win. Mag. 25-inch bbls. Weight: 8 to 9.5 lbs. Sights: express rear; ramp front. Checkered walnut stock and forearm. Made 1967 to date.
Standard calibers $5295
375 H&H Mag. (disc. 1988),458 Win. Mag **6450**

Krieghoff Ulm Over/Under Rifle $8650
Same general specifications as Teck model, except has sidelocks with leaf arabesque engraving. Made 1963 to date.

Krieghoff ULM-Primus Over/Under Rifle $11,500
Deluxe version of Ulm model, has detachable sidelocks, higher grade engraving and stock wood. Made 1963 to date.

LAKEFIELD ARMS LTD.
Ontario, Canada

Lakefield Model 64B Semiautomatic Rifle $120
Caliber: 22 LR. 10-shot magazine. 20-inch bbl. Weight: 5.5 lbs. 40 inches overall. Bead front sight, adj. rear. Grooved receiver for scope mounts. Stamped checkering on walnut-finished hardwood stock with Monte Carlo cheekpiece. Made 1990 to date.

Lakefield Model 90B Bolt-Action Target Rifle ... $325
Caliber: 22 LR. 5-shot magazine. 21-inch bbl. w/snow cap. 39.63 inches overall. Weight: 8.25 lbs. Adj. receiver peep sight; globe front w/colored inserts. Receiver drilled and tapped for scope mounts. Biathlon-style natural finished hardwood stock w/shooting rails, hand stop and butthook. Made 1991 to date.

Lakefield Model 91T/91TR Bolt-Action Target Rifle
Calibers: 22 Short, Long, LR. 25-inch bbl. 43.63 inches overall. Weight: 8 lbs. Adj. rear peep sight; globe front w/inserts. Receiver drilled and tapped for scope mounts. Walnut finished hardwood stock w/shooting rails and hand stop. **Model 91TR** is a 5-shot clip-fed repeater. Made 1991 to date.
Model 91T Single Shot $295
Model 91TR Repeater (22 LR only) **315**

Lakefield Model 92S Target Rifle $250
Same general specifications as Model 90B, except with conventional target-style stock. 8 lbs. No sights, but drilled and tapped for scope mounts.

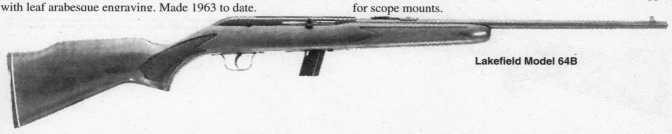

Lakefield Model 64B

RIFLES

Lakefield Model 92S

Lakefield Mark I

Lakefield Mark I Bolt-Action Rifle $90
Calibers: 22 Short, Long, LR. Single-shot. 20.5-inch bbl. (19-inch Youth Model); available in smoothbore. Weight: 5.5 lbs. 39.5 inches overall. Bead front sight; adj. rear. Grooved receiver for scope mounts. Checkered walnut-finished hardwood stock w/Monte Carlo and pistol grip. Blued finish. Made 1990 to date.

Lakefield Mark II Bolt-Action Rifle
Same general specifications as the Mark I, except in the repeater version with 10-shot clip magazine in 22 LR only.

Mark II Standard . . . . $ 95
Mark II Youth (19-inch barrel) 95
Mark II Left-hand 105

LAURONA RIFLES
Mfd. in Eibar, Spain
Imported by Galaxy Imports, Victoria, TX

Laurona Model 2000X O/U Express Rifle
Calibers: 30-06, 8×57 JRS, 8×75 JR, 375 H&H, 9.3×74R 5-shot magazine. 24-inch separated bbls. Weight: 8.5 lbs. Quarter rib drilled and tapped for scope mount. Open sights. Matte black chrome finish. Monte Carlo-style checkered walnut buttstock; tulip forearm. Made 1993 to date.

Standard Calibers $2250
Magnum Calibers 2795

L.A.R. MANUFACTURING, INC.
West Jordan, Utah

L.A.R. Big Boar Competitor Bolt-Action Rifle . . $1695
Single-shot, bull-pup action. Caliber: 50 BMG. 36-inch bbl. 45.5 inches overall. Weight: 28.4 lbs. Made 1994 to date.

LUNA RIFLE
Mehlis, Germany
Manufactured by Ernst Friedr. Büchel

Luna Single-Shot Target Rifle $895
Falling block action. Calibers: 22 LR, 22 Hornet. 29-inch bbl. Weight: about 8.25 lbs. Sights: micrometer peep rear tang; open rear; ramp front. Cheekpiece stock w/full pistol grip, semibeavertail forearm, checkered, swivels. Made before WWII.

MAGNUM RESEARCH, INC.
Minneapolis, Minnesota

Magnum Research Mountain Eagle
Bolt-Action Rifle $1050
Calibers: 270 Win., 280 Rem., 7mm Rem. Mag., 30-06, 300 Win. Mag., 338 Win. Mag. 5-shot (Std.) or 4-shot (Mag.). 24-inch bbl. 44 inches overall. Weight: 7.75 lbs. Receiver drilled and tapped for scope mount; no sights. Blued finish. Fiberglass composite stock. 1000 made in 1994.

Luna Single-Shot Target Rifle

Magnum Research
Mountain Eagle Bolt-Action Rifle

MANNLICHER SPORTING RIFLES
Steyr, Austria
Manufactured by Steyr-Daimler-Puch, A.-G.

In 1967, Steyr-Daimler-Puch introduced a series of sporting rifles with a bolt action that is a departure from the Mannlicher-Schoenauer system of earlier models. In the latter, the action is locked by lugs symmetrically arranged behind the bolt head as well as by placing the bolt handle ahead of the right flank of the receiver, the rear section of which is open on top for backward movement of the bolt handle. The current action, made in four lengths to accommodate different ranges of cartridges, has a closed-top receiver; the bolt locking lugs are located toward the rear of the bolt (behind the magazine), and the Mannlicher-Schoenauer rotary magazine has been redesigned as a detachable box type of Makrolon.

Mannlicher Model L Carbine **$1025**
Same general specifications as Model SL Carbine, except has type "L" action, weighs about 6.2 lbs. Calibers same as for Model L Rifle. Made 1968 to date.

Mannlicher Model L Rifle **$1095**
Same general specifications as Model SL Rifle, except has type "L" action, weighs about 6.3 lbs. Calibers: 22-250, 5.6×57 (discontinued 1991), 243 Win., 6mm Rem. 308 Win. Made 1968 to date.

Mannlicher Model L Varmint Rifle. **$1065**
Same general specifications as Model SL Varmint Rifle except has type "L" action. Calibers: 22-250, 243 Win., 308 Win. Made 1969 to date.

Mannlicher Model Luxus Bolt-Action Rifle
Same general specifications as Models L and M, except with 3-shot detachable box magazine and single-set trigger. Full or half-stock with low-luster oil or high-gloss lacquer finish.
Full stock **$1395**
Half stock **1295**

Mannlicher Model M Carbine
Same general specifications as Model SL Carbine except has type "M" action, stock w/recoil pad, weighs about 6.8 lbs. Made 1969 to date. Left-hand version w/additional 6.5×55 and 9.3×62 calibers introduced in 1977.
Right-hand Carbine **$1050**
Left-hand Carbine **1395**

Mannlicher Model M Professional Rifle **$995**
Same as standard Model M Rifle, except has synthetic (Cycolac) stock, weighs about 7.5 lbs. Calibers: 6.5×55, 6.5×57, 270 Win., 7×57, 7×64, 7.5 Swiss, 30-06, 8×57JS, 9.3×62. Introduced 1977.

Mannlicher Model M Rifle
Same general specifications as Model SL Rifle, except w/type "M" action, stock w/forend tip and recoil pad; weighs about 6.9 lbs. Calibers: 6.5×57, 270 Win., 7×57, 7×64, 30-06, 8×57JS,

Mannlicher Model L Rifle

Mannlicher Model M Carbine

Mannlicher Model M Professional

Mannlicher Model M Rifle

Mannlicher Model SL Carbine

Mannlicher Model SL Rifle

Mannlicher Model M Rifle *(Cont.)*

9.3×62. Made 1969 to date. Left-hand version also in calibers 6.5×55 and 7.5 Swiss intro. 1977.

Right-hand Rifle . . . . **$ 975**
Left-hand Rifle **1395**

Mannlicher Model S Rifle **$995**

Same general specifications as Model SL Rifle, except has type "S" action, 4-round magazine, 25.63-inch bbl., stock with forend tip and recoil pad, weighs about 8.4 lbs. Calibers: 6.5×68, 257 Weatherby Mag., 264 Win. Mag., 7mm Rem. Mag., 300 Win. Mag., 300 H&H Mag., 308 Norma Mag., 8×68S, 338 Win. Mag., 9.3×64, 375 H&H Mag. Made 1970 to date.

Mannlicher Model SL Carbine **$995**

Same general specifications as Model SL Rifle, except has 20-inch bbl. and full-length stock, weighs about 6 lbs. Made 1968 to date.

Mannlicher Model SL Rifle **$960**

Steyr-Mannlicher SL bolt action. Calibers: 222 Rem., 222 Rem., 222 Rem. Mag., 223 Rem. 5-shot rotary magazine, detachable. 23.63-inch bbl. Weight: about 6 lbs. Single- or double-set trigger (mechanisms interchangeable). Sights: open rear; hooded ramp front. Half stock of European walnut w/Monte Carlo comb and cheekpiece, skip-checkered forearm and pistol grip, rubber buttpad, QD swivels. Made 1967 to date.

Mannlicher Model SL Rifle
w/Single-Set Trigger

**Mannlicher Model SSG
Match Target Rifle**

Mannlicher Model SL Varmint Rifle **$1025**
Same general specifications as Model SL Rifle, except caliber
222 Rem. only, has 25.63-inch heavy bbl., no sights, weighs
about 7.92 lbs. Made 1969 to date.

Mannlicher Model SSG Match Target Rifle
Type "L" action. Caliber: 308 Win. (7.62×51 NATO). 5- or 10-
round magazine, single-shot plug. 25.5-inch heavy bbl. Weight:
10.25 lbs. Single trigger. Sights: micrometer peep rear; globe
front. Target stock, European walnut or synthetic, with full pistol
grip, wide forearm w/swivel rail, adj. rubber buttplate. Made
1969 to date.
W/walnut stock **$1595**
W/synthetic stock **1295**

Mannlicher Model S/T Rifle **$1150**
Same as Model S Rifle, except has heavy 25.63-inch bbl.,
weighs about 9 lbs. Calibers: 9.3×64, 375 H&H Mag., 458 Win.
Mag. Option of 23.63-inch bbl. in latter caliber. Made 1975 to
date.

**Mannlicher-Schoenauer Model 1903 Bolt-Action
Sporting Carbine** **$895**
Caliber: 6.5×53mm (referred to in some European gun cata-
logs as 6.7×53mm, following the Austrian practice of designating calibers by bullet diameter). 5-shot rotary magazine.
450mm (17.7-inch) bbl. Weight: about 6.5 lbs. Double-set
trigger. Sights: two-leaf rear; ramp front. Full-length sporting
stock w/cheekpiece, pistol grip, trap buttplate, swivels. Pre-
WWII.

Mannlicher-Schoenauer Model 1905 Carbine . . . **$795**
Same as Model 1903, except caliber 9×56mm and has 19.7-inch
bbl., weighs about 6.75 lbs. Pre-WWII.

Mannlicher-Schoenauer Model 1908 Carbine . . . **$825**
Same as Model 1905, except calibers 7×57mm and 8×56mm
Pre-WWII.

—————————— *NOTE* ——————————

**Certain Mannlicher-Schoenauer models were produced before
WWII. Manufacture of sporting rifles and carbines was resumed
at the Steyr-Daimler-Puch plant in Austria in 1950 during which
time the Model 1950 rifles and carbines were introduced.**

Mannlicher-Schoenauer Model 1910 Carbine . . . **$895**
Same as Model 1905, except in 9.5×57mm. Pre-WWII.

Mannlicher-Schoenauer Model 1924 Carbine . . . **$795**
Same as Model 1905, except caliber 30-06 (7.62×63mm). Pre-
WWII.

**Mannlicher-Schoenauer Model 1950
Bolt-Action Sporting Rifle** **$695**
Calibers: 257 Roberts, 270 Win., 30-06. 5-shot rotary magazine.
24-inch bbl. Weight: about 7.25 lbs. Single trigger or double-set
trigger. Redesigned low bolt handle, shotgun-type safety. Sights:
folding leaf open rear; hooded ramp front. Improved half-length
stock w/cheekpiece, pistol grip, checkered, ebony forend tip,
swivels. Made 1950-52.

RIFLES

**Mannlicher-Schoenauer Model 1903
Sporting Carbine**

**Mannlicher-Schoenauer
Model 1905 Carbine**

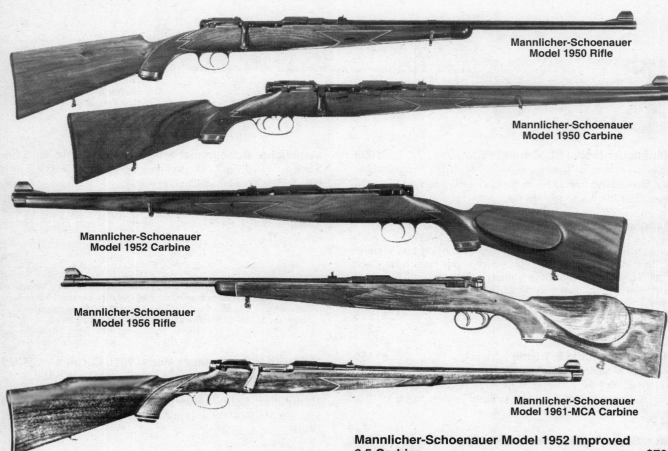

Mannlicher-Schoenauer
Model 1950 Rifle

Mannlicher-Schoenauer
Model 1950 Carbine

Mannlicher-Schoenauer
Model 1952 Carbine

Mannlicher-Schoenauer
Model 1956 Rifle

Mannlicher-Schoenauer
Model 1961-MCA Carbine

Mannlicher-Schoenauer Model 1950 Carbine . . . $750
Same general specifications as Model 1950 Rifle except has 20-inch bbl., full-length stock, weighs about 7 lbs. Made 1950-1952.

Mannlicher-Schoenauer Model 1950 6.5 Carbine . . $725
Same as other Model 1950 Carbines except caliber 6.5×53mm, has 18.25-inch bbl., weighs 6.75 lbs. Made 1950-1952.

Mannlicher-Schoenauer Model 1952 Improved Carbine $850
Same as Model 1950 Carbine except has swept-back bolt handle, redesigned stock. Calibers: 257, 270, 7mm, 30-06. Made 1952-1956.

Mannlicher-Schoenauer Model 1952 Improved 6.5 Carbine $795
Same as Model 1952 Carbine except caliber 6.5×53mm, has 18.25-inch bbl. Made 1952-56.

Mannlicher-Schoenauer Model 1952 Improved Sporting Rifle $650
Same as Model 1950 except has swept-back bolt handle redesigned stock. Calibers: 257, 270, 30-06, 9.3×62mm. Made 1952-56 and imported exclusively by Stoeger Arms Corp.

Mannlicher-Schoenauer Model 1956 Custom Carbine $695
Same general specifications as Models 1950 and 1952 Carbines, except has redesigned stock with high comb. Drilled and tapped for scope mounts. Calibers: 243, 6.5mm, 257, 270, 7mm, 30-06, 308. Made 1956-60.

Mannlicher-Schoenauer
High Velocity Sporting Rifle

Mannlicher-Schoenauer
M72 L/M Carbine

Mannlicher-Schoenauer Model 1956 Custom Sporting Rifle $595
Same general specifications as Models 1950 and 1952 except 22-inch bbl., redesigned stock with high comb. Calibers: 243 and 30-06. Made 1956-60.

Mannlicher-Schoenauer Carbine, Model 1961-MCA $695
Same as Model 1956 Carbine, except has universal Monte Carlo design stock. Calibers: 243 Win., 6.5mm, 270, 308, 30-06. Made 1961-71.

Mannlicher-Schoenauer Rifle, Model 1961-MCA . $675
Same as Model 1956 Rifle, except has universal Monte Carlo design stock. Calibers: 243, 270, 30-06. Made 1961-1971.

Mannlicher-Schoenauer High Velocity Bolt-Action Sporting Rifle $1200
Calibers: 7×64 Brenneke, 30-06 (7.62×63), 8×60 Magnum, 9.3×62, 10.75×68mm. 23.6-inch bbl. Weight: about 7.5 lbs. Sights: British-style 3-leaf open rear; ramp front. Half-length sporting stock w/cheek-piece, pistol grip, checkered, trap buttplate, swivels. Also produced in takedown model. Pre-WWII.

Mannlicher-Schoenauer M72 Model L/M Carbine $695
Same general specifications as M72 Model L/M Rifle except has 20-inch bbl. and full-length stock, weighs about 7.2 lbs. Made 1972 to date.

Mannlicher-Schoenauer M72 Model L/M Rifle . . $795
M72 bolt action, type L/M receiver front-locking bolt internal rotary magazine (5-round). Calibers: 22-250, 5.6×57, 6mm Rem., 243 Win., 6.5×57, 270 Win., 7×57, 7×64, 308 Win., 30-06. 23.63-inch bbl. Weight: about 7.3 lbs. Single- or double-set trigger (mechanisms interchangeable). Sights: open rear; hooded ramp front. Half stock of European walnut, checkered forearm and pistol grip, Monte Carlo cheekpiece, rosewood forend tip, recoil pad, QD swivels. Made 1972 to date.

Mannlicher-Schoenauer M72 Model S Rifle $750
Same general specifications as M72 Model L/M Rifle, except has Magnum action, 4-round magazine, 25.63-inch bbl., weighs about 8.6 lbs. Calibers: 6.5×68, 7mm Rem. Mag., 8×68S, 9.3×64, 375 H&H Mag. Made 1972 to date.

Mannlicher-Schoenauer M72 Model S/T Rifle . . . $995
Same as M72 Model S Rifle, except has heavy 25.63-inch bbl., weighs about 9.3 lbs. Calibers: 300 Win. Mag. 9.3×64, 375 H&H Mag., 458 Win. Mag. Option of 23.63-inch bbl. in latter caliber. Made 1975 to date.

MARLIN FIREARMS CO.
North Haven, Connecticut

Marlin Model 9 Semiautomatic Carbine
Calibers: 9mm Parabellum. 12-shot magazine. 16.5-inch bbl. 35.5 inches overall. Weight: 6.75 lbs. Manual bolt hold-open.

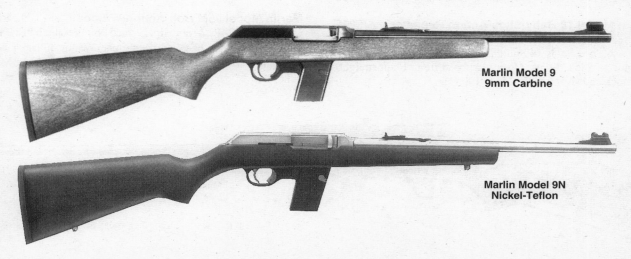

Marlin Model 9
9mm Carbine

Marlin Model 9N
Nickel-Teflon

RIFLES

Marlin Model 15Y "Little Buckaroo"

Marlin Model 15YN

Marlin Model 20

Marlin Model 9 Semiautomatic Carbine *(Cont.)*

Sights: hooded post front; adj. open rear. Walnut-finished hardwood stock w/rubber buttpad. Blued or nickel-Teflon finish. Made 1985 to date.

Model 9 .... **$225**
Model 9N (Nickel-Teflon) **275**

Marlin Model 15Y/15YN

Bolt-action, single-shot "Little Buckaroo" rifle. Caliber: 22 Short, Long or LR. 16.25-inch bbl. Weight: 4.25 lbs. Thumb safety. Ramp front sight; adj. open rear. One-piece walnut Monte Carlo stock w/full pistol grip. Made 1984-88. Reintroduced in 1989 as Model 15YN.

Model 15Y .... **$ 90**
Model 15YN **100**

Marlin Model 18 Baby Slide-Action Repeater ... $225

Exposed hammer. Solid frame. Caliber: 22 LR, Long Short. Tubular magazine holds 14 Short. 20-inch bbl., round or octagon. Weight: 3.75 lbs. Sights: Open rear; bead front. Plain straight-grip stock and slide handle. Made 1906-09.

Marlin Model 20 Slide-Action Repeating Rifle . . $240

Exposed hammer. Takedown. Caliber: 22 LR, Long, Short. Tubular magazine: half-length holds 15 Short, 12 Long, 10 LR; full-length holds 25 Short, 20 Long, 18 LR. 24-inch octagon bbl. Weight: about 5 lbs. Sights: open rear; bead front. Plain straight-grip stock, grooved slide handle. Made 1907-22. *Note:* After 1920 was designated "Model 20-S."

Marlin Model 25 Bolt-Action Rifle $105

Caliber: 22 Short, Long or LR. 7-shot clip. 22-inch bbl. Weight: 5.5 lbs. Ramp front sight, adj. open rear. One-piece walnut Monte Carlo stock w/full pistol grip Mar-Shield® finish. Made 1984-1988.

Marlin Model 25 Slide-Action Repeater $255

Exposed hammer. Takedown. Caliber: 22 Short (also handles 22 CB Caps). Tubular magazine holds 15 Short. 23-inch bbl. Weight: about 4 lbs. Sights: open rear; beaded front. Plain straight-grip stock and slide handle. Made 1909-10.

Marlin Model 25M Bolt-Action W/Scope $120

Caliber: 22 WMR. 7-shot clip. 22-inch bbl. Weight: 6 lbs. Ramp front sight w/brass bead, adj. open rear. Walnut-finished stock w/Monte Carlo styling and full pistol grip. Sling swivels. Made 1986-88.

Marlin Model 25 Bolt-Action Rifle

**Marlin Model 25MB
Midget Magnum**

Marlin Model 25MB Midget Magnum $115
Bolt action. Caliber: 22 WMR. 7-shot capacity. 16.25-inch bbl. Weight: 4.75 lbs. Walnut-finished Monte Carlo-style stock w/full pistol grip and abbreviated forend. Sights: ramp front w/brass bead, adj. open rear. Thumb safety. Made 1986-88.

Marlin Model 25MN/25N Bolt-Action Rifle
Caliber: 22 WMR (Model 25MN) or 22 LR (Model 25N). 7-shot clip magazine. 22-inch bbl. 41 inches overall. Weight: 5.5 to 6 lbs. Adj. open rear sight, ramp front; receiver grooved for scope mounts. One piece walnut-finished hardwood Monte Carlo stock w/pistol grip. Made 1989 to date.
Marlin Model 25MN $125
Marlin Model 25N 115

Marlin Model 27 Slide-Action Repeating Rifle .. $245
Exposed hammer. Takedown. Calibers: 25-20, 32-20. ⅔ magazine (tubular) holds 7 shots. 24-inch octagon bbl. Weight: about 5.75 lbs. Sights: open rear; bead front. Plain straight-grip stock, grooved slide handle. Made 1910-16.

Marlin Model 27S $250
Same as Model 27, except has round bbl., also chambered for 25 Stevens R.F. Made 1920-32.

Marlin Model 29 Slide-Action Repeater $260
Similar to Model 20, has 23-inch round bbl., half magazine only, weighs about 5.75 lbs. **Model 37** is same type except has 24-inch bbl. and full magazine. Made 1913-16.

Marlin Model 30AS Lever Action $195
Caliber: 30/30 Win. 6-shot tubular magazine. 20-inch bbl. with Micro-Groove rifling. 38.25 inches overall. Weight: 7 lbs. Brass bead front sight, adj. rear. Solid top receiver, offset hammer spur for scope use. Walnut-finished hardwood stock w/pistol grip. Mar-Shield® finish. Made 1984 to date.

Marlin Model 32 Slide-Action Repeater $350
Hammerless. Takedown. Caliber: 22 LR, Long, Short. ⅔ tubular magazine holds 15 Short, 12 Long, 10 LR; full magazine, 25 Short, 20 Long, 18 LR. 24-inch octagon bbl. Weight: about 5.5 lbs. Sights: open rear; bead front. Plain pistol-grip stock, grooved slide handle. Made 1914-15.

Marlin Model 36 Lever-Action Repeating Carbine $295
Calibers: 30-30, 32 Special. 6-shot tubular magazine. 20-inch bbl. Weight: about 6.5 lbs. Sights: Open rear; bead front. Pistol-grip stock, semibeavertail forearm w/carbine bbl. band. Made 1936-48. *Note:* In 1936, this was designated "Model 1936."

Marlin Model 36 Sporting Carbine $315
Same as Model 36A rifle except has 20-inch bbl., weighs 6.25 lbs.

Marlin Model 36A/36A-DL Lever-Action Repeating Rifle
Same as Model 36 Carbine, except has ⅔ magazine holding 5 cartridges, 24-inch bbl., weighs 6.75 lbs., has hooded front sight,

RIFLES

Marlin Model 27

Marlin Model 29

Marlin Model 38

Marlin Model 36A/36A-DL *(Cont.)*

semibeavertail forearm. Model 36A-DL has deluxe checkered stock, swivels and sling. Made 1938-48.

Model 36A Standard **$210**
Model 36A-DL (Deluxe) **280**

Marlin Model 38 Slide-Action Repeating Rifle . . **$245**

Hammerless. Takedown. Caliber: 22 LR, Long, Short. ⅔ magazine (tubular) holds 15 Short, 12 Long, 10 LR. 24-inch

Marlin Model 38 Slide-Action Repeating Rifle *(Cont.)*

octagon or round bbls. Weight: about 5.5 lbs. Sights: open rear; bead front. Plain shotgun-type pistol-grip buttstock w/hard rubber buttplate, grooved slide handle. Ivory bead front sight; adj. rear. About 20,000 Model 38 rifles were made between 1920-30. *See* photo preceding page.

Marlin Model 39 Carbine

**Marlin Model 39 Carbine
90th Anniversary Carbine**

Marlin Model 39 Century Ltd.

**Marlin Model 39 Rifle
Original First Issue**

**Marlin Model 39A
90th Anniversary Rifle**

Marlin Model 39 — ADL

Marlin Model 39AS

Marlin Model 39 Carbine $185
Same as Model 39M, except has lightweight bbl., ¾ magazine (capacity: 18 Short, 14 Long, 12 LR), slimmer forearm. Weight: 5.25 lbs. Made 1963-67.

Marlin Model 39 90th Anniversary Carbine $595
Carbine version of 90th Anniversary Model 39A. 500 made in 1960. Value is for carbine in new, unfired condition.

Marlin 39 Century Ltd. $285
Commemorative version of Model 39A. Receiver inlaid with brass medallion, Marlin Centennial 1870-1970. Square lever. 20-inch octagon bbl. Fancy walnut straight-grip stock and forearm; brass forend cap, buttplate, nameplate in buttstock. 35,388 made in 1970.

Marlin Model 39 Lever-Action Repeater $1495
Takedown. Casehardened receiver. Caliber: 22 LR, Long, Short. Tubular magazine holds 25 Short, 20 Long, 18 LR. 24-inch octagon bbl. Weight: about 5.75 lbs. Sights: open rear; bead front. Plain pistol-grip stock and forearm. Made 1922-38.

Marlin Model 39A $395
General specifications same as Model 39, except has blued receiver, round bbl., heavier stock with semibeavertail forearm, weighs about 6.5 lbs. Made 1938-60.

Marlin Model 39A 90th Anniversary Rifle
Commemorates Marlin's 90th anniversary. Same general specifications as Golden 39A, except has chrome-plated bbl. and action, stock and forearm of select walnut finely checkered, carved figure of a squirrel on right side of buttstock. 500 made in 1960. Value is for rifle in new, unfired condition.
Model 39A 90th Anniversary Rifle $575
Model 39-ADL (Blued Bbl./Action, 1960-63) 250

Marlin Model 39A Article II Rifle $275
Commemorates National Rifle Association Centennial 1871-1971. "The Right to Bear Arms" medallion inlaid in receiver. Similar to Model 39A. Magazine capacity: 26 Short, 21 Long, 19 LR. 24-inch octagon bbl. Fancy walnut pistol-grip stock and forearm; brass forend cap, buttplate. 6,244 made in 1971.

Marlin Golden 39A/39AS Rifle
Same as Model 39A, except has gold-plated trigger, hooded ramp front sight, sling swivels. Made 1960-87 (39A); Model 39AS currently manufactured.
Golden 39A $195
Golden 39AS (W/Hammer Block Safety) 215

Marlin Model 39A "Mountie" Lever-Action Repeating Rifle $210
Same as Model 39A, except has lighter, straight-grip stock, slimmer forearm. Weight: 6.25 lbs. Made 1953-60.

Marlin Model 39A Octagon $485
Same as Golden 39A, except has oct. bbl., plain bead front sight, slimmer stock and forearm, no pistol-grip cap or swivels. Made 1973.

Marlin Model 39D $195
Same as Model 39M, except has pistol-grip stock, forearm with bbl. band. Made 1970-74.

Marlin 39M Article II Carbine $225
Same as 39A Article II Rifle, except has straight-grip buttstock, square lever, 20-inch octagon bbl., reduced magazine capacity. 3,824 made in 1971.

Marlin Golden 39M
Calibers: 22 Short, Long and LR. Tubular magazine holds 21 Short, 16 Long or 15 LR cartridges. 20-inch bbl. 36 inches overall. Weight: about 6 lbs. Gold-plated trigger. Hooded ramp front sight, adj. folding semi-buckhorn rear. Two-piece, straight-grip American black walnut stock. Sling swivels. Mar-Shield® finish. Made 1960-87.
Golden 39M $190
Model 39M Octagon (octagonal bbl., plain bead front sight, no swivels, made 1973) 250

Marlin Model 39M "Mountie" Carbine $220
Same as Model 39A "Mountie" Rifle, except has 20-inch bbl. and reduced magazine capacity: 21 Short, 16 Long, 15 LR. Weight: 6 lbs. Made 1954-60.

Marlin Model 39TDS Takedown Carbine

Marlin Model 45

Marlin Model 39TDS Carbine **$250**
Same general specifications as Model 39M, except takedown style with 16.5-inch bbl. and reduced magazine capacity. 32.63 inches overall. Weight: 5.25 lbs. Made 1988 to date.

Marlin Model 45 . . . . **$235**
Semiautomatic action. Caliber: 45 Auto.7-shot clip.16.5-inch bbl. 35.5 inches overall. Weight: 6.75 lbs. Manual bolt hold-open. Sights: ramp front sight w/brass bead, adj. folding rear. Receiver drilled and tapped for scope mount. Walnut-finished hardwood stock. Made 1986 to date.

Marlin Model 49/49DL Autoloading Rifle
Same as Model 99C, except has two-piece stock, checkered after 1970. Made 1968-71. **Model 49DL** has scrollwork on sides of receiver, checkered stock and forearm; made 1971-78.
Model 49 . . . . **$120**
Model 49DL **130**

Marlin Model 50/50E Autoloading Rifle
Takedown. Caliber: 22 LR. 6-shot detachable box magazine. 22-inch bbl. Weight: about 6 lbs. Sights: open rear; bead front; **Model 50E** has peep rear sight, hooded front. Plain pistol-grip stock, forearm with finger grooves. Made 1931-34.
Model 50 . . . . **$130**
Model 50E **150**

Marlin Model 56 Levermatic Rifle **$145**
Same as Model 57 except clip-loading. Magazine holds eight rounds. Weight: about 5.75 lbs. Made 1955-64.

Marlin Model 57 Levermatic Rifle **$160**
Lever action. Caliber: 22 LR, 22 Long, 22 Short. Tubular magazine holds 19 LR, 21 Long, 27 Short. 22-inch bbl. Weight: about 6.25 lbs. Sights: open rear, adj. for windage and elevation; hooded ramp front. Monte Carlo-style stock with pistol grip. Made 1959-65.

Marlin Model 57M Levermatic **$190**
Same as Model 57, except chambered for 22 WMR cartridge, has 24-inch bbl., 15-shot tubular magazine, and weighs 6.4 lbs. Monte Carlo style pistol-grip stock; no checkering. Made 1960-1969.

Marlin Model 60 Semiautomatic Rifle **$95**
Caliber: 22 LR. 14-shot tubular magazine. 22-inch bbl. 40.5 inches overall. Weight: 5.5 lbs. Grooved receiver. Ramp front sight with removable hood; adj. open rear. Anodized receiver w/blued bbl. Monte Carlo-style walnut-finished hardwood stock w/Mar-Shield® finish. Made 1981 to date. *Note:* Marketed 1960-1980 under the Glenfield promotion logo, and with slightly different stock configuration.

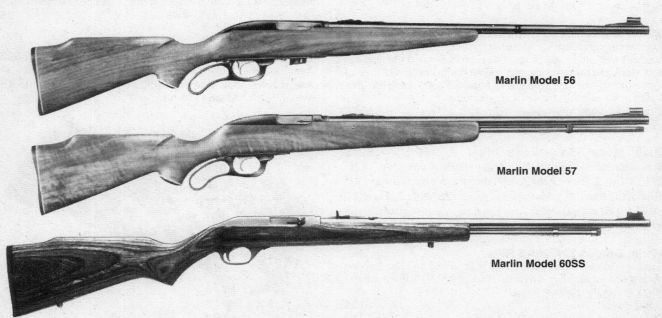

Marlin Model 56

Marlin Model 57

Marlin Model 60SS

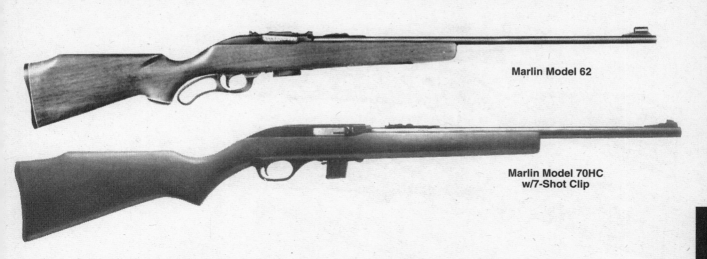

Marlin Model 62

Marlin Model 70HC
w/7-Shot Clip

Marlin Model 60SS Semiautomatic Rifle $155
Same general specifications as the Model 60, except w/stainless bbl. and magazine tube; laminated black/gray Maine birch stock w/nickel-plated swivel studs. Made 1993 to date.

Marlin Model 62 Levermatic Rifle $275
Lever action. Calibers: 256 Magnum, 30 Carbine. 4-shot clip magazine. 23-inch bbl. Weight: 7 lbs. Sights: open rear; hooded ramp front. Monte Carlo-style stock w/pistol grip, swivels and sling. Made in 256 Magnum 1963-66; in 30 Carbine 1966-69.

Marlin Model 65 Bolt-Action Single-Shot Rifle . . . $115
Takedown. Caliber: 22 LR, Long, Short. 24-inch bbl. Weight: about 5 lbs. Sights: open rear; bead front. Plain pistol-grip stock with grooved forearm. Made 1932-38. **Model 65E** is same as Model 65, except has rear peep sight and hooded front sight.

Marlin Model 70HC Semiautomatic $115
Caliber: 22 LR. 7- and 15-shot magazine. 18-inch bbl. Weight: 5.5 lbs. 36.75 inches overall. Ramp front sight; adj. open rear. Grooved receiver for scope mounts. Walnut-finished hardwood stock w/Monte Carlo and pistol grip.

Marlin Model 70P Semiautomatic $120
"Papoose" takedown. Caliber: 22 LR. 7-shot clip. 16.25-inch bbl. 35.25 inches overall. Weight: 3.75 lbs. Sights: ramp front, adj. open rear. Side ejection, manual bolt hold-open. Cross-bolt safety. Walnut-finished hard-wood stock w/abbreviated forend, pistol grip. Made 1984 to date.

Marlin Model 75C Semiautomatic $125
Caliber: 22 LR. 13-shot tubular magazine. 18-inch bbl. 36.5 inches overall. Weight: 5 lbs. Side ejection. Cross-bolt safety. Sights: ramp-mounted blade front; adj. open rear. Monte Carlo-style walnut-finished hardwood stock w/pistol grip. Made 1975 to date.

Marlin Model 80 Bolt-Action Repeating Rifle
Takedown. Caliber: 22 LR, Long, Short. 8-shot detachable box magazine. 24-inch bbl. Weight: about 6 lbs. Sights: open rear; bead front. Plain pistol-grip stock. Made 1934-39. **Model 80E,** w/peep rear sight; hooded front, made 1934-40.
Model 80 Standard $110
Model 80E **105**

Marlin Model 70P

Marlin Model 75C

Marlin Model 80C

Marlin Model 80DL

Marlin Model 81DL

Marlin Model 88-C

Marlin Model 89-C

Marlin Model 80C/80DL Bolt-Action Repeater

Improved version of Model 80. **Model 80C** has bead from sight, semibeavertail forearm; made 1940-70. **Model 80DL** has peep rear sight; hooded blade front sight on ramp, swivels; made 1940-65.

Model 80C **$100**
Model 80DL **105**

Marlin Model 81/81E Bolt-Action Repeater

Takedown. Caliber: 22 LR, Long, Short. Tubular magazine holds 24 Short, 20 Long, 18 LR. 24-inch bbl. Weight: about 6.25 lbs. Sights: open rear, bead front. Plain pistol-grip stock. Made 1937-40. **Model 81E** has peep rear sight; hooded front with ramp.

Model 81 . . . . **$115**
Model 81E **135**

Marlin Model 81C/81DL Bolt-Action Repeater

Improved version of Model 81 with same general specifications. **Model 81C** has bead front sight, semibeavertail forearm; made 1940-70. **Model 81 DL** has peep rear sight hooded front, swivels; discontinued 1965.

Model 81C **$115**
Model 81DL **125**

Marlin Model 88-C/88-DL Autoloading Rifle

Takedown. Caliber: 22 LR. Tubular magazine in buttstock holds 14 cartridges. 24-inch bbl. Weight: about 6.75 lbs. Sights: open rear; hooded front. Plain pistol-grip stock. Made 1947-56. **Model 88-DL** has receiver peep sight, checkered stock and sling swivels, made 1953-56.

Model 88-C **$130**
Model 88-DL **135**

Marlin Model 93 Musket

Marlin Model 93
Lever-Action Rifle

Marlin Model 94
Sporting Carbine

Marlin Model 89-C/89-DL Autoloading Rifle

Clip magazine version of Model 88-C. 7-shot clip (12-shot in later models); other specifications same. Made 1950-61. **Model 89-DL** has receiver peep sight, sling swivels.

Model 89-C **$125**
Model 89-DL **155**

Marlin Model 92 Lever-Action Repeating Rifle . $1095

Calibers: 22 Short, Long, LR; 32 Short, Long (rimfire or center-fire by changing firing pin). Tubular magazines: holding 25 Short, 20 Long, 18 LR (22); 17 Short, 14 Long (32); 16-inch bbl. model has shorter magazine holding 15 Short, 12 Long, 10 LR. Bbl. lengths: 16 (22 cal. only) 24, 26, 28 inches. Weight: with 24-inch bbl., about 5.5 lbs. Sights: open rear; blade front. Plain straight-grip stock and forearm. Made 1892-1916. *Note:* Originally designated "Model 1892." However, like many other models of the day, the first two digits of the date were eventually dropped.

Marlin Model 93/93SC Carbine

Same as Standard Model 93 Rifle, except in calibers 30-30 and 32 Special only. Model 93 has 7-shot magazine. 20-inch round bbl., carbine sights, weighs about 6.75 lbs. Model 93SC has ⅔ magazine holding 5 shots, weighs 6.5 lbs.

Model 93 Carbine **$1295**
Model 93SC Sporting Carbine **775**

Marlin Model 93 Lever-Action Repeating Rifle . $1150

Solid frame or takedown. Calibers: 25-36 Marlin, 30-30, 32 Special, 32-40, 38-55. Tubular magazine holds 10 cartridges. 26-inch round or octagon bbl. standard; also made with 28-, 30- and 32-inch bbls. Weight: about 7.25 lbs. Sights: open rear; bead front. Plain straight-grip stock and forearm. Made 1893-1936. *Note:* Before 1915 designated "Model 1893."

Marlin Model 93 Musket $1195

Same as Standard Model 93, except has 30-inch bbl., angular bayonet, ramrod under bbl., musket stock, full-length military-style forearm. Weight: 8 lbs. Made 1893-1915.

Marlin Model 94 Lever-Action Repeating Rifle . $1295

Solid frame or takedown. Calibers: 25-20, 32-20, 38-40, 44-40. 10-shot tubular magazine. 24-inch round or octagon bbl. Weight: about 7 lbs. Sights open rear; bead front. Plain straight-grip stock and forearm (also available with pistol-grip stock). Made 1894-1934. *Note:* Before 1906 designated "Model 1894."

Marlin Model 97 Lever-Action Repeating Rifle . $1350

Takedown. Caliber: 22 LR, Long, Short. Tubular magazine; full length holds 25 Short, 20 Long, 18 LR; half length holds 16 Short, 12 Long and 10 LR. Bbl. lengths: 16, 24, 26, 28 inches. Weight: about 6 lbs. Sights: open rear; bead front. Plain straight-grip stock and forearm (also avail. w/pistol-grip stock). Made 1897-1922. *Note:* Before 1905, this Marlin rifle was designated "Marlin Model 1897," but appeared in the 1907 Marlin catalog the the "97."

Marlin Model 98 Autoloading Rifle $145

Solid frame. Caliber: 22 LR. Tubular magazine holds 15 cartridges. 22-inch bbl. Weight: about 6.75 lbs. Sights: open rear; hooded ramp front. Monte Carlo stock w/cheekpiece. Made 1950-61. *See* photo next page.

Marlin Model 99 Autoloading Rifle $155

Caliber: 22 LR. Tubular magazine holds 18 cartridges. 22-inch bbl. Weight: about 5.5 lbs. Sights: open rear; hooded ramp front. Plain pistol-grip stock. Made 1959-61.

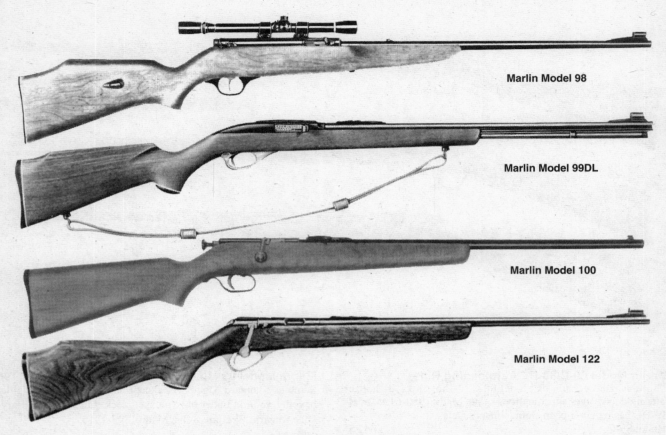

Marlin Model 98

Marlin Model 99DL

Marlin Model 100

Marlin Model 122

Marlin Model 99C $165
Same as Model 99 except has gold-plated trigger, receiver
grooved for tip-off scope mounts, Monte Carlo stock (checkered
in later production). Made 1962-78.

Marlin Model 99DL $195
Same as Model 99 except has gold-plated trigger, jeweled breech
bolt, Monte Carlo stock w/pistol grip, swivels and sling. Made
1960-65.

Marlin Model 99M1 Carbine $210
Same as Model 99C except styled after U.S. 30M1 Carbine; 9-
shot tubular magazine, 18-inch bbl. Sights: open rear; military-
style ramp front; carbine stock w/handguard and bbl. band, sling
swivels. Weight: 4.5 lbs. Made 1966-79.

Marlin Model 100 Bolt-Action Single-Shot Rifle . . $100
Takedown. Caliber: 22 LR, Long, Short. 24-inch bbl. Weight:
about 4.5 lbs. Sights: open rear; bead front. Plain pistol-grip
stock. Made 1936-60.

Marlin Model 100SB $175
Same as Model 100 except smoothbore for use with 22 shot cartridges, shotgun sight. Made 1936-41.

Marlin Model 100 Tom Mix Special $500
Same as Model 100 except has peep rear sight; hooded front;
sling. Made 1936-46.

Marlin Model 101 . . . . $105
Improved version of Model 100 with same general specifications
except has stock with beavertail forearm, weighs about 5 lbs. Introduced 1951; discontinued.

Marlin Model 101 DL $125
Same as Model 101 except has peep rear sight; hooded front,
swivels. Discontinued.

**Marlin Model 122 Single-Shot Junior
Target Rifle** $105
Bolt action. Caliber: 22 LR, 22 Long, 22 Short. 22-inch bbl.
Weight: about 5 lbs. Sights: open rear; hooded ramp front. Monte
Carlo stock w/pistol grip, swivels, sling. Made 1961-65.

Marlin Model 322 Bolt-Action Varmint Rifle $450
Sako short Mauser action. Caliber: 222 Rem. 3-shot clip magazine. 24-inch medium weight bbl. Checkered stock. Sights: two-
position peep rear; hooded ramp front. Weight: about 7.5 lbs.
Made 1954-57.

Marlin Model 336 Marauder $325
Same as Model 336 Texan Carbine except has 16.25-inch bbl.,
weighs about 6.25 lbs. Made 1963-64. *See* photo next page.

Marlin Model 336 Micro Groove Zipper $525
General specifications same as Model 336 Sporting Carbine, except caliber 219 Zipper. Made 1955-61.

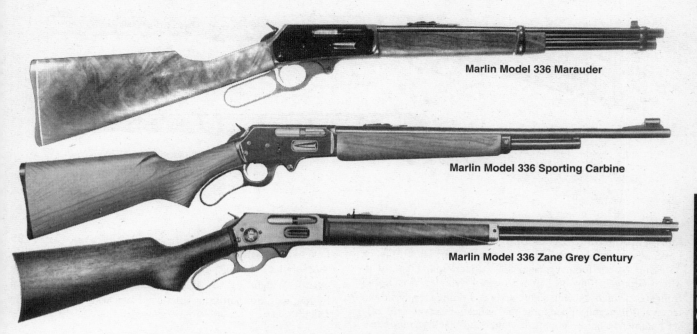

Marlin Model 336 Marauder

Marlin Model 336 Sporting Carbine

Marlin Model 336 Zane Grey Century

Marlin Model 336 Octagon $260

Same as Model 336T, except chambered for 30-30 WCF only and fitted with 22-inch octagon bbl. Blade front sight; open rear. Made 1973 only.

Marlin Model 336 Sporting Carbine $225

Same as Model 336A rifle, except has 20-inch bbl., weighs 6.25 lbs. Made 1948-63.

Marlin Model 336 Zane Grey Century $325

Similar to Model 336A, except has 22-inch octagonal bbl., caliber 30-30, Zane Grey Centennial 1872-1972 medallion inlaid in receiver; select walnut stock with classic pistol grip and forearm; brass buttplate, forend cap. Weight: 7 lbs. 10,000 total production (numbered ZG1 through ZG10,000). Made 1972 only.

Marlin Model 336A Lever-Action Rifle $225

Improved version of Model 36A Rifle with same general specifications, has improved action with round breech bolt. Calibers: 30-30, 32 Special (discontinued 1963), 35 Rem. (introduced 1952). Made 1948-63; reintroduced 1973, discontinued 1980.

Marlin Model 336A-DL $395

Same as Model 336A Rifle except has deluxe checkered stock and forearm, swivels and sling. Made 1948-63.

Marlin Model 336C Lever-Action Carbine $230

Improved version of Model 36 Carbine with same general specifications, has improved action with round breech bolt. Original calibers: 30-30 and 32 Win. Spec. Made 1948-83. *Note:* Caliber 35 Rem. introduced 1953. Caliber 32 Winchester Special discontinued 1963.

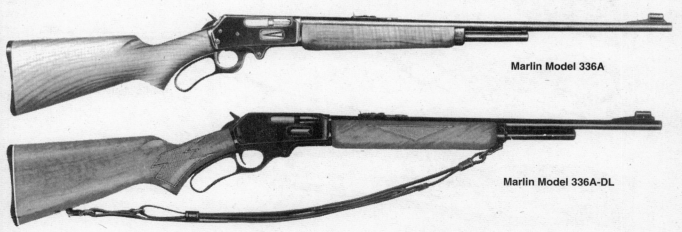

Marlin Model 336A

Marlin Model 336A-DL

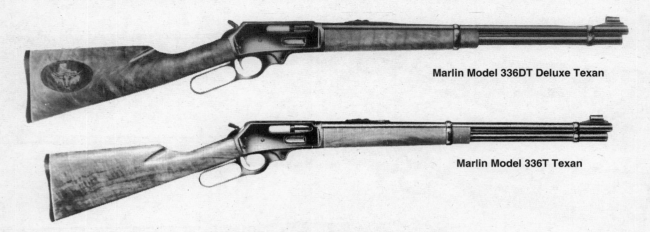

Marlin Model 336DT Deluxe Texan

Marlin Model 336T Texan

Marlin Model 336CS W/Scope **$295**
Lever action with hammer block safety. Caliber: 30/30 Win. or
35 Rem. 6-shot tubular magazine. 20-inch round bbl. with
Micro-Groove rifling. 38.5 inches overall. Weight: 7 lbs. Ramp
front sight with hood, adj. semibuckhorn folding rear. Solid top
receiver drilled and tapped for scope mount or receiver sight; offset hammer spur for scope use. American black walnut stock
w/pistol grip, fluted comb. Mar-Shield® finish. Made 1984 to
date.

Marlin Model 336DT Deluxe Texan **$285**
Same as Model 336T, except has select walnut stock and fore-
arm, hand-carved longhorn steer and map of Texas on buttstock.
Made 1962-64.

Marlin Model 336T Texan Carbine **$200**
Same as Model 336 Carbine, except has straight-grip stock and is
not available in caliber 32 Special. Made 1953-83. Caliber 44
Magnum made 1963-67.

Marlin Model 336TS **$195**
Lever action with hammer block safety. Caliber: 30-30 Win. 6-
shot tubular magazine. 18.5-inch Micro-Groove bbl. 37 inches
overall. Weight: 6.5 lbs. Ramp front sight, adj. semibuckhorn
folding rear. Straight-grip American black walnut stock. Made
1983-87.

Marlin Model 444 Lever-Action Repeating Rifle . . **$255**
Action similar to Model 336. Caliber: 444 Marlin. 4-shot tubular magazine. 24-inch bbl. Weigh: 7.5 lbs. Sights: open
rear; hooded ramp front. Monte Carlo stock w/straight grip,
recoil pad. Carbine-style forearm w/bbl. band. Swivels, sling.
Made 1965-71.

Marlin 444 Sporter **$275**
Same as Model 444 Rifle, except has 22-inch bbl., pistol-grip
stock and forearm as on Model 336A, recoil pad, QD swivels and
sling. Made 1972-83.

Marlin Model 336TS Carbine

Marlin Model 444SS Rifle

Marlin Model 455 Sporter

Marlin Model 444SS $315
Same general specifications as Model 444, except has hammer safety. Made 1984 to date.

Marlin Model 455 Bolt-Action Sporter $335
FN Mauser action with Sako trigger. Calibers: 270, 30-06, 308. 5-shot box magazine. 24-inch medium weight stainless-steel bbl. Monte Carlo stock w/cheekpiece, checkered pistol grip and forearm. Lyman 48 receiver sight; hooded ramp front. Weight: about 8.5 lbs. Made 1957-59.

Marlin Model 780 Bolt-Action Repeater Series
Caliber: 22 LR, Long, Short. 7-shot clip magazine. 22-inch bbl. Weight: 5.5 to 6 lbs. Sights: open rear; hooded ramp front. Re-

Marlin Model 780 Bolt-Action Repeater Series *(Cont.)*
ceiver grooved for scope mounting. Monte Carlo stock w/checkered pistol grip and forearm. Made 1971-88.
Model 780 Standard . . . . $ 95
Model 781 (w/17-shot tubular magazine) 95
Model 782 (22 WMR, w/swivels, sling) 120
Model 783 (w/12-shot tubular magazine) 125

Marlin Model 880 Bolt-Action Repeater Series
Caliber: 22 rimfire. 7-shot magazine. 22-inch bbl. 41 inches overall. Weight: 5.5 to 6 lbs. Hooded ramp front sight; adj. folding rear. Grooved receiver for scope mounts. Checkered Monte Carlo-style walnut stock w/ QD studs and rubber recoil pad. Made 1989 to date.

RIFLES

Marlin Model 780

Marlin Model 781

Marlin Model 783

Marlin Model 782L

Marlin Model 883N

Marlin Model 880 Bolt-Action Repeater Series *(Cont.)*
Model 880 (22 LR) **$130**
Model 881 (w/7-shot tubular magazine **135**
Model 882 (22 WMR) **140**
Model 882L (w/laminated hardwood stock) **150**
Model 883 (22 WMR w/12-shot tubular magazine) **145**
Model 883N (w/nickel-teflon finish) **165**
Model 883SS (stainless w/laminated stock) **175**

Marlin Model 980 22 Magnum **$125**
Bolt action. Caliber: 22 WMR. 8-shot clip magazine. 24-inch bbl. Weight: about 6 lbs. Sights: open rear; hooded ramp front. Monte Carlo stock, swivels, sling. Made 1962-70.

Marlin Model 989 Autoloading Rifle **$110**
Caliber: 22 LR. 7-shot clip magazine. 22-inch bbl. Weight: about 5.5 lbs. Sights: open rear; hooded ramp front. Monte Carlo walnut stock w/pistol grip. Made 1962-66.

Marlin Model 989M2 Carbine **$115**
Same as Model 99M1, except clip-loading, 7-shot magazine. Made 1966-79.

Marlin Model 922 Magnum Self-Loading Rifle . . **$250**
Similar to the Model 9, except chambered for 22 WMR. 7-shot magazine. 20.5-inch bbl. 39.5 inches overall. Weight: 6.5 lbs. American black walnut stock with Monte Carlo. Blued finish. Made 1993 to date.

Marlin Model 990 Semiautomatic
Caliber: 22 LR. 17-shot tubular magazine. 22-inch bbl. 40.75 inches overall. Weight: about 5.5 lbs. Side ejection. Cross-bolt safety. Ramp front sight w/brass bead; adj. semibuckhorn folding rear. Receiver grooved for scope mount. Monte Carlo-style American black walnut stock w/checkered pistol grip and forend. Made 1979-87.
Model 990 Semiautomatic **$110**
Model 990L (w/14 Rounds, Laminated hardwood
    stock, QD studs, Black recoil pad; 1992 to date) **135**

Marlin Model 980

Marlin Model 989

Marlin Model 989M2

Marlin Model 990

Marlin Model 990L

Marlin Model 995

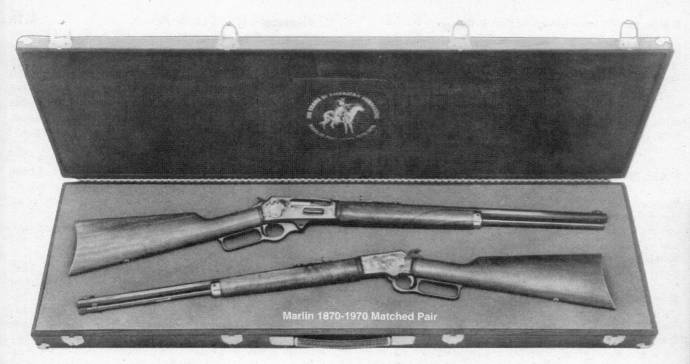

Marlin 1870-1970 Matched Pair

Marlin Model 995 Semiautomatic **$125**
Caliber: 22 LR. 7-shot clip magazine. 18-inch bbl. 36.75 inches overall. Weight: about 5 lbs. Cross-bolt safety. Sights: ramp front w/brass bead; adj. folding semibuckhorn rear. Monte Carlo-style American black walnut stock w/checkered pistol grip and forend. Made 1979 to date.

Marlin 1870-1970 Centennial Matched Pair, Models 336 and 39 . . . . **$1495**
Presentation grade rifles in luggage-style case. Matching serial numbers. Fancy walnut straight-grip buttstock and forearm brass buttplate and forend cap. Engraved receiver w/inlaid medallion; square lever. 20-inch octagon bbl. **Model 336:** 30-30, 7-shot, 7 lbs. **Model 39:** 22 Short, Long, LR, tubular magazine holds 21 Short, 16 Long, 15 LR. 1,000 sets produced. Made 1970. Value is for rifles in new, unfired condition. *See* illustration above.

Marlin Model 1892 Lever-Action Rifle
See Marlin Model 92.

Marlin Model 1893 Lever-Action Rifle
See Marlin Model 93.

Marlin Model 1894 Carbine
Replica of original Model 94. Caliber: 44 Rem. 10-shot magazine. 20-inch round bbl. Weight: 6 lbs. Sight: open rear; ramp front. Straight-grip stock. Made 1969-84.
Standard Model 1894 Carbine **$285**
Model 1894 Octagon (made 1973) **275**
Model 1894 Sporter (w/22-inch bbl., made 1973) **310**

Marlin Model 1894 Carbine

Marlin Model 1894 CL

Marlin Model 1894 Lever-Action Rifle

See Marlin Model 94 Lever-Action Rifle that was listed previously under this section.

Marlin 1894CL Classic $290

Calibers: 218 Bee, 25-20 Win., 32-20 Win. 6-shot tubular magazine. 22-inch bbl. 38.75 inches overall. Weight: 6.25 lbs. Adj. semibuckhorn folding rear sight, brass bead front. Receiver tapped for scope mounts. Straight-grip American black walnut stock with Mar-Shield® finish. Made 1988 to date.

Marlin Model 1894CS Lever Action $275

Caliber: 357 Magnum, 38 Special. 9-shot tubular magazine. 18.5-inch bbl. 36 inches overall. Weight: 6 lbs. Side ejection. Hammer block safety. Square finger lever. Bead front sight, adj. semibuckhorn folding rear. Offset hammer spur for scope use. Two-piece straight-grip American black walnut stock w/white buttplate spacer. Mar-Shield® finish. Made 1984 to date. *See* photo preceding page.

Marlin Model 1894M Lever Action $210

Caliber: 22 WMR. 11-shot tubular magazine. 20-inch bbl. Weight: 6.25 lbs. Sights: ramp front w/brass bead and Wide-Scan hood; adj. semibuckhorn folding rear. Offset hammer spur for scope use. Straight-grip American black walnut stock w/white buttplate spacer. Squared finger lever. Made 1986-88.

Marlin Model 1894S Lever Action $275

Calibers: 41 Mag., 44 Rem. Mag., 44 S&W Special, 45 Colt. 10-shot tubular magazine. 20-inch bbl. 37.5 inches overall. Weight: 6 lbs. Sights and stock same as Model 1894M. Made 1984 to date.

Marlin Model 1895 45-70 Repeater $275

Model 336-type action. Caliber: 45-70 Government. 4-shot magazine. 22-inch bbl. Weight: about 7 lbs. Sights: open rear; bead front. Straight-grip stock, forearm w/metal end cap, QD swivels, leather sling. Made 1972-79.

Marlin Model 1895 Lever-Action Repeater $1495

Solid frame or takedown. Calibers: 33 WCF, 38-56, 40-65, 40-70, 40-82, 45-70. 9-shot tubular magazine. 24-inch round or octagon bbl. standard (other lengths available). Weight: about 8 lbs. Sights: open rear; bead front. Plain stock and forearm (also available w/pistol-grip stock). Made 1895-1915.

Marlin Model 1895SS Lever Action $295

Caliber: 45-70 Govt. 4-shot tubular magazine. 22-inch bbl. with Micro-Groove rifling. 40.5 inches overall. Weight: 7.5 lbs. Ramp front sight w/brass bead and Wide-Scan hood; adj. semibuckhorn folding rear. Solid top receiver tapped for scope mount or receiver sight. Off-set hammer spur for scope use. Two-piece American black walnut stock w/fluted comb, pistol grip, sling swivels. Made 1984 to date.

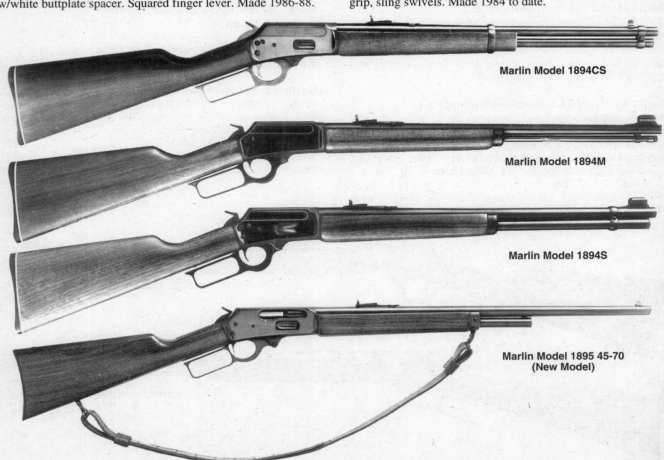

Marlin Model 1894CS

Marlin Model 1894M

Marlin Model 1894S

Marlin Model 1895 45-70 (New Model)

**Marlin Model 1895 Rifle
(Old Model — 1895 - 1915)**

Marlin Model 1897 Lever-Action Rifle
See Marlin Model 97.

Marlin Model 1936 Lever-Action Carbine
See Marlin Model 36.

MMarlin Model 2000 Target Rifle **$425**
Bolt-action single-shot. Caliber: 22 LR. Optional 5-shot adapter kit available. 22-inch bbl. 41 inches overall. Weight: 8 lbs. Globe front sight, adj. peep rear. Textured composite Kevlar stock. Made 1991 to date.

Marlin Model A-1E **$175**
Same as Model A-1, except has peep rear sight; hooded front.

Marlin Model MR-7 Bolt-Action Rifle **$425**
Calibers: 270 Win. and 30-06, 4-shot magazine. 22-inch bbl., 43.31 inches overall. Weight: 7 lbs., 9.5 oz. Checkered American walnut stock with recoil pad and sling-swivel studs. Jeweled bolt. Made from 1996 to date.

Marlin Model 2000

Marlin Model A-1 Autoloader

Marlin Model A-1 Autoloading Rifle **$150**
Takedown. Caliber: 22 LR. 6-shot detachable box magazine. 24-inch bbl. Weight: about 6 lbs. Open rear sight. Plain pistol-grip stock. Made 1935-46.

Marlin Model A-1C Autoloading Rifle **$155**
Improved version of Model A-1 w/same general specifications, stock w/semibeavertail forend. Made 1940-46.

Marlin Model A-1DL **$185**
Same as Model A-lC, except has peep rear sight; hooded front, swivels.

Marlin-Glenfield Model 10 . . . . **$80**
Same as Marlin Model 101, except has walnut-finished hardwood stock. Made 1966-79. *Note:* Later production has hot-iron wood-stamped pistol grip to simulate checkering/carving; plain forend.

Marlin-Glenfield Model 20 . . . . **$80**
Same as Marlin Model 80/780, except has bead front sight, walnut-finished hardwood stock. Made 1966 to date. *Note:* Recent production has stamped pistol grip to simulate checkering; plain forend.

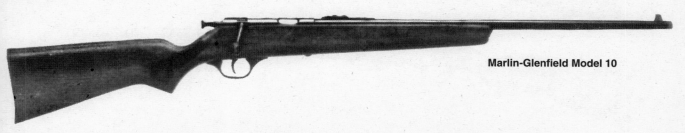

Marlin-Glenfield Model 10

Marlin-Glenfield Model 30A

Marlin-Glenfield Model 60

Marlin-Glenfield Model 30 . . . . **$175**
Same as Marlin Model 336C, except chambered for 30-30 only,
has 4-shot magazine, plainer stock and forearm of walnut-
finished hardwood. Made 1966-68.

Marlin-Glenfield Model 30A **$185**
Same as Marlin Model 336C, except chambered for 30-30 only,
has checkered stock of walnut-finished hardwood. Made 1969 to
date.

Marlin-Glenfield Model 36G **$225**
Same as Marlin Model 336C, except chambered for 30-30 only,
has 5-shot magazine, plainer stock. Made 1960-65.

Marlin-Glenfield Model 60 . . . . **$70**
Same as Marlin Model 99C, except has walnut-finished hardwood stock. Made 1960-80.

Marlin-Glenfield Model 70 . . . . **$75**
Same as Marlin Model 989M2, except has walnut-finished hardwood stock; no handguard. Made 1966-69.

Marlin-Glenfield Model 80G **$75**
Same as Marlin Model 80C, except has plainer stock, bead front
sight. Made 1960-65.

Marlin-Glenfield Model 81G **$80**
Same as Marlin Model 81C, except has plainer stock, bead front
sight. Made 1960-65.

Marlin-Glenfield Model 99G **$85**
Same as Marlin Model 99C, except has plainer stock, bead front
sight. Made 1960-65.

Marlin-Glenfield Model 101G **$70**
Same as Marlin Model 101, except has plainer stock. Made
1960-65.

Marlin-Glenfield Model 989G Autoloading Rifle . . **$70**
Same as Marlin Model 989, except has plain stock, bead front
sight. Made 1962-64.

Marlin-Glenfield Model 70

Marlin-Glenfield Model 80G

MAUSER SPORTING RIFLES
Oberndorf am Neckar, Germany
Manufactured by Mauser-Werke GmbH

Before the end of WWI, the name of the Mauser firm was "Waffenfabrik Mauser A.-G." Shortly after WWI, it was changed to "Mauser-Werke A.-G." This may be used as a general clue to the age of genuine Original-Mauser sporting rifles made before WWII, because all bear either of these firm names as well as the "Mauser" banner trademark.

The first four rifles listed were manufactured before WWI. Those that follow were produced between World Wars I and II. The early Mauser models can generally be identified by the pistol grip, which is rounded instead of capped, and the M/98 military-type magazine floorplate and catch, the later models have hinged magazine floorplate with lever or button release.

PRE-WORLD WAR I MODELS

Mauser Bolt-Action Sporting Carbine **$795**
Calibers: 6.5×54, 6.5×58, 7×57, 8×57, 957mm. 19.75-inch bbl. Weight: about 7 lbs. Full-stocked to muzzle. Other specifications same as for standard rifle.

Mauser Bolt-Action Sporting Rifle **$650**
Calibers: 6.5×55, 6.5×58, 7×57, 8×57, 9×57, 9.3×62 10.75×68.5-shot box magazine, 23.5-inch bbl. Weight. 7 to 7.5 lbs. Double-set trigger. Sights: tangent curve rear; ramp front. Pistol-grip stock, forearm w/schnabel tip, swivels.

**Mauser Bolt-Action Sporting Rifle,
Military Type** **$495**
So called because of "stepped" M/98-type bbl., military front sight and double-pull trigger. Calibers: 7×57, 8×57, 9×57mm. Other specifications same as for standard rifle.

**Mauser Bolt-Action Sporting Rifle,
Short Model** **$650**
Calibers: 6.5×54, 8×51mm. 19.75-inch bbl. Weight about 6.25 lbs. Other specifications same as for standard rifle.

PRE-WORLD WAR II MODELS

**Mauser Model DSM34 Bolt-Action Single-Shot
Sporting Rifle** **$375**
Also called "Sport-model." Caliber: 22 LR. 26-inch bbl. Weight: about 7.75 lbs. Sights: tangent curve open rear; barleycorn front. M/98 military-type stock, swivels. Intro. c. 1935.

**Mauser Model EL320 Bolt-Action Single-Shot
Sporting Rifle** **$345**
Caliber: 22 LR. 23.5-inch bbl. Weight: about 4.25 lbs. Sights: adj. open rear; bead front. Sporting stock w/checkered pistol grip, swivels.

**Mauser Model EN310 Bolt-Action Single-Shot
Sporting Rifle** **$325**
Caliber: 22 LR. ("22 Lang fur Buchsen.") 19.75-inch bbl. Weight: about 4 lbs. Sights: fixed open rear, blade front. Plain pistol-grip stock.

**Mauser Model ES340 Bolt-Action Single-Shot
Target Rifle** **$350**
Caliber: 22 LR. 25.5-inch bbl. Weight: about 6.5 lbs. Sights: tangent curve rear; ramp front. Sporting stock w/checkered pistol grip and grooved forearm, swivels.

**Mauser Model ES340B Bolt-Action Single-Shot
Target Rifle** **$375**
Caliber: 22 LR. 26.75-inch bbl. Weight: about 8 lbs. Sights: tangent curve open rear; ramp front. Plain pistol-grip stock, swivels.

NOTE

The "B" series of Mauser 22 rifles (Model ES340B, MS350B, etc.) were improved versions of their corresponding models and were introduced about 1935.

**Mauser Model ES350 Bolt-Action Single-Shot
Target Rifle** **$495**
"Meistershaftsbuchse" (Championship Rifle). Caliber: 22 LR. 27.5-inch bbl. Weight: about 7.75 lbs. Sights: open micrometer rear; ramp front. Target stock w/checkered pistol grip and forearm, grip cap, swivels.

Mauser Model ES340

Mauser Model ES350

Mauser MS420

Mauser Standard Model

**Mauser Model ES350B Bolt-Action Single-Shot
Target Rifle** **$445**
Same general specifications as Model MS350B except single
shot, weighs about 8.25 lbs.

**Mauser Model KKW Bolt-Action Single-Shot
Target Rifle** **$395**
Caliber: 22 LR. 26-inch bbl. Weight: about 8.75 lbs. Sights: tangent curve open rear; barleycorn front. M/98 military-type stock,
swivels. *Note:* This rifle has an improved design Mauser 22 action w/separate nonrotating bolt head. In addition to being produced for commercial sale, this model was used as a training rifle
by the German armed forces; it was also made by Walther and
Gustloff. Introduced just before WWII.

**Mauser Model M410 Bolt-Action Repeating
Sporting Rifle** **$425**
Caliber: 22 LR. 5-shot detachable box magazine. 23.5-inch bbl.
Weight: about 5 lbs. Sights: tangent curve open rear; ramp front.
Sporting stock w/checkered pistol grip, swivels.

**Mauser Model MM410B Bolt-Action Repeating
Sporting Rifle** **$695**
Caliber: 22 LR. 5-shot detachable box magazine. 23.5-inch bbl.
Weight: about 6.25 lbs. Sights: tangent curve open rear; ramp
front. Lightweight sporting stock w/checkered pistol grip, swiv-
els.

**Mauser Model MS350B Bolt-Action Repeating
Target Rifle** **$675**
Caliber: 22 LR. 5-shot detachable box magazine. Receiver and
bbl. grooved for detachable rear sight or scope. 26.75-inch bbl.
Weight: about 8.5 lbs. Sights: micrometer open rear; ramp front.
Target stock w/checkered pistol grip and forearm, grip cap, sling
swivels.

**Mauser Model MS420 Bolt-Action Repeating
Sporting Rifle** **$695**
Caliber: 22 LR. 5-shot detachable box magazine. 25.5-inch bbl.
Weight: about 6.5 lbs. Sights: tangent curve open rear; ramp
front. Sporting stock w/checkered pistol grip, grooved forearm
swivels.

**Mauser Model MS420B Bolt-Action Repeating
Target Rifle** **$625**
Caliber: 22 LR. 5-shot detachable box magazine. 26.75-inch bbl.
Weight: about 8 lbs. Sights: tangent curve open rear; ramp front.
Target stock w/checkered pistol grip, grooved forearm, swivels.

Mauser Standard Model Rifle **$475**
Refined version of the German Service Kar. 98k. Straight bolt
handle. Calibers: 7mm Mauser (7×57mm) 7.9mm Mauser
(8×57mm). 5-shot box magazine. 23.5-inch bbl. Weight: about
8.5 lbs. Sights: blade front; adj. rear. Walnut stock of M/98
military-type. *Note:* These rifles were made for commercial sale
and are of the high quality found in the Oberndorf Mauser sporters. They bear the Mauser trademark on the receiver ring.

Mauser Type "A" Bolt-Action Sporting Rifle . . **$1195**
Special British Model. Calibers: 7×57, 30-06 (7.62×63) 8×60,
9×57, 9.3×62mm. 5-shot box magazine. 23.5-inch round bbl.
Weight: about 7.25 lbs. Military-type single trigger. Sights: express rear; hooded ramp front. Circassian walnut sporting stock
w/checkered pistol grip and forearm, with or w/o cheekpiece,
buffalo horn forend tip and grip cap, detachable swivels. Variations: octagon bbl., double-set trigger, shotgun-type safety, folding peep rear sight, tangent curve rear sight, three-leaf rear sight.

**Mauser Type "A" Bolt-Action Sporting Rifle,
Magnum Model** **$1250**
Same general specifications as standard Type "A," except has
Magnum action, weighs 7.5 to 8.5 lbs. Calibers: 280 Ross, 318
Westley Richards Express, 10.75×68mm, 404 Nitro Express.

**Mauser Type "A" Bolt-Action Sporting Rifle,
Short Model** **$1050**
Same as standard Type "A," except has short action, 21.5-inch
round bbl., weighs about 6 lbs. Calibers: 250-3000, 6.5×54,
8×51mm.

Mauser Type "B" Bolt-Action Sporting Rifle . . . **$950**
Normal Model. Calibers: 7×57, 30-06 (7.62×63), 8×57, 8×60,
9×57, 9.3×62, 10.7568mm. 5-shot box magazine. 23.5-inch
round bbl. Weight: about 7.25 lbs. Double-set trigger. Sights:
three-leaf rear, ramp front. Fine walnut stock w/checkered pistol
grip, schnabel forend tip, cheekpiece, grip cap, swivels. Varia-

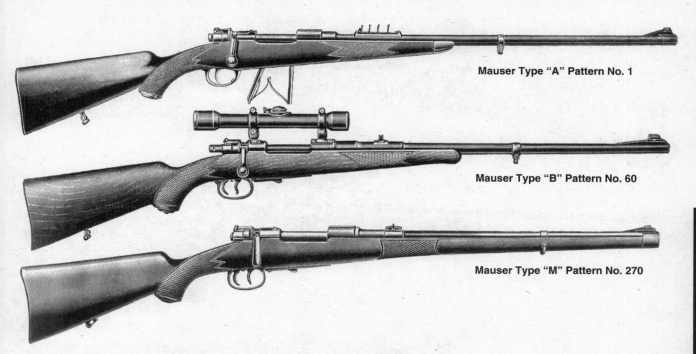

Mauser Type "A" Pattern No. 1

Mauser Type "B" Pattern No. 60

Mauser Type "M" Pattern No. 270

Mauser Type "B" Bolt-Action Sporting Rifle *(Cont.)*

tions: octagon or half-octagon bbl., military-type single trigger, shotgun-type trigger, shotgun-type safety, folding peep rear sight, tangent curve rear sight, telescopic sight.

Mauser Type "K" Bolt-Action Sporting Rifle . . $1595

Light Short Model. Same specifications as Normal Type "B" model except has short action, 21.5-inch round bbl., weighs about 6 lbs. Calibers: 250-3000, 6.5×54, 8×51mm.

Mauser Type "M" Bolt-Action Sporting Carbine . . $895

Calibers: 6.5×54, 7×57, 30-06 (7.62×63), 8×51, 8×60, 9×57mm. 5-shot box magazine. 19.75-inch round bbl. Weight: 6 to 6.75 lbs. Double-set trigger, flat bolt handle. Sights: three-leaf rear; ramp front. Stocked to muzzle, cheekpiece, checkered pistol grip and forearm, grip cap, steel forend cap, swivels. Variations: military-type single trigger, shotgun-type trigger, shotgun-type safety, tangent curve rear sight, telescopic sight.

NOTE

Production of original Mauser sporting rifles (66 Series) resumed at the Oberndorf plant in 1965 by Mauser-Jagdwaffen GmbH, now Mauser-Werke Oberndorf GmbH. The Series 2000-3000-4000 rifles, however, were made for Mauser by Friedrich Wilhelm Heym Gewehrfabrik, Muennerstadt, West Germany.

Mauser Type "S" Bolt-Action Sporting Carbine $925

Calibers: 6.5×54 7×57, 8×51, 8×60, 9×57mm. 5-shot box magazine. 19.75-inch round bbl. Weight: about 6 to 6.75 lbs. Double-set trigger. Sights: three-leaf rear; ramp front. Stocked to muzzle, schnabel forend tip, cheekpiece, checkered pistol grip w/cap, swivels. Variations: same as listed for Normal Model Type "B."

POST-WORLD WAR II MODELS

Mauser Model 66S Bolt-Action Standard Sporting Rifle

Telescopic short action. Bbls. interchangeable within caliber group. Single- or double-set trigger (interchangeable). Calibers: 243 Win., 6.5×57, 270 Win., 7×64, 308 Win., 30-06. 3-round magazine. 23.6-inch bbl. (25.6-inch in 7×64). Weight: about 7.3 lbs. (7.5 lbs. in 7×64). Sights: adj. open rear, hooded ramp front. Select European walnut stock, Monte Carlo w/cheekpiece, rosewood forend tip and pistol-grip cap, skip checkering, recoil pad, sling swivels. Made 1965 to date, export to U.S. discontinued 1974. *Note: U.S.* designation, 1971-73, was "Model 660."

With one bbl. $1195
Extra bbl. assembly **500**

Mauser Model 66S Standard

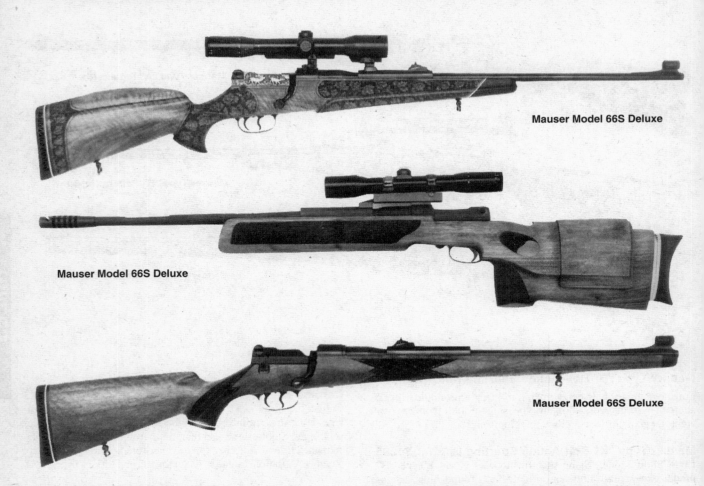

Mauser Model 66S Deluxe

Mauser Model 66S Deluxe

Mauser Model 66S Deluxe

Mauser Model 66S Deluxe Sporter

On special order, Model 66S rifles and carbines are available with elaborate engraving, gold and silver inlays and carved stocks of the finest select walnut. Added value is upward of **$1000.**

Mauser Model 66S Ultra

Same general specifications as Model 66S Standard, except has 20.9-inch bbl., weighs about 6.8 lbs.

With one bbl. **$1295**
Extra bbl. assembly   500

Mauser Model 66SG Big Game

Same general specifications as Model 66S Standard, except has 25.6-inch bbl., weighs about 9.3 lbs. Calibers: 375 H&H Mag., 458 Win. Mag. *Note: U.S.* designation, 1971-73, was "Model 660 Safari."

With one bbl. **$1450**
Extra bbl. assembly   550

Mauser Model 66SH High Performance

Same general specifications as Model 66S Standard, except has 25.6-inch bbl., weighs about 7.5 pounds (9.3 pounds in 9.3×64). Calibers: 6.5×68, 7mm Rem. Mag., 7mm S.E.v. Hofe, 300 Win. Mag., 8×68S, 9.3×64.

With one bbl. **$1050**
Extra bbl. assembly   500

Mauser Model 66SP Super Match Bolt-Action Target Rifle **$2550**

Telescopic short action. Adj. single-stage trigger. Caliber: 308 Win. (chambering for other cartridges available on special order). 3-shot magazine. 27.6-inch heavy bbl. with muzzle brake, dovetail rib for special scope mount. Weight: about 12 lbs. Target stock with wide and deep forearm, full pistol grip, thumbhole adj. cheekpiece, adj. rubber buttplate.

Mauser Model 66ST Carbine

Same general specifications as Model 66S Standard, except has 20.9-inch bbl., full-length stock, weighs about 7 lbs.

With one bbl. **$1095**
Extra bbl. assembly   500

Mauser Model 83 Bolt-Action Rifle **$1895**

Centerfire single-shot, bolt-action rifle for 300-meter competition. Caliber: 308 Win. 25.5-inch fluted bbl. Weight: 10.5 lbs. Adj. micrometer rear sight globe front. Fully adj. competition stock. Discontinued 1988.

Mauser Model 99 Classic Bolt-Action Rifle

Calibers: 243 Win., 25-06, 270 Win., 30-06, 308 Win., 257 Wby., 270 Wby., 7mm Rem. Mag., 300 Win., 300 Wby. 375 H&H. 4-shot magazine (standard), 3-shot (Magnum). Bbl.: 24-inch (standard) or 26-inch (Magnum). 44 inches overall (stan-

Mauser Model 99

Mauser Model 201

Mauser Model 3000

Mauser Model 4000

Mauser Model 99 Classic Rifle *(Cont.)*

dard). Weight: 8 lbs. No sights. Checkered European walnut stock with rosewood grip cap available in Classic and Monte Carlo styles with High-Luster or oil finish. Discontinued importing 1994.

Standard Classic or Monte Carlo (Oil Finish) **$895**
Magnum Classic or Monte Carlo (Oil Finish) 945
Standard Classic or Monte Carlo (H-L Finish) 925
Magnum Classic or Monte Carlo (H-L Finish) 995

Mauser Model 107 Bolt-Action Rifle **$275**

Caliber: 22 LR. Mag. 5-shot magazine. 21.5-inch bbl. 40 inches overall. Weight: 5 lbs. Receiver drilled and tapped for rail scope mounts. Hooded front sight, adj. rear. Discontinued importing 1994.

Mauser Model 201/201 Luxus Bolt-Action Rifle

Calibers: 22 LR, 22 Win. Mag. 5-shot magazine. 21-inch bbl. 40 inches overall. Weight: 6.5 lbs. Receiver drilled and tapped for scope mounts. Sights optional. Checkered walnut-stained beech stock with Monte Carlo. Model 201 Luxus has checkered European walnut stock QD swivels, rosewood forend and rubber recoil pad. Made 1989 to date. Discontinued importing 1994.

Model 201 Standard **$450**
Model 201 Magnum 495
Model 201 Luxus Standard 575
Model 201 Luxus Magnum 625

Mauser Model 2000 Bolt-Action Sporting Rifle . . **$295**

Modified Mauser-type action. Calibers: 270 Win., 308 Win., 30-06. 5-shot magazine. 24-inch bbl. Weight: about 7.5 lbs. Sights: folding leaf rear; hooded ramp front. Checkered walnut stock w/Monte Carlo comb and cheekpiece, forend tip, sling swivels. Made 1969-71. *Note:* Model 2000 is similar in appearance to Model 3000.

Mauser Model 3000 Bolt-Action Sporting Rifle . . **$445**

Modified Mauser-type action. Calibers: 243 Win., 270 Win., 308 Win., 30-06. 5-shot magazine. 22-inch bbl. Weight: about 7 lbs. No sights. Select European walnut stock, Monte Carlo style w/cheekpiece, rosewood forend tip and pistol-grip cap, skip checkering, recoil pad, sling swivels. Made 1971-74.

Mauser Model 3000 Magnum **$495**

Same general specifications as standard Model 3000, except has 3-shot magazine, 26-inch bbl., weighs about 8 lbs. Calibers: 7mm Rem. Mag., 300 Win. Mag., 375 H&H Mag.

Mauser Model 4000 Varmint Rifle **$395**

Same general specifications as standard Model 3000, except w/smaller action, folding leaf rear sight; hooded ramp front, rubber buttplate instead of recoil pad, weighs about 6.75 lbs. Calibers: 222 Rem., 223 Rem. 22-inch bbl. Select European walnut stock with rosewood forend tip and pistol-grip cap. French checkering and sling swivels.

McMILLAN GUN WORKS
Phoenix, Arizona
Now owned by Harris Gunworks

See Harris Gunworks.

GEBRÜDER MERKEL
Suhl, Germany

For Merkel combination guns and drillings, *see* listings under Merkel shotguns.

Merkel Model 220

Merkel Over/Under Rifles ("Bock-Doppelbüchsen")
Calibers: 5.6×35 Vierling, 6.5×58r5, 7×57r5, 8×57JR, 8×60R Magnum, 9.3×53r5, 9.3×72r5, 9.3×74r5, 10.3×60R as well as most of the British calibers for African and Indian big game. Various bbl. lengths, weights. In general, specifications correspond to those of Merkel over/under shotguns. Values of these over/under rifles (in calibers for which ammunition is obtainable) are about the same as those of comparable shotgun models. Currently manufactured. For more specific data, *see* Merkel shotgun models indicated below.

Model 220	$ 6,250
Model 220E	7,295
Model 221	5,950
Model 221E	7,850
Model 320	6,500
Model 320E	12,000
Model 321	13,250
Model 321E	14,000
Model 322	14,500
Model 323	15,500
Model 324	17,500

MEXICAN MILITARY RIFLE
Mfd. by Government Arsenal, Mexico, D.F.

Mexican Model 1936 Mauser Military Rifle $175
Same as the German Kar.98k with minor variations, has U.S. M/1903 Springfield-type knurled cocking piece.

MIDLAND RIFLES
Gibbs Rifle Company, Inc.
Martinsburg, WV

Midland rifles were developed around the Springfield 1903 bolt system and have an established reputation throughout the world as well-built, lightweight sporting rifles.

Midland Model 2100 Bolt-Action Rifle $290
Calibers: 22-250, 243 Win., 6mm Rem., 270 Win., 6.5×55, 7×57, 7×64, 308 Win., and 30-06. 4-shot magazine. 22-inch bbl., 43 inches overall. Weight: 7 lbs. Flip-up rear sight; hooded ramp front. Finely finished and checkered walnut stock with pistol-grip cap and sling swivels. Steel recoil bar. Action drilled and tapped for scope mounts.

Midland Model 2600 Bolt-Action Rifle $275
Same general specifications as the Model 2100 except no pistol-grip cap, and stock is walnut-finished hardwood.

Midland Model 2700 Lightweight Rifle $330
Same general specifications as the Model 2100 except the weight of this rifle as been reduced by utilizing a tapered bbl., anodized aluminum trigger housing and lightened stock. Weight: 6.5 lbs.

MITCHELL ARMS. INC.
Santa Ana, California

Mitchell Model 15/22 Semiautomatic
High Standard-style action. Caliber: 22 LR. 15-shot magazine (10-shot after 10/13/94). 20.5-inch bbl. 37.5 inches overall. Weight: 6.25 lbs. Ramp front sight; adj. open rear. Blued finish. Mahogany stock; Monte Carlo-style American walnut stock on Deluxe Model. Made 1994 to date.

Model 15/22 SP (Special) w/plastic buttplate	$ 70
Model 15/22 Carbine	105
Model 15/22D Deluxe	125

Midland Model 2700 Lightweight

**Mitchell Model 15/22
Carbine**

Mitchell Model 9300 Series Bolt-Action Rifle

Calibers: 22 LR, 22 Mag. 5- or 10-shot magazine. 22.5-inch bbl. 40.75 inches overall. Weight: 6.5 lbs. Beaded ramp front sight; adj. open rear. Blued finish. American walnut stock. Made 1994-95.

9301 (22 LR, Checkered, Rosewood Caps) **$185**
9302 (22 Mag., Checkered, Rosewood Caps) **195**
9303 (22 LR, Plain Stock) **145**
9304 (22 Mag., Checkered Stock, No Rosewood Caps) . . . **155**
9305 (22 LR, Special Stock) **125**

Mitchell AK-22 Semiautomatic Rifle $245

Replica of the AK-47 rifle. Calibers: 22 LR, 22 WMR. 20-shot magazine (22 LR), 10-shot (22 WMR). 18-inch bbl. 36 inches overall. Weight: 6.5 lbs. Sights: post front; open adj. rear. European walnut stock and forend. Matte black finish. Made 1985-94.

Mitchell CAR-15 22 Semiautomatic Rifle $250

Replica of the AR-15 CAR rifle. Caliber: 22 LR. 15-shot magazine. 16.25-inch bbl. 32 inches overall. Sights: adj. post front; adj. aperture rear. Telescoping buttstock and ventilated forend. Matte black finish. Made 1990-94.

Mitchell Galil 22 Semiautomatic Rifle $250

Replica of the Israeli Galil rifle. Calibers: 22 LR, 22 WMR. 20-shot magazine (22 LR), 10-shot (22 WMR). 18-inch bbl. 36 inches overall. Weight: 6.5 lbs. Sights: adj. post front; rear adj. for windage. Folding metal stock with European walnut grip and forend. Matte black finish. Made 1987-93.

Mitchell M-16A 22 Semiautomatic Rifle $245

Replica of the AR-15 rifle. Caliber: 22 LR. 15-shot magazine. 20.5-inch bbl. 38.5 inches overall. Weight: 7 lbs. Sights: adj. post front, adj. aperture rear. Black composition stock and forend. Matte black finish. Made 1990-94.

Mitchell MAS 22 Semiautomatic Rifle $255

Replica of the French MAS bullpup rifle. Caliber: 22 LR. 20-shot magazine. 18-inch bbl. 28 inches overall. Weight: 7.5 lbs. Sights: adj. post front, folding aperture rear. European walnut buttstock and forend. Matte black finish. Made 1987-93.

Mitchell PPS Semiautomatic Rifle

Caliber: 22 LR. 20-shot magazine, 50-shot drum. 16.5-inch bbl. 33.5 inches overall. Weight: 5.5 lbs. Sights: blade front; adj. rear. European walnut stock with ventilated bbl. shroud. Matte black finish. Made 1989-94.

Model PPS (20-shot) **$270**
Model PPS/50 (50-shot drum) **350**

O.F. MOSSBERG & SONS, INC.
North Haven, Connecticut

Mossberg Model 10 Bolt-Action Single-Shot Rifle $105

Takedown. Caliber: 22 LR, Long, Short. 22-inch bbl. Weight: about 4 lbs. Sights: open rear; bead front. Plain pistol-grip stock w/swivels, sling. Made 1933-35.

Mossberg Model 14 Bolt-Action Single-Shot Rifle $110

Takedown. Caliber: 22 LR, Long, Short. 24-inch bbl. Weight: about 5.25 lbs. Sights: peep rear; hooded ramp front. Plain pistol-grip stock with semibeavertail forearm, 1.25-inch swivels. Made 1934-35.

Mossberg Model 20 Bolt-Action Single-Shot Rifle $115

Takedown. Caliber: 22 LR, Long, Short. 24-inch bbl. Weight: about 4.5 lbs. Sights: open rear; bead front. Plain pistol-grip stock and forearm with finger grooves, sling and swivels. Made 1933-35.

RIFLES

Mossberg Model 25

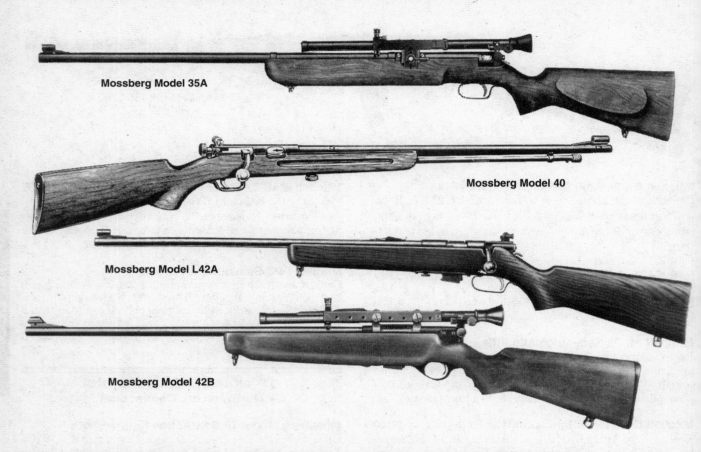

Mossberg Model 35A

Mossberg Model 40

Mossberg Model L42A

Mossberg Model 42B

Mossberg Model 25/25A Bolt-Action Single-Shot Rifle
Takedown. Caliber: 22 LR, Long, Short. 24-inch bbl. Weight: about 5 lbs. Sights: peep rear; hooded ramp front. Plain pistol-grip stock w/semibeavertail forearm. 1.25-inch swivels. Made 1935-36.
Model 25 . . . . **$100**
Model 25A (Improved Model 25, 1936-38) **125**

Mossberg Model 26B/26C Bolt-Action Single-Shot
Takedown. Caliber: 22 LR, Long, Short. 26-inch bbl. Weight: about 5.5 lbs. Sights; Rear, micrometer click peep or open; hooded ramp front. Plain pistol-grip stock swivels. Made 1938-41.
Model 26B **$125**
Model 26C (No rear sight/swivels) **100**

Mossberg Model 30 Bolt-Action Single-Shot Rifle **$100**
Takedown. Caliber: 22 LR, Long, Short. 24-inch bbl. Weight: about 4.5 lbs. Sights: peep rear; bead front, on hooded ramp. Plain pistol-grip stock, forearm with finger grooves. Made 1933-35.

Mossberg Model 34 Bolt-Action Single-Shot Rifle **$110**
Takedown. Caliber: 22 LR, Long, Short. 24-inch bbl. Weight: 5.5 lbs. Sights: peep rear; hooded ramp front. Plain pistol-grip stock w/semibeavertail forearm, 1.25-inch swivels. Made 1934-35.

Mossberg Model 35 Target Grade Bolt-Action Single-Shot Rifle **$220**
Caliber: 22 LR. 26-inch heavy bbl. Weight: about 8.25 lbs. Sights: micrometer click rear peep; hooded ramp front. Large target stock w/full pistol grip, cheekpiece, full beavertail forearm, 1.25-inch swivels. Made 1935-37.

Mossberg Model 35A Bolt-Action Single-Shot Rifle **$225**
Caliber: 22 LR. 26-inch heavy bbl. Weight: about 8.25 lbs. Sights: micrometer click peep rear; hooded front. Target stock w/cheekpiece full pistol grip and forearm, 1.25-inch sling swivels. Made 1937-38.

Mossberg Model 35A-LS **$235**
Caliber 22 LR. Same as Model 35A but with Lyman 57 rear sight, 17A front. Target stock with checkpiece, full pistol grip and forearm.

Mossberg Model 35B **$200**
Same specifications as Model 44B, except single shot. Made 1938-40.

Mossberg Model 40 Bolt-Action Repeater **$95**
Takedown. Caliber: 22 LR, Long, Short, 16-round tubular magazine. 24-inch bbl. Weight: about 5 lbs. Sights: peep rear; bead front, on hooded ramp. Plain pistol-grip stock, forearm with finger grooves. Made 1933-35.

Mossberg Model 42C

Mossberg Model L-43

Mossberg Model 43B

Mossberg Model 44US

Mossberg Model 42 Bolt-Action Repeater $100
Takedown. Caliber: 22 LR, Long, Short. 7-shot detachable box magazine. 24-inch bbl. Weight: about 5 lbs. Sights: receiver peep, open rear; hooded ramp front. Pistol-grip stock. 1.25-inch swivels. Made 1935-37.

Mossberg Model 42A/L42A Bolt-Action Repeaters
Takedown. Caliber: 22 LR, Long, Short. 7-shot detachable box magazine. 24-inch bbl. Weight: about 5 lbs. Sights: receiver peep, open rear; ramp front. Plain pistol-grip stock. Made 1937-38. **Model L42A,** made 1937-1941, has left-hand action.

Model 42A $115
Model L42A   150

Mossberg Model 42B/42C Bolt-Action Repeaters
Takedown. Caliber: 22 LR, Long, Short. 5-shot detachable box magazine. 24-inch bbl. Weight: about 6 lbs. Sights: micrometer click receiver peep, open rear hooded ramp front. Plain pistol-grip stock, swivels. Made 1938-41.

Model 42B $100
Model 42C (No rear peep sight)   95

Mossberg Model 42M Bolt-Action Repeater $145
Caliber: 22 LR, Long, Short. 7-shot detachable box magazine. 23-inch bbl. Weight: about 6.75 lbs. Sights: microclick receiver peep, open rear; hooded ramp front. Two-piece Mannlicher-type stock w/cheekpiece and pistol grip, swivels. Made 1940-50.

Mossberg Model 43/L43 Bolt-Action Repeaters . . . $215
Speedlock, adj. trigger pull. Caliber: 22 LR. 7-shot detachable box magazine. 26-inch heavy bbl. Weight: about 8.25 lbs. Sights: Lyman 57 rear; selective aperture front. Target stock w/cheekpiece, full pistol grip, beavertail forearm, adj. front swivel. Made 1937-38. Model L43 is same as Model 43 except has left-hand action.

Mossberg Model 43B $225
Same as Model 44B, except with Lyman 57 receiver sight and 17A front sight. Made 1938-39.

Mossberg Model 44 Bolt-Action Repeater $135
Takedown. Caliber: 22 LR, Long, Short. Tubular magazine holds 16 LR. 24-inch bbl. Weight: 6 lbs. Sights: peep rear; hooded ramp front. Plain pistol-grip stock w/semibeavertail forearm, 1.25-inch swivels. Made 1934-35. *Note:* Do not confuse this rifle with the later Models 44B and 44US, which are clip repeaters.

Mossberg Model 44B Bolt-Action Target Rifle . . $200
Caliber: 22 LR. 7-shot detachable box magazine. Made 1938-1941.

Mossberg Model 44US Bolt-Action Repeater . . . $185
Caliber: 22 LR. 7-shot detachable box magazine. 26-inch heavy bbl. Weight: about 8.5 lbs. Sights: micrometer click receiver peep, hooded front. Target stock, swivels. Made 1943-48. *Note:* This model was used as a training rifle by the U.S. Armed Forces during WWII.

Mossberg Model L45A
Left-Hand Model

Mossberg Model 45B

Mossberg Model 45 Bolt-Action Repeater $140

Takedown. Caliber: 22 LR, Long, Short. Tubular magazine
holds 15 LR, 18 Long, 22 Short. 24-inch bbl. Weight: about 6.75
lbs. Sights: rear peep; hooded ramp front. Plain pistol-grip stock,
1.25-inch swivels. Made 1935-1937.

Mossberg Model 45A, L45A, 45AC Bolt-Action Repeaters

Takedown. Caliber: 22 LR, Long, Short. Tubular magazine
holds 15 LR, 18 Long, 22 Short. 24-inch bbl. Weight: about 6.75
lbs. Sights: receiver peep, open rear; hooded blade front sight
mounted on ramp. Plain pistol-grip stock, 1.25-inch sling swivels. Made 1937-1938.

Model 45A **$130**
Model L45A (Left-Hand Action) **175**
Model 45AC (No receiver peep sight) **115**

Mossberg Model 45B/45C Bolt-Action Repeaters

Takedown. Caliber: 22 LR, Long, Short. Tubular magazine
holds 15 LR, 18 Long, 22 Short. 24-inch bbl. Weight: about
6.25 lbs. Open rear sight; hooded blade front sight, mounted
on ramp. Plain pistol-grip stock w/sling swivels. Made 1938-
1940.

Model 45B **$125**
Model 45C (No sights, made 1935-37) **110**

Mossberg Model 46 Bolt-Action Repeater $140

Takedown. Caliber: 22 LR, Long, Short. Tubular magazine
holds 15 LR, 18 Long, 22 Short. 26-inch bbl. Weight: 7.5 lbs.
Sights: a micrometer click rear peep; hooded ramp front. Pistol-
grip stock w/cheekpiece, full beavertail forearm, 1.25-inch swivels. Made 1935-1937.

Mossberg Model 46A, 46A-LS, L46A-LS Bolt-Action Repeaters

Takedown. Caliber: 22 LR, Long, Short. Tubular magazine
holds 15 LR, 18 Long, 22 Short. 26-inch bbl. Weight: about 7.25
lbs. Sights: micrometer click receiver peep, open rear; hooded
ramp front. Pistol-grip stock w/cheekpiece and beavertail forearm, quick-detachable swivels. Made 1937-1938.

Model 46A **$135**
Model 46A-LS (w/Lyman 57 Receiver Sight) **180**
Model L46A-LS (Left-hand Action) **245**

Mossberg Model 46B Bolt-Action Repeater $115

Takedown. Caliber: 22 LR, Long, Short. Tubular magazine
holds 15 LR, 18 Long, 22 Short. 26-inch bbl. Weight: about 7 lbs.
Sights: micrometer click receiver peep open rear, hooded front.
Plain pistol-grip stock w/cheekpiece, swivels. *Note:* Postwar
version of this model has full magazine holding 20 LR, 23 Long,
30 Short. Made 1938-1950.

Mossberg Model L46A-LS

Mossberg Model 46B

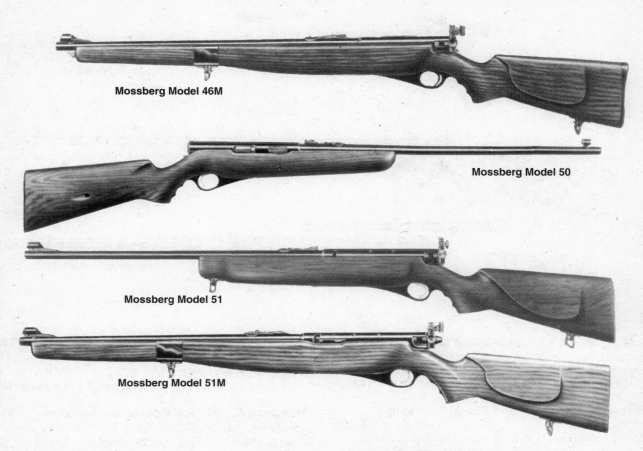

Mossberg Model 46M

Mossberg Model 50

Mossberg Model 51

Mossberg Model 51M

Mossberg Model 46BT $155
Same as Model 46B, except has heavier bbl. and stock weighs 7.75 lbs. Made 1938-39.

Mossberg Model 46C $115
Same as Model 46 except has a heavier bbl. and stock than that model, weighs 8.5 lbs. Made 1936-37.

Mossberg Model 46M Bolt-Action Repeater $140
Caliber: 22 LR, Long, Short. Tubular magazine holds 22 Short, 18 Long, 15 LR. 23-inch bbl. Weight: about 7 lbs. Sights: microclick receiver peep, open rear; hooded ramp front. Two-piece Mannlicher-type stock w/cheekpiece and pistol grip, swivels. Made 1940-52.

Mossberg Model 50 Autoloading Rifle $135
Same as Model 51, except has plain stock w/o beavertail cheekpiece, swivels or receiver peep sight. Made 1939-1942.

Mossberg Model 51 Autoloading Rifle $150
Takedown. Caliber: 22 LR. 15-shot tubular magazine in buttstock. 24-inch bbl. Weight: about 7.25 lbs. Sights: micrometer click receiver peep, open rear; hooded ramp front. Cheekpiece stock w/full pistol grip and beavertail forearm, swivels. Made 1939 only.

Mossberg Model 51M Autoloading Rifle $155
Caliber: 22 LR. 15-shot tubular magazine. 20-inch bbl. Weight: about 7 lbs. Sights: microclick receiver peep, open rear; hooded ramp front. Two-piece Mannlicher-type stock w/pistol grip and cheekpiece, hard-rubber buttplate and sling swivels. Made 1939-1946.

Mossberg Model 140B Sporter-Target Rifle $140
Same as Model 140K, except has peep rear sight, hooded ramp front sight. Made 1957-1958.

Mossberg Model 140B

Mossberg Model 140K

Mossberg Model 144LS

Mossberg Model 146B

Mossberg Model 140K Bolt-Action Repeater . . . $120
Caliber: 22 LR, 22 Long, 22 Short. 7-shot clip magazine. 24.5-inch bbl. Weight: 5.75 lbs. Sights: open rear; bead front. Monte Carlo stock w/cheekpiece and pistol grip, sling swivels. Made 1955-58.

Mossberg Model 142-A Bolt-Action Repeating Carbine $150
Caliber: 22 Short Long, LR. 7-shot detachable box magazine.18-inch bbl. Weight: about 6 lbs. Sights: peep rear, military-type front. Monte Carlo stock w/pistol grip, hinged forearm pulls down to form hand grip, sling swivels mounted on left side of stock. Made 1949-57.

Mossberg Model 142K $100
Same as Model 142, except has open rear sight. Made 1953-57.

Mossberg Model 144 Bolt-Action Target Rifle . . $190
Caliber: 22 LR. 7-shot detachable box magazine. 26-inch heavy bbl. Weight: about 8 lbs. Sights: microclick receiver peep; hooded front. Pistol-grip target stock w/beavertail forearm, adj. hand stop, swivels. Made 1949-54. *Note:* This model designation was resumed c.1973 to replace the Model 144LS, and then discontinued again in 1985.

Mossberg Model 144LS $225
Same as Model 144 except has Lyman 57MS or Mossberg S331 receiver sight and Lyman 17A front sight. Made 1954 to date. *Note:* This model since c.1973 has been marketed as Model 144.

Mossberg Model 146B Bolt-Action Repeater . . . $140
Takedown. Caliber: 22 LR, Long, Short. Tubular magazine holds 30 Short, 23 Long, 20 LR. 26-inch bbl. Weight: about 7 lbs. Sights: micrometer click rear peep, open rear; hooded front. Plain stock with pistol grip, Monte Carlo comb and cheekpiece, knob forend tip, swivels. Made 1949-54.

Mossberg Model 151K $130
Same as Model 151M except has 24-inch bbl., weighs about 6 pounds, w/o peep sight, plain stock w/Monte Carlo comb and cheekpiece, pistol-grip knob, forend tip, w/o swivels. Made 1950-51.

Mossberg Model 151M Autoloading Rifle $155
Improved version of Model 51M with same general specifications, complete action is instantly removable without use of tools. Made 1946-58.

Mossberg Model 151K

Mossberg Model 151M

Mossberg Model 152

Mossberg Model 320B

Mossberg Model 320K

Mossberg Model 333

Mossberg Model 340B

Mossberg Model 340K

Mossberg Model 152 Autoloading Carbine $150
Caliber: 22 LR. 7-shot detachable box magazine. 18-inch bbl. Weight: about 5 lbs. Sights: peep rear; military-type front. Monte Carlo stock w/pistol grip, hinged forearm pulls down to form hand grip, sling mounted on swivels on left side of stock. Made 1948-57.

Mossberg Model 152K $120
Same as Model 152, except w/open instead of peep rear sight. Made 1950-57.

Mossberg Model 320B Boy Scout Target Rifle . . $125
Same as Model 340K, except single shot w/auto. safety. Made 1960-71.

Mossberg Model 320K Hammerless Bolt-Action Single-Shot $100
Same as Model 346K except single shot, has drop-in loading platform, automatic safety. Weight: about 5.75 lbs. Made 1958-60.

Mossberg Model 321 B $115
Same as Model 321K, except has receiver peep sight. Made 1972-75.

Mossberg Model 321K Bolt-Action Single-Shot . . $120
Same as Model 341, except single shot. Made 1972-80.

Mossberg Model 333 Autoloading Carbine $130
Caliber: 22 LR. 15-shot tubular magazine. 20-inch bbl. Weight: about 6.25 lbs. Sights: open rear; ramp front. Monte Carlo stock w/checkered pistol grip and forearm, bbl. band, swivels. Made 1972-73.

Mossberg Model 340B Target Sporter $135
Same as Model 340K, except has peep rear sight, hooded ramp front sight. Made 1958-81.

Mossberg Model 340K Hammerless Bolt-Action Repeater $130
Same as Model 346K, except clip type, 7-shot magazine. Made 1958-71.

Mossberg Model 341

Mossberg Model 342K Carbine

Mossberg Model 346B

Mossberg Model 346K

Mossberg Model 350K Clip

Mossberg Model 351K Sporter

Mossberg Model 340M **$195**
Same as Model 340K, except has 18.5-inch bbl., Mannlicher-style stock with swivels and sling. Weight: 5.25 lbs. Made 1970-71.

Mossberg Model 341 Bolt-Action Repeater **$95**
Caliber: 22 Short, Long, LR. 7-shot clip magazine. 24-inch bbl. Weight: 6.5 lbs. Sights: open rear, ramp front. Monte Carlo stock w/checkered pistol grip and forearm, sling swivels. Made 1972 to date.

Mossberg Model 342K Hammerless Bolt-Action Carbine **$100**
Same as Model 340K, except has 18-inch bbl., stock has no cheekpiece, extension forend is hinged, pulls down to form hand grip-sling swivels and web strap on left side of stock. Weight: about 5 lbs. Made 1958-1974.

Mossberg Model 346B **$130**
Same as Model 346K, except has peep rear sight, hooded ramp front sight. Made 1958-1967.

Mossberg Model 346K Hammerless Bolt-Action Repeater **$115**
Caliber: 22 Short, Long, LR. Tubular magazine holds 25 Short, 20 Long, 18 LR. 24-inch bbl. Weight: about 6.5 lbs. Sights: open rear; bead front. Walnut stock w/Monte Carlo comb, cheekpiece, pistol grip, sling swivels. Made 1958-71.

Mossberg Model 350K Autoloading Rifle — Clip Type **$105**
Caliber: 22 Short (high speed), Long, LR. 7-shot clip magazine. 23.5-inch bbl. Weight: about 6 lbs. Sights: open rear; bead front. Monte Carlo stock w/pistol grip. Made 1958-71.

Mossberg Model 351C Automatic Carbine **$135**
Same as Model 351K, except has 18.5-inch bbl., Western carbine-style stock w/barrel band and sling swivels. Weight: 5.5 lbs. Made 1965-71.

Mossberg Model 351K Automatic Sporter **$125**
Caliber: 22 LR. 15-shot tubular magazine in buttstock. 24-inch bbl. Weight: about 6 lbs. Sights: open rear; bead front. Monte Carlo stock w/pistol grip. Made 1960-71.

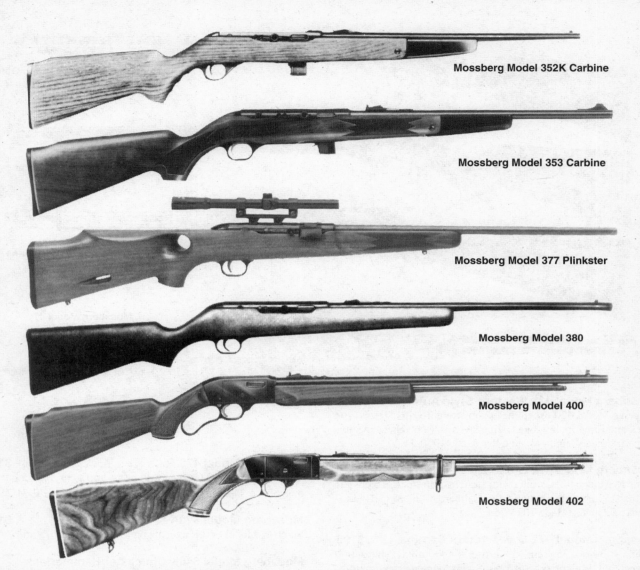

Mossberg Model 352K Carbine

Mossberg Model 353 Carbine

Mossberg Model 377 Plinkster

Mossberg Model 380

Mossberg Model 400

Mossberg Model 402

RIFLES

Mossberg Model 352K Autoloading Carbine . . . **$115**
Caliber: 22 Short, Long, LR. 7-shot clip magazine. 18-inch bbl. Weight: about 5 lbs. Sights: open rear; bead front. Monte Carlo stock w/pistol grip; extension forend of Tenite is hinged, pulls down to form hand grip; sling swivels, web strap. Made 1958-71.

Mossberg Model 353 Autoloading Carbine **$125**
Caliber: 22 LR. 7-shot clip magazine. 18-inch bbl. Weight: about 5 lbs. Sights: open rear; ramp front. Monte Carlo stock w/checkered pistol grip and forearm; black Tenite extension forend pulls down to form hand grip. Made 1972-85.

Mossberg Model 377 Plinkster Autoloader **$145**
Caliber: 22 LR. 15-shot tubular magazine. 20-inch bbl. Weight: about 6.25 lbs. 4× scope sight. Thumbhole stock with rollover cheekpiece, Monte Carlo comb, checkered forearm; molded of modified polystyrene foam in walnut finish; sling swivel studs. Introduced 1977.

Mossberg Model 380 Semiautomatic Rifle **$120**
Caliber: 22 LR. 15-shot buttstock magazine. 20-inch bbl. Weight: 5.5 lbs. Sights: open rear; bead front. Made 1980-85.

Mossberg Model 400 Palomino Lever Action . . . **$175**
Hammerless. Caliber: 22 Short, Long, LR. Tubular magazine holds 20 Short, 17 Long, 15 LR. 24-inch bbl. Weight: about 5.5 lbs. Sights; open rear; bead front. Monte Carlo stock w/checkered pistol grip; beavertail forearm. Made 1959-64.

Mossberg Model 402 Palomino Carbine **$180**
Same as Model 400, except has 18.5-inch (1961-64) or 20-inch bbl. (1964-71), forearm with bbl. band, swivels; magazine holds two less rounds. Weight: about 4.75 lbs. Made 1961-71.

Mossberg Model 430 Automatic Rifle **$115**
Caliber: 22 LR. 18-shot tubular magazine. 24-inch bbl. Weight: about 6.25 lbs. Sights: open rear; bead front. Monte Carlo stock w/checkered pistol grip; checkered forearm. Made 1970-71.

Mossberg Model 472 Brush Gun

Mossberg Model 472 Carbine
(Pistol Grip)

Mossberg Model 472 Carbine
(Straight Grip)

Mossberg Model 472
One in Five Thousand

Mossberg Model 432 Western-Style Auto $110
Same as Model 430 except has plain straight-grip carbine-type
stock and forearm, bbl. band, sling swivels. Magazine capacity:
15 cartridges. Weight: about 6 lbs. Made 1970-71.

Mossberg Model 472 Brush Gun $175
Same as Model 472 Carbine with straight-grip stock, except has
18-inch bbl., weighs about 6.5 lbs. Caliber: 30-30. Magazine capacity: 5 rounds. Made 1974-76.

Mossberg Model 472 Lever-Action Carbine $195
Calibers: 30-30, 35 Rem. centerfire. 6-shot tubular magazine.
20-inch bbl. Weight: 6.75 to 7 lbs. Sights: open rear; ramp front.
Pistol-grip or straight-grip stock, forearm w/bbl. band; sling
swivels on pistol-grip model saddle ring on straight-grip model.
Made 1972-79.

Mossberg Model 472 One in Five Thousand . . . $325
Same as Model 472 Brush Gun, except has Indian scenes etched on
receiver; brass buttplate, saddle ring and bbl. bands, gold-plated
trigger-bright blued finish-select walnut stock and forearm. Limited
edition of 5,000; serial numbered 1 to 5,000. Made in 1974.

Mossberg Model 472 Rifle $165
Same as Model 472 Carbine with pistol-grip stock, except has 24-
inch bbl., 5-shot magazine, weighs about 7 lbs. Made 1974-76.

Mossberg Model 620K $110
Same as Model 640K, except single shot. Made 1960-64.

Mossberg Model 640K Chuckster Hammerless
Bolt-Action Rifle $125
Caliber: 22 WMR. 5-shot detachable clip magazine. 24-inch bbl.
Weight: about 6 lbs. Sights: open rear; bead front. Monte Carlo
stock w/cheekpiece, pistol grip, sling swivels. Made 1959-84.

Mossberg Model 640KS $130
Deluxe version of Model 640K, has select walnut stock hand
checkering; gold-plated front sight, rear sight elevator, and trigger. Made 1960-64.

Mossberg Model 640K

Mossberg Model 640KS

Mossberg Model 640M

Mossberg Model 642K

Mossberg Model 800

Mossberg Model 800D

Mossberg Model 800M

RIFLES

Mossberg Model 640M **$195**
Similar to Model 640K, except chambered for 22 WMR; has 20-inch bbl., Mannlicher-style stock w/Monte Carlo comb and cheekpiece, swivels. Made 1967-73.

Mossberg Model 642K **$175**
Same as Model 640K, except has 18.5-inch bbl., forearm with black Tenite extension that pulls down to form hand grip. Made 1961-64.

Mossberg Model 800 Bolt-Action
Centerfire Rifle **$175**
Calibers: 222 Rem., 22-250, 243 Win., 308 Win. 4-shot magazine, 3-shot in 222. 22-inch bbl. Weight: about 7.5 lbs. Sights: folding leaf rear; ramp front. Monte Carlo stock w/cheekpiece, checkered pistol grip and forearm, sling swivels. Made 1967-79.

Mossberg Model 800D Super Grade **$295**
Deluxe version of Model 800, except has stock w/rollover comb and cheekpiece, rosewood forend tip and pistol-grip cap. Weight: about 6.75 lbs. Chambered for all calibers listed for the Model 800 except for 222 Rem. Sling swivels. Made 1970-1973.

Mossberg Model 800M **$265**
Same as Model 800, except has flat bolt handle, 20-inch bbl., Mannlicher-style stock. Weight: 6.5 lbs. Calibers: 22-250, 243 Win., 308 Win. Made 1969-72.

Mossberg Model 800VT Varmint/Target **$235**
Similar to Model 800, except has 24-inch heavy bbl., no sights. Weight: about 9.5 lbs. Calibers: 222 Rem., 22-250, 243 Win. Made 1968-79.

Mossberg Model 810

Mossberg Model 810 Bolt-Action Centerfire Rifle

Calibers: 270 Win., 30-06, 7mm Rem. Mag., 338 Win. Mag. Detachable box magazine (1970-75) or an internal magazine with hinged floorplate (1972 to date). Capacity: 4-shot in 270 and 30-06, 3-shot in Magnums. 22-inch bbl. in 270 and 30-06, 24-inch in Magnums. Weight: 7.5 to 8 lbs. Sights: leaf rear; ramp front. Stock w/Monte Carlo comb and cheekpiece, checkered pistol grip and forearm, grip cap, sling swivels. Made 1970-79.

Standard calibers **$260**
Magnum calibers **295**

Mossberg Model 1500 Mountaineer Grade I
Centerfire Rifle **$245**

Calibers: 223, 243, 270, 30-06, 7mm Mag. 22-inch or 24-inch (7mm Mag.) bbl. Weight: 7 lbs. 10 oz. Hardwood walnut finished checkered stock. Sights: hooded ramp front w/gold bead; fully adj. rear. Drilled and tapped for scope mounts. Sling swivel studs. Made 1987-88.

Mossberg Model 1500 Varmint Bolt-Action Rifle

Same as Model 1500 Grade I, except with 22-inch heavy bbl. Chambered in 222, 22-250, 223 only. High-luster blued finish or Parkerized satin finished stock. Imported from Japan 1982 to date.

High-Luster Blue **$300**
Parkerized Satin Finish **340**

Mossberg Model 1700LS Classic Hunter
Bolt-Action Rifle **$355**

Same as Model 1500 Grade I, except w/checkered classic-style stock and schnabel forend. Chambered in 243, 270, 30-06 only. Imported from Japan 1983 to date.

Mossberg Model B Bolt-Action Rifle **$125**

Takedown. Caliber: 22 LR, Long, Short. Single shot. 22-inch bbl. Sights: open rear; bead front. Plain pistol-grip stock. Made 1930-32.

Mossberg Model K Slide-Action Repeater **$215**

Hammerless. Takedown. Caliber: 22 LR, Long, Short. Tubular magazine holds 20 Short, 16 Long, 14 LR. 22-inch bbl. Weight: about 5 lbs. Sights: open rear; bead front. Plain straight-grip stock. Grooved slide handle. Made 1922-31.

Mossberg Models L42A, L43, L45A, L46A-LS

See Models 42A, 43, 45A and 46A-LS respectively; "L" refers to a left-hand version of those rifles.

Mossberg Model L Single-Shot Rifle **$325**

Martini-type falling-block lever action. Takedown. Caliber: 22 LR, Long, Short. 24-inch bbl. Weight: about 5 lbs. Sights: open rear; bead front. Plain pistol-grip stock and forearm. Made 1929-32.

Mossberg Model M Slide-Action Repeater **$210**

Specifications same as for Model K except has 24-inch octagon bbl., pistol-grip stock, weighs about 5.5 lbs. Made 1928-31.

Mossberg Model R Bolt-Action Repeater **$205**

Takedown. Caliber: 22 LR, Long, Short. Tubular magazine. 24-inch bbl. Sights: open rear; bead front. Plain pistol-grip stock. Made 1930-32.

MUSGRAVE MFRS. & DIST. (PTY) LTD.
Bloemfontein, South Africa

The following Musgrave bolt-action rifles were manufactured 1971-76.

Musgrave Premier NR5 Bolt-Action
Hunting Rifle **$350**

Calibers: 243 Win., 270 Win., 30-06, 308 Win., 7mm Rem. Mag. 5-shot magazine. 25.5-inch bbl. Weight: 8.25 lbs. Furnished w/o sights, but drilled and tapped for scope mount. Select walnut

Mossberg Model L

Mossberg Model R

Musgrave Premier NR5

Musgrave RSA NR1

Musgrave Valiant NR6

Musgrave Premier NR5 Bolt-Action Hunting Rifle *(Cont.)*

Monte Carlo stock w/cheekpiece, checkered pistol grip and forearm, contrasting pistol-grip cap and forend tip, recoil pad, swivel studs.

Musgrave RSA NR1 Bolt-Action Single-Shot Target Rifle **$345**

Caliber: 308 Win. (7.62mm NATO). 26.4-inch heavy bbl. Weight: about 10 lbs. Sights: aperture receiver; tunnel front. Walnut target stock w/beavertail forearm, handguard, bbl. band, rubber buttplate, sling swivels.

Musgrave Valiant NR6 Hunting Rifle **$295**

Similar to Premier, except has 24-inch bbl.; stock w/straight comb, skip French-style checkering, no grip cap or forend tip. Sights: leaf rear; hooded ramp front bead sight. Weight: 7.75 lbs. unloaded.

MUSKETEER RIFLES
Washington, D.C.
Mfd. by Firearms International Corp.

Musketeer Mauser Sporter **$315**
FN Mauser bolt action. Calibers: 243, 25-06, 270, 264 Mag., 308, 30-06, 7mm Mag., 300 Win. Mag. Magazine holds 5 standard, 3 Magnum cartridges. 24-inch bbl. Weight: about 7.25 lbs. No sights. Monte Carlo stock w/checkered pistol grip and forearm, swivels. Made 1963-72.

NAVY ARMS CO.
Martinsburg, WV (formerly Ridgefield, NJ)

Navy Arms 45-70 Mauser Carbine **$175**
Same as 45-70 Mauser Rifle, except has 18-inch bbl., straight-grip stock with low comb, weighs about 7.5 lbs. Discontinued.

Musketeer Mauser

Navy Arms 45-70 Mauser

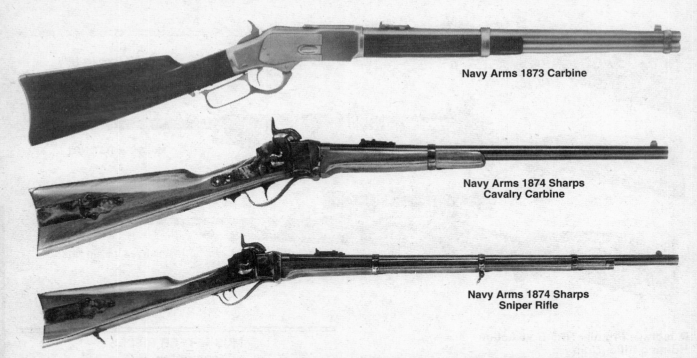

Navy Arms 1873 Carbine

Navy Arms 1874 Sharps Cavalry Carbine

Navy Arms 1874 Sharps Sniper Rifle

Navy Arms 45-70 Mauser Rifle $160
Siamese Mauser bolt action. Caliber: 45-70 Gov't. 3-round magazine. 24- or 26-inch bbl. Weight: about 8.5 lbs. with 26-inch bbl. Sights: open rear; ramp front. Checkered stock w/Monte Carlo comb. Intro.1973; discontinued.

Navy Arms 1873 Carbine $555
Similar to Model 1873 Rifle, except has blued receiver, 10-shot magazine, 19-inch round bbl., carbine-style forearm w/bbl. band, weighs about 6.75 lbs. Discontinued. Reissued in 1991 in 44-40 or 45 Colt.

Navy Arms Model 1873 Lever Action Rifle $580
Replica of Winchester Model 1873. Casehardened receiver. Calibers: 22 LR, 357 Magnum, 44-40. 15-shot magazine. 24-inch octagon bbl. Weight: about 8 lbs. Sights: open rear; blade front. Straight-grip stock, forearm w/end cap. Discontinued. Reissued in 1991 in 44-40 or 45 Colt with 12-shot magazine. Discontinued 1994.

Navy Arms 1873 Trapper's Model $595
Same as Model 1873 Carbine, except has 16.5-inch bbl., 8-shot magazine, weighs about 6.25 lbs. Discontinued.

Navy Arms 1874 Sharps Cavalry Carbine $455
Replica of Sharps 1874 Cavalry Carbine. Similar to the Sniper Model, except w/22-inch bbl. and carbine stock. Caliber: 45-70. Imported 1994 to date.

Navy Arms 1874 Sharps Sniper Rifle
Replica of Sharps 1874 Sharpshooter's Rifle. Caliber: 45-70. Falling breech, single shot. 30-inch bbl. 46.75 inches overall. Weight: 8.5 lbs. Double-set triggers. Color casehardened receiver. Blade front sight; rear sight w/elevation leaf. Polished blued bbl. Military three-band stock w/patch box. Imported 1994 to date.
Infantry Model (Single Trigger) $655
Sniper Model (DST) 695

Navy Arms Engraved Models
Yellowboy and Model 1873 rifles and carbines are available in deluxe models with select walnut stocks and forearms and engraving in three grades. Grade "A" has delicate scrollwork in limited areas. Grade "B" is more elaborate with about 40 percent coverage. Grade "C" has highest grade engraving. Add to value:
Grade "A" $100
Grade "B" 135
Grade "C" 350

Navy Arms Martini Target Rifle

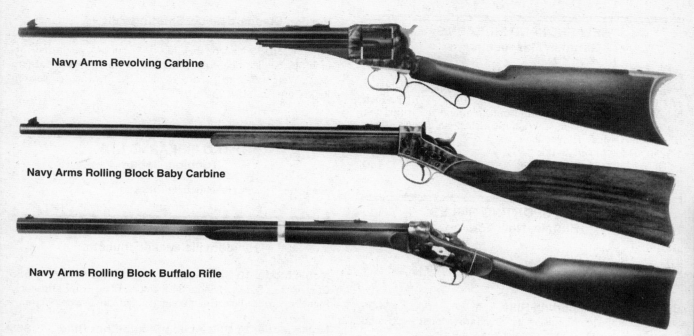

Navy Arms Revolving Carbine

Navy Arms Rolling Block Baby Carbine

Navy Arms Rolling Block Buffalo Rifle

Navy Arms Martini Target Rifle $340
Martini single-shot action. Calibers: 444 Marlin, 45-70. 26- or 30-inch half-octagon or full-octagon bbl. Weight: about 9 lbs. with 26-inch bbl. Sights: Creedmore tang peep, open middle, blade front. Stock w/cheekpiece and pistol grip, forearm with schnabel tip, both checkered. Introduced 1972; discontinued.

Navy Arms Revolving Carbine $435
Action resembles that of Remington Model 1875 Revolver. Casehardened frame. Calibers: 357 Magnum, 44-40, 45 Colt. 6-shot cylinder. 20-inch bbl. Weight: about 5 lbs. Sights: open rear; blade front. Straight-grip stock brass trigger guard and buttplate. Intro. 1968; discont.

Navy Arms Rolling Block Baby Carbine $195
Replica of small Remington Rolling Block single-shot action. Casehardened frame, brass trigger guard. Calibers: 22 LR, 22 Hornet, 357 Magnum, 44-40. 20-inch octagon or 22-inch round bbl. Weight: about 5 lbs. Sights: open rear; blade front. Straight-grip stock, plain forearm, brass buttplate. Made 1968-81.

Navy Arms Rolling Block Buffalo Carbine $295
Same as Buffalo Rifle, except has 18-inch bbl., weighs about 10 lbs.

Navy Arms Rolling Block Buffalo Rifle $325
Replica Remington Rolling Block single-shot action. Casehardened frame, brass trigger guard. Calibers: 444 Marlin, 45-70, 50-70. 26- or 30-inch heavy half-octagon or full-octagon bbl. Weight: 11 to 12 lbs. Sights: open rear; blade front. Straight-grip stock w/brass buttplate, forearm w/brass bbl. band. Made 1971 to date.

Navy Arms Rolling Block Creedmoor Rifle $495
Same as Buffalo Rifle, except calibers 45-70 and 50-70 only, 28- or 30-inch heavy half-octagon or full-octagon bbl., Creedmoor tang peep sight.

Navy Arms Yellowboy Carbine $425
Similar to Yellowboy Rifle, except has 19-inch bbl., 10-shot magazine (14-shot in 22 Long Rifle), carbine-style forearm. Weight: about 6.75 lbs. Discontinued. Reissued 1991 in 44-40 only.

Navy Arms Yellowboy Lever-Action Repeater . . $495
Replica of Winchester Model 1866. Calibers: 38 Special, 44-40. 15-shot magazine. 24-inch octagon bbl. Weight: about 8 lbs. Sights; folding leaf rear; blade front. Straight-grip stock, forearm w/end cap. Intro. 1966; discontinued. Reissued 1991 in 44-40 only w/12-shot magazine and adj. ladder-style rear sight.

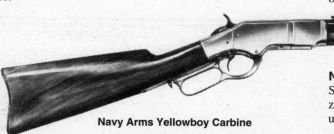

Navy Arms Yellowboy Trapper's Model $425
Same as Yellowboy Carbine, except has 16.5-inch bbl., magazine holds two fewer rounds, weighs about 6.25 lbs. Discontinued.

Navy Arms Yellowboy Carbine

NEW ENGLAND FIREARMS
Gardner, Massachusetts

New England Firearms Handi-Rifle
Single-shot, break-open action with side-lever release. Calibers: 22 Hornet, 22-250, 223, 243, 270, 30-30, 30-06, 45-70. 22-inch bbl. Weight: 7 lbs. Sights: ramp front; folding rear. Drilled and tapped for scope mounts. Walnut-finished hardwood stock. Blued finish. Made 1989 to date.
22-250, 243, 270 and 30-06 . . . . **$150**
22 Hornet, 223, 30-30 and 45-70 . . . .   **140**

NEWTON SPORTING RIFLES
Buffalo, New York

Mfd. by Newton Arms Co., Charles Newton Rifles Corp. and Buffalo Newton Rifle Co.

Buffalo Newton Sporting Rifle **$695**
Same general specifications as Standard Model — Second Type. Made c. 1922-32 by Buffalo Newton Rifle Co.

Newton-Mauser Sporting Rifle **$625**
Mauser (Oberndorf) action. Caliber: 256 Newton. 5-shot box magazine, hinged floorplate. Double-set triggers. 24-inch bbl. Open rear sight, ramp front sight. Sporting stock with checkered pistol grip. Weight: about 7 lbs. Made c. 1914 by Newton Arms Co.

**Newton Standard Model Sporting Rifle —
First Type** **$795**
Newton bolt action, interrupted screw-type breech-locking mechanism, double-set triggers. Calibers: 22, 256, 280, 30, 33, 35 Newton- 30-06. 24-inch bbl. Sights: open rear or cocking-piece peep; ramp front. Checkered pistol-grip stock. Weight: 7 to 8 lbs., depending on caliber. Made c. 1916-18 by Newton Arms Co.

**Newton Standard Model Sporting Rifle —
Second Type** **$735**
Newton bolt action, improved design; distinguished by reversed-set trigger and 1917-Enfield-type bolt handle. Calib-

**Newton Standard Model Sporting Rifle —
Second Type (Cont.)**
ers: 256, 30, 35 Newton and 30-06. 5-shot box magazine. 24-inch bbl. Sights: open rear; ramp front. Checkered pistol-grip stock. Weight: 7.75 to 8.25 lbs. Made c. 1921 by Charles Newton Rifle Corp.

NIKKO FIREARMS LTD.
Tochiga, Japan

See listings under Golden Eagle Rifles.

NOBLE MFG. CO.
Haydenville, Massachusetts

Noble Model 10 Bolt-Action Single-Shot Rifle . . . **$65**
Caliber: 22 LR, Long, Short. 24-inch bbl. Plain pistol-grip stock. Sights: open rear, bead front. Weight: about 4 lbs. Made 1955-58.

Noble Model 20 Bolt-Action Single-Shot Rifle . . . **$65**
Manually cocked. Caliber: 22 LR, Long, Short. 22-inch bbl. Weight: about 5 lbs. Sights: open rear; bead front. Walnut stock w/pistol grip. Made 1958-63.

Noble Model 33 Slide-Action Repeater **$70**
Hammerless. Caliber: 22 LR, Long, Short. Tubular magazine holds 21 Short, 17 Long, 15 LR. 24-inch bbl. Weight: 6 lbs. Sights: open rear; bead front. Tenite stock and slide handle. Made 1949-53.

Noble Model 33A **$65**
Same general specifications as Model 33 except has wood stock and slide handle. Made 1953-55.

Noble Model 222 Bolt-Action Single-Shot Rifle . . . **$75**
Manually cocked. Caliber: 22 LR, Long, Short. Barrel integral w/receiver. Overall length: 38 inches. Weight: about 5 lbs. Sights: interchangeable V-notch and peep rear; ramp front. Scope mounting base. Pistol-grip stock. Made 1958-71.

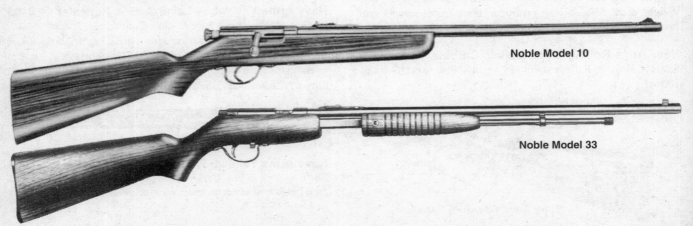

Noble Model 10

Noble Model 33

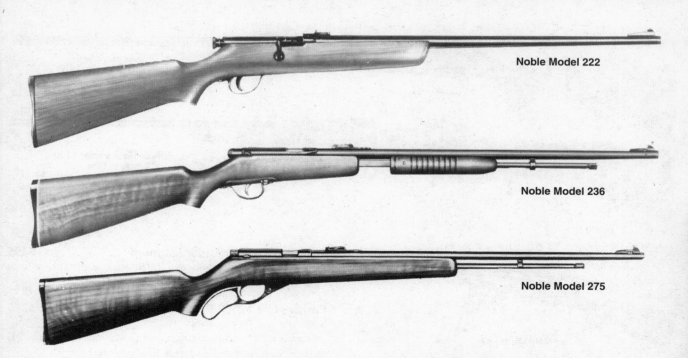

Noble Model 222

Noble Model 236

Noble Model 275

Noble Model 236 Slide-Action Repeating Rifle . . . $85

Hammerless. Caliber: 22 Short, Long, LR. Tubular magazine holds 21 Short, 17 Long, 15 LR. 24-inch bbl. Weight: about 5.5 lbs. Sights: open rear; ramp front. Pistol-grip stock, grooved slide handle. Made 1951 to date.

Noble Model 275 Lever-Action Rifle $100

Hammerless. Caliber: 22 Short, Long, LR. Tubular magazine holds 21 Short, 17 Long, 15 LR. 24-inch bbl. Weight: about 5.5 lbs. Sights: open rear; ramp front. Stock w/semipistol grip. Made 1958-71.

PARKER-HALE LIMITED
Birmingham, England

Parker-Hale Model 81 African $655

Same general specifications as Model 81 Classic, except in caliber 375 H&H only. Sights: African express rear; hooded blade front. Barrel-band swivel. All-steel trigger guard. Checkered European walnut stock w/pistol grip and recoil pad. Engraved receiver. Imported since 1986.

Parker-Hale Model 81 Classic Bolt-Action Rifle . . $495

Calibers: 22-250, 243 Win., 270 Win., 6mm Rem., 6.5×55, 7×57, 7×64, 308 Win., 30-06, 300 Win. Mag., 7mm Rem. Mag. 4-shot magazine. 24-inch bbl. Weight: 7.75 lbs. Sights: adj. open rear, hooded ramp front. Checkered pistol-grip stock of European walnut. Imported since 1984.

Parker-Hale Model 85 Sniper Rifle $1325

Caliber: 308 Win. 10- or 20-shot M-14-type magazine. 24.25-inch bbl. 45 inches overall. Weight: 12.5 lbs. Blade front sight, folding aperture rear. McMillan fiberglass stock w/detachable bipod. Made 1992 to date.

Parker-Hale Model 87 Bolt-Action Repeating
Target Rifle $950

Calibers: 243 Win., 6.5×55, 308 Win., 30-06 Springfield, 300 Win. Mag. 5-shot detachable box magazine. 26-inch bbl. 45 inches overall. Weight: 10 lbs. No sights; grooved for target-style scope mounts. Stippled walnut stock w/adj. buttplate. Sling swivel studs. Parkerized finish. Folding bipod.

Parker-Hale Model 81 Classic

Parker-Hale Model 1100
Lightweight

Parker-Hale Model 1200
Super Clip

Parker-Hale Model 87

Parker-Hale Model 1000 Standard Rifle **$295**
Calibers: 22-250, 243 Win., 270 Win., 6mm Rem., 308 Win., 30-06. 4-shot magazine. Bolt action. 22-inch or 24-inch (22-250) bbl. 43 inches overall. 7.25 lbs. Checkered walnut Monte Carlo-style stock with satin finish. Imported 1984-88.

**Parker-Hale Model 1100 Lightweight
Bolt-Action Rifle** **$365**
Same general specifications as the Model 1000 Standard except w/22-inch lightweight profile bbl., hollow bolt handle, alloy trigger guard and floorplate, 6.5 lbs., schnabel forend. Imported since 1984.

Parker-Hale Model 1100M African Magnum Rifle . . **$595**
Same as Model 1000 Standard, except w/24-inch bbl. in calibers 404 Jeffery, 458 Win. Mag. Weight: 9.5 lbs. Sights: adj. rear; hooded post front. Imported since 1984.

**Parker-Hale Model 1200 Super Clip
Bolt-Action Rifle** **$425**
Same as Model 1200 Super, except w/detachable box magazine in calibers 243 Win., 6mm Rem., 270 Win. 30-06 and 308 Win., 300 Win. Mag., 7mm Rem. Mag. Imported from England since 1984.

**Parker-Hale 1200 Super Bolt-Action
Sporting Rifle** **$395**
Mauser-type bolt action. Calibers: 22-250, 243 Win., 6mm Rem., 25-06, 270 Win., 30-06, 308 Win. 4-shot magazine. 24-inch bbl. Weight: 7.25 lbs. Sights: folding open rear, hooded ramp front. European walnut stock w/rollover Monte Carlo cheekpiece, rosewood forend tip and pistol-grip cap, skip checkering, recoil pad, sling swivels. Made 1968 to date.

Parker-Hale 1200 Super Magnum **$495**
Same general specifications as 1200 Super, except calibers 7mm Rem. Mag. and 300 Win. Mag., 3-shot magazine.

Parker-Hale 1200P Presentation **$395**
Same general specifications as 1200 Super, except has scroll-engraved action, trigger guard and floorplate, no sights. QD swivels. Calibers: 243 Win. and 30-06. Made 1969-75.

Parker-Hale 1200V Varmint **$385**
Same general specifications as 1200 Super, except has 24-inch heavy bbl., no sights, weighs 9.5 lbs. Calibers: 22-250, 6mm Rem., 25-06, 243 Win. Made 1969 to date.

Parker-Hale Model 1300C Scout **$465**
Calibers: 243, 308 Win. 10-round magazine. 20-inch bbl. w/muzzle brake. 41 inches overall. Weight: 8.5 lbs. No sights, drilled and tapped for scope. Checkered laminated birch stock w/QD swivels. Made 1992 to date.

Parker-Hale Model 2700 Lightweight **$295**
Same general specifications as Model 2100 Midland, except w/tapered lightweight bbl. and aluminum trigger guard. Weight: 6.5 lbs. Made 1992 to date.

PEDERSEN CUSTOM GUNS
North Haven, Connecticut
Division of O.F. Mossberg & Sons, Inc.

Pedersen Model 3000 Grade I Bolt-Action Rifle . . **$795**
Richly engraved with silver inlays, full-fancy American black walnut stock. Mossberg Model 810 action. Calibers: 270 Win., 30-06, 7mm Rem. Mag., 338 Win. Mag. 3-shot magazine, hinged floorplate. 22-inch bbl. in 270 and 30-06, 24-inch in Magnums. Weight: 7 to 8 lbs. Sights: open rear; hooded ramp front. Monte Carlo stock w/roll-over cheekpiece, wraparound hand checkering on pistol grip and forearm, rosewood pistol-grip cap and forend tip, recoil pad or steel buttplate with trap, detachable swivels. Made 1973-75.

Pedersen Model 3000 Grade I

Pedersen Model 3000 Grade III

Pedersen Model 3000 Grade II **$595**
Same as Model 3000 Grade I, except less elaborate engraving, no inlays, fancy grade walnut stock with recoil pad. Made 1973-75.

Pedersen Model 3000 Grade III **$495**
Same as Model 3000 Grade I, except no engraving or inlays, select grade walnut stock w/recoil pad. Made 1973-74.

**Pedersen Model 4700 Custom
Deluxe Lever-Action Rifle** **$195**
Mossberg Model 472 action. Calibers: 30-30, 35 Rem. 5-shot tubular magazine. 24-inch bbl. Weight: 7.5 lbs. Sights: open rear, hooded ramp front. Hand-finished black walnut stock and beavertail forearm, barrel band swivels. Made 1975.

J.C. PENNEY CO., INC.
Dallas, Texas

Firearms sold under the J.C. Penney label were mfd. by Marlin, High Standard, Stevens, Savage and Springfield.

J.C. Penney Model 2025 Bolt-Action Repeater . . . **$50**
Takedown. Caliber: 22 RF. 8-shot detachable box magazine. 24-inch bbl. Weight: about 6 lbs. Sights: open rear; bead front. Plain pistol-grip stock. Mfd. by Marlin.

J.C. Penney Model 2035 Bolt-Action Repeater . . . **$50**
Takedown. Caliber: 22 RF. 8-shot detachable box magazine. 24-inch bbl. Weight: about 6 lbs. Sights: open rear; bead front. Plain pistol-grip stock. Mfd. by Marlin.

J.C. Penney Model 2935 Lever-Action Rifle **$145**
Same general specifications as Marlin Model 336.

**J.C. Penney Model 6400 Bolt-Action
Centerfire Rifle** **$120**
Same general specifications as Savage Model 340.

J.C. Penney Model 6660 Autoloading Rifle **$75**
Caliber: 22 RF. Tubular magazine. 22-inch bbl. Weight: about 5.5 lbs. Sights: open rear; hooded ramp front. Plain pistol-grip stock. Mfd. by Marlin.

PLAINFIELD MACHINE COMPANY
Dunellen, New Jersey

Plainfield M-1 Carbine **$150**
Same as U.S. Carbine, Cal. 30, M-1, except also available in caliber 5.7mm (22 with necked-down 30 Carbine cartridge case). Current production has ventilated metal handguard and barrel band w/o bayonet lug; earlier models have standard military-type fittings. Made 1960-77.

Plainfield M-1 Carbine, Commando Model **$175**
Same as M-1 Carbine, except has paratrooper-type stock w/telescoping wire shoulderpiece. Made 1960-77.

Plainfield M-1 Carbine, Military Sporter **$150**
Same as M-1 Carbine, except has unslotted buttstock and wood handguard. Made 1960-77.

Plainfield M-1 Deluxe Sporter **$175**
Same as M-1 Carbine, except has Monte Carlo sporting stock Made 1960-73.

Plainfield M-1 Carbine

RIFLES

Polish Model 1929 Mauser

POLISH MILITARY RIFLES
Manufactured by Government Arsenals at Radom and Warsaw, Poland

**Polish Model 1898 (Karabin 98, K98) Mauser
Military Carbine** **$175**
Same, except for minor details, as the German Kar. 98a. First
manufactured during early 1920s.

**Polish Model 1898 (Karabin 98, WZ98A) Mauser
Military Rifle** **$120**
Same, except for minor details, as the German Gew. 98 used in
WWI. Manufacture began c. 1921.

**Polish Model 1929 (Karabin 29, WZ29) Mauser
Military Rifle** **$175**
Same except for minor details, as the Czech Model 24. Mfd.
1929 thru WWII. A similar model produced during German occupation was designated Gew. 29/40.

WILLIAM POWELL & SON LTD.
Birmingham, England

Powell Double-Barrel Rifle **$25,000**
Boxlock. Made to order in any caliber during the time that the rifle was manufactured. Bbls.: Made to order in any legal length,
but 26 inches recommended. Highest grade French walnut buttstock and forearm with fine checkering. Metal is elaborately engraved. Imported by Stoeger about 1938-51.

Powell Bolt-Action Rifle **$2100**
Mauser-type bolt action. Calibers: 6×54 through 375 H&H
Magnum. 3- and 4-shot shot magazine, depending upon chambering. 24-inch bbl. Weight: 7.5 to 8.75 lbs. Sights: folding
leaf rear; hooded ramp front. Cheekpiece stock, checkered
forearm and pistol grip, swivels. Imported by Stoeger about
1938-51.

JAMES PURDEY & SONS LTD.
London, England

Purdey Double Rifle **$43,500**
Sidelock action, hammerless, ejectors. Almost any caliber is available but the following are the most popular: 375 Flanged Magnum
Nitro Express, 500/465 Nitro Express 470 Nitro Express, 577 Nitro Express. 25.5-inch bbls. (25-inch in 375). Weight: 9.5 to 12.75
lbs. Sights: folding leaf rear; ramp front. Cheekpiece stock, checkered forearm and pistol grip, recoil pad, swivels. Currently manufactured to indivual measurements and specifications; same
general specifications apply to pre-WWII model.

Purdey Bolt-Action Rifle **$4650**
Mauser-type bolt action. Calibers: 7×57, 300 H&H Magnum,
375 H&H Magnum, 10.75×73. 3-shot magazine. 24-inch bbl.
Weight: 7.5 to 8.75 lbs. Sights: folding leaf rear; hooded ramp
front. Cheekpiece stock, checkered forearm and pistol grip,
swivels. Currently manufactured; same general specifications
apply to pre-WWII model.

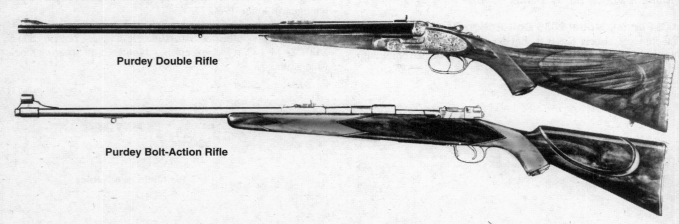

Purdey Double Rifle

Purdey Bolt-Action Rifle

Remington No. 2 Single-Shot Rifle

Remington No. 3 Single-Shot Rifle

REMINGTON ARMS COMPANY
Ilion, New York

To facilitate locating Remington firearms, models are grouped into four categories: Single-shot rifles, bolt-action repeating rifles, slide-action (pump) rifles, and semiautomatic rifles. For a complete listing, please refer to the index.

Remington Single-Shot Rifles

Remington No. 1 Sporting Rifle **$695**
Single-Shot, rolling-blcok action. Calibers: 40-50, 40-70, 44-77, 50-45, 50-70 Gov't. centerfire and 44 Long, 44 Extra Long, 45-70, 46 Long, 46 Extra Long, 50-70 rimfire. Bbl. lengths: 28- or 30-inch part octagon. Weight: 5 to 7.5 lbs. Sights: folding leaf rear sight; sporting front, dovetail bases. Plain walnut straight stock; flanged-top, semicarbine buttplate. Plain walnut forend with thin rounded front end. Made 1868 to 1902.

Remington No. 1½ Sporting Rifle **$795**
Single-Shot, rolling-blcok action. Calibers: 22 Short, Long, or Extra Long. 25 Stevens, 32, and 38 rimfire cartridges. 32-20, 38-40 and 44-40 centerfire. Bbl. lengths: 24-, 26-, 28- or 30-inch part octagon. Remaining features similar to Remington No. 1. Made from 1869 to 1902.

Remington No. 2 Sporting Rifle
Single-shot, rolling-block action. Calibers: 22, 25, 32, 38, 44 rimfire or centerfire. Bbl. lengths: 24, 26, 28 or 30 inches. Weight: 5 to 6 lbs. Sights: open rear; bead front. Straight-grip sporting stock and knobtip forearm of walnut. Made 1873-1910.
Calibers: 22, 25, 32 . . . . **$595**
Calibers: 38, 44 . . . . **675**

Remington No. 3 Creedmoor and
Schuetzen Rifles . . . . **$5000+**
Produced in a variety of styles and calibers, these are collector's items and bring far higher prices than the sporting types. The Schuetzen Special, which has an under-lever action, is especially rare — perhaps less than 100 having been made.

Remington No. 3 High Power Rifle
Single shot. Hepburn falling-block action w/side lever. Calibers: 30-30, 30-40, 32 Special, 32-40, 38-55, 38-72 (high-power cartridges). Bbl. lengths: 26-, 28-, 30-inch. Weight: about 8 lbs. Open sporting sights. Checkered pistol-grip stock and forearm. Made 1893-1907.
Calibers: 30-30, 30-40, 32 Special, 32-40 . . . . **$1425**
Calibers: 38-55, 38-72 . . . . **1750**

Remington No. 3 Sporting Rifle **$1050**
Single shot. Hepburn falling-block action w/side lever. Calibers: 22 WCF, 22 Extra Long, 25-20 Stevens, 25-21 Stevens, 25-25 Stevens, 32 WCF, 32-40 Ballard & Marlin, 32-40 Rem., 38 WCF, 38-40 Rem., 38-50 Rem., 38-55 Ballard & Marlin, 40-60 Ballard & Marlin, 40-60 WCF, 40-65 Rem. Straight, 40-82 WCF, 45-70 Gov., 45-90 WCF, also was supplied on special order in bottle-necked 40-50, 40-70, 40-90, 44-77, 44-90, 44-105, 50-70 Gov., 50-90 Sharps Straight. Bbl. lengths: 26-inch (22, 25, 32 cal. only), 28-inch, 30-inch; half-octagon or full-octagon. Weight: 8 to 10 lbs. Sights: open rear; blade front. Checkered pistol-grip stock and forearm. Made 1880 to c. 1911.

Remington No. 4 Single-Shot Rifle **$425**
Rolling-block action. Solid frame or takedown. Calibers: 22 Short and Long,22 LR, 25 Stevens R.F., 32 Short and Long R.F. 22.5-inch octagon bbl., 24-inch available in 32 caliber only.

Remington No. 4

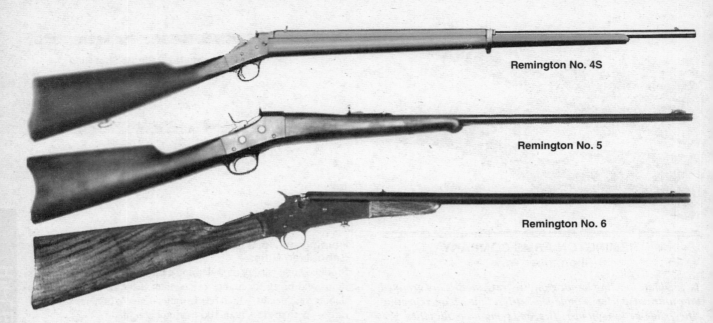

Remington No. 4S

Remington No. 5

Remington No. 6

Remington No. 4 Single-Shot Rifle *(Cont.)*

Weight: about 4.5 lbs. Sights: open rear; blade front. Plain walnut stock and forearm. Made 1890-1933.

Remington No. 4S Military Model 22
Single-Shot Rifle $795

Rolling-block action. Calibers: 22 Short only, 22 LR only. 28-inch bbl. Weight: about 5 lbs. Sights: military-type rear; blade front. Military-type stock w/handguard, stacking swivel, sling. Has a bayonet stud on the barrel; bayonet and scabbard were regularly supplied. *Note:* At one time the "Military Model" was the official rifle of the Boy Scouts of America and was called the "Boy Scout Rifle." Made 1913-33.

Remington No. 5 Special Single-Shot Rifle

Single-shot, rolling-block action. Calibers: 7mm Mauser, 30-30, 30-40 Krag, 303 British, 32-40, 32 Special, 38-55 (high-power cartridges). Bbl. lengths: 24, 26 and 28 inches. Weight: about 7 lbs. Open sporting sights. Plain straight-grip stock and forearm. Made 1902-18. *Note:* Models 1897 and 1902 Military Rifles, intended for the export market, are almost identical with the No. 5 except for 30-inch bbl. full military stock and weight (about 8.5 pounds); a carbine was also supplied. The military rifles were produced in caliber 8mm Lebel for France, 7.62mm Russian for Russia and 7mm Mauser for the Central and South American

Remington No. 5 Special Single-Shot Rifle *(Cont.)*

government trade. At one time, Remington also offered these military models to retail buyers.

Sporting Model	**$395**
Military Model	250

Remington No. 6 Takedown Rifle $310

Single-shot, rolling-block action. Calibers: 22 Short, 22 Long, 22 LR, 32 Short/Long RF. 20-inch bbl. Weight: avg. 4 lbs. Sights: open front and rear; tang peep. Plain straight-grip stock, forearm. Made 1901-33.

Remington No. 7 Target and Sporting Rifle $695

Single shot. Rolling-block Army Pistol frame. Calibers: 22 Short, 22 LR, 25 Stevens R.F. (other calibers as available in No. 2 Rifle were supplied on special order). Half-octagon bbls.: 24-, 26-, 28-inch. Weight: about 6 lbs. Sights: Lyman combination rear; Beach combination front. Fancy walnut stock and forearm, Swiss buttplate available as an extra. Made 1903-11.

Remington Model 33 Bolt-Action
Single-Shot Rifle $120

Takedown. Caliber: 22 Short, Long, LR. 24-inch bbl. Weight: about 4.5 lbs. Sights: open rear, bead front. Plain, pistol-grip stock, forearm with grasping grooves. Made 1931-36.

Remington No. 7 Target

**Remington Model 33
Single-Shot Rifle**

Remington Model 33 NRA Junior Target Rifle . . $150
Same as Model 33 Standard, except has Lyman peep rear sight, Patridge-type front sight, 0.88-inch sling and swivels, weighs about 5 lbs.

Remington Model 40X Centerfire Rifle $395
Specifications same as for Model 40X Rimfire (heavy-weight). Calibers: 222 Rem., 222 Rem. Mag., 7.62mm NATO, 30-06 (others were available on special order). Made 1961-64. Value shown is for rifle w/o sights.

Remington Model 40X Heavyweight Bolt-Action Target Rifle (Rimfire)
Caliber: 22 LR. Single shot. Action similar to Model 722. Click adj. trigger. 28-inch heavy bbl. Redfield Olympic sights. Scope bases. High-comb target stock bedding device, adj. swivel, rubber buttplate. Weight: 12.75 lbs. Made 1955-1964.
With sights $410
Without sights 325

Remington Model 40-X Sporter $1395
Same general specifications as Model 700 C Custom (*see* that listing in this section of the Rifle Section), except in caliber 22 LR. Made 1972-77.

Remington Model 40X Standard Barrel
Same as Model 40X Heavyweight except has lighter bbl. Weight: 10.75 lbs.
With sights . . . ., ... $350
Without sights 325

Remington Model 40-XB Centerfire Match Rifle . . $695
Bolt action, single shot. Calibers: 222 Rem., 222 Rem. Mag., 223 Rem., 22-250, 6×47mm, 6mm Rem., 243 Win., 25-06, 7mm Rem. Mag., 30-06, 308 Win. (7.62mm NATO), 30-338, 300 Win. Mag. 27.25-inch standard or heavy bbl. Target stock w/adj. front swivel block on guide rail, rubber buttplate. Weight w/o sights: standard bbl., 9.25 lbs.; heavy bbl., 11.25 lbs. Value shown is for rifle without sights. Made 1964 to date.

Remington Model 40-XB Rangemaster Centerfire
Single-shot target rifle with same basic specifications as Model 40-XB Centerfire Match. Additional calibers in 220 Swift, 6mm BR Rem. and 7mm BR Rem., and stainless bbl. only. American walnut or Kevlar (weighs 1 lb. less) target stock with forend stop. Discontinued 1994.
Model 40-XB Right-hand Model $790
Model 40-XB Left-hand Model 835
For 2-oz. trigger, **add** 100
Model 40-XB KS (Kevlar Stock, R.H.) 905
Model 40-XB KS (Kevlar Stock, L.H.) 950
For 2-oz. trigger, **add** 100
For Repeater Model, **add** 80

Remington Model 40-XB Rangemaster Rimfire Match Rifle $425
Bolt action, single shot. Caliber: 22 LR. 28-inch standard or heavy bbl. Target stock with adj. front swivel block on guide rail, rubber buttplate. Weight w/o sights: standard bbl., 10 lbs.; heavy bbl., 11.25 lbs. Value shown is for rifle without sights. Made 1964-74.

**Remington Model 40X
Standard Rimfire**

**Remington Model 40-XB
Centerfire**

**Remington Model 40-XB
Rimfire**

RIFLES

Remington Model 40-XB
Varmint Special

Remington Model 40-XBBR

Remington Model 40-XC

Remington Model 40-XB Varmint Special Rifle . . $785
Same general specifications as Model 40-XB Repeater, except
has synthetic stock of Kevlar. Made 1987-94.

Remington Model 40-XBBR Bench Rest Rifle
Bolt action, single shot. Calibers: 222 Rem., 222 Rem. Mag., 223
Rem., 6×47mm, 308 Win. (7.62mm NATO). 20- or 26-inch un-
blued stainless-steel bbl. Supplied w/o sights. Weight: with 20-
inch bbl. 9.25 lbs., with 26-inch bbl.,12 lbs. (heavy Varmint
class; 7.25 lbs. w/Kevlar stock (light Varmint class). Made 1969
to date.
Model 40-XBBR $650
Model 40-XBBR KS (Kevlar Stock) (disc.) 980

Remington Model 40-XC National Match Course Rifle
Bolt-action repeater. Caliber: 308 Win. (7.62mm NATO). 5-shot
magazine, clip slot in receiver. 24-inch bbl. Supplied w/o sights.
Weight: 11 lbs. Thumb groove stock w/adj. hand stop and sling
swivel, adj. buttplate. Made 1974 to date.
Model 40-XC $795
Model 40-XC KS (Kevlar Stock) (disc. 1994) 960

Remington Model 40-XR Custom Sporter Rifle
Caliber: 22 RF. 24-inch contoured bbl. Supplied w/o sights.
Made in four grades of checkering, engraving and other custom
features. Made 1987 to date.
Grade I . . . . $ 880
Grade II 1595
Grade III 2195
Grade IV 3850

Remington Model 40-XR Rimfire Position Rifle
Bolt action, single shot. Caliber: 22 LR. 24-inch heavy bbl. Supplied w/o sights. Weight: about 10 lbs. Position-style stock
w/thumb groove, adj. hand stop and sling swivel on guide rail,
adj. buttplate. Made 1974 to date.
Model 40-XR $895
Model 40-XR KS (Kevlar Stock) 950

Remington Model 41A Targetmaster Bolt-Action
Single-Shot Rifle $165
Takedown. Caliber: 22 Short, Long, LR. 27-inch bbl. Weight:
about 5.5 lbs. Sights: open rear; bead front. Plain pistol-grip
stock. Made 1936-40.

Remington Model 40-XR
Custom Sporter Grade II

Remington Model 40-XR
Rimfire Position Rifle

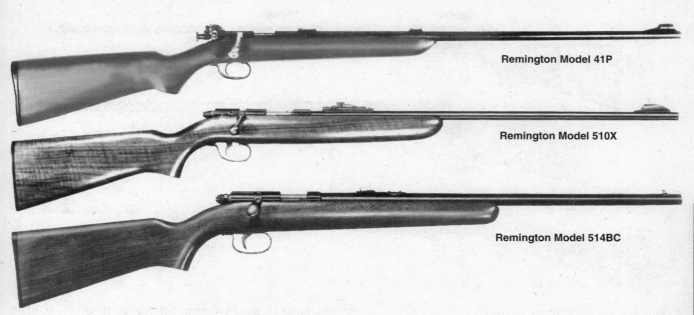

Remington Model 41P

Remington Model 510X

Remington Model 514BC

Remington Model 41AS $175
Same as Model 41A, except chambered for 22 Remington Special (22 W.R.F.).

Remington Model 41P $130
Same as Model 41A, except has peep rear sight, hooded front sight.

Remington Model 41SB $220
Same as Model 41A, except smoothbore for use with shot cartridges.

Remington Model 510A Targetmaster
Bolt-Action Single-Shot Rifle $195
Takedown. Caliber: 22 Short, Long, LR. 25-inch bbl. Weight: about 5.5 lbs. Sights: open rear; bead front. Plain pistol-grip stock. Made 1939-62.

Remington Model 510P $150
Same as Model 510A, except has peep rear sight, Patridge front, on ramp.

Remington Model 510SB $250
Same as Model 510A, except smoothbore for use with shot cartridges, shotgun bead front sight, no rear sight.

Remington Model 510X Bolt-Action
Single-Shot Rifle $160
Same as Model 510A, except improved sights. Mfd.1964-66.

Remington Model 514 Bolt-Action Single-Shot . . $135
Takedown. Caliber: 22 Short, Long, LR. 24-inch bbl. Weight: 4.75 lbs. Sights: open rear; bead front. Plain pistol-grip stock. Made 1948-71.

Remington Model 514BC Boy's Carbine $175
Same as Model 514 except has 21-inch bbl., 1-inch shorter stock. Made 1961-71.

Remington Model 514P $200
Same as Model 514, except has receiver peep sight.

Remington Model 540-X Rimfire Target Rifle . . . $265
Bolt-action, single-shot. Caliber: 22 R. 26-inch heavy bbl. Supplied w/o sights. Weight: about 8 lbs. Target stock w/Monte Carlo cheekpiece and thumb groove, guide rail for hand stop and swivel, adj. buttplate. Made 1969-74.

Remington Model 540-XR Position Rifle $285
Bolt-action, single-shot. Caliber: 22 LR. 26-inch medium-weight bbl. Supplied w/o sights. Weight: 8 lbs. 13 oz. Position-

Remington Model 540-X

RIFLES

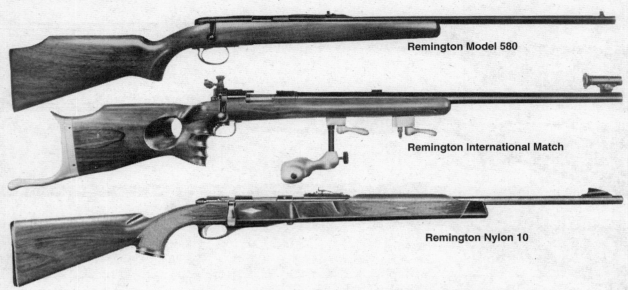

Remington Model 580

Remington International Match

Remington Nylon 10

Remington Model 540-XR *(Cont.)*

style stock w/thumb groove, guide rail for hand stop and swivel, adj. buttplate. Made 1974-84.

Remington Model 540-XRJR $295
Same as Model 540-XR, except 1.75-inch shorter stock. Made 1974-84.

Remington Model 580 Bolt-Action Single-Shot . . $115
Caliber: 22 Short, Long, LR. 24-inch bbl. Weight: 4.75 lbs. Sights: bead front; U-notch rear. Monte Carlo stock. Made 1967-78.

Remington Model 580BR Boy's Rifle $125
Same as Model 580, except has 1-inch shorter stock. Made 1971-78.

Remington Model 580SB Smooth Bore $145
Same as Model 580, except smooth bore for 22 Long Rifle shot cartridges. Made 1967-78.

Remington International Free Rifle $695
Same as Model 40-XB rimfire and centerfire, except has "free rifle"-type stock with adj. buttplate and hook, adj. palmrest, movable front sling swivel, 2-oz. trigger. Weight: about 15 lbs. Made 1964-74. Value shown is for rifle with professionally finished stock, no sights.

Remington International Match Free Rifle $795
Calibers: 22 LR, 222 Rem., 222 Rem. Mag., 7.62mm NATO, 30-06 (others were available on special order). Model 40X-type bolt action, single shot. 2-oz. adj. trigger. 28-inch heavy bbl. Weight: about 15.5 lbs. "Free rifle"-style stock with thumbhole (furnished semifinished by mfr.); interchangeable and adj. rubber buttplate and hook buttplate, adj. palmrest, sling swivel. Made 1961-64. Value shown is for rifle with professionally finished stock, no sights.

Remington Nylon 10 Bolt-Action
Single-Shot Rifle $85
Caliber: 22 Short, Long, LR. 19.13-inch bbl. Weight: 4.25 lbs. Open rear sight; ramped blade front. Receiver grooved for scope mount. Brown nylon stock. Made 1962-1966.

Bolt-Action Repeating Rifles

Remington Model Seven (7) CF Bolt-Action Rifle
Calibers: 17 Rem., 222 Rem., 223 Rem., 243 Win., 6mm Rem., 7mm-08 Rem., 308 Win. Magazine capacity: 5-shot in 17 Rem., 222 Rem., 223 Rem., 4-shot in other calibers. 18.5-inch bbl. Weight: 6.5 lbs. Walnut stock checkering, and recoil pad. Made 1983 to date. 223 Rem. added in 1984.
Standard calibers except 17 Rem. **$395**
Caliber 17 Rem. 415

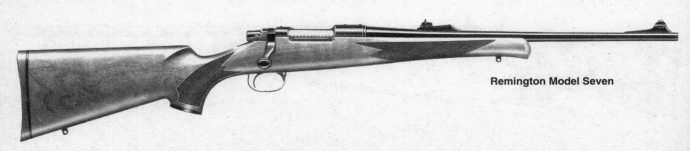

Remington Model Seven

Remington Model Seven FS

Remington Model Seven KS Custom Rifle

RIFLES

Remington Model Seven (7) FS Rifle $425
Calibers: 243, 7mm-08 Rem., 308 Win. 18.5-inch bbl. 37.5
inches overall. Weight: 5.25 lbs. Hand layup fiberglass stock, reinforced with DuPont Kevlar at points of bedding and stress.
Made 1987-90.

Remington Model Seven (7) KS Rifle $645
Calibers: 223 Rem., 7mm-08, 308, 35 Rem. and 350 Rem. Mag.
20-inch bbl. Custom made in Remington's Custom shop with
Kevlar stock. Made 1987 to date.

Remington Model Seven (7) MS Custom Rifle . . $695
Similar to the standard Model 7, except fitted with a laminated
full Mannlicher-style stock. Weight: 6.75 lbs. Calibers: 222
Rem., 22-250, 243, 6mm Rem.,7mm-08, 308, 350 Rem. Additional calibers available on special order. Made 1993 to date.

Remington Model Seven (7) SS Rifle $385
Same as Model 7, except 20-inch stainless bbl., receiver and bolt;
black synthetic stock. Calibers: 243, 7mm-08 or 308. Made 1994
to date.

Remington Model Seven (7) Youth Rifle $310
Similar to the standard Model 7, except fitted with hardwood
stock with a 12.19-inch pull. Calibers: 243, 6mm, 7mm-08 only.
Made 1993 to date.

**Remington Model 30A Bolt-Action
Express Rifle** $415
Standard Grade. Modified M/1917 Enfield Action. Calibers: 25,
30, 32 and 35 Rem., 7mm Mauser, 30-06. 5-shot box magazine.
22-inch bbl. Weight: about 7.25 lbs. Sights: open rear; bead
front. Walnut stock w/checkered pistol grip and forearm. Made
1921-40. *Note:* Early Model 30s had a slender forend with schnabel tip, military-type double-pull trigger.

Remington Model 30R Carbine $495
Same as Model 30A, except has 20-inch bbl., plain stock weighs
about 7 lbs.

Remington Model 30S Sporting Rifle $555
Special Grade. Same action as Model 30A. Calibers: 257 Roberts,
7mm Mauser, 30-06. 5-shot box magazine. 24-inch bbl. Weight:
about 8 lbs. Lyman #48 Receiver sight, bead front sight. Special
high comb stock with long, full forearm, checkered. Made 1930-40.

Remington Model 30A

Remington Model 30R

Remington Model 30S

Remington Model 34

Remington Model 37 (1937)

Remington Model 37 (1940)

Remington Model 34 Bolt-Action Repeater $135
Takedown. Caliber: 22 Short, Long, LR. Tubular magazine holds 22 Short, 17 Long or 15 LR. 24-inch bbl. Weight: 5.25 lbs. Sights: open rear; bead front. Plain, pistol-grip stock, forearm w/grasping grooves. Made 1932-36.

Remington Model 34 NRA Target Rifle $195
Same as Model 34 Standard, except has Lyman peep rear sight, Patridge-type front sight, .88-inch sling and swivels, weighs about 5.75 lbs.

Remington Model 37 Rangemaster Bolt-Action Target Rifle (I)
Model of 1937. Caliber: 22 LR. 5-shot box magazine, single shot adapter also supplied as standard equipment. 28-inch heavy bbl. Weight: about 12 lbs. Remington front and rear sights, scope bases. Target stock, swivels, sling. *Note:* Original 1937 model had a stock with outside bbl. hand similar in appearance to that of the old-style Winchester Model 52, forearm design was modified and bbl. band eliminated in 1938. Made 1937-40.
With factory sights $455
Without sights 325

Remington Model 37 Rangemaster Bolt-Action Target Rifle (II)
Model of 1940. Same as Model of 1937, except has "Miracle" trigger mechanism and Randle design stock with high comb, full pistol grip and wide beavertail forend. Made 1940-54.
With factory sights $525
Without sights 445

Remington Model 40-XB Centerfire Repeater ... $775
Same as Model 40-XB Centerfire except 5-shot repeater. Calibers: 222 Rem., 222 Rem. Mag., 223 Rem., 22-250, 6×47mm, 6mm Rem., 243 Win., 308 Win. (7.62mm NATO). Heavy bbl. only. Discontinued.

Remington Model 78 Sportsman Bolt-Action Rifle $225
Similar to Model 700 ADL, except with straight-comb walnut-finished hardwood stock in calibers 223 Rem., 243 Win, 270 Win., 30-06 Springfield and 308 Win. 22-inch bbl. Weight: 7 lbs. Adj. sights. Made 1984-91.

Remington Model 341A Sportsmaster Bolt-Action Repeater $135
Takedown. Caliber: 22 Short, Long, LR. Tubular magazine holds 22 Short, 17 Long, 15 LR. 27-inch bbl. Weight: about 6 lbs. Sights; open rear; bead front. Plain pistol-grip stock. Made 1936-40.

Remington Model 341P $160
Same as Model 341A, except has peep rear sight, hooded front sight.

Remington Model 341SB $275
Same as Model 341A, except smoothbore for use with shot cartridges.

Remington Model 78 Sportsman

Remington Model 341A

Remington Model 511A Scoremaster Bolt-Action Box Magazine Repeater $140

Takedown. Caliber: 22 Short, Long, LR.6-shot detachable box magazine. 25-inch bbl. Weight: about 5.5 lbs. Sights: open rear; bead front. Plain pistol-grip stock. Made 1939-62.

Remington Model 511P $125

Same as Model 511A, except has peep rear sight, Patridge-type blade front, on ramp.

Remington Model 511X Bolt-Action Repeater . . $150

Clip type. Same as Model 511A, except improved sights. Made 1964-66.

Remington Model 512A Sportsmaster Bolt-Action Repeater $145

Takedown. Caliber: 22 Short, Long, LR. Tubular magazine holds 22 Short, 17 Long, 15 LR. 25-inch bbl. Weight: about 5.75 lbs. Sights: open rear; bead front. Plain pistol-grip stock w/semibeavertail forend. Made 1940-62.

Remington Model 512P $185

Same as Model 512A, except has peep rear sight, blade front, on ramp.

Remington Model 512X Bolt-Action Repeater . . $195

Tubular magazine type. Same as Model 512A, except has improved sights. Made 1964-66.

Remington Model 513S Bolt-Action Rifle $365

Caliber: 22 LR. 6-shot detachable box magazine. 27-inch bbl. Weight: about 6.75 lbs. Marble open rear sight, Patridge-type front. Checkered sporter stock. Made 1941-56.

Remington Model 513TR Matchmaster Bolt-Action Target Rifle $250

Caliber: 22 LR. 6-shot detachable box magazine. 27-inch bbl. Weight: about 9 lbs. Sights: Redfield No. 75 rear; globe front. Target stock. Sling and swivels. Made 1941-69.

RIFLES

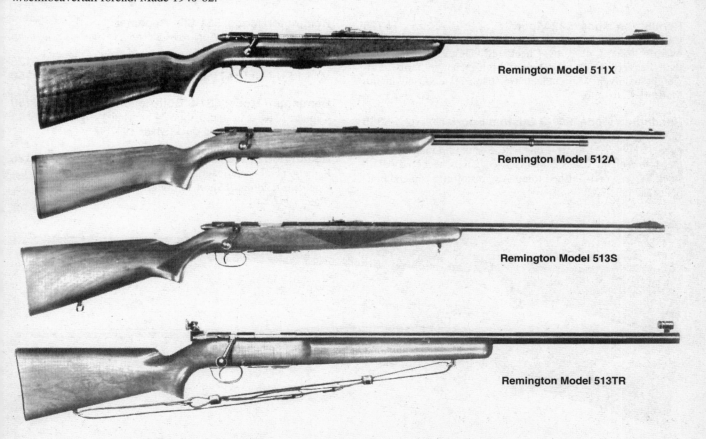

Remington Model 511X

Remington Model 512A

Remington Model 513S

Remington Model 513TR

Remington Model 521TL

Remington Model 541-S

Remington Model 541-T

Reminaton Model 521TL Junior Target Bolt-Action Repeater $225
Takedown. Caliber: 22 LR. 6-shot detachable box magazine. 25-inch bbl. Weight: about 7 lbs. Sights: Lyman No. 57RS rear; dovetailed blade front. Target stock. Sling and swivels. Made 1947-69.

Remington Model 522 Viper $125
Calibers: 22 LR. 10-shot magazine. 20-inch bbl. 40 inches overall. Weight: 4.63 lbs. Checkered black PET resin stock with beavertail forend. Dupont high-tech synthetic light-weight receiver. Matte black finish on all exposed metal. Made 1993 to date.

Remington Model 541-S Custom Sporter $365
Bolt-action repeater. Scroll engraving on receiver and trigger guard. Caliber: 22 Short, Long, LR. 5-shot clip magazine. 24-inch bbl. Weight: 5.5 lbs. Supplied w/o sights. Checkered walnut stock w/rosewood-finished forend tip, pistol-grip cap and butt-plate. Made 1972-84.

Remington Model 541-T Bolt-Action Rifle
Caliber: 22 RF. Clip-fed, 5-shot. 24-inch bbl. Weight: 5.88 lbs. Checkered walnut stock. Made 1986 to date; heavy bbl. model introduced in 1993.
Model 541-T Standard $250
Model 541-T HB Heavy bbl. 295

Remington Model 581 Clip Repeater
Same general specifications as Model 580, except has 5-shot clip magazine. Made 1967-84.
Model 581 . . . . $125
Model 581 Left Hand (made 1969-1984) 150

Remington Model 581-S Bolt-Action Rifle $150
Caliber: 22 RF. Clip-fed, 5-shot. 24-inch bbl. Weight: about 4.75 lbs. Plain walnut-colored stock. Made 1987-92.

Remington Model 582 Tubular Repeater $125
Same general specifications as Model 580, except has tubular magazine holding 20 Short, 15 Long, 14 LR. Weight: about 5 lbs. Made 1967-84.

Remington Model 581

Remington Model 581-S

Remington Model 582

Remington Model 591

Remington Model 592

Remington Model 591 Bolt-Action Clip Repeater $175
Caliber: 5mm Rimfire Magnum. 4-shot clip magazine. 24-inch bbl. Weight: 5 lbs. Sights: bead front; U-notch rear. Monte Carlo stock. Made 1970-73.

Remington Model 592 Tubular Repeater $165
Same as Model 591, except has tubular magazine holding 10 rounds, weighs 5.5 lbs. Made 1970-73.

Remington Model 600 Bolt-Action Carbine $495
Calibers: 222 Rem., 6mm Rem., 243 Win., 308 Win., 35 Rem. 5-shot box magazine (6-shot in 222 Rem.). 18.5-inch bbl. with ventilated rib. Weight: 6 lbs. Sights: open rear; blade ramp front. Monte Carlo stock w/pistol grip. Made 1964-67.

Remington Model 600 Magnum $625
Same as Model 600, except calibers 6.5mm Rem. Mag. and 350 Rem. Mag., 4-shot magazine, special Magnum-type bbl. with racket for scope back-up, laminated walnut and beech stock w/recoil pad. QD swivels and sling; weight: about 6.5 lbs. Made 1965-67.

Remington Model 600 Montana Territorial Centennial $755
Same as Model 600, except has commemorative medallion embedded in buttstock. Made 1964. Value is for rifle in new, unfired condition.

Remington Model 660 Bolt-Action Carbine $425
Calibers: 222 Rem., 6mm Rem., 243 Win., 308 Win. 5-shot box magazine (6-shot in 222). 20-inch bbl. Weight: 6.5 lbs. Sights: open rear; bead front, on ramp. Monte Carlo stock, checkered, black pistol-grip cap and forend tip. Made 1968-71.

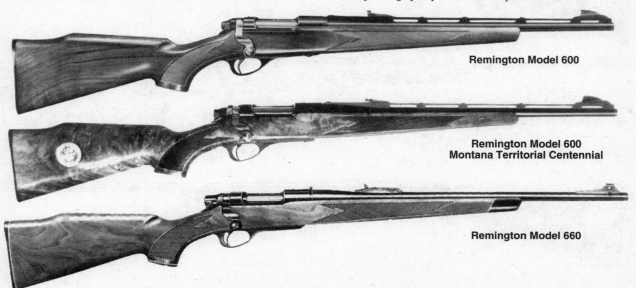

Remington Model 600

Remington Model 600
Montana Territorial Centennial

Remington Model 660

RIFLES

Remington Model 660 Magnum **$575**
Same as Model 660, except calibers 6.5mm Rem. Mag. and 350
Rem. Mag., 4-shot magazine, laminated walnut-and-beech stock
with recoil pad, QD swivels and sling. Made 1968-71.

Remington Model 700 ADL Centerfire Rifle **$285**
Calibers: 22-250, 222 Rem., 25-06, 6mm Rem., 243 Win., 270
Win., 30-06, 308 Win., 7mm Rem. Mag. Magazine capacity: 6-
shot in 222 Rem.; 4-shot in 7mm Rem. Mag. 5-shot in other
calibers. Bbl. lengths: 24-inch in 22-250, 222 Rem., 25-06, 7mm
Rem. Mag.; 22-inch in other calibers. Weight: 7 lbs. standard;
7.5 lbs. in 7mm Rem. Mag. Sights: ramp front; sliding ramp open
rear. Monte Carlo stock w/cheekpiece, skip checkering, recoil
pad on Magnum. Laminated stock also avail. Made 1962-93.

Remington Model 700 BDL Centerfire Rifle
Same as Model 700 ADL, except has hinged floorplate hooded
ramp front sight, stock w/black forend tip and pistol-grip cap, cut
checkering, QD swivels and sling. Additional calibers: 17 Rem.,
223 Rem., 264 Win. Mag., 7mm-08, 280, 300 Sav., 300 Win.

Remington Model 700 BDL Centerfire Rifle *(Cont.)*
Mag., 8mm Rem. Mag., 338 Win. Mag., 35 Whelen. All have 24-
inch bbls. Magnums have 4-shot magazine, recoil pad, weighs
7.5 pounds; 17 Rem. has 6-shot magazine, weighs 7 lbs. Made
1962 to date. Made 1973 to date.

Standard calibers except 17 Rem.	**$385**
Magnum calibers and 17 Rem.	**425**
Left-hand, 270 Win. and 30-06	**395**
Left-hand, 7mm Rem. Mag.	**400**

Remington Model 700 BDL European Rifle
Same general specifications as Model 700 BDL, except has oil-
finished walnut stock. Calibers: 243, 270, 7mm-08, 7mm Mag.,
280 Rem., 30-06. Made 1993 to date.

Standard Calibers	**$395**
Magnum Calibers	**415**

Remington Model 700 BDL SS Bolt-Action Rifle
Same as Model 700 BDL, except w/24-inch stainless barrel, receiver and bolt plus black synthetic stock. Calibers: 223 Rem.,

Remington Model 700 ADL

Remington Model 700 ADL
w/Laminated Stock

Remington Model 700 BDL

Remington Model 700 ADL
Left Hand

Remington Model 700 BDL Magnum

Remington Model 700 BDL SS *(Cont.)*

243 Win., 6mm Rem., 25-06 Rem., 270 Win. 280 Rem., 7mm-08, 7mm Rem. Mag., 7mm Wby. Mag., 30-06, 300 Win., 308 Win., 338 Win. Mag. Made 1992 to date.

Standard Calibers **$425**
Magnum Calibers, **add** 30
Detachable Box Magazine, **add** 30

Remington Model 700 BDL Varmint Special **$395**

Same as Model 700 BDL, except has 24-inch heavy bbl., no sights, weighs 9 lbs. (8.75 lbs. in 308 Win.). Calibers: 22-250, 222 Rem., 223 Rem., 25-06, 6mm Rem., 243 Win., 308 Win. Made 1967-94.

Remington Model 700 Classic

Same general specifications as Model 700 BDL, except has "Classic" stock of high-quality walnut with full-pattern cut-checkering, special satin wood finish; schnabel forend. Brown

Remington Model 700 Classic *(Cont.)*

rubber buttpad. Hinged floorplate. No sights. Weight: 7 lbs. Also chambered for "Classic" cartridges such as 257 Roberts and 250-3000. Intro. 1981.

Standard Calibers **$355**
Magnum Calibers 385

Remington Model 700 Custom Bolt-Action Rifle

Same general specifications as Model 700 BDL, except custom built, and available in choice of grades — each with higher quality wood, different checkering patterns, engraving, high-gloss blued finish. Introduced in 1965.

Model 700 C Grade I . . . . **$ 895**
Model 700 C Grade II 1595
Model 700 C Grade III 2450
Model 700 C Grade IV 3950
Model 700 D Peerless 1395
Model 700 F Premier 2655

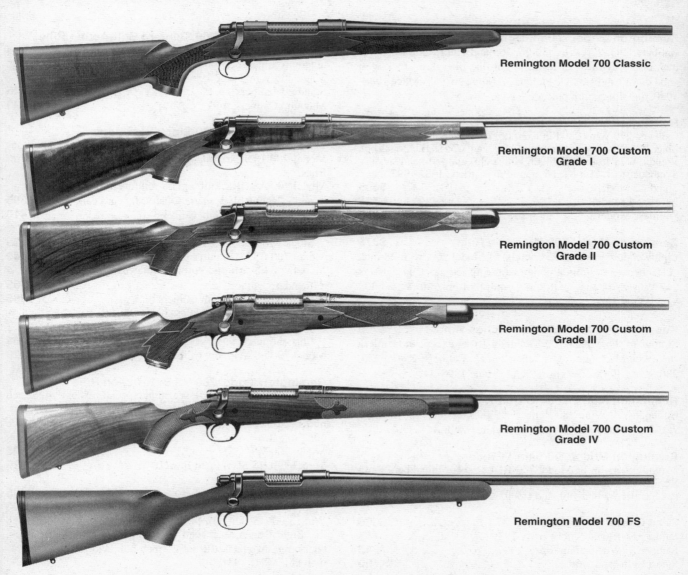

Remington Model 700 Classic

Remington Model 700 Custom Grade I

Remington Model 700 Custom Grade II

Remington Model 700 Custom Grade III

Remington Model 700 Custom Grade IV

Remington Model 700 FS

RIFLES

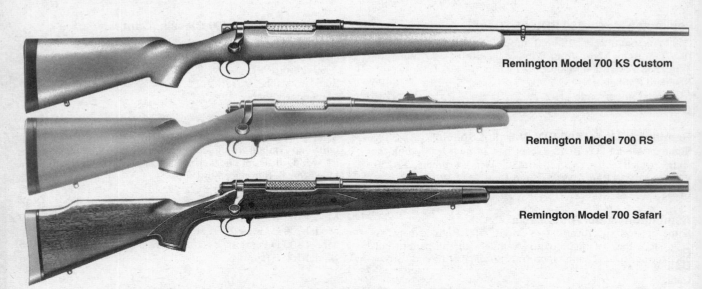

Remington Model 700 KS Custom

Remington Model 700 RS

Remington Model 700 Safari

Remington Model 700 FS Bolt-Action Rifle **$435**
Calibers: 243, 270 Win., 30-06, 308 and 7mm Rem. Mag. 22-inch bbl. Weight: 6.25 lbs. Straight-line fiberglass stock with solid black English-style buttpad and sling swivels. Made 1987-1990. *See* illustration preceding page.

Remington Model 700 KS Custom Mountain Rifle
Calibers: 270 Win., 280 Rem., 30-06, 7mm Rem. Mag., 300 Win. Mag., 338 Win. Mag., 8mm Rem. Mag. and 375 H&H. 22-inch bbl. Weight: 6.75 lbs. Available in both right- and left-hand models. Synthetic stock with Kevlar aramid fiber. Made 1987-1993.
Standard Model **$695**
Left-hand Model 725
Stainless Model 825

Remington Model 700 Mountain Rifle **$375**
Lightweight version (6.75 pounds) of Model 700, with 22-inch bbl., checkered straight-comb satin-finished stock in calibers 243 Win., 270 Win., 280 Rem., 7mm-08 Rem., 30-06 and 308 Win. Made 1986 to date.

Remington 700 MTRSS Bolt-Action Rifle **$400**
Similar to the Model 700 Mountain Rifle, except in stainless steel with black textured synthetic stock. Calibers: 25-06, 270, 280 Rem., 30-06. Weighs 6.25 lbs. Made 1993-94.

Remington Model 700 RS Bolt-Action Rifle **$370**
Calibers: 270 Win., 280 Rem. and 30-06. 22-inch bbl. Weight: 7.25 lbs. Stock made of Du Pont Rynite. Made 1987-90.

Remington Model 700 Safari Grade
Magnum version of Model 700 BDL, except in calibers 8mm Rem. Mag., 375 H&H Mag., 416 Rem. Mag. and 458 Win. Mag., has heavier 24-inch bbl. and stock, weighs 9 lbs. Made 1962 to date.
Safari Classic/Monte Carlo **$665**
Safari KS (Kevlar Stock) intro. 1989 765
Safari KS (Wood-grain) intro. 1992 845
Safari Left-hand, **add** 50

Remington Model 700 Sendero Bolt-Action Rifle
Same as Model 700 VS, except chambered in long action and magnum calibers: 25-06 Rem., 270 Win., 280 Rem., 7mm Rem. Mag., 300 Win. Made 1994 to date.
Standard Calibers **$445**
Magnum Calibers, **add** 25

Remington Model 700 Stock Variations
The following rifles have the same general specifications as Model 700 BDL, except with different stock options and finishes.
Model 700 AS (Black fiberglass-reinforced resin stock; nonreflective black matte finish) Standard calibers ... **$395**
Model 700 AS, Magnum calibers 410
Model 700 CS (Mossy Oak Bottomland Camo Synthetic Stock w/black matte finish) Standard calibers 425
Model 700 CS, Magnum calibers 440
Model 700 LS (Multi-colored laminated stock) Standard calibers 365
Model 700 LS, Magnum calibers 385
Model 700 SS (Matte stainless bbl. and action, Black synthetic stock) Standard calibers (discontinued 1994) 400
Model 700 SS Magnum calibers 420

Remington Model 700 VS Bolt-Action Rifle
Same as Model 700 BDL Varmint Special, except w/26-inch stainless bbl., receiver and bolt; black synthetic stock w/aluminum bedding block. Calibers: 22-250, 220 Swift, 223, 308. Made 1992 to date.
Model 700 VS **$425**
Model 700 VS SF (Fluted Barrel) 525

Remington Model 720A Bolt-Action High Power .. **$925**
Modified M/1917 Enfield action. Calibers: 257 Roberts, 270 Win., 30-06. 5-shot box magazine. 22-inch bbl. Weight: about 8 lbs. Sights: open rear; bead front, on ramp. Pistol-grip stock, checkered. **Model 720R** has 20-inch bbl.; **Model 720S** has 24-inch bbl. Made 1941.

Remington Model 721A Deluxe

Remington Model 722A

Remington Model 721A Standard Grade Bolt-Action High-Power Rifle $295

Calibers: 264 Win., 270 Win., 30-06. 4-shot box magazine. 24-inch bbl. Weight: about 7.25 lbs. Sights: open rear; bead front, on ramp. Plain sporting stock. Made 1948-62.

Remington Model 721A 300 Magnum Standard Grade $495

Caliber: 300 H&H Magnum. Same as standard model, except has 26-inch heavy bbl., 3-shot magazine, recoil pads, weighs 8.25 lbs.

Remington Model 721ADL/BDL Deluxe

Same as Model 721A Standard or Magnum, except has deluxe checkered stock and/or select wood.

Model 721ADL Deluxe Grade	**$355**
Model 721ADL 300 Magnum Deluxe	475
Model 721BDL Deluxe Special Grade	425
Model 721BDL 300 Magnum Deluxe	450

Remington Model 722A Standard Grade Sporter

Same as Model 721A Bolt-Action, except shorter action in calibers 257 Roberts, 308 Win., 300 Savage, weighs 7 lbs. Made 1948-62. Caliber 222 Rem. (26-inch bbl., 5-shot magazine, 8 lbs.) introduced in 1950; caliber 244 Rem. (4-round capacity) introduced 1955.

Standard calibers	**$265**
222 Rem. Standard Grade	295
244 Rem. Standard Grade	280

Remington Model 722ADL Deluxe Grade

Same as Model 722A, except has deluxe checkered stock.

Standard Calibers	**$325**
222 Rem. Deluxe Grade	350
244 Rem. Deluxe Grade	375

Remington Model 722BDL Deluxe Special Grade

Same as Model 722ADL, except select wood.

Standard Calibers	**$395**
222 Rem. Deluxe Special Grade	425
224 Rem. Deluxe Special Grade	445

Remington Model 725 Kodiak Magnum Rifle .. $2695

Similar to Model 725ADL. Calibers: 375 H&H Mag., 458 Win. Mag. 3-shot magazine. 26-inch bbl. with recoil reducer built into muzzle. Weight: about 9 lbs. Deluxe, reinforced Monte Carlo stock with recoil pad, black forend tip swivels, sling. Less than 100 made in 1961.

Remington Model 725ADL Bolt-Action Repeating Rifle $570

Calibers: 222, 243, 244, 270, 280, 30-06. 4-shot box magazine (5-shot in 222). 22-inch bbl. (24-inch in 222). Weight: about 7 lbs. Sights: open rear, hooded ramp front. Monte Carlo comb stock w/pistol grip, checkered, swivels. Made 1958-61.

Remington Model 788 Centerfire Bolt-Action

Calibers: 222 Rem., 22-250, 223 Rem., 6mm Rem., 243 Win., 308 Win., 30-30, 44 Rem. Mag. 3-shot clip magazine (4-shot in 222 and 223 Rem.). 24-inch bbl. in 22s, 22-inch in other calibers. Weight: 7.5 lbs. with 24-inch bbl.; 7.25 lbs. with 22-inch bbl. Sights: blade front, on ramp; U-notch rear. Plain Monte Carlo stock. Made 1967-84.

Standard R.H. Model	**$275**
Left Hand (6mm Rem. and 308 Win. only made 1972-79)	295

Remington Nylon 11 Bolt-Action Repeater $90

Clip type. Caliber: 22 Short, Long, LR. 6- or 10-shot clip mag. 19.63-inch bbl. Weight: 4.5 lbs. Sights: open rear; blade front. Nylon stock. Made 1962-66.

Remington Nylon 12 Bolt-Action Repeater $90

Same as Nylon 11 except has tubular magazine holding 22 Short, 17 Long, 15 LR. Made 1962-66.

RIFLES

Remington Nylon 12

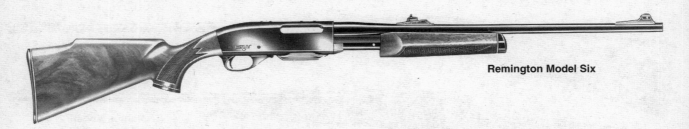

Remington Model Six

Slide- and Lever-Action Rifles

Remington Model Six (6) Slide-Action Repeater .. **$325**
Hammerless. Calibers: 6mm Rem., 243 Win., 270 Win. 7mm
Express Rem., 30-06, 308 Win. 22-inch bbl. Weight: 7.5 lbs.
Checkered Monte Carlo stock and forearm. Made 1981-88.

**Remington Model Six (6) Slide-Action Repeater,
Peerless Grade** **$1295**
Same as Model Six Standard, except has engraved receiver.
Made 1981-88.

**Remington Model Six (6) Slide-Action Repeater,
Premier Grade** **$3750**
Same as Model Six Standard, except has engraved receiver with
gold inlay. Made 1981-88.

**Remington Model 12A, 12B, 12C, 12CS Slide-Action
Repeaters**
Standard Grade. Hammerless. Takedown. Caliber: 22 Short,
Long or LR. Tubular magazine holds 15 Short, 12 Long or 10 LR
cartridges. 22- or 24-inch round or octagonal bbl. Open rear
sight, bead front. Plain, half-pistol-grip stock and grooved slide
handle of walnut. Made 1909-36.
Model 12A **$295**
Model 12B (22 Short only w/octagon bbl.) **310**
Model 12C (w/24-inch octagon bbl.) **335**
Model 12CS (22 WRF w/24-inch octagon bbl.) **295**

**Remington Model 14A High Power Slide-Action
Repeating Rifle** **$350**
Standard Grade. Hammerless. Takedown. Calibers: 25, 30, 32
and 35 Rem. 5-shot tubular magazine. 22-inch bbl. Weight:
about 6.75 lbs. Sights: open rear; bead front. Plain, half-pistol-
grip stock and grooved slide handle of walnut. Made 1912-35.

Remington Model 14R Carbine **$375**
Same as Model 14A except has 18.5-inch bbl., straight-grip
stock, weighs about 6 lbs.

Remington Model 14 ½ Carbine **$695**
Same as Model 14.5 Rifle, except has 9-shot magazine, 18.5-
inch bbl.

Remington Model 14½ Rifle **$725**
Similar to Model 14A, except calibers 38-40 and 44-40, 11-shot
full magazine, 22.5-inch bbl. Made 1912 to early 1920s.

Remington Model 25A Slide-Action Repeater .. **$325**
Standard Grade. Hammerless. Takedown. Calibers: 25-20, 32-
20. 10-shot tubular magazine. 24-inch bbl. Weight: about 5.5 lbs.
Sights: open rear; bead front. Plain, pistol-grip stock, grooved
slide handle. Made 1923-36

Remington Model 25R Carbine **$425**
Same as Model 25A, except has 18-inch bbl. 6-shot magazine,
straight-grip stock, weighs about 4.5 lbs.

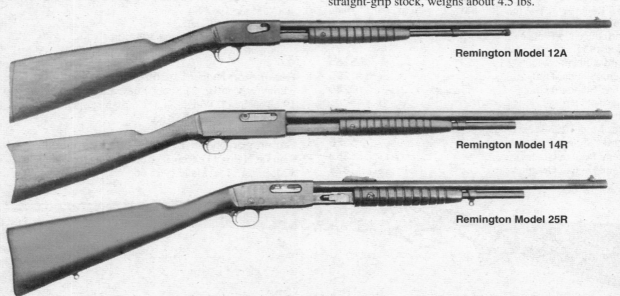

Remington Model 12A

Remington Model 14R

Remington Model 25R

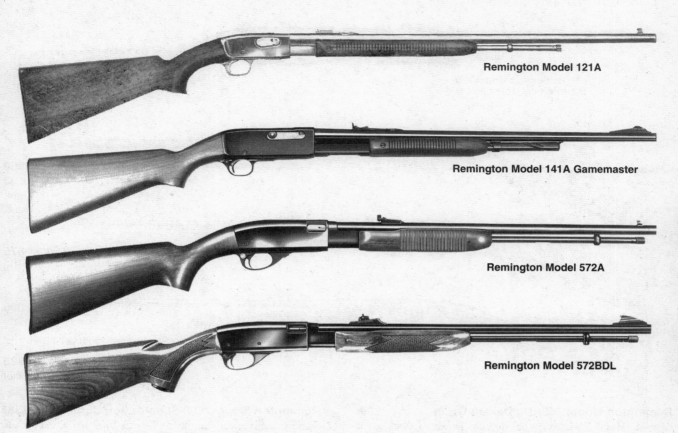

Remington Model 121A

Remington Model 141A Gamemaster

Remington Model 572A

Remington Model 572BDL

Remington Model 121A Fieldmaster Slide-Action Repeater **$265**
Standard Grade. Hammerless. Takedown. Caliber: 22 Short, Long, LR. Tubular magazine holds 20 Short, 15 Long or 14 LR cartridges. 24-inch round bbl. Weight: 6 lbs. Plain, pistol-grip stock and grooved semibeavertail slide handle. Made 1936-54.

Remington Model 121S **$325**
Same as Model 121A, except chambered for 22 Remington Special (22 W.R.F.). Magazine holds 12 rounds. Disc.

Remington Model 121SB **$395**
Same as Model 121A, except smoothbore. Discontinued.

Remington Model 141A Gamemaster Slide-Action Repeater **$295**
Standard Grade. Hammerless. Takedown. Calibers: 30, 32 and 35 Rem. 5-shot tubular magazine. 24-inch bbl. Weight: about 7.75 lbs. Sights: open rear; bead front, on ramp. Plain, pistol-grip stock, semibeavertail forend (slide-handle). Made 1936-50.

Remington Model 572A Fieldmaster Slide-Action Repeater **$150**
Hammerless. Caliber: 22 Short, Long, LR. Tubular magazine holds 20 Short, 17 Long, 15 LR. 23-inch bbl. Weight: about 5.5 lbs. Sights: open rear; ramp front. Pistol-grip stock, grooved forearm. Made 1955-88.

Remington Model 572BDL Deluxe **$185**
Same as Model 572A, except has blade ramp front sight, sliding ramp rear; checkered stock and forearm. Made 1966 to date.

Remington Model 572SB Smooth Bore **$250**
Same as Model 572A except smooth bore for 22 LR shot cartridges. Made 1961 to date.

Remington Model 760 Bicentennial Commemorative **$595**
Same as Model 760, except has commemorative inscription on receiver. Made 1976. *See* illustration next page.

Remington Model 760 Carbine **$375**
Same as Model 760 Rifle, except made in calibers 270 Win., 280 Rem., 30-06 and 308 Win. only, has 18.5-inch bbl., weighs 7.25 lbs. Made 1961-80. *See* illustration next page.

Remington Model 760 Gamemaster Standard Grade Slide-Action Repeating Rifle **$300**
Hammerless. Calibers: 223 Rem., 6mm Rem., 243 Win., 257 Roberts, 270 Win. 280 Rem., 30-06, 300 Sav., 308 Win., 35 Rem. 22-inch bbl. Weight: about 7.5 lbs. Sights: open rear; bead front, on ramp. Plain pistol-grip stock, grooved slide handle on early models, current production has checkered stock and slide handle. Made 1952-80. *See* illustration next page.

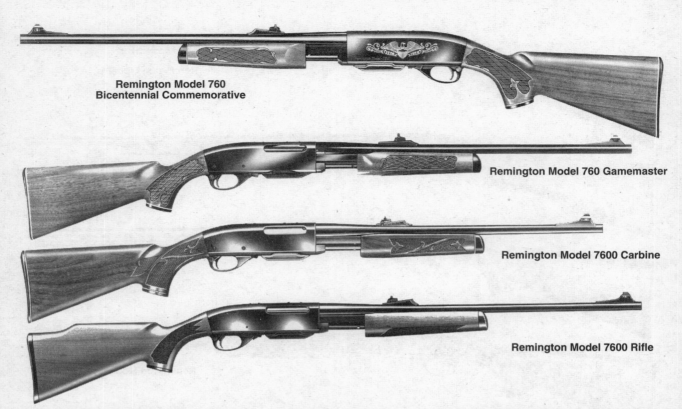

Remington Model 760
Bicentennial Commemorative

Remington Model 760 Gamemaster

Remington Model 7600 Carbine

Remington Model 7600 Rifle

Remington Model 760ADL Deluxe Grade $395
Same as Model 760, except has deluxe checkered stock, standard or high comb, grip cap, sling swivels. Made 1953-63.

Remington Model 760BDL Custom Deluxe $320
Same as Model 760 Rifle, except made in calibers 270, 30-06 and 308 only, has Monte Carlo cheekpiece stock forearm with black tip, basket-weave checkering. Available also in left-hand model. Made 1953-80.

Remington Model 760D Peerless Grade $1290
Same as Model 760, except scroll engraved, fancy wood. Made 1953-80.

Remington Model 760F Premier Grade $2790
Same as Model 760, except extensively engraved with game scenes and scroll, finest grade wood. Also available with receiver inlaid with gold; adds 50 percent to value. Made 1953-80.

Remington Model 7600 Slide-Action Carbine . . . $335
Same general specifications as Model 7600 Rifle, except has 18.5-inch bbl. and weighs 7.25 lbs. Made 1987 to date.

Remington Model 7600 Slide-Action Rifle $345
Similar to Model Six, except has lower grade finishes. Made 1981 to date.

Remington Model 7600 Special Purpose $325
Same general specification as the Model 7600, except chambered only in 270 or 30-06. Special Purpose matte black finish on all exposed metal. American walnut stock with SP nonglare finish.

Remington Nylon 76 Lever-Action Repeater . . . $250
Short-throw lever action. Caliber: 22 LR, 14-shot buttstock tubular magazine. Weight: 4 lbs. Black or brown nylon stock and forend. Made 1962-64. Remington's only lever-action rifle.

Remington Nylon 76 Lever-Action Rifle

Remington Sportsman 76

Remington Sportsman 76 Slide-Action Rifle **$245**
Caliber: 30-06, 4-shot magazine. 22-inch bbl. Weight: 7.5 lbs.
Open rear sight; front blade mounted on ramp. Uncheckered
hardwood stock and forend. Made 1985-87.

Semiautomatic Rifles

Remington Model Four (4) Autoloading Rifle
Hammerless. Calibers: 6mm Rem., 243 Win., 270 Win. 7mm
Express Rem., 30-06, 308 Win. 22-inch bbl. Weight: 7.5 lbs.
Sights: open rear; bead front, on ramp. Monte Carlo checkered
stock and forearm. Made 1981-88.
Standard . . . . **$ 345**
Peerless Grade (Engr. receiver) **1295**
Premier Grade (Engr. receiver, gold inlay) **2850**

Remington Model Four Diamond Anniversary Ltd. Edition
Same as Model Four Standard, except has engraved receiver
w/inscription, checkered high-grade walnut stock and forend.
Only 1,500 produced. Made 1981 only.
Standard Grade . . . . **$ 895**
Peerless Grade **1720**
Premier Grade **3540**
Premier Gold Grade **5250**

Remington Model 8A Autoloading Rifle **$395**
Standard Grade. Takedown. Calibers: 25, 30, 32 and 35 Rem.
Five-shot, clip-loaded magazine. 22-inch bbl. Weight: 7.75
lbs. Sights: adj. and dovetailed open rear; dovetailed bead
front. Half-moon metal buttplate on plain straight-grip walnut
stock; plain walnut forearm with thin curved end. Made 1906-
1936.

Remington Model 16 Autoloading Rifle **$275**
Takedown. Closely resembles the Winchester Model 03 semiautomatic rifle. Calibers: 22 Short, 22 LR, 22 Rem. Auto. 15-shot
tubular magazine in buttstock. 22-inch bbl. Weight: 5.75 lbs.
Sights: open rear; dovetailed bead front. Plain straight-grip stock
and forearm. Made 1914-1928. *Note:* In 1918 this model was
discontinued in all calibers except 22 Rem. Auto; specifications
given are for that. *See* illustration next page.

Remington Model 24A Autoloading Rifle **$290**
Standard Grade. Takedown. Calibers: 22 Short only, 22 LR
only. Tubular magazine in buttstock, holds 15 Short or 10 LR.
21-inch bbl. Weight: about 5 lbs. Sights: dovetailed adj. open
rear; dovetailed bead front. Plain walnut straight-grip buttstock; plain walnut forearm. Made 1922-35. *See* illustration
next page.

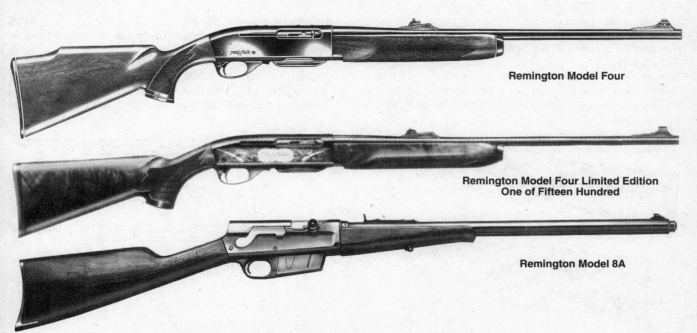

Remington Model Four

Remington Model Four Limited Edition One of Fifteen Hundred

Remington Model 8A

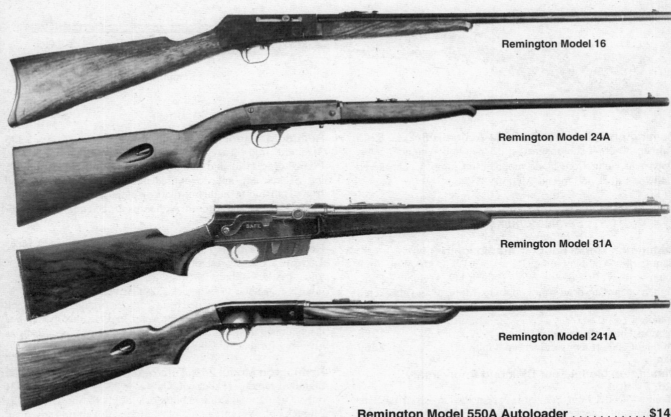

Remington Model 16

Remington Model 24A

Remington Model 81A

Remington Model 241A

Remington Model 81A Woodsmaster Autoloader **$350**
Standard Grade. Takedown. Calibers: 30, 32 and 35 Rem., 300 Sav. 5-shot box magazine (not detachable). 22-inch bbl. Weight: 8.25 lbs. Sights: open rear; bead front. Plain walnut pistol-grip stock, forearm. Made 1936-50.

Remington Model 241A Speedmaster Autoloader **$275**
Standard Grade. Takedown. Calibers: 22 Short only, 22 LR only. Tubular magazine in buttstock, holds 15 Short or 10 LR. 24-inch bbl. Weight: about 6 lbs. Sights; open rear, bead front. Plain walnut stock and forearm. Made 1935-51.

Remington Model 550A Autoloader **$145**
Has "Power Piston" or floating chamber, which permits interchangeable use of 22 Short, Long or LR cartridges. Tubular magazine holds 22 Short, 17 Long, 15 LR. 24-inch bbl. Weight: about 6.25 lbs. Sights: open rear; bead front. Plain, one-piece pistol-grip stock. Made 1941-71.

Remington Model 550P **$155**
Same as Model 550A, except has peep rear sight, blade front, on ramp.

Remington Model 550-2G **$195**
"Gallery Special." Same as Model 550A, except has 22-inch bbl., screweye for counter chain and fired shell deflector.

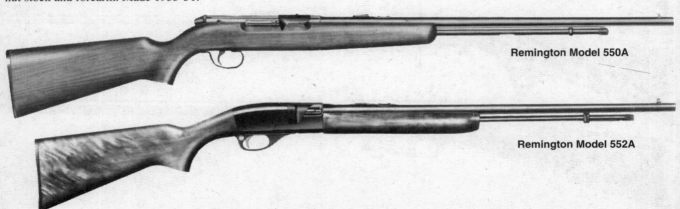

Remington Model 550A

Remington Model 552A

Remington 552 BDL

Remington Model 552A Speedmaster Autoloader $150
Caliber: 22 Short, Long, LR. Tubular magazine holds 20 Short, 17 Long, 15 LR. 25-inch bbl. Weight: about 5.5 lbs. Sights: open rear; bead front. Pistol-grip stock, semibeavertail forearm. Made 1957-88.

Remington Model 552BDL Deluxe $175
Same as Model 552A, except has checkered walnut stock and forearm. Made 1966 to date.

Remington Model 552C Carbine $160
Same as Model 552A, except has 21-inch bbl. Made 1961-77.

Remington Model 552GS Gallery Special $175
Same as Model 552A, except chambered for 22 Short only. Made 1957-77.

Remington Model 740A Woodsmaster Autoloader Rifle $295
Standard Grade. Gas-operated. Calibers: 30-06 or 308. 4-shot detachable box magazine. 22-inch bbl. Weight: about 7.5 lbs. Plain pistol-grip stock, semibeavertail forend with finger grooves. Sights: open rear; ramp front. Made 1955-60.

Remington Model 740ADL/BDL Deluxe
Same as Model 740A, except has deluxe checkered stock, standard or high comb, grip cap, sling swivels. Model 740 BDL also has select wood. Made 1955-60.
Model 740 ADL Deluxe Grade $325
Model 740 BDL Deluxe Special Grade 350

Remington Model 742 Bicentennial Commemorative $550
Same as Model 742 Woodsmaster rifle, except has commemorative inscription on receiver. Made 1876.

Remington Model 742 Canadian Centennial $565
Same as Model 742 rifle, except has commemorative inscription on receiver. Made 1967. Value is for rifle in new, unfired condition.

Remington Model 742 Carbine $380
Same as Model 742 Woodsmaster Rifle, except made in calibers 30-06 and 308 only, has 18.5-inch bbl., weighs 6.75 lbs. Made 1961-80.

RIFLES

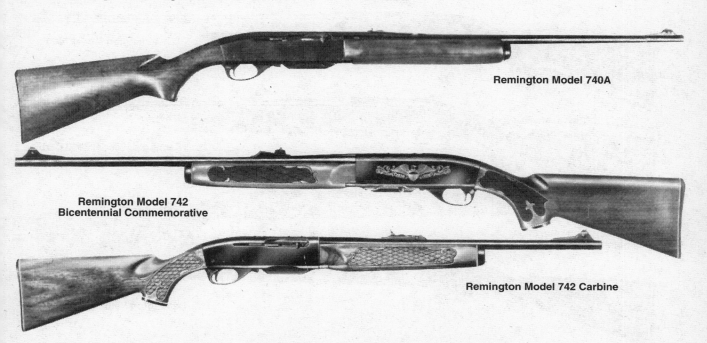

Remington Model 740A

Remington Model 742 Bicentennial Commemorative

Remington Model 742 Carbine

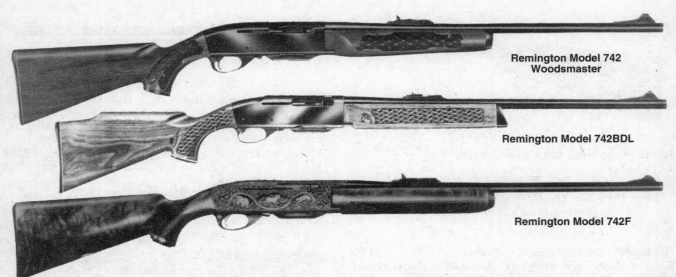

Remington Model 742
Woodsmaster

Remington Model 742BDL

Remington Model 742F

Remington Model 742 Woodsmaster Automatic Big Game Rifle $300

Gas-operated semiautomatic. Calibers: 6mm Rem., 243 Win., 280 Rem., 30-06, 308 Win. 4-shot clip magazine. 22-inch bbl. Weight: 7.5 lbs. Sights: open rear; bead front, on ramp. Checkered pistol-grip stock and forearm. Made 1960-80.

Remington Model 742BDL Custom Deluxe $350

Same as Model 742 Rifle, except made in calibers 30-06 and 308 only, has Monte Carlo cheekpiece stock, forearm with black tip, basket-weave checkering. Available in left-hand model. Made 1966-80.

Remington Model 742D Peerless Grade $1295

Same as Model 742 except scroll engraved, fancy wood. Made 1961-80.

Remington Model 742F Premier Grade $2850

Same as Model 742 except extensively engraved with game scenes and scroll, finest grade wood. Also available with receiver inlaid with gold; adds 50 percent to value. Made 1961-1980.

Remington Model 7400 Autoloader $365

Similar to Model Four, except has lower grade finishes. Made 1981 to date.

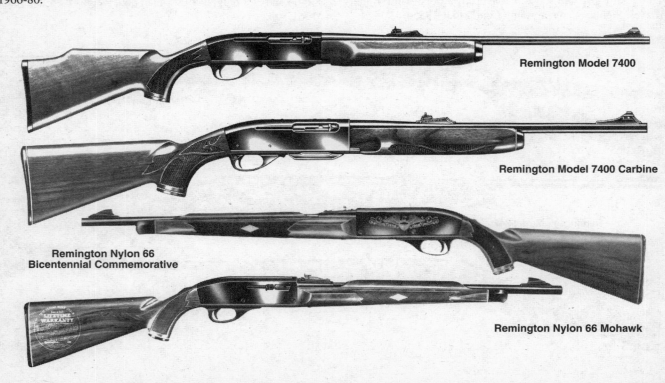

Remington Model 7400

Remington Model 7400 Carbine

Remington Nylon 66
Bicentennial Commemorative

Remington Nylon 66 Mohawk

Remington Sportsman 74

Remington Model 7400 Carbine $375
Caliber: 30-06 only. Similar to the Model 7400 rifle except has 18.5-inch bbl. and weighs 7.25 lbs. Made 1988 to date. *See* illustration preceding page.

Remington Model 7400 Special Purpose $375
Same general specification as the Model 7400, except chambered only in 270 or 30-06. Special Purpose matte black finish on metal. American walnut stock with SP nonglare finish.

Remington Nylon 66 Apache Black $130
Same as Nylon 66 Mohawk Brown, except bbl. and receiver cover chrome-plated, black stock. Made 1962-84.

Remington Nylon 66 Bicentennial Commemorative $155
Same as Nylon 66 except has commemorative inscription on receiver. Made 1976. *See* illustration preceding page.

Remington Nylon 66 GS Gallery Special $95
Same as Nylon 66 Mohawk Brown except chambered for 22 Short only. Made 1959-80.

Remington Nylon 66MB Autoloading Rifle $125
Similar to the early production Nylon 66 Black Apache, except with blued bbl. and receiver cover. Made 1978 to date.

Remington Nylon 66 Mohawk Brown Autoloader . . $95
Caliber: 22 LR. Tubular magazine in buttstock holds 14 rounds. 19.5-inch bbl. Weight: about 4 lbs. Sights: open rear; blade front. Brown nylon stock and forearm. *See* illustration preceding page. Made 1959 to date.

Remington Nylon 77 Clip Repeater $150
Same as Nylon 66, except has 5-shot clip magazine. Made 1970-71.

Remington Sportsman 74 Autoloading Rifle $265
Caliber: 30-06, 4-shot magazine. 22-inch bbl. Uncheckered buttstock and forend. Open rear sight; ramped blade front sight.

JOHN RIGBY & CO.
London, England

Rigby 275 Lightweight Magazine Rifle . . . . . . $4000+
Same as standard 275 rifle, except has 21-inch bbl. and weighs only 6.75 lbs.

Rigby 275 Magazine Rifle

Rigby 275 Magazine Sporting Rifle . . . . $5000+
Mauser action. Caliber: 275 High Velocity or 7×57mm 5-shot box magazine. 25-inch bbl. Weight: about 7.5 lbs. Sights: folding leaf rear; bead front. Sporting stock w/half-pistol grip, checkered. Specifications given are those of current model; however, in general, they apply also to prewar model.

Rigby 350 Magnum

Rigby 350 Magnum Magazine Sporting Rifle . . $3595
Mauser action. Caliber: 350 Magnum. 5-shot box magazine. 24-inch bbl. Weight: about 7.75 lbs. Sights: folding leaf rear; bead front. Sporting stock with full pistol grip, checkered. Currently mfd.

Rigby 416 Big Game Magazine Sporting Rifle . . $6000+
Mauser action. Caliber: 416 Big Game. 4-shot box magazine. 24-inch bbl. Weight: 9 to 9.25 lbs. Sights: folding leaf rear; bead front. Sporting stock with full pistol grip, checkered. Currently mfd.

Rigby Best Quality Hammerless Ejector Double Rifle $39,000
Sidelocks. Calibers: 275 Magnum, 350 Magnum, 470 Nitro Express. 24- to 28-inch bbls. Weight: 7.5 to 10.5 lbs. Sights: folding leaf rear; bead front. Checkered pistol-grip stock and forearm.

Rigby Second Quality Hammerless Ejector Double Rifle $15,000
Same general specifications as Best Quality double rifle, except boxlock.

Rigby Third Quality Hammerless Ejector Double Rifle $9900
Same as Second Quality double rifle, except plainer finish and not of as high quality.

ROSS RIFLE CO.
Quebec, Canada

Ross Model 1910 Bolt-Action Sporting Rifle ... **$225**
Straight-pull bolt action with interrupted-screw-type lugs. Calibers: 280 Ross, 303 British. 4-shot or 5-shot magazine. Bbl. lengths: 22, 24, 26 inches. Sights: two-leaf open rear; bead front. Checkered sporting stock. Weight: about 7 lbs. Made c. 1910 to end of World War I. *Note:* Most firearm authorities agree that this and other Ross models with interrupted-screw-type lugs are unsafe to fire.

ROSSI RIFLES
Sao Leopoldo, Brazil
Manufactured by Amadeo Rossi, S.A.

Rossi 62 Gallery Model SAC Carbine
Same as standard Gallery Model, except in 22 LR only with 16.25-inch bbl.; weighs 5.5 lbs. Made 1975 to date.
Blued Finish **$145**
Nickel Finish **165**

Rossi 62 Gallery Model Magnum **$145**
Same as standard Gallery Model, except chambered for 22 WMR, 10-shot magazine. Made 1975 to date.

Rossi 62 Gallery Model Slide-Action Repeater
Similar to Winchester Model 62. Calibers: 22 LR, Long, Short or 22 WMR. Tubular magazine holds 13 LR, 16 Long, 20 Short. 23-inch bbl. 39.25 inches overall. Weight: 5.75 lbs. Sights: open

Rossi 62 Gallery *(Cont.)*
rear; bead front. Straight-grip stock, grooved slide handle. Blued or nickel finish. Made 1970 to date.
Blued Finish **$150**
Nickel Finish **175**

Rossi Lever-Action Carbine

Rossi Lever-Action Carbine Engraved Model . . **$250**
Same as standard model, except has engraved action. Made 1981 to date.

Rossi Lever-Action Carbine **$225**
Similar to Winchester Model 92. Caliber: 357 Mag. Tubular magazine. 20-inch bbl. Weight: 5.75 lbs. Sights: open rear; bead front. Straight-grip walnut stock. Made 1978 to date.

RUGER RIFLES
Southport, Connecticut
Manufactured by Sturm, Ruger & Co.

Ruger Number One (1) Light Sporter **$395**
Same as No. 1 Standard, except has 22-inch bbl., folding leaf rear sight on quarter-rib and ramp front sight, Henry pattern forearm.

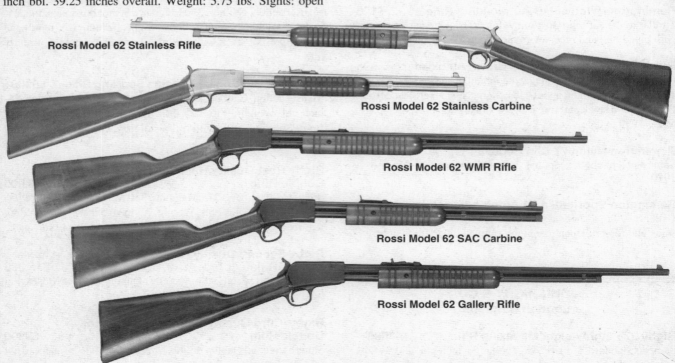

Rossi Model 62 Stainless Rifle

Rossi Model 62 Stainless Carbine

Rossi Model 62 WMR Rifle

Rossi Model 62 SAC Carbine

Rossi Model 62 Gallery Rifle

Ruger No. 1 Light Sporter

Ruger No. 1 Medium Sporter

Ruger Number One (1) Medium Sporter $395
Same as No. 1 Light Sporter, except has 26-inch bbl. 22-inch in 45-70); weight is 8 lbs (7.25 lbs. in 45-70). Calibers: 7mm Rem. Mag., 300 Win. Mag., 45-70. Made 1966 to date.

Ruger Number One (1) "North Americans" Presentation Rifle $52,000
Same general specifications as the Ruger No. 1 Standard, except highly customized with elaborate engravings, carvings, fine-line checkering and gold inlays. A series of 21 is planned, each rifle depicting a North American big-game animal, chambered in the caliber appropriate to the game. Stock is of Northern California English walnut. Comes in trunk-style Huey case with Leupold scope and other accessories.

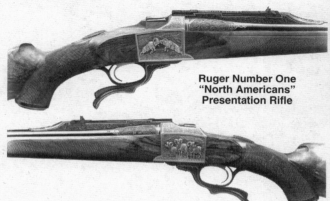

Ruger Number One "North Americans" Presentation Rifle

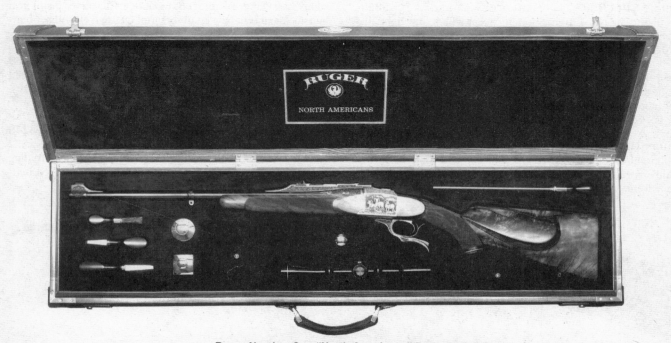

Ruger Number One "North Americans" Presentation Set

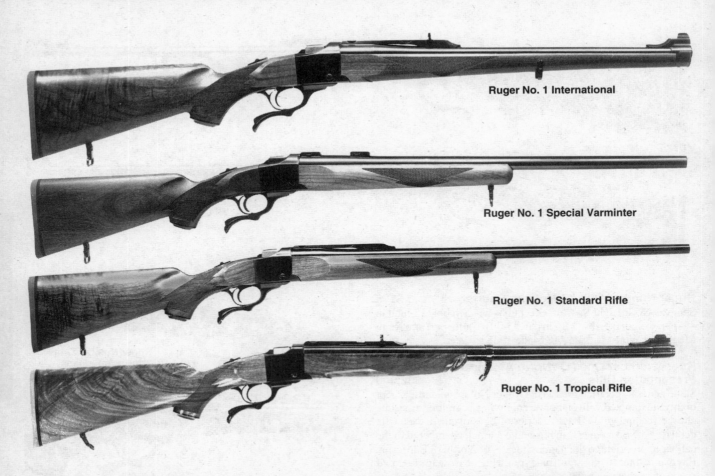

Ruger No. 1 International

Ruger No. 1 Special Varminter

Ruger No. 1 Standard Rifle

Ruger No. 1 Tropical Rifle

Ruger Number One (1) RSI Internaltional Single-Shot Rifle $395
Similar to the No. 1 Light Sporter, except with lightweight 20-inch bbl. and full Mannlicher-style forend, in calibers 243 Win., 270 Win., 7×57mm, 30-06. Weight: 7.25 lbs.

Ruger Number One (1) Special Varminter $425
Same as No. 1 Standard, except has heavy 24-inch bbl. with target scope bases, no quarter-rib. Weight: 9 lbs. Calibers: 22-250, 25-06, 7mm Rem. Mag., 300 Win. Mag. Made 1966 to date.

Ruger Number One (1) Standard Rifle $385
Falling-block single-shot action with Farquharson-type lever. Calibers: 22-250, 243 Win., 6mm Rem., 25-06, 270 Win., 30-06, 7mm Rem. Mag., 300 Win. Mag. 26-inch bbl. Weight: 8 lbs. No

Ruger Number One (1) Standard Rifle *(Cont.)*
sights, has quarter-rib for scope mounting. Checkered pistol-grip buttstock and semibeavertail forearm, QD swivels, rubber buttplate. Made 1966 to date.

Ruger Number One (1) Tropical Rifle $480
Same as No. 1 Light Sporter, except has heavy 24-inch bbl.; calibers are 375 H&H Mag. and 458 Win. Mag. Weight: 8.25 lbs. for 375; 9 lbs. for 458. Made 1966-94.

Ruger Number Three (3) Single-Shot Carbine . . $245
Falling-block action with American-style lever. Calibers: 22 Hornet 30-40, 45-70. 22-inch bbl. Weight: 6 lbs. Sights: folding leaf rear; gold bead front. Carbine-style stock w/curved buttplate, forearm with bbl. band. Made 1972-86.

Ruger No. 3 Single-Shot Carbine

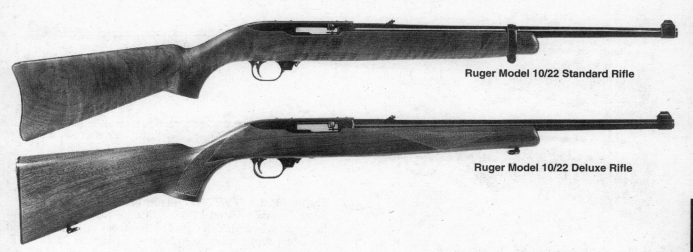

Ruger Model 10/22 Standard Rifle

Ruger Model 10/22 Deluxe Rifle

Ruger Model 10/22 Autoloading Carbine

Caliber: 22 LR. Detachable 10-shot rotary magazine. 18.5-inch bbl. Weight: 5 lbs. Sights: folding leaf rear; bead front. Carbine-style stock with bbl. band and curved buttplate (walnut stock discontinued 1980). Made 1964 to date. International and Sporter versions discontinued 1971.

10/22 Standard Carbine (Walnut stock)	**$175**
10/22 Int'l (w/Mannlicher-style stock, swivels) Discontinued 1971	**425**
10/22 RB (Birch stock, Blued)	**125**
K10/22 RB (Birch stock, Stainless)	**150**
10/22 Sporter (Monte Carlo stock, flat buttplate sling swivels). Discontinued 1971	**165**
10/22 SP Deluxe Sporter (w/Checkered stock Flat buttplate, sling swivels; made since 1966)	**185**
10/22 RBI Int'l (Blued); made since 1994	**175**

Ruger Model 44 Autoloading Carbine

Gas-operated. Caliber: 44 Magnum. 4-shot tubular magazine (with magazine release button since 1967). 18.5-inch bbl. Weight: 5.75 lbs. Sights: folding leaf rear; gold bead front. Carbine-style stock w/bbl. band and curved buttplate. Made 1961-86. International and Sporter versions discontinued 1971.

Model 44 Standard Autoloading Carbine **$365**

Ruger Model 44 Autoloading Carbine *(Cont.)*

Model 44 Int'l (w/Mannlicher-style stock, swivels) . . .	**550**
Model 44 Sporter (w/Monte Carlo stock, flat buttplate, sling swivels	**360**
Model 44RS Carbine (w/Rear peep sight, sling swivels; disc. 1978)	**345**

Ruger Model 77 Bolt-Action Rifle

Receiver with integral scope mount base or with round top. Short stroke or magnum length action (depending on caliber) in the former type receiver, magnum only in the latter. Calibers: 22-250, 220 Swift, 6mm Rem., 243 Win., 200-3000, 25-06, 257 Roberts, 270 Win., 7×57mm, 7mm Rem. Mag., 280 Rem., 308 Win., 30-06, 300 Win. Mag. 338 Win. Mag., 458 Win. Mag. 5-shot magazine standard, 4-shot in 220 Swift, 3-shot in magnum calibers. 22-, 24- or 26-inch bbl. (depending on caliber). Weight: about 7 lbs.; 458 Mag. model, 8.75 lbs. Round-top model furnished w/folding leaf rear sight and ramp front; integral base model furnished w/scope rings,with or w/o open sights. Stock w/checkered pistol grip and forearm, pistol-grip cap, rubber recoil pad, QD swivel studs. Made 1968 to date.

Model 77, integral base, no sights	**$335**
Model 77, 338 Win Mag.	**385**

Ruger Model 44 Carbine

Ruger Model 77 Round Top Receiver

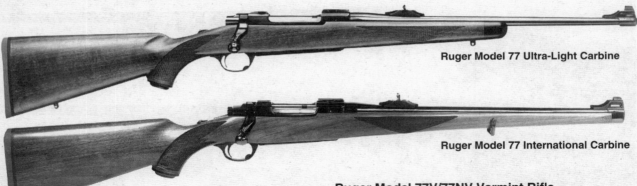

Ruger Model 77 Ultra-Light Carbine

Ruger Model 77 International Carbine

Ruger Model 77 Bolt-Action Rifle *(Cont.)*

Model 77RL Ultra Light, no sights, 20-inch
    ultralight bbl., 6 lbs. (1983 to date) **$375**
Model 77RS, integral base, open sights   365
Model 77RS, 338 Win. Mag., 458 Win. Mag. with
    standard stock   395
Model 77RS, 458 Win. Mag. with fancy Circassian
    walnut stock   550
Model 77RSI International, Mannlicher stock,
    short action, 18.5-inch bbl., 7 lbs.   395
Model 77ST, round top, open sights   345
Model 77ST, 338 Win. Mag.   395

Ruger Model 77 (M-77) Ultra Light Carbine **$350**

Bolt action. Calibers: 270, 30-06, 243, 308. 18.5-inch bbl. About
39 inches overall. Weight: 6 lbs. Hand-checkered American walnut stock with pistol grip. Open sights and equipped with Ruger
Integral Scope bases with one-inch Ruger rings. Sling swivels.
Made 1986 to date.

Ruger Model 77V/77NV Varmint Rifle

Same as standard Model 77 with integral base receiver, except
has heavy 24-inch (26-inch in 220 Swift) bbl. drilled and tapped
for target scope bases. Weight: 9 lbs. Calibers: 22-250, 220
Swift, 243 Win., 6mm Rem., 25-06, 308. Made 1968-92. Model
M77NV with laminated American stock introduced in 1992.
Model 77V **$385**
Model 77NV   465

Ruger Model 77 Mark II All-Weather Rifle **$380**

Revised Model 77 action. Same general specifications as Model
M-77 Mark II, except with stainless bbl. and action. Zytel
injection-molded stock. Calibers: 223, 243, 270, 308, 30-06,
7mm Mag., 300 Win. Mag., 338 Win. Mag. Made 1990 to date.

Ruger Model 77 Mark II Bolt-Action Rifle

Revised Model 77 action. Same general specifications as Model
M-77, except with new 3-position safety and fixed blade ejector
system. Calibers 223 and 6.5×55 Swedish also available.
Model M77 MKIIR, SA, no sights **$365**
Model M77 MKIIRS, SA, sights   395
Model M77 MKIIRL, SA, 20-inch bbl   380
Model M77 MKIILR, LA, left-hand   365

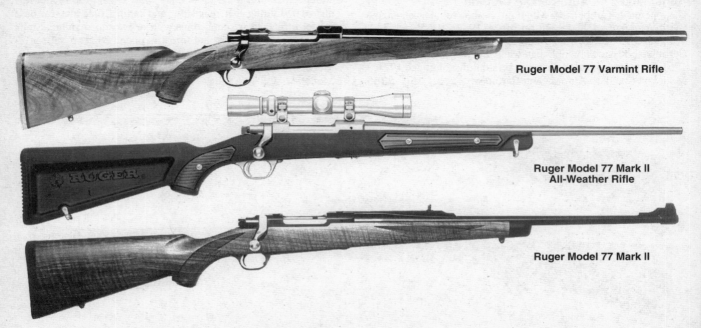

Ruger Model 77 Varmint Rifle

Ruger Model 77 Mark II
All-Weather Rifle

Ruger Model 77 Mark II

Ruger Model 77/22 Rimfire

Ruger Model 77 Mark II (V2B) Target Rifle $435
Similar to the Model 77 Varmint Rifle, except with laminated American hardwood stock with flat forearm and no checkering. Calibers: 22 PPC, 22-250, 220 Swift, 223, 6mm PPC 25-06, 308. 26-inch bbl. 44 inches overall. Weight: 9.25 lbs. Made 1992 to date.

Ruger Model 77 Mark II (EXP) Express Rifle $995
Calibers: 270, 30-06, 7mm Rem. Mag., 300 Win. Mag. 4-shot magazine. 22-inch bbl. with integral rib. Weight: 7.5 lbs. Ramp front sight, adj. leaf rear. Checkered walnut stock with steel grip cap and black recoil pad. Blued finish. Made 1991 to date.

Ruger Model 77 Mark II (RSM) Magnum Rifle . . . $1095
Calibers: 375 H&H, 404 Jeffery, (4-shot magazine); 416 Rigby, 458 Win. Mag.(3-shot magazine). 26-inch bbl. with integral rib. Weight: 9.75 lbs. (375, 404); 10.25 lbs. (416, 458). Sights: ramp front; three-leaf Express rear. Checkered Circassian walnut stock with steel-grip cap and recoil pad. Blued finish. Made 1989 to date.

Ruger Model 77/22 Hornet Bolt-Action Rifle
Mini-Sporter built on the 77/22 action in caliber 22 Hornet. 6-shot rotary magazine. 20- inch bbl. 40 inches overall. Weight: 6 lbs. Receiver machined for Ruger rings (included). Beaded front sight and open adj. rear, or no sights. Blued or stainless finish. Checkered American walnut stock. Made 1994 to date.
Model 77/22RH (rings, no sights) **$300**
Model 77/22RSH (rings & sights) **315**
Model 77/22VH (S/S rings, no sights) **370**

Ruger Model 77/22 Rimfire Bolt-Action Rifle
Calibers: 22 LR or 22 WMR. 10-shot (22 LR) or 9-shot (22 WMR) rotary magazine. 20-inch bbl. 39.75 inches overall. Weight: 5.75 lbs. Integral scope bases; with or w/o sights. Checkered American walnut or Zytel injection-molded stock. Stainless or blued finish. Made 1983 to date. (Blued); stainless introduced 1989.
77/22 R, rings, no sights, walnut stock **$265**
77/22 RS, rings, sights, walnut. **275**
77/22 RP, rings, no sights, synthetic stock **220**
77/22 RSP, rings, sights, synthetic stock **235**
K77/22 RP, S/S rings, no sights, synthetic **275**
K77/22 RSP, S/S, rings, sights, synthetic **285**
77/22 RM, 22 WMR, rings, no sights, walnut **260**
77/22 RSM, 22 WMR, rings, sights, walnut **275**
K77/22 SMP, 22 WMR, S/S, rings, sights, syn. **290**
K77/22 RMP, 22 WMR, S/S, no sights, syn. **325**
K77/22 VBZ, 22 WMR, no sights, syn. (1993) **280**

Ruger Mini-14 Semiautomatic Rifle
Gas-operated. Caliber: 223 Rem. (5.56mm). 5-, 10- or 20-shot box magazine. 18.5-inch bbl. Weight: about 6.5 lbs. Sights: peep rear; blade front mounted on removable barrel band. Pistol-grip stock w/curved buttplate, handguard. Made 1976 to date.
Mini-14/5 Blued **$385**
K-Mini-14/5 Stainless Steel **400**
Mini-14/5F Blued, Folding Stock **550**
K-Mini-14/5F Stainless, Folding Stock **600**
Mini-14 Ranch Rifle, Scope Model, 6.25 lbs. **375**
K-Mini-1H Ranch Rifle, Scope Model, Stainless **495**

Ruger Mini-14 Semiautomatic

Ruger Mini-14 with Folding Stock

Ruger Mini-Thirty Autoloader

Ruger Mini-Thirty (30) Autoloader
Caliber: 7.62 × 39mm. 5-shot detachable magazine. 18.5-inch bbl. 37.25 inches overall. Weight: 7 lbs. 3 oz. Designed for use with telescopic sights. Walnut stained stock. Sights: Peep rear; blade front mounted on bbl. band. Blued or stainless finish. Made 1986 to date.

Blued Finish **$400**
Stainless Finish **435**

Russian Model 1891 Mosin

RUSSIAN MILITARY RIFLES
Principal U.S.S.R. Arms Plant is located at Tula

Russian Model 1891 Mosin Military Rifle $95
Nagant system bolt action. Caliber: 7.62mm Russian. 5-shot box magazine. 31.5-inch bbl. Weight: about 9 lbs. Sights: open rear; blade front. Full stock w/straight grip. Specifications given are for WWII version; earlier types differ slightly. Note: In 1916, Remington Arms Co. and New England Westinghouse Co. produced 250,000 of these rifles on a contract from the Imperial Russian Government. Few were delivered

Russian Model 1891 Mosin Military Rifle *(Cont.)*
to Russia and the balance bought by the U.S. Government for training in 1918. Eventually, many of these rifles were sold to N.R.A. members for about $3 each by the director of Civilian Marksmanship.

Russian Tokarev Model 40 Semiautomatic
Military Rifle $495
Gas-operated. Caliber: 7.62mm Russian. 10-shot detachable box magazine. 24.5-inch bbl. Muzzle brake. Weight: about 9 lbs. Sights: leaf rear, hooded post front. Full stock w/pistol grip. Differences among Models 1938,1940 and 1941 are minor.

Sako Model 73

Sako Model 74 Carbine

SAKO RIFLES
Riihimaki, Finland
Manufactured by Oy Sako AB

Sako Model 72 . . . . $655
Single model designation replacing Vixen Sporter, Vixen Carbine, Vixen Heavy Barrel, Forester Sporter, Forester Carbine,

Sako Model 72 *(Cont.)*
Forester Heavy Barrel, Finnbear Sporter, and Finnbear Carbine, with same specifications except all but heavy barrel models fitted with open rear sight. Values same as for corresponding earlier models. Made 1972-74.

Sako Model 73 Lever-Action Rifle $745
Same as Finnwolf, except has 3-shot clip magazine, flush floorplate; stock has no cheekpiece. Made 1973-75.

Sako Model 74 Super Sporter

Sako Model 74 Super Rimfire

Sako Classic

Sako Deluxe Lightweight

Sako Model 74 Carbine **$495**
Long Mauser-type bolt action. Caliber: 30-06. 5-shot magazine. 20-inch bbl. Weight: about 7.5 lbs. No sights. Checkered Mannlicher-type full stock of European walnut, Monte Carlo cheekpiece. Made 1974-78.

Sako Model 74 Heavy Barrel Rifle, Long Action . . **$525**
Same specifications as with short action, except has 24-inch heavy bbl., weighs about 8.75 lbs.; magnum has 4-shot magazine. Calibers: 25-06, 7mm Rem. Mag. Made 1974-78.

**Sako Model 74 Heavy Barrel Rifle,
Medium Action** **$545**
Same specifications as with short action, except has 23-inch heavy bbl., weighs about 8.5 lbs. Calibers: 220 Swift, 22-250, 243 Win., 308 Win. Made 1974-78.

**Sako Model 74 Heavy Barrel Rifle,
Short Action** **$560**
Mauser-type bolt action. Calibers: 222 Rem., 223 Rem. 5-shot magazine. 23.5-inch heavy bbl. Weight: about 8.25 lbs. No sights. Target-style checkered European walnut stock w/beavertail forearm. Made 1974-78.

Sako Model 74 Super Sporter, Long Action **$535**
Same specifications as with short action, except has 24-inch bbl., weighs about 8 lbs.; magnums have 4-shot magazine, recoil pad. Calibers: 25-06, 270 Win. 7mm Rem. Mag., 30-06, 300 Win. Mag., 338 Win. Mag., 375 H&H Mag. Made 1974-78.

Sako Model 74 Super Sporter, Medium Action . . **$595**
Same specifications as with short action, except weight is 7.25 lbs. Calibers: 220 Swift, 22-250, 243 Win. Made 1974-78.

Sako Model 74 Super Sporter, Short Action **$615**
Mauser-type bolt action. Calibers: 222 Rem., 223 Rem. 5-shot magazine. 23.5-inch bbl. Weight: about 6.5 lbs. No sights. Checkered European walnut stock with Monte Carlo cheekpiece, QD swivel studs. Made 1974, now discontinued.

Sako Model 78 Super Hornet Sporter **$425**
Same specifications as Model 78 Rimfire, except caliber 22 Hornet, 4-shot magazine. Intro. 1977; disc. 1987.

Sako Model 78 Super Rimfire Sporter **$345**
Bolt action. Caliber: 22 LR. 5-shot magazine. 22.5-inch bbl. Weight, about 6.75 lbs. No sights. Checkered European walnut stock, Monte Carlo cheekpiece. Introduced 1977; discontinued.

Sako Classic Bolt-Action Rifle
Medium Action (243. Win.) or Long Action (270 Win. 30-06, 7mm Rem. Mag.). American walnut stock. Made 1980-86. Reintroduced in 1993 with matte lacquer finish stock, 22- or 24-inch bbl., overall length of 42 to 44 inches, weight 6.88 to 7.25 lbs.
Standard Calibers **$670**
Magnum Caliber **695**
Left-Hand Models **735**

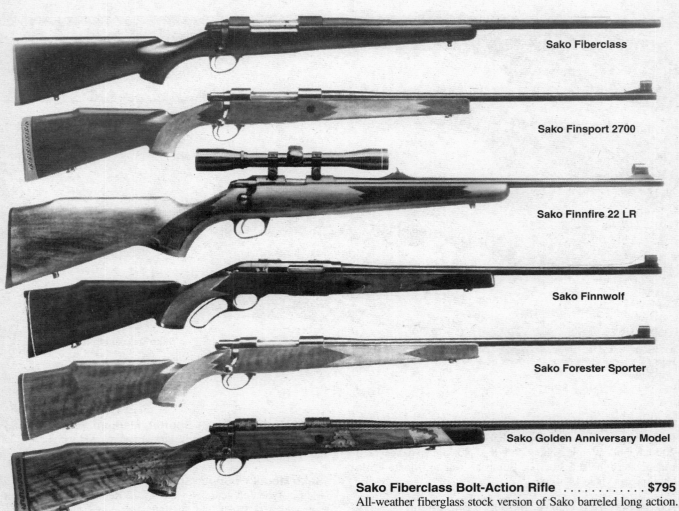

Sako Fiberclass

Sako Finsport 2700

Sako Finnfire 22 LR

Sako Finnwolf

Sako Forester Sporter

Sako Golden Anniversary Model

Sako Deluxe Grade AI **$625**
Same specifications as Standard Grade, except with 22 lines to
the inch French checkering, rosewood grip cap and forend tip,
semibeavertail forend.

Sako Deluxe Grade AII **$650**
Same specifications as Standard Grade, except with 22 lines per
inch French checkering, rosewood grip cap and forend tip,
semibeavertail forend.

Sako Deluxe Grade AIII **$895**
Same specifications as with standard, except with French checkering, rosewood grip cap and forend tip, semibeavertail forend.

Sako Deluxe Lightweight Bolt-Action Rifle **$845**
Same general specifications as Hunter Lightweight, except has
beautifully grained French walnut stock; superb high-gloss finish, fine hand-cut checkering, rosewood forend tip and grip cap.
Introduced 1985. *See* illustration preceding page.

Sako Fiberclass Bolt-Action Rifle **$795**
All-weather fiberglass stock version of Sako barreled long action.
Calibers: 25-06, 270, 30-06, 7mm Rem. Mag., 300 Win. Mag., 338
Win. Mag., 375 H&H Mag. Bbl. length: 22.5 inches. Overall length:
44.25 inches. Weight: 7.25 lbs. Made 1984 to date.

Sako Finnbear Carbine **$720**
Same as Finnbear Sporter, except has 20-inch bbl., Mannlicher-
type full stock. Made 1971.

Sako Finnbear Sporter **$695**
Long Mauser-type bolt action. Calibers: 25-06, 264 Mag. 270,
30-06, 300 Win. Mag., 338 Mag., 7mm Mag., 375 H&H Mag.
Magazine holds 5 standard or 4 magnum cartridges. 24-inch bbl.
Weight: about 7 lbs. Hooded ramp front sight. Sporter stock
w/Monte Carlo cheekpiece, checkered pistol grip and forearm,
recoil pad, swivels. Made 1961-71.

Sako Finnfire Bolt-Action Rifle **$495**
Mini-Sporter built for rimfires on a scaled-down Sako design.
Caliber: 22 LR. 5- or 10-shot magazine. 22-inch bbl. 39.5 inches
overall. Weight: 5.25 lbs. Receiver machined for 11mm dovetail
scope rings. Beaded blade front sight, open adj. rear. Blued finish. Checkered European walnut stock. Imported 1994 to date.

Sako Hunter Lightweight

Sako Mannlicher-Style Carbine

Sako Sporter Deluxe

Sako Finnwolf Lever-Action Rifle **$775**
Hammerless. Calibers: 243 Win., 308 Win. 4-shot clip magazine. 23-inch bbl. Weight: 6.75 lbs. Hooded ramp front sight. Sporter stock w/Monte Carlo cheekpiece, checkered pistol grip and forearm, swivels (available w/right- or left-hand stock). Made 1963-72.

Sako Finsport 2700 . . . . **$715**
Bolt-action centerfire rifle. Calibers: 270, 30-06, 7mm Rem. Mag., 300 Win. Mag. Bbl. length: 24 inches. Weight: 8 lbs. Made 1984-1986.

Sako Forester Carbine **$630**
Same as Forester Sporter, except has 20-inch bbl., Mannlicher-type full stock. Made 1958-71.

Sako Forester Heavy Barrel **$595**
Same as Forester Sporter, except has 24-inch heavy bbl. weighs 7.5 lbs. Made 1958-71.

Sako Forester Sporter **$580**
Medium-length Mauser-type bolt action. Calibers: 22-250, 243 Win., 308 Win. 5-shot magazine. 23-inch bbl. Weight: 6.5 lbs. Hooded ramp front sight. Sporter stock w/Monte Carlo cheekpiece, checkered pistol grip and forearm, swivels. Made 1957-71.

Sako Golden Anniversary Model **$1850**
Special presentation-grade rifle issued in 1973 to commemorate Sako's 50th anniversary. 1,000 (numbered 1 to 1,000) made. Same specifications as Deluxe Sporter, long action, 7mm Rem. Mag. Receiver, trigger guard and floorplate decorated w/gold oak leaf and acorn motif. Stock of select European walnut, checkering bordered w/hand-carved oak leaf pattern.

Sako High-Power Mauser Sporting Rifle **$535**
FN Mauser action. Calibers: 270, 30-06. 5-shot magazine. 24-inch bbl. Sights: open rear leaf; Patridge front; hooded ramp. Checkered stock w/Monte Carlo comb and cheekpiece. Weight: about 7.5 lbs. Made 1950-57.

Sako Hunter Lightweight Bolt-Action Rifle
5- or 6-shot magazine. Bbl. length: 21.5 inches, AI; 22 inches, AII; 22.5 inches, AIII. Overall length: 42.25-44.5 inches. Weight: 5.75 lbs., AI; 6.75 lbs. AII; 7.25 lbs., AIII. Monte Carlo-style European walnut stock, oil finished. Hand-checkered pistol grip and forend. Introduced 1985. Left-hand version introduced 1987.

AI (Short Action) 17 Rem.	$ 595
222 Rem., 223 Rem.	610
AII (Medium Action)	
22-250 Rem., 243 Win., 308 Win.	525
AIII (Long Action) 25-06 Rem., 270 Win., 30-06	580
338 Win. Mag.	660
375 H&H Mag.	710
Left-hand Model (Standard Cal.)	930
Magnum Calibers	1070

Sako Laminated Stock Bolt-Action Rifles
Similar in style and specifications to the Hunter Grade, except with stock of resin-bonded, hardwood veneers. Available 18 calibers in AI (Short), AII (Medium) or AV action, left-handed version in 10 calibers, AV only. Introduced in 1987.

Short or Medium Action	$750
Long Action/Magnum	775

Sako Magnum Mauser **$970**
Similar specifications as Standard Model, except has recoil pad and redesigned longer AIII action to handle longer magnum cartridges. Calibers: 300 H&H Magnum, 375 H&H Magnum, standard at time of introduction.

Sako Mannlicher-Style Carbine
Similar to the Hunter Model, except with full Mannlicher-style stock and 18.5-inch bbl. Weighs 7.5 lbs. Chambered in 243, 25-06, 270, 308, 30-06, 7mm Rem. Mag., 300 Win. Mag., 338 Win. Mag., 375 H&H. Introduced in 1977.

Standard Calibers	$860
Magnum Calibers (except 375)	895
375 H&H	900

Sako Safari Grade **$1695**
Classic bolt action. Calibers: 300 Win. Mag., 338 Win. Mag.,
375 H&H. Oil-finished European walnut stock with hand-
checkering. Barrel band swivel, express-type sight rib; satin or
matte blue finish. Introduced in 1980.

Sako Sporter Deluxe **$725**
Same as Vixen, Forester, Finnbear and Model 74, except has fancy
French walnut stock w/skip checkering, rosewood forend tip and
pistol-grip cap, recoil pad, inlaid trigger guard and floorplate. *See illustration preceding page.*

Sako Standard Grade AI **$540**
Short bolt action. Calibers: 17 Rem.,222 Rem.,223 Rem. 5-shot
magazine. 23.5-inch bbl. Weight: about 6.5 pounds. No sights.
Checkered European walnut stock w/Monte Carlo cheekpiece,
QD swivel studs. Made 1978 to date.

Sako Standard Grade AII **$550**
Medium bolt action. Calibers: 22-250 Rem., 243 Win., 308 Win.
23.5-inch bbl. in 22-250; 23-inch bbl. in other calibers. 5-shot
magazine. Weight: about 7.25 pounds. Checkered European
walnut stock w/Monte Carlo cheekpiece, QD swivel studs. Made
1978-85.

Sako Standard Grade AIII **$595**
Long bolt action. Calibers: 25-06 Rem., 270 Win., 30-06, 7mm
Rem. Mag., 300 Win. Mag., 338 Win. Mag., 375 H&H. 24-inch
bbl. 4-shot magazine. Weight: 8 lbs. Made 1978-84.

Sako Super Deluxe Rifle **$1650**
Available in AI, AII, AIII action calibers. Select European walnut stock, hand-checkered, deep oak leaf hand-engraved design.

Sako TRG-21

Sako TRG-S

Sako Vixen Carbine

Sako Vixen Heavy Barrel

Sako Vixen Sporter

Sako TRG-21 Target Rifle $2850
Caliber: 308 Win 10-shot magazine. 25.75-inch stainless heavy bbl. 46.5 inches overall. Weight: 10.5 lbs. No sights. Optional Q/D scope mount with 1-inch or 30mm rings. Reinforced polyurethane stock w/adj. cheekpiece and buttplate. Two-stage adj. trigger. Introduced in 1993.

Sako TRG-S Bolt-Action Rifle
Calibers: 243, 7mm-08, 270, 30-06, 7mm Rem. Mag., 300 Win. Mag., 338 Win. Mag. 5-shot magazine (standard calibers), 4-shot (magnum), 22- or 24-inch bbl. 45.5 inches overall. Weight: 7.75 lbs. No sights. Reinforced polyurethane stock w/Monte Carlo. Introduced in 1993.
Standard Calibers $500
Magnum Calibers 560

Sako Vixen Carbine $695
Same as Vixen Sporter, except has 20-inch bbl., Mannlicher-type full stock. Made 1947-71.

Sako Vixen Heavy Barrel $725
Same as Vixen Sporter, except calibers 222 Rem., 222 Rem. Mag., 223 Rem., heavy bbl., target-style stock w/beavertail forearm. Weight: 7.5 lbs. Made 1947-71.

Sako Vixen Sporter $755
Short Mauser-type bolt action. Calibers: 218 Bee, 22 Hornet, 222 Rem., 222 Rem. Mag., 223 Rem. 5-shot magazine. 23.5-inch bbl. Weight: 6.5 lbs. Hooded ramp front sight. Sporter stock w/Monte Carlo cheekpiece, checkered pistol grip and forearm, swivels. Made 1946-71.

J. P. SAUER & SOHN
Suhl, Germany
Imported by G.U., Inc. (Simmons Enterprises)

Sauer Mauser Bolt-Action Sporting Rifle $995
Calibers: 7×57 and 8×57mm most common, but these rifles were produced in a variety of calibers, including most of the popular Continental numbers as well as our 30-06. 5-shot box magazine. 22- or 24-inch Krupp steel bbl., half-octagon with raised matted rib. Double-set trigger. Weight: about 7.5 lbs. Sights: three-leaf open rear; ramp front. Sporting stock w/cheekpiece, checkered pistol grip, raised side-panels, schnabel tip, swivels. Also made w/20-inch bbl. and full-length stock. Mfd before WWII.

Sauer Model S-90 Bolt-Action Rifles
Calibers: 243 Win., 308 Win. (Short action); 25-06, 270 Win.,30-06 (Medium action); 7mm Rem. Mag.,300 Win. Mag., 300 Wby., 338 Win., 375 H&H (Magnum action). 4-shot (standard) or 3-shot magazine (magnum). Bbl. length: 20-inch (Stutzen), 24-inch. Weight: 7 lbs. 6 oz. to 10 lbs. 12 oz. (Safari). Adj. open rear sights; ramp front. Checkered American or European walnut stock with a variety of finishes. Monte Carlo cheekpiece. Made 1986 to date.
S-90 Lux $795
S-90 Safari 895
S-90 Stutzen 870
S-90 Supreme 995

Sauer Model 200 Bolt-Action Rifles
Calibers: 243 Win., 25-06, 270 Win., 30-06, 308 Win. Box magazine. 24-inch (American) or 26-inch (European) interchangeable bbl. Weight: 6.75 to 7.75 lbs. American Model has checkered European walnut straight stock w/satin oil finish, no sights. European Model has Monte Carlo cheekpiece, contrasting forend and pistol grip cap w/high-gloss finish; with sights. Made late 1980s.
American/European Models $695
Left-hand Model 750

SAVAGE INDUSTRIES
Westfield, Massachusetts
Formerly of Utica, New York

Savage Model 3 Bolt-Action Single-Shot Rifle . . $135
Takedown. Caliber: 22 Short, Long, LR. 26-inch bbl. on prewar rifles, postwar production has 24-inch bbl. Weight: about 5 lbs. Sights: open rear; bead front. Plain pistol-grip stock. Made 1933-52.

Savage Model 3S $175
Same as Model 3, except has peep rear sight, hooded front. Made 1933-42.

Savage Model 3ST $180
Same as Model 3S, except fitted with swivels and sling. Made 1933-42.

Savage Model 4 Bolt-Action Repeater $115
Takedown. Caliber: 22 Short, Long, LR. 5-shot detachable box magazine. 24-inch bbl. Weight: about 5.5 lbs. Sights: open rear; bead front. Checkered pistol-grip stock on prewar models, early production had grooved forearm; postwar rifles have plain stocks. Made 1933-65.

Savage Model 3

Savage Model 4

Savage Model 5

Savage Model 6

Savage Model 19 NRA (1933)

Savage Model 20

Savage Model 4M **$125**
Same as Model 4, except chambered for 22 Rimfire Magnum.
Made 1961-65.

Savage Model 4S **$145**
Same as Model 4, except has peep rear sight, hooded front. Made
1933-42.

Savage Model 5 Bolt-Action Repeater **$135**
Same as Model 4 except has tubular magazine (holds 21 Short,
17 Long, 15 LR), weighs about 6 lbs. Made 1936-61.

Savage Model 5S **$140**
Same as Model 5, except has peep rear sight, hooded front. Made
1936-42.

Savage Model 6 Autoloading Rifle **$165**
Takedown. Caliber: 22 Short, Long, LR. Tubular magazine
holds 21 Short, 17 Long, 15 LR. 24-inch bbl. Weight: about 6 lbs.
Sights: open rear; bead front. Checkered pistol-grip stock on prewar models, postwar rifles have plain stocks. Made 1938-68.

Savage Model 6S **$180**
Same as Model 6, except has peep rear sight, bead front. Made
1938-42.

Savage Model 7 Autoloading Rifle **$150**
Same general specifications as Model 6, except has 5-shot detachable box magazine. Made 1939-51.

Savage Model 7S **$175**
Same as Model 7, except has peep rear sight, hooded front. Made
1938-42.

Savage Model 19 Bolt-Action Target Rifle **$225**
Model of 1933. Speed lock. Caliber: 22 LR. 5-shot detachable
box magazine. 25-inch bbl. Weight: about 8 lbs. Adj. rear peep
sight, blade front on early models, later production equipped
w/extension rear sight, hooded front. Target stock w/full pistol
grip and beavertail forearm. Made 1933-46.

Savage Model 19 NRA Bolt-Action Match Rifle . . **$295**
Model of 1919. Caliber: 22 LR. 5-shot detachable box magazine.
25-inch bbl. Weight: about 7 lbs. Sights: adj. rear peep; blade
front. Full military stock w/pistol grip. Made 1919-33.

Savage Model 19H **$395**
Same as standard Model 19 (1933), except chambered for 22
Hornet, has Model 23D-type bolt mechanism, loading port and
magazine. Made 1933-42.

Savage Model 19L **$250**
Same as standard Model 19 (1933), except equipped w/Lyman
48Y receiver sight, 17A front sight. Made 1933-42.

Savage Model 19M **$275**
Same as standard Model 19 (1933), except has heavy 28-inch
bbl. with scope bases, weighs about 9.25 lbs. Made 1933-42.

Savage Model 20-1926 Hi-Power
Bolt-Action Rifle **$365**
Same as Model 1920, except has 24-inch medium weight bbl.,
improved stock, Lyman 54 rear peep sight, weighs about 7 lbs.
Made 1926-29.

Savage Model 23A Bolt-Action Sporting Rifle . . . **$190**
Caliber: 22 LR. 5-shot detachable box magazine. 23-inch bbl.
Weight: about 6 lbs. Sights: open rear, blade or bead front. Plain
pistol-grip stock with slender forearm and schnabel tip. Made
1923-33.

Savage Model 23AA

Savage Model 29

Savage Model 23AA $250
Model of 1933. Improved version of the Model 23A with same general specifications, except has speed lock, improved stock, weighs about 6.5 lbs. Made 1933-42.

Savage Model 23B $215
Same as Model 23A, except caliber 25-20, 25-inch bbl. Model of 1933 has improved stock w/full forearm instead of the slender forearm w/schnabel found on earlier production. Weight: about 6.5 lbs. Made 1923-42.

Savage Model 23C $225
Same as Model 23B, except caliber 32/20. Made 1923-42.

Savage Model 23D $285
Same as Model 23B, except caliber 22 Hornet. Made 1933-47.

Savage Model 25 Slide-Action Repeater $325
Takedown. Hammerless. Caliber: 22 Short, Long, LR. Tubular magazine holds 20 Short, 17 Long, 15 LR. 24-inch octagon bbl. Weight: about 5.75 pounds. Sights: open rear; blade front. Plain pistol-grip stock, grooved slide handle. Made 1925-29.

Savage Model 29 Slide-Action Repeater $300
Takedown. Hammerless. Caliber: 22 Short, Long, LR. Tubular magazine holds 20 Short, 17 Long, 15 LR. 24-inch bbl., octagon on prewar, round on postwar production. Weight: about 5.5 lbs. Sights: open rear; bead front. Stock w/checkered pistol grip and slide handle on prewar, plain stock and grooved forearm on postwar production. Made 1929-67.

Savage Model 40 Bolt-Action Sporting Rifle . . . $250
Standard Grade. Calibers: 250/3000, 300 Sav., 30/30, 30/06. 4-shot detachable box magazine. 22-inch bbl. in calibers 250/3000 and 30/30; 24-inch in 300 Sav. and 30/06. Weight: about 7.5 lbs. Sights: open rear; bead front, on ramp. Plain pistol-grip stock w/tapered forearm and schnabel tip. Made 1928-40.

Savage Model 45 Super Sporter $350
Special Grade. Same as Model 40, except has checkered pistol grip and forearm, Lyman No. 40 receiver sight. Made 1928-40.

Savage Model 60 Autoloading Rifle $115
Caliber: 22 LR. 15-shot tubular magazine. 20-inch bbl. Weight: 6 lbs. Sights: open rear, ramp front. Monte Carlo stock of walnut w/checkered pistol grip and forearm. Made 1969-72.

RIFLES

Savage Model 40

Savage Model 45

Savage Model 60

Savage Model 63K

Savage Model 71
"Stevens Favorite"

Savage Model 90

Savage Model 63K Key Lock Bolt-Action Single-Shot Rifle $75
Trigger locked with key. Caliber: 22 Short, Long, LR. 18-inch bbl. Weight: 4 lbs. Sights: open rear; hooded ramp front. Full-length stock w/pistol grip, swivels. Made 1970-72.

Savage Model 63KM $90
Same as Model 63K, except chambered for 22 WMR. Made 1970-72.

Savage Model 71 "Stevens Favorite" Single-Shot Lever-Action Rifle $150
Replica of the original Stevens Favorite issued as a tribute to Joshua Stevens, "Father of 22 Hunting." Caliber: 22 LR. 22-inch full-octagon bbl. Brass-plated hammer and lever. Sights: open rear; brass blade front. Weight: 4.5 lbs. Plain straight-grip buttstock and schnabel forend; brass commemorative medallion inlaid in butt-stock, brass crescent-shaped buttplate. 10,000 produced. Made in 1971 only. Value is for new, unfired specimen.

Savage Model 90 Autoloading Carbine $120
Similar to Model 60, except has 16.5-inch bbl.,10-shot tubular magazine, folding leaf rear sight, bead front, carbine-style stock of uncheckered walnut with bbl. band and sling swivels. Weight: 5.75 lbs. Made 1969-72.

Savage Model 99 Lever-Action Repeater
Introduced in 1899, this model has been produced in a variety of styles and calibers. Original designation "Model 1899" was changed to "Model 99" c.1920. Earlier rifles and carbines — similar to Models 99A, 99B and 99H — were supplied in calibers 25-35, 30-30, 303 Sav., 32-40 and 38-55. Post-WWII Models 99A, 99C 99CD 99DE, 99DL 99F and 99PE have top tang safety other 99s have slide safety on right side of trigger guard. Models 99C and 99CD have detachable box magazine instead of traditional Model 99 rotary magazine.

Savage Model 99A (I) $525
Hammerless. Solid frame. Calibers: 30/30, 300 Sav., 303 Sav. Five-shot rotary magazine. 24-inch bbl. Weight: about 7.25 lbs. Sights: open rear; bead front, on ramp. Plain straight-grip stock, tapered forearm. Made 1920-36.

Savage Model 99A (II) $350
Current model. Similar to original Model 99A, except has top tang safety, 22-inch bbl., folding leaf rear sight, no crescent buttplate. Calibers: 243 Win., 250 Sav., 300 Sav., 308 Win. Made 1971-82.

Savage Model 99B $650
Takedown. Otherwise same as Model 99A, except weight about 7.5 lbs. Made 1920-36.

Savage Model 99A
First Issue

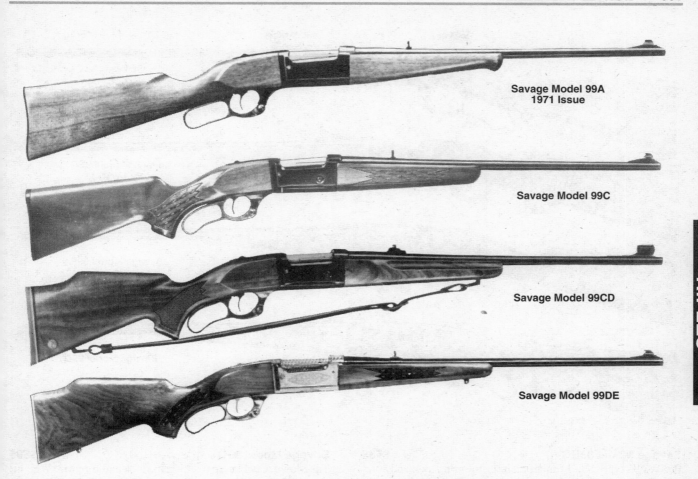

Savage Model 99A
1971 Issue

Savage Model 99C

Savage Model 99CD

Savage Model 99DE

RIFLES

Savage Model 99C **$425**
Current model. Same as Model 99F, except has clip magazine instead of rotary. Calibers: 243 Win., 284 Win., 308 Win. (4-shot detachable magazine holds one round less in 284). Weight: about 6.75 lbs. Made 1965 to date.

Savage Model 99CD **$395**
Deluxe version of Model 99C. Calibers: 243 Win.,250 Sav., 308 Win. Hooded ramp front sight. Weight: 8.25 lbs. Stock w/Monte Carlo comb and cheekpiece, checkered pistol grip, grooved forearm, swivels and sling. Made 1975 to 81.

Savage Model 99DE Citation Grade **$525**
Same as Model 99PE, except has less elaborate engraving. Made 1968-70.

Savage Model 99DL Deluxe **$295**
Postwar model. Calibers: 243 Win., 308 Win. Same as Model 99F, except has high comb Monte Carlo stock, sling swivels. Weight: about 6.75 lbs. Made 1960-73.

Savage Model 99E Carbine (I) **$675**
Pre-WWII type. Solid frame. Calibers: 22 Hi-Power, 250/3000, 30/30, 300 Sav., 303 Sav. with 22-inch bbl.; 300 Sav. 24-inch. Weight: about 7 lbs. Other specifications same as Model 99A. Made 1920-36.

Savage Model 99E Carbine (II) **$275**
Current model. Solid frame. Calibers: 250 Sav., 243 Win., 300 Sav., 308 Win. 20- or 22-inch bbl. Checkered pistol-grip stock and forearm. Made 1960-89.

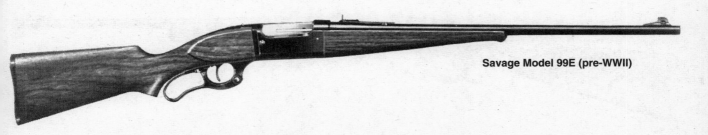

Savage Model 99E (pre-WWII)

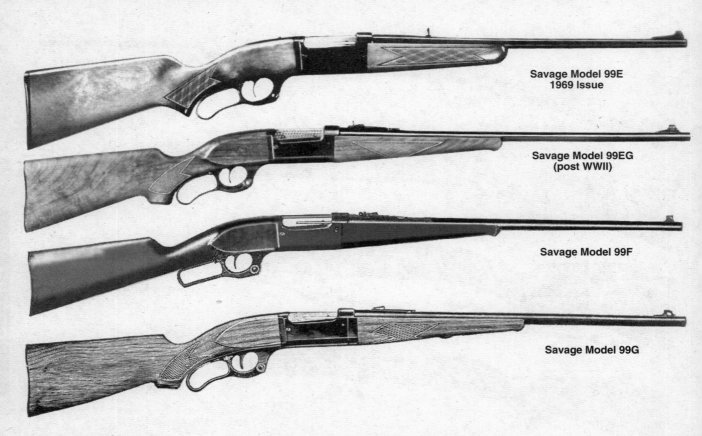

Savage Model 99E
1969 Issue

Savage Model 99EG
(post WWII)

Savage Model 99F

Savage Model 99G

Savage Model 99EG (I) **$535**
Pre-WWII type. Solid frame. Plain pistol-grip stock and forearm. Otherwise same as Model G. Made 1936-41.

Savage Model 99EG (II) **$495**
Post-WWII type. Same as prewar model, except has checkered stock and forearm. Calibers: 250 Sav., 300 Sav., 308 Win. (introduced 1955), 243 Win., and 358 Win. Made 1946-60.

Savage Model 99F Featherweight (I) **$595**
Pre-WWII type. Takedown. Specifications same as Model 99E, except weighs about 6.5 pounds. Made 1920-1942.

Savage Model 99F Featherweight (II) **$325**
Postwar model. Solid frame. Calibers: 243 Win., 300 Sav., 308 Win. 22-inch bbl. Checkered pistol-grip stock and forearm. Weight: about 6.5 lbs. Made 1955-73.

Savage Model 99G **$595**
Takedown. Checkered pistol-grip stock and forearm. Weight: about 7.25 lbs. Other specifications same as Model 99E. Made 1920-42.

Savage Model 99H Carbine **$495**
Solid frame. Calibers: 250/3000, 30/30, 303 Sav. 20-inch special weight bbl. Walnut carbine stock w/metal buttplate; walnut forearm w/bbl. band. Weight: about 6.5 lbs. Open rear sights; ramped blade front sight. Other specifications same as Model 99A. Made 1931-42.

Savage Model 99K **$1350**
Deluxe version of Model G with same specifications, except has fancy stock and engraving on receiver and bbl., Lyman peep rear sight, folding middle. Made 1931-42.

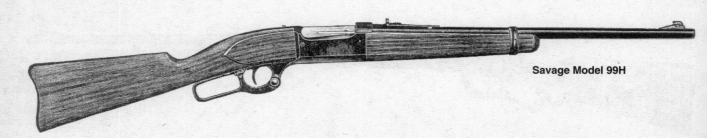

Savage Model 99H

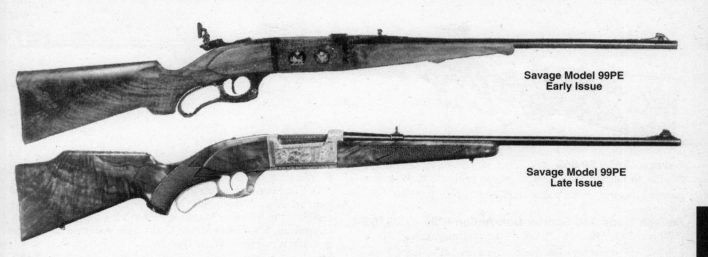

**Savage Model 99PE
Early Issue**

**Savage Model 99PE
Late Issue**

Savage Model 99PE Presentation Grade $1395
Same as Model 99DL, except has engraved receiver (game scenes on sides), tang and lever, fancy walnut Monte Carlo stock and forearm with hand checkering, QD swivels. Calibers: 243, 284, 308. Made 1968-70.

Savage Model 99R (I) $575
Pre-WWII type. Solid frame. Calibers: 250/3000 with 22-inch bbl.; 300 Sav. with 24-inch bbl. Weight: about 7.5 lbs. Special large pistol-grip stock and forearm, checkered. General specifications same as other Model 99 rifles. Made 1936-42.

Savage Model 99R (II) $450
Post-WWII type. Same as prewar model, except made with 24-inch bbl. only, has screw eyes for sling swivels. Calibers: 250 Sav., 300 Sav., 308 Win., 243 Win. and 358 Win. Made 1946-60.

Savage Model 99RS (I) $550
Pre-WWII type. Same as prewar Model 99R, except equipped w/Lyman rear peep sight and folding middle sight, quick detachable swivels and sling. Made 1936-42.

Savage Model 99RS (II) $395
Post-WWII type. Same as postwar Model 99RS, except equipped w/Redfield 70LH receiver sight, blank in middle sight slot. Made 1946-58.

Savage Model 99T $435
Featherweight. Solid frame. Calibers: 22 Hi-Power, 30/30, 303 Sav. with 20-inch bbl.; 300 Sav. with 22-inch bbl. Checkered pistol-grip stock and beavertail forearm. Weight: about 7 lbs. General specifications same as other Model 99 rifles. Made 1936-42.

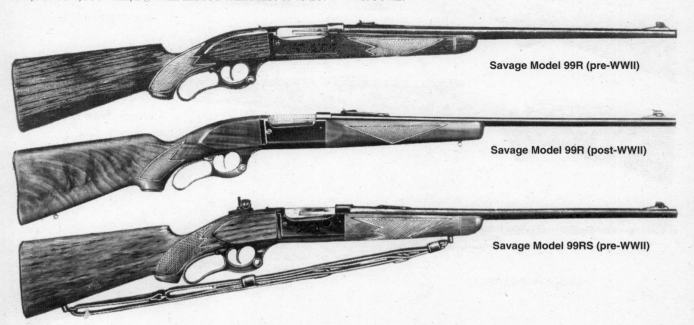

Savage Model 99R (pre-WWII)

Savage Model 99R (post-WWII)

Savage Model 99RS (pre-WWII)

Savage Model 99T

Savage Model 99-358 . . . . **$385**
Similar to current Model 99A, except caliber 358 Win. has
grooved forearm, recoil pad, swivel studs. Made 1977-80.

Savage Model 110 Sporter Bolt-Action Rifle . . . **$160**
Calibers: 243, 270, 308, 30-06. 4-shot box magazine. 22-inch
bbl. Weight: about 6.75 lbs. Sights: open rear; ramp front. Standard sporter stock with pistol grip checkered. Made 1958-1963.

Savage Model 110B Bolt-Action Rifle
Same as Model 110E, except with checkered select walnut
Monte Carlo-style stock (early models) or brown laminated
stock (late models). Calibers: 243 Win., 270 Win. 30-06, 7mm
Rem. Mag., 338 Win. Mag. Made 1976 to date.
Early Model **$235**
Laminated Stock Model **275**

Savage Model 110BL **$295**
Same as Model 110B, except has left-hand action.

Savage Model 110C
Calibers: 22-250, 243, 25-06, 270, 308, 30-06, 7mm Rem. Mag.,
300 Win. Mag. 4-shot detachable clip magazine (3-shot in Magnum calibers). 22-inch bbl. (24-inch in 22-250 Magnum calibers). Weight: 6.75 lbs., Magnum, 7.75 to 8 lbs. Sights: open rear;
ramp front. Checkered Monte Carlo-style walnut stock (Magnum has recoil pad). Made 1966-88.
Standard Calibers **$285**
Magnum Calibers **295**

Savage Model 110CL
Same as Model 110C, except has left-hand action. (Available
only in 243 Win., 30-06, 270 and 7mm Mag.)
Standard Calibers **$275**
Magnum Calibers **295**

Savage 110CY Youth/Ladies Rifle **$265**
Same as Model 110 G except with walnut-finished hardwood
stock with 12.5-inch pull. Calibers: 243 and 300 Savage. Made
1991 to date.

Savage Model 110

Savage Model 110B

Savage Model 110BL

Savage Model 110C

Savage Model 110E

Savage Model 110D

Similar to Model 110C, except has internal magazine with hinged floorplate. Calibers: 243 Win., 270 Win., 30-06, 7mm Rem. Mag., 300 Win. Mag. Made 1972-88.

Standard Calibers **$260**
Magnum Calibers 295

Savage Model 110DL

Same as Model 110D, except has left-hand action. Discontinued.

Standard Calibers **$270**
Magnum Calibers 295

Savage Model 110E **$225**

Calibers: 22-250, 223 Rem., 243, 270 Win.,308, 7mm Rem. Mag., 30-06. 4-shot box magazine (3-shot in Magnum). 20- or 22-inch bbl. (24-inch stainless steel in Magnum). Weight: 6.75 lbs.; Magnum, 7.75 lbs. Sights: open rear; ramp front. Plain Monte Carlo stock on early production; current models have checkered stocks of walnut-finished hardwood (Magnum has recoil pad). Made 1963 to date.

Savage Model 110EL **$225**

Same as Model 110E, except has left-hand action, made in 30-06 and 7mm Rem. Mag. only. Made 1969-73.

Savage Model 110F/110K Bolt-Action Rifle

Same as Model 110E, except **Model** 110F has black Rynite® synthetic stock, swivel studs; made 1988 to date. **Model** 110K has laminated camouflage stock; made 1986 to date.

Model 110F, Adj. Sights **$275**
Model 110FNS, No Sights 285
Model 110K Standard Calibers 295
Model 110K Magnum Calibers 335

Savage Model 110FP Police Rifle **$295**

Calibers: 223, 308 Win. 4-shot magazine. 24-inch bbl. 45.5 inches overall. Weight: 9 lbs. Black Rynite composition stock. Matte blue finish. Made 1990 to date.

Savage 110G Bolt-Action Rifle

Calibers: 223, 22-250, 243, 270, 7mm Rem. Mag., 308 Win., 30-06, 300 Win. Mag. 5-shot (standard) or 4-shot magazine (magnum). 22- or 24-inch bbl. 42.38 overall (standard). Weight: 6.75 to 7.5 lbs. Ramp front sight, adj. rear. Checkered walnut-finished hardwood stock with rubber recoil pad. Made 1989 to date.

Model 110G Standard Calibers **$255**
Model 110G Magnum Calibers 280
Model 110GLNS, Left-hand, No Sights 305

Savage Model 110GV Varmint Rifle **$295**

Similar to the Model 110 G, except fitted with medium-weight varmint bbl. with no sights. Receiver drilled and tapped for scope mount. Calibers 22-250 and 223 only. Made 1989 to date.

Savage Model 110M Magnum

Same as Model 110MC, except calibers: 7mm Rem. Mag. 264, 300 and 338 Win. 24-inch bbl. Stock with recoil pad. Weight: 7.75 to 8 lbs. Made 1963-69.

Model 110M Magnum **$235**
Model 110ML Magnum, Left-Hand Action 260

Savage Model 110MC

Same as Model 110, except has Monte Carlo-style stock. Calibers: 22-250, 243, 270, 308, 30-06. 24-inch bbl. in 22-250. Made 1959-69.

Model 110MC **$160**
Model 110MCL w/Left-hand Action 170

Savage Model 110 MCL

Savage Model 110P

Savage Model 110PE

Savage Model 110P Premier Grade
Calibers: 243 Win., 7mm Rem. Mag., 30-06. 4-shot magazine (3-shot in Magnum). 22-inch bbl. (24-inch stainless steel in Magnum). Weight: 7 lbs.; Magnum, 7.75 lbs. Sights: open rear folding leaf; ramp front. French walnut stock w/Monte Carlo comb and cheekpiece, rosewood forend tip and pistol-grip cap, skip checkering, sling swivels (Magnum has recoil pad). Made 1964-70.
Calibers 243 Win. and 30-06 . . . . **$335**
Caliber 7mm Rem. Mag. **385**

Savage Model 110PE Presentation Grade
Same as Model 110P, except has engraved receiver, floorplate and trigger guard, stock of choice grade French walnut. Made 1968-70.
Calibers 243 and 30-06 . . . . **$525**
Caliber 7mm Rem. Mag. **585**

Savage Model 110PEL Presentation Grade
Same as Model 110PE, except has left-hand action.
Calibers 243 and 30-06 . . . . **$675**
Caliber 7mm Rem. Mag. **695**

Savage Model 110PL Premier Grade
Same as Model 110P, except has left-hand action.
Calibers 243 Win. and 30-06 . . . . **$335**
Caliber 7mm Rem. Mag. **385**

Savage Model 110S/110V
Same as Model 110E, except **Model 110S** in 308 Win. only; **Model 110V** in 22-250 and 223 Rem. w/heavy 2-inch barrel, 47 inches overall, 9 pounds. Discont. 1989.
Model 110S **$275**
Model 110V **295**

Savage Model 111 Chieftain Bolt-Action Rifle
Calibers: 243 Win., 270 Win., 7×57mm, 7mm Rem. Mag. 30-06. 4-shot clip magazine (3-shot in Magnum). 22-inch bbl. (24-inch in Magnum). Weight: 7.5 lbs., 8.25 lbs. Magnum. Sights: leaf rear; hooded ramp front. Select walnut stock w/Monte Carlo comb and cheekpiece, checkered, pistol-grip cap, QD swivels and sling. Made 1974-79.
Standard calibers **$295**
Caliber 7mm Rem. Mag. **335**

Savage Models 111 F, 111 FC, 111 FNS Classic Hunters
Similar to the Model 111G, except with graphite/fiberglass composition stock. Weight: 6.25 lbs. Made 1994 to date.
Model 111F (Box Mag., Right/Left Hand) **$260**
Model 111FC (Detachable Magazine) **290**
Model 111FNS (Box Mag., No Sights, R/L Hand) **260**

Savage Models 111 G, 111 GC, 111 GNS Classic Hunters
Calibers: 22-250 Rem., 223 Rem., 243 Win., 25-06 Rem. 250 Sav., 270 Win., 7mm-08 Rem., 7mm Rem. Mag., 30-06, 300 Sav., 300 Win. Mag., 308 Win., 338 Win. 22- or 24-inch bbl. Weight: 7 lbs. Ramp front sight, adj. open rear. Walnut-finished hardwood stock. Blued finish. Made 1994 to date.
Model 111G (Box Mag., Right/Left Hand) **$265**
Model 111GC (Detachable Mag., R/L Hand) **285**
Model 111GNS (Box Mag., No Sights) **255**

Savage Model 112BV, 112BVSS Heavy Varmint Rifles
Similar to the Model 110G, except fitted with 26-inch heavy bbl. Laminated wood stock with high comb. Calibers 22-250 and 223 only.
Model 112BV (Made 1993-94) **$375**
Model 112BVSS (Fluted stainless bbl.; made
   since 1994) **395**

Savage Model 111 Chieftain

Savage Model 111F

Savage Model 112V

Savage Model 116FCSAK

Savage Model 112FV, 112FVS, 112FVSS Varmint Rifles

Similar to the Model 110G, except fitted with 26-inch heavy bbl. and Dupont Rynite stock. Calibers: 22-250, 223 and 220 Swift (112FVS only). Blued or stainless finish. Made 1991-94.

Model 112FV (blued) **$250**
Model 112FVS (blued, single shot) **275**
Model 112FVSS (stainless) **375**

Savage Model 112V Varmint Rifle **$305**

Bolt action, single shot. Caliber: 220 Swift, 222 Rem., 223 Rem., 22-250, 243 Win., 25-06. 26-inch heavy bbl. with scope bases. Supplied w/o sights. Weight: 9.25 lbs. Select walnut stock in varmint style w/checkered pistol grip, high comb, QD sling swivels. Made 1975-79.

Savage Model 114CU Classic Ultra **$375**

Calibers: 270 Win., 7mm Rem. Mag., 30-06, 300 Win. Mag. 22- or 24-inch bbl. Weight: 7 lbs. Ramp front sight; adj. open rear. Checkered select walnut stock w/oil finish, red buttpad. High-luster blued finish. Made 1991 to date.

Savage Models 116FSAK, 116FCSAK Bolt-Action Rifles

Similar to the Model 116FSK, except in calibers 270 Win., 30-06, 7mm Mag., 300 Win. Mag., 338 Win. Mag. Fluted 22-inch stainless bbl. w/adj. muzzle brake. Weight: 6.5 lbs. Made 1994 to date.

Model 116FSAK **$385**
Model 116FCSAK (Detachable Mag.) **445**

Savage Models 116FSC, 116FSS Bolt-Action Rifles

Improved Model 110 with satin stainless action and bbl. Calibers: 223, 243, 270, 30-06, 7mm Rem. Mag., 300 Win. Mag., 338 Win. Mag. 22- or 24-inch bbl. 4- or 5-shot capacity. Weight: about 7.5 lbs. Black Rynite® stock w/recoil pad and swivel studs. Receiver drilled and tapped for scope mounts, no sights. Made 1991 to date.

Model 116FSS **$375**
Model 116FSC, Detachable Magazine **395**

Savage 116FSK Kodiak Rifle **$395**

Similar to the Model 116FSS, except with 22-inch bbl. chambered for 338 Win. Mag. only. "Shock Suppressor" recoil reducer. Made 1993 to date.

Savage Model 116SE Safari Express **$695**

Calibers: 300 Win. Mag., 338 Win., 425 Express, 458 Win. Mag. 24-inch stainless bbl. fitted w/adj. muzzle brake. 45.5 inches overall. Weight: 8.5 lbs. Ramp front sight; 3-leaf Express rear. Checkered select walnut stock. Stainless finish. Made 1994 to date.

Savage Model 170 Pump-Action Centerfire Rifle. . . **$190**

Calibers: 30-30, 35 Rem. 3-shot tubular magazine. 22-inch bbl. Weight: 6.75 lbs. Sights: folding leaf rear; ramp front. Select walnut stock w/checkered pistol grip Monte Carlo comb, grooved slide handle. Made 1970-81.

Savage Model 170C Carbine **$195**

Same as Model 170 Rifle, except has 18.5-inch bbl., straight comb stock, weighs 6 lbs.; caliber 30-30 only. Made 1974-81.

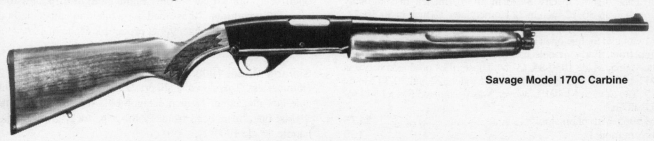

Savage Model 170C Carbine

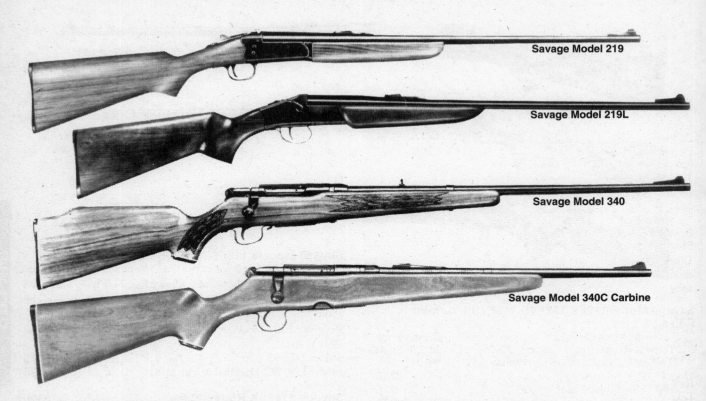

Savage Model 219

Savage Model 219L

Savage Model 340

Savage Model 340C Carbine

Savage Model 219 Single-Shot Rifle

Hammerless. Takedown. Shotgun-type action with top lever. Calibers: 22 Hornet, 25-20, 32-20, 30-30. 26-inch bbl. Weight: about 6 lbs. Sights: open rear; bead front. Plain pistol-grip stock and forearm. Made 1938-65.

Model 219 . . . . **$175**
Model 219L (w/side lever, made 1965-67) **125**

Savage Model 221-229 Utility Guns

Same as Model 219, except in various calibers, supplied in combination with an interchangeable shotgun bbl. All versions discontinued.

Model 221 (30-30,12-ga. 30-inch bbl.) **$140**
Model 222 (30-30,16-ga. 28-inch bbl.) **125**
Model 223 (30-30, 20-ga. 28-inch bbl.) **110**
Model 227 (22 Hornet, 12-ga. 30-inch bbl.) **150**
Model 228 (22 Hornet, 16-ga. 28-inch bbl.) **145**
Model 229 (22 Hornet, 20-ga. 28-inch bbl.) **140**

Savage Model 340 Bolt-Action Repeater

Calibers: 22 Hornet, 222 Rem., 223 Rem., 225 Win., 30-30. Clip magazine; 4-shot capacity (3-shot in 30-30). Bbl. lengths: originally 20-inch in 30-30, 22-inch in 22 Hornet; later 22-inch in 30-30, 24-inch in other calibers. Weight: 6.5 to 7.5 lbs. depending on caliber and vintage. Sights: open rear (folding leaf on recent production); ramp front. Early models had plain pistol-grip stock checkered since 1965. Made 1950-85. (*Note:* Those rifles produced between 1947-1950 were 22 Hornet Stevens Model 322 and 30-30 Model 325. The Savage Model, however, was designated Model 340 for all calibers.)

Pre-1965 with plain stock **$175**
Current model **160**

Savage Model 340C Carbine **$185**

Same as Model 340, except caliber 30-30, 18.5-inch bbl. Weight: about 6 lbs. Made 1962-64.

Savage Model 340S Deluxe **$225**

Same as Model 340, except has checkered stock, screw eyes for sling, peep rear sight, hooded front. Made 1955-60.

Savage Model 342 . . . . **$250**

Designation, 1950 to 1955, of Model 340 22 Hornet.

Savage Model 342S Deluxe **$275**

Designation, 1950 to 1955, of Model 340S 22 Hornet.

Savage Anniversary Model 1895 Lever-Action Rifle **$475**

Replica of Savage Model 1895 Hammerless Lever-Action Rifle issued to commemorate the 75th anniversary (1895-1970) of Savage Arms. Caliber: 308 Win. 5-shot rotary magazine.24-inch full-octagon bbl. Engraved receiver. Brass-plated lever. Sights: open rear; brass blade front. Plain straight-grip buttstock, schnabel-type forend; brass medallion inlaid in buttstock, brass crescent-shaped buttplate. 9,999 produced. Made in 1970 only. Value is for new, unfired specimen.

Savage Model 1903 Slide-Action Repeater **$225**

Hammerless. Takedown. Caliber: 22 Short, Long, LR. Detachable box magazine. 24-inch octagon bbl. Weight: about 5 lbs. Sights: open rear; bead front. Pistol-grip stock, grooved slide handle. Made 1903-21.

Savage Model 1895 Replica

Savage Model 1904 Bolt-Action Single-Shot Rifle $100
Takedown. Caliber: 22 Short, Long, LR. 18-inch bbl. Weight: about 3 lbs. Sights: open rear; bead front. Plain, straight-grip, one-piece stock. Made 1904-17.

Savage Model 1905 Bolt-Action Single-Shot Rifle $100
Takedown. Caliber: 22 Short, Long, LR. 22-inch bbl. Weight: about 5 lbs. Sights: open rear; bead front. Plain, straight-grip one-piece stock. Made 1905-19.

Savage Model 1909 Slide Action Repeater $195
Hammerless. Takedown. Similar to Model 1903, except has 20-inch round bbl., plain stock and forearm, weighs about 4.75 lbs. Made 1909-15.

Savage Model 1912 Autoloading Rifle $325
Takedown. Caliber: 22 LR only. 7-shot detachable box magazine. 20-inch bbl. Weight: about 4.5 lbs. Sights: open rear, bead front. Plain straight-grip stock and forearm. Made 1912-16.

Savage Model 1914 Slide-Action Repeater $265
Hammerless. Takedown. Caliber: 22 Short, Long, LR. Tubular magazine holds 20 Short, 17 Long, 15 LR. 24-inch octagon bbl. Weight: about 5.75 lbs. Sights: open rear; bead front. Plain pistol-grip stock, grooved slide handle. Made 1914-24.

--- NOTE ---

In 1965, Savage began the importation of rifles manufactured by J. G. Anschutz GmbH, Ulm, West Germany. Models designated "Savage/Anschutz" are listed in this section, those marketed in the U.S. under the "Anschutz" name are included in that firm's listings. Anschutz rifles are now distributed in the U.S. by Precision Sales Int'l., Westfield, Mass. *See* "Anschutz" for detailed specifications.

Savage Model 1920 Hi-Power Bolt-Action Rifle $400
Short Mauser-type action. Calibers: 250/3000, 300 Sav: 5-shot box magazine. 22-inch bbl. in 250 cal.; 24-inch in 300 cal. Weight: about 6 lbs. Sights: open rear; bead front. Checkered pistol-grip stock w/slender forearm and schnabel tip. Made 1920-26.

Savage/Anschutz Mark 10 Bolt-Action Target Rifle $295
Single shot. Caliber: 22 LR. 26-inch bbl. Weight: 8.5 lbs. Sights: Anschutz micrometer rear; globe front. Target stock w/full pistol grip and cheekpiece, adj. hand stop and swivel. Made 1967-72.

Savage/Anschutz Mark 10D $300
Same as Mark 10, except has redesigned stock with Monte Carlo comb, different rear sight. Weight: 7.75 lbs. Made 1972.

Savage/Anschutz Model 54 Custom Sporter . . . $515
Same as Anschutz Model 1422D.

Savage/Anschutz Model 54M $550
Same as Anschutz Model 1522D.

Savage/Anschutz Model 64 Bolt-Action Target Rifle $395
Same as Anschutz Model 1403.

Savage/Anschutz Model 153 Bolt-Action Sporter $395
Caliber: 222 Rem. 3-shot clip magazine. 24-inch bbl. Sights: folding leaf open rear; hooded ramp front. Weight: 6.75 lbs. French walnut stock w/cheekpiece, skip checkering, rosewood forend tip and grip cap, swivels. Made 1964-67.

Savage/Anschutz Model 153S $495
Same as Model 153, except has double-set trigger. Made 1965-67.

Savage/Anschutz Model 164 Custom Sporter . . . $250
Same as Anschutz Model 1416.

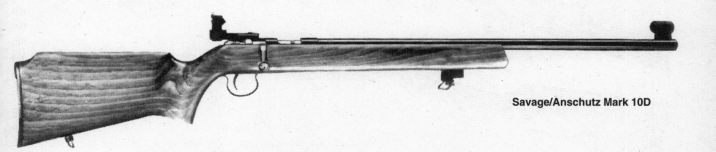

Savage/Anschutz Mark 10D

RIFLES

Savage-Stevens Model 34

Savage-Stevens Model 35

Savage/Anschutz Model 164M $295
Same as Anschutz Model 1516.

Savage/Anschutz Model 184 Sporter $315
Same as Anschutz Model 1441.

Savage-Stevens Model 34 Bolt-Action Repeater . . $85
Caliber: 22 Short, Long, LR. 5-shot clip magazine. 20-inch bbl. Weight: 5.5 lbs. Sights: open rear; bead front. Checkered stock w/Monte Carlo comb. Made 1969-81.

Savage-Stevens Model 34M $90
Same as Model 34, except chambered for 22 WMR. Made 1969-73.

Savage-Stevens Model 35 . . . . $80
Bolt-action repeater. Caliber: 22 LR. 6-shot clip magazine. 22-inch bbl. Weight: about 5 lbs. Sights: open rear; ramp front. Monte Carlo stock w/checkered pistol grip and forearm. Made 1982 to date.

Savage-Stevens Model 35M $90
Same as Model 35, except chambered for 22 WMR. Made 1982 to date.

Savage-Stevens Model 46 Bolt-Action Rifle $95
Caliber: 22 Short, Long, LR. Tubular magazine holds 22 Short, 17 Long, 15 LR. 20-inch bbl. Weight: 5 lbs. Plain pistol-grip stock on early production; later models have Monte Carlo stock w/checkering. Made 1969-73.

Savage-Stevens Model 65 Bolt-Action Rifle $90
Caliber: 22 Short, Long, LR. 5-shot clip magazine. 20-inch bbl. Weight: 5 lbs. Sights: open rear; ramp front. Monte Carlo stock w/checkered pistol grip and forearm. Made 1969-73.

Savage-Stevens Model 65M $105
Same as Model 65, except chambered for 22 WMR, has 22-inch bbl., weighs 5.25 lbs. Made 1969-81.

Savage-Stevens Model 46

Savage-Stevens Model 65

Savage-Stevens Model 72 Crackshot

Savage-Stevens Model 73

Savage-Stevens Model 80

Savage-Stevens Model 72 Crackshot Single-Shot Lever-Action Rifle $110
Falling-block action. Casehardened frame. Caliber: 22 Short, Long, LR. 22-inch octagon bbl. Weight: 4.5 lbs. Sights: open rear; bead front. Plain straight-grip stock and forend of walnut. Made 1772 to date.

Savage-Stevens Model 73 Bolt-Action Single-Shot $75
Caliber: 22 Short, Long, LR. 20-inch bbl. Weight: 4.75 lbs. Sights: open rear; bead front. Plain pistol-grip stock. Made 1965-80.

Savage-Stevens 73Y Youth Model $85
Same as Model 73, except has 18-inch bbl., 1.5-inch shorter butt-stock, weighs 4.5 lbs. Made 1965-80.

Savage-Stevens Model 74 Little Favorite $130
Same as Model 72 Crackshot, except has black-finished frame, 22-inch round bbl., walnut-finished hardwood stock. Weight: 4.75 lbs. Made 1972-74.

Savage-Stevens Model 80 Autoloading Rifle . . . $120
Caliber: 22 LR. 15-shot tubular magazine. 20-inch bbl. Weight: 6 lbs. Sights: open rear, bead front. Monte Carlo stock of walnut w/checkered pistol grip and forearm. Made 1976 to date. *(Note: This rifle is essentially the same as Model 60 of 1969-72, except for a different style of checkering, side instead of top safety and plain bead instead of ramp front sight.)*

Savage-Stevens Model 88 Autoloading Rifle . . . $125
Similar to Model 60, except has walnut-finished hardwood stock, plain bead front sight; weight, 5.75 lbs. Made 1969-72.

Savage-Stevens Model 89 Single-Shot Lever-Action Carbine $100
Martini-type action. Caliber: 22 Short, Long, LR. 18.5-inch bbl. Weight: 5 lbs. Sights: open rear; bead front. Western-style carbine stock w/straight grip, forearm with bbl. band. Made 1976-89.

Savage-Stevens Model 987-T Autoloading Rifle $120
Caliber: 22 LR. 15-shot tubular magazine. 20-inch bbl. Weight: 6 lbs. Sights: open rear; ramp front. Monte Carlo stock w/checkered pistol grip and forearm. Made 1981-89.

Savage "Stevens Favorite"
See **Savage Model 71.**

RIFLES

Savage-Stevens Model 89

Savage-Stevens Model 987-T

SCHULTZ & LARSEN GEVAERFABRIK
Otterup, Denmark

Schultz & Larsen Match Rifle No. 47 . . . . **$585**
Caliber: 22 LR. Bolt action, single shot, set trigger. 28.5-inch heavy bbl. Weight: about 14 lbs. Sights: micrometer receiver, globe front. Free-rifle stock w/cheekpiece, thumbhole, adj. Schuetzen-type buttplate, swivels, palmrest.

Schultz & Larsen Free Rifle Model 54 . . . . **$765**
Calibers: 6.5×55mm or any standard American centerfire caliber. Schultz & Larsen M54 bolt action, single shot, set trigger. 27.5-inch heavy bbl. Weight: about 15.5 lbs. Sights: micrometer receiver; globe front. Free-rifle stock w/cheekpiece, thumbhole, adj. Schuetzen-type buttplate, swivels, palmrest.

Schultz & Larsen Model 54J Sporting Rifle **$635**
Calibers: 270 Win., 30-06, 7×61 Sharpe & Hart. Schultz & Larsen bolt action. 3-shot magazine. 24-inch bbl. in 270 and 30-06, 26-inch in 7×61 S&H. Checkered stock w/ Monte Carlo comb and cheekpiece. Value shown is for rifle less sights.

SEARS, ROEBUCK & COMPANY
Chicago, Illinois

The most encountered brands or model designations used by Sears are J. C. Higgins and Ted Williams. Firearms sold under these designations have been mfd. by various firms including Winchester, Marlin, Savage, Mossberg, etc.

Sears Model 2C Bolt-Action Rifle **$85**
Caliber: 22RF. 7-shot clip mag. 21-inch bbl. Weight: 5 lbs. Sights: open rear; ramp front. Plain Monte Carlo stock. Mfd. by Win.

Sears Model 42 Bolt-Action Repeater **$80**
Takedown. Caliber: 22RF. 8-shot detachable box magazine. 24-inch bbl. Weight: 6 lbs. Sights: open rear; bead front. Plain pistol-grip stock. Mfd. by Marlin.

Sears Model 42DL Bolt-Action Repeater **$85**
Same general specifications as Model 42 except fancier grade w/peep sight, hooded front sight and swivels.

Sears Model 44DL Lever-Action Rifle **$140**
Caliber: 22RF. Tubular magazine holds 19 LR cartridges. 22-inch bbl. Weight: 6.25 lbs. Sights: open rear; hooded ramp front. Monte Carlo-style stock w/pistol grip. Mfd. by Marlin.

Sears Model 53 Bolt-Action Rifle **$195**
Calibers: 243, 270, 308, 30-06. 4-shot magazine. 22-inch bbl. Weight: 6.75 lbs. Sights: open rear; ramp front. Standard sporter stock w/pistol grip, checkered. Mfd. by Savage.

Sears Model 54 Lever-Action Rifle **$150**
Similar general specifications as Winchester Model 94 carbine. Made in 30-30 caliber only. Mfd. by Winchester.

Sears Model 103 Series Bolt-Action Repeater . . . **$85**
Same general specifications as Model 103.2 with minor changes. Mfd. by Marlin.

Sears Model 103.2 Bolt-Action Repeater **$85**
Takedown. Caliber: 22RF. 8-shot detachable box magazine. 24-inch bbl. Weight: 6 lbs. Sights: open rear; bead front. Plain pistol-grip stock. Mfd. by Marlin.

R. F. SEDGLEY, INC.
Philadelphia, Pennsylvania

Sedgley Springfield Sporter **$950**
Springfield '03 bolt action. Calibers: 220 Swift, 218 Bee, 22-3000, R2, 22-4000, 22 Hornet, 25-35, 250-3000, 257 Roberts, 270 Win., 7mm, 30-06. 24-inch bbl. Weight: 7.5 lbs. Sights: Lyman No. 48 receiver; bead front on matted ramp. Checkered walnut stock, grip cap, sling swivels. Discontinued 1941.

Sedgley Springfield Left-Hand Sporter **$1025**
Bolt action reversed for left-handed shooter; otherwise the same as standard Sedgley Springfield Sporter.

Sedgley Springfield Mannlicher-Type Sporter . . **$1195**
Same as the standard Sedgley Springfield Sporter, except has 20-inch bbl., Mannlicher-type full stock w/cheekpiece, weighs 7.75 lbs.

Sedgley Springfield Sporter

Sedgley Springfield Left-Hand

Sedgley Springfield Mannlicher

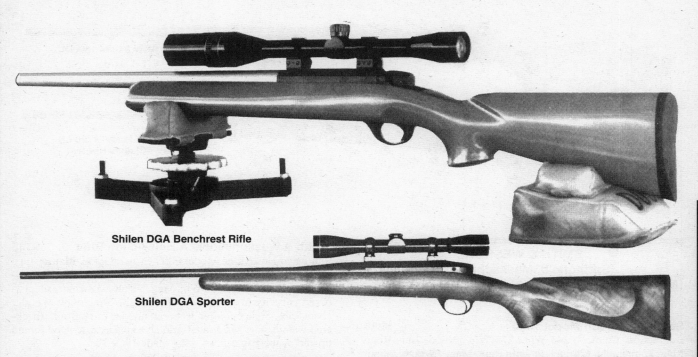

Shilen DGA Benchrest Rifle

Shilen DGA Sporter

SHILEN RIFLES, INC.
Ennis, Texas

Shilen DGA Benchrest Rifle **$925**
DGA single-shot bolt action. Calibers as listed for Sporter. 26-inch medium-heavy or heavy bbl. Weight: from 10.5 lbs. No sights. Fiberglass or walnut stock, classic or thumbhole pattern. Currently manufactured.

Shilen DGA Sporter **$895**
DGA bolt action. Calibers: 17 Rem.,222 Rem.,223 Rem. 22-250, 220 Swift, 6mm Rem., 243 Win., 250 Sav., 257 Roberts, 284 Win., 308 Win., 358 Win. 3-shot blind magazine. 24-inch bbl. Average weight: 7.5 lbs. No sights. Select Claro walnut stock w/cheekpiece, pistol grip, sling swivel studs. Currently manufactured.

Shilen DGA Varminter **$850**
Same as Sporter, except has 25-inch medium-heavy bbl. Weight: about 9 lbs.

SIG SWISS INDUSTRIAL COMPANY
Neuhausen-Rhine Falls, Switzerland

SIG-AMT Semiautomatic Rifle **$4500**
Caliber: 308 Win.(7.62 NATO). 5, 10, or 20-shot magazine. 18.5-inch bbl. w/flash suppressor. Weight: 9.5 lbs. Sights: adj. aperture rear, post front. Walnut buttstock and forend with synthetic pistol grip. Imported 1980s.

SIG-AMT Sporting Rifle **$2800**
Semiautomatic version of SG510-4 automatic assault rifle based on Swiss Army SIGW57. Roller-delayed blowback action. Caliber: 7.62×51mm NATO (308 Win.). 5-, 10- and 20-round magazines. 19-inch bbl. Weight: about 10 lbs. Sights, aperture rear, post front. Wood buttstock and forearm, folding bipod. Made 1960-74.

SIG-PE57 Semiautomatic Rifle **$3750**
Caliber: 7.65 Swiss. 24-shot magazine. 23.75-inch bbl. Weight: 12.5 lbs. Sights: adj. aperture rear; post front. High-impact synthetic stock. Imported from Switzerland during the 1980s.

Shilen DGA Varminter

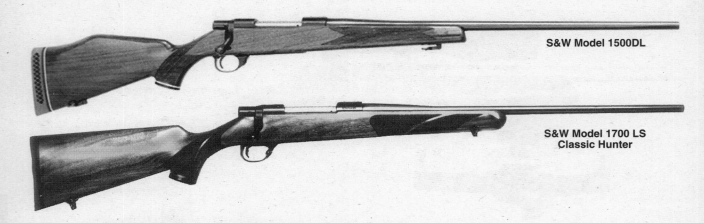

S&W Model 1500DL

S&W Model 1700 LS Classic Hunter

SMITH & WESSON
Springfield, Massachusetts
Mfd. by Husqvarna Vapenfabrik A.B., Huskvarna, Sweden

Smith & Wesson Model 1500 . . . . $285
Bolt action. Calibers: 243 Win., 270 Win., 30-06, 7mm Rem. Mag. 22-inch bbl. (24-inch in 7mm Rem. Mag.). Weight: about 7.5 lbs. American walnut stock w/Monte Carlo comb and cheekpiece, cut checkering. Sights: open rear, hooded ramp, gold bead front. Introduced in 1979, this model was also produced by Mossberg (*see* separate listings); now discontinued.

Smith & Wesson Model 1500DL Deluxe $315
Same as standard model, except w/o sights; has engine-turned bolt, decorative scroll on floorplate, French checkering.

Smith & Wesson Model 1700 LS
"Classic Hunter" $350
Bolt action. Calibers: 243 Win., 270 Win., 30-06, 5-shot magazine. 22-inch bbl. Weight: 7.5 lbs. Solid recoil pad, no sights, Schnabel forend, checkered walnut stock. Introduced 1983.

Smith & Wesson Model A Bolt-Action Rifle $335
Similar to Husqvarna Model 9000 Crown Grade. Mauser-type bolt action. Calibers: 22-250, 243 Win., 270 Win., 308 Win., 30-06, 7mm Rem. Mag., 300 Win. Mag. 5-shot magazine, except 3-round capacity in latter two calibers. 23.75-inch bbl. Weight: about 7 lbs. Sights: folding leaf rear; hooded ramp front. Checkered walnut stock w/Monte Carlo cheekpiece, rosewood forend tip and pistol-grip cap, swivels. Made 1969-72.

Smith & Wesson Model B $325
Same as Model A, except has 20.25-inch extra-light bbl., Monte Carlo cheekpiece w/schnabel-style forearm, weighs about 6 lbs. 10 oz. Calibers: 243 Win., 30-06.

Smith & Wesson Model C $325
Same as Model B, except has cheekpiece stock w/straight comb.

Smith & Wesson Model D $415
Same as Model C, except has full-length Mannlicher-style forearm.

Smith & Wesson Model E $450
Same as Model B, except has full-length Mannlicher-style forearm.

Springfield Armory BM59

SPRINGFIELD, INC.
Colona, Illinois
(formerly Springfield Armory of Geneseo, Ill.)

This is a private firm, not to be confused with the former U.S. Government facility in Springfield, Mass.

Springfield Armory BM-59 Semiautomatic Rifle
Gas-operated. Caliber: 308 Win. (7.62mm NATO). 20-shot detachable box magazine. 19.3-inch bbl. with flash suppressor. About 43 inches overall. Weight: 9.25 lbs. Adj. military aperture rear sight, square post front; direct and indirect grenade launcher sights. European walnut stock w/handguard or folding buttstock (Alpine Paratrooper). Made 1981 to date. *See* illustration preceding page.
Standard Model $1795
Paratrooper Model 1950

Springfield Armory M-1 Garand Semiautomatic Rifle
Gas-operated. Calibers: 308 Win. (7.62 NATO), 30-06. 8-shot stripper clip. 24-inch bbl. 43.5 inches overall. Weight: 9.5 lbs. Adj. aperture rear sight, military square blade front. Standard "Issuegrade" walnut stock or folding buttstock. Made 1979 to date.
Standard Model . . . . $ 775
National Match 950
Ultra Match 995
Sniper Model 1095
Paratrooper with folding stock 995

Springfield Armory Match M1A
Same as Standard MIA, except has National Match grade bbl. with modified flash suppressor, National Match sights, turned trigger pull, gas system assembly in one unit, modified mainspring guide glass-bedded walnut stock. Super Match M1A has premium-grade heavy bbl. (weighs 10 lbs).
Match M1A $1095
Super Match M1A 1250

Springfield Armory Standard M1A Semiautomatic
Gas-operated. Similar to U.S. M14 service rifle, except has no provision for automatic firing. Caliber: 7.65mm NATO (308

Springfield Armory Standard M1A *(Cont.)*
Win.). 5-, 10- or 20-round detachable box magazine. 25.13-inch bbl with flash suppressor. Weight: about 9 lbs. Sights: adj. aperture rear; blade front. Fiberglass, birch or walnut stock, fiberglass handguard, sling swivels. Made 1974 to date.
W/fiberglass or birch stock $695
W/walnut stock 765

SQUIRES BINGHAM CO., INC.
Makati, Rizal, Philippines

Squires Bingham Model 14D Deluxe Bolt-Action
Repeating Rifle $125
Caliber: 22 LR. 5-shot box magazine. 24-inch bbl. Sights: V-notch rear; hooded ramp front. Receiver grooved for scope mounting. Pulong Dalaga stock with contrasting forend tip and grip cap, checkered forearm and pistol grip. Weight: about 6 lbs. Currently mfd.

Squires Bingham Model 15 . . . . $150
Same as Model 14D, except chambered for 22 WMR. Currently mfd.

Squires Bingham Model M16 Semiautomatic
Rifle $175
Styled after U.S. M16 military rifle. Caliber: 22 LR. 15-shot box magazine. 19.5-inch bbl. w/muzzle brake/flash hider. Rear sight in carrying handle, post front on high ramp. Black-painted mahogany buttstock and forearm. Weight: about 6.5 lbs. Currently mfd.

Squires Bingham Model M20D Deluxe
Semiautomatic Rifle $180
Caliber: 22 LR. 15-shot box magazine. 19.5-inch bbl. w/muzzle brake/flash hider. Sights: V-notch rear; blade front. Receiver grooved for scope mounting. Pulong Dalaga stock w/contrasting forend tip and grip cap, checkered forearm/pistol grip. Weight: about 6 lbs. Currently mfd.

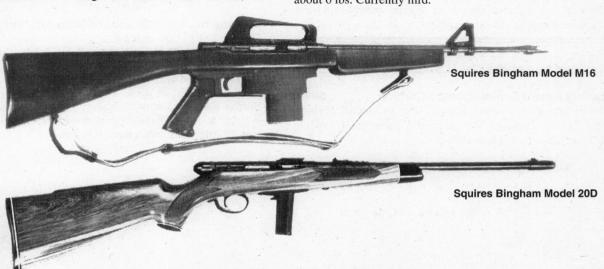

Squires Bingham Model M16

Squires Bingham Model 20D

RIFLES

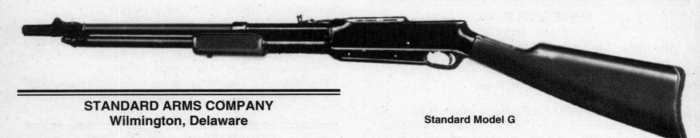

Standard Model G

STANDARD ARMS COMPANY
Wilmington, Delaware

Standard Model G Automatic Rifle **$425**
Gas-operated. Autoloading. Hammerless. Takedown. Calibers: 25-35, 30-30, 25 Rem., 30 Rem., 35 Rem. Magazine capacity: 4 rounds in 35 Rem., 5 rounds in other calibers. 22.38-inch bbl. Weight: about 7.75 lbs. Sights: open sporting rear; ivory bead front. Shotgun-type stock. Made c. 1910. *Note:* This was the first gas-operated rifle manufactured in the U.S. While essentially an autoloader, the gas port can be closed and the rifle operated as a slide-action repeater.

Standard Model M Hand-Operated Rifle **$295**
Slide-action repeater with same general specifications as Model G, except lacks autoloading feature. Weight: about 7 lbs.

Star Rolling Block Carbine

STAR
Eibar, Spain
Mfd. by Bonifacio Echeverria, S.A.

Star Rolling Block Carbine **$160**
Single-shot action similar to Remington Rolling Block. Calibers: 30-30, 357 Mag. ,44 Mag. 20-inch bbl. Weight: about 6 lbs. Sights: folding leaf rear; ramp front. Walnut straight-grip stock w/crescent buttplate, forearm with bbl. band. Made 1973-75.

STERLING
Imported by Lanchester U.S.A., Inc., Dallas, Texas

Sterling Mark 6 Semiautomatic Carbine **$695**
Caliber: 9mm Para. 34-shot magazine. Bbl.: 16.1 inches. Weight: about 7.5 lbs. Flip-type rear peep sight, ramp front. Folding metal skeleton stock. Made 1983-94.

J. STEVENS ARMS CO.
Chicopee Falls, Massachusetts
Div. of Savage Industries, Westfield, Mass.

J. Stevens Arms eventually became a division of Savage Industries. Consequently, the "Stevens" brand name is used for some rifles by Savage; *see* separate Savage-Stevens listings under Savage.

Stevens No. 12 Marksman Single-Shot Rifle . . . **$145**
Lever action, tip-up. Takedown. Calibers: 22 LR, 25 R.F., 32 R.F. 22-inch bbl. Plain straight-grip stock, small tapered forearm.

Stevens No. 14 Little Scout Single-Shot Rifle . . . **$125**
Caliber: 22 RF. 18-inch bbl. One-piece slab stock readily distinguishes it from the No. 14½ that follows. Made 1906-1910.

Stevens No. 14½ Little Scout Single-Shot Rifle **$150**
Rolling block. Takedown. Caliber: 22 LR. 18- or 20-inch bbl. Weight: about 2.75 lbs. Sights: open rear; blade front. Plain straight-grip stock, small tapered forearm.

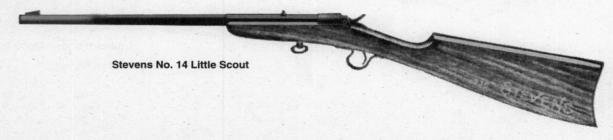

Stevens No. 14 Little Scout

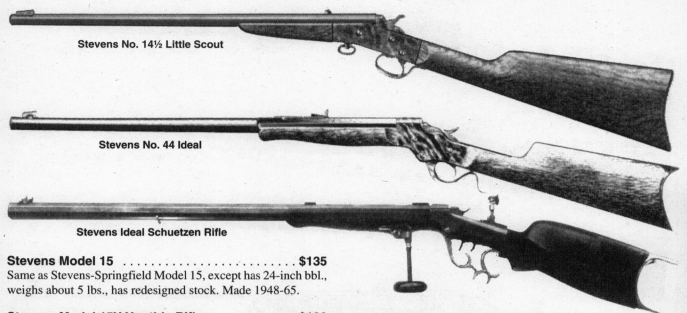

Stevens No. 14½ Little Scout

Stevens No. 44 Ideal

Stevens Ideal Schuetzen Rifle

Stevens Model 15 . . . . $135
Same as Stevens-Springfield Model 15, except has 24-inch bbl., weighs about 5 lbs., has redesigned stock. Made 1948-65.

Stevens Model 15Y Youth's Rifle $130
Same as Model 15, except has 21-inch bbl., short buttstock, weighs about 4.75 lbs. Made 1958-65.

Stevens No. 44 Ideal Single-Shot Rifle $625
Rolling block. Lever action. Takedown. Calibers: 22 LR 25 R.F., 32 R.F., 25-20 S.S., 32-20, 32-40, 38-40, 38-55, 44-40. Bbl. lengths: 24-inch, 26-inch (round, half-octagon, full-octagon). Weight: about 7 lbs with 26-inch round bbl. Sights: open rear; Rocky Mountain front. Plain straight-grip stock and forearm. Made 1894-32.

Stevens No. 44½ Ideal Single-Shot Rifle $745
Falling-block lever-action rifle. Aside from the new design action introduced in 1903, the specifications of this model are the same as those of Model 44. Model 44½ discontinued about 1916.

Stevens Nos. 45 to 54 Ideal Single-Shot Rifles
These are the higher-grade models, differing from the standard No. 44 and 44½ chiefly in finish, engraving, set triggers, levers, bbls., stock, etc. The Schuetzen types (including the "Stevens-Pope" models) are in this series. These are the higher grade models, differing from the standard No. 44 and No. 44 ½ chiefly in finish, engraving set triggers, levers, barrels, stocks, etc. The Schuetzen types (including the "Stevens-Pope" models) are in this series. Model Nos. 45 to 54 wre introduced about 1896 and originally had the No. 44-type rolling-block action, which was superseded in 1903 by the No. 44½ falling-block action.

Stevens Model 66 Bolt-Action Repeating Rifle . . $115
Takedown. Caliber: 22 Short, Long, LR. Tubular magazine holds 13 LR, 15 Long, 19 Short. 24-inch bbl. Weight: about 5 lbs. Sights: open rear, bead front. Plain pistol-grip stock w/grooved forearm. Made 1931-35.

Stevens No. 70 Visible Loading Slide-Action Repeating Rifle $225
Exposed hammer. Caliber: 22 LR, Long, Short. Tubular magazine holds 11 LR, 13 Long, 15 Short. 22-inch bbl. Weight: about 4.5 lbs. Sights: open rear; bead front. Plain straight-grip stock, grooved slide handle. Made 1907-34. *Note:* Nos. 70½, 71, 71½, 72, 72½ are essentially the same as No. 70, differing chiefly in bbl. length or sight equipment.

Stevens Model 87 Autoloading Rifle $150
Takedown. Caliber: 22 LR. 15-shot tubular magazine. 24-inch bbl. (20-inch on current model). Weight: about 6 pounds. Sights: open rear, bead front. Pistol-grip stock. Made 1938 to date. *Note:* This model originally bore the "Springfield" brand name, discontinued in 1948.

Stevens Model 322 Hi-Power Bolt-Action Carbine $225
Caliber: 22 Hornet. 4-shot detachable box magazine. 21-inch bbl. Weight: about 6.75 lbs. Sights: open rear; ramp front. Pistol-grip stock. Made 1947-1950. (*See* Savage Models 340, 342.)

Stevens Model 87

Stevens No. 414 Armory Model

Stevens Model 416

Stevens Model 53

Stevens Model 055

Stevens Model 056

Stevens Model 322-S $275
Same as Model 325, except has peep rear sight. (*See* Savage
Models 340S, 342S.)

**Stevens Model 325 Hi-Power Bolt-Action
Carbine** $225
Caliber: 30-30. 3-shot detachable box magazine. 21-inch bbl.
Weight: about 6.75 lbs. Sights: open rear; bead front. Plain
pistol-grip stock. Made 1947-50. (*See* Savage Model 340.)

Stevens Model 325-S $265
Same as Model 325, except has peep rear sight. (*See* Savage
Model 340S.)

**Stevens No. 414 Armory Model
Single-Shot Rifle** $425
No. 44-type lever action. Calibers: 22 LR only, 22 Short only.
26-inch bbl. Weight: about 8 lbs. Sights: Lyman receiver peep;
blade front. Plain straight-grip stock, military-type forearm,
swivels. Made 1912-32.

Stevens Model 416 Bolt-Action Target Rifle . . . $215
Caliber: 22 LR. 5-shot detachable box magazine. 26-inch heavy
bbl. Weight: about 9.5 lbs. Sights: receiver peep; hooded front.
Target stock, swivels, sling. Made 1937-49.

**Stevens No. 419 Junior Target Model Bolt-Action
Single-Shot Rifle** $235
Takedown. Caliber: 22 LR. 26-inch bbl. Weight: about 5.5 lbs.
Sights: Lyman No. 55 rear peep; blade front. Plain junior target
stock w/pistol grip and grooved forearm, swivels, sling. Made
1932-36.

**Stevens Buckhorn Model 053 Bolt-Action Single-
Shot Rifle** $110
Takedown. Calibers: 22 Short, Long, LR, 22 WMR. 25 Stevens
R.F. 24-inch bbl. Weight: about 5.5 lbs. Sights: receiver peep;
open middle; hooded front. Sporting stock w/pistol grip and
black forend tip. Made 1935-48.

Stevens Buckhorn Model 53 . . . . $125
Same as Buckhorn Model 053, except has open rear sight and
plain bead front sight. *See* illustration preceding page.

Stevens Buckhorn Model 055 . . . . $140
Takedown. Same as the Model 056 except single-shot action and
weighs 5.5 lbs. *See* illustration preceding page.

**Stevens Buckhorn Model 056 Bolt-Action
Repeating Rifle** $150
Takedown. Caliber: 22 LR, Long, Short. 5-shot detachable box
magazine. 24-inch bbl. Weight: about 6 lbs. Sights: receiver peep,
open middle, hooded front. Sporting stock w/pistol grip and black
forend tip. Made 1935-48.

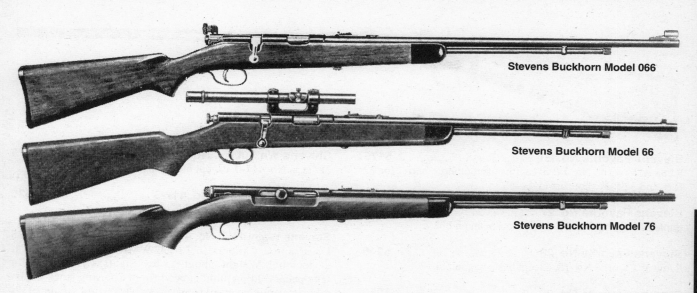

Stevens Buckhorn Model 066

Stevens Buckhorn Model 66

Stevens Buckhorn Model 76

Stevens Buckhorn Model 56 . . . . **$115**
Same as Buckhorn Model 056, except has open rear sight and plain bead front sight.

Stevens Buckhorn No. 057 . . . . **$110**
Same as Buckhorn Model 076, except has 5-shot detachable box magazine. Made 1939-48.

Stevens Buckhorn No. 57 . . . . **$125**
Same as Buckhorn Model 76, except has 5-shot detachable box magazine. Made 1939-48.

**Stevens Buckhorn Model 066 Bolt-Action
Repeating Rifle** **$150**
Takedown. Caliber: 22 LR, Long, Short. Tubular magazine holds 21 Short, 17 Long, 15 LR. 24-inch bbl. Weight: about 6 lbs. Sights: receiver peep; open middle; hooded front. Sporting stock w/pistol grip and black forend tip. Made 1935-48.

Stevens Buckhorn Model 66 . . . . **$115**
Same as Buckhorn Model 066, except has open rear sight, plain bead front sight.

Stevens Buckhorn No. 076 Autoloading Rifle . . **$150**
Takedown. Caliber: 22 LR. 15-shot tubular magazine. 24-inch bbl. Weight: about 6 lbs. Sights: receiver peep; open middle; hooded front. Sporting stock w/pistol grip, black forend tip. Made 1938-48.

Stevens Buckhorn No. 76 . . . . **$145**
Same as Buckhorn No. 076, except has open rear sight, plain bead front sight.

Stevens Crack Shot No. 26 Single-Shot Rifle . . . **$155**
Lever action. Takedown. Calibers: 22 LR, 32 R.F.18-inch or 22-inch bbl. Weight: about 3.25 lbs. Sights: open rear; blade front. Plain straight-grip stock, small tapered forearm. Made 1913-39.

Stevens Crack Shot No. 26½ **$180**
Same as Crack Shot No.26, except has smoothbore bbl. for shot cartridges.

Stevens Favorite No. 17 Single-Shot Rifle **$165**
Lever action. Takedown. Calibers: 22 LR, 25 R.F., 32 R.F. 24-inch round bbl., other lengths were available. Weight: about 4.5 lbs. Sights: open rear; Rocky Mountain front. Plain straight-grip stock, small tapered forearm. Made 1894-1935.

Stevens Favorite No. 18 . . . . **$245**
Same as Favorite No. 17 except has Vernier peep rear sight, leaf middle sight, Beach combination front sight.

Stevens Favorite No. 19 . . . . **$275**
Same as Favorite No. 17 except has Lyman combination rear sight, leaf sight, Lyman front sight.

Stevens Crack Shot No. 26

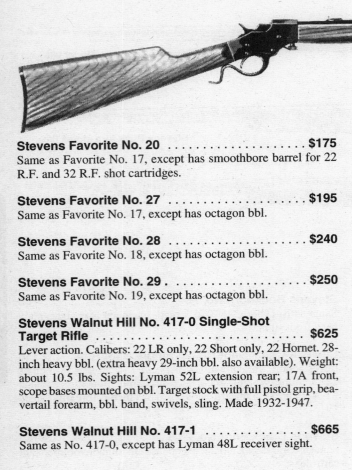

Stevens Favorite No. 27

Stevens Favorite No. 20 . . . . $175
Same as Favorite No. 17, except has smoothbore barrel for 22 R.F. and 32 R.F. shot cartridges.

Stevens Favorite No. 27 . . . . $195
Same as Favorite No. 17, except has octagon bbl.

Stevens Favorite No. 28 . . . . $240
Same as Favorite No. 18, except has octagon bbl.

Stevens Favorite No. 29 . . . . $250
Same as Favorite No. 19, except has octagon bbl.

Stevens Walnut Hill No. 417-0 Single-Shot Target Rifle $625
Lever action. Calibers: 22 LR only, 22 Short only, 22 Hornet. 28-inch heavy bbl. (extra heavy 29-inch bbl. also available). Weight: about 10.5 lbs. Sights: Lyman 52L extension rear; 17A front, scope bases mounted on bbl. Target stock with full pistol grip, beavertail forearm, bbl. band, swivels, sling. Made 1932-1947.

Stevens Walnut Hill No. 417-1 . . . . $665
Same as No. 417-0, except has Lyman 48L receiver sight.

Stevens Walnut Hill No. 417-2 . . . . $775
Same as No. 417-0, except has Lyman No. 144 tang sight.

Stevens Walnut Hill No. 417-3 . . . . $625
Same as No. 417-0, except w/o sights.

Stevens Walnut Hill No. 417½ Single-Shot Rifle . . $695
Lever action. Calibers: 22 LR, 22 WMR, 25 R.F., 22 Hornet. 28-inch bbl. Weight: about 8.5 lbs. Sights: Lyman No. 144 tang peep, folding middle; bead front. Sporting stock w/pistol grip, semibeavertail forearm, swivels, sling. Made 1932-1940.

Stevens Walnut Hill No. 418 Single-Shot Rifle . . $415
Lever action. Takedown. Calibers: 22 LR only, 22 Short only. 26-inch bbl. Weight: about 6.5 lbs. Sights: Lyman No. 144 tang peep; blade front. Pistol-grip stock, semibeavertail forearm, swivels, sling. Made 1932-40.

Stevens Walnut Hill No. 418½ $485
Same as No. 418, except also available in calibers 22 WMR and 25 Stevens R.F., has Lyman No. 2A tang peep sight, bead front sight.

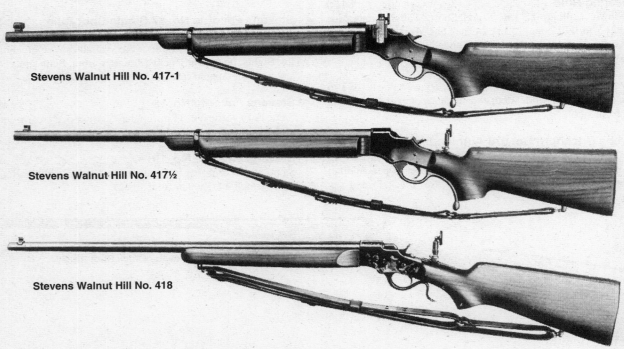

Stevens Walnut Hill No. 417-1

Stevens Walnut Hill No. 417½

Stevens Walnut Hill No. 418

Stevens-Springfield Model 15

Stevens-Springfield Model 83

Stevens-Springfield Model 15 Single-Shot Bolt-Action Rifle **$125**
Takedown. Caliber: 22 LR, Long, Short. 22-inch bbl. Weight: about 4 lbs. Sights: open rear, bead front. Plain pistol-grip stock. Made 1937-48.

Stevens-Springfield Model 82 Bolt-Action Single-Shot Rifle **$110**
Takedown. Caliber: 22 LR, Long, Short. 22-inch bbl. Weight: 4 lbs. Sights: open rear; gold bead front. Plain pistol-grip stock w/grooved forearm. Made 1935-39.

Stevens-Springfield Model 83 Bolt-Action Single-Shot Rifle **$110**
Takedown. Calibers: 22 LR, Long, Short; 22 WMR, 25 Stevens R.F. 24-inch bbl. Weight: about 4.5 lbs. Sights: peep rear; open middle; hooded front. Plain pistol-grip stock w/grooved forearm. Made 1935-39.

Stevens-Springfield Model 84 . . . . **$130**
Same as Model 86, except has 5-shot detachable box magazine. Pre-1948 rifles of this model were designated Springfield Model 84, later known as Stevens Model 84. Made 1940-65.

Stevens-Springfield Model 84-S (084) **$135**
Same as Model 84, except has peep rear sight and hooded front sight. Pre-1948 rifles of this model were designated Springfield Model 084, later known as Stevens Model 84-S. Discontinued.

Stevens-Springfield Model 85 . . . . **$165**
Same as Stevens Model 87, except has 5-shot detachable box magazine. Made 1939 to date. Pre-1948 rifles of this model were designated Springfield Model 85, currently known as Stevens Model 85. *See* illustration next page.

Stevens-Springfield Model 85-S (085) **$150**
Same as Model 85, except has peep rear sight and hooded front sight. Pre-1948 models were designated Springfield Model 085; also known as Stevens Model 85-S. *See* illustration next page.

Stevens-Springfield Model 86 Bolt-Action Repeater **$115**
Takedown. Caliber: 22 LR, Long, Short. Tubular magazine holds 15 LR, 17 Long, 21 Short. 24-inch bbl. Weight: about 6 lbs. Sights: open rear, gold bead front. Pistol-grip stock, black forend tip on later production. Made 1935-65. *Note:* The "Springfield" brand name was discontinued in 1948.

Stevens-Springfield Model 86-S (086) **$125**
Same as Model 86, except has peep rear sight and hooded front sight. Pre-1948 rifles of this model were designated as Springfield Model 086, later known as Stevens Model 86-S. Discontinued.

Stevens-Springfield Model 87-S (087) **$145**
Same as Stevens Model 87, except has peep rear sight and hooded front sight. Pre-1948 rifles of this model were designated as Springfield Model 087, later known as Stevens Model 87-S. Disc.

RIFLES

Stevens-Springfield Model 83

Stevens-Springfield Model 84

Stevens-Springfield Model 85

Stevens-Springfield Model 86-S

STEYR-DAIMLER-PUCH A.-G.
Steyr, Austria

See also listings under Mannlicher.

Steyr AUG-SA Semiautomatic Rifle **$3595**
Gas-operated. Caliber: 223 Rem. (5.56mm). 30- or 40-shot magazine. 20-inch bbl. standard; optional 16-inch or 24-inch heavy bbl. w/folding bipod. 31 inches overall. Weight: 8.5 lbs. Sights: Integral 1.5X scope and mount. Green high-impact synthetic stock w/folding vertical grip.

Steyr Small Bore Carbine **$425**
Bolt-action repeater. Caliber: 22 LR. 5-shot detachable box magazine. 19.5-inch bbl. Sights: leaf rear; hooded bead front. Mannlicher-type stock, checkered, swivels. Made 1953-67.

STOEGER RIFLE
Mfd. by Franz Jaeger & Co., Suhl, Germany; dist. in the U.S. by A. F. Stoeger, Inc., New York, N.Y.

Stoeger Hornet Rifle **$895**
Same as Herold Rifle. *See* listing of that rifle for specifications. Imported during the 1930s.

THOMPSON/CENTER ARMS
Rochester, New Hampshire

Thompson/Center Contender Carbine
Calibers: 22 LR, 22 Hornet, 222 Rem., 223 Rem., 7mm T.C.U., 7×30 Waters, 30-30 Win., 35 Rem., 44 Mag., 357 Rem. Max. and 410 bore. 21-inch interchangeable bbls. 35 inches overall. Adj. iron sights. Checkered American walnut or Rynite stock and forend. Made 1985 to date.
Standard Model (rifle calibers) **$335**
Standard Model (410 bore) 350
Rynite Stock Model (rifle calibers) 295
Rynite Stock Model (410 bore) 335
Extra Bbls. (rifle calibers) 155
Extra Bbls. (410 bore) 175
Youth Model (all calibers and 410 bore) 285

Thompson/Center Contender Carbine Survival System **$495**
Similar to the standard Contender Carbine with Rynite stock and forend. Comes with two 16.25-inch bbls., chambered in 223 and 45/.410 bore. Camo Cordura case.

Steyr Small Bore Carbine

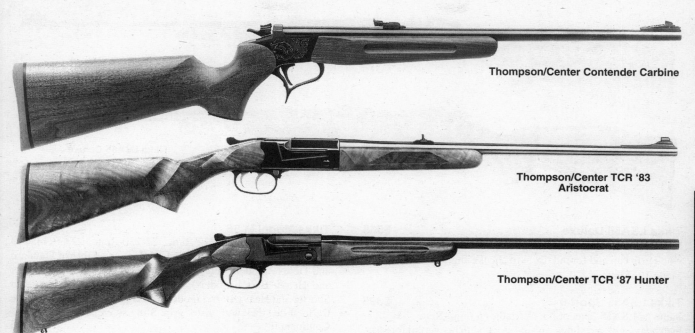

Thompson/Center Contender Carbine

Thompson/Center TCR '83 Aristocrat

Thompson/Center TCR '87 Hunter

RIFLES

Thompson/Center Stainless Contender Carbine

Same as the standard Contender Carbine Model, except stainless steel w/blued sights. Calibers: 22 LR, 22 Hornet, 223 Rem., 7-30 Waters, 30-30 Win., .410 Ga. Walnut or Rynite stock and forend. Made 1993 to date.

Walnut Stock Model **$395**
Rynite Stock Model 375
Youth Stock Model 350

Thompson/Center TCR '83 Aristocrat Model

Break frame, overlever action. Calibers: 223 Rem., 22/250 Rem., 243 Win., 7mm Rem. Mag., 30-06 Springfield. Interchangeable bbls.: 23 inches in length. Weight: 6 lbs., 14 oz. American walnut stock and forearm, checkered, black rubber recoil pad, cheekpiece. Made 1983-87.

TCR '83 Standard Model **$295**
TCR '83 Aristocrat 365

Thompson/Center TCR '87 Hunter Rifle

Similar to TCR '83, except in calibers 22 Hornet, 222 Rem., 223 Rem., 22-250 Rem., 243 Win., 270 Win., 7mm-08, 308 Win., 30-

Thompson/Center TCR '87 Hunter Rifle *(Cont.)*

06, 32-40 Win. Also 12-ga. slug and 10- and 12-ga. field bbls. 23-inch standard or 25.88-inch heavy bbl. interchangeable.39.5 to 43.38 inches overall. Weight: 6 lbs. 14 oz. to 7.5 lbs. Iron sights optional. Checkered American black walnut buttstock w/fluted end. Discontinued 1993.

Standard Model **$375**
Extra Bbl. (rifle calibers and 10- or 12-ga. Field) 190
Extra Bbl. (12-ga. slug) 225

TIKKA RIFLES
Produced in Italy by Armi Marocchi
Imported by Stoeger Industries, Inc.

Tikka Model 412S Double Rifle **$1075**
Formerly Valmet. Calibers: 308 Win., 30-06, 9.3×74R; automatic ejectors on 9.3×74R only. 24-inch bbl. 40 inches overall. Weight: 8.5 lbs. European walnut stock. Automatic ejectors. Manufactured in Italy from 1990 to date.

Tikka Model 412S Double Rifle

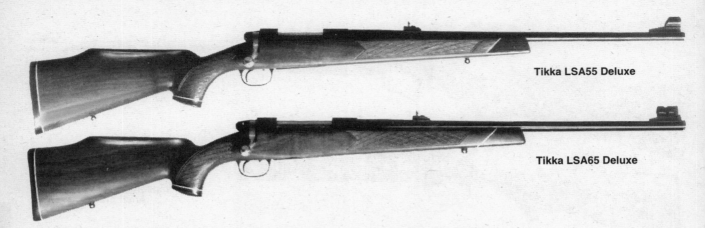

Tikka LSA55 Deluxe

Tikka LSA65 Deluxe

Tikka LSA55 Deluxe **$365**
Same as LSA55 Standard, except has rollover cheekpiece, rosewood grip cap and forend tip, skip checkering, high-luster blue. Made 1965-88.

Tikka LSA55 Sporter **$395**
Same as LSA55, except not available in 6mm Rem., has 22.8-inch heavy bbl., no sights, special stock with beavertail forearm, weighs about 9 lbs. Made 1965-88.

Tikka LSA55 Standard Bolt Action Repeater . . . **$350**
Mauser-type action. Calibers: 222 Rem., 22-250, 6mm Rem. Mag., 243 Win., 308 Win. 3-shot clip magazine. 22.8-inch bbl. Weight: 6.8 lbs. Sights: folding leaf rear; hooded ramp front. Checkered walnut stock w/Monte Carlo cheekpiece, swivels. Made 1965-88.

Tikka LSA65 Deluxe **$380**
Same as LSA65 Standard, except has special features of LSA55 Deluxe. Made 1970-88.

Tikka LSA65 Standard **$330**
Same as LSA55 Standard, except calibers: 25-06, 6.5×55 270 Win., 30-06. 5-shot magazine, 22-inch bbl., weighs 7.5 lbs. Made 1970-88.

Tikka Model M 55
Bolt action. Calibers: 222 Rem., 22-250 Rem., 223 Rem. 243 Win., 308 Win. (6mm Rem. and 17 Rem. available in Standard and Deluxe models only). 23.2-inch bbl. (24.8-inch in Sporter and Heavy Barrel models). 42.8 inches overall (44 inches in Sporter and Heavy Barrel models). Weight: 7.25 to 9 lbs. Monte Carlo-style stock with pistol grip. Sling swivels.

Continental	**$495**
Deluxe Model	500
Sporter	475
Sporter with sights	495
Standard	450
Super Sporter	540
Super Sporter with sights	575
Trapper	465

Tikka Model M 65
Bolt action. Calibers: 25-06, 270 Win., 308 Win., 30-06, 7mm Rem. Mag., 300 Win. Mag. (Sporter and Heavy Bbl. models in 270 Win., 308 Win. and 30-06 only). 22.4-inch bbl. (24.8-inch in Sporter and Heavy Bbl. models). 43.2 inches overall (44 inches in Sporter, 44.8 inches in Heavy Bbl.). Weight: 7.5 to 9.9 lbs. Monte Carlo-style stock w/pistol grip. Discontinued 1989.

Continental	**$530**
Deluxe Magnum	540
Deluxe Model	495

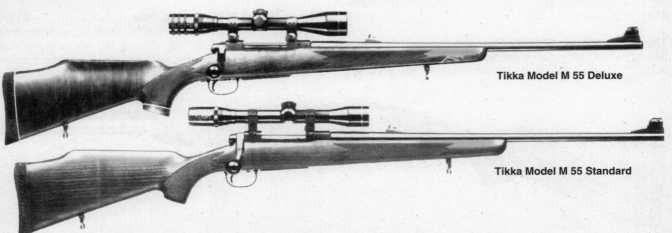

Tikka Model M 55 Deluxe

Tikka Model M 55 Standard

Tikka Model M 65 Sporter

Tikka Continental/Varmint

Tikka New Generation

Tikka Premium Grade Rifle

Tikka Model M 65 *(Cont.)*

Magnum **$485**
Sporter 470
Sporter with sights 525
Standard 450
Super Sporter 575
Super Sporter with sights 595
Super Sporter Master 730

Tikka Model M 65 Wildboar **$525**
Same general specifications as Model M 65, except 20.8-inch
bbl., overall length of 41.6 inches and weight of 7.5 lbs. Discontinued 1989.

Tikka Continental **$695**
Calibers: 223 Rem., 22-250 Rem., 243 Win., 308 Win. Overall
length: 43.75 inches. Weight 8.5 lbs. Prone-type stock and extra
wide forend for varmint or target shooting. Made 1991 to date.

Tikka New Generation **$575**
Bolt action. Calibers: 223 Rem., 22-250 Rem., 243 Win. 270
Win., 308 Win., 30-06, 7mm Rem. Mag., 300 Win. Mag., and
338 Win. Mag. 3- and 5-round magazines. 22-inch bbl.; 24
inches in Magnum. Weight: 7 lbs. 2 oz. Checkered walnut stock.
Oversized trigger guard. Made 1989 to date.

Tikka Model M 65 Wildboar

Tikka Whitetail/Battue

Tikka Premium Grade **$635**
Bolt action. Calibers: 223 Rem., 22-250 Rem., 243 Win. 270
Win., 308 Win., 30-06, 7mm Rem. Mag., 300 Win. Mag. and 338
Win. Mag. 3- and 5-round magazine. Hand-checkered with matte
lacquer stock and rollover cheekpiece. Rosewood pistol-grip cap
and forend tip. Deep blued bbl. Made 1990 to date.

Tikka Whitetail Battue **$575**
Calibers: 308 Win., 270 Win., 30-06, 7mm Mag., 300 Win.
Mag., 338 Win. Mag. 20.5-inch bbl. 40.5 inches overall.
Weight: 7 lbs. Sights: wide V-shaped rear; hooded front. Op-
tional 3-round detachable magazine. Matte lacquer stock.
Made 1991 to date.

Uberti Model 1873 Carbine

UBERTI USA, INC.
Lakeville, Connecticut

Uberti Model 1866 Sporting Rifle
Replica of Winchester Model 1866 lever-action repeater. Calibers: 22 LR, 22 WMR, 38 Spec., 44-40, 45 LC. 24.25-inch octagonal bbl. 43.25 inches overall. Weight: 8.25 lbs. Blade front sight,
rear elevation leaf. Brass frame and buttplate. Bbl., magazine
tube, other metal parts blued. Walnut buttstock and forearm.
Model 1866 Rifle **$495**
Model 1866 Carbine (19-inch Round Bbl.) **485**
Model 1866 Trapper (16-inch Bbl.) **470**

Uberti Model 1873 Sporting Rifle
Replica of Winchester Model 1873 lever-action repeater. Calib-
ers: 22 LR, 22 WMR, 38 Spec., 357 Mag., 44-40, 45 LC. 24.25-
or 30-inch octagonal bbl. 43.25 inches overall. Weight: 8 lbs.
Blade front sight; adj. open rear. Color casehardened frame. Bbl.,
magazine tube, hammer, lever and buttplate blued. Walnut butt-
stock and forearm.
Model 1873 Rifle **$555**
Model 1873 Carbine (19-inch Round Bbl.) **525**
Model 1873 Trapper (16-inch Bbl.) **495**

Uberti Henry Rifle
Replica of Henry lever-action repeating rifle. Calibers: 44-40, 45
LC. 24.5-inch half-octagon bbl. 43.75 inches overall. Weight:
9.25 lbs. Blade front sight; rear sight adj. for elevation. Brass
frame, buttplate and magazine follower. Bbl., magazine tube and
remaining parts blued. Walnut buttstock.
Henry Rifle **$550**
Henry Carbine (22.5-inch Bbl.) **525**
Henry Trapper (16- or 18-inch Bbl.) **560**

ULTRA-HI PRODUCTS COMPANY
Hawthorne, New Jersey

**Ultra-Hi Model 2200 Single-Shot
Bolt-Action Rifle** **$100**
Caliber: 22 LR, Long, Short. 23-inch bbl. Weight: about 5 lbs.
Sights: open rear; blade front. Monte Carlo stock w/pistol grip.
Made in Japan. Introduced 1977; disc.

Ultra-Hi Model 2200

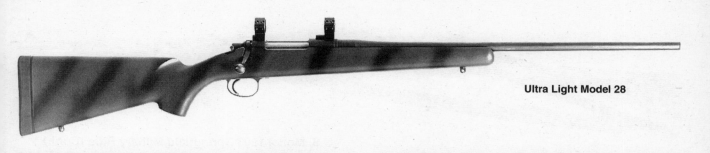

Ultra Light Model 28

ULTRA LIGHT ARMS COMPANY
Granville, West Virginia

Ultra Light Arms Model 20 Bolt-Action Rifle
Calibers: 22-250 Rem., 243 Win., 6mm Rem., 250-3000 Savage, 257 Roberts, 257 Ack., 7mm Mauser, 7mm Ack., 7mm-08 Rem., 284 Win., 300 Savage, 308 Win., 358 Win. Box magazine. 22-inch ultra light bbl. Weight: 4.75 lbs. No sights. Synthetic stock of Kevlar or graphite finished seven different colors. Nonglare matte or bright metal finish. Medium-length action available L.H. models.
Standard Model **$1570**
Left-hand Model **1655**

Ultra Light Arms Model 20S Bolt-Action Rifle
Same general specifications as the Model 20, except w/short action in calibers 17 Rem., 222 Rem., 223 Rem., 22 Hornet only.
Standard Model **$1595**
Left-hand Model **1695**

Ultra Light Arms Model 24 Bolt-Action Rifle
Same general specifications as the Model 20, except w/long action in calibers 25-06, 270 Win., 30-06 and 7mm Express only.
Standard Model **$1655**
Left-hand Model **1730**

Ultra Light Arms Model 28 Bolt-Action Rifle . . . $1850
Same general specifications as the Model 20, except w/long Magnum action in calibers 264 Win. Mag., 7mm Rem. Mag., 300 Win. Mag., 338 Win. Mag. only. Offered w/recoil arrestor. Left-hand model available.

Ultra Light Arms Model 40 Bolt-Action Rifle
Similar to the Model 28, except in calibers 300 Wby. and 416 Rigby. Weight: 5.5 lbs. Made 1994 to date.
Standard Model **$1850**
Left Hand, **add** **150**

UNIQUE RIFLE
Hendaye, France
Mfd. by Manufacture d'Armes des Pyrénées Francaises

Unique T66 Match Rifle **$5395**
Single-shot bolt-action rifle. Caliber: 22 LR. 25.5-inch bbl. Weight: about 10.5 lbs. Sights: micrometer aperture rear; globe front. French walnut target stock w/Monte Carlo comb, bull pistol grip, wide and deep forearm, stippled grip surfaces, adj. swivel on accessory track, adj. rubber buttplate. Made 1966 to date.

U.S. MILITARY RIFLES
Mfd. by Springfield Armory, Remington Arms Co., Winchester Repeating Arms Co., Inland Mfg. Div. of G.M.C., and other contractors. *See* notes.

Unless otherwise indicated, the following U.S. Military rifles were mfd. at Springfield Armory, Springfield, Mass.

U.S. Model 1898 Krag-Jorgensen Carbine **$750**
Same general specifications as Model 1898 Rifle, except has 22-inch bbl., weighs about 8 lbs., carbine-type stock. *Note:* The foregoing specifications apply, in general, to Carbine Models 1896 and 1899, which differed from Model 1898 only in minor details.

U.S. Model 1898 Krag-Jorgensen Military Rifle . . **$495**
Bolt action. Caliber: 30-40 Krag. 5-shot hinged box magazine. 30-inch bbl. Weight: about 9 lbs. Sights: adj. rear; blade front. Military-type stock, straight grip. *Note:* The foregoing specifications apply, in general, to Rifle Models 1892 and 1896, which differed from Model 1898.

U.S. Model 1898 Krag Rifle

U.S. Model 1903 Springfield

U.S. Model 1903 Mark I Springfield $745
Same as Standard Model 1903, except altered to permit use of the Pedersen Device. This device, officially designated "U.S. Automatic Pistol Model 1918," converted the M/1903 to a semiautomatic weapon firing a 30 caliber cartridge similar to the 32 automatic pistol ammunition. Mark I rifles have a slot milled in the left side of the receiver to serve as an ejection port when the Pedersen Device was in use; these rifles were also fitted with a special sear and cutoff. Some 65,000 of these devices were manufactured and presumably a like number of M/1903 rifles converted to handle them. During the early 1930s all Pedersen Devices were ordered destroyed and the Mark I rifles were reconverted by replacement of the special sear and cut-off with standard components. Some 20-odd specimens are known to have escaped destruction and are in government museums and private collections. Probably more are extant. Rarely is a Pedersen Device offered for sale, so a current value cannot be assigned. However, many of the altered rifles were bought by members of the National Rifle Association through the Director of Civilian Marksmanship. Value shown is for the Mark I rifle without the Pedersen Device.

U.S. Model 1903 National Match Springfield $995
Same general specifications as the Standard Model 1903, except specially selected with star-gauged bbl., Type C pistol-grip stock, polished bolt assembly; early types have headless firing pin assembly and reversed safety lock. Produced especially for target shooting.

U.S. Model 1903 Springfield Military Rifle
Modified Mauser-type bolt action. Caliber: 30-06. 5-shot box magazine. 23.79-inch bbl. Weight: about 8.75 lbs. Sights: adj. rear; blade front. Military-type stock straight grip. *Note:* M/1903 rifles of Springfield manufacture with serial numbers under 800,000 (1903-1918) have casehardened receivers; those between 800,000 and 1,275,767 (1918-1927) were double-heat-treated; rifles numbered over 1,275,767 have nickel-steel bolts and receivers. Rock Island production from No. 1 to 285,507 have case-

U.S. Model 1903 Springfield Military Rifle *(Cont.)*
hardened receivers. Improved heat treatment was adopted in May 1918 with No. 285,207; about three months later with No. 319,921 the use of nickel steel was begun, but the production of some double-heat-treated carbon-steel receivers and bolts continued. Made 1903-1930 at Springfield Armory; during WWI, M/1903 rifles were also made at Rock Island Arsenal, Rock Island, Ill.

W/casehardened receiver $185
W/double-heat-treated receiver 225
W/nickel steel receiver 350

U.S. Model 1903 Springfield Sporter $995
Same general specifications as the National Match, except has sporting design stock, Lyman No. 48 receiver sight.

U.S. Model 1903 Style T Springfield Match Rifle . . $1155
Same specifications as the Springfield Sporter, except has heavy bbl. (26-, 28- or 30-inch), scope bases, globe front sight, weighs about 12.5 lbs. with 26-inch bbl.

U.S. Model 1903 Type A Springfield Free Rifle . . . $1390
Same as Style T, except made with 28-inch bbl. only, has Swiss buttplate, weighs about 13.25 lbs.

U.S. Model 1903 Type B Springfield Free Rifle . . $1655
Same as Type A, except has cheekpiece stock, palmrest, Woodie double-set triggers, Garand fast firing pin, weighs about 14.75 lbs.

U.S. Model 1903-A1 Springfield
Same general specifications as Model 1903, except may have Type C pistol-grip stock adopted in 1930. The last Springfields produced at the Springfield Armory were of this type, final serial number was 1,532,878 made in 1939. *Note:* Late in 1941, the Remington Arms Co., Ilion, N.Y., began production under government contract of Springfield rifles of this type with a few minor modifications. These rifles are numbered 3,000,001-3,348,085 and were manufactured before the adoption of Model 1903-A3.

Springfield manufacture $365
Remington manufacture 315

U.S. Model 1903 Springfield Sporter

U.S. Model 1903-A1 Springfield

U.S. Model 1903-A3 Springfield

U.S. Model 1903-A3 Springfield **$395**
Same general specifications as Model 1903-A1, except modified
to permit increased production and lower cost; may have either
straight-grip or pistol-grip stock, bolt is not interchangeable with
earlier types, has receiver peep sight, many parts are stamped
sheet steel, including the trigger guard and magazine assembly.
Quality of these rifles, lower than that of other 1903 Springfields,
reflects the emergency conditions under which they were produced. Mfd. during WWII by Remington Arms Co. and L. C.
Smith Corona Typewriters, Inc.

U.S. Model 1922-M1 22 Springfield Target Rifle . . **$855**
Modified Model 1903. Caliber: 22 LR. 5-shot detachable box
magazine. 24.5-inch bbl. Weight: about 9 lbs. Sights: Lyman
No. 48C receiver, blade front. Sporting-type stock similar to
that of the Model 1903 Springfield Sporter. Issued 1927.
Note: The earlier Model 1922, which is seldom encountered,
differs from the foregoing chiefly in the bolt mechanism and
magazine.

U.S. M2 22 Springfield Target Rifle **$850**
Same general specifications as Model 1922-M1, except has
speedlock, improved bolt assembly adj. for headspace. *Note:*
These improvements were later incorporated in many rifles of
the preceding models (M1922, M1922MI) and arms so converted were marked "M1922M2" or "M1922MII."

U.S. Rifle, Caliber 30, M1 (Garand) Mil. Rifle **$725**
Clip-fed, gas-operated, air-cooled semiautomatic. Uses a clip
containing 8 rounds. 24-inch bbl. Weight: w/o bayonet, 9.5 lbs.
Sights: adj. peep rear; blade front w/guards. Pistol-grip stock,
handguards. Made 1937-57. *Note:* Garand rifles have also been
produced by Winchester Repeating Arms Co., Harrington &
Richardson Arms Co., and International Harvester Co. Deduct
25% for arsenal-assembled mismatches.

U.S. Rifle, Caliber 30, M1, National Match **$1150**
Accurized target version of the Garand. Glass-bedded stock;
match grade bbl., sights, gas cylinder. "NM" stamped on bbl. forward of handguard.

NOTE

The U.S. Model 1917 Enfield was mfd. 1917-18 by Remington Arms
Co. of Delaware (later Midvale Steel & Ordnance Co.), Eddystone,
PA; Remington Arms Co., Ilion, NY; Winchester Repeating Arms
Co., New Haven, CT.

U.S. Model 1917 Enfield Military Rifle **$275**
Modified Mauser-type bolt action. Caliber: 30-06. 5-shot box
magazine. 26-inch bbl. Weight: about 9.25 lbs. Sights: adj. rear;
blade front w/guards. Military-type stock w/semi-pistol grip.
This design originated in Great Britain as their "Pattern '14" and
was mfd. in caliber 303 for the British Government in three U.S.

U.S. Rifle Cal. 30 M1 (Garand)

U.S. Model 1917 Enfield

U.S. Carbine Cal. 30 M1

U.S. Model 1917 Enfield Military Rifle *(Cont.)*

plants. In 1917, the U.S. Government contracted with these firms to produce the same rifle in caliber 30-06; over two million of these Model 1917 Enfields were mfd. While no more were produced after WWI, the U.S. supplied over a million of them to Great Britain during WWII.

U.S. Carbine, Caliber 30, M1 . . . . $525

Gas-operated (short-stroke piston), semiautomatic. 15- or 30-round detachable box magazine. 18-inch bbl. Weight: about 5.5 lbs. Sights: adj. rear; blade front sight w/guards. Pistol-grip stock w/handguard, side-mounted web sling. Made 1942-45. In 1963, 150,000 surplus M1 Carbines were sold at $20 each to members of the National Rifle Assn. by the Dept. of the Army. *Note:* For Winchester and Rock-Ola, add 30%; for Irwin Pedersen, add 80%. Quality Hardware did not complete its production run. Guns produced by other manufacturers were marked "Unquality" & command premium prices.

NOTE
The WWII-vintaqe 30-caliber U.S. Carbine was mfd. by Inland Mfg. Div. of G.M.C., Dayton, OH; Winchester Repeating Arms Co., New Haven, CT, and other contractors: International Business Machines Corp., Poughkeepsie, NY; National Postal Meter Co., Rochester, NY; Quality Hardware & Machine Co., and Rock-Ola Co., Chicago, IL; Saginaw Steering Gear Div. of G.M.C., Saginaw, M1; Standard Products Co., Port Clinton, OH; Underwood-Elliott-Fisher Co., Hartford, CT.

U.S. REPEATING ARMS CO.

See **Winchester Rifle listings.**

UNIVERSAL SPORTING GOODS, INC.
Miami, Florida

Universal Deluxe Carbine $195
Same as standard model, except also available in caliber 256, has deluxe walnut Monte Carlo stock and handguard. Made 1965 to date.

Universal Standard M-1 Carbine $180
Same as U.S. Carbine, Cal.30, M1, except may have either wood or metal handguard, bbl. band with or w/o bayonet lug; 5-shot magazine standard. Made 1964 to date.

UZI CARBINE
Mfd. by Israel Military Industries, Israel

Uzi Semiautomatic Model B Carbine $995
Calibers: 9mm Parabellum, 41 Action Express, 45 ACP. 20- to 50-round magazine. 16.1-inch bbl. Weight: 8.4 lbs. Metal folding stock. Front post-type sight, open rear, both adjustable. Imported by Action Arms 1983-89.

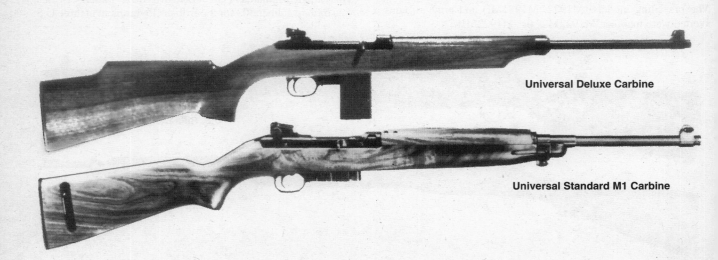

Universal Deluxe Carbine

Universal Standard M1 Carbine

Uzi Carbine

VALMET OY
Jyväskylä, Finland

Valmet M-62S Semiautomatic Rifle **$1195**
Semiautomatic version of Finnish M-62 automatic assault rifle based on Russian AK-47. Gas-operated rotating-bolt action. Caliber: 7.62mm×39 Russian. 15- and 30-round magazines. 16.63-inch bbl. Weight: about 8 lbs. w/metal stock. Sights: tangent aperture rear; hooded blade front w/luminous flip-up post for low-light use. Tubular steel or wood stock. Introduced 1962, discontinued.

Valmet M-71S **$995**
Same specifications as M-62S, except caliber 5.56mm×45 (223 Rem.), has open rear sight, reinforced resin or wood stock, weighs 7.75 lbs. with former. Made 1971 to date.

Valmet M-76 Semiautomatic Rifle
Semiautomatic assault rifle. Gas-operated, rotating bolt action. Caliber: 223 Rem. 15- and 30-shot magazines. Made 1984 to date.
Wooden stock . . . . **$ 925**
Folding stock **1195**

Valmet M-78 Semiautomatic Rifle **$1155**
Caliber: 7.62×51 (NATO). 24.13-inch bbl. Overall length: 43.25 inches. Weight: 10.5 lbs.

Valmet M-82 Semiautomatic Carbine **$1690**
Caliber: 223 Rem. 15- or 30-shot magazine. 17-inch bbl. 27 inches overall. Weight: 7.75 lbs.

Valmet Model 412 S Double Rifle **$795**
Boxlock. Manual or automatic extraction. Calibers: 243, 308, 30-06, 375 Win., 9.3×74R. Bbls.: 24-inch over/under. Weight: 8.63 lbs. American walnut checkered stock and forend.

Valmet Hunter Semiautomatic Rifle **$755**
Similar to the M-78, except in calibers 223 Rem. (5.56mm), 243 Win., 308 Win. (7.62 NATO) and 30-06. 5-, 9- or 15-shot magazine. 20.5-inch plain bbl. 42 inches overall. Weight: 8 lbs. Sights: adj. 412 combination scope mount/rear; blade front, mounted on gas tube. Checkered European walnut buttstock and extended checkered forend and handguard. Imported since 1986.

Valmet M-62S

Valmet Hunter

Vickers Jubilee Model

VICKERS LTD.
Crayford, Kent, England

Vickers Empire Model **$325**
Similar to Jubilee Model, except has 27- or 30-inch bbl., straight-grip stock, weighs about 9.25 lbs. with 30-inch bbl. Made before WWII.

Vickers Jubilee Model Single-Shot Target Rifle . . **$395**
Round-receiver Martini-type action. Caliber: 22 LR. 28-inch heavy bbl. Weight: about 9.5 lbs. Sights: Parker-Hale No.2 front; Perfection rear peep. One-piece target stock w/full forearm and pistol grip. Made before WWII.

VOERE, VOELTER & COMPANY
Vaehrenbach, Germany

Mauser-Werke acquired Voere in 1987 and all models are now marketed under new designations.

Voere Model 1007 Biathlon Repeater **$255**
Caliber: 22 LR. 5-shot magazine. 19.5-inch bbl. 39 inches overall. Weight: 5.5 lb. Sights: adj. rear, blade front. Plain beechwood stock. Imported 1984-86.

Voere Model 1013 Bolt-Action Repeater **$445**
Same as Model 1007, except with military-style stock in 22 WMR caliber. Double-set triggers optional. Imported 1984-86 by KDF, Inc.

Voere Model 2107 Bolt-Action Repeater
Caliber: 22 LR. 5 or 8-shot magazine. 19.5-inch bbl. 41 inches overall. Weight: 6 lbs. Sights: adj. rear sight, hooded front. European hardwood Monte Carlo-style stock. Imported 1986 by KDF, Inc.
Standard Model **$195**
Deluxe Model **225**

WALTHER RIFLES
Mfd. by the German firms of Waffenfabrik Walther and Carl Walther Sportwaffenfabrik

The following Walther rifles were mfd. before WWII by Waffenfabrik Walther, Zella-Mehlis (Thür.), Germany.

Walther Model 1 Autoloading Rifle (Light) **$335**
Similar to Standard Model 2, but with 20-inch bbl., lighter stock, weighs about 4.5 lbs.

Walther Model 2 Autoloading Rifle **$445**
Bolt action, may be used as autoloader, manually operated repeater or single shot. Caliber: 22 LR. 5- or 9-shot detachable box magazine. 24.5-inch bbl. Weight: about 7 lbs. Sights: tangent-curve rear; ramp front. Sporting stock w/checkered pistol grip, grooved forearm, swivels. Discontinued.

Walther Olympic Bolt-Action Match Rifle **$925**
Single-shot. Caliber: 22 LR. 26-inch heavy bbl. Weight: about 13 lbs. Sights: micrometer extension rear; interchangeable front. Target stock w/checkered pistol grip, thumbhole, full beavertail forearm covered w/corrugated rubber, palmrest, adj. Swiss-type buttplate, swivels. Discontinued.

Walther Model 1

Walther Model 2

Walther Model GX-1

Walther Model KKM-S

Walther Model U.I.T. Super Match

Walther Model V Bolt-Action Single-Shot Rifle . . $390
Caliber: 22 LR. 26-inch bbl. Weight: about 7 lbs. Sights: open rear; ramp front. Plain pistol-grip stock w/grooved forearm. Discontinued.

Walther Model V Meisterbüchse (Champion) . . . $435
Same as standard Model V, except has micrometer open rear sight and checkered pistol grip. Discontinued.

Post WWII Models

The Walther rifles listed below have been manufactured since WWII by Carl Walther Sportwaffenfabrik, Ulm (Donau), Germany.

Walther Model GX-1 Free Rifle $1355
Bolt action, single shot. Caliber: 22 LR. 25.5-inch heavy bbl. Weight: 15.9 lbs. Sights: micrometer aperture rear; globe front. Thumbhole stock w/adj. cheekpiece and buttplate w/removable hook, accessory rail. Left-hand stock available. Accessories furnished include hand stop and sling swivel, palmrest, counterweight assembly.

Walther Model KKJ Sporter $525
Bolt action. Caliber: 22 LR. 5-shot box magazine. 22.5-inch bbl. Weight: 5.5 lbs. Sights: open rear; hooded ramp front. Stock w/cheekpiece, checkered pistol grip and forearm, sling swivels. Discontinued.

Walther Model KKJ-Ho $665
Same as Model KKJ, except chambered for 22 Hornet. Discontinued.

Walther Model KKJ-Ma $495
Same as Model KKJ, except chambered for 22 WMR. Discontinued.

Walther Model KKM International Match Rifle . . $825
Bolt action, single shot. Caliber: 22 LR. 28-inch heavy bbl. Weight: 15.5 lbs. Sights: micrometer aperture rear; globe front. Thumbhole stock w/high comb, adj. hook buttplate, accessory rail. Left-hand stock available. Discontinued.

Walther Model KKM-S $795
Same specifications as Model KKM, except has adj. cheekpiece. Discontinued.

Walther Moving Target Match Rifle $625
Bolt action, single shot. Caliber: 22 LR. 23.6-inch bbl. w/weight. Weight: 8.6 lbs. Supplied w/o sights. Thumbhole stock w/adj. cheekpiece and buttplate. Left-hand stock available.

Walther Prone 400 Target Rifle $695
Bolt action, single shot. Caliber: 22 LR. 25.5-inch heavy bbl. Weight: 10.25 lbs. Supplied w/o sights. Prone stock w/adj. cheekpiece and buttplate, accessory rail. Left-hand stock available. Discontinued.

Walther Model SSV Varmint Rifle **$550**
Bolt action, single shot. Calibers: 22 LR, 22 Hornet. 25.5-inch bbl. Weight: 6.75 lbs. Supplied w/o sights. Monte Carlo stock w/high cheekpiece, full pistol grip and forearm. Discontinued.

Walther Model U.I.T. Special Match Rifle **$870**
Bolt action, single shot. Caliber: 22 LR. 25.5-inch bbl. Weight: 10.2 lbs. Sights: Micrometer aperture rear; globe front. Target stock w/high comb, adj. buttplate, accessory rail. Left-hand stock avail. Discontinued 1993.

Walther Model U.I.T. Super Match Rifle **$925**
Bolt action, single shot. Caliber: 22 LR. 25.5-inch heavy bbl. Weight: 10.2 lbs. Micrometer aperture rear; globe front. Target stock w/support for off-hand shooting, high comb, adj. buttplate and swivel. Left-hand stock available. Discontinued 1993.

MONTGOMERY WARD
Chicago, Illinois
Western Field and Hercules Models

Firearms under the "private label" names of Western Field and Hercules are manufactured by such firms as Mossberg, Stevens, Marlin, and Savage for distribution and sale by Montgomery Ward.

Montgomery Ward Model 14M-497B Western Field Bolt-Action Rifle **$80**
Caliber: 22 RF. 7-shot detachable box magazine. 24-inch bbl. Weight: about 5 lbs. Sights: receiver peep; open rear; hooded ramp front. Pistol-grip stock. Mfd. by Mossberg.

Montgomery Ward Model M771 Western Field Lever-Action Rifle **$155**
Calibers: 30-30, 35 Rem. 6-shot tubular magazine. 20-inch bbl. Weight: 6.75 lbs. Sights: open rear; ramp front. Pistol-grip or straight stock, forearm w/barrel band. Mfd. by Mossberg.

Montgomery Ward Model M772 Western Field Lever-Action Rifle **$175**
Calibers: 30-30, 35 Rem. 6-shot tubular magazine. 20-inch bbl. Weight: 6.75 lbs. Sights: open rear; ramp front. Pistol-grip or straight stock, forearm with bbl. band. Mfd. by Mossberg.

Montgomery Ward Model M775 Bolt-Action Rifle **$190**
Calibers: 222 Rem., 22-250, 243 Win., 308 Win. 4-shot magazine. Weight: about 7.5 lbs. Sights: folding leaf rear; ramp front. Monte Carlo stock w/cheekpiece, pistol grip. Mfd by Mossberg.

Montgomery Ward Model M776 Bolt-Action Rifle **$195**
Calibers: 222 Rem., 22-250, 243 Win., 308 Win. 4-shot magazine. Weight: about 7.5 lbs. Sights: folding leaf rear; ramp front. Monte Carlo stock w/cheekpiece, pistol grip. Mfd. by Mossberg.

Montgomery Ward Model M778 Lever-Action Rifle **$165**
Calibers: 30-30, 35 Rem. 6-shot tubular magazine. 20-inch bbl. Weight: 6.75 lbs. Sights: open rear; ramp front. Pistol-grip or straight stock, forearm w/bbl. band. Mfd. by Mossberg.

Montgomery Ward Model M780 Bolt-Action Rifle **$195**
Calibers: 222 Rem., 22-250, 243 Win., 308 Win. 4-shot magazine. Weight: about 7.5 lbs. Sights: folding leaf rear; ramp front. Monte Carlo stock w/cheekpiece, pistol grip. Mfd. by Mossberg.

Montgomery Ward Model M782 Bolt-Action Rifle **$195**
Same general specifications as Model M780.

Montgomery Ward Model M808 . . . . **$85**
Takedown. Caliber: 22RF. 15-shot tubular magazine. Bbls.: 20- and 24-inch. Weight: about 6 lbs. Sights: open rear; bead front. Pistol-grip stock. Mfd. by Stevens.

Montgomery Ward Model M832 Bolt-Action Rifle . **$90**
Caliber: 22 RF. 7-shot clip magazine. 24-inch bbl. Weight: 6.5 lbs. Sights: open rear; ramp front. Mfd. by Mossberg.

Montgomery Ward Model M836 . . . . **$95**
Takedown. Caliber: 22RF. 15-shot tubular magazine. Bbls.: 20- and 24-inch. Weight: about 6 lbs. Sights: open rear; bead front. Pistol-grip stock. Mfd. by Stevens.

Montgomery Ward Model M865 Lever-Action Carbine **$120**
Hammerless. Caliber: 22RF. Tubular magazine. Made with both 18.5-inch and 20-inch bbls., forearm with bbl. band, swivels. Weight: about 5 lbs. Mfd. by Mossberg.

Montgomery Ward Model M894 Autoloading Carbine **$115**
Caliber: 22 RF. 15-shot tubular magazine. 20-inch bbl. Weight: about 6 lbs. Sights: open rear; ramp front. Monte Carlo stock w/pistol grip. Mfd. by Mossberg.

Montgomery Ward Model M-SD57 . . . . **$90**
Takedown. Caliber: 22RF. 15-shot tubular magazine. Bbls.: 20- and 24-inch. Weight: about 6 lbs. Sights: open rear; bead front. Pistol-grip stock. Mfd. by Stevens.

WEATHERBY, INC.
South Gate, California

Weatherby Classicmark I Rifle
Same general specifications as Mark V, except with checkered select American Claro walnut stock with oil finish and presentation recoil pad. Satin metal finish. Made 1992-93.

Calibers 240 to 300 Wby.	**$750**
Caliber 340 Wby.	795
Caliber 378 Wby.	825
Caliber 416 Wby.	895
Caliber 460 Wby.	950

Weatherby Classicmark I

Weatherby Crown Custom Rifle

Weatherby Classicmark II Rifle
Same general specifications as Classicmark I, except with checkered select American walnut stock with oil finish steel grip cap and Old English recoil pad. Satin metal finish. Right-hand only. Made 1992-93.

Calibers 240 to 340 Wby. (26-inch bbl.)	**$1150**
Caliber 378 Wby.	1225
Caliber 416 Wby.	1350
Caliber 460 Wby.	1425

Weatherby Crown Custom Rifle . . . . $2400+
Calibers: 240, 30-06, 257, 270, 7mm, 300, and 340. Bbl.: made to order. Super fancy walnut stock. Also available w/engraved barraled action including gold animal overlay.

Weatherby Deluxe 378 Magnum Rifle $1790
Same general specifications as Deluxe Magnum in other calibers, except caliber 378 W. M. Schultz & Larsen action; 26-inch bbl. Discontinued 1958.

Weatherby Deluxe Magnum Rifle $1290
Calibers: 220 Rocket, 257 Weatherby Mag., 270 W.M. 7mm W.M., 300 W.M., 375 W.M. Specially processed FN Mauser action. 24-inch bbl. (26-inch in 375 cal.). Monte Carlo-style stock with cheekpiece, black forend tip, grip cap, checkered pistol grip and forearm, quick-detachable sling swivels. Value shown is for rifle w/o sights. Discontinued 1958.

Weatherby Deluxe Rifle $995
Same general specifications as Deluxe Magnum, except chambered for standard calibers such as 270, 30-06, etc. Discontinued 1958.

Weatherby Fiberguard™ Rifle $425
Same general specifications as Vanguard except for fiberglass stock and matte metal finish.

Weatherby Fibermark™ Rifle $895
Same general specifications as Mark V except with molded fiberglass stock, finished in a nonglare black wrinkle finish. The metal is finished in a non-glare matte finish. Discontinued 1993.

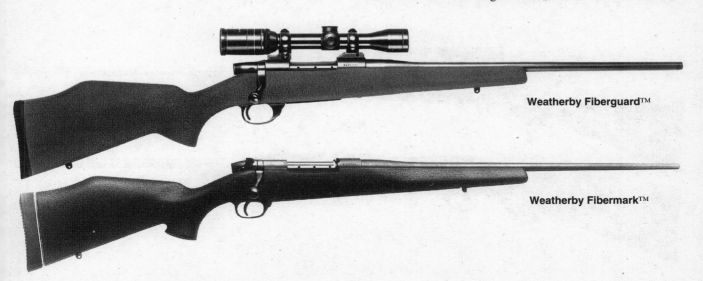

Weatherby Fiberguard™

Weatherby Fibermark™

RIFLES

Weatherby Mark V Deluxe

Weatherby Mark V Euromark

Weatherby Mark V Deluxe Bolt Action Sporting Rifle

Mark V action, right or left hand. Calibers: 22-250, 30-06- 224 Weatherby Varmintmaster; 240, 257, 270, 7mm, 300, 340, 378, 416, 460 Weatherby Magnums. Box magazine holds 2 to 5 cartridges depending on caliber. 24- or 26-inch bbl. Weight: 6.5 to 10.5 lbs. Monte Carlo-style stock with cheekpiece, skip checkering, forend tip, pistol-grip cap, recoil pad, QD swivels. Values shown are for rifles w/o sights. Made in Germany 1958-69; in Japan 1970-94.

Calibers 22-250, 224	**$795**
Caliber 378 Weatherby Magnum	895
Caliber 460 Weatherby Magnum	995
Other calibers	675
Add for left-hand action	100

Deduct 30% if Japanese-made

Weatherby Mark V Euromark Bolt-Action Rifle .. $995

Same general specifications as other Mark V rifles, except has hand-rubbed, satin oil finish Claro walnut stock and nonglare special process blue matte barreled action. Left-hand models available. Made 1986-93; reintro. 1995.

Weatherby Mark V Lazermark Rifle $945

Same general specifications as Mark V except with lazer-carved stock.

Weatherby Mark V Safari Grade Rifle $1695

Same general specifications as Mark V except extra capacity magazine, bbl. sling swivel, and express rear sight typical "Safari" style.

Weatherby Mark V Sporter Rifle

Sporter version of the Mark V, with low-luster metal finish. Stock without grip cap or forend tip. No sights. Made 1993 to date.

Calibers 257 to 300 Wby	**$550**
34() Weatherby	565
375 H&H	655
Other Non-Wby. Calibers	500

Weatherby Mark XXII Deluxe 22 Automatic Sporter Clip-fed Model $295

Semiautomatic with single-shot selector. Caliber: 22 LR. 5- and 10-shot clip magazines. 24-inch bbl. Weight: 6 lbs. Sights: folding leaf open rear; ramp front. Monte Carlo-type stock w/cheekpiece, pistol grip, forend tip, grip cap, skip checkering, QD swivels. Introduced 1964. Made in Italy 1964-69; in Japan, 1970-1981; in the U.S., 1982-90.

Weatherby Mark V Lazermark

Weatherby Mark V Safari Grade

Weatherby Mark XXII Clip-fed

Weatherby Mark XXII, Tubular Magazine Model . . **$275**
Same as Mark XXII, Clip-fed Model, except has 15-shot tubular magazine. Made in Japan 1973-81; in the U.S.,1882-90.

Weatherby Vanguard (I) Bolt-Action Sporting Ritle
Mauser-type action. Calibers: 243 Win., 25-06, 270 Win., 7mm Rem. Mag., 30-06, 300 Win. Mag. 5-shot magazine; (3-shot in Magnum calibers).24-inch bbl. Weight: 7 lbs. 14 oz. No sights. Monte Carlo-type stock w/cheekpiece, rosewood forend tip and pistol-grip cap, checkering, rubber buttpad, QD swivels. Made in Japan i970-84.
Vanguard Standard **$325**
Vanguard VGL (w/shorter 20-inch bbl., plain checkered
   stock matte finish, 6.5 lbs **335**
Vanguard VGS (wj24-inch bbl., plain checkered stock,
   matte finish **355**
Vanguard VGX (w/higher grade finish) **395**

Weatherby Vanguard Classic I Rifle **$365**
Same general specifications as Vanguard VGX Deluxe, except with hand-checkered classic-style stock, black buttpad and satin finish. Calibers 223 Rem., 243 Win. 270 Win., 7mm-08, 7mm Rem. Mag., 30-06 and 308 Win. Made 1989-94.

Weatherby Vanguard Classic II Rifle **$575**
Same general specifications as Vanguard VGX Deluxe, except custom checkered classic-style American walnut stock with black forend tip, grip cap and solid black recoil pad, satin finish. Made 1989-94.

Weatherby Vanguard VGX Deluxe **$515**
Calibers: 22-250 Rem., 243 Rem., 270 Wby. Mag., 270 Win., 7mm Rem. Mag., 30-06, 300 Win. Mag., 300 Wby. Mag., 338 Win. Mag. 3- or 5-round capacity. 24-inch bbl. About 44 inches overall. Weight: 7 to 8.5 lbs. Custom checkered American walnut stock with Monte Carlo and recoil pad. Rosewood forend tip and pistol-grip cap. High-luster finish. Discontinued 1994.

Weatherby Varmintmaster Bolt-Action Rifle **$895**
Calibers: 224 Wby., 22-250, 4-shot magazine. 26-inch bbl. 45 inches overall. Weight: 7.75 lbs. Checkered walnut stock. No sights. Discontinued.

Weatherby Weathermark Rifle
Same general specifications as Classicmark, except with checkered black Weathermark™ composite stock. Mark V bolt action. Calibers: 240, 257, 270, 300, 340, 378, 416 and 460 Weatherby Magnums; plus 270 Win., 7mm Rem. Mag., 30-06 and 375 H&H Mag. Weight: 8 to 10 lbs. Right-hand only. Made 1992 to date.
Calibers 257 to 300 Wby **$475**
Caliber 340 Weatherby **495**
375 H&H **595**
Other non-Wby. calibers **455**

Weatherby Weathermark Alaskan Rifle **$635**
Same general specifications as the Weathermark, except with nonglare electroless nickel finish. Right-hand only. Made 1992 to date.

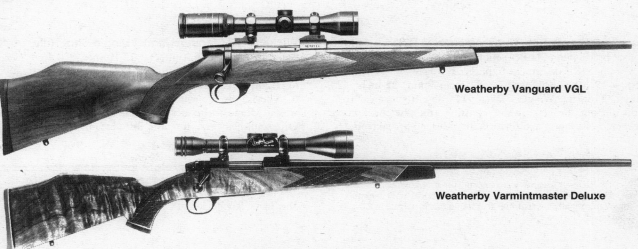

Weatherby Vanguard VGL

Weatherby Varmintmaster Deluxe

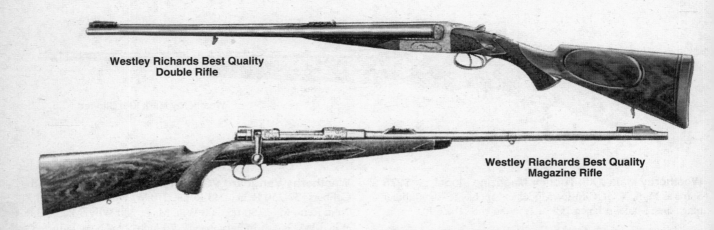

Westley Richards Best Quality
Double Rifle

Westley Riachards Best Quality
Magazine Rifle

WESTERN FIELD RIFLES

See listings under "W" for Montgomery Ward.

WESTLEY RICHARDS & CO., LTD.
London, England

Westley Richards Best Quality Double Rifle . . **$29,500**
Boxlock, hammerless, ejector. Hand-detachable locks. Calibers:
30-06, 318 Accelerated Express, 375 Mag., 425 Mag. Express,
465 Nitro Express, 470 Nitro Express. 25-inch bbls. Weight: 8.5
to 11 lbs. Sights: leaf rear; hooded front. French walnut stock
w/cheekpiece, checkered pistol grip and forend.

Wickliffe '76 Standard
Single-Shot Rifle

Westley Richards Best Quality Magazine Rifle . . **$6,890**
Mauser or Magnum Mauser action. Calibers: 7mm High Velocity, 30-06, 318 Accelerated Express, 375 Mag., 404 Nitro Express, 425 Mag. Bbl. lengths: 24-inch; 7mm, 22-inch; 425
caliber, 25-inch. Weight 7.25 to 9.25 lbs. Sights: leaf rear;
hooded front. French walnut sporting stock w/cheekpiece,
checkered pistol grip and forearm, horn forend tip, swivels.

NOTE

Westley Richards firearms were custom built for individual customers. Although the calibers listed under each model were the most
common, virtually any cartridge that would fit and operate in the action could be had on special order.

WICKLIFFE RIFLES
Wickliffe, Ohio
Mfd. by Triple S Development Co., Inc.

Wickliffe '76 Commemorative Model **$650**
Limited edition of 100. Same as Deluxe Model, except has filled
etching on receiver sidewalls, U.S. silver dollar inlaid in stock, 26-
inch bbl. only, comes in presentation case. Made in 1976 only.

Wickliffe '76 Deluxe Model **$395**
Same as Standard Model, except 22-inch bbl. in 30-06 only, has
high-luster blued finish, fancy-grade figured American walnut
stock with nickel silver grip cap.

Wickliffe '76 Standard Model Single-Shot Rifle . . **$335**
Falling-block action. Calibers: 22 Hornet, 223 Rem., 22-250,
243 Win., 25-06, 308 Win., 30-06, 45-70. 22-inch lightweight
bbl. (243 and 308 only) or 26-inch heavy sporter bbl. Weight:
6.75 or 8.5 lbs., depending on bbl. No sights. Select American
walnut Monte Carlo stock with right or left cheekpiece and pistol
grip, semi-beavertail forearm. Introduced 1976; discontinued.

TED WILLIAMS RIFLES

See Sears, Roebuck and Company.

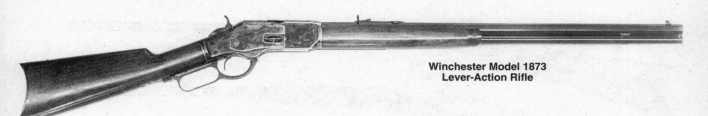

**Winchester Model 1873
Lever-Action Rifle**

WINCHESTER RIFLES
Winchester Repeating Arms Company
New Haven, Connecticut

Early Models 1873 – 1918

NOTE

Most Winchester rifles manufactured prior to 1918 used the date of approximate manufacture as the Model number. For example, the Model 1894 repeating rifle was manufactured from 1894 to 1937. When Winchester started using two-digit model numbers after 1918, the "18" was dropped and the rifle was then called the Model 94. The Model 1892 was called the Model 92, etc.

Winchester Model 1873 Lever-Action Carbine . . **$3295**
Same as Standard Model 1873 Rifle, except has 20-inch bbl., 12-shot magazine, weighs 7.25 lbs.

Winchester Model 1873 Lever-Action Rifle **$2750**
Calibers: 32-20, 38-40, 44-40; a few were chambered for 22 rimfire. 15-shot magazine, also made with 6-shot half magazine. 24-inch bbl. (round, half-octagon, octagon). Weight: about 8.5 lbs. Sights: open rear; bead or blade front. Plain straight-grip stock and forearm. Made 1873-1924. 720,610 rifles of this model were mfd.

**Close-up of barrel engraving on Winchester Model 1873
One of One Thousand.**

**Winchester Model 1873 — One of One
Thousand** . . . . **$50,000+**
During the late 1870s Winchester offered Model 1873 rifles of superior accuracy and extra finish, designated "One of One Thousand" grade, at $100. These rifles are marked "1 of 1000" or "One of One Thousand." Only 136 of this model are known to have been manufactured. This is one of the rarest of shoulder arms and, because so very few have been sold in recent years, it is extremely difficult to assign a value; however, in the author's opinion, an "excellent" specimen would probably bring a price upward of $50,000.

**Alternate barrel inscription designating a Winchester
Model 1873 "1 of 1000."**

Winchester Model 1873 Special Sporting Rifle . . **$3295**
Same as Standard Model 1873 Rifle, except this type has receiver casehardened in colors, pistol-grip stock of select walnut, octagon bbl. only.

Winchester Model 1885 Single-Shot Rifle
Designed by John M. Browning, this falling-block, lever-action rifle was manufactured from 1885 to 1920 in a variety of models and chambered for most of the popular cartridges of the period — both rimfire and centerfire — from 22 to 50 caliber. There are two basic styles of frames, low-wall and high-wall. The low-wall was chambered only for the lower-powered cartridges, while the high-wall was supplied in all calibers and made in three basic types: the standard model for No. 3 and heavier barrels is the type commonly encountered; the thin-walled version was supplied with No. 1 and No. 2 light barrels and the thick-walled action in the heavier calibers. Made in both solid frame and takedown versions.

Barrels were available in five weights ranging from the lightweight No. 1 to the extra heavy No. 5 in round, half-octagon and full-octagon styles. Many other variations were also offered.

**Winchester Model 1885 High-Wall
Sporting Rifle** **$1425**
Solid frame or takedown. No. 3, 30-inch bbl., standard. Weight: 9.5 lbs. Standard trigger and lever. Open rear sights; blade front sight. Plain stock and forend.

**Winchester Model 1885 Low-Wall
Sporting Rifle** **$925**
Solid frame. No. 1, 28-inch round or octagon bbl. Weight: 7 lbs. Open rear sight; blade front sight. Plain stock and forend.

Winchester Model 1885 Scheutzen Rifle **$3995**
Solid frame or takedown. High-wall action. Scheutzen double-set trigger. Spur finger lever. No. 3, 30-inch octagon bbl. Weight: 12 lbs. Vernier rear peep sight; wind-gauge front sight. Fancy walnut Scheutzen stock with checkered pistol-grip and forend. Scheutzen buttplate; adj. palmrest.

Winchester Model 1885 Special Sporting Rifle . . **$1295**
Same general specifications as the standard high-wall model except with checkered fancy walnut stock and forend.

RIFLES

Winchester Model 1885
Sporting Rifle

Winchester Model 1885
Schuetzen Rifle

Winchester Model 1885 Musket

Winchester Model 1885 Single-Shot Musket $950
Solid frame. Low-wall. Calibers: 22 Short and Long Rifle. 28-inch round bbl. Weight: 8.6 lbs. Lyman rear peep sight; blade front sight. Military-type stock and forend. *Note:* The U.S. Government purchased a large quantity of these muskets during World War I for training purposes.

Winchester Model 1885 Single-Shot "Winder" Musket $695
Solid frame or takedown. High-wall. Plain trigger. 28-inch round bbl. Weight: 8.5 lbs. Musket rear sight; blade front sight. Military-type stock and forend w/bbl. band and sling stud/rings.

Winchester Model 1886 Lever-Action Rifle
Solid frame or takedown. Calibers: 33 Win., 38-56, 38-70, 40-65, 40-70, 40-82, 45-70, 45-90, 50-100, 50-110. The 33 Win. and 45-70 were the last calibers in which this model was supplied. 8-shot tubular magaine; also 4-shot half-magazine. 26-inch bbl. (round, half-octagon, octagon). Weight: 7.5 lbs. Sights: open rear; bead or blade front. Plain straight-grip stock and forend or standard models. Made 1886-1935.
Standard Model................................. $3150
Takedown Model 3500
Deluxe Model (pistol grip and high-quality walnut) ... 6000

Winchester Model 1886 Saddle-Ring Carbine .. $8250
Same as standard rifle, except with 22-inch bbl., carbine buttstock and forend. Carbine rear sight. Saddle ring on left side of receiver.

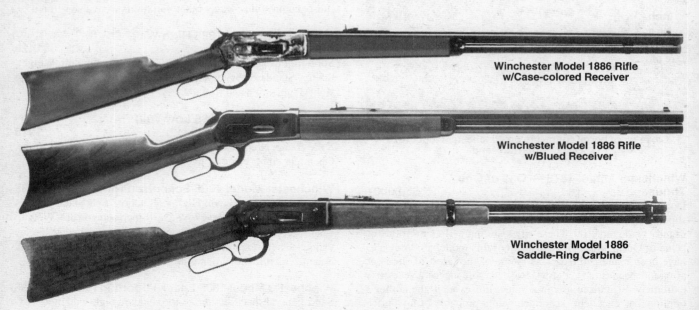

Winchester Model 1886 Rifle
w/Case-colored Receiver

Winchester Model 1886 Rifle
w/Blued Receiver

Winchester Model 1886
Saddle-Ring Carbine

Winchester Model 1890

Winchester Model 1892 Rifle

Winchester Model 1890 Slide-Action Rifle

Visible hammer. Calibers: 22 Short, Long, LR; 22 WRF (not interchangeable). Tubular magazine holds 15 Short, 12 Long, 11 LR; 12 WRF. 24-inch octagon bbl. Weight: 5.75 lbs. Sights: open rear; bead front. Plain straight-grip stock, grooved slide handle. Originally solid frame; after No. 15,499, all rifles of this model were takedown type. Fancy checkered pistol-grip stock, nickel-steel bbl. supplied at extra cost, which can also increase the value by 100% or more. Made 1890-1932.

Blue	$ 695
Blue (22 WRF)	1150
Case-Colored Receiver	3550

Winchester Model 1892 Lever-Action Rifle $1650

Solid frame or takedown. Calibers: 25-20, 32-20, 38-40, 44-40. 13-shot tubular magazine; also 7-shot half-magazine. 24-inch bbl. (round, octagon, half-octagon). Weight: from 6.75 lbs. up. Sights: open rear; bead front. Plain straight-grip stock and forend. Pistol-grip fancy walnut stocks were available at extra cost and also doubles the value of the current value for standard models.

Winchester Model 1892 Saddle-Ring Carbine . . $1595

Same general specifications as the Model 1892 rifle except carbine buttstock, forend and sights. 20-inch bbl. Saddle ring on left side of receiver.

Winchester Model 1894 Lever-Action Rifle $1295

Solid frame or takedown. Calibers: 25-35, 30-30, 32-40, 32 Special, 38-55. 7-shot tubular magazine or 4-shot half-magazine. 26-inch bbl. (round, octagon, half-octagon). Weight: about 7.35 lbs. Sights: open rear; bead front. Plain straight-grip stock and forearm on standard model; crescent-shaped or shotgun-style buttplate. Made 1894-1937. *See* also Winchester Model 94 for later variations of this Model.

Winchester Model 1894 Lever-Action Deluxe . . $2450

Same general specifications as the standard rifle except checkered pistol-grip buttstock and forend using high-grade walnut. Engraved versions are considerably higher in value.

Winchester Model 1894 Saddle-Ring Carbine . . $1850

Same general specifications as the Model 1894 standard rifle except 20-inch bbl., carbine buttstock, forend, and sights. Saddle ring on left side of receiver. Weighs about 6.5 lbs.

Winchester Model 1894 Standard Carbine $995

Same general specifications as Saddle-Ringle Carbine except shotgun type buttstock and plate, no saddle ring, standard open rear sight. Sometimes called "Eastern Carbine." *See* also Winchester Model 94 carbine.

Winchester Model 1894 Rifle

Winchester Model 1894 Fancy-Grade Takedown Rifle

Winchester Model 1894 Saddle-Ring Carbine

Winchester Model 1895 Carbine

Winchester Model 1895 Rifle

Winchester Lee Sporting Rifle

Winchester Model 1895 Lever-Action Carbine . . **$1895**
Same as Model 95 Standard Rifle (below), except has 22-inch bbl., carbine-style buttstock and forend, weighs about 8 lbs., calibers 30-40 Krag, 30-03, 30-06 and 303, solid frame only.

Winchester Model 1895 Lever-Action Rifle **$1400**
Calibers: 30-40 Krag, 30-03, 30-06, 303 British, 7.62mm Russian, 35 Win., 38-72, 40-72, 405 Win. 4-shot box magazine, except 30-40 and 303, which have 5-shot magazines. Bbl. lengths: 24-, 26-, 28-inches (round, half-octagon, octagon). Weight: about 8.5 lbs. Sights: open rear; bead or blade front. Plain straight-grip stock and forend (standard). Both solid frame and takedowns avail. Made 1897-1931.

Winchester Model (1897) Lee Bolt-Action Rifle
Straight-pull bolt action. Caliber: 236 U.S. Navy, 5-shot box magazine, clip loaded. 24- and 28-inch bbl. Weight: 7.5 to 8.5 lbs. Sights: folding leaf rear sight on musket; open sporting sight on sporting rifle.
Musket Model **$895**
Sporting Rifle **950**

**Winchester Model 1900 Bolt-Action
Single-Shot Rifle** **$325**
Takedown. Caliber: 22 Short and Long. 18-inch bbl. Weight: 2.75 lbs. Open rear sight; blade front sight. One-piece, straight-grip stock. Made from 1899 to 1902.

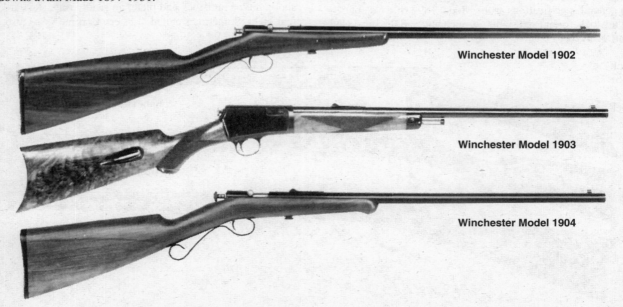

Winchester Model 1902

Winchester Model 1903

Winchester Model 1904

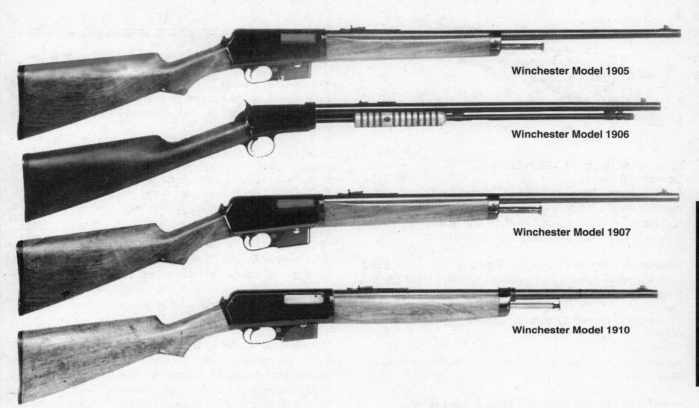

Winchester Model 1905

Winchester Model 1906

Winchester Model 1907

Winchester Model 1910

RIFLES

Winchester Model 1902 Bolt-Action Single-Shot Rifle $295
Takedown. Basically the same as Model 1900 with minor improvements. Calibers: 22 Short and Long, 22 Extra Long, 22 LR. Weight: 3 lbs. Made 1902-1931. *See* photo opposite page.

Winchester Model 1903 Self-Loading Rifle $325
Takedown. Caliber: 22 WRA. 10-shot tubular magazine in buttstock. 20-inch bbl. Weight: 5.75 lbs. Sights: open rear; bead front. Plain straight-grip stock and forearm (fancy grade illustrated). Made 1903-36. *See* photo opposite page.

Winchester Model (1904) 99 Thumb-Trigger Bolt-Action Single-Shot Rifle $525
Takedown. Same as Model 1902 except fired by pressing a button behind the cocking piece. Made 1904-1923.

Winchester Model 1904 Bolt-Action Single-Shot Rifle $225
Similar to Model 1902. Takedown. Caliber: 22 Short, Long Extra Long, LR. 21-inch bbl. Weight: 4 lbs. Made 1904-1931. *See* photo opposite page.

Winchester Model 1905 Self-Loading Rifle $525
Takedown. Calibers: 32 Win. S.L., 35 Win. S.L. 5- or 10-shot detachable box magazine. 22-inch bbl. Weight: 7.5 lbs. Sights: open rear; bead front. Plain pistol-grip stock and forearm. Made 1905-1920.

Winchester Model 1906 Slide-Action Repeater . . $550
Takedown. Visible hammer. Caliber: 22 Short, Long, LR. Tubular magazine holds 20 Short, 16 Long or 14 LR. 20-inch bbl. Weight: 5 lbs. Sights: open rear; bead front. Straight-grip stock and grooved forearm. Made 1906-1932.

Winchester Model 1907 Self-Loading Rifle $4950
Takedown. Caliber: 351 Win. S.L. 5- or 10-shot detachable box magazine. 20-inch bbl. Weight: 7.75 lbs. Sights: open rear; bead front. Plain pistol-grip stock and forearm. Made 1907-1957.

Winchester Model 1910 Self-Loading Rifle $595
Takedown. Caliber: 401 Win. S.L. 4-shot detachable box magazine. 20-inch bbl. Weight: 8.5 lbs. Sights: open rear; bead front. Plain pistol-grip stock and forearm. Made 1910-1936.

NOTE

Following WWI, Winchester had financial difficulties and like many other firearm firms of the day, failed. However, Winchester continued to operate in the hands of receivers. Then, in 1931, The Western Cartridge Co. — under the leadership of John Olin — purchased all assets of the firm. After that, Winchester leaped ahead of all other firms of the day in firearm and ammunition development.

The first sporting firearm to come out of the Winchester plant after WWI was the Model 20 shotgun, but this was quickly followed by the famous Model 52 bolt-action rifle. This was also a time when Winchester dropped the four-digit model numbers and began using two-digit numbers instead. This model-numbering procedure, with one exception (Model 677), continued for the next several years.

Winchester Model 43 Special Grade

Winchester Model 43 Bolt-Action Sporting Rifle $550
Standard Grade. Calibers: 218 Bee, 22 Hornet, 25-20, 32-20 (latter two discontinued 1950). 3-shot detachable box magazine. 24-inch bbl. Weight: 6 lbs. Sights: open rear, bead front on hooded ramp. Plain pistol-grip stock with swivels. Made 1949-1957.

Winchester Model 43 Special Grade $650
Same as Standard Model 43, except has checkered pistol grip and forearm, grip cap.

Winchester Model 47 Bolt-Action Single-Shot Rifle $235
Caliber: 22 Short, Long, LR. 25-inch bbl. Weight: 5.5 lbs. Sights: peep or open rear; bead front. Plain pistol-grip stock. Made 1949-1954.

Winchester Model 52 Bolt-Action Target Rifle
Standard bbl. First type. Caliber: 22 LR. 5-shot box magazine. 28-inch bbl. Weight: 8.75 lbs. Sights: folding leaf peep rear; blade front sight; standard sights various other combinations available. Scope bases. Semi-military-type target stock w/pistol grip; original model has grasping grooves in forearm; higher comb and semibeavertail forearm on later models. Numerous changes were made in this model, the most important was the adoption of the speed lock in 1929; Model 52 rifles produced before this change are generally referred to as "slow lock" models. Last arms of this type bore serial numbers followed by the letter "A." Made 1919-1937.
Slow Lock Model $525
Speed Lock Model 595

Winchester Model 52 Heavy Barrel $625
First type. Speed lock. Same general specifications as Standard Model 52 of this type, except has heavier bbl., Lyman 17G front sight, weighs 10 lbs.

Winchester Model 52 International Match Rifle
Similar to Model 52-D Heavy Barrel, except has special lead-lapped bbl., laminated "free rifle" style stock with high comb, thumbhole, hook buttplate, accessory rail, handstop/swivel assembly, palmrest. Weight: 13.5 lbs. Made 1969-1978.
With standard trigger $660
With Kenyon or I.S.U. trigger 775

Winchester Model 52 International Prone $950
Similar to Model 52-D Heavy Barrel, except has special lead-lapped bbl., prone stock with fuller pistol grip rollover cheek-piece removable for bore-cleaning. Weight 11.5 lbs. Made 1975 to date.

Winchester Model 52 Sporting Rifle $1850
First type. Same as Standard Model 52 of this type, except has lightweight 24-inch bbl., Lyman No. 48 receiver sight and gold bead front sight on hooded ramp, deluxe checkered sporting stock with cheekpiece, black forend tip, etc. Weight: 7.75 lbs.

Winchester Model 52-B Bolt-Action Rifle
Standard bbl. Extensively redesigned action. Supplied with choice of "Target" stock, an improved version of the previous Model 52 stock, or "Marksman" stock with high comb, full pistol grip and beavertail forearm. Weight: 9 lbs. Offered with a wide choice of target sight combinations (Lyman, Marble-Goss, Red-field, Vaver, Winchester), value shown is for rifle less sight equipment. Other specifications as shown for first type. Made 1935-1947. Reintroduced by U.S. Repeating Arms Co. in 1993.
Sporting Model $1795
Target Model 595
USRAC Sporting Model 435

Winchester Model 47

Winchester Model 52 Standard Barrel

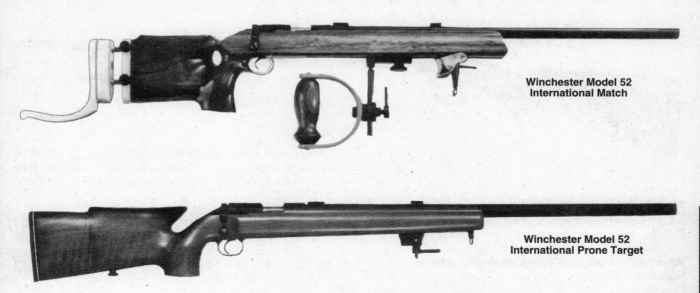

Winchester Model 52
International Match

Winchester Model 52
International Prone Target

Winchester Model 52-B Bull Gun/Heavy Barrel . . $625
Same specifications as Standard Model 52-B, except Bull Gun has extra heavy bbl., Marksman stock only, weighs 12 lbs. Heavy Bbl. model weighs 11 lbs.

Winchester Model 52-C Bolt-Action Rifle
Improved action with "Micro-Motion" trigger mechanism and new-type "Marksman" stock. General specifications same as shown for previous models. Made 1947-1961, Bull Gun from 1952. Value shown is for rifle less sights.

Bull Gun (Extra Heavy Barrel, wt. 12 lbs.)	**$595**
Standard Barrel (Wt. 9.75 lbs.)	**575**
Target Model (Heavy Barrel)	**585**

Winchester Model 52-D Bolt-Action
Target Rifle $625
Redesigned Model 52 action, Single-Shot. Caliber: 22 LR. 28-inch standard or heavy bbl., free-floating, with blocks for standard target scopes. Weight: with standard bbl., 9.75 lbs., with heavy barrel, 11 lbs. Restyled Marksman stock with accessory channel and forend stop, rubber buttplate. Made 1961-1978. Value shown is for rifle without sights.

Winchester Model 53 Lever-Action Repeater . . $1595
Modification of Model 92. Solid frame or takedown. Calibers: 25-20, 32-20, 44-40. 6-shot tubular half-magazine in solid frame model. 7-shot in takedown. 22-inch nickel steel bbl. Weight: 5.5

Winchester Model 52-B
Standard Barrel

Winchester Model 52-B Sporter

Winchester Model 52-C
Heavy Barrel

Winchester Model 53

Winchester Model 53 *(Cont.)*

to 6.5 lbs. Sights: open rear; bead front. Redesigned straight-grip stock and forearm. Made 1924-1932.

Winchester Model 54 Bolt-Action High Power Sporting Rifle (I) $575

First type. Calibers: 270 Win., 7×57mm, 30-30, 30-06, 7.65×53mm, 9×57mm. 5-shot box magazine. 24-inch bbl. Weight: 7.75 lbs. Sights: open rear; bead front. Checkered stock w/pistol grip, tapered forearm w/schnabel tip. This type has two-piece firing pin. Made 1925-1930.

Winchester Model 54 Bolt-Action High Power Sporting Rifle (II) $650

Standard Grade. Improved type with speed lock and one-piece firing pin. Calibers: 22 Hornet, 220 Swift, 250/3000, 257 Roberts, 270 Win., 7×57mm, 30-06. 5-shot box magazine. 24-inch bbl., 26-inch in cal. 220 Swift. Weight: about 8 lbs. Sights: open rear, bead front on ramp. NRA-type stock w/checkered pistol grip and forearm. Made 1930-36. **Add** $200 for 22 Hornet caliber.

Winchester Model 54 Carbine (I) $650

First type. Same as Model 54 rifle, except has 20-inch bbl., plain lightweight stock with grasping grooves in forearm. Weight: 7.25 lbs.

Winchester Model 54 Carbine (II) $695

Improved type. Same as Model 54 Standard Grade Sporting Rifle of this type, except has 20-inch bbl. Weight: about 7.5 lbs. This model may have either NRA-type stock or the lightweight stock found on the first-type Model 54 Carbine.

Winchester Model 54 National Match Rifle $825

Same as Standard Model 54, except has Lyman sights, scope bases, Marksman-type target stock, weighs 9.5 lbs. Same calibers as Standard Model.

Winchester Model 54 Sniper's Match Rifle $895

Similar to the earlier Model 54 Sniper's Rifle, except has Marksman-type target stock, scope bases, weighs 12.5 lbs. Available in same calibers as Model 54 Standard Grade.

Winchester Model 54 Sniper's Rifle $775

Same as Standard Model 54, except has heavy 26-inch bbl., Lyman #48 rear peep sight and blade front sight semi-military stock, weighs 11.75 pounds, cal. 30-06 only.

Winchester Model 54 Rifle

Winchester Model 54 Carbine

Winchester Model 54 Rifle
22 Hornet Model

Winchester Model 54 Super Grade

Winchester Model 54 Super Grade **$950**
Same as Standard Model 54 Sporter, except has deluxe stock with cheekpiece, black forend tip, pistol-grip cap, quick detachable swivels, 1-inch sling strap.

Winchester Model 54 Target Rifle **$825**
Same as Standard Model 54, except has 24-inch medium-weight bbl. (26-inch in cal. 220 Swift), Lyman sights, scope bases, Marksman-type target stock, weighs 10.5 lbs., same calibers as Standard Model.

Winchester Model 55 "Automatic" Single-Shot . . . **$225**
Caliber: 22 Short, Long, LR. 22-inch bbl. Sights: open rear, bead front. One-piece walnut stock. Weight: about 5.5 lbs. Made 1958-1960.

Winchester Model 55 Lever-Action Repeater
Modification of Model 94. Solid frame or takedown. Calibers: 25-35, 30-30, 32 Win. Special. 3-shot tubular half magazine. 24-inch nickel steel bbl. Weight: about 7 lbs. Sights: open rear; bead front. Made 1924-1932.
Straight Grip . . . . **$ 950**
Pistol Grip **1700**

Winchester Model 56 Bolt-Action Sporting Rifle . . **$495**
Solid frame. Caliber: 22 LR, 22 Short. 5- or 10-shot detachable box magazine. 22-inch bbl. Weight: 4.75 lbs. Sights: open rear; bead front. Plain pistol-grip stock with schnabel forend. Made 1926-29.

Winchester Model 57 Bolt-Action Target Rifle . . **$525**
Solid frame. Same as Model 56, except available (until 1929) in 22 Short as well as LR with 5- or 10-shot magazine. Has semi-military style target stock, bbl. band on forend, swivels and web sling, Lyman peep rear sight, blade front sight, weighs 5 lbs. Mfd. 1926-1936.

Winchester Model 58 Bolt-Action Single-Shot . . **$250**
Similar to Model 02. Takedown. Caliber. 22 Short, Long LR. 18-inch bbl. Weight: 3 lbs. Sights, open rear; blade front. Plain, flat, straight-grip hardwood stock. Not serial numbered. Made 1928-1931. *See* photo next page.

Winchester Model 59 Bolt-Action Single-Shot . . **$425**
Improved version of Model 58, has 23-inch bbl., redesigned stock w/pistol grip, weighs 4.5 lbs. Made 1930.

RIFLES

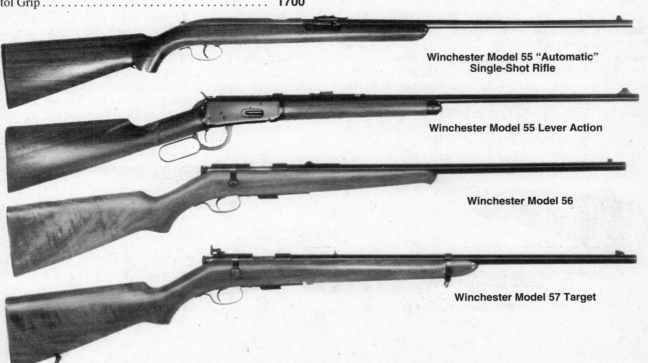

Winchester Model 55 "Automatic" Single-Shot Rifle

Winchester Model 55 Lever Action

Winchester Model 56

Winchester Model 57 Target

Winchester Model 58

Winchester Model 59

Winchester Model 60A

Winchester Model 60 Bolt-Action Single-Shot . . $225
Redesign of Model 59. Caliber: 22 Short, Long, LR. 23-inch bbl. (27-inch after 1933). Weight: 4.25 lbs. Sights: open rear, blade front. Plain stock w/pistol grip. Made 1930-34.

Winchester Model 60A Target Rifle $475
Essentially the same as Model 60, except has Lyman peep rear sight and square top front sight, semi-military target stock and web sling, weighs 5.5 lbs. Made 1932-39.

Winchester Model 61 Hammerless
Slide-Action Repeater $525
Takedown. Caliber: 22 Short, Long, LR. Tubular magazine holds 20 Short, 16 Long, 14 LR. 24-inch round bbl. Weight: 5.5 lbs. Sights: open rear; bead front. Plain pistol-grip stock, grooved semibeavertail slide handle. Also available with 24-inch full-octagon bbl. and only calibers 22 LR, 22 Short or 22 WRF. Made 1932-1963. *Note:* Octagon barrel model commands higher prices (disc. 1943-44); assembled until 1948.

Winchester Model 61 Magnum $625
Same as Standard Model 61, except chambered for 22 WMR; magazine holds 12 rounds. Made 1960-63.

Winchester Model 62 Visible Hammer
Slide-Action Repeater $475
Modernized version of Model 1890. Caliber: 22 Short, Long, LR. 23-inch bbl. Weight: 5.5 lbs. Plain straight-grip stock, grooved semibeavertail slide handle. Also available in Gallery Model chambered for 22 Short only. Made 1932-1959. *Note:* Pre-WWII model (small forearm) commands 25% higher price.

Winchester Model 63 Self-Loading Rifle $525
Takedown. Caliber: 22 LR High Speed only. 10-shot tubular magazine in buttstock. 23-inch bbl. Weight: 5.5 lbs. Sights: open rear, bead front. Plain pistol-grip stock and forearm. Originally available with 20-inch bbl. as well as 23-inch. Made 1933-1959. *See* photo top of next page.

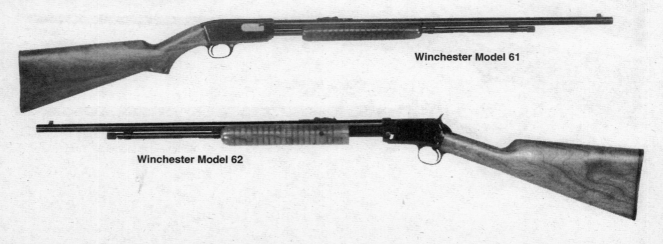

Winchester Model 61

Winchester Model 62

Winchester Model 63

Winchester Model 64 Deer Rifle $1795

Same as Standard Model 64, calibers 30-30 and 32 Win. Special, except has checkered pistol grip and semibeavertail forearm, swivels and sling, weighs 7.75 lbs. Made 1933-1956.

Winchester Model 64 Lever-Action Repeater

Standard Grade. Improved version of Models 94 and 55. Solid frame. Calibers: 25-35, 30-30, 32 Win. Special. 5-shot tubular two-thirds magazine. 20- or 24-inch bbl. Weight: about 7 lbs. Sights: open rear; bead front on ramp w/sight cover. Plain pistol-grip stock and forearm. Made 1933-1956. Production resumed in 1972 (caliber 30-30, 24-inch bbl.); discontinued 1974.

Original model $595
1972-74 model 395

Winchester Model 64 — 219 Zipper $1895

Same as Standard Grade Model 64, except has 26-inch bbl., peep rear sight. Made 1937-1947.

Winchester Model 65 Lever-Action Repeater . . $1695

Improved version of Model 53. Solid frame. Calibers: 25-20 and 32-20. Six-shot tubular half-magazine. 22-inch bbl. Weight: 6.5 lbs. Sights: open rear, bead front on ramp base. Plain pistol-grip stock and forearm. Made 1933-1947.

Winchester Model 65 — 218 Bee $1995

Same as Standard Model 65, except has 24-inch bbl., peep rear sight. Made 1938-1947.

Winchester Model 67 Bolt-Action
Single-Shot Rifle $150

Takedown. Calibers: 22 Short, Long, LR, 22 LR shot (smoothbore), 22 WRF. 27-inch bbl. Weight: 5 lbs. Sights: open rear, bead front. Plain pistol-grip stock (original model had grasping grooves in forearm). Made 1934-1963. *See* illustration next page.

RIFLES

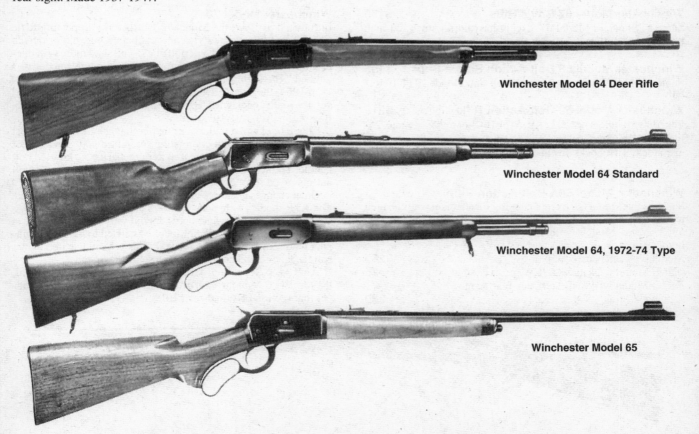

Winchester Model 64 Deer Rifle

Winchester Model 64 Standard

Winchester Model 64, 1972-74 Type

Winchester Model 65

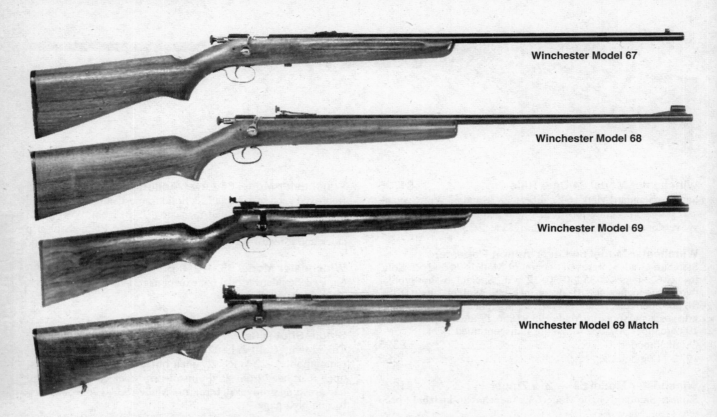

Winchester Model 67

Winchester Model 68

Winchester Model 69

Winchester Model 69 Match

Winchester Model 67 Boy's Rifle **$175**
Same as Standard Model 67, except has shorter stock, 20-inch bbl., weighs 4.25 lbs.

Winchester Model 68 Bolt-Action Single-Shot . . **$195**
Same as Model 67, except has rear peep sight. Made 1934-1946.

Winchester Model 69 Bolt-Action Rifle **$215**
Takedown. Caliber: 22 S, L, LR. 5- or 10-shot box magazine. 25-inch bbl. Weight: 5.5 lbs. Peep or open rear sight. Plain pistol-grip stock. Rifle cocks on closing motion of the bolt. Made 1935-1937.

Winchester Model 69A Bolt-Action Rifle
Same as the Model 69, except cocking mechanism was changed to cock the rifle by the opening motion of the bolt. Made 1937-1963. *Note:* Models with grooved receivers command 20% higher prices.
Model 69A Standard **$265**
Match Model w/Lyman #57EW receiver sight. **325**
Target Model w/Winchester peep rear sight,
  swivels, sling **350**

Winchester Model 70
Introduced in 1937, the Model 70 Bolt-Action Repeating Rifle was offered in several styles and calibers. Only minor design changes were made over a period of 27 years, and more than one-half million of these rifles were sold. The original model was dubbed "The Rifleman's Rifle."

In 1964, the original Model 70 was superseded by a revised version with redesigned action, improved bolt, swaged (free-floating) barrel, restyled stock.

This model again underwent major changes in 1972 — most visible: new stock with contrasting forend tip and grip cap, cut checkering (instead of impressed as in predecessor) knurled bolt handle. The action was machined from a solid block of steel with barrels made from chrome molybdenum steel.

Other changes in the design and style of the Model 70 continued. The XTR models were added in 1978 along with the Model 70A, the latter omitting the white liners, forend caps and floor plates. In 1981, an XTR Featherweight Model was added to the line, beginning with serial number G1,440,000. This version featured lighter barrels, fancy-checkered stocks with schnabel forend.

After U.S. Repeating Arms took over the Winchester plant, the Model 70 went through even more changes as described under that section of Winchester rifles.

Winchester Model 70
Basic Post WWII Model

**Winchester Model 70
Pre-1964 Standard Model**

PRE-1964 MODEL 70

Winchester Model 70 African Rifle **$3355**
Same general specifications as Super Grade Model 70, except has 25-inch bbl., 3-shot magazine, Monte Carlo stock with recoil pad. Weight: about 9.5 lbs. Caliber: 458 Winchester Magnum. Made 1956–1963.

Winchester Model 70 Alaskan **$1550**
Same as Standard Model 70, except calibers 338 Win. Mag., 375 H&H Mag.; 3-shot magazine in 338, 4-shot in 375 caliber; 25-inch bbl.; stock with recoil pad. Weight: 8 lbs. in 338; 8.75 lbs. in 375 caliber. Made 1960–63.

Winchester Model 70 Bull Gun **$2150**
Same as Standard Model 70, except has heavy 28-inch bbl., scope bases, Marksman stock, weighs 13.25 lbs., caliber 300 H&H Magnum and 30-06 only. Disc. 1963.

Winchester Model 70 Featherweight Sporter . . . **$925**
Same as Standard Model 70, except has redesigned stock and 22-inch bbl., aluminum trigger guard, floorplate and buttplate. Calibers: 243 Win., 264 Win. Mag., 270 Win., 308 Win., 30-06, 358 Win. Weight: about 6.5 lbs. Made 1952–1963.

NOTE

On December 22, 1931, the Winchester Repeating Arms Company was purchased by Western Cartridge Company, but continued to operate under the same Winchester name until December 31, 1938, when the name was changed to:

**WINCHESTER REPEATING ARMS COMPANY
Division of Western Cartridge Company**

Winchester Model 70 National Match Rifle **$1155**
Same as Standard Model 70, except has scope bases, Marksman-type target stock, weighs 9.5 lbs., caliber 30-06 only. Discontinued 1960.

Winchester Model 70 Standard Grade **$875**
Calibers: 22 Hornet, 220 Swift, 243 Win., 250-3000, 257 Roberts, 270 Win., 7×57mm, 30-06, 308 Win., 300 H&H Mag., 375 H&H Mag. 5-shot box magazine (4-shot in Magnum calibers). 24-inch bbl. standard; 26-inch in 220 Swift and 300 Mag.; 25-inch in 375 Mag.; at one time a 20-inch bbl. was available. Sights: open rear; hooded ramp front. Checkered walnut stock; Monte Carlo comb standard on later production. Weight: from 7.75 pounds depending on caliber and bbl. length. Made 1937–1963.

Winchester Model 70 Super Grade **$1995**
Same as Standard Grade Model 70, except has deluxe stock w/cheekpiece, black forend tip, pistol-grip cap, quick detachable swivels, sling. Discontinued 1960.

**Winchester Model 70 Super Grade
Featherweight** **$1695**
Same as Standard Grade Featherweight except has deluxe stock w/cheekpiece, black forend tip, pistol-grip cap, quick detachable swivels, sling. Discontinued 1960. *Note:* SG-FWs are rare but, unless documented, will not command premium price of $2800–$3500; price here reflects "All" (incl. nondocumented transactions).

Winchester Model 70 Target Rifle **$1595**
Same as Standard Model 70, except has 24-inch medium-weight bbl., scope bases, Marksman stock, weight about 10.5 lbs. Originally offered in all of the Model 70 calibers, this rifle was available later in calibers 243 Win. and 30-06. Discontinued 1963.

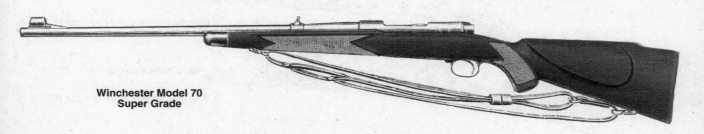

**Winchester Model 70
Super Grade**

RIFLES

Winchester Model 70 Standard Weight
Target Rifle

Winchester Model 70 Heavy Weight
Target Rifle

Winchester Model 70 Bull Gun

Winchester Model 70 Target Heavy Weights ... **$1595**
Same general specifications as Standard Model 70 except with
either 24- or 26-inch heavy weight bbl. and weighs 10.5 lbs. No
checkering. 243 and 30-06 calibers.

Winchester Model 70 Target Bull Barrel **$2150**
Same general specifications as Standard Model 70 except 28-
inch heavy weight bbl. and chambered for either 30-06 or 300
H&H Mag. Drilled and tapped for front sight base. Receiver slotted for clip loading. Weight: 13.25 lbs.

Winchester Model 70 Varmint Rifle **$945**
Same general specifications as Standard Model 70, except has
26-inch heavy bbl., scope bases, special varminter stock. Calibers: 220 Swift, 243 Win. Made 1956–1963.

Winchester Model 70 Westerner **$980**
Same as Standard Model 70, except calibers 264 Win. Mag., 300
Win. Mag.; 3-shot magazine; 26-inch bbl. in former caliber, 24-
inch in latter. Weight: about 8.25 lbs. Made 1960–63.

1964-TYPE MODEL 70

Winchester Model 70 African **$660**
Caliber: 458 Win. Mag. 3-shot magazine. 22-inch bbl. Weight:
8.5 lbs. Special "African" sights. Monte Carlo stock with ebony
forend tip, hand-checkering, twin stock-reinforcing bolts, recoil
pad, QD swivels. Made 1964–1971.

Winchester Model 70 Deluxe **$595**
Calibers: 243, 270 Win., 30-06, 300 Win. Mag. 5-shot box maga-
zine (3-shot in Magnum). 22-inch bbl. (24-inch in Magnum).
Weight: 7.5 lbs. Sights: open rear; hooded ramp front. Monte
Carlo stock w/ebony forend tip, hand-checkering, QD swivels,
recoil pad on Magnum. Made 1964–1971.

**Winchester Model 70 International Army
Match Rifle** **$625**
Caliber: 308 Win. (7.62 NATO). 5-shot box magazine. 24-inch
heavy barrel. Externally adj. trigger. Weight: 11 lbs. ISU stock
w/military oil finish, forearm rail for standard accessories, verti-

Winchester Model 70 African (1964)

Winchester Model 70 Deluxe (1964)

**Winchester Model 70
International Army Match (1964)**

Winchester Model 70 International Army Match Rifle *(Cont.)*

cally adj. buttplate. Made in 1971. Value shown is for rifle w/o sights.

Winchester Model 70 Magnum

Calibers: 7mm Rem. Mag.; 264, 300, 338 Win. Mag.; 375 H&H Mag. 3-shot magazine. 24-inch bbl. Weight: 7.75 to 8.5 lbs. Sights: open rear; hooded ramp front. Monte Carlo stock w/cheekpiece, checkering, twin stock-reinforcing bolts, recoil pad, swivels. Made 1964–1971.

Caliber 375 H&H Mag.............................. **$525**
Other calibers **350**

Winchester Model 70 Mannlicher **$495**

Calibers: 243, 270, 308 Win., 30-06. 5-shot box magazine. 19-inch bbl. Sights: open rear; hooded ramp front. Weight: 7.5 lbs. Mannlicher-style stock w/Monte Carlo comb and cheekpiece, checkering, steel forend cap, QD sling swivels. Made 1969–1971.

Winchester Model 70 Standard **$425**

Calibers: 22-250, 222 Rem., 225, 243, 270, 308 Win., 30-06. 5-shot box magazine. 22-inch bbl. Weight: 7.5 lbs. Sights: open rear; hooded ramp front. Monte Carlo stock w/cheekpiece, checkering, swivels. Made 1964–1971.

Winchester Model 70 Target **$595**

Calibers: 308 Win. (7.62 NATO) and 30-06. 5-shot box magazine. 24-inch heavy bbl. Blocks for target scope. No factory sights installed, but drilled and tapped for front and rear sights. Weight: 10.25 lbs. High-comb Marksman-style stock, aluminum hand stop, swivels. Straight-grain, one-piece stock with sling swivels, but no checkering. Made 1964–1971.

Winchester Model 70 Varmint **$575**

Same as Model 70 Standard, except has 24-inch target weight bbl., blocks for target scope. No factory sights installed, but drilled and tapped for front and rear sights. Available in calibers 22-250, 222 Rem., and 243 Win. only. Weight: 9.75 lbs. Made 1964–1971.

RIFLES

Winchester Model 70 Mannlicher (1964)

Winchester Model 70 Standard (1964)

Winchester Model 70 Target (1964)

Winchester Model 70 African (1972)

Winchester Model 70 Featherweight

1972-TYPE MODEL 70

Winchester Model 70 African $645
Similar to Model 70 Magnum, except caliber 458 Win. Mag.; has 22-inch bbl., special African open rear sight, reinforced stock with ebony forend tip, detachable swivels and sling; front sling swivel stud attached to bbl. Weight: about 8.5 lbs. Made 1972 to date.

Winchester Model 70 Classic SM
Similar to the Model 70 Classic Sporter, except with checkered black composite stock and matte metal finish. Made 1994 to date.

Standard Model	$335
In caliber 375 H&H.	395
With BOSS, **add**	90
With Open Sights, **add**	35

Winchester Model 70 Classic Sporter
Similar to the Model 70 Sporter, except has pre-64-style action w/controlled round feeding, classic-style stock. Optional open sights. Made 1994 to date.

Standard Model	$360
With BOSS, **add**	90
With Open Sights, **add**	35

Winchester Model 70 Classic Stainless
Similar to the Model 70 Classic Sporter, except with matte stainless steel finish. Weight: 8 lbs. No open sights, except 375 H&H. Made 1994 to date.

Standard Model	$360
In caliber 375 H&H.	395
With BOSS, **add**	90

Winchester Model 70 Custom Sharpshooter . . . $1250
Calibers: 22-250, 223, 308 Win., 300 Win. Mag. 24- or 26-inch bbl. 44.5 inches overall (24-inch bbl.). Weight: 11 lbs. Custom fitted, hand-honed action. McMillan A-2 target-style stock. Matte blue finish. Made 1992 to date.

Winchester Model 70 Custom Sporting Sharpshooter $1195
Similar to the Custom Sharpshooter Model, except has McMillan sporter-style gray composite stock. Stainless 24- or 26-inch bbl. with blued receiver. Calibers: 270, 7mm STW, 300 Win. Mag. Made 1993 to date.

Winchester Model 70 Golden 50th Anniversary Edition Bolt-Action Rifle $955
Caliber: 300 Win. 3-shot magazine. 24-inch bbl. 44.5 inches overall. Weight: 7.75 lbs. Checkered American walnut stock.

Winchester Model 70
Golden 50th Anniversary Rifle

Winchester Model 70 Featherweight Classic

Winchester Model 70 Lightweight

Winchester Model 70 Magnum

Winchester Model 70 Carbine

Winchester Model 70 Golden 50th Anniversary Edition Bolt-Action Rifle *(Cont.)*

Hand-engraved American scroll pattern on bbl., receiver, magazine cover, trigger guard and pistol-grip cap. Sights: adj. rear; hooded front ramp. Inscription on bbl. reads "The Rifleman's Rifle 1937–1987." Only 500 made 1986–87.

Winchester Model 70 Featherweight Classic. . . . $425
Similar to the Model 70 XTR Featherweight, except with controlled-round feeding system. Calibers: 270, 280 and 30-06. Made 1992 to date.

Winchester Model 70 International Army Match . . $750
Caliber: 308 Win. (7.62mm NATO). 5-shot magazine, clip slot in receiver bridge. 24-inch heavy barrel. Weight: 11 lbs. No sights, but drilled and tapped for front and rear iron sights, and/or scope mounts. ISU target stock. Introduced 1973; discont.

Winchester Model 70 Lightweight Bolt-Action Rifle $345
Calibers: 22-250 and 223 Rem.; 243, 270 and 308 Win.; 30-06 Springfield. 5-shot mag. capacity (6-shot 223 Rem.). 22-inch barrel. 42 to 42.5 inches overall. Weight: 6 to 6.25 lbs. Checkered classic straight stock. Sling swivel studs. Made 1986 to date.

Winchester Model 70 Magnum
Same as Model 70, except has 3-shot magazine, 24-inch bbl., reinforced stock with recoil pad. Weight: about 7.75 pounds (except 8.5 pounds in 375 H&H Mag.). Calibers: 264 Win. Mag., 7mm Rem. Mag., 300 Win. Mag., 338 Win. Mag., 375 H&H Mag. Made 1972 to date.
375 H&H Magnum $445
Other Magnum calibers. 395

Winchester Model 70 Standard $325
Same as Model 70A, except has 5-shot magazine, Monte Carlo stock with cheekpiece, black forend tip and pistol-grip cap with white spacers, checkered pistol grip and forearm, detachable sling swivels. Same calibers plus 225 Win. Made 1972 to date.

Winchester Model 70 Standard Carbine $330
Same general specifications as Standard Model 70 except 19-inch bbl. and weighs 7.25 lbs. Shallow recoil pad. Walnut stock and forend with traditional Model 70 checkering. Swivel studs. No sights, but drilled and tapped for scope mount.

Winchester Model 70 Sporter DBM
Same general specifications as Model 70 Sporter SSM, except with detachable box magazine. Calibers: 22-250 (discontinued 1994), 223 (discontinued 1994), 243 (discontinued 1994), 270, 7mm Rem. Mag., 308 (discontinued 1994), 30-06, 300 Win. Mag. Made 1992 to date.
Model 70 DBM $375
Model 70 DBM-S 395

Winchester Model 70 Stainless Sporter SSM . . . $395
Same general specifications as Model 70 XTR Sporter, except with checkered black composite stock and matte finished receiver, bbl. and other metal parts. Calibers: 270, 7mm Rem. Mag., 30-06, 300 Win. Mag., 338 Win. Mag. Weight: 7.75 lbs. Made 1992 to date.

Winchester Model 70 Super Grade $495
Calibers: 270, 7mm Rem. Mag., 30-06, 300 Win. Mag., 338 Win. Mag. 5-shot magazine (standard), 3-shot (magnum). 24-inch bbl. 44.5 inches overall. Weight: 7.75 lbs. Checkered walnut stock with sculptured cheekpiece and tapered forend. Scope bases and

Winchester Model 70 Varmint

Winchester Model 70 Win-Cam

Winchester Model 70 Winlite

Winchester Model 70 Win-Tuff

Winchester Model 70 Super Grade *(Cont.)*

rings, no sights. Controlled-round feeding system. Made 1990 to date.

Winchester Model 70 Target $555

Calibers: 30-06 and 308 Win. (7.62mm NATO). 5-shot magazine. 26-inch heavy bbl. Weight: 10.5 lbs. No sights, but drilled and tapped for scope mount and also open sights. High-comb Marksman-style target stock, aluminum hand stop, swivels. Made 1972 to date.

Winchester Model 70 Ultra Match $595

Similar to Model 70 Target, but custom grade; has 26-inch heavy bbl. with deep counterbore, glass bedding, externally adj. trigger. Made 1972 to date.

Winchester Model 70 Varmint (Heavy Barrel)

Same as Model 70 Standard, except has medium-heavy, counter-bored 26-inch bbl., no sights, stock with less drop. Weight: 9 lbs. Calibers: 22-250 Rem., 223 Rem., 243 Win., 308 Win. Made 1972 to date. **Model 70 SHB**, in 308 Win. only with black synthetic stock and matte blue receiver/bbl., made 1992 to date.

Model 70 Varmint $435
Model 70 SHB (Synthetic Heavy Barrel) 475

Winchester Model 70 Win-Cam Rifle $365

Caliber: 270 Win. and 30-06 Springfield. 24-inch barrel. Camouflage one-piece laminated stock. Recoil pad. Drilled and tapped for scope. Made 1986 to date.

Winchester Model 70 Winlite Bolt-Action Rifle . . $485

Calibers: 270 Win., 280 Rem., 30-06 Springfield, 7mm Rem., 300 Win. Mag., and 338 Win. Mag. 5-shot magazine; 3-shot for Magnum calibers. 22-inch bbl.; 24-inch for Magnum calibers. 42.5 inches overall; 44.5, Magnum calibers. Weight: 6.25 to 7 lbs. Fiberglass stock with rubber recoil pad, sling swivel studs. Made 1986 to date.

Winchester Model 70 Win-Tuff Bolt-Action Rifle

Calibers: 22-250, 223, 243, 270, 308 and 30-06 Springfield. 22-inch bbl. Weight: 6.25–7 lbs. Laminated dye-shaded brown wood stock with recoil pad. Barrel drilled and tapped for scope. Swivel studs. FWT Model made 1986–1994. LW Model introduced in 1992.

Featherweight Model $395
Lightweight Model (Made 1992–93) 345

Winchester Model 70 XTR Featherweight $365

Similar to Standard Win. Model 70, except lightweight American walnut stock with classic schnabel forend, checkered. 22-inch bbl., hooded blade front sight, folding leaf rear sight. Stainless-steel magazine follower. Weight: 6.75 lbs. Made 1984 to date.

Winchester Model 70 XTR Sporter Rifle $375

Calibers: 264 Win. Mag., 7mm Rem. Mag., 300 Win. Mag., 200 Weatherby Mag., and 338 Win. Mag. 3-shot magazine. 24-inch barrel. 44.5 inches overall. Weight: 7.75 lbs. Walnut Monte Carlo stock. Rubber buttpad. Receiver tapped and drilled for scope mounting. Made 1986 to date.

Winchester Model 70 XTR Sporter

Winchester Model 70A

Winchester Model 70 XTR Sporter Magnum $395

Calibers: 264 Win. Mag., 7mm Rem. Mag., 300 Win. Mag., 338 Win. Mag. 3-shot magazine. 24-inch bbl. 44.5 inches overall. Weight: 7.75 lbs. No sights furnished, optional adj. folding leaf rear; hooded ramp. Receiver drilled and tapped for scope. Checkered American walnut Monte Carlo-style stock with satin finish. Made 1986 to date.

Winchester Model 70 XTR Sporter Varmint $375

Same general specifications as Model 70 XTR Sporter, except in calibers 223, 22-250, 243 only. Checkered American walnut Monte Carlo-style stock w/cheekpiece.

Winchester Model 70 Characteristics

Winchester Model 70 First Model I
(Serial Numbers 1 – 80,000)

First manufactured in 1936; first sold in 1937. Receiver drilled for Lyman No. 57W or No. 48WJS receiver peep sights. Also drilled and tapped for Lyman or Fecker scope-sight block. Weight w/24-inch bbl. in all calibers except .375 H&H Mag.: 8.25 lbs. 9 lbs. in H&H Mag. Early type safety located on bolt top. Production of this model ended in 1942 at about serial number 80,000 due to World War II.

Winchester Model 70 Second Model
(Serial Numbers 80,000 – 350,000)

All civilian production of Winchester Model 70 rifles halted during World War II. Production resumed in 1947 with an improved safety and integral front-sight ramp. Serial numbers started at around 80,000. This model type was produced until 1954, ending around serial number 350,000.

Winchester Model 70 Third Model
(Serial Numbers 350,000 – 400,000)

This variety was manufactured from 1954 to 1960 and retained many features of the Second Model, except that a folding rear sight replaced the earlier type and front-sight ramps were brazed onto the bbl. rather than being an integral part of the bbl.

The Model 70 Featherweight Rifle was introduced in 1954 in 308 WCF caliber. It was fitted with a light 22-inch bbl. and was also available with either a Monte Carlo or Standard stock.

Winchester Model 70A $285

Calibers: 222 Rem., 22-250, 243 Win., 25-06, 270 Win., 30-06, 308 Win. 4-shot magazine. 22-inch bbl. (except 24- or 26-inch in 25-06). Weight: about 7.5 lbs. Sights: open rear; hooded ramp front. Monte Carlo stock with checkered pistol grip and forearm, sling swivels. Made 1972 to date.

Winchester Model 70A Magnum $315

Same as Model 70A, except has 3-shot magazine, 24-inch bbl., recoil pad. Weight: about 7.75 lbs. Calibers: 264 Win. Mag., 7mm Rem. Mag., 300 Win. Mag. Made 1972 to date.

Winchester Model 70 Third Model
(Serial Numbers 350,000 – 400,000) (Cont.)

The 243 Win. cartridge was added in 1955 in all grades of the Winchester Model 70 except the National Match and Bull Gun models. The 358 Win cartridge was also introduced in 1955, along with a new Varmint model chambered for the 243 caliber only.

Winchester Model 70 Fourth Model
(Serial Numbers 400,000 – 500,000)

Different markings were inscribed on the barrels of these models and new magnum calibers were added; that is, 264 Win Mag., 338 Win. Mag, and 458 Win. Mag. All bbls. of this variation were about 0.13 inch shorter than previous ones. The 22 Hornet and 257 Roberts were discontinued in 1962; the 358 Win. caliber in 1963.

Winchester Model 70 Fifth Model
(Serial Numbers 500,000 to about 570,000)

These rifles may be recognized by slightly smaller checkering patterns along with slightly smaller lightweight stocks. Featherweight bbls. were marked "Featherweight." Webbed recoil pads were furnished on magnum calibers.

Post-1964 Winchester Model 70 Rifles

In 1964, the Winchester-Western Division of Olin Industries claimed that they were losing money on every Model 70 they produced. Both labor and material costs had increased to a level

Winchester Model 70 Characteristics (Cont.)
Post-1964 Models

that could no longer be ignored. Other models followed suit. Consequently, sweeping changes were made to the entire Winchester line. Many of the older, less popular, models were discontinued. Models that were to remain in production were modified for lower production costs.

1964 Winchester Model 70 Rifles
(Serial Numbers 570,000 to about 700,000)

The first version of the "New Model 70s" utilized a free-floating barrel, swaged rifle bore, new stock and sights, new type of bolt and receiver, and a different finish throughout on both the wood and metal parts. The featherweight grade was dropped, but six other grades were available in this new line:

- Standard
- Deluxe (Replaced Previous Super Grade)
- Magnum
- Varmint
- Target
- African

1966 Winchester Model 70 Rifles
(Serial Numbers 700,000-G to about 1,005,000)

In general, this group of Model 70s had fancier wood checkering, cross-bolt stock reinforcement, improved wood finish, along with an improved action.

One cross-bolt reinforcement was used on standard guns. Magnum calibers, however, used an additional forward cross-bolt along with a red recoil pad.

The free-floating barrel clearance forward of the breech taper was reduced in thickness. Impressed checkering was used on the deluxe models until 1968. Hand checkering was once again used on deluxe and carbine models in 1969; the big, red "W" was removed from all grip caps. A new red safety-indicator and undercut cheekpiece was introduced in 1971.

1972 Winchester Model 70 Rifles
(Serial Numbers G1,005,000 to about G1,360,000)

Both the barrels and receivers for this variety of Model 70s were made from chrome molybdenum (C-M) steel. The barrels were tapered with spiral rifling ranging in length from 22 to 24 inches. Calibers 222 Rem., 225 Win. 22-250, 243 Win., 25-06, 270, 308 Win., 30-06 and 458 WM used the 22-inch length, while the following calibers used the 24-inch length: 222 Rem., 22-250, 243 Win., 264 Win. Mag., 7mm Mag., 300 and 375 H&H Mag. The 225 Win caliber was dropped in 1973; Mannlicher stocks were also discontinued in 1973.

The receiver for this variety of Model 70s was machined from a block of C-M steel. A new improved anti-bind bolt was introduced along with a new type of ejector.

Other improvements included hand-cut checkering, pistol-grip stocks with pistol-grip and dark forend caps. An improved satin wood finished was also utilized.

1978 Winchester Model 70 Rifles
(Serial Numbers began around G1,360,000)

This variety of Model 70 was similar to the 1972 version except that a new XTR style was added which featured high-luster wood and metal finishes, fine-cut checkering, and similar embellish-

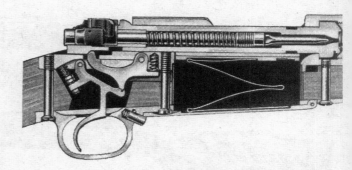

Cross-sectional view of the pre-1964 Winchester Model 70's speed lock action. This action cocks on the opening movement of the bolt with polished, smooth-functioning cams and guide lug, insuring fast and smooth operation.

ments. All Model 70 rifles made during this period used the XTR style; no standard models were available.

In 1981, beginning with serial number G1,440,000 (approximately), a Featherweight version of the Model 70 XTR was introduced. The receiver was identical to the 1978 XTR, but lighter barrels were fitted. Stocks were changed to a lighter design with larger scroll checkering patterns and a Schnabel forend with no Monte Carlo comb. A satin sheen stock finish on the featherweight version replaced the high-luster finish used on the other XTR models.

A new style red buttplate with thick, black rubber liner was used on the featherweight models. The grip cap was also redesigned for this model.

U.S. Repeating Arms Model 70s — 1982 to date

In the early 1980s, negotiations began between Olin Industries and an employee-based corporation. The result of these negotiations ended with Olin selling all tools, machinery, supplies, etc. at the New Haven plant to the newly-formed corporation which was eventually named *U.S. Repeating Arms Company.* Furthermore, U.S. Repeating Arms Company purchased the right to use the Winchester name and logo.

Winchester Model 70s went through very few changes the first two years after the transistion. However, in 1984, the Featherweight Model 70 XTR rifles were offered in a new short action for 22-250 Rem., 223 Rem., 243 Win. and 308 Win. calibers, in addition to their standard action which was used for the longer cartridges. A new Model 70 lightweight carbine was also introduced this same year.

Two additional models were introduced in 1985 — the Model 70 Lightweight Mini-Carbine Short Action and the Model 70 XTR Sporter Varmint; but this was just the beginning. The Model 70 Winlite appeared in the 1986 "Winchester" catalog, along with two economy versions of the Model 70 — the Winchester Ranger and the Ranger Youth Carbine. Five or six different versions of the Winchester Model 70 had been sufficient for 28 years (1937 - 1964). Now, changes in design and the addition of new models each year seemed to be necessary to keep the rifle alive.

New models were added, old models dropped, changed in design, etc. on a regular basis. The trend continues. Still, the Winchester Model 70 Bolt-Action Repeating Rifle — in any of its variations — is the most popular bolt-action rifle ever built.

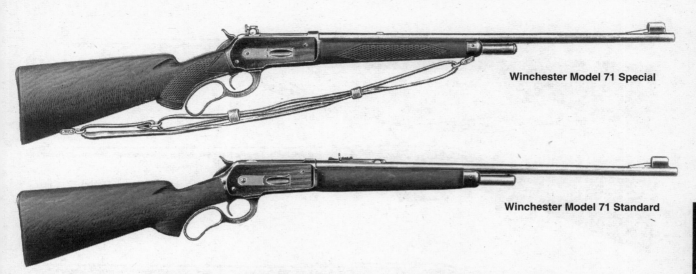

Winchester Model 71 Special

Winchester Model 71 Standard

Winchester Model 71 Lever-Action Repeater

Solid frame. Caliber: 348 Win. 4-shot tubular magazine. 20- or 24-inch bbl. Weight: 8 lbs. Sights: open or peep rear; bead front on ramp w/hood. Walnut stock. Made 1935–1957.

Special Grade (checkered pistol grip and forearm, grip cap, quick-detachable swivels and sling	**$1200**
Special Grade Carbine (20-inch bbl.; disc. 1940)	**1895**
Standard Grade (lacks checkering, grip cap, sling and swivels)	**815**
Standard Grade Carbine (20-inch bbl.; disc. 1940)	**1400**

Winchester Model 72 Bolt-Action Repeater $245

Tubular magazine. Takedown. Caliber: 22 Short, Long, LR. Magazine holds 20 Short, 16 Long or 15 LR. 25-inch bbl. Weight: 5.75 lbs. Sights: peep or open rear; bead front. Plain pistol-grip stock. Made 1938–1959.

Winchester Model 73 Lever-Action Repeater

See Model 1873 rifles, carbines, "One of One Thousand" and other variations of this model at the beginning of Winchester Rifle Section. *Note:* The Winchester Model 1873 was the first lever-action repeating rifle bearing the Winchester name.

Winchester Model 74 Self-Loading Rifle $195

Takedown. Calibers: 22 Short only, 22 LR only. Tubular magazine in buttstock holds 20 Short, 14 LR. 24-inch bbl. Weight: 6.25 lbs. Sights: open rear; bead front. Plain pistol-grip stock, one-piece. Made 1939–1955.

Winchester Model 75 Sporting Rifle $625

Same as Model 75 Target, except has 24-inch bbl., checkered sporter stock, open rear sight; bead front on hooded ramp, weighs 5.5 lbs.

Winchester Model 72

Winchester Model 74

Winchester Model 75 Sporting

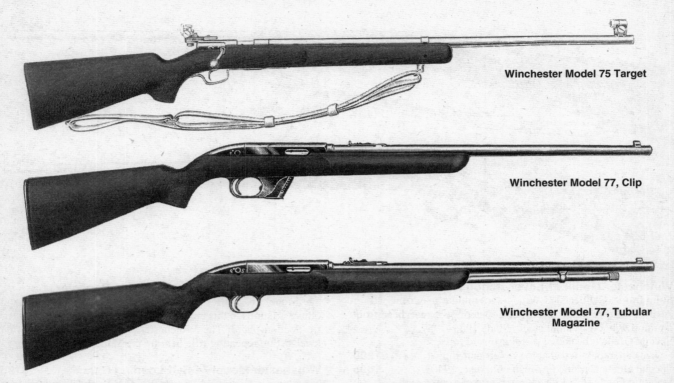

Winchester Model 75 Target

Winchester Model 77, Clip

Winchester Model 77, Tubular Magazine

Winchester Model 75 Target Rifle. $395
Caliber: 22 LR. 5- or 10-shot box magazine. 28-inch bbl. Weight: 8.75 lbs. Target sights (Lyman, Redfield or Winchester). Target stock w/pistol grip and semibeavertail forearm, swivels and sling. Made 1938–1959.

Winchester Model 77 Semiautomatic Rifle, Clip Type $165
Solid frame. Caliber: 22 LR. 8-shot clip magazine. 22-inch bbl. Weight: about 5.5 lbs. Sights: open rear; bead front. Plain, one-piece pistol-grip stock. Made 1955–1963.

Winchester Model 77, Tubular Magazine Type . . $175
Same as Model 77. Clip type, except has tubular magazine holding 15 rounds. Made 1955–1963.

Winchester Model 86 Carbine and Rifle
See Model 1886 at beginning of Winchester Rifle Section.

Winchester Model 88 Carbine $525
Same as Model 88 Rifle, except has 19-inch bbl., plain carbine-style stock and forearm with bbl. band. Weight: 7 lbs. Made 1968–1973.

Winchester Model 88 Lever-Action Rifle $465
Hammerless. Calibers: 243 Win., 284 Win., 308 Win., 358 Win. 4-shot box magazine. 3-shot in pre-1963 models and in 284. 22-inch bbl. Weight: about 7.25 lbs. One-piece walnut stock with pistol grip, swivels (1965 and later models have basket-weave ornamentation instead of checkering). Made 1955–1973. *Note:* 243 and 358 introduced 1956, latter discontinued 1964; 284 introduced 1963.

Winchester Model 94 Antique Carbine. $245
Same as standard Post-64 Model 94 Carbine, except has decorative scrollwork and casehardened receiver, brass-plated loading gate, saddle ring; caliber 30-30 only. Made 1964–1984.

Winchester Model 88 Lever-Action Rifle Pre-1965

Winchester Model 94 Carbine
Post-WW II, Pre-1964

Winchester Model 94 Carbine
Same as Model 1894 Rifle, except 20-inch round bbl., 6-shot full-length magazine. Weight: about 6.5 lbs. Originally made in calibers 25-35, 30-30, 32 Special and 38-55. Original version discontinued 1964. *See* 1894 Models at beginning of Winchester Rifle Section.
Pre-World War II (under No. 1,300,000) **$995**
Postwar, pre-1964 (under No. 2,700,000) **550**

Winchester Model 94 Classic Carbine **$295**
Same as Canadian Centennial '67 Commemorative Carbine, except without commemorative details; has scroll-engraved receiver, gold-plated loading gate. Made 1968–1970.

Winchester Model 94 Classic Rifle **$295**
Same as Model 67 Rifle, except without commemorative details; has scroll-engraved receiver, gold-plated loading gate. Made 1968–1970.

Winchester Model 94 Deluxe Carbine **$345**
Caliber: 30-30. 6-shot magazine. 20-inch bbl. 37.75 inches overall. Weight: 6.5 lbs. Semi-fancy American walnut stock with rubber buttpad, long forearm and specially cut checkering. Engraved with "Deluxe" script. Made 1987 to date.

Winchester Model 94 Long Barrel Rifle **$245**
Caliber: 30-30. 7-round magazine. 24-inch bbl. 41.75 inches overall. Weight: 7 lbs. American walnut stock. Blade front sight. Made 1987 to date.

Winchester Model 94 Trapper **$225**
Same as Winchester Model 94 Carbine, except 16-inch bbl. and weighs 6 lbs. 2 oz. Made 1980 to date.

Winchester Model 94 Win-Tuff Rifle **$235**
Caliber: 30-30. 6-round magazine. 20-inch bbl. 37.75 inches overall. Weight: 6.5 lbs. Brown laminated wood stock. Made 1987 to date.

Winchester Model 94 Wrangler II Angle Eject Carbine **$245**
Same as standard Model 94 Carbine, except has 16-inch bbl., engraved receiver and chambered for 38-55 Win. Introduced by U.S. Repeating Arms.

Winchester Model 94 XTR Big Bore **$250**
Modified Model 94 action for added strength. Caliber: 375 Win. 20-inch bbl. Rubber buttpad. Checkered stock and forearm. Weight: 6.5 lbs. Made 1978 to date. *See* photo next page.

RIFLES

**Winchester Model 94
Long Barrel Rifle**

**Winchester Model 94
Win-Tuff**

**Winchester Model 94
Wrangler II Angle Eject**

Winchester Model 94 XTR Big Bore

Winchester Model 94 XTR 7-30 Waters

Winchester Model 94 XTR in 7-30 Waters Lever-Action Rifle $225
Same general specifications as standard Angle Eject M94 except chambered for 7-30 Waters cartridge and has 24-inch bbl. Weight: 7 lbs. Made 1985 to date by U.S. Repeating Arms.

MODEL 94 COMMEMORATIVES

Values indicated are for commemorative Winchesters in new condition.

Winchester Model 94 Alaskan Purchase Centennial Commemorative Carbine $1595
Same as Wyoming issue, except different medallion and inscription. 1,501 made in 1967.

Winchester Model 94 Antlered Game $495
Standard Model 94 action. Gold-colored medallion inlaid in stock. Antique gold-plated receiver, lever tang and bbl. bands. Medallion and receiver engraved with elk, moose, deer and caribou. 20.5-inch bbl. Curved steel buttplate. In 30-30 caliber. 19,999 made in 1978.

Winchester Model 94 Bicentennial '76 Carbine . . $595
Same as Standard Model 94 Carbine, except caliber 30-30 only; antique silver-finished, engraved receiver; stock and forearm of fancy walnut, checkered, Bicentennial medallion embedded in buttstock, curved buttplate. 20,000 made in 1976.

Winchester Model 94 Buffalo Bill Commemorative
Same as Centennial '66 Rifle, except receiver is black-chromed, scroll-engraved and bears name "Buffalo Bill"; hammer, trigger, loading gate, saddle ring, forearm cap, and buttplate are nickel-plated; Buffalo Bill Memorial Assn. commemorative medallion embedded in buttstock; "Buffalo Bill Commemorative" inscribed on bbl., facsimile signature "W.F. Cody, Chief of Scouts" on tang. Carbine has 20-inch bbl., 6-shot magazine, 7-lb. weight. Made in 1968.

Carbine	**$395**
Rifle	445
Matched Carbine/Rifle Set (120,751 made)	895

Winchester Canadian Centennial '67 Commemorative
Same as Centennial '66 Rifle, except receiver engraved — with maple leaves — mand forearm cap are black-chromed, buttplate is blued, commemorative inscription in gold on barrel and top tang: "Canadian Centennial 1867–1967." Carbine has 20-inch bbl., 6-shot magazine, 7-lb. weight. Made in 1967.

Carbine	**$350**
Rifle	375
Matched Carbine/Rifle Set (90,398 made)	795

Winchester Centennial '66 Commemorative
Commemorates Winchester's 100th anniversary. Standard Model 94 action. Caliber: 30-30. Full-length magazine holds 8 rounds. 26-inch octagon bbl. Weight: 8 lbs. Gold-plated receiver and forearm cap. Sights: open rear; post front. Saddle ring. Wal-

Winchester Centennial '66 Commemorative

**Winchester Model 94
Chief Crazy Horse Commemorative**

Winchester Centennial '66 Commemorative *(Cont.)*

nut buttstock and forearm with high-gloss finish, solid brass butt-plate. Commemorative inscription on bbl. and top tang of receiver. Made in 1966.

Carbine **$395**
Rifle. **425**
Matched Carbine/Rifle Set (100,478 made) **895**

Winchester Model 94 Cheyenne Comm. $750

Available in Canada only. Same as Standard Model 94 Carbine, except chambered for 44-40. 11,225 made in 1977.

Winchester Model 94 Chief Crazy Horse Commemorative $510

Cailber: 38-55, 7-shot tubular magazine. 24-inch bbl., 41.75 inches overall. Walnut stock with medallion of the United Sioux Tribes; buttstock and forend also decorated with brass tacks. Engraved receiver. Open rear sights; bead front sight. 19,999 made in 1983.

Winchester Model 94 Colt Commemorative Carbine Set $2595

Standard Model 94 action. Caliber: 44-40 Win. 20-inch bbl. Weight: 6.25 lbs. Features a horse-and-rider trademark and distinctive WC monogram in gold etching on left side of receiver. Sold in set with Colt Single Action Revolver chambered for same caliber.

Winchester Model 94 Cowboy Commemorative Carbine $475

Same as Standard Model 94 Carbine, except caliber 30-30 only; nickel-plated receiver, tangs, lever, bbl. bands; engraved receiver, "Cowboy Commemorative" on bbl., commemorative medallion embedded in buttstock; curved buttplate. 20,915 made in 1970. Nickel-silver medallion inlaid in stock. Antique silver-plated receiver engraved with scenes of the old frontier. Checkered walnut stock and forearm. 19,999 made in 1979.

Winchester Model 94 Golden Spike Commemorative Carbine $375

Same as Standard Model 94 Carbine, except caliber 30-30 only; gold-plated receiver, tangs and bbl. bands; engraved receiver, commemorative medallion embedded in stock. 64,758 made in 1969.

Winchester Model 94 Illinois Sesquicentennial Commemorative Carbine $395

Same as Standard Model 94 Carbine, except caliber 30-30 only; gold-plated buttplate, trigger, loading gate, and saddle ring; receiver engraved with profile of Lincoln, commemorative inscription on receiver, bbl.; souvenir medallion embedded in stock. 31,124 made in 1968.

Winchester Model 94 Legendary Frontiersmen Commemorative $525

Standard Model 94 action. Caliber: 39-55. 24-inch round bbl. Nickel-silver medallion inlaid in stock. Antique silver-plated receiver engraved with scenes of the old frontier. Checkered walnut stock and forearm. 19,999 made in 1979.

Winchester Model 94 Legendary Lawmen Commemorative $525

Same as Standard Model 94 Carbine, except 30-30 only; antique silver-plated receiver engraved with action law-enforcement scenes. 16-inch Trapper bbl., antique silver-plated bbl. bands. 19,999 made in 1978.

Winchester Model 94 Lone Star Commemorative

Same as Theodore Roosevelt Rifle, except yellow-gold plating; "Lone Star" engraving on receiver and bbl., commemorative medallion embedded in buttstock. Made in 1970.

Rifle. **$450**
Matched Carbine/Rifle Set (30,669 made) **995**

**Winchester Colt
Commemorative Set**

Winchester Model 94 NRA Centennial Rifle

Winchester Model 94 NRA Centennial Musket . . **$395**
Commemorates 100th anniversary of National Rifle Association of America. Standard Model 94 action. Caliber: 30-30. 7-shot magazine. 26-inch bbl. Sights: military folding rear; blade front. Black chrome-finished receiver engraved "NRA 1871–1971" plus scrollwork. Barrel inscribed "NRA Centennial Musket." Musket-style buttstock and full-length forearm; commemorative medallion embedded in buttstock. Weight: 7.13 lbs. Made in 1971.

Winchester Model 94 NRA Centennial Rifle. **$395**
Same as Model 94 Rifle, except has commemorative details as in NRA Centennial Musket (barrel inscribed "NRA Centennial Rifle"); caliber 30-30, 24-inch bbl., QD sling swivels. Made in 1971.

Winchester Model 94 NRA Centennial Matched Set **$850**
Rifle and musket were offered in sets with consecutive serial numbers. *Note:* Production figures not available. These rifles offered in Winchester's 1972 catalog.

Winchester Model 94 Nebraska Centennial Commemorative Carbine. **$1325**
Same as Standard Model 94 Carbine, except caliber 30-30 only; gold-plated hammer, loading gate, bbl. band, and buttplate; souvenir medallion embedded in stock, commemorative inscription on bbl. 2,500 made in 1966.

Winchester Model 94 Theodore Roosevelt Commemorative Rifle/Carbine
Standard Model 94 action. Caliber: 30-30. Rifle has 6-shot half-magazine, 26-inch octagon bbl., 7.5-lb. weight. Carbine has 6-shot full magazine, 20-inch bbl., 7-lb. weight. White gold-plated receiver, upper tang, and forend cap; receiver engraved with American Eagle, "26th President 1901–1909," and Roosevelt's signature. Commemorative medallion embedded in buttstock. Saddle ring. Half pistol grip, contoured lever. Made in 1969.
Carbine **$395**
Rifle. 425
Matched Set (49,505 made) 850

Winchester Model 94 Texas Ranger Association Carbine. **$2400**
Same as Texas Ranger Commemorative Model 94, except special edition of 150 carbines, numbered 1 through 150, with hand-checkered full-fancy walnut stock and forearm. Sold only through Texas Ranger Association. Made in 1973.

Winchester Model 94 Texas Ranger Commemorative Carbine. **$745**
Same as Standard Model 94 Carbine, except caliber 30-30 only, stock and forearm of semi-fancy walnut, replica of Texas Ranger star embedded in buttstock, curved buttplate. 5,000 made in 1973.

Winchester Model 94 John Wayne Comm. **$925**
Standard Model 94 action. Caliber: 32-40. 18.5-inch bbl. Receiver is pewter-plated with engraving of Indian attack and cattle

**Winchester Model 94
John Wayne Carbine**

**Winchester Model 94
Wells Fargo Carbine**

Winchester Model 100 Autoloading Rifle

Winchester Model 94 John Wayne Comm. *(Cont.)*

drive scenes. Oversized bow on lever. Nickel-silver medallion in buttstock bears a bas-relief portrait of Wayne. Selected American walnut stock with deep-cut checkering. Introduced by U.S. Repeating Arms.

Winchester Model 94 Wells Fargo & Co. Commemorative Carbine $525

Same as Standard Model 94 Carbine, except 30-30 only; antique silver-finished, engraved receiver; stock and forearm of fancy walnut, checkered, curved buttplate. Nickel-silver stagecoach medallion (inscribed "Wells Fargo & Co. —1852–1977—125 Years") embedded in buttstock. 20,000 made in 1977.

Winchester Model 94 Oliver F. Winchester Commemorative $595

Standard Model 94 action. Caliber: 38-55. 24-inch octagonal bbl. Receiver is satin gold-plated with distinctive engravings. Stock and forearm semi-fancy American walnut with high grade checkering. 19,999 made in 1980.

Winchester Model 94 Wyoming Diamond Jubilee Commemorative Carbine $1495

Same as Standard Model 94 Carbine, except caliber 30-30 only, receiver engraved and casehardened in colors, brass saddle ring and loading gate, souvenir medallion embedded in buttstock, commemorative inscription on bbl. 1,500 made in 1964.

Winchester Model 100 Autoloading Rifle $405

Gas-operated semiautomatic. Calibers: 243, 284, 308 Win. 4-shot clip magazine (3-shot in 284). 22-inch bbl. Weight: 7.25 lbs. Sights: open rear; hooded ramp front. One-piece stock w/pistol grip, basket-weave checkering, grip cap, sling swivels. Made 1961–1973.

Winchester Model 100 Carbine $450

Same as Model 100 Rifle, except has 19-inch bbl., plain carbine-style stock and forearm with bbl. band. Weight: 7 lbs. Made 1967–1973.

Winchester Model 121 Deluxe $125

Same as Model 121 Standard, except has ramp front sight, stock with fluted comb and sling swivels. Made 1967–1973.

RIFLES

Winchester Model 121 Deluxe

Winchester Model 131

Winchester Model 141

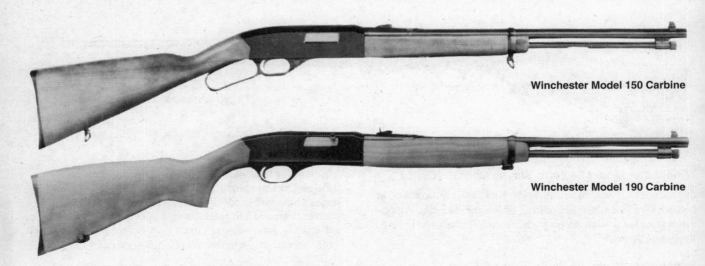

Winchester Model 150 Carbine

Winchester Model 190 Carbine

Winchester Model 121 Standard Bolt-Action Single Shot **$120**
Caliber: 22 Short, Long, LR. 20.75-inch bbl. Weight: 5 lbs. Sights: open rear; bead front. Monte Carlo-style stock. Made 1967–1973.

Winchester Model 121 Youth **$125**
Same as Model 121 Standard, except has 1.25-inch shorter stock. Made 1967–1973.

Winchester Model 131 Bolt-Action Repeater **$135**
Caliber: 22 Short, Long or LR. 7-shot clip magazine. 20.75-inch bbl. Weight: 5 lbs. Sights: open rear; ramp front. Plain Monte Carlo stock. Made 1967–1973. *See* photo preceding page.

Winchester Model 135 . . . . **$125**
Same as Model 131, except chambered for 22 WMR cartridge. Magazine holds 5 rounds. Made in 1967.

Winchester Model 141 Bolt-Action Tubular Repeater **$140**
Same as Model 131, except has tubular magazine in buttstock; holds 19 Short, 15 Long, 13 LR. Made 1967–1973. *See* photo preceding page.

Winchester Model 145 . . . . **$140**
Same as Model 141, except chambered for 22 WMR; magazine holds 9 rounds. Made in 1967.

Winchester Model 150 Lever-Action Carbine . . . **$110**
Same as Model 250, except has straight loop lever, plain carbine-style straight-grip stock and forearm with bbl. band. Made 1967–1973.

Winchester Model 190 Carbine **$120**
Same as Model 190 rifle, except has carbine-style forearm with bbl. band. Made 1967–1973.

Winchester Model 190 Semiautomatic Rifle **$105**
Same as current Model 290, except has plain stock and forearm. Made 1966–1978.

Winchester Model 250 Deluxe Rifle **$150**
Same as Model 250 Standard Rifle, except has fancy walnut Monte Carlo stock and forearm, sling swivels. Made 1965–1971.

Winchester Model 250 Standard Lever-Action Rifle **$120**
Hammerless. Caliber: 22 Short, Long or LR. Tubular magazine holds 21 Short, 17 Long, 15 LR. 20.5-inch bbl. Sights: open rear; ramp front. Weight: about 5 lbs. Plain stock and forearm on early production; later model has checkering. Made 1963–1973.

Winchester Model 255 Deluxe Rifle **$150**
Same as Model 250 Deluxe Rifle, except chambered for 22 WMR cartridge. Magazine holds 11 rounds. Made 1965–1973.

Winchester Model 250 Standard

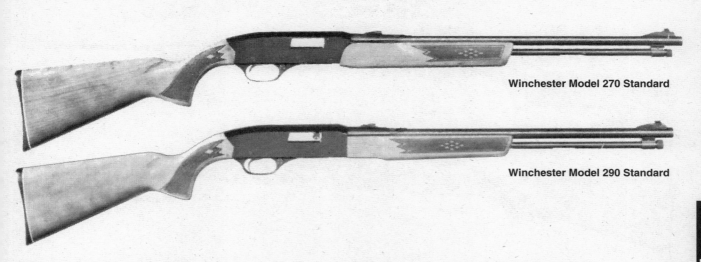

Winchester Model 270 Standard

Winchester Model 290 Standard

Winchester Model 255 Standard Rifle $130
Same as Model 250 Standard Rifle, except chambered for 22 WMR cartridge. Magazine holds 11 rounds. Made 1964–1970.

Winchester Model 270 Deluxe Rifle $125
Same as Model 270 Standard Rifle, except has fancy walnut Monte Carlo stock and forearm. Made 1965–1973.

Winchester Model 270 Standard Slide-Action Rifle $105
Hammerless. Caliber: 22 Short, Long or LR. Tubular magazine holds 21 Short, 17 Long, 15 LR. 20.5-inch bbl. Sights: open rear; ramp front. Weight: about 5 lbs. Early production had plain walnut stock and forearm (slide handle); latter also furnished in plastic (Cycolac); last model has checkering. Made 1963–1973.

Winchester Model 275 Deluxe Rifle $165
Same as Model 270 Deluxe Rifle, except chambered for 22 WMR cartridge. Tubular magazine holds 11 rounds. Made 1965–1970.

Winchester Model 275 Standard Rifle $125
Same as Model 270 Standard Rifle, except chambered for 22 WMR cartridge. Magazine holds 11 rounds. Made 1964–1970.

Winchester Model 290 Deluxe Rifle $175
Same as Model 290 Standard Rifle, except has fancy walnut Monte Carlo stock and forearm. Made 1965–1973.

Winchester Model 290 Standard Semiautomatic Rifle
Caliber: 22 Long or LR. Tubular magazine holds 17 Long, 15 LR. 20.5-inch bbl. Sights: open rear; ramp front. Weight: about 5 lbs. Plain stock and forearm on early production; current model has checkering. Made 1963–1977.
W/plain stock/forearm. $175
W/checkered stock/forearm. **210**

Winchester Model 310 Bolt-Action Single Shot . . . $195
Caliber: 22 Short, Long, LR. 22-inch bbl. Weight: 5.63 lbs. Sights: open rear; ramp front. Monte Carlo stock w/checkered pistol grip and forearm, sling swivels. Made 1972–75.

Winchester Model 310

Winchester Model 320

Winchester Model 490

Winchester Model 670

Winchester Model 670 Magnum

Winchester Model 320 Bolt-Action Repeater **$295**
Same as Model 310, except has 5-shot clip magazine. Made 1972–74. *See* photo preceding page.

Winchester Model 490 Semiautomatic Rifle **$250**
Caliber: 22 LR. 5-shot clip magazine. 22-inch bbl. Weight: 6 lbs. Sights: folding leaf rear; hooded ramp front. One-piece walnut stock w/checkered pistol grip and forearm. Made 1975–77.

Winchester Model 670 Bolt-Action Sporting Rifle **$250**
Calibers: 225 Win., 243 Win., 270 Win., 30-06, 308 Win. 4-shot magazine. 22-inch bbl. Weight: 7 lbs. Sights: open rear; ramp front. Monte Carlo stock w/checkered pistol grip and forearm. Made 1967–1973.

Winchester Model 670 Carbine **$275**
Same as Model 670 Rifle, except has 19-inch bbl. Weight: 6.75 lbs. Calibers: 243 Win., 270 Win., 30-06. Made 1967–1970.

Winchester Model 670 Magnum **$295**
Same as Model 670 Rifle, except has 24-inch bbl., reinforced stock with recoil pad with slightly different checkering pattern. Weight: 7.25 lbs. Calibers: 264 Win. Mag., 7mm Rem. Mag., 300 Win. Mag. Open rear sight; ramp front sight with hood. Made 1967–1970.

Winchester Model 770 Bolt-Action Sporting Rifle **$295**
Model 70-type action. Calibers: 22-250, 222 Rem., 243, 270 Win., 30-06. 4-shot box magazine. 22-inch bbl. Sights: open rear; hooded ramp front. Weight: 7.13 lbs. Monte Carlo stock, checkered pistol grip and forend; sling swivels. Made 1969–1971.

Winchester Model 770 Magnum **$315**
Same as Standard Model 770, except 24-inch bbl., weight 7.25 lbs., recoil pad. Calibers: 7mm Rem. Mag., 264 and 300 Win. Mag. Made 1969–1971.

Winchester Model 770

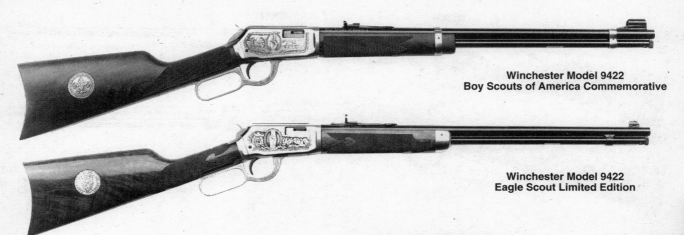

**Winchester Model 9422
Boy Scouts of America Commemorative**

**Winchester Model 9422
Eagle Scout Limited Edition**

Winchester Model 9422 Boy Scouts of America Commemorative $500

Standard Model 9422 action. Caliber: 22RF. 20.5-inch round bbl. Receiver roll-engraved and plated in antique pewter, illustrating the Boy Scout oath and law. Frame carries inscription, "1910–1985." "Boy Scouts of America" inscribed on right side of bbl. Checkered stock and forearm of American walnut with satin finish. A maximum of 15,000 were produced by U.S. Repeating Arms beginning with serial number BSA1.

Winchester Model 9422 Eagle Scout Commemorative $2195

Standard Model 9422 action. Caliber: 22 RF. Same general specifications as Boy Scout model except different engraving, jeweled bolt, antique gold-plated forearm cap and brass magazine tube. Only 1,000 were made by U.S. Repeating Arms bearing serial number Eagle 1 through Eagle 1,000.

Winchester Model 9422 Lever-Action Carbine . . $245

Styled after Model 94. Caliber: 22 Short, Long, LR. Tubular magazine holds 21 Short, 17 Long, 15 LR. 20.5-inch bbl. Weight: 6.25 lbs. Sights: open rear; hooded ramp front. Carbine-style stock and forearm, bbl. band. Made 1972 to date.

Winchester Model 9422M $295

Same as Model 9422, except chambered for 22 WMR; magazine holds 11 rounds. Stock options: Walnut, Win-Cam (laminated green), Win-Tuff (laminated brown). Made 1972 to date.

Winchester Model 9422 Win-Cam $260

Caliber: 22 RF. 11-shot magazine. 20.5-inch bbl. 37.13 inches overall. Weight: 6.25 lbs. Laminated non-glare green-shaded stock and forend. Made 1987 to date.

Winchester Model 9422 XTR Classic $275

Same general specifications as standard Model 9422, except has pistol-grip stock and weighs 6.5 lbs.

Winchester Double Xpress Rifle $2150

Over/under double rifle. Caliber: 30-06. 23.5-inch bbl. Weight: 8.5 lbs. Made for Olin Corp. by Olin-Kodensha in Japan. Introduced 1982.

Winchester Ranger Bolt-Action Carbine $260

Calibers: 223 Rem., 243 Win., 270, 30-06, 7mm Rem. (discontinued 1985), Mag. 3- and 4-shot magazine. Bbl.: 24-inch in 7mm; 22-inch in 270 and 30-06. Open sights. American hardwood stock. Made 1985 to date by U.S. Repeating Arms.

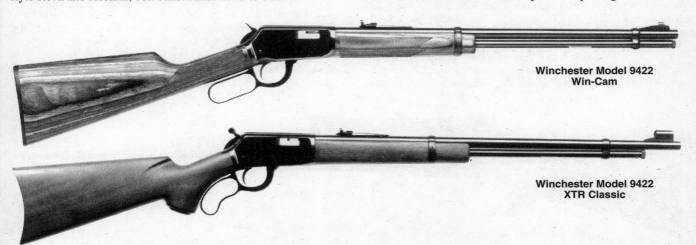

**Winchester Model 9422
Win-Cam**

**Winchester Model 9422
XTR Classic**

Winchester Ranger Bolt-Action Rifle

Winchester Ranger Lever-Action Rifle

Winchester Ranger Youth Bolt-Action Carbine . . $265
Calibers: 223 (discontinued 1989), 243, and 308 Win. 4- and 5-shot magazine. Bbl.: 20-inch. Weight: 5.75 lbs. American hardwood stock. Open rear sight. Made 1985 to date by U.S. Repeating Arms.

Winchester Ranger Lever-Action
Carbine **$185**
Caliber: 30-30. 5-shot tubular magazine. Bbl.: 20-inch round. Weight: 6.5 lbs. American hardwood stock. Economy version of Model 94. Made 1985 to date by U.S. Repeating Arms.

WINSLOW ARMS COMPANYWINSLOW ARMS COMPANY
Camden, South Carolina

Winslow Bolt-Action Sporting Rifle
Action: FN Supreme Mauser, Mark X Mauser, Remington 700 and 788, Sako, Winchester 70. *Standard calibers:* 17-222, 17-223, 222 Rem., 22-250, 243 Win., 6mm Rem., 25-06, 257 Roberts, 270 Win., 7×57, 280 Rem., 284 Win., 308 Win., 358 Win. *Magnum calibers:* 17-222 Mag., 257 Weatherby, 264 Win., 270 Weath., 7mm Rem., 7mm Weath., 300 H&H, 300 Weath., 300 Win., 308 Norma, 8mm Rem., 338 Win., 358 Norma, 375 H&H, 375 Weath., 458 Win. 3-shot magazine in standard calibers, 2-shot in magnum. 24-inch barrel in standard calibers, 26-inch in magnum. Weight: with 24-inch bbl., 7 to 7.5 lbs.; with 26-inch bbl., 8 to 9 lbs. No sights. Stocks: "Bushmaster" with slender pistol grip and beavertail forearm, "Plainsmaster" with full curl pistol grip and flat forearm; both styles have

Winslow Bolt-Action Sporting Rifle *(Cont.)*
Monte Carlo cheekpiece; rosewood forend tip and pistol-grip cap, recoil pad, QD swivels; woods used include walnut, maple, myrtle. There are eight grades—Commander, Regal, Regent, Regimental, Royal, Imperial, Emperor— ascending order of quality of wood, carving, inlays, engraving. Values shown are for basic rifle in each grade; extras such as special fancy wood, more elaborate carving, inlays and engraving can increase these figures considerably. Made 1962–1989.

Commander Grade	$ 495
Regal Grade	585
Regent Grade	695
Regimental Grade	895
Crown Grade.	1200
Royal Grade	1400
Imperial Grade	3000
Emperor Grade	5500

ZEPHYR DOUBLE RIFLES
Manufactured by Victor Sarasqueta Company
Eibar, Spain

Zephyr Double Rifle **$16,000**
Boxlock. Calibers: Available in practically every caliber from .22 Hornet to .505 Gibbs. Bbls.: 22 to 28 inches standard, but any lengths were available on special order. Weight: 7 lbs. for the smaller caliber up to 12 or more lbs. for the larger calibers. Checkered Spanish walnut stock and beavertail forearm. Receiver engraved with scroll patterns. Imported by Stoeger from about 1938 to1951.

Winslow Crown Grade

Section III
SHOTGUNS

ALDENS SHOTGUN
Chicago, Illinois

Aldens Model 670 Chieftain Slide Action **$165**
Hammerless. Gauges: 12, 20 and others. 3-shot tubular magazine. Bbl.: 26- to 30-inch; various chokes. Weight: 6.25 to 7.5 lbs. depending on bbl. length and ga. Walnut-finished hardwood stock.

AMERICAN ARMS
N. Kansas City, Missouri

See also Franchi Shotguns.

American Arms Bristol Over/Under **$560**
Boxlock with Greener crossbolt and false engraved sideplates. Gauges: 12, 20; 3-inch chambers. Bbls.: 26-, 30-, or 32-inch vent-rib in various choke combinations. Single selective trigger. Checkered walnut stock and forend. Imported 1986 to 1989.

American Arms Brittany Hammerless Double **$570**
Boxlock with engraved case-colored receiver. Single selective trigger. Selective automatic ejectors. Gauges: 12, 20. 3-inch chambers. Bbls.: 25- or 27-inch with screw in choke tubes (IC/M/F). Weight: 6.5 pounds (20 ga.). Checkered English-style walnut stock with semibeavertail forearm or pistol-grip stock with high-gloss finish. Imported from 1989 to date.

American Arms Camper Special

American Arms Camper Special. **$85**
Similar to the Single Barrel, except a takedown model with 21-inch bbl., M choke and pistol-grip stock. Made in 1989 only.

NOTE

The following abbreviations are used throughout this section when referring to chokes: Cyl.=Cylinder; F=Full; IC=Improved Cylinder; IM=Improved Modified; M=Modified; SK=Skeet.

American Arms Combo **$155**
Similar to the Single-Barrel model, except available with interchangeable rifle and shotgun bbls. 22 LR/20-ga. shotgun or 22 Hornet/12-ga. shotgun. Rifle bbl. has adj. rear sights; blade-type front sight. Made in 1989.

American Arms Derby Hammerless Double **$645**
Sidelock with engraved sideplates. Single non-selective trigger. Selective automatic ejectors. Gauges: 12, 20. 3 inch chambers. Bbls.: 26-inch (IC/M) or 28-inch (M/ F). Weight: 6 lbs. (20 ga.). Checkered English-style walnut stock and splinter forearm with hand-rubbed oil finish. Engraved frame/sideplates w/antique silver finish. Imported 1986 to 1994.

American Arms Bristol Over/Under

American Arms Derby

American Arms Gentry/York

American Arms Silver

American Arms WS/SS Hammerless

American Arms Gentry Hammerless Double
Color casehardened boxlock receiver with scroll engraving. Double triggers. Extractors. Gauges: 12, 16, 20, 28, .410. 3-inch chambers (16 and 28 have 2.75-inch). Bbls.: 26-inch (IC/M) or 28-inch (M/F, 12, 16 and 20). Weight: 6.75 lbs. (12 ga.). Checkered walnut buttstock with pistol grip and beavertail forearm; both with semi-gloss oil finish. Imported from 1987 to date.

12, 16 or 20 Gauge	$455
28 or .410 Gauge	500

American Arms Grulla #2 Hammerless Double
True sidelock with engraved detachable sideplates. Double triggers. Extractors and cocking indicators. Gauges: 12 and 20 w/2.75-inch chambers; 28 and .410 with 3-inch. Bbls.: 26-inch (IC/M) or 28-inch (M/F, 12 and 28 ga. only). Weight: 6.25 lbs. (12 gauge). English-style walnut stock and splinter forearm w/hand-rubbed oil finish and checkered grip, forearm and butt. Imported 1989 to 1995.

Standard Model	$2400
Two-barrel Set	2975

American Arms Silver I Over/Under
Boxlock. Single selective trigger. Extractors. Gauges: 12, 20 and .410 with 3-inch chambers; 28 with 2.75 inch. Bbls.: 26-inch (IC/M), 28-inch (M/F, i2 and 20 ga. only). Weight: 6.75 lbs. (12 ga.). Checkered walnut stock and forearm. Antique-silver receiver with scroll engraving. Imported from 1987 to date.

12 or 20 Gauge	$410
28 or .410 Gauge	450

American Arms Silver II Over/Under
Similar to Model Silver I, except with selective automatic ejectors and 26-inch barrels with screw-in tubes (12 and 20 ga.). Fixed chokes (28 and .410). Made 1987 to date.

12 or 20 Gauge	$540
28 or .410	560
Two-barrel Set	825

American Arms Silver Lite Over/Under
Similar to Model Silver II, except with blued, engraved alloy receiver. Available in 12 and 20 gauge only. Imported from 1990 to 1992.

Standard Model	$525
Two-barrel Set	830

American Arms Silver Skeet/Trap $700
Similar to the Silver II Model, except has 28-inch (Skeet) or 30-inch (Trap) ported barrels with target-style rib and mid-bead sight. Imported from 1992 to date.

American Arms Silver Sporting Over/Under $645
Boxlock. Single selective trigger. Selective automatic ejectors. Gauges: 12, 2.75-inch chambers. Bbls.: 28-inch with Franchoke tubes: SK, IC, M and F. Weight: 7.5 lbs. Checkered walnut stock and forearm. Special broadway rib and vented side ribs. Engraved receiver with chrome-nickel finish. Imported from 1990 to date.

American Arms Single-Shot Shotgun $85
Break-open action. Gauges: 12, 20, .410, 3-inch chamber. Weight: about 6.5 lbs. Bead front sight. Walnut-finished hardwood stock with checkered grip and forend. Made from 1988 to 1990.

American Arms Slugger Single-Shot Shotgun . . . $95
Similar to the Single-Shot model, except in 12 and 20 ga. only with 24-inch slug bbl. Rifle-type sights and recoil pad. Made from 1989 to 1990.

American Arms TS/OU 12 Shotgun $540
Turkey Special. Boxlock. Single selective trigger. Selective automatic ejectors. Gauge: 12, 3.5-inch chambers. Bbls.: 24-inch O/U with screw-in choke tubes (IC, M, F). Weight: 6 lbs. 15 oz. Checkered European walnut stock and beavertail forearm. Matte blue metal finish. Imported 1987 to date.

American Arms TS/SS 10 Hammerless Double . . $595
Turkey Special. Same general specifications as Model WS/SS 10, except with 26-inch side-by-side bbls., screw-in choke tubes (F/F) and chambered for 10-ga. 3.5-inch shells. Weight: 10 lbs. 13 oz. Imported 1987 to 1993.

American Arms TS/SS 12 Hammerless Double . . $495
Same general specifications as Model WS/SS 10, except in 12 gauge with 26-inch side-by-side bbls. and 3 screw-in choke tubes (IC/M/F). Weight: 7 lbs. 6 oz. Imported 1987 to date.

American Arms WS/OU 12 Shotgun $495
Waterfowl Special. Boxlock. Single selective trigger. Selective automatic ejectors. Gauge: 12; 3.5-inch chambers. Bbls.: 28-inch O/U with screw-in tubes (IC/M/F). Weight: 7 lbs. Checkered European walnut stock and beavertail forearm. Matte blue metal finish. Imported 1987 to date.

American Arms WS/SS 10 Hammerless Double . . . $595
Waterfowl Special. Boxlock. Double triggers. Extractors. Gauge: 10; 3.5-inch chambers. Bbls.: 32-inch side/side choked F/F. Weight: about 11 lbs. Checkered walnut stock and beavertail forearm with satin finish. Parkerized metal finish. Imported from 1987 to 1995.

American Arms WT/OU 10 Shotgun $750
Same general specifications as Model WS/OU 12, except chambered for 10-ga. 3.5-inch shells. Extractors. Satin wood finish and matte blue metal. Imported 1987 to date.

SHOTGUNS

Armalite AR-17

ARMALITE, INC.
Costa Mesa, California

Armalite AR-17 Golden Gun **$545**
Recoil-operated semiautomatic. High-test aluminum barrel and receiver housing. 12 ga. only. 2-shot. 24-inch bbl. with interchangeable choke tubes: IC/M/F. Weight: 5.6 lbs. Polycarbonate stock and forearm recoil pad. Gold anodized finish standard, also made with black finish. Made 1964-65. Less than 2,000 produced.

ARMSPORT, INC.
Miami, Florida

Armsport Models 1050,1053,1054 Hammerless Doubles
Side-by-side with engraved receiver, double triggers and extractors. Gauges: 12, 20, .410- 3-inch chambers. **Model 1050:** 12 ga., 28-inch bbl., M/F choke. **Model 1053:** 20 ga., 26-inch bbl., I/M choke. **Model 1054:** .410 ga., 26-inch bbl., I/M. Weight: 6 lbs. (12 ga.). European walnut buttstock and forend. Made in Italy. Importation discontinued 1993.
Model 1050 .... **$555**
Model 1053 .... **600**
Model 1054 .... **615**

Armsport Model 1125 Single-Shot Shotgun **$75**
Bottom-opening lever. Gauges: 12, 20. 3-inch chambers. Bead front sight. Plain stock and forend. Made 1987 to 1989.

Armsport Model 2700 Goose Gun
Similar to the 2700 Standard Model, except 10 ga. w/2-inch chambers. Double triggers with 28-inch bbl. choked IC/M or 32-inch bbl., F/F. 12mm wide vent rib. Weight: 9.5 lbs. Canada geese engraved on receiver. Antiqued silver-finished action. Checkered European walnut stock w/rubber recoil pad. Made in Italy 1986 to 1993.
With Fixed Chokes **$810**
With Choke Tubes **875**

Armsport Model 2700 Over/Under Series
Hammerless, takedown shotgun with engraved receiver. Selective single or double triggers. Gauges: 10, 12, 20, 28 and .410. Bbl.: 26-or 28-inch with fixed chokes or choke tubes. Weight: 8 lbs. Checkered European walnut buttstock and forend. Made in Italy. Importation discontinued 1993.
Model 2705 (.410, DT, fixed chokes) **$535**
Model 2730/31 (Boss-style action, SST Choke tubes) ... **595**
Model 2733/35 (Boss-style action, extractors) **595**
Model 2741 (Boss-style action, ejectors) **745**
Model 2742 Sporting Clays (12 ga./choke tubes) **595**
Model 2744 Sporting Clays (20 ga./choke tubes) **595**
Model 2750 Sporting Clays (12 ga./sideplates) **685**
Model 2751 Sporting Clays (20 ga./sideplates) **685**

Armsport Model 2755 Slide-Action Shotgun
Gauge: 12 w/3-inch chamber. Tubular magazine. Bbls.: 28- or 30-inch w/fixed choke or choke tubes. Weight: 7 lbs. European walnut stock. Made in Italy 1986-87.
Standard Model, Fixed choke **$275**
Standard Model, Choke Tubes **345**
Police Model, 20-inch Bbl........................ **250**

Armsport Model 1050

Armsport Model 1125

Armsport Model 2741

Armsport Model 2900 Tri-Barrel

Armsport Model 2900 Tri-Barrel Shotgun $2450

Boxlock. Double triggers with top-tang bbl. selector. Extractors. Gauge: 12; 3-inch chambers. Bbls.: 28-inch (IC, M and F). Weight: 7.75 lbs. Checkered European walnut stock and forearm. Engraved silver receiver. Imported from 1986 to 1993.

ASTRA SHOTGUNS
Guernica, Spain
Manufactured by Unceta y Compania

Astra Model 650 Over/Under Shotgun

Hammerless, takedown with double triggers. 12 gauge w/ ¾-inch chambers. Bbls.: 28-inch (M/F or SK/SK); 30-inch (M/F). Weight: 6.75 lbs. Checkered European walnut buttstock and forend.

With Extractors	$450
With Ejectors	545

Astra Model 750 Over/Under Shotgun

Similar to the Model 650, except with selective single trigger and ejectors. Made in field, Skeet and Trap configurations since 1980.

Field Model w/Extractors	$500
Field Model w/Ejectors	595
Trap or Skeet	710

AYA (AGUIRRE Y ARANZABAL)
Eibar, Spain
Previously Manufactured by Diarm

AyA Model 1 Hammerless Double

A Holland & Holland sidelock similar to the Model 2 except in 12 and 20 ga. only, with special engraving and exhibition-grade wood. Weight: 5-8 lbs., depending on ga. Imported since 1992 by Armes de Chasse.

Model 1 w/Single Trigger (Early Importation)	$2795
Model 1 w/Double Triggers	2395
Two Bbl. Set, add	2150

AyA Model 2 Hammerless Double

Sidelock action with selective single or double triggers automatic ejectors and safety. Gauges: 12, 20, 28, (2.75-inch chambers); .410 (3-inch chambers). Bbls.: 26- or 28-inch w/various fixed choke combinations. Weight: 7 lbs. (12 ga.). English-style straight walnut buttstock and splinter forend. Imported since 1992 by Armes de Chasse.

12 or 20 ga. w/Double Triggers	$1450
12 or 20 ga. w/Single Trigger	1525
28 or .410 ga. w/Double Triggers	1600
28 or .410 ga. w/Double Trigger	1750
Two-bbl. Set	2150

AyA Model 4 Hammerless Double

Lightweight Anson & Deely boxlock with a scalloped frame. Gauges: 12, 16, 20, 28, and .410. Bbls.: 25- to 28-inch with concave rib. Importation discontinued 1987 and resumed in 1992 by Armes de Chasse.

12 Gauge	$645
16 Gauge (early importation)	470
20 Gauge	635
28 Gauge	695
.410 Bore	745
Deluxe Grades, **add**	500

AyA Model 37 Super Over/Under Shotgun $2595

Sidelock. automatic ejectors. Selective single trigger. Made in all gauges, bbl. lengths and chokes. Vent-rib bbls. Elaborately engraved. Checkered stock (w/straight or pistol grip) and forend. Discontinued 1895.

AyA Model Super A Over/Under Shotgun $4595

Similar to the Standard Model 37 Super except has nickel steel frame and fitted with detachable sidelocks engraved with game scenes. Importation discontinued 1987 and resumed 1992 by Armes de Chasse.

AyA Model 53E $1695

Same general specifications as Model 117, except more elaborate engraving and select figured wood. Importation discontinued 1987 and resumed in 1992 by Armes de Chasse.

AyA Model 56 Hammerless Double

Pigeon weight Holland & Holland sidelock with Purdey-style third lug and sideclips. Gauges: 12, 16, 20. Receiver has fine-line scroll and rosette engraving; gold-plated locks. Importation discontinued 1987 and resumed 1992 by Armes de Chasse.

12 Gauge	$2770
16 Gauge (early importation)	2160
20 Gauge (early importation)	2895

AyA Model 53E

SHOTGUNS

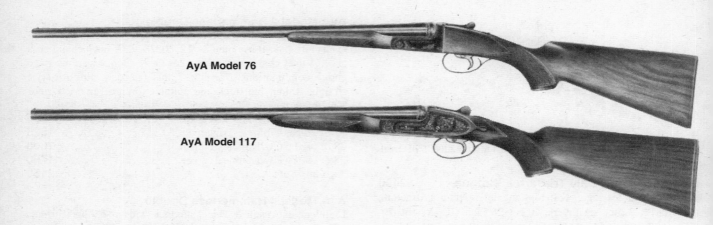

AyA Model 76

AyA Model 117

AyA Model 76 Hammerless Double **$550**
Anson & Deeley boxlock. Auto ejectors. Selective single trigger.
Gauges: 12, 20 (3-inch). Bbls.: 26-, 28-, 30-inch (latter in 12 ga.
only), any standard choke combination. Checkered pistol-grip
stock/beavertail forend. Disc.

AyA Model 76—.410 Gauge **$610**
Same general specifications as 12 and 20 gauge Model 76, except chambered for 3-inch shells in .410, has extractors, double
triggers, 26-inch bbls. only, English-style stock with straight
grip and small forend. Discontinued.

AyA Model 117 Hammerless Double **$825**
Holland & Holland-type sidelocks, hand-detachable. Engraved
action. Automatic ejectors. Selective single trigger. Gauges: 12,
20 (3-inch). Bbls.: 26-, 27-, 28-, 30-inch; 27- and 30-inch in 12
ga. only; any standard choke combination. Checkered pistol-grip
stock and beavertail forend of select walnut. Manufactured in
1985.

AyA Bolero **$350**
Same general specifications as Matador except non-selective
single trigger and extractors. Gauges: 12 16, 20, 20 Magnum (3-
inch), .410 (3-inch). *Note:* This model, prior to 1956, was designated F. I. Model 400 by the importer. Made 1955-1963.

AyA Contento Over/Under Shotgun
Boxlock with Woodward side lugs and double internal bolts.
Gauges: 12 (2.75-inch chambers). Bbls.: 26-, 28-inch field; 30-,
32-inch trap; either fixed chokes as required or screw-in choke
tubes. Hand-checkered European Walnut stock and forend.
Single-selective trigger and automatic ejectors.

AyA Contento Over/Under Shotgun *(Cont.)*
M.K.1 Field . . . . **$ 575**
M.K.2 . . . .   **725**
M.K.3 . . . .   **1260**
Add for interchangeable single bbl. **400**

AyA Matador Hammerless Double **$425**
Anson & Deeley boxlock. Selective automatic ejectors. Selective single trigger. Gauges: 12, 16, 20, 20 Magnum (3-inch).
Bbls.: 26-, 28-, 30-inch; any standard choke combination.
Weight: 6.5 to 7.5 lbs., depending on ga. and bbl. length. Checkered pistol-grip stock and beavertail forend. *Note:* This model,
prior to 1956, was designated F. I. Model 400E by the U.S. importer, Firearms Int'l. Corp. of Washington, D.C. Made 1955-
1963.

AyA Matador II **$495**
Improved version of Matador with same general specifications,
except has vent-rib barrels. Made 1964-69.

AyA Matador III **$710**
Same general specifications as AyA Matador II. Made 1970-
1985.

BAIKAL SHOTGUNS

See K.B.I, Inc.

AyA Matador II

Baker Black Beauty Special

BAKER SHOTGUNS
Batavia, New York
Made 1903-1933 by Baker Gun Company

Baker Batavia Ejector $775
Same general specifications as the Batavia Leader, except higher quality and finer finish throughout; has Damascus or homotensile steel bbls., checkered pistol-grip stock and forearm of select walnut; automatic ejectors standard; 12 and 16 ga. only.

Baker Batavia Leader Hammerless Double
Sidelock. Plain extractors or automatic ejectors. Double triggers. Gauges: 12, 16, 20. Bbls.: 26- to 32-inch; any standard boring. Weight: about 7.75 lbs. (12 ga. with 30-inch bbls.). Checkered pistol-grip stock and forearm.
With Plain Extractors $415
With Automatic Ejectors 450

Baker Batavia Special $325
Same general specifications as the Batavia Leader, except plainer finish, 12 and 16 ga. only; has plain extractors, homotensile steel bbls.

Baker Black Beauty Special
Same general specifications as the Batavia Leader, except higher quality and finer finish throughout; has line engraving, special steel bbls., select walnut stock w/straight, full or half-pistol grip.
With Plain Extractors $715
With Automatic Ejectors 795

Baker Grade R
High-grade gun with same general specifications as the Batavia Leader, except has fine Damascus or Krupp fluid steel bbls., engraving in line, scroll and game scene designs, checkered stock and forearm of fancy European walnut; 12 and 16 ga. only.
Non-ejector $1000
With Automatic Ejectors 1200

Baker Grade S
Same general specifications as the Batavia Leader, except higher quality and finer finish throughout; has Flui-tempered steel bbls., line and scroll engraving, checkered stock with half-pistol grip and forearm of semifancy imported walnut; 10, 12 and 16 ga.
Non-ejector $765
With Automatic Ejectors 985

Baker Paragon, Expert and Deluxe Grades
Made to order only, these are the higher grades of Baker hammerless sidelock double-bbl. shotguns. After 1909, the Paragon Grade, as well as the Expert and Deluxe introduced that year, had a cross bolt in addition to the regular Baker system taper wedge fastening. There are early Paragon guns with Damascus bbls. and some are non-ejector, but this grade was also produced with automatic ejectors and with the finest fluid steel bbls., in lengths to 34 inches, standard on Expert and Deluxe guns.

Differences among the three models are in overall quality, finish, elaborateness of engraving and grade of fancy figured walnut in the stock and forearm; Expert and Deluxe wood may be carved as well as checkered. Choice of straight, full or half-pistol grip was offered. A single trigger was available in the two higher grades. The Paragon was available in 10 ga.

SHOTGUNS

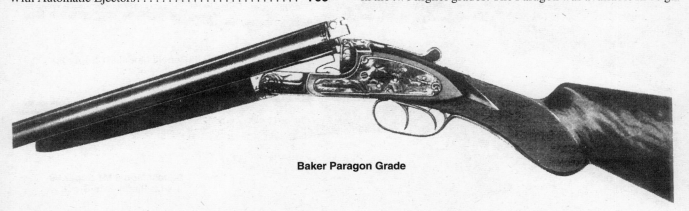

Baker Paragon Grade

Baker Paragon, Expert and Deluxe Grades *(Cont.)*

(Damascus bbls. only), this and the other two models were regularly produced in 12, 16 and 20 ga.

Paragon Grade, Non-ejector	$1525
Paragon Grade, Automatic Ejectors	1625
Expert Grade	2495
Deluxe Grade	3725
For Single Trigger, **add**	250

BELKNAP SHOTGUNS
Louisville, Kentucky

Belknap Model B-63 Single-Shot Shotgun $85
Takedown. Visible hammer. Automatic ejector. Gauges: 12, 20 and .410. Bbls.: 26- to 36-inch, F choke. Weight: average 6 lbs. Plain pistol-grip stock and forearm.

Belknap Model B-63E Single-Shot Shotgun $85
Same general specifications as Model B-68, except has side lever opening instead of top lever.

Belknap Model B-64 Slide-Action Shotgun $175
Hammerless. Gauges: 12, 16, 20 and .410. 3-shot tubular magazine. Various bbl. lengths and chokes from 26-inch to 30-inch. Weight: 6.25 to 7.5 lbs. Walnut-finished hardwood stock.

Belknap Model B-65C Autoloading Shotgun $285
Browning-type lightweight alloy receiver. 12 gauge only. 4-shot tubular magazine. Bbl.: plain, 28-inch. Weight: about 8.25 lbs. Discontinued 1949.

Belknap Model B-68 Single-Shot Shotgun $95
Takedown. Visible hammer. Automatic ejector. Gauges: 12, 16, 20 and .410. Bbls.: 26-inch to 36-inch; F choke. Weight: 6 lbs. Plain pistol-grip stock and forearm.

BENELLI SHOTGUNS
Urbino, Italy

Benelli Model 121 M1 Military/Police Autoloading Shotgun $365
Gauge: 12. 7-shot magazine. 19.75-inch bbl. 39.75 inches overall. Cylinder choke, 2.75-inch chamber. Weight: 7.4 lbs. Matte black finish and European hardwood stock. Post front sight, fixed buckhorn rear sight. Made in 1985.

Benelli Model Black Eagle Autoloading Shotgun
Two-piece aluminum and steel receiver. Gauge: 12; 3-inch chamber. 4-shot magazine. Screw-in choke tubes (SK, IC, M, IM, F). Bbls.: ventilated rib; 21, 24, 26 or 28 inches w/bead front sight; 24-inch rifled slug. 42.5 to 49.5 inches overall. Weight: 7.25 lbs. (28-inch bbl.). Matte black lower receiver with blued upper receiver and bbl. Checkered walnut stock with high-gloss finish and drop adjustment. Made from 1989 to date.

Competition Model	$675
Slug Model (Discontinued 1992)	495
Standard Model (Discontinued 1992)	475

Benelli Model Black Eagle Executive
Custom Black Eagle Series. Montefeltro-style rotating bolt with three locking lugs. All steel tower receiver engraved and gold inlayed by Bottega Incisione di Cesare Giovanelli. 12 gauge only. 21-, 24-, 26-, or 28-inch vent-rib bbl. w/5 screw-in choke tubes (Type I) or fixed chokes. Custom deluxe walnut stock and forend. Built to customer specifications on special order.

Executive Type I	$2825
Executive Type II	3295
Executive Type III	3850

Benelli Model M1 Super 90 Defense Autoloader . . $525
Same general specifications as Model Super 90, except w/pistol-grip stock. Available with Ghost-Ring sight option. Made from 1986 to date.

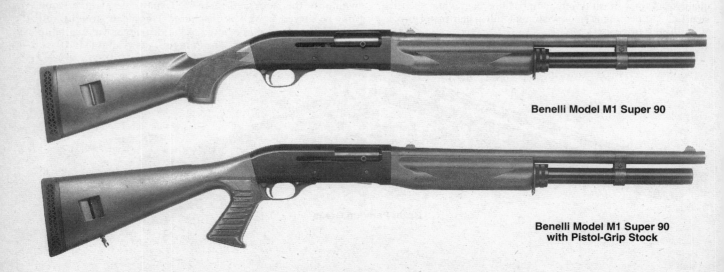

Benelli Model M1 Super 90

**Benelli Model M1 Super 90
with Pistol-Grip Stock**

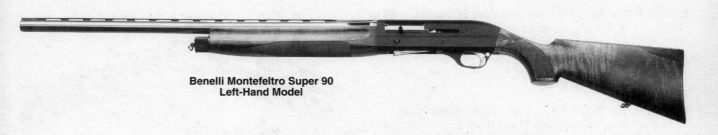

**Benelli Montefeltro Super 90
Left-Hand Model**

Benelli Model M1 Super 90 Entry Autoloader . . . $600
Same gen. specifications as Model Super 90, except w/5-shot magazine. 14-inch bbl. 35.5 inches overall. Weight: 6.5 lbs. Standard or pistol-grip stock. Made 1992 to date. *Special permit required for under 18 inch bbl.*

Benelli Model M1 Super 90 Field
Inertia-recoil semiautomatic shotgun. Gauge: 12; 3-inch chamber. 3-shot magazine. Bbl.: 21, 24, 26 or 28 inches. 42.5 to 49.5 inches overall. Choke: SK, IC, M, IM, F. Matte receiver. Standard polymer stock or satin walnut (26- or 28-inch bbl. only). Bead front sight. Made from 1990 to date.
With Polymer Stock $460
With Walnut Stock 480

Benelli Model M1 Super 90 Slug Autoloader
Same general specifications as M1 Super 90 Field, except w/5-shot magazine. 18.5-inch bbl. Cylinder bore. 39.75 inches overall. Weight: 6.5 lbs. Polymer standard stock. Rifle or Ghost-Ring sights. Made from 1986 to date.
With Rifle Sights $550
With Ghost-Ring Sights 595

Benelli Model M1 Super 90 Sporting Special Autoloader $575
Same general specifications as M1 Super 90 Field, except w/18.5-inch bbl. 39.75 inches overall. Weight: 6.5 lbs. Ghost-ring sights. Polymer stock. Made from 1994 to date.

Benelli Model M1 Super 90 Tactical Autoloader . . $625
Same general specifications as M1 Super 90 Field, except w/18.5-inch bbl. 5-shot magazine. IC, M, or F choke. 39.75 inches overall. Weight: 6.5 lbs. Rifle or Ghost-Ring sights. Polymer pistol-grip or standard stock. Made from 1994 to date.

Benelli Model M3 Super 90 Pump/Autoloader
Inertia-recoil semiautomatic and/or pump action. Gauge: 12. 7-shot magazine. Cylinder choke. 19.75-inch bbl. 41 inches overall (31 inches folded). Weight: 7 to 7.5 lbs. Matte black finish. Stock: standard synthetic, pistol-grip or folding tubular steel. Standard rifle or Ghost-Ring sights. Made from 1989 to

Benelli Model M3 Super 90 Pump/Autoloader *(Cont.)*
date. *Caution: Increasing the magazine capacity to more than 5 rounds in M3 shotguns w/pistol-grip stocks violates provisions of the 1994 Crime Bill. This model may be used legally only by the military and law-enforcement agencies.*
Standard Model $685
Pistol-grip Model 750
With Folding Stock 795
With Laser Sight 995
For Ghost Ring Sights, **add** 50

Benelli Montefeltro Super 90 Semiautomatic
Same general specifications as Model M1 Super 90, except has checkered walnut stock with high-gloss finish. Bbls.: 21, 24, 26 or 28 inches, with screw-in choke tubes (IC, M, IM, F). Weight: 7.5 lbs. Blued finish. Imported from 1987 to date.
Standard Model $595
Slug Model (Discontinued 1992) 625
Turkey Model 615
Uplander Model 625
Left-hand Model 650

Benelli Model SL 121V Semiauto Shotgun $325
Gauge: 12. 5-shot capacity. Bbls.: 26-, 28- and 30-inch. 26-inch choked M, IM, IC, 28-inch, F, M, IM; 30-inch, F choke (Mag.). Straight walnut stock with hand-checkered pistol grip and forend. Ventilated rib. Made in 1985.

Benelli Model SL 121V Slug Shotgun $350
Same general specifications as Benelli SL 121V, except designed for rifled slugs and equipped with rifle sights. Made in 1985.

Benelli Model SL 123V Semiauto Shotgun $375
Gauge: 12. 26- and 28-inch bbls. 26-inch choked IM, M, IC; 28-inch choked F, IM, M. Made in 1985.

Benelli Model SL 201 Semiautomatic Shotgun . . $320
Gauge: 20. 26-inch bbl. Mod. choke. Weight: 5 lbs., 10 oz. Ventilated rib. Made in 1985.

SHOTGUNS

Benelli Model SL121V

Benelli Model Super 90 Autoloading Shotgun . . $515
Gauge: 12. 7-shot magazine. Cylinder choke. 19.75-inch bbl. 39.75 inches overall. Weight: 7 lbs. 4 oz. to 7 lbs. 10 oz. Matte black finish. Stock and forend made of fiberglass reinforced polymer. Sights: post front, fixed buckhorn rear, drift adj. Introduced 1985; discontinued.

Benelli Super Black Eagle Autoloading Shotgun
Same general specifications as Model Black Eagle, except with 3.5-inch chamber that accepts 2.75-, 3- and 3.5-inch shells. 2-shot magazine (3.5-inch), 3-shot magazine (2.75- or 3-inch). High-gloss or satin finish stock. Matte black or blued metal finish. Made from 1991 to date.
Custom Slug Model $675
Standard Model 695

BERETTA USA CORP.
Accokeek, Maryland

Manufactured by Fabbrica D'Armi Pietro Beretta S.p.A. in the Gardone Valtrompia (Brescia), Italy

Beretta Model 57E

Beretta Model 57E Over-and-Under
Same general specifications as Golden Snipe, but higher quality throughout. Made 1955-1967.
With Non-selective Single Trigger $650
With Selective Single Trigger. 795

Beretta Model 409PB

Beretta Model 409PB Hammerless Double $695
Boxlock. Double triggers. Plain extractors. Gauges: 12, 16, 20, 28. Bbls.: 27.5-, 28.5- and 30-inch, IC/M choke or M/F choke. Weight: from 5.5 to 7.75 lbs., depending on gauge and bbl. length. Straight or pistol-grip stock and beavertail forearm, checkered. Made 1934-1964.

Beretta Model 410, 10-Gauge Magnum $950
Same as Model 410E, except heavier construction. Plain extractors. Double triggers. 10-gauge Magnum, 3.5-inch chambers. 32-inch bbls., both F choke. Weight: about 10 lbs. Checkered pistol-grip stock and forearm, recoil pad. Made 1934-1984.

Beretta Model 410E

Beretta Model 410E $765
Same general specifications as Model 409PB, except has automatic ejectors and is of higher quality throughout. Made 1934-1964.

Beretta Model 411E $1125
Same general specifications as Model 409PB except has sideplates, automatic ejectors and is of higher quality throughout. Made 1934-1964.

Beretta Model 424

Beretta Model 424 Hammerless Double $725
Boxlock. Light border engraving. Plain extractors. Gauges: 12, 20; chambers 2.75-inch in former, 3-inch in latter. Bbls.: 28-inch M/F choke, 26-inch IC/M choke. Weight: 5 lbs. 14 oz. to 6 lbs. 10 oz., depending on gauge and bbl. length. English-style straight-grip stock and forearm, checkered. Made 1977-1984.

Beretta Model 426E

Beretta Model 426E $950
Same as Model 424, except action body is finely engraved, silver pigeon inlaid in top lever; has selective automatic ejectors and selective single trigger, stock and forearm of select European walnut. Made 1977-1984.

Beretta Model 452 Hammerless Double
Custom English-style sidelock. Single, non-selective trigger or double triggers. Manual safety. Selective automatic ejectors. Gauge: 12; 2.75- or 3-inch chambers. Bbls.: 26, 28 or 30 inches choked to customers specifications. Weight: 6.75 lbs. Checkered high-grade walnut stock. Receiver with coin-silver finish.
Model 452 Standard $18,250
Model 452 EELL 24,925

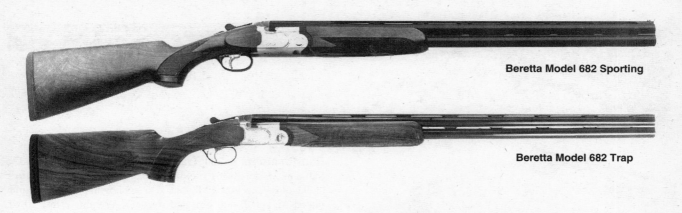

Beretta Model 682 Sporting

Beretta Model 682 Trap

Beretta Model 625 S/S Hammerless Double
Boxlock. Gauges: 12 or 20. Bbls.: 26-, 28- or 30-inch w/fixed choke combinations. Single selective or double triggers w/extractors. Checkered English-style buttstock and forend. Made 1984-87.
With Double Triggers **$725**
With Single Selective Trigger. 850

Beretta Model 626 S/S Hammerless Double
Field Grade side-by-side. Boxlock action w/single selective trigger, extractors and automatic safety. Gauges: 12 (2.75-inch chambers); 20 (3-inch chambers). Bbls.: 26- or 28-inch with Mobilchoke® or various fixed-choke combinations. Weight: 6.75 lbs. (12 ga.). Bright chrome finish. Checkered European walnut buttstock and forend in straight English style. Made 1985-1994.
Model 626 Field (Discontinued 1988) . . . . **$ 795**
Model 626 (3.5-inch Magnum, Disc. 1993) 1095
Model 626 Onyx 925

Beretta Model 627 S/S Hammerless Double
Same as Model 626 S/S, except w/engraved sideplates and pistol-grip or straight English-style stock. Made 1985-1994.
Model 627 EL Field. **$1925**
Model 627 EELL 3555

Beretta Model 682 Over/Under Shotgun
Hammerless takedown with single selective trigger. Gauges: 12, 20, 28, .410. Bbls.: 26- to 34-inch with fixed chokes or Mobilchoke® tubes. Checkered European walnut buttstock/forend in various grades and configurations.
Model 682 Comp Trap Standard **$1955**
Model 682 Comp Trap Top Single 2050
Model 682 Comp Trap Pigeon 2350
Model 682 Comp Trap Combo. 2725
Model 682 Comp Skeet 1495
Model 682 Comp Skeet 2-Bbl. Set 3195
Model 682 Comp Skeet 4-Bbl. Set 3250
Model 682 Continental Sport and Sporting Model 1795
Model 682 Sporting Combo 2350
Model 682 Super Pigeon Trap 1790
Model 682 Super Sport 1925
Model 682 Super Trap 2050
Model 682 Super Trap Combo 2690
Model 682 Super Trap Top Single 2195
Model 682 Super Trap Unsingle 1755

Beretta Model 686 Essential O/U Shotgun **$720**
Boxlock action. Gauge: 12; 3-inch chambers. 26- or 28-inch bbls. w/ventilated rib. Chokes: F, M, IC or MC3 Mobilchoke®. 45.7 inches overall. Weight: 6.7 lbs. Checkered American walnut pistol-grip buttstock and forend. Matte black receiver; high-gloss blued bbls. and trigger guard. Made 1994 to date.

Beretta Model 686 Over/Under Shotgun
Low-profile improved boxlock action. Single selective trigger. Selective automatic ejectors. Gauges: 12, 20, 28 with 3.5- 3- or 2.75-inch chambers, depending upon ga. Bbls.: 26-, 28-, 30-inch w/fixed chokes or Mobilchoke® tubes. Weight: 5.75 to 7.5 lbs. Checkered American walnut stock and forearm of various qualities, depending upon model. Receiver finishes also vary, but all have blued bbls. Sideplates to simulate sidelock action on EL models.
Model 686 Field, Onyx . . . . **$ 925**
Model 686 (3.5-inch Mag., Disc. 1993) 1125
Model 686 EL, English 1495
Model 686 EL Gold Perdiz 1695
Model 686 L Silver Perdiz. 1050
Model 686 Skeet 1125
Model 686 Sporting (Disc. 1993) 895
Model 686 Sporting Onyx 875
Model 686 Sporting Onyx Gold (Disc. 1993) 995
Model 686 Sporting Combo 1755
Model 686 Two-bbl. Set 1525
Model 686 Ultralight 995

Beretta Model 687 Over/Under Shotgun
Same as Model 686, except with decorative sideplates and varying grades of engraving and game-scene motifs. *See* photos next page.
Model 687L Field **$1290**
Model 687 L Onyx (Disc. 1991) 895
Model 687 EL 1955
Model 687 EL Small Frame 2290
Model 687 EELL 2920
Model 687 EELL Combo 3890
Model 687 EELL Sporter, Trap Skeet 3550
Model 687 EELL Skeet 4-bbl. Set 6150
Model 687 Sporting 1495
Model 687 Sporting Combo 2350

Beretta Model 687EL

Beretta Model 687ELL

Beretta Model 1200 Semiautoloading Shotgun

Short recoil action. Gauge: 12; 2.75- or 3-inch chamber. 6-shot magazine. 24-, 26- or 28-inch vent-rib bbl. w/fixed chokes or Mobilchoke® tubes. Weight: 7.25 lbs. Matte black finish. Adj. technopolymer stock and forend. Made from 1988 to date.

Model 1200 w/Fixed Choke (Disc. 1989)	**$415**
Model 1200 Riot (Disc. 1989)	**465**
Model 1201 w/Mobilchoke®	**375**
Model 1201 Riot	**450**

Beretta Model A-301 Autoloading Shotgun $355

Field Gun. Gas-operated. Scroll-decorated receiver. Gauge: 12 or 20; 2.75-inch chamber in former, 3-inch in latter. 3-shot magazine. Bbl.: ventilated rib; 28-inch F or M choke, 26-inch IC. Weight: 6 lbs. 5 oz. – 6 lbs. 14 oz., depending on gauge and bbl. length. Checkered pistol grip stock/forearm. Made 1977-1982.

Beretta Model A-301 Magnum $395

Same as Model A-301 Field Gun, except chambered for 12 ga. 3-inch Magnum shells, 30-inch F choke bbl. only, stock with recoil pad. Weight: 7.25 lbs.

Beretta Model A-301 Skeet Gun $400

Same as Model A-301 Field Gun, except 26-inch bbl. SK choke only, skeet-style stock, gold-plated trigger.

Beretta Model A-301 Slug Gun $350

Same as Model A-301 Field Gun, except has plain 22-inch bbl., slug choke, with rifle sights. Weight: 6 lbs. 14 oz.

Beretta Model A-301 Trap Gun $375

Same as Model A-301 Field Gun, except has 30-inch bbl. in F choke only, checkered Monte Carlo stock with recoil pad, gold-plated trigger. Blued bbl. and receiver. Weight: 7 lbs. 10 oz. Made 1978-1982.

Beretta Model A-302 Semiautoloading Shotgun

Similar to gas-operated Model 301. Hammerless, takedown shotgun with tubular magazine and Mag-Action that handles both 2.75- and 3-inch Magnum shells. Gauge: 12 or 20; 2.75- or 3-inch Mag. chambers. Bbl.: vent or plain; 22-inch/Slug (12 ga.); 26-inch/IC (12 or 20) 28-inch/M (20 ga.), 28-inch/Multi-choke (12 or 20 ga.) 30-inch/F (12 ga.). Weight: 6.5 lbs., 20 ga.; 7.25. lbs., 12 ga. Blued/ black finish. Checkered European walnut, pistol-grip stock and forend. Made 1983 to c. 1987.

Standard Model with Fixed Choke	**$355**
Standard Model with Multi-choke	**400**

Beretta Model A-302 Super Lusso $1825

A custom A-302 in presentation grade with hand-engraved receiver and custom select walnut stock.

Beretta Model A-303 Semiautoloader

Similar to Model 302, except with target specifications in Trap, Skeet and Youth configurations, and weighs 6.5 to 8 lbs. Made from 1983 to date.

Field and Upland Models	**$395**
Skeet and Trap (Discontinued 1994)	**400**
Slug Model (Discontinued 1992)	**455**
Sporting Clays	**495**
Super Skeet	**675**
Super Trap	**660**
Waterfowl/Turkey (Discontinued 1992)	**435**
For Mobilchoke®, add	**50**

Beretta Model A-303 Youth Gun $400

Locked-breech, gas-operated action. Gauges: 12 and 20; 2-shot magazine. Bbls.: 24, 26, 28, 30 or 32 inches, vent rib. Weight: 7 lbs. (12 ga.), 6 lbs. (20 ga.). Crossbolt safety. Length of pull shortened to 12.5 inches. Made 1988 to date.

Beretta Model A-303

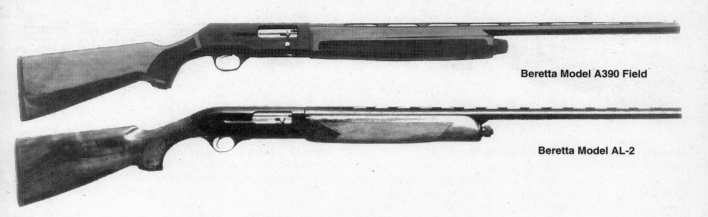

Beretta Model A390 Field

Beretta Model AL-2

Beretta Model A-390 Semiautoloading Shotgun

Gas-operated, self-regulating action designed to handle any size load. Gauge: 12; 3-inch chamber. 3-shot magazine. Bbl.: 24, 26, 28 or 30 inches w/vent rib and Mobilchoke® tubes. Weight: 7.5 lbs. Select walnut stock w/adj. comb. Blued or matte black finish. Made 1992 to date.

Standard Model	**$455**
Field Model	**465**
Deluxe Model	**475**
For Mobilchoke®, **add**.	**50**

Beretta Model A-390 Super Target

Similar to the Model 390 Field, except in 12 gauge only with 2.75-inch chamber. Skeet: 28-inch ported bbl. with wide vent rib and fixed choke (SK). Trap: 30- or 32-inch with Mobilchoke® tubes. Weight: 7.5 lbs. Fully adj. buttstock. Made from 1993 to date.

Super Trap Model	**$645**
Super Skeet Model	**615**
For Mobilchoke®, **add**.	**50**

Beretta Model AL-1 Field Gun $355

Same as Model AL-2 gas-operated Field Gun, except has bbl. without rib, no engraving on receiver. Made 1971-73.

Beretta Model AL-2 Autoloading Shotgun

Field Gun. Gas-operated. Engraved receiver (1968 version, 12 gauge only, had no engraving). Gauge: 12 or 20. 2.75-inch chamber. 3-shot magazine. Bbls.: vent rib; 30-inch F choke, 28-inch F or M choke, 26-inch IC. Weight: 6.5 to 7.25 pounds, depending on gauge and bbl. length. Checkered pistol-grip stock and forearm. Made 1968-1975.

With Plain Receiver	**$285**
With Engraved Receiver	**440**

Beretta Model AL-2 Magnum. $355

Same as Model AL-2 Field Gun, except chambered for 12 gauge 3-inch Magnum shells; 30-inch F or 28-inch M choke bbl. only. Weight: about 8 lbs. Made 1973-75.

Beretta Model AL-2 Skeet Gun $335

Same as Model AL-2 Field Gun, except has wide rib, 26-inch bbl. in SK choke only, checkered pistol-grip stock and beavertail forearm. Made 1969-1975.

Beretta Model AL-2 Trap Gun $325

Same as Model AL-2 Field Gun, except has wide rib, 30 inch bbl. in F choke only, beavertail forearm. Monte Carlo stock with recoil pad. Weight: about 7.75 lbs. Made 1969-1975.

Beretta Model AL-3

Similar to corresponding AL-2 models in design and general specifications. Made 1975-76.

Field Model	**$335**
Magnum Model	**345**
Skeet Model	**350**
Trap Model	**315**

Beretta Model AL-3 Deluxe Trap Gun $685

Same as standard Model AL-3 Trap Gun, except has fully engraved receiver, gold-plated trigger and safety, stock and forearm of premium grade European walnut, gold monogram escutcheon inlaid in buttstock. Made 1975-76.

Beretta Model ASE 90 Over-and-Under Shotgun

Competition-style receiver with coin-silver finish and gold inlay featuring drop-out trigger group. Gauge: 12; 2.75-inch chamber. Bbls.: 28- or 30-inch w/fixed or Mobilchoke® tubes; vent rib. Weight: 8.5 pounds (30-inch bbl.). Checkered high-grade walnut stock. Made 1992 to 1994.

Pigeon, Skeet, Trap Models	**$5850**
Sporting Clays Model	**5995**

Beretta Model Asel

Beretta Model Asel Over-and-Under Shotgun . . $1190

Boxlock. Single non-selective trigger. Selective automatic ejectors. Gauges: 12, 20. Bbls.: 26-, 28-, 30-inch; IC and M choke or M and F choke. Weight: about 5.75 lbs., 20 ga.; about 7 lbs., 12 ga. Checkered pistol-grip stock and forearm. Made 1947-1964.

SHOTGUNS

Beretta Model BL-1

Beretta Model BL-1/BL-2 Over/Under

Boxlock. Plain extractors. Double triggers. 12 gauge, 2.75-inch chambers only. Bbls.: 30- and 28-inch M/F choke, 26-inch IC/M choke. Weight: 6.75-7 lbs., depending on bbl. length. Checkered pistol-grip stock and forearm. Made 1968-1973.

Model BL-1 . . . . **$325**
Model BL-2 (Single Selective Trigger) **375**

Beretta Model BL-2/S **$365**

Similar to Model BL-1, except has selective "Speed-Trigger," vent-rib bbls., 2.75- or 3-inch chambers. Weight: 7-7.5 lbs. Made 1974-76.

Beretta Model BL-3 . . . . **$555**

Same as Model BL-1, except has deluxe engraved receiver, selective single trigger, vent-rib bbls., 12 or 20 gauge, 2.75-inch or 3-inch chambers in former, 3-inch in latter. Weight: 6-7.5 lbs. depending on gauge and bbl. length. Made 1968-76.

Beretta Models BL-4, BL-5 and BL-6

Higher grade versions of Model BL-3 with more elaborate engraving and fancier wood; Model BL-6 has sideplates. Selective automatic ejectors standard. Made 1968-1976. (Model BL-6 introduced in 1973).

Model BL-4 . . . . **$ 675**
Model BL-5 . . . . **895**
Model BL-6 . . . . **1125**

Beretta Series BL Skeet Guns

Models BL-3, BL-4, BL-5 and BL-6 with standard features of their respective grades plus wider rib and skeet-style stock, 26-inch bbls. SK choked. Weight: 6 – 7.25 lbs. depending on ga.

Model BL-3 Skeet Gun . . . . **$ 600**
Model BL-4 Skeet Gun **750**
Model BL-5 Skeet Gun **925**
Model BL-6 Skeet Gun **1255**

Beretta Series BL Trap Guns

Models BL-3, BL-4, BL-5 and BL-6 with standard features of their respective grades plus wider rib and Monte Carlo stock with recoil pad; 30-inch bbls., improved M/F or both F choke. Weight: about 7.5 lbs.

Model BL-3 Trap Gun . . . . **$ 580**
Model BL-4 Trap Gun **690**
Model BL-5 Trap Gun **890**
Model BL-6 Trap Gun **1195**

Beretta Model FS-1

Beretta Model FS-1 Folding Single **$145**

Formerly "Companion." Folds to length of bbl. Hammerless. Underlever. Gauge: 12, 16, 20, 28 or .410. Bbl.: 30-inch in 12 ga., 28-inch in 16 and 20 ga.; 26-inch in 28 and .410 ga.; all F choke. Checkered semipistol-grip stock/forearm. Weight: 4.5-5.5 lbs. depending on gauge. Discontinued 1971.

Beretta Golden Snipe Over-and-Under

Same as Silver Snipe, except has automatic ejectors, ventilated rib is standard feature. Made 1959-1967.

With Non-selective Single Trigger **$625**
Extra for Selective Single Trigger **100**

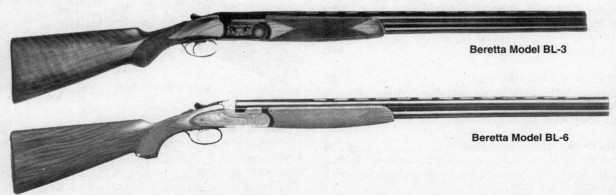

Beretta Model BL-3

Beretta Model BL-6

Beretta Model GR-2

Beretta Model GR-2 Hammerless Double $595

Boxlock. Plain extractors. Double triggers. Gauges: 12, 20; 2.75-inch chambers in former, 3-inch in latter. Bbls.: vent rib; 30-inch M/F choke (12 ga. only); 28-inch M/F choke, 26-inch IC/M choke. Weight: 6.5 to 7.5 lbs. depending on gauge and bbl. length. Checkered pistol-grip stock and forearm. Made 1968-1976.

Beretta Model GR-3 .... $675

Same as Model GR-2, except has selective single trigger chambered for 12-ga. 3-inch or 2.75-inch shells. Magnum model has 30-inch M/F choke bbl., recoil pad. Weight: about 8 lbs. Made 1968-1976.

Beretta Model GR-4 .... $725

Same as Model GR-2, except has automatic ejectors and selective single trigger, higher grade engraving and wood. 12 ga., 2.75-inch chambers only. Made 1968-1976.

Beretta Grade 100 Over-and-Under Shotgun ... $1495

Sidelock. Double triggers. Automatic ejectors. 12 ga. only. Bbls.: 26-, 28-, 30-inch, any standard boring. Weight: about 7.5 lbs. Checkered stock and forend, straight or pistol grip. Discontinued.

Beretta Grade 200 .... $1995

Same general specifications as Grade 100 except higher quality, bores and action parts hard chrome-plated. Discontinued.

Beretta Mark II Single-Barrel Trap Gun $450

Boxlock action similar to that of Series "BL" Over-and-Unders. Engraved receiver. Automatic ejector. 12 ga. only. 32- or 34-inch bbl. with wide vent rib. Weight: about 8.5 lbs. Monte Carlo stock with pistol grip and recoil pad, beavertail forearm. Made 1972-76.

Beretta Model S55B Over-and-Under Shotgun .. $475

Boxlock. Plain extractors. Selective single trigger. Gauges: 12, 20; 2.75- or 3-inch chambers in former, 3-inch in latter. Bbls. vent rib; 30-inch M/F choke or both F choke in 12-ga. 3-inch Magnum only; 28-inch M/F choke; 26 inch IC/M choke. Weight: 6.5 to 7.5 lbs. depending on gauge and bbl. length. Checkered pistol-grip stock and forearm. Introduced in 1977.

Beretta Model S56E $550

Same as Model S55B, except has scroll-engraved receiver selective automatic ejectors. Introduced in 1977.

Beretta Model S58 Skeet Gun $705

Same as Model S56E, except has 26-inch bbls. of Boehler Antinit Anticorro steel, SK choked, with wide vent rib; skeet-style stock and forearm. Weight: 7.5 lbs. Introduced in 1977.

Beretta Model S58 Trap Gun $665

Same as Model S58 Skeet Gun, except has 30-inch bbls. bored IM/F Trap, Monte Carlo stock with recoil pad. Weight: 7 lbs. 10 oz. Introduced in 1977.

Beretta Silver Hawk Featherweight Hammerless Double-Barrel Shotgun

Boxlock. Double triggers or non-selective single trigger. Plain extractor. Gauges: 12, 16, 20, 28, 12 Mag. Bbls.: 26- to 32-inch with high matted rib, all standard choke combinations. Weight: 7 lbs. (12 ga. w/26-inch bbls.). Checkered walnut stock with beavertail forearm. Discontinued 1967. *See* Photo next page.

With Double Triggers $465
For Non-selective Single Trigger, **add** 65

SHOTGUNS

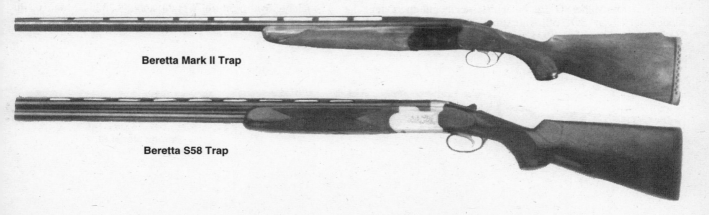

Beretta Mark II Trap

Beretta S58 Trap

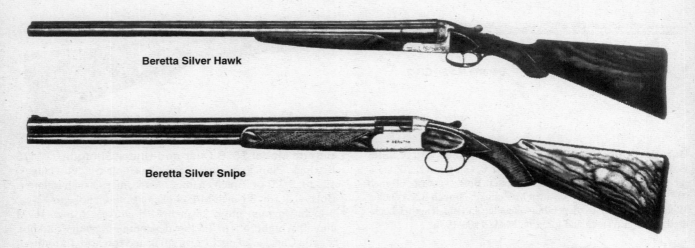

Beretta Silver Hawk

Beretta Silver Snipe

Beretta Silver Snipe Over-and-Under Shotgun

Boxlock. Non-selective or selective single trigger. Plain extractor. Gauges: 12, 20, 12 Mag., 20 Mag. Bbls.: 26-, 28-, 30-inch; plain or vent rib; chokes IC/M, M/F, SK #1 and #2, F/F. Weight: from about 6 lbs. in 20 ga. to 8.5 lbs. in 12 ga. (Trap gun). Checkered walnut pistol-grip stock and forearm. Made 1955-1967.

With Plain Bbl., Non-selective Trigger **$395**
With Vent-rib Bbl., Non-sel. Single Trigger **455**
For Selective Single Trigger, **add** **65**

Beretta Model SL-2 Pump Gun **$285**

Hammerless. Takedown. 12 gauge only. 3-shot magazine. Bbls.: vent rib; 30-inch F choke, 28-inch M, 26-inch IC. Weight: about 7-7.25 lbs., depending on bbl. length. Checkered pistol-grip stock and forearm. Made 1968-1971.

Beretta Series "SO" Over-and-Under Shotguns

Sidelock. Selective automatic ejectors. Selective single trigger or double triggers. 12 gauge only, 2.75- or 3-inch chambers. Bbls.: vent rib (wide type on skeet and trap guns); 26-, 27-, 29-, 30-inch; any combination of standard chokes. Weight: 7 to 7.75 lbs., depending on bbl. length, style of stock and density of wood. Stock and forearm of select walnut, finely checkered; straight or pistol grip, field, skeet and trap guns have appropriate styles of stock and forearm. Models differ chiefly in quality of wood and grade of engraving. Models SO-3EL, SO-3EELL, SO4 and SO-5 have hand-detachable locks. "SO-4" is used to designate skeet and trap models derived from Model SO-3EL but with less elaborate engraving. Models SO3EL and SO-3EELL are similar to the earlier SO-4 and SO-5, respectively. Made 1933 to date.

Beretta Model "SO" *(Cont.)*

Model SO-2 (Discontinued 1986) **$4025**
Model SO-3 (Discontinued 1986) **5890**
Model SO-3EELL (Discontinued) **8550**
Model SO-4 Skeet or Trap Gun (Disc. 1986) **6495**
Model SO-4 (pre-1977) or SO-3EL (Disc.) **6295**
Model SO-5 Sporting, Skeet or Trap **9600**

Beretta Models SO-6 and SO-9 Premium Grade Shotguns

High-grade over/unders in the SO series. Gauges: 12 only (SO-6); 12, 20, 28 and .410 (SO-9). Fixed or Mobilchoke® (12 ga. only). Sidelock action. Silver or casehardened receiver (SO-6); English custom hand-engraved scroll or game scenes (SO-9). Supplied with leather case and accessories. Made from about 1990 to date.

SO-6 Over/Under **$11,200**
SO-9 Over/Under **19,700**

Beretta Model SO-7 S/S Double **$18,800**

Side-by-side shotgun with same general specifications as SO Series over/unders, except higher grade with more elaborate engraving, fancier wood. Made 1948 to c. 1990.

Beretta Model TR-1 Single-Shot Trap Gun **$245**

Hammerless. Underlever action. Engraved frame. 12 gauge only. 32-inch bbl. with vent rib. Weight: about 8.25 lbs. Monte Carlo stock with pistol grip and recoil pad, beavertail forearm. Made 1968-1971.

Beretta Model SL-2

Beretta Model TR-2........................ **$275**
Same as Model TR-1, except has extended ventilated rib. Made 1969-1973.

Beretta Vittoria Pintail Semiautoloader **$450**

Beretta Victoria Pintail *(Cont.)*
Short Montefeltro-type recoil action. Gauge: 12; 3-inch chamber. Bbl.: 24-inch slug, 24- or 26-inch vent rib w/Mobilchoke® tubes. Weight: 7 lbs. Checkered walnut stock/forend. Matte finish on both metal and wood. Made 1993 to date.

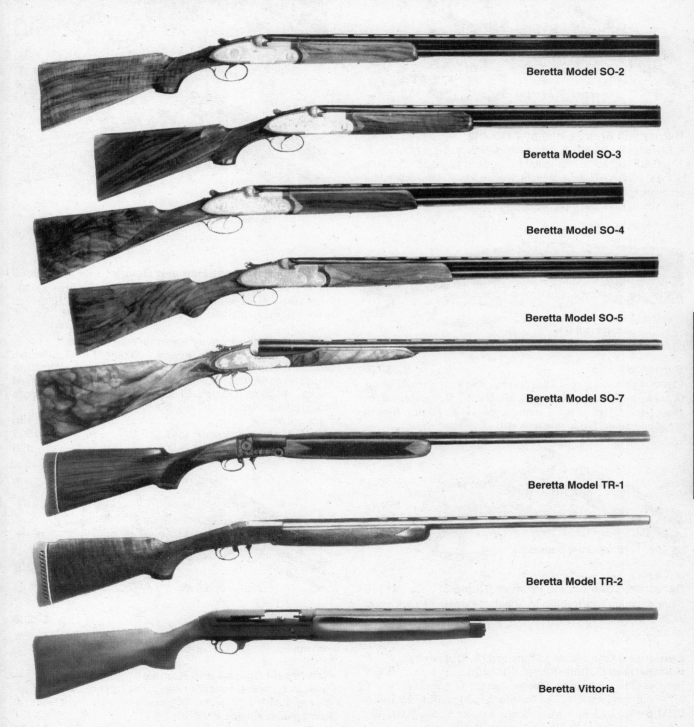

Beretta Model SO-2

Beretta Model SO-3

Beretta Model SO-4

Beretta Model SO-5

Beretta Model SO-7

Beretta Model TR-1

Beretta Model TR-2

Beretta Vittoria

VINCENZO BERNARDELLI
Gardone V.T. (Brescia), Italy

Bernardelli Brescia

Bernardelli Brescia Hammer Double **$725**
Back-action sidelock. Plain extractors. Double triggers. Gauges: 12, 20. Bbls.: 27.5 or 29.5-inch M/F choke in 12 gauge, 25.5-inch IC/M choke in 20 gauge. Weight: from 5.75 to 7 lbs., depending on gauge and bbl. length. English-style stock and forearm, checkered. No longer imported.

Bernardelli Elio

Bernardelli Elio **$925**
Lightweight game gun, 12 gauge only, with same general specifications as Standard Gamecock (S. Uberto 1), except weighs about 6 to 6.25 lbs., has automatic ejectors, fine English-pattern scroll engraving. No longer imported.

Bernardelli Gamecock

Bernardelli Gamecock, Premier (Rome 3) **$1195**
Same general specifications as Standard Gamecock (S. Uberto 1), except has sideplates, auto ejectors, single trigger. Currently manufactured.

Bernardelli Gamecock, Standard (S. Uberto 1)
Hammerless Double-Barrel Shotgun **$995**
Boxlock. Plain extractors. Double triggers. Gauges: 12, 16, 20; 2.75-inch chambers in 12 and 16, 3-inch in 20 ga. Bbls. 25.5-inch IC/M choke; 27.5-inch M/F choke. Weight: 5.75-6.5 lbs., depending on ga. and bbl. length. English-style straight-grip stock and forearm, checkered. No longer imported.

Bernardelli Standard Gamecock

Bernardelli Gardone

Bernardelli Gardone Hammer Double **$2065**
Same general specifications as Brescia, except for higher grade engraving and wood, but not as high as the Italia. Half-cock safety. Discontinued 1956.

Bernardelli Hemingway Hammerless Double
Boxlock. Single or double triggers with hinged front. Selective automatic ejectors. Gauges: 12 and 20 w/2.75- or 3-inch chambers, 16 and 28 w/2.75-inch. Bbls.: 23.5- to 28-inch with fixed chokes. Weight: 6.25 lbs. Checkered English-style European walnut stock. Silvered and engraved receiver.
Standard Model **$1395**
Deluxe Model w/Sideplates (Disc. 1993) 1595
For Single Trigger, **add** 75

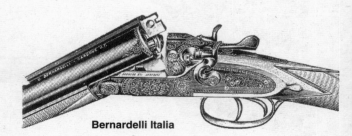

Bernardelli Italia

Bernardelli Italia **$2200**
Same general specifications as Brescia, except higher grade engraving and wood. Discontinued 1986.

Bernardelli Roma 4 and Roma 6
Same as Premier Gamecock (Rome 3), except higher grade engraving and wood, double triggers. Currently manufactured; Roma 6 discontinued 1993.
Roma 4 . . . . **$1095**
Roma 6 1150

Bernardelli Roma 6

Bernardelli S. Uberto 2

Bernadelli S. Uberto 2 . . . . $995
Same as Standard Gamecock (S. Uberto 1), except higher grade engraving and wood. Currently manufactured.

Bernardelli S. Uberto F.S.

Bernardelli S. Uberto F.S. $1255
Same as Standard Gamecock, except with higher grade engraving, wood and has auto ejectors. Currently manufactured.

Bernardelli V.B. Holland Liscio

Bernardelli V.B. Holland Liscio Deluxe Hammerless Double Barrel Shotgun $6950
Holland & Holland-type sidelock action. Auto ejectors. Double triggers.12 gauge only. Any bbl. length, chokes. Checkered stock (straight or pistol grip) and forearm. Currently manufactured.

BOSS & COMPANY
London, England

Boss Double Barrel

Boss Hammerless Double-Barrel Shotgun . . . $25,000
Sidelock. Automatic ejectors. Double triggers, non-selective or selective single trigger. Made in all gauges, bbl. lengths and chokes. Checkered stock and forend, straight or pistol grip.

Boss Hammerless Over/Under Shotgun $38,500
Sidelock. Automatic ejectors. Selective single trigger. Made in all gauges, bbl. lengths and chokes. Checkered stock and forend, straight or pistol grip. Discontinued.

ERNESTO BREDA
Milan, Italy

Breda Autoloading Shotgun
Recoil-operated. 12 gauge, 2.75-inch chamber. 4-shell tubular magazine. Bbls.: 25.5- and 27.5-inch, plain, matted or vent rib, IC, M or F choke; current model has 26-inch vent-rib bbl. with interchangeable choke tubes. Weight: about 7.25 lbs. Checkered straight or pistol-grip stock and forearm. Discontinued 1988.
W/Plain Bbl. $355
W/Raised Matted-rib Bbl. 395
W/Ventilated-rib Bbl. 415
W/Vent Rib, Interchangeable Choke Tubes. 430

Breda Autoloading Shotgun

SHOTGUNS

Breda Magnum

Same general specifications as standard model, except chambered for 12-gauge 3-inch Magnum, 3-shot magazine; latest model has 29-inch vent-rib bbl. Disc. 1988.
W/Plain Bbl. **$465**
W/Ventilated-rib Bbl. **475**

BRNO SHOTGUNS
Manufactured in Czechoslovakia

Brno 500 Over/Under Shotgun $625

Hammerless boxlock with double triggers and ejectors.12 gauge w/2.75-inch chambers. 27.5-inch bbls. choked M/F. Weight: 7 lbs. Checkered walnut stock with classic style cheekpiece.

Brno 500 Series O/U Combination Guns

Similar to the 500 Series over/under shotgun, except lower bbl. chambered in rifle calibers.
Model 571 12/6×65R (Disc. 1993) . . . . $ 695
Model 572 12/7×65R (Imported since 1992) **725**
Model 584 12/7×57R (Imported since 1992) **695**
Super Series, **add** **100**
Super Series 3-Bbl. Set (Disc. 1991) **1695**

Brno CZ 581 Over/Under Shotgun $570

Hammerless boxlock with double triggers, ejectors and automatic safety. 12 gauge w/2.75- or 3-inch chambers. 28-inch bbls. choked M/F. Weight: 7.5 lbs. Checkered walnut stock.

Brno Super Over/Under Shotgun $695

Hammerless sidelock with selective single or double triggers and ejectors. 12 gauge w/2.75- or 3-inch chambers. 27.5-inch bbls. choked M and F. Weight: 7.25 lbs. Checkered European walnut stock with classic-style cheekpiece.

Brno ZH 300 Series Over/Under Shotguns

Hammerless boxlock with double triggers. Gauge: 12 or 16 w/2.75- or 3-inch chambers. Bbls.: 26, 27.5 or 30 inches; choked M/F. Weight: 7 lbs. Skip-line checkered walnut stock with classic-style cheekpiece.
Model 300 (Discontinued 1993) $415
Model 301 Field (Discontinued 1991) **425**
Model 302 Skeet (Discontinued 1992) **475**
Model 303 Trap (Discontinued 1992) **495**

Brno ZH 300 Series O/U Combination Guns

Similar to the 300 Series over/under shotgun, except lower bbl. chambered in rifle calibers.
Model 300 Combo 8-Bbl. Set (Disc. 1991) **$2995**
Model 304 12 Ga./7×57R (Disc. 1995) **525**
Model 305 12 Ga./5.6×52R (Disc. 1993) **595**
Model 306 12 Ga./5.6×50R (Disc. 1993) **625**
Model 307 12 Ga./22 Hornet (Imported since 1995) . . . **550**
Model 324 16 Ga./7×57R (Disc. 1987). **500**

Brno ZP 149 Hammerless Double

Sidelock action with double triggers, automatic ejectors and automatic safety.12 gauge w/2.75- or 3-inch chambers. 28.5-inch bbls. choked M/F. Weight: 7.25 lbs. Checkered walnut buttstock with cheekpiece.
Standard Model **$475**
Engraved Model **520**

BROWNING SHOTGUNS
Morgan (formerly Ogden), Utah

Designated "American" Browning because they were produced in Ilion, New York, the following Remington-made Brownings are almost identical to the Remington Model 11 A and Sportsman and the Browning Auto-5. They are the only Browning shotguns manufactured in the U.S. during the 20th century and were made for Browning Arms when production was suspended in Belgium because of WW II.

AMERICAN BROWNING SHOTGUNS

American Browning Grade I Autoloader $365

Recoil-operated. Gauges: 12, 16, 20. 2- or 4-shell tubular magazine. Plain bbl., 26- to 32-inch, any standard boring. Weight: about 6.88 lbs. (20 ga.) to 8 lbs. (12 ga.). Checkered pistol-grip stock and forearm. Made 1940-49.

American Browning Special

Same general specifications as Grade I, except supplied with raised matted rib or vent rib. Discont. 1949.
With raised matted rib **$425**
With ventilated rib **465**

American Browning Grade I

American Browning Special

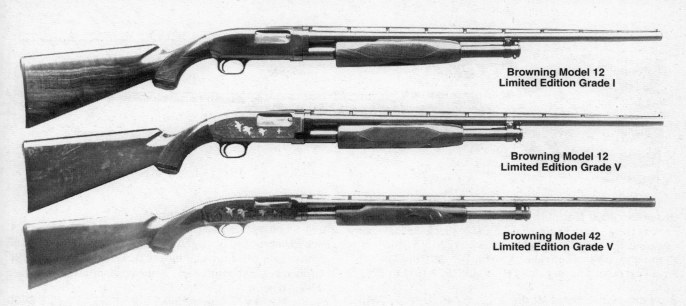

Browning Model 12
Limited Edition Grade I

Browning Model 12
Limited Edition Grade V

Browning Model 42
Limited Edition Grade V

American Browning Special Skeet Model **$525**
Same general specifications as Grade I, except has 26-inch bbl.
with vent rib and Cutts Compensator. Discontinued 1949.

American Browning Utility Field Gun **$345**
Same general specifications as Grade I, except has 28-inch plain
bbl. with Poly Choke. Discontinued 1949.

Browning Model 12 Pump Shotgun

Special limited edition Winchester Model 12. Gauge: 20 or 28.
Five-shot tubular magazine. 26-inch bbl., M choke. 45 inches
overall. Weight: about 7 lbs. Grade I has blued receiver, checkered walnut stock with matte finish. Grade V has engraved receiver, checkered deluxe walnut stock with high-gloss finish.
Made 1988-1992.

Grade I, 20 Gauge (8600)	**$425**
Grade I, 28 Gauge	445
Grade V, 20 Gauge (4000)	755
Grade V, 28 Gauge	790

Browning Model 42 Limited Edition Shotgun

Special limited edition Winchester Model 42 pump shotgun.
Same general specifications as Model 12, except with smaller
frame in .410 ga. and 3-inch chamber. Made 1991-93.

Grade I (6000 produced)	**$555**
Grade V (6000 produced)	855

NOTE

Fabrique Nationale Herstal (formerly Fabrique Nationale d'Armes
de Guerre) of Herstal, Belgium, is the longtime manufacturer of
Browning shotguns, dating back to 1900. Miroku Firearms Mfg. Co.
of Tokyo, Japan, bought into the Browning company and has, since
the early 1970s, undertaken some of the production. The following
shotguns were manufactured for Browning by these two firms.

Browning 2000 Buck Special **$315**
Same as Field Model, except has 24-inch plain bbl. Bored for rifled slug and buck shot, fitted with rifle sights (open rear, ramp
front). 12 ga., 2.75-inch or 3-inch chamber; 20 ga., 2.75-inch
chamber. Weight: 12 ga., 7 lbs. 8 oz.; 20 ga., 6 lbs. 10 oz. Made
1974-1981 by FN.

Browning 2000 Gas Automatic Shotgun, Field Model

Gas-operated. Gauge: 12 or 20. 2.75-inch chamber. 4-shot magazine. Bbl.: 26-, 28-, 30-inch, any standard choke plain matted
bbl. (12 ga. only) or vent rib. Weight: 6 lbs. 11 oz.-7 lbs. 12 oz.
depending on gauge and bbl. length. Checkered pistol-grip
stock/forearm. Made 1974-1981 by FN.

With Plain Matted Bbl.	**$335**
With Vent-rib Bbl.	350

SHOTGUNS

Browning 2000 Field Model

Browning Model A-500

Browning Automatic-5
Buck Special

Browning 2000 Magnum Model $350
Same as Field Model, except chambered for 3-inch shells, 3-shot magazine. Bbl.: 26- (20 ga. only), 28-, 30- or 32-inch (latter two 12 ga. only); any standard choke; vent rib. Weight: 6 lbs. 11 oz.-7 lbs. 13 oz. depending on ga. and bbl. Made 1974-1981 by FN.

Browning 2000 Skeet Model $345
Same as Field Model, except has skeet-style stock with recoil pad, 26-inch vent-rib bbl., SK choke. 12 or 20 ga., 2.75-inch chamber. Weight: 8 lbs. 1 oz. (12 ga.); 6 lbs. 12 oz.(20 ga.) Made 1974-1981 by FN.

Browning 2000 Trap Model $345
Same as Field Model except has Monte Carlo stock with recoil pad, 30- or 32-inch bbl. w/high-post vent rib and receiver extension, M/I/F chokes. 12 ga., 2.75-inch chamber. Weight: about 8 lbs. 5 oz. Made 1974-1981 by FN.

Browning A-500G Gas-Operated Semiautomatic
Same general specifications as Browning Model A-500R except gas-operated. Made 1990 to 1993.
Buck Special $435
Hunting Model 445

Browning A-500G Sporting Clays $445
Same general specifications as Model A-500G except has matte blued receiver with "Sporting Clays" logo. 28- or 30-inch bbl. w/Invector choke tubes. Made 1992 to 1993.

Browning A-500R Semiautomatic
Recoil-operated. Gauge: 12. 26- to 30-inch vent-rib bbls. 24-inch Buck Special. Invector choke tube system. 2.75- or 3-inch Magnum cartridges. Weight: 7 lbs. 3 oz.-8 lbs. 2 oz. Cross-bolt safety. Gold-plated trigger. Scroll-engraved receiver. Gloss-finished walnut stock and forend. Made by FN from 1987 to 1993.
Hunting Model $455
Buck Special 495

Browning A-Bolt Series Shotgun
Bolt-action repeating single-barrel shotgun. 12 ga. only with 3-inch chambers, 2-shot magazine. 22- or 23-inch rifled bbl., with or without a rifled invector tube. Checkered walnut or graphite/fiberglass composite stock. Matte black metal finish. Made 1995 to date.
Stalker Model w/Composite Stock $450
Hunter Model w/Walnut stock 475
With Rifled Bbl., **add** 50
With Open Sights, **add** 25

Browning Autoloading Shotguns, Grade III and IV
These higher grade models differ from the Standard or Grade I in general quality, grade of wood, checkering, engraving, etc., otherwise specifications are the same. Grade IV guns, sometimes called Midas Grade, are inlaid with yellow and green gold. Discontinued in 1940.
Grade III, Plain Bbl. $2300
Grade IV, Plain Bbl. 3700
For Raised Matte-rib Bbl., **add** 225
For Vent-rib Bbl., **add** 450

Browning Automatic-5, Buck Special Models
Same as Light 12, Magnum 12, Light 20, Magnum 20, in respective gauges, except 24-inch plain bbl. bored for rifled slug and buckshot, fitted with rifle sights (open rear, ramp front). Weight: 6.13-8.25 lbs. depending on gauge. Made 1964-1976 by FN, since then by Miroku.
FN Manufacture, with Plain Bbl. $525
Miroku Manufacture 465

Browning Automatic-5 Classic $750
Gauge: 12. 5-shot capacity. 28-inch vent-rib bbl./M choke. 2.75-inch chamber. Engraved silver gray receiver. Gold-plated trigger. Cross-bolt safety. High-grade, hand checkered select American walnut stock w/rounded pistol grip. 5,000 issued; made in Japan in 1984, engraved in Belgium.

Browning Automatic-5 Classic

Browning Automatic-5 Gold Classic

Browning Automatic-5 Gold Classic $2895

Same general specifications as Automatic-5 Classic, except engraved receiver inlaid with gold. Pearl border on stock and forend plus fine-line hand-checkering. Each gun numbered "1 of Five Hundred," etc. 500 issued in 1984; made in Belgium.

Browning Automatic-5, Light 12

12 gauge only. Same general specifications as Standard Model, except lightweight (about 7.25 lbs.), has gold-plated trigger. Guns without rib have striped matting on top of bbl. Fixed chokes or Invector tubes. Made 1948-1976 by FN, since then by Miroku.

FN Manufacture, Plain Bbl.	$450
FN Manufacture, Raised Matte Rib	525
FN Manufacture, Ventilated Rib	575
Miroku Manufacture, Vent Rib, Fixed Choke	450
Miroku manufacture, Vent Rib, Invectors	495

Browning Automatic-5, Light 20

Same general specifications as Standard Model, except lightweight and 20 gauge. Bbl.: 26- or 28-inch; plain or vent rib. Weight: about 6.25-6.5 lbs. depending on bbl. Made 1958-1976 by FN, since then by Miroku.

FN Manufacture, Plain Bbl.	$515
FN Manufacture, Vent-rib Bbl.	555
Miroku Manufacture, Vent Rib, Fixed Choke	415
Miroku Manufacture, Vent Rib, Invectors	475

Browning Automatic-5, Magnum 12 Gauge

Same general specifications as Standard Model. Chambered for 3-inch Magnum 12-gauge shells. Bbl.: 28-inch M/F, 30- or 32-inch F/F, plain or vent rib. Weight: 8.5-9 lbs. depending on bbl. Buttstock has recoil pad. Made 1958-1976 by FN, since then by Miroku. Fixed chokes or Invector tubes.

FN Manufacture, Plain Bbl.	$535
FN Manufacture, Vent-rib Bbl.	580
Miroku Manufacture, Vent Rib, Fixed Chokes.........	435
Miroku Manufacture, Vent Rib, Invectors	495

Browning Automatic-5, Magnum 20 Gauge

Same general specifications as Standard Model, except chambered for 3-inch Magnum 20-ga. shell. Bbl.: 26- or 28-inch, plain or vent rib. Weight: 7 lbs. 5 oz.-7 lbs. 7 oz. depending on bbl. Made 1967-1976 by FN, since then by Miroku.

FN Manufacture, Plain Bbl.	$545
FN Manufacture, Vent-rib Bbl.	575
Miroku Manufacture, Vent Rib, Invectors	450

Browning Automatic-5, Skeet Model

12 gauge only. Same general specifications as Light 12. Bbl.: 26-or 28-inch, plain or vent rib, SK choke. Weight: 7 lbs. 5 oz.-7 lbs. 10 oz. depending on bbl. Made by FN prior to 1976, since then by Miroku.

FN Manufacture, Plain Bbl.	$495
FN Manufacture, Vent-rib Bbl.	525
Miroku Manufacture, Vent-rib Bbl.	395

Browning Automatic-5 Stalker

Same general specifications as Automatic-5 Light and Magnum models, except with matte blue finish and black graphite fiberglass stock and forearm. Made 1992 to date.

Light Model	$495
Magnum Model	525

Browning Automatic-5, Standard (Grade I)

Recoil-operated. Gauge: 12 or 16 (16-gauge guns made prior to WW II were chambered for $2\frac{9}{16}$-inch shells; standard 16 discontinued 1964). 4-shell magazine in 5-shot model, prewar guns were also available in 3-shot model. Bbls.: 26- to 32-inch; plain, raised matted or vent rib; choice of standard chokes. Weight: about 8 lbs., 12 ga.,7.5 lbs., 16 ga. Checkered pistol-grip stock and forearm. *(Note:* Browning Special, discontinued about 1940.)* Made 1900-1973 by FN.

Grade I, Plain Bbl.	$395
Grade I or Browning Special, Raised Matted Rib......	505
Grade I or Browning Special, Vent Rib	520

Browning Automatic-5, Sweet 16

16 gauge only. Same general specifications as Standard Model, except lightweight (about 6.75 lbs.), has goldplated trigger. Guns without rib have striped matting on top of bbl. Made 1937-1976 by FN.

With Plain Bbl.	$450
With Raised Matted or Ventilated Rib	495

Browning Auto-5, Sweet Sixteen New Model ... $495

Reissue of popular 16-gauge Hunting Model with 5-shot capacity, 2.75-inch chamber, scroll-engraved blued receiver, high-gloss French walnut stock with rounded pistol grip. 26- or 28-inch vent-rib bbl. F choke tube. Weight: 7 lbs. 5 oz. Reintroduced 1987-1993.

Browning Automatic-5, Sweet Sixteen New Model

SHOTGUNS

Browning Model B-80 Upland Special

Browning Automatic-5, Trap Model **$550**
12 gauge only. Same general specifications as Standard Model, except has trap-style stock, 30-inch vent-rib bbl. F choke. Weight: 8.5 lbs. Discontinued 1971.

Browning Model B-80 Gas-Operated Automatic
Gauge: 12 or 20; 2.75-inch chamber. 4-shot magazine. Bbl.: 26-, 28- or 30-inch, any standard choke, vent-rib bbl. with fixed chokes or Invector tubes. Weight: 6 lbs. 12 oz.-8 lbs. 1 oz. depending on gauge and bbl. Checkered pistol-grip stock and forearm. Made 1981-87.
Model B-80 Standard **$395**
Model B-80 Magnum (3-inch Mag.) **425**

Browning Model B-80 Plus **$435**
Same general specifications as Browning Model B-80, except chambered for 3-inch shotshells. Made in 1988 only.

Browning Model B-80 Superlight **$395**
Same as Standard Model, except weighs 1 lb. less.

Browning Model B-80 Upland Special **$405**
Gauge: 12 or 20. 22-inch vent-rib bbl. Invector choke tube system. 2.75-inch chambers. 42 inches overall. Weight: 5 lbs. 7 oz. (20 ga.); 6 lbs. 10 oz. (12 ga.). German nickel silver sight bead. Cross-bolt safety. Checkered walnut straight-grip stock and forend. Discontinued 1988.

Browning BPS Game Gun Deer Special **$375**
Same general specifications as Standard BPS Model, except has 20.5-inch bbl. w/adj. rifle-style sights. Solid scope mounting system. Checkered walnut stock with sling swivel studs. Made from 1992 to date.

Browning BPS Game Gun Turkey Special **$360**
Same general specifications as Standard BPS Model, except with matte blue metal finish and satin-finished stock. Gauges: 10, 3.5-inch chamber,12, 3- or 3.5-inch. Bbls.: 22-, 28-, 30-inch w/Extra-Full Invector choke system. Receiver drilled and tapped for scope. Made 1992 to date.

Browning BPS Pigeon Grade **$495**
Same general specifications as Standard BPS Model, except with select grade walnut stock and gold-trimmed receiver. Available in 12 ga. only with 26- or 28-inch vent-rib bbl. Made 1992 to date.

Browning BPS Pump Invector Stalker
Same general specifications as BPS Pump Shotgun, except in 10 and 12 ga. with Invector choke system, 22-, 26-, 28- or 30-inch bbls.; matte blue metal finish with matte black stock. Made 1987 to date.
12-Gauge Model (3-inch) **$355**
10- & 12-Gauge Model (3.5-inch) **450**

Browning BPS Pump Shotgun
Takedown. Gauges: 10, 12 (3.5-inch chamber); 12 or 20 (3-inch), 2.75-inch in 28 gauge and target models. Bbls.: 22-, 24-, 26-, 28-, 30-, or 32-inch; fixed choke or Invector tubes. Weight: 7.5 lbs. (with 28-inch bbl.). Checkered select walnut pistol-grip stock and semibeavertail forearm, recoil pad. Introduced in 1977. Made by Miroku.
Hunting Model (10 or 12 ga., 3.5") **$450**
Hunting, Upland (12 or 20 ga.) **350**
Buck Special (10 or 12 ga., 3.5") **460**
Buck Special (12 or 20 ga.) **350**
With Fixed Choke, **deduct** **50**

Browning BPS Youth and Ladies' Model
Lightweight (6 lbs. 11 oz.) version of BPS Pump Shotgun in 20 gauge with 22-inch bbl. and floating vent rib, F choke (invector) tube. Made 1986 to date.
Standard Invector Model (Disc. 1994) **$345**
Invector Plus Model **345**

Browning BSA 10 Semiautomatic Shotgun
Gas-operated short-stroke action. 10 gauge; 3.5-inch chamber. 5-shot magazine. Bbls.: 26-, 28-or 30-inch with Invector tubes and vent rib. Weight: 10.5 lbs. Checkered select walnut buttstock and forend. Blued finish. Made 1993 to date. *Note:* Although introduced as the BSA 10, this model is now marketed as the Gold Series. *See* separate listing for pricing.

Browning BPS Youth and Ladies' Model

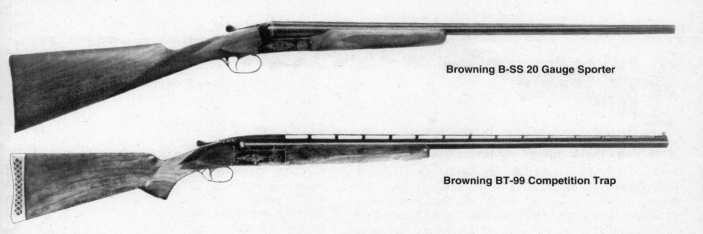

Browning B-SS 20 Gauge Sporter

Browning BT-99 Competition Trap

Browning B-SS Side-by-Side **$550**
Boxlock. Automatic ejectors. Non-selective single trigger. Gauges: 12, 20, 3-inch chambers. Bbls. 26-, 28-, or 30-inch (latter in 12 gauge only); IC/M, M/F, or F/F chokes; matte solid rib. Weight (w/28-inch bbls.): 12 ga., 7 lbs. 5 oz., 20 ga., 7 lbs. Checkered straight-grip stock and beavertail forearm. Made 1972-1987 by Miroku.

Browning B-SS Side-by-Side Sidelock **$1575**
Same general specifications as B-SS boxlock models, except sidelock version available in 26- or 28-inch bbl. lengths. 26-inch choked IC/M; 28-inch, M/F. Double triggers. Satin grayed receiver engraved with rosettes and scrolls. German nickel-silver sight bead. Weight: 6.25 lbs. to 6 lbs. 11 oz. 12 ga. made in 1983; 20 ga. made in 1984.

Browning B-SS S/S 20 Gauge Sporter **$575**
Same as standard B-SS 20 gauge, except has selective single trigger, straight-grip stock. Introduced 1977. Discontinued 1987.

Browning BT-99 Competition Trap Special
Same as BT-99, except has super-high wide rib and standard Monte Carlo or fully adj. stock. Available w/adj. choke or Invector Plus tubes with optional porting. Made 1976 to date.
Grade I w/Fixed Choke (Disc. 1992) **$685**
Grade I w/Invectors 850
Grade I Stainless (Disc. 1994) 895

Browning BT-99 Grade I Single Bbl. Trap **$575**
Boxlock. Automatic ejector. 12 gauge only. 32- or 34-inch vent-rib bbl., M, IM or F choke. Weight: about 8 lbs. Checkered pistol-grip stock and beavertail forearm, recoil pad. Made 1971-76 by Miroku.

Browning BT-99 Max
Boxlock. 12 ga. only w/ejector selector and no safety. 32- or 34-inch ported bbl. with high post vent-rib. Checkered select walnut butt-stock and finger-grooved forend with high luster finish. Engraved receiver with blued or stainless metal finish. Made 1995-96.
Blued . . . . **$ 895**
Stainless 1155

Browning BT-99 Plus
Similar to the BT-99 Competition, except with Browning Recoil Reduction System. Made 1989-1995.
Grade I . . . . **$ 995**
Pigeon Grade 1075
Signature Grade 1045
Stainless Model 1135
Golden Clays 2195

Browning BT-99 Plus Micro **$1095**
Same general specifications as BT-99 Plus, except scaled down for smaller shooters. 30-inch bbl. with adj. rib and Browning's recoil reducer system. Made 1991 to date.

BT-100 Single-Shot Trap
Similar to the BT-99 Max except w/additional stock options and removable trigger group. Made 1995 to 1994.
Blued . . . . **$ 995**
Stainless 1295
Thumbhole Stock, **add** 275
Removable Trigger Group, **add** 450
Fixed Choke, **deduct** 50

Browning Citori Hunting Over/Under Models . . . **$695**
Boxlock. Gauges: 12,16, 20, 28 and .410. Bbl. lengths: 24-, 26-, 28-, or 30-inch with vent rib. Chokes: M/F or invector (30-inch

Browning Citori O/U
Hunting Model

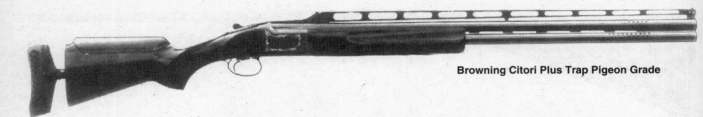

Browning Citori Plus Trap Pigeon Grade

Browning Citori Hunting Over/Under Models *(Cont.)*

bbl.); invector, M/F or IC/M (other bbl. lengths). Overall length ranges from 41-47 inches. 2.75-, 3- or 3-inch Mag. loads, depending on gauge. Weight: 5.75 lbs. to 7 lbs. 13 oz. Single selective, gold-plated trigger. Medium raised German nickel-silver sight bead. Checkered, rounded pistol-grip walnut stock with beavertail forend. Prices vary with the different grades. Made from 1973 to date by Miroku.

Browning Citori Lightning O/U Models

Same general specifications as the Citori Hunting Models except with classic Browning rounded pistol-grip stock.

Grade I . . . . $ 625
Grade III 950
Grade VI 1350

Browning Citori Skeet Gun

Same as Hunting Model, except has skeet-style stock and forearm, 26- or 28-inch bbls., both bored SK choke. Available with either standard vent rib or special target-type, high-post, wide vent rib. Weight (with 26-inch bbls.): 12 ga., 8 pounds; 20 ga., 7 lbs. Made 1974 to date by Miroku.

Grade I . . . . $ 895
Grade III 990
Grade VI (Disc. 1995) 1495
4-Bbl. Set, Grade I 2875
4-Bbl. Set, Grade II 3295
4-Bbl. Set, Grade VI (Disc. 1995) 3575

Browning Citori Sporting Clays

Same general specifications as Hunting Model except engraved, with gold-filled logos identifying each model.

GTI Model (Disc. 1995) . . . . $ 950
Lightning Model 895
Micro Citori Lightning Model (w/low rib) 850
Special Model 895
Ultra Model (Previously GTI) 990
Model 425 Grade I 995
Model 325 Grade II (Disc. 1994) 1025
Model 802 Sporter (ES) Extended Swing 1095

Browning Citori Sporting Clays (Cont.)

For Golden Grade **add** **$900**
For Pigeon Grade **add** **100**
For 2 Barrel Set **add** **850**
For Adjustable Stock **add** **200**
For High Rib **add** **80**
For Ported Barrels **add** **55**

Browning Citori Superlight O/U Shotguns

Similar to the Citori Hunting Model, except with straight-grip stock and schnabel forend tip. Made by Miroku 1982 to date.

Grade I, Fixed Choke . . . . $ 695
Grade I, Invector 725
Garde III, 12 and 20 ga. 995
Grade III, 28 and 410 ga. 1255
Grade VI, 12 and 20 ga. 1455
Grade VI, 28 and 410 ga. 1725

Browning Citori Trap Gun

Same as Hunting Model, except 12 ga. only, has Monte Carlo or fully adjustable stock and beavertail forend, trap-style recoil pad; 20- or 32-inch bbls.; M/F, IM/F, or F/F. Available with either standard vent rib or special target-type, high-post, wide vent rib. Weight: 8 lbs. Made from 1974 to date by Miroku.

Citori Plus Trap $1025
Citori Plus Trap w/ported bbl. 1095
Grade I 975
Grade III 1095
Grade VI (Disc. 1994) 1450

Browning Citori Upland Special O/U Shotgun . . . $725

A shortened version of the Hunting Model, fitted with 24-inch bbls. and straight-grip stock.

Browning Double Automatic (Steel Receiver)

Short recoil system. Takedown. 12 ga. only. Two shots. Bbls.: 26-, 28-, 30-inch; any standard choke. Checkered pistol-grip stock and forend. Weight: about 7.75 lbs. Made 1955-1961.

With plain bbl. $465
With recessed-rib bbl. 590

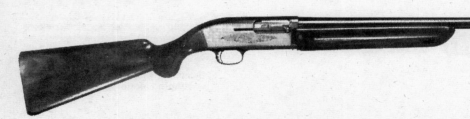

**Browning Double Automatic
Standard Grade**

Browning Gold Hunter

Browning Liège O/U

Browning Gold Hunter Series Autoloading Shotgun
Self-cleaning, gas-operated, short-stroke action. Gauges: 10 (3.5-inch chamber); 12 or 20 (3-inch chamber). 26-, 28-, or 30-inch bbl. w/Invector or Invector Plus choke tubes. Checkered walnut or graphite/fiberglass composite stock. Polished or matte black metal finish. Made 1994 to date

Gold Hunter Model w/Walnut Stock	**$455**
Gold Stalker Model w/Composite Stock	**480**
Gold 10 Hunter w/Walnut Stock	**695**
Gold 10 Stalker w/Composite Stock	**725**

Browning Liège Over/Under Shotgun $725
Boxlock. Automatic ejectors. Non-selective single trigger. 12 gauge only. Bbls.: 26.5-, 28-, or 30-inch; 2.75-inch chambers in 26.5- and 28-inch, 3-inch in 30-inch, IC/M, M/F, or F/F chokes; vent rib. Weight: 7 lbs. 4 oz. to 7 lbs. 14 oz., depending on bbls. Checkered pistol-grip stock and forearm. Made 1973-75 by FN.

Browning Lightning Sporting Clays
Similar to the standard Citori Lightning Model, except Classic-style stock with rounded pistol grip. 30-inch back-bored bbls. with Invector Plus tubes. Receiver with "Lightning Sporting Clays Edition" logo. Made 1989 to date.

Standard Model	**$895**
Pigeon Grade	**975**

Browning Over/Under Classic $1650
Gauge: 20, 2.75-inch chambers. 26-inch blued bbls. choked IC/M. Gold-plated, single selective trigger. Manual, top-tang-mounted safety. Engraved receiver. High grade, select American walnut straight-grip stock with schnabel forend. Fine-line checkering with pearl borders. High-gloss finish. 5,000 issued in 1986; made in Japan, engraved in Belgium.

**Browning Over/Under
Gold Classic**

Browning Over/Under Gold Classic $3995
Same general specifications as Over/Under Classic, except more elaborate engravings, enhanced in gold, including profile of John M. Browning. Fine oil finish. 500 issued; made in 1986 in Belgium.

Browning Recoilless Trap Shotgun
The action and bbl. are driven forward when firing to achieve 70 percent less recoil. 12 gauge, 2.75-inch chamber. 30-inch bbl. with Invector Plus tubes; adjustable vent rib. 51.63 inches overall. Weight: 9 lbs. Adj. checkered walnut buttstock and forend. Blued finish. Made from 1993 to date.

Standard Model	**$1200**
Micro Model (27-inch bbl.)	**1250**

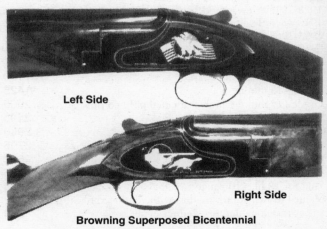

Left Side

Right Side

Browning Superposed Bicentennial

Browning Superposed Bicentennial
Commemorative $12,950
Special limited edition issued to commemorate U.S. Bicentennial. 51 guns, one for each state in the Union plus one for Washington, D.C. Receiver with sideplates has engraved and gold-inlaid hunter and wild turkey on right side, U.S. flag and bald eagle on left side, together with state markings inlaid in gold, on blued background. Checkered straight-grip stock and schnabel-style forearm of highly figured American walnut. Velvet-lined wooden presentation case. Made in 1976 by FN. Value shown is for gun in new, unfired condition.

SHOTGUNS

Browning Superposed BROADway 12 Trap

Browning Superposed BROADway 12 Trap . . . $1525
Same as standard Trap Gun, except has 30- or 32-inch bbls. with wider BROADway rib. Discontinued 1976.

Browning Superposed Shotguns, Hunting Models
Over/under boxlock. Selective automatic ejectors. Selective single trigger; earlier models (worth 25 % less) supplied with double triggers, twin selective triggers or non-selective single trigger. Gauges: 12, 20 (intro. 1949, 3-inch chambers in later production), 28, .410 (latter two ga. intro. 1960). Bbls.: 26.5-,28-,30-,32-inch, raised matted or vent rib, prewar Lightning Model made without ribbed bbl., postwar version supplied only with vent rib; any combination of standard chokes. Weight (w/26.5-inch vent-rib bbls.): *Standard 12,* 7 lbs. 11 oz.; *Lightning 12,* 7 lbs. 6 oz.; *Standard 20,* 6 lbs. 8 oz.; *Lightning 20,* 6 lbs. 4 oz.; *Lightning 28,* 6 lbs. 7 oz.; *Lightning .410,* 6 lbs. 10 oz. Checkered pistol-grip stock/forearm.

Higher grades — Pigeon, Pointer, Diana, Midas, Grade VI — differ from standard Grade I models in overall quality, engraving, wood and checkering, otherwise, specifications are the same. Midas Grade and Grade VI guns are richly gold-inlaid. Made by FN 1928-1976. Prewar models may be considered as discontinued in 1940 when Belgium was occupied by Germany. Grade VI offered 1955-1960. Pointer Grade discontinued in 1966, Grade I Standard in 1973, Pigeon Grade in 1974. Lightning Grade I, Diana and Midas Grades were not offered after 1976.

Grade I Standard	$1150
Grade I Lightning	1425
Grade I Lightning, prewar, matted bbl., no rib	2000
Grade II—Pigeon	2495
Grade III—Pointer	2950
Grade IV—Diana	3795
Grade V—Midas	4650
Grade VI	6295
Add for 28 or .410 gauge	995
Values shown are for models with ventilated rib, if gun has raised matted rib, **deduct**	200

Grade IV Diana (Postwar)

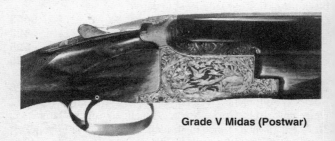

Grade V Midas (Postwar)

Browning Superposed Lightning and Superlight Models (Reissue)
Reissue of popular 12-and 20-gauge superposed shotguns. Lightning models available in 26.5- and 28-inch bbl. lengths with 2.75- or 3-inch chambering, full pistol grip. Superlight models available in 26.5-inch bbl. lengths with 2.75-inch chambering only, and straight-grip stock with schnabel forend. Both have hand-engraved receivers, fine-line checkering, gold-plated single selective trigger, automatic selective ejectors, manual safety. Weight: 6 to 7.5 lbs. Reintroduced 1985-86.

Grade II, Pigeon	$2595
Grade III, Pointer	2995
Grade IV, Diana	3195
Grade V, Midas	4195

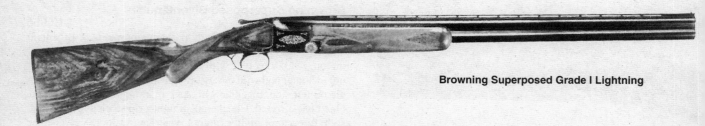

Browning Superposed Grade I Lightning

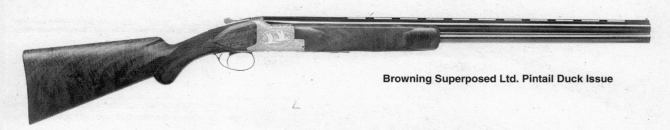

Browning Superposed Ltd. Pintail Duck Issue

Browning Superposed Magnum $1350
Same as Grade I, except chambered for 12-ga. 3-inch shells, 30-inch vent-rib bbls., stock with recoil pad. Weight: about 8.25 lbs. Discontinued 1976.

Browning Superposed Ltd. Black Duck Issue . . $4600
Gauge: 12. Superposed Lightning action. 28-inch vent-rib bbls. Choked M/F. 2.75-inch chambers. Weight: 7 lbs. 6 oz. Gold inlaid receiver and trigger guard engraved with Black Duck scenes. Gold-plated, single selective trigger. Top-tang mounted manual safety. Automatic, selective ejectors. Front and center ivory sights. High-grade, hand-checkered, hand-oiled select walnut stock and forend. 500 issued in 1983.

Browning Superposed Ltd. Mallard Duck Issue . . $4650
Same general specifications as Ltd. Black Duck Issue, except Mallard Duck scenes engraved on receiver and trigger guard, dark French walnut stock with rounded pistol grip. 500 issued in 1981.

Browning Superposed Ltd. Pintail Duck Issue . . $4650
Same general specifications as Ltd. Black Duck Issue, except Pintail Duck scenes engraved on receiver and trigger guard, stock is of dark French walnut with rounded pistol grip. 500 issued in 1982.

Browning Superposed, Presentation Grades
Custom versions of Super-Light, Lightning Hunting, Trap and Skeet Models, with same general specifications as those of standard guns, but of higher overall quality. The four Presentation Grades differ in receiver finish (grayed or blued), engraving gold inlays, wood and checkering Presentation 4 has sideplates. Made by FN, these models were introduced in 1977.

Presentation 1	$3200
Presentation 1, gold-inlaid	3600
Presentation 2	3800
Presentation 2, gold-inlaid	4600
Presentation 3, gold-inlaid	5520
Presentation 4	6500
Presentation 4, gold-inlaid	7500

Browning Superposed Skeet Guns, Grade I
Same as standard Lightning 12, 20, 28 and .410 Hunting Models, except has skeet-style stock and forearm, 26.5- or 28-inch vent-rib bbls. with SK choke. Available also in All Gauge Skeet Set: Lightning 12 with one removable forearm and three extra sets of bbls. in 20, 28 and .410 gauge in fitted luggage case. Discontinued 1976.

12 or 20 gauge	$1495
28 or .410 gauge	1795
All Gauge Skeet Set	4250

Browning Superposed Super-Light Model $1425
Ultralight field gun version of Standard Lightning Model has classic straight-grip stock and slimmer forearm. Available only in 12 and 20 gauges (2.75-inch chambers), with 26.5-inch vent-rib bbls. Weight: 6.5 lbs., 12 ga.; 6 lbs., 20 ga. Made 1967-1976.

Browning Superposed Trap Gun $1475
Same as Grade I, except has trap-style stock, beavertail forearm, 30-inch vent-rib bbls., 12 gauge only. Discont. 1976.

Browning Twelvette Double Automatic
Lightweight version of Double Automatic with same general specifications except aluminum receiver. Bbl. with plain matted top or vent rib. Weight: 6.75 to 7 lbs., depending on bbl. Receiver is finished in black w/gold engraving; 1956-1961 receivers were also anodized in gray, brown and green w/silver engraving. Made 1955-1971.

With Plain Bbl.	$425
With Vent-rib Bbl.	525

Browning Twentyweight Double Automatic
Same as Twelvette, but ¾ lb. lighter. 26.5-inch Bbl. only. Made 1956-1971.

With Plain Bbl.	$450
With Vent-rib Bbl.	595

NOTE

The following markings are used to indicate chokes on Browning shotguns: *=Full, *– - Improved Modified, ** = Modified, **– = Improved Cylinder, **S = Skeet, and *** - Cylinder

---

SHOTGUNS

Browning Twelvette
Double Automatic

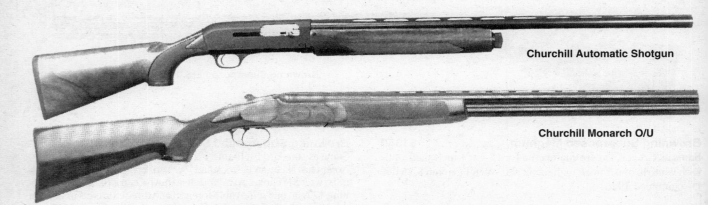

Churchill Automatic Shotgun

Churchill Monarch O/U

CHURCHILL SHOTGUNS
Italy and Spain
Imported by Ellett Brothers, Inc., Chapin, SC; previously by Kassnar Imports, Inc., Harrisburg, PA

Churchill Automatic Shotgun
Gas-operated. Gauge: 12, 2.75- or 3-inch. 5-shot magazine with cutoff. Bbl.: 24-, 25-, 26-, 28-inch with ICT Choke tubes. Checkered walnut stock with satin finish. Made 1990-1994.
Standard Model $425
Turkey Model 450

Churchill Monarch Over/Under Shotgun
Hammerless, takedown with engraved receiver. Selective single or double triggers. Gauges: 12, 20, 28, .410; 3-inch chambers. Bbls.: 25- or 26-inch (IC/M); 28-inch (M/F). Weight: 6.5-7.5 lbs. Checkered European walnut buttstock and forend. Made in Italy 1986-1993.
With Double Triggers $365
With Single Trigger 425

Churchill Regent Over/Under Shotguns
Gauges: 12 or 20; 2.75-inch chambers. 27-inch bbls. w/interchangeable choke tubes and wide vent rib. Single selective trigger, selective automatic ejectors. Checkered pistol-grip stock in fancy walnut. Imported from Italy 1984-88.
Regent V $825
Regent VII w/Sideplates 950

Churchill Regent Side-by-Side Shotguns
12 gauge s/s. 25-, 27- or 28-inch bbls. w/fixed choke or interchangeable choke tubes. Double triggers. Automatic top tang safety. Double safety sidelock, engraved antique silver receiver.

Churchill Regent Side-by-Side Shotguns *(Cont.)*
Automatic selective ejectors. Oil-finished English-style stock of extra select European walnut. Imported from Spain 1984-1993.
Regent Standard $650
Regent VI, Sidelock 775

Churchill Regent Skeet $675
12 or 20 gauge with 2.75-inch chambers. Selective automatic ejectors, single-selective trigger. 26-inch over/under bbls. w/vent rib. Weight: 7 lbs. Made in Italy 1984-88.

Churchill Regent Trap $685
12-gauge competition shotgun w/2.75-inch chambers. 30 inch over/under bbls. choked IM/F, vent side ribs. Weight: 8 lbs. Selective automatic ejectors, single selective trigger. Checkered Monte Carlo stock with Supercushion recoil pad. Made in Italy 1984-88.

Churchill Sporting Clays Over/Under $695
Same general specifications as Windsor IV, except in 12 ga. only w/28-inch ported bbls. and choke tubes. Selective automatic ejectors. Weight: 7.5 lbs. Made from 1992-94.

Churchill Windsor Over/Under Shotguns
Hammerless, boxlock with engraved receiver, selective single trigger. Extractors or ejectors. Gauges: 12, 20, 28 or .410; 3-inch chambers. Bbls.: 24 to 30 inches w/fixed chokes or choke tubes. Weight: 6 lbs. 3 oz. (Flyweight) to 7 lbs. 10 oz. (12 ga.). Checkered straight (Flyweight) or pistol-grip stock and forend of European walnut. Imported from Italy 1984-1993.
Windsor III w/Fixed Chokes $500
Windsor III w/Choke Tubes 550
Windsor IV w/Fixed Chokes (Disc. 1993) 555
Windsor IV w/Choke Tubes 695

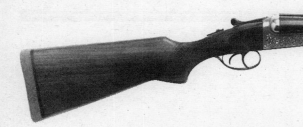

**Churchill Windsor Grade
Side-by-Side Shotgun**

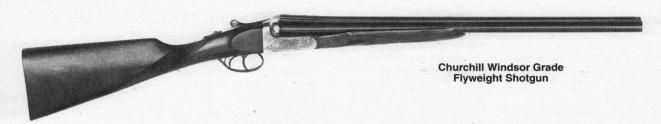

**Churchill Windsor Grade
Flyweight Shotgun**

Churchill Windsor Side-by-Side Shotguns

Boxlock action with double triggers, ejectors or extractors and automatic safety. Gauges: 10, (3.5-inch chambers); 12, 20, 28, .410 (3-inch chambers), 16 (2.75-inch chambers). Bbls.: 23 to 32 inches w/various fixed choke or choke tube combinations. Weight: 5 lbs. 12 oz. (Flyweight) to 11.5 lbs. (10 ga.). European walnut buttstock and forend. Imported from Spain 1984-1990.

Windsor I 10 ga. **$550**
Windsor I 12 thru .410 ga. 465
Windsor II 12 or 20 ga. 450

E.J. CHURCHILL, LTD.
Surrey (previously London), England

All of the E.J. Churchill shotguns listed below are no longer imported.

E.J. Churchill Field Model Hammerless Double

Sidelock Hammerless ejector gun with same general specifications as Premiere Model but of lower quality.

With Double Triggers **$7950**
Selective Single Trigger, **add** 400

E.J. Churchill Premiere Quality Hammerless Double

Sidelock. Automatic ejectors. Double triggers or selective single trigger. Gauges: 12, 16, 20, 28. Bbls.: 25-, 28- 30-, 32-inch; any degree of boring. Weight: 5-8 lbs. depending on gauge and bbl. length. Checkered stock and forend, straight or pistol grip.

With Double Triggers **$14,500**
Selective Single Trigger, **extra** 900

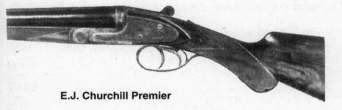

E.J. Churchill Premier

E.J. Churchill Premiere Quality Under-and-Over Shotgun

Sidelock. Automatic ejectors. Double triggers or selective single trigger. Gauges: 12, 16, 20, 28. Bbls.: 25-, 28-, 30-, 32-inch, any degree of boring. Weight: 5-8 lbs. depending on gauge and bbl. length. Checkered stock and forend, straight or pistol grip.

With Double Triggers. **$14,995**
Selective Single Trigger, **add**. 700
Raised Vent Rib, **add**. 400

E.J. Churchill Utility Model Hammerless Double Barrel

Anson & Deeley boxlock action. Double triggers or single trigger. Gauges: 12, 16, 20, 28, .410. Bbls.: 25-, 28-, 30-, 32-inch, any degree of boring. Weight: 4.5-8 lbs. depending on ga. and bbl. length. Checkered stock and forend, straight or pistol grip.

With Double Triggers **$4350**
Selective Single Trigger, **add** 400

E.J. Churchill XXV Premiere Hammerless

Double **$12,500**
Sidelock. Assisted opening. Automatic ejectors. Double triggers. Gauges: 12, 20. 25-inch bbls. w/narrow, quick-sighting rib; any standard choke combination. English-style straight-grip stock and forearm, checkered.

E.J. Churchill XXV Imperial **$9750**
Similar to XXV Premiere, but no assisted opening feature.

E.J. Churchill XXV Hercules **$7695**
Boxlock, otherwise specs same as for XXV Premiere.

E.J. Churchill XXV Regal **$4250**
Similar to XXV Hercules, but without assisted opening feature. Gauges: 12, 20, 28, .410.

CLASSIC DOUBLES
Tochigi, Japan

Imported by Classic Doubles International, St. Louis, MO, and previously by Olin as Winchester Models 101 and 23.

Classic Model 101 Over/Under Shotgun

Boxlock. Engraved receiver w/single selective trigger, auto ejectors and combination bbl. selector and safety. Gauges: 12, 20, 28 or .410, 2.75-, 3-inch chambers. 25.5- 28- or 30-inch vent-rib bbls. Weight: 6.25 – 7.75 lbs. Checkered French walnut stock and forearm. Imported 1987-1990.

Classic I Field **$1295**
Classic II Field 1500
Classic Sporter 1550
Classic Sporter Combo 2450
Classic Trap 1200
Classic Trap Single 1295
Classic Trap Combo 1950
Classic Skeet 1450
Classic Skeet 4-Bbl. Set 3795
Classic Waterfowler 1095
For Grade II (28 Ga.), **add** 750
For Grade II (.410 Ga.), **add**. 250

SHOTGUNS

Classic Model 201 Side-by-Side Shotgun

Boxlock. Single selective trigger, automatic safety and selective ejectors. Gauges: 12 or 20; 3-inch chambers. 26- or 28-inch vent-rib bbl., fixed chokes or internal tubes. Weight: 6 to 7 lbs. Checkered French walnut stock and forearm. Imported 1987-1990.

Field Model $1295
Skeet Model   1595
For Internal Choke Tubes, **add**   100

Classic Model 201 Small Bore Set $3855

Same general specifications as the Classic Model 201, except with smaller frame, in 28 ga. (IC/M) and .410 (F/M). Weight: 6-6.5 lbs. Imported 1987-1990.

COGSWELL & HARRISON, LTD.
London, England

Cogswell & Harrison Ambassador Hammerless Double-Barrel Shotgun $3195

Boxlock. Sideplates with game scene or rose scroll engraving. Automatic ejectors. Double triggers. Gauges: 12, 16, 20. Bbls.: 26-, 28-, 30-inch; any choke combination. Checkered straight-grip stock and forearm. Currently manufactured.

Cogswell & Harrison Avant Tout Series Hammerless Double-Barrel Shotguns

Boxlock. Sideplates (except Avant Tout III Grade). Automatic ejectors. Double triggers or single trigger (selective or non-selective). Gauges: 12, 16, 20. Bbls.: 25-, 27.5-, 30-inch, any choke combination. Checkered stock and forend, straight grip standard. Made in three models— Avant Tout I or Konor, Avant Tout II or Sandhurst, Avant Tout III or Rex—which differ chiefly in overall quality engraving, grade of wood, checkering, etc.; general specifications are the same. Discontinued.

Avant Tout I $2350
Avant Tout II   2325
Avant Tout III   1915
Single Trigger, Non-selective, **add**   225
Single Trigger, Selective, **add**   300

Cogswell & Harrison Best Quality Hammerless Victor Model

Cogswell & Harrison Best Quality Hammerless Sidelock Double Barrel Shotgun

Hand-detachable locks. Automatic ejectors. Double triggers or single trigger (selective or non-selective). Gauges: 12, 16, 20. Bbls.: 25-, 26-, 28-, 30-inch, any choke combination. Checkered stock and forend, straight grip standard.

Victor Model $6855
Primic Model (Discontinued)   4395
Single Trigger, Non-selective, **add**   225
Single Trigger, Selective, **add**   300

Cogswell & Harrison Huntic Model Hammerless Double

Sidelock. Automatic ejectors. Double triggers or single trigger (selective or non-selective). Gauges: 12, 16, 20. Bbls.: 25-, 27.5-, 30-inch; any choke combination. Checkered stock and forend, straight grip standard. Discontinued.

With Double Triggers $3250
Single Trigger, Non-selective, **add**   225
Single Trigger, Selective, **add**   300

Cogswell & Harrison Markor Hammerless Double

Boxlock. Non-ejector or ejector. Double triggers. Gauges: 12, 16, 20. Bbls.: 27.5 or 30-inch; any choke combination. Checkered stock and forend, straight grip standard. Discontinued.

Non-ejector $1325
Ejector Model   1695

Cogswell & Harrison Regency Hammerless Double $2550

Anson & Deeley boxlock action. Automatic ejectors. Double triggers. Gauges: 12, 16, 20. Bbls.: 26-, 28-, 30-inch, any choke combination. Checkered straight-grip stock and forearm. Introduced in 1970 to commemorate the firm's bicentenary, this model has deep scroll engraving and the name "Regency" inlaid in gold on the rib. Currently manufactured.

COLT INDUSTRIES
Hartford, Connecticut

Colt Auto Shotguns were made by Luigi Franchi S.p.A. and are similar to corresponding models of that manufacturer.

Colt Auto Shotgun — Magnum

Same as Standard Auto, except steel receiver, handles 3-inch Magnum shells, 30- and 32-inch bbls. in 12 ga., 28-inch in 20 ga. Weight: 12 ga., about 8.25 lbs. Made 1964-66.

With Plain Bbl. $345
With Solid-rib Bbl.   375
With Ventilated-rib Bbl.   395

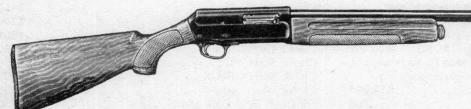

Colt Auto Shotgun – Ultra Light Standard

Colt Custom Hammerless Double

Colt Standard Pump

Colt Auto Shotgun — Magnum Custom
Same as Magnum, except has engraved receiver, select walnut stock and forearm. Made 1964-66.
With Solid-rib Bbl. **$425**
With Ventilated-rib Bbl. **475**

Colt Auto Shotgun — Ultra Light Custom
Same as Standard Auto, except has engraved receiver, select walnut stock and forearm. Made 1964-66.
With Solid-rib Bbl. **$350**
With Ventilated-rib Bbl. **375**

Colt Auto Shotgun — Ultra Light Standard
Recoil-operated. Takedown. Alloy receiver. Gauges: 12, 20. Magazine holds 4 shells. Bbls.: plain, solid or vent rib, chrome-lined; 26-inch IC or M choke, 28-inch M or F choke, 30-inch F choke, 32-inch F choke. Weight: 12 ga., about 6.25 lbs. Checkered pistol-grip stock and forearm. Made 1964-66.
With Plain Bbl. **$245**
With Solid-rib Bbl. **275**
With Vent-rib Bbl. **295**

Colt Custom Hammerless Double **$595**
Boxlock. Double triggers. Auto ejectors. Gauges: 12 Mag., 16. Bbls.: 26-inch IC/M; 28-inch M/F; 30-inch F/F. Weight: 12 ga., about 7.5 lbs. Checkered pistol-grip stock and beavertail forearm. Made in 1961.

Colt-Sauer Drilling

Coltsman Custom Pump **$320**
Same as Standard Pump shotgun except has checkered stock, vent-rib bbl. Weight: about 6.5 lbs. Made 1961-63 by Manufrance.

Coltsman Standard Pump Shotgun **$295**
Takedown. Gauges: 12, 16, 20. Magazine holds 4 shells. Bbls.: 26-inch IC; 28-inch M or F choke; 30-inch F choke. Weight: about 6 lbs. Plain pistol-grip stock and forearm. Made 1961-65 by Manufrance.

Colt-Sauer Drilling **$3295**
Three-bbl. combination gun. Boxlock. Set rifle trigger. Tang bbl. selector, automatic rear sight positioner. 12 ga. over 30-06 or 243 rifle bbl. 25-inch bbls., F and M choke. Weight: about 8 lbs. Folding leaf rear sight, blade front with brass bead. Checkered pistol-grip stock and beavertail forearm, recoil-pad. Made 1974 to date by J. P. Sauer & Sohn, Eckernförde, Germany.

CONNECTICUT VALLEY CLASSICS
Westport, Connecticut

CVC Classic Field Over/Under **$1495**
Similar to the standard Classic Sporter Over/Under Model, except w/30-inch bbls. only and non-reflective matte blued finish on both bbls. and receiver for Waterfowler; other Grades with different degrees of embellishment; Grade I the lowest and Grade III the highest. Made 1993 to date.
Grade I **$1755**
Grade II.. **1895**
Grade III **2065**
Waterfowler **1695**

CVC Classic Sporter Over/Under
Gauge: 12; 3-inch chamber. Bbls.: 28-, 30- or 32-inch w/ screw-in tubes. Weight: 7.75 lbs. Engraved stainless or nitrided receiver; blued bbls. Checkered American black walnut butt-stock and forend with low-luster satin finish. Made from 1993 to date.
Classic Sporter **$1595**
Stainless Classic Sporter......................... **1895**

SHOTGUNS

Daly Commander Over/Under

CHARLES DALY, INC.
New York, New York

The pre-WWII Charles Daly shotguns, with the exception of the Commander, were manufactured by various firms in Suhl, Germany. The postwar guns, except for the Novamatic series and the current models distributed by Outdoor Sports Headquarters, were produced by Miroku Firearms Mfg. Co., Tokyo.

Charles Daly Commander Over/Under Shotgun
Daly pattern Anson & Deeley system boxlock action. Automatic ejectors. Double triggers or Miller selective single trigger. Gauges: 12, 16, 20, 28, .410. Bbls.: 26- to 30-inch, IC/M or M/F choke. Weight: 5.25 to 7.25 lbs. depending on ga. and bbl. length. Checkered stock and forend, straight or pistol grip. The two models, 100 and 200, differ in general quality, grade of wood, checkering, engraving, etc.; otherwise specs are the same. Made in Belgium c. 1939.

Model 100	$390
Model 200	525
Miller Single Trigger, **add**	100

**Daly Hammerless Double—
Regent Diamond**

Charles Daly Hammerless Double-Barrel Shotgun
Daly pattern Anson & Deeley system boxlock action. Automatic ejectors—except "Superior Quality" is non-ejector. Double triggers. Gauges: 10, 12, 16, 20, 28, .410. Bbls.: 26- to 32-inch, any combination of chokes. Weight: from 4 to 8.5 lbs. depending on ga. and bbl. length. Checkered pistol-grip stock and forend. The four grades—Regent Diamond, Diamond, Empire, Superior—differ in general quality, grade of wood, checkering, engraving, etc.; otherwise specifications are the same. Discontinued about 1933.

Diamond Quality	$8450
Empire Quality	3895
Regent Diamond Quality	9950
Superior Quality	995

Charles Daly Hammerless Drilling (Three Barrel Gun)
Daly pattern Anson & Deeley system boxlock action. Plain extractors. Double triggers, front single set for rifle bbl. Gauges: 12, 16, 20, 25-20, 25-35, 30-30 rifle bbl. Supplied in various bbl. lengths and weights. Checkered pistol-grip stock and forend. Auto rear sight operated by rifle bbl. selector. The three grades — Regent Diamond, Diamond, Superior—differ in general quality, grade of wood, checkering, engraving, etc.; otherwise, specs are the same. Discont. about 1933.

Diamond Quality	$4695
Regent Diamond Quality	8950
Superior Quality	2595

Charles Daly Hammerless Double— Empire Grade $545
Boxlock. Plain extractors. Non-selective single trigger. Gauges: 12, 16, 20; 3-inch chambers in 12 and 20, 2.75-inch in 16 ga. Bbls.: vent rib; 26-, 28-, 30-inch (latter in 12 ga. only); IC/M, M/F, F/F. Weight: 6 to 7.75 lbs., depending on ga. and bbls. Checkered pistol-grip stock and beavertail forearm. Made 1968-1971.

Charles Daly 1974 Wildlife Commemorative ... $1695
Limited issue of 500 guns. Similar to Diamond Grade over/under. 12-ga. trap and skeet models only. Duck scene engraved on right side of receiver, fine scroll on left side. Made in 1974.

Charles Daly Novamatic Lightweight Autoloader
Same as Breda. Recoil-operated. Takedown.12 ga., 2.75-inch chamber. 4-shell tubular magazine. Bbls.: plain vent rib; 26-inch IC or Quick-Choke w/three interchangeable tubes, 28-inch M or F choke. Weight (w/26-inch vent-rib bbl.): 7 lbs. 6 oz. Checkered pistol-grip stock and forearm. Made 1968 by Ernesto Breda, Milan, Italy.

With Plain Bbl.	$350
With Vent-rib Bbl.	395
For Quick-Choke, **add**	20

Charles Daly Novamatic Super Lightweight
Lighter version of Novamatic Lightweight. Gauges: 12, 20. Weight (with 26-inch vent-rib bbl.): 12 ga., 6 lbs. 10 oz.; 20 ga., 6 lbs. SK choke available in 26-inch vent-rib bbl. 28-inch bbls. in 12 ga. only. Quick-Choke in 20 ga. w/plain bbl. Made 1968 by Ernesto Breda, Milan, Italy.

12 Ga., Plain Bbl.	$345
12 Ga., Vent-rib Bbl.	375
20 Ga., Plain Bbl.	310
20 Ga., Plain Bbl. w/Quick-Choke	325
20 Ga., Vent-rib Bbl.	345

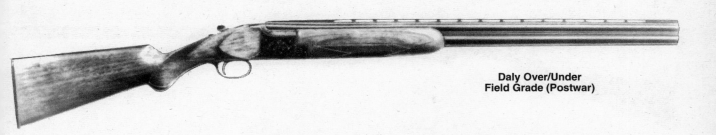

**Daly Over/Under
Field Grade (Postwar)**

Charles Daly Novamatic Super Lightweight 20-Gauge Magnum $345
Same as Novamatic Super Lightweight 20, except 3-inch chamber, has 3-shell magazine, 28-inch vent-rib bbl., F choke.

Charles Daly Novamatic 12-Gauge Magnum . . . $350
Same as Novamatic Lightweight, except chambered for 12-ga. Magnum 3-inch shell, has 3-shell magazine, 30-inch vent-rib bbl., F choke, and stock w/recoil pad. Weight: 7.75 lbs.

Charles Daly Novamatic Trap Gun $375
Same as Novamatic Lightweight, except has 30-inch vent rib bbl., F choke and Monte Carlo stock w/recoil pad. Weight: 7.75 lbs.

Charles Daly Over/Under Shotguns (Prewar)
Daly-pattern Anson & Deeley-system boxlock action. Sideplates. Auto ejectors. Double triggers. Gauges: 12, 16, 20. Supplied in various bbl. lengths and weights. Checkered pistol-grip stock and forend. The two grades — Diamond and Empire — differ in general quality, grade of wood, checkering, engraving, etc.; otherwise specifications are the same. Discontinued about 1933.
Diamond Quality $4395
Empire Quality 3295

Charles Daly Over/Under Shotguns (Postwar)
Boxlock. Auto ejectors or selective auto/manual ejection. Selective single trigger. Gauges: 12, 12 Magnum (3- inch chambers), 20 (3-inch chambers), 28, .410. Bbls.: vent rib; 26-, 28-, 30-inch; standard choke combinations. Weight: 6 to 8 lbs. depending on ga. and bbls. Select walnut stock with pistol grip, fluted forearm checkered; Monte Carlo comb on trap guns; recoil pad on 12-ga. Mag. and trap models. The various grades differ in quality of engraving and wood. Made 1963-1976.
Diamond Grade $955
Field Grade 550
Superior Grade 695
Venture Grade 525

Charles Daly Sextuple Model Single-Barrel Trap Gun
Daly pattern Anson & Deeley system boxlock action. Six locking bolts. Auto ejector. 12 ga. only. Bbls.: 30-, 32-, 34-inch, vent rib. Weight: 7.5 to 8.25 lbs. Checkered pistol-grip stock and forend. The two models made — Empire and Regent Diamond — differ in general quality, grade of wood, checkering, engraving, etc., otherwise specs are the same. Discontinued about 1933.
Regent Diamond Quality $2850
Empire Quality 1995

Charles Daly Single-Shot Trap Gun
Daly pattern Anson & Deeley system boxlock action. Auto ejector. 12 ga. only. Bbls.: 30-, 32-, 34-inch, vent rib. Weight: 7.5 to 8.25 lbs. Checkered pistol-grip stock and forend. This model was made in Empire Quality only. Discontinued about 1933.
Diamond Grade $2790
Empire Grade 2135

Charles Daly Superior Grade Single-Shot Trap . . $595
Boxlock. Automatic ejector. 12 ga. only. 32- or 34-inch vent-rib bbl., F choke. Weight: about 8 lbs. Monte Carlo stock w/pistol grip and recoil pad, beavertail forearm, checkered. Made 1968-1976.

NOTE

The following Charles Daly shotguns are distributed in the U.S. by Outdoor Sports Headquarters, Dayton Ohio. The Daly semi-auto guns are currently manufactured in Japan, while the o/u models are produced in Italy and Spain.

Charles Daly Diamond Grade Over/Under
Boxlock. Single selective trigger. Selective automatic ejectors. Gauges: 12 and 20, 3-inch chambers (2.75 target grade). Bbls.: 26-, 27- or 30-inch w/fixed chokes or screw-in tubes. Weight: 7 lbs. Checkered European walnut stock and forearm with oil finish. Engraved antique silver receiver and blued bbls. Made 1984-1990.
Standard Model $595
Skeet Model 650
Trap Model 695

Charles Daly DSS Hammerless Double $525
Boxlock. Single selective trigger. Selective automatic ejectors. Gauges: 12 and 20; 3-inch chambers. 26-inch bbls. w/screw-in choke tubes. Weight: 6.75 lbs. Checkered walnut pistol-grip stock and semibeavertail forearm w/recoil pad. Engraved antique silver receiver and blued bbls. Made from 1990 to date.

Charles Daly Field Grade Over/Under $385
Boxlock. Single selective trigger. Extractors. Gauges: 12 and 20; 3-inch chambers. Bbls.: 26-inch, IC/M; 28-inch, M/F. Weight: 6.75 lbs. (12 ga.). Checkered walnut stock and forearm w/semi-gloss finish and recoil pad. Engraved color-casehardened receiver and blued bbls. Made from 1989 to date.

Charles Daly Field Semiauto Shotgun $310
Recoil-operated. Takedown. 12-ga. and 12-ga. Magnum. Bbls.: 27- and 30-inch; vent rib. Made 1982-88.

SHOTGUNS

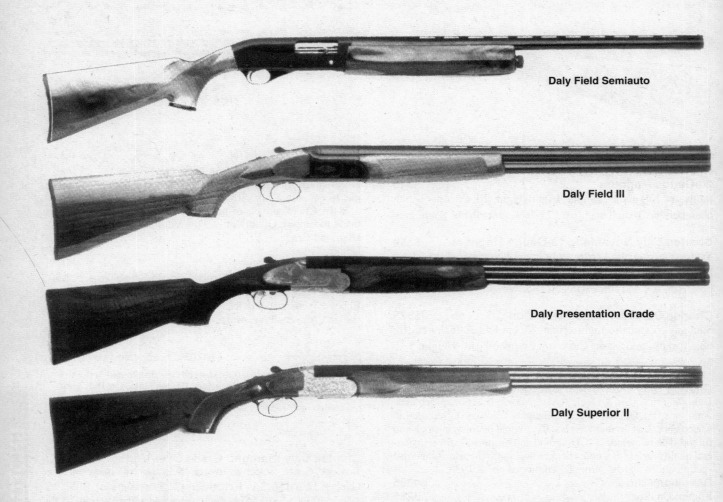

Daly Field Semiauto

Daly Field III

Daly Presentation Grade

Daly Superior II

Charles Daly Field III Over/Under Shotgun $395
Boxlock. Plain extractors. Non-selective single trigger. Gauges:
12 or 20. Bbls.: vent rib; 26- and 28-inch; IC/M, M/F. Weight: 6
to 7.75 lbs. depending on ga. and bbls. Chrome-molybdenum
steel bbls. Checkered pistol-grip stock and forearm. Made from
1982 to date.

Charles Daly Lux Over/Under $565
Similar to the Field Grade, except with selective automatic ejectors and choke tubes. Gauges: 12, 20, 28 and .410. Receiver with
antique silver finish and blued bbls. Made from 1989 to date.

Charles Daly Multi-XII Self-loading Shotgun . . . $395
Similar to the gas-operated field semiauto, except with new
Multi-Action gas system designed to shoot all loads without adjustment. 12 ga. w/3-inch chamber. 27-inch bbl. w/Invector
choke tubes, vent rib. Made in Japan from 1987 to date.

Charles Daly Over/Under Presentation Grade . . . $795
Purdey double cross-bolt locks. Single selective trigger. Gauges:
12 or 20. Bbls.: chrome-molybdenum steel, rectified, honed and
internally chromed, 27-inch vent rib. Hand-checkered deluxe
European walnut stock. Made 1982-86.

Charles Daly Over/Under Superior II Shotgun . . . $555
Boxlock. Plain extractors. Non-selective single trigger. Gauges:
12 or 20. Bbls.: chrome-molybdenum vent rib 26-,28-, 30-inch,
latter in Magnum only, assorted chokes. Silver engraved receiver. Checkered pistol-grip stock and forearm. Made from
1982 to date.

Charles Daly Sporting Clays Over/Under $695
Similar to the Field Grade, except in 12 ga. only w/ported bbls.
and internal choke tubes. Made from 1990 to date.

DARNE S.A.
Saint-Etienne, France

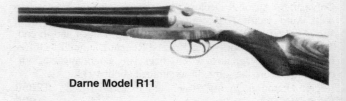

Darne Model R11

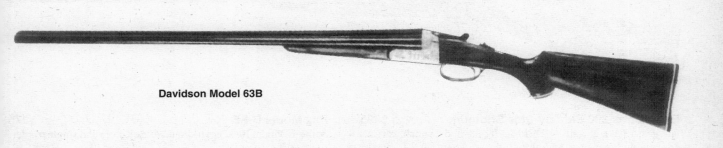

Davidson Model 63B

Darne Hammerless Double-Barrel Shotguns

Sliding-breech action w/fixed bbls. Auto ejectors. Double triggers. Gauges: 12, 16, 20, 28; also 12 and 20 Magnum with 3-inch chambers. Bbls.: 27.5-inch standard, 25.5- to 31.5-inch lengths available; any standard choke combination. Weight: 5.5 to 7 lbs., depending on ga. and bbl. length. Checkered straight-grip or pistol-grip stock and forearm. The various models differ in grade of engraving and wood. Currently manufactured.

Model R11 (Bird Hunter)	$ 875
Model R15 (Pheasant Hunter)	1925
Model R16 (Magnum)	1495
Model V19 (Quail Hunter)	2850
Model V22	3500
Model V Hors Série No. 1	6500

DAVIDSON GUNS
Mfd. by Fabrica de Armas ILJA, Eibar, Spain; distributed by Davidson Firearms Co., Greensboro, North Carolina

Davidson Model 63B Double-Barrel Shotgun . . . $250

Anson & Deeley boxlock action. Frame-engraved and nickel plated. Plain extractors. Auto safety. Double triggers. Gauges: 12, 16, 20, 28, .410. Bbl. lengths: 25 (.410 only), 26, 28, 30 inches (latter 12 ga. only). Chokes: IC/ M, M/F, F/F. Weight: 5 lbs. 11 oz. (.410) to 7 lbs. (12 ga.). Checkered pistol-grip stock and forearm of European walnut. Made from 1963 to date.

Davidson Model 63B Magnum

Similar to standard Model 63B, except chambered for 10 ga. 3.5-inch, 12 and 20 ga. 3-inch Magnum shells; 10 ga. has 32-inch bbls., choked F/F. Weight: 10 lb. 10 oz. Made from 1963 to date.

12-and 20-gauge Magnum	$335
10-gauge Magnum	395

Davidson Model 69SL Double-Barrel Shotgun . . $415

Sidelock action w/detachable sideplates, engraved and nickel-plated. Plain extractors. Auto safety. Double triggers. 12 and 20 ga. Bbls.: 26-inch IC/M, 28-inch M/F. Weight: 12 ga., 7 lbs., 20 ga., 6.5 lbs. Pistol-grip stock and forearm of European walnut, checkered. Made 1963-1976.

Davidson Model 73 Stagecoach
Hammer Double $265

Sidelock action with detachable sideplates and exposed hammers. Plain extractors. Double triggers. Gauges: 12, 20, 3-inch chambers. 20-inch bbls, M/F chokes. Weight: 7 lbs., 12 ga.; 6.5 lbs., 20 ga. Checkered pistol-grip stock and forearm. Made from 1976 to date.

EXEL ARMS OF AMERICA
Gardner, Massachusetts

Exel Series 100 Over/Under Shotgun

Gauge: 12. Single selective trigger. Selective auto ejectors. Hand-checkered European walnut stock with full pistol grip, tulip forend. Black metal finish. Chambered for 2.75-inch shells (Model 103 for 3-inch). Weight: 6. 88 to 7.88 lbs. Discontinued 1988.

Model 101, 26-inch bbl., IC/M	$375
Model 102, 28-inch bbl., IC/IM	380
Model 103, 30-inch bbl., M/F	395
Model 104, 28-inch bbl., IC/IM	435
Model 105, 28-inch bbl., 5 choke tubes	550
Model 106, 28-inch bbl., 5 choke tubes	660
Model 107 Trap, 30-inch bbl., Full + 5 tubes	695

SHOTGUNS

Exel Model 101 Over/Under

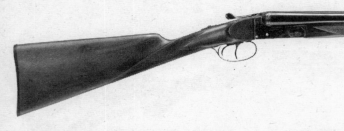

Exel Model 200 Side-by-Side

Exel Series 200 Side-by-Side Shotgun $395
Gauges: 12, 20, 28 and .410. Bbls.: 26-, 27- and 28-inch; various choke combinations. Weight: 7 lbs. average. American or European-style stock and forend. Made 1985 to 1987.

Exel Series 300 Over/Under Shotgun $460
Gauge: 12. Bbls.: 26-, 28- and 29-inch. Non-glare black-chrome matte finish. Weight: 7 lbs. average. Selective auto ejectors, engraved receiver. Hand-checkered European walnut stock and forend. Made 1985-1986.

FOX SHOTGUNS
Made by A. H. Fox Gun Co., Philadelphia, PA, 1903 to 1930, and since then by Savage Arms, originally of Utica, NY, now of Westfield, MA. In 1993 Connecticut Manufacturing Co. of New Britain, CT, reintroduced selected models.

Values shown are for 12 and 16 ga. doubles made by A. H. Fox. Twenty gauge guns often are valued up to 75% higher. Savage-made Fox models generally bring prices 25% lower. With the exception of Model B, production of Fox shotguns was discontinued about 1942.

Fox Model B Hammerless Double $235
Boxlock. Double triggers. Plain extractor. Gauges: 12, 16, 20, .410. 24- to 30-inch bbls., vent rib on current production; chokes: M/F, C/M, F/F (.410 only). Weight: about 7.5 lbs., 12 ga. Checkered pistol-grip stock and forend. Made about 1940-1985.

Fox Model B-DE $275
Same as Model B-ST except frame finished in satin chrome, select walnut buttstock with checkered pistol grip and beavertail forearm. Made 1965-66.

Fox Model B-DL $315
Same as Model B-ST except frame finished in satin chrome, select walnut buttstock with checkered pistol grip side panels, beavertail forearm. Made 1962-66.

Fox Model B-SE $375
Same as Model B except has selective ejectors and single trigger. Made 1966-1989.

Fox Model B-ST $255
Same as Model B except has non-selective single trigger. Made 1955-1966.

Fox Hammerless Double-Barrel Shotguns
The higher grades have the same general specifications as the standard Sterlingworth model with differences chiefly in workmanship and materials. Higher grade models are stocked in fine select walnut; quantity and quality of engraving increases with grade and price. Except for Grade A, all other grades have auto ejectors.

Grade A	$ 1,425
Grade AE	1,725
Grade BE	2,750
Grade CE	3,595
Grade DE	7,655
Grade FE	15,550
Grade XE	5,250
Fox-Kautzky selective single trigger, **extra**	300
Ventilated rib, **extra**	400
Beavertail forearm, **extra**	200

Fox Single-Barrel Trap Guns
Boxlock. Auto ejector. 12 ga. only. 30- or 32-inch vent-rib bbl. Weight: 7.5 to 8 lbs. Trap-style stock and forearm of select walnut, checkered, recoil pad optional. The four grades differ chiefly in quality of wood and engraving; Grade M guns, built to order, have finest Circassian walnut. Stock and receiver are elaborately engraved and inlaid with gold. Discontinued 1942. *Note:* In 1932 the Fox Trap Gun was redesigned and those manufactured after that date have a stock with full pistol grip and Monte Carlo comb; at the same time frame was changed to permit the rib line to extend across it to the rear.

Grade JE	$2795
Grade KE	3595
Grade LE	4950
Grade ME	9500

Fox Model B

Fox "Skeeter" Double-Barrel Shotgun $2595
Boxlock. Gauge: 12 or 20. Bbls.: 28 inches w/full-length vent rib. Weight: approx. 7 lbs. Buttstock and beavertail forend of select American walnut, finely checkered. Soft rubber recoil pad and ivory bead sights. Made in early 1930s.

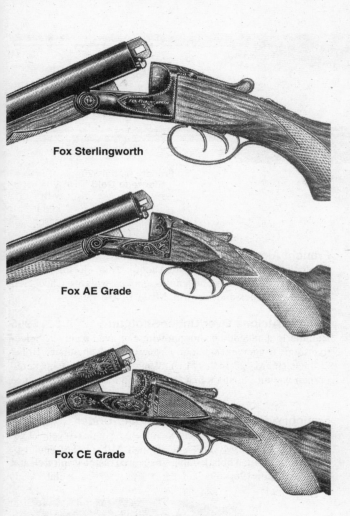

Fox Sterlingworth

Fox AE Grade

Fox CE Grade

Fox Sterlingworth Deluxe
Same general specifications as Sterlingworth, except 32-inch bbl. also available, recoil pad, ivory bead sights.

With plain extractors................................$1295
With automatic ejectors 1595

Fox Sterlingworth Hammerless Double
Boxlock. Double triggers (Fox-Kautzky selective single trigger extra). Plain extractors (auto ejectors extra). Gauges: 12,16, 20. Bbl. lengths: 26-, 28-, 30-inch; chokes F/F, M/F, C/M (any combination of C to F choke borings was available at no extra cost). Weight: 12 ga., 6.88 to 8.25 lbs.; 16 ga., 6 to 7 lbs.; 20 ga., 5.75 to 6.75 lbs. Checkered pistol-grip stock and forearm.

With plain extractors $1155
With automatic ejectors 1495
Selective single trigger, **extra** 300

Fox Sterlingworth Skeet and Upland Game Gun
Same general specifications as the standard Sterlingworth except has 26- or 28-inch bbls. with skeet boring only, straight-grip stock. Weight: 7 lbs., 12 ga.

With plain extractors...............................$1550
With automatic ejectors 1895

Super Fox HE Grade $2995
Long-range gun made in 12 ga. only (chambered for 3-inch shells on order), 30- or 32-inch full choke bbls., auto ejectors standard. Weight: 8.75 to 9.75 lbs. General specifications same as standard Sterlingworth.

NOTE

> The following A.H. Fox Shotguns were reintroduced by the Connecticut Manufacturing Co. (New Britain, CT) in 1993.

CMC Fox Hammerless Double-Barrel Shotguns
High-grade doubles similar to the original Fox models. 20 ga. only. 26-, 28- or 30-inch bbls. Double triggers automatic safety and ejectors. Weight: 5.5 to 7 lbs. Custom Circassian walnut stock with hand-rubbed oil finish. Custom stock configuration: straight, semi- or full pistol-grip stock w/traditional pad, hard rubber plate checkered or skeleton butt; schnabel, splinter or beavertail forend. Made 1993 to date.

CE Grade . . . . $ 5,295
XE Grade 7,550
DE Grade 9,995
FE Grade 15,995
Exhibition Grade 20,950

LUIGI FRANCHI S.P.A.
Brescia, Italy

Franchi 48/AL Ultra Light Shotgun
Recoil-operated, takedown, hammerless shotgun with tubular magazine. Gauges: 12 or 20 (2.75-inch); 12-ga. Magnum (3-inch chamber). Bbls.: 24- to 32-inch w/various choke combinations. Weight: 5 lbs. 2 oz. (20 ga.) to 6.25 lbs. (12 ga.). Checkered pistol-grip walnut stock and forend with high-gloss finish.

Standard Model...................................$365
Hunter or Magnum Models 395

Franchi Model 500 Standard Autoloader $315
Gas-operated. 12 gauge. 4-shot magazine. Bbls.: 26-, 28-inch; vent rib; IC, M, IM, F chokes. Weight: about 7 lbs. Checkered pistol-grip stock and forearm. Made 1976-1980. *See* photo next page.

Franchi Model 520 Deluxe $350
Same as Model 500, except higher grade with engraved receiver. Made 1975-79. *See* photo next page.

Franchi Model 520 Eldorado Gold $695
Same as Model 520, except custom grade with engraved and gold-inlaid receiver, finer quality wood. Intro. 1977. *See* photo next page.

SHOTGUNS

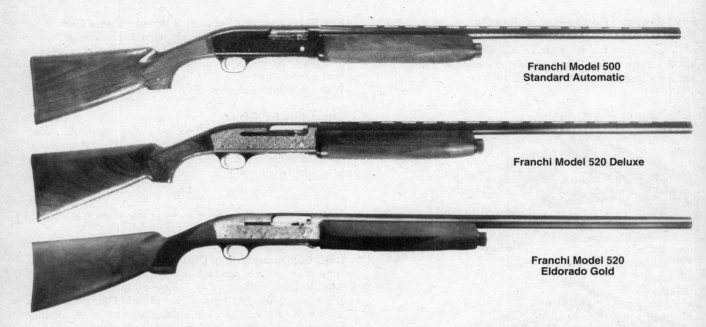

Franchi Model 500
Standard Automatic

Franchi Model 520 Deluxe

Franchi Model 520
Eldorado Gold

Franchi Model 2003 Trap Over/Under $1065
Boxlock. Auto ejectors. Selective single trigger. 12 gauge. Bbls.: 30-, 32-inch IM/F, F/F, high-vent rib. Weight (with 30-inch bbl.): 8.25 lbs. Checkered walnut beavertail forearm and stock with straight or Monte Carlo comb, recoil pad. Luggage-type carrying case. Introduced 1976; discontinued.

Franchi Model 2004 Trap Single Barrel $1095
Same as Model 2003, except single bbl., 32- or 34-inch full choke. Weight (with 32-inch bbl.): 8.25 lbs. Introduced 1976; discontinued.

Franchi Model 2005 Combination Trap $1575
Model 2004/2005 type gun with two sets of bbls., single and over/under. Introduced 1976; discontinued.

Franchi Model 2005/3 Combination Trap $1995
Model 2004/2005 type gun with three sets of bbls., any combination of single and over/under. Introduced 1976; discontinued.

Franchi Model 3000/2 Combination Trap $2475
Boxlock. Automatic ejectors. Selective single trigger. 12 ga. only. Bbls.: 32-inch over/under choked F/IM, 34-inch underbarrel M choke; high vent rib. Weight (with 32-inch bbls.): 8 lbs. 6 oz. Choice of six different castoff buttstocks. Introduced 1979; discontinued.

Franchi Airone Hammerless Double $1100
Boxlock. Anson & Deeley system action. Auto ejectors. Double triggers. 12 ga. Various bbl. lengths, chokes, weights. Checkered straight-grip stock and forearm. Made 1940-1950.

Franchi Alcione Over/Under Shotgun $995
Hammerless, takedown shotgun with engraved receiver. Selective single trigger and ejectors. 12 ga. w/3-inch chambers. Bbls.: 26-inch (IC/M, 28-inch (M/F). Weight: 6.75 lbs. Checkered French walnut buttstock and forend. Imported from Italy since 1982.

Franchi Aristocrat Field Model Over/Under $495
Boxlock. Selective auto ejectors. Selective single trigger. 12 ga. Bbls.: 26-inch IC/M; 28- and 30-inch M/F choke, vent rib. Weight (w/26-inch bbls.): 7 lbs. Checkered pistol-grip stock and forearm. Made 1960-69.

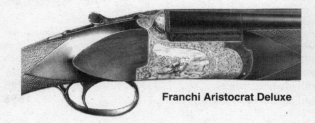

Franchi Aristocrat Deluxe

Franchi 2004 Trap

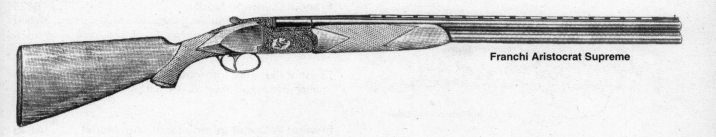

Franchi Aristocrat Supreme

Franchi Aristocrat Deluxe and Supreme Grades
Available in Field, Skeet and Trap Models with the same general specifications as standard guns of these types. Deluxe and Supreme Grades are of higher quality with stock and forearm of select walnut, elaborate relief engraving on receiver, trigger guard, tang and top lever. Supreme game birds inlaid in gold. Made 1960-66.
Deluxe Grade . . . . $ 880
Supreme Grade 1195

Franchi Aristocrat Imperial and Monte Carlo Grades
Custom guns made in Field, Skeet and Trap Models with the same general specifications as standard for these types. Imperial and Monte Carlo Grades are of highest quality with stock and forearm of select walnut, fine engraving — elaborate on the latter grade. Made 1967-69.
Imperial Grade $2195
Monte Carlo Grade 3095

Franchi Aristocrat Magnum Model $475
Same as Field Model, except chambered for 3-inch shells, has 32-inch bbls. choked F/F; stock has recoil pad. Weight: about 8 lbs. Made 1962-65.

Franchi Aristocrat Silver King. $575
Available in Field, Magnum, Meet and Trap models with the same general specifications as standard guns of these types. Silver King has stock and forearm of select walnut more elaborately engraved silver-finished receiver. Made 1962-69.

Franchi Aristocrat Skeet Model $545
Same general specifications as Field Model, except made only with 26-inch vent-rib bbls. with SK chokes #1 and #2, skeet-style stock and forearm. Weight: about 7.5 lbs. Later production had wider (l0mm) rib. Made 1960-69.

Franchi Aristocrat Trap Model $565
Same general specifications as Field Model, except made only with 30-inch vent-rib bbls., M/F choke, trap-style stock with recoil pad, beavertail forearm. Later production had Monte Carlo comb, 10mm rib. Made 1960-69.

Franchi Astore Hammerless Double $795
Boxlock. Anson & Deeley system action. Plain extractors. Double triggers. 12 ga. Various bbl. lengths, chokes, weights. Checkered straight-grip stock and forearm. Made 1937-1960.

Franchi Astore II

Franchi Astore II $995
Similar to Astore S, but not as high grade. Furnished with either plain extractors or auto ejectors, double triggers, pistol-grip stock. Bbls.: 27-inch IC/IM; 28-inch M/F chokes. Currently manufactured for Franchi in Spain.

Franchi Astore S

Franchi Astore S $1895
Same as Astore, except has higher grade wood, fine engraving. Automatic ejectors, single trigger, 28-inch bbl. (M/F or IM/F choke) are standard on current production. Discontinued.

Franchi Crown Grade

SHOTGUNS

Franchi Diamond Grade

Franchi Crown, Diamond and Imperial Grade Autoloaders

Same general specifications as Standard Model, except these are custom guns of the highest quality. Crown Grade has hunting scene engraving, Diamond Grade has silver-inlaid scroll engraving; Imperial Grade has elaborately engraved hunting scenes with figures inlaid in gold. Stock and forearm of fancy walnut. Made 1954-1975.

Crown Grade	**$1395**
Diamond Grade	1795
Imperial Grade	2295

Franchi Dynamic-12

Same general specifications and appearance as Standard Model, except 12 ga. only, has heavier steel receiver. Weight: about 7.25 lbs. Made 1965-1972.

With plain barrel	**$310**
With ventilated rib	340

Franchi Dynamic-12 Slug Gun $340

Same as standard Slug Gun, except 12 ga. only, has heavier steel receiver. Made 1965-1972.

Franchi Dynamic-12 Skeet Gun $395

Same general specifications and appearance as Standard Model, except has heavier steel receiver, made only in 12 ga. with 26-inch vent-rib bbl., SK choke, stock and forearm of extra fancy walnut. Made 1965-1972.

Franchi Eldorado Model $425

Same general specifications as Standard Model except highest grade with gold-filled engraving, stock and forearm of select walnut, furnished with vent-rib bbl. only. Made 1954-1975.

Franchi Falconet International Skeet Model $925

Similar to Standard Skeet Model, but higher grade. Made 1970-1974.

Franchi Falconet International Trap Model $945

Similar to Standard Trap Model, but higher grade; with straight or Monte Carlo comb stock. Made 1970-1974.

Franchi Falconet Over/Under Field Models

Boxlock. Auto ejectors. Selective single trigger. Gauges: 12, 16, 20, 28, .410. Bbls.: 24-, 26-, 28-, 30-inch; vent rib. Chokes: C/IC, IC/M, M/F. Weight: from about 6 lbs. Engraved lightweight alloy receiver, light-colored in Buckskin Model, blued in Ebony Model, pickled silver in Silver Model. Checkered walnut stock and forearm. Made 1968-1975.

Buckskin or Ebony Model	**$495**
Silver Model	560

Franchi Falconet Standard Skeet Model $855

Same general specifications as Field Models, except made only with 26-inch bbls. with SK chokes #1 and #2, wide vent rib, color-casehardened receiver skeet-style stock and forearm. Weight: 12 ga., about 7.75 lbs. Made 1970-74.

Franchi Falconet Standard Trap Model $845

Same general specifications as Field Models, except made only in 12 ga. with 30-inch bbls., choked M/F, wide vent rib, color-casehardened receiver, Monte Carlo trap style stock and forearm, recoil pad. Weight: about 8 lbs. Made 1970-74.

Franchi Hammerless Sidelock Doubles

Hand-detachable locks. Self-opening action. Auto ejectors. Double triggers or single trigger. Gauges: 12,16, 20. Bbl. lengths, chokes, weights according to customer's specifications.

Franchi Eldorado

Franchi Imperial Montecarlo Extra Sidelock Double

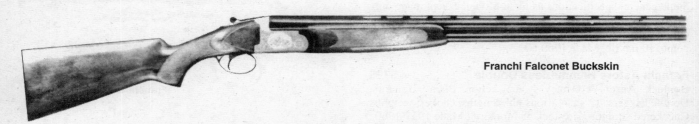

Franchi Falconet Buckskin

**Franchi Hunter Model
w/Ventilated Rib**

Franchi Hammerless Sidelock Doubles *(Cont.)*

Checkered stock and forend, straight or pistol grip. Made in six grades — Condor, Imperiale, Imperiale S, Imperiale Montecarlo No. 5, Imperiale Montecarlo No.11, Imperiale Montecarlo Extra — which differ chiefly in overall quality, engraving, grade of wood, checkering, etc.; general specifications are the same. Only the Imperiale Montecarlo Extra Grade is currently manufactured.

Condor Grade	**$ 6,525**
Imperiale, Imperiale S Grades	**8,795**
Imperiale Montecarlo Grades No. 5, 11	**12,595**
Imperiale Montecarlo Extra Grade	**14,650**

Franchi Hunter Model

Same general specifications as Standard Model except higher grade with engraved receiver; furnished with ribbed bbl. only. Made 1950 to 1990.

With solid rib	**$345**
With ventilated rib	**350**

Franchi Hunter Model Magnum **$395**

Same as Standard Model Magnum, except higher grade with engraved receiver, vent-rib bbl. only. Formerly designated "Wildfowler Model." Made 1954-73.

Franchi Peregrine Model 400 . . . . **$495**

Same general specifications as Model 451, except has steel receiver. Weight (with 26.5-inch bbl.): 6 lbs. 15 oz. Made 1975-78.

Franchi Peregrine Model 451 Over-and-Under . . **$530**

Boxlock. Lightweight alloy receiver. Automatic ejectors. Selective single trigger. 12 ga. Bbls.: 26.5-, 28-inch; choked C/IC, IC/M, M/F; vent rib. Weight (with 26.5-inch bbls.): 6 lbs. 1 oz. Checkered pistol-grip stock and forearm. Made 1975-78.

Franchi PG-80 Gas-Operated Semiautomatic Shotgun

Gas-operated, takedown, hammerless shotgun with tubular magazine. 12 ga. w/2.75-inch chamber. 5-shot magazine. Bbls.: 24 to 30 inches w/vent rib. Weight: 7.5 lbs. Gold-plated trigger.

Franchi PG-80 *(Cont.)*

Checkered pistol-grip stock and forend of European walnut. Imported from Italy 1985-1990.

Prestige Model	**$435**
Elite Model	**495**

Franchi Skeet Gun **$395**

Same general specifications and appearance as Standard Model, except made only with 26-inch vent-rib bbl., SK choke. Stock and forearm of extra fancy walnut. Made 1972-74.

Franchi Slug Gun **$335**

Same as Standard Model, except has 22-inch plain bbl., Cyl. bore, folding leaf open rear sight, gold bead front sight. Made 1960 to date.

Franchi Standard Model Autoloader

Recoil operated. Light alloy receiver. Gauges: 12, 20. 4-shot magazine. Bbls.: 26-, 28-, 30-inch; plain, solid or vent rib, IC/ M, F chokes. Weight: 12 ga., about 6.25 lbs. 20 ga., 5.13 lbs. Checkered pistol-grip stock and forearm. Made 1950 to date.

With plain barrel	**$310**
With solid rib	**335**
With ventilated rib	**360**

Franchi Standard Model Magnum

Same general specifications as Standard Model, except has 3-inch chamber, 32-inch (12 ga.) or 28-inch (20 ga.) F choke bbl., recoil pad. Weight: 12 ga., 8.25 lbs.; 20 ga., 6 lbs. Formerly designated "Superange Model." Made 1954-1988.

With plain barrel	**$355**
With ventilated rib	**375**

Franchi Turkey Gun **$400**

Same as Standard Model Magnum, except higher grade with turkey scene engraved receiver, 12 ga. only, 36-inch matted-rib bbl., Extra Full choke. Made 1963-65.

NOTE: **The Franchi shotguns that follow on the next page are currently imported by American Arms, Inc.**

Franchi Slug Gun

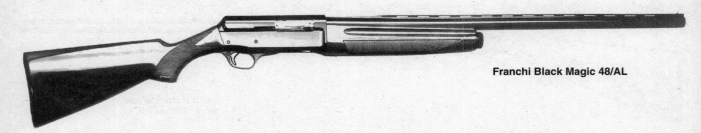

Franchi Black Magic 48/AL

Franchi Black Magic 48/AL Semiautomatic

Similar to the Franchi Model 48/AL, except with Franchoke screw-in tubes and matte black receiver with Black Magic logo. Gauge: 12 or 20, 2.75-inch chamber. Bbls.: 24-, 26-, 28-inch with vent rib; 24-inch rifled slug with sights. Weight: 5.2 lbs. (20 ga.). Checkered walnut buttstock and forend. Blued finish.

Standard Model **$425**
Slug Barrel Model **455**

Franchi Falconet 2000 Over/Under **$975**

Boxlock. Single selective trigger. Selective automatic ejectors. Gauge: 12, 2.75-inch chambers. Bbls.: 26-inch w/Franchoke tubes; IC/M/F. Weight: 6 lbs. Checkered walnut stock and forearm. Engraved silver receiver w/gold-plated game scene. Imported from 1992 to 1993.

Franchi LAW-12 Shotgun **$495**

Similar to the SPAS-12 Model, except gas-operated semiautomatic action only, ambidextrous safety, decocking lever and adjustable sights. Made 1983-1994.

Franchi SPAS-12 Shotgun

Selective operating system functions as a gas-operated semiautomatic or pump action. Gauge: 12, 2.75-inch chamber. 7-shot magazine. Bbl.: 21.5 inches with cylinder bore and muzzle protector or optional screw-in choke tubes, matte finish. 41 inches overall with fixed stock. Weight: 8.75 lbs. Blade front sight, aperture rear sight. Folding or black nylon buttstock with pistol grip and forend, non-reflective anodized finish. Made 1983-1994.

Fixed Stock Model **$895**
Folding Stock Model **825**
Optional Choke Tubes, **add** **100**

Franchi Sporting 2000 Over/Under **$925**

Similar to the Franchi Falconet 2000. Boxlock. Single selective trigger. Selective automatic ejectors. Gauge: 12; 2.75-inch chambers. Ported 28-inch bbls., w/vent rib. Weight: 7.75 lbs. Blued receiver. Bead front sight. Checkered walnut stock and forearm; plastic composition buttplate. Imported from 1992 to 1993.

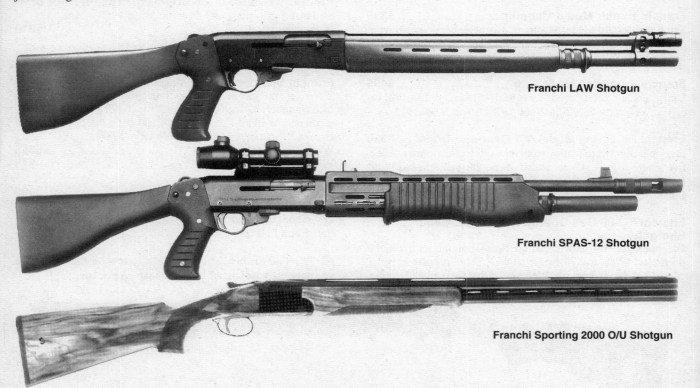

Franchi LAW Shotgun

Franchi SPAS-12 Shotgun

Franchi Sporting 2000 O/U Shotgun

AUGUSTE FRANCOTTE & CIE., S.A.
Liège, Belgium

Francotte shotguns for many years were distributed in the U.S. by Abercrombie & Fitch of New York City. This firm has used a series of model designations for Francotte guns which do not correspond to those of the manufacturer. Because so many Francotte owners refer to their guns by the A & F model names and numbers, the A & F series is included in a listing separate from that of the standard Francotte numbers.

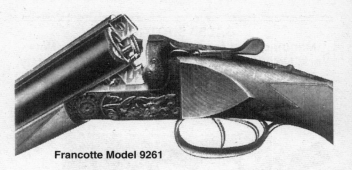

Francotte Model 9261

Francotte Model 6886

Francotte Model 8446

Francotte Boxlock Hammerless Doubles

Anson & Deeley system. Side clips. Greener crossbolt on Models 6886, 8446, 4996 and 9261; square crossbolt on Model 6930, Greener-Scott crossbolt on Model 8457, Purdey bolt on Models 11/18E and 10/18E/628. Auto ejectors. Double triggers. Made in all standard gauges, barrel lengths, chokes, weights. Checkered stock and forend straight or pistol grip. The eight models listed vary chiefly in fastening as described above, finish and engraving, etc.; general specifications are the same. All except Model 10/18E/628 are discontinued.

Model 6886	$2690
Model 8446 ("Francotte Special"), 6930, 4996	2995
Model 8457, 9261 ("Francotte Original"), 11/18E	3850
Model 10/18E/628	4895

Francotte Model 10/18E/62B

Francotte Boxlock Hammerless Doubles — A & F Series

Boxlock, Anson & Deeley type. Crossbolt. Sideplate on all except Knockabout Model. Side clips. Auto ejectors. Double triggers. Gauges: 12, 16, 20, 28, .410. Bbls.: 26- to 32-inch in 12 ga., 26- and 28-inch in other ga.; any boring. Weight: 4.75 to 8 lbs. depending on ga. and bbl. length. Checkered stock and forend; straight, half or full pistol grip. The seven grades — No. 45 Eagle Grade, No. 30, No. 25, No. 20, No. 14, Jubilee Model, Knockabout Model — differ chiefly in overall quality, engraving, grade of wood, checkering, etc.; general specifications are the same. Discontinued.

No. 14	$1695
No. 20	2595
No. 25	2995
No. 30	4750
No. 45 Eagle Grade	5795
Jubilee Model	4100
Knockabout Model	1655

Francotte Boxlock Hammerless Doubles (Sideplates)

Anson & Deeley system. Reinforced frame with side clips. Purdey-type bolt except on Model 8455 which has Greener crossbolt. Auto ejectors. Double triggers. Made in all standard gauges, bbl. lengths, chokes, weights. Checkered stock and forend, straight or pistol grip. Models 10594, 8455 and 6982 are of equal quality, differing chiefly in style of engraving; Model 9/40E/38321 is a higher grade gun in all details and has fine English-style engraving. Currently manufactured.

Models 10594, 8455, 6982	$3895
Model 9/40E/38321	4750

Francotte Fine Over/Under Shotgun $9000

Model 9/40.SE. Boxlock, Anson & Deeley system. Auto ejectors. Double triggers. Made in all standard gauges; bbl. length, boring to order. Weight: about 6.75 lbs. 12 ga. Checkered stock and forend, straight or pistol grip. Currently manufactured.

Francotte Fine Sidelock Hammerless Double . . $19,250

Model 120.HE/328. Automatic ejectors. Double triggers. Made in all standard ga.; bbl. length, boring, weight to order. Checkered stock and forend, straight or pistol grip. Currently manufactured.

Francotte Half-Fine Over/Under Shotgun $7925

Model SOB.E/11082. Boxlock, Anson & Deeley system. Auto ejectors. Double triggers. Made in all standard gauges; barrel length, boring to order. Checkered stock and forend, straight or pistol grip. *Note:* This model is similar to No. 9/40.SE, except gen. quality lower. Discontinued.

SHOTGUNS

GALEF SHOTGUNS
Manufactured for J. L. Galef & Son, Inc., New York, New York, by M. A. V. I., Gardone F. T., Italy, by Zabala Hermanos, Eiquetta, Spain, and by Antonio Zoli, Gardone V. T., Italy

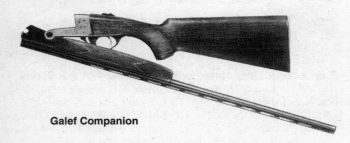

Galef Companion

Galef Companion Folding Single-Barrel Shotgun
Hammerless. Underlever. Gauges: 12 Mag., 16, 20 Mag., 28, .410. Bbls.: 26-inch (.410 only), 28-inch (12, 16, 20, 28), 30-inch (12-ga. Only); F choke; plain or vent rib. Weight: 4.5 lbs. for .410 to 5 lbs. 9 oz. for 12 ga. Checkered pistol-grip stock and forearm. Made by M. A. V. I. from 1968 to date.
With plain bbl. . . . . $ 95
With ventilated rib 125

Galef Golden Snipe $445
Same as Silver Snipe, except has selective automatic ejectors. Made by Antonio Zoli 1968 to date.

Galef Monte Carlo Trap Single-Barrel Shotgun . . $195
Hammerless. Underlever. Plain extractor. 12 ga. 32-inch bbl., F choke, vent rib. Weight: about 8.25 lbs. Checkered pistol-grip stock with Monte Carlo comb and recoil pad, beavertail forearm. Introduced by M. A. V. I. in 1968; discontinued.

Galef Silver Hawk Hammerless Double $395
Boxlock. Plain extractors. Double triggers. Gauges: 12, 20; 3-inch chambers. Bbls.: 26-, 28-, 30-inch (latter in 12 ga. only);

Galef Silver Hawk Hammerless Double *(Cont.)*
IC/M, M/F chokes. Weight: 12 ga. with 26-inch bbls., 6 lbs. 6 oz. Checkered walnut pistol-grip stock and beavertail forearm. Made by Antonio Zoli 1968-1972.

Galef Silver Snipe Over/Under Shotgun $415
Boxlock. Plain extractors. Single trigger. Gauges: 12, 20; 3-inch chambers. Bbls: 26-, 28-, 30-inch (latter in 12 ga. only); IC/M, M/F chokes; vent rib. Weight: 12 ga. with 28-inch bbls., 6.5 lbs. Checkered walnut pistol-grip stock and forearm. Introduced by Antonio Zoli in 1968; disc.

Galef Zabala Hammerless Double-Barrel Shotgun
Boxlock. Plain extractors. Double triggers. Gauges: 10 Mag., 12 Mag., 16, 20 Mag., 28, .410. Bbls.: 22-, 26-, 28-, 30-, 32-inch; IC/IC, IC/M, M/F chokes. Weight: 12 ga. with 28-inch bbls., 7.75 lbs. Checkered walnut pistol-grip stock and beavertail forearm, recoil pad. Made by Zabala from 1972 to date.
10 gauge $235
Other gauges 175

GAMBA S. p. A.
Gardone V. T. (Brescia), Italy

Gamba Daytona Competition Over/Under
Boxlock with Boss-style locking system. Anatomical single trigger; optional adj., single-selective release trigger. Selective automatic ejectors. Gauge: 12 or 20; 2.75- or 3-inch chambers. Bbls.: 26.75-, 28-, 30- or 32-inch choked SK/SK, IM/F or M/F. Weight: 7.5 to 8.5 lbs. Black or chrome receiver with blued bbls. Checkered select walnut stock and forearm with oil finish. Imported by Heckler & Koch until 1992.
American Trap Model $4,045
Pigeon, Skeet, Trap Models. 4,745
Sporting Model 3,995
Sideplate Model 9,625
Engraved Models . . . . 7500 to 10,000
Sidelock Model 19,750

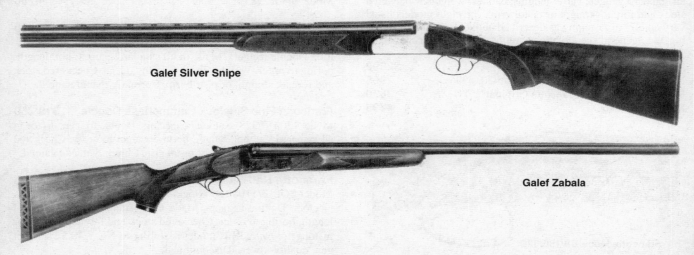

Galef Silver Snipe

Galef Zabala

Garbi Model 200

GARBI SHOTGUNS
Eibar, Spain

Garbi Model 100 Sidelock Shotgun **$2855**
Gauges: 12, 16, 20 and 28. Bbls.: 25-, 28-, 30-inch. Action: Holland & Holland pattern sidelock; automatic ejectors and double trigger. Weight: 5 lbs. 6 oz. to 7 lbs. 7 oz. English-style straight grip stock with fine-line hand-checkered butt; classic forend. Made 1985 to date.

Garbi Model 101 Sidelock Shotgun **$3375**
Same general specifications as Model 100, except the sidelocks are handcrafted with hand-engraved receiver; select walnut straight-grip stock.

Garbi Model 102 Sidelock Shotgun **$3895**
Similar to the Model 101, except with large scroll engraving. Made 1985-1993.

Garbi Model 103 Hammerless Double
Similar to Model 100, except with Purdey-type, higher grade engraving.
Model 103A **$3895**
Model 103B 5950

Garbi Model 200 Hammerless Double **$5895**
Similar to Model 100, except with double heavy-duty locks. Continental-style floral and scroll engraving. Checkered deluxe walnut stock and forearm.

GARCIA CORPORATION
Teaneck, New Jersey

Garcia Bronco 22/.410 O/U Combination **$95**
Swing-out action. Takedown. 18.5-inch bbls.; 22 LR over, .410 ga. under. Weight: 4.5 lbs. One-piece stock and receiver, crackle finish. Intro. 1976; discontinued.

Garcia Bronco .410 Single Shot **$75**
Swing-out action. Takedown. .410 ga. 18.5-inch bbl. Weight: 3.5 lbs. One-piece stock and receiver, crackle finish. Intro. In 1967; discontinued.

GOLDEN EAGLE FIREARMS INC.
Houston, Texas
Mfd. By Nikko Firearms Ltd., Tochigi, Japan

Golden Eagle Model 5000 Grade I Field O/U **$775**
Receiver engraved and inlaid with gold eagle head. Boxlock. Auto ejectors. Selective single trigger. Gauges: 12, 20; 2.75- or 3-inch chambers, 12 ga., 3-inch, 20 ga. Bbls.: 26-, 28-, 30-inch (latter only in 12-ga. 3-inch Mag.); IC/M, M/F chokes; vent rib. Weight: 6.25 lbs., 20 ga.; 7.25 lbs., 12 ga.; 8 lbs., 12-ga. Mag. Checkered pistol-grip stock and semibeavertail forearm. Imported 1975-1982. *Note:* Guns marketed 1975-76 under the Nikko brand name have white receivers; since 1976 are blued.

SHOTGUNS

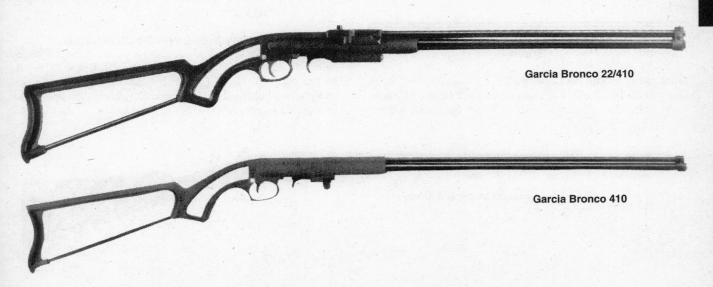

Garcia Bronco 22/410

Garcia Bronco 410

**Golden Eagle Model 5000
Grade II Field**

Golden Eagle Model 5000 Grade I Skeet **$795**
Same as Field Model, except has 26- or 28-inch bbls. with wide (11 mm) vent rib, SK choked. Imported 1975-1982.

Golden Eagle Model 5000 Grade I Trap **$815**
Same as Field Model, except has 30-, or 32-inch bbls. with wide (11 mm) vent rib (M/F, IM/F, F/F chokes), trap-style stock with recoil pad. Imported 1975-1982.

Golden Eagle Model 5000 Grade II Field **$825**
Same as Grade I Field Model, except higher grade with fancier wood, more elaborate engraving and "screaming eagle" inlaid in gold. Imported 1975-1982.

Golden Eagle Model 5000 Grade II Skeet **$865**
Same as Grade I Skeet Model, except higher grade with fancier wood, more elaborate engraving and "screaming eagle" inlaid in gold; inertia trigger, vent side ribs. Imported 1975-1982.

Golden Eagle Model 5000 Grade II Trap **$875**
Same as Grade I Trap Model, except higher grade with fancier wood, more elaborate engraving and "screaming eagle" inlaid in gold; inertia trigger, vent side ribs. Imported 1975-1982.

Golden Eagle Model 5000 Grade III Grandee . . . **$1995**
Best grade, available in Field, Skeet and Trap Models with same general specifications as lower grades. Has sideplates with game scene engraving, scroll on frame and bbls., fancy wood (Monte Carlo comb, full pistol grip and recoil pad on Trap Model). Made 1976 to 1982.

GOROSABEL SHOTGUNS
Spain

Gorosabel Model 503 Shotgun **$695**
Gauges: 12, 16, 20 and .410. Action: Anson & Deely-style box-lock. Bbls.: 26-, 27-, and 28-inch. Select European walnut,

Gorosabel Model 503 Shotgun *(Cont.)*

English or pistol grip, sliver or beavertail forend, hand-checkering. Scalloped frame and scroll engraving. Intro. 1985; discontinued.

Gorosabel Model 504 Shotgun **$750**
Gauge: 12 or 20. Action: Holland & Holland-style sidelock. Bbl.: 26-, 27-, or 28-inch. Select European walnut, English or pistol grip, sliver or beavertail forend, hand-checkering. Holland-style large scroll engraving. Inro. 1985; discontinued.

Gorosabel Model 505 Shotgun **$995**
Gauge: 12 or 20. Action: Holland & Holland-style sidelock. Bbls.: 26-, 27-, or 28-inch. Select European walnut, English or pistol grip, sliver or beavertail forend, hand-checkering. Purdey-style fine scroll and rose engraving. Intro. 1985; discontinued.

STEPHEN GRANT
London, England

**Grant Best Quality Self-Opener Double-Barrel
Shotgun** **$10,225**
Sidelock, self-opener. Gauges: 12, 16 and 20. Bbls.: 25 to 30 inches standard. Highest grade English or European walnut straight-grip buttstock and forearm with Greener type lever. Imported by Stoeger in the 1950s.

**Grant Best Quality Side-Lever Double-Barrel
Shotgun** **$9995**
Sidelock, self-lever. Gauges: 12, 16 and 20. Bbls.: 25 to 30 inches standard. Highest grade English or European walnut straight-grip buttstock and forearm with Greener type lever. Imported by Stoeger in the 1950s.

Gorosabel Model 503 Shotgun

W. W. GREENER, LTD.
Birmingham, England

Greener Empire

Greener Jubilee

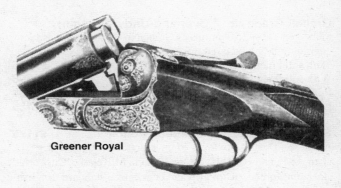

Greener Royal

Greener Empire Model Hammerless Doubles

Boxlock. Non-ejector or with automatic ejectors. Double triggers. 12 ga. only (2.75-inch or 3-inch chamber). Bbls.: 28- to 32-inch; any choke combination. Weight: from 7.25 to 7.75 lbs. depending on bbl. length. Checkered stock and forend, straight- or half-pistol grip. Also furnished in "Empire Deluxe Grade," this model has same general specs, but deluxe finish.

Empire Model, non-ejector	**$1550**
Empire Model, ejector	**1775**
Empire Deluxe Model, non-ejector	**1795**
Empire Deluxe Model, ejector	**1995**

Greener Far-Killer

Greener Far-Killer Model Grade FH35 Hammerless Double-Barrel Shotgun

Boxlock. Non-ejector or with automatic ejectors. Double triggers. Gauges: 12 (2.75-inch or 3-inch), 10, 8. Bbls.: 28-, 30- or 32-inch. Weight: 7.5 to 9 lbs. in 12 ga. Checkered stock, forend; straight or half-pistol grip.

Non-ejector, 12 ga.	**$2295**
Ejector, 12 ga.	**3150**
Non-ejector, 10 or 8 ga.	**2495**
Ejector, 10 or 8 ga.	**3295**

Greener G. P. (General Purpose) Single Barrel . . **$450**

Greener Improved Martini Lever Action. Takedown. Ejector. 12 ga. only. Bbl. lengths: 26-, 30-, 32-inch. M or F choke. Weight: 6.25 to 6.75 lbs. depending on bbl. length. Checkered straight-grip stock and forearm.

Greener Hammerless Ejector Double-Barrel Shotguns

Boxlock. Auto ejectors. Double triggers, non-selective or selective single trigger. Gauges: 12, 16, 20, 28, .410 (two latter gauges not supplied in Grades DH40 and DH35). Bbls.: 26-, 28-, 30-inch; any choke combination. Weight: from 4.75 to 8 lbs. Depending on ga. and bbl. length. Checkered stock and forend, straight- or half-pistol grip. The Royal, Crown, Sovereign and Jubilee Models differ in quality, engraving, grade of wood, checkering, etc. General specifications are the same.

Royal Model Grade DH75	**$3995**
Crown Model Grade DH55.	**2950**
Sovereign Model Grade DH40	**2595**
Jubilee Model Grade DH35	**2150**
Selective single trigger, extra	**330**
Non-selective single trigger, extra	**250**

GREIFELT & COMPANY
Suhl, Germany

Greifelt Grade No. 1 Over-and-Under Shotgun

Anson & Deeley boxlock, Kersten fastening. Auto ejectors. Double triggers or single trigger. Elaborately engraved. Gauges: 12, 16, 20, 28, .410. Bbls.: 26- to 32-inch, any combination of chokes, vent or solid matted rib. Weight: 4.25 to 8.25 lbs. depending on ga. and bbl. length. Straight- or pistol-grip stock, Purdey-type forend, both checkered. Manufactured prior to World War II.

With solid matted-rib bbl., except .410	**$2995**
With solid matted-rib bbl., .410 ga.	**3500**
Extra for ventilated rib	**380**
Extra for single trigger	**425**

SHOTGUNS

Greifelt Grade No. 1 O/U

Greifelt Grade No. 3 Over-and-Under Shotgun

Same general specifications as Grade No. 1 except not as fancy engraving. Manufactured prior to World War II.

With solid matted-rib bbl., except .410 . . . . $2595
With solid matted-rib bbl., .410 ga. 2695
Extra for ventilated rib 380
Extra for single trigger 425

Greifelt Model 22 Hammerless Double. $1175
Anson & Deeley boxlock. Plain extractors. Double triggers. Gauges: 12 and 16. Bbls.: 28- or 30-inch, M/F choke. Checkered stock and forend, pistol grip and cheekpiece standard, English-style stock also supplied. Manufactured since World War II.

Greifelt Model 22E Hammerless Double $2195
Same as Model 22, except has automatic ejectors.

Greifelt Model 103 Hammlerless Double $1695
Anson & Deeley boxlock. Plain extractors. Double triggers. Gauges: 12 and 16. Bbls.: 28- or 30-inch, M and F choke. Checkered stock and forend, pistol grip and cheekpiece standard, English-style stock also supplied. Manufactured since World War II.

Greifelt Model 103E Hammerless Double $1795
Same as Model 103, except has automatic ejectors.

Greifelt Model 143E Over-and-Under Shotgun

General specifications same as prewar Grade No. 1 Over-and-Under except this model is not supplied in 28 and .410 ga. or with 32-inch bbls. Model 143E is not as high quality as the Grade No. 1 gun. Mfd. Since World War II.

With raised matted rib, double triggers $1950
With ventilated rib, selective single trigger 2795

Greifelt Hammerless Drilling (Three Barrel
Combination Gun) $2950
Boxlock. Plain extractors. Double triggers, front single set for rifle bbl. Gauges: 12, 16, 20; rifle bbl. in any caliber adapted to this type of gun. 26-inch bbls. Weight: about 7.5 lbs. Auto rear sight operated by rifle bbl. selector. Checkered stock and forearm, pistol grip and cheekpiece standard. Manufactured prior to WW II. *Note:* Value shown is for guns chambered for cartridges readily obtainable; if rifle bbl. is an odd foreign caliber, value will be considerably less.

Greifelt Over-and-Under Combination Gun

Similar in design to this maker's over-and-under shotguns. Gauges: 12, 16, 20, 28, .410; rifle bbl. in any caliber adapted to this type of gun. Bbls.: 24- or 26-inch, solid matted rib. Weight: from 4.75 to 7.25 lbs. Folding rear sight. Manufactured prior to WWII. *Note:* Values shown are for gauges other than .410 with rifle bbl. Chambered for a cartridge readily obtainable; if in an odd foreign caliber, value will be considerably less. .410 ga. increases in value by about 50%.

With nonautomatic ejector $4850
With automatic ejector 5250

HARRINGTON & RICHARDSON ARMS COMPANY
Gardner, Massachusetts
Now H&R 1871, Inc.

In 1986, all H&R operations were discontinued. In 1992, the firm was purchased by New England Firearms of Gardner, Mass., and the H&R line was divided. Models are now manufactured under that banner as well as H&R 1871, Inc.

H&R No. 3 Hammerless

Harrington & Richardson No. 3 Hammerless
Single-Shot Shotgun $90
Takedown. Automatic ejector. Gauges: 12, 16, 20, .410. Bbls.: plain, 26- to 32-inch, F choke. Weight: 6.5 to 7.25 lbs. depending on ga. and bbl. length. Plain pistol-grip stock and forend. Disc. 1942.

H&R No. 5 Standard Lightweight

Harrington & Richardson No. 5 Standard
Lightweight Hammer Single $100
Takedown. Auto ejector. Gauges: 24, 28, .410, 14mm. Bbls.: 26- or 28-inch, F choke. Weight: about 4 to 4.75 lbs. Plain pistol-grip stock/forend. Disc. 1942.

H&R No. 6 Heavy Breech

Harrington & Richardson No. 6 Heavy Breech Single-Shot Hammer Shotgun $100
Takedown. Automatic ejector. Gauges: 10, 12, 16, 20. Bbls.: plain, 28- to 36-inch, F choke. Weight: about 7 to 7.25 lbs. Plain stock and forend. Disc. 1942.

H&R No. 7 Bay Series

Harrington & Richardson No. 7 or 9 Bay State Single-Shot Hammer Shotgun $110
Takedown. Automatic ejector. Gauges: 12, 16, 20, .410. Bbls.: plain 26- to 32-inch, F choke. Weight: 5.5 to 6.5 lbs. depending on ga. and bbl. length. Plain pistol-grip stock and forend. Discontinued 1942.

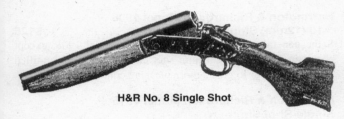

H&R No. 8 Single Shot

Harrington & Richardson No. 8 Standard Single-Shot Hammer Shotgun $135
Takedown. Automatic ejector. Gauges: 12, 16, 20, 24, 28, .410. Bbl.: plain, 26- to 32-inch, F choke. Weight: 5.5 to 6.5 lbs. depending on ga. and bbl. length. Plain pistol-grip stock and forend. Made 1908-1942.

Harrington & Richardson Model 348 Gamester Bolt-Action Shotgun. $95
Takedown. 12 and 16 ga. 2-shot tubular magazine, 28-inch bbl, F choke. Plain pistol-grip stock. Weight: about 7.5 lbs. Made 1949-1954.

Harrington & Richardson Model 349 Gamester Deluxe $110
Same as Model 348, except has 26-inch bbl. With adj. choke device, recoil pad. Made 1953-55.

Harrington & Richardson model 351 Huntsman Bolt-Action Shotgun $125
Takedown. 12 and 16 ga. 2-shot tubular magazine. Pushbutton safety. 26-inch bbl. with H&R variable choke. Weight: about 6.75 lbs. Monte Carlo stock with recoil pad. Made 1956-58.

Harrington & Richardson Model 400 Pump $175
Hammerless. Gauges: 12, 16, 20. Tubular magazine holds 4 shells. 28-inch bbl., F choke. Weight: about 7.25 lbs. Plain pistol-grip stock (recoil pad in 12 and 16 ga.), grooved slide handle. Made 1955-1967.

Harington & Richardson Model 401 . . . . $175
Same as Model 400, except has H&R variable choke. Made 1956-1963.

Harrington & Richardson Model 402 . . . . $185
Similar to Model 400, except .410 ga., weighs about 5.5 lbs. Made 1959-1967.

Harrington & Richardson Model 403 Autoloading Shotgun. $200
Takedown. .410 ga. Tubular magazine holds four shells. 26-inch bbl., F choke. Weight: about 5.75 lbs. Plain pistol-grip stock and forearm. Made in 1964.

Harrington & Richardson Model 404/404C. $225
Boxlock. Plain extractors. Double triggers. Gauges: 12, 20, .410. Bbls.: 28-inch in 12 ga. (M/F choke), 26-inch in 20 ga. (IC/M and .410 (F/F). Weight: 5.5 to 7.25 lbs. Plain walnut-finished hardwood stock and forend on Model 404; 404C checkered. Made in Brazil by Amadeo Rossi 1969-1972. *See* photo next page.

Harrington & Richardson Model 440 Pump $145
Hammerless. Gauges: 12, 16, 20. 2.75-inch chamber in 16 ga., 3-inch in 12 and 20 ga. 3-shot magazine. Bbls.: 26-, 28-, 30-inch; IC, M, F choke. Weight: 6.25 lbs. Plain pistol-grip stock and slide handle, recoil pad. Made 1968-1973. *See* photo next page.

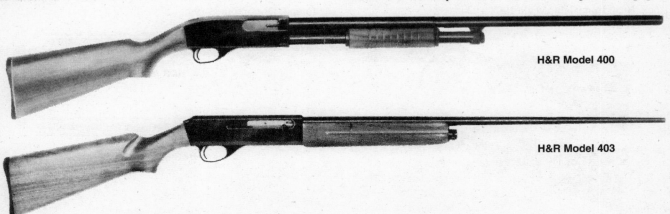

H&R Model 400

H&R Model 403

SHOTGUNS

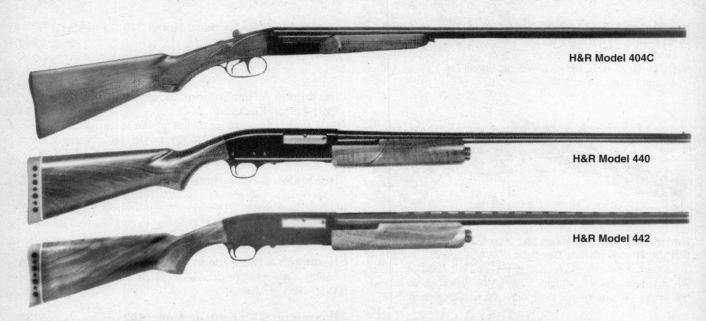

H&R Model 404C

H&R Model 440

H&R Model 442

Harrington & Richardson Model 442 . . . . $185
Same as Model 440, except has vent-rib bbl., checkered stock
and forearm, weighs 6.75 lbs. Made 1969-1973.

Harrington & Richardson Model 1212 Field. $295
Boxlock. Plain extractors. Selective single trigger. 12 ga., 2.75-
inch chambers. 28-inch bbls., IC/IM, vent rib. Weight: 7 lbs.
Checkered walnut pistol-gip stock and fluted forearm. Made
1976-1980 by Lanber Arms S. A., Zaldibar (Vizcaya), Spain.

**Harrington & Richardson Model 1212
Waterfowl Gun** $350
Same as Field Gun, except chambered for 12-ga, 3-inch Mag.
Shells, has 30-inch bbls., M/F chokes, stock and recoil pad,
weighs, 7.5 lbs. Made 1976-1980.

**Harrington & Richardson Model 1908
Single-Shot Shotgun** $115
Takedown. Automatic ejector. Gauges: 12, 16, 24 and 28. Bbls.:
26- to 32-inch, F choke. Weight: 5.25 to 6.5 lbs., depending on
ga. and bbl. length. Casehardened receiver. Plain pistol-grip
stock. Bead front sight. Made 1908-1934.

**Harrington & Richardson Model 1908
.410 (12mm) Single-Shot Shotgun** $125
Same general specifications as standard Model 1908, except
chambered for .410 or 12mm shot cartridge with bbl. milled
down at receiver to give a more pleasing contour.

**Harrington & Richardson Model 1915
Single-Shot Shotgun**
Takedown. Both nonauto and auto ejectors available. Gauges:
24, 28, .410, 14mm and 12mm. Bbls.: 26- or 28-inch, F choke.
Weight: 4 to 4.75 lbs., depending on ga. and bbl. length. Plain
black walnut stock with semipistol grip.
24 ga. $165
28 , .410 ga. 135

Harrington & Richardson Folding Gun $135
Single barrel hammer shotgun hinged at the front of the frame,
the bbl. folds down against the stock. *Light Frame Model*:
gauges — 28, 14mm, .410; 22-inch bbl.; weighs about 4.5 lbs.
Heavy Frame Model: gauges — 12, 16, 20, 28, .410; 26-inch
bbl.; weighs from 5.75 to 6.5 lbs. Plain pistol-grip stock and
forend. Discontinued 1942.

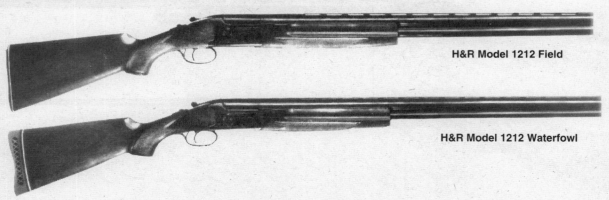

H&R Model 1212 Field

H&R Model 1212 Waterfowl

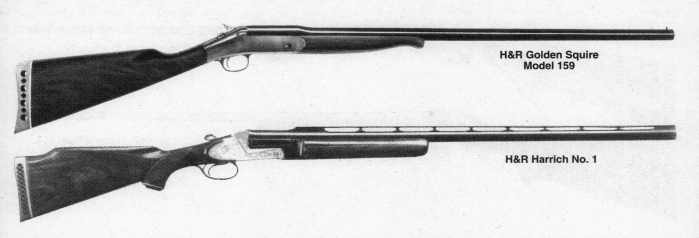

H&R Golden Squire
Model 159

H&R Harrich No. 1

**Harrington & Richardson Golden Squire Model 159
Single-Barrel Hammer Shotgun** $100
Hammerless. Side lever. Automatic ejection. Gauges: 12, 20.
Bbls: 30-inch in 12 ga., 28-inch in 20 ga., both F choke. Weight:
about 6.5 lbs. Straight-grip stock with recoil pad, forearm with
schnabel. Made 1964-66.

**Harrington & Richardson Golden Squire Jr.
Model 459** $115
Same as Model 159, except gauges 20 and .410, 26-inch bbl.,
youth-size stock. Made in 1964.

**Harrington & Richardson Harrich No. 1
Single-Barrel Trap Gun** $1750
Anson & Deeley-type locking system with Kersten top locks and
double underlocking lugs. Sideplates engraved with hunting
scenes. 12 ga. Bbls.: 32-, 34-inch; F choke; high vent rib.
Weight: 8.5 lbs. Checkered monte Carlo stock with pistol grip
and recoil pad, beavertail forearm, of select walnut. Made in Fer-
lach, Austria, 1971-75.

**Harrington & Richardson "Top Rib"
Single-Barrel Shotgun** $165
Takedown. Auto ejector. Gauges: 12, 16 and 20. Bbls.: 28- to 30-
inch, F choke with full-length matted top rib. Weight: 6.5 to 7 lbs.
depending on ga. and barrel length. Black walnut pistol-grip
stock (capped) and forend; both checkered. Flexible rubber buttplate. Made during 1930s.

**Harrington & Richardson Topper No. 48
Single-Barrel Hammer Shotgun** $125
Similar to old Model 8 Standard. Takedown. Top lever. Auto
ejector. Gauges: 12, 16, 20, .410. Bbls.: plain; 26- to 30-inch; M
or F choke. Weight: 5.5 to 6.5 lbs. depending on ga. and bbl.
length. Plain pistol-grip stock and forend. Made 1946-1957.

**Harrington & Richardson Topper Model 099
Deluxe** $110
Same as Model 158, except has matte nickel finish, semipistol
grip walnut-finished American hardwood stock; semibeavertail
forearm; 12, 16, 20, and .410 ga. Made 1982-86.

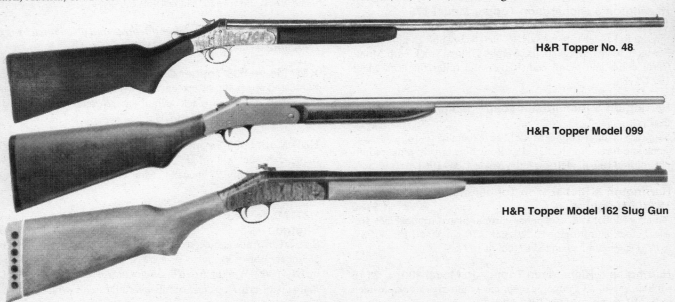

H&R Topper No. 48

H&R Topper Model 099

H&R Topper Model 162 Slug Gun

SHOTGUNS

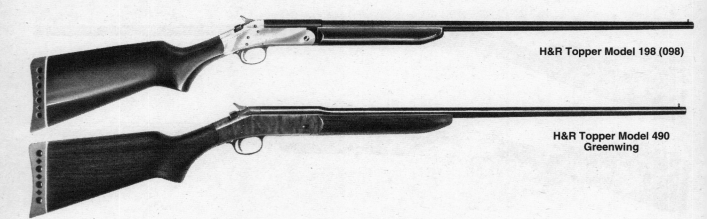

H&R Topper Model 198 (098)

H&R Topper Model 490 Greenwing

Harrington & Richardson Topper Model 148 Single-Shot Hammer Shotgun **$110**
Takedown. Side lever. Auto ejection. Gauges: 12, 16, 20, .410. Bbls.: 12 ga., 30-, 32- and 36-inch; 16 ga., 28- and 30-inch; 20 and .410 ga., 28-inch; F choke. Weight: 5 to 6.5 lbs. Plain pistol-grip stock and forend, recoil pad. Made 1958-61.

Harrington & Richardson Topper Model 158 (058) Single-Shot Hammer Shotgun **$115**
Takedown. Side lever. Automatic ejection. Gauges: 12, 20, .410 (2.75-inch and 3-inch shells); 16 (2.75-inch). Barrel length and choke combinations: 12 ga., 36-inch/F, 32-inch/F, 30-inch/F, 28-inch/F or M; .410, 28-inch/F. Weight: about 5.5 lbs. Plain pistol-grip stock and forend, recoil pad. Made 1962-1981. *Note:* Designation changed to 058 in 1974.

Harrington & Richardson Topper Model 162 Slug Gun **$135**
Same as Topper Model 158, except has 24-inch bbl., Cyl. bore, with rifle sights. Made 1968-1986. *See* photo preceding page.

Harrington & Richardson Topper Model 176 10 Gauge Magnum **$145**
Similar to Model 158, but has 36-inch heavy bbl. chambered for 3.5-inch 10- ga. Mag. shells, weighs 10 lbs.; stock with Monte Carlo comb and recoil pad, longer and fuller forearm. Made 1977-1986.

Harrington & Richardson Topper Model 188 Deluxe **$125**
Same as standard Topper Model 148, except has chromed frame, stock and forend in black, red, yellow, blue, green, pink, or purple colored finish. .410 ga. only. Made 1958-1961.

Harrington & Richardson Topper Model 198 (098) Deluxe **$130**
Same as Model 158, except has chrome-plated frame, black finished stock and forend; 12, 20 and .410 ga. Made 1962-1981. *Note:* Designation changed to 098 in 1974.

Harrington & Richardson Topper Jr. Model 480 . . . **$115**
Similar to No. 48 Topper, except has youth-size stock, 26-inch bbl, .410 ga. only. Made 1958-1961.

Harrington & Richardson Topper No. 488 Deluxe . . **$110**
Same as standard No. 48 Topper, except chrome-plated frame, black lacquered stock and forend, recoil pad. Discontinued 1957.

Harrington & Richardson Topper Model 490 . . . . **$115**
Same as Model 158, except has youth-size stock (3 inches shorter), 26-inch bbl.; 20 and 28 gauge (M choke), .410 (F). Made 1962-1986.

Harrington & Richardson Topper Model 490 Greenwing **$130**
Same as the Model 490, except has a special high-polished finish. Made 1981-86.

Harrington & Richardson Topper Jr. Model 580 . . . **$100**
Same as Model 480, except has colored stocks as on Model 188. Made 1958-1961.

Harrington 7 Richardson Topper Model 590 . . . . **$105**
Same as Model 490, except has chrome-plated frame, black finished stock and forend. Made 1962-63.

The following models are manufactured and distributed by the reorganized company of H&R 1871, Inc.

H&R Model 098 Topper Classic Youth **$95**
Same as Topper Junior, except also available in 28 ga. and has checkered American black walnut stock/forend w/satin finish and recoil pad. Made 1991 to date.

H&R Model 098 Topper Deluxe **$95**
Same as Model 098 Single Shot Hammer, except in 12 ga., 3-inch chamber only. 28-inch bbl.; Mod. choke tube. Made 1992 to date.

H&R Model 098 Topper Hammer Single-Shot Shotgun **$80**
Side lever. Automatic ejector. Gauges: 12, 20 and .410; 3-inch chamber. Bbls.: 28-inch, (12 ga./M); 26-inch, (20 ga./M); 26-inch (.410/F). Weight: 5 to 6 lbs. Satin nickel receiver, blued bbl. Plain pistol-grip stock and semibeavertail forend w/black finish. Reintroduced 1992.

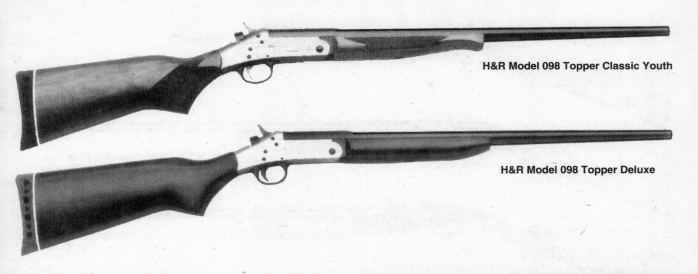

H&R Model 098 Topper Classic Youth

H&R Model 098 Topper Deluxe

H&R Model 098 Topper Junior **$85**
Same as Model 098, except has youth-size stock and 22-inch bbl.
20 or .410 ga. only. Made 1991 to date.

H&R Model .410 Tamer Shotgun **$95**
Takedown. Topper-style single-shot, side lever action w/auto
ejector. Gauge: .410; 3-inch chamber. 19.5-inch bbl. 33 inches
overall. Weight: 5.75 lbs. Black polymer thumbhole stock designed to hold 4 extra shotshells. Matte electroless nickel finish.
Made 1994 to date.

H&R Model N. W. T. F. Turkey Mag
Same as Model 098 Single-Shot Hammer, except w/24-inch
bbl., 3.5-inch chamber w/screw-in choke tube. Weight: 6 lbs.
American hardwood stock, Mossy Oak camo finish. Made 1991
to date.
NWTF Turkey Mag. **$120**
NWTF Youth Turkey Mag. **115**

HERCULES SHOTGUNS

See Listings under "W" for Montgomery Ward.

HEYM SHOTGUNS
Münnerstadt, Germany

**Heym Model 22S "Safety" Shotgun/Rifle
Combination** **$2595**
Gauges: 16 and 20. Calibers: 22 Mag., 22 Hornet, 222 Rem.,
222 Rem. Mag., 5.6×50R Mag., 6.5×57R, 7×57R, 243 Win. 24-inch
bbls. 40 inches overall. Weight: about 5.5 lbs. Single-set trigger.
Left-side bbl. selector. Integral dovetail base for scope mounting. Arabesque engraving. Walnut stock. Discontinued 1993.

Heym Model 55 BF Shotgun/Rifle Combo **$5125**
Gauges: 12, 16 and 20. Calibers: 5.6×50R Mag., 6.5×57R,
7×57R, 7×65R, 243 Win., 308 Win., 30-06. 25-inch bbls. 42
inches overall. Weight: about 6.75 lbs. Black satin-finished,
corrosion-resistant bbls. of Krupps special steel. Hand-
checkered walnut stock with long pistol grip. Hand-engraved
leaf scroll. German cheekpiece. Discontinued 1988.

J. C. Higgins Shotguns

See Sears, Roebuck & Company.

SHOTGUNS

RIGHT: Heym Model 22S "Safety"
Shotgun/Rifle Combination
Gun

Heym Model 55 BF Shotgun/Rifle

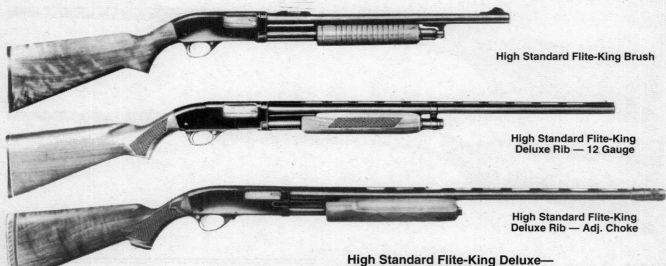

High Standard Flite-King Brush

High Standard Flite-King
Deluxe Rib — 12 Gauge

High Standard Flite-King
Deluxe Rib — Adj. Choke

HIGH STANDARD SPORTING ARMS
East Hartford, Connecticut
Formerly High Standard Mfg. Corp. of
Hamden, Conn.

In 1966, High Standard introduced new series of Flite-King Pumps and Supermatic autoloaders, both readily identifiable by the damascened bolt and restyled checkering. To avoid confusion, these models are designated "Series II" in this text. This is not an official factory designation. Operation of this firm was discontinued in 1984.

High Standard Flite-King Brush—12 Gauge $200
Same as Flite-King Field 12, except has 18- or 20-inch bbl. (cylinder bore) with rifle sights. Made 1962-64.

High Standard Flite-King Brush Deluxe $235
Same as Flite-King Brush, except has adj. peep rear sight, checkered pistol grip, recoil pad, fluted slide handle, swivels and sling. Not available with 18 inch bbl. Made 1964-66.

High Standard Flite-King Brush (Series II) $205
Same as Flite-King Deluxe 12 (II), except has 20-inch bbl., cylinder bore, with rifle sights. Weight: 7 lbs. Made 1966-1975.

High Standard Flite-King Brush Deluxe (II) $250
Same as Flite-King Brush (II), except has adj. peep rear sight, swivels and sling. Made 1966-1975.

High Standard Flite-King Deluxe—12 Ga. (Series II)
Hammerless. 5-shot magazine. Bbls.: plain; 27-inch with adj. choke. 26-inch IC, 28-inch M or F. 30-inch F choke. Weight: about 7.25 lbs. Checkered pistol-grip stock and forearm, recoil pad. Made 1966-1975.
With adj. choke **$265**
Without adj. choke **240**

High Standard Flite-King Deluxe—
20, 28, .410 Gauge (Series II) $225
Same as Flite-King Deluxe 12 (II), except chambered for 20 and .410 ga. 3-inch shell, 28 ga. 2.75-inch shell; plain bbl. in IC (20), M (20, 28), F choke (20, 28, .410) Weight: about 6 lbs. Made 1966-1975.

High Standard Flite-King Deluxe Rib—12 Ga. . . . $275
Same as Flite-King Field 12, except vent-rib bbl. (28 inch M or F. 30-inch F), checkered stock and forearm Made 1961-66.

High Standard Flite-King Deluxe Rib—12 Gauge (II)
Same as Flite-King Deluxe 12 (II), except has vent-rib bbl., available in 27-inch with adj. choke, 28-inch M or F, 30-inch F choke. Made 1966-1975.
With adj. choke **$300**
Without adj. choke **275**

High Standard Flite-King Deluxe Rib—20 Ga. . . $265
Same as Flite-King Field 20, except vent-rib bbl. (28 inch M or F), checkered stock and slide handle. Made 1962-66.

High Standard Flite-King Deluxe Rib—
20, 28, .410 Ga. (Series II)
Same as Flite-King Deluxe 20, 28, .410 (II), except 20 ga. available with 27-inch adj. choke, 28-inch M or F choke. Weight: about 6.25 lbs. Made 1966-1975.
With adj. Choke **$300**
Without adj. Choke **295**

High Standard Flite-King Deluxe Skeet Gun—
12 Gauge (Series II) $255
Same as Flite-King Deluxe Rib 12 (II), except available only with 26-inch vent-rib bbl., SK choke, recoil pad optional. Made 1966-1975.

High Standard Flite-King Deluxe Skeet Gun—
20, 28, 410 Gauge (Series II) $300
Same as Flite-King Deluxe Rib 20, 28, .410 (II) except available only with 26-inch vent-rib bbl., SK choke. Made 1966-1975.

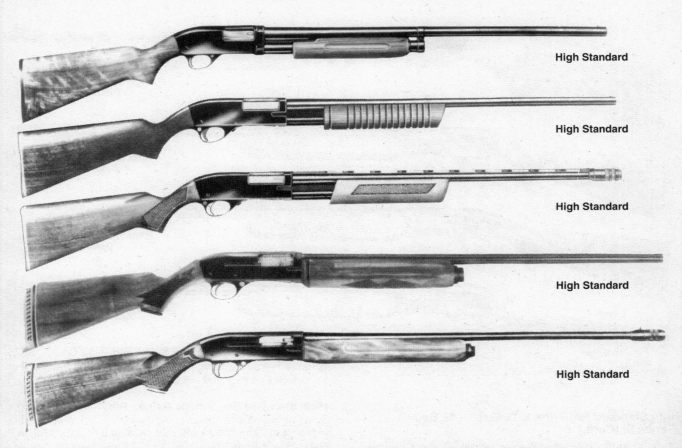

High Standard

High Standard

High Standard

High Standard

High Standard

High Standard Flite-King Deluxe Trap Gun (II) . . **$255**
Same as Flite-King Deluxe Rib 12 (II), except available only with 30-inch vent-rib bbl., F choke; trap-style stock. Made 1966-75.

High Standard Flite-King Field Pump—12 Ga. . . **$215**
Hammerless. Magazine holds 5 shells. Bbls.: 26-inch IC, 28-inch M or F, 30-inch F choke. Weight: 7.25 lbs. Plain pistol-grip stock and slide handle. Made 1960-66.

High Standard Flite-King Field Pump—20 Ga. . . **$195**
Hammerless. Chambered for 3-inch Magnum shells, also handles 2.75-inch. Magazine holds four shells. Bbls.: 26-inch IC, 28-inch M or F choke. Weight: about 6 lbs. Plain pistol-grip stock and slide handle. Made 1961-66.

High Standard Flite-King Pump Shotguns—16 Gauge
Same general specifications as Flite-King 12, except not available in Brush, Skeet and Trap Models, or 30-inch bbl. Values same as for 12-ga. guns. Made 1961-65.

High Standard Flite-King Pump Shotguns—.410 Ga.
Same general specifications as Flite-King 20, except not available in Special and Trophy Models, or with other than 26-inch Full choke barrel. Values same as for 20-ga. guns. Made 1962-66.

High Standard Flite-King Skeet—12 Gauge **$300**
Same as Flite-King Deluxe Rib, except 26-inch vent-rib bbl., with SK choke. Made 1962-66.

High Standard Flite-King Special—12 Gauge . . . **$215**
Same as Flite-King Field 12, except has 27-inch bbl. with adj. choke. Made 1960-66.

High Standard Flite-King Special—20 Gauge . . . **$220**
Same as Flite-King Field 20, except has 27-inch bbl. with adj. choke. Made 1961-66.

High Standard Flite-King Trap—12 Gauge **$315**
Same as Flite-King Deluxe Rib 12, except 30-inch vent-rib bbl., F choke, special trap stock with recoil pad. Made 1962-66.

High Standard Flite-King Trophy—12 Gauge . . . **$300**
Same as Flite-King Deluxe Rib 12, except has 27-inch vent-rib bbl. with adj. choke. Made 1960-66.

High Standard Flite-King Trophy—20 Gauge . . . **$305**
Same as Flite-King Deluxe Rib 20, except has 27-inch vent-rib bbl. with adj. choke. Made 1962-66.

High Standard Supermatic Deer Gun **$275**
Same as Supermatic Field 12, except has 22-inch bbl. (cylinder bore) with rifle sights, checkered stock and forearm, recoil pad. Weight: 7.75 lbs. Made in 1965.

High Standard Supermatic Deluxe—12 Ga. (Series II)
Gas-operated autoloader. 4-shot magazine. Bbls.: plain; 27-inch with adj. choke (discontinued about 1970); 26-inch IC, 28-inch

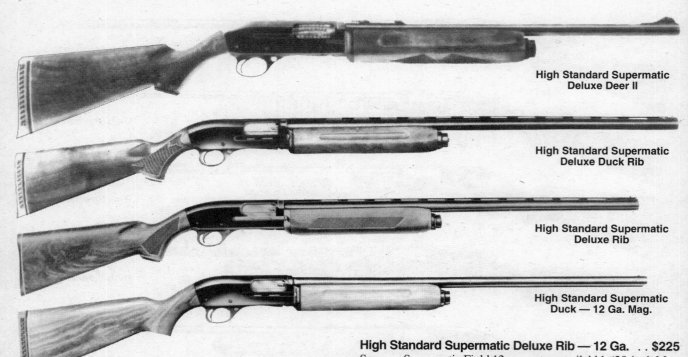

High Standard Supermatic
Deluxe Deer II

High Standard Supermatic
Deluxe Duck Rib

High Standard Supermatic
Deluxe Rib

High Standard Supermatic
Duck — 12 Ga. Mag.

High Standard Supermatic Deluxe — 12 Ga. (Series II) (Cont.)

M or F. 30-inch F choke. Weight: about 7.5 lbs. Checkered pistol-grip stock and forearm, recoil pad. Made 1966-1975.
With adj. choke **$300**
Without adj. choke 255

High Standard Supermatic Deluxe — 20 Ga. (Series II)
Same as Supermatic Deluxe 12 (II), except chambered for 20 ga. 3-inch shell; bbls. available in 27-inch with adj. choke (discontinued about 1970), 26-inch IC, 28-inch M or F choke. Weight: about 7 lbs. Made 1966-1975.
With adj. choke **$215**
Without adj. choke 255

High Standard Supermatic Deluxe Deer Gun (II) . . $325
Same as Supermatic Deluxe 12 (II), except has 22-inch bbl., cylinder bore, with rifle sights. Weight: 7.75 lbs. Made 1966-1974.

High Standard Supermatic Deluxe Duck— 12 Gauge Magnum (Series II) $225
Same as Supermatic Deluxe 12 (II), except chambered for 3-inch Magnum shelf, 3-shot magazine, 30-inch plain bbl., F choke. Weight: 8 lbs. Made 1966-1974.

High Standard Supermatic Deluxe Duck Rib — 12 Gauge Magnum (Series II) $255
Same as Supermatic Deluxe Rib 12 (II), except chambered for 3-inch Magnum shell, 3-shot magazine; 30-inch vent-rib bbl., F choke. Weight: 8 lbs. Made 1966-1975.

High Standard Supermatic Deluxe Rib — 12 Ga. . . $225
Same as Supermatic Field 12, except vent-rib bbl. (28-inch M or F, 30-inch F), checkered stock and forearm. Made 1961-66.

High Standard Supermatic Deluxe Rib — 12 Gauge (II)
Same as Supermatic Deluxe 12 (II), except has vent-rib bbl.; available in 27-inch with adj. choke, 28-inch M or F, 30-inch F choke. Made 1966-1975.
With adj. choke **$265**
Without adj. choke 240

High Standard Supermatic Deluxe Rib — 20 Ga. . . $265
Same as Supermatic Field 20, except vent-rib bbl. (28-inch M or F), checkered stock and forearm. Made 1963-66.

High Standard Supermatic Deluxe Rib — 20 Ga. (II)
Same as Supermatic Deluxe 20 (II), except has vent-rib bbl. Made 1966-1975.
With adj. choke **$255**
Without adj. choke 235

High Standard Supermatic Deluxe Skeet Gun — 12 Gauge (Series II) **$255**
Same as Supermatic Deluxe Rib 12 (II), except available only with 26-inch vent-rib bbl., SK choke. Made 19661975.

High Standard Supermatic Deluxe Skeet Gun — 20 Gauge (Series II) **$265**
Same as Supermatic Deluxe Rib 20 (II), except available only with 26-inch vent-rib bbl., SK choke. Made 1966-1975.

High Standard Supermatic Deluxe Trap Gun (Series II) **$275**
Same as Supermatic Deluxe Rib 12 (II), except available only with 30-inch vent-rib bbl., Full choke; trap-style stock. Made 1966-1975.

High Standard Supermatic
Duck Rib — 12 Gauge

High Standard Supermatic Duck—12 Ga. Mag. . . . $255

Same as Supermatic Field 12, except chambered for 3-inch Magnum shell, 30-inch F choke bbl., recoil pad. Made 1961-66.

High Standard Supermatic Duck Rib—12 Gauge Magnum $275

Same as Supermatic Duck 12 Magnum, except has vent-rib bbl., checkered stock and forearm. Made 1961-66.

High Standard Supermatic Field Autoloading Shotgun—12 Gauge $195

Gas-operated. Magazine holds four shells. Bbls.: 26-inch IC, 28-inch M or F choke, 30-inch F choke. Weight: about 7.5 lbs. Plain pistol-grip stock and forearm. Made 1960-66.

High Standard Supermatic Field Autoloading Shotgun—20 Gauge $215

Gas-operated. Chambered for 3-inch Magnum shells, also handles 2.75-inch. Magazine holds three shells. Bbls.: 26-inch IC, 28-inch M or F choke. Weight: about 7 lbs. Plain pistol-grip stock and forearm. Made 1963-66.

High Standard Supermatic Shadow Automatic . . $290

Gas-operated. Gauge: 12, 20, 2.75- or 3-inch chamber in 12 ga., 3-inch in 20 ga. Magazine holds four 2.75-inch shells, three 3-inch. Bbls.: full-size airflow rib; 26-inch (IC or SK choke), 28-inch (M, IM or F), 30-inch (trap or F choke), 12-ga. 3-inch Magnum available only in 30-inch F choke; 20 ga. not available in 30-inch. Weight: 12 ga., 7 lbs. Checkered walnut stock and forearm. Made 1974-75 by Caspoll Int'l., Inc., Tokyo.

High Standard Supermatic Shadow Indy O/U . . . $825

Boxlock. Fully engraved receiver. Selective auto ejectors. Selective single trigger. 12 ga. 2.75-inch chambers. Bbls.: full-size airflow rib; 27.5 inch both SK choke, 29.75-inch IM/F or F/F. Weight: with 29.75-inch bbls., 8 lbs. 2 oz. Pistol-grip stock with recoil pad, ventilated forearm, skip checkering. Made 1974-75 by Caspoll Int'l., Inc., Tokyo.

High Standard Supermatic Shadow Seven $675

Same general specifications as Shadow Indy, except has conventional vent rib, less elaborate engraving, standard checkering forearm is not vented, no recoil pad. 27.5-inch bbls.; also available in IC/M, M/F choke. Made 1974-75.

SHOTGUNS

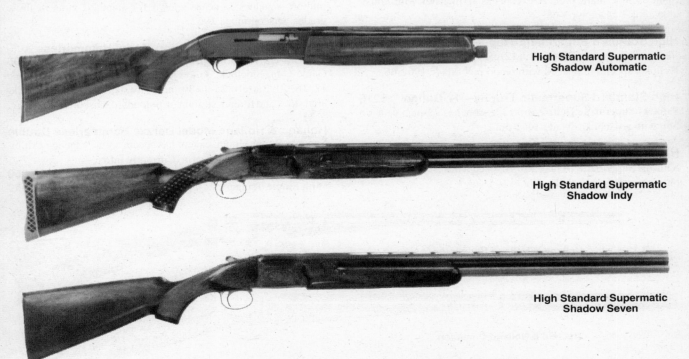

High Standard Supermatic
Shadow Automatic

High Standard Supermatic
Shadow Indy

High Standard Supermatic
Shadow Seven

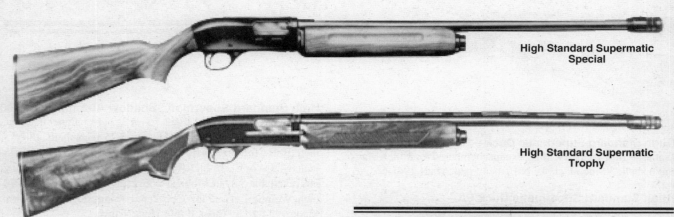

High Standard Supermatic Special

High Standard Supermatic Trophy

High Standard Supermatic Skeet — 12 Gauge . . $205
Same as Supermatic Deluxe Rib 12, except 26-inch vent-rib bbl. with SK choke. Made 1962-66.

High Standard Supermatic Skeet — 20 Gauge . . $230
Same as Supermatic Deluxe Rib 20, except 26-inch vent-rib bbl. with SK choke. Made 1964-66.

High Standard Supermatic Special — 12 Gauge . . $200
Same as Supermatic Field 12, except has 27-inch bbl. with adjustable choke. Made 1960-66.

High Standard Supermatic Special — 20 Gauge . . $210
Same as Supermatic Field 20 except has 27-inch bbl. with adjustable choke. Made i963-66.

High Standard Supermatic Trap — 12 Gauge . . . $215
Same as Supermatic Deluxe Rib 12, except 30-inch vent-rib bbl., F choke, special trap stock with recoil pad. Made 1962-66.

High Standard Supermatic Trophy—12 Gauge . . $215
Same as Supermatic Deluxe Rib 12, except has 27-inch vent-rib bbl. with adj. choke. Made 1961-66.

High Standard Supermatic Trophy—20 Gauge . . $225
Same as Supermatic Deluxe Rib 20, except has 27-inch vent-rib bbl. with adjustable choke. Made 1963-66.

HOLLAND & HOLLAND, LTD.
London, England

Holland & Holland Badminton Model Hammerless Double-Barrel Shotgun. Originally No. 2 Grade
General specifications same as Royal Model except without self-opening action. Made as a Game Gun or Pigeon and Wildfowl Gun. Made from 1902 to date.
With double triggers **$8350**
With single trigger **9250**

Holland & Holland Centenary Model Hammerless Double-Barrel Shotgun
Lightweight (5.5 lbs.). 12 ga. game gun designed for 2-inch shell. Made in four grades—Model Deluxe, Royal, Badminton, Dominion — values same as shown for standard guns in those grades. Discontinued 1962.

Holland & Holland Dominion Model Hammerless Double-Barrel Shotgun **$4695**
Game Gun. Sidelock. Auto ejectors. Double triggers. Gauges: 12, 16, 20. Barrels: 25- to 30-inch, any standard boring. Checkered stock and forend, straight grip standard. Discontinued 1967.

Holland & Holland Model Deluxe Hammerless Double
Same as Royal Model, except has special engraving and exhibition grade stock and forearm. Currently mfd.
With Double Triggers **$25,950**
With Single Trigger **27,950**

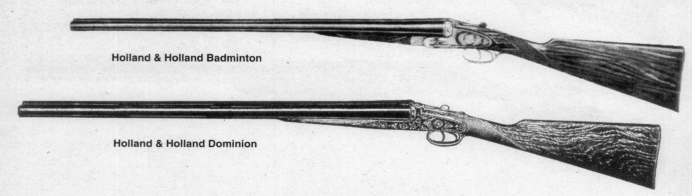

Holland & Holland Badminton

Holland & Holland Dominion

**Holland & Holland Royal
Double-Barrel Shotgun**

Holland & Holland Northwood Model Hammerless Double-Barrel Shotgun $5295

Anson & Deeley system boxlock. Auto ejectors. Double triggers. Gauges: 12, 16, 20, 28 in Game Model; 28 ga. not offered in Pigeon Model; Wildfowl Model in 12 ga. only (3-inch chambers available). Bbls.: 28-inch standard in Game and Pigeon Models, 30-inch in Wildfowl Model; other lengths, any standard choke combination available. Weight: from 5 to 7.75 lbs. depending on ga. and barrels. Checkered straight-grip or pistol-grip stock and forearm. Discontinued.

Holland & Holland Riviera Model Pigeon Gun . . $10,500

Same as Badminton Model but supplied with two sets of bbls., double triggers. Discontinued 1967.

**Holland & Holland Royal Model
Hammerless Double**

Holland & Holland Royal Model Hammerless Double

Self-opening. Sidelocks hand-detachable. Auto ejectors. Double triggers or single trigger. Gauges: 12, 16, 20, 28 .410. Built to customer's specifications as to bbl. length, chokes, etc. Made as a Game Gun or Pigeon and Wildfowl Gun, the latter having treble-grip action and side clips. Checkered stock and forend, straight grip standard. Made from 1885 to date.

With Double Triggers $25,250
With Single Trigger 28,750

Holland & Holland Royal Model Under-and-Over

Sidelocks, hand-detachable. Auto ejectors. Double triggers or single trigger. 12 ga. Built to customer's specifications as to bbl. length, chokes, etc. Made as a Game Gun or Pigeon and Wildfowl Gun. Checkered stock and forend, straight grip standard. *Note:* In 1951 Holland & Holland introduced its New Model Under/Over with an improved, narrower action body. Discont. 1960.

New Model (Double Triggers) $25,000
New Model (Single Trigger) 27,500
Old Model (Double Triggers) 17,500
Old Model (Single Trigger) 19,500

Holland & Holland Single-Shot Super Trap Gun

Anson & Deeley system boxlock. Auto ejector. No safety. 12 ga. Bbls.: wide vent rib, 30- or 32-inch, with Extra Full choke. Weight: about 8.75 lbs. Monte Carlo stock with pistol grip and recoil pad, full beavertail forearm. Models differ in grade of engraving and wood. Discontinued.

Standard Grade $4750
Deluxe Grade 6850
Exhibition Grade 8950

HUNTER ARMS COMPANY
Fulton, New York

Hunter Fulton

Hunter Fulton Hammerless Double-Barrel Shotgun

Boxlock. Plain extractors. Double triggers or non-selective single trigger. Gauges: 12 16, 20. Bbls.: 26- to 32-inch various choke combinations. Weight: about 7 lbs. Checkered pistol-grip stock and forearm. Discont. 1948.

With Double Triggers $325
With Single Trigger 550

Hunter Special

Hunter Special Hammerless Double-Barrel Shotgun

Boxlock. Plain extractors. Double triggers or non-selective single trigger. Gauges: 12,16, 20. Bbls.: 26- to 30-inch various choke combinations. Weight: 6.5 to 7.25 lbs. depending on barrel length and gauge. Checkered full pistol-grip stock and forearm. Discont. 1948.

With Double Triggers $525
With Single Trigger 610

SHOTGUNS

IGA SHOTGUNS
Wayne, New Jersey
Distributed by Stoeger Industries, Inc.

IGA Coach Gun
Gauges: 12, 20 and .410. 20-inch side-by-side bbls. Chokes: IC/M. 3-inch chambers. Weight: 6.5 lbs. Double triggers. Automatic safety. Hand-rubbed oil-finished pistol grip hardwood stock and forend with hand checkering. Made 1983 to date.

Blued Finish **$265**
Chrome Finish. **300**
W/Engraved Stock **285**

IGA Condor I O/U Single-Trigger Shotgun
Gauges: 12 or 20. 26- or 28-inch bbls. of chrome-molybdenum steel. Chokes: Fixed — M/F or IC/M; screw-in choke tubes (12 ga. only). 3-inch chambers. Weight: 6.75 to 7 lbs. Sighting rib with anti-glare surface. Hand checkered hardwood pistol-grip stock and forend. Made from 1983 to date.

With fixed chokes **$290**
With Screw-in Tubes **350**

IGA Condor II O/U Double-Trigger Shotgun $275
Same general specifications as the Condor I Over/Under except with double triggers and fixed chokes only; 26-inch bbls., IC/M; 28-inch bbls., M/F.

IGA Condor Supreme. $450
Same general specifications as Condor I except upgraded with fine-checkered Brazilian walnut buttstock and forend, a matte-laquered finish, and a massive monoblock that joins the bbls. in a solid one-piece assembly at the breech end. Bbls. formulated for use with steel shot. Automatic ejectors. Made 1996 to date.

IGA Deluxe Hunter Clay Shotgun
Same general specifications and values as IGA Condor Supreme. Made 1997 to date.

IGA Era 2000 O/U Shotgun $425
Gauge: 12 w/3-inch chambers. 26- or 28-inch bbls. of chrome-molybdenum steel with screw-in choke tubes. Extractors. Manual safety. (Mechanical triggers.) Weight: 7 lbs. Checkered Brazilian hardwood stock with oil finish. Made 1992-95.

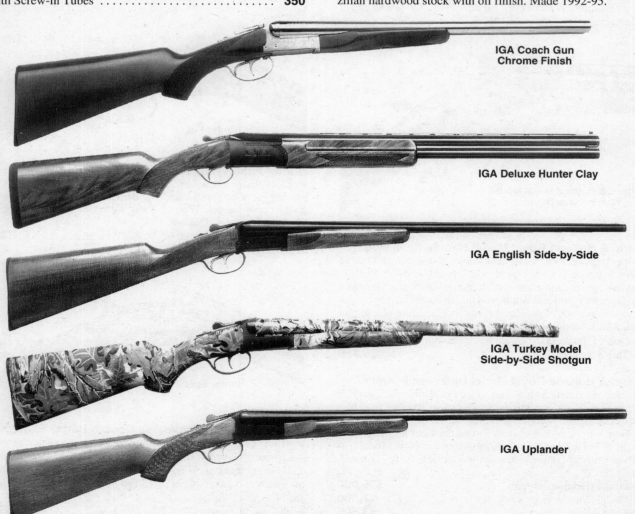

IGA Coach Gun Chrome Finish

IGA Deluxe Hunter Clay

IGA English Side-by-Side

IGA Turkey Model Side-by-Side Shotgun

IGA Uplander

IGA Reuna Single-Shot Shotgun

Visible hammer. Under-lever release. Gauges: 12, 20 and .410; 3-inch chambers. 26- or 28-inch bbls. w/fixed chokes or screw-in choke tubes (12 ga. only). Extractors. Weight: 5.25 to 6.5 lbs. Plain Brazilian hardwood stock and semibeavertail forend. Made from 1992 to date.

W/Fixed Choke	**$ 85**
W/Choke Tubes	**145**

IGA Uplander Side-by-Side Shotgun

Gauges: 12, 20, 28 and .410. 26- or 28-inch bbls. of chrome-molybdenum steel. Various fixed-choke combinations; screw-in choke tubes (12 ga. only). 3-inch chambers (2.75inch in 28 ga.). Weight: 6.25 to 7 lbs. Double triggers. Automatic safety. Matte-finished solid sighting rib. Hand-rubbed, oil-finished pistol-grip stock and forend w/hand checkering. Made from 1983 to date.

With fixed chokes	**$275**
With Screw-in Tubes	**305**
English Model & Turkey Model (straight grip)	**310**
Ladies Model	**315**
Youth Model	**285**

ITHACA GUN COMPANY
King Ferry (formerly Ithaca), New York
Now Ithaca Acquisition Corp./Ithaca Gun Co.

Ithaca Model 37 Bicentennial Commemorative . . $395

Limited to issue of 1976. Similar to Model 37 Supreme, except has special Bicentennial design etched on receiver, full-fancy walnut stock and slide handle. Serial numbers U.S.A. 0001 to U.S.A. 1976. Originally issued with presentation case with cast pewter belt buckle. Made in 1976. Value is for gun in new, unfired condition.

Ithaca Model 37 English Ultra $355

Same general specifications as Model 37 Ultralite, except straight buttstock, 25-inch Rot-Forged vent-rib bbl. Made 1984-1987.

Ithaca Model 37 Featherlight Standard Grade Slide-Action Repeating Shotgun

Adaptation of the earlier Remington Model 17, a Browning design patented in 1915. Hammerless. Takedown. Gauges: 12, 16 (discontinued 1973), 20. 4-shell magazine. Bbl. lengths: 26-, 28-, 30-inch (the latter in 12 ga. only); standard chokes. Weight: from 5.75` to 7.5 lbs. depending on gauge and bbl. length. Checkered pistolgrip stock and slide handle. Some guns made in the 1950s and 1960s have grooved slide handle; plain or checkered pistol grip. Made 1937-1984.

Standard w/checkered pistol grip	**$230**
W/plain stock	**200**
Model 37D Deluxe (1954-1977)	**285**
Model 37DV Deluxe Vent Rib (1962-1984)	**315**
Model 37R Deluxe Solid Rib (1955-1961)	**215**
Model 37V Standard Vent Rib (1962-1984)	**265**

Ithaca Model 37 Field Grade Mag. w/Tubes $295

Same general specifications as Model 37 Featherlight, except 32-inch bbl. and detachable choke tubes. Vent-rib bbl. Made 1984-87.

Ithaca Model 37 $5000 Grade $5795

Custom built, elaborately engraved and inlaid with gold, hand-finished working parts, stock and forend of select figured walnut. General specifications same as standard Model 37. *Note:* The same gun was designated the $1000 Grade prior to World War II. Made 1937-1967.

Ithaca Model 37 Standard Deerslayer. $285

Same as Model 37 Standard, except has 20- or 26-inch bbl. bored for rifled slugs, rifle-type open rear sight and ramp front sight. Weight: 5.75 to 6.5 lbs. depending on ga. and bbl. length. Made 1959 to date.

Ithaca Model 37 Super Deluxe Deerslayer $325

Formerly "Deluxe Deerslayer." Same as Model 37 Standard Deerslayer, except has stock and slide handle of fancy walnut. Made from 1962 to date.

**Ithaca Model 37
English Ultra**

**Ithaca Model 37
Lightweight Standard**

**Ithaca Model 37
Super Deluxe Deerslayer**

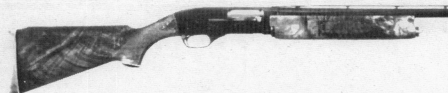

Ithaca Model 37 Supreme

Ithaca Model 37 Supreme Grade $485
Available in Skeet or Trap Gun, similar to Model 37T. Made from 1967 to date.

Ithaca Model 37 Ultralite
Same general specifications as Model 37 Featherlight, except streamlined forend, gold trigger, Sid Bell grip cap and vent rib. Weight: 5 to 5.75 lbs. Made 1984-87.
Standard $325
With Choke Tubes 355

Ithaca Model 37R Solid Rib Grade
Same general specifications as the Model 37 Featherlight except has a raised solid rib, adding about ¼ pound of weight. Made 1937-1967.
With checkered grip and slide handle $300
With plain stock 295

Ithaca Model 37S Skeet Grade $465
Same general specifications as the Model 37 Featherlight, except has vent rib and large extension-type forend; weighs about ½ lb. more. Made 1937-1955.

Ithaca Model 37T Target Grade $450
Same general specifications as Model 37 Featherlight, except has vent-rib bbl., checkered stock and slide handle of fancy walnut (choice of skeet- or trap-style stock). *Note:* This model replaced Model 37S Skeet and Model 37T Trap. Made 1955-1961.

Ithaca Model 37T Trap Grade $465
Same general specifications as Model 37S, except has straighter trap-style stock of select walnut, recoil pad; weighs about ½ lb. more. Made 1937-1955.

Ithaca Model 51 Deerslayer $295
Same as Model 51 Standard, except has 24-inch plain bbl. with slug boring, rifle sights, recoil pad. Weight: about 7.25 lbs. Made 1972-1984.

Ithaca Model 51 Deluxe Skeet Grade $395
Same as Model 51 Standard, except 26-inch vent-rib bbl. only, SK choke, skeet-style stock, semi-fancy wood. Weight: about 8 lbs. Made 1970-1987.

Ithaca Model 51 Deluxe Trap Grade
Same as Model 51 Standard, except 12 ga. only, 30-inch bbl. with broad floating rib, F choke, trap-style stock w/straight or Monte Carlo comb, semifancy wood, recoil pad. Weight: about 8 lbs. Made 1970-1987.
With straight stock $315
With Monte Carlo stock 345

Ithaca Model 51 Standard Automatic Shotgun
Gas-operated. Gauges: 12, 20. 3-shot. Bbls.: plain or vent rib, 30-inch F choke (12 ga. only), 28-inch F or M, 26-inch IC. Weight: 7.25-7.75 lbs. depending on ga. and bbl. Checkered pistol-grip stock, forearm. Made 1970-1980. Still avail. in 12 and 20 ga., 28-inch M choke only.
With plain barrel $230
With ventilated rib 275

Ithaca Model 51 Standard Magnum
Same as Model 51 Standard, except has 3-inch chamber, handles Magnum shells only; 30-inch bbl. in 12 ga., 28-inch in 20 ga., F or M choke, stock with recoil pad. Weight: 7.75-8 lbs. Made 1972 to date.
With plain barrel (discontinued 1976) $250
With ventilated rib 295

Ithaca Model 51A Turkey Gun $325
Same general specifications as standard Model 51 Magnum, except 26-inch bbl. and matte finish. Disc. 1986.

Ithaca Model 66 Long Tom $100
Same as Model 66 Standard, except has 36-inch F choke bbl., 12 ga. only, checkered stock and recoil pad standard. Made 1969-1974.

Ithaca Model 66 Standard Supersingle Lever
Single shot. Hand-cocked hammer. Gauges: 12 (discont. 1974), 20, .410, 3-inch chambers. Bbls.: 12 ga., 30-inch F choke, 28-inch F or M; 20 ga., 28-inch F or M; .410, 26-inch F. Weight: about 7 lbs. Plain or checkered straight-grip stock, plain forend. Made 1963-1978.
Standard Model $125
Vent Rib Model (20 ga., checkered stock, recoil
    pad, 1969-1974) 145
Youth Model (20 & .410 ga., 26-inch bbl., shorter
    stock, recoil pad, 1965-1978) 115

Ithaca Model 51 Deluxe Trap

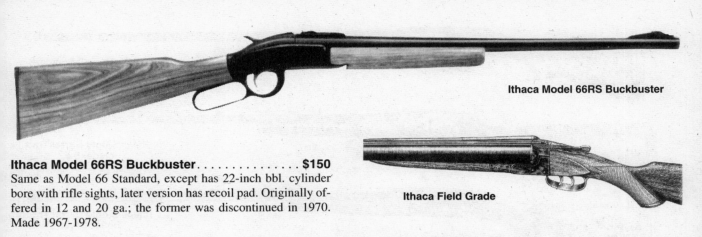

Ithaca Model 66RS Buckbuster

Ithaca Model 66RS Buckbuster **$150**
Same as Model 66 Standard, except has 22-inch bbl. cylinder
bore with rifle sights, later version has recoil pad. Originally offered in 12 and 20 ga.; the former was discontinued in 1970.
Made 1967-1978.

Previously issued as the Ithaca Model 37, the Model 87 guns
listed below are now made available through the Ithaca Acqui-
sition Corp.

Ithaca Model 87 Deerslayer Shotgun
Gauges: 12 or 20, 3-inch chamber. Bbls.: 18.5-, 20- or 25-inch
(w/special or rifled bore). Weight: 6 to 6.75 lbs. Ramp blade
front sight, adjustable rear. Receiver grooved for scope. Checkered American walnut pistol-grip stock and forearm. Made from
1988 to date.

Basic Model	**$275**
Basic Field Combo (w/extra 28-inch bbl.)	345
Deluxe Model	325
Deluxe Combo (w/extra 28-inch bbl.)	410
DSPS Model (8-shot)	280
Field Model	240
Monte Carlo Model	255
Ultra Model (discontinued 1991)	295

Ithaca Model 87 Deerslayer II Rifled Shotgun . . . $360
Similar to the Standard Deerslayer Model, except with solid
frame construction and 25-inch rifled bbl. Monte Carlo stock.
Made from 1988 to date.

Ithaca Model 87 Ultralite Field Pump Shotgun . . $295
Gauges: 12 and 20; 2.75-inch chambers. 25-inch bbl. with choke
tube. Weight: 5 to 6 lbs. Made 1988-1990.

Ithaca Model 87 Field Grade
Gauge: 12 or 20.; 3-inch chamber. 5-shot magazine. Fixed
chokes or screw-in choke tubes (IC, M, F). Bbls.: 18.5-inch
(M&P); 20- and 25-inch (Combo); 26-, 28-, 30-inch vent rib.
Weight: 5 to 7 lbs. Made from 1988 to date.

Basic Field Model	**$290**
Camo Model	365
Deluxe Model	340
Deluxe Combo Model	375
English Model	295
Hand Grip Model (w/polymer pistol-grip)	325
M&P Model	280
Supreme Model	595
Turkey Model	295
Ultra Deluxe Model (discontinued 1992)	365
Ultra Deluxe Model (discontinued 1992)	335

Ithaca Field Grade

Ithaca No. 2

Ithaca No. 4

Ithaca Hammerless Double-Barrel Shotguns
Boxlock. Plain extractors, auto ejectors standard on the "E" grades.
Double triggers, non-selective or selective single trigger extra.
Gauges: Magnum 10, 12; 12, 16, 20, 28, .410. Bbls.: 26- to 32-inch,
any standard boring. Weight: 5.75 (.410) to 10.5 lbs. (Magnum 10).
Checkered pistol-grip stock and forearm standard. Higher grades
differ from Field Grade in quality of workmanship, grade of wood,
checkering, engraving, etc.; general specifications are the same. Ithaca doubles made before 1925 (serial number 425,000) the rotary
bolt and a stronger frame were adopted. Values shown are for this
latter type; earlier models valued about 50% lower. Smaller gauge
guns may command up to 75% higher. Discontinued 1948.

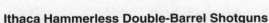

Field Grade	$ 650
No. 1 Grade.	695
No. 2 Grade.	950
No. 3 Grade	1,200
No. 4E Grade (ejector)	2,495
No. 5E Grade (ejector)	3,295
No. 7E Grade (ejector)	9,995
$2000 (prewar $1000) Grade (ejector and selective single trigger standard)	8,595

Extras:

Magnum 10 or 12 gauge (in other than the four highest grades), **add**	$200
Automatic ejectors (Grades No. 1, 2, 3, w/ejectors are designated No. 1E, 2E, 3E), **add**	200

SHOTGUNS

Ithaca Mag-10 Standard

Ithaca Single-Barrel Trap Model 5-E

Ithaca Single-Barrel Trap "Dollar Grade"

Ithaca Hammerless Double-Barrel Shotguns (*Cont.*)

Selective single trigger, **add**	**$150**
Non-selective single trigger, **add**	100
Beavertail forend (Field No. 1 or 2), **add**	150
Beavertail forend (No. 3 or 4), **add**	175
Beavertail forend (No. 5, 7 or $2000 Grade), **add**	250
Ventilated rib (No. 4, 5, 7 or $2000 Grade), **add**	250
Ventilated rib (lower grades), **add**	175

Ithaca LSA-55 Turkey Gun. $500

Over/under shotgun/rifle combination. Boxlock. Exposed hammer. Plain extractor. Single trigger. 12 ga./222 Rem. 24.5-inch ribbed bbls. (rifle bbl. has muzzle brake). Weight: about 7 lbs. Folding leaf rear sight, bead front sight. Checkered Monte Carlo stock and forearm. Made 1970-77 by Oy Tikkakoski AB, Finland.

Ithaca Mag-10 Automatic Shotgun

Gas-operated. 10 ga. 3.5-inch Magnum. 3-shot. 32-inch plain (Standard Grade only) or vent-rib bbl. F choke. Weight: 11 lbs., plain bbl.; 11.5 lbs., vent rib. Standard Grade has plain stock and forearm. Deluxe and Supreme Grades have checkering, semifancy and fancy wood respectively, and stud swivel. All have recoil pad. Deluxe and Supreme Grades made 1974-1982. Standard Grade introduced in 1977. All grades discontinued 1986.

Camo Model	**$650**
Deluxe Grade	695
Roadblocker	595
Standard Grade, plain barrel	530
Standard Grade, ventilated rib	625
Standard Grade, with tubes	695
Supreme Grade	840

Ithaca Single-Shot Trap, Flues and Knick Models

Boxlock. Hammerless. Ejector. 12 ga. only. Bbl. lengths: 30-, 32-, 34-inch (32-inch only in Victory Grade). Vent rib. Weight: about 8 lbs. Checkered pistol-grip stock and forend. Grades differ only in quality of workmanship, engraving, checkering, wood, etc. Flues Model, serial numbers under 400,000, made 1908-1921. Triple-bolted Knick Model, serial numbers above 400,000, made since 1921. Victory Model discontinued in 1938, No. 7-E in 1964, No. 4-E in 1976, No. 5-E in 1986, Dollar Grade in 1991. Values shown are for Knick Model; Flues Model guns bring prices about 50% lower.

Victory Grade	**$　895**
No. 4-E	1,295
No. 5-E	2,650
No. 7-E	4,795
$5000 Grade (prewar $1000 Grade)	8,850
Sousa Grade	10,000

NOTE

The following Ithaca-Perazzi shotguns were manufactured by Manifattura Armi Perazzi, Brescia, Italy. *See* also separate Perazzi listings.

Ithaca-Perazzi Competition I Skeet. $2855

Boxlock. Auto ejectors. Single trigger. 12 ga. 26.75-inch vent-rib bbls. SK choke w/integral muzzle brake. Weight: about 7.75 lbs. Checkered skeet-style pistol-grip buttstock and forearm; recoil pad. Made 1969-1974.

Ithaca-Perazzi Competition Trap I O/U

Boxlock. Auto ejectors. Single trigger. 12 ga. 30- or 32-inch vent-rib bbls. IM/F choke. Weight: about 8.5 lbs. Checkered pistol-grip stock, forearm; recoil pad. Made 1969-1974.

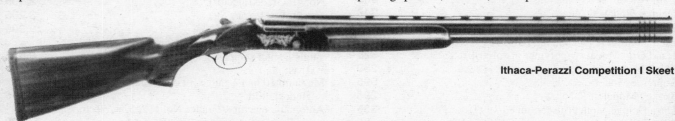

Ithaca-Perazzi Competition I Skeet

Ithaca Perazzi Competition I Trap

Ithaca-Perazzi Competition I Trap Single Barrel . . $1950

Boxlock. Auto ejection. 12 ga. 32- or 34-inch bbl., vent rib, F choke. Weight: 8.5 lbs. Checkered Monte Carlo stock and beavertail forearm, recoil pad. Made 1973-78.

Ithaca-Perazzi Competition IV Trap Gun $2395

Boxlock. Auto ejection. 12 ga. 32- or 34-inch bbl. With high, wide vent rib, four interchangeable choke tubes (Extra Full, F, IM, M). Weight: about 8.75 lbs. Checkered Monte Carlo stock and beavertail forearm, recoil pad. Fitted case. Made 1977-78.

Ithaca-Perazzi Light Game O/U Field $2895

Boxlock. Auto ejectaors. Single trigger. 12 ga. 27.5-inch vent-rib bbls., M/F or IC/M choke. Weight: 6.75 lbs. Checkered field-style stock and forearm. Made 1972-74.

Ithaca Perazzi Mirage Live Bird $3250

Same as Mirage Trap, except has 28-inch bbls., M and Extra Full choke, speial stock and forearm for live bird shooting. Weight: about 8 lbs. Made 1973-78.

Ithaca-Perazzi Mirage Skeet $2750

Same as Mirage Trap, except has 28-inch bbls. with integral muzzle brakes, SK choke, skeet-stype stock and forearm. Weight: about 8 lbs. Made 1973-78.

Ithaca-Perazzi Mirage Trap $2850

Same general specifications as MX-8 Trap, except has tapered rib. Made 1973-78.

Ithaca-Perazzi MT-6 Skeet $2795

Same as MT-6 Trap, except has 28-inch bbls. with two skeet choke tubes instead of Extra Full and F, skeet-style stock and forearm. Weight: about 8 lbs. Made 1976-78.

Ithaca-Perazzi MT-6 Trap Combo $3595

MT-6 with extra single under bbl. with high-rise aluminum vent rib, 32- or 34-inch; seven interchanageable choke tubes (IC through Extra Full). Fitted case. Made 1977-78.

Ithaca-Perazzi MT-6 Trap Over/Under $2495

Boxlock. Auto selective ejectors. Non-selective single trigger. 12 ga. Barrels separated, wide vent rib, 30-or 32-inch, five interchangeable choke tubes (Extra full, F, IM, M, IC). Weight: about 8.5 lbs. Checkered pistol-grip stock/forearm, recoil pad. Fitted case. Made 1976-78.

Ithaca-Perazzi MX-8 Trap Combo $3950

MX-8 with extra single bbl., vent rib, 32- or 34-inch, F choke, forearm; two trigger groups included. Made 1973-78.

Ithaca-Perazzi MX-8 Trap Over/Under $2895

Boxlock. Auto selective ejectors. Non-selective single trigger. 12 ga. Bbls.: high vent rib; 30- or 32-inch, IM/F choke. Weight: 8.25 to 8.5 lbs. Checkered Monte Carlo stock and forearm, recoil pad. Made 1969-1978.

Ithaca-Perazzi Single-Barrel Trap Gun $1925

Boxlock. Auto ejection. 12 ga. 34-inch vent-rib bbl., F choke. Weight: abaout 8.5 lbs. Checkered pistol-grip stock, forearm; recoil pad. Made 1971-72.

NOTE

The following Ithaca- SKB shotguns, manufactured by SKB Arms Company, Tokyo, Japan, were distributed in the U.S. by Ithaca Gun Company 1966-1976. *See* also listings under SKB.

SHOTGUNS

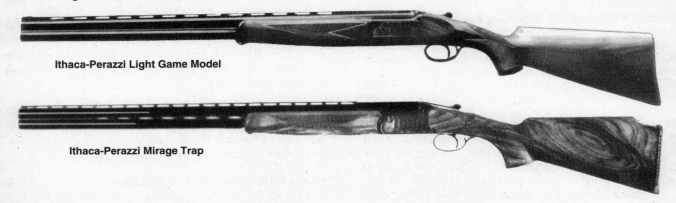

Ithaca-Perazzi Light Game Model

Ithaca-Perazzi Mirage Trap

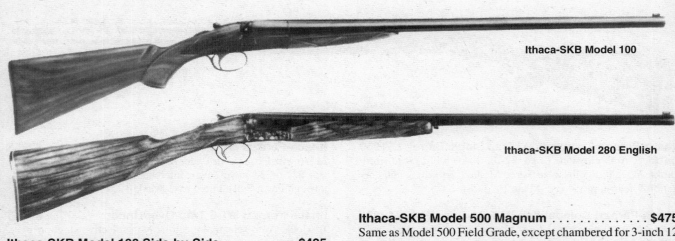

Ithaca-SKB Model 100

Ithaca-SKB Model 280 English

Ithaca-SKB Model 100 Side-by-Side **$425**
Boxlock. Plain extractors. Selective single trigger. Auto safety.
Gauges: 12 and 20; 2.75-inch and 3-inch chambers respectively.
Bbls.: 30-inch, F/F (12 ga. only); 28-inch, F/M; 26-inch, IC/M
(12 ga. only); 25-inch, IC/M (20 ga. only). Weight: 12 ga., about
7 lbs.; 20 ga., about 6 lbs. Checkered stock and forend. Made
1966-1976.

Ithaca-SKB Model 150 Field Grade **$450**
Same as Model 100, except has fancier scroll engraving, beavertail forearm. Made 1972-74.

Ithaca-SKB Model 200E Field Grade S/S **$550**
Same as Model 100, except auto selective ejectors, engraved and
silver-plated frame, gold-plated nameplate and trigger,
beavertail forearm. Made 1966-1976.

Ithaca-SKB Model 200E Skeet Gun **$595**
Same as Model 200E Field Grade, except 26-inch (12 ga.) and
25-inch (20 ga./2.75-inch chambers) bbls., SK choke; nonautomatic safety and recoil pad. Made 1966-1976.

Ithaca-SKB Model 280 English **$695**
Same as Model 200E, except has scrolled game scene engraving
on frame, English-style straight-grip stock; 30-inch bbls. not
available; special quail gun in 20 ga. has 25-inch bbls., both
bored IC. Made 1971-76.

Ithaca-SKB Model 300 Standard Automatic Shotgun
Recoil-operated. Gauges: 12, 20 (3-inch). 5-shot. Bbls.: plain or
vent rib; 30-inch F choke (12 ga. only), 28-inch F or M, 26-inch
IC. Weight: about 7 lbs. Checkered pistol-grip stock and fore-
arm. Made 1968-1972.
With plain barrel **$235**
With ventilated rib 265

Ithaca-SKB Model 500 Field Grade O/U **$425**
Boxlock. Auto selective ejectors. Selective single trigger.
Nonautomatic safety. Gauges: 12 and 20; 2.75-inch and 3-inch
chambers respectively. Vent-rib bbls.: 30-inch M/F (12 ga.
only); 28-inch M/F; 26-inch IC/M. Weight: 12 ga., about 7.5 lbs;
20 ga., about 6.5 lbs. Checkered stock and forearm. Made 1966-
1976.

Ithaca-SKB Model 500 Magnum **$475**
Same as Model 500 Field Grade, except chambered for 3-inch 12
ga. shells, has 30-inch bbls., IM/F choke. Weight: about 8 lbs.
Made 1973-76.

Ithaca-SKB Model 600 Doubles Gun **$585**
Same as Model 600 Trap Grade, except specially choked for 21-
yard first target, 30-yard second. Made 1973-75.

Ithaca-SKB Model 600 Field Grade **$525**
Same as Model 500, except has silver-plated frame, higher grade
wood. Made 1969-1976.

Ithaca-SKB Model 600 Magnum **$545**
Same as Model 600 Field Grade, except chambered for 3-inch 12
ga. shells; has 30-inch bbls., IM/F choke. Weight: 8.5 lbs. Made
1969-72.

Ithaca-SKB Model 600 Skeet Grade
Same as Model 500, except also available in 28 and .410 ga., has
silver-plated frame, higher grade wood, recoil pad, 26- or 28-
inch bbls. (28-inch only in 28 and .410), SK choke. Weight: 7 to
7.75 lbs. depending on ga. and bbl. length. Made 1966-1976.
12 or 20 gauge **$550**
28 or .410 gauge 625

Ithaca-SKB Model 600 Skeet Combo Set **$1525**
Model 600 Skeet Grade with matched set of 20, 28 and .410 ga.
bbls., 28-inch, fitted case. Made 1970-76.

Ithaca-SKB Model 600 Trap Grade O/U **$565**
Same as Model 500, except 12 ga. only, has silver-plated frame,
30- or 32-inch bbls. choked F/F or F/IM, choice of Monte Carlo
or straight stock of higher grade wood, recoil pad. Weight: about
8 lbs. Made 1966-1976.

Ithaca-SKB Model 680 English **$595**
Same as Model 600 Field Grade, except has intricate scroll engraving, English-style straight-grip stock and forearm of extra-
fine walnut; 30-inch bbls. not available. Made 1973-76.

Ithaca-SKB Model 700 Doubles Gun **$775**
Same as Model 700 Trap Grade, except choked for 21-yard first
target, 30-yard second target. Made 1973-75.

Ithaca-SKB Model 700 Skeet Grade

Ithaca-SKB Model 900 Deluxe

Ithaca-SKB Model 700 Skeet Combo Set $1895
Model 700 Skeet Grade with matched set of 20, 28 and .410 ga. bbls., 28-inch fitted case. Made 1970-71.

Ithaca-SKB Model 700 Skeet Grade $750
Same as Model 600 Skeet Grade, except not available in 28 and .410 ga., has more elaborate scroll engraving, extra-wide rib, higher grade wood. Made 1969-1975.

Ithaca-SKB Model 700 Trap Grade $765
Same as Model 600 Trap Grade, except has more elaborate scroll engraving, extra-wide rib, higher grade wood. Made 1969-1975.

Ithaca-SKB Model 900 Deluxe Automatic $315
Same as Model 300, except has game scene etched and gold-filled on receiver, vent rib standard. Made 1968-1972.

Ithaca-SKB Model 900 Slug Gun $285
Same as Model 900 Deluxe, except has 24-inch plain bbl. with slug boring, rifle sights. Weight: about 6.5 lbs. Made 1970-72.

Ithaca-SKB Century Single-Shot Trap Gun $525
Boxlock. Auto ejector. 12 ga. Bbls.: 32- or 34-inch, vent rib, F choke. Weight: about 8 lbs. Checkered walnut stock with pistol grip, straight or Monte Carlo comb, recoil pad, beavertail forearm. Made 1973-74.

Ithaca-SKB Century II $575
Boxlock. Auto ejector. 12 ga. Bbls: 32- or 34-inch, vent rib, F choke. Weight: 8.25 lbs. Improved version of Century. Same general specifications, except has higher comb on checkered stock stock, reverse-taper beavertail forearm with redesigned locking iron. Made 1975-76.

Ithaca-SKB Model XL300 Standard Automatic
Gas-operated. Gauges: 12, 20 (3-inch). 5-shot. Bbls.: plain or vent rib; 30-inch F choke (12 ga. only), 28-inch F or M, 26-inch IC. Weight: 6 to 7.5 lbs. depending on ga. and bbl. Checkered pistol-grip stock, forearm. Made 1972-76.
With plain barrel $215
With ventilated rib 235

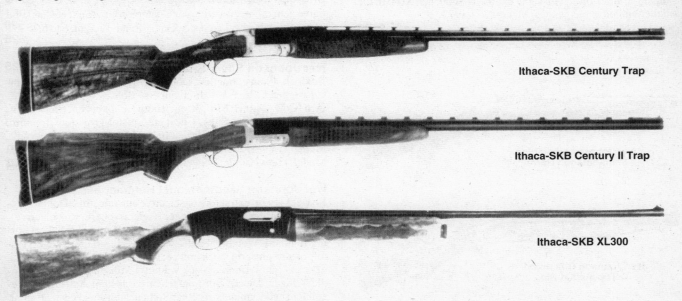

Ithaca-SKB Century Trap

Ithaca-SKB Century II Trap

Ithaca-SKB XL300

SHOTGUNS

Ithaca-SKB Model XL900 Deluxe Automatic $275
Same as Model XL300, except has game scene finished in silver on receiver, vent rib standard. Made 1972-76.

Ithaca-SKB Model XL900 Skeet Grade $335
Gas-operated. Gauges: 12, 20 (3-inch). 5-shot tubular magazine. Same as Model XL900 Deluxe, except has scrolled receiver finished in black chrome, 26-inch bbl. only, SK choke, skeet-style stock. Weight: 7 or 7.5 lbs. depending on ga. Made 1972-76.

Ithaca-SKB Model XL900 Slug Gun $295
Same as Model XL900 Deluxe, except has 24-inch plain bbl. with slug boring, rifle sights. Weight: 6.5 or 7 lbs. depending on ga. Made 1972-76.

Ithaca-SKB Model XL900 Trap Grade $345
Same as Model XL900 Deluxe, except 12 ga. only, has scrolled receiver finished in black chrome, 30-inch bbl. only, IM or F choke, trap style with straight or Monte Carlo comb, recoil pad. Weight: about 7.75 lbs. Made 1972-76.

Iver Johnson Hercules Hammerless

IVER JOHNSON'S ARMS & CYCLE WORKS
Fitchburg, Massachusetts
Currently a division of the American Military Arms Corp.
Jacksonville, Arkansas

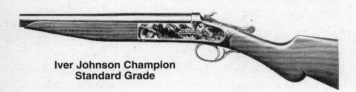

Iver Johnson Champion Standard Grade

Iver Johnson Champion Grade Single-Shot Hammer Shotgun
Auto ejector. Gauges: 12,16, 20, 28 and .410. Bbls.: 26- to 36-inch, F choke. Weight: 5.75 to 7.5 lbs. depending on ga. and bbl. length. Plain pistol-grip stock and forend. Extras include checkered stock and forend, pistol-grip cap and knob forend. Known as Model 36. Also made in a Semi-Octagon Breech, Top Matted and Jacketed Breech (extra heavy) model. Made in Champion Lightweight as Model 39 in gauges 24, 28, 32 and .410, 44 and 45 caliber, 12 and 14mm with same extras — $200, add $100 in the smaller and obsolete gauges. Made 1909-1973.
Standard Model $150
Semi-Octagon Breech 245
Top Matted Rib (Disc. 1948) 230

Iver Johnson Champion Semi-octagon Barrel

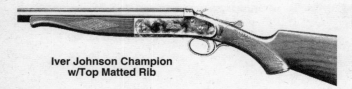

Iver Johnson Champion w/Top Matted Rib

Iver Johnson Hercules Grade Hammerless Double
Boxlock. (Some made with false sideplates.) Plain extractors and auto ejectors. Double or Miller Single triggers (both selective or non-selective). Gauges: 12, 16, 20 and .410. Bbl. lengths: 26- to 32-inch, all chokes. Weight: 5.75 to 7.75 lbs. depending on gauge and bbl. length. Checkered stock and forend. Straight grip in .410 ga. with both 2.5- and 3-inch chambers. Extras include Miller Single Trigger, Jostam Anti-Flinch Recoil Pad and Lyman Ivory Sights at extra cost. Discontinued 1946.
With double triggers, extractors $495
With double triggers, automatic ejectors 595
Extra for non-selective single trigger 100
Extra for selective single trigger 135
Extra for .410 gauge 185

Iver Johnson Matted Rib Single-Shot Hammer Shotgun in Smaller Gauges $275
Same general specifications as Champion Grade except has solid matted top rib, checkered stock and forend. Weight: 6 to 6.75 lbs. Discontinued 1948.

Iver Johnson Silver Shadow Over/Under Shotgun
Boxlock. Plain extractors. Double triggers or non-selective single trigger.12 ga., 3-inch chambers. Bbls.: 26-inch IC/M; 28-inch IC/M, 28-inch M/F; 30-inch both F choke; vent rib. Weight: w/28-inch bbls., 7.5 lbs. Checkered pistol-grip stock/forearm. Made by F. Marocchi, Brescia Italy 1973-78.
Model 412 w/Double Triggers $400
Model 422 w/Single Trigger 440

Iver Johnson Skeeter Model Hammerless Double
Boxlock. Plain extractors or selective auto ejectors. Double triggers or Miller Single Trigger (selective or non-selective). Gauges: 12, 16, 20, 28 and .410. 26- or 28-inch bbls., skeet boring standard. Weight: about 7.5 lbs.; less in smaller gauges. Pistol- or straight-grip stock and beavertail forend, both checkered, of select fancy-figured black walnut. Extras include Miller Single Trigger, selective or non-selective, Jostam Anti-Flinch Recoil Pad and Lyman Ivory Rear Sight at additional cost. Discont. 1942.

Iver Johnson Skeeter

Iver Johnson Skeeter Model *(Cont.)*

With Double Triggers, plain extractors . . . . $ 895
With Double Triggers, automatic ejectors 1095
Extra for non-selective single trigger 100
Extra for selective single trigger 135
Extra for .410 gauge 200
Extra for 28 gauge 300

Iver Johnaon Special Trap Single-Shot Hammer Shotgun $295
Auto ejector. 12 ga. only. 32-inch bbl. with vent rib, F choke. Checkered pistol-grip stock and forend. Weight: about 7.5 lbs. Discontinued 1942.

Iver Johnson Super Trap Hammerless Double
Boxlock. Plain extractors. Double trigger or Miller single trigger (slective or non-selective), 12 ga. only, F choke 32-inch bbl., vent rib. Weight: 8.5 lbs. Checkered pistol-grip stock and bevertail forend, recoil pad, Discontinued 1942.
With Double Triggers $850
Extra for Non-selective Single Trigger 250
Extra for Selective Single Trigger 300

KBI INC. SHOTGUNS
Harrisburg, Pennsylvania

KBI/Baikal Hammerless Double $275
Boxlock. Double triggers with extractors. 12 ga.; 2.75-inch chambers. Bbls.: 26-inch, IC/M; 28-inch, M/F w/fixed chokes. Weight: 6.75 lbs. Made in Russia.

KBI/Baikal Over/Under $350
Boxlock. Single selective trigger with automatic ejectors or double triggers with extractors. Gauge: 12 or 20; 2.75-inch chambers. Bbls.: 26-inch, IC/M; 28-inch, M/F; fixed chokes or screw-in choke tubes. Weight: 7 lbs. Checkered European walnut stock and forearm. Made in Russia.

KBI/Baikal Single Shot $265
Hammerless. Automatic ejector. Manual safety. Gauges: 12 (2.75-inch chamber), 20 or .410 with 3-inch. Bbls.: 26-, 28-inch with fixed chokes (IC, M, F). Weight: 5.5 to 6 lbs. Made in Russia.

KBI/Fias Grade I Over/Under
Boxlock. Single selective trigger. Gauges: 12, 20, 28, .410; 3-inch chambers. Bbls.: 26-inch IC/M; 28-inch M/F; screw-in choke tubes. Weight: 6.5 to 7.5 lbs. Checkered European walnut stock and forearm. Engraved receiver and blued finish.
12 Gauge Model $375
20 Gauge Model 450
28 and .410 Models 560

KBI/Kassnar Grade II Side-by-Side Shotgun $415
Gauges: 10, 12, 20, 28 and .410. 26- to 32-inch chromed bbls. Weight: 5 lbs. (.410 ga.) to 9 lbs. (10 ga.). Double-hinged triggers. Automatic top tang safety. Extractors. Casehardened antique silver receiver w/fine scroll engraving. Checkered European walnut stock. Discontinued 1990.

KBI/Omega Over-Under
Boxlock. Single selective trigger. Gauges: 12, 20, 28, .410; 3-inch chambers. Bbls.: 26- or 28-inch vent-rib with fixed chokes (IC/M or M/F). Automatic safety. Weight: 6 to 7.5 lbs. Checkered European walnut stock and forearm. Discontinued 1992.
Deluxe Model (12 ga. only) $350
Standard Model 300

KESSLER ARMS CORP.
Silver Creek, New York

Kessler Lever-Matic Repeating Shotgun $135
Lever action. Takedown. Gauges: 12, 16, 20; three-shot magazine. Bbls.: 26-, 28-, 30-inch; F choke. Plain pistol-grip stock, recoil pad. Weight: 7 to 7.75 lbs. Discont. 1953.

Kessler Three Shot Bolt-Action Repeater $75
Takedown. Gauges: 12, 16, 20. Two-shell detachable box magazine. Bbls.: 28-inch in 12 and 16 ga.; 26-inch in 20 ga.; F choke. Weight: 6.25 to 7.25 lbs. depending on ga. and bbl. length. Plain one-piece pistol-grip stock, recoil pad. Made 1951-53.

KBI/Baikal Over/Under

SHOTGUNS

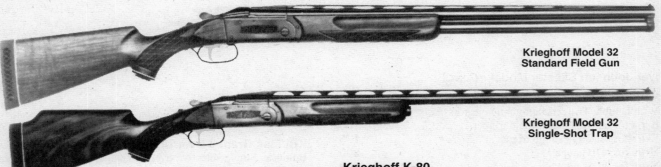

**Krieghoff Model 32
Standard Field Gun**

**Krieghoff Model 32
Single-Shot Trap**

H. KRIEGHOFF JAGD UND
SPORTWAFFENFABRIK
Ulm (Donau), West Germany

Krieghoff Model 32 Four-Barrel Skeet Set
Over/under w/four sets of matched bbls.: 12, 20, 28 and .410 ga., in fitted case. Available in six grades that differ in quality of engraving and wood. Discontinued 1979.

Standard Grade	$ 8,590
München Grade	9,750
San Remo Grade	10,500
Monte Carlo Grade	15,950
Crown Grade	17,500
Super Crown Grade	19,755
Exhibition Grade	29,950

Krieghoff Model 32 Standard Grade Over/Under
Similar to prewar Remington Model 23. Boxlock. Auto ejector. Single trigger. Gauges: 12, 20, 28, .410. Bbls.: vent rib, 26.5- to 32-inch, any chokes. Weight: 12 ga. Field gun with 28-inch bbls., about 7.5 lbs. Checkered pistol-grip stock and forearm of select walnut; available in field, skeet and trap styles. Made 1958-1981.

With one set of bbls.	$1995
Low-rib Two-Bbl. Trap Combo	2995
Vandalia (high-rib) Two-Bbl. Trap Combo	3995

Krieghoff Model 32 Standard Grade
Single-Shot Trap Gun **$1495**
Same action as over/under. 12 ga. 32- or 34-inch bbl. with high vent-rib on bbl.; M, IM, or F choke. Checkered Monte Carlo buttstock with thick cushioned recoil pad, beavertail forearm. Disc. 1979.

Krieghoff K-80
Refined and enhanced version of the Model 32. Single selective mechanical trigger, adj. for position; release trigger optional. Fixed chokes or screw-in choke tubes. Interchangeable front bbl. Hangers to adjust point of impact. Quick-removable stock. Color casehardened or satin grey finished receiver; aluminum alloy receiver on lightweight models. Available in standard plus five engraved grades. Made 1980 to date. Standard grade shown except where noted.

SKEET MODELS
Skeet International	$4950
Skeet Special	4595
Skeet Standard Model	3950
Skeet w/Tubla Chokes	4750

SKEET SETS
Standard Grade 2-Bbl. Set	$ 6,550
Standard Grade 4-Bbl. Set	8,595
Bavaria Grade 4-Bbl. Set	12,250
Danube Grade 4-Bbl. Set	15,950
Gold Target Grade 4-Bbl. Set	18,750

SPORTING MODELS
Pigeon	$4695
Sporting Clays	4950

TRAP MODELS
Trap Combo	$6995
Trap Single	4950
Trap Standard	4595
Trap Unsingle	5145
RT Models (Removable Trigger) **Add**	1385

Krieghoff Model KS-5 Single-Barrel Trap
Boxlock with no sliding top-latch. Adjustable or optional release trigger. Gauge: 12; 2.75-inch chamber. Bbl.: 32-, 34-inch w/fixed choke or screw-in tubes. Weight: 8.5 lbs. Adjustable or Monte Carlo European walnut stock. Blued or nickel receiver. Made from 1980 to date. Redesigned and streamlined in 1993.

**Krieghoff Model K-80
w/Screw-In Choke Tubes**

**Krieghoff Model K-80
Trap Unsingle**

Krieghoff Model KS-5 Single-Barrel Trap *(Cont.)*

Standard Model w/Fixed Chokes	**$2190**
Standard Model w/Tubes	2595
Special Model w/Adj. Rib & Stock	2750
Special Model w/Adj. Rib & Stock, Tubes	3295

**Krieghoff Neptun
Drilling**

Krieghoff Neptun Drilling **$9550**

Same general specifications as Trumpf model, except has sidelocks with hunting scene engraving. Currently manufactured.

Krieghoff Neptun-Primus Drilling **$10,950**

Deluxe version of Neptun model; has detachable sidelocks, higher grade engraving and fancier wood. Currently manufactured.

Krieghoff Teck Over/Under Rifle-Shotgun **$4995**

Boxlock. Kersten double crossbolt system. Steel or dural receiver. Split extractor or ejector for shotgun bbl. Single or double triggers. Gauges: 12, 16, 20; latter with either 2.75- or 3-inch chamber. Calibers: 22 Hornet, 222 Rem., 222 Rem. Mag., 7×57r5, 7×64, 7×65r5, 30-30, 300 Win. Mag., 30-6, 308, 9.3×74R. 25-inch bbls. With solid rib, folding leaf rear sight, post or bead front sight; over bbl. is shotgun, under bbl. rifle (later fixed or interchangeable; extra rifle bbl., $175). Weight: 7.9 to 9.5 lbs. depending on type of receiver and caliber. Checkered pistol-grip stock with cheekpiece and semibeavertail forearm of figured walnut, sling swivels. Made 1967 to date. *Note:* This combination gun is similar in appearance to the same model shotgun.

Krieghoff Teck Over/Under Shotgun **$3820**

Boxlock. Kersten double crossbolt system. Auto ejector. Single or double triggers. Gauges: 12, 16, 20; latter with either 2.75- or 3-inch chambers. 28-inch vent-rib bbl., M/F choke. Weight: about 7 lbs. Checkered walnut pistol-grip stock and forearm. Made 1967-1989.

Krieghoff Trumpf Drilling **$5595**

Boxlock. Steel or dural receiver. Split extractor or ejector for shotgun bbls. Double triggers. Gauges: 12, 16, 20; latter with either 2.75- or 3-inch chambers. Calibers: 243, 6.5×57r5, 7×57r5, 7×65r5, 30-06; other calibers available. 25-inch bbls. with solid rib, folding leaf rear sight, post or bead front sight; rifle bbl. soldered or free floating. Weight: 6.6 to 7.5 lbs. depending on type of receiver, ga. And caliber. Checkered pistol-grip stock with cheekpiece and forearm of figured walnut, sling swivels. Made 1953 to date.

Krieghoff Ulm Over/Under Rifle-Shotgun **$8595**

Same general specifications as Teck model, except has sidelocks with leaf arabesque engraving. Made from 1963 to date. *Note:* This combination gun is similar in appearance to the same model shotgun.

Krieghoff Ulm Over/Under Shotgun **$7395**

Same general specifications as Teck model, except has sidelocks with leaf arabesque engraving. Made 1958 to date.

Krieghoff ULM-P Live Pigeon Gun

Sidelock. Gauge: 12. 28- and 30-inch bbls. Chokes: F/IM. Weight: 8 lbs. Oil-finished, fancy English walnut stock w/semibeavertail forearm. Light scrollwork engraving. Tapered, vent rib. Made from 1983 to date.

Bavaria	**$12,500**
Standard	9250

**Krieghoff ULM
Over/Under**

Krieghoff Ulm-Primus Over/Under **$8295**

Deluxe version of Ulm model; detachable sidelocks, higher grade engraving and fancier wood. Made 1958 to date.

Krieghoff Ulm-Primus O/U Rifle-Shotgun **$9255**

Deluxe version of Ulm model; has detachable sidelocks, higher grade engraving and fancier wood. Made 1963 to date. *Note:* This combination gun is similar in appearance to the same model shotgun.

SHOTGUNS

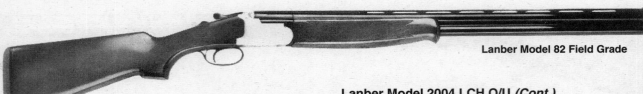

Lanber Model 82 Field Grade

Krieghoff ULM-S Skeet Gun
Sidelock. Gauge: 12. Bbl.: 28-inch. Chokes: skeet/skeet. Other specifications similar to the Model ULM-P. Made 1983-86.
Bavaria **$7595**
Standard **5995**

Krieghoff ULM-T O/U Live Trap Gun
Over/under sidelock. Gauge: 12. 30-inch bbl. Tapered vent rib. Chokes: IM/F; optional screw-in choke. Custom grade versions command a higher price. Discontinued 1986.
Bavaria **$7350**
Standard **5895**

Krieghoff Ultra O/U Rifle-Shotgun
Deluxe Over/Under combination with 25-inch vent-rib bbls. Chambered 12 ga. only and various rifle calibers for lower bbl. Kickspanner design permits cocking with thumb safety. Satin receiver. Weight: 6 lbs. Made from 1985 to date.
Ultra O/U Combination **$2595**
Ultra B w/Selective Front Trigger **2795**

LANBER SHOTGUNS
Spain

Lanber Model 82 O/U Shotgun **$425**
Boxlock. Gauge: 12 or 20; 3-inch chambers. 26- or 28-inch vent-rib bbls. with ejectors and fixed chokes. Weight: 7 lbs. 2 oz. Double or single-selective trigger. Engraved silvered receiver. Checkered European walnut stock and forearm. Imported 1994.

Lanber Model 844 MST Magnum O/U **$350**
Field grade. Gauge: 12. 3-inch Mag. chambers. 30-inch flat vent-rib bbls. Chokes: M/F. Weight: 7 lbs. 7 oz. Single selective trigger. Blued bbls. and engraved receiver. European walnut stock with hand-checkered pistol grip and forend. Made 1984-86.

Lanber Model 2004 LCH O/U **$525**
Field grade. Gauge: 12. 2.75-inch chambers. 28-inch flat vent-rib bbls. 5 interchangeable choke tubes: Cyl, IC, M, IM, F.

Lanber Model 2004 LCH O/U *(Cont.)*
Weight: about 7 lbs. Single selective trigger. Engraved silver receiver with fine-line scroll. Walnut stock with checkered pistol grip and forend. Rubber recoil pad. Imported 1984-86.

Lanber 2008 LCH O/U Skeet **$630**
Same as Model 2004 LCH except 28-inch bbls. w/5 interchangeable choke tubes. Imported 1984-86.

Lanber Model 2009 LCH O/U Skeet **$675**
Gauge: 12. 30-inch vent-rib bbls. 3 interchangeable choke tubes: M, IM, F. Manual safety. Other specifications same as Model 2008 LCH Skeet. Imported 1984-86.

CHARLES LANCASTER
London, England

Lancaster "Twelve-Twenty" Double-Barrel Shotgun **$12,250**
Sidelock, self-opener. Gauge: 12. Bbls.: 24 to 30 inches standard. Weight: about 5.75 lbs. Elaborate metal engraving. Highest quality English or French walnut buttstock and forearm. Imported by Stoeger in the 1950s.

JOSEPH LANG & SONS
London, England

Highest Quality Over/Under Shotgun **$14,600**
Sidelock. Gauges: 12, 16, 20, 28 and .410. Bbls.: 25 to 30 inches standard. Highest grade English or French walnut buttstock and forearm. Selective single trigger. Imported by Stoeger in 1950s.

LAURONA SHOTGUNS
Spain

Laurona Grand Trap Combo
Same general specifications as Model 300, except supplied with 29-inch over/under bbls., screw-in choke tubes and 34-inch single barrel. Discontinued 1992.
Model GTO (top single) **$1695**
Model GTU (bottom single) **1695**
Extra Field O/U bbls. (12 or 20 ga.), **add** **560**

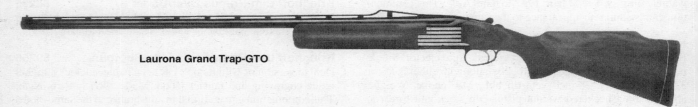

Laurona Grand Trap-GTO

Laurona Silhouette 300 Over/Under
Boxlock. Single selective trigger. Selective automatic ejectors. Gauge: 12; 2.75-, 3- or 3.5-inch chambers. 28- or 29-inch vent-rib bbls. with flush or knurled choke tubes. Weight: 7.75 to 8 lbs. Checkered pistol-grip European walnut stock and beavertail forend. Engraved receiver with silvered finish and black chrome bbls. Made 1988-1992.

Model 300 Sporting Clays	$ 995
Model 300 Trap	1025
Model 300 Trap, Single	1095
Model 300 Ultra-Magnum	975

Laurona Super Model Over/Under Shotguns
Boxlock. Single selective or twin single triggers. Selective automatic ejectors. Gauges: 12 or 20; 2.75- or 3-inch chambers. 26-, 28- or 29-inch vent-rib bbls. with fixed chokes or screw-in choke tubes. Weight: 7 to 7.25 lbs. Checkered pistol-grip European walnut stock. Engraved receiver with silvered finish and black chrome bbls. Made from 1985 to date.

Model 82 super Game (discontinued)	$ 825
Model 83 MG Super Game	925
Model 84 S Super Trap	1025
Model 85 MG Super Game	935
Model 85 MG 2-Bbl. Set	1325
Model 85 MS Special Sporting (discontinued)	995
Model 85 MS Super Trap	1025
Model 85 MS Pigeon	995
Model 85 S Super Skeet	995

LEBEAU-COURALLY SHOTGUNS
Belgium

Lebeau-Courally Boxlock Side-by-Side
Shotguns ... $9550
Gauges: 12, 16, 20 and 28. 26- to 30-inch bbls. Weight: 6.5 lbs. average. Checkered, hand-rubbed, oil-finished, straight-grip stock of French walnut. Classic forend. Made from 1986 to date.

LEFEVER ARMS COMPANY
Syracuse and Ithaca, N.Y.

Lefever sidelock hammerless double-barrel shotguns were made by Lefever Arms Company of Syracuse, New York, from about 1885-1915 (serial numbers 1 to 70,000) when the firm was sold to Ithaca Gun Company of Ithaca, New York. Production of these models was continued at the Ithaca plant until 1919 (serial numbers 70,001 to 72,000). Grades listed are those that appear in the last catalog of the Lefever Gun Company, Syracuse. In 1921, Ithaca introduced the boxlock Lefever Nitro Special double, followed in 1934 by the Lefever Grade A; there also were two single barrel Lefevers made from 1927-1942. Manufacture of Lefever brand shotguns was discontinued in 1948. *Note:* "New Lefever" boxlock shotguns made circa 1904-1906 by D. M. Lefever Company, Bowling Green, Ohio, are included in a separate listing.

Lefever A Grade Hammerless Double-Barrel Shotgun
Boxlock. Plain extractors or auto ejector. Single or double triggers. Gauges: 12, 16, 20, .410. Bbls.: 26-32 inches, standard chokes. Weight: about 7 lbs. in 12 ga. Checkered pistol-grip stock and forearm. Made 1934-1942.

Lefever A Grade Boxlock

Lefever A Grade Hammerless (Cont.)
With Plain Extractors, Double Triggers	$750
Extra for Automatic Ejector	100
Extra for Single Trigger	100
Extra for Beavertail Forearm	75

Lefever A Grade Skeet Model ... $1095
Same as A Grade, except standard features include auto ejector, single trigger, beavertail forearm; 26-inch bbls., skeet boring. Discontinued 1942.

Lefever Single-Shot Trap

Lefever Hammerless Single-Shot Trap Gun $455
Boxlock. Ejector. 12 ga. only. 30- or 32-inch bbl.; vent rib. Weight: about 8 lbs. Checkered pistol-grip stock and forend, recoil pad. Made 1927-1942.

Lefever Long Range Hammerless Single-Barrel Field Gun ... $275
Boxlock. Plain extractor. Gauges: 12, 16, 20, .410. Bbl. lengths: 26-32 inches. Weight: 5.5 to 7 lbs. depending on ga. and bbl. length. Checkered pistol-grip stock and forend. Made 1927-1942.

Lefever Nitro Special Hammerless Double
Boxlock. Plain extractors. Single or double triggers. Gauges: 12, 16, 20, .410. Bbls.: 26- to 32-inch, standard chokes. Weight: about 7 lbs. in 12 ga. Checkered pistol-grip stock and forend. Made 1921-1948.
With Double Triggers	$475
With Single Trigger	595

Lefever Sidelock Hammerless Doubles
Plain extractors or auto ejectors. Double triggers or selective single trigger. Gauges: 10, 12, 16, 20. Bbls.: 26-32 inches; standard choke combinations. Weight: 5.75 to 10.5 lbs. depending on ga. and bbl. length. Checkered walnut straight-grip or pistol-grip stock and forearm. Grades differ chiefly in quality of workmanship, engraving, wood, checkering, etc.; general specifications are the same. DS and DSE Grade guns lack the cocking indicators found on all other models. Suffix "E" means model has auto ejector; also standard on A, AA, Optimus, and Thousand Dollar Grade guns.
H Grade	$ 1295
HE Grade	1855
G Grade	1595
GE Grade	2150

SHOTGUNS

Lefever DE Grade

Left Sideplate of Lefever CE Grade

F Grade	$ 1,690
FE Grade	2,425
E Grade	2,290
EE Grade	3,395
D Grade	2,495
DE Grade	3,955
DS Grade	1055
DSE Grade	1,295
C Grade	4,150
CE Grade	6,995
B Grade	4,950
BE Grade	8,395
A Grade	16,000
AA Grade	22,000
Optimus Grade	28,500
Thousand Dollar Grade	42,500
Extra for single trigger	650

**Left Sideplate
Lefever BE Grade**

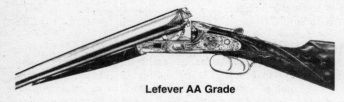

Lefever AA Grade

Lefever Optimus Grade

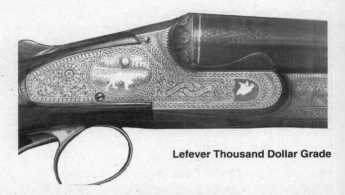

Lefever Thousand Dollar Grade

D. M. LEFEVER COMPANY
Bowling Green, Ohio

In 1901, D. M. "Uncle Dan" Lefever, founder of the Lefever Arms Company, withdrew from that firm to organize D. M. Lefever, Sons & Company (later D. M. Lefever Company) to manufacture the "New Lefever" boxlock double- and single-barrel shotguns. These were produced at Bowling Green, Ohio, from about 1904-1906, when Dan Lefever died and the factory closed permanently. Grades listed are those that appear in the last catalog of D. M. Lefever Co.

D. M. Lefever Hammerless Double-Barrel Shotguns

"New Lefever." Boxlock. Auto ejector standard on all grades except O Excelsior, which was regularly supplied with plain extractors (auto ejector offered as an extra). Double triggers or selective single trigger (latter standard on Uncle Dan Grade, extra on all others). Gauges: 12, 16, 20. Bbls.: any length and choke combination. Weight: 5.5 to 8 lbs. depending on ga. and bbl. length. Checkered walnut straight-grip or pistol-grip stock and forearm. Grades differ chiefly in quality of workmanship, engraving, wood, checkering, etc.; general specifications are the same.

O Excelsior Grade with plain extractors	$ 2,550
O Excelsior Grade with automatic ejectors	2,895
No. 9, F Grade	3,595
No. 8, E Grade	4,375
No. 6, C Grade	5,195
No. 5, B Grade	6,895
No. 4, AA Grade	10,000
Uncle Dan Grade	15,000
Extra for single trigger	400

D. M. Lefever Single-Barrel Trap Gun $4995

Boxlock. Auto ejector. 12 ga. only. Bbls.: 26- to 32 inches, F choke. Weight: 6.5 to 8 lbs., depending on bbl. length. Checkered walnut pistol-grip stock and forearm.

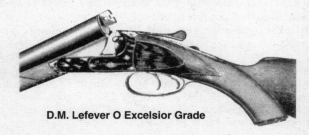

D.M. Lefever O Excelsior Grade

Magtech Model 586.2 VR w/Vent Rib

MAGTECH SHOTGUNS
San Antonio, Texas
Mfd. By CBC in Brazil

Magtech Model 586.2 Slide-Action Shotgun
Gauge: 12; 3-inch chamber. 19-, 26- or 28-inch bbl.; fixed chokes or integral tubes. 46.5 inches overall. Weight: 8.5 lbs. Double-action slide bars. Brazilian hardwood stock. Polished blued finish. Imported 1992 to date.

Model 586.2 F (28-inch Bbl., Fixed Choke)	$165
Model 586.2 P (19-inch Plain Bbl., Cyl. Bore)	175
Model 586.2 S (24-inch Bbbl., Rifle Sights, Cyl. Bore	170
Model 586.2 VR (Vent Rib w/Tubes)	190

MARLIN FIREARMS CO.
North Haven (formerly New Haven), Conn.

Marlin Model 16 Visible Hammer Slide-Action Repeater
Takedown. 16 ga. 5-shell tubular magazine. Bbls.: 26- or 28-inch, standard chokes. Weight: about 6.25 lbs. Pistol-grip stock, grooved slide handle; checkering on higher grades. Difference among grades is in quality of wood, engraving on Grades C and D. Made 1904-10.

Grade A	$325
Grade B	425
Grade C	535
Grade D	1095

Marlin Model 17 Brush Gun $295
Same as Model 17 Standard, except has 26-inch bbl., cylinder bore. Weight: about 7 lbs. Made 1906-08.

Marlin Model 17 Riot Gun $305
Same as Model 17 Standard, except has 20-inch bbl., cylinder bore. Weight: about 6.88 lbs. Made 1906-08.

Marlin Model 17 Standard Visible Hammer Slide-Action Repeater $295
Solid frame. 12 ga. 5-shot tubular magazine. Bbls.: 30- or 32-inch, F choke. Weight: about 7.5 lbs. Straight-grip stock, grooved slide handle. Made 1906-08.

Marlin Model 19 Visible Hammer Slide-Action Repeater
Similar to Model 1898, but improved, lighter weight, with two extractors, matted sighting groove on receiver top. Weight: about 7 lbs. Made 1906-07.

Grade A	$ 285
Grade B	405
Grade C	535
Grade D	1125

Marlin Model 21 Trap Visible Hammer Slide-Action Repeater
Similar to Model 19 with same general specifications, except has straight-grip stock. Made 1907-09.

Grade A	$ 295
Grade B	435
Grade C	550
Grade D	1125

Marlin Model 24 Visible Hammer Slide-Action Repeater
Similar to Model 19, but has improved takedown system and auto recoil safety lock, solid matted rib on frame. Weight: about 7.5 lbs. Made 1908-15.

Grade A	$ 305
Grade B	455
Grade C	565
Grade D	1160

Marlin Model 26 Brush Gun $245
Same as Model 26 Standard, except has 26-inch bbl., cylinder bore. Weight: about 7 lbs. Made 1909-15.

Marlin Model 26 Riot Gun $215
Same as Model 26 Standard, except has 20-inch bbl., cylinder bore. Weight: about 6.88 lbs. Made 1909-15.

Marlin Model 26 Standard Visible Hammer Slide-Action Repeater $235
Similar to Model 24 Grade A, except solid frame and straight-grip stock. 30- or 32-inch full choke bbl. Weight: about 7.13 lbs. Made from 1909-15.

Marlin Model 28 Hammerless Slide-Action Repeater
Takedown. 12 ga. 5-shot tubular magazine. Bbls.: 26-, 28-, 30-, 32-inch, standard chokes; matted-top bbl. except on Model 28D

Marlin Model 17 Standard

SHOTGUNS

Marlin Model 28B

Marlin Model 30 Grade D

Marlin Model 28 Hammerless Slide-Action *(Cont.)*

which has solid matted rib. Weight: about 8 lbs. Pistol-grip stock, grooved slide handle; checkering on higher grades. Grades differ in quality of wood, engraving on Models 28C and 28D. Made 1913-22; all but Model 28A discont. in 1915.

Model 28A	$ 295
Model 28B	425
Model 28C	550
Model 28D	1195

Marlin Model 28T Trap Gun $535

Same as Model 28, except has 30-inch matted-rib bbl., F choke, straight-grip stock with high-fluted comb of fancy walnut, checkered. Made in 1915.

Marlin Model 28TS Trap Gun $295

Same as Model 28T, except has matted-top bbl., plainer stock. Made in 1915.

Marlin Model 30 Field Gun $285

Same as Model 30 Grade B, except has 25-inch bbl., M choke, straight-grip stock. Made 1913-14.

Marlin Model 30 Visible Hammer Slide-Action Repeater

Similar to Model 16, but with Model 24 improvements. Made 1910-14.

Grade A	$ 295
Grade B	425
Grade C	545
Grade D	1210

Marlin Models 30A, 30B, 30C, 30D

Same as Model 30; designations were changed in 1915. Also available in 20 ga. with 25- or 28-inch bbl., matted-top bbl. on all grades. Suffixes "A," "B," "C" and "D" correspond to former grades. Made in 1915.

Model 30A	$ 320
Model 30B	400
Model 30C	595
Model 30D	1075

Marlin Model 31 Hammerless Slide-Action Repeater

Similar to Model 28, except scaled down for 16 and 20 ga. Bbls.: 25-inch (20 ga. only), 26-inch (16 ga. only), 28-inch, all with matted top, standard chokes. Weight: 16 ga., about 6.75 lbs.; 20 ga., about 6 lbs. Pistol-grip stock, grooved slide handle; checkering on higher grades; straight-grip stock optional on Model 31D. Made 1915-1917; Model 31A until 1922.

Model 31A	$ 315
Model 31B	425
Model 31C	550
Model 31D	1200

Marlin Model 31F Field Gun $400

Same as Model 31B, except has 25-inch bbl., M choke, straight- or pistol-grip stock. Made 1915-17.

Marlin Model 42A Visible Hammer Slide-Action Repeater $245

Similar to pre-World War I Model 24 Grade A with same general specifications, but not of as high quality. Made from 1922-34.

Marlin Model 43 Hammerless Slide-Action Repeater

Similar to pre-World War I Models 28A, 28T and 28TS, with same general specifications, but not of as high quality. Made 1923-30.

Model 43A	$250
Model 43T	500
Model 43TS	525

Marlin Model 43A

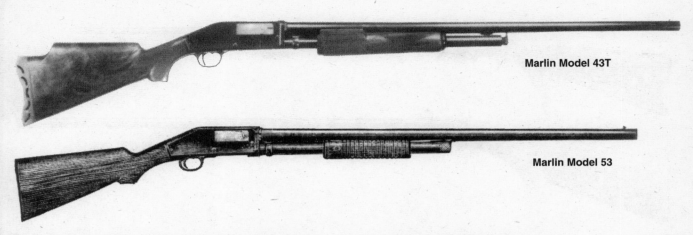

Marlin Model 43T

Marlin Model 53

Marlin Model 44 Hammerless Slide-Action Repeater
Similar to pre-World War I Model 31A, with same general specifications, but not of as high quality. 20 ga. only. Model 44A is a standard grade field gun. Model 44S Special Grade has checkered stock and slide handle of fancy walnut. Made 1923-35.
Model 44A **$300**
Model 44S **415**

Marlin Model 49 Visible Hammer Slide-Action Repeating Shotgun **$375**
Economy version of Model 42A, offered as a bonus on the purchase of four shares of Marlin stock. About 3000 were made 1925-28.

Marlin Model 53 Hammerless Slide-Action Repeater **$305**
Similar to Model 43A, with same general specifications. Made 1929-30.

Marlin Model 55 Goose Gun **$175**
Same as Model 55 Hunter, except chambered for 12-ga. 3-inch Magnum shell, has 36-inch bbl., F choke, swivels and sling. Weight: about 8 lbs. Made 1962 to date.

Marlin Model 55 Hunter Bolt-Action Repeater
Takedown. Gauges: 12, 16, 20. 2-shot clip magazine. 28-inch bbl. (26-inch in 20 ga.), F or adj. choke. Plain pistol-grip stock; 12 ga. has recoil pad. Weight: about 7.25 lbs.; 20 ga., 6.5 lbs. Made 1954-65.
With plain barrel . . . . **$ 95**
With adjustable choke **115**

Marlin Model 55 Swamp Gun **$100**
Same as Model 55 Hunter except chambered for 12-ga. 3-inch Magnum shell, has shorter 20.5-inch bbl. with adj. choke, sling swivels and slightly better-quality stock. Weight: about 6.5 lbs. Made 1963-65.

SHOTGUNS

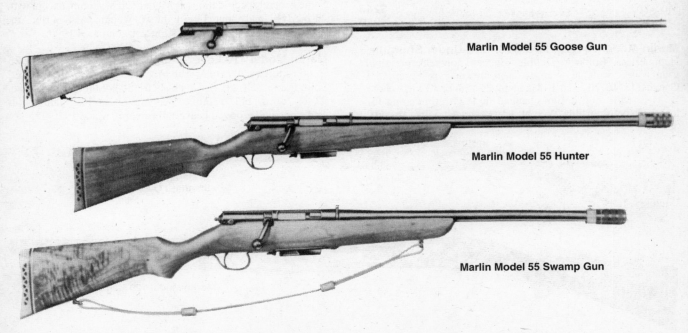

Marlin Model 55 Goose Gun

Marlin Model 55 Hunter

Marlin Model 55 Swamp Gun

Marlin Model 59

Marlin Model 60

Marlin Model 55S Slug Gun $135
Same as Model 55 Goose Gun, except has 24-inch bbl., cylinder bore, rifle sights. Weight: about 7.5 lbs. Made 1974-79.

Marlin Model 59 Auto-Safe Bolt-Action Single ... $85
Takedown. Auto thumb safety, .410 ga. 24-inch bbl., F choke. Weight: about 5 lbs. Plain pistol-grip stock. Made 1959-61.

Marlin Model 60 Single-Shot Shotgun $190
Visible hammer. Takedown. Boxlock. Automatic ejector. 12 ga. 30- or 32-inch bbl., F choke. Weight: about 6.5 lbs. Pistol-grip stock, beavertail forearm. *Note:* Only about 600 were produced in 1923.

Marlin Model 63 Hammerless Slide-Action Repeater
Similar to Models 43A and 43T with same general specifications. Model 63TS Trap Special is same as Model 63T Trap Gun except stock style and dimensions to order. Made 1931-35.
Model 63A $245
Model 63T or 63TS 350

Marlin Model 90 Standard Over-and-Under Shotgun
Hammerless. Boxlock. Double triggers; non-selective single trigger was available as an extra on prewar guns except .410. Gauges: 12, 16, 20, .410. Bbls.: plain; 26-, 28- or 30-inch; chokes IC/M or M/F; bbl. design changed in 1949, eliminating full-length rib between bbls. Weight: 12 ga., about 7.5 lbs.; 16 and 20

Marlin Model 90 *(Cont.)*
ga., about 6.25 lbs. Checkered pistol-grip stock and forearm, recoil pad standard on prewar guns. Postwar production: Model 90-DT (double trigger), Model 90-ST (single trigger). Made 1937-58.
With double triggers $395
With single trigger 495

Marlin Model 120 Magnum Slide-Action Repeater $235
Hammerless. Takedown. 12 ga. (3-inch). 4-shot tubular magazine. Bbls.: 26-inch vent rib, IC; 28-inch vent rib M choke; 30-inch vent rib, F choke; 38-inch plain, F choke; 40-inch plain, F choke; 26-inch slug bbl. with rifle sights, IC. Weight: about 7.75 lbs. Checkered pistol-grip stock and forearm, recoil pad. Made 1971-85.

Marlin Model 120 Slug Gun $215
Same general specifications as Model 120 Magnum, except with 20-inch bbl. and about .5 lbs. lighter in weight. No vent rib. Adj. rear rifle sights; hooded front sight. Discontinued 1990.

Marlin Model 410 Lever-Action Repeater $625
Action similar to that of Marlin Model 93 rifle. Visible hammer. Solid frame. .410 ga. (2.5-inch shell). 5-shot tubular magazine. 22- or 26-inch bbl., F choke. Weight: about 6 lbs. Plain pistol-grip stock and grooved beavertail forearm. Made 1929-32.

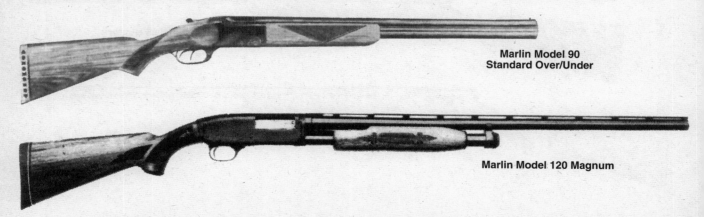

Marlin Model 90
Standard Over/Under

Marlin Model 120 Magnum

Marlin Model 410

Marlin Model 512 Slugmaster

Marlin Model 55-10
Super Goose 10

Marlin Model 512 Slugmaster Shotgun $225
Bolt-action repeater. Gauge: 12; 3-inch chamber, 2-shot magazine. 21-inch rifled bbl. w/adj. open sight. Weight: 8 lbs. Walnut-finished birch stock. Made 1994 to date.

Marlin Model 1898 Visible Hammer Slide-Action Repeater
Takedown. 12 ga. 5-shell tubular magazine. Bbls.: 26-, 28-, 30-, 32-inch; standard chokes. Weight: about 7.25 lbs. Pistol-grip stock, grooved slide handle; checkering on higher grades. Difference among grades is in quality of wood, engraving on Grades C and D. Made 1898-05. *Note:* This was the first Marlin shotgun.

Grade A (Field)	$ 300
Grade B	505
Grade C	695
Grade D	1650

Marlin Model 55-10 Super Goose 10 .... $175
Similar to Model 55 Goose Gun, except chambered for 10 ga. 3.5-inch Magnum shell, has 34-inch heavy bbl., F choke. Weight: about 10.5 lbs. Made 1976-85.

Marlin Premier Mark I Slide-Action Repeater ... $175
Hammerless. Takedown. 12 ga. Magazine holds 3 shells. Bbls.: 30-inch F choke, 28-inch M, 26-inch IC or SK choke. Weight: about 6 lbs. Plain pistol-grip stock and forearm. Made in France 1960-63.

Marlin Premier Mark II and IV
Same action and mechanism as Premier Mark I, except engraved receiver (Mark IV is more elaborate), checkered stock and forearm, fancier wood, ventilated rib and similar refinements. Made 1960-63.

Premier Mark II	$205
Premier Mark IV (plain barrel)	275
Premier Mark IV (vent-rib barrel)	325

SHOTGUNS

Marlin Premier Mark I

Marlin Premier Mark IV

Marlin-Glenfield Model 50

Marlin-Glenfield Model 50 Bolt-Action Repeater . . $65

Similar to Model 55 Hunter, except chambered for 12-or 20-ga., 3-inch Magnum shell; has 28-inch bbl. in 12 ga., 26-inch in 20 ga., F choke. Made 1966-74.

Marlin-Glenfield 778 Slide-Action Repeater

Hammerless. 12 ga. 2.75-inch or 3-inch. 4-shot tubular magazine. Bbls.: 26-inch IC, 28-inch M, 30-inch F, 38-inch MXR, 20-inch slug bbl. Weight: 7.75 lbs. Checkered pistol grip. Made from 1979-84.

With plain barrel **$140**

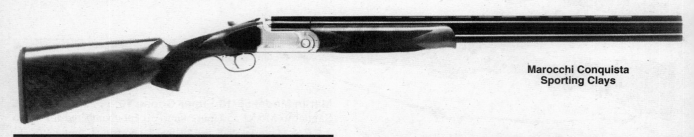

**Marocchi Conquista
Sporting Clays**

MAROCCHI SHOTGUNS
Brescia, Italy
Imported by Precision Sales International of Westfield, MA

Marocchi Conquista Model O/U Shotgun

Boxlock. Gauge: 12; 2.75-inch chambers. 28-, 30- or 32-inch vent-rib bbl. Fixed choke or internal tubes. 44.38 to 48 inches overall. Weight: 7.5 to 8.25 lbs. Adj. single-selective trigger. Checkered American walnut stock w/recoil pad. Imported since 1994.

Lady Sport Garde I	**$1295**
Lady Sport Grade II	1495
Lady Sport Grade III	2295
Skeet Model Grade I	1235
Skeet Model Grade II	1550
Skeet Model Grade III	2350
Sporting Clays Grade I	1245
Sporting Clays Grade II	1465
Sporting Clays Grade III	2250
Trap Model Grade I	1295
Trap Model Grade II	1560
Trap Model Grade III	2395
Left-Handed Model, **add**	100

MAVERICK ARMS, INC.
Eagle Pass, Texas

Maverick Model 60 Autoloading Shotgun

Gauge: 12, 2.75- or 3-inch chamber. 5-round capacity. Bbls.: Magnum or non-Magnum; 24- or 28-inch with fixed choke or screw-in tubes, plain or vent rib; blued. Weight: 7.25 lbs. Black synthetic buttstock and forend. Made from 1993 to date.

Standard Model	**$160**
Combo Model w/extra 18.5" bbl.	205
Turkey/Deer Model (w/Ghost Ring sights)	225

Maverick Model 88 Bullpup **$225**

Gauge: 12; 3-inch chamber. Bbl.: 18.5-inch w/fixed choke, blued. Weight: 9.5 lbs. Dual safeties: grip style and crossbolt. Fixed sights in carrying handle. High-impact black synthetic stock; trigger-forward bullpup configuration with twin pistol-grip design. Made from 1991 to date.

Maverick Model 88 Pump Shotgun

Gauge: 12; 2.75- or 3-inch chamber. Bbl.: 28 inches/M or 30 inches/F w/fixed choke or screw-in integral tubes; plain or vent rib, blued. Weight: 7.25 lbs. Bead front sight. Black syn-

**Maverick Model 60
Turkey/Deer Combo**

**Maverick Model 88 Pump
Vent Rib**

Maverick Model 88 Pump Shotgun *(Cont.)*

thetic or wood buttstock and forend; forend grooved. Made from 1989 to date.

Synthetic stock w/plain bbl.	**$150**
Synthetic stock w/vent-rib bbl.	**160**
Synthetic Combo w/18.5" bbl.	**180**
Wood stock w/vent-rib bbl./tubes	**175**
Wood Combo w/vent-rib bbl./tubes	**215**

Maverick Model 91 Pump Shotgun

Same as Model 88, except with 2.75-, 3- or 3.5-inch chamber, 28-inch bbl. W/ACCU-F choke, crossbolt safety and synthetic stock only.

Synthetic stock w/plain bbl.	**$185**
Synthetic stock w/vent-rib bbl.	**210**

Maverick Model HS410 Pump Shotgun

Similar to the Model 88, except in .410 bore with 3-inch chamber. Blued 18.5-inch bbl. with muzzle brake. Weight: 6.25 lbs. Optional laser sight. Synthetic stock. Made from 1993 to date. A similar gun is marketed by Mossberg under the same model designation.

Standard Model	**$175**
Laser Model	**290**

GEBRÜDER MERKEL
Suhl, Germany

Merkel Model 8 Hammerless Double **$895**

Anson & Deeley boxlock action with Greener double-bbl. hook lock. Double triggers. Extractors. Automatic safety. Gauges: 12, 16, 20; 2.75- or 3-inch chambers. 26-or 28-inch bbls. with fixed standard chokes. Checkered European walnut stock, pistol-grip or English-style with or without cheekpiece. Scroll engraved receiver with tinted marble finish.

Merkel Model 47LSC Sporting Clays S/S **$2195**

Anson & Deeley boxlock action w/single-selective adj. trigger, cocking indicators and manual safety. Gauge: 12; 3-inch chambers. 28-inch bbls.w/Briley choke tubes and H&H style ejectors. Weight: 7.25 lbs. Color cashardened receiver w/Arabesque engraving. Checkered select-grade walnut stock, beavertail forearm. Imported 1993-1994.

Merkel Model 47S

Merkel Models 47S, 147S, 247S, 347S, 447S
Hammerless Sidelocks

Same general specifications as Model 147E except has sidelocks engraved with arabesques, borders, scrolls or game scenes in varying degrees of elaborateness.

Model 47S	**$3255**
Model 147S	**4395**
Model 247S	**3995**
Model 347S	**4550**
Model 447S	**4895**

Merkel Model 100 Over-and-Under Shotgun

Hammerless. Boxlock. Greener crossbolt. Plain extractor. Double triggers. Gauges: 12, 16, 20. Made with plain or ribbed bbls. in various lengths and chokes. Plain finish no engraving. Check-

Merkel Model 447S

SHOTGUNS

Merkel Model 100 Over-and-Under Shotgun *(Cont.)*

ered forend and stock with pistol grip and cheekpiece or English style. Made prior to WWII.

With plain bbl. **$1155**
With ribbed bbl. **1195**

Merkel Models 101 and 101E Over/Unders

Same as Model 100, except ribbed bbl. standard, has separate extractors (ejectors on Model 101E), English engraving. Made prior to World War II.

Model 101 . . . . **$1250**
Model 101E **1350**

Merkel Model 147E

Merkel Model 122

Merkel Model 122 Hammerless Double **$2995**
Similar to the Model 147S except with nonremovable sidelocks, in gauges 12, 16 or 20. Imported since 1993.

Merkel Model 122E Hammerless Sidelock **$3195**
Similar to the Model 122 except w/removable sidelocks and cocking indicators. Importation discontinued 1992.

Merkel Model 127 Hammerless Sidelock **$15,750**
Holland & Holland system, hand-detachable locks. Auto ejectors. Double triggers. Made in all standard gauges, bbl. lengths and chokes. Checkered forend and pistol-grip stock; available with cheekpiece or English style buttstock. Elaborate engraving. Made prior to WW II.

Merkel Model 130 Hammerless Boxlock
Double **$8500**
Anson & Deeley system. Sideplates. Auto ejectors. Double triggers. Elaborate hunting scene or arabesque engraving. Made in all standard gauges, various bbl. lengths and chokes. Checkered forend and stock with pistol grip and cheekpiece or English style. Made prior to WW II.

Merkel Model 147E Hammerless Boxlock
Double-Barrel Shotgun **$1595**
Anson & Deeley system. Auto ejectors. Double triggers. Gauges: 12, 16, 20 (3-inch chambers available in 12 and 20 ga.). Bbls.: 26-inch standard, other lengths available; any standard choke combination. Weight: about 6.5 lbs. Checkered straight-grip stock and forearm. Discontinued 1989.

Merkel Models 200, 200E, 201, 201E, 202 and 202E Over-and-Under Shotguns

Hammerless. Boxlock. Kersten double crossbolt. Scalloped frame. Sideplates on Models 202 and 202E. Arabesque or hunting engraving supplied on all except Models 200 and 200E. "E" models have ejectors, others have separate extractors. Signal pins. Double triggers. Gauges: 12, 16, 20, 24, 28, 32 (last three not available in postwar guns). Ribbed bbls. in various lengths and chokes. Weight: 5.75 to 7.5 lbs. depending on bbl. length and gauge. Checkered forend and stock with pistol grip and cheekpiece or English style. The 200, 201, and 202 differ in overall quality, engraving, wood, checkering, etc.; aside from the faux sideplates on Models 202 and 202E, general specifications are the same. Models 200, 201, 202, and 202E, all made before WW II, are discontinued. Model 202E is still in production.

Model 200 . . . . **$1295**
Model 200E **2350**
Model 200 ES Skeet **3695**
Model 200ET Trap **3550**
Model 200 SC Sporting Clays **3955**
Model 201 (Discontinued) **1625**
Model 201E (Pre-WW II) **1895**
Model 201E (post-WW II) **3495**
Model 201 ES Skeet **5595**
Model 201 ET Trap. **5550**
Model 202 (Discontinued) **2495**
Model 202E (Pre-WW II) **2795**
Model 202 E (Post-WW II) **5395**

Merkel Model 200E

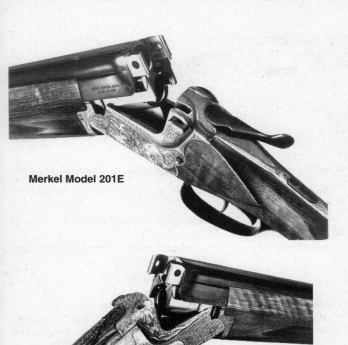

Merkel Model 201E

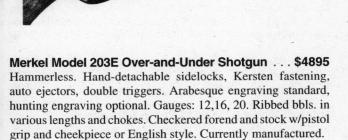

Merkel Model 203E

Merkel Model 303E

Merkel Model 203E Over-and-Under Shotgun . . . $4895

Hammerless. Hand-detachable sidelocks, Kersten fastening, auto ejectors, double triggers. Arabesque engraving standard, hunting engraving optional. Gauges: 12,16, 20. Ribbed bbls. in various lengths and chokes. Checkered forend and stock w/pistol grip and cheekpiece or English style. Currently manufactured.

Merkel Model 204E Over-and-Under Shotgun . . $4500

Similar to Model 203E; has Merkel sidelocks, fine English engraving. Made prior to World War II.

Merkel Models 300, 300E, 301, 301E and 302 O/U

Merkel-Anson system boxlock. Kersten double crossbolt, two underlugs, scalloped frame, sideplates on Model 302. Arabesque or hunting engraving. "E" models and Model 302 have auto ejectors, others have separate extractors. Signal pins. Double triggers. Gauges: 12, 16, 20, 24, 28, 32. Ribbed bbls. in various lengths and chokes. Checkered forend and stock with pistol grip and cheekpiece or English style. Grades 300, 301 and 302 differ in overall quality, engraving, wood, checkering, etc.; aside from the dummy sideplates on Model 302, general specifications are the same. Manufactured prior to World War II.

Model 300	$1850
Model 300E	1995
Model 301	4095
Model 301E	4875
Model 302	6795

Merkel Model 303E Over/Under Shotgun $11,900

Similar to Model 203E. Has Kersten crossbolt, double underlugs, Holland & Holland-type hand-detachable sidelocks, auto ejectors. This is a finer gun than Model 203E. Currently manufactured.

Merkel Model 304E Over/Under Shotgun $14,750

Special version of the Model 303E-type, but higher quality throughout. This is the top grade Merkel over/under. Currently manufactured.

Merkel Models 400, 400E, 401, 401E Over/Unders

Similar to Model 101 except have Kersten double crossbolt, arabesque engraving on Models 400 and 400E, hunting engraving on Models 401 and 401E, finer general quality. "E" models have Merkel ejectors, others have separate extractors. Made prior to World War II.

Model 400	$1295
Model 400E	1425
Model 401	1450
Model 401E	1725

Merkel Over-and-Under Combination Guns ("Bock-Büchsflinten")

Shotgun bbl. over, rifle bbl. under. Gauges: 12,16, 20; calibers: 5.6×35 Vierling, 7×57r5, 8×57JR, 8X60R Magnum, 9.3×53r5, 9.3×72r5, 9.3×74R and others. Various bbl. lengths, chokes and weights. Other specifications and values correspond to those of Merkel over/under shotguns listed below. Currently manufactured. Model 210 & 211 series discontinued 1992.

Models 410, 410E, 411E . . . . . . *see* shotgun Models 400, 400E, 401, 401E respectively

Models 210, 210E, 211, 211E, 212, 212E . . . . . *see* shotgun Models 200, 200E, 201, 201E, 202, 202E

SHOTGUNS

NOTE

Merkel over/under guns were often supplied with accessory barrels, interchangeable to convert the gun into an arm of another type; for example, a set might consist of one pair each of shotgun, rifle and combination gun barrels. Each pair of interchangeable barrels has a value of approximately one-third that of the gun with which they are supplied.

Miida Model 612

Merkel Anson Drillings

Three-bbl. combination guns; usually made with double shotgun bbls., over rifle bbl., although "Doppelbüchsdrillingen" were made with two rifle bbls. over and shotgun bbl. under. Hammerless. Boxlock. Anson & Deeley system. Side clips. Plain extractors. Double triggers. Gauges: 12, 16, 20; rifle calibers: 7×57r5, 8×57JR and 9.3×74R are most common, but other calibers from 5.6mm to 10.75mm available. Bbls.: standard drilling 25.6 inches; short drilling, 21.6 inches. Checkered pistol-grip stock and forend. The three models listed differ chiefly in overall quality, grade of wood, etc.; general specifications are the same. Made prior to WW II.

Model 144 . . . . **$7000**
Model 142 . . . . **4500**
Model 145 . . . . **3500**

MIIDA SHOTGUNS
Manufactured for Marubeni America Corp., New York, N.Y., by Olin-Kodensha Co., Tochigi, Japan

Miida Model 612 Field Grade Over-and-Under . . **$780**

Boxlock. Auto ejectors. Selective single trigger. 12 ga. Bbls.: vent rib; 26-inch, IC/M; 28-inch, M/F choke. Weight: with 26-inch bbl., 6 lbs.11 oz. Checkered pistol-grip stock and forearm. Made 1972-74.

Miida Model 2100 Skeet Gun **$850**

Similar to Model 612, except has more elaborate engraving on frame (50 percent coverage), skeet-style stock and forearm of select grade wood; 27-inch vent-rib bbls., SK choke. Weight: 7 lbs. 11 oz. Made 1972-74.

Miida Model 2200T Trap Gun, Model 2200S Skeet Gun **$895**

Similar to Model 612, except more elaborate engraving on frame (60 percent coverage), trap- or skeet-style stock and semibeavertail forearm of fancy walnut, recoil pad on trap stock. Bbls.: wide vent rib; 29.75-inch, IM/F choke on Trap Gun; 27-inch, SK choke on Skeet Gun. Weight: Trap, 7 lbs. 14 oz.; Skeet, 7 lbs. 11 oz. Made 1972-74.

Miida Model 2300T Trap Gun, Model 2300S Skeet Gun **$950**

Same as Models 2200T and 2200S, except more elaborate engraving on frame (70% coverage). Made 1972-74.

Miida Grandee Model GRT/IRS Trap/Skeet Gun . . **$2195**

Boxlock with sideplates. Frame, breech ends of bbls., trigger guard and locking lever fully engraved and gold inlaid. Auto ejectors. Selective single trigger. 12 ga. Bbls.: wide vent rib; 29-

Miida Grandee Model GRT/IRS Trap/Skeet Gun *(Cont.)*

inch, F choke on Trap Gun; 27-inch, SK choke on Skeet Gun. Weight: Trap, 7 lbs. 14 oz.; Skeet, 7 lbs. 11 oz. Trap- or skeet-style stock and semibeavertail forearm of extra fancy wood, recoil pad on trap stock. Made 1972-74.

MITCHELL ARMS
Santa Ana, California

Mitchell Model 9104/9105 Pump Shotguns

Slide action in Field/Riot configuration. Gauge: 12; 5-shot tubular magazine. 20-inch bbl.; fixed choke or screw-in tubes. Weight: 6.5 lbs. Plain walnut stock. Made 1994 to date.

Model 9104 (w/Plain Bbl.) **$185**
Model 9105 (w/Rifle Sight) **195**
With Choke Tubes, **add** **20**

Mitchell Model 9108/9109 Pump Shotgun

Slide action in Military/Police/Riot configuration. Gauge: 12, 7-shot tubular magazine. 20-inch bbl.; fixed choke or screw-in tubes. Weight: 6.5 lbs. Plain walnut stock and grooved slide handle w/brown, green or black finish. Blued metal. Made 1994 to date.

Model 9108 (w/Plain Bbl.) **$190**
Model 9109 (w/Rifle Sights) **205**
With Choke tubes, **add** **20**

Mitchell Model 9111/9113 Pump Shotgun

Slide action in Military/Police/Riot configuration. Gauge: 12; 6-shot tubular magazine. 18.5-inch bbl.; fixed choke or screw-in tubes. Weight: 6.5 lbs. Synthetic or plain walnut stock and grooved slide handle w/brown, green or black finish. Blued metal. Made 1994 to date.

Model 9111 (w/Plain Bbl.) **$185**
Model 9113 (w/Rifle Sights) **205**
With Choke Tubes, **add** **20**

Mitchell Model 9114/9114FS

Slide action in Military/Police/Riot configuration. Gauge: 12; 7-shot tubular magazine. 20-inch bbl.; fixed choke or screw-in tubes. Weight: 6.5-7 lbs. Synthetic pistol-grip or folding stock. Blued metal. Made 1994 to date.

Model 9114 . . . . **$225**
Model 9114FS **250**

Mitchell Model 9115/911FS Pump Shotgun **$250**

Slide action in Military/Police/Riot configuration. Gauge: 12; 6-shot tubular magazine. 18.5-inch bbl. w/heat-shield hand guard; Weight: 7 lbs. Gray synthetic stock and slide handle. Parkerized metal. Made 1994 to date.

Mossberg Model 83D

MONTGOMERY WARD
See shotgun listings under "W"

MORRONE SHOTGUN
**Manufactured by Rhode Island Arms Company
Hope Valley, RI**

Morrone Standard Model 46 Over-and-Under . . . **$725**
Boxlock. Plain extractors. Non-selective single trigger. Gauges: 12, 20. Bbls.: plain, vent rib; 26-inch IC/M; 28-inch M/F choke. Weight: about 7 lbs., 12 ga.; 6 lbs., 20 ga. Checkered straight- or pistol-grip stock and forearm. Made 1949-53. *Note:* Less than 500 of these guns were produced, about 50 in 20 ga., a few had vent-rib bbls. Value shown is for 12 ga. w/plain bbls.; the rare 20 ga. and vent-rib types should bring considerably more.

O. F. MOSSBERG & SONS, INC.
**North Haven, Connecticut
Formerly of New Haven, Conn.**

Mossberg Model 83D or 183D **$100**
3-shot. Takedown. .410-bore only. 2-shell fixed top-loading magazine. 23-inch bbl. w/two interchangeable choke tubes (M/F). Later production had 24-inch bbl. Plain one-piece pistol-grip stock. Weight: about 5.5 lbs. Originally designated Model 83D, changed in 1947 to Model 183D. Made 1940-1971.

**Mossberg Model 85D or 185D Bolt-Action
Repeating Shotgun** **$85**
Takedown. 3-shot. 20 ga. only. 2-shell detachable box magazine. 25-inch bbl., three interchangeable choke tubes (F, M, IC). Later production had 26-inch bbl. with F/IC choke tubes. Weight: about 6.25 lbs. Plain one-piece, pistol-grip stock. Originally designated Model 85D changed in 1947 to Model 185D. Made 1940-71.

Mossberg Model 183K **$95**
Same as Model 183D, except has 25-inch bbl. w/variable C-Lect-Choke instead of interchangeable choke tubes. Made 1953-86.

Mossberg Model 185K **$100**
Same as Model 185D, except has variable C-Lect-Choke instead of interchangeable choke tubes. Made 1950-63.

Mossberg Model 190D **$95**
Same as Model 185D, except in 16 ga. Weight: about 6 lbs. Made 1955-71.

Mossberg Model 850

Mossberg Model 183K

Mossberg Model 185K

Mossberg Model 190D

Mossberg Model 195D

Mossberg Model 190K $105
Takedown. 3-shot; 2-shell magazine and one shell in chamber.
Same as Model 185K, except in 16 ga. Weight: about 6.75 lbs.
Made 1956-63.

Mossberg Model 195D $110
Takedown. 3-shot; 2-shell magazine and one shell in chamber.
Same as Model 185D, except in 12 ga. Weight: about 6.75 lbs.
Made 1955-71.

Mossberg Model 195K $105
Takedown. 3-shot; 2-shell magazine and one shell in chamber.
Same as Model 185K, except in 12 ga. Weight: about 7.5 lbs.
Made 1956-63.

Mossberg Model 200D $115
Same as Model 200K, except w/two interchangeable choke
tubes instead of C-Lect-Choke. Made 1955-59.

Mossberg Model 200K Slide-Action Repeater . . $115
12 ga. 3-shot detachable box magazine. 28-inch bbl. C-Lect-
Choke. Plain pistol-grip stock. Black nylon slide handle.
Weight: about 7.5 lbs. Made 1955-59.

Mossberg Model 385K $100
Same as Model 395K, except 20 ga. (3-inch), 26-inch bbl. w/C-
Lect-Choke. Weight: about 6.25 lbs.

Mossberg Model 390K $115
Same as Model 395K, except 16 ga. (2.75-inch). Made 1963-74.

Mossberg Model 395K Bolt-Action Repeater . . . $100
Takedown. 3-shot (detachable-clip magazine holds two
shells).12 ga. (3-inch chamber). 28-inch bbl. w/C-Lect-Choke.
Weight: about 7.5 lbs. Monte Carlo stock with recoil pad. Made
1963-83.

Mossberg Model 395S Slugster $130
Same as Model 395K, except has 24-inch bbl., cylinder bore, rifle sights, swivels and web sling. Weight: about 7 lbs. Made
1968-81.

Mossberg Model 500 Accu-Choke Shotgun $225
Pump. Gauge: 12. 24- or 28-inch bbl. Weight: 7.25 lbs. Checkered walnut-finished wood stock w/ventilated recoil pad. Available with synthetic field or Speed-feed stocks. Drilled and tapped
receivers, swivels and camo sling on camo models. Made from
1987 to date.

Mossberg Model 500 Bantam Shotgun $185
Same as Model 500 Sporting Pump, except 20 or .410 ga. only.
22-inch w/ACCU-Choke tubes or 24-inch w/F choke; vent rib.
Scaled-down checkered hardwood stock. Made from 1992 to
date.

Mossberg 500 Bullpup

Mossberg Model 500 Bullpup Shotgun $370
Pump. Gauge: 12. 6- or 8-shot capacity. Bbl.: 18.5 to 20 inches.
26.5 and 28.5 inches overall. Weight: about 9.5 lbs. Multiple independent safety systems. Dual pistol grips, rubber recoil pad.
Fully enclosed rifle-type sights. Synthetic stock. Ventilated bbl.
heat shield. Made 1987-90.

Mossberg Model 500 Accu-Choke

Mossberg Model 500 Camo Pump

Mossberg Model 500 Camo Pump

Same as Model 500 Sporting Pump, except 12 ga. only. Receiver drilled and tapped. QD swivels and camo sling. Special camouflage finish.

Standard Model **$195**
Combo Model (w/extra Slugster bbl.) **250**

Mossberg Model 500 Camper

Mossberg Model 500 Camper $200

Same general specifications as Model 500 Field Grade, except .410 bore, 6-shot magazine, 18.5-inch plain Cyl. bore bbl. Synthetic pistol grip and camo carrying case. Made 1986-90.

Mossberg Model 500 Field Grade Hammerless Slide Action Repeater

Pre-1977 type. Takedown. Gauges: 12, 16, 20, .410. 3-inch chamber (2.75-inch in 16 ga.). Tubular magazine holds five 2.75-inch shells or four three-inch. Bbls.: plain- 30-inch regular or heavy Magnum, F choke (12 ga. only); 28-inch, M or F; 26-inch, IC or adj. C-Lect-Choke; 24-inch Slugster, cylinder bore, w/rifle sights. Weight: 5.75 to lbs. Plain pistol-grip stock w/recoil pad grooved slide handle. After 1973, these guns have checkered stock and slide handle, Models 500AM and 500AS have receivers etched with game scenes. The latter has swivels and sling. Made 1962-76.

Model 500A, 12 gauge **$185**
Model 500AM, 12 gauge, heavy Magnum bbl. **200**
Model 500AK, 12 gauge, C-Lect-Choke **225**
Model 500AS, 12 gauge, Slugster **220**
Model 500B 16 gauge **200**
Model 500Bk, 16 gauge, C-Lect-Choke **235**
Model 500BS, 16 gauge, Slugster **225**
Model 500C 20 gauge **200**
Model 500ck, 20 gauge, C-Lect-Choke **240**
Model 500CS, 20 gauge, Slugster **225**
Model 500E, .410 gauge **240**
Model 500EK, .410 gauge, C-Lect-Choke **275**

Mossberg Model 500 "L" Series

"L" in model designation. Same as pre-1977 Model 500 Field Grade, except not available in 16 ga., has receiver etched with different game scenes; Accu-Choke w/three interchangeable tubes (IC, M, F) standard, restyled stock and slide handle. Bbls.: plain or vent rib; 30- or 32-inch, heavy, F choke (12 ga. Magnum and vent rib only); 28-inch, Accu-Choke (12 and 20 ga.); 26-inch F choke (.410 bore only); 18.5-inch (12 ga. only), 24-inch (12 and 20 ga.) Slugster with rifle sights, cylinder bore. Weight: 6 to 8.5 lbs. Intro. 1977.

Model 500ALD, 12 gauge, plain bbl. (Disc. 1980) **$210**
Model 500ALDR, 12 gauge, vent rib **250**
Model 500ALMR, 12 ga., Heavy Duck Gun
  (Disc. 1980) **250**
Model 500ALS, 12 gauge, Slugster (Disc. 1981) **200**
Model 500CLD, 20 gauge, plain bbl. (Disc. 1980) **200**
Model 500CLDR, 20 gauge, vent rib **250**
Model 500CLS, 20 gauge, Slugster (Disc. 1980) **250**
Model 500EL, .410 gauge, plain bbl. (Disc. 1980) **215**
Model 500ELR, .410 gauge, vent rib **250**

Mossberg Model 500 Mariner

Mossberg Model 500 Mariner Shotgun $265

Slide action. Gauge: 12. 18.5 or 20-inch bbl. 6-shot and 8-shot respectively. Weight: 7.25 lbs. High-strength synthetic buttstock and forend. Available in extra round-carrying speedfeed synthetic buttstock. All metal treated for protection against saltwater corrosion. Intro. 1987.

Mossberg Model 500 Muzzleloader Combo $275

Same as Model 500 Sporting Pump, except w/extra 24-inch rifled 50-caliber muzzleloading bbl. w/ram rod. Made from 1992 to date.

Mossberg Model 500 Persuader Law Enforcement Shotgun

Similar to pre-1977 Model 500 Field Grade, except 12 ga. only, 6- or 8-shot, has 18.5- or 20-inch plain bbl., cylinder bore, either shotgun or rifle sights, plain pistol-grip stock and grooved slide handle, sling swivels. Special Model 500ATP8-SP has bayonet lug, Parkerized finish. Currently manufactured.

SHOTGUNS

Mossberg Model 500 Persuader

Mossberg Model 500 Persuader *(Cont.)*

Model 500ATP6, 6-shot, 18.5-inch bbl., shotgun sights . . **$185**
Model 500ATP6CN, 6-shot, nickel finish, "Cruiser"
pistol grip **190**
Model 500ATP6N, 6-shot, nickel finish, 2.75- or 3-inch
Mag. shells **190**
Model 500ATP6S, 6-shot, 18.5" bbl., rifle sights **185**
Model 500ATP8, 8-shot, 20-inch bbl., shotgun sights . . **205**
Model 500ATP8S, 8-shot, 20-inch bbl., rifle sights . . . **215**
Model 500ATP8-SP Special Enforcement **250**
Model 500 Bullpup **375**
Model 500 Security Combo Pack **150**
Model 500 Cruiser with pistol grip **155**

Mossberg Model 500 Pigeon Grade

Same as Model 500 Super Grade, except higher quality w/fancy wood, floating vent rib; field gun hunting dog etching, trap and skeet guns have scroll etching. Bbls.: 30-inch, F choke (12 ga. only); 28-inch, M choke; 26-inch, SK choke or C-Lect-Choke. Made 1971-75.
Model 500APR, 12 ga., Field, Trap or Skeet **$350**
Model 500APKR, 12 gauge, Field Gun, C-Lect-Choke . . **360**
Model 500 APTR, 12 gauge, Trap Gun, Monte
Carlo stock **425**
Model 500CPR, 20 gauge, Field or Skeet Gun **365**
Model 500EPR, .410 gauge, Field or Skeet Gun **375**

Mossberg Model 500 Pump Combo Shotgun . . . $245

Gauges: 12 and 20. 24- and 28-inch bbl. w/adj. rifle sights. Weight: 7 to 7.25 lbs. Available w/blued or camo finish. Drilled and tapped receiver w/sling swivels and a camo web sling. Made from 1987 to date.

Mossberg Model 500 Pump Slugster Shotgun

Gauge: 12. 24-inch bbl. w/adj. rifle sights. Weight: 7 lbs. Camo finish. Drilled and tapped receiver w/camo sling and swivels. Made 1987 to date.
Standard Barrel Model **$195**
Rifled Barrel Model **220**
Rifled Barrel w/Integral Scope Mount **240**

Mossberg Model 500 Regal Slide-Action Repeater

Similar to regular Model 500 except higher quality workmanship throughout. Gauges: 12 and 20. Bbls.: 26- and 28-inch w/various chokes, or Accu-Choke. Weight: 6.75 to 7.5 lbs. Checkered walnut stock and forearm. Made 1985 to date.
Model 500 with Accu-Choke **$185**
Model 500 with fixed choke **170**

Mossberg Model 500 Sporting Pump

Gauges: 12, 20 or .410, 2.75- or 3-inch chamber. Bbls.: 22 to 28 inches w/fixed choke or screw-in tubes; plain or vent rib. Weight: 6.25 to 7.25 lbs. White bead front sight, brass midbead. Checkered hardwood buttstock and forend w/walnut finish.
Standard Model **$190**
Field Combo (w/extra Slugster bbl.) **245**

Mossberg Model 500 Super Grade

Same as pre-1977 Model 500 Field Grade, except not made in 16 ga., has vent-rib bbl., checkered pistol grip and slide handle. Made 1965-76.
Model 500AR, 12 gauge **$195**
Model 500AMR, 12 gauge, heavy Magnum bbl. **220**
Model 500AKR, 12 gauge, C-Lect-Choke **225**
Model 500CR 20 gauge **210**
Model 500CKk, 20 gauge, C-Lect-Choke **295**
Model 500ER, .410 gauge **190**
Model 500EKR, .410 gauge, C-Lect-Choke **240**

Mossberg Model 500 Turkey/Deer Combo $255

Pump (slide action). Gauge: 12. 20- and 24-inch bbls. Weight: 7.25 lbs. Drilled and tapped receiver, camo sling and swivels. Adj. rifle sights and camo finish. Vent rib. Made from 1987 to date.

Mossberg Model 500 Turkey Gun $260

Same as Model 500 Camo Pump, except w/24-inch ACCU-Choke bbl. w/extra full choke tube and Ghost Ring sights. Made from 1992 to date.

Mossberg Model 500 Turkey/Deer Combo

Mossberg Model 590 Military

Mossberg Model 500 Waterfowl/Deer Combo . . $265
Same general specifications as the Turkey/Deer Combo except with either 28- or 30-inch bbl. along with the 24-inch bbl. Made from 1987 to date.

Mossberg Model 500ATR Super Grade Trap . . $290
Same as pre-1977 Model 500 Field Grade, except 12 ga. only w/vent-rib bbl.; 30-inch F choke, checkered Monte Carlo stock w/recoil pad, beavertail forearm (slide handle). Made 1968-71.

Mossberg Model 500DSPR Duck Stamp
Commemorative $645
Limited edition of 1000 to commemorate the Migratory Bird Hunting Stamp Program. Same as Model 500DSPR Pigeon Grade 12-Gauge Magnum Heavy Duck Gun w/heavy 30-inch vent-rib bbl., F choke; receiver has special Wood Duck etching. Gun accompanied by a special wall plaque. Made in 1975. *Note:* Value is for gun in new, unfired condition.

Mossberg Model 590 Military Security $275
Same general specifications as the Model 590 Military except there is no heat shield and gun has short pistol-grip style instead of buttstock. Weight: about 6.75 lbs. Made from 1987 to date.

Mossberg Model 590 Military Shotgun
Slide-action. Gauge: 12. 9-shot capacity. 20-inch bbl. Weight: about 7 lbs. Synthetic or hardwood buttstock and forend. Ventilated bbl. heat shields. Equipped with bayonet lug. Blue or Parkerized finish. Made from 1987 to date.

Synthetic Model, blued	$265
Synthetic Model Parkerized	285
Speedfeed Model, blued	280
Speedfeed Model, Parkerized	285
Intimidator Model w/Laser Sight, blued	365
Intimidator Model w/Laser Sight, Parkerized	375
For Ghost Ring Sight, **add**	50

Mossberg Model 595 Bolt-Action Repeater $135
12 ga. only. 4-shot detachable magazine. 18.5-inch bbl. Weight: about 7 lbs. Walnut finished stock w/recoil pad and sling swivels. Made 1985-86.

Mossberg Model 712 Autoloading Shotgun $250
Gas-operated, takedown, hammerless shotgun with 5-shot (4-shot w/3-inch chamber) tubular magazine. 12 ga. Bbls.: 28-inch vent rib or 24-inch plain bbl. Slugster w/rifle sights; ACCU-Choke tube system. Weight: 7.5 lbs. Plain alloy receiver, top-mounted ambidextrous safety. Checkered walnut stained hardwood stock with recoil pad. Imported from Japan 1988-90.

Mossberg Model 835 Field Pump Shotgun
Similar to the Model 9600 Regal, except has walnut-stained hardwood stock and one ACCU-Choke tube only.

StandardModel	$215
Turkey Model	225
Combo Model (24- & 28-inch bbls.)	245

Mossberg Model 835 "NWTF" Ulti-Mag™
Shotgun $375
National Wild Turkey Federation pump-action. Gauge: 12, 3.5-inch chamber. 24-inch vent-rib bbl. with four ACCU-MAG chokes. Realtree® Camo finish. QD swivel and post. Made 1989-1993.

Mossberg Model 835 Regal Ulti-Mag Pump
Gauge: 12, 3.5-inch chamber. Bbls.: 24- or 28-inch vent-rib w/ACCU-Choke screw-in tubes. Weight: 7.75 lbs. White bead front, brass mid-bead. Checkered hardwood or synthetic stock with camo finish.

Special Model	$225
Standard Model	280
Camo Synthetic Model	300
Combo Model	325

SHOTGUNS

Mossberg Model 595

Mossberg Model 1000 Junior

Mossberg Model 1000 Autoloading Shotgun
Gas-operated, takedown, hammerless shotgun with tubular magazine. Gauges: 12, 20; 2.75- or 3-inch chamber. Bbls.: 22- to 30-inch vent rib w/fixed choke or ACCU-Choke tubes; or 22-inch plain bbl, Slugster w/rifle sights. Weight: 6.5 to 7.5 lbs. Scroll-engraved alloy receiver, crossbolt-type safety. Checkered American walnut buttstock and forend. Imported from Japan.
Junior Model, 20 ga., 22-inch bbl. **$345**
Standard Model with Fixed Choke **355**
Standard Model with Choke Tubes **375**

Mossberg Model 1000 Super Autoloading Shotgun
Similar to Model 1000, but in 12 ga. only w/3-inch chamber and new gas metering system. Bbls.: 26-, 28- or 30-inch vent rib with ACCU-Choke tubes.
Standard Model w/Choke Tubes **$395**
Waterfowler Model (Parkerized) **425**

Mossberg Model 1000S Super Skeet **$495**
Similar to Model 1000 in 12 or 20 ga., except w/all-steel receiver and vented jug-type choke for reduced muzzle jump. Bright-point front sight and brass mid-bead. 1 and 2 oz. forend cap weights.

Mossberg Model 5500 Autoloading Shotgun
Gas-operated. Takedown. 12 ga. only. 4-shot magazine (3-shot with 3-inch shells). Bbls.: 18.5- to 30-inch; various chokes. Checkered walnut finished hardwood. Made 1985-86.
Model 5500 w/ACCU-Choke **$250**
Model 5500 Modified Junior **255**
Model 5500 Slugster **265**
Model 5500 12 gauge **225**
Model 5500 Guardian **215**

Mossberg Model 5500 MKII Autoloading Shotgun
Same as Model 5500, except equipped w/two Accu-Choke bbls.: 26-inch ported for non-Magnum 2.75-inch shells; 28-inch for Magnum loads. Made 1988-93.
Standard Model **$240**
Camo Model **275**
NTWF Mossy Oak Model **285**

Mossberg Model 6000 Auto Shotgun **$240**
Similar to the Model 9200 Regal, except has 28-inch vent-rib bbl. w/mod. ACCU-Choke tube only. Made from 1993 to date.

Mossberg Model 9200 Camo Shotgun
Similar to the Model 9200 Regal, except has synthetic stock and forend and is completely finished in camouflage pattern (incl. bbl.). Made from 1993 to date.
Standard Model (OFM Camo) **$295**
Turkey Model (Mossy Oak® camo) **325**
Combo Model (24- & 28-inch bbls. w/OFM Camo) . . . **375**

Mossberg Model 9200 Regal Autoloader
Gauge: 12; 3-inch chamber. Bbls.: 24- to 28-inch w/ACCU-Choke tubes; plain or vent rib. Weight: 7.25 to 7.5 lbs. Checkered hardwood buttstock and forend w/walnut finish. Made from 1992 to date.
Model 9200 w/ACCU-Choke **$280**
Model 9200 w/rifled bbl. **295**
Model 9200 Combo (w/extra Slugster bbl.) **330**

Mossberg Model 9200 USST Autoloader **$280**
Similar to the Model 9200 Regal, except has 26-inch vent-rib bbl. w/ACCU-Choke tubes. "United States Shooting Team" engraved on receiver. Made from 1993 to date.

Mossberg Model HS410 Home Security Pump Shotgun
Gauge: .410; 3-inch chamber. Bbl.: 18.5-inch with muzzle brake; blued. Weight: 6.25 lbs. Synthetic stock and pistol-grip slide. Optional laser sight. Made from 1990 to date. A similar version of this gun is marketed by Maverick Arms under the same model designation.
Standard Model **$190**
Laser Model **340**

Mossberg "New Haven Brand" Shotguns
Promotional models, similar to their standard guns but plainer in finish, are marketed by Mossberg under the "New Haven" brand name. Values generally are about 20 percent lower than for corresponding standard models.

Mossberg Model 5500 Guardian

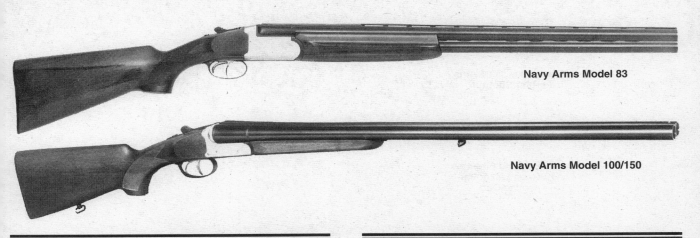

Navy Arms Model 83

Navy Arms Model 100/150

NAVY ARMS SHOTGUNS
Ridgefield, New Jersey

Navy Arms Model 83/93 Bird Hunter Over/Under
Hammerless. Boxlock, engraved receiver. Gauges: 12 and 20; 3-inch chambers. Bbls.: 28-inch chrome lined with double vent-rib construction. Checkered European walnut stock and forearm. Gold plated triggers. Made 1984-90.
Model 83 w/Extractors $245
Model 93 w/Ejectors 275

Navy Arms Model 95/96 Over/Under Shotgun
Same as the Model 83/93, except w/five interchangeable choke tubes. Imported from Italy. Discontinued 1990.
Model 95 w/Extractors $325
Model 96 w/Ejectors 395

Navy Arms Model 100/150 Field Hunter Double-Barrel Shotgun
Boxlock. Gauges: 12 and 20. Bbls.: 28-inch chrome lined. Checkered European walnut stock and forearm. Made 1984-90.
Model 100 . . . . $295
Model 150 (auto ejectors) 375

Navy Arms Model 410 Over/Under Shotgun $240
Hammerless, takedown shotgun with engraved chrome receiver. Single trigger. .410 ga. w/3-inch chambers. Bbls.: 26-inch (F/F or SK/SK); vent rib. Weight: 6.25 lbs. Checkered European walnut buttstock and forend. Imported from Italy since 1986.

NEW ENGLAND FIREARMS
Gardner, Massachusetts

New England Firearms Handi-Gun $150
Single-shot, break-open action w/side-lever release; two-barrel set. Rifle bbl.: Most calibers from .22 Hornet through .45-70. Gauges: 12, 20, .410. 22-inch bbls. M choke. Blued or electroless nickel finish. Made 1989-1993.

New England Firearms NWTF Turkey Special . . $150
Similar to Turkey and Goose Model except has 24-inch plain bbl. w/screw-in Turkey full choke tube. Mossy Oak Camo finish on entire gun. Made from 1992 to date.

New England Firearms Pardner Shotgun
Takedown. Side lever. Single bbl. Gauges: 12, 20 and .410 w/3-inch chamber; 16 and 28 w/2.75-inch chamber. Bbl.: 26- or 28-inch, plain; fixed choke. Weight: 5-6 lbs. Bead front sight. Pistol grip-style hardwood stock with walnut finish. Made from 1988 to date.
Standard Model $75
Youth Model 80

New England Firearms Tracker Slug Gun
Similar to Pardner Model, except in 12 or 20 ga. only. Bbl.: 24-inch w/cylinder choke or rifled slug (Tracker II). Weight: 6 lbs. American hardwood stock w/walnut or camo finish, schnabel forend, sling swivel studs. Made from 1992 to date.
Tracker Slug . . . . $ 95
Tracker II (rifled bore) 100

SHOTGUNS

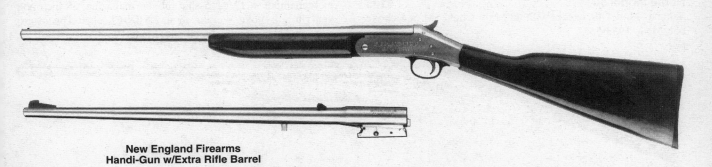

**New England Firearms
Handi-Gun w/Extra Rifle Barrel**

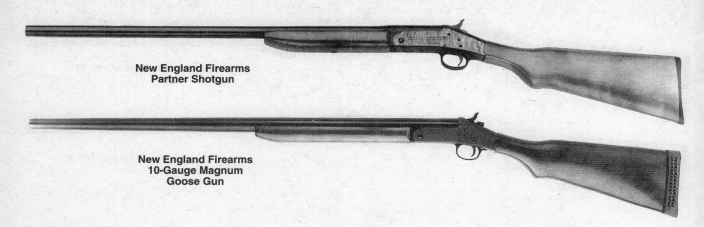

New England Firearms
Partner Shotgun

New England Firearms
10-Gauge Magnum
Goose Gun

New England Firearms Turkey and Goose Gun

Similar to Pardner Model, except chambered in 10 ga. w/3.5-inch chamber. 28-inch plain barrel w/F choke. Weight: 9.5 lbs. American hardwood stock w/walnut or camo finish. Made from 1992 to date.

Standard Model $110
Camo Model 120

NIKKO FIREARMS LTD.
Tochigi, Japan

See listings under Golden Eagle Firearms, Inc.

NOBLE MANUFACTURING company
Haydenville, Massachusetts

Noble Series 602 and 70 are similar in appearance to the corresponding Model 66 guns.

Noble Model 40 Hammerless Slide-Action Repeating Shotgun $110

Solid frame. 12 ga. only. 5-shell tubular magazine. 28-inch bbl. w/ventilated Multi-Choke. Weight: about 7.5 lbs. Plain pistol-grip stock, grooved slide handle. Made 1950-55.

Noble Model 50 .... $105

Same as Model 40, except without Multi-Choke. M or F choke bbl. Made 1953-55.

Noble Key Lock
Fire Control Mechanism
Supplied with
Models 66,166L, 602

Noble Model 60 Hammerless Slide-Action Repeating Shotgun $155

Solid frame. 12 and 16 ga. 5-shot tubular magazine. 28-inch bbl. w/adj. choke. Plain pistol-grip stock w/recoil pad, grooved slide handle. Weight: about 7.5 lbs. Made 1955-66.

Noble Model 65 .... $135

Same as Model 60, except without adj. choke and recoil pad. M or F choke bbl. Made 1955-66. *See* photo next page.

Noble Model 66CLP $125

Same as Model 66RCLP, except has plain bbl. Introduced in 1967. Discontinued.

Noble Model 66RCLP Hammerless Slide-Action Repeating Shotgun $165

Solid frame. Key lock fire control mechanism. Gauges: 12, 16. 3-inch chamber in 12 ga. 5-shot tubular magazine. 28-inch bbl., vent rib, adj. choke. Weight: about 7.5 lbs. Checkered pistol-grip stock and slide handle, recoil pad. Made 1967-70.

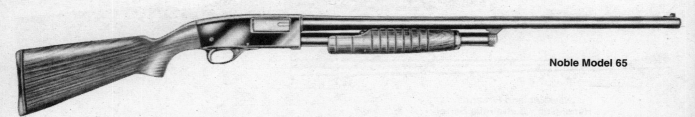

Noble Model 65

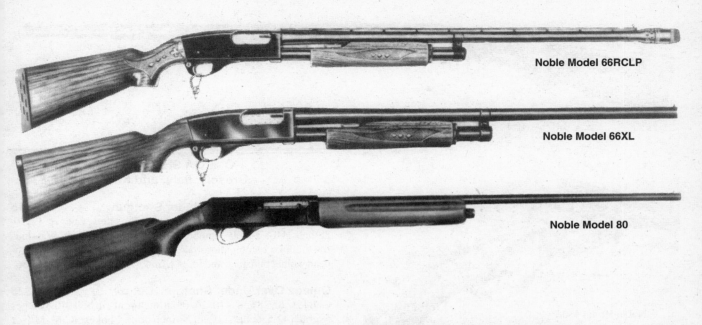

Noble Model 66RCLP

Noble Model 66XL

Noble Model 80

Noble Model 66RLP **$145**
Same as Model 66RCLP, except with F or M choke. Made 1967-1970.

Noble Model 66XL **$125**
Same as Model 66RCLP, except has plain bbl., F or M choke slide handle only checkered, no recoil pad. Made 1967-70.

Noble Model 70CLP Hammerless Slide-Action Repeating Shotgun **$150**
Solid frame. .410 gauge. Magazine holds 5 shells. 26-inch bbl. w/adj. choke. Weight: about 6 lbs. Checkered buttstock and forearm, recoil pad. Made 1958-70.

Noble Model 70RCLP **$165**
Same as Model 70CLP, except has vent rib. Made 1967-70.

Noble Model 70RLP **$150**
Same as Model 70CLP, except has vent rib and no adj. choke. Made 1967-70.

Noble Model 70XL. **$105**
Same as Model 70CLP, except without adj. choke and checkering on buttstock. Made 1958-70.

Noble Model 80 Autoloading Shotgun **$225**
Recoil-operated. .410 ga. Magazine holds three 3-inch shells, four 2.5-inch shells. 26-inch bbl., full choke. Weight: about 6 lbs. Plain pistol-grip stock and fluted forearm. Made 1964-66.

Noble Model 166L Deergun **$230**
Solid frame. Key lock fire control mechanism. 12 ga. 2.75-inch chamber. 5-shot tubular magazine. 24-inch plain bbl., specially bored for rifled slug. Lyman peep rear sight, post ramp front sight. Receiver dovetailed for scope mounting. Weight: about 7.25 lbs. Checkered pistol-grip stock and slide handle, swivels and carrying strap. Made 1967-70.

Noble Model 420 Hammerless Double **$310**
Boxlock. Plain extractors. Double triggers. Gauges: 12 ga. 3-inch mag.; 16 ga.; 20 ga. 3-inch mag.; .410 ga. Bbls.: 28-inch, except .410 in 26-inch, M/F choke. Weight: about 6.75 lbs. Engraved frame. Checkered walnut stock and forearm. Made 1958-70.

Noble Model 450E Hammerless Double **$395**
Boxlock. Engraved frame. Selective auto ejectors. Double triggers. Gauges: 12, 16, 20. 3-inch chambers in 12 and 20 ga. 28-inch bbls., M/F choke. Weight: about 6 lbs. 14 oz., 12 ga. Checkered pistol-grip stock and beavertail forearm, recoil pad. Made 1967-70.

SHOTGUNS

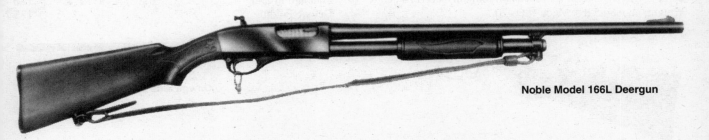

Noble Model 166L Deergun

Noble Model 420

Nobel Model 450E

Noble Model 602CLP $155
Same as Model 602RCLP, except has plain bbl. Made 1958-70.

**Noble Model 602RCLP Hammerless
Slide-Action Repeating Shotgun** $185
Solid frame. Key lock fire control mechanism. 20 ga. 3-inch
chamber. 5-shot tubular magazine. 28-inch bbl., vent rib, adj.
choke. Weight: about 6.5 lbs. Checkered pistol-grip stock/slide
handle, recoil pad. Made 1967-70.

Noble Model 602RLP $165
Same as Model 602RCLP, except without adj. choke, bored F or
M choke. Made 1967-70.

Noble Model 602XL $125
Same as Model 602RCLP, except has plain bbl., F or M choke,
slide handle only checkered, no recoil pad. Made 1958-70.

Noble Model 662 . . . . $175
Same as Model 602CLP, except has aluminum receiver and bbl..
Weight: about 4.5 lbs. Made 1966-70.

OMEGA SHOTGUNS
Brescia, Italy, and Korea

Omega Folding Over/Under Shotgun $315
Hammerless. Single trigger with automatic safety. Gauges: 12, 20,
28 and .410; 3-inch chambers. Bbls.: 26- or 28-inch w/various
fixed choke combinations. Weight: 5.5-6 lbs. Checkered European walnut buttstock and forend. Imported from Italy since 1986.

Omega Over/Under Shotgun, Deluxe $325
Gauges: 20, 28 and .410. 26- or 28-inch vent-rib bbls. 40.5 inches
overall (42.5 inches, 20 ga., 28-inch bbl.). Chokes: IC/M, M/F or
F/F (.410). Weight: about 5.5 -6 lbs. Single trigger. Automatic
safety. European walnut stock w/checkered pistol grip and tulip
forend. Made in Italy from 1984 to date.

Omega Side-by-Side Shotgun, Deluxe $185
Same general specifications as the Standard Side-by-Side except
has checkered European walnut stock and low bbl. rib. Made in
Italy from 1984 to date.

Omega Side-by-Side Shotgun, Standard $165
Gauge: .410. 26-inch bbl. 40.5 inches overall. Choked F/F. Weight:
5.5 lbs. Double trigger. Manual safety. Checkered beechwood stock
and semi-pistol grip. Made in Italy from 1984 to date.

Omega Single-Shot Shotgun, Deluxe $105
Same general specifications as the Standard Single Bbl. except
has checkered walnut stock, top lever break, fully blued receiver,
vent rib. Made in Korea from 1984 to date.

Omega Single-Shot Shotgun, Standard
Gauges: 12, 16, 20, 28 and .410. Bbl. lengths: 26-,28- or 30-inch.
Weight: 5 lbs. 4 oz.-5 lbs. 11 oz. Indonesian walnut stock. Matte-
chromed receiver and top lever break. Made in Korea from 1984
to date.
Standard Fixed . . . . $ 80
Standard Folding 125
Deluxe Folding 175

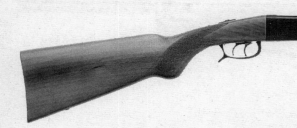

Omega Side-by-Side Shotgun, Deluxe

Parker A-1 Special

PARKER BROTHERS
Meriden, Connecticut

This firm was taken over by Remington Arms Company in 1934 and its production facilities moved to Remington's Ilion, New York, plant.

Parker Hammerless Double-Barrel Shotguns

Grades V.H.E. through A-1 Special. Boxlock. Auto ejectors. Double triggers or selective single trigger. Gauges: 10, 12, 16, 20, 28, .410. Bbls.: 26- to 32-inch, any standard boring. Weight: 6.88-8.5 lbs.,12 ga. Stock and forearm of select walnut, checkered; straight, half-or full-pistol grip. Grades differ only in quality of workmanship, grade of wood, engraving, checkering, etc.; general specifications are the same for all. Discontinued about 1940.

V.H.E. Grade, 12 or 16 gauge	$ 2,695
V.H.E. Grade, 20 gauge	3,850
V.H.E. Grade, 28 gauge	14,500
G.H.E. Grade, 12 or 16 gauge	3,695
G.H.E. Grade, 20 gauge	4,150
G.H.E. Grade, 28 gauge	6,500
G.H.E. Grade, .410 gauge	17,500
D.H.E. Grade, 12 or 16 gauge	4,995
D.H.E. Grade, 20 gauge	5,855
D.H.E. Grade, 28 gauge	12,500
D.H.E. Grade, .410 gauge	19,500
C.H.E. Grade, 12 or 16 gauge	7,425
C.H.E. Grade, 20 gauge	8,450
C.H.E. Grade, 28 gauge	17,500
C.H.E. Grade, .410 gauge	35,250
B.H.E. Grade, 12 or 16 gauge	8,655
B.H.E. Grade, 20 gauge	11,995
B.H.E. Grade, 28 gauge	18,500
B.H.E. Grade, .410 gauge	22,750
A.H.E. Grade, 12 or 16 gauge	16,250
A.H.E. Grade, 20 gauge	22,750
A.H.E. Grade, 28 gauge	29,500
A.A.H.E. Grade, 12 or 16 gauge	29,950
A.A.H.E. Grade, 20 gauge	47,000
A.A.H.E. Grade, 28 gauge	75,500
A-1 Special Grade, 12 or 16 gauge	68,000
A-1 Special Grade, 20 gauge	90,000
A-1 Special Grade, 28 gauge	130,000

For *non-ejector guns*, **deduct** 30 percent from values shown.
Vent-rib barrels, **add** 20 percent to values shown.

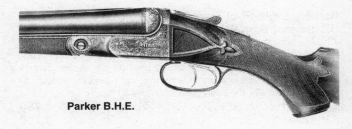

Parker B.H.E.

Parker C.H.E.

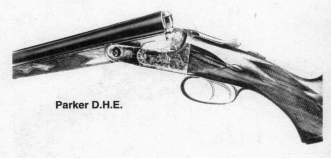

Parker D.H.E.

Parker G.H.E.

SHOTGUNS

Parker A.H.E.

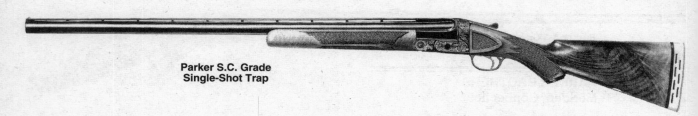

**Parker S.C. Grade
Single-Shot Trap**

Parker Single-Shot Trap Guns

Hammerless. Boxlock. Ejector. 12 ga. only. Bbl. lengths: 30-, 32-, 34-inch, any boring, vent rib. Weight: 7.5-8.5 lbs. Stock and forearm of select walnut, checkered; straight, half-or full-pistol grip. The five grades differ only in quality of workmanship, grade of wood, checkering, engraving, etc.; general specifications same for all. Discontinued about 1940.

S.C. Grade	$ 2,850
S.B. Grade	3,700
S.A. Grade	4,700
S.A.A. Grade	5,800
S.A.1 Special	19,000

Parker Skeet Gun

Same as other Parker doubles from Grade V.H.E. up, except selective single trigger and beavertail forearm are standard on this model, as are 26-inch bbls., SK choke. Discontinued about 1940. Values are 20 percent higher.

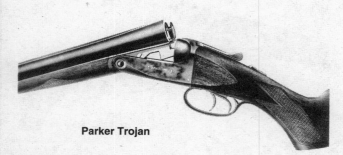

Parker Trojan

Parker Trojan Hammerless Double-Barrel Shotgun

Boxlock. Plain extractors. Double trigger or single trigger. Gauges: 12, 16, 20. Bbls.: 30-inch both F choke (12 ga. only), 26- or 28-inch M and F choke. Weight: 6.25-7.75 lbs. Checkered pistol-grip stock and forearm. Discont. 1939.

12 or 16 gauge	$1595
20 gauge	2850

PARKER REPRODUCTIONS
Middlesex, New Jersey

Parker Hammerless Double-Barrel Shotguns

Reproduction of the original Parker boxlock. Single selective trigger or double triggers. Selective automatic ejectors. Automatic safety. Gauges: 12, 16, 20 or 28; 2.75- or 3-inch chambers. Bbls.: 26- or 28-inch choked SK/SK, IC/M, M/F. Weight: 5.5-7 lbs. Checkered English-style or pistol-grip American walnut stock w/beavertail or splinter forend and checkered skeleton buttplate. Color casehardened receiver with game scenes and scroll engraving. Imported from Japan 1984 to date.

D Grade	$ 2,395
D Grade 2-barrel set	3,550
B Grade Bank Note Limited Edition	3,295
B Grade 2-barrel set	4,750
B Grade 3-barrel set	5,595
A-1 Special Grade	6,995
A-1 Special Grade 2-barrel set	7,950
A-1 Special Grade Custom Engraved	8,995
A-1 Special Grade 3-barrel set	10,500

PARKER-HALE SHOTGUNS
Mfd. by Ignacio Ugartechea, Spain

Parker-Hale Model 645A (American)
Side-by-Side Shotgun $695

Gauges: 12, 16 and 20. Boxlock action. 26- and 28-inch bbls. Chokes: IC/M, M/F. Weight: 6 lbs. average. Single non-selective trigger. Automatic safety. Hand-checkered pistol grip walnut stock w/beavertail forend. Raised matted rib. English scroll-design engraved receiver. Discontinued 1990.

Parker-Hale Model 645E (English) Side-by-Side Shotgun

Same general specifications as the Model 645A, except double triggers, straight grip, splinter forend, checkered butt and concave rib. Discontinued 1990.

Parker-Hale Model 545A

Parker-Hale Model 645E

Parker-Hale Model 645E (English) Side-by-Side Shotgun *(Cont.)*

MODEL 645E
12, 16, 20 ga. with 26- or 28-inch bbl. $750
28, .410 ga. with 27-inch bbl. 795
MODEL 645E-XXV
12, 16, 20 ga. with 25-inch bbl. 725
28, .410 ga. with 25-inch bbl. 795

PEDERSEN CUSTOM GUNS
North Haven, Connecticut
Division of O. F. Mossberg & Sons, Inc.

Pedersen Model 1000 Over/Under Hunting Shotgun
Boxlock. Auto ejectors. Selective single trigger. Gauges: 12, 20. 2.75-inch chambers in 12 ga., 3-inch in 20 ga. Bbls.: vent rib; 30-inch M/F (12 ga. only); 28-inch IC/M (12 ga. only), M/F; 26-inch IC/M. Checkered pistol-grip stock and forearm. Grade I is the higher quality gun with custom stock dimensions, fancier wood, more elaborate engraving, silver inlays. Made 1973-75.
Grade I $1895
Grade II 1525

Pedersen Model 1000 Magnum
Same as Model 1000 Hunting Gun, except chambered for 12-ga. Magnum 3-inch shells, 30-inch bbls., IM/F choke. Made 1973-75.
Grade I $1950
Grade II 1595

Pedersen Model 1000 Skeet Gun
Same as Model 1000 Hunting Gun, except has skeet-style stock; 26- and 28-inch bbls. (12 ga. only), SK choke. Made 1973-75.

Pedersen Model 1000 Skeet Gun *(Cont.)*
Grade I $2050
Grade II 1650

Pedersen Model 1000 Trap Gun
Same as Model 1000 Hunting Gun, except 12 ga. only, has Monte Carlo trap-style stock, 30- or 32-inch bbls., M/F or IM/F choke. Made 1973-75.
Grade I $1995
Grade II 1495

Pedersen Model 1500 O/U Hunting Shotgun $550
Boxlock. Auto ejectors. Selective single trigger. 12 ga. 2.75- or 3-inch chambers. Bbls.: vent rib; 26-inch IC/M; 28- and 30-inch M/F; Magnum has 30-inch, IM/F choke. Weight. 7-7.5 lbs., depending on bbl. length. Checkered pistol-grip stock and forearm. Made 1973-75.

Pedersen Model 1500 Skeet Gun $595
Same as Model 1500 Hunting Gun, except has skeet-style stock, 27-inch bbls., SK choke. Made 1973-75.

Pedersen Model 1500 Trap Gun $595
Same as Model 1500 Hunting Gun, except has Monte Carlo trap-style stock, 30- or 32-inch bbls., M/F or IM/F chokes. Made 1973-75.

Pedersen Model 2000 Hammerless Double
Boxlock. Auto ejectors. Selective single trigger. Gauges: 12, 20. 2.75-inch chambers in 12 ga., 3-inch in 20 ga. Bbls.: vent rib; 30-inch M/F (12 ga. only); 28-inch M/F, 26-inch IC/M choke. Checkered pistol-grip stock and forearm. Grade I is the higher quality gun w/custom dimensions, fancier wood, more elaborate engraving, silver inlays. Made 1973-74.

SHOTGUNS

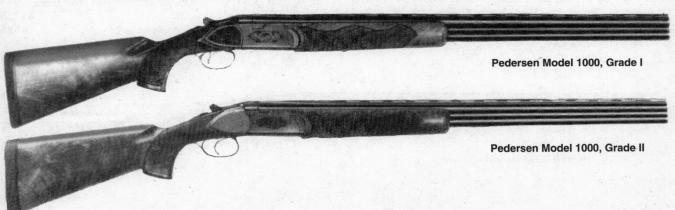

Pedersen Model 1000, Grade I

Pedersen Model 1000, Grade II

Pedersen Model 2000 Hammerless Double *(Cont.)*

Grade I **$1595**
Grade II **1295**

Pedersen Model 2500 Hammerless Double **$380**

Boxlock. Auto ejectors. Selective single trigger. Gauges: 12, 20. 2.75-inch chambers in 12 ga., 3-inch in 20 ga. Bbls.: vent rib; 28-inch M/F; 26-inch IC/M choke. Checkered pistol-grip stock and forearm. Made 1973-74.

Pedersen Model 4000 Hammerless Slide-Action Repeating Shotgun **$380**

Custom version of Mossberg Model 500. Full-coverage floral engraving on receiver. Gauges: 12, 20, .410. 3-inch chamber. Bbls.: vent rib; 26-inch IC or SK choke; 28-inch F or M; 30-inch F. Weight: 6-8 lbs. depending on ga. and bbl. Checkered stock and slide handle of select wood. Made in 1975.

Pedersen Model 4000 Trap Gun **$365**

Same as standard Model 4000, except 12 ga. only, has 30-inch F choke bbl., Monte Carlo trap-style stock w/recoil pad. Made in 1975.

Pedersen Model 4500 . . . . **$325**

Same as Model 4000, except has simpler scroll engraving. Made in 1975.

Pedersen Model 4500 Trap Gun **$350**

Same as Model 4000 Trap Gun, except has simpler scroll engraving. Made in 1975.

J. C. PENNEY CO., INC.
Dallas, Texas

J. C. Penney Model 4011 Autoloading Shotgun . . . **$175**

Hammerless. 5-shot magazine. Bbls.: 26-inch IC; 28-inch M or F; 30-inch F choke. Weight: 7.25 lbs. Plain pistol-grip stock and slide handle.

J. C. Penney Model 6610 Single-Shot Shotgun . . **$80**

Hammerless. Takedown. Auto ejector. Gauges: 12, 16, 20 and .410. Bbl. length: 28-36 inches. Weight: about 6 lbs. Plain pistol-grip stock and forearm.

J. C. Penney Model 6630 Bolt-Action Shotgun . . . **$110**

Takedown. Gauges: 12, 16, 20. 2-shot clip magazine. 26- and 28-inch bbl. lengths; with or without adj. choke. Plain pistol-grip stock. Weight: about 7.25 lbs.

J. C. Penney Model 6670 Slide-Action Shotgun . . . **$130**

Hammerless. Gauges: 12, 16, 20, and .410. 3-shot tubular magazine. Bbls.: 26- to 30-inch; various chokes. Weight: 6.25-7.25 lbs. Walnut finished hardwood stock.

J. C. Penney Model 6870 Slide-Action Shotgun **$195**

Hammerless. Gauges: 12, 16, 20, .410. 4-shot magazine. Bbls.: vent rib; 26- to 30-inch, various chokes. Weight: average 6.5 lbs. Plain pistol-grip stock.

PERAZZI SHOTGUNS
Manufactured by Manifattura Armi Perazzi, Brescia, Italy

See **also listings under Ithaca-Perazzi.**

Perazzi DB81 Over/Under Trap **$4650**

Gauge: 12; 2.75-inch chambers. 29.5- or 31.5-inch bbls. w/wide vent rib; M/F chokes. Weight: 8 lbs. 6 oz. Detachable and interchangeable trigger with flat V-springs. Bead front sight. Interchangeable and custom-made checkered stock; beavertail forend. Made from 1988 to date.

Perazzi DB81 Single-Shot Trap **$3850**

Same general specifications as the DB81 Over/Under, except in single bbl. version w/32- or 34-inch wide vent-rib bbl., F choke. Made from 1988 to date.

NOTE

Prices shown reflect Standard Grade values, except where noted. For SC3 Grade add 70%, for SCO Grade add 190% and for SHO Grade add 500%.

Perazzi Grand American 88 Special Single Trap

Same general specifications as MX8 Special Single Trap, except w/high ramped rib. Fixed choke or screw-in choke tubes.
Model 88 Standard **$4255**
Model 88 w/Interchangeable Choke Tubes **4595**

Perazzi DB81 Over/Under Trap

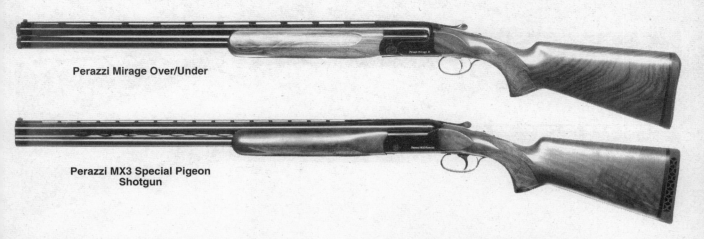

Perazzi Mirage Over/Under

Perazzi MX3 Special Pigeon Shotgun

Perazzi Mirage Over/Under Shotgun

Gauge: 12; 2.75-inch chambers. Bbls.: 27.63-, 29.5- or 31.5-inch vent-rib w/fixed chokes or screw-in choke tubes. Single selective trigger. Weight: 7 to 7.75 lbs. Interchangeable and custom-made checkered buttstock and forend.

Competition Trap, Skeet, Pigeon, Sporting . . . . $ 4,800
Skeet 4-Barrel Sets 12,400
Competition Special (w/adj. 4-position trigger) **add** . 400

Perazzi MX1 Over/Under Shotgun

Similar to Model MX8, except w/ramp-style, tapered rib and modified stock configuration.

Competition Trap, Skeet, Pigeon & Sporting $3600
MX1C (w/Choke Tubes) 3750
MX1B (w/Flat Low-Rib) 3560

Perazzi MX2 Over/Under Shotgun

Similar to Model MX8, except w/broad high-ramped competition rib.

Competition-Trap, Skeet, Pigeon & Sporting $3750
MX2C (w/choke tubes) 3750

Perazzi MX3 Over/Under Shotgun

Similar to Model MX8, except w/ramp-style, tapered rib and modified stock configuration.

Competition Trap, Skeet, Pigeon & Sporting $3595
Competition Special (w/adj. 4-position trigger) **add** . . 300
Game Models 3195
Combo O/U plus SB 3950
SB Trap 32- or 34-inch 2695
Skeet 4-bbl. sets 8950
Skeet Special 4-bbl. sets 9555

Perazzi MX3 Special Pigeon Shotgun $4250

Gauge: 12; 2.75-inch chambers. 29.5- or 31.5-inch vent-rib bbl.; IC/M and extra full chokes. Weight: 8 lbs. 6 oz. Detachable and interchangeable trigger group w/flat V-springs. Bead front sight. Interchangeable and custom-made checkered stock for live pigeon shoots; splinter forend. Made from 1991 to date.

Perazzi MX4 Over/Under Shotgun

Similar to Model MX3 in appearance and shares the MX8 locking system. Detachable, adj. 4-position trigger standard. Interchangeable choke tubes optional.

Competition Trap, Skeet, Pigeon & Sporting $3650
MX4C (w/Choke Tubes) 3895

Perazzi MX5 Over/Under Game Gun

Similar to Model MX8, except in hunting configuration chambered in 12 or 20 ga. Non-detachable single selective trigger.
MX5 Standard $2495
MX5C (w/Choke Tubes) 2750

Perazzi MX7 Over/Under Shotgun $4575

Similar to Model MX12, except w/MX3-style receiver and top-mounted trigger selector. Bbls.: 28.73-, 2.5-, 31.5-inch w/vent rib; screw-in choke tubes. Made from 1992 to date.

Perazzi MX8 Over/Under Shotgun

Gauge: 12, 2.75-inch chambers. Bbls.: 27.63-, 29.5- or 31.5-inch vent-rib w/fixed chokes or screw-in choke tubes. Weight: 7 to 8.5 lbs. Interchangeable and custom-made checkered stock; beavertail forend. Special models have detachable and interchangeable 4-position trigger group w/flat V-springs. Made from 1988 to date.

SHOTGUNS

Perazzi MX8

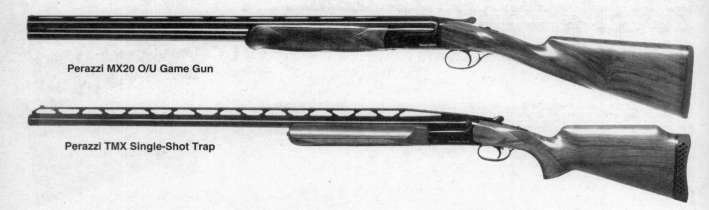

Perazzi MX20 O/U Game Gun

Perazzi TMX Single-Shot Trap

Perazzi MX8 Over/Under Shotgun *(Cont.)*

MX8 Standard	**$3695**
MX8 Special (adj. 4-pos. trigger)	3795
MX8 Special Single (32- or 34-inch bbl.)	3595
MX8 Special Combo	7390

Perazzi MX8/20 Over/Under Snotgun $3850

Similar to the Model MX8, except w/smaller frame and custom stock. Available in sporting or game configurations with fixed chokes or screw-in tubes. Made from 1993 to date.

Perazzi MX9 Over/Under Shotgun $5995

Gauge: 12; 2.75-inch chambers. Bbls.: 29.5- or 30.5-inch w/choke tubes and vent side rib. Selective trigger. Checkered walnut stock w/adj. cheekpiece. Available in single bbl., combo, O/U trap, skeet, pigeon and sporting models. Made from 1993 to date.

Perazzi MX10 Over/Under Shotgun $7595

Similar to the Model MX9, except w/fixed chokes and different rib configuration. Made from 1993 to date.

Perazzi MX12 Over/Under Game Gun

Gauge: 12, 2.75-inch chambers. Bbls.: 26-, 27.63-, 28.38- or 29.5-inch, vent-rib, fixed chokes or screw-in choke tubes. Non-detachable single selective trigger group w/coil springs. Weight: 7.25 lbs. Interchangeable and custom-made checkered stock; schnabel forend.

MX12 Standard	**$3850**
MX12C (w/Choke Tubes)	4250

Perazzi MX20 O/U Game Gun

Gauges: 20, 28 and .410; 2.75- or 3-inch chambers. 26-inch vent-rib bbls., M/F chokes or screw-in chokes. Auto selective ejectors. Selective single trigger. Weight: 6 lbs. 6 oz. Non-detachable coil-spring trigger. Bead front sight. Interchangeable and custom-made checkered stock w/schnabel forend. Made from 1988 to date

Standard Grade	**$ 3,995**
Standard Grade w/Gold Outline	6,950
MX20C w/Choke Tubes	4,295
SC3 Grade	7,500
SCO Grade	10,350

Perazzi MX28 Over/Under Game Gun $10,950

Similar to the Model MX12, except chambered in 28 ga. w/26-inch bbls. fitted to smaller frame. Made from 1993 to date.

Perazzi MX410 Over/Under Game Gun $10,950

Similar to the Model MX12, except in .410 bore w/3-inch chambers, 26-inch bbls. fitted to smaller frame. Made from 1993 to date.

Perazzi TM1 Special Single-Shot Trap $3455

Gauge: 12- 2.75-inch chambers. 32- or 34-inch bbl. w/wide vent rib; full choke. Weight: 8 lbs. 6 oz. Detachable and interchangeable trigger group with coil springs. Bead front sight. Interchangeable and custom-made stock w/checkered pistol grip and beavertail forend. Made from 1988 to date.

Perazzi TMX Special Single-Shot Trap $3590

Same general specifications as Model TM1 Special, except w/ultra-high rib. Interchangeable choke tubes optional.

PIOTTI SHOTGUNS
Italy

Piotti King No. 1 Sidelock **$12,995**
Gauges: 10, 12, 16, 20, 28 and .410. 25- to 30-inch bbls. (12 ga.), 25- to 28-inch (other ga.). Weight: about 5 lbs. (.410) to 8 lbs. (12 ga.) Holland & Holland pattern sidelock. Double triggers standard. Coin finish or color casehardened. Level file-cut rib. Full-coverage scroll engraving, gold inlays. Hand-rubbed, oil-finished, straight-grip stock with checkered butt, splinter forend.

Piotti King Extra Side-by-Side Shotgun **$17,250**
Same general specifications as the Piotti King No. 1, except has choice of engraving, gold inlays plus stock is of exhibition grade wood.

Piotti Lunik Sidelock Shotgun **$13,250**
Same general specifications as the Monte Carlo model except has level, file-cut rib. Renaissance-style, large scroll engraving in relief, gold crown in top lever, gold name, and gold crest in forearm, finely figured wood.

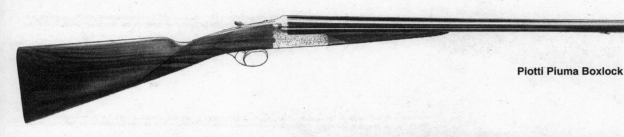

Piotti Piuma Boxlock

Piotti Monte Carlo Sidelock Shotgun $8455

Gauges: 10, 12, 16, 20, 28 or .410. Bbls.: 25- to 30-inch. Holland & Holland pattern sidelock. Weight: 5-8 lbs. Automatic ejectors. Double triggers. Hand-rubbed oil-finished straight-grip stock with checkered butt. Choice of Purdey-style scroll and rosette or Holland & Holland-style large scroll engraving.

Piotti Piuma Boxlock Side-by-Side Shotgun .. $8395

Same general specifications as the Monte Carlo model, except has Anson & Deeley boxlock action w/demi-bloc bbls., scalloped frame. Standard scroll and rosette engraving. Hand-rubbed, oil-finished straight-grip stock.

WILLIAM POWELL & SON LTD.
Birmingham, England

Powell No. 1 Best Grade Double-Barrel
Shotgun $25,000

Sidelock. Gauges: Made to order, with 12, 16 and 20 the most common. Bbls.: Made to order in any length, but 28 inches was recommended. Highest grade French walnut buttstock and forearm with fine checkering. Metal elaborately engraved. Imported by Stoeger about 1938-51.

Powell No. 2 Best Grade Double $20,000

Same general specifications as the Powell No. 1, except plain finish without engraving. Imported by Stoeger about 1938-51.

Powell No. 6 Crown Grade Double $8000

Boxlock. Gauges: Made to order, with 12, 16 and 20 the most common. Bbls.: Made to order, but 28 inches was recommended. Highest grade French walnut buttstock and forearm w/fine checkering. Metal elaborately engraved. Uses Anson & Deeley locks. Imported by Stoeger about 1938-51.

Powell Number 7 Aristocrat

Powell No. 7 Aristocrat Grade Double $2500

Same general specifications as the Powell No. 6, except w/lower quality wood and metal engraving.

PRECISION SPORTS SHOTGUNS
Cortland, New York
Manufactured by Ignacio Ugartechea, Spain

Precision Sports 600 Series American Hammerless Doubles

Boxlock. Single selective trigger. Selective automatic ejectors. Automatic safety. Gauges: 12, 16, 20, 28, .410; 2.75- or 3-inch chambers. Bbls.: 26-,27- or 28-inch w/raised matte rib; choked IC/M or M/F. Weight: 5.75-7 lbs. Checkered pistol-grip walnut buttstock with beavertail forend. Engraved silvered receiver with blued bbls. Imported from Spain 1986 to date.

640A (12, 16, 20 ga. w/extractors)	$625
640A (28, .410 ga. w/extractors)	750
640 Slug Gun (12 ga. w/extractors)	735
645A (12, 16, 20 ga. w/ejectors)	695
645A (28 .410 ga. w/ejectors)	850
645A (20/28 ga. two-bbl. set)	995
650A (12 ga. w/extractors, choke tubes)	655
655A (12 ga. w/ejectors, choke tubes)	725

Precision Sports 600 Series English Hammerless Doubles

Boxlock. Same general specifications as American 600 Series, except w/double triggers and concave rib. Checkered English-style walnut stock w/splinter forend, straight grip and oil finish.

640E (12, 16, 20 ga. w/extractors)	$555
640E (28, .410 ga. w/extractors)	625
640 Slug Gun (12 ga. w/extractors)	735
645E (12, 16, 20 ga. w/ejectors)	750
645E (28 .410 ga. w/ejectors)	715
645E (20/28 ga. two-bbl. set)	945
650E (12 ga. w/extractors, choke tubes)	650
655E (12 ga. w/ejectors, choke tubes)	695

Precision Sports Model 640M Magnum 10 Hammerless Double

Similar to Model 640E, except in 10 ga. w/3.5-inch Mag. chambers. Bbls.: 26-, 30-, 32-inch choked F/F.

Model 640M Big Ten, Turkey	$655
Model 640M Goose Gun	675

Precision Sports Model 645E-XXV Hammerless Double

Similar to Model 645E, except w/25-inch bbl. and Churchill-style rib.

645E-XXV (12, 16, 20 ga. w/ejectors)	$725
645E-XXV (28, .410 ga. w/ejectors)	795

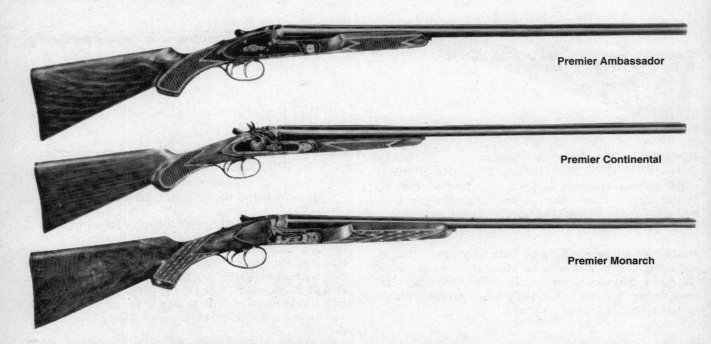

Premier Ambassador

Premier Continental

Premier Monarch

PREMIER SHOTGUNS

Premier shotguns have been produced by various gunmakers in Europe.

Premier Ambassador Model Field Grade Hammerless Double-Barrel Shotgun $350

Sidelock. Plain extractors. Double triggers. Gauges: 12, 16, 20, .410. 3-inch chambers in 20 and .410 ga., 2.75- inch in 12 and 16 ga. Bbls.: 26-inch in .410 ga., 28 inch in other ga.; choked M/F. Weight: 6 lbs.3 oz.-7 lbs.3 oz. depending on gauge. Checkered pistol-grip stock and beavertail forearm. Intro. in 1957; discontinued.

Premier Brush King $250

Same as standard Regent Model, except chambered for 12 (2.75-inch) and 20 ga. (3-inch) only; has 22-inch bbls., IC/M choke, straight-grip stock. Weight: 6 lbs. 3 oz. in 12 ga.; 5 lbs. 12 oz. in 20 ga. Introduced in 1959; discontinued.

Premier Conbnental Model Field Grade Hammer Double-Barrel Shotgun $350

Sidelock. Exposed hammers. Plain extractors. Double triggers. Gauges: 12, 16, 20, .410. 3-inch chambers in 20 and .410 ga., 2.75-inch in 12 and 16 ga. Bbls.: 26-inch in .410 ga.; 28-inch in other ga.; choked M/F. Weight: 6 lbs. 3 oz.-7 lbs. 3 oz. depending on gauge. Checkered pistol-grip stock and English-style forearm. Introduced in 1957; discontinued.

Premier Monarch Supreme Grade Hammerless Double-Barrel Shotgun $375

Boxlock. Auto ejectors. Double triggers. Gauges: 12, 20. 2.75-inch chambers in 12 ga., 3-inch in 20 ga. Bbls.: 28-inch M/F; 26-inch IC/M choke. Weight: 6 lbs. 6 oz.-7 lbs. 2 oz. depending on gauge and bbl. Checkered pistol-grip stock and beavertail forearm of fancy walnut. Introduced in 1959; discontinued.

Premier Presentation Custom Grade $895

Similar to Monarch model, but made to order, of higher quality with hunting scene engraving gold and silver inlaid, fancier wood. Introduced in 1959; discontinued.

Premier Regent 10-Gauge Magnum Express . . . $295

Same as standard Regent Model, except chambered for 10-ga. Magnum 3.5-inch shells, has heavier construction, 32-inch bbls. choked F/F, stock with recoil pad. Weight: 11.25 lbs. Introduced in 1957; discontinued.

Premier Regent 12-Gauge Magnum Express . . . $265

Same as standard Regent Model, except chambered for 12-ga. Magnum 3-inch shells, has 30-inch bbls. choked F and F, stock with recoil pad. Weight: 7.25 lbs. Introduced in 1957; discontinued.

Premier Regent Model Field Grade Hammerless Double-Barrel Shotgun $225

Boxlock. Plain extractors. Double triggers. Gauges: 12,16, 20, 28, .410. 3-inch chambers in 20 and .410 ga., 2.75-inch in other gauges. Bbls.: 26-inch IC/M, M/F (28 and .410 ga. only); 28-inch M/F; 30-inch M/F (12 ga. only). Weight: 6 lbs. 2 oz.-7 lbs. 4 oz. depending on gauge and bbl. Checkered pistol-grip stock and beavertail forearm. Introduced in 1955; discontinued.

JAMES PURDEY & SONS, LTD.
London, England

Purdey Hammerless Double-Barrel Shotgun

Sidelock. Auto ejectors. Single or double triggers. Gauges: 12, 16, 20. Bbls.: 26-, 27-, 28-, 30-inch (latter in 12 ga. only); any boring, any shape or style of rib. Weight: 5.25 -5.5 lbs. depending on model, gauge and bbl length. Checkered stock and forearm, straight grip standard, pistol-grip also available. Purdey

Purdey Hammerless Double

Purdey Over/Under

Purdey Single-Shot Trap

Purdey Hammerless Double-Barrel Shotgun *(Cont.)*

guns of this type have been made from about 1880 to date. Models include: Game Gun Featherweight Game Gun, Two-Inch Gun (chambered for 12 ga. 2-inch shells), Pigeon Gun (w/3rd fastening and side clips), values of all models are the same.
With double triggers **$31,500**
With single trigger 34,550

Purdey Over/Under Shotgun

Sidelock. Auto ejectors. Single or double triggers. Gauges: 12 16, 20. Bbls.: 26-, 27-, 28-, 30-inch (latter in 12 ga. only); any boring, any style rib. Weight: 6-7.5 pounds depending on gauge and bbl. length. Checkered stock and forend, straight or pistol grip. Prior to WW II, the Purdey Over-and-Under Gun was made

Purdey Over/Under Shotgun *(Cont.)*

with a Purdey action; since the war James Purdey & Sons have acquired the business of James Woodward & Sons and all Purdey over/under guns are now built on the Woodward principle. General specifications of both types are the same.
With Purdey action, double triggers **$39,000**
With Woodward action, double triggers 42,000
Single trigger, **extra** 1,000

Purdey Single-Barrel Trap Gun **$9,300**
Sidelock. Mechanical features similar to those of the over/under model with Purdey action. 12 ga. only. Built to customer's specifications. Made prior to World War II.

SHOTGUNS

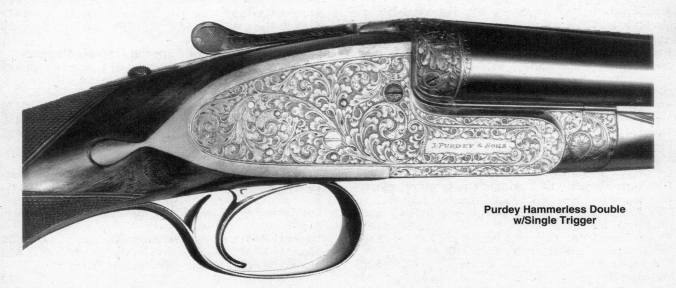

J. PURDEY & SONS

Purdey Hammerless Double
w/Single Trigger

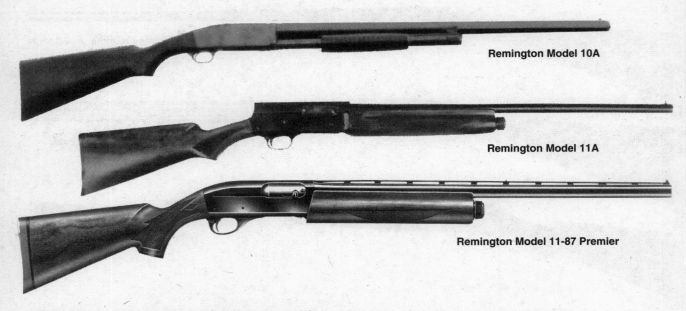

Remington Model 10A

Remington Model 11A

Remington Model 11-87 Premier

REMINGTON ARMS CO.
Ilion, New York

Eliphalet Remington Jr. began making long arms with his father in 1816. In 1828 they moved their facility to Ilion, N.Y., where it remained a family-run business for decades. As the family died, other people bought controlling interests and today, still a successful gunmaking company, it is a subsidiary of the du Pont Corporation.

Remington Model 10A Standard Grade
Slide-Action Repeating Shotgun $275
Hammerless. Takedown. 6-shot. 12 ga. only. 5-shell tubular magazine. Bbls.: plain; 26- to 32-inch; choked F, M or Cyl. Weight: about 7.5 lbs. Plain pistol-grip stock, grooved slide handle. Made 1907-29.

Remington Model 11 Special, Tournament, Expert and Premier Grade Guns
These higher grade models differ from the Model 11A in general quality, grade of wood, checkering, engraving, etc. General specifications are the same.

Model 11B Special Grade	$ 425
Model 11D Tournament Grade	850
Model 11E Expert Grade	1250
Model 11F Premier Grade	2195

Remington Model 11A Standard Grade Autoloader
Hammerless Browning type. 5-shot. Takedown. Gauges: 12, 16, 20. Tubular magazine holds four shells. Bbls.: plain, solid or vent rib, lengths from 26-32 inches, F, M, IC, Cyl., SK chokes. Weight: about 8 lbs., 12 ga.; 7.5 lbs., 16 ga.; 7.25 lbs., 20 ga. Checkered pistol grip and forend. Made 1905-49.

With plain barrel	$255
With solid-rib barrel	345
With ventilated-rib barrel	365

Remington Model 11R Riot Gun $275
Same as Model 11A Standard Grade, except has 20-inch plain barrel, 12 ga. only. Remington Model 11-48. *See* Remington Sportsman-48 Series.

Remington Model 11-87 Premier Autoloader
Gas-operated. Hammerless. Gauge: 12; 3-inch chamber. Bbl.: 26-, 28- or 30-inch with REM choke. Weight: 8.13- 8.38 lbs., depending on bbl. length. Checkered walnut stock and forend in satin finish. Made 1987 to date.

Premier Deer Gun	$395
Premier Deer Gun w/Cantilever scope mount	470
Premier Skeet	650
Premier Sporting Clays	520
Premier Standard Autoloader	425
Premier Trap	475
For Left-Hand Models, **add**	50

Remington Model 11-87 Special Purpose Magnum
Same general specifications Model 11-87 Premier, except with non-reflective wood finish and Parkerized metal. 21-, 26- or 28-inch vent-rib bbl. with REM Choke tubes. Made 1987-93.

Model 11-87 SP Field Magnum	$470
Model 11-87 SP Deer Gun (w/21-inch bbl.)	450
Model 11-87 SP Deer Gun w/cantilever scope mount	495

Remington 11-87 SPS Magnum
Same general specifications Model 11-87 Special Purpose Magnum, except with synthetic buttstock and forend. 21-, 26- or 28-inch vent-rib bbl. with REM Choke tubes. Matte black or Mossy Oak Camo finish (except NWTF Turkey Gun). Made 1990 to date.

Model 11-87 SPS Magnum (Matte black)	$450
Model 11-87 SPS Camo (Mossy Oak Camo)	495
Model 11-87 NWTF Turkey Gun (Brown Trebark) Discontinued 1993	520
Model 11-87 SPST Turkey Gun (Matte black)	475

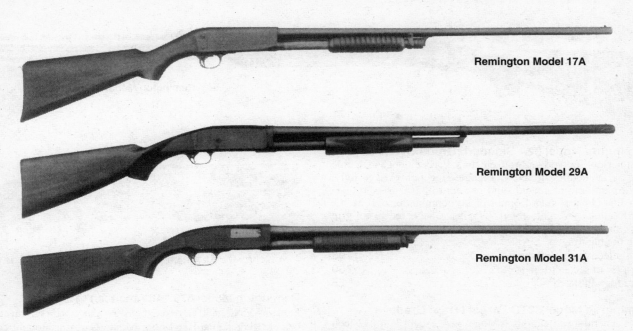

Remington Model 17A

Remington Model 29A

Remington Model 31A

Remington Model 17A Standard Grade Slide-Action Repeating Shotgun $365

Hammerless. Takedown. 5-shot. 20 ga. only. 4-shell tubular magazine. Bbls.: plain; 26- to 32-inch; choked F, M or Cyl. Weight: about 5.75 lbs. Plain pistol-grip stock, grooved slide handle. Made 1921-33. *Note:* The present Ithaca Model 37 is an adaptation of this Browning design.

Remington Model 29A Standard Grade Slide-Action Repeating Shotgun $350

Hammerless. Takedown. 6-shot. 12 ga. only. 5-shell tubular magazine. Bbls.: plain- 26- to 32-inch, choked F, M or Cyl. Weight: about 7.5 lbs. Checkered pistol-grip stock and slide handle. Made 1929-33.

Remington Model 29T Target Grade $360

Same general specifications as Model 29A, except has trap-style stock with straight grip, extension slide handle, vent-rib bbl. Discontinued 1933.

Remington Model 31 Skeet Grade

Same general specifications as Model 31A, except has 26-inch bbl. with raised solid or vent rib, SK choke, checkered pistol-grip stock and beavertail forend. Weight: about 8 lbs., 12 ga. Made 1932-1939.

With raised solid rib	$395
With ventilated rib	495

Remington Model 31 Special, Tournament, Expert and Premier Grade Guns

These higher grade models differ from the Model 31A in general quality, grade of wood, checkering, engraving, etc. General specifications are the same.

Model 31B Special Grade	$ 450
Model 31D Tournament Grade	775
Model 31E Expert Grade	1095
Model 31F Premier Grade	1200

Remington Model 31A Slide-Action Repeater

Hammerless. Takedown. 3- or 5-shot. Gauges: 12, 16, 20. Tubular magazine. Bbls.: plain, solid or vent rib; lengths from 26 -32 inches; F, M, IC, C or SK choke. Weight: about 7.5 lbs., 12 ga.; 6.75 lbs., 16 ga.; 6.5 lbs., 20 ga. Earlier models have checkered pistol-grip stock and slide handle; later models have plain stock and grooved slide handle. Made 1931-49.

Model 31A with plain barrel	$325
Model 31A with solid-rib barrel	395
Model 31A with vent-rib barrel	425
Model 31H Hunters' Special w/sporting-style stock . . .	395
Model 31R Riot Gun w/20-inch plain bbl., 12 ga.	225

Remington Model 31S Trap Special/31TC Trap Grade

Same general specifications as Model 31A, except 12 ga. only, has 30- or 32-inch vent-rib bbl., F choke, checkered trap stock with full pistol grip and recoil pad, checkered extension beavertail forend. Weight: about 8 lbs. (Trap Special has solid-rib bbl., half pistol-grip stock with standard walnut forend).

Model 31S Trap Special	$425
Model 31TC Trap Grade	595

Remington Model 32 Skeet Grade

Same general specifications as Model 32A, except 26- or 28-inch bbl., SK choke, beavertail forend, selective single trigger only. Weight: about 7.5 lbs. Made 1932-42.

With plain barrels	$1550
With raised solid rib	1695
With ventilated rib	1850

Remington Model 32 Tournament, Expert and Premier Grade Guns

These higher grade models differ from the Model 32A in general quality, grade of wood, checkering, engraving, etc. General specifications are the same. Made 1932-42.

Model 32D Tournament Grade	$ 2,995
Model 32E Expert Grade	3,795
Model 32F Premier Grade	10,000

SHOTGUNS

Remington Model 32TC Trap

Remington Model 32A Standard Grade Over/Under

Hammerless. Takedown. Auto ejectors. Early model had double triggers, later built with selective single trigger only. 12 ga. only. Bbls.: plain, raised matted solid or vent rib; 26-, 28-, 30-, 32-inch; F/M choke standard, option of any combination of F, M, IC, C, SK choke. Weight: about 7.75 lbs. Checkered pistol-grip stock and forend. Made 1932-42.

With double triggers $1595
With selective single trigger 1795
Extra for raised solid rib 200
Extra for ventilated rib 25

Remington Model 32TC Target (Trap) Grade

Same general specifications as Model 32A, except 30- or 32-inch vent-rib bbl., F choke, trap-style stock with chleckered pistol-grip and beavertail forend. Weight: about 8 lbs. Made l932-42.

With double triggers $2495
With selective single trigger 3655

Remington Model 89 (1989) $950

Hammers. Circular action. Gauges: 10,12, 16. 28- to 32-inch bls.; steel or damascus twist. Weight 7-10 lbs. Made 1889-1908.

Remington Model 90-T Single-Shot Trap $2350

Gauge: 12; 2.75-inch chambers. 30-, 32- or 34-inch vent-rib bbl. with fixed chokes or screw-in REM Chokes; ported or non-ported. Weight: 8.25 lbs. Checkered American walnut standard or Monte Carlo stock with low-luster finish. Engraved sideplates and drop-out trigger group optional. Made 1990 to date.

NOTE

In 1980 Remington changed the stock styling for all Model 870 Shotguns.

**Remington Model 870
"All American" Trap**

Remington Model 870 "All American" Trap Gun . . $725

Same as Model 870TB, except custom grade with engraved receiver, trigger guard and bbl.; Monte Carlo or straight-comb stock and forend of fancy walnut; available only with 30-inch F choke bbl. Made 1972-77.

Remington Model 870 Competition Trap $495

Based on standard Model 870 receiver, except is single-shot with gas-assisted recoil-reducing system, new choke design, a high step-up vent rib, and redesigned stock, forend with cut checkering and a satin finish. Weight: 8.5 lbs. Made 1981 to date.

Remington Model 870 Deer Gun Brushmaster Deluxe

Same as Model 870 Standard Deer Gun, except available in 20 ga. as well as 12, has cut-checkered, satin-finished American walnut stock and forend, recoil pad.

Right-Hand Model $295
Left-Hand Model 345

Remington Model 870 Deer Gun Standard $295

Same as Model 870 Wingmaster Riot Gun, except has rifle-type sights.

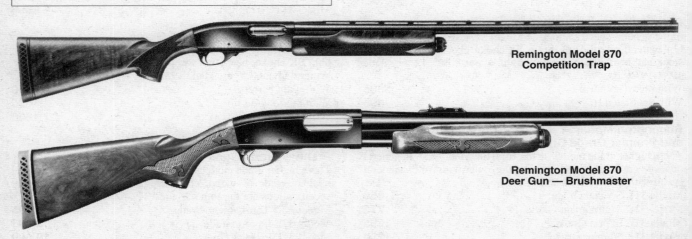

**Remington Model 870
Competition Trap**

**Remington Model 870
Deer Gun — Brushmaster**

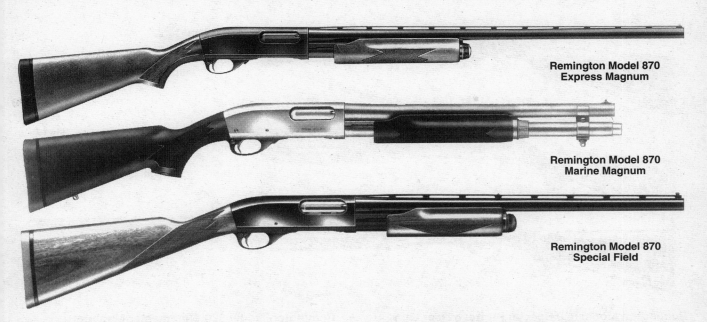

Remington Model 870
Express Magnum

Remington Model 870
Marine Magnum

Remington Model 870
Special Field

Remington Model 870 Express

Same general specifications Model 870 Wingmaster, except has low-luster walnut-finished hardwood stock with pressed checkering and black recoil pad. Gauges: 12, 20 or .410- 3-inch chambers. Bbls.: 26- or 28-inch vent-rib with REM Choke; 25-inch vent-rib with fixed choke (.410 only). Black oxide metal finish. Made 1987 to date.

Model 870 Express (12 or 20 ga., REM Choke) **$200**
Model 870 Express (.410 w/fixed choke) 215
Express Combo (w/extra 20-inch Deer Bbl.) 270

Remington Model 870 Express Deer Gun

Same general specifications as Model 870 Express, except in 12 ga. only, 20-inch bbl. with fixed IC choke, adj. rifle sights and Monte Carlo stock. Made 1991 to date.

Express Deer Gun w/standard barrel **$205**
Express Deer Gun w/fully rifled barrel 230

Remington Model 870 Express Turkey Gun **$220**

Same general specifications as Model 870 Express, except has 21-inch vent-rib bbl. and Turkey Extra-Full REM choke. Made 1991 to date.

Remington Model 870 Express Youth Gun **$250**

Same general specifications as Model 870 Express, except has scaled-down stock with 12.5-inch pull and 21-inch vent-rib bbl. with REM choke. Made 1991 to date.

Remington Model 870 Lightweight

Same as standard Model 870, but with scaled-down receiver and lightweight mahogany stock; 20 ga. only. 2.75-inch chamber. Bbls.: plain or vent rib; 26-inch, IC; 28-inch, M or F choke. REM choke available from 1987. Weight 5.75 lbs. w/26-inch plain bbl. American walnut stock and forend with satin or Hi-gloss finish. Made 1972 to date.

With plain barrel **$235**
With ventilated-rib barrel 260
With REM choke barrel 340

Remington Model 870 Lightweight Magnum

Same as Model 870 Lightweight, but chambered for 20 ga. Magnum 3-inch shell; 28-inch bbl., plain or vent rib, F choke. Weight: 6 lbs. with plain bbl. Made 1972 to date.

With plain barrel **$295**
With ventilated-rib barrel 325

Remington Model 870 Magnum Duck Gun

Same as Model 870 Field Gun, except has 3-inch chamber 12 and 20 gauge Magnum only. 28- or 30-inch bbl., plain or vent rib, M or F choke, recoil pad. Weight: about 7 or 6.75 lbs. Made 1964 to date.

With plain barrel **$295**
With ventilated-rib barrel 310

Remington Model 870 Marine Magnum **$295**

Same general specifications as Model 870 Wingmaster except with 7-shot magazine, 18-inch plain bbl. with fixed IC choke, bead front sight and electroless nickel finish. Made 1992 to date.

Remington Model 870 Mississippi Magnum
Duck Gun **$320**

Same as Remington Model 870 Magnum Duck Gun except has 32-inch bbl. Engraved receiver, "Ducks Unlimited." Made in 1983.

Remington Model 870 SA Skeet Gun,
Small Bore **$295**

Similar to Wingmaster Model 870SA, exeept chambered for 28 and .410 ga. (2.5-inch chamber for latter); 25- inch vent-rib bbl., SK choke. Weight: 6 lbs., 28 ga.; 6.5 lbs., .410. Made 1969-82.

Remington Model 870 Special Field Shotgun . . . **$325**

Pump action. Hammerless. Gauge: 12 or 20. 21-inch vent-rib bbl. with REM choke. 41.5 inches overall. Weight: 6-7 lbs. Straight-grip checkered walnut stock and forend. Made 1987 to date.

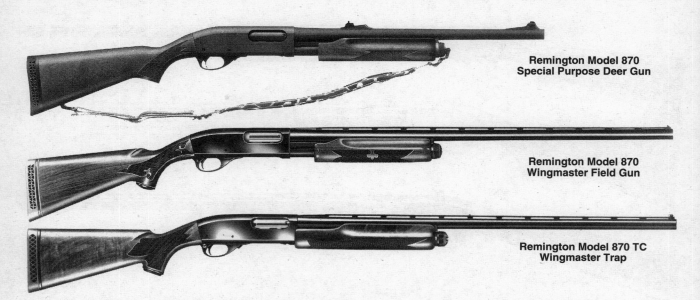

Remington Model 870
Special Purpose Deer Gun

Remington Model 870
Wingmaster Field Gun

Remington Model 870 TC
Wingmaster Trap

Remington Model 870 Special Purpose Deer Gun

Similar to Special Purpose Magnum, except with 20-inch IC choke, rifle sights. Matte black oxide and Parkerized finish. Oil-finished, checkered buttstock and forend with recoil pad. Made 1986 to date.

Model 870 SP Deer Gun **$330**
Model 870 SP Deer Gun, cantilever scope mount 365

Remington Model 870 Special Purpose Magnum. **$295**

Similar to the 870 Magnum Duck Gun, except with 26-, 28- or 30-inch vent-rib REM Choke bbl.12 ga. only; 3-inch chamber. Oil-finished field-grade stock with recoil pad, QD swivels and Cordura sling. Made 1985 to date.

Remington Model 870 SPS Magnum

Same general specifications Model 870 Special Purpose Magnum, except with synthetic stock and forend. 26- or 28-inch vent-rib bbl. with REM Choke tubes. Matte black or Mossy Oak Camo finish. Made 1991 to date.

Model 870 SPS Magnum (black syn. stock) **$270**
Model 870 SPS-T Camo (Mossy Oak Camo) 280

Remington Model 870 Wingmaster Field Gun

Same general specifications as Model 870AP, except checkered stock and forend. Later models have REM choke systems in 12 ga. Made 1964 to date.

With plain barrel **$270**
With ventilated-rib barrel 295

Remington Model 870 Wingmaster Field Gun, Small Bore

Same as standard Model 870, but scaled down. Gauges: 20, 28, .410. 25-inch bbl., plain or vent rib; IC, M or F choke, 26-, 28-inch (20 ga.) vent rib with REM Choke tubes. Weight: 5.5-6.25 lbs. depending on gauge and bbl. Made 1969 to date.

With plain barrel **$325**
With ventilated-rib barrel 340
With REM Choke 350

Remington Model 870 Wingmaster Magnum Deluxe Grade **$325**

Same as Model 870 Magnum Standard Grade, except has checkered stock and extension beavertail forearm, bbl. with matted top surface. Discontinued in 1963.

Remington Model 870 Wingmaster Magnum Standard Grade **$285**

Same as Model 870AP, except chambered for 12 ga. 3-inch Magnum, 30-inch F choke bbl., recoil pad. Weight: about 8.25 lbs. Made 1955-63.

Remington Model 870 Wingmaster REM Choke Series

Hammerless, takedown with blued all-steel receiver. Gauges: 12, 20; 3-inch chamber. Tubular magazine. Bbls.: 21-, 26-, 28-inch vent-rib with REM Choke. Weight: 7.5 lbs. (12 ga.). Satin-finished, checkered walnut buttstock and forend with recoil pad. Right- or left-hand models. Made 1986 to date.

Standard Model, 12 ga. **$305**
Standard Model, 20 ga. 315
Youth Model, 21-inch barrel 310

Remington Model 870ADL Wingmaster Deluxe Grade

Same general specifications as Wingmaster Model 870AP except has pistol-grip stock and extension beavertail forend, both finely checkered; matted top surface or vent-rib bbl. Made 1950-63.

With matted top-surface barrel **$220**
With ventilated-rib barrel 245

Remington Model 870AP Wingmaster Standard Grade

Hammerless. Takedown. Gauges: 12, 16, 20. Tubular magazine holds four shells. Bbls.: plain, matted top surface or vent rib; 26-inch IC, 28-inch M or F choke, 30-inch F choke (12 ga. only). Weight: about 7 lbs., 12 ga.; 6.75 lbs., 16 ga.; 6.5 lbs., 20 ga. Plain pistol-grip stock, grooved forend. Made 1950-63.

With plain barrel **$200**
With matted top-surface barrel 210
With ventilated-rib barrel 230
Left-hand model 240

Remington Model 870BDL Wingmaster Deluxe Special

Same as Model 870ADL, except select American walnut stock and forend. Made 1950-63.

With matted top-surface barrel **$275**
With ventilated-rib barrel **305**

Remington Model 870D, 870F Wingmaster Tournament and Premier Grade Guns

These higher grade models differ from the Model 870AP in general quality, grade of wood, checkering, engraving, etc. General operating specifications are essentially the same. Made 1950 to date.

Model 870D Tournament Grade **$1895**
Model 870F Premier Grade **4250**
Model 870F Premier Grade with gold inlay **5990**

Remington Model 870R Wingmaster Riot Gun . . **$280**

Same as Model 870AP, except 20-inch bbl., IC choke, 12 ga. only.

Remington Model 870SA Wingmaster Skeet Gun

Same general specifications as Model 870AP, except has 26-inch vent-rib bbl., SK choke, ivory bead front sight, metal bead rear sight, pistol-grip stock and extension beavertail forend. Weight: 6.75 to 7.5 lbs. depending on gauge. Made 1950-82.

Model 870SA Skeet Grade (Disc. 1982) .... **$ 275**
Model 870SC Skeet Target Grade (Disc 1980) **425**
Model 870SD Skeet Tournament Grade **1250**
Model 870SF Skeet Premier Grade **2495**

Remington Model 870TB Wingmaster Trap Special **$335**

Same general specifications as Model 870AP Wingmaster except has 28- or 30-inch vent-rib bbl., F choke, metal bead front sight, no rear sight. "Special" grade trap-style stock and forend, both checkered, recoil pad. Weight: about 8 lbs. Made 1950-81.

Remington Model 870TC Trap

Same general specifications Model 870TC Wingmaster except with REM Choke high-rib vent bbl. Redesigned satin finished stock and forend with cut-checkering. Made 1987 to date.

Model 870 TC Trap (Standard) **$460**
Model 870 TC Trap (Monte Carlo) **475**

Remington Model 870TC Wingmaster Trap Grade

Same as Model 870TB, except higher grade walnut in stock and forend, has both front and rear sights. Made 1950-79. Model 870 TC reissued in 1987. See separate listing.

Model 870TC Trap Grade .... **$ 425**
Model 870TD Trap Tournament Grade **1295**
Model 870TF Trap Premier Grade **2550**

Remington Model 878A Automaster **$225**

Gas-operated Autoloader. 12 ga., 3-shot magazine. Bbls.: 26-inch IC, 28-inch M choke, 30-inch F choke. Weight: about 7 lbs. Plain pistol-grip stock and forearm. Made 1959-62.

NOTE: New stock checkering patterns and receiver scroll markings were incorporated on all standard Model 1100 field, magnum, skeet and trap models in 1979.

Remington Model 1100 Automatic Field Gun

Gas-operated. Hammerless. Takedown. Gauges: 12, 16, 20. Bbls.: plain or vent. rib; 30-inch F, 28-inch M or F, 26-inch IC; or REM choke tubes. Weight: average 7.25-7.5 lbs. depending on ga. and bbl. length. Checkered walnut pistol-grip stock and forearm in high-gloss finish. Made 1963 to date. 16 ga. discontinued.

With plain barrel **$295**
With ventilated-rib barrel **335**
REM choke model **375**
REM chokes, Left-hand action **395**

Remington Model 1100 Deer Gun **$400**

Same as Model 1100 Field Gun, except has 22-inch barrel, IC, with rifle-type sights; 12 and 20 ga. only; recoil pad. Weight: about 7.25 lbs. Made 1963 to date.

SHOTGUNS

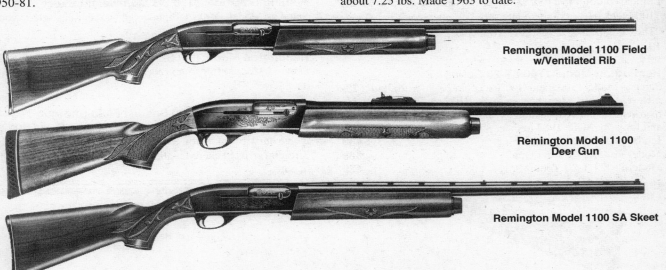

Remington Model 1100 Field
w/Ventilated Rib

Remington Model 1100
Deer Gun

Remington Model 1100 SA Skeet

Remington Model 1100 Ducks Unlimited Atlantic Commemorative $660
Limited production for one year. Similar specifications to Model 1100 Field, except with 32-inch F choke, vent-rib bbl. 12-ga. Magnum only. Made in 1982.

Remington Model 1100 Ducks Unlimited "The Chesapeake" Commemorative $495
Limited edition 1 to 2400. Same general specifications as Model 1100 Field, except sequentially serial numbered with markings "The Chesapeake." 12-ga. Magnum with 30-inch F choke, vent-rib bbl. Made in 1981.

Remington Model 1100 Field Grade, Small Bore
Same as standard Model 1100, but scaled down. Gauges: 28, .410.25-inch bbl., plain or vent rib; IC, M or F choke. Weight: 6.25-7 lbs. depending on gauge and bbl. Made 1969 to date.
With plain barrel **$380**
With ventilated rib **395**

Remington Model 1100 Lightweight
Same as standard Model 1100, but scaled-down receiver and lightweight mahogany stock; 20 ga. only, 2.75-inch chamber. Bbls.: plain or vent rib; 26-inch IC; 28-inch M and F choke. Weight: 6.25 lbs. Made 1971 to date.
With plain barrel **$370**
With ventilated rib **400**

Remington Model 1100 Lightweight Magnum
Same as Model 1100 Lightweight, but chambered for 20 gauge Magnum 3-inch shell; 28-inch bbl., plain or vent rib, F choke. Weight: 6.5 lbs. Made 1971 to date.
With plain barrel **$400**
With ventilated rib **420**
With choke tubes **450**

Remington Model 1100 LT-20 Ducks Unlimited Special Commemorative $495
Limited edition 1 to 2400. Same general specifications as Model 1100 Field, except sequentially serial numbered with markings "The Chesapeake." 20 ga. only. 26-inch IC, vent-rib bbl. Made in 1981.

Remington Model 1100 LT-20 Series
Same as Model 1100 Field Gun, except in 20 ga. with shorter 23-inch vent-rib bbl., straight-grip stock. REM choke series has 21-inch vent-rib bbl., choke tubes. Weight: 6.25 lbs. Checkered grip and forearm. Made 1983 to date.
Model 1100 LT-20 Special **$430**
Model 1100 LT-20 Deer Gun **395**
Model 1100 LT-20 Youth **425**

Remington Model 1100 Magnum $350
Limited production. Similar to the Model 1100 Field, except with 26-inch F choke, vent-rib bbl. and 3-inch chamber. Made in 1981.

Remington Model 1100 Magnum Duck Gun
Same as Model 1100 Field Gun, except has 3-inch chamber,12 and 20 ga. Mag. only. 30-inch plain or vent-rib bbl. in 12 ga., 28-inch in 20 ga.; M or F choke. Recoil pad. Weight: about 7.75 lbs. Made 1963 to date.
With plain barrel **$295**
With ventilated-rib barrel **335**

Remington Model 1100 One of 3000 Field $925
Limited edition, numbered 1 to 3000. Similar to Model 1100 Field, except with fancy wood and gold-trimmed etched hunting scenes on receiver. 12 gauge with 28-inch Mod., vent-rib bbl. Made in 1980.

Remington Model 1100 SA Skeet Gun
Same as Model 1100 Field Gun, 12 and 20 ga., except has 26-inch vent-rib bbl., SK choke or with Cutts Compensator. Weight: 7.25-7.5 lbs. Made 1963 to date.
With skeet-choked barrel **$390**
With Cutts Comp **410**
Left-hand action **425**

Remington Model 1100 SA Lightweight Skeet . . $375
Same as Model 1100 Lightweight, except has skeet-style stock and forearm, 26-inch vent-rib bbl., SK choke. Made 1971 to date.

Remington Model 1100 SA Skeet Small Bore . . $415
Similar to standard Model 1100SA, except chambered for 28 and .410 ga. (2.5-inch chamber for latter); 25-inch vent-rib bbl., SK choke. Weight: 6.75 lbs., 28 ga.; 7.25 lbs., .410. Made 1969 to date.

Remington Model 1100 SB Lightweight Skeet . . $395
Same as Model 1100SA Lightweight, except has select wood. Introduced in 1977.

Remington Model ll00 SB Skeet Gun $375
Same as Model 1100SA, except has select wood. Made 1963 to date.

Remington Model 1100 Special Field Shotgun . . $410
Gas-operated. 5-shot. Hammerless. Gauges: 12 and 20. 21-inch vent-rib bbl. with REM choke. Weight: 6.5-7.25 lbs. Straight-grip checkered walnut stock and forend. Made 1987 to date.

**Remington Model 100
Special Field**

**Remington Model 1100
Tournament Trap**

Remington Model 1100 SP Magnum

Same as Model 1100 Field, except 12 ga. only with 3-inch chambers. Bbls.: 26- or 30-inch F choke; or 26-inch with REM Choke tubes; vent rib. Non-reflective matte black, Parkerized bbl. and receiver. Satin-finished stock and forend. Made 1981 to date.

With Fixed Choke **$395**
With REM Choke **410**

Remington Model 1100 Tournament and Premier

These higher grade guns differ from standard models in overall quality, grade of wood, checkering, engraving, gold inlays, etc. General specifications are the same. Made 1963 to date.

Model 1100D Tournament **$1590**
Model 1100F Premier **2995**
Model 1100F Premier with gold inlay **4295**

Remington Model 1100 Tournament Skeet **$425**

Similar to Model 1100 Field, except with 26-inch bbl. SK choke. Gauges: 12, LT-20, 28, and .410. Features select walnut stocks and new cut-checkering patterns. Made 1979-89.

Remington Model 1100 Tournament Trap

Similar to Model 1100 Field Gun, except with 30-inch F or M trap bbls. 12-ga. Features select walnut stocks with cut-checkering patterns. Made 1979 to date.

D Grade **$1495**
F Grade **2995**
F Grade w/Gold Inlay **4150**

Remington Model 1100TA Trap Gun **$360**

Similar to Model 1100TB Trap Gun, except with regular-grade stocks. Available in both left- and right-hand versions. Made 1979 to date.

Remington Model 1100TB Trap Gun

Same as Model 1100 Field Gun, except has special trap stock, straight or Monte Carlo comb, recoil pad; 30-inch vent-rib bbl., F or M trap choke; 12 ga. only. Weight: 8.25 lbs. Made 1963-79.

With straight stock **$395**
With Monte Carlo stock **415**

Remington Model 1900 Hammerless Double . . . **$655**

Improved version of Model 1894. Boxlock. Auto ejector. Double triggers. Gauges: 10, 12, 16. Bbls.: 28 to 32 inches. Value shown is for standard grade with ordnance steel bbls. Made 1900-1910.

Remington Model 3200 Competition Skeet Gun **$1425**

Same as Model 3200 Skeet Gun, except has gilded scrollwork on frame, engraved forend latch plate and trigger guard, select fancy wood. Made 1973-84.

Remington Model 3200 Competition Skeet Set . . **$5195**

Similar specifications to Model 3200 Field. 12-ga. O/U with additional, interchangeable bbls. in 20, 28, and .410 ga. Cased. Made 1980-84.

Remington Model 3200 Competition Trap Gun . . . **$1625**

Same as Model 3200 Trap Gun, except has gilded scrollwork on frame, engraved forend latch plate and trigger guard, select fancy wood. Made 1973-84.

Remington Model 3200 Field Grade Magnum . . **$1390**

Same as Model 3200 Field, except chambered for 12 ga. mag. 3-inch shell- 30-inch bbls., M and F or both F choke. Made 1975-84.

Remington Model 3200 Field Grade O/U **$995**

Boxlock. Auto ejectors. Selective single trigger. 12 ga. 2.75-inch chambers. Bbls.: vent rib, 26- and 28-inch M/F; 30-inch IC/M. Weight: about 7.75 lbs. with 26-inch bbls. Checkered pistol-grip stock/forearm. Made 1973-78.

Remington Model 3200 "One of 1000" Skeet . . **$2150**

Same as Model 3200 "One of 1000" Trap, except has 26- or 28-inch bbls., SK choke, skeet-style stock and forearm. Made in 1974.

Remington Model 3200 "One of 1000" Trap . . . **$2195**

Limited edition numbered 1 to 1000. Same general specifications as Model 3200 Trap Gun, but has frame, trigger guard and forend latch elaborately engraved (designation "One of 1,000" on frame side), stock and forearm of high grade walnut. Supplied in carrying case. Made in 1973.

SHOTGUNS

**Remington Model 3200
"One of 1000" Skeet**

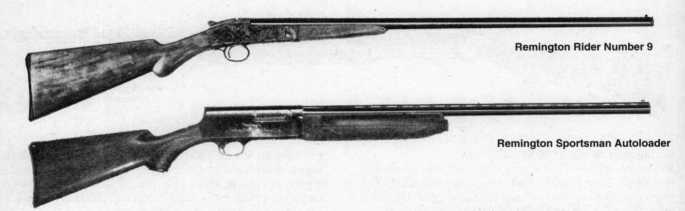

Remington Rider Number 9

Remington Sportsman Autoloader

Remington Model 3200 Skeet Gun $1150
Same as Model 3200 Field Grade, except skeet-style stock and full beavertail forearm, 26- or 28-inch bbls., SK choke. Made 1973-80.

Remington Model 3200 Special Trap Gun $995
Same as Model 3200 Trap Gun, except has select fancy-grade wood and other minor refinements. Made 1973-84.

Remington Model 3200 Trap Gun $1175
Same as Model 3200 Field Grade, except trap-style stock w/Monte Carlo or straight comb, select wood, beavertail forearm, 30- or 32-inch bbls. w/ventilated rib, IM/F or F/F chokes. Made 1973-1977.

Remington Rider No. 9 Single-Shot Shotgun ... $295
Improved version of No. 3 Single Barrel Shotgun made in the late 1800s. Semihammerless. Gauges 10, 12, 16, 20, 24, 28. 30- to 32-inch plain bbl. Weight: about 6 lbs. Plain pistol-grip stock and forearm. Auto ejector. Made 1902-10.

Remington SP-10 Magnum $695
Takedown. Gas-operated with stainless steel piston. 10 ga., 3.5-inch chamber. Bbls.: 26- or 30-inch vent-rib with REM Choke screw-in tubes. Weight: 11 to 11.25 lbs. Metal bead front. Checkered walnut stock with satin finish. Made 1989 to date.

Remington SP-10 Magnum Turkey Combo $995
Same general specifications as Model SP-10 Magnum, except has extra 22-inch REM Choke bbl. with M, F and Turkey Extra-Full tubes. Rifle sights. QD swivels and camo sling. Made 1991 to date.

Remington Sportsman A Standard Grade Autoloader
Same general specifications as Model 11A, except magazine holds two shells. Also available in "B" Special Grade, "D" Tournament Grade, "E" Expert Grade, "F" Premier Grade. Made 1931-48. Same values as for Model 11A.

Remington Sportsman Skeet Gun
Same general specifications as the Sportsman A, except has 26-inch bbl. (plain, solid or vent rib), SK choke, beavertail forend. Discont. 1949.
With plain barrel **$350**
With solid-rib barrel **435**
With ventilated-rib barrel **465**

Remington Sportsman-48A Standard Grade 3-Shot Autoloader
Streamlined receiver. Hammerless. Takedown. Gauges: 12, 16, 20. Tubular magazine holds two shells. Bbls.: plain, matted top surface or vent rib; 26-inch IC, 28-inch M or F choke, 30-inch F choke (12 ga. only). Weight: about 7.5 lbs., 12 ga.; 6.25 lbs., 16 ga.; 6.5 lbs., 20 ga. Pistol-grip stock, grooved forend, both checkered. Made 1949-59.
With plain bbl.................................. **$295**
With matted top-surface bbl.................... **325**
With ventilated-rib bbl. **345**

Remington Sportsman-48 B, D, F Special, Tournament and Premier Grade Guns
These higher grade models differ from the Sportsman-48A in general quality, grade of wood, checkering, engraving, etc. General specifications are the same. Made 1949-59.
Sportsman-48B Special Grade .... **$ 355**
Sportsman-48D Tournament Grade **755**
Sportsman-48F Premier Grade **1690**

Remington Sportsman-48A

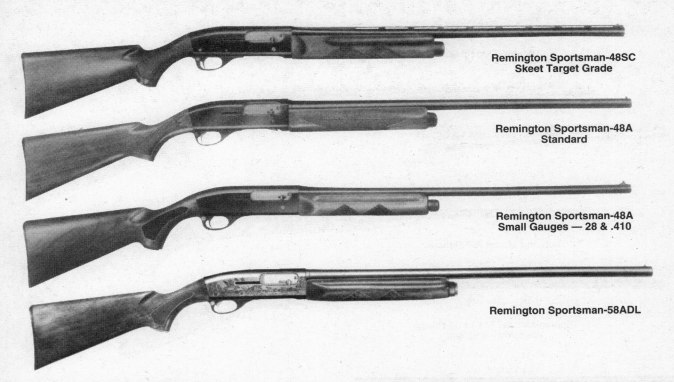

Remington Sportsman-48SC
Skeet Target Grade

Remington Sportsman-48A
Standard

Remington Sportsman-48A
Small Gauges — 28 & .410

Remington Sportsman-58ADL

Remington Sportsman-48SA Skeet Gun

Same general specifications as Sportsman-48A, except has 26-inch bbl. with matted top surface or vent rib, SK choke, ivory bead front sight, metal bead rear sight. Made 1949-60.

With matted top-surface barrel	**$ 265**
With ventilated-rib barrel	**325**
Sportsman-48SC Skeet Target Grade	**400**
Sportsman-48SD Skeet Tournament Grade	**695**
Sportsman-48SF Skeet Premier Grade	**1695**

Remington Model 11-48A Riot Gun $255

Same as Model 11-48A, except 20-inch plain barrel and 12 ga. only. Discontinued in 1969.

Remington Model 11-48A Standard Grade 4-Shot Autoloader .410 & 28 Gauge

Same general specifications as Sportsman-48A, except gauge, 3-shell magazine, 25-inch bbl. Weight: about 6.25 lbs. 28 ga. introduced 1952, .410 in 1954. Discontinued in 1969. Prices same as shown for Sportsman-48A.

Remington Model 11-48A Standard Grade 5-Shot Autoloader

Same general specifications as Sportsman-48A, except magazine holds four shells, forend not grooved. Also available in Special Grade (11-48B), Tournament Grade (11-48D) and Premier Grade (11-48F). Made 1949-1969. Prices same as shown for Sportsman-48A.

Remington Model 11-48SA 28 Gauge Skeet $325

Same general specifications as Model 11-48A 28 Gauge except has 25-inch vent-rib bbl., SK choke. 28 ga. introduced 1952, .410 in 1954.

Remington Sportsman-58 Skeet Target, Tournament and Premier Grades

These higher grade models differ from the Sportsman-58SA in general quality, grade of wood, checkering, engraving, and other refinements. General operating and physical specifications are the same.

Sportsman-58C Skeet Target Grade	**$ 500**
Sportsman-58D Skeet Tournament Grade	**695**
Sportsman-58SF Skeet Premier Grade	**1255**

Remington Sportsman-58 Tournament and Premier

These higher grade models differ from the Sportsman-58ADL with vent-rib bbl. in general quality, grade of wood, checkering, engraving, etc. General specifications are the same.

Sportsman-58D Tournament Grade	**$ 800**
Sportsman-58F Premier Grade	**1400**

Remington Sportsman-58ADL Autoloader

Deluxe Grade. Gas-operated. 12 ga. 3-shot magazine. Bbls.: plain or vent rib, 26-, 28- or 30-inch; IC, M or F choke, or Remington Special Skeet choke. Weight: about 7 lbs. Checkered pistol-grip stock and forearm. Made 1956-64.

With plain barrel	**$295**
With ventilated-rib barrel	**325**

Remington Sportsman-58BDL Deluxe Special Grade

Same as Model 58ADL, except select grade wood.

With plain barrel	**$300**
With ventilated-rib barrel	**345**

Remington Sportsman-58SA Skeet Grade $330

Same general specifications as Model 58ADL with vent-rib bbl., except special skeet stock and forearm.

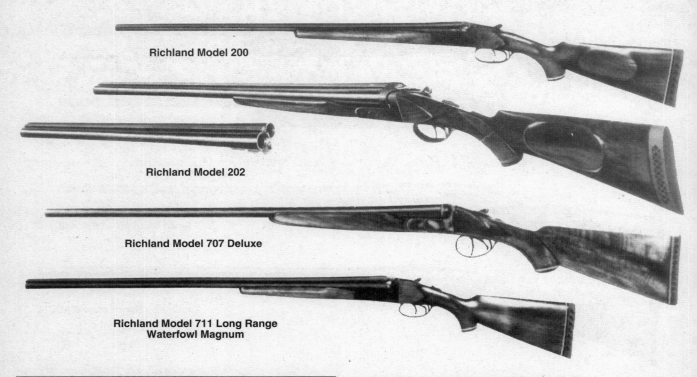

Richland Model 200

Richland Model 202

Richland Model 707 Deluxe

Richland Model 711 Long Range
Waterfowl Magnum

REVELATION SHOTGUNS
See Western Auto listings.

RICHLAND ARMS COMPANY
Blissfield, Michigan
Manufactured in Italy and Spain

Richland Model 200 Field Grade Double **$295**
Hammerless, boxlock, Anson & Deeley-type. Plain extractors. Double triggers. Gauges: 12, 16, 20, 28, .410 (3-inch chambers in 20 and .410; others have 2.75-inch). Bbls.: 28-inch M/F choke, 26-inch IC/M; .410 with 26-inch M/F only; 22-inch IC/M in 20 ga. only. Weight: 6 lbs. 2 oz. to 7 lbs. 4 oz. Checkered walnut stock with cheekpiece, pistol grip, recoil pad; beavertail forend. Made in Spain 1963 to date.

Richland Model 202 All-Purpose Field Gun **$355**
Hammerless, boxlock, Anson & Deeley-type. Same as Model 200, except has two sets of barrels same gauge. 12 ga.: 30-inch bbls. F/F, 3-inch chambers; 26-inch bbls. IC/M, 2.75-inch chambers. 20 gauge: 28-inch bbls. M/F; 22-inch bbls. IC/M, 3-inch chambers. Made 1963 to date.

Richland Model 707 Deluxe Field Gun **$310**
Hammerless, boxlock, triple bolting system. Plain extractors. Double triggers. Gauges: 12, 2.75-inch chambers; 20, 3-inch chambers. Bbls.: 12 ga., 28-inch M/F, 26-inch IC/M; 20 ga., 30-inch F/F, 28-inch M/F, 26-inch IC/M. Weight: 6 lbs. 4 oz. to 6 lbs. 15 oz. Checkered walnut stock and forend, recoil pad. Made 1963-72.

Richland Model 711 Long Range Waterfowl Magnum Double Barrel Shotgun
Hammerless, boxlock, Anson & Deeley-type, Purdey triple lock. Plain extractors. Double triggers. Auto safety. Gauges: 10, 3.5-inch chambers; 12, 3-inch chambers. Bbls.: 10 ga., 32-inch; 12 ga., 30-inch; F/F. Weight: 10 ga., 11 pounds; 12 ga., 7.75 lbs. Checkered walnut stock and beavertail forend; recoil pad. Made in Spain 1963 to date.
10 Gauge Magnum **$345**
12 Gauge Magnum **275**

Richland Model 808 Over-and-Under Gun **$375**
Boxlock. Plain extractors. Non-selective single trigger. 12 ga. only. Bbls. (Vickers steel): 30-inch F/F; 28-inch M/F; 26-inch IC/M. Weight: 6 lbs. 12 oz. to 7 lbs. 3 oz. Checkered walnut stock/forend. Made in Italy 1963-68.

Richland Model 808
Over/Under

JOHN RIGBY & COMPANY
London, England

Rigby Hammerless Box Lock Double-Barrel Shotguns
Auto ejectors. Double triggers. Made in all gauges, barrel lengths and chokes. Checkered stock and forend, straight grip standard. Made in two grades: Sackville and Chatsworth. These guns differ in general quality, engraving, etc.; specifications are the same.

Sackville Grade $5125
Chatsworth Grade 3850

Rigby Regal Sidelock

Rigby Hammerless Side Lock Double-Barrel Shotguns
Auto ejectors. Double triggers. Made in all gauges, barrel lengths and chokes. Checkered stock and forend, straight grip standard. Made in two grades: Regal (best quality) and Sandringham; these guns differ in general quality, engraving, etc., specifications are the same.

Regal Grade $9000
Sandringham Grade 6595

AMADEO ROSSI, S.A.
Sao Leopoldo, Brazil

Rossi Hammerless Double Barrel Shotgun $265
Boxlock. Plain extractors. Double triggers. 12 ga. 3-inch chambers. Bbls.: 26-inch IC/M; 28-inch M/F choke. Weight: 7 to 7.5 lbs. Pistol-grip stock and beavertail forearm, uncheckered. Made 1974 to date. *Note:* H&R Model 404 (1969-72) is same gun.

Rossi Overland Hammer Double $225
Sidelock. Plain extractors. Double triggers. Gauges: 12, .410; 3-inch chambers. Bbls.: 20-inch, IC/M in 12 g.; 26-inch, F/F choke in .410. Weight: 7 lbs., 12 ga.; 6 lbs. .410. Pistol-grip stock and beavertail forearm, uncheckered. *Note:* Because of its resemblance to the short-barreled doubles carried by guards riding shotgun on 19th-century stagecoaches, the 12 ga. version originally was called the "Coach Gun." Made 1968-89.

ROTTWEIL SHOTGUNS
West Germany

Rottweil Model 72 Over/Under Shotgun $1595
Hammerless, takedown with engraved receiver. 12 ga.; 2.75-inch chambers. 26.75-inch bbls. with SK/SK chokes. Weight: 7.5 lbs. Interchangeable trigger groups and buttstocks. Checkered French walnut buttstock and forend. Imported from West Germany.

Rottweil Model 650 Field O/U Shotgun $620
Breech action. Gauge: 12. 28-inch bbls. Six screw-in choke tubes. Automatic ejectors. Engraved receiver. Checkered pistol grip stock. Made 1984-86.

Rottweil American Skeet $1550
Boxlock action. Gauge: 12. 27-inch vent-rib bbls. 44.5 inches overall. SK chokes. Weight: 7.5 lbs. Designed for tube sets. Hand-checkered European walnut stock with modified forend. Made 1984-87.

Rottweil International Trap Shotgun $1595
Boxlock action. Gauge: 12. 30-inch bbls. 48.5 inches overall. Weight: 8 lbs. Choked IM/F. Selective single trigger. Metal bead front sight. Checkered European walnut stock w/pistol grip. Engraved action. Made 1984-87.

Rossi Hammerless Double

Rossi Overland Double

Rottweil American Skeet

SHOTGUNS

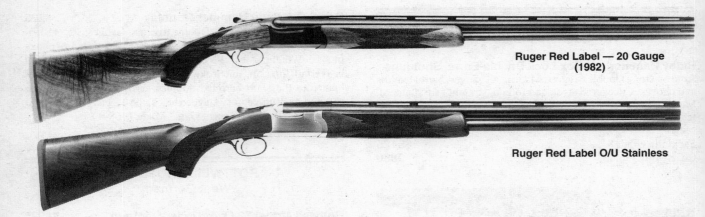

Ruger Red Label — 20 Gauge
(1982)

Ruger Red Label O/U Stainless

RUGER SHOTGUN
Southport, Connecticut
Manufactured by Sturm, Ruger & Company

Ruger Plain Grade Red Label Over/Under **$745**
Boxlock. Auto ejectors. Selective single trigger. 20 ga. 3-inch
chambers. 26-inch vent-rib bbl., IC/M or SK choke. Weight:
about 7 lbs. Checkered pistol-grip stock and forearm. Introduced
in 1977, 12 ga. version 1982. Chambers: 2.75- and 3-inch. Bbls.:
26-, 28- and 30-inch. Weight: about 7.5 lbs.

Ruger Red Label Over/Under Stainless
Gauges: 12 and 20; 3-inch chambers. Bbls.: 26- or 28-inch. Various
chokes, fixed or screw-in tubes. Weight: 7 to 7.5 lbs. Single selec-
tive trigger. Selective automatic ejectors. Automatic top safety.
Standard gold bead front sight. Pistol-grip or English-style Ameri-
can walnut stock w/hand-cut checkering. Made 1985 to date.
W/Fixed Chokes **$800**
W/Screw-in Tubes **895**

Ruger Red Label "Woodside" Over/Under **$745**
Similar to the Red Label O/U Stainless except in 12 ga. only
with wooden sideplaate extensions. Made 1995 to date.

Ruger Sporting Clays Over/Under Stainless . . **$920**
Similar to the Red Label O/U Stainless, except in 12 ga. only
w/30-inch vent-rib bbls., no side ribs; back-bored w/screw-in
choke tubes (not interchangeable w/other Red Label O/U models). Brass front and mid-rib beads. Made 1992 to date.

VICTOR SARASQUETA, S. A.
Eibar, Spain

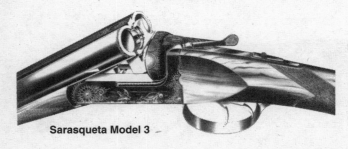

Sarasqueta Model 3

Sarasqueta Model 3 Hammerless Boxlock Double-Barrel Shotgun
Plain extractors or auto ejectors. Double triggers. Gauges: 12,
16, 20. Made in various bbl. lengths, chokes and weights. Checkered stock and forend, straight grip standard. Currently manufactured.
Model 3, plain extractors **$465**
Model 3E, automatic ejectors **550**

Sarasqueta Model 6E

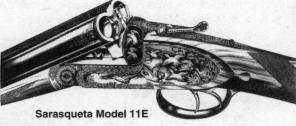

Sarasqueta Model 11E

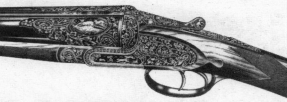

Sarasqueta Model 12E

Sarasqueta Hammerless Sidelock Doubles
Automatic ejectors (except on Models 4 and 203 which have
plain extractors). Double triggers. Gauges: 12, 16, 20. Barrel
lengths, chokes and weights made to order. Checkered stock and
forend, straight grip standard. Models differ chiefly in overall

Sarasqueta Hammerless Sidelock Doubles (Cont.)

quality, engraving, grade of wood, checkering, etc.; general specifications are the same. Currently manufactured.

Model 4	$ 575
Model 4E	625
Model 203	575
Model 203E	625
Model 6E	725
Model 7E	740
Model 10E	1555
Model 11E	1650
Model 12E	1895

J. P. SAUER & SOHN
Eckernförde, Germany
Formerly located in Suhl, Germany

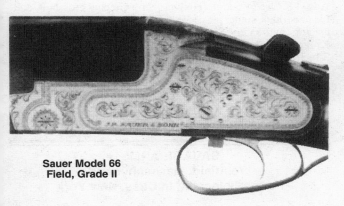

**Sauer Model 66
Field, Grade II**

**Sauer Model 66
Field, Grade III**

Sauer Model 66 Over/Under Field Gun

Purdey-system action with Holland & Holland-type sidelocks. Selective single trigger. Selective auto ejectors. Automatic safety. Available in three grades of engraving. 12 ga. only. Krupp-Special steel bbls. w/vent rib 28-inch, M/F choke. Weight: about 7.25 lbs. Checkered walnut stock and forend; recoil pad. Made 1966-75.

Grade I	$1600
Grade II	2100
Grade III	2900

Sauer Model 66 Over/Under Skeet Gun

Same as Model 66 Field Gun, except 26-inch bbls. with wide vent rib, SK choked- skeet-style stock and ventilated beavertail forearm; nonautomatic safety. Made 1966-75.

Grade I	$1595
Grade II	2050
Grade III	2895

Sauer Model 66 Over/Under Trap Gun

Same as Model 66 Skeet Gun, except has 30-inch bbls. choked F/F or M/F; trap-style stock. Values same as for Skeet Model. Made 1966-75.

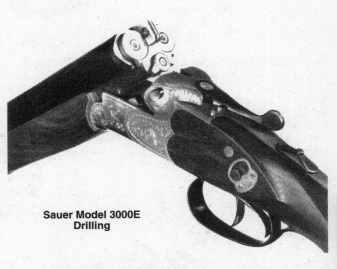

**Sauer Model 3000E
Drilling**

Sauer Model 3000E Drilling

Combination rifle and double barrel shotgun. Blitz action with Greener crossbolt, double underlugs, separate rifle cartridge extractor, front set trigger, firing pin indicators, Greener side safety, sear slide selector locks right shotgun bbl. for firing rifle bbl. Gauge/calibers: 12 ga. (2.75-inch chambers); 222, 243, 30-06, 7×65R. 25-inch Krupp-Special steel bbls.; M/F choke automatic folding leaf rear rifle sight. Weight: 6.5 to 7.25 lbs. depending on rifle caliber. Checkered walnut stock and forend; pistol grip, M Monte Carlo comb and cheekpiece, sling swivels. Standard Model with arabesque engraving; Deluxe Model with hunting scenes engraved on action. Currently manufactured. *Note: Also* see listing under Colt.

Standard Model	$2955
Deluxe Model	3990

Sauer Artemis Double-Barrel Shotgun

Holland & Holland-type sidelock with Greener crossbolt double underlugs, double sear safeties, selective single trigger, selective auto ejectors. Grade I with fine-line engraving, Grade II with full English arabesque engraving. 12 ga. (2.75-inch chambers). Krupp-Special steel bbls., 28-inch, M/F choke. Weight: about 6.5 lbs. Checkered walnut pistol-grip stock and beavertail forend; recoil pad. Made 1966-77.

Grade I	$3995
Grade II	4950

SHOTGUNS

Sauer BBF Combination
Rifle/Shotgun

Sauer Royal Double

Sauer BBF Over/Under Combination Rifle/Shotgun

Blitz action with Kersten lock, front set trigger fires rifle bbl., slide-operated sear safety. Gauge/calibers: 16 ga.; 30-30, 30-06,7×65R.25-inch Krupp-Special steel bbls.; shotgun bbl. F choke, folding-leaf rear sight. Weight: about 6 lbs. Checkered walnut stock and forend; pistol grip, mod. Monte Carlo comb and cheekpiece, sling swivels. Standard Model with arabesque engraving; Deluxe Model with hunting scenes engraved on action. Currently manufactured.

Standard Model **$1850**
Deluxe Model **2295**

Sauer Royal Double-Barrel Shotguns

Anson & Deeley action (boxlock) with Greener crossbolt, double underlugs, signal pins, selective single trigger, selective auto ejectors, auto safety. Scalloped frame with arabesque engraving. Krupp-Special steel bbls. Gauges: 12, 2.75-inch chambers, 20, 3-inch chambers. Bbls.: 30-inch (12 ga. only) and 28-inch, M/F 26-inch (20 ga. only), IC/M. Weight: 12 ga., about 6.5 lbs.; 20 ga., 6 lbs. Checkered walnut pistol-grip stock and beavertail forend; recoil pad. Made 1955-77.

Standard Model **$1295**
20 Gauge **1795**

Sauer Rex I
Single-Shot Shotgun

Sauer Rex I Single-Shot Shotgun **$175**

Gauges: 12, 16, 20. 24.5-inch bbl.; Weight: 5.8 lbs. Hardwood buttstock and forend.

SAVAGE ARMS
Westfield, Massachusetts
Formerly located in Utica, New York

Savage Model 24 22-.410 O/U Combination **$130**
Same as Stevens No. 22-.410, has walnut stock and forearm. Made 1950-65.

Savage Model 24C Camper's Companion **$145**
Same as Model 24FG, except made in 22 Magnum/20 ga. only; has 20-inch bbls., shotgun tube Cyl. bore. Weight: 5.75 lbs. Trap in butt provides ammunition storage; comes with carrying case. Made 1972-89.

Savage Model 24D **$185**
Same as Models 24DL and 24MDL, except frame has black or casehardened finish. Game scene decoration of frame eliminated in 1974; forearm uncheckered after 1976. Made 1970-88.

Savage Model 24
First Issue

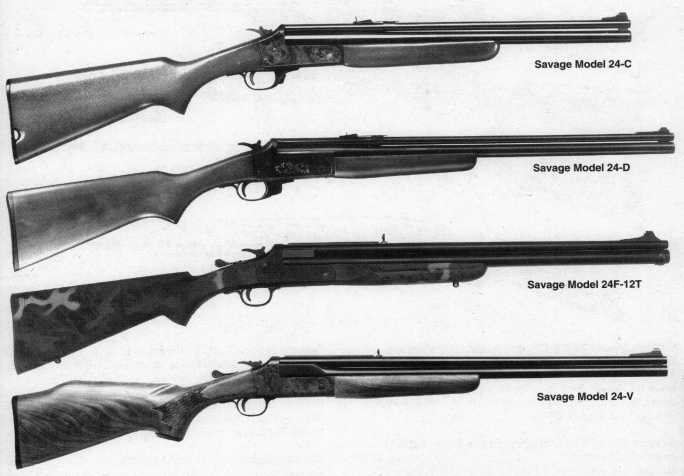

Savage Model 24-C

Savage Model 24-D

Savage Model 24F-12T

Savage Model 24-V

Savage Model 24DL $195
Same general specifications as Model 24S, except top lever opening; satin-chrome-finished frame decorated with game scenes,
checkered Monte Carlo stock and forearm. Made 1965-69.

Savage Model 24F-12T Turkey Gun $255
12- or 20-ga. shotgun bbl./22 Hornet, 223 or 30-30 caliber rifle.
24-inch blued bbls., 3-inch chambers, extra removable F choke
tube. Hammer block safety. Color casehardened frame. du Pont
Rynite® camo stock. Swivel studs. Made 1989 to date.

Savage Model 24FG Field Grade $125
Same general specifications as Model 24S, except top lever
opening. Made 1972 to date.

Savage Model 24MDL $140
Same as Model 24DL, except rifle bbl. chambered for 22 WMR.
Made 1965-69.

Savage Model 24MS $125
Same as Model 24S, except rifle bbl. chambered for 22 WMR.
Made 1965-71.

Savage Model 24S Over/Under Combination . . . $140
Boxlock. Visible hammer. Side lever opening. Plain extractors.
Single trigger. 20 ga. or .410 bore shotgun bbl. under 22 LR bbl.,
24-inch. Open rear sight, ramp front, dovetail for scope mount-
ing. Weight: about 6.75 lbs. Plain pistol-grip stock and forearm.
Made 1965-71.

Savage Model 24V $235
Similar to Model 24D, except 20 ga. under 222 Rem., 22 Rem.,
357 Mag., 22 Hornet or 30-30 rifle bbl. Made 1971-89.

**Savage Model 24-VS
Camper/Survival**

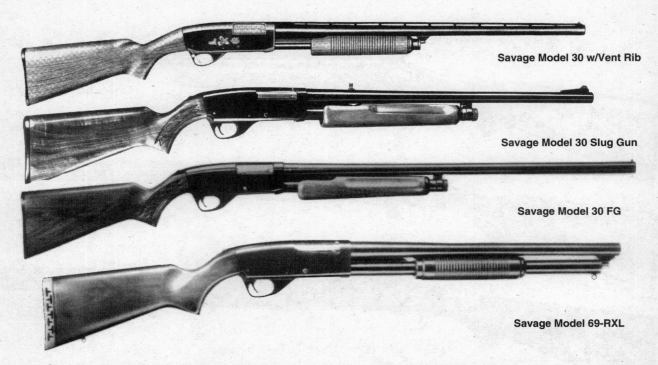

Savage Model 30 w/Vent Rib

Savage Model 30 Slug Gun

Savage Model 30 FG

Savage Model 69-RXL

Savage Model 24-VS Camper/Survival/Centerfire Rifle/Shotgun $195
Similar to Model 24V except 357 Rem. Mag. over 20 ga. Nickel finish full-length stock and accessory pistol-grip stock. Overall length: 36 inches with full stock; 26 inches w/pistol grip. Weight: about 6.5 lbs. Made 1983-88.

Savage Model 28A Standard Grade Slide-Action Repeating Shotgun $225
Hammerless. Takedown. 12 ga. 5-shell tubular magazine. Plain bbl., lengths: 26-,28-, 30-, 32-inches, choked C/M/F. Weight: about 7.5 lbs. with 30-inch bbl. Plain pistol-grip stock, grooved slide handle. Made 1928-31.

Savage Model 28B $235
Raised matted rib; otherwise the same as Model 28A.

Savage Model 28D Trap Grade $300
Same general specifications as Model 28A, except has 30-inch F choke bbl. w/matted rib, trap-style stock w/checkered pistol grip, checkered slide handle of select walnut.

Savage Model 30 Solid Frame Hammerless Slide-Action Shotgun $180
Gauges: 12, 16, 20, .410. 2.75-inch chamber in 16 ga., 3- inch in other ga. Magazine holds four 2.75-inch shells or three 3-inch shells. Bbls.: vent rib; 26-, 28-, 30-inch; IC, M, F choke. Weight: average 6.25 to 6.75 lbs. depending on ga. Plain pistol-grip stock (checkered on later production), grooved slide handle. Made 1958-70.

Savage Model 30 Takedown Slug Gun $175
Same as Model 30FG, except 21-inch Cyl. bore bbl. with rifle sights. Made 1971-79.

Savage Model 30AC Solid Frame $195
Same as Model 30 Solid Frame, except has 26-inch bbl. with adj. choke; 12 ga. only. Made 1959-70.

Savage Model 30AC Takedown $175
Same as Model 30FG, except has 26-inch bbl. with adj. choke; 12 and 20 ga. only. Made 1971-72.

Savage Model 30ACL Solid Frame $195
Same as Model 30AC Solid Frame, except left-hand model with ejection port and safety on left side; 12 ga. only. Made 1960-64.

Savage Model 30D Takedown $175
Deluxe Grade. Same as Model 30FG, except has receiver engraved with game scene, vent-rib bbl., recoil pad. Made 1971 to date.

Savage Model 30FG Takedown Hammerless Slide-Action Shotgun $145
Field Grade. Gauges: 12, 20, .410. 3-inch chamber. Magazine holds four 2.75-inch shells or three 3-inch shells. Bbls.: plain; 26-inch F choke (.410 ga. only); 28-inch M/F choke; 30-inch F choke (12 ga. only). Weight: average 7 to 7.75 lbs. depending on gauge. Checkered pistol-grip stock, fluted slide handle. Made 1970-79.

Savage Model 30L Solid Frame $170
Same as Model 30 Solid Frame, except left-handed model with ejection port and safety on left side; 12 ga. only. Made 1959-70.

Savage Model 30T Solid Frame Trap and Duck . . $195
Same as Model 30 Solid Frame, except only in 12 ga. w/30-inch F choke bbl.; has Monte Carlo stock with recoil pad, weighs about 8 lbs. Made 1963-70.

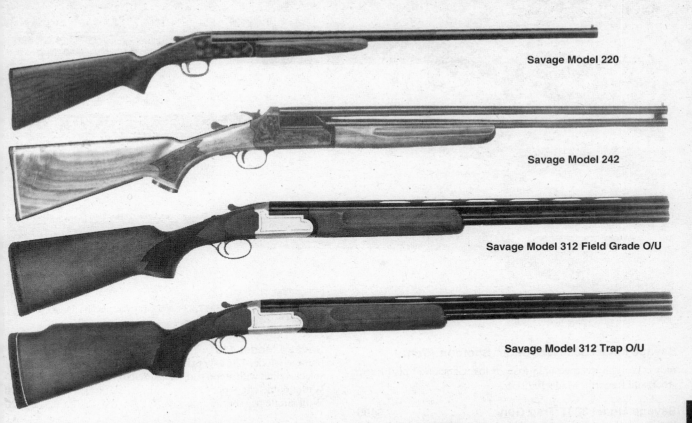

Savage Model 220

Savage Model 242

Savage Model 312 Field Grade O/U

Savage Model 312 Trap O/U

Savage Model 30T Takedown Trap Gun **$175**
Same as Model 30D, except only in 12 ga. w/30-inch F choke bbl. Monte Carlo stock with recoil pad. Made 1970-73.

Savage Model 69-RXL Slide-Action Shotgun . . . **$165**
Hammerless, side ejection top tang safe for left- or right-hand use. 12 ga. chambered for 2.75- and 3-inch magnum shells. 18.25-inch bbl. Tubular magazine holds 6 rounds (one less for 3-inch mag). Walnut finish hardwood stock with recoil pad, grooved operating handle. Weight: about 6.5 lbs. Made 1982 to date. *See* photo preceding page.

Savage Model 220 Single-Barrel Shotgun **$125**
Hammerless. Takedown. Auto ejector. Gauges: 12,16, 20 .410. Single shot. Bbl. lengths: 12 ga., 28- to 36-inch, 16 ga., 28- to 32-inch; 20 ga., 26- to 32-inch; .410 bore, 26-and 28-inch. F choke. Weight: about 6 lbs. Plain pistol-grip stock and wide forearm. Made 1938-65.

Savage Model 220AC **$150**
Same as Model 220, except has Savage adj. choke.

Savage Model 220L **$120**
Same general specifications as Model 220, except has side lever opening instead of top lever. Made 1965-72.

Savage Model 220P **$135**
Same as Model 220, except has Poly Choke built integrally with bbl., made in 12 ga. with 30-inch bbl., 16 and 20 ga. with 28-inch bbl., not made in .410 bore; has recoil pad.

Savage Model 242 Over/Under Shotgun **$285**
Similar to Model 24D, except both bbls. .410 bore, F choke. Weight: about 7 lbs. Made 1977-80.

Savage Model 312 Field Grade O/U **$495**
Gauge: 12; 2.75- or 3-inch chambers. 26- or 28-inch bbls. w/vent rib; F/M/IC chokes. 43 or 45 inches overall. Weight: 7 lbs. Internal hammers. Top tang safety. American walnut stock with checkered pistol grip and recoil pad. Made 1990-93.

Savage Model 312 Sporting Clays O/U **$525**
Same as Model 312 Field Grade, except furnished with #1 and #2 skeet tubes and 28-inch bbls. only. Made 1990-93.

Savage Model 312 Trap Over/Under **$530**
Same as Model 312 Field Grade, except with 30-inch bbls. only, Monte Carlo buttstock and weight of 7.5 lbs. Made 1990-93.

Savage Model 330 Over/Under Shotgun **$425**
Boxlock. Plain extractors. Selective single trigger. Gauges: 12, 20. 2.75-inch chambers in 12 ga., 3-inch in 20 gauge. Bbls.: 26-inch IC/M; 28-inch M/F; 30-inch M/F choke (12 ga. only). Weight: 6.25 to 7.25 lbs., depending on gauge. Checkered pistol-grip stock and forearm. Made 1969-78.

Savage Model 333 Over/Under Shotgun **$525**
Boxlock. Auto ejectors. Selective single trigger. Gauges: 12, 20. 2.75-inch chambers in 12 ga., 3-inch in 20 ga. Bbls.: vent rib; 26-inch SK choke, lC/M; 28-inch M/F; 30-inch M/F choke (12 ga.

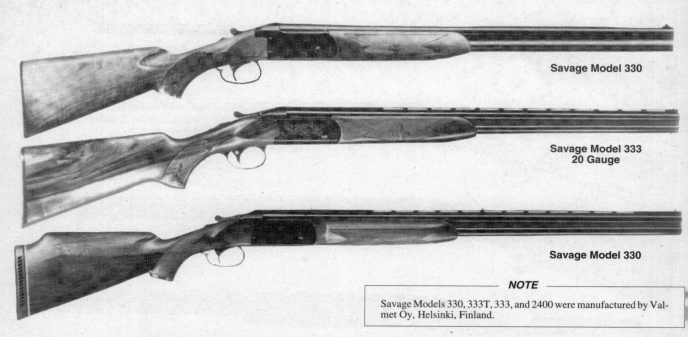

Savage Model 330

Savage Model 333
20 Gauge

Savage Model 330

Savage Model 333 Over/Under Shotgun *(Cont.)*

only). Weight: average 6.25 to 7.25 lbs. Checkered pistol-grip stock and forearm. Made 1973-79.

Savage Model 333T Trap Gun $495
Similar to Model 330, except only in 12 ga. with 30-inch vent-rib bbls., IM/F choke; Monte Carlo stock w/recoil pad. Weight: 7.75 lbs. Made 1972-79.

Savage Model 420 Over/Under Shotgun
Boxlock. Hammerless. Takedown. Automatic safety. Double triggers or non-selective single trigger. Gauges: 12, 16, 20. Bbls.: plain, 26- to 30-inch (the latter in 12 ga. only); choked M/F, C/IC. Weight with 28-inch bbls.: 12 ga., 7.75 lbs.; 16 ga., 7.5 lbs.; 20 ga., 6.75 lbs. Plain pistol-grip stock and forearm. Made 1938-42.
With double triggers $495
With single trigger 575

Savage Model 430
Same as Model 420, except has matted top bbl., checkered stock of select walnut with recoil pad, checkered forearm. Made 1938-42.
With double triggers $550
With single trigger 600

Savage Model 440 Over/Under Shotgun $475
Boxlock. Plain extractors. Selective single trigger. Gauges: 12, 20. 2.75-inch chambers in 12 ga., 3-inch in 20 ga. Bbls.: vent rib; 26-inch SK choke, IC/M; 28-inch M/F; 30-inch M/F choke (12 ga. only). Weight: average 6 to 6.5 lbs. depending on ga. Made 1968-72.

Savage Model 440T Trap Gun $465
Similar to Model 440, except only in 12 ga. with 30-inch bbls., extra-wide vent rib, IM/F choke. Trap-style Monte Carlo stock and semibeavertail forearm of select walnut, recoil pad. Weight: 7.5 lbs. Made 1969-72.

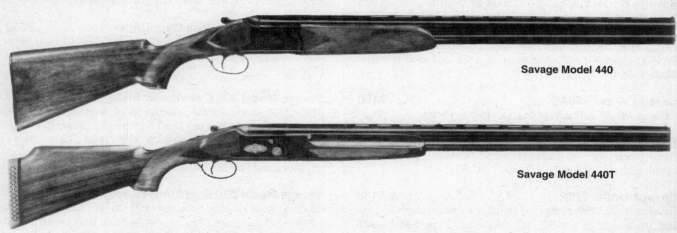

Savage Model 440

Savage Model 440T

Savage Model 550

Savage Model 444 Deluxe Over/Under Shotgun . . $525
Similar to Model 440, except has auto ejectors, select walnut stock and semibeavertail forearm. Made 1969-72.

Savage Model 550 Hammerless Double $235
Boxlock. Auto ejectors. Non-selective single trigger. Gauges: 12, 20. 2.75-inch chamber in 12 ga., 3-inch in 20 ga. Bbls.: vent rib; 26-inch IC/M; 28-inch M/F; 30-inch M/F choke (12 ga. only). Weight: 7 to 8 lbs. Checkered pistol-grip stock and semibeavertail forearm. Made 1971-73.

Savage Model 720 Standard Grade 5-Shot Autoloading Shotgun $250
Browning type. Takedown. 12 and 16 ga. 4-shell tubular magazine. Bbl.: plain; 26- to 32-inch (the latter in 12 ga. only); choked C, M, F. Weight: about 8.25 lbs., 12 ga. with 30-inch bbl.; 16 ga., about .5 lb. lighter. Checkered pistol-grip stock and forearm. Made 1930-49.

Savage Model 726 Upland Sporter Grade 3-Shot Autoloading Shotgun $240
Same as Model 720, except has 2-shell magazine capacity. Made 1931-49.

Savage Model 740C Skeet Gun $295
Same as Model 726, except has special skeet stock and full beavertail forearm, equipped with Cutts Compensator bbl. length overall with spreader tube is about 24.5 inches. Made 1936-49.

Savage Model 745 Lightweight Autoloader $210
Three- or five-shot model. Same general specifications as Model 720, except has lightweight alloy receiver, 12 ga.only, 28-inch plain bbl. Weight: about 6.75 lbs. Made 1940-49.

Savage Model 750 Automatic Shotgun $210
Browning-type autoloader. Takedown. 12 ga. 4-shot tubular magazine. Bbls.: 28-inch F or M choke; 26-inch IC. Weight: about 7.25 lbs. Checkered walnut pistol-grip stock and grooved forearm. Made 1960-67.

Savage Model 750-AC $275
Same as Model 750, except has 26-inch bbl. with adj. choke. Made 1964-67.

Savage Model 750-SC $250
Same as Model 750, except has 26-inch bbl. with Savage Super Choke. Made 1962-63.

Savage Model 755 Standard Grade Autoloader . . . $215
Streamlined receiver. Takedown.12 and 16 ga. 4-shell tubular magazine (a three-shot model with magazine capacity of two shells was also produced until 1951). Bbl.: plain, 30-inch F choke (12 ga. only), 28-inch F or M, 26-inch IC. Weight: about 8.25 lbs., 12 ga. Checkered pistol-grip stock and forearm. Made 1949-58.

Savage Model 755-SC $200
Same as Model 755, except has 26-inch bbl. w/recoil-reducing, adj. Savage Super Choke.

SHOTGUNS

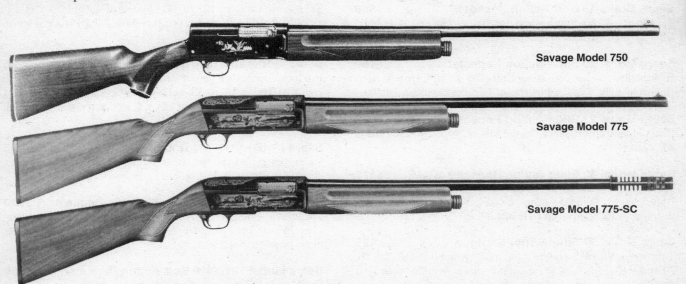

Savage Model 750

Savage Model 775

Savage Model 775-SC

**Savage Model 2400
Over/Under Combination Gun**

Savage Model 775 Lightweight $210
Same general specifications as Model 755, except has light-weight alloy receiver and weighs about 6.73 lbs. Made 1950-65.

Savage Model 775-SC $210
Same as Model 775, except has 26-inch bbl. with Savage Super Choke.

Savage Model 2400 Over/Under Combination . . $595
Boxlock action similar to that of Model 330. Plain extractors. Selective single trigger. 12-ga. (2.75-inch chamber) shotgun bbl., F choke, over 308 Win. or 222 Rem. rifle bbl.; 23.5-inch; solid matted rib with blade front sight and folding leaf rear, dovetail for scope mounting. Weight: about 7.5 lbs. Monte Carlo stock w/pistol grip and recoil pad, semibeavertail forearm, checkered. Made 1975-79 by Valmet.

SEARS, ROEBUCK & COMPANY
Chicago, Illinois
J. C. Higgins and Ted Williams Models

Although they do not correspond to specific models below the names Ted Williams and J. C. Higgins have been used to designate various Sears shotguns at various times.

Sears Model 18 Bolt-Action Repeater $80
Takedown. 3-shot top-loading magazine. Gauge: .410 only. Bbl.: 25-inch w/variable choke. Weight: about 5.75 lbs.

Sears Model 20 Slide-Action Repeater $160
Hammerless. 5-shot magazine. Bbls.: 26- to 30-inch w/various chokes. Weight: 7.25 lbs. Plain pistol-grip stock and slide handle.

Sears Model 21 Slide-Action Repeater $185
Same general specifications as the Model 20 except vent rib and adj. choke.

Sears Model 30 Slide-Action Repeater $175
Hammerless. Gauges: 12, 16, 20 and .410. 4-shot magazine. Bbls.: 26- to 30-inch, various chokes. Weight: 6.5 lbs. Plain pistol-grip stock, grooved slide handle.

Sears Model 97 Single-Shot Shotgun $65
Takedown. Visible hammer. Automatic ejector. Gauges: 12, 16, 20 and .410. Bbls.: 26- to 36-inch, F choke. Weight: average 6 lbs. Plain pistol-grip stock and forearm.

Sears Model 97-AC Single-Shot Shotgun $80
Same general specifications as Model 97 except fancier stock and forearm.

Sears Model 101.7 Double-Barrel Shotgun $160
Boxlock. Double triggers. Gauges: 12, 16, 20, .410. Bbls.: 26- to 32-inch, choked M and F. Weight: from 6 to 7.5 lbs. Plain stock and forend.

Sears Model 101.7C Double-Barrel Shotgun . . . $175
Same general specifications as Model 101.7, except checkered stock and forearm.

Sears Model 101.25 Bolt-Action Shotgun $80
Takedown. .410 gauge. 5-shell tubular magazine. 24-inch bbl., F choke. Weight: about 6 lbs. Plain, one-piece pistol-grip stock.

Sears Model 101.40 Single-Shot Shotgun $65
Takedown. Visible hammer. Automatic ejector. Gauges: 12, 16, 20 and .410. Bbls.: 26- to 36-inch, F choke. Weight: average 6 lbs. Plain pistol-grip stock and forearm.

Sears Model 101.1120 Bolt-Action Repeater $80
Takedown. .410 ga. 24-inch bbl., F choke. Weight: about 5 lbs. Plain one-piece pistol-grip stock.

Sears Model 101.1380 Bolt-Action Repeater $90
Takedown. Gauges: 12, 16, 20. 2-shell detachable box magazine. 26-inch bbl., F choke. Weight: about 7 lbs. Plain one-piece pistol-grip stock.

Sears Model 101.1610 Double-Barrel Shotgun . . $235
Boxlock. Double triggers. Plain extractors. Gauges: 12, 16, 20 and .410. Bbls.: 24- to 30-inch. Various chokes, but mostly M and F. Weight: about 7.5 lbs, 12 ga. Checkered pistol-grip stock and forearm.

Sears Model 101.1701 Double-Barrel Shotgun . . $245
Same general specifications as Model 101.1610 except satin chrome frame and select walnut stock and forearm.

Sears Model 101.5350-D Bolt-Action Repeater . . . $80
Takedown. Gauges: 12, 16, 20. 2-shell detachable box magazine. 26-inch bbl., F choke. Weight: about 7.25 lbs. Plain one-piece pistol-grip stock.

Sears Model 101.5410 Bolt-Action Repeater $80
Same general specifications as Model 101.5350-D.

Sears Model 103.720 Bolt-Action Repeater **$75**
Takedown. Automatic thumb safety. .410 ga. 24-inch bbl., F choke. Weight: about 5 lbs. Plain pistol-grip stock.

Sears Model 103.740 Bolt-Action Repeater **$75**
Same general specifications as Model 103.720.

Sears Model 200 Slide-Action Repeater **$165**
Front-locking rotary bolt. Takedown. 4-shot magazine. Gauges: 12, 16 and 20. Bbl.: plain or vent rib. Weight: 6.5 to 7.25 lbs. Checkered pistol grip and forearm.

Sears Model 300 Autoloading Shotgun **$195**
Gas-operated. Front-locking rotary bolt. Takedown. 2-shot magazine. Gauges: 12, 16, 20. Bbl.: plain or vent rib. Various chokes. Weight: 6.5 to 7.5 lbs. Checkered pistol-grip stock and forearm, recoil pad.

Sears Model 5100 Double-Barrel Shotgun **$150**
Boxlock. Double triggers. Gauges: 12,16, 20, .410. Bbls.: 26- to 32-inch, IC/M, M/F, and F/F chokes depending on ga. Weight: 6 to 7.5 lbs.

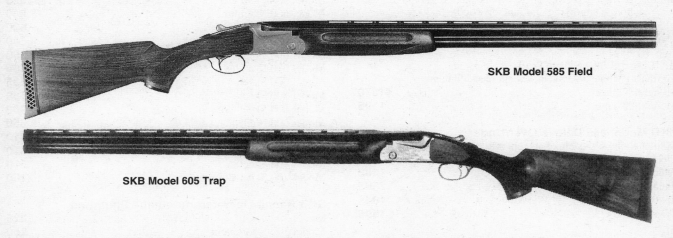

SKB Model 585 Field

SKB Model 605 Trap

SKB ARMS COMPANY
Tokyo, Japan

SKB Models 300 and 400 Side-by-Side Doubles
Similar to Model 200E, except higher grade. Models 300 and 400 differ in that the latter has more elaborate engraving and fancier wood.
Model 300 . . . . **$625**
Model 400 795

SKB Model 400 Skeet **$825**
Similar to Model 200E Skeet, except higher grade with more elaborate engraving and full fancy wood.

SKB Model 480 English **$865**
Similar to Model 280 English, except higher grade with more elaborate engraving and full fancy wood.

SKB Model 500 Small Gauge O/U Shotgun **$550**
Similar to Model 500, except gauges 28 and .410; has 28-inch vent-rib bbls., M/F chokes. Weight: about 6.5 lbs.

SKB Model 505 O/U Shotgun
Blued boxlock action. Gauge: 12, 20, 28 and .410. Bbls.: 26-, 28, 30-inch; IC/M, M/F or inner choke tubes. 45.19 inches overall. Weight: 6.6 to 7.4 lbs. Hand checkered walnut stock. Metal bead front sight, ejectors, single selective trigger. Introduced 1988.
Standard Model . . . . **$ 795**
Two-bbl. Field Set. 1250

SKB Model 585 Deluxe Over/Under Shotgun
Boxlock. Gauges: 12, 20, 28 and .410; 2.75-or 3-inch chambers. Bbls.: 26-, 28-, 30-, 32- or 34-inch with vent rib; fixed chokes or Inter-choke tubes. Weight: 6.5 to 8.5 lbs. Single selective trigger. Selective automatic ejectors. Manual safety. Checkered walnut stock in standard or Monte Carlo style. Silver nitride finish with engraved game scenes. Made 1987 to date.
Field, Skeet, Trap Grade . . . . **$ 790**
Field Grade, two-bbl. set 1395
Skeet Set (20, 28, .410 ga.) 1895
Sporting Clays 825
Trap Combo (two-bbl.) 1395

SKB Model 600 Small Gauge **$675**
Same as Model 500 Small Gauge, except higher grade with more elaborate engraving and fancier wood.

SKB Model 605 Trap O/U Shotgun **$895**
Similar to the Model 505 except has silvered, engraved receiver. Introduced 1988.

SKB Model 685 Deluxe Over/Under
Similar to the 585 Deluxe, except with semi-fancy American walnut stock. Gold trigger and jeweled barrel block. Silvered receiver with fine engraving.
Field, Skeet, Trap Grade . . . . **$ 895**
Field Grade, two-bbl. set 1395
Skeet Set 1995
Sporting Clays 925
Trap Combo. two bbl. 1595

SHOTGUNS

SKB Model 885 Trap

SKB Model 800 Skeet/Trap Over/Under

Similar to Model 700 Skeet and Trap, except higher grade with more elaborate engraving and fancier wood.

Model 800 Skeet **$870**
Model 800 Trap **895**

SKB Model 880 Skeet/Trap

Similar to Model 800 Skeet, except has sideplates.

Model 880 Skeet **$1070**
Model 880 Trap **1195**

SKB Model 885 Deluxe Over/Under

Similar to the 685 Deluxe, except with engraved sideplates.

Field, Skeet, Trap Grade . . . . **$ 995**
Field Grade, two-bbl. set **1395**
Skeet Set **2595**
Sporting Clays **1045**
Trap Combo **1695**

The following SKB shotguns were distributed by Ithaca Gun Co. 1966-76. For specific data, please see corresponding listings under Ithaca.

SKB Century Single-Barrel Trap Gun

The SKB catalog does not differentiate between Century and Century II; however, specifications of current Century are those of Ithaca-SKB Century II.

Century **$495**
Century II **595**

SKB Gas-operated Automatic Shotguns

Model XL300 with plain barrel **$265**
Model XL300 with vent rib **295**
Model XL900 . . . . **325**
Model XL900 Trap **370**
Model XL900 Skeet **345**
Model XL900 Slug **290**
Model 1300 Upland, Slug **375**
Model 1900 Field, Trap, Slug **445**

SKB Over/Under Shotguns

Model 500 Field **$525**
Model 500 Magnum **540**
Model 600 Field **630**
Model 600 Magnum **640**
Model 600 Trap **650**
Model 600 Doubles **650**
Model 600 Skeet—12 or 20 gauge **635**
Model 600 Skeet—28 or .410 . . . . **650**
Model 600 Skeet Combo **1900**
Model 600 English **650**
Model 700 Trap **810**
Model 700 Doubles **810**
Model 700 Skeet **810**
Model 700 Skeet Combo **2100**

SKB Recoil-Operated Automatic Shotguns

Model 300—with plain barrel **$225**
Model 300—with vent rib **250**
Model 900 . . . . **335**
Model 900 Slug **295**

SKB Side-by-Side Double-Barrel Shotguns

Model 100 . . . . **$385**
Model 150 . . . . **395**
Model 200E **525**
Model 200E Skeet **560**
Model 280 English **595**

SILE SHOTGUNS
Sile Distributors
New York, NY

Sile Field Master II O/U Shotgun **$450**
Gauge: 12, 3-inch chambers. 28-inch bbl., IC, M, IM, F choke tubes. 45.25 inches overall. Weight: 7.25 lbs. Satin-finished walnut, checkered stock and forend. Introduced 1989.

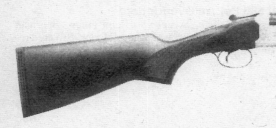

Sile Field Master II

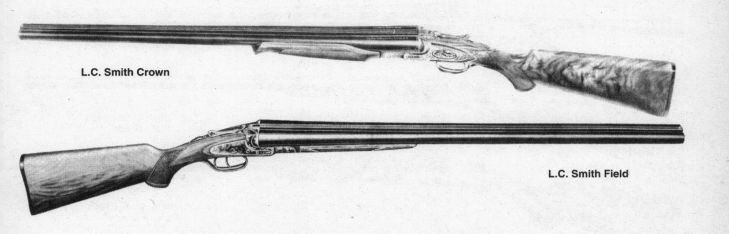

L.C. Smith Crown

L.C. Smith Field

L. C. SMITH SHOTGUNS
Made 1890-1945 by Hunter Arms Company, Fulton, N.Y.; 1946-51 and 1968-73 by Marlin Firearms Company, New Haven, Conn.

L. C. Smith Double-Barrel Shotguns

Values shown are for L. C. Smith doubles made by Hunter. Those of 1946-51 Marlin manufacture generally bring prices about ⅓ lower. Smaller gauge models, especially in the higher grades, command premium prices: up to 50 percent more for 20 gauge, up to 200 percent for .410 gauge.

Crown Grade, double triggers, automatic ejectors	**$ 4,600**
Crown Grade, selective single trigger, automatic ejectors	**4,850**
Deluxe Grade, selective single trigger, automatic ejectors	**15,195**
Field Grade, double triggers, plain extractors	**995**
Field Grade, double triggers, auto ejectors	**1,195**
Field Grade, non-selective single trigger, plain extractors	**1,125**
Field Grade, selective single trigger, automatic ejectors	**1,170**
Ideal Grade, double triggers, plain extractors	**1,500**
Ideal Grade, double triggers, automatic ejectors	**1,695**
Ideal Grade, selective single trigger, automatic ejectors	**1,950**
Monogram Grade, selective single trigger, automatic ejectors	**9,595**
Olympic Grade, selective single trigger, automatic ejectors	**1,790**
Premier Grade, selective single trigger automatic ejectors	**11,550**
Skeet Special, non-selective single trigger, automatic ejectors	**1,640**
Skeet Special, sel. single trigger, auto ejectors	**1,695**
.410 Ga.	**12,200**
Specialty Grade, double triggers, auto ejectors	**2,895**
Specialty Grade, selective single trigger, automatic ejectors	**3,300**
Trap Grade, sel. single trigger, auto ejectors	**1,295**

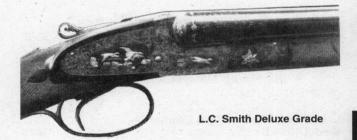

L.C. Smith Deluxe Grade

L C. Smith Hammerless Double-Barrel Shotguns

Sidelock. Auto ejectors standard on higher grades, extra on Field and Ideal Grades. Double triggers or Hunter single trigger (non-selective or selective). Gauges: 12, 16, 20, .410. Bbls.: 26- to 32-inch, any standard boring. Weight: 6.5 to 8.25 lbs., 12 ga. Checkered stock and forend; choice of straight, half or full pistol grip, beavertail or standard-type forend. Grades differ only in quality of workmanship, wood, checkering, engraving, etc. Same general specifications apply to all. Manufacture of these L. C. Smith guns was discontinued in 1951. Production of Field Grade 12 ga. was resumed 1968-73. *Note:* L. C. Smith Shotguns manufactured by the Hunter Arms Co. 1890-13 were designated by numerals to indicate grade, with the exception of Pigeon and Monogram.

00 Grade	**$ 1,025**
0 Grade	**1,350**
1 Grade	**1,500**
2 Grade	**1,700**
3 Grade	**2,350**
Pigeon	**3,000**
4 Grade	**5,500**
5 Grade	**5,750**
Monogram	**8,500**
A1	**3,500**
A2	**8,400**
A3	**+15,000**

SHOTGUNS

L.C. Smith Ideal Grade

L.C. Smith Model 1968
Field Grade

L.C. Smith Model 1968
Deluxe Grade

L. C. Smith Hammerless Double Model 1968
Field Grade **$595**
"Re-creation" of the original L. C. Smith double. Sidelock. Plain
extractors. Double triggers. 12 ga. 28-inch vent-rib bbls., M/F
choke. Weight: about 6.75 lbs. Checkered pistol-grip stock and
forearm. Made 1968-73.

L. C. Smith Hammerless Double
Model 1968 Deluxe **$645**
Same as 1968 Field Grade, except has Simmons floating vent rib,
beavertail forearm. Made 1971-73.

L. C. Smith Single-Shot Trap Guns
Boxlock. Hammerless. Auto ejector.12 gauge only. Bbl. lengths:
32- or 34-inch. Vent rib. Weight: 8 to 8.25 lbs. Checkered pistol-
grip stock and forend, recoil pad. Grades vary in quality of workmanship, wood, engraving, etc.; general specifications are the
same. Discont. 1951. *Note:* Values shown are for L. C. Smith single-barrel trap guns made by Hunter. Those of Marlin manufacture generally bring prices about one-third lower.

Olympic Grade	$ 1375
Specialty Grade	1695
Crown Grade	3195
Monogram Grade	4395
Premier Grade	7075
Deluxe Grade	1,115

SMITH & WESSON SHOTGUNS
Springfield, Massachusetts
Mfd. by Howa Machinery, Ltd., Nagoya, Japan

In 1985 Smith and Wesson sold its shotgun operation to O. F.
Mossberg & Sons, Inc.

Smith & Wesson Model 916 Slide-Action Repeater
Hammerless. Solid frame. Gauges: 12, 16, 20. 3-inch chamber in
12 and 20 ga. 5-shot tubular magazine. Bbls.: plain or vent rib; 20-
inch C (12 ga., plain only); 26-inch IC- 28-inch M or F; 30-inch F
choke (12 ga. only). Weight: with 28-inch plain bbl., 7.25 lbs.
Plain pistol-grip stock, fluted slide handle. Made 1972-81.
With plain bbl. **$155**
With ventilated-rib bbl. **195**

Smith & Wesson Model 916T
Same as Model 916, except takedown, 12 ga. only. Not available
with 20-inch bbl. Made 1976-81.
With plain bbl. **$175**
With ventilated-rib bbl. **195**

Smith & Wesson Model 1000 Autoloader **$315**
Gas-operated. Takedown. Gauges: 12, 20. 2.75-inch chamber in
12 ga., 3-inch in 20 ga. 4-shot magazine. Bbls.: vent rib, 26-inch

L.C. Smith Single-Shot Trap Gun

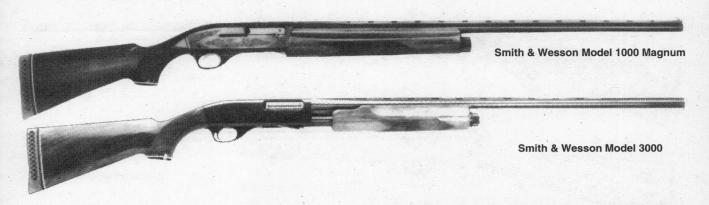

Smith & Wesson Model 1000 Magnum

Smith & Wesson Model 3000

Smith & Wesson Model 1000 Autoloader *(Cont.)*

SK choke, IC; 28-inch M or F; 30-inch F choke (12 ga. only). Weight: with 28-inch bbl., 6.5 lbs. in 20 ga.,7.5 lbs. in 12 ga. Checkered pistol-grip stock and forearm. Made 1972 to date.

Smith & Wesson Model 1000 Magnum $395

Same as standard Model 1000, except chambered for 12 ga. magnum, 3-inch shells; 30-inch bbl. only, M or F choke; stock with recoil pad. Weight: about 8 lbs. Introduced in 1977.

Smith & Wesson Model 1000P $325

Same general specifications as Model C 3000 Slide Action, but an earlier version.

Smith & Wesson Model 3000 Slide Action $295

Hammerless. 20-ga. Bbls.: 26-inch IC; 28-inch M or F. Chambered for 3-inch magnum and 2.75-inch loads. American walnut stock and forearm. Checkered pistol grip and forearm. Introduced 1982.

SPRINGFIELD ARMS
Built by Savage Arms Company, Utica, New York

Springfield Double-Barrel Hammer Shotgun . . . $325

Gauges: 12 and 16. Bbls.: 28 to 32 inches. In 12 ga., 32-inch model, both bbls. have F choke. All other gauges and barrel lengths are left barrel Full, right barrel Mod. Weight: 7.25 to 8.25 lbs., depending on gauge and barrel length. Black walnut checkered buttstock and forend. Discontinued 1934.

SQUIRES BINGHAM CO., INC.
Makati, Rizal, Philippines

Squires Bingham Model 30 Pump Shotgun $160

Hammerless. 12 ga. 5-shot magazine. Bbl.: 20-inch Cyl.; 28-inch M; 30-inch F choke. Weight: about 7 lbs. Pulong Dalaga stock and slide handle. Currently manufactured.

J. STEVENS ARMS COMPANY
Chicopee Falls, Massachusetts
Division of Savage Arms Corporation

Stevens No. 20 "Favorite" Shotgun $350

Calibers: 22 and 32 Shot. Smoothbore bbl. Blade front sight; no rear. Made 1893-1939.

Stevens No. 39 New Model Pocket Shotgun $525

Gauge: .410. Calibers: 38-40 Shot, 44-40 Shot. Bbls.: 10, 12, 15 or 18 inches, half-octagonal smoothbore. Shotgun sights. Made 1895-1906.

Stevens No. 22-.410 Over/Under Combination Gun

22 caliber rifle barrel over .410 bore shotgun barrel. Visible hammer. Takedown. Single trigger. 24-inch bbls., shotgun bbl. F choke. Weight: about 6 lbs. Open rear sight and ramp front sight of sporting rifle type. Plain pistol-grip stock and forearm; originally supplied with walnut stock and forearm. "Tenite" (plastic) was used in later production. Made 1938-50. *Note:* This gun is now manufactured as the Savage Model 24.

With wood stock and forearm $185
With Tenite stock and forearm 145

SHOTGUNS

Squires Bingham Model 30 Pump Shotgun

Stevens Model 51

Stevens Model 58

Stevens Model 58-410

Stevens Model 51 Bolt-Action Shotgun **$85**
Single shot. Takedown. .410 ga. 24-inch bbl., F choke. Weight: about 4.75 lbs. Plain one-piece pistol-grip stock. checkered on later models. Made 1962-71.

Stevens Model 58 Bolt-Action Repeater **$105**
Takedown. Gauges: 12, 16, 20. 2-shell detachable box magazine. 26-inch bbl., F choke. Weight: about 7.25 lbs. Plain one-piece pistol-grip stock on early models w/takedown screw on bottom of forend. Made 1933-1981. *Note:* Later production models have 3-inch chamber in 20 ga., checkered stock with recoil pad.

Stevens Model 58-.410 Bolt-Action Repeater **$95**
Takedown. .410 ga. 3-shell detachable box magazine. 24-inch bbl., F choke. Weight: about 5.5 lbs. Plain one-piece pistol-grip stock, checkered on later production. Made 1937-1981.

Stevens Model 59 Bolt-Action Repeater **$135**
Takedown. .410 ga. 5-shell tubular magazine. 24-inch bbl., F choke. Weight: about 6 lbs. Plain, one-piece pistol-grip stock, checkered on later production. Made 1934-73.

Stevens Model 67 Pump Shotgun
Hammerless, side-ejection solid-steel receiver. Gauges: 12, 20 and .410, 2.75- or 3-inch shells. Bbls.: 21-, 26-, 28- 30-inch with fixed chokes or interchangeable choke tubes, plain or vent rib. Weight: 6.25 to 7.5 lbs. Optional rifle sights. Walnut-finished hardwood stock with corn cob-style forend.

Standard Model, Plain Bbl.	**$200**
Standard Model, Vent Rib	225
Standard Model, w/Choke Tubes	235
Slug Model w/Rifle Sights	195
Lobo Model, Matte Finish	215
Youth Model, 20 ga.	185
Camo Model. w/Choke Tubes	260

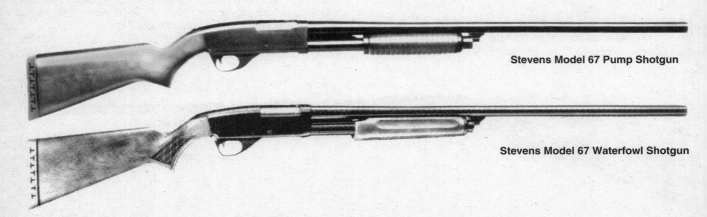

Stevens Model 67 Pump Shotgun

Stevens Model 67 Waterfowl Shotgun

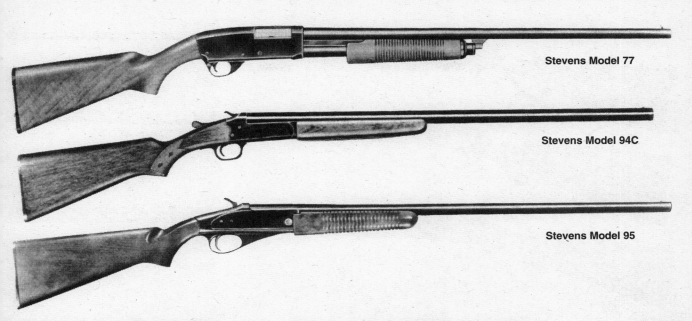

Stevens Model 77

Stevens Model 94C

Stevens Model 95

Stevens Model 67 Waterfowl Shotgun **$235**
Hammerless. Gauge: 12. 3-shot tubular magazine. Walnut finished hardwood stock. Weight: about 7.5 lbs. Made 1972-89.

Stevens Model 77 Slide-Action Repeater **$215**
Solid frame. Gauges: 12, 16, 20. 5-shot tubular magazine. Bbls.: 26-inch IC, 28-inch M or F choke. Weight: about 7.5 lbs. Plain pistol-grip stock with recoil pad, grooved slide handle. Made 1954-71.

Stevens Model 77-AC **$235**
Same as Model 77, except has Savage Super Choke.

Stevens Model 79-VR Super Value **$225**
Hammerless, side ejection. Bbl.: chambered for 2.75-inch and 3-inch mag. shells. 12, 20, and .410 ga. vent rib. Walnut finished hardwood stock with checkering on grip. Weight: 6.75-7 lbs. Made 1979 to date.

Stevens Model 94 Single-Shot Shotgun **$105**
Takedown. Visible hammer. Auto ejector. Gauges: 12, 16, 20, 28, .410. Bbls.: 26-, 28-, 30-, 32-, 36-inch, F choke. Weight: about 6 lbs. depending on gauge and barrel. Plain pistol-grip stock and forearm. Made 1939-61.

Stevens Model 94C **$125**
Same as Model 94, except has checkered stock, fluted forearm on late production. Made 1965 to date.

Stevens Model 94Y Youth Gun **$130**
Same as Model 94, except made in 20 and .410 ga. only; has 26-inch F choke bbl., 12.5-inch buttstock with recoil pad; checkered pistol grip and fluted forend on late production. Made 1959 to date.

Stevens Model 95 Single-Shot Shotgun **$90**
Solid frame. Visible hammer. Plain extractor. 12 ga. 3-inch chamber. Bbls.: 28-inch M- 30-inch F choke. Weight: about 7.25 lbs. Plain pistol-grip stock, grooved forearm. Made 1965-69.

Stevens Model 107 Single-Shot Hammer Shotgun **$85**
Takedown. Auto ejector. Gauges: 12, 16, 20, .410. Bbl. lengths: 28- and 30-inch (12 and 16 ga.), 28-inch (20 ga.), 26-inch (.410); F choke only. Weight: about 6 lbs., 12 bore ga. Plain pistol-grip stock and forearm. Made about 1937-53.

Stevens Model 124 Cross Bolt Repeater **$140**
Hammerless. Solid frame. 12 ga. only. 2-shot tubular magazine. 28-inch bbl.; IC, M or F choke. Weight: about 7 lbs. Tenite stock and forearm. Made 1947-52.

Stevens Model 240 Over-and-Under Shotgun . . **$510**
Visible hammer. Takedown. Double triggers. .410 ga. 26-inch bbls., F choke. Weight: 6 lbs. Tenite (plastic) pistol-grip stock and forearm. Made 1940-49.

SHOTGUNS

Stevens Model 124

Stevens Model 258

Stevens Model 311

Stevens Model 530

Stevens Model 258 Bolt-Action Repeater **$95**
Takedown. 20-gauge. 2-shell detachable box magazine. 26-inch barrel, Full choke. Weight: about 6.25 lbs. Plain one-piece pistol-grip stock. Made 1937-65.

Stevens-Springfield Model 311 Hammerless Double
Same general specifications as Stevens Model 530, except earlier production has plain stock and forearm; checkered on current guns. Originally produced as a "Springfield" gun, this model became a part of the "Stevens" line in 1948 when the "Springfield" brand name was discontinued. Made 1931-89.
Pre-WW II **$335**
Post-WW II **295**

Stevens Model 311 -R Hammerless Double **$255**
Same general specifications as Stevens Model 311 except compact design for law enforcement use. Bbls.: 18.25-inch 12 gauge with solid rib, chambered for 2.75 and 3-inch Mag. shells. Double triggers and auto top tang safety. Walnut finished hardwood stock with recoil pad and semibeavertail forend. Weight: about 6.75 lbs. Made 1982-89.

Stevens Model 530 Hammerless Double **$265**
Boxlock. Double triggers. Gauges: 12, 16, 20, .410. Bbl. lengths: 26- to 32-inch; choked M/F, C/M, F/F. Weight: 6 to 7.5 pounds depending on gauge and barrel length. Checkered pistol-grip stock and forearm; some early models with recoil pad. Made 1936-54.

Stevens Model 530M **$240**
Same as Model 530, except has Tenite (plastic) stock and forearm. Discontinued about 1947.

Stevens Model 530ST Double Gun **$255**
Same as Model 530, except has non-selective single trigger. Discontinued.

Stevens Model 620 Hammerless Slide Action Repeating Shotgun **$225**
Takedown. Gauges: 12, 16, 20. 5-shell tubular magazine. Bbl. lengths: 26-, 28-, 30-, 32-inch; choked F, M IC, C. Weight: about 7.75 lbs., 12 ga.; 7.25 lbs., 16 ga.- 6 lbs., 20 ga. Checkered pistol-grip stock and slide handle. Made 1927-53.

Stevens Model 620

Stevens Model 820

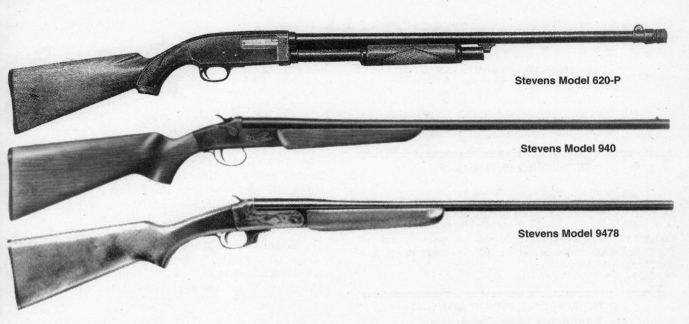

Stevens Model 620-P

Stevens Model 940

Stevens Model 9478

Stevens Model 620-C $225
Same specifications as Model 620 except equipped with Cutts Compensator and two choke tubes.

Stevens Model 620-P $235
Same specifications as Model 620 equipped with Aero-Dyne Poly Choke and 27-inch bbl.

Stevens Model 620-PV $235
Same specifications as Model 620 except equipped with ventilated Poly Choke and 27-inch bbl.

Stevens Model 621 . . . . $275
Same as Model 620, except has raised solid matted-rib barrel. Discontinued.

Stevens Model 820 Hammerless Slide-Action Repeating Shotgun $210
Solid frame. 12 gauge only. 5-shell tubular magazine. 28-inch barrel; IC, M or F choke. Weight: about 7.5 lbs. Plain pistol-grip stock, grooved slide handle. Early models furnished w/Tenite buttstock and forend. Made 1949-54.

Stevens Model 820-SC $235
Same as Model 820, except has Savage Super Choke.

Stevens Model 940 Single-Shot Shotgun $95
Same general specifications as Model 94, except has side lever opening instead of top lever. Made 1961-70.

Stevens Model 940Y Youth Gun $110
Same general specifications as Model 94Y, except has side lever opening instead of top lever. Made 1961-70.

Stevens Model 9478 . . . . $95
Takedown. Visible hammer. Automatic ejector. Gauges: 12, 20, .410. Bbls.: 26-, 28-, 30-, 36-inch; Full choke. Weight: average 6 pounds depending on gauge and barrel. Plain pistol-grip stock and forearm. Made 1978-85.

Stevens-Springfield Model 311 . . . . $295
Same specifications as Stevens Model 311.

Stevens-Springfield Model 5151 . . . . $325
Same specifications as the Stevens Model 311 except with checkered grip and forend; equipped with recoil pad and two Ivoroid sights.

SHOTGUNS

STOEGER SHOTGUNS
See IGA Shotguns

-Stevens-Springfield Model 5151

Tecni-Mec Model SPL 640
Folding Shotgun

TECNI-MEC SHOTGUNS
Italy

Tecni-Mec Model SPL 640 Folding Shotgun . . . **$365**
Gauges: 12, 16, 20, 24, 28, 32 and .410 bore. 26-inch bbl.
Chokes: IC/IM. Weight: 6.5 lbs. Checkered walnut pistol-grip
stock and forend. Engraved receiver. Available with double triggers. Made 1988 to 1994.

THOMPSON/CENTER ARMS
Rochester, New Hampshire

Thompson/Center Contender
.410 Carbine

Thompson/Center Contender .410 Ga. Carbine . . **$295**
Gauge: .410 smoothbore. 21-inch vent-rib bbl. 34.75 inches
overall. Weight: about 5.25 lbs. Bead front sight. Rynite® stock
and forend. Made 1991 to date.

Thompson/Center Model '87 Hunter Shotgun . . . **$325**
Single shot. Gauge: 10 or 12; 3.5-inch chamber. 25-inch field
bbl. with F choke. Weight 8 lbs. Bead front sight. American
black walnut stock with recoil pad. Drop at heel .9 inch. Made
1987 to 1992.

Thompson/Center Model '87 Hunter Slug **$345**
Gauge: 10 (3.5-inch chamber) or 12 (3-inch chamber). Same
general specifications as Model '87 Hunter Shotgun, except with
22-inch slug (rifled) bbl. and rifle sights. Made 1987 to 1992.

TIKKA SHOTGUNS
Riihimaki, Finland
Manufactured by Sako; formerly by Valmet

Tikka M 07 Shotgun/Rifle Combination **$795**
Gauge/caliber: 12/222 Rem. Shotgun bbl.: about 25 inches; rifle
bbl.: about 22.75 inches. 40.66 inches overall. Weight: about 7
lbs. Dovetailed for telescopic sight. Single trigger with selector
between the bbls. Vent rib. Monte Carlo-style walnut stock with
checkered pistol grip and forend. Made 1965-87.

Tikka M 77 Over/Under Shotgun **$995**
Gauge: 12. 27-inch vent-rib bbls. Approx. 44 inches overall.
Weight: about 7.25 lbs. Bbl. selector. Ejectors. Monte Carlo-
style walnut stock with checkered pistol grip and forend; rollover
cheekpiece. Made 1977-87.

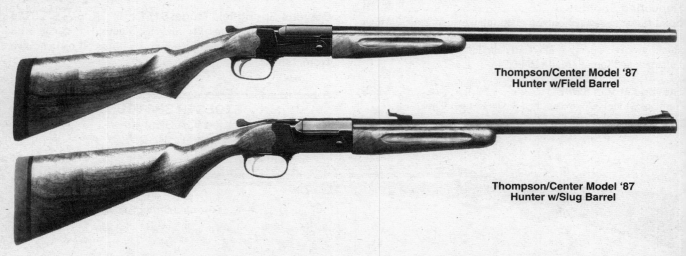

Thompson/Center Model '87
Hunter w/Field Barrel

Thompson/Center Model '87
Hunter w/Slug Barrel

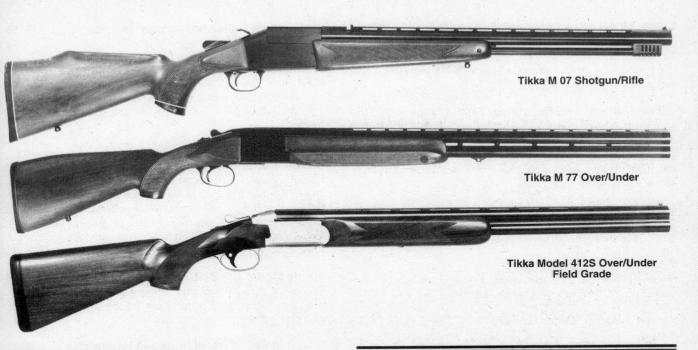

Tikka M 07 Shotgun/Rifle

Tikka M 77 Over/Under

Tikka Model 412S Over/Under
Field Grade

Tikka Model 412S Over/Under
Gauge: 12; 3-inch chambers. 24-, 26-, 28- or 30-inch blued
chrome-lined bbls. with five integral stainless steel choke tubes.
Weight: 7.25 to 7.5 lbs. Matte nickel receiver. Select American
walnut stock with checkered pistol grip and forend. (Same as the
former Valmet Model 412.) Manufactured in Italy by arrange-
ment with Marocchi from 1990 to 1993.
Field Model $850
Sporting Clays Model 925

Tikka M 77K Shotgun/Rifle Combination $1050
Gauge: 12/70. Calibers: 222 Rem., 5.6×52r5, 6.5×55, 7×57r5,
7×65r5, 308 Win. Vent-rib bbls.: about 25 inches (shotgun; almost 23 inches (rifle). 42.3 inches overall. Weight: about 7.5 lbs.
Double triggers. Monte Carlo-style walnut stock with checkered
pistol grip and forend; rollover cheekpiece. Made 1977-86.

SHOTGUNS OF ULM
Ulm, West Germany

See listings under Krieghoff.

U.S. REPEATING ARMS CO.
New Haven, Connecticut

See **Winchester Shotgun listings.**

VALMET OY
Jyväskylä, Finland

*See also Savage Models 330, 333T, 333 and 2400, which are
Valmet guns.*

Valmet Lion Over-and-Under Shotgun $365
Boxlock. Selective single trigger. Plain extractors.12 ga. only.
Bbls.: 26-inch IC/M; 28-inch M/F, 30-inch M/F, F/F. Weight:
about 7 lbs. Checkered pistol-grip stock and forearm. Made
1947-68.

Valmet Model 412 K Over/Under Field Shotgun . . $645
Hammerless. 12-ga., 3-inch chamber. 36-inch bbl., F/F chokes.
American walnut Monte Carlo stock. Made 1982-87.

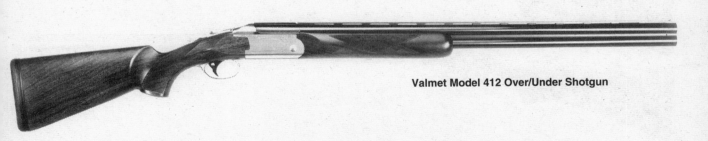

Valmet Model 412 Over/Under Shotgun

SHOTGUNS

Valmet Model 412 K Shotgun/Rifle Combination . . $775
Similar to Model 412 K, except bottom bbl. chambered for either 222 Rem., 223 Rem., 243 Win., 308 Win. or 30-06. 12-ga. shotgun bbl. with IM choke. Monte Carlo American walnut stock, recoil pad.

Valmet Model 412 KE Over/Under Field Shotgun . . $615
12-ga. chambered for 2.75-inch shells 26-inch bbl., IC/M chokes; 28-inch bbl., M/F chokes; 12-ga. chambered for 3-inch shells, 30-inch bbl., M/F chokes. 20-ga. (3-inch shells); 26-inch bbl. IC/M chokes; 28-inch bbl., M/ F chokes. American walnut Monte Carlo stock.

Valmet Model 412 KE Skeet $665
Similar to Model 412 K, except Skeet stock and chokes. 12 and 20 ga. Discontinued 1989.

Valmet Model 412 KE Trap $695
Similar to Model 412 K Field, except trap stock, recoil pad. 30-inch bbls., IM/F chokes. Discontinued 1989.

Valmet 3-Barrel Set for Model 412 . . . . $1795

MONTGOMERY WARD
Chicago, Illinois
Western Field and Hercules Models

Although they do not correspond to specific models below, the names Western Field and Hercules have been used to designate various Montgomery Ward shotguns at various times.

Wards Model 25 Slide-Action Repeater $160
Solid frame. 12 ga. only. 2- or 5-shot tubular magazine. 28-inch bbl., various chokes. Weight: about 7.5 lbs. Plain pistol-grip stock, grooved slide handle.

Wards Model 40 Over/Under Shotgun $595
Hammerless. Boxlock. Double triggers. Gauges: 12, l6, 20, .410. Bbls.: plain; 26- to 30-inch, various chokes. Checkered pistol-grip stock and forearm.

Wards Model 40N Slide-Action Repeater $165
Same general specifications as Model 25.

Wards (Western Field) Model 50 Pumpgun $170
Solid frame. Gauges: 12 and 16. 2- and 5-shot magazine. 26-, 28- or 30-inch bbl., 48 inches overall w/28-inch bbl. Weight: 7.25 - 7.75 lbs. Metal bead front sight. Walnut stock and grooved forend.

**Wards (Western Field) Model 52
Double-Barrel Shotgun** $225
Hammerless coil-spring action. Gauges: 12, 16, 20 and .410. 26-, 28-, or 30-inch bbls., 42 to 46 inches overall, depending upon bbl. length. Weight: 6 (.410 ga. w/26-inch bbl.) to 7.25 lbs. (12 ga. w/30-inch bbls.), depending upon gauge and bbl. length. Casehardened receiver; blued bbls. Plain buttstock and forend. Made circa 1954.

Wards Model 172 Bolt-Action Shotgun $85
Takedown. 2-shot detachable clip magazine. 12 ga. 28-inch bbl. with variable choke. Weight: about 7.5 lbs. Monte Carlo stock with recoil pad.

Wards Model 550A Slide-Action Repeater $225
Takedown. Gauges: 12, 16, 20, .410. 5-shot tubular magazine. Bbls.: plain, 26- to 30-inch, various chokes. Weight: 6 (.410 ga. w/26-inch bbl.) to 8 lbs. (12 ga. w/30-inch bbls.). Plain pistol-grip stock and grooved slide handle.

Wards Model SB300 Double-Barrel Shotgun . . . $235
Same general specifications as Model SD52A.

Wards Model SB312 Double-Barrel Shotgun . . . $250
Boxlock. Double triggers. Plain extractors. Gauges: 12, 16, 20, .410. Bbls.: 24- to 30-inch. Various chokes. Weight, about 7.5 lbs. in 12 ga.; 6.5 lbs in .410 ga. Checkered pistol-grip stock and forearm.

Wards Model SD52A Double-Barrel Shotgun . . . $195
Boxlock. Double triggers. Plain extractors. Gauges: 12, 16, 20, .410. Bbls.: 26- to 32-inch, various chokes. Plain forend and pistol-grip buttstock. Weight: 6 (.410 ga., 26-inch bbls.) to 7.5 lbs. (12 ga., 32-inch bbls.).

Wards Western Field Model 50

Wards Western Field Model 52

Weatherby Model 82

WEATHERBY, INC.
South Gate, California

Weatherby Model 82 Autoloading Shotgun
Hammerless, gas-operated. 12 ga. only. Bbls.: 22- to 30-inch, various integral chokes. Weight: 7.5 lbs. Checkered walnut stock and forearm. Made 1982-89.
Standard Autoloading Shotgun **$365**
BuckMaster Auto Slug w/rifle sights (1986-90) **390**

Weatherby Model 92 Slide-Action Shotgun
Hammerless, short-stroke action. 12 ga.; 3-inch chamber. Tubular magazine. Bbls.: 22-, 26-, 28-, 30-inch with fixed choke or IMC choke tubes; plain or vent rib with rifle sights. Weight: 7.5 lbs. Engraved, matte black receiver and blued barrel. Checkered high-gloss buttstock and forend. Imported from Japan since 1982.
Standard Model 92 . . . . **$275**
BuckMaster Pump Slug w/rifle sights (intro. 1986) **295**

Weatherby Athena Over/Under Shotgun
Engraved boxlock action with Greener crossbolt and sideplates. Gauges: 12, 20, 28 and .410; 2.75- or 3.5-inch chambers. Bbls.: 26-, 28-, 30- or 32-inch with fixed or IMC Multi-choke tubes. Weight: 6.75 to 7.38 lbs. Single selective trigger. Selective auto ejectors. Top tang safety. Checkered Claro walnut stock and forearm with high-luster finish. Made 1982 to date.

Weatherby Athena Over/Under Shotgun *(Cont.)*
Field Model w/IMC Multi-choke (12 or 20 ga.). **$1150**
Field Model w/Fixed Chokes (28 or .410 ga.) **1295**
Skeet Model w/Fixed Chokes (12 or 20 ga.) **1275**
Skeet Model w/Fixed Chokes (28 or .410 ga.) **1425**
Master Skeet Tube Set **2195**
Trap Model w/IMC Tubes **1195**
Grade V (1993 to date) **1595**

Weatherby Centurion Automatic Shotgun
Gas-operated. Takedown. 12 ga. 2.75-inch chamber. 3-shot magazine. Bbls.: vent ribs; 26-inch SK, IC or M 28-inch M or F; 30-inch Full choke. Weight: with 28-inch bbl., 7 lbs. 10.5 oz. Checkered pistol-grip stock and forearm, recoil pad. Made in Japan 1972-81.
Centurion Field Grade **$325**
Centurion Trap Gun (30-inch Full choke bbl.) **320**
Centurion Deluxe (etched receiver, fancy wood) **360**

Weatherby Olympian Over/Under Shotgun
Gauges: 12 and 20. 2.75- (12 ga.) and 3-inch (20 ga.) chambers. Bbls.: 26-, 28-, 30, and 32-inch. Weight: 6.75 - 8.75 lbs. America walnut stock and forend.
Field Model **$710**
Skeet Model **730**
Trap Model **725**

SHOTGUNS

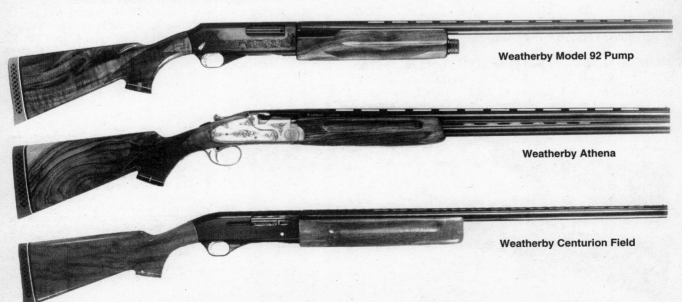

Weatherby Model 92 Pump

Weatherby Athena

Weatherby Centurion Field

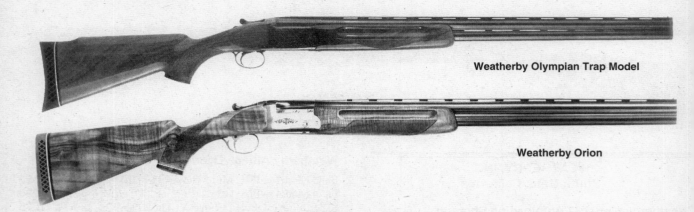

Weatherby Olympian Trap Model

Weatherby Orion

Weatherby Orion Over/Under Shotgun

Boxlock with Greener crossbolt. Gauges: 12, 20, 28 and .410; 2.75- or 3-inch chambers. Bbls.: 26-, 28, 30-, 32- or 34-inch with fixed or IMC Multi-choke tubes. Weight: 6.5 to 9 lbs. Single selective trigger. Selective auto ejectors. Top tang safety. Checkered, high-gloss pistol-grip Claro walnut stock and forearm. Finish: Grade I, plain blued receive; Grade II, engraved blued receiver; Grade III, silver gray receiver. Made 1982 to date.

Orion I Field w/IMC (12 or 20 ga.)	**$770**
Orion II Field w/IMC (12 or 20 ga.)	**845**
Orion III Field w/IMC (12 or 20 ga.)	**870**
Skeet II w/Fixed Chokes	**895**
Sporting Clays II	**945**
Trap II	**920**

Weatherby Patrician Slide-Action Shotgun

Hammerless. Takedown. 12 ga. 2.75-inch chamber. 4 shot tubular magazine. Bbls.: vent rib; 26-inch, SK, IC M; 28-inch, M F; 30-inch, F choke. Weight: with 28-inch bbl., 7 lbs. 7 oz. Checkered pistol-grip stock and slide handle, recoil pad. Made in Japan 1972-82.

Patrician Field Grade	**$250**
Patrician Deluxe (etched receiver, fancy grade wood)	**295**
Patrician Trap Gun (30-inch F choke bbl.)	**260**

Weatherby Regency Field Grade O/U Shotgun . . $790

Boxlock with sideplates, elaborately engraved. Auto ejectors. Selective single trigger. Gauges: 12, 20. 2.75-inch chamber in 12 ga., 3-inch in 20 ga. Bbls.: vent rib; 26-inch SK, IC/M, M/F (20

Weatherby Regency Over/Under Shotgun *(Cont.)*

ga. only); 28-inch SK, IC/M, M/F; 30-inch M/F (12 ga only). Weight with 28-inch Bbls.: 7 lbs. 6 oz., 12 ga.; 6 lbs. 14 oz., 20 ga. Checkered pistol-grip stock and forearm of fancy walnut. Made in Italy 1965-82.

Weatherby Regency Trap Gun $695

Similar to Regency Field Grade, except has trap-style stock with straight or Monte Carlo comb. Bbls. have vent side ribs and high, wide vent top rib; 30- or 32-inch, M/F, IM/F or F/F chokes. Weight: with 32-inch bbls., 8 lbs. Made in Italy 1965-1982.

WESTERN ARMS CORP.
Ithaca, New York
Division of Ithaca Gun Company

Western Long Range Hammerless Double

Boxlock. Plain extractors. Single or double triggers. Gauges: 12, 16, 20, .410. Bbls.: 26- to 32-inch, M/F choke standard. Weight: 7.5 lbs., 12 ga. Plain pistol-grip stock and forend. Made 1929-46.

With double triggers	**$275**
With single trigger	**350**

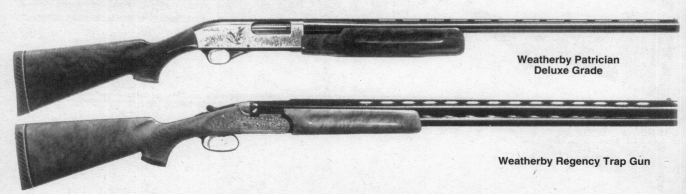

Weatherby Patrician Deluxe Grade

Weatherby Regency Trap Gun

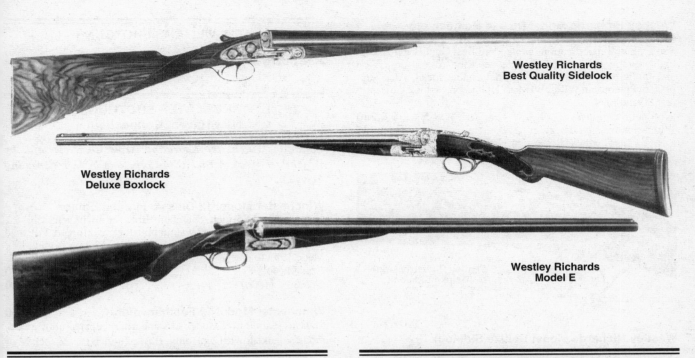

Westley Richards
Best Quality Sidelock

Westley Richards
Deluxe Boxlock

Westley Richards
Model E

WESTERN AUTO SHOTGUNS
Kansas City, Missouri

Revelation Model 300H Slide-Action Repeater . . **$205**
Gauges: 12,16, 20, .410. 4-shot tubular magazine. Bbls.: 26- to 30-inch, various chokes. Weight: about 7 lbs. Plain pistol-grip stock, grooved slide handle.

Revelation Model 310A Slide-Action Repeater . . **$200**
Takedown. 12 ga. 5-shot tubular magazine. Bbls.: 28- and 30-inch. Weight: about 7.5 lbs. Plain pistol-grip stock.

Revelation Model 310B Slide-Action Repeater . . **$175**
Same general specifications as Model 310A except chambered for 16 ga.

Revelation Model 310C Slide-Action Repeater . . **$210**
Same general specifications as Model 310A except chambered for 20 ga.

Revelation Model 310E Slide-Action Repeater . . **$220**
Same general specifications as Model 310A except chambered for .410 bore.

Revelation Model 325BK Bolt-Action Repeater . . **$85**
Takedown. 2-shot detachable clip magazine. 20 ga. 26-inch bbl. with variable choke. Weight: 6.25 lbs.

WESTERN FIELD SHOTGUNS

See "W" for listings under Montgomery Ward.

WESTLEY RICHARDS & CO., LTD.
Birmingham, England

The Pigeon and Wildfowl Gun, available in all of the Westley Richards models except the Ovundo, has the same general specifications as the corresponding standard field gun, except has magnum action of extra strength and treble bolting, chambered for 12 gauae only (2.75- or 3-inch); 30-inch Full choke barrels standard. Weight: about 8 lbs. The manufacturer warns that 12-gauge magnum shells should not be used in their standard weight double-barrel shotguns.

Westley Richards Best Quality Boxlock Hammerless Double-Barrel Shotgun
Boxlock. Hand-detachable locks and hinged cover plate. Selective ejectors. Double triggers or selective single trigger. Gauges: 12, 16, 20. Barrel lengths and boring to order. Weight: 5.5 to 6.25 lbs. depending on ga. and bbl. length. Checkered stock and forend, straight or half-pistol grip. Also supplied in Pigeon and Wildfowl Model with same values. Made from 1899 to date.
With double triggers **$10,500**
With selective single trigger **11,000**

Westley Richards Best Quality Sidelock Hammerless Double-Barrel Shotgun
Hand-detachable sidelocks. Selective ejectors. Double triggers or selective single trigger. Gauges: 12, 16, 20, 28, .410. Bbl. lengths and boring to order. Weight: 4.75 to 6.75 lbs., depending on ga. and bbl. length. Checkered stock and forend, straight or half-pistol grip. Also supplied in Pigeon and Wildfowl Model with same values. Currently manufactured.
With double triggers **$19,225**
With selective single trigger **21,000**

Westley Richards Model Deluxe Boxlock Hammerless Double-Barrel Shotgun

Same general specifications as standard Best Quality gun except higher quality throughout. Has Westley Richards top-projection and treble-bite lever-work, hand-detachable locks. Also supplied in Pigeon and Wildfowl Model with same values. Currently manufactured.

With double triggers . . . . $ 8,950
With selective single trigger   10,000

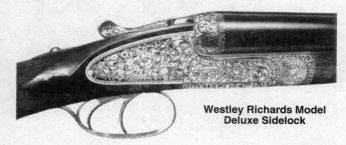

**Westley Richards Model
Deluxe Sidelock**

Westley Richards Model Deluxe Sidelock

Same as Best Quality Sidelock, except higher grade engraving and wood. Currently manufactured.

With double triggers $20,000
With single trigger   24,000

Westley Richards Model E Hammerless Double

Anson & Deeley-type boxlock action. Selective ejector or non-ejector. Double triggers. Gauges: 12, 16, 20. Barrel lengths and boring to order. Weight: 5.5 to 7.25 lbs. depending on type, ga. and bbl. length. Checkered stock and forend, straight or half-pistol grip. Also supplied in Pigeon and Wildfowl Model with same values. Currently manufactured.

Ejector model $3795
Non-ejector model   3300

Westley Richards Ovundo (Over/Under) $14,995

Hammerless. Boxlock. Hand-detachable locks. Dummy side-plates. Selective ejectors. Selective single trigger. 12 ga. Barrel lengths and boring to order. Checkered stock/ forend, straight or half-pistol grip. Mfd. before WW II.

TED WILLIAMS SHOTGUNS

See Sears shotguns.

WINCHESTER SHOTGUNS
New Haven, Connecticut

Formerly Winchester Repeating Arms Co. Now mfd. by Winchester-Western Div., Olin Corp., and by U.S. Repeating Arms Co.

Winchester Model 12 Classic Limited Edition

Gauge: 20; 2.75-inch chamber. Bbl.: 26-inch vent rib; IC. Weight: 7 lbs. Checkered walnut buttstock and forend. Polished blue finish (Grade I) or engraved with gold inlays (Grade IV). Made 1993 to date.

Grade I (4000) . . . . $ 670
Grade IV (1000)   1090

Winchester Model 12 Featherweight $460

Same as Plain Barrel Model 12 Standard, except has alloy guard, modified takedown. 12 ga. only. Bbls.: 26-inch IC; 28-inch M or F; 30-inch F choke. Weight: about 6.75 lbs. Made 1959-62.

Winchester Model 12 Field Gun, 1972 Type $565

Same general specifications as Standard Model 12. 12 ga. only. 26-, 28- or 30-inch vent-rib bbl., standard chokes. Engine-turned bolt and carrier. Hand-checkered stock/slide handle of semi-fancy walnut. Made 1972-75.

Winchester Model 12 Heavy Duck Gun $725

12 ga. only, chambered for 3-inch shells. Same general specifications as Standard Grade, except 30- or 32-inch plain full choke bbl. only, 3-shot magazine, recoil pad. Weight: about 8.75 lbs. Discontinued 1964.

Winchester Model 12 Heavy Duck Gun, Matte Rib $870

Same as Plain Barrel Model 12 Heavy Duck Gun, except has solid raised matted rib and weighs a few ounces more. Discontinued 1959.

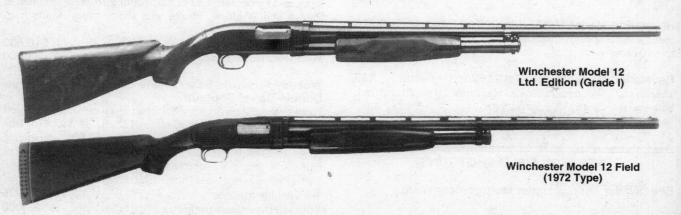

**Winchester Model 12
Ltd. Edition (Grade I)**

**Winchester Model 12 Field
(1972 Type)**

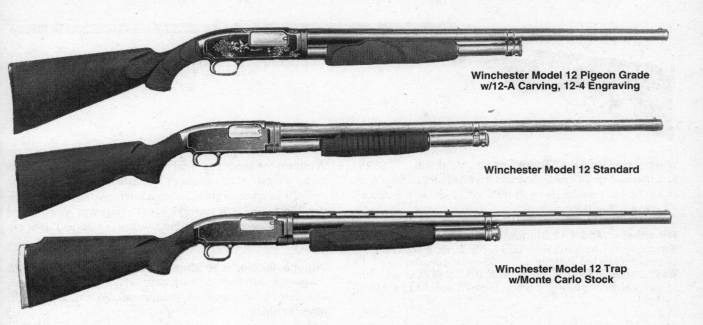

Winchester Model 12 Pigeon Grade
w/12-A Carving, 12-4 Engraving

Winchester Model 12 Standard

Winchester Model 12 Trap
w/Monte Carlo Stock

Winchester Model 12 Pigeon Grade

Deluxe versions of the regular Model 12 Standard or Field Gun, Duck Gun, Skeet Gun and Trap Gun made on special order. This grade has finer finish throughout, hand-smoothed action, engine-turned breech bolt and carrier, stock and extension slide handle of high grade walnut, fancy checkering, stock dimensions to individual specifications. Engraving and carving available at extra cost ranging from about $135 to over $1000. Discont. 1965.

Field Gun, plain bbl.	**$1150**
Field Gun, vent rib	**1395**
Skeet Gun, matted rib	**1450**
Skeet Gun, vent rib	**1595**
Skeet Gun, Cutts Compensator	**995**
Trap Gun, matted rib	**1350**
Trap Gun, vent rib	**1425**

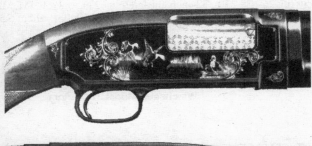

**Winchester Model 12
12-4 Engraving**

Winchester Model 12 Riot Gun $550

Same general specifications as Plain Barrel Model 12 Standard, except has 20-inch cylinder bore bbl.,12 gauge only. Made 1918-1963.

Winchester Model 12 Skeet Gun $850

Gauges: 12, 16, 20, 28. 5-shot tubular magazine. 26-inch matted rib bbl., SK choke. Weight: about 7.75 lbs., 12 ga.; 6.75 lbs., other gauges. Bradley red or ivory bead front sight. Winchester 94B middle sight. Checkered pistol-grip stock and extension slide handle. Discont. after WWII.

Winchester Model 12 Skeet Gun, Cutts Compensator $775

Same general specifications as standard Model 12 Skeet Gun, except has plain bbl. fitted with Cutts Compensator, 26 inches overall. Discont. 1954.

Winchester Model 12 Skeet Gun, Plain Barrel . . $745

Same general specifications as standard Model 12 Skeet except w/no rib.

Winchester Model 12 Skeet Gun, Vent Rib $1095

Same general specifications as standard Model 12 Skeet Gun, except has 26-inch bbl. with vent rib, 12 and 20 ga. Discontinued in 1965.

Winchester Model 12 Skeet Gun, 1972 Type . . . $725

Same gen. specifications as Standard Model 12. 12 ga. only. 26-inch vent-rib bbl., SK choke. Engine-turned bolt and carrier. Hand-checkered skeet-style stock and slide handle of choice walnut, recoil pad. Made 1972-75.

Winchester Model 12 Standard Gr., Matted Rib . . . $750

Same general specifications as Plain Bbl. Model 12 Standard, except has solid raised matted rib. Discontinued after World War II.

Winchester Model 20 Single-Shot Shotgun

Winchester Model 12 Standard Gr., Vent Rib . . . $825
Same general specifications as Plain Barrel Model 12 Standard, except has vent rib. 26.75- or 30-inch bbl.,12 ga. only. Discont. after World War II.

Winchester Model 12 Standard Slide-Action Repeater
Hammerless. Takedown. Gauges: 12, 16, 20, 28. 6-shell tubular magazine. Plain bbl. Lengths: 26- to 32-inches; choked F to Cyl. Weight: about 7.5 lbs., 12 ga. 30-inch, 6.5 lbs. in other ga. with 28-inch bbl. Plain pistol-grip stock, grooved slide handle. Made 1912-64.

28 gauge	**$2995**
12-ga., 28-inch bbl. (Full)	**595**
Other gauges, etc.	**575**

Winchester Model 12 Super Pigeon Grade $1995
Custom version of Model 12 with same general specifications as standard models. 12 ga. only. 26-, 28- or 30-inch vent-rib bbl., any standard choke. Engraved receiver. Hand-smoothed and fitted action. Full fancy walnut stock and forearm made to individual order. Made 1965-72.

Winchester Model 12 Trap Gun
Same general specifications as standard Model 12, except has straighter stock, checkered pistol grip and extension slide handle, recoil pad, 30-inch matted-rib bbl., F choke, 12 ga. only. Discont. after World War II; vent-rib model discontinued 1965. *See illustration previous page.*

Matted-rib bbl.	**$850**
With straight stock, vent rib	**950**
With Monte Carlo stock, vent rib	**995**

Winchester Model 12 Trap Gun, 1972 Type $695
Same general specifications as Standard Model 12. 12 gauge only. 30-inch vent-rib bbl., F choke. Engine-turned bolt and carrier. Hand-checkered trap-style stock (straight or Monte Carlo comb) and slide handle of select walnut, recoil pad. Intro. in 1972. Discontinued.

Winchester Model 20 Single-Shot Hammer Gun . . $375
Takedown. .410 bore. 2.5-inch chamber. 26-inch bbl., F choke. Checkered pistol-grip stock and forearm. Weight: about 6 lbs. Made 1919-24.

Winchester Model 21 Custom, Pigeon, Grand American
Since 1959, the Model 21 has been offered only in deluxe models: Custom, Pigeon, Grand American — on special order. General specifications same as for Model 21 standard models, except these custom guns have full fancy American walnut stock and forearm with fancy checkering, finely polished and hand-smoothed working parts, etc.; engraving inlays, carved stocks and other extras are available at additional cost. Made 1960 to date.

Custom Grade	**$ 5,500**
Pigeon Grade	**7,500**
Grand American	**16,500**

Winchester Model 21 Double-Barrel Field Gun
Hammerless. Boxlock. Automatic safety. Double triggers or selective single trigger, selective or non-selective ejection (all postwar Model 21 shotguns have selective single trigger and selective ejection). Gauges: 12,16, 20. Bbls.: raised matted rib or vent rib; 26-, 28-, 30-, 32-inch, the latter in 12 ga. only; F, IM, M, IC, SK chokes. Weight: 7.5 lbs., 12 ga. w/30-inch bbl.; about 6.5

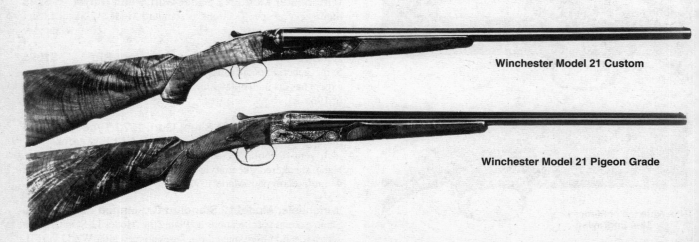

Winchester Model 21 Custom

Winchester Model 21 Pigeon Grade

Winchester Model 23

Winchester Model 24

Winchester Model 25

Winchester Model 21 Double-Barrel Field Gun *(Cont.)*

lbs. 16 or 20 ga. w/28-inch bbl. Checkered pistol- or straight-grip stock, regular or beavertail forend. Made 1930-58.

With double trigger, non-selective ejection	**$2795**
With double trigger, selective ejection	2995
With selective single trigger, non-selective ejection . .	3250
With selective single trigger, selective ejection	3400
Extra for vent rib	500

Winchester Model 21 Duck Gun

Same general specifications as Model 21 Field Gun, except chambered for 12 ga. 3-inch shells, 30- or 32-inch bbls. only, F choke, selective single trigger, selective ejection, pistol-grip stock with recoil pad, beavertail forearm, both checkered. Discont. 1958.

With matted-rib barrels	**$2995**
With vent-rib barrels	3250

Winchester Model 21 Skeet Gun

Same general specifications as Model 21 Standard, except has 26- or 28-inch bbls. only, SK chokes No. 1 and 2 Bradley red bead front sight, selective single trigger, selective ejection, nonauto safety, checkered pistol- or straight-grip stock without buttplate or pad (wood butt checkered), checkered beavertail forearm. Discont. 1958.

With matted-rib barrels	**$3600**
With vent-rib barrels	4200

Winchester Model 21 Trap Gun

Same general specifications as Model 21 Standard, except has 30- or 32-inch bbls. only, F choke, selective single trigger, selective ejection, nonauto safety, checkered pistol-or straight-grip stock with recoil pad, checkered beavertail forearm. Discont. 1958.

With matted-rib barrels	**$3575**
With vent-rib barrels	4200

Winchester Model 23 Side-by-Side Shotgun

Boxlock. Single trigger. Automatic safety. Gauges: 12, 20, 28, .410. Bbls.: 25.5-, 26-, 28-inch with fixed chokes or Winchoke tubes. Weight: 5.88 to 7 lbs. Checkered American walnut buttstock and forend. Made in 1979 for Olin at its Olin-Kodensha facility, Japan.

Classic 23 — Gold inlay, Engraved	**$1500**
Custom 23 — Plain receiver, Winchoke system	895
Heavy Duck 23 — Standard	1225
Lightweight 23 — Classic Style	1215
Light Duck 23 — Standard	1150
Light Duck 23 — 12 ga. Golden Quail	1350
Light Duck 23 — .410 Golden Quail	1995
Custom Set 23 — 20 & 28 gauge	3560

Winchester Model 24 Hammerless Double **$495**

Boxlock. Double triggers. Plain extractors. Auto safety. Gauges: 12, 16, 20. Bbls.: 26-inch IC/M; 28-inch M/F (also IC/M in 12 ga. only); 30-inch M and F in 12 ga. only. Weight: about 7.5 lbs., 12 ga. Metal bead front sight. Plain pistol-grip stock, semibeavertail forearm. Made 1939-57.

Winchester Model 25 Riot Gun **$345**

Same as Model 25 Standard, except has 20-inch cylinder bore bbl., 12 ga. only. Made 1949-55.

Winchester Model 25 Slide-Action Repeater . . . **$410**

Hammerless. Solid frame. 12 ga. only. 4-shell tubular magazine. 28-in. Plain bbl.; IC, M or F choke. Weight: about 7.5 lbs. Metal bead front sight. Plain pistol-grip stock, grooved slide handle. Made 1949-55.

Winchester Model 36 Single-Shot Bolt Action . . **$295**

Takedown. Uses 9mm Short or Long shot or ball cartridges interchangeably. 18-inch bbl. Plain stock. Weight: about 3 lbs. Made 1920-27. *See* illustration next page.

SHOTGUNS

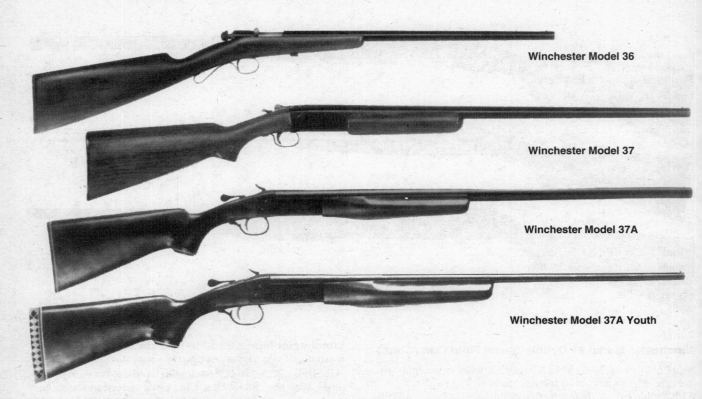

Winchester Model 36

Winchester Model 37

Winchester Model 37A

Winchester Model 37A Youth

Winchester Model 37 Single-Shot Shotgun
Semi-hammerless. Auto ejection. Takedown. Gauges: 12, 16, 20, 28, .410. Bbl. lengths: 28-, 30-, 32-inch in all gauges except .410; 26- or 28-inch in .410; all barrels plain with F choke. Weight: about 6.5 pounds, 12 ga. Made 1937-63.

12 Gauge	**$225**
28 Gauge	795
Other Gauges	150

Winchester Model 37A Single Shot Shotgun . . . $125
Similar to Model 370, except has engraved receiver and gold trigger, checkered pistol-grip stock, fluted forearm; 16 ga. available with 30-inch bbl. only. Made 1973-80.

Winchester Model 37A Youth $135
Similar to Model 370 Youth, except has engraved receiver and gold trigger, checkered pistol-grip stock, fluted forearm. Made 1973-80.

Winchester Model 40 Skeet Gun $795
Same general specifications as Model 40 Standard, except has 24-inch plain bbl. w/Cutts Compensator and screw-in choke tube, checkered forearm and pistol grip, grip cap. Made 1940-1941.

Winchester Model 40 Standard Autoloader $545
Streamlined receiver. Hammerless. Takedown. 12 ga. only. 4-shot tubular magazine. 28- or 30-inch bbl.; M or F choke. Weight: about 8 lbs. Bead sight on ramp. Plain pistol-grip stock, semibeavertail forearm. Made 1940-41.

Winchester Model 41 Single-Shot Bolt Action
Takedown. .410 bore. 2.5-inch chamber (chambered for 3-inch shells after 1932). 24-inch bbl., F choke. Plain straight stock standard. Also made in deluxe version. Made 1920-34.

Standard Model	**$525**
Deluxe Model	600

Winchester Model 40 Skeet

Winchester Model 41 Deluxe

**Winchester Model 42 Classic
Limited Edition**

Winchester Model 42 Standard

Winchester Model 42 Classic Ltd. Edition **$1250**
Gauge: .410 with 2.75-inch chamber. Bbl.: 26-inch vent rib; F choke. Weight: 7 lbs. Checkered walnut buttstock and forend. Engraved blue with gold inlays. Limited production of 850. Made 1993 to date.

Winchester Model 42 Deluxe **$2100**
Same general specifications as the Model 42 Standard, except has vent rib, finer finish throughout, hand-smoothed action, engine-turned breech bolt and carrier, stock and extension slide handle of high grade walnut, fancy checkering, stock dimensions to individual specifications. Engraving and carving were offered at extra cost. Made 1933-63.

Winchester Model 42 Skeet Gun **$1750**
Same general specifications as Model 42 Standard, except has checkered straight or pistol-grip stock and extension slide handle, 26- or 28-inch matted-rib bbl., SK choke. *Note:* Some Model 42 Skeet Guns are chambered for 2.5-inch shells only. Discont. 1963.

**Winchester Model 42 Standard Grade,
Matt Rib** **$1450**
Same general specifications as Plain Bbl. Model 42, except has solid raised matted rib. Discont. 1963.

Winchester Model 42 Standard **$995**
Hammerless. Takedown. .410 bore (3- or 2.5-inch shell). Tubular magazine holds five 3-inch or six 2.5-inch shells. 26- or 28-inch plain bbl.; cylinder bore, M or F choke. Weight: about 6 lbs. Plain pistol-grip stock; grooved slide handle. Made 1933-63.

Winchester Model 50 Field Gun, Vent Rib **$375**
Same as Model 50 Standard, except has vent rib.

Winchester Model 50 Skeet Gun **$460**
Same as Model 50 Standard, except has 26-inch vent-rib bbl. with SK choke, skeet-style stock of select walnut.

Winchester Model 50 Standard Grade **$360**
Non-recoiling bbl. and independent chamber. Gauges: 12 and 20. 2-shot tubular magazine. Bbl.: 12 ga. — 26-, 28-, 30-inch; 20 ga. — 26-, 28-inch; IC, SK, M, F choke. Checkered pistol-grip stock and forearm. Weight: about 7.75 lbs. Made 1954-61.

Winchester Model 50 Trap Gun **$475**
Same as Model 50 Standard, except 12 ga. only, has 30-inch vent-rib bbl. with F choke, Monte Carlo stock of select walnut.

Winchester Model 59 Autoloading Shotgun **$435**
Gauge: 12. Magazine holds two shells. Alloy receiver. Win-Lite steel and fiberglass bbl.: 26-inch IC, 28-inch M or F choke, 30-inch F choke; also furnished with 26-inch bbl. with Versalite choke (interchangeable F, M, IC tubes; one supplied with gun). Weight: about 6.5 lbs. Checkered pistol-grip stock and forearm. Made 1959-65.

SHOTGUNS

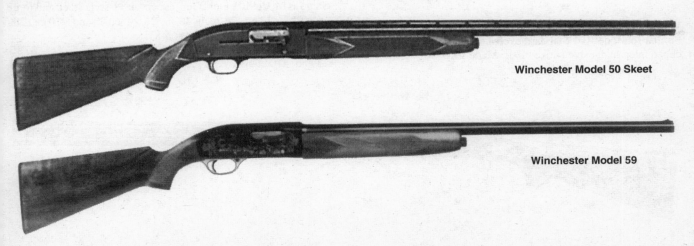

Winchester Model 50 Skeet

Winchester Model 59

Winchester Model 97 Riot Gun

Winchester Model 97 Riot Gun $495

Takedown or solid frame. Same general specifications as standard Model 97, except 12 ga. only, 20-inch cylinder bore bbl. Made 1897-1957.

Winchester Model 97 Trap, Tournament and Pigeon

These higher grade models offer higher overall quality than the standard grade. Discont. 1939.

Trap Gun **$695**
Tournament Grade **825**
Pigeon Grade **995**

Winchester Model 97 Trench Gun $1295

Solid frame. Same as Model 97 Riot Gun, except has handguard and is equipped with a bayonet. World War I government issue, 1917-18.

Winchester Model 97 Slide-Action Repeater ... $395

Standard Grade. Takedown or solid frame. Gauges: 12 and 16. 5-shell tubular magazine. Bbl.: plain; 26 to 32 inches, the latter in 12 ga. only; choked F to Cyl. Weight: about 7.75 lbs. (12 ga. w/28-inch barrel). Plain pistol-grip stock, grooved slide handle. Made 1897-1957.

NOTE

All Winchester Model 101s are mfd. for Olin Corp. at its Olin-Kodensha facility in Tochigi, Japan. Production for Olin Corp. stopped in Nov. 1987. Importation of Model 101s was continued by Classic Doubles under that logo until 1990. *See* separate heading for additional data.

Winchester Model 101 Diamond Grade Target .. $1295

Similar to Model 101 Standard except silvered frame and Winchoke interchangeable choke tubes. Made 1981-90.

Winchester Model 101 Field Gun Over/Under

Boxlock. Engraved receiver. Auto ejectors. Single selective trigger. Combination bbl. selector and safety. Gauges: 12 and 28, 2.75-inch chambers; 20 and .410, 3-inch chambers. Vent-rib bbls.: 30- (12 ga. only) and 26.5-inch, IC/M. Weight: 6.25 to 7.75 lbs. depending on gauge and bbl. length. Hand-checkered French walnut stock and forearm. Made 1963-81; gauges other than 12 intro. 1966.

12 and 20 gauge **$695**
28 and .410 gauge **875**

Winchester Model 101 Grand European $1295

Similar to Model 101 Pigeon Grade except silvered frame and Winchoke interchangeable choke tubes. Made 1981-1987.

Winchester Model 101 Magnum Field Gun $710

Same as Model 101 Field Gun, except chambered for 12 or 20 ga. 3-inch magnum shells only, 30-inch bbls. (F/F or M/F), recoil pad. Made 1966-81.

Winchester Model 101 Pigeon Grade

Same general specifications as standard Model 101 Field and Skeet, except higher grade with more elaborately engraved satin gray steel receiver, fancier wood and finer checkering. 12 and 20 ga. only. Made 1974-81.

Field Gun .... **$ 875**
Skeet Gun **995**
Trap Gun with straight stock **995**
Trap Gun with Monte Carlo stock **1295**

Winchester Model 101 Skeet Gun

Same as Model 101 Field Gun, except skeet-style stock and forearm. Bbls.: 12 ga., 26-inch- 20 ga., 26.5-inch 28 and .410 ga., 28-inch; all SK choked. Made 1966-81.

12 and 20 gauge **$795**
28 and .410 gauge **810**

Winchester Model 101 Waterfowl

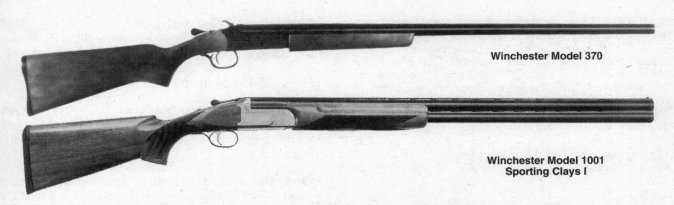

Winchester Model 370

Winchester Model 1001
Sporting Clays I

Winchester Model 101 Waterfowl $1025

Similar to Model 101 Magnum Field, except silvered frame and Winchoke interchangeable choke tubes. Made 1981 to date. *See photo preceding page.*

Winchester Model 370 Single-Shot Shotgun $95

Visible hammer. Auto ejector. Takedown. Gauges: 12, 16, 20, 28, .410. 2.75-inch chambers in 16 and 28 ga., 3-inch in other ga. Bbls.: 12 ga., 30-, 32- or 36-inch, 16 ga; 30- or 32-inch; 20 and 28 ga., 28-inch; .410 bore, 26-inch, all F choke. Weight: 5.5-6.25 lbs. Plain pistol-grip stock and forearm. Made 1968-73.

Winchester Model 370 Youth $105

Same as standard Model 370, except has 26-inch bbl. and 12.5-inch stock with recoil pad; 20 gauge with IM choke, .410 bore with F choke. Made 1968-73.

Winchester Model 1001 O/U Shotgun

Boxlock. 12 ga., 2.75- or 3-inch chambers. Bbls.: 28- or 30-inch vent rib; WinPlus choke tubes. Weight: 7-7.75 lbs. Checkered walnut buttstock and forend. Blued finish with scroll engraved receiver. Made 1993 to date.
Field Model (28" bbl., 3") $795
Sporting Clays I (28" bbl.) 895
Sporting Clays II (30" bbl.) 895

Winchester Model 1200 Deer Gun $200

Same as standard Model 1200, except has special 22-inch bbl. with rifle-type sights, for rifled slug or buckshot; 12 ga. only. Weight: 6.5 lbs. Made 1965-74.

Winchester Model 1200 Defender Slide-Action Security Shotgun $195

Hammerless. 12 and 20 ga. (3-inch chambers). 18-inch bbl. 8-shot capacity. Low-glare blued finish. Weight: 6.75 lbs. Made 1984 to date by U. S. Repeating Arms.

Winchester Model 1200 Field Gun — Magnum

Same as standard Model 1200, except chambered for 3-inch 12 and 20 ga. magnum shells; plain or vent-rib bbl., 28- or 30-inch, F choke. Weight: 7.38 to 7.88 lbs. Made 1964-83.
With plain bbl. $200
With vent-rib bbl. 210
Add for Winchester Recoil Reduction System 50

Winchester Model 1200 Pistol Grip Defender $195

Same general specifications as standard Model 1200, except has 18-inch bbl., 7-shot magazine and pistol grip. Mfd. by U. S. Repeating Arms.

Winchester Model 1200 Police $195

Same general specifications as 1200 Defender, except has rifle-type front and rear sights. Stainless-steel bbl. and satin chrome finish on all external metal parts.

Winchester Model 1200 Skeet Gun $195

Same as standard Model 1200, except 12 and 20 ga. only; has 2-shot magazine, specially tuned trigger, 26-inch vent-rib bbl. SK choke, semi-fancy walnut stock and forearm. Weight: 7.25 to 7.5 lbs. Made 1965-73. Also avail. 1966-70 with Winchester Recoil Reduction System (add $50 to value).

SHOTGUNS

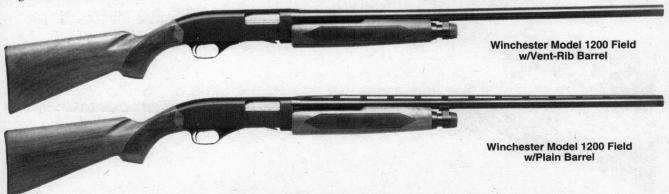

Winchester Model 1200 Field
w/Vent-Rib Barrel

Winchester Model 1200 Field
w/Plain Barrel

Winchester Model 1200 Slide-Action Field Gun

Front-locking rotary bolt. Takedown. 4-shot magazine. Gauges: 12, 16, 20 (2.75-inch chamber). Bbl.: plain or vent rib; 26-, 28-, 30-inch; IC, M, F choke or with Win-choke (interchangeable tubes IC-M-F). Weight: 6.5 to 7.25 lbs. Checkered pistol-grip stock and forearm (slide handle), recoil pad; also avail. 1966-70 w/Winchester Recoil Reduction System (Cycolac stock). Made 1964-83.

With plain bbl.	**$185**
With vent-rib bbl.	205
Add for Winchester Recoil Reduction System	50
Add for Winchoke	25

Winchester Model 1200 Stainless

Winchester Model 1200 Stainless $260

Same as standard Model 1200 Defender, except has stainless-steel bbl. and special bright chrome finish on external metal parts.

Winchester Model 1200 Trap Gun

Same as standard Model 1200, except 12 gauge only. Has 2-shot magazine, 30-inch vent-rib bbl., Full choke or 28-inch with Win-choke. Semi-fancy walnut stock, straight Made 1965-73. Also available 1966-70 with Winchester Recoil Reduction System.

With straight-trap stock	**$275**
With Monte Carlo stock	325
Add for Winchester Recoil Reduction System	50
Add for Winchoke	25

Winchester Model 1300 CamoPack $325

Gauge: 12.3-inch Magnum. 5-shot magazine. Bbls.: 30-and 22-inch with Winchoke system. Weight: 7 lbs. Laminated stock with Win-Cam camouflage green, cut checkering, recoil pad, swivels and sling. Made 1987.

Winchester Model 1300 Deer Gun $295

Same as standard Model 1300, except has special 24.13-inch bbl. with rifle-type sights, for rifled slug or buckshot; 12 ga. only. Weight: 6.5 lbs.

Winchester Model 1300 Deluxe Slide-Action Pump

Gauges: 12 and 20; 3-inch chamber. 5-shot magazine. Bbl.: 22, 26 or 28 inches with vent rib; Winchoke tubes. Weight: 6.5 lbs. Checkered walnut buttstock and forend. Polished blued finish with roll-engraved receiver. Made 1984 to date.

Model 1300 Deluxe	**$280**
Model 1300 Ladies/Youth (22-inch bbl.)	235

Winchester Model 1300 Featherweight Slide-Action Shotgun $265

Hammerless. Takedown. 4-shot magazine. Gauges: 12 and 20 (3-inch chambers). Bbl.: 22-inch vent rib. Weight: 6.38 lbs. Checkered walnut buttstock, grooved slide handle. Made 1985 to date.

Winchester Model 1300 Ranger Series

Gauges: 12 and 20; 3-inch chamber. 5-shot magazine. Bbl.: 22-(Rifled), 26- or 28-inches with vent rib; Winchoke tubes. Weight: 7.25 lbs. Walnut-finished hardwood buttstock and forend. Blued finish. Made 1984 to date.

Standard Model	**$220**
Combo Model	275
Rifled Deer Combo (D&T w/rings & bases)	290

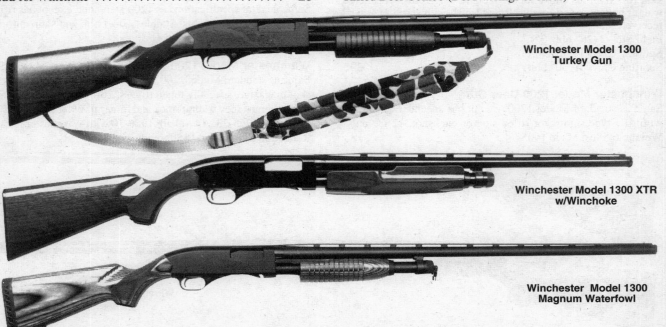

Winchester Model 1300 Turkey Gun

Winchester Model 1300 XTR w/Winchoke

Winchester Model 1300 Magnum Waterfowl

Winchester Model 1300 Slug Hunter

Similar to the Model 1300, except has 22-inch rifled bbl. with rifle sights and walnut stock.

Hunter Model	**$335**
Whitetails Unlimited Model	**340**

Winchester Model 1300 Turkey Slide-Action . . . $250

Same general specifications as Model 1300 Featherweight, except low-luster finish on walnut stock and forearm; nonglare matte finish on receiver, bbl. and exterior metal surfaces.

Winchester Model 1300 Turkey Win-Cam $295

Same as Model 1300 CamoPack, except has only one 22-inch bbl. Made 1987 to date.

Winchester Model 1300 Waterfowl Slide-Action Shotgun $275

Same general specifications as Model 1300 Featherweight, except 30-inch bbl. Weight: 7 lbs. Made 1985-92.

Winchester Model 1300 XTR Slide-Action $305

Hammerless. Takedown. 4-shot magazine. Gauges: 12 and 20 (3-inch chambers). Bbl.: plain or vent rib; 28-inch bbls.; Winchoke (interchangeable tubes IC-M-F). Weight: about 7 lbs.

NOTE

Model 1400 shotguns were available in left-hand versions (ejection port and safety on left side), with values the same as for right-hand models. In 1968, Model 1400 was replaced by Model 1400 Mark ll, which is the same gun with an improved action release and restyled checkering on stock and forearm. Both models are listed here as there is a slight difference in value.

Winchester Model 1400 Automatic Field Gun

Gas-operated. Front-locking rotary bolt. Takedown. 2-shot magazine. Gauges: 12, 16, 20 (2.75-inch chamber). Bbl.: plain or vent rib; 26-,28-,30-inch; IC, M, F choke, or with Winchoke (interchangeable tubes IC-M-F). Weight: 6.5 to 7.25 lbs. Checkered pistol-grip stock and forearm, recoil pad, also available with Winchester Recoil Reduction System (Cycolac stock). Made 1964-68.

With plain bbl.	**$250**
With vent-rib bbl.	**275**
Add for Winchester Recoil Reduction System	**75**
Add for Winchoke	**25**

Winchester Model 1400 Deer Gun $225

Same as standard Model 1400, except has special 22-inch bbl. with rifle-type sights, for rifle slug or buckshot; 12 ga. only. Weight: 6.25 lbs. Made 1965-68.

Winchester Model 1400 Mark II Deer Gun $275

Same general specifications as Model 1400 Deer Gun. Made 1968-73.

Winchester Model 1400 Mark II Field Gun

Same general specifications as Model 1400 Field Gun, except not chambered for 16 gauge; Winchester Recoil Reduction System not available after 1970- only 28-inch barrels w/Winchoke offered after 1973. Made 1968-78.

With plain bbl.	**$240**
With plain bbl. and Winchoke	**260**
With vent-rib bbl.	**275**
With vent-rib bbl. and Winchoke	**295**
Add for Winchester Recoil Reduction System	**75**

Winchester Model 1400 Mark II Skeet Gun $340

Same general specifications as Model 1400 Skeet Gun. Made 1968-73.

Winchester Model 1400 Mark II Trap Gun

Same general specifications as Model 1400 Trap Gun, except also furnished with 28-inch bbl. and Winchoke. Winchester Recoil Reduction System not available after 1970. Made 1968-73.

With straight stock	**$340**
With Monte Carlo stock	**375**
Add for Winchester Recoil Reduction System	**75**
Add for Winchoke	**25**

Winchester Model 1400 Mark II Utility Skeet $245

Same general specifications as Model 1400 Mark II Skeet Gun, except has stock and forearm of field grade walnut. Made 1970-73.

Winchester Model 1400 Mark II Utility Trap $265

Same as Model 1400 Mark II Trap Gun, except has Monte Carlo stock/forearm of field grade walnut. Made 1970-73.

Winchester Model 1400 Skeet Gun $275

Same as standard Model 1400, except 12 and 20 ga. only, 26-inch vent-rib bbl., SK choke, semi-fancy walnut stock and forearm. Weight: 7.25 to 7.5 lbs. Made 1965-68. Also available with Winchester Recoil Reduction System (add $50 to value).

SHOTGUNS

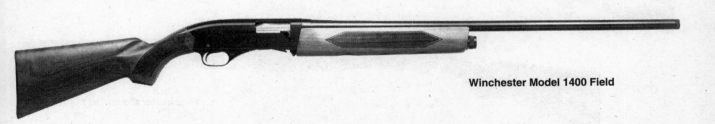

Winchester Model 1400 Field

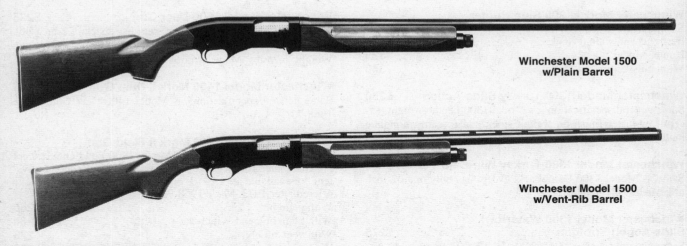

Winchester Model 1500
w/Plain Barrel

Winchester Model 1500
w/Vent-Rib Barrel

Winchester Model 1400 Trap Gun

Same as standard Model 1400, except 12 ga. only with 30-inch vent-rib bbl., F choke. Semi-fancy walnut stock, straight or Monte Carlo trap style. Also available with Winchester Recoil Reduction System. Weight: about 8.25 lbs. Made 1965-68.

With straight stock $325
With Monte Carlo stock   360
Add for Winchester Recoil Reduction System   75

Winchester Model 1500 XTR Semiautomatic . . . $305

Gas-operated. Gauges: 12 and 20 (2.75-inch chambers). Bbl.: plain or vent rib; 28-inch; Winchoke (interchangeable tubes IC-M-F). American walnut stock and forend; checkered grip and forend. Weight: 7.25 lbs.

Winchester Model 1901 Lever-Action Repeater . . $1195

Same general specifications as Model 1887 of which this is a redesigned version. 10 ga. only. Made 1901-20.

Winchester Model 1911 Autoloading Shotgun . . $425

Hammerless. Takedown. 12 gauge only. 4-shell tubular magazine. Bbl.: plain, 26- to 32-inch, standard borings. Weight: about 8.5 lbs. Plain or checkered pistol-grip stock and forearm. Made 1911-25.

Winchester Pistol Grip
Stainless Marine

Winchester Pistol Grip Stainless Marine $225

Same general specifications as standard Model 1200, except has 18-inch bbl., 6-shot magazine and pistol grip. Mfd. by U. S. Repeating Arms.

Winchester Pistol Grip Stainless Police $225

Same general specifications as standard Model 1200, except has 18-inch bbl., 6-shot magazine and pistol grip. Mfd. by U. S. Repeating Arms.

Winchester Quail Special O/U Small Frame . . . $1295

Same specifications as small-frame Model 101, except in 28 and .410 ga. with 3-inch chambers. 25.5-inch bbls. with choke tubes (28 ga.) or M/F chokes (.410). Imported from Japan in 1987.

Winchester Model 1901

Winchester Model 1911

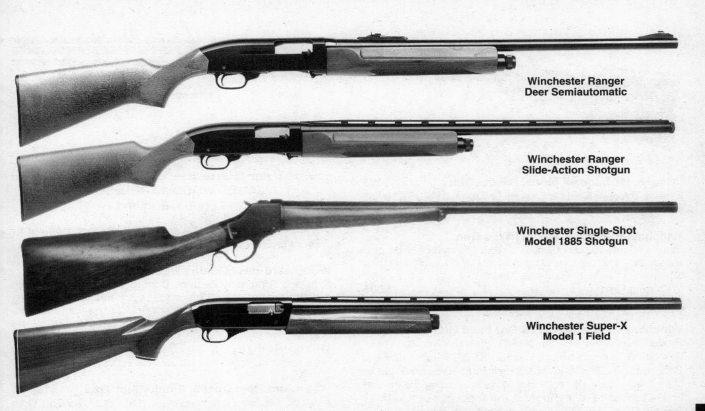

Winchester Ranger
Deer Semiautomatic

Winchester Ranger
Slide-Action Shotgun

Winchester Single-Shot
Model 1885 Shotgun

Winchester Super-X
Model 1 Field

Winchester Ranger Combination Shotgun **$225**
Same as Ranger Deer Combination, except has one 28-inch vent-rib bbl. with M choke and one 18-inch Police Cyl. bore. Made 1987 to date.

Winchester Ranger Deer Combination **$240**
Gauge: 12, 3-inch Magnum. 3-shot magazine. Bbl.: 24-inch Cyl. bore deer bbl. and 28-inch vent-rib bbl. with Winchoke system. Weight: 7.25 lbs. Made 1987 to date.

Winchester Ranger Semiautomatic **$195**
Gauges: 12, 20. 2-shot magazine. 28-inch vent-rib bbl. with F choke. Overall length: 48.63 inches. Weight: 7 to 7.25 lbs. Walnut finish, hardwood stock and forearm with cut checkering. Made 1984 to date by U. S. Repeating Arms.

Winchester Ranger Semiauto Deer Shotgun . . . **$210**
Same general specifications as Ranger Semiautomatic except 24.13-inch plain bbl. with rifle sights. Mfd. by U.S. Repeating Arms.

Winchester Ranger Slide-Action Shotgun **$180**
Hammerless. 12 and 20 ga.; 3-inch chambers. Walnut finished hardwood stock, ribbed forearm. 28-inch vent-rib bbl.; Winchoke system. Weight: 7.25 lbs. Made 1982 to date by U. S. Repeating Arms.

Winchester Ranger Youth Slide-Action **$175**
Same general specifications as standard Ranger Slide-Action except chambered for 20 ga. only, has 4-shot magazine, recoil pad on buttstock and weighs 6.5 lbs. Mfd. by U. S. Repeating Arms.

Winchester Shotgun/Rifle Combination **$1995**
12-ga. Winchoke bbl. on top and rifle bbl. chambered for 30-06 on bottom (over/under). 25-inch bbls. Engraved receiver. Hand checkered walnut stock and forend. Weight: 8.5 lbs. Mfd. for Olin Corp. in Japan.

Winchester Single-Shot 1885 Shotgun **$1150**
Falling-block action, same as Model 1885 Rifle. Highwall receiver. Solid frame or takedown. 20 ga. 3-inch chamber. 26-inch bbl.; plain, matted or matted rib; Cyl. bore, M or F choke. Weight: about 5.5 lbs. Straught-grip stock and forearm. Made 1914-16.

**Winchester Stainless Marine Slide-Action
Security Shotgun** **$275**
Hammerless. 12 ga. only. 18-inch bbl. of ordnance stainless steel. 7-shot capacity. Weight: 7 lbs. Made 1984 to date by U. S. Repeating Arms.

**Winchester Stainless Police Slide-Action
Security Shotgun** **$275**
Hammerless. 12 ga. only. 18-inch ordnance stainless steel bbl. accommodates gas launchers. Rifle-type sights. Made from 1984 to date by U.S. Repeating Arms.

Winchester Super-X Model I Auto Field Gun . . . **$375**
Gas-operated. Takedown.12 ga. 2.75-inch chamber 4-shot magazine. Bbl.: vent-rib 26-inch IC; 28-inch M or F; 30-inch F choke. Weight about 7 lbs. Checkered pistol-grip stock and forearm. Made 1974-84.

Winchester Xpert Model 96 Field

Winchester Super-X Model I Skeet Gun $495
Same as Super-X Field Gun, except has 26-inch bbl., SK choke, skeet-style stock and forearm of select walnut. Made 1974-84.

Winchester Super-X Model I Trap Gun
Same as Super-X Field Gun, except has 30-inch bbl., IM or F choke, trap-style stock (straight or Monte Carlo comb) and forearm of select walnut, recoil pad. Made 1974-84.
With straight stock $395
With Monte Carlo stock 450

Winchester Xpert Model 96 O/U Field Gun $575
Boxlock action similar to Model 101. Plain receiver. Auto ejectors. Selective single trigger. Gauges: 12, 20. 3-inch chambers. Bbl.: vent rib; 26-inch IC/M; 28-inch M/F, 30-inch F/F choke (12 ga. only). Weight: 6.25 to 8.25 lbs. depending on ga. and bbls. Checkered pistol-grip stock and forearm. Made 1976-81 for Olin Corp. at its Olin-Kodensha facility in Japan.

Winchester Xpert Model 96 Skeet Gun $600
Same as Xpert Field Gun, except has 2.75-inch chambers, 27-inch bbls., SK choke, skeet-style stock and forearm. Made 1976-1981.

Winchester Xpert Model 96 Trap Gun
Same as Xpert Field Gun, except 12 ga. only, 2.75-inch chambers, has 30-inch bbls., IM/F or F/F choke, trap-style stock (straight or Monte Carlo comb) with recoil pad. Made 1976-81.
With straight stock $580
With Monte Carlo stock 595

JAMES WOODWARD & SONS
London, England

The business of James Woodward & Sons was acquired by James Purdey & Sons after World War II.

Woodward Best Quality Hammerless Double
Sidelock. Automatic ejectors. Double triggers or single trigger. Built to order in all standard gauges, bbl. lengths, boring and other specifications; made as a field gun, pigeon and wildfowl gun, skeet gun or trap gun. Manufactured prior to World War II.
With double triggers $19,250
With single trigger 20,500

Woodward Best Quality Single-Shot Trap ... $10,925
Sidelock. Mechanical features of the Under and Over Gun. vent-rib bbl. 12 ga. only. Built to customers' specifications and measurements, including type and amount of checkering, carving, and engraving. Made prior to World War II.

Woodward Best Quality Over/Under Shotgun
Sidelock. Automatic ejectors. Double triggers or single trigger. Built to order in all standard gauges, bbl. lengths, boring and other specifications, including Special Trap Grade with vent rib. Woodward introduced this type of gun in 1908. Made until World War II. *See* listing of Purdey Over/Under Gun.
With double triggers $24,500
Single trigger, extra 1,000

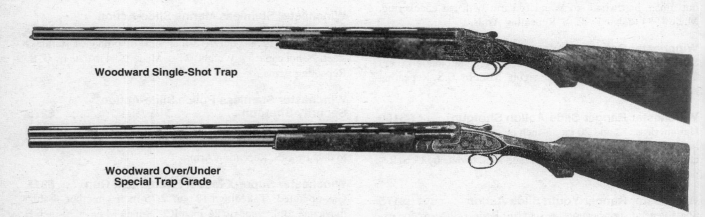

Woodward Single-Shot Trap

Woodward Over/Under
Special Trap Grade

ZEPHYR SHOTGUNS
Manufactured by Victor Sarasqueta Company, Eibar, Spain

Zephyr Model 1 Over/Under Shotgun **$925**
Same general specifications as Field Model O/U, except with more elaborate engraving, finer wood and checkering. Imported by Stoeger 1930s-51.

Zephyr Model 2 Over/Under Shotgun **$1155**
Sidelock. Auto ejectors. Gauges: 12, 16, 20, 28 and .410. Bbls.: 25 to 30 inches most common. Modest scroll engraving on receiver and sideplates. Checkered, straight-grain select walnut buttstock and forend. Imported by Stoeger 1930s-51.

Zephyr Model 3 Over/Under Shotgun **$1615**
Same general specifications as Zephyr Model 2 O/U, except with more elaborate engraving, finer wood and checkering. Imported by Stoeger 1930s-51.

Zephyr Model 400E Field Grade Double-Barrel Shotgun
Anson & Deeley boxlock system. Gauges: 12 16, 20, 28 and .410. Bbls.:25 to 30 inches. Weight: 4.5 lbs. (.410) to 6.25 lbs. (12 ga.). Checkered French walnut buttstock and forearm. Modest scroll engraving on bbls., receiver and trigger guard. Imported by Stoeger 1930s-50s.

12, 16 or 20 gauge	$1150
28 or .410 gauge	1290
Add for selective single trigger	200

Zephyr Model 401 E Skeet Grade Double-Barrel Shotgun
Same general specifications as Field Grade (above), except with beavertail forearm. Bbls.:25 to 28 inches. Imported by Stoeger 1930s-50s.

12, 16 or 20 gauge	$1420
28 or .410 gauge	1550
Extra for selective single trigger	350
Extra for nonselective single trigger	250

Zephyr Model 402E Deluxe Double-Barrel Shotgun **$1730**
Same general specifications as Model 400E Field Grade except for custom refinements. The action was carefully hand-honed for smoother operation; finer, elaborate engraving throughout plus higher quality wood in stock and forearm. Imported by Stoeger 1930s-50s.

Zephyr Crown Grade

Zephyr Crown Grade **$1200**
Boxlock. Gauges: 12, 16, 20, 28 and .410. Bbls.: 25 to 30 inches standard, but any lengths could be ordered. Weight: 6 lbs. 4 oz. (.410) to 7 lbs. 4 oz. (12 ga.). Checkered Spanish walnut stock and beavertail forearm. Receiver engraved with scroll patterns. Imported by Stoeger 1938-51.

Zephyr Field Model Over/Under Shotgun **$645**
Anson & Deeley boxlock. Auto ejectors. Gauges: 12, 16 and 20. Bbls.: 25 to 30 inches standard- full-length matt rib. Double triggers. Checkered buttstock and forend. Light scroll engraving on receiver. Imported by Stoeger 1930s-51.

Zephyr Honker Single-Shot Shotgun **$895**
Sidelock. Gauge: 10; 3.5-inch magnum. 36-inch vent-rib barrel w/F choke. Weight: 10.5 lbs. Checkered select Spanish walnut buttstock and beavertail forend; recoil pad. Imported by Stoeger 1950s-72.

Zephyr Pinehurst Double-Barrel Shotgun **$895**
Boxlock. Gauges: 12, 16, 20, 28 and .410. Bbls.: 25 to 28 inches most common. Checkered, select walnut buttstock and forend. Selective single trigger and auto ejectors. Imported by Stoeger 1950s-72.

Zephyr Premier Grade

Zephyr Premier Grade Double-Barrel Shotgun . . **$2000**
Sidelock. Gauges: 12, 16, 20, 28 and .410. Bbls.: any length, but 25 to 30 inches most popular. Weight: 4.5 lbs. (.410) to 7 lbs. (12 ga.). Checkered high-grade French walnut buttstock and forend. Imported by Stoeger 1930s-51.

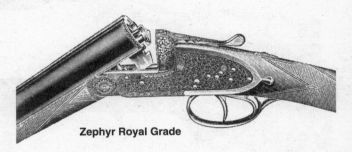
Zephyr Royal Grade

Zephyr Royal Grade Double-Barrel Shotgun . . **$3000**
Same general specifications as the Premier Grade, except with more elaborate engraving, finer checkering and wood. Imported by Stoeger 1930s-51.

SHOTGUNS

Zephyr Sterlingworth II Double-Barrel Shotgun . . . $995
Genuine sidelocks with color-casehardened sideplates. Gauges: 12, 16, 20 and .410. Bbls.: 25 to 30 inches. Weight: 6 lbs. 4 oz. (.410) to 7 lbs. 4 oz. (12 ga.). Select Spanish walnut buttstock and beavertail forearm. Light scroll engraving on receiver and sideplates. Automatic, sliding-tang safety. Imported by Stoeger 1950s-72.

Zephyr Thunderbird Double-Barrel Shotgun . . $1150
Sidelock. Gauges: 12 and 10 Magnum. Bbls.: 32-inch, both F choke. Weight: 8 lbs. 8 oz. (12 ga.), 12 lbs. (10 ga.). Receiver elaborately engraved with waterfowl scenes. Checkered select Spanish walnut buttstock and beavertail forend. Plain extractors, double triggers. Imported by Stoeger 1950-72.

Zephyr Upland King Double-Barrel Shotgun . . $1125
Sidelock. Gauges: 12, 16, 20, 28 and .410. Bbls.: 25 to 28 inches most popular. Checkered buttstock and forend of select walnut. Selective single trigger and auto ejectors. Imported by Stoeger 1950-72.

Zephyr Uplander Double-Barrel Shotgun $1050
Same general specifications as the Zephyr Sterlingworth II, except with selective auto ejectors and highly polished sideplates. Imported by Stoeger 1951-72.

Zephyr Woodlander II Double-Barrel Shotgun . . . $545
Boxlock. Gauges: 12, 20 and .410. Bbls.:25 to 30 inches. Weight: 6 lbs. 4 oz. (.410) to 7 lbs. 4 oz. (12 ga.). Checkered Spanish walnut stock and beavertail forearm. Engraved receiver. Imported by Stoeger 1950-72.

ANGELO ZOLI
Mississauga, Ontario, Canada

Angelo Zoli Alley Cleaner S/S Shotgun $550
Gauges: 12 and 20. 20-inch bbl. 26.5 inches overall. Weight: 7 lbs. average. Chokes: F/M, F, IM, M, IC, SK. Chrome-lined barrels. Walnut stock and engraved action. Made 1986-87.

Angelo Zoli Apache O/U Field Shotgun $425
Gauge: 12. Chokes: F/M, F, IM, M, IC, SK. 20-inch bbl. Short vent rib. Weight: 7.5 lbs. Checkered walnut stock and forearm. Lever action. Pistol grip. Made 1986-88.

Angelo Zoli Daino I Folding Single Shot $135
Gauges: 12, 20 and .410. 28- or 30-inch bbl. Weight: 6 lbs. average. Choke: Full. Chrome-lined barrel, vent rib. Pistol-grip walnut stock. Engraved action. Made 1986-88.

Angelo Zoli HK 2000 Semiautomatic Shotgun . . $525
Gauge: 12. 5-shot capacity. Bbls.: 24-, 26-, 28- and 30-inch; vent rib. Weight: 6.5 to 7.5 lbs. Checkered walnut stock and forearm. Glossy finish. Pistol grip. Engraved receiver. Made 1988.

Angelo Zoli Patricia Side-by-Side Shotguns . . $1200
Gauge: .410 only. 28-inch bbl. Choke: F/M. Weight: 5.5 lbs. Automatic ejectors; Zoli single selective trigger, boxlock. Hand-checkered walnut stock with English straight grip, splinter forearm. Made 1986-88.

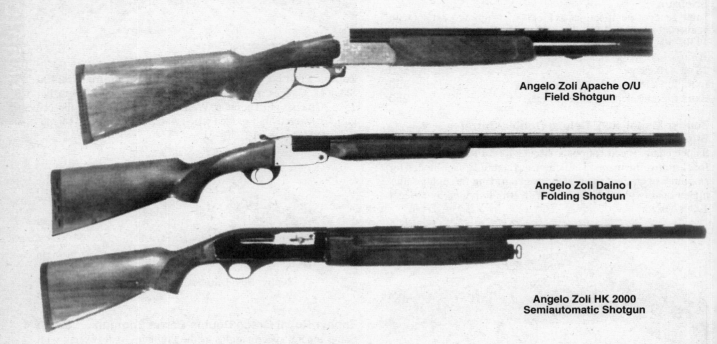

**Angelo Zoli Apache O/U
Field Shotgun**

**Angelo Zoli Daino I
Folding Shotgun**

**Angelo Zoli HK 2000
Semiautomatic Shotgun**

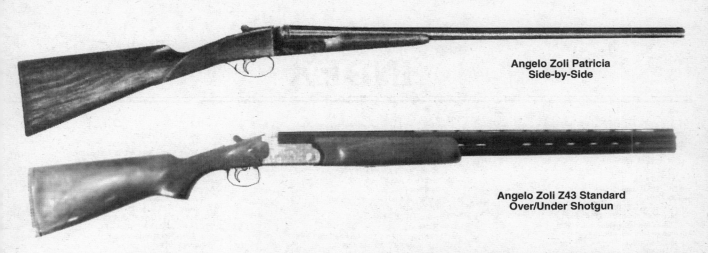

**Angelo Zoli Patricia
Side-by-Side**

**Angelo Zoli Z43 Standard
Over/Under Shotgun**

Angelo Zoli Saint George O/U Competition Trap Combo $1060

Gauge: 12. 30- and 32-inch vent rib barrels. Weight: 8 lbs. Single selective trigger. Oil-finished, pistol-grip walnut stock. Made 1986-88.

Angelo Zoli Silver Snipe Over/Under Shotgun . . $705

Purdey-type boxlock with crossbolt. Selective single trigger. Gauges: 12, 20; 3-inch chambers. Bbls.: 26-, 28- or 30-inch with a variety of choke combinations. Weight: 5.75 to 6.75 lbs. Checkered European walnut buttstock and forend. Made in Italy.

Angelo Zoli Z43 Standard O/U Shotgun $420

Gauge: 12 or 20. 26-, 28- or 30-inch bbls. Chokes: F/M, M/IC Weight: 6.75 to 8 lbs. vent lateral ribs, standard extractors, single non-selective trigger. Glossy-finished walnut stock and forearm. Automatic safety. Made 1986-88.

ANTONIO ZOLI, U.S.A., INC.
Fort Wayne, Indiana
Manufactured in Italy

Antonio Zoli Silver Falcon O/U $795

Gauges: 12 and 20; 3-inch chambers. 26- or 28-inch blued barrels. Weight: 6.25 to 7.25 lbs. Antiqued silver finish on receiver. Pistol-grip stock of Turkish Circassian walnut with polyurethane-type finish. Imported 1989-1990.

Antonio Zoli Uplander Side/Side Shotgun $745

Gauges: 12 and 20. Casehardened receiver. Checkered oil-finished, hand-rubbed stock of Turkish Circassian walnut; splinter forend. Imported 1989-90.

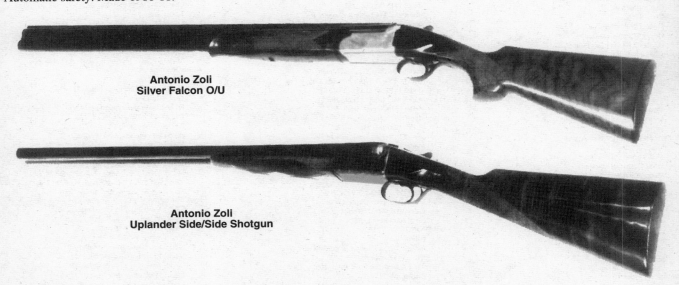

**Antonio Zoli
Silver Falcon O/U**

**Antonio Zoli
Uplander Side/Side Shotgun**

SHOTGUNS

INDEX